Public Law

Other Titles in the Textbook Series

Cretney's Family Law
Employment Law
Environment Law
Criminal Law
Land Law
Tort
Contract

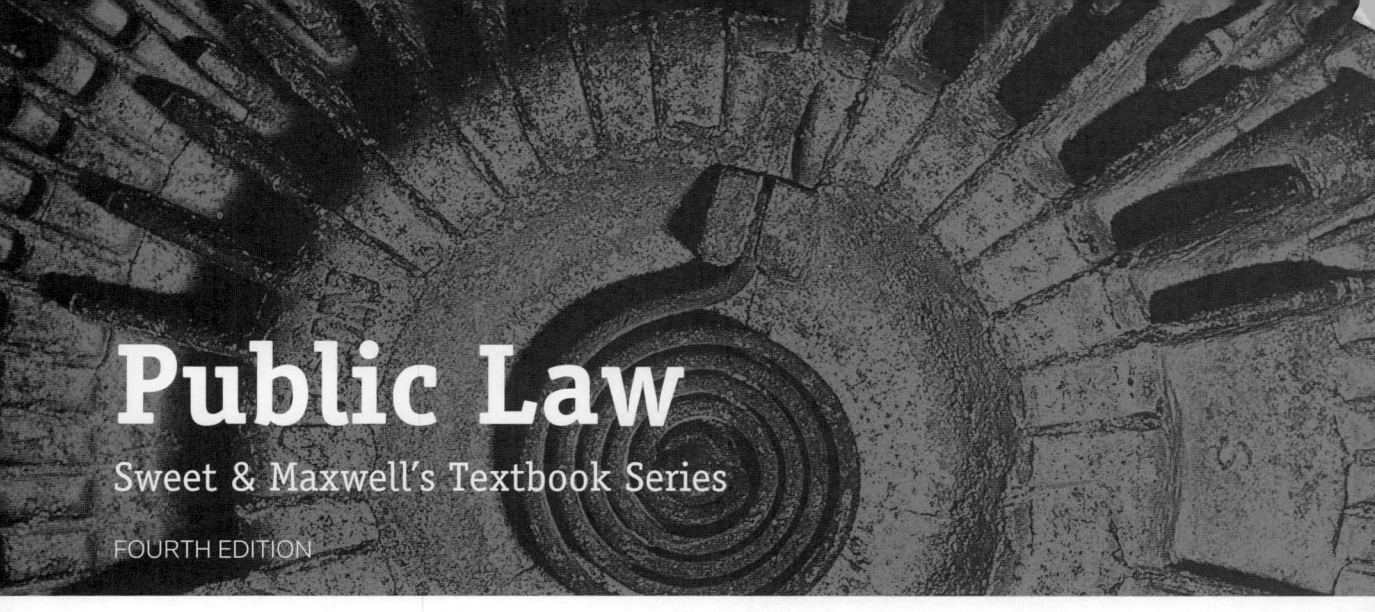

Public Law

Sweet & Maxwell's Textbook Series

FOURTH EDITION

by
John F. McEldowney, LL.B., Ph.D.
Professor of Law at the University of Warwick

SWEET & MAXWELL
LONDON • 2016

First edition 1994
Reprinted 1995
Second edition 1998
Third edition 2002
Fourth edition 2016

Published in 2016 by
Thomson Reuters (Professional) UK Limited
trading as Sweet & Maxwell, Friars House,
160 Blackfriars Road, London, SE1 8EZ
(Registered in England & Wales, Company No 1679046.
Registered Office and address for service: 2nd floor,
1 Mark Square, Leonard Street, London EC2A 4EG

For further information on our products and services,
visit www.sweetandmaxwell.co.uk

Typeset by Servis Filmsetting Ltd, Stockport, Cheshire
Printed and bound by CPI Group (UK) Ltd, Croydon, CR0 4YY

No natural forests were destroyed to make this product;
only farmed timber was used and re-planted.

A CIP catalogue record for this book is available from the British Library.

ISBN: 978-0-41403-818-9

Thomson Reuters and the Thomson Reuters logo are trademarks of Thomson Reuters.
Sweet & Maxwell ® is a registered trademark of Thomson Reuters (Professional) UK Limited.

All rights reserved. Crown copyright material is reproduced with the
permission of the Controller of HMSO and the Queen's Printer for Scotland.

No part of this publication may be reproduced or transmitted in any form or by any means, or stored in any retrieval system of any nature without prior written permission, except for permitted fair dealing under the Copyright, Designs and Patents Act 1988, or in accordance with the terms of a licence issued by the Copyright Licensing Agency in respect of photocopying and/or reprographic reproduction. Application for permission for other use of copyright material including permission to reproduce extracts in other published works shall be made to the publishers. Full acknowledgement of author, publisher and source must be given.

© 2016 John F. McEldowney

Dedication

For Sharron and Emma

Guide to the Book

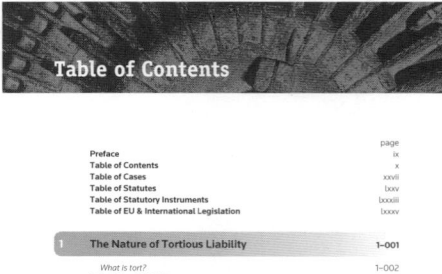

Table of Contents
The Table of Contents provides you with an at a glance overview of the coverage for each chapter.

Table of Cases
The Table of Cases provides you with a handy list of all cases referred to througout this book.

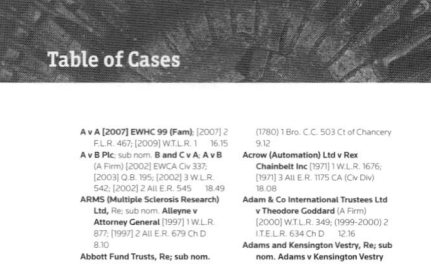

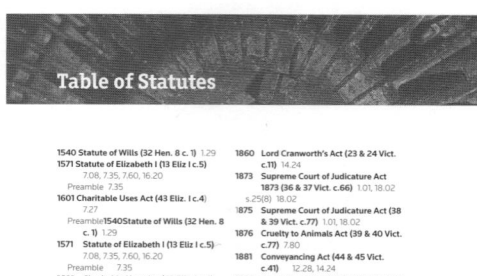

Table of Statutes
The Table of Statutes provides you a handy list of all statutes referred to throughout this book.

Key Cases
All cases are highlighted making your research of the subject easier.

Key Extracts
Key extracts are boxed throughout to make them easily identifiable.

Paragraph Numbering
Paragraph numbering helps you move between sections and references with ease.

Footnotes
Footnotes help minimise text distractions while providing access to relevant supplementary material.

Preface

Fundamental constitutional reforms have not diminished in scale or intensity since 1997. Five years after the election of the first peacetime coalition government in 2010 that ended in May 2015 with the election of a Conservative majority government, constitutional change continues. Major financial cuts in public expenditure and across the public sector as a result of the 2008 financial crisis represent a major and overriding influence driving reform today. There is a reshaping of the regulatory state as well as a "re-balancing" of constitutional actors and systems. There is evidence that the constitutional landscape of the state itself is being withdrawn through devolutionary and decentralising pressures, and greater financial autonomy away from Westminster. Economic considerations are likely to be a dominant influence in shaping our constitutional arrangements for some time to come. Theoretical and normative considerations are in evidence in recent public law scholarship. The contour of power between the citizen, the state and the boundaries of the rule of law is under intense debate. Public lawyers in practice face drastic reductions in legal aid and increasing court fees with significant consequences. It is the pace of change as well as the substantive nature of many changes that has proved demanding to assess. Uncertainties overshadow many contemporary issues and consideration of the future direction of public law. There is debate about the UK's continued membership of the European Union, the role of the Human Rights Act 1998 and the effectiveness of Parliament amidst widespread distrust of politicians. The election of the Conservative majority-led government in May 2015 brings proposals for far-reaching constitutional reforms including the possibility of repeal of the Human Rights Act 1998 and its replacement with a British Bill of Rights. The "in out" referendum in June 2016 on the referendum question: Should the UK remain a member of the European Union or leave the European Union? resulted in a decision to leave the EU with major constitutional consequences for the UK and the EU. Further changes in devolution arrangements for the four nations are likely. There is an ever increasing tension between protecting civil liberties and addressing terrorism. Increased intelligence and surveillance is likely to be demanded while at the same time upholding a liberal and free society.

The 800 years anniversary of Magna Carta in 2015 provides a suitable opportunity to assess the role of public law in the UK and to take account of its transformation and future direction. It is clear that the subject is in a state of flux and it is likely to remain so into the future. This sets significant challenges. Many questions about the scope, content and future direction of public law and how the subject is taught are raised by the changes. It is hoped that the new edition of this book will provide readers with an explanation and analysis of the public law of the UK including the impact of constitutional reforms. The decisions of the Administrative Court and the availability of rights under the European Convention on Human Rights under the Human Rights Act 1998 continue to have far-reaching significance. Judges may declare legislation incompatible with the Convention and Parliament is provided with a fast-track procedure to alter legislation to bring the law into compatibility. The UK's Supreme Court is influenced by the jurisprudence of the European Court of Human Rights in Strasbourg.

There are major innovations in parliamentary reform. Some were put in place some years ago, for example the formation of the House of Lords Select Committee on the Constitution to keep under review the operation of the constitution and to consider the constitutional implications of public bills coming before the House. Others are more recent such as the election of chairs of Select Committees by MPs following the recommendations of the Public Administration Committee (Chair Tony Wright) in 2009. This has marked a major step forward in select committee scrutiny of the Executive. The establishment of the Parliamentary Commission on Banking Standards in 2012 (Chair Andrew Tyrie) is another example. This has additional powers and rights not normally given to Select Committees and involves members from the Lords and Commons. It has provided a useful model for the future growth in committee scrutiny. In 2012, the Liaison Committee in its review of select committees sought greater clarity in their role and powers. The Joint Committee in Human Rights and its legal adviser provides a useful source of standards and legal advice to law makers at a time of political and economic uncertainty. Still other reforms are in the planning stages such as proposed changes to the powers of local government including greater financial autonomy. Reform of the House of Lords is still being debated. The Strathclyde Review (December 2015) of the relationship between the House of Commons and the House of Lords over the decision of the House of Lords to twice amend a motion and decline to implement a statutory instrument to implement the Government's policy on tax credits, is likely to raise questions about the general powers of the House of Lords. More generally, the House of Commons Political and Constitutional Reform Committee (2014) produced a codified form of the UK's Constitution as well as a Draft Bill containing a written constitution for the UK may provide a useful blue- print for a written constitution, though this is unlikely in the short term.

The courts are also active in the development of case law, particularly with an enlarged jurisdiction under the Human Rights Act 1998. Substantial legislative changes dominate the influences on public law today. Significantly, these include: the Constitutional Reform and Governance Act 2010; Disability Act 2010; Local Government Act 2011; European Union Act 2011; Localism Act 2011 and Fixed Term Parliaments Act 2011; Crime and Courts Act 2013; Defamation Act 2013; Scottish Independence Referendum 2013; Wales Act 2014; House of Lords Reform Act 2014; Local Audit and Accountability Act 2014; Deregulation Act 2015; Modern Slavery Act 2015; Serious Crime Act 2015; and Recall of MPs Act 2015.

It is inevitable that for reasons of space, the main focus of the book is on the public law that is applicable to England. Developments in Scotland, Wales and Northern Ireland under devolution are examined and points of comparison are made whenever relevant. It is increasingly clear that the asymmetrical nature of our constitutional arrangements today gives rise to a developing specialism in each jurisdiction and will inevitably lead to greater diversity in the legal and constitutional arrangements in the UK. Increasingly the UK's constitutional arrangements appear to become focused on a predominantly English constitution and less regard for any consequences for the Union.

Proposals for devolution to mega cities and regions in England are likely to increase diversity in public sector delivery in the UK. At the time of writing there are bills before Parliament on Scotland, the Scotland Bill 2015/16 and on further devolution to local authorities, the Cities and Local Government Devolution Bill 2015/16. Significant reforms are planned in the area of data and communications in the Draft Investigatory Powers Bill in November 2015. Clauses 72 and 73 of the Bill provide a power for the Secretary of State to require the retention of communications data and including IP addresses, internet connection records and e mail addresses. There is considerable controversy over the use of such powers and their application to communications data.

The scale of the constitutional and administrative reforms set out above, have resulted in a number of substantial changes and re-writing of major parts of this book. First the format has been altered to accommodate a student focus in learning about public law. There is the addition of a section at the end of each chapter highlighting the key issues and conclusions. The bibliographical section has been supplemented. At the end of each chapter there is a section on additional reading.

There has been some re-organisation of the book necessitated by new developments. Attention is given to the impact the devolved system of government, with additional powers to Scotland, will have on the UK. There are proposals and discussion about future changes such as powers associated with devolution to Scotland including enhanced financial autonomy, and perhaps further powers to Wales and Northern Ireland and suggestions for devolution to England and "Mega Cities". The chapter on local government has taken account of some of the recent changes in the governance of local authorities.

Chapter 12 on public finance is a revised version of J. F. McEldowney's, "Public Expenditure and the Control of Public Finance" in J. Jowell, D. Oliver and C. O'Cinneide (eds), *The Changing Constitution* (Oxford: Oxford University Press, 2015), pp.350–377.

Finally, I would like to thank Sweet & Maxwell who provided support in the work of producing the book. I am also grateful to the University of Warwick for a term of sabbatical leave. I am most grateful to my colleagues for their support and most of all to Sharron and Emma for their advice and understanding.

April 2016

Contents

Preface ix
Table of Cases xxv
Table of Statutes lix
Table of Statutory Instruments lxxvii

Part I General Introduction

1 The Public Law of the United Kingdom: Definition and Scope   1-001
    A: Introduction   1-001
    B: The Aims and Functions of Public Law   1-005
    C: Evolving and Changing Public Law   1-011
    D: Constitutional Reform in its Historical Context   1-021
    E: The essential characteristics of the United Kingdom's Constitution   1-027
    F: Summary and Conclusions   1-033
    Further Reading

2 The Asymmetrical Constitution: The Structure of the United Kingdom   2-001
    A: Introduction   2-001
    B: The sources of constitutional law and the composition of the United Kingdom   2-002
        England   2-007
        Wales   2-011
        Scotland   2-013
        Ireland   2-021
    C: Devolution   2-034
        Administrative devolution   2-035
        Proposals for devolution in the 1970s   2-038
        Devolution Acts of 1998 and their significance   2-041
    D: Devolution in Scotland, Wales and Northern Ireland   2-045
        General   2-045
        Some common characteristics of devolution   2-047
        The Electorate in Wales and Scotland   2-055
        The Electorate in Northern Ireland   2-056

The Electorate in London	2-057
E: Devolution in England	2-065
England	2-065
London	2-066
English regions	2-068
F: Devolution in Wales	2-069
The Government of Wales Acts 1998 and 2006	2-069
The Silk Commission Review: Finance and Legislation	2-076
The Draft Wales Bill 2015–16	2-080
G: Devolution in Scotland	2-081
The Scotland Act 1998	2-082
The Scotland Act 2012	2-087
The Role of the Courts	2-089
The Scottish referendum and the Smith Commission Agreement	2-090
The Scotland Bill 2015/16	2-092
H: Devolution in Northern Ireland	2-094
Northern Ireland	2-094
I: The Northern Ireland Act 1998	2-095
J: Co-ordinating Devolution and the UK Parliament	2-101
The West Lothian question and English votes for English laws	2-102
Legislative Consent Motions	2-110
Parliamentary Procedures and Select and Grand Committees	2-112
The constitutional implications of UK devolution	2-118
The Supreme Court and the Judicial Committee of the Privy Council	2-121
The Commonwealth Charter	2-124
K: Europe and the Europeanisation of UK law	2-126
The European Commission	2-130
The Council of the European Union	2-137
The European Council	2-141
The European Parliament	2-142
The European Court of Justice	2-146
The European Court of Auditors	2-151
L: Sovereignty and the United Kingdom Parliament	2-155
M: The Future Constitutional Arrangements in the UK: Some Conclusions	2-164
N: Summary and Conclusions	2-166
Further Reading	
3 Parliament	3-001
A: Introduction	3-001
B: Parliament, Government and the Doctrine of the Separation of Powers	3-010

C: Parliament's Role	3-020
D: Procedures and processes in enacting legislation	3-039
Pre-legislative scrutiny	3-041
Post-legislative scrutiny	3-042
Forms of Legislation	3-044
English Votes for English Laws	3-049
Private Members' Bills	3-050
Private Bills	3-054
Hybrid Bills	3-056
E: Drafting and Interpreting Legislation	3-068
(i) The Literal Rule	3-078
(ii) The Golden Rule	3-079
(iii) The Mischief Rule	3-080
(iv) The Ejusdem Generis Rule	3-081
(v) Human rights as an aid to interpretation	3-082
(vi) "Constitutional statutes" and their interpretation	3-085
F: The Deregulation Agenda	3-089
Debate and scrutiny	3-092
G: Parliament—Fulfilling Public Expectations?	3-105
Parliament and Public Engagement	3-108
Parliament, the Crown and prerogative	3-109
H: The House of Lords	3-119
I: The Salisbury Convention: The House of Commons and House of Lords at work	3-132
J: Reforming the House of Lords?	3-134
Before 1999	3-135
After the House of Lords Act 1999	3-142
The Strathclyde Review (December 2015)	3-150
Composition	3-151
Select Committees	3-153
K: Parliamentary Privileges	3-157
The nature of Privileges	3-157
Regulating financial and other interests	3-170
L: Summary and Conclusions	3-175
Further Reading	
4 Government	**4-001**
A: Introduction	4-001
B: Governing under the UK's Constitution	4-005
C: Defining Central and Local Government	4-019
D: Crown and Prerogative	4-028
Definition and Review	4-028

E: The Prerogative in Foreign Affairs	4–056
F: The Crown and the Government	4–067
The personal powers of the Sovereign	4–070
G: Cabinet and Prime Minister	4–075
Powers and functions	4–075
Special advisers	4–110
Collective and individual ministerial responsibility	4–111
The Scott Report and ministerial responsibility	4–117
Collective responsibility	4–141
H: The Civil Service	4–151
Definition	4–152
Role and function of the Civil Service	4–162
I: Summary and Conclusions	4–170
Further Reading	

5   The Rule of Law and Constitutional Conventions   5–001

A: Introduction	5–001
B: Conventions	5–007
C: The Rule of Law	5–043
D: Contemporary Debate on Judicial Discretion, the Rule of Law and the Sovereignty of Parliament	5–065
E: Summary and Conclusions	5–074
Further Reading	

6   An Introduction to Administrative Law   6–001

A: Introduction	6–003
B: Administrative Law and Administration in its Historical Perspective	6–014
State intervention and legislation	6–023
Courts, lawyers and legal techniques	6–036
Allocation of functions	6–060
C: Legislation, Guidance, Codes of Practice and Delegated Legislation	6–065
D: Prerogative Powers, Licences and Contracts	6–076
E: Central and Local Government	6–093
Types of agencies	6–099
Fringe organisations and statutory bodies	6–101
F: Courts	6–109
The Judiciary and the Administration of Justice	6–109
The development of judicial review	6–142
G: The Human Rights Act 1998	6–156
H: Tribunals and Inquiries	6–163
I: Summary and Conclusions	6–184
Further Reading	

PART II Public Law, Politics, Ideas and Influences

7 The Electorate, Politics and the Constitution — 7–001
  A: Introduction — 7–001
  B: What are Electoral Systems Intended to Achieve? — 7–005
  C: Parliamentary Democracy, Origins, Ideas and Influences — 7–014
    Dicey, parliamentary sovereignty and popular democracy — 7–018
    Parliamentary franchise 1832–1948 — 7–030
  D: The Electorate — 7–039
    The Electoral Registration and Administration Act 2013 and individual registration — 7–044
    Constituency boundaries — 7–045
    The Electoral Commission — 7–066
  E: Election Campaign and Finance — 7–068
    Registration — 7–068
    Election expenses and accounting requirements — 7–070
    Elections and the Media — 7–072
    "Purdah" at central and local elections and referendums — 7–084
    Europe — 7–088
  F: Manifesto, Mandate and Pressure Groups — 7–092
    Manifesto and mandate — 7–092
    Pressure groups — 7–110
  G: Electoral Reform — 7–122
    First Past the Post — 7–123
    The aims and objectives of the electoral system — 7–130
  H: Single Transferable Vote — 7–137
    Regional List System — 7–140
    Additional Member System — 7–142
    Supplementary Vote — 7–144
    Alternative Vote — 7–146
  I: Referendums — 7–153
  J: Summary and Conclusions — 7–163
  Further Reading

8 Public Law and Legal Thought — 8–001
  A: Introduction — 8–001
  B: Contemporary Issues and Debates — 8–004
  C: The Common Law Tradition — 8–017
  D: The Historical Legacy — 8–040
  E: The Science of Law — 8–051
  F: Dicey and his Contemporaries — 8–068
  G: Public Law and Political Change — 8–089

H: Public Law in the Twenty-First Century	8–106
I: Human Rights and Public Law	8–111
J: Summary and Conclusions	8–121
Further Reading	

9 The European Union — 9–001

A: Introduction	9–001
Economic governance	9–004
Competitiveness	9–005
Sovereignty	9–006
Social benefits and free movement	9–007
B: Evolving Europe	9–013
Membership of the European Union	9–015
C: Evaluating Membership of the European Union	9–023
D: The European Union Institutions and Structures	9–026
Council and Commission	9–028
The Commission	9–034
The European Council	9–039
The European Parliament	9–041
The Court of Justice of the European Union	9–047
E: The Jurisprudence of the European Court	9–053
F: Sources of European Union Law	9–070
G: The European Court of Auditors	9–086
H: Europeanisation and the Creation of a European Public Law	9–091
I: The European Convention on Human Rights and Fundamental Freedoms and European Union Law	9–096
J: Conclusions and Summary	9–103
Further Reading	

PART III Government, Regulation and Accountability

10 Government and Accountability — 10–001

A: Introduction	10–001
B: Accountability Defined	10–005
C: The Scott Report and Parliament	10–019
D: The Party System	10–023
E: The Role of Parliament	10–037
Scrutiny and passage of legislation	10–041
Pre- and post-legislative scrutiny	10–052
Select committees	10–054
F: Parliamentary reform: The way forward?	10–070

  Parliamentary debate and ministerial responsibility   10-072
 G: Government and the Crown   10-079
  Ministers and public interest immunity   10-079
 H: Government and Secrecy   10-112
 I: Summary and Conclusions   10-128
 Further Reading

11 Beyond New Public Management and the State   11-001
 A: Introduction   11-001
 B: Civil Service: Evolution, Change and the Managing of Government   11-007
 C: Management Techniques: New Public Management and beyond   11-012
 D: The Development of Agencies   11-019
 E: Agencies, Accountability and Control   11-034
 F: Civil Servants and Ministers   11-052
 G: Formulating Systems of Accountability   11-057
 H: BSE—a Case Study of Crisis Management, Policy Making and Problem Solving   11-063
 I: Beyond New Public Management and the Future   11-074
 J: Summary and Conclusions   11-086
 Further Reading

12 Public Finance   12-001
 A: Introduction   12-001
 B: The System of Planning and Financial Control   12-004
  Public revenue   12-006
  The Treasury, planning and financial control   12-013
  The Accounting Officer   12-023
 C: Planning and Controlling Public Expenditure   12-028
  The Bank of England   12-032
  The Private Finance Initiative   12-037
 D: Devolution and Funding of the Scottish Parliament, National Assembly for Wales and the Northern Ireland Assembly   12-041
 E: Parliament and the Control of Public Expenditure   12-048
  Supply procedures and the Consolidated Fund   12-054
  The Treasury and departmental controls over public expenditure   12-063
 F: Resource Accounting   12-070
 G: The Contingencies Fund   12-073
 H: The Committee of Public Accounts (PAC), Select Committees and the Comptroller and Auditor General (C & AG) and Audit   12-077
  Certification audit   12-085
  Value for money examinations   12-088
 I: The Courts   12-096

J: Summary and Conclusions ... 12–099
Further Reading

13 Local Government ... 13–001
A: Introduction ... 13–001
B: Transforming Local Government in an Era of Change ... 13–006
    Phase One: 1979–1997 ... 13–007
    Phase two: 1997–2002 ... 13–010
    Phase three: The era of Localism under the Localism Act 2011 and decentralisation strategies ... 13–018
    The Influence of the "Big Society" ... 13–019
C: Local Authorities, Organisation and Structure ... 13–020
    England ... 13–021
    London ... 13–021
    The modern functions of local authorities ... 13–024
    The Cities and Local Government Devolution Act 2016 ... 13–031
    Elections ... 13–032
D: Change and Structure in Local Government ... 13–040
    Structure and organisation ... 13–040
    Competitive tendering for local authority services ... 13–046
    Private finance initiative projects ... 13–049
    Central-local government relations ... 13–050
    Local Authority Finance ... 13–051
E: Judicial Oversight and Local Authority Activities ... 13–068
    Controls over local government expenditure ... 13–079
F: Audit and Accountability ... 13–096
G: Summary and Conclusions ... 13–103
Further Reading

14 Privatisation and Regulation ... 14–001
A: Introduction ... 14–001
B: Nationalisation Policy and Structures ... 14–006
C: Privatisation Policy and Objectives ... 14–010
D: Regulation Structures and Techniques ... 14–014
    The Role of the Courts ... 14–016
E: Regulating and Privatising the Utilities ... 14–020
    British Telecom ... 14–020
    The Office of Communications Act 2002 ... 14–026
    Energy and natural resources utilities ... 14–027
    Gas ... 14–028
    Electricity ... 14–045
    The Utilities Act 2000 ... 14–057

Water	14–061
The Water Act 2014	14–071
F: The Broader Regulatory Structure: Learning from Experience	14–074
G: Summary and Conclusions	14–082
Further Reading	

Part IV Citizens' Grievances, Human Rights and Civil Liberties

15 Citizens' Grievances — 15–001
- A: Introduction — 15–001
- B: Informal Mechanisms of Complaint and MPs — 15–006
- C: Tribunals and Inquiries — 15–013
    - *Tribunals* — 15–013
    - *The Leggatt Review of the Tribunal System* — 15–025
    - *The Tribunals Court and Enforcement Act 2007* — 15–026
- D: Inquiries — 15–034
    - *The Inquiries Act 2005* — 15–068
    - *The Chilcot Inquiry* — 15–070
    - *The Independent Inquiry into Child Sexual Abuse (Lowell Goddard)* — 15–071
    - *Inspectorates* — 15–072
- E: Ombudsmen: Local and Central — 15–073
    - *Central Government* — 15–073
    - *Local Commissioners for Administration* — 15–101
    - *The European Ombudsman* — 15–115
    - *Reforming the Ombudsman System* — 15–116
- F: Summary and Conclusions — 15–118
- Further Reading

16 Human Rights and Civil Liberties — 16–001
- A: Introduction — 16–001
- B: The Human Rights Act 1998 — 16–004
    - *The method of incorporation of the European Convention on Human Rights* — 16–004
    - *Parliament and the Human Rights Act* — 16–010
    - *The scope of the Human Rights Act 1998* — 16–012
    - *Territorial scope and the theatre of war* — 16–015
    - *The Human Rights Act and public bodies* — 16–021
    - *Interpreting the Human Rights Act 1998 and policy considerations* — 16–027
- C: The European Convention on Human Rights — 16–041
    - *Citizens' rights and citizenship* — 16–066
- D: Religion and Race — 16–078

Human rights and euthanasia	16–084
Freedom of religion and the criminal law	16–090
E: Work	16–102
F: Immigration, Citizenship and Extradition	16–107
Citizenship and the right of abode	16–107
Immigration rules and procedures	16–113
Asylum	16–115
Refugee or humanitarian protection	16–122
The Immigration Bill 2015–16	16–122
Deportation	16–123
G: Personal Freedom and Police powers	16–125
Arrest	16–131
Search and seizure	16–139
Interrogation of suspects	16–142
Accountability of the police	16–152
Complaints against the police	16–155
Reform proposals and work in progress	16–161
H: Summary and Conclusions	16–162
Further Reading	

17 Judicial Review 17–001

A: Introduction	17–001
B: The Classification of Administrative Decision-making	17–008
Statutory appeals	17–014
The application for judicial review: public and private Law	17–021
Judicial review: overall policy and trends	17–051
Grounds for review	17–059
Ultra vires and excess of jurisdiction	17–062
C: Abuse of Discretion	17–092
D: Proportionality	17–103
E: Legitimate Expectations	17–107
F: Natural Justice	17–110
The duty to act fairly	17–113
G: Excluding Judicial Review	17–129
H: What is the Impact of Public Law Litigation?	17–140
I: Summary and Conclusions	17–142
Further Reading	

18 Remedies 18–001

A: Introduction	18–001
B: Forms of Relief	18–003
C: The Law of Standing	18–011

Standing in private law	18–017
Standing in public law	18–021
Pressure groups and standing	18–033
Rules of standing and the role of the courts	18–053
D: Public Law Remedies	18–059
Procedural matters	18–059
The discretionary nature of remedies	18–067
Void and voidable administrative action	18–073
Certiorari (a Quashing Order), Prohibition (a Prohibiting Order) and Mandamus (a Mandatory Order)	18–077
Habeas Corpus	18–086
E: Private Law Remedies	18–089
Declaration and injunction	18–090
The Crown	18–104
Discovery, damages and restitution	18–106
Tort and contract liability of public authorities	18–108
F: Summary and Conclusions	18–117
Further Reading	

PART V Public Law and Conflict

19 Public Order and The Freedom of Assembly — 19–001

A: Introduction	19–001
B: Historical Perspectives	19–006
C: Police Powers	19–012
Public meetings and assemblies	19–012
Public processions	19–014
Breach of the peace	19–043
Offences under the Public Order Act 1986	19–054
The management of demonstrations and techniques of "kettling"	19–072
Police organisation and accountability	19–073
The Intelligence Services' functions and policing	19–088
D: Military Powers, States of Emergency and Terrorism	19–092
Legal liability and the use of force	19–110
The Terrorism Act 2000	19–118
Police and Investigative powers in response to terrorism	19–126
Control orders	19–134
Terrorism and human rights	19–140
UK Judicial Scrutiny over information obtained abroad and the Norwich Pharmacal Principle	19–142
Closed Material Procedure and the Justice and Security Act 2013	19–147

E: Summary and Conclusions   19–153
Further Reading

20 Secrecy, Freedom of Expression And The State   20-001
  A: Introduction   20-001
  B: Open Government and Official Secrets   20-007
      Official secrets legislation   20-017
  C: The Security Services   20-041
      The Draft Investigatory Powers Bill 2015/16   20-072
  D: Press and Media   20-078
      The BBC   20-094
      Charter renewal and the BBC   20-102
      Commercial broadcasting   20-103
  E: Freedom of Expression   20-110
      The Public Interest Disclosure Act 1998 and the Freedom of Information Act 2000   20-110
      The Evolving Criminal Law   20-119
      The Defamation Act 2013   20-127
      Contempt of court   20-131
  F: Summary and Conclusions   20-140
  Further Reading

21 Public Law in the Twenty-First Century   21-001
  A: Introduction   21-001
  B: Continuity and Change—the Developing Constitution   21-009
      Constitutional reforms and future directions   21-012
  C: A Written Constitution for the UK?   21-018
      English votes of English laws and implications for the legislative process   21-025
  D: Public Law Scholarship   21-029
  Further Reading

Bibliography   *825*
Index   *845*

Table of Cases

A (Children) (Conjoined Twins: Medical Treatment) (No.1), Re [2001] Fam. 147; [2001] 2 W.L.R. 480; [2000] 4 All E.R. 961; [2001] 1 F.L.R. 1; [2000] 3 F.C.R. 577; [2000] H.R.L.R. 721; [2001] U.K.H.R.R. 1; 9 B.H.R.C. 261; [2000] Lloyd's Rep. Med. 425; (2001) 57 B.M.L.R. 1; [2001] Crim. L.R. 400; [2001] Fam. Law 18; (2000) 150 N.L.J. 1453   18-055

A v Secretary of State for the Home Department [2004] UKHL 56; [2005] 2 A.C. 68; [2005] 2 W.L.R. 87; [2005] 3 All E.R. 169; [2005] H.R.L.R. 1; [2005] U.K.H.R.R. 175; 17 B.H.R.C. 496; [2005] Imm. A.R. 103; (2005) 155 N.L.J. 23; (2005) 149 S.J.L.B. 28   16-011, 16-019, 19-141, 19-148

A v United Kingdom (3455/05) (2009) 49 E.H.R.R. 29; 26 B.H.R.C. 1   19-148, 19-151

AB v Home Department. *See* R. (on the application of AB) v Secretary of State for the Home Department

Abbassy v Commissioner of Police of the Metropolis [1990] 1 W.L.R. 385; [1990] 1 All E.R. 193; (1990) 90 Cr. App. R. 250; [1990] R.T.R. 164; (1989) 139 N.L.J. 1266.   16-134

Adams v Scottish Ministers 2003 S.C. 171; 2003 S.L.T. 366; 2002 S.C.L.R. 881; [2002] U.K.H.R.R. 1189; 2002 G.W.D. 26-879   21-051

Air Canada v Secretary of State for Trade (No.2) [1983] 2 A.C. 394; [1983] 2 W.L.R. 494; [1983] 1 All E.R. 910   18-106

Airedale NHS Trust v Bland [1993] A.C. 789; [1993] 2 W.L.R. 316; [1993] 1 All E.R. 821; [1993] 1 F.L.R. 1026; [1994] 1 F.C.R. 485; [1993] 4 Med. L.R. 39; (1993) 12 B.M.L.R. 64; [1993] Fam. Law 473; (1993) 143 N.L.J. 199   16-084

Al-Jedda v United Kingdom (27021/08) (2011) 53 E.H.R.R. 23; 30 B.H.R.C. 637   16-016

Al-Skeini v Defence Secretary. *See* R. (on the application of Al-Skeini) v Secretary of State for Defence

Al-Skeini v United Kingdom (55721/07) (2011) 53 E.H.R.R. 18; 30 B.H.R.C. 561; [2011] Inquest L.R. 73   16-015, 16-016

Alfred Crompton Amusement Machines Ltd v Customs and Excise Commissioners (No.2) [1974] A.C. 405; [1973] 3 W.L.R. 268; [1972] 1 W.L.R. 833; [1973] 2 All E.R. 1169; (1973) 117 S.J. 602   10-085

Ambrose v Harris [2011] UKSC 43; [2011] 1 W.L.R. 2435; 2012 S.C. (U.K.S.C.) 53; 2011 S.L.T. 1005; 2011 S.C.L. 866; 2011 S.C.C.R. 651; [2012] H.R.L.R. 1; [2011] U.K.H.R.R. 1159; (2011) 108(40) L.S.G. 21; 2011 G.W.D. 31-667   3-083

American Cyanamid Co v Ethicon Ltd [1975] A.C. 396; [1975] 2 W.L.R. 316; [1975] 1 All E.R. 504; [1975] F.S.R. 101; [1975] R.P.C. 513; (1975) 119 S.J. 136   18-097

Amministrazione delle Finanze dello Stato v Simmenthal SpA (106/77) EU:C:1978:49; [1978] E.C.R. 629; [1978] 3 C.M.L.R. 263   2-161

Animal Defenders International v United Kingdom. *See* R. (on the application of Animal Defenders International) v Secretary of State for Culture, Media and Sport

Anisminic Ltd v Foreign Compensation Commission [1969] 2 A.C. 147; [1969] 2 W.L.R. 163; [1969] 1 All E.R. 208; (1968) 113 S.J. 55   17–086, 17–087, 17–135, 18–075

Anns v Merton LBC [1978] A.C. 728; [1977] 2 W.L.R. 1024; [1977] 2 All E.R. 492; 75 L.G.R. 555; (1977) 243 E.G. 523; (1988) 4 Const. L.J. 100; [1977] J.P.L. 514; (1987) 84 L.S.G. 319; (1987) 137 N.L.J. 794; (1977) 121 S.J. 377   18–110

Anufrijeva v Southwark LBC [2003] EWCA Civ 1406; [2004] Q.B. 1124; [2004] 2 W.L.R. 603; [2004] 1 All E.R. 833; [2004] 1 F.L.R. 8; [2003] 3 F.C.R. 673; [2004] H.R.L.R. 1; [2004] U.K.H.R.R. 1; 15 B.H.R.C. 526; [2004] H.L.R. 22; [2004] B.L.G.R. 184; (2003) 6 C.C.L. Rep. 415; [2004] Fam. Law 12; (2003) 100(44) L.S.G. 30   18–115

Arthur JS Hall and Co v Simmons [2002] 1 A.C. 615; [2000] 3 W.L.R. 543; [2000] 3 All E.R. 673; [2000] B.L.R. 407; [2000] E.C.C. 487; [2000] 2 F.L.R. 545; [2000] 2 F.C.R. 673; [2001] P.N.L.R. 6; [2000] Fam. Law 806; [2000] E.G. 99 (C.S.); (2000) 97(32) L.S.G. 38; (2000) 150 N.L.J. 1147; (2000) 144 S.J.L.B. 238; [2000] N.P.C. 87   6–139

Associated Picture Houses Ltd v Wednesbury Corp [1948] 1 K.B. 223; [1947] 2 All E.R. 680; (1947) 63 T.L.R. 623; (1948) 112 J.P. 55; 45 L.G.R. 635; [1948] L.J.R. 190; (1947) 177 L.T. 641; (1948) 92 S.J. 26   1–013, 5–063, 13–068, 13–092, 17–096, 17–097, 17–100—17–104, 17–107, 20–068

Aston Canlow and Wilmcote with Billesley Parochial Church Council v Wallbank [2003] UKHL 37; [2004] 1 A.C. 546; [2003] 3 W.L.R. 283; [2003] 3 All E.R. 1213; [2003] H.R.L.R. 28; [2003] U.K.H.R.R. 919; [2003] 27 E.G. 137 (C.S.); (2003) 100(33) L.S.G. 28; (2003) 153 N.L.J. 1030; (2003) 147 S.J.L.B. 812; [2003] N.P.C. 80   16–022, 16–026

Attorney General v Associated Newspapers Group Plc [1989] 1 W.L.R. 322; [1989] 1 All E.R. 604; [1989] C.O.D. 256; (1988) 138 N.L.J. Rep. 305; (1988) 132 S.J. 1639   20–136

Attorney General v Associated Newspapers Ltd [2012] EWHC 2029 (Admin); [2012] A.C.D. 98   20–139

Attorney General v Bates (1606) 2 St. Tr. 371   2–019

Attorney General v Blake [2001] 1 A.C. 268; [2000] 3 W.L.R. 625; [2000] 4 All E.R. 385; [2000] 2 All E.R. (Comm) 487; [2001] I.R.L.R. 36; [2001] Emp. L.R. 329; [2000] E.M.L.R. 949; (2000) 23(12) I.P.D. 23098; (2000) 97(32) L.S.G. 37; (2000) 150 N.L.J. 1230; (2000) 144 S.J.L.B. 242   4–147, 20–040

Attorney General v Crayford UDC [1962] Ch. 575; [1962] 2 W.L.R. 998; [1962] 2 All E.R. 147; [1962] 1 Lloyd's Rep. 163; (1962) 126 J.P. 308; 60 L.G.R. 261; (1962) 106 S.J. 175   17–067

Attorney General v De Keysers Royal Hotel Ltd. *See* De Keyser's Royal Hotel Ltd, Re

Attorney General v Fulham Corp [1921] 1 Ch. 440 Ch D   17–064

Attorney General v Guardian Newspapers Ltd (No.1) [1987] 1 W.L.R. 1248; [1987] 3 All E.R. 316; [1989] 2 F.S.R. 81; (1987) 84 L.S.G. 2689; (1987) 137 N.L.J. 785; (1987) 131 S.J. 1122   4–146

Attorney General v Guardian Newspapers Ltd (No.2). See Attorney General v Observer Ltd

Attorney General v Jonathan Cape Ltd [1976] Q.B. 752; [1975] 3 W.L.R. 606; [1975] 3 All E.R. 484; (1975) 119 S.J. 696   4-085, 4-143—4-146, 5-004, 5-014, 10-089, 10-116, 20-016, 20-034

Attorney General v MGN Ltd [2011] EWHC 2074 (Admin); [2012] 1 W.L.R. 2408; [2012] 1 Cr. App. R. 1; [2012] E.M.L.R. 9; [2012] A.C.D. 13; (2011) 155(32) S.J.L.B. 23   20-139

Attorney General v New Statesman and Nation Publishing Co [1981] Q.B. 1; [1980] 2 W.L.R. 246; [1980] 1 All E.R. 644; (1980) 70 Cr. App. R. 193; [1980] Crim. L.R. 236; (1980) 124 S.J. 101   20-136

Attorney General v News Groups Newspapers Ltd [1989] Q.B. 110; [1988] 3 W.L.R. 163; [1988] 2 All E.R. 906; (1988) 87 Cr. App. R. 323; (1988) 138 N.L.J. Rep. 55; (1988) 132 S.J. 934   20-136

Attorney General v Observer Ltd [1990] 1 A.C. 109; [1988] 3 W.L.R. 776; [1988] 3 All E.R. 545; [1989] 2 F.S.R. 181; (1988) 85(42) L.S.G. 45; (1988) 138 N.L.J. Rep. 296; (1988) 132 S.J. 1496   4-146, 10-117, 11-018, 20-016, 20-034, 20-038, 20-039, 20-041, 20-045

Attorney General v Times Newspapers Ltd [1974] A.C. 273; [1973] 3 W.L.R. 298; [1973] 3 All E.R. 54; (1973) 117 S.J. 617   16-055, 20-131

Attorney General for Northern Ireland's Reference (No.1 of 1975) [1977] A.C. 105; [1976] 3 W.L.R. 235; [1976] 2 All E.R. 937; (1976) 120 S.J. 524   19-097

Auckland Harbour Board v The King [1925] A.C. 318 PC (NZ)   12-096

Austin v Commissioner of Police of the Metropolis [2009] UKHL 5; [2009] 1 A.C. 564; [2009] 2 W.L.R. 372; [2009] 3 All E.R. 455; [2009] H.R.L.R. 16; [2009] U.K.H.R.R. 581; 26 B.H.R.C. 642; [2009] Po. L.R. 66; (2009) 153(4) S.J.L.B. 29   19-072

Austin v United Kingdom (39692/09) (2012) 55 E.H.R.R. 14; 32 B.H.R.C. 618; [2012] Crim. L.R. 544   19-072

AXA General Insurance Ltd, Petitioners [2011] UKSC 46; [2012] 1 A.C. 868; [2011] 3 W.L.R. 871; 2012 S.C. (U.K.S.C.) 122; 2011 S.L.T. 1061; [2012] H.R.L.R. 3; [2011] U.K.H.R.R. 1221; (2011) 122 B.M.L.R. 149; (2011) 108(41) L.S.G. 22   2-061, 2-063, 2-165, 21-051

Axa General Insurance v Lord Advocate. See AXA General Insurance Ltd, Petitioners

Ayr Harbour Trustees v Oswald (1883) 8 App. Cas. 623; (1883) 10 R. (H.L.) 85   17-073

B v Chief Constable of Northern Ireland [2015] EWHC 3691 (Admin); [2016] A.C.D. 30   19-111

Bank Mellat v HM Treasury [2010] EWCA Civ 483; [2012] Q.B. 91; [2010] 3 W.L.R. 1090; [2010] U.K.H.R.R. 760; [2010] Lloyd's Rep. F.C. 499   19-148

Bank Mellat v HM Treasury [2013] UKSC 38; [2014] A.C. 700; [2013] 4 All E.R. 495; [2013] Lloyd's Rep. F.C. 557   19-152

Bank Mellat v HM Treasury [2015] EWHC 1258 (Comm); [2016] 1 All E.R. (Comm) 766   19-152

Barraclough v Brown [1897] A.C. 615 HL   18-093

Barrett v Enfield LBC [2001] 2 A.C. 550; [1999] 3 W.L.R. 79; [1999] 3 All E.R. 193; [1999] 2 F.L.R. 426; [1999] 2 F.C.R. 434; (1999) 1 L.G.L.R. 829; [1999] B.L.G.R. 473; (1999) 11 Admin. L.R. 839; [1999] Ed. C.R. 833; (1999) 2 C.C.L. Rep.

203; [1999] P.I.Q.R. P272; (1999) 49 B.M.L.R. 1; [1999] Fam. Law 622; (1999) 96(28) L.S.G. 27; (1999) 143 S.J.L.B. 183   18–110
Barrs v Bethell [1982] Ch. 294; [1981] 3 W.L.R. 874; [1982] 1 All E.R. 106; 81 L.G.R. 269; (1981) 125 S.J. 808   18–020
Beatty v Gillbanks (1882) 15 Cox C.C. 138; (1882) L.R. QBD 308 QBD   19–035, 19–036
Belfast City Council v Miss Behavin' Ltd [2007] UKHL 19; [2007] 1 W.L.R. 1420; [2007] 3 All E.R. 1007; [2007] N.I. 89; [2007] H.R.L.R. 26; [2008] B.L.G.R. 127; [2007] L.L.R. 312; (2007) 104(19) L.S.G. 27; (2007) 151 S.J.L.B. 575   17–105
Belmarsh Case. *See* A v Secretary of State for the Home Department
Benwell, Ex p. *See* R. v Secretary of State for the Home Department Ex p. Benwell
Board of Education v Rice [1911] A.C. 179   8–087
Boddington v British Transport Police [1999] 2 A.C. 143; [1998] 2 W.L.R. 639; [1998] 2 All E.R. 203; (1998) 162 J.P. 455; (1998) 10 Admin. L.R. 321; (1998) 148 N.L.J. 515   17–042, 17–049
Bourgoin SA v Ministry of Agriculture [1986] Q.B. 716; [1985] 3 W.L.R. 1027; [1985] 3 All E.R. 585; [1986] 1 C.M.L.R. 267; (1985) 82 L.S.G. 3435   18–111
Bowden v South West Water Services [1999] 3 C.M.L.R. 180; [1999] Eu. L.R. 573; [1999] Env. L.R. 438   2–161
Bowles v Bank of England [1913] 1 Ch. 57 Ch D   12–007, 12–097
Bowman v United Kingdom (24839/94) (1998) 26 E.H.R.R. 1; 4 B.H.R.C. 25; [1998] H.R.C.D. 273   7–077
Boyce v Paddington Corp [1903] 1 Ch. 109 Ch D   18–017, 18–020
British Oxygen Co Ltd v Minister of Technology [1971] A.C. 610; [1969] 2 W.L.R. 892; [1970] 3 W.L.R. 488; [1970] 3 All E.R. 165   12–007
British Railways Board v Pickin [1974] A.C. 765; [1974] 2 W.L.R. 208; [1974] 1 All E.R. 609; (1974) 118 S.J. 134   3–060
British Steel Corporation v Granada Television Ltd [1981] A.C. 1096; [1980] 3 W.L.R. 774; [1981] 1 All E.R. 417; (1980) 124 S.J. 812   20–138
British Steel Plc v Customs and Excise Commissioners (No.1) [1997] 2 All E.R. 366   17–041
Broadmoor Hospital v Hyde, *Times*, March 18, 1994; *Independent*, March 4, 1994   20–138
Brogan v United Kingdom (A/145-B) (1989) 11 E.H.R.R. 117   16–064
Bromley LBC v Greater London Council [1983] 1 A.C. 768; [1982] 2 W.L.R. 92; [1982] 1 All E.R. 153; (1982) 126 S.J. 16   7–099, 7–101, 13–074, 13–098, 17–066, 17–073, 17–096
Brooks v Commissioner of Police of the Metropolis [2005] UKHL 24; [2005] 1 W.L.R. 1495; [2005] 2 All E.R. 489; [2005] Po. L.R. 157; (2005) 155 N.L.J. 653   8–116
Bulmer v Bollinger [1974] Ch. 401; [1974] 3 W.L.R. 202; [1974] 2 All E.R. 1226; [1974] 2 C.M.L.R. 91; [1974] F.S.R. 334; [1975] R.P.C. 321; (1974) 118 S.J. 404   9–056
Burmah Oil Co (Burma Trading) Ltd v Lord Advocate [1965] A.C. 75; [1964] 2 W.L.R. 1231; [1964] 2 All E.R. 348; 1964 S.C. (H.L.) 117; 1964 S.L.T. 218; (1964) 108 S.J. 401   4–028, 4–054, 19–109
Burmah Oil Co Ltd v Bank of England [1980] A.C. 1090; [1979] 3 W.L.R. 722; [1979] 3 All E.R. 700; (1979) 123 S.J. 786   10–090, 10–093, 10–094, 12–007

Bushell v Secretary of State for the
    Environment [1981] A.C. 75; [1980] 3
    W.L.R. 22; [1980] 2 All E.R. 608; 78
    L.G.R. 269; (1980) 40 P. & C.R. 51; [1980]
    J.P.L. 458; (1981) 125 S.J. 168   17–116
Cambridge Water Co Ltd v Eastern Counties
    Leather Plc [1994] 2 A.C. 264; [1994] 2
    W.L.R. 53; [1994] 1 All E.R. 53; [1994] 1
    Lloyd's Rep. 261; [1994] Env. L.R. 105;
    [1993] E.G. 211 (C.S.); (1994) 144 N.L.J.
    15; (1994) 138 S.J.L.B. 24   18–110
Campbell and Cosans v United Kingdom
    (7511/76) (1982) 4 E.H.R.R. 293
    ECHR   16–052
Campbell and Fell v United Kingdom (A/80)
    (1985) 7 E.H.R.R. 165   16–050
Campbell v MGN Ltd (No.2) [2005] UKHL
    61; [2005] 1 W.L.R. 3394; [2005] 4 All
    E.R. 793; [2006] 1 Costs L.R. 120; [2006]
    E.M.L.R. 1; [2006] H.R.L.R. 2; 21 B.H.R.C.
    516; (2005) 102(42) L.S.G. 23; (2005)
    155 N.L.J. 1633   8–114
Canon Selwyn, Ex p. (1872) 36 JP Journal
    54   2–032
Carltona v Commissioners of Works [1943] 2
    All E.R. 560 CA   17–071
Case of Monopolies. See Darcy v Allin
Case of Proclamations, 77 E.R. 1352;
    (1610) 12 Co. Rep. 74; (1610) 2 St. Tr.
    723   2–019, 4–029, 4–045
Case of Prohibition del Roy (1607) 12 Co.
    Rep. 63   2–019
Chandler v DPP [1964] A.C. 763; [1962] 3
    W.L.R. 694; [1962] 3 All E.R. 142; (1962)
    46 Cr. App. R. 347; (1962) 106 S.J.
    588   20–019, 20–020
Chichester DC v Searle. See South
    Buckinghamshire DC v Porter (No.1)
Chief Adjudication Officer v Foster [1993]
    A.C. 754; [1993] 2 W.L.R. 292; [1993] 1
    All E.R. 705; [1993] C.O.D. 259; (1993)
    137 S.J.L.B. 36   3–084, 17–016

Chiron Corp v Murex Diagnostics Ltd (No.8)
    [1995] All E.R. (E.C.) 88; [1995] F.S.R.
    309   9–058
Clifford, Re [1921] 2 A.C. 570 HL   19–097
Cocks v Thanet DC [1983] 2 A.C. 286; [1982]
    3 W.L.R. 1121; [1982] 3 All E.R. 1135;
    (1983) 6 H.L.R. 15; 81 L.G.R. 81; [1984]
    R.V.R. 31; (1982) 126 S.J. 820   17–031,
    17–033, 17–039
Colhoun v Friel 1996 S.L.T. 1252
    HCJ   19–043
Commission of the European Communities
    v United Kingdom (C–222/94)
    EU:C:1996:314; [1996] E.C.R. I-4025;
    [1996] 3 C.M.L.R. 793; [1997] E.M.L.R.
    1   2–133
Commission of the European Communities
    v United Kingdom (C–382/92)
    EU:C:1994:233; [1994] E.C.R. I-2435;
    [1995] 1 C.M.L.R. 345; [1994] I.C.R. 664;
    [1994] I.R.L.R. 392   2–133
Commission of the European Communities
    v United Kingdom (C–61/81)
    EU:C:1996:314; [1982] E.C.R. 2601;
    [1982] 3 C.M.L.R. 284; [1982] I.C.R.
    578   2–133
Commission of the European Communities
    v United Kingdom (C–98/01) [2003]
    E.C.R. I-4641; [2003] 2 C.M.L.R. 19;
    [2003] All E.R. (EC) 878; [2003] C.E.C.
    425   2–133
Congreve v Home Office [1976] Q.B. 629;
    [1976] 2 W.L.R. 291; [1976] 1 All E.R. 697;
    (1975) 119 S.J. 847   12–008, 12–097,
    15–084, 18–007
Conservative and Unionist Central Office
    v Burrell [1982] 1 W.L.R. 522; [1982] 2
    All E.R. 1; [1982] S.T.C. 317; 55 T.C. 671;
    [1981] T.R. 543   7–084
Conway v Rimmer [1968] A.C. 910; [1968] 2
    W.L.R. 998; [1968] 1 All E.R. 874; (1968)
    112 S.J. 191   10–088, 10–090

Copeland v Ministry of Defence Unreported 19 May 1999 Northern Ireland   19-114

Corporate Officer of the House of Commons v Information Commissioner [2008] EWHC 1084 (Admin); [2009] 3 All E.R. 403; [2008] A.C.D. 71; (2008) 105(23) L.S.G. 24; (2008) 158 N.L.J. 751   3-174, 20-118

Costello v Chief Constable of Derbyshire [2001] EWCA Civ 381; [2001] 1 W.L.R. 1437; [2001] 3 All E.R. 150; [2001] 2 Lloyd's Rep. 216; [2001] Po. L.R. 83   16-155

Costello v Chief Constable of Northumbria [1999] 1 All E.R. 550; [1999] I.C.R. 752; (1999) 11 Admin. L.R. 81; (1999) 163 J.P.N. 634; (1998) 148 N.L.J. 1880   8-116

Council of Civil Service Unions v Minister for the Civil Service [1985] A.C. 374; [1984] 3 W.L.R. 1174; [1984] 3 All E.R. 935; [1985] I.C.R. 14; [1985] I.R.L.R. 28; (1985) 82 L.S.G. 437; (1984) 128 S.J. 837   1-013, 4-037, 4-046, 4-051, 4-158, 6-077, 6-151, 9-084, 16-058, 17-060, 17-096, 17-103, 17-107, 17-110, 17-116

Courage Ltd v Crehan (C-453/99) EU:C:2001:465; [2002] Q.B. 507; [2001] 3 W.L.R. 1646; [2001] E.C.R. I-6297; [2002] U.K.C.L.R. 171; [2001] 5 C.M.L.R. 28; [2001] All E.R. (EC) 886; [2001] C.E.C. 297; [2002] I.C.R. 457   2-161

Credit Suisse v Allerdale BC [1997] Q.B. 306; [1996] 3 W.L.R. 894; [1996] 4 All E.R. 129; [1996] 2 Lloyd's Rep. 241; [1996] 5 Bank. L.R. 249; (1997) 161 J.P. Rep. 88   6-087, 6-089, 13-071, 17-063

Credit Suisse v Waltham Forest LBC [1997] Q.B. 362; [1996] 3 W.L.R. 943; [1996] 4 All E.R. 176; (1997) 29 H.L.R. 115; 94 L.G.R. 686; (1997) 9 Admin. L.R. 517   6-089

Crossman Diaries case. *See* Attorney General v Jonathan Cape Ltd

D v National Society for the Prevention of Cruelty to Children [1978] A.C. 171; [1977] 2 W.L.R. 201; [1977] 1 All E.R. 589; 76 L.G.R. 5; (1977) 121 S.J. 119   10-095

Darcy v Allin, 77 E.R. 1260; (1602) 11 Co. Rep. 84b   2-019

Davy v Spelthorne BC [1984] A.C. 262; [1983] 3 W.L.R. 742; [1983] 3 All E.R. 278; 82 L.G.R. 193; (1984) 47 P. & C.R. 310; [1984] J.P.L. 269; (1983) 133 N.L.J. 1015; (1983) 127 S.J. 733   17-032, 17-033, 17-034

de Freitas v Permanent Secretary of the Ministry of Agriculture, Fisheries, Lands and Housing [1999] 1 A.C. 69; [1998] 3 W.L.R. 675; 4 B.H.R.C. 563; (1998) 142 S.J.L.B. 219 PC (Antigua and Barbuda)   17-105

De Keyser's Royal Hotel Ltd, Re [1920] A.C. 508 HL   4-053

Department for Education and Skills v Information Commissioner and Evening Standard (AP) EA/2006/006   20-117

Department of Constitutional Affairs v O'Brien [2013] UKSC 6; [2013] 1 W.L.R. 522; [2013] 2 All E.R. 1; [2013] I.C.R. 499; [2013] I.R.L.R. 315; [2013] Pens. L.R. 129   2-147, 9-066

Derbyshire CC v Times Newspapers Ltd [1992] Q.B. 770; [1992] 3 W.L.R. 28; [1992] 3 All E.R. 65; 90 L.G.R. 221; (1992) 4 Admin. L.R. 469; [1992] C.O.D. 305; (1992) 142 N.L.J. 276   13-075

Dimes v Grand Junction Canal Proprietors, 10 E.R. 301; (1852) 3 H.L. Cas. 759 HL   17-125

Director General of Fair Trading v Proprietary Association of Great Britain [2001] 1 W.L.R. 700; [2001] U.K.C.L.R. 550; [2001] I.C.R. 564; [2001] H.R.L.R. 17;

[2001] U.K.H.R.R. 429; (2001) 3 L.G.L.R. 32; (2001) 98(7) L.S.G. 40; (2001) 151 N.L.J. 17; (2001) 145 S.J.L.B. 29   16–013, 17–127

Doody v Secretary of State for the Home Department. *See* R. v Secretary of State for the Home Department Ex p. Doody

Douglas v Hello! Ltd (No.1) [2001] Q.B. 967; [2001] 2 W.L.R. 992; [2001] 2 All E.R. 289; [2001] E.M.L.R. 9; [2001] 1 F.L.R. 982; [2002] 1 F.C.R. 289; [2001] H.R.L.R. 26; [2001] U.K.H.R.R. 223; 9 B.H.R.C. 543; [2001] F.S.R. 40   8–114, 16–012, 20–004

Doyle v Northumbria Probation Committee [1991] 1 W.L.R. 1340; [1991] 4 All E.R. 294; [1992] I.C.R. 121; (1992) 89(7) L.S.G. 28; (1991) 141 N.L.J. 855   17–044, 17–045

DPP v Whyte [1972] A.C. 849; [1972] 3 W.L.R. 410; [1972] 3 All E.R. 12; (1973) 57 Cr. App. R. 74; [1972] Crim. L.R. 556; (1972) 116 S.J. 583   16–075

Dudgeon v United Kingdom (A/45) (1981) 4 E.H.R.R. 149 ECHR   16–053

Duncan v Cammell Laird & Co Ltd [1942] A.C. 624; [1942] 1 All E.R. 587; (1942) 73 Ll. L. Rep. 109; (1942) 86 S.J. 287   10–086, 10–088

Duncan v Jones [1936] 1 K.B. 218 KBD   19–039

Dyson v Attorney General [1911] 1 K.B. 410 CA   18–091

Earl Spencer v United Kingdom (28851/95) (1998) 25 E.H.R.R. CD 105   8–114, 20–004

East Riding of Yorkshire Council v Gibson [2000] 3 C.M.L.R. 329; [2000] I.C.R. 890; [2000] I.R.L.R. 598   9–054

Eba v Advocate General for Scotland [2011] UKSC 29; [2012] 1 A.C. 710; [2011] 3 W.L.R. 149; [2011] P.T.S.R. 1095; [2011] S.T.C. 1705; 2012 S.C. (U.K.S.C.) 1; 2011 S.L.T. 768; [2011] Imm. A.R. 745; [2011] S.T.I. 1941; (2011) 108(27) L.S.G. 24; (2011) 161 N.L.J. 917   6–175, 15–028

Edwards (Inspector of Taxes) v Bairstow [1956] A.C. 14; [1955] 3 W.L.R. 410; [1955] 3 All E.R. 48; 48 R. & I.T. 534; 36 T.C. 207; (1955) 34 A.T.C. 198; [1955] T.R. 209; (1955) 99 S.J. 558   17–019

Emmott v Minister for Social Welfare (C-208/90) EU:C:1991:333; [1991] E.C.R. I-4269; [1991] 3 C.M.L.R. 894; [1993] I.C.R. 8; [1991] I.R.L.R. 387   2–161

English v Emery Reimbold and Strick Ltd [2002] EWCA Civ 605; [2002] 1 W.L.R. 2409; [2002] 3 All E.R. 385; [2002] C.P.L.R. 520; [2003] I.R.L.R. 710; [2002] U.K.H.R.R. 957; (2002) 99(22) L.S.G. 34; (2002) 152 N.L.J. 758; (2002) 146 S.J.L.B. 123   17–124

Entick v Carrington, 95 E.R. 807; (1765) 2 Wils. K.B. 275; (1765) 19 St. Tr. 1030   5–059, 5–065, 8–049, 19–090

Esso Petroleum Co Ltd v Southport Corp [1954] 2 Q.B. 182; [1954] 3 W.L.R. 200; [1954] 2 All E.R. 561; [1954] 1 Lloyd's Rep. 446; (1954) 118 J.P. 411; 52 L.G.R. 404; (1954) 98 S.J. 472   19–019

Findlay v United Kingdom (22107/93) (1996) 21 E.H.R.R. CD7   19–100

Findlay v United Kingdom (22107/93) (1997) 24 E.H.R.R. 221   19–102

Foreign and Commonwealth Office v Information Commissioner (EA/2007/0047)   20–118

Foster v British Gas (C-188/89) EU:C:1990:313; [1991] 1 Q.B. 405; [1991] 2 W.L.R. 258; [1990] 3 All E.R. 897; [1990] E.C.R. I-3313; [1990] 2 C.M.L.R. 833; [1991] I.C.R. 84; [1990] I.R.L.R. 353; [1990] Pens. L.R. 189   9–074, 14–019

Foster v Chief Adjudication Officer. *See* Chief Adjudication Officer v Foster

Francome v Mirror Group Newspapers Ltd [1984] 1 W.L.R. 892; [1984] 2 All E.R. 408; (1984) 81 L.S.G. 2225; (1984) 128 S.J. 484   1-012

Francovich v Italy (C-6/90 and C-9/90) EU:C:1991:428; [1991] E.C.R. I-5357; [1993] 2 C.M.L.R. 66; [1995] I.C.R. 722; [1992] I.R.L.R. 84   2-161, 5-065, 9-076, 9-081, 18-051

Franklin v Minister of Town and Country Planning [1948] A.C. 87; [1947] 2 All E.R. 289; (1947) 63 T.L.R. 446; (1947) 111 J.P. 497; 45 L.G.R. 581; [1947] L.J.R. 1440   17-125

Garden Cottage Foods v Milk Marketing Board [1984] A.C. 130; [1983] 3 W.L.R. 143; [1983] 2 All E.R. 770; [1983] Com. L.R. 198; [1983] 3 C.M.L.R. 43; [1984] F.S.R. 23; (1983) 127 S.J. 460   2-161

Gaskin v United Kingdom (A/160) [1990] 1 F.L.R. 167; (1990) 12 E.H.R.R. 36   16-054

GCHQ Case. *See* Council of Civil Service Unions v Minister for the Civil Service

Geddis v Bann Reservoir Proprietors (1878) L.R. 3 App. Cas. 430 HL   18-109

Germany v Council of the European Union (C-122/95) [1998] E.C.R. I-973; [1998] 3 C.M.L.R. 570   2-161

Ghaidan v Godin Mendoza [2004] UKHL 30; [2004] 2 A.C. 557; [2004] 3 W.L.R. 113; [2004] 3 All E.R. 411; [2004] 2 F.L.R. 600; [2004] 2 F.C.R. 481; [2004] H.R.L.R. 31; [2004] U.K.H.R.R. 827; 16 B.H.R.C. 671; [2004] H.L.R. 46; [2005] 1 P. & C.R. 18; [2005] L. & T.R. 3; [2004] 2 E.G.L.R. 132; [2004] Fam. Law 641; [2004] 27 E.G. 128 (C.S.); (2004) 101(27) L.S.G. 30; (2004) 154 N.L.J. 1013; (2004) 148 S.J.L.B. 792; [2004] N.P.C. 100; [2004] 2 P. & C.R. DG17   6-007, 8-120

Gibson v East Riding Council. *See* East Riding of Yorkshire Council v Gibson

Gillan v United Kingdom (4158/05) (2010) 50 E.H.R.R. 45; 28 B.H.R.C. 420; [2010] Crim. L.R. 415; (2010) 160 N.L.J. 104   19-125

Gillick v West Norfolk and Wisbech AHA [1986] A.C. 112; [1985] 3 W.L.R. 830; [1985] 3 All E.R. 402; [1986] Crim. L.R. 113; (1985) 82 L.S.G. 3531; (1985) 135 N.L.J. 1055; (1985) 129 S.J. 738   17-045, 18-055, 18-092

Glasgow Corp v Central Land Board 1956 S.C. (H.L.) 1; 1956 S.L.T. 41; [1956] J.P.L. 442   10-086

Godden v Hales (1686) 11 State Tr. 1166   2-019

Golder v United Kingdom (A/18) (1975) 1 E.H.R.R. 524 ECHR   16-050

Goodwin v United Kingdom (17488/90) (1996) 22 E.H.R.R. 123; 1 B.H.R.C. 81   20-138

Gouriet v Union of Post Office Workers [1978] A.C. 435; [1977] 3 W.L.R. 300; [1977] 3 All E.R. 70; (1977) 121 S.J. 543   18-016, 18-019, 18-102

Grad v Finanzamt Traunstein (9/70) EU:C:1970:78; [1970] E.C.R. 825; [1971] C.M.L.R. 1   9-072

Greens v United Kingdom (60041/08) (2011) 53 E.H.R.R. 21; [2010] 2 Prison L.R. 22; (2010) 160 N.L.J. 1685   21-050

Grieve v Douglas-Home 1965 S.C. 315; 1965 S.L.T. 186   7-076

H Lavender & Son Ltd v Minister of Housing and Local Government [1970] 1 W.L.R. 1231; [1970] 3 All E.R. 871; 68 L.G.R. 408; (1970) 114 S.J. 636   17-071

H v Lord Advocate [2012] UKSC 24; [2013] 1 A.C. 413; [2012] 3 W.L.R. 151; [2012] 4 All E.R. 600; 2012 S.C. (U.K.S.C.) 308; 2012 S.L.T. 799; 2012 S.C.L. 635; 2012

S.C.C.R. 562; [2012] H.R.L.R. 24; (2012) 109(27) L.S.G. 19; 2012 G.W.D. 21–432
Halford v Sharples [1992] 1 W.L.R. 736; [1992] 3 All E.R. 624; [1992] I.C.R. 583 10–096, 19–080
Hamilton v Al Fayed (No.1) [2001] 1 A.C. 395; [2000] 2 W.L.R. 609; [2000] 2 All E.R. 224; [2000] E.M.L.R. 531; (2000) 97(14) L.S.G. 43; (2000) 144 S.J.L.B. 157 3–165, 4–139, 10–021
Hammersmith and Fulham LBC v Secretary of State for the Environment [1991] 1 A.C. 521; [1990] 3 W.L.R. 898; [1990] 3 All E.R. 589; 89 L.G.R. 129; [1990] R.V.R. 188; (1991) 155 L.G. Rev. 48; (1990) 140 N.L.J. 1422; (1990) 134 S.J. 1226 13–081, 13–082
Handyside v United Kingdom (A/24) (1979–80) 1 E.H.R.R. 737 ECHR 16–056, 16–067
Hanningfield v Chief Constable of Essex [2013] EWHC 243 (QB); [2013] 1 W.L.R. 3632 16–133
Hatton v United Kingdom (36022/97) (2003) 37 E.H.R.R. 28; 15 B.H.R.C. 259 16–035
Hayes v Chief Constable of Merseyside [2011] EWCA Civ 911; [2012] 1 W.L.R. 517; [2011] 2 Cr. App. R. 30; [2012] Crim. L.R. 35 16–133
Hazell v Hammersmith and Fulham LBC [1992] 2 A.C. 1; [1991] 2 W.L.R. 372; [1991] 1 All E.R. 545; 89 L.G.R. 271; (1991) 3 Admin. L.R. 549; [1991] R.V.R. 28; (1991) 155 J.P.N. 527; (1991) 155 L.G. Rev. 527; (1991) 88(8) L.S.G. 36; (1991) 141 N.L.J. 127 6–086, 6–087, 13–084, 13–099, 17–062, 17–063
Health and Safety Executive v Wolverhampton City Council [2012] UKSC 34; [2012] 1 W.L.R. 2264; [2012] 4 All E.R. 429; [2012] P.T.S.R. 1362; [2012] B.L.G.R. 843; [2013] J.P.L. 43; [2012] 30 E.G. 74 (C.S.); (2012) 162 N.L.J. 1000; (2012) 156(29) S.J.L.B. 27 6–161, 16–039, 16–040, 17–141
Hedley Byrne & Co Ltd v Heller & Partners Ltd [1964] A.C. 465; [1963] 3 W.L.R. 101; [1963] 2 All E.R. 575; [1963] 1 Lloyd's Rep. 485; (1963) 107 S.J. 454 8–116
Hertsmere BC v Harty. *See* South Buckinghamshire DC v Porter (No.1)
Heydon's Case, 74 E.R. 67; (1586) 1 Leo. 72; (1584) 3 Co. Rep. 7a 3–080
Hill v Chief Constable of West Yorkshire [1989] A.C. 53; [1988] 2 W.L.R. 1049; [1988] 2 All E.R. 238; (1988) 152 L.G. Rev. 709; (1988) 85(20) L.S.G. 34; (1988) 138 N.L.J. Rep. 126; (1988) 132 S.J. 700 8–115, 8–116, 16–154, 18–110
Hipperson v Electoral Registration Officer for the District of Newbury [1985] Q.B. 1060; [1985] 3 W.L.R. 61; [1985] 2 All E.R. 456; 83 L.G.R. 638; (1985) 82 L.S.G. 2247; (1985) 129 S.J. 432 7–040
Hirst v Chief Constable of West Yorkshire (1987) 85 Cr. App. R. 143; (1987) 151 J.P. 304; [1987] Crim. L.R. 330; (1987) 151 L.G. Rev. 130 19–014, 19–015
Hirst v HM Attorney General. *See* R. (on the application of Pearson) v Secretary of State for the Home Department
Hirst v United Kingdom (74025/01) (2006) 42 E.H.R.R. 41; 19 B.H.R.C. 546; [2006] 1 Prison L.R. 220; (2005) 155 N.L.J. 1551 3–083, 8–113, 21–050
HK (An Infant), Re [1967] 2 Q.B. 617; [1967] 2 W.L.R. 962; [1967] 1 All E.R. 226; (1967) 111 S.J. 296 17–114
HM Treasury v Information Commissioner [2009] EWHC 1811 (Admin); [2010] Q.B. 563; [2010] 2 W.L.R. 931; [2010] 2 All E.R. 55; [2009] A.C.D. 73 10–127

Hoechst Marion Roussel Ltd v Kirin-Amgen Inc Unreported 21 March 2002 HL   1-020
Home Office v Harman [1983] 1 A.C. 280; [1982] 2 W.L.R. 338; [1982] 1 All E.R. 532; (1982) 126 S.J. 136   20-032
Home Secretary v AP [2010] UKSC 24; [2011] 2 A.C. 1; [2010] 3 W.L.R. 51; [2010] 4 All E.R. 245; [2010] H.R.L.R. 25; [2010] U.K.H.R.R. 748; 29 B.H.R.C. 296; (2010) 107(26) L.S.G. 17; (2010) 160 N.L.J. 903   19-134
Hone v Maze Prison Visitors. See R. v Board of Visitors of the Maze Prison Ex p. Hone
Hood v United Kingdom (27267/95) (2000) 29 E.H.R.R. 365   19-102
Hounslow LBC v Powell [2011] UKSC 8; [2011] 2 A.C. 186; [2011] 2 W.L.R. 287; [2011] 2 All E.R. 129; [2011] P.T.S.R. 512; [2011] H.R.L.R. 18; [2011] U.K.H.R.R. 548; [2011] H.L.R. 23; [2011] B.L.G.R. 363; [2011] 1 P. & C.R. 20; [2011] 9 E.G. 164 (C.S.); (2011) 155(8) S.J.L.B. 31; [2011] N.P.C. 24   8-120
Houston v BBC 1995 S.C. 433; 1995 S.L.T. 1305 Ct of Session   20-107
Howell v Falmouth Boat Construction Co Ltd [1951] A.C. 837; [1951] 2 All E.R. 278; [1951] 2 Lloyd's Rep. 45; [1951] 2 T.L.R. 151; (1951) 95 S.J. 413   17-079
Huang v Secretary of State for the Home Department [2007] UKHL 11; [2007] 2 A.C. 167; [2007] 2 W.L.R. 581; [2007] 4 All E.R. 15; [2007] 1 F.L.R. 2021; [2007] H.R.L.R. 22; [2007] U.K.H.R.R. 759; 24 B.H.R.C. 74; [2007] Imm. A.R. 571; [2007] I.N.L.R. 314; [2007] Fam. Law 587; (2007) 151 S.J.L.B. 435   17-105
Hubbard v Pitt [1976] Q.B. 142; [1975] 3 W.L.R. 201; [1975] 3 All E.R. 1; [1975] I.C.R. 308; (1975) 119 S.J. 393   19-003
Ireland v United Kingdom (A/25) (1979-80) 2 E.H.R.R. 25   9-096, 16-061
Jackson v Attorney General. See R. (on the application of Jackson) v Attorney General
Jephson v Labour Party [1996] I.R.L.R. 116   7-068
John Calder Publications Ltd v Powell [1965] 1 Q.B. 509; [1965] 2 W.L.R. 138; [1965] 1 All E.R. 159; (1965) 129 J.P. 136; (1965) 109 S.J. 71   16-068
John v Express Newspapers [2000] 1 W.L.R. 1931; [2000] 3 All E.R. 257; [2000] E.M.L.R. 606; (2000) 97(21) L.S.G. 38; (2000) 150 N.L.J. 615; (2000) 144 S.J.L.B. 217   20-138
Johnston v Chief Constable of the Royal Ulster Constabulary (C-222/84) EU:C:1986:206; [1987] Q.B. 129; [1986] 3 W.L.R. 1038; [1986] 3 All E.R. 135; [1986] E.C.R. 1651; [1986] 3 C.M.L.R. 240; [1987] I.C.R. 83; [1986] I.R.L.R. 263; (1987) 84 L.S.G. 188; (1986) 130 S.J. 953   9-072, 9-107, 17-136
Joyce v Sengupta [1993] 1 W.L.R. 337; [1993] 1 All E.R. 897; (1992) 142 N.L.J. 1306; (1992) 136 S.J.L.B. 274   20-093
Kadi v Council of the European Union (C-402/05 P) [2009] 1 A.C. 1225; [2009] 3 W.L.R. 872; [2008] E.C.R. I-6351; [2008] 3 C.M.L.R. 41; [2010] All E.R. (EC) 1105; [2009] Lloyd's Rep. F.C. 95   2-161
Kaye v Robertson [1991] F.S.R. 62   8-114, 20-004
Kennedy v Information Commissioner [2014] UKSC 20; [2015] A.C. 455; [2014] 2 W.L.R. 808; [2014] 2 All E.R. 847; [2014] E.M.L.R. 19; [2014] H.R.L.R. 14; (2014) 158(13) S.J.L.B. 37   17-059
Kent v Griffiths [2001] Q.B. 36; [2000] 2 W.L.R. 1158; [2000] 2 All E.R. 474;

[2000] P.I.Q.R. P57; [2000] Lloyd's Rep. Med. 109; (2000) 97(7) L.S.G. 41; (2000) 150 N.L.J. 195; (2000) 144 S.J.L.B. 106   8–116

Khan v United Kingdom (35394/97) (2001) 31 E.H.R.R. 45; 8 B.H.R.C. 310; [2000] Po. L.R. 156; [2000] Crim. L.R. 684   19–091

Kirklees MBC v Wickes Building Supplies Ltd [1993] A.C. 227; [1992] 3 W.L.R. 170; [1992] 3 All E.R. 717; [1992] 2 C.M.L.R. 765; 90 L.G.R. 391; (1992) 142 N.L.J. 967; [1992] N.P.C. 86   13–073, 18–015

Knuller v DPP [1973] A.C. 435; [1972] 3 W.L.R. 143; [1972] 2 All E.R. 898; (1972) 56 Cr. App. R. 633; [1975] Crim. L.R. 704; (1972) 116 S.J. 545   16–075

Kruse v Johnson [1898] 2 Q.B. 91 QBD   17–098

L v Birmingham City Council [2007] UKHL 27; [2008] 1 A.C. 95; [2007] 3 W.L.R. 112; [2007] 3 All E.R. 957; [2007] H.R.L.R. 32; [2008] U.K.H.R.R. 346; [2007] H.L.R. 44; [2008] B.L.G.R. 273; (2007) 10 C.C.L. Rep. 505; [2007] LS Law Medical 472; (2007) 96 B.M.L.R. 1; (2007) 104(27) L.S.G. 29; (2007) 157 N.L.J. 938; (2007) 151 S.J.L.B. 860; [2007] N.P.C. 75   16–024

Laker Airways Ltd v Department of Trade [1977] Q.B. 643; [1977] 2 W.L.R. 234; [1977] 2 All E.R. 182; (1976) 121 S.J. 52   4–028, 4–058, 14–077, 17–065

Lam v United Kingdom, 5 July 2001 ECHR   1–014, 18–066

Lever (Finance) Ltd v Westminster Corp [1971] 1 Q.B. 222; [1970] 3 W.L.R. 732; [1970] 3 All E.R. 496; 68 L.G.R. 757; (1970) 21 P. & C.R. 778; [1971] J.P.L. 115; (1970) 114 S.J. 651   17–080, 17–081

Lewis v Chief Constable of South Wales [1991] 1 All E.R. 206   16–132

Liversidge v Anderson [1942] A.C. 206; [1941] 3 All E.R. 338 HL   19–109

Lloyd v McMahon [1987] A.C. 625; [1987] 2 W.L.R. 821; [1987] 1 All E.R. 1118; 85 L.G.R. 545; [1987] R.V.R. 58; (1987) 84 L.S.G. 1240; (1987) 137 N.L.J. 265; (1987) 131 S.J. 409   17–015

Lonrho Plc v Tebbit [1992] 4 All E.R. 280; [1992] B.C.C. 779; [1993] B.C.L.C. 96   10–009

Loutchansky v Times Newspapers Ltd (No.1) [2001] EWCA Civ 536; [2002] Q.B. 321; [2001] 3 W.L.R. 404; [2001] 4 All E.R. 115; [2001] E.M.L.R. 26; (2001) 151 N.L.J. 643   20–125

Loutchansky v Times Newspapers Ltd (No.2) [2001] EWCA Civ 1805; [2002] Q.B. 783; [2002] 2 W.L.R. 640; [2002] 1 All E.R. 652; [2002] E.M.L.R. 14; [2002] Masons C.L.R. 35; (2002) 99(6) L.S.G. 30; (2001) 145 S.J.L.B. 277   20–126

M v Home Office [1994] 1 A.C. 377; [1993] 3 W.L.R. 433; [1993] 3 All E.R. 537; (1995) 7 Admin. L.R. 113; (1993) 90(37) L.S.G. 50; (1993) 143 N.L.J. 1099; (1993) 137 S.J.L.B. 199   3–014, 4–023, 4–035, 9–083, 10–009, 10–084, 18–105

McCall v Poulton [2008] EWCA Civ 1313; [2009] C.P. Rep. 15; [2009] R.T.R. 11; [2009] 1 C.M.L.R. 45; [2009] Eu. L.R. 383; [2009] Lloyd's Rep. I.R. 454; [2009] P.I.Q.R. P8   9–064

McCann, Farrell and Savage v United Kingdom (A/324) (1996) 21 E.H.R.R. 97   16–060, 19–117

McClaren v Home Office [1990] I.C.R. 824; [1990] I.R.L.R. 338; (1990) 2 Admin. L.R. 652; [1990] C.O.D. 257; (1990) 87(17) L.S.G. 31; (1990) 134 S.J. 90   4–160, 17–045

McConnell v Chief Constable of Greater Manchester [1990] 1 W.L.R. 364; [1990]

1 All E.R. 423; (1990) 91 Cr. App. R. 88; (1990) 154 J.P.N. 62; (1990) 87(6) L.S.G. 41; (1990) 134 S.J. 457   19–049
MacCormick v Lord Advocate 1953 S.C. 396; 1953 S.L.T. 255   2–017, 2–018
McEldowney v Forde [1971] A.C. 632; [1969] 3 W.L.R. 179; [1969] 2 All E.R. 1039; [1970] N.I. 11; (1969) 113 S.J. 565   19–109
McGuigan v Ministry of Defence [1982] 19 N.I.J.B. CA (Civ Div).   19–113
McLaughlin v Ministry of Defence (1978) 7 N.I.J.B   19–114
McLeod v Commissioner of Police of the Metropolis [1994] 4 All E.R. 553   16–141
McLeod v United Kingdom (24755/94) [1998] 2 F.L.R. 1048; [1999] 1 F.C.R. 193; (1999) 27 E.H.R.R. 493; 5 B.H.R.C. 364; [1999] Crim. L.R. 155; [1998] H.R.C.D. 878; [1998] Fam. Law 734   16–141
McShane v United Kingdom (43290/98) (2002) 35 E.H.R.R. 23   19–117
Madzimbamuto v Lardner-Burke [1969] 1 A.C. 645; [1968] 3 W.L.R. 1229; [1968] 3 All E.R. 561; (1968) 112 S.J. 1007   5–012
Makanjuola v Commissioner of Police of the Metropolis [1992] 3 All E.R. 617   10–096, 10–097, 10–098
Malone v Commissioner of Police of the Metropolis (No.2) [1979] Ch. 344; [1979] 2 W.L.R. 700; [1979] 2 All E.R. 620; (1979) 69 Cr. App. R. 168; (1979) 123 S.J. 303   4–045, 6–076
Malone v United Kingdom (A/82) (1985) 7 E.H.R.R. 14 ECHR   16–059, 20–065
Mandalia v Secretary of State for the Home Department [2015] UKSC 59; [2015] 1 W.L.R. 4546; [2016] Imm. A.R. 180   17–059, 17–109
Marcic v Thames Water Utilities Ltd [2003] UKHL 66; [2004] 2 A.C. 42; [2003] 3 W.L.R. 1603; [2004] 1 All E.R. 135; [2004] B.L.R. 1; 91 Con. L.R. 1; [2004] Env. L.R. 25; [2004] H.R.L.R. 10; [2004] U.K.H.R.R. 253; [2003] 50 E.G. 95 (C.S.); (2004) 101(4) L.S.G. 32; (2003) 153 N.L.J. 1869; (2003) 147 S.J.L.B. 1429; [2003] N.P.C. 150   16–033, 16–035, 18–114
Maritime Electric Co v General Dairies Ltd [1937] A.C. 610; [1937] 1 All E.R. 748 PC (Canada)   17–075
Marks v Beyfus (1890) 25 Q.B.D. 494 CA   10–102
Marshall v Southampton and South West Hampshire AHA (Teaching) (152/84) EU:C:1986:84; [1994] Q.B. 126; [1993] 3 W.L.R. 1054; [1993] 4 All E.R. 586; [1993] E.C.R. I-4367; [1993] 3 C.M.L.R. 293; [1993] I.C.R. 893; [1993] I.R.L.R. 445   9–073, 14–019
Mercury Communications Ltd v Director General of Telecommunications [1996] 1 W.L.R. 48; [1996] 1 All E.R. 575; [1995] C.L.C. 266; [1998] Masons C.L.R. Rep. 39   14–017, 17–037
Metropolitan Police Commissioner v Caldwell. See R. v Caldwell (James)
Metropolitan Properties Co (FGC) Ltd v Lannon [1969] 1 Q.B. 577; [1968] 3 W.L.R. 694; [1968] 3 All E.R. 304; (1968) 19 P. & C.R. 856; [1968] R.V.R. 490; (1968) 112 S.J. 585   17–125
Metzger v Department of Health and Social Security [1978] 1 W.L.R. 1046; [1978] 3 All E.R. 753; (1978) 122 S.J. 572   12–096
Michael v Chief Constable of South Wales Police [2015] UKSC 2; [2015] A.C. 1732; [2015] 2 W.L.R. 343; [2015] 2 All E.R. 635; [2015] H.R.L.R. 8; [2015] Med. L.R. 171; [2015] Inquest L.R. 78   8–116, 18–110
Mullaney v Chief Constable of the West Midlands [2001] EWCA Civ 700; [2001] Po. L.R. 150   8–116

Murphy v Brentwood DC [1991] 1 A.C. 398; [1990] 3 W.L.R. 414; [1990] 2 All E.R. 908; [1990] 2 Lloyd's Rep. 467; 50 B.L.R. 1; 21 Con. L.R. 1; (1990) 22 H.L.R. 502; 89 L.G.R. 24; (1991) 3 Admin. L.R. 37; (1990) 6 Const. L.J. 304; (1990) 154 L.G. Rev. 1010; [1990] E.G. 105 (C.S.); (1990) 87(30) L.S.G. 15; (1990) 134 S.J. 1076   18–110

Murray v Express Newspapers Plc [2008] EWCA Civ 446; [2009] Ch. 481; [2008] 3 W.L.R. 1360; [2008] E.C.D.R. 12; [2008] E.M.L.R. 12; [2008] 2 F.L.R. 599; [2008] 3 F.C.R. 661; [2008] H.R.L.R. 33; [2008] U.K.H.R.R. 736; [2008] Fam. Law 732; (2008) 105(20) L.S.G. 23; (2008) 158 N.L.J. 706; (2008) 152(19) S.J.L.B. 31   8–114

N v Secretary of State for the Home Department [2005] UKHL 31; [2005] 2 A.C. 296; [2005] 2 W.L.R. 1124; [2005] 4 All E.R. 1017; [2005] H.R.L.R. 22; [2005] U.K.H.R.R. 862; [2005] Imm. A.R. 353; [2005] I.N.L.R. 388; (2005) 84 B.M.L.R. 126; (2005) 102(24) L.S.G. 35; (2005) 155 N.L.J. 748   16–007

Nagy v Weston [1965] 1 W.L.R. 280; [1965] 1 All E.R. 78; (1965) 129 J.P. 104; (1965) 109 S.J. 215   19–014

Neilson v Laugharne [1981] Q.B. 736; [1981] 2 W.L.R. 537; [1981] 1 All E.R. 829; (1981) 125 S.J. 202   10–105

Newsgroup Newspapers Ltd v Society of Graphical and Allied Trades SOGAT) 1982 [1987] I.C.R. 181; [1986] I.R.L.R. 337; (1986) 136 N.L.J. 893   19–028

Norwich Pharmacal Co v Customs and Excise Commissioners [1974] A.C. 133; [1973] 3 W.L.R. 164; [1973] 2 All E.R. 943; [1973] F.S.R. 365; [1974] R.P.C. 101; (1973) 117 S.J. 567   19–143—19–146

NS v Home Secretary. *See* R. (on the application of NS) v Secretary of State for the Home Department (C-411/10)

Nwabueze v General Medical Council [2000] 1 W.L.R. 1760; (2000) 56 B.M.L.R. 106   17–127

O'Brien v Department of Constitutional Affairs. *See* Department of Constitutional Affairs v O'Brien

O'Hara v Chief Constable of the RUC [1997] A.C. 286; [1997] 2 W.L.R. 1; [1997] 1 All E.R. 129; [1996] N.I. 8; [1997] 1 Cr. App. R. 447; [1997] Crim. L.R. 432; (1997) 94(2) L.S.G. 26; (1996) 146 N.L.J. 1852; (1997) 141 S.J.L.B. 20   19–075

O'Reilly v Mackman [1983] 2 A.C. 237; [1982] 3 W.L.R. 1096; [1982] 3 All E.R. 1124; (1982) 126 S.J. 820   1–013, 14–018, 17–029, 17–031, 17–032, 17–034, 17–036—17–041, 17–043, 17–044, 17–046, 17–049, 17–090, 18–059, 18–079, 18–089, 18–090, 18–106

Office of Government Commerce v Information Commissioner [2008] EWHC 774 (Admin); [2010] Q.B. 98; [2009] 3 W.L.R. 627; [2008] A.C.D. 54   3–075

OFT v Abbey National Plc [2009] UKSC 6; [2010] 1 A.C. 696; [2009] 3 W.L.R. 1215; [2010] 1 All E.R. 667; [2010] 2 All E.R. (Comm) 945; [2010] 1 Lloyd's Rep. 281; [2010] 1 C.M.L.R. 44; [2010] Eu. L.R. 309; (2009) 159 N.L.J. 1702; (2009) 153(45) S.J.L.B. 28   2–147, 9–064

Osman v United Kingdom (23452/94) [1999] 1 F.L.R. 193; (2000) 29 E.H.R.R. 245; 5 B.H.R.C. 293; (1999) 1 L.G.L.R. 431; (1999) 11 Admin. L.R. 200; [2000] Inquest L.R. 101; [1999] Crim. L.R. 82; [1998] H.R.C.D. 966; [1999] Fam. Law 86; (1999) 163 J.P.N. 297   8–115, 8–116, 18–110

Padfield v Minister of Agriculture, Fisheries and Food [1968] A.C. 997; [1968] 2 W.L.R. 924; [1968] 1 All E.R. 694; (1968) 112 S.J. 171   1–013, 17–093, 17–094, 17–097, 18–083

Page v Hull University Visitor. *See* R. v Lord President of the Privy Council Ex p. Page

Palacegate Properties Ltd v Camden LBC (2001) 3 L.G.L.R. 18; (2001) 82 P. & C.R. 17; [2000] 4 P.L.R. 59; [2001] J.P.L. 373 (Note); [2001] A.C.D. 23   17–091

Parkins v Sodexho Ltd [2001] UKEAT 1239; [2002] I.R.L.R. 109   5–031, 16–106

Parliamentary Privilege Act 1770, In Re [1958] A.C. 331; [1958] 2 W.L.R. 912; [1958] 2 All E.R. 329; (1958) 102 S.J. 380   4–139, 10–021

Patel v University of Bradford Senate [1978] 1 W.L.R. 1488; [1978] 3 All E.R. 841; (1978) 122 S.J. 791   17–131

Pearlman v Keepers and Governors of Harrow School [1979] Q.B. 56; [1978] 3 W.L.R. 736; [1979] 1 All E.R. 365; (1979) 38 P. & C.R. 136; (1978) 247 E.G. 1173; [1978] J.P.L. 829   17–089, 17–090

Pepper v Hart [1993] A.C. 593; [1992] 3 W.L.R. 1032; [1993] 1 All E.R. 42; [1992] S.T.C. 898; [1993] I.C.R. 291; [1993] I.R.L.R. 33; [1993] R.V.R. 127; (1993) 143 N.L.J. 17; [1992] N.P.C. 154   3–067, 3–074, 3–084, 3–166, 12–010, 12–096, 17–010

Pergamon Press Ltd, Re [1971] Ch. 388; [1970] 3 W.L.R. 792; [1970] 3 All E.R. 535; (1970) 114 S.J. 569   17–114, 17–116

Persey v Secretary of State for Environment, Food and Rural Affairs. *See* R. (on the application of Persey) v Secretary of State for the Environment, Food and Rural Affairs

Pham v Secretary of State for the Home Department [2015] UKSC 19; [2015] 1 W.L.R. 1591; [2015] 3 All E.R. 1015; [2015] 2 C.M.L.R. 49; [2015] Imm. A.R. 950; [2015] I.N.L.R. 593   2–150, 2–163, 9–067, 17–028, , 17–102, 17–106 , 17–142, 21–049

Pickin v British Railways Board. *See* British Railways Board v Pickin

Pickstone v Freemans Plc [1989] A.C. 66; [1988] 3 W.L.R. 265; [1988] 2 All E.R. 803; [1988] 3 C.M.L.R. 221; [1988] I.C.R. 697; [1988] I.R.L.R. 357; (1988) 138 N.L.J. Rep. 193   17–010

Pickwell v Camden LBC [1983] Q.B. 962; [1983] 2 W.L.R. 583; [1983] 1 All E.R. 602; 80 L.G.R. 798; (1982) 126 S.J. 397   13–092

Piddington v Bates [1961] 1 W.L.R. 162; [1960] 3 All E.R. 660; (1961) 105 S.J. 110   19–039

Pigs Marketing Board (Northern Ireland) v Redmond (83/78): EU:C:1978:214; [1978] E.C.R. 2347; [1979] 1 C.M.L.R. 177   9–056, 9–062

Pinochet (No.2). *See* R. v Bow Street Metropolitan Stipendiary Magistrate Ex p. Pinochet Ugarte (No.2)

Porter v Magill [2001] UKHL 67; [2002] 2 A.C. 357; [2002] 2 W.L.R. 37; [2002] 1 All E.R. 465; [2002] H.R.L.R. 16; [2002] H.L.R. 16; [2002] B.L.G.R. 51; (2001) 151 N.L.J. 1886; [2001] N.P.C. 184   7–108, 13–100

Practice Direction (CA: Citation of Authorities) [2001] 1 W.L.R. 1001; [2001] 2 All E.R. 510; [2001] 1 Lloyd's Rep. 725; [2001] C.P.L.R. 301; [2001] 1 F.C.R. 764; (2001) 145 S.J.L.B. 132   6–009

Practice Statement (Admin Ct: Administration of Justice) [2002] 1 W.L.R. 810; [2002] 1 All E.R. 633; [2002] A.C.D. 64   1–011, 6–146, 17–021, 18–057

Prebble v Television New Zealand Ltd [1995] 1 A.C. 321; [1994] 3 W.L.R. 970; [1994] 3 All E.R. 407; (1994) 91(39) L.S.G. 38; (1994) 144 N.L.J. 1131; (1994) 138 S.J.L.B. 175   3-074, 3-165, 4-139, 10-021

Pretty v United Kingdom (2346/02) [2002] 2 F.L.R. 45; [2002] 2 F.C.R. 97; (2002) 35 E.H.R.R. 1; 12 B.H.R.C. 149; (2002) 66 B.M.L.R. 147; [2002] Fam. Law 588; (2002) 152 N.L.J. 707   16-084

Prince v Secretary of State for Scotland 1985 S.C. 8; 1985 S.L.T. 74; [1984] 1 C.M.L.R. 723   7-093

Puhlhoffer v Hillingdon LBC. *See* R. v Hillingdon LBC Ex p. Puhlhofer

Pyx Granite Ltd v Ministry of Housing and Local Government [1960] A.C. 260; [1959] 3 W.L.R. 346; [1959] 3 All E.R. 1; (1959) 123 J.P. 429; 58 L.G.R. 1; (1959) 10 P. & C.R. 319; (1959) 103 S.J. 633   18-093

R. v Adams [1957] Crim. L.R. 365   16-084

R. v Alladice (1988) 87 Cr. App. R. 380; [1988] Crim. L.R. 608; (1988) 138 N.L.J. Rep. 141   16-144

R. v Anderson; R. v Oz [1972] 1 Q.B. 304; [1971] 3 W.L.R. 939; [1971] 3 All E.R. 1152; (1972) 56 Cr. App. R. 115; [1972] Crim. L.R. 40; (1971) 115 S.J. 847   16-067, 16-068

R. v Barnet LBC Ex p. Shah [1983] 2 A.C. 309; [1983] 2 W.L.R. 16; [1983] 1 All E.R. 226; 81 L.G.R. 305; (1983) 133 N.L.J. 61; (1983) 127 S.J. 36   18-078

R. v Bedwellty Justices Ex p. Williams [1997] A.C. 225; [1996] 3 W.L.R. 361; [1996] 3 All E.R. 737; [1996] 2 Cr. App. R. 594; (1996) 160 J.P. 549; (1996) 8 Admin. L.R. 643; [1996] Crim. L.R. 906; [1997] C.O.D. 54; (1996) 160 J.P.N. 696; (1996) 93(34) L.S.G. 34; (1996) 146 N.L.J. 1149; (1996) 140 S.J.L.B. 192   17-089

R. v Blaue (Robert Konrad) [1975] 1 W.L.R. 1411; [1975] 3 All E.R. 446; (1975) 61 Cr. App. R. 271; [1975] Crim. L.R. 648; (1975) 119 S.J. 589   16-090

R. v Board of Visitors of the Maze Prison Ex p. Hone [1988] A.C. 379; [1988] 2 W.L.R. 177; [1988] 1 All E.R. 321; (1988) 132 S.J. 158   15-018, 17-121

R. v Boundary Commission for England Ex p. Gateshead BC; R. v Boundary Commission for England Ex p. Foot [1983] Q.B. 600; [1983] 2 W.L.R. 458; [1983] 1 All E.R. 1099; (1983) 127 S.J. 155   7-049, 7-060, 7-061, 7-063

R. v Bow Street Magistrates Court Ex p. Choudhury [1991] 1 Q.B. 429; [1990] 3 W.L.R. 986; [1991] 1 All E.R. 306; (1990) 91 Cr. App. R. 393; [1990] Crim. L.R. 711; [1990] C.O.D. 305; (1990) 87(24) L.S.G. 40; (1990) 140 N.L.J. 782   16-081

R. v Bow Street Metropolitan Stipendiary Magistrate Ex p. Pinochet Ugarte (No.1) [2000] 1 A.C. 61; [1998] 3 W.L.R. 1456; [1998] 4 All E.R. 897; 5 B.H.R.C. 209; (1998) 94(48) L.S.G. 31; (1998) 148 N.L.J. 1808   4-066

R. v Bow Street Metropolitan Stipendiary Magistrate Ex p. Pinochet Ugarte (No.2) [2000] 1 A.C. 119; [1999] 2 W.L.R. 272; [1999] 1 All E.R. 577; 6 B.H.R.C. 1; (1999) 11 Admin. L.R. 57; (1999) 96(6) L.S.G. 33; (1999) 149 N.L.J. 88   4-066, 6-132, 17-127, 17-128

R. v Brent HA Ex p. Francis [1985] Q.B. 869; [1984] 3 W.L.R. 1317; [1985] 1 All E.R. 74; (1985) 82 L.S.G. 36; (1984) 128 S.J. 815   13-041

R. v Broadcasting Complaints Commission Ex p. Barclay [1997] E.M.L.R. 62; (1997) 9 Admin. L.R. 265; [1997] C.O.D. 57   3-082

R. v Broadcasting Complaints Commission
Ex p. Owen [1985] Q.B. 1153; [1985]
2 W.L.R. 1025; [1985] 2 All E.R.
522   7-079
R. v Broadcasting Standards Commission Ex
p. BBC [2001] Q.B. 885; [2000] 3 W.L.R.
1327; [2000] 3 All E.R. 989; [2001]
B.C.C. 432; [2001] 1 B.C.L.C. 244; [2000]
E.M.L.R. 587; [2000] H.R.L.R. 374;
[2000] U.K.H.R.R. 624; [2000] C.O.D.
322; (2000) 97(17) L.S.G. 32; (2000) 144
S.J.L.B. 204   20-107
R. v Brown [1996] A.C. 543; [1996] 2 W.L.R.
203; [1996] 1 All E.R. 545; [1996] 2 Cr.
App. R. 72; [1997] E.C.C. 105; [1998]
Masons C.L.R. Rep. 108; [1996] Crim.
L.R. 408; (1996) 93(10) L.S.G. 21; (1996)
146 N.L.J. 209; (1996) 140 S.J.L.B.
66   8-114, 20-004
R. v Caldwell (James) [1982] A.C. 341; [1981]
2 W.L.R. 509; [1981] 1 All E.R. 961; (1981)
73 Cr. App. R. 13; [1981] Crim. L.R. 392;
(1981) 125 S.J. 239   19-018
R. v Camden LBC Ex p. Gillan (1989) 21
H.L.R. 114; [1989] C.O.D. 196; (1990) 154
L.G. Rev. 234   18-082
R. v Chaytor [2010] UKSC 52; [2011] 1 A.C.
684; [2010] 3 W.L.R. 1707; [2011] 1 All
E.R. 805   3-162, 3-163
R. v Chief Constable of Devon and Cornwall
Ex p. Central Electricity Generating
Board [1982] Q.B. 458; [1981] 3 W.L.R.
967; [1981] 3 All E.R. 826   19-045,
19-047
R. v Chief Constable of Devon and Cornwall
Ex p. Hay [1996] 2 All E.R. 711   17-100
R. v Chief Constable of Merseyside Ex p.
Calveley [1986] Q.B. 424; [1986] 2
W.L.R. 144; [1986] 1 All E.R. 257; [1986]
I.R.L.R. 177   18-067
R. v Chief Constable of the West Midlands
Ex p. Wiley [1995] 1 A.C. 274; [1994] 3
W.L.R. 433; [1994] 3 All E.R. 420; [1995]
1 Cr. App. R. 342; [1994] C.O.D. 520;
(1994) 91(40) L.S.G. 35; (1994) 144 N.L.J.
1008; (1994) 138 S.J.L.B. 156   10-095,
10-101, 10-106, 10-107
R. v Civil Service Appeal Board Ex p. Bruce
[1988] 3 All E.R. 686; [1988] I.C.R.
649   4-160
R. v Civil Service Appeal Board Ex p.
Cunningham [1991] 4 All E.R. 310;
[1992] I.C.R. 817; [1992] I.C.R. 816; [1991]
I.R.L.R. 297; [1991] C.O.D. 478; (1991) 141
N.L.J. 455   4-159
R. v Clegg [1995] 1 A.C. 482; [1995] 2 W.L.R.
80; [1995] 1 All E.R. 334; [1995] 1 Cr.
App. R. 507; [1995] Crim. L.R. 418;
(1995) 92(8) L.S.G. 39; (1995) 145 N.L.J.
87   19-116
R. v Commissioner for Local Administration
Ex p. Croydon LBC [1989] 1 All E.R.
1033; 87 L.G.R. 221; [1989] C.O.D. 226;
(1989) 153 L.G. Rev. 131   15-110, 15-111,
15-113
R. v Commissioner for Local Administration
Ex p. H (A Minor) (1999) 1 L.G.L.R. 932;
[1999] C.O.D. 382; (1999) 96(5) L.S.G.
37; (1999) 143 S.J.L.B. 39   15-112
R. v Commissioner of Police of the
Metropolis Ex p. Blackburn (No.1) [1968]
2 Q.B. 118; [1968] 2 W.L.R. 893; [1968] 1
All E.R. 763; (1968) 112 S.J. 112   18-082,
18-084
R. v Commissioners of Income Tax (1888) 21
Q.B.D. 313 CA   6-020
R. v Criminal Injuries Compensation Board
Ex p. Lain [1967] 2 Q.B. 864; [1967] 3
W.L.R. 348; [1967] 2 All E.R. 770; (1967)
111 S.J. 331   18-078
R. v Crisp (1919) 83 J.P. 121   20-021
R. v Customs and Excise Commissioners Ex
p. Cook [1970] 1 W.L.R. 450; [1970] 1 All
E.R. 1068; (1969) 114 S.J. 34   18-085

R. v Dairy Produce Quota Tribunal for England and Wales Ex p. Caswell [1990] 2 A.C. 738; [1990] 2 W.L.R. 1320; [1990] 2 All E.R. 434; (1990) 2 Admin. L.R. 765; [1990] C.O.D. 243; (1990) 140 N.L.J. 742   18-062

R. v Davis [1993] 1 W.L.R. 613; [1993] 2 All E.R. 643; (1993) 97 Cr. App. R. 110; (1993) 137 S.J.L.B. 19   10-104

R. v Derbyshire C Ex p. Noble [1990] I.C.R. 808; [1990] I.R.L.R. 332   17-045

R. v Director General of Gas Supply Ex p. Smith CO/1398/88   14-018

R. v Director of Government Communications Headquarters Ex p. Hodges Times, July 26, 1988; Independent, July 21, 1988 QBD   20-044

R. v Disciplinary Committee of the Jockey Club Ex p. Aga Khan [1993] 1 W.L.R. 909; [1993] 2 All E.R. 853; [1993] C.O.D. 234; (1993) 143 N.L.J. 163   17-023, 17-133

R. v DPP Ex p. Kebilene [2000] 2 A.C. 326; [1999] 3 W.L.R. 972; [1999] 4 All E.R. 801; [2000] 1 Cr. App. R. 275; [2000] H.R.L.R. 93; [2000] U.K.H.R.R. 176; (2000) 2 L.G.L.R. 697; (1999) 11 Admin. L.R. 1026; [2000] Crim. L.R. 486; (1999) 96(43) L.S.G. 32   3-083, 6-007

R. v East Berkshire HA Ex p. Walsh [1985] Q.B. 152; [1984] 3 W.L.R. 818; [1984] 3 All E.R. 425; [1984] I.C.R. 743; [1984] I.R.L.R. 278   17-043

R. v Electricity Commissioners Ex p. London Electricity Joint Committee Co (1920) Ltd [1924] 1 K.B. 171 CA   18-006, 18-077

R. v Fulling [1987] Q.B. 426; [1987] 2 W.L.R. 923; [1987] 2 All E.R. 65; (1987) 85 Cr. App. R. 136; (1987) 151 J.P. 485; [1987] Crim. L.R. 492; (1987) 151 J.P.N. 364; (1987) 131 S.J. 408   16-148

R. v Gough [1993] A.C. 646; [1993] 2 W.L.R. 883; [1993] 2 All E.R. 724; (1993) 97 Cr. App. R. 188; (1993) 157 J.P. 612; [1993] Crim. L.R. 886; (1993) 157 J.P.N. 394; (1993) 143 N.L.J. 775; (1993) 137 S.J.L.B. 168   17-127

R. v Governor of Brixton Prison Ex p. Osman (No.1) [1991] 1 W.L.R. 281; [1992] 1 All E.R. 108; (1991) 93 Cr. App. R. 202; [1991] Crim. L.R. 533   10-102, 10-105

R. v H [2004] UKHL 3; [2004] 2 A.C. 134; [2004] 2 W.L.R. 335; [2004] 1 All E.R. 1269; [2004] 2 Cr. App. R. 10; [2004] H.R.L.R. 20; 16 B.H.R.C. 332; (2004) 101(8) L.S.G. 29; (2004) 148 S.J.L.B. 183   19-142

R. v Hammersmith and Fulham LBC Ex p. Burkett [2002] UKHL 23; [2002] 1 W.L.R. 1593; [2002] 3 All E.R. 97; [2002] C.P. Rep. 66; [2003] Env. L.R. 6; [2003] 1 P. & C.R. 3; [2002] 2 P.L.R. 90; [2002] J.P.L. 1346; [2002] A.C.D. 81; [2002] 22 E.G. 136 (C.S.); (2002) 99(27) L.S.G. 34; (2002) 152 N.L.J. 847; (2002) 146 S.J.L.B. 137; [2002] N.P.C. 75   15-112, 18-064

R. v Hammersmith and Fulham LBC Ex p. People Before Profit 80 L.G.R. 322; (1983) 45 P. & C.R. 364; [1981] J.P.L. 869   18-033

R. v Hampden (1637) 3 St. Tr. 825   2-019

R. v Hastings Board of Health 122 E.R. 1243; (1865) 6 B. & S. 401 KB   18-078

R. v Henderson Unreported November 1992   15-042

R. v Henn [1981] A.C. 850; (1980) 71 Cr. App. R. 44; [1980] 2 C.M.L.R. 229; [1980] F.S.R. 382; (1980) 124 S.J. 290   9-056, 9-060

R. v Higher Education Funding Council Ex p. Institute of Dental Surgery [1994] 1 W.L.R. 242; [1994] 1 All E.R. 651; [1994] E.L.R. 506; [1994] C.O.D. 147   17-123

R. v Hillingdon LBC Ex p. Puhlhofer [1986] A.C. 484; [1986] 2 W.L.R. 259; [1986] 1 All E.R. 467; [1986] 1 F.L.R. 22; (1986) 18 H.L.R. 158; [1986] Fam. Law 218; (1986) 83 L.S.G. 785; (1986) 136 N.L.J. 140; (1986) 130 S.J. 143   17–043, 18–067

R. v Hillingdon LBC Ex p. Royco Homes Ltd [1974] Q.B. 720; [1974] 2 W.L.R. 805; [1974] 2 All E.R. 643; 72 L.G.R. 516; (1974) 28 P. & C.R. 251; (1974) 118 S.J. 389   18–069, 18–078

R. v HM Coroner for East Kent Ex p. Spooner (1987) 3 B.C.C. 636; (1989) 88 Cr. App. R. 10; (1988) 152 J.P. 115; (1988) 152 J.P.N. 94   15–038

R. v HM Coroner for Greater Manchester Ex p. Tal [1985] Q.B. 67; [1984] 3 W.L.R. 643; [1984] 3 All E.R. 240; [1984] Crim. L.R. 557; (1984) 128 S.J. 500   17–090

R. v Howell [1982] Q.B. 416; [1981] 3 W.L.R. 501; [1981] 3 All E.R. 383; (1981) 73 Cr. App. R. 31; [1981] Crim. L.R. 697; (1981) 125 S.J. 462   19–043, 19–046, 19–047

R. v Human Fertilisation and Embryology Authority Ex p. Blood [1999] Fam. 151; [1997] 2 W.L.R. 806; [1997] 2 All E.R. 687; [1997] 2 C.M.L.R. 591; [1997] Eu. L.R. 370; [1997] 2 F.L.R. 742; [1997] 2 F.C.R. 501; (1997) 35 B.M.L.R. 1; [1997] C.O.D. 261; [1997] Fam. Law 401; (1997) 147 N.L.J. 253   16–065

R. v Independent Television Commission Ex p. Virgin Television Ltd [1996] E.M.L.R. 318 Div Ct   14–017

R. v Inland Revenue Commissioners Ex p. MFK Underwriting Agents Ltd [1990] 1 W.L.R. 1545; [1990] 1 All E.R. 91; [1990] S.T.C. 873; 62 T.C. 607; [1990] C.O.D. 143; (1989) 139 N.L.J. 1343   17–108

R. v Inland Revenue Commissioners Ex p. National Federation of Self-Employed and Small Businesses Ltd [1982] A.C. 617; [1981] 2 W.L.R. 722; [1981] 2 All E.R. 93; [1981] S.T.C. 260; 55 T.C. 133; (1981) 125 S.J. 325   5–036, 6–005, 15–085, 18–026

R. v Inner London Education Authority Ex p. Brunyate [1989] 1 W.L.R. 542; [1989] 2 All E.R. 417; 87 L.G.R. 725; (1989) 1 Admin. L.R. 65; (1989) 153 L.G. Rev. 929; (1989) 133 S.J. 749   17–069

R. v Inspectorate of Pollution Ex p. Greenpeace Ltd (No.1) [1994] 1 W.L.R. 570; [1994] 4 All E.R. 321   17–005

R. v Inspectorate of Pollution Ex p. Greenpeace Ltd (No.1) [1994] 1 W.L.R. 570; [1994] 4 All E.R. 321   18–047

R. v International Stock Exchange Ex p. Else (1982) Ltd [1993] Q.B. 534; [1993] 2 W.L.R. 70; [1993] 1 All E.R. 420; [1993] B.C.C. 11; [1993] B.C.L.C. 834; [1993] 2 C.M.L.R. 677; (1994) 6 Admin. L.R. 67; [1993] C.O.D. 236   2–147, 9–057

R. v Jordan and Tyndall [1963] Crim. L.R. 124 CCA   19–012

R. v Lambert (Steven) [2001] UKHL 37; [2002] 2 A.C. 545; [2001] 3 W.L.R. 206; [2001] 3 All E.R. 577; [2002] 1 All E.R. 2; [2001] 2 Cr. App. R. 28; [2001] H.R.L.R. 55; [2001] U.K.H.R.R. 1074; [2001] Crim. L.R. 806; (2001) 98(33) L.S.G. 29; (2001) 145 S.J.L.B. 174   3–083, 16–027

R. v Lambeth LBC Ex p. Crookes (1997) 29 H.L.R. 28; [1996] C.O.D. 398 QBD   15–112

R. v Lewes Justices Ex p. Home Secretary. See Rogers v Secretary of State for the Home Department

R. v Lewisham Union [1897] 1 Q.B. 498 QBD   18–084

R. v Liverpool City Council Ex p. Liverpool Taxi Fleet Operators Association [1975] 1 W.L.R. 701; [1975] 1 All E.R. 379; 73 L.G.R. 143; (1974) 119 S.J. 166   13–041

R. v Liverpool Corp Ex p. Liverpool Taxi Fleet Operators Association [1972] 2 Q.B. 299; [1972] 2 W.L.R. 1262; [1972] 2 All E.R. 589; 71 L.G.R. 387; (1972) 116 S.J. 201   18–081

R. v Local Commissioner for Administration for England Ex p. Eastleigh BC [1988] Q.B. 855; [1988] 3 W.L.R. 113; [1988] 3 All E.R. 151; 86 L.G.R. 491; (1988) 152 L.G. Rev. 890; [1988] E.G. 28 (C.S.); (1988) 132 S.J. 564   15–109, 15–110, 15–113

R. v Local Commissioner for Administration for the North and East Area of England Ex p. Bradford City Council [1979] Q.B. 287; [1979] 2 W.L.R. 1; [1979] 2 All E.R. 881; 77 L.G.R. 305; [1978] J.P.L. 767; (1978) 122 S.J. 573   15–103

R. v Local Commissioner for Administration in North and North East England Ex p. Liverpool City Council [2001] 1 All E.R. 462; (2000) 2 L.G.L.R. 603; [2000] B.L.G.R. 571; [2000] N.P.C. 18   15–112

R. v Local Government Board Ex p. Arlidge [1915] A.C. 120 HL   8–087, 17–071

R. v Lord Chancellor Ex p. Child Poverty Action Group [1999] 1 W.L.R. 347; [1998] 2 All E.R. 755; [1998] C.O.D. 267; (1998) 148 N.L.J. 20   18–057

R. v Lord Chancellor Ex p. Witham [1998] Q.B. 575; [1998] 2 W.L.R. 849; [1997] 2 All E.R. 779; [1997] C.O.D. 291; (1997) 147 N.L.J. 378; (1997) 141 S.J.L.B. 82   5–061

R. v Lord Chancellors Department Ex p. Nangle [1992] 1 All E.R. 897; [1991] I.C.R. 743; [1991] I.R.L.R. 343; [1991] C.O.D. 484   17–043

R. v Lord President of the Privy Council Ex p. Page [1993] A.C. 682; [1992] 3 W.L.R. 1112; [1993] 1 All E.R. 97; [1993] I.C.R. 114; (1993) 143 N.L.J. 15; (1993) 137 S.J.L.B. 45   17–131, 18–080

R. v Mahroof (Abdul) (1989) 88 Cr. App. R. 317 CA (Civ Div)   19–060

R. v Ministry of Agriculture, Fisheries and Food Ex p. Hamble (Offshore) Fisheries Ltd [1995] 2 All E.R. 714; [1995] 1 C.M.L.R. 533; (1995) 7 Admin. L.R. 637; [1995] C.O.D. 114   17–107

R. v Ministry of Defence Ex p. Smith [1996] Q.B. 517; [1996] 2 W.L.R. 305; [1996] 1 All E.R. 257; [1996] I.C.R. 740; [1996] I.R.L.R. 100; (1996) 8 Admin. L.R. 29; [1996] C.O.D. 237; (1995) 145 N.L.J. 1689   4–037, 17–104

R. v Monopolies and Mergers Commission Ex p. Argyll Group Plc [1986] 1 W.L.R. 763; [1986] 2 All E.R. 257; (1986) 2 B.C.C. 99086   17–069, 18–071

R. v National Insurance Commissioner Ex p. Viscusi [1974] 1 W.L.R. 646; [1974] 2 All E.R. 724; 16 K.I.R. 197; (1974) 118 S.J. 346   15–024

R. v North and East Devon Health Authority Ex p. Coughlan [2001] Q.B. 213; [2000] 2 W.L.R. 622; [2000] 3 All E.R. 850; (2000) 2 L.G.L.R. 1; [1999] B.L.G.R. 703; (1999) 2 C.C.L. Rep. 285; [1999] Lloyd's Rep. Med. 306; (2000) 51 B.M.L.R. 1; [1999] C.O.D. 340; (1999) 96(31) L.S.G. 39; (1999) 143 S.J.L.B. 213   17–108

R. v Oz. *See* R. v Anderson

R. v Paddington Valuation Officer Ex p. Peachey Property Corporation Ltd (No.2) [1966] 1 Q.B. 380; [1965] 3 W.L.R. 426; [1965] 2 All E.R. 836; (1965) 129 J.P. 447; 63 L.G.R. 353; [1965] R.A. 177; [1965] R.V.R. 384; 11 R.R.C. 141; (1965) 109 S.J. 475   18–078

R. v Panel on Take-overs and Mergers Ex p. Datafin [1987] Q.B. 815; [1987] 2 W.L.R. 699; [1987] 1 All E.R. 564; (1987) 3 B.C.C. 10; [1987] B.C.L.C. 104; [1987] 1 F.T.L.R.

181; (1987) 131 S.J. 23   6-090, 14-018, 17-133

R. v Parchment [1989] Crim. L.R. 290   16-137

R. v Parliamentary Commissioner for Administration Ex p. Dyer [1994] 1 W.L.R. 621; [1994] 1 All E.R. 375; [1994] C.O.D. 331; (1993) 137 S.J.L.B. 259   15-099, 15-113

R. v Plymouth Justice Ex p. Rogers [1982] Q.B. 863; [1982] 3 W.L.R. 1; [1982] 2 All E.R. 175; (1982) 75 Cr. App. R. 64; [1982] 3 C.M.L.R. 221; (1982) 126 S.J. 308   9-056

R. v Ponting [1985] Crim. L.R. 318 CCC   4-147

R. v Radio Authority Ex p. Bull [1998] Q.B. 294; [1997] 3 W.L.R. 1094; [1997] 2 All E.R. 561; [1997] E.M.L.R. 201; [1997] C.O.D. 382; (1997) 147 N.L.J. 489   17-011

R. v Rahman [2008] EWCA Crim 1465; [2008] 4 All E.R. 661; [2009] 1 Cr. App. R. (S.) 70; [2008] Crim. L.R. 906; (2008) 105(28) L.S.G. 15; (2008) 152(29) S.J.L.B. 32   20-121

R. v Registrar General Ex p. Segerdal [1970] 2 Q.B. 697; [1970] 3 W.L.R. 479; [1970] 3 All E.R. 886; (1970) 114 S.J. 703   16-079

R. v Reid [1992] 1 W.L.R. 793; [1992] 3 All E.R. 673; (1992) 95 Cr. App. R. 391; (1994) 158 J.P. 517; [1992] R.T.R. 341; (1994) 158 J.P.N. 452; (1992) 89(34) L.S.G. 40; (1992) 136 S.J.L.B. 253   9-084

R. v Samuel [1988] Q.B. 615; [1988] 2 W.L.R. 920; [1988] 2 All E.R. 135; (1988) 87 Cr. App. R. 232; [1988] Crim. L.R. 299; (1988) 152 J.P.N. 238   16-143, 16-144

R. v Secretary of State for Education and Science Ex p. Avon CC [1991] 1 Q.B. 558; [1991] 2 W.L.R. 702; [1991] 1 All E.R. 282; 89 L.G.R. 121; (1991) 3 Admin. L.R. 17; [1990] C.O.D. 349; (1990) 140 N.L.J. 781   6-149, 7-102

R. v Secretary of State for Employment Ex p. Equal Opportunities Commission [1995] 1 A.C. 1; [1994] 2 W.L.R. 409; [1994] 1 All E.R. 910; [1995] 1 C.M.L.R. 391; [1994] I.C.R. 317; [1994] I.R.L.R. 176; 92 L.G.R. 360; [1994] C.O.D. 301; (1994) 91(18) L.S.G. 43; (1994) 144 N.L.J. 358; (1994) 138 S.J.L.B. 84   9-079

R. v Secretary of State for Foreign and Commonwealth Affairs Ex p. World Development Movement Ltd [1995] 1 W.L.R. 386; [1995] 1 All E.R. 611; [1995] C.O.D. 211; (1995) 145 N.L.J. 51   12-024, 12-068, 12-097, 17-005, 18-039, 18-042

R. v Secretary of State for Foreign and Commonwealth Affairs Ex p. Everett [1989] Q.B. 811; [1989] 2 W.L.R. 224; [1989] 1 All E.R. 655; [1989] Imm. A.R. 155; [1989] C.O.D. 291; (1989) 86(8) L.S.G. 43; (1989) 133 S.J. 151   4-060

R. v Secretary of State for Health Ex p. Wagstaff [2001] 1 W.L.R. 292; [2002] All E.R (D) 1021 Div Ct   17-122

R. v Secretary of State for Home Affairs Ex p. Lees [1941] 1 K.B. 72 CA   19-109

R. v Secretary of State for the Environment Ex p. Kirkstall Valley Campaign Ltd [1996] 3 All E.R. 304; [1997] 1 P.L.R. 8; [1996] J.P.L. 1042; [1996] C.O.D. 337; (1996) 160 J.P. Rep. 699; [1996] E.G. 46 (C.S.); (1996) 146 N.L.J. 478; [1996] N.P.C. 41   17-121

R. v Secretary of State for the Environment Ex p. Lancashire CC [1994] 4 All E.R. 165; 93 L.G.R. 29; [1994] C.O.D. 347; (1994) 158 L.G. Rev. 541; (1994) 91(9) L.S.G. 40; (1994) 138 S.J.L.B. 53   13-022

R. v Secretary of State for the Environment Ex p. Nottinghamshire CC [1986] A.C. 240; [1986] 2 W.L.R. 1; [1986] 1 All E.R. 199; 84 L.G.R. 305; (1986) 83 L.S.G. 359; (1985) 135 N.L.J. 1257; (1986) 130 S.J. 36   5-004, 7-101, 13-077, 17-012, 17-096

R. v Secretary of State for the Environment Ex p. Ostler [1977] Q.B. 122; [1976] 3 W.L.R. 288; [1976] 3 All E.R. 90; 75 L.G.R. 45; (1976) 32 P. & C.R. 166; (1976) 238 E.G. 971; [1976] J.P.L. 301; (1976) 120 S.J. 332   17-139

R. v Secretary of State for the Environment Ex p. Rose Theatre Trust Co [1990] 1 Q.B. 504; [1990] 2 W.L.R. 186; [1990] 1 All E.R. 754; (1990) 59 P. & C.R. 257; [1990] 1 P.L.R. 39; [1990] J.P.L. 360; [1990] C.O.D. 186; [1989] E.G. 107 (C.S.); (1990) 87(6) L.S.G. 41; (1990) 134 S.J. 425   18-034, 18-036, 18-049, 18-103, 18-117

R. v Secretary of State for the Environment, Transport and the Regions Ex p. Challenger [2001] Env. L.R. 12; [2000] H.R.L.R. 630; [2000] C.O.D. 448   3-083

R. v Secretary of State for the Home Department Ex p. Benwell [1985] Q.B. 554; [1984] 3 W.L.R. 843; [1984] 3 All E.R. 854; [1984] I.C.R. 723; [1985] I.R.L.R. 6; (1984) 81 L.S.G. 2544; (1984) 128 S.J. 703.   17-043

R. v Secretary of State for the Home Department Ex p. Brind [1991] 1 A.C. 696; [1991] 2 W.L.R. 588; [1991] 1 All E.R. 720; (1991) 3 Admin. L.R. 486; (1991) 141 N.L.J. 199; (1991) 135 S.J. 250   17-011, 17-103, 20-097

R. v Secretary of State for the Home Department Ex p. Dew [1987] 1 W.L.R. 881; [1987] 2 All E.R. 1049; (1987) 84 L.S.G. 1967; (1987) 131 S.J. 658   17-043

R. v Secretary of State for the Home Department Ex p. Doody [1994] 1 A.C. 531; [1993] 3 W.L.R. 154; [1993] 3 All E.R. 92; (1995) 7 Admin. L.R. 1; (1993) 143 N.L.J. 991   17-124

R. v Secretary of State for the Home Department Ex p. Doorga [1990] Imm. A.R. 98; [1990] C.O.D. 109 CA (Civ Div)   18-023

R. v Secretary of State for the Home Department Ex p. Fire Brigades Union [1995] 2 A.C. 513; [1995] 2 W.L.R. 464; [1995] 2 All E.R. 244; (1995) 7 Admin. L.R. 473; [1995] P.I.Q.R. P228; (1995) 145 N.L.J. 521; (1995) 139 S.J.L.B. 109   4-039, 4-048

R. v Secretary of State for the Home Department Ex p. Gallagher [1996] 2 C.M.L.R. 951   2-161

R. v Secretary of State for the Home Department Ex p. Hosenball [1977] 1 W.L.R. 766; [1977] 3 All E.R. 452; (1977) 121 S.J. 255   17-116

R. v Secretary of State for the Home Department Ex p. Khawaja [1984] A.C. 74; [1983] 2 W.L.R. 321; [1983] 1 All E.R. 765; [1982] Imm. A.R. 139; (1983) 127 S.J. 137   18-087

R. v Secretary of State for the Home Department Ex p. Leech (No.2) [1994] Q.B. 198; [1993] 3 W.L.R. 1125; [1993] 4 All E.R. 539; (1993) 137 S.J.L.B. 173   3-081

R. v Secretary of State for the Home Department Ex p. McWhirter (1969) 119 N.L.J. 926   7-048

R. v Secretary of State for the Home Department Ex p. Muboyai [1992] Q.B. 244; [1991] 3 W.L.R. 442; [1991] 4 All E.R. 72; [1992] C.O.D. 37   18-088

R. v Secretary of State for the Home Department Ex p. Northumbria Police

Authority [1989] Q.B. 26; [1988] 2 W.L.R. 590; [1988] 1 All E.R. 556; (1988) 152 L.G. Rev. 308   4-044, 4-046, 4-052, 6-079, 19-081

R. v Secretary of State for the Home Department Ex p. Oladehinde [1991] 1 A.C. 254; [1990] 3 W.L.R. 797; [1990] 3 All E.R. 393; (1991) 3 Admin. L.R. 393; (1990) 140 N.L.J. 1498; (1990) 134 S.J. 1264   17-071

R. v Secretary of State for the Home Department Ex p. Onibiyo [1996] Q.B. 768; [1996] 2 W.L.R. 490; [1996] 2 All E.R. 901; [1996] Imm. A.R. 370; (1996) 93(17) L.S.G. 30; (1996) 140 S.J.L.B. 109   17-100, 17-101

R. v Secretary of State for the Home Department Ex p. Pierson [1998] A.C. 539; [1997] 3 W.L.R. 492; [1997] 3 All E.R. 577; (1997) 94(37) L.S.G. 41; (1997) 147 N.L.J. 1238; (1997) 141 S.J.L.B. 212   5-071

R. v Secretary of State for the Home Department Ex p. Quinn (Refusal to Remit Sentence) [2000] Prison L.R. 222; [2001] A.C.D. 45 QBD   4-037

R. v Secretary of State for the Home Department Ex p. Simms [2000] 2 A.C. 115; [1999] 3 W.L.R. 328; [1999] 3 All E.R. 400; [1999] E.M.L.R. 689; 7 B.H.R.C. 411; (1999) 11 Admin. L.R. 961; [1999] Prison L.R. 82; [1999] C.O.D. 520; (1999) 96(30) L.S.G. 28; (1999) 149 N.L.J. 1073; (1999) 143 S.J.L.B. 212   15-019

R. v Secretary of State for the Home Department Ex p. Sivakumaran [1988] A.C. 958; [1988] 2 W.L.R. 92; [1988] 1 All E.R. 193; [1988] Imm. A.R. 147; (1988) 85(6) L.S.G. 37; (1988) 132 S.J. 22   16-116

R. v Secretary of State for the Home Department Ex p. Swati [1986] 1 W.L.R. 477; [1986] 1 All E.R. 717; [1986] Imm. A.R. 88; (1986) 83 L.S.G. 780; (1986) 136 N.L.J. 189; (1986) 130 S.J. 186   18-067

R. v Secretary of State for the Home Department Ex p. Swati [1986] 1 W.L.R. 477; [1986] 1 All E.R. 717; [1986] Imm. A.R. 88; (1986) 83 L.S.G. 780; (1986) 136 N.L.J. 189; (1986) 130 S.J. 186   17-043

R. v Secretary of State for the Home Department Ex p. Tarrant [1985] Q.B. 251; [1984] 2 W.L.R. 613; [1984] 1 All E.R. 799; (1984) 81 L.S.G. 1045; (1984) S.J. 223   17-121

R. v Secretary of State for Trade and Industry Ex p. Lonrho [1989] 1 W.L.R. 525; [1989] 2 All E.R. 609; (1989) 5 B.C.C. 633; (1989) 139 N.L.J. 717; (1989) 133 S.J. 724   14-018, 17-012

R. v Secretary of State for Trade and Industry Ex p. Vardy [1993] 1 C.M.L.R. 721; [1993] I.C.R. 720; [1993] I.R.L.R. 104; (1994) 6 Admin. L.R. 1   14-018

R. v Secretary of State for Transport Ex p. Factortame Ltd (No.1) [1990] 2 A.C. 85; [1989] 2 W.L.R. 997; [1989] 2 All E.R. 692; [1989] 3 C.M.L.R. 1; [1989] C.O.D. 531; (1989) 139 N.L.J. 715   9-065, 9-068, 9-079, 9-080, 9-081, 9-084, 16-006, 18-051, 18-105

R. v Secretary of State for Transport Ex p. Factortame Ltd (No.2) [1991] 1 A.C. 603; [1990] 3 W.L.R. 818; [1991] 1 All E.R. 70; [1991] 1 Lloyd's Rep. 10; [1990] 3 C.M.L.R. 375; (1991) 3 Admin. L.R. 333; (1990) 140 N.L.J. 1457; (1990) 134 S.J. 1189   2-159–2-161, 3-060, 3-087, 5-065, 6-184, 9-065 , 18-105

R. v Senior [1899] 1 Q.B. 283 Crown Cases Reserved   16-091

R. v Shayler [2002] UKHL 11; [2003] 1 A.C. 247; [2002] 2 W.L.R. 754; [2002] 2 All E.R. 477; [2002] H.R.L.R. 33; [2002]

U.K.H.R.R. 603; [2002] A.C.D. 58; (2002) 99(17) L.S.G. 34; (2002) 146 S.J.L.B. 84   20–040
R. v Stanley [1965] 2 Q.B. 327; [1965] 2 W.L.R. 917; [1965] 1 All E.R. 1035; (1965) 49 Cr. App. R. 175; (1965) 129 J.P. 279; (1965) 109 S.J. 193   16–075
R. v University of Liverpool Ex p. Caesar Gordon [1991] 1 Q.B. 124; [1990] 3 W.L.R. 667; [1990] 3 All E.R. 821; (1991) 3 Admin. L.R. 101; [1991] C.O.D. 23   19–013, 19–029
R. v Visitors to the Inns of Court Ex p. Calder [1994] Q.B. 1; [1993] 3 W.L.R. 287; [1993] 2 All E.R. 876; [1993] C.O.D. 242; (1993) 143 N.L.J. 164   17–132
R. v Waltham Forest LBC Ex p. Baxter [1988] Q.B. 419; [1988] 2 W.L.R. 257; [1987] 3 All E.R. 671; 86 L.G.R. 254; [1988] R.V.R. 6; (1987) 137 N.L.J. 947; (1988) 132 S.J. 227   13–044, 17–070
R. v Waltham Forest LBC Ex p. Waltham Forest Ratepayers Action Group (1988) 152 L.G. Rev. 96   17–070
R. v Wandsworth LBC Ex p. Beckwith [1996] 1 W.L.R. 60; [1996] 1 All E.R. 129; [1996] 1 F.C.R. 504; 94 L.G.R. 77; (1996) 8 Admin. L.R. 242; (1996) 30 B.M.L.R. 105; (1996) 93(2) L.S.G. 28; (1996) 140 S.J.L.B. 27   17–062
R. v Wandsworth LBC Ex p. Mansoor [1997] Q.B. 953; [1996] 3 W.L.R. 282; [1996] 3 All E.R. 913; [1996] 3 F.C.R. 289; (1997) 29 H.L.R. 801; (1996) 160 J.P. Rep. 1020; (1996) 160 J.P.N. 786; (1996) 140 S.J.L.B. 158   17–101
R. v Ward [1993] 1 W.L.R. 619; [1993] 2 All E.R. 577; (1993) 96 Cr. App. R. 1; [1993] Crim. L.R. 312; (1992) 89(27) L.S.G. 34; (1992) 142 N.L.J. 859; (1992) 136 S.J.L.B. 191   10–104
R. (on the application of AB) v Secretary of State for the Home Department [2013] EWHC 3453 (Admin); [2014] 2 C.M.L.R. 22   9–100
R. (on the application of Abbasi) v Foreign Secretary [2002] EWCA Civ 1598; [2003] U.K.H.R.R. 76; (2002) 99(47) L.S.G. 29   6–080
R. (on the application of Al-Jedda) v Defence Secretary [2007] UKHL 58; [2008] 1 A.C. 332; [2008] 2 W.L.R. 31; [2008] 3 All E.R. 28; [2008] H.R.L.R. 13; [2008] U.K.H.R.R. 244; 24 B.H.R.C. 569; (2008) 152(1) S.J.L.B. 22   16–016
R. (on the application of Al-Skeini) v Secretary of State for Defence [2007] UKHL 26; [2008] 1 A.C. 153; [2007] 3 W.L.R. 33; [2007] 3 All E.R. 685; [2007] H.R.L.R. 31; [2007] U.K.H.R.R. 955; 22 B.H.R.C. 518; [2007] Inquest L.R. 168; (2007) 104(26) L.S.G. 34; (2007) 157 N.L.J. 894; (2007) 151 S.J.L.B. 809   16–015
R. (on the application of Alconbury Developments Ltd) v Secretary of State for the Environment, Transport and the Regions [2001] UKHL 23; [2003] 2 A.C. 295; [2001] 2 W.L.R. 1389; [2001] 2 All E.R. 929; [2002] Env. L.R. 12; [2001] H.R.L.R. 45; [2001] U.K.H.R.R. 728; (2001) 3 L.G.L.R. 38; (2001) 82 P. & C.R. 40; [2001] 2 P.L.R. 76; [2001] J.P.L. 920; [2001] 20 E.G. 228 (C.S.); (2001) 98(24) L.S.G. 45; (2001) 151 N.L.J. 727; (2001) 145 S.J.L.B. 140; [2001] N.P.C. 90   1–017, 6–156, 6–157, 6–160, 16–029, 16–031, 16–032, 16–039, 18–047, 18–109
R. (on the application of Animal Defenders International) v Secretary of State for Culture, Media and Sport [2013] E.M.L.R. 28; (2013) 57 E.H.R.R. 21; 34 B.H.R.C. 137; (2013) 163(7564) N.L.J. 20   20–104

R. (on the application of Bancoult) v Foreign Secretary (No.2) [2008] UKHL 61; [2009] 1 A.C. 453; [2008] 3 W.L.R. 955; [2008] 4 All E.R. 1055; (2008) 105(42) L.S.G. 20; (2008) 158 N.L.J. 1530; (2008) 152(41) S.J.L.B. 29   4-051, 17-060

R. (on the application of Bancoult) v Secretary of State for the Foreign and Commonwealth Office [2001] Q.B. 1067; [2001] 2 W.L.R. 1219; [2001] A.C.D. 18; (2000) 97(47) L.S.G. 39   4-037

R. (on the application of Berky) v Newport City Council [2012] EWCA Civ 378; [2012] 2 C.M.L.R. 44; [2012] Env. L.R. 35; [2012] B.L.G.R. 592; [2012] 2 P. & C.R. 12; [2012] 14 E.G. 62 (C.S.); [2013] P.T.S.R. D1   17-029

R. (on the application of Bhatt Murphy) v The Independent Assessor [2008] EWCA Civ 755; (2008) 152(29) S.J.L.B. 29   17-108

R. (on the application of Bibi) v Newham Council [2001] EWCA Civ 607; [2002] 1 W.L.R. 237; (2001) 33 H.L.R. 84; (2001) 98(23) L.S.G. 38; [2001] N.P.C. 83   17-108

R. (on the application of Boughton) v HM Treasury [2006] EWCA Civ 504; [2006] B.T.C. 460   12-096

R. (on the application of Bradley) v Work and Pensions Secretary [2008] EWCA Civ 36; [2009] Q.B. 114; [2008] 3 W.L.R. 1059; [2008] 3 All E.R. 1116; [2008] Pens. L.R. 103   15-100

R. (on the application of C) v Mental Health Review Tribunal [2001] EWCA Civ 1110; [2002] 1 W.L.R. 176; [2002] 2 F.C.R. 181; (2001) 4 C.C.L. Rep. 284; [2001] Lloyd's Rep. Med. 450; [2001] M.H.L.R. 110; (2001) 98(29) L.S.G. 39; (2001) 145 S.J.L.B. 167   16-027

R. (on the application of Camelot UK Lotteries Ltd) v Gambling Commission [2012] EWHC 2391 (Admin); [2013] P.T.S.R. 729; [2012] L.L.R. 930   18-062

R. (on the application of Cart) v Upper Tribunal [2011] UKSC 28; [2012] 1 A.C. 663; [2011] 3 W.L.R. 107; [2011] 4 All E.R. 127; [2011] P.T.S.R. 1053; [2011] S.T.C. 1659; [2012] 1 F.L.R. 997; [2011] Imm. A.R. 704; [2011] M.H.L.R. 196; [2012] Fam. Law 398; [2011] S.T.I. 1943; (2011) 161 N.L.J. 916; (2011) 155(25) S.J.L.B. 35   1-015, 6-175, 15-028

R. (on the application of Chester) v Secretary of State for Justice [2013] UKSC 63; [2014] A.C. 271; [2013] 3 W.L.R. 1076; [2014] 1 All E.R. 683; 2014 S.C. (U.K.S.C.) 25; 2014 S.L.T. 143; [2014] 1 C.M.L.R. 45; [2014] H.R.L.R. 3; 2013 G.W.D. 34-676   21-014

R. (on the application of ClientEarth) v Secretary of State for the Environment, Food and Rural Affairs (C-04/13) [2015] 1 C.M.L.R. 55; [2015] Env. L.R. 17   2-150

R. (on the application of ClientEarth) v Secretary of State for the Environment, Food and Rural Affairs [2015] UKSC 28; [2015] 4 All E.R. 724; [2015] P.T.S.R. 909; [2015] 3 C.M.L.R. 15; [2015] Env. L.R. D7   6-004, 18-048, 21-048

R. (on the application of Consumer Council for the Postal Services) v Postal Services Commission [2007] EWCA Civ 167; (2007) 104(12) L.S.G. 34   17-143

R. (on the application of Corner House Research) v Director of Serious Fraud Office [2008] UKHL 60; [2009] 1 A.C. 756; [2008] 3 W.L.R. 568; [2008] 4 All E.R. 927; [2008] Lloyd's Rep. F.C. 537; [2009] Crim. L.R. 46; (2008) 158 N.L.J. 1149; (2008) 152(32) S.J.L.B. 29   3-018, 5-072, 6-160, 18-047, 18-109

R. (on the application of Corner House) v Director of the Serious Fraud Office [2008] EWHC 246 (Admin); [2008] C.P. Rep. 20; [2008] A.C.D. 63   16-039

R. (on the application of Cowl) v Plymouth Council [2001] EWCA Civ 1935; [2002] 1 W.L.R. 803; [2002] C.P. Rep. 18; (2002) 5 C.C.L. Rep. 42; [2002] A.C.D. 11; [2002] Fam. Law 265; (2002) 99(8) L.S.G. 35; (2002) 146 S.J.L.B. 27   18-002

R. (on the application of D) v Worcestershire CC [2013] EWHC 2490 (Admin); [2013] B.L.G.R. 741; (2013) 16 C.C.L. Rep. 323   12-097

R. (on the application of Daly) v Secretary of State for the Home Department [2001] UKHL 26; [2001] 2 A.C. 532; [2001] 2 W.L.R. 1622; [2001] 3 All E.R. 433; [2001] H.R.L.R. 49; [2001] U.K.H.R.R. 887; [2001] Prison L.R. 322; [2001] A.C.D. 79; (2001) 98(26) L.S.G. 43; (2001) 145 S.J.L.B. 156   1-013, 17-102, 17-104

R. (on the application of Davis) v Secretary of State for the Home Department [2015] EWHC 2092 (Admin); [2016] 1 C.M.L.R. 13; [2015] H.R.L.R. 14; [2016] Crim. L.R. 48   20-072

R. (on the application of Equitable Members Action Group) v HM Treasury [2009] EWHC 2495 (Admin); (2009) 159 N.L.J. 1514   15-100

R. (on the application of Evans) v Attorney General [2015] UKSC 21; [2015] A.C. 1787; [2015] 2 W.L.R. 813; [2015] 4 All E.R. 395; [2015] 2 C.M.L.R. 43; [2015] Env. L.R. 34; [2015] F.S.R. 26   1-012, 3-118, 20-006, 20-115, 20-117

R. (on the application of Faulkner) v Justice Secretary [2011] EWCA Civ 349; [2011] H.R.L.R. 23; [2011] A.C.D. 101; (2011) 108(15) L.S.G. 20   18-116

R. (on the application of G1) v Secretary of State for the Home Department [2012] EWCA Civ 867; [2013] Q.B. 1008; [2013] 2 W.L.R. 1277; [2012] 4 All E.R. 987; [2012] 3 C.M.L.R. 36   2-150, 9-067

R. (on the application of Gentle) v Prime Minister [2008] UKHL 20; [2008] 1 A.C. 1356; [2008] 2 W.L.R. 879; [2008] 3 All E.R. 1; [2008] H.R.L.R. 27; [2008] U.K.H.R.R. 822; 27 B.H.R.C. 1; (2008) 105(16) L.S.G. 28; (2008) 152(16) S.J.L.B. 28   6-080

R. (on the application of Gillan) v Commissioner of Police of the Metropolis [2006] UKHL 12; [2006] 2 A.C. 307; [2006] 2 W.L.R. 537; [2006] 4 All E.R. 1041; [2006] 2 Cr. App. R. 36; [2006] H.R.L.R. 18; [2006] U.K.H.R.R. 740; 21 B.H.R.C. 202; [2006] Po. L.R. 26; [2006] Crim. L.R. 752; (2006) 150 S.J.L.B. 366   19-125

R. (on the application of Greenfield) v Home Secretary [2005] UKHL 14; [2005] 1 W.L.R. 673; [2005] 2 All E.R. 240; [2005] H.R.L.R. 13; [2005] U.K.H.R.R. 323; 18 B.H.R.C. 252; [2005] 2 Prison L.R. 129; (2005) 102(16) L.S.G. 30; (2005) 155 N.L.J. 298   18-115, 18-116

R. (on the application of H) v Mental Health Review Tribunal for North and East London Region [2001] EWCA Civ 415; [2002] Q.B. 1; [2001] 3 W.L.R. 512; [2001] H.R.L.R. 36; [2001] U.K.H.R.R. 717; (2001) 4 C.C.L. Rep. 119; [2001] Lloyd's Rep. Med. 302; (2001) 61 B.M.L.R. 163; [2001] M.H.L.R. 48; [2001] A.C.D. 78; (2001) 98(21) L.S.G. 40; (2001) 145 S.J.L.B. 108   6-157, 16-027

R. (on the application of HS2 Action Alliance Ltd) v Secretary of State for Transport [2014] EWCA Civ 1578; [2015] P.T.S.R.

1025; [2015] J.P.L. 555   3-085, 3-087, 5-068

R. (on the application of Jackson) v Attorney General [2005] UKHL 56; [2006] 1 A.C. 262; [2005] 3 W.L.R. 733; [2005] 4 All E.R. 1253; (2005) 155 N.L.J. 1600; [2005] N.P.C. 116   3-075, 3-087, 3-131, 5-070, 6-160, 6-184, 16-039, 18-047, 18-109, 21-047

R. (on the application of KM) v Cambridgeshire CC [2012] UKSC 23; [2012] 3 All E.R. 1218; [2012] P.T.S.R. 1189; [2012] B.L.G.R. 913; (2012) 15 C.C.L. Rep. 374; (2012) 126 B.M.L.R. 186; (2012) 162 N.L.J. 780   12-097

R. (on the application of Lichniak) v Secretary of State for the Home Department [2001] EWHC Admin 294; [2002] Q.B. 296; [2001] 3 W.L.R. 933; [2001] 4 All E.R. 934; [2001] H.R.L.R. 43; [2001] Prison L.R. 271; (2001) 98(24) L.S.G. 43; (2001) 145 S.J.L.B. 127   17-003

R. (on the application of Lumba) v Home Secretary [2011] UKSC 12; [2012] 1 A.C. 245; [2011] 2 W.L.R. 671; [2011] 4 All E.R. 1; [2011] U.K.H.R.R. 437; (2011) 108(14) L.S.G. 20; (2011) 155(12) S.J.L.B. 30   18-108

R. (on the application of MA) v Work and Pensions Secretary [2013] EWHC 2213 (QB); [2013] P.T.S.R. 1521; [2013] Eq. L.R. 972   17-115

R. (on the application of Macrae) v County of Herefordshire DC [2012] EWCA Civ 457; [2012] L.L.R. 720; [2012] J.P.L. 1356   1-015

R. (on the application of Mahmood) v Secretary of State for the Home Dept [2001] 1 W.L.R. 840; [2001] 1 F.L.R. 756; [2001] 2 F.C.R. 63; [2001] H.R.L.R. 14; [2001] U.K.H.R.R. 307; [2001] Imm. A.R. 229; [2001] I.N.L.R. 1; (2001) 3 L.G.L.R. 23; [2001] A.C.D. 38; [2001] Fam. Law 257   17-102

R. (on the application of McDonald) v Kensington and Chelsea RLBC [2011] UKSC 33; [2011] 4 All E.R. 881; [2011] P.T.S.R. 1266; [2011] H.R.L.R. 36; [2011] Eq. L.R. 974; [2012] B.L.G.R. 107; (2011) 14 C.C.L. Rep. 341; (2011) 121 B.M.L.R. 164; (2011) 108(29) L.S.G. 17; (2011) 161 N.L.J. 1026; (2011) 155(27) S.J.L.B. 39   12-097

R. (on the application of MK) v Barking and Dagenham LB Council [2013] EWHC 3486 (Admin).   13-093

R. (on the application of Mohamed) v Secretary of State for Foreign and Commonwealth Affairs [2010] EWCA Civ 65; [2011] Q.B. 218; [2010] 3 W.L.R. 554; [2010] 4 All E.R. 91   10-111, 19-142

R. (on the application of Moos) v Commissioner of Police of the Metropolis [2012] EWCA Civ 12   19-072

R. (on the application of Morgan Grenfell) v Special Commissioners of Income Tax [2002] UKHL 21; [2003] 1 A.C. 563; [2002] 2 W.L.R. 1299; [2002] 3 All E.R. 1; [2002] S.T.C. 786; [2002] H.R.L.R. 42; 74 T.C. 511; [2002] B.T.C. 223; 4 I.T.L. Rep. 809; [2002] S.T.I. 806; (2002) 99(25) L.S.G. 35; (2002) 146 S.J.L.B. 126; [2002] N.P.C. 70   12-096

R. (on the application of Mullins) v Appeal Board of the Jockey Club (No.1) [2005] EWHC 2197 (Admin); [2006] L.L.R. 151; [2006] A.C.D. 2   17-023

R. (on the application of Nadarajah) v Secretary of State for the Home Department [2005] EWCA Civ 1363   17-107, 17-109

R. (on the application of New College London Ltd) v Secretary of State for the Home Department [2013] UKSC 51;

R. (on the application of Nicklinson) v [2013] 1 W.L.R. 2358; [2013] 4 All E.R. 195; [2013] P.T.S.R. 995; [2014] Imm. A.R. 151; [2014] I.N.L.R. 66   6-092

R. (on the application of Nicklinson) v Ministry of Justice [2014] UKSC 38; [2015] A.C. 657; [2014] 3 W.L.R. 200; [2014] 3 All E.R. 843; [2014] 3 F.C.R. 1; [2014] H.R.L.R. 17; 36 B.H.R.C. 465; (2014) 139 B.M.L.R. 1   16-084, 16-085, 21-014

R. (on the application of NS) v Secretary of State for the Home Department (C-411/10) [2013] Q.B. 102; [2012] 3 W.L.R. 1374; [2012] 2 C.M.L.R. 9; [2012] All E.R. (EC) 1011; (2012) 109(29) L.S.G. 26   9-100

R. (on the application of O) v Secretary of State for International Development [2014] EWHC 2371 (QB)   6-004, 6-145

R. (on the application of Pearson) v Secretary of State for the Home Department [2001] EWHC Admin 239; [2001] H.R.L.R. 39   16-008

R. (on the application of Pelling) v Bow County Court (No.2) [2001] U.K.H.R.R. 165; [2001] A.C.D. 1 QBD   18-058

R. (on the application of Persey) v Secretary of State for the Environment, Food and Rural Affairs [2002] EWHC 371 (Admin); [2003] Q.B. 794; [2002] 3 W.L.R. 704; (2002) 99(18) L.S.G. 37; (2002) 146 S.J.L.B. 92; [2002] N.P.C. 44   17-122

R. (on the application of Pretty) v DPP. *See* Pretty v United Kingdom (2346/02)

R. (on the application of Pro-Life Alliance) v BBC [2003] UKHL 23; [2004] 1 A.C. 185; [2003] 2 W.L.R. 1403; [2003] 2 All E.R. 977; [2003] E.M.L.R. 23; [2003] H.R.L.R. 26; [2003] U.K.H.R.R. 758; [2003] A.C.D. 65; (2003) 100(26) L.S.G. 35; (2003) 153 N.L.J. 823; (2003) 147 S.J.L.B. 595   20-108

R. (on the application of Q) v Secretary of State for the Home Department [2003] EWHC 195 (Admin); (2003) 100(15) L.S.G. 26   6-137

R. (on the application of Quila) v Home Secretary [2011] UKSC 45; [2012] 1 A.C. 621; [2011] 3 W.L.R. 836; [2012] 1 All E.R. 1011; [2012] 1 F.L.R. 788; [2011] 3 F.C.R. 575; [2012] H.R.L.R. 2; [2011] U.K.H.R.R. 1347; 33 B.H.R.C. 381; [2012] Imm. A.R. 135; [2011] I.N.L.R. 698; [2012] Fam. Law 21; (2011) 108(41) L.S.G. 15; (2011) 155(39) S.J.L.B. 31   1-013, 17-105

R. (on the application of Quinn) v Secretary of State for the Home Department. *See* R. v Secretary of State for the Home Department Ex p. Quinn (Refusal to Remit Sentence)

R. (on the application of Reilly) v Secretary of State for Work and Pensions [2013] UKSC 68; [2014] A.C. 453; [2013] 3 W.L.R. 1276; [2014] 1 All E.R. 505   16-010

R. (on the application of Reilly) v Secretary of State for Work and Pensions [2014] EWHC 2182 (Admin); [2015] Q.B. 573; [2015] 2 W.L.R. 309   16-010

R. (on the application of Rowe) v Revenue and Customs Commissioners [2015] EWHC 2293 (Admin); [2015] B.T.C. 27   17-107, 17-108

R. (on the application of Royal College of Nursing) v Secretary of State for the Home Department [2010] EWHC 2761 (Admin); [2011] P.T.S.R. 1193; [2011] 2 F.L.R. 1399; [2011] U.K.H.R.R. 309; (2011) 117 B.M.L.R. 10; [2011] Fam. Law 231; (2010) 154(46) S.J.L.B. 30   16-010

R. (on the application of Sandiford) v Secretary of State for Foreign and Commonwealth Affairs [2014] UKSC 44;

[2014] 1 W.L.R. 2697; [2014] 4 All E.R. 843; [2014] H.R.L.R. 21   4-051
R. (on the application of Sarkandi) v Secretary of State for Foreign and Commonwealth Affairs [2015] EWCA Civ 687   19-157
R. (on the application of SB) v Denbigh High School Governors [2006] UKHL 15; [2007] 1 A.C. 100; [2006] 2 W.L.R. 719; [2006] 2 All E.R. 487; [2006] 1 F.C.R. 613; [2006] H.R.L.R. 21; [2006] U.K.H.R.R. 708; 23 B.H.R.C. 276; [2006] E.L.R. 273; (2006) 103(14) L.S.G. 29; (2006) 156 N.L.J. 552   1-013, 17-105
R. (on the application of Smith) v Oxfordshire Assistant Deputy Coroner [2010] UKSC 29; [2011] 1 A.C. 1; [2010] 3 W.L.R. 223; [2010] 3 All E.R. 1067; [2010] H.R.L.R. 28; [2010] U.K.H.R.R. 1020; 29 B.H.R.C. 497; [2010] Inquest L.R. 119; (2010) 107(28) L.S.G. 17; (2010) 160 N.L.J. 973; (2010) 154(26) S.J.L.B. 28   16-016
R. (on the application of Spath Holme Ltd) v Secretary of State for the Environment, Transport and the Regions [2001] 2 A.C. 349; [2001] 2 W.L.R. 15; [2001] 1 All E.R. 195; (2001) 33 H.L.R. 31; [2001] 1 E.G.L.R. 129; [2000] E.G. 152 (C.S.); (2001) 98(8) L.S.G. 44; (2000) 150 N.L.J. 1855; (2001) 145 S.J.L.B. 39; [2000] N.P.C. 139   3-088
R. (on the application of SRM Global Master Fund LP) v Treasury Commission. *See* SRM Global Masters Fund LP v Treasury Commissioner
R. (on the application of T, JB and AW) v Chief Constable of Greater Manchester, Secretary of State for the Home Department and Secretary of State for Justice [2014] UKSC 35; [2015] A.C. 49; [2014] 3 W.L.R. 96; [2014] 4 All E.R. 159; [2014] 2 Cr. App. R. 24; 38 B.H.R.C. 505   16-010

R. (on the application of TG) v Lambeth LBC [2011] EWCA Civ 526; [2011] 4 All E.R. 453; [2012] P.T.S.R. 364; [2011] 2 F.L.R. 1007; [2011] 2 F.C.R. 443; [2011] H.L.R. 33; [2011] B.L.G.R. 889; (2011) 14 C.C.L. Rep. 366; [2011] Fam. Law 808   18-115

R. (on the application of Transport for London) v London Underground Ltd [2001] EWHC Admin 637; Times, August 2, 2001   12-038

R. (on the application of Ullah) v Special Adjudicator [2004] UKHL 26; [2004] 2 A.C. 323; [2004] 3 W.L.R. 23; [2004] 3 All E.R. 785; [2004] H.R.L.R. 33; [2004] U.K.H.R.R. 995; [2004] Imm. A.R. 419; [2004] I.N.L.R. 381; (2004) 101(28) L.S.G. 33; (2004) 154 N.L.J. 985; (2004) 148 S.J.L.B. 762   3-083, 16-007

R. (on the application of Vetterlein) v Hampshire CC [2001] EWHC Admin 560; [2002] Env. L.R. 8; [2002] 1 P. & C.R. 31; [2002] J.P.L. 289   16-032

R. (on the application of W) v Birmingham City Council [2011] EWHC 1147 (Admin); [2011] Eq. L.R. 721; [2012] B.L.G.R. 1; (2011) 14 C.C.L. Rep. 516; (2011) 120 B.M.L.R. 134; [2011] A.C.D. 84.   12-097

R. (on the application of Weaver) v London and Quadrant Housing Trust [2009] EWCA Civ 587; [2010] 1 W.L.R. 363; [2009] 4 All E.R. 865; [2010] P.T.S.R. 1; [2009] H.R.L.R. 29; [2009] U.K.H.R.R. 1371; [2009] H.L.R. 40; [2009] B.L.G.R. 962; [2009] L. & T.R. 26; [2009] 25 E.G. 137 (C.S.); (2009) 153(25) S.J.L.B. 30; [2009] N.P.C. 81   16-025

R. (on the application of Wheeler) v Office of the Prime Minister [2008] EWHC 1409 (Admin); [2008] A.C.D. 70; (2008) 105(26) L.S.G. 22   7-106

R. (on the application of Wilkinson) v IRC [2005] UKHL 30; [2005] 1 W.L.R. 1718; [2006] 1 All E.R. 529; [2006] S.T.C. 270; [2005] U.K.H.R.R. 704; 77 T.C. 78; [2005] S.T.I. 904; (2005) 102(25) L.S.G. 33   12–096

Rabone v Pennine Care NHS Foundation Trust [2012] UKSC 2; [2012] 2 A.C. 72; [2012] 2 W.L.R. 381; [2012] 2 All E.R. 381; [2012] P.T.S.R. 497; [2012] H.R.L.R. 10; 33 B.H.R.C. 208; (2012) 15 C.C.L. Rep. 13; [2012] Med. L.R. 221; (2012) 124 B.M.L.R. 148; [2012] M.H.L.R. 66; [2012] Inquest L.R. 1; (2012) 162 N.L.J. 261; (2012) 156(6) S.J.L.B. 31   18–115

Recovery of Medical Costs for Asbestos Diseases (Wales) Bill, Re [2015] UKSC 3; [2015] A.C. 1016; [2015] 2 W.L.R. 481; [2015] 2 All E.R. 899; [2015] H.R.L.R. 9; [2015] Lloyd's Rep. I.R. 474; (2015) 143 B.M.L.R. 1   21–052

Recovery of Medical Costs for Asbestos Diseases (Wales) Bill: reference by the Counsel General for Wales and the Association of British Insurers [2015] UKSC 3; [2015] A.C. 1016   2–064

Reference Re Amendment of the Constitution of Canada (1982) 125 D.L.R. (3d) 1   5–004, 5–016

Reynolds v Times Newspapers Ltd [2001] 2 A.C. 127; [1999] 3 W.L.R. 1010; [1999] 4 All E.R. 609; [2000] E.M.L.R. 1; [2000] H.R.L.R. 134; 7 B.H.R.C. 289; (1999) 96(45) L.S.G. 34; (1999) 149 N.L.J. 1697; (1999) 143 S.J.L.B. 270   20–128

Ridge v Baldwin [1964] A.C. 40; [1963] 2 W.L.R. 935; [1963] 2 All E.R. 66; (1963) 127 J.P. 295; (1963) 127 J.P. 251; 61 L.G.R. 369; 37 A.L.J. 140; 234 L.T. 423; 113 L.J. 716; (1963) 107 S.J. 313   1–013, 8–100, 14–016, 17–119, 18–078

Roberts v Hopwood [1925] A.C. 578 HL   13–092, 13–096, 17–095

Robertson v Minister of Pensions [1949] 1 K.B. 227; [1948] 2 All E.R. 767; 64 T.L.R. 526; [1949] L.J.R. 323; (1948) 92 S.J. 603   17–078

Robinson v Secretary of State for Northern Ireland [2002] UKHL 32; [2002] N.I. 390   2–064

Roe v Wade 410 U.S. 113 (1973)   1–028, 6–156

Rogers v Secretary of State for the Home Department; R. v Lewes Justices Ex p. Secretary of State for the Home Department [1973] A.C. 388; [1972] 3 W.L.R. 279; [1972] 2 All E.R. 1057; (1972) 116 S.J. 696   10–085, 10–103

Rondel v Worsley [1969] 1 A.C. 191; [1967] 1 W.L.R. 142; [1967] 3 W.L.R. 1666; [1967] 3 All E.R. 993; (1967) 111 S.J. 927   8–115

Roquette Freres SA v Council of Ministers of the European Communities (138/79) [1980] E.C.R. 3333   2–145

Rost v Edwards [1990] 2 Q.B. 460; [1990] 2 W.L.R. 1280; [1990] 2 All E.R. 641; (1990) 87(12) L.S.G. 42   3–162, 4–139, 10–021

Rowling v Takaro Properties Ltd [1988] A.C. 473; [1988] 2 W.L.R. 418; [1988] 1 All E.R. 163   10–009

Roy v Kensington and Chelsea and Westminster Family Practitioner Committee [1992] 1 A.C. 624; [1992] 2 W.L.R. 239; [1992] 1 All E.R. 705; [1992] I.R.L.R. 233; (1992) 4 Admin. L.R. 649; [1992] 3 Med. L.R. 177; (1992) 142 N.L.J. 240; (1992) 136 S.J.L.B. 63   17–034, 17–048

Royal College of Nursing v Secretary of State for the Home Department. See R. (on the application of Royal College

of Nursing) v Secretary of State for the Home Department
Rugby Football Union v Consolidated Information Services Ltd [2012] UKSC 55; [2012] 1 W.L.R. 3333; [2013] 1 All E.R. 928; [2013] 1 C.M.L.R. 56; [2013] E.M.L.R. 25; [2013] H.R.L.R. 8; [2012] Info. T.L.R. 353; [2013] F.S.R. 23; (2012) 162 N.L.J. 1504; (2012) 156(45) S.J.L.B. 31   9–100
Russell v Duke of Norfolk [1949] 1 All E.R. 109; 65 T.L.R. 225; (1949) 93 S.J. 132   17–111
Rylands v Fletcher (1868) L.R. 3 H.L. 330   16–034
Sarkandi v Secretary of State for Foreign and Commonwealth Affairs. See R. (on the application of Sarkandi) v Secretary of State for Foreign and Commonwealth Affairs
Scoppola v Italy (126/05) [2013] 1 Costs L.O. 62; (2013) 56 E.H.R.R. 19; 33 B.H.R.C. 126   8–113, 16–009
Secretary of State for Defence v Guardian Newspapers Ltd [1985] A.C. 339; [1984] 3 W.L.R. 986; [1984] 3 All E.R. 601; (1984) 81 L.S.G. 3426; (1984) 128 S.J. 571   20–133
Secretary of State for Education and Science v Tameside MBC [1977] A.C. 1014; [1976] 3 W.L.R. 641; [1976] 3 All E.R. 665; (1976) 120 S.J. 735   7–100, 13–068, 13–069, 17–134
Secretary of State for the Home Department v AF [2009] UKHL 28; [2010] 2 A.C. 269; [2009] 3 W.L.R. 74; [2009] 3 All E.R. 643; [2009] H.R.L.R. 26; [2009] U.K.H.R.R. 1177; 26 B.H.R.C. 738; (2009) 106(25) L.S.G. 14   3–083
Secretary of State for the Home Department v MB [2007] UKHL 46; [2008] 1 A.C. 440; [2007] 3 W.L.R. 681; [2008] 1 All E.R. 657; [2008] H.R.L.R. 6; [2008] U.K.H.R.R. 119; [2008] Crim. L.R. 491; (2007) 157 N.L.J. 1577; (2007) 151 S.J.L.B. 1437   19–148
Seven Bishops' Case (1688) 12 St. Tr. 371   2–019
Silver v United Kingdom (A/161) (1983) 5 E.H.R.R. 347 ECHR   16–050
Sinclair Gardens Investments (Kensington) Ltd, Re [2015] EWCA Civ 1247; [2016] 1 P. & C.R. 14; [2016] R.V.R. 125   15–029
Sirros v Moore [1975] Q.B. 118; [1974] 3 W.L.R. 459; [1974] 3 All E.R. 776; (1974) 118 S.J. 661   6–138
Smith v Chief Constable of Sussex [2008] UKHL 50; [2009] 1 A.C. 225; [2008] 3 W.L.R. 593; [2008] 3 All E.R. 977; [2009] 1 Cr. App. R. 12; [2008] H.R.L.R. 44; [2008] U.K.H.R.R. 967; [2009] P.I.Q.R. P2; [2009] LS Law Medical 1; [2008] Inquest L.R. 176; [2008] Po. L.R. 151; (2008) 152(32) S.J.L.B. 31   8–116
Smith v East Elloe Rural DC [1956] A.C. 736; [1956] 2 W.L.R. 888; [1956] 1 All E.R. 855; (1956) 120 J.P. 263; 54 L.G.R. 233; (1956) 6 P. & C.R. 102; (1956) 100 S.J. 282   17–138
Smith v Ministry of Defence 2013] UKSC 41; [2014] A.C. 52; [2013] 3 W.L.R. 69; [2013] 4 All E.R. 794; [2013] H.R.L.R. 27; 35 B.H.R.C. 711; [2014] P.I.Q.R. P2; [2013] Inquest L.R. 135   16–016, 18–116
Solihull MBC v Maxfern Ltd [1977] 1 W.L.R. 127; [1977] 2 All E.R. 177; 75 L.G.R. 327; [1977] J.P.L. 171   13–070
South Buckinghamshire DC v Porter (No.1); Chichester DC v Searle; Wrexham CBC v Berry; Hertsmere BC v Harty [2003] UKHL 26; [2003] 2 A.C. 558; [2003] 2 W.L.R. 1547; [2003] 3 All E.R. 1; [2003] H.R.L.R. 27; [2003] U.K.H.R.R. 1344; [2003] B.L.G.R. 449; [2003] 2 P.L.R.

101; [2003] J.P.L. 1412; [2003] 23 E.G. 135 (C.S.); (2003) 100(22) L.S.G. 32; (2003) 147 S.J.L.B. 626; [2003] N.P.C. 70   6-157, 16-036, 16-037

South East Asia Firebricks Sdn. Bhd. v Non-Metallic Mineral Products [1981] A.C. 363; [1980] 3 W.L.R. 318; [1980] 2 All E.R. 689; (1980) 124 S.J. 496   17-090

South Place Ethical Society, Re; sub nom. Barralet v Attorney General [1980] 1 W.L.R. 1565; [1980] 3 All E.R. 918; 54 T.C. 446; [1980] T.R. 217; (1980) 124 S.J. 774   16-079

Southport Corp v Esso Petroleum. *See* Esso Petroleum Co Ltd v Southport Corp

Spycatcher litigation. *See* Attorney General v Observer Ltd (No.2)

SRM Global Masters Fund LP v Treasury Commissioner [2009] EWCA Civ 788; [2010] B.C.C. 558; [2009] U.K.H.R.R. 1219   6-160, 16-039, 18-047, 18-109

Starrs v Ruxton 2000 J.C. 208; 2000 S.L.T. 42; 1999 S.C.C.R. 1052; [2000] H.R.L.R. 191; [2000] U.K.H.R.R. 78; 8 B.H.R.C. 1; 1999 G.W.D. 37-1793   16-027

Steed v Secretary of State for the Home Department [2000] 1 W.L.R. 1169; [2000] 3 All E.R. 226; (2000) 97(23) L.S.G. 40   17-042

Steel v United Kingdom (24838/94) (1999) 28 E.H.R.R. 603; 5 B.H.R.C. 339; [1998] Crim. L.R. 893; [1998] H.R.C.D. 872   19-001

Steeples v Derbyshire CC [1985] 1 W.L.R. 256; [1984] 3 All E.R. 468; [1981] J.P.L. 582; (1985) 82 L.S.G. 358   18-018

Stockdale v Haringey LBC 88 L.G.R. 7; [1989] R.A. 107; (1990) 154 L.G. Rev. 91   13-077

Sunday Times v United Kingdom (A/30) (1979-80) 2 E.H.R.R. 245; (1979) 76 L.S.G. 328   16-055, 20-132

Sydney Municipal Council v Campbell [1925] A.C. 338 PC (Aus)   17-092

Tariq v Home Office [2011] UKSC 35; [2012] 1 A.C. 452; [2011] 3 W.L.R. 322; [2012] 1 All E.R. 58; [2012] 1 C.M.L.R. 2; [2011] I.C.R. 938; [2011] I.R.L.R. 843; [2011] H.R.L.R. 37; [2011] U.K.H.R.R. 1060   19-149

Taylor v Lawrence 2002] EWCA Civ 90; [2003] Q.B. 528; [2002] 3 W.L.R. 640; [2002] 2 All E.R. 353; [2002] C.P. Rep. 29; (2002) 99(12) L.S.G. 35; (2002) 152 N.L.J. 221; (2002) 146 S.J.L.B. 50   17-128

Teare v O'Callaghan (1982) 4 E.H.R.R. 232   16-052

Thoburn v Sunderland City Council [2002] EWHC 195 (Admin); [2003] Q.B. 151; [2002] 3 W.L.R. 247; [2002] 4 All E.R. 156; (2002) 166 J.P. 257; [2002] 1 C.M.L.R. 50; [2002] Eu. L.R. 253; [2002] L.L.R. 548; (2002) 99(15) L.S.G. 35; (2002) 152 N.L.J. 312; (2002) 146 S.J.L.B. 69   3-087, 5-070, 6-160, 16-039, 18-047, 18-109, 21-049

Thomas v Chief Adjudication Officer [1991] 2 Q.B. 164; [1991] 2 W.L.R. 886; [1991] 3 All E.R. 315; [1990] 3 C.M.L.R. 611; [1990] I.R.L.R. 436   9-079

Thomas v National Union of Mineworkers (South Wales Area) [1986] Ch. 20; [1985] 2 W.L.R. 1081; [1985] 2 All E.R. 1; [1985] I.C.R. 886; (1985) 82 L.S.G. 1938; (1985) 129 S.J. 416   19-028

Thomas v Sawkins [1935] 2 K.B. 249; [1935] All E.R. Rep. 655 KBD   19-052

Thomas v Sorrell (1674) Vaugh. 330   2-019

Thomas v University of Bradford [1987] A.C. 795; [1987] 2 W.L.R. 677; [1987] 1 All E.R. 834; [1987] I.C.R. 245; (1987) 84 L.S.G. 980; (1987) 137 N.L.J. 220; (1987) 131 S.J. 296   17-131

Tisdell v Combe 112 E.R. 667; (1838) 7 Ad. & El. 788   20–133

Torfaen BC v B&Q Plc (C–145/88) EU:C:1989:593; [1990] 2 Q.B. 19; [1990] 2 W.L.R. 1330; [1990] 1 All E.R. 129; [1989] E.C.R. 3851; [1990] 1 C.M.L.R. 337; [1990] C.O.D. 141; (1990) 134 S.J. 908   9–079

TP v United Kingdom (28945/95) [2001] 2 F.L.R. 549; [2001] 2 F.C.R. 289; (2002) 34 E.H.R.R. 2; (2001) 3 L.G.L.R. 52; (2001) 4 C.C.L. Rep. 398; [2001] Fam. Law 59   8–116

Tyrer v United Kingdom (A/26) (1979–80) 2 E.H.R.R. 1 ECHR   16–051

Uniplex (UK) Ltd v NHS Business Services (C–406/08) EU:C:2010:45; [2010] P.T.S.R. 1377; [2010] 2 C.M.L.R. 47   1–014, 17–027, 18–066

United Kingdom v Council of the European Union (C–84/94)EU:C:1996:431; [1996] E.C.R. I-5755; [1996] 3 C.M.L.R. 671; [1996] All E.R. (EC) 877; [1997] I.C.R. 443; [1997] I.R.L.R. 30   9–054

Van Colle v Chief Constable of Hertfordshire [2008] UKHL 50; [2009] 1 A.C. 225; [2008] 3 W.L.R. 593; [2008] 3 All E.R. 977; [2009] 1 Cr. App. R. 12; [2008] H.R.L.R. 44; [2008] U.K.H.R.R. 967; [2009] P.I.Q.R. P2; [2009] LS Law Medical 1; [2008] Inquest L.R. 176; [2008] Po. L.R. 151; (2008) 152(32) S.J.L.B. 31   8–116

Van Duyn v Home Office (41/74) EU:C:1974:133; [1975] Ch. 358; [1975] 2 W.L.R. 760; [1975] 3 All E.R. 190; [1974] E.C.R. 1337; [1975] 1 C.M.L.R. 1; (1974) 119 S.J. 302   9–072

Van Gend en Loos v Nederlandse Administratie der Belastingen (26/62) EU:C:1963:1; [1963] E.C.R. 1; [1963] C.M.L.R. 105   9–065

Venables v News Group Newspapers Ltd [2001] Fam. 430; [2001] 2 W.L.R. 1038; [2001] 1 All E.R. 908; [2001] E.M.L.R. 10; [2001] 1 F.L.R. 791; [2002] 1 F.C.R. 333; [2001] H.R.L.R. 19; [2001] U.K.H.R.R. 628; 9 B.H.R.C. 587; [2001] Fam. Law 258; (2001) 98(12) L.S.G. 41; (2001) 151 N.L.J. 57; (2001) 145 S.J.L.B. 43   16–012

Von Colson v Land Nordrhein-Westfahlen (C–14/83) EU:C:1984:153 [1984] E.C.R. 1891; [1986] 2 C.M.L.R. 430   9–075

Wandsworth LBC v Winder [1985] A.C. 461; [1984] 3 W.L.R. 1254; [1984] 3 All E.R. 976; (1985) 17 H.L.R. 196; 83 L.G.R. 143; (1985) 82 L.S.G. 201; (1985) 135 N.L.J. 381; (1984) 128 S.J. 838   17–039, 17–040

Webb v Chief Constable of Merseyside [2000] Q.B. 427; [2000] 2 W.L.R. 546; [2000] 1 All E.R. 209; (1999) 96(47) L.S.G. 33; (2000) 144 S.J.L.B. 9   16–155

Western Fish Products Ltd v Penwith DC [1981] 2 All E.R. 204; 77 L.G.R. 185; (1979) 38 P. & C.R. 7; [1978] J.P.L. 627; (1978) 122 S.J. 471   17–076, 17–077, 17–079, 17–081

Whaley v Lord Watson of Invergowrie 2000 S.C. 340; 2000 S.L.T. 475; 2000 S.C.L.R. 279; 2000 G.W.D. 8–272   2–089

Wheeler v Leicester City Council [1985] A.C. 1054; [1985] 3 W.L.R. 335; [1985] 2 All E.R. 1106; 83 L.G.R. 725; (1985) 129 S.J. 558   17–097

Williams v Bedwelty Justices. See R. v Bedwellty Justices Ex p. Williams

Wilson v First County Trust Limited (No.2) [2003] UKHL 40; [2004] 1 A.C. 816; [2003] 3 W.L.R. 568; [2003] 4 All E.R. 97; [2003] 2 All E.R. (Comm) 491; [2003] H.R.L.R. 33; [2003] U.K.H.R.R. 1085; (2003) 100(35) L.S.G. 39; (2003) 147 S.J.L.B. 872   3–075, 6–156

Wise v Dunning [1902] 1 K.B. 167 KBD   19-038
Woolwich Building Society v IRC (No.2) [1993] A.C. 70; [1992] 3 W.L.R. 366; [1992] 3 All E.R. 737; [1992] S.T.C. 657; (1993) 5 Admin. L.R. 265; 65 T.C. 265; (1992) 142 N.L.J. 1196; (1992) 136 S.J.L.B. 230   12-009, 12-010; 12-096, 18-107
Worringham and Humphreys v Lloyds" Bank Ltd (No.2) [1982] 1 W.L.R. 841; [1982] 3 All E.R. 373; [1982] I.C.R. 299; [1982] I.R.L.R. 74; (1982) 126 S.J. 99   16-103
Wrexham v Berry. *See* South Buckinghamshire DC v Porter (No.1)

X v United Kingdom (A/46) (1982) 4 E.H.R.R. 188 ECHR   16-057, 18-086
X Ltd v Morgan-Grampian (Publishers) Ltd [1991] 1 A.C. 1; [1990] 2 W.L.R. 1000; [1990] 2 All E.R. 1; (1990) 87(17) L.S.G. 28; (1990) 140 N.L.J. 553; (1990) 134 S.J. 546   20-134
Young v United Kingdom (A/44) [1982] E.C.C. 264; [1981] I.R.L.R. 408; (1982) 4 E.H.R.R. 38   16-058
Z v United Kingdom (29392/95) [2001] 2 F.L.R. 612; [2001] 2 F.C.R. 246; (2002) 34 E.H.R.R. 3; 10 B.H.R.C. 384; (2001) 3 L.G.L.R. 51; (2001) 4 C.C.L. Rep. 310; [2001] Fam. Law 583   8-115, 8-116

Table of Statutes

1215 Magna Carta 1–031, 2–007, 3–021, 5–002, 5–045
1284 Statute of Wales 2–011
1494 Poynings Law 2–024
1535 Laws in Wales Act (c.26) 2–011
1535 Vagabonds Act 13–055
1597 Poor Relief Act 13–055
1601 Poor Relief Act (c.2) 6–051, 13–055
1627 Petition of Right (c.1) 3–024
1688 Bill of Rights (c.2) 1–031, 2–007, 2–008, 3–024, 3–112, 3–159
   art.9 3–165, 4–139, 10–021
1689 Bill of Rights 8–043, 12–008, 12–049, 12–097
   art.4 12–049
1700 Act of Settlement (c.2) 2–007, 2–008, 3–115
1701 Act of Settlement 8–043
1707 Union with England Act (c.7) 2–014, 2–025, 8–043
   art.1 2–017, 2–031
1715 Septennial Act (c.38) 3–026
1743 Poor Relief Act (c.38) 6–051
1800 Act of Union (Ireland) Act (c.38) 2–032
1801 Enclosure Act (c.109) 6–043
1814 Treason Act (c.146)
   s.1 3–115
1832 Representation of the People Act (c.45) 3–027, 3–032, 6–016, 7–030, 7–033, 7–034, 7–112, 8–065
1833 Judicial Committee Act (c.41) 2–121
1835 Municipal Corporations Act 3–032, 6–034
1840 Parliamentary Papers Act (c.9) 3–166
1843 Libel Act (c.96)
   s.5 20–123
1844 Factories Act (c.15) 6–029
1844 Judicial Committee Act (c.69) 2–121
1844 Poor Law Amendment Act (c.101) 6–052
1845 General Enclosure Act 6–045
1847 Town Police Clauses Act (c.89)
   s.28 19–049
1848 Treason Felony Act (c.12) 3–115
1848 Summary Jurisdiction Act (c.43) 6–058
1855 Places of Worship Registration Act (c.81) 16–078
1855 Metropolis Local Management Act (c.120) 2–003
   s.62 17–095
1857 Obscene Publications Act (c.83) 16–073
1857 Summary Proceedings Act 6–057
1860 Petitions of Right Act (c.34) 10–082, 10–083
1861 Offences Against the Person Act (c.100) 3–030, 19–061
1866 Exchequer and Audit Departments Act (c.39) 6–048, 12–069, 12–081
   s.22 12–022
1866 Poor Law Amendment Act (c.113) 13–55
1867 British North American Act (c.3) 5–015

TABLE OF STATUTES

1867 Representation of the People Act (c.102)   3–027, 7–035, 7–036, 8–065
1872 Parks Regulations Act (c.15)   19–028
1875 Public Health Act (c.79)   19–028
1876 Appellate Jurisdiction Act (c.59)   3–151, 6–115
1879 District Auditors Act (c.6)   6–053
1882 Municipal Corporations Act (c.50)
    s.191(4)   17–119
1883 Corrupt and Illegal Practices Prevention Act (c.51)   7–070
1884 Representation of the People Act (c.3)   7–036
1886 Riot (Damages) Act (c.38)   19–059
1888 Local Government Act (c.41)   3–032
1889 Official Secrets Act (c.52)   20–017
1893 Rules Publication Act (c.66)   10–050
1894 Merchant Shipping Act (c.60)
    s.466   15–037
1894 Local Government Act (c.73)   6–046
1898 Prison Act (c.41)   15–018
1905 Sydney Corporation Amendment Act   17–092
1906 Open Spaces Act (c.25)
    s.15   19–028
1909 Electric Lighting Act (c.34)   15–063
1911 Parliament Act (c.13)   1–031, 3–087, 3–122, 3–123, 3–125, 3–129—3–131, 5–070, 7–153, 12–049
    s.1   3–126
    s.7   7–045
1911 Official Secrets Act (c.28)   4–154, 11–075, 20–017
    s.1   20–019, 20–026
      (1)   20–018
    s.2   10–114, 10–115, 20–021, 20–023, 20–024, 20–029
      (1)   20–022
    s.9   20–091
1911 National Insurance Act (c.55)   6–165
1913 Trade Union Act (c.30)
    s.3(1)(b)   7–083
1914 Government of Ireland Act (c.90)   3–129
1914 Welsh Church Act (c.91)   3–129
1919 Church of England (Assembly) Powers Act (c.76)   6–067
1920 Indemnity Act (c.48)   19–104
1920 Emergency Powers Act (c.55)   6–066, 19–093, 19–103
1920 Government of Ireland Act (c.67)   2–027, 2–028, 2–030, 2–034, 2–038, 2–094, 5–013, 7–053
    s.75   2–027
1920 Official Secrets Act (c.75)   11–075, 20–017
1921 Tribunals of Inquiry (Evidence) Act (c.7)   4–118, 6–133, 6–182, 15–041, 15–043, 15–045, 15–048, 15–068
1921 Exchequer and Audit Departments Act (c.52)   12–069
1922 Irish Free State Constitution Act (c.1)   2–027
1922 Irish Free State (Consequential Provisions) Act (c.2)   2–027
1922 Irish Free State (Agreement) Act (c.4)   2–027
1931 Statute of Westminster (c.4)   5–015, 5–016
    s.4   5–035
1932 Chancel Repairs Act (c.20)   16–022
1933 Administration of Justice (Miscellaneous Provisions) Acts (c.36)   6–144, 18–006
1934 Factories Act   14–015
1936 His Majesty's Declaration of Abdication Act (c.3)   3–116
1936 Public Order Act (c.6)   19–006, 19–011, 19–030
    s.1   19–013
    s.2   19–013

s.3 19-030	1949 House of Commons (Redistribution of Seats) Act (c.66) 7-048, 7-049
s.5 19-051, 19-054, 19-062, 19-063	1949 Parliament Act (c.103) 1-031, 3-087, 3-122, 3-125, 3-126, 3-129, 3-131, 5-070, 12-049, 21-047
1938 Administration of Justice (Miscellaneous Provisions) Acts (c.63) 6-144	1950 Foreign Compensation Act (c.12)
s.7 18-006	s.4(4) 17-086, 17-135
1939 Emergency Powers (Defence) Act (c.62) 19-106	1950 Shops Act (c.28) 13-070, 13-073
1939 Import, Export and Customs Powers (Defence) Act (c.69) 4-119, 19-107	s.47 13-073
	1952 Civil List Act (c.37) 3-116, 4-067
1939 Official Secrets Act (c.121) 11-075, 20-017	1952 Prison Act (c.52) 4-160, 15-018
	1953 Post Office Act (c.36)
1940 Emergency Powers (Defence) Act (c.20) 19-106	s.11 16-075
	1953 Royal Titles Act (c.9) 2-018
1944 Education Act (c.31) 17-069	1957 Electricity Act (c.48) 14-046
s.9(1) 16-081	1957 Housing Act (c.56) 17-039
s.68 17-134	s.111(1) 17-067
1945 Representation of the People Act (c.5) 7-038	1958 Life Peerages Act (c.21) 3-151
	1958 House of Commons (Redistribution of Seats) Act (c.26) 7-048, 7-049
1945 Statutory Orders (Special Procedure) Act (c.18) 6-045, 6-067	1958 Agricultural Marketing Act (c.47) 17-094
1946 Statutory Instruments Act (c.36) 10-045, 10-050	s.19 17-093
s.5 10-046	1958 Public Records Act (c.51)
1946 New Towns (c.68) 17-125	s.5(1) 20-013
1946 National Insurance Act 6-169	1958 Tribunals and Inquiries Act (c.66) 6-173, 15-014, 15-040
1947 Crown Proceedings Act (c.44) 4-034, 6-020, 6-04, 10-082, 10-083	1959 Street Offences Act (c.57)
	s.7(3) 16-132
s.2 18-108	1959 Obscene Publications Act (c.66) 16-056, 16-067—16-072, 16-075
s.21(1) 18-104	
s.28 10-087	s.2 16-071
1947 Town and Country Planning Act (c.51) 18-003	s.3 16-073
	1959 Mental Health Act (c.72)
1948 National Insurance Act (c.29) 6-169	s.66(3) 16-057
1948 British Nationality Act (c.56) 16-108	1960 Public Bodies (Admission to Meetings) Act (c.67) 13-041
1948 Representation of the People Act (c.65) 7-038	1962 Commonwealth Immigrants Act (c.21) 16-108
1949 Wireless Telegraphy Act (c.54) 12-008, 12-097	1964 Emergency Powers Act (c.38) 19-093, 19-094, 19-103

TABLE OF STATUTES

1964 Police Act (c.48) 4–047, 6–079, 19–011, 19–079
  s.28 19–082
  s.41 19–081
  s.49 16–156, 16–159
  s.51(3) 19–034
1964 Obscene Publications Act (c.74) 16–071
  s.1(2) 16–070
  s.2 16–071
1964 Diplomatic Privileges Act (c.81) 4–066
1965 War Damage Act (c.18) 4–054, 19–109
1965 Law Commission Act (c.22) 3–069
1965 Race Relations Act (c.73) 16–093, 16–094, 16–100, 20–120
1966 Local Government Act (c.42) 13–057
  s.11 13–030
1967 General Rates Act (c.9) 13–055
1967 Parliamentary Commissioner Act (c.13) 15–075, 15–078, 15–080, 15–086, 15–102
  s.5(2) 15–084
    (5) 15–099
  s.6(3) 15–091
    (4) 15–091
  s.7(2) 15–099
  s.8 15–092
    (4) 4–085, 15–092
  s.10 15–093
    (3) 15–093
  s.12(3) 15–087
  Sch.2 15–078
1967 Public Records Act (c.44) 20–013
1967 Criminal Law Act (c.58)
  s.3 19–096, 19–112, 19–113
1967 Abortion Act (c.87)
  s.4 16–091
1968 Provisional Collection of Taxes Act (c.2) 12–007, 12–059, 12–097
1968 National Loans Act (c.13) 3–126, 12–012
1968 Consular Relations Act (c.18) 4–066
1968 Theatres Act (c.54) 16–077
  s.4 20–122
  s.6 20–122
1968 Theft Act (c.60) 21–011
1968 Race Relations Act (c.71) 16–093—16–095
1968 Town and Country Planning Act (c.72) 15–063
1969 Representation of the People Act (c.15) 7–039
  s.9(4) 7–076
  s.75(1)(c) 7–076
1969 Post Office Act (c.48)
  s.80 20–065
1970 Equal Pay Act (c.41) 2–133, 4–156, 16–102, 16–103
1971 Unsolicited Goods and Services Act (c.30)
  s.4 16–074
1971 Misuse of Drugs Act (c.38) 16–139
  s.23 16–131
1971 Tribunals and Inquiries Act (c.62) 6–173
  s.11 15–040
1971 Civil Aviation Act (c.75) 4–058, 14–077, 17–0
1971 Immigration Act (c.77) 10–072, 16–108, 16–109, 16–111, 16–123, 17–071
  s.1 16–113
    (3) 16–132
  s.2 16–113
  s.3(2) 6–092, 16–111, 16–113
1971 Town and Country Planning Act (c.78) 18–003
  Pt II 15–052
1972 Civil List Act (c.7) 3–116, 4–067
1972 Superannuation Act (c.11) 4–154
1972 Road Traffic Act (c.20) 19–034

1972	Gas Act (c.60) 9-074	1974	Lord Chancellor (Tenure of Office and Discharge of Ecclesiastical Functions) Act (c.25) 16-079
1972	European Communities Act (c.68) 1-031, 3-087, 5-070, 9-013, 16-006, 21-049	1974	Northern Ireland Act (c.28) 2-029
	s.2 2-155	1974	Finance Act (c.30) 15-094
	(1) 2-156	1974	Health and Safety at Work Act (c.37) 6-068
	(2) 2-156		s.16 6-068
	(4) 2-155, 2-157		s.17 6-068
	s.3 2-155	1974	Trade Union and Labour Relations Act (c.52) 16-058
1972	Local Government Act (c.70) 6-066, 6-088, 13-032, 15-050		s.15 19-040
	s.111 6-087, 13-030, 17-062, 17-063	1974	Rehabilitation of Offenders Act (c.53) 16-010
	(1) 6-086, 13-085, 13-087	1975	Finance Act (c.7) 15-094
	s.137 13-030	1975	Social Security Act (c.14) 9-079, 12-096
	s.222 13-070, 13-073	1975	House of Commons Disqualification Act (c.24) 4-019, 4-084
	(1) 18-015	1975	Ministers of the Crown Act (c.26) 4-019
	s.235 19-028	1975	Ministerial and other Salaries Act (c.27) 4-084
	s.236 2-075	1975	Referendum Act (c.33) 7-155
	s.250 15-058	1975	Sex Discrimination Act (c.65) 4-156, 7-068, 16-102, 16-104
	Sch.13 6-086, 6-087, 17-062		Pt II 16-104
	Pt 1 13-087	1975	Civil List Act (c.82) 3-116, 4-067
1972	Northern Ireland (Border Poll) Act 7-154	1976	Local Government (Miscellaneous Provisions) Act (c.57)
1973	Northern Ireland Assembly Act (c.17) 2-038		s.19(1) 6-087
1973	National Health Service Reorganisation Act (c.32) 15-080	1976	Motorcycle Crash Helmets (Religious Exemption) Act (c.62) 16-083
1973	Northern Ireland Constitution Act (c.36) 2-038, 7-154	1976	Race Relations Act (c.74) 4-156, 16-093—16-095, 16-097, 16-100, 16-104, 20-120
1973	Fair Trading Act (c.41)		s.1 16-100
	Sch.8 14-034		s.5 16-093
	Sch.9 14-037		ss.35—38 16-100
1973	Government Trading Funds Act (c.63) 11-048, 11-050, 12-022, 12-048	1976	Planning Inquiries (Attendance of Public) Act 15-053
	s.2 11-050		
	s.4(6) 12-022		
1974	Local Government Act (c.7) 15-101, 15-109		
1974	Contingencies Fund Act (c.18) 12-073		

1977	Housing (Homeless Persons) Act (c.48) 17-031, 17-033, 17-043, 18-067		s.2 20-136
			(2) 20-138
			s.10 20-133, 20-134
1978	European Assembly Elections Act (c.10) 7-089		Sch.1 20-136
1981	Senior Courts Act (c.54) 1-013, 6-008, 6-066, 6-145, 17-024, 18-005
1978	State Immunity Act (c.33) 4-066
1978	Protection of Children Act (c.37) 16-076		s.31 1-013, 6-145, 17-024, 17-025, 17-029, 18-001, 18-005, 18-052, 18-063
1978	Employment Protection Consolidation Act (c.44) 18-094
Pt V 4-156		(2) 18-104
s.138 4-156		(3) 6-008, 18-026, 18-026
1978	Scotland Act (c.51) 2-081, 7-156		(3C–3F) 17-026, 17-056, 18-061
1978	Wales Act (c.52) 7-156		(5) 6-013
1979	Customs and Excise Management Act (c.2)		(6) 17-028, 18-060
			(7) 18-060
s.49 16-074	1981	British Nationality Act (c.61) 4-059, 16-109, 16-111, 16-123
1979	Ancient Monuments and Archaeological Areas Act (c.46)
			s.6 16-111
s.1 18-036		s.39(2) 16-111
1980	Child Care Act (c.5)		s.40(2) 17-028
s.26 15-039		Sch.1 16-111
1980	Education Act (c.20)	1981	Acquisition of Land Act (c.67) 15-049, 17-138
s.6(3)(a)   16-082
s.13 16-082		s.23 17-018
1980	Employment Act (c.42) 6-074	1981	Broadcasting Act (c.68) 17-103
s.3(8) 19-040	1982	Civil Aviation Act (c.16) 14-077
s.16(1) 19-040	1982	Oil and Gas (Enterprise) Act (c.23) 14-038
1980	Overseas Development and Co-operation Act (c.63) 18-044
	1982	Local Government (Miscellaneous Provisions) Act (c.30) 16-076
s.1   18-042
(1) 18-043	1982	Local Government Finance Act (c.32) 13-059, 17-015
1980	Local Government Planning and Land Act (c.65) 13-058, 13-059
Pt III 13-047		Pt III 13-096
Pt VI 13-057		s.19 6-052
1980	Highways Act (c.66) 19-011		s.20 6-052
s.137 19-014		s.25(d) 18-014
1981	British Telecommunications Act (c.38) 14-020	1982	Northern Ireland Act (c.38) 2-029
1982	Mental Health (Amendment) Act (c.51) 16-057
1981	Contempt of Court Act (c.49) 6-140, 16-048, 20-132
1983	Representation of the People Act (c.2) 7-040, 7-068, 13-037

s.1   7-039
s.75   7-077
s.93   7-075
s.95   19-028
s.96   19-028
1983   British Nationality (Falkland Islands) Act (c.6)   16-111
1983   National Audit Act (c.44)   3-050, 12-081
　s.6   12-088
　Sch.4   12-081
1983   Medical Act (c.54)   2-123
1984   Prevention of Terrorism (Temporary Provisions) Act (c.8)   4-052, 16-064
1984   Telecommunications Act (c.12)   14-020, 14-021, 14-023, 14-024, 17-037, 20-072
　s.1   14-021
1984   Dentists Act (c.24)   2-123
　s.27   15-016
1984   County Courts Act (c.28)
　s.75   6-066
1984   Rates Act (c.33)   13-060, 13-079
1984   Data Protection Act (c.35)   10-119, 15-001
1984   Video Recordings Act (c.39)   16-076
1984   Trade Union Act (c.49)   7-071
1984   Police and Criminal Evidence Act (c.60)   6-073, 15-004, 16-127, 16-129, 16-130, 16-135, 16-138, 16-139, 16-142, 16-146, 16-149, 19-132, 20-053, 20-072, 20-091
　Pt II   16-140
　s.1   16-139
　s.8   16-140
　s.9   16-140
　s.18   16-141
　s.24   16-131, 16-132, 16-133
　　(3)   16-133
　ss.24—26   19-049
　s.25   19-049
　s.26   16-132, 19-049

　s.32   16-141
　ss.50—60   16-146
　s.58   16-125
　　(1)   16-142
　s.61   16-136
　s.62   16-136
　s.66   16-129
　s.76   16-147
　　(8)   16-148
　ss.76—78   16-146
　s.78   16-146
　ss.83—100   16-156
　Sch.2   16-132
1985   Companies Act (c.6)   12-072
1985   Company Securities (Insider Dealing) Act (c.8)   15-036
1985   Cinemas Act (c.13)   16-076
1985   Hong Kong Act (c.15)   16-111
1985   Prosecution of Offences Act (c.23)   16-125, 16-127, 19-074
　s.23   4-041
1985   Local Government (Access to Information) Act (c.43)   13-042, 20-005
1985   Representation of the People Act (c.50)   7-039, 7-068
　ss.1—3   7-039
　Sch.4 para.38   19-028
1985   Local Government Act (c.51)   6-096
1985   Interception of Communications Act (c.56)   4-045, 6-076, 16-048, 20-065, 20-066, 20-068, 20-069, 20-070
　s.1(3)   20-071
　s.2   20-066
　s.65   20-071
1985   Sporting Events (Control of Alcohol etc.) Act (c.57)   16-132, 19-041
1986   Local Government Act (c.10)
　s.4   7-084
1986   Drugs Trafficking Offences Act (c.32)   19-132

1986	Gas Act (c.44) 14-030—14-033, 14-038, 14-060	1987	Immigration (Carriers' Liability) Act (c.24) 16-114
1986	Social Security Act (c.50) 17-017	1987	Northern Ireland (Emergency Provisions) Act (c.30)

1986   Gas Act (c.44)   14-030—14-033, 14-038, 14-060
1986   Social Security Act (c.50)   17-017
1986   Parliamentary Constituencies Act (c.56)   7-050
   Sch.2   7-050
      r.1   7-050
      r.2   7-050
      r.3   7-050
      r.4   7-054—7-057, 7-060, 7-061, 7-063, 7-064
      rr.4—6   7-050
      r.5   7-054, 7-055, 7-057—5-061, 7-063, 7-064
      r.7   7-050
   Sch.3   15-079
1986   Financial Services Act (c.60)
   s.177(1)   15-036
1986   Education (No.2) Act (c.61)   19-013, 19-029
   s.43   19-013
      (2)   16-083
1986   Public Order Act (c.64)   3-069, 4-052, 16-101, 19-005, 19-011, 19-026, 19-054, 19-059, 19-065, 19-066, 19-071, 19-073, 20-120
   Pt I   19-030
   Pt III   16-100
   s.1   19-055
   s.2   19-060, 19-061
   s.3   19-061
      (6)   1-132
   s.4   19-051, 19-060, 19-062, 19-063
      (a)   19-063
   s.5   19-064, 19-065
      (4)   19-065
   s.8   19-057
   s.11   19-030, 19-066
   s.12   19-030, 19-067
   s.14   19-030
   s.17   20-120

1987   Immigration (Carriers' Liability) Act (c.24)   16-114
1987   Northern Ireland (Emergency Provisions) Act (c.30)
   s.5   16-062
1987   Access to Personal Files Act (c.37)   20-005
1987   Parliamentary and Health Service Commissioners Act (c.39)   15-078
1987   Channel Tunnel Act (c.53)   15-066
1988   Local Government Act (c.9)   6-085, 13-007, 13-048, 15-102
   s.30   18-014
   Sch.4   18-014
1988   Merchant Shipping Act (c.12)   2-159, 9-080
   s.14   9-081, 9-083
1988   Immigration Act (c.14)   16-123
1988   Employment Act (c.19)
   s.1   16-083
1988   Access to Medical Reports Act (c.28)   10-123, 20-005
1988   Environment and Safety Information Act (c.30)   20-005
1988   Criminal Justice Act (c.33)   4-039, 4-048
   Pt VII   4-039
   s.108   4-038
   s.134   4-066
   s.139   16-139
   s.140   16-139
   s.171   4-039
1988   Legal Aid Act (c.34)
   s.18(4)   18-072
1988   Education Reform Act (c.40)   6-149, 13-048
   s.2(1)(a)   16-081
      (8)   16-081
   s.6   16-081
   s.7   16-081
      (1)   16-081
   s.202   16-083

1988 Local Government Finance Act (c.41) 13-063	s.5 15-106
1988 Copyright, Designs and Patents Act (c.48) 20-111	s.26 15-105
	s.31 15-102
1988 Road Traffic Act (c.52)	1990 Town and Country Planning Act (c.8)
s.163 16-131	s.78 18-003
1989 Prevention of Terrorism (Temporary Provisions) Act (c.4) 19-103, 19-119	s.97 6-161, 16-040
	s.187B 16-036
s.16 19-132	s.288 6-147
s.17 19-132	1990 Access to Health Records Act (c.23) 20-005
s.18A 19-122	
Sch.5 19-132	1990 Government Trading Act (c.30) 11-048, 11-050, 12-012, 12-022
Sch.7 19-132	
1989 Security Services Act (c.5) 19-088, 19-089, 20-051, 20-052, 20-056, 20-057, 20-059, 20-063	
	1990 Human Fertilisation and Embryology Act (c.37) 14-075, 16-065
s.3 20-051	1990 Courts and Legal Services Act (c.41) 6-118, 6-138
1989 Official Secrets Act (c.6) 4-154, 11-052, 11-075, 15-071, 20-023, 20-024, 20-026, 20-028—20-030, 20-040, 20-046, 20-047	
	s.110 15-083
	1990 Broadcasting Act (c.42) 20-103
	s.92(2)(a)(i) 17-011
s.1 4-147, 20-040, 20-047	1990 Environmental Protection Act (c.43) 15-072
(2) 20-047	
(3) 20-048	1990 Import and Export Control Act (c.45) 19-107
ss.1-4 20-025	
s.2(2)b 20-049	1991 War Crimes Act (c.13) 3-130
s.4 20-040	1991 Local Government Finance (Publicity for Auditors Reports) Act (c.15) 13-007
s.8 20-027	
1989 Water Act (c.15) 14-061, 14-062, 14-067	
	1991 Football (Offences) Act (c.19) 19-041
s.230(3) 14-064	
1989 Electricity Act (c.29) 14-040, 14-049, 14-050, 14-053, 14-054, 14-056, 14-060	1991 Northern Ireland (Emergency Provisions) Act (c.24)
	Pt IV 19-133
Pt III 14-056	Sch.3 19-133
s.36 14-055	1991 Child Support Act (c.48) 11-037
s.96 14-050, 14-056	1991 Water Industry Act (c.56) 14-062, 14-070, 16-034
1989 Football Spectators Act (c.37) 19-041	
	s.18 16-034
1989 Local Government and Housing Act (c.42) 13-030, 13-045, 13-048, 13-063, 15-102	s.22 16-034
	s.37 14-062
	s.94 14-062

TABLE OF STATUTES

1992 Local Government Finance Act
(c.14)   13–066, 13–067
  Pt 2   18–112
  s.1   6–096
  s.54   6–096
1992 Local Government Act
(c.19)   6–085, 13–008, 13–022,
13–034
  Pt II   13–033
  s.13(6)   13–022
1992 Competition and Service (Utilities)
Act (c.43)   14–005, 14–025, 14–041,
14–056, 14–070
  s.39   14–070
1992 Tribunals and Inquiries Act
(c.53)   6–173, 15–040
1992 Civil Service (Management of
Functions) Act (c.61)   4–157
1993 British Coal and British Rail
(Transfer Proposals) Act
(c.2)   14–012
1993 Judicial Pensions and Retirement Act
(c.8)   6–126
1993 Osteopaths Act (c.21)   2–123,
14–075
1993 Asylum and Immigration Appeals Act
(c.23)   16–115, 17–017, 17–043
  s.3   16–116
  s.8   16–116
  s.9   16–116
1993 Video Recordings Act (c.24)   16–076
1993 Local Government (Amendment) Act
(c.27)   13–030
1993 Representation of the People Act
(c.29)
  s.59   7–039
1993 European Communities
(Amendment) Act (c.32)   2–127
1993 Education Act (c.35)
  ss.266—269   15–103
  Sch.16   15–103
1993 Welsh Language Act (c.38)   2–012

1993 European Parliamentary Elections
Act (c.41)   7–089
1993 Railways Act (c.43)   6–105, 14–012
1993 Health Service Commissioners Act
(c.46)   15–081
1994 Intelligence Services Act
(c.13)   19–088, 20–047, 20–057,
20–063, 20–072
  s.1(1)   20–057
  s.3(1)   20–057
  s.9(4)   20–058
  s.10(7)   19–088
1994 Local Government (Wales) Act
(c.19)   13–020
1994 Coal Industry Act (c.21)   14–012
1994 Police and Magistrates' Courts Act
(c.29)   19–084
1994 Criminal Justice and Public Order
Act (c.33)   16–126, 16–128, 19–005,
19–011, 19–084
  Pt IV   19–027
  Pt V   19–021, 19–052
  ss.34—39   16–150
1994 Local Government etc (Scotland) Act
(c.39)   13–020
1994 Deregulation and Contracting Out
Act (c.40)   3–089, 6–070, 6–071,
14–043
  Pt 1 Ch.1   6–070
1995 Environment Act (c.25)   14–062
1995 Child Support Act (c.34)   11–037
1995 Gas Act (c.45)   14–038, 14–039,
14–060
1995 Town and Country Planning (Costs of
Inquiries etc.) Act (c.49)   15–052
1995 Disability Discrimination Act
(c.50)   16–106
1995 Criminal Injuries Compensation Act
(c.53)   4–039
1996 Northern Ireland (Entry to
Negotiations, etc.) Act (c.11)   2–033
1996 Reserved Forces Act (c.14)   19–101

1996	Police Act (c.16) 15–004, 19–076, 19–084	1998	Greater London Authority (Referendum) Act (c.3) 2–066
	Pt IV 16–159	1998	Bank of England Act (c.11) 12–032
	Sch.2 para.1(1) 19–085		Pt 1 12–034
1996	Employment Rights Act (c.18) 20–112		s.4 12–032
	s.43J 5–031	1998	Northern Ireland (Elections) Act (c.12) 2–033
1996	Northern Ireland (Emergency Provisions) Act (c.22) 19–119	1998	Public Interest Disclosure Act (c.23) 4–166, 5–031, 16–106, 20–110, 20–112
	Pt IV 19–133	1998	Data Protection Act (c.29) 15–004, 19–088, 20–005, 20–113, 20–113, 20–140
1996	Criminal Procedure and Investigations Act (c.25) 10–109, 16–128, 20–040		s.28 4–085
1996	Defamation Act (c.31) 3–165, 20–124	1998	Crime and Disorder Act (c.37) 3–048, 16–128, 19–053
	s.13 3–165, 3–166, 4–140, 10–022		s.36 3–115
1996	Security Services Act (c.35) 19–089—19–091, 20–052, 20–062, 20–063	1998	Government of Wales Act (c.38) 2–043, 2–069, 2–070, 2–071, 2–073, 12–044
1996	Armed Forces Act (c.46) 19–100		Pt III 2–043
1996	Asylum and Immigration Act (c.49) 16–115—16–118, 17–017		s.22 2–070
	s.4 16–118		s.107 2–059
	s.7 16–118	1998	Competition Act (c.41) 14–003
	s.8 16–119	1998	Human Rights Act (c.42) I-001, IV-001, 1–003, 1–010, 1–011, 1–013, 1–017, 1–027, 1–028, 1–031, 2–059, 2–060, 2–165, 3–048, 3–067, 3–082, 3–132, 4–007, 4–037, 4–147, 5–043, 5–064, 5–067, 5–073, 6–002, 6–007, 6–011, 6–080, 6–121, 6–129, 6–131, 6–146, 6–155—6–160, 6–184, 7–039, 7–077, 8–014, 8–111, 8–114, 8–117, 8–120, 10–122, 10–123, 11–085, 12–096, 15–001, 15–013, 15–019, 15–057, 15–099, 15–118, 16–001—16–003, 16–005—16–007, 16–009—16–012, 16–015, 16–021, 16–025, 16–027, 16–036, 16–041, 16–125, 16–162, 17–003, 17–102, 17–143, 18–001, 18–064, 18–115, 18–116, 18–121, 19–001, 19–122,
	s.9 16–118		
1996	Broadcasting Act (c.55) 20–103, 20–105		
1996	Public Order (Amendment) Act (c.59) 19–065		
1997	Northern Ireland Arms Decommissioning Act (c.7) 2–033		
1997	Protection from Harassment Act (c.40)		
	s.4 19–020		
	s.5 19–020		
1997	Police Act (c.50) 16–010, 19–041, 19–083, 19–091, 20–070		
	Pt IV 16–156		
1997	Special Immigration Appeals Commission Act (c.68) 19–147, 19–151		

19–153, 19–159, 20–002—20–005, 20–008, 20–040, 20–107, 20–125, 20–140, 21–002, 21–003, 21–004, 21–014, 21–036, 21–058
s.2   3–083, 16–007, 17–013
s.3   3–067, 3–166, 6–156, 16–006, 21–014
(1)   8–120
s.4   16–006, 21–014
(2)   17–013
s.6   6–156, 16–012, 16–014, 16–021, 16–024, 18–022
(3)(b)   16–021
(5)   16–021
s.7   6–156, 16–013, 16–021, 18–022
s.8   16–014
(4)   6–156
s.10   3–067, 16–006
s.12   16–026
s.13   16–026
s.19   3–067, 16–007
Sch.2   16–006
1998   Scotland Act (c.46)   2–020, 2–042, 2–059, 2–070, 2–082, 2–083, 2–085, 2–088, 2–089, 12–044
s.28   2–084
(5)   2–089
(7)   2–106, 2–110
s.29   2–059
s.30(2)   2–083
s.33   2–075
s.57   2–059
Sch.4   2–083
Sch.5   2–042, 2–083, 12–043
1998   Northern Ireland Act (c.47)   2–032, 2–033, 2–094, 2–095, 2–097, 12–044
s.1   2–030
s.6   2–059
s.24   2–059
Sch.4A Pt 1A   2–097
s.3C   2–097

1998   Registration of Political Parties Act (c.48)   7–068
1999   European Parliamentary Elections Act (c.1)   3–130, 7–089
1999   Disability Rights Commission Act (c.17)   16–106
1999   Football (Offences and Disorder) Act (c.21)   19–041
ss.1—5   19–041
1999   Employment Relations Act (c.26)   4–166
1999   Local Government Act (c.27)   13–010, 13–013, 21–012
s.30   13–013
Sch.1   13–013
1999   Food Standards Act (c.28)   6–072
s.22   6–072
s.23   6–072
1999   Greater London Authority Act (c.29)   2–003, 2–057, 2–066
Pt 1   2–010
Pt VI   19–076
Pt VII   19–076
1999   Immigration and Asylum Act (c.33)   16–115—16–117, 16–119, 16–120, 17–017
s.4   16–119
s.14   16–123
s.22   16–119
s.65   16–120
ss.74—78   16–120
s.84   16–119
1999   House of Lords Act (c.34)   3–002, 3–142
2000   Northern Ireland Act (c.1)   2–033, 2–044
2000   Representation of the People Act (c.2)   7–039, 7–40, 7–041
2000   Armed Forces Discipline Act (c.4)   19–101
2000   Crown Prosecution Inspectorate Act (c.10)   19–074

2000	Terrorism Act (c.11) 15–029, 19–118, 19–119, 19–122, 19–133, 20–072
	Pt II 19–121, 19–122
	Pt III 19–121, 19–122
	Pt V 19–122, 19–123, 19–132
	s.1 19–118, 19–119
	s.5 19–121
	s.19 19–122, 20–137
	(3) 20–137
	s.24 19–121
	s.25 19–125
	s.41 19–122—19–124
	Sch.6 19–121
	Sch.7 19–132
	Sch.8 19–132
2000	Child Support, Pensions and Social Security Act (c.19) 11–037
2000	Government Resources and Accounts Act (c.20) 12–015, 12–023, 12–069, 12–072
2000	Local Government Act (c.22) 13–007, 13–014, 13–040, 21–022
	Pt II 13–016
	Pt III 13–016
	s.2 13–030
2000	Regulation of Investigatory Powers Act (c.23) 15–029, 16–128, 19–091, 20–064, 20–070
	Pt II 20–064
	Pt III 20–064, 20–070
	s.1 20–070
2000	Football (Disorder) Act (c.25) 19–041
	s.2 19–041
2000	Utilities Act (c.27) 6–073, 6–083, 14–003, 14–005, 14–027, 14–057, 14–059, 14–060, 14–083, 15–004
2000	Health Service Commissioners (Amendment) Act (c.28) 15–082
2000	Race Relations (Amendment) Act (c.34) 16–101
2000	Freedom of Information Act (c.36) 1–011, 3–042, 3–174, 4–013, 4–085, 5–031, 10–053, 10–123, 10–127, 10–129, 11–075, 15–004, 15–011, 19–088, 20–002, 20–005, 20–008, 20–110, 20–113, 20–115, 20–116, 20–140
	Pt I 20–113
	Pt II 20–114
	s.1 10–124, 20–113
	s.2(2) 20–005
	s.14 10–124
	s.18 10–126
	s.23 20–005
	ss.26—29 20–114
	ss.32—35 20–114
	s.35 20–117
	(1) 10–127
	ss.38—39 20–114
	ss.42—44 20–114
	s.44 20–114
	s.53 3–118, 20–006
	Sch.1 20–113
2000	Transport Act (c.38) 14–004, 14–012
2000	Political Parties, Elections and Referendums Act (c.41) 7–039
	Pt I 7–066
	Pt III 7–068, 7–070
	Pt IV 7–068, 7–070
	Pt VII 7–158
	s.125 7–084, 7–085
	s.139 7–071
	s.140 7–071
	s.144 7–077
2000	Sexual Offences (Amendment) Act (c.44) 3–130
2000	Bail, Judicial Appointments etc. (Scotland) Act (asp 9) 6–121
2001	Regulatory Reform Act (c.6) 3–091, 6–070, 6–071

TABLE OF STATUTES

2001 Criminal Justice and Police Act (c.16)   16–128, 19–020, 19–053
   s.57   16–155
2001 Anti-Terrorism, Crime and Security Act (c.24)   7–108, 16–017, 19–140
   Pt 4   16–018, 19–140
   s.23   16–019, 19–140
2002 Sex Discrimination (Election Candidates) Act (c.2)   7–068
2002 British Overseas Territories Act (c.8)   16–112
2002 Land Registration Act (c.9)   16–022
2002 Office of Communications Act (c.11)   14–003, 14–026
2002 Football (Disorder) (Amendment) Act (c.12)   19–042
2002 Electoral Fraud (Northern Ireland) Act (c.13)   7–043
2002 Export Control Act (c.28)   19–107
2002 Proceeds of Crime Act (c.29)   11–051
2002 Police Reform Act (c.30)   5–031, 16–156
2002 Enterprise Act (c.40)   15–029
2002 Freedom of Information (Scotland) Act (asp 13)   20–116
2003 Communications Act (c.21)   14–026, 20–103
   s.333   7–073, 20–107
2003 Criminal Justice Act (c.44)
   s.30   16–135
     (1)   16–135
   s.41   16–136
   s.42   16–136
2004 Gangmasters (Licensing) Act (c.11)   20–052
2004 Hunting Act (c.37)   3–087, 3–130, 3–131, 5–070, 21–047
2005 Prevention of Terrorism Act (c.2)   16–011, 16–019, 16–020, 19–134, 19–141, 19–147
   s.1   19–134
   s.6   19–134
2005 Constitutional Reform Act (c.4)   1–027, 5–008, 5–043, 6–008, 6–112, 6–117—6–119, 6–173, 15–026
   s.3   6–121
     (6)   6–121
   s.5(1)   6–122
   Sch.11(1) para.1   6–008
2005 Mental Capacity Act (c.5)   3–042, 10–053
2005 Inquiries Act (c.12)   3–042, 6–133, 6–182, 10–053, 15–068, 15–069, 15–071
2005 Serious Organised Crime and Police Act (c.15)   19–028
2005 Gambling Act (c.19)   3–042
2006 Racial and Religious Hatred Act (c.1)   16–101
2006 Terrorism Act (c.11)   19–124, 20–120, 20–121
   Pt I   19–129
   Pt IV   19–126
   s.1   20–120
   s.2   20–121
     (13)   20–121
   s.20(3)(a)   20–120
   s.43   19–125
   s.44   19–125
   s.55   19–127
     (3)   19–127
   s.56   19–128
   s.57   19–128
     (3)   19–128
   s.58   19–129
   s.58A   19–129
2006 Government of Wales Act (c.32)   2–069, 2–070, 2–071, 2–073
   Pt 4   2–072, 2–073
   s.45   2–071
   Sch.5   2–070

2006	Wireless Telegraphy Act (c.36) 20-072
2006	Safeguarding Vulnerable Groups Act (c.47) 16-010
2006	Charities Act (c.50) 3-042
2006	Legislative Reform Act (c.51) 3-091
2006	Armed Forces Act (c.52) 4-062
2007	Tribunals, Courts and Enforcement Act (c.15) 1-013, 1-015, 6-173, 15-026
s.13	15-027
s.14	15-027
2007	Pensions Act (c.22) 10-053
2007	Sustainable Communities Act (c.23) 13-019
2007	Greater London Authority Act (c.24) 2-010, 2-066
2008	Regulatory Enforcement and Sanctions Act (c.13) 14-079
2008	Health and Social Care Act (c.14)
s.145	16-025
2008	Counter-Terrorism Act (c.28) 16-011, 19-129, 19-147
2008	Planning Act (c.29) 15-067
2009	Banking Act (c.1) 12-064, 12-103
s.5	12-103
s.10	12-103
s.74	12-025, 12-103
s.75	12-025
2009	Northern Ireland Act (c.3)
Sch.1 s.4(3)	2-097
2009	Business Rate Supplements Act (c.7) 2-067
2009	Political Parties and Elections Act (c.12) 7-070
Sch.9	7-071
2009	Parliamentary Standards Act (c.13) 10-037, 20-118, 21-011
2009	Law Commission Act (c.14) 3-071
2009	Perpetuities and Accumulations Act (c.18) 3-072
2009	Local Democracy, Economic Development and Construction Act (c.20) 2-068, 13-002
2009	Coroners and Justice Act (c.25) 15-011
s.73	20-119
2009	Damages (Asbestos-related Conditions) (Scotland) Act (asp 4) 2-061, 21-050
2010	Fiscal Responsibility Act (c.3) 12-015, 12-099
2010	Third Parties (Rights Against Insurers) Act (c.10) 3-072
2010	Equality Act (c.15) I-001, 1-010, 7-069, 11-085
2010	Bribery Act (c.23) 4-165, 11-055, 11-058
2010	Constitutional Reform and Governance Act (c.25) 1-027, 3-110, 4-040, 4-110, 4-152, 4-158, 4-161, 11-006, 11-053, 12-051, 12-099
2010	Equitable Life (Payments) Act (c.34) 15-100
2011	Parliamentary Voting System and Constituencies Act (c.1) 7-050
2011	Budget Responsibility and National Audit Act (c.4) 12-015, 12-017, 12-082, 12-099
s.1	12-015
2011	European Union Act (c.12) 1-031, 3-065, 7-160, 9-068, 21-002
2011	Police Reform and Social Responsibility Act (c.13) 2-010, 2-066, 2-068, 16-152, 16-153, 16-157, 19-077, 19-079
2011	Fixed Term Parliaments Act (c.14) I-001, 3-010, 3-110, 4-036, 4-064, 4-071, 7-013, 7-045, 7-084, 7-098, 12-059, 21-002
2011	Sovereign Grant Act (c.15) 3-116, 4-068
s.6	4-068

TABLE OF STATUTES

2011 Localism Act (c.20)   1-031, 2-010, 2-066, 2-067, 4-026, 6-094, 7-159, 11-084, 13-002, 13-018, 13-019, 13-029, 13-103, 15-114, 21-002, 21-020
2011 Terrorism Prevention and Investigation Measures Act (c.23)   19-135, 19-138
   s.6(4)   19-135
      (10)   19-135
   s.8   19-136
   s.9(6)   19-137
   s.16   19-138
   ss.16—20   19-138
2011 Public Bodies Act (c.24)   2-010, 2-066, 3-091, 6-101, 6-177, 15-031
2012 Health and Social Care Act (c.7)   11-083, 14-075
2012 Protection of Freedoms Act (c.9)   1-031, 15-001, 16-010, 19-123
   s.47A(2)   19-125
      (3)   19-125
      (5)   19-125
   s.59   19-125
2012 Scotland Act (c.11)   2-076, 2-077, 2-084—2-087, 2-090, 2-092, 12-046
2012 Financial Services Act (c.21)   1-011, 12-035
2013 Public Service Pensions Act (c.2)   4-084
2013 Electoral Registration and Administration Act (c.6)   7-043, 7-050
2013 Jobseekers (Back to Work Schemes) Act (c.17)   16-010
2013 Justice and Security Act (c.18)   19-088, 19-147, 19-157, 19-159, 20-059
   Pt 2   10-111, 19-088, 19-150
   s.6   19-150, 19-151
   s.9   19-151
   s.12   19-151
2013 Crime and Courts Act (c.22)   6-117, 20-088
   s.23   17-054
   s.57   19-063
2013 Enterprise and Regulatory Reform Act (c.24)   5-031, 16-106, 20-088
2013 Defamation Act (c.26)   20-127
   s.1   20-127
   s.4   20-128
   s.5   20-129
   s.6   20-130
   s.8   20-130
   s.11   20-130
2013 Financial Services (Banking Reform) Act (c.33)   12-020
2013 Scottish Independence Referendum Act (asp 14)   7-087
2014 Local Audit and Accountability Act (c.2)   6-053, 12-084, 13-004, 13-102
2014 Water Act (c.21)   14-071, 14-072
2014 Immigration Act (c.22)   16-122, 16-124
   Pt 2   16-124
2014 Care Act (c.23)   14-075
2014 House of Lords Reform Act (c.24)   3-134, 3-151
2014 Data Retention and Investigatory Powers Act (c.27)   19-005, 20-072
   Pt 5   19-139
   Pt 6   19-139
   Pt 7   19-139
   s.1   20-072
2014 Wales Act (c.29)   2-076
2015 Criminal Justice and Courts Act (c.2)   6-155
   s.84(2)   17-026, 17-056, 18-061
2015 Counter-Terrorism and Security Act (c.6)   4-061, 19-005, 19-013, 19-138, 19-139, 19-154

Pt 1	19–138
Pt 2	19–138
Pt 3	20–072
2015	International Development (Official Development Assistance Target) Act (c.12) 4–011
2015	House of Lords (Expulsion and Suspension) Act (c.14) 3–151
2015	Deregulation Act (c.20) 6–071, 20–102
2015	Corporation Tax (Northern Ireland) Act (c.21) 2–100
2015	House of Commons Commission Act (c.24) 3–038
2015	Small Business, Enterprise and Employment Act (c.26) 16–106
2015	Modern Slavery Act (c.30) 3–041, 6–105, 10–052, 15–001, 20–052
2015	European Union Referendum Act (c.36) 7–003, 9–002
2016	Cities and Local Government Devolution Act (c.1) 2–068, 13–002, 13–031
2016	Scotland Act (c.11) 2–088

Table of Statutory Instruments

1952 Trafalgar Square Regulations (SI 1952/776) 19–028
1965 Rules of the Supreme Court (SI 1965/1776) 17–024, 18–004, 18–006
    Ord.5 r.2 18–090
        r.4 18–090
    Ord.15 r.16 18–090, 18–091
    Ord.25 r.5 18–091
    Ord.53 1–013, 6–145, 17–021, 17–024, 17–025, 17–029, 17–030, 17–031, 17–034, 17–040, 17–044, 17–047, 17–048, 18–001, 18–004, 18–005, 18–009, 18–010, 18–021, 18–025, 18–028, 18–052, 18–059, 18–060, 18–063, 18–081, 18–084, 18–086, 18–089, 18–095, 18–096, 18–100, 18–103, 18–106, 19–050
        r.3(10) 18–104
        r.4 18–060
        r.9(5) 17–047
1972 Northern Ireland Movement of Pigs Regulations 9-062
1975 Rehabilitation of Offenders Act 1974 (Exceptions) Order (SI 1975/1023) 16–010
1976 Building Regulations (SI 1976/1676) 15–109
1977 Police (Appeal) Rules (SI 1977/759) 18–067
1982 Homosexual Offences (Northern Ireland) Order (SI 1982/1536) 16–048, 16–053
1983 Equal Pay (Amendment) Regulations (SI 1983/1794) 2–133
1985 Police (Complaints) (General) Regulations (SI 1985/520) 16–156
1988 Town and Country Planning (Inquiries Procedure) Rules (SI 1988/944) 15–040
    r.16(4) 15–056
       (5) 15–056
1990 Immigration Rules 16–123
1992 Environmental Information Regulations (SI 1992/3240) 10–123
1994 Immigration Rules 16–115—16–117
1995 Police Regulations (SI 1995/215) 18–067
1995 Town and Country Planning (General Permitted Development) Order (SI 1995/418) 15–109
1996 Asylum Appeals (Procedure) Rules (SI 1996/2070) 16–117
1998 Civil Procedure Rules (SI 1998/3132) 6–008, 6–066, 18–002
   Pt 8 1–013
   Pt 30 6–012
   r.52 6–147
   Pt 54 1–013, 6–145, 17–021, 18–001
   r.54 6–147, 17–029
   r.54.4 6–008
   r.54.12 6–148
   r.54.19 6–012
   r.54.20 6–012
1999 National Assembly for Wales (Transfer of Functions) Order (SI 1999/672) 2–070
1999 Police (Conduct) Regulations (SI 1999/730) 15–004

1999	Prosecution of Offences Act 1985 (Specified Proceedings) Order (SI 1999/904) 16–125	2010	Family Procedure Rules (SI 2010/2955) 20–139
2000	Immigration and Asylum Appeals (Procedure) Rules (SI 2000/2333) 16–120	2012	Civil Procedure (Amendment No.2) Rules (SI 2012/2208) 6–175
2003	Privacy and Electronic Communications (EC Directive) Regulations (SI 2003/2426) 15–012, 20–113	2013	Rehabilitation of Offenders Act 1974 (Exceptions) Order 1975 (Amendment) (England and Wales) Order (SI 2013/1198) 16–010
2004	Environmental Information Regulations (SI 2004/3391) 15–012	2013	Civil Procedure (Amendment No.4) Rules (SI 2013/1412) 6–147, 6–148
2006	Public Contracts Regulations (SI 2006/5) 6–147	2013	Supreme Court (Judicial Appointments) Regulations (SI 2013/2193) 6–117
2008	Export Control Order (SI 2008/3231) 19–107	2013	Defamation (Operators of Websites Regulations (SI 2013/3028) 20–129
2010	Data Protection (Monetary Penalties) (Maximum Penalty and Notices) Regulations (SI 2010/31) 20–113	2014	Civil Legal Aid (Remuneration) (Amendment) (No.3) Regulations (SI 2014/607) 17–057
		2015	Transfer of Functions (Information and Public Records) Order (SI 2015/1897) 20–014

Part I

General Introduction

Part I provides a general introduction to public law setting out a definition of the subject and the scope of the book.[1] The sources of constitutional and administrative law are examined and explained. This part of the book contains an outline of the subject setting out the main principles of constitutional law including the powers of Parliament, government and the courts, and briefly examines the development of administrative law and the impact of the Human Rights Act 1998 and the Equality Act 2010. The public law of the UK is a reflection of many of the underlining social, political and economic factors that are found in the UK. Martin Loughlin makes the pertinent point:

> "Once extolled as a standing wonder, the British Constitution today can evoke bewilderment and sometimes even derision. Many now find the idea of a constitution that has grown organically in response to economic, political and social changes rather puzzling."[2]

Instead of consolidating and slowing down, the pace of change affecting the UK's constitutional arrangements appears to be under renewed review and political pressures. Many of the present-day contemporary changes are as a consequence of economic austerity following the financial crisis in 2008 and a growth in public debt as a percentage of GDP.[3] Pressure on public spending has led to large cuts in public sector finances. The role of the state and public funding of many aspects of service delivery is under intense scrutiny with reductions in funding courts, legal aid and many aspects of public welfare. Tony Prosser has recently identified what he terms "the economic constitution"[4] that reminds us that public law applies to areas

---

1 Peter Leyland, *The Constitution of the / Kingdom*, 2nd edn (Oxford: Hart Publishers, 2012).
2 Martin Loughlin, *The British Constitution* (Oxford: Oxford University Press, 2013), p.1.
3 Institute for Fiscal Studies, *The IFS Green Budget 2015* (London: Institute for Fiscal Studies, 2015).
4 Tony Prosser, *The Economic Constitution* (Oxford: Oxford University Press, 2014).

of economic management, public finance, and the regulation of many services and institutions that advance constitutional norms within patterns of economic activity. Economic instruments are increasingly important within the boundaries of "hard" and "soft" law. Oversight through audit and scrutiny are also relevant and important. Increasingly the Judiciary are important in terms of interpretation but also in defining boundaries and settling legality. Parliament and regulatory agencies and institutions provide different forms of accountability and political oversight. The economic constitution is a useful perspective that emphasises the interdependence of the market, the state and the delivery of many public and private services. Managing the economy enables the government to make far reaching and significant decisions using different techniques and strategies to engage with constitutional norms as well as institutions.

The relationship between the citizen and the state is being recalibrated. Overshadowing many of our constitutional liberties are questions about terrorism and striking a proportionate balance in addressing the terrorist threat while maintaining and protecting civil liberties. The election of a coalition government in 2010 and the Fixed Term Parliaments Act 2011 which introduced a five year fixed term parliament, is a reflection of changes in mainstream party politics, necessitated by the fact that no one single party had an overall majority. The implications of coalition government for public law are still being evaluated.[5] The May 2015 election has resulted in a Conservative led majority government. Political intrusion into the working of many aspects of the UK's constitution has become accepted often leaving checks and balances on executive power weak and ineffective. The UK's constitution is highly unusual as it is largely unwritten, reliant on self-restraint and in reality much of the exercise of power is far removed from judicial scrutiny. Constitutional actors and institutions such as Parliament, the courts and judges have come under intense media scrutiny particularly the actions, salaries and expenses of individual peers and MPs. Economic considerations mixed with European scepticism has also fuelled political discussion about human rights, devolution and membership of the EU. Many view the current state of the UK's constitutional arrangements with some anxiety and that current debates about devolution and the EU are evidence of a "constitutional crossroads".[6] It is clear that the greater transfer of powers to Scotland will transform the current relationship between England, Wales, and Northern Ireland. This raises issues about "English votes for English laws" and opens up debates about financial arrangements between the devolved governments.[7] It will also raise serious questions about how far the United Kingdom Parliament will be able to supervise and oversee the devolved arrangements. The referendum on EU membership on 23 June 2016 is also capable of redefining the UK especially as there is a division of opinion in Scotland, Northern Ireland with a vote to remain compared to England and Wales with a vote to leave.

---

5   See Richard Rawlings, "A Coalition Government in Westminster" in J. Jowell, D. Oliver and C. O'Cinneide, *The Changing Constitution*, 8th edn (Oxford: Oxford University Press, 2015), pp.194–221.
6   See the Report of an Independent Commission, *A Constitutional Crossroads: Ways forward for the United Kingdom*, The Bingham Centre, London May, 2015.
7   See House of Commons Briefing Paper, *English votes for English laws* 7339 (2 December 2015).

1

The Public Law of the United Kingdom: Definition and Scope

A: Introduction

It is first necessary to define not only public law, but also, what public law is intended to achieve.[1] The term public law may at first appear unusual. Many writers and textbooks[2] prefer to refer to public law in terms of constitutional and administrative law. In the common law tradition, historically the categorisation of constitutional law was distinguished from administrative law. Often the two branches of constitutional and administrative law were seen as distinct and poorly integrated, a reflection of the absence of a codified or written constitution. There may also have been a reluctance to use the term public law as it is a term used in civil law systems and commonly found in continental jurisprudence influenced by Roman Law. Under a civil law system a clear distinction is drawn between public and private law for two reasons: because of a separate system of courts and because of differences in the development of codes and in the conceptual framework of analysis.[3] As Elliott and Feldman have usefully noted

1–001

---

1 Perhaps the most revealing analysis is to be found in Walter Bagehot's view: "There is a great difficulty in the way of a writer who attempts to sketch a living Constitution—a Constitution that is in actual work and power. The difficulty is that the subject is in constant change. An historical writer does not feel this difficulty: he deals only with the past; he can say definitely, the Constitution worked in such and such a manner in the year at which he begins, and in a manner in such and such respects different in the year at which he ends; he begins with a definitive point of time and ends with one also. But a contemporary writer who tries to paint what is before him is puzzled and perplexed: what he sees is changing daily". Walter Bagehot, "Introduction to the second edition", *The English Constitution*, 2nd edn (London: H. S. King, 1872).
2 See A. W. Bradley and K. D. Ewing, C.J.S. Knight, *Constitutional and Administrative Law* 16th edn (London: Longman, 2014).
3 See, R. C. Van Caenegem, *An Historical Introduction to Western Constitutional Law* (Cambridge: Cambridge University Press, 1995).

THE PUBLIC LAW OF THE UNITED KINGDOM: DEFINITION AND SCOPE

> "public law is concerned with the state – its structures, the actions and interactions of its institutions and people who operate them, the principles and mechanisms on which it runs – and its relationship with other entities and individuals inside and outside the state."[4]

1-002 The importance of public law is increasingly being recognised, not only as a subject in its own right, but also for the conceptual framework and analysis which it brings to the understanding of all aspects of power[5] and how power is exercised and a growing recognition that many of its historical attributes—conventions and understandings are being slowly eroded. This leaves considerable space for politics and politicians to fill every orifice of the constitution with consequences for courts, Parliament and citizen. The English common law has developed significantly since the nineteenth century. Increasingly it is influenced by membership of the EU. Still further, the recent election of a majority Conservative Government in May 2015 is likely to continue to engage constitutional change that is capable of reshaping the public law of the UK and potentially the UK's membership of the EU. The relationship between England and the devolved nations is likely to have long-term constitutional significance in terms of the future of the UK. The subject of this book has progressed enormously so that today it is more accurate to understand constitutional and administrative law as linked together and as part of the relationship between the judicial, executive and legislative elements of the constitution.

1-003 Public law has now evolved sufficiently in the UK to make it desirable to distinguish between public and private law matters when it comes to litigation in the courts. Even so there is no precise divide between public law and private law. The Human Rights Act 1998 requires consideration of the nature of a public body as distinct from a private body. Private law mainly concerns the parties in a dispute over tort, contract or property law. A large part of private law is based on the law of tort covering civil liability for wrongfully inflicted injury. It is possible to regard public law as broadly referring to the relationship between the citizen and the state. The liability of public authorities for actions in tort law is also relevant especially in terms of compensation in respect of examples such as the National Health Authority. Public law is a composite of different aspects of the constitutional and administrative system in this country. This gives public law a unique and distinctive conceptual focus. In one part it is focused on institutions such as Parliament, the government and the courts. Surrounding the question as to how these institutions perform their constitutional role are public law issues such as: the relationship between aspects of the state and the citizen; the intricacies of systems of accountability and models of participation and electoral representation. Public law, however, is equally concerned with individual rights and how the rules of good administration are applied. It defines how government may exercise powers and how government may be controlled. It defines political and legal powers. The scope and remit of public law is found in

---

4 Mark Elliott and David Feldman (eds), *The Cambridge Public Law* (Cambridge: Cambridge University Press, 2015), p.1.
5 Dawn Oliver, "Common Values in Public and Private Law and the Public/Private Divide"' [1997] *Public Law* 630. Martin Loughlin, *The British Constitution* (Oxford: Hart Publishers, 2013).

the requirements of judicial review in terms of legality, fairness, and rationality that provides a synergy with the rule of law. Public law also sets standards for public life and administration. In the absence of a single written documentary form of a constitution, the sources for public law are found in a plethora of conventions, rules and understandings as well as formal statutory and prerogative powers.

Constitutional reforms over the past two decades will undoubtedly influence the future development of public law as a conceptual subject. Public law offers a homogenous view of constitutional and administrative law. Thus it could be argued that all public powers however exercised and by whoever should be amenable to review and scrutiny.[6] Wade and Forsyth have noted that "in the context of the rule of law, the aim is to subordinate the government to the ordinary law of the land".[7] This has important significance in the form of accountability that is to be used especially if there is an increase in judicial scrutiny and a decrease in Parliamentary control and effectiveness. Public law seeks to address not only the administrative rules developed by the judges, but also the relationship between those rules and government accountability. The historical distinction to be drawn between constitutional and administrative law appears to emphasise the evolutionary way the UK developed its constitutional arrangements. This may not reflect the reality of today. The English common law is likely to maintain its own distinctive qualities but, under the influence of codified systems of law, provide its unique contribution to problem-solving. It may not be possible to assimilate fully civil and common law systems and the difficulties in achieving this may prove counter-productive.[8] Each system may inform the other and the outcome a composite of each other with elements of adversarial and inquisitorial techniques in case management systems.

B: The Aims and Functions of Public Law

What are the aims of public law? The question is frequently asked of subjects such as tort, contract, criminal law or environmental law yet this fundamental question as to the role and function of public law is hardly considered. The answer is to be found in the assortment of aims and objectives associated with defining how government is accountable and representative. Controls exercised by Parliament and the courts are intended to provide citizens with assurances about the way government makes decisions and transparency is a key element in

---

6   There is a discussion among contract lawyers between those in favour of a law of obligations and others who see contract as a distinct area of law built on mutual promises of the parties. A. Burrows, "Contract, Tort and Restitution—A Satisfactory Division or Not?" (1983) *Law Quarterly Review*. More generally, see E. McKendrick, *Contract Law*, 4th edn (London: Macmillan, 2000).
7   H. W. R. Wade and C. F. Forsyth, *Administrative Law*, 8th edn (Oxford: Oxford University Press, 2000), p.31.
8   J. W. F. Allison, *A Continental Distinction in the Common Law* (Oxford: Oxford University Press, 1999).

public confidence. Public law is required to provide that transparency, both *a priori* and *ex post* through the systems of accountability that are in place. Public law is intended to ensure that citizens' rights are protected and that good administration is supported. Internal systems of accountability need to be distinguished from external systems. The former is concerned with internal systems of audit, rules and conventions that apply to the exercise of ministerial discretion.[9] The latter takes the form of external controls through Parliament, the courts, the media and public opinion.

A striking feature of the UK's present-day constitutional arrangements is its vulnerability and therefore its dependency on executive self-restraint irrespective of the form of government in power-coalition or majority led. This stems from the overwhelming presumption in English law, at least until relatively recently, that if the action or decision is not categorically prohibited it is assumed to be legal. Political control is often overpowering as political party rivalries compete for election. Government authority and power is assumed on the basis that the executive may do anything unless prohibited by statute. An equally familiar presumption was that the protection of rights is intended to protect minorities, while the protection of the majority is afforded by Parliament. In that way majoritarian democracy assumes that the casting of one vote in favour of a particular proposition commands the respect of the loser, even if the margins are so close as to be meaningless. The culture of majority government provides a superficial gloss that the winner may take all and there is little to prevent that abuse. Fairness grounded in the analogy of good sportsmanship expects self-restraint to be offered in the spirit of compromise and to find a way to accommodate the interests of the loser. In the eighteenth and nineteenth centuries deference to authority including government and the monarchy provided cohesion. In an age where deference has diminished, institutions have had to depend on persuasion rather than their status. The liberty of the nation also depended on assuming good stewardship by the holder of public office. Today this cannot be taken for granted and in most cases the public interest requires that the holder of public office exercises powers in an accountable way. Press and media attention intrude into the private and public lives of public figures. Increasing demands for transparency and verifiable outputs such as league tables and standards are an attempt to address public disquiet and mistrust. A generation of mistrust in politicians may led to an unhealthy scepticism about political life of even voting at elections. This may not be easily redressed even when standards in public life are made legally enforceable. There is a discernible trend that is likely to expand public law into new areas and through a variety of regulatory techniques there is potential for an expansion in the supervisory role of the courts that fills in the gaps left in the system of accountability. There is also a continuing search for some form of "constitutionalism" in UK public law scholarship.[10] This has an

---

9 John F. McEldowney, "The Control of Public Expenditure" in *The Changing Constitution* (J. Jowell and D. Oliver (eds), 4th edn (Oxford: Oxford University Press, 2001), pp.190–228; and the new edition J. Jowell, D. Oliver and C. O'Cinneide, *The Changing Constitution*, 8th edn (Oxford: Oxford University Press, 2015), pp.350–377.

10 Thomas Poole, "Tilting at Windmills? Truth and illusion in 'The Political constitution'" (2007) 70 *Modern Law Review* 250. Mark D. Walters, "Dicey on writing the 'Law of the Constitution'. (2012) *Oxford Journal of Legal Studies* 21. Jeremy Waldron, *Law and Disagreements* (Oxford: Oxford University Press, 1999), pp. 88–118. See

understandable rationale in attempting to advance under a non-written constitution the formulation of ideas and principles to guide restraints on unfettered political power.[11] It may also act as an "umbrella" term to cover arrangements between the Judiciary, Parliament and government covering such subjects as the sovereignty of Parliament, the rule of law, rights, legality and fairness. There is also a continuing quest for an adequate theoretical underpinning of the contours of what defines public law.[12] The UK is undergoing a period of constitutional change if not a potential constitutional revolution in the light of permanent devolution and potentially a re-negotiated EU membership. This may bring into question its pragmatic and incremental approach to change that builds on historical foundations rather than starting from a fresh perspective. The emergence of an English constitutional focus is likely as the distinctions between devolved nations intensifies. This is already apparent, for example, in the case of planning law where there are divergencies between the four nations.[13] This suggests, that out of necessity there will be specialisms developing within each nation that will have to be accommodated.

The UK's traditional approach is that there are remedies available to the individual that might address the exceptional case where there is a lapse of judgment or an error in the actions of a public official. The general presumption is that the ordinary law and self-restraint are sufficient to control arbitrariness. The high dependency on executive self-restraint is also part of the history of the nation and the culture of the people. It is clear that the pre-eminent concern in Britain is political convenience to allow the party in power to govern, a reflection of the way the balance between the different elements of the constitution is expected to be struck.

The pre-eminence afforded to political decision-making creates another dimension to defining public law and that is in setting the limits on economic power. Extensive economic powers through a diaspora of economic instruments such as the system of budgeting, and the borrowing of money are in the hands of the executive. As Page and Daintith[14] explain, economic powers are effectively under government control:

> "The executive can do this because basic principles of our constitution recognise it as an autonomous body which can manage its own resources save where Parliament ordains otherwise, and give it co-

---

Richard Stacey, "Democratic jurisprudence and judicial review: Waldron's contribution to political positivism" (2010) *Oxford Journal of Legal Studies* 749. See the discussion about Waldron's views in Mark Tushnet, "How different are Waldron's and Fallon's core cases for and against judicial review?" (2010) *Oxford Journal of legal Studies* 49.

11 J. W. F. Allison, "The Spirits of the Constitution" in N. Bamforth and P. Leyland (eds), *Accountability in the Contemporary Constitution* (Oxford: Oxford University Press, 2013), pp.27–56.
12 Jo Eric Khusal Murkens, "The quest for constitutionalism in UK public law discourse" (2009) *Oxford Journal of Legal Studies* 427–456.
13 House of Commons Library, *Comparison of the planning systems in the four UK countries*, Briefing Paper 07459 (20 January 2016).
14 T. Daintith and A. Page, *The Executive in the Constitution* (Oxford: Oxford University Press, 1999), p.398. See T. Daintith, "Law as a Policy Instrument: Comparative Perspectives" in *Law as an Instrument of Economic Policy: Comparative and Critical Approaches* (T. Daintith (ed), (Berlin: W. de Gruyter, 1988), pp.3–55.

> ordinate power with Parliament in the all-important area of public expenditure."

1-009 Public law has developed beyond the understanding of the accretion of political power and defining the limits of power. Having developed a system of remedies from medieval times and ensured the economic liberty of commerce and contractual relationships in the eighteenth and nineteenth centuries, legislation has pushed the frontiers of public law to develop individual rights.

1-010 The Human Rights Act 1998 and supporting legislation such as the Equality Act 2010 define public law in terms of individual rights and their protection through law. Giving legal priority to rights in this way marks a profound shift to the judicial element of the constitution. This triumph of judicial power over the other parts of the constitution vests legal rules, with a higher authority than the political process. In securing the promotion of legal rules, the question facing judges is: how is judicial power in the hands of appointed judges to be made compatible with the democratic process? Contemporary criticisms of the Human Rights Act have suggested that it has given too much discretion to the Judiciary and there are objections about how decisions made in Strasbourg appear to be too influential in the interpretation of Convention rights in defined examples such as the rights of prisoners to vote in elections.[15]

C: Evolving and Changing Public Law

1-011 The public law of the UK is defined by the prevailing constitutional order, the government and the various institutions of the state, the rights of the citizen and membership of the EU. As Mark Elliott has noted we live in a "multidimensional constitution"[16] with a variety of powers and responsibilities dispersed through numerous institutions and organisations. This extends from formal legislation, cases and binding legal procedures to "soft law" including a diaspora of circulars, regulations and rules. The distinction between hard and soft law is not sharply defined but relates to the day-to-day functioning of administrative decisions and good governance.[17] A striking feature of public law today is the growth in legislation. A House of Lords Library Note has estimated from 1983 to 2012 there have been 132 government Acts on matters relating to the constitution.[18] During the same period education, health, criminal justice and immigration

---

15 *Hirst v UK (No.2)* (2006) 42 EHRRI 41.
16 Mark Elliott, "legislative supremacy in a multidimensional constitution" in M. Elliott and D. Feldman (eds), *The Cambridge Public Law* (Cambridge: Cambridge University Press, 2015), pp.73–95.
17 Richard Rawlings, "Soft Law never dies" in M. Elliott and D. Feldman (eds), *The Cambridge Public Law* (Cambridge: Cambridge University Press, 2015), pp.215–233.
18 House of Lords Library Note Volume of Legislation LLN 2013/008 (11 May 2013).

received statutory support through legislation.[19] The pattern of legislative growth continues and has intensified as more constitutionally significant legislation is passed.

Local government has many statutory powers and responsibilities. Since 1998 there have been devolved powers to the Scottish Parliament, the Welsh Assembly, the Northern Ireland Assembly and since 1999 there has been an elected mayor for London. The public law of the UK has advanced considerably.[20] There are several reasons for this. Fundamental constitutional reforms have embraced changes to the electoral system, a more independent Bank of England with the responsibility of adjusting interest rates removed from the government of the day, financial and banking regulation transferred from the Financial Services Authority (FSA) to the Bank of England has resulted in a new system of financial regulation under the Financial Services Act 2012. This includes the establishment of the Financial Policy Committee, responsible for macro-prudential regulation and testing the resilience of the financial system of the UK economy; the Prudential Regulation Authority, an independent subsidiary of the Bank of England responsible for micro-prudential regulation of financial institutions and assessing balance sheet risk and the regulation of around 1700 financial firms[21]; and the Financial Conduct Authority responsible for the conduct of business and markets regulation. The latter supervises firms in the UK providing financial products and services in both the UK and for international customers.[22] The new arrangements give a pivotal role to the Bank of England and seek to adopt a preventative stance to avoid and prevent another financial crisis. The Bank of England and Financial Services Bill 2015/16 (HL) makes provisions for the reform of financial regulation, including the Prudential Regulatory Authority becoming a committee of the Bank of England, thus the Bank has wide responsibilities for financial supervision.[23] There are also reforms to the House of Lords, and strategies to modernise almost every aspect of government institutions and procedures. The Freedom of Information Act 2000 has made a considerable difference in allowing access to government information. There are changes to the criminal justice system, tribunals and inquiries, and to the management of the courts system. The Human Rights Act 1998, which came fully into force in October 2000 remains controversial and the newly elected Conservative Government in May 2015 has promised a British Bill of Rights.[24] One of the

---

19 There were 36 statutes on education, 37 on health, 110 on criminal justice and 11 on immigration.
20 See K. D. Ewing, "The Unbalanced Constitution" in *Sceptical Essays on Human Rights* (T. Campbell, K. D. Ewing and A. Tomkins (eds), (Oxford: Oxford University Press, 2001), p.103.
21 The Prudential Regulation Authority is required to promote the safety and soundness of firms and also to ensure that policyholders are protected. See House of Commons Library Research Papers: *The Independent Commission on Banking: The Vickers Report*, SNBT 6171 (30 December 2013); House of Commons Library Research Papers: *Banking executives' remuneration in the UK* SNBT-6204 (13 January 2013); and HL Paper 27-II (19 June 2013).
22 See House of Commons Library Research Papers, *LIBOR, Public Inquiries and FCA disciplinary powers* SN/BT/6376 (29 July 2014).
23 House of Commons Library, *The Bank of England and Financial Services Bill 2015/16*, No.7476 (28 January 2016).
24 *Practice Statement (Admin Ct: Administration of Justice)* [2002] 1 W.L.R. 810; [2002] 1 All E.R. 633 QBD. It is noted that from 2 October to 31 December 2001 some 19 per cent of judicial review cases raised an issue of human rights. In numerical terms judicial review receipts for 2001 showed an overall increase of 11 per cent on 2000.

10 THE PUBLIC LAW OF THE UNITED KINGDOM: DEFINITION AND SCOPE

concerns about the Human Rights Act is that elected ministers may become more subservient to the courts because of increased judicial controls.

1-012 In conceptual terms, public law has developed its own technical rules and procedures and techniques of analysis. In academic terms, public law has broadly defined terms of reference including the academic discourse from lawyers, economists, historians and political scientists. There is also a significant judicial contribution. This may come from the interpretation of the intention of Parliament in the rules of statutory interpretation and the various decided cases. Perhaps noteworthy is the development of administrative law that is largely a product of judicial creativity and self-regulation. Since the 1960s there has been a remarkable judicial self-confidence in defining and articulating the role of the courts in public law matters. As Lord Donaldson remarked in 1984[25]:

> "Parliamentary democracy as we know it is based in the rule of law. That requires all citizens to obey the law, unless and until it can be changed by due process. There are no privileged classes to whom it does not apply."

More recently, Lord Hughes in the Supreme Court made clear how balances between the role of the courts and Parliamentary intention should be calculated[26]:

> "The rule of law is of the first importance. But it is an integral part of the rule of law that courts give effect to Parliamentary intention. The rule of law is not the same as a rule that courts must always prevail, no matter what the statute says."

The Supreme Court allowed the publication of private and personal correspondence of Prince Charles to previous governments, despite the Attorney General claiming that this was not in the public interest and that Prince Charles's private views as the heir to the Throne should not be made public to ensure the Prince's political neutrality which was essential when he would succeed the Throne.

1-013 Changes in judicial attitudes, towards developing the common law in the direction of rights defined more broadly, came through a series of landmark cases in the 1960s. Since then, English administrative law has developed incrementally. *Ridge v Baldwin*,[27] *Padfield v Minister of Agriculture, Fisheries and Food*,[28] and the development of *Wednesbury*[29] unreasonableness enabled the courts to adopt a proactive approach. Instead of relying on instances of past failure in order to develop a systematic approach to administrative law, the courts

---

25 *Francome v Mirror Group Newspapers Ltd* [1984] 1 W.L.R. 892; [1984] 2 All E.R. 408 CA (Civ Div) at [412].
26 *R. (on the application of Evans) v Attorney General)* [2015] UKSC 21; [2015] A.C. 1787 at [154].
27 [1964] A.C. 40; [1963] 2 W.L.R. 935 HL.
28 [1968] A.C. 997; [1968] 2 W.L.R. 924 HL.
29 [1948] 1 K.B. 223; [1947] 2 All E.R. 680 CA.

filled in, through their own initiative, gaps left by legislative neglect. The result was clear: a self-confident Judiciary that was prepared to fashion new tools for the development of judicial review. In 1977, Order 53 was introduced, streamlining mechanisms and procedures for the application for judicial review.[30] This has been modified by the new CPR Pt 8 and a new Pt 54, and from 2 October 2000 this is the legal foundation for judicial review along with s.31 of the Senior Courts Act 1981.[31] Two landmark decisions showed the extent of judicial self-confidence. In *O'Reilly v Mackman*[32] the House of Lords established that the Divisional Bench of the High Court (now the Administrative Court) had exclusive (subject to certain exceptions) jurisdiction over administrative law matters. In the *Council of Civil Service Unions* decision,[33] the House of Lords engaged in a form of judicial codification of common law principles. The grounds for judicial review included unreasonableness, irrationality, proportionality, and procedural impropriety. The higher standards required under the Human Rights Act 1998[34] have seen noticeable advances in developing the intensity of judicial review.[35]

As a result of both creative judicial activism and legislation, judges have developed a wide discretion as to when to uphold a judicial review. This flexibility, allowing the courts the power to exclude unmeritorious cases at an early stage, saves time and creates a specialised jurisdiction for the administrative courts. The use of time limits so that applications for judicial review should be made promptly,[36] is subject to much judicial and political debate on how "promptly" should be interpreted. The European Court of Justice decision in *Uniplex (UK) Ltd, v NHS Business Services Authority*[37] cast doubt on whether setting time limits and the requirement of promptness was always compatible with access to justice. However, the European Court of Human Rights subsequently found that the use of "promptness" to set a time limit on cases being taken to court was compatible with art.6 of the European Convention of Human Rights.[38] The standing of the applicant is determined by the substantial merits of the applicant's case. The courts have a discretion whether or not to grant any remedy.

The role of the courts must also be placed in the context of the development of an extensive jurisdiction by statutory tribunals. The Tribunals, Courts and Enforcement Act 2007 provides a new framework for the reform of tribunals and under proposals undertaken by the Leggatt review.[39] Broadly Leggatt's reforms provided much needed organisation for tribunals

---

30 *Administrative Court Guidance: Applying for Judicial Review* (2014–15)
31 The renamed Superior Courts Act 1981 has become the Senior Courts Act 1981. See the Tribunals, Courts and Enforcement Act 2007 for the new Upper Tribunal to exercise judicial review powers.
32 [1983] 2 A.C. 237; [1982] 3 W.L.R. 1096 HL.
33 *Council of Civil Service Unions v Minister for the Civil Service* [1985] A.C. 374; [1984] 3 W.L.R. 1174 HL.
34 *R v Secretary of State for the Home Department Ex p. Daly* [2001] 2 W.L.R. 1622; [2001] UKHL 26.
35 *R. (on the application of Quila) v Home Secretary* [2011] UKSC 45; *R. (on the application of SB) v Denbigh High School Governors* [2006] UKHL 15.
36 This had been set at 3 months as a working rule but in planning cases six weeks is the new rule.
37 Case C-406/08 [2010] 2 C.M.L.R. 47.
38 *Lam v UK* (ECHR) 5 July 2001 and the discussion in *R. (on the application of Macrae) v County of Herefordshire DC* [2012] EWCA Civ 457.
39 See Sir Andrew Leggatt, Tribunals for users-one system one service (2001).

with a first-tier system subdivided into subject matter with a single route for a single appellate division. A unique aspect was to give the Upper Tier tribunal in specified cases a so called "judicial review" power that follows similar powers given to the Administrative Court.[40]

1-016 The extension of the role of the courts is also part of a larger question of how law is increasingly being used to regulate market power and, through regulatory reform, increase accountability over the newly privatised utility industries. The scale of this challenge provides public law with perhaps its most formidable challenge ranging as it does across different economic instruments and policy considerations related to the economy, and the size of the public sector. Sensitive issues such as migration and refugees have come to the fore. It may also impinge on the perceptions of politicians that there is an increasing juridification of decision-making. This may make a public lawyer's interpretation of the UK's constitution highly contested. Some scholars[41] see the definition of the constitution largely based on identifying the sources of the constitution, applying statutory interpretation and considering the range of values and standards that are prescriptive of how government behaves as well as on how politicians perform their tasks. Other scholars are concerned with the moral values that underpin the constitution and is focused on how legal discourse is integrated into the broader social sciences. Underpinning this discussion there are those that prefer to see the constitution as a product of political underpinnings that do much to inform and evaluate how public law is to be interpreted and understood.[42]

1-017 Added to this is a rights-based analysis of how rights may allow legal challenge and create changes in the law. In substantive and legal terms there is an administrative court with an exclusive jurisdiction to hear applications for judicial review. Judicial review or administrative law requires its own distinct rules and procedures. The Human Rights Act 1998 provides citizens with enforceable rights and enables the Judiciary broadly defined powers to interpret and review potentially all public power in whatever way it may be defined. Lord Hoffman in the House of Lords in *Alconbury*[43] explained the role of the courts under the Human Rights Act 1998 that has defined a form of judicial self-restraint in interpreting the Act:

> "There is no conflict between human rights and the democratic principle. Respect for human rights requires that certain basic rights of individuals should not be capable in any circumstances of being overridden by the majority, even if they think that the public interest so requires. Other rights should be capable of being overridden only in very restricted circumstances. These are rights which belong to

---
40 R. (on the application of Cart) v Upper Tribunal [2011] UKSC 28; [2012] 1 A.C. 663.
41 See Stuart Lakin, "Defending and Contesting the Sovereignty of Law: The Public Lawyer as Interpretivist" (2015) MLR 549–70.
42 See T. R. S. Allen, *The Sovereignty of Law: Freedom, Constitution and Common law* (Oxford: Oxford University Press, 2013) for a full discussion of the issues underpinning public law scholarship.
43 R (on the application of Alconbury Developments Ltd) v Secretary of State for the Environment, Transport and the Regions [2001] UKHL 23; [2001] 2 All E.R. 929 at [980] para.70.

> individuals simply by virtue of their humanity, independently of any utilitarian calculation. The protection of these basic rights from majority decision requires that independent and impartial tribunals should have the power to decide whether legislation infringes them and either (as in the United States) to declare such legislation invalid or (as in the United Kingdom) to declare that it is incompatible with the governing human rights instrument. But outside these basic rights there are many decisions which have to be made every day. . . in which the only fair method of decision is by some person or body accountable to the electorate."

There remains a marked reluctance to introduce a wholly written constitution in the absence of a political will to do so. Amid the calls for change, respect is given to the continuity of many existing practices and institutions. This is the unique quality of the UK's constitutional arrangements: its enduring ability to change, survive and re-invent itself. This flexibility is a remarkable feature of constitutional arrangements that may be traced back to early medieval history but are capable of adapting and supporting a modern system of government. There is an equal reluctance to embrace the codification that is the hallmark of a civil law system. For these reasons the problem focus and approach of the common law will retain its enduring qualities and most likely adapt to change incrementally without a "revolution".

There are a number of purposes for seeking to define constitutional arrangements. In formal terms it is clear that defining a country's constitutional arrangements helps to explain the relationship between the citizen and the state. A constitution helps determine how the state may exercise its powers and duties, how duties may be enforced and how the citizen may exercise rights. A constitution defines and sets out the relationship between the main organs of government which in the British context means the Crown, Cabinet, Parliament and the courts. A constitution may also influence how government may govern and may provide for accountability over government activities. A country's constitution may reflect the character of its people, their beliefs, "norms"', prejudices and preferences. It may also in turn help to shape and inform attitudes to government, law and relations with other countries.

At the outset it is helpful to categorise the UK's constitutional arrangements. There is much benefit to be gained from the perspective of political scientists. Professor Wheare wrote[44] that in defining a constitution, there may exist six points of classification: written and unwritten; rigid and flexible; supreme and subordinate; federal and unitary; separated powers and fused powers; republican and monarchical. Adopting Wheare's classifications it is at once apparent that the UK has a unitary constitution—though some would say that because of devolution, a union state. It is also clear that the UK's constitution is a flexible, monarchical constitution

---

44 K. C. Wheare, *Modern Constitutions*, 2nd edn (Oxford, Oxford University Press, 1966), pp.4–8. Graham Gee, "The political constitutionalism of JAG Griffith" *Legal Studies* (2008) 28(1), pp.20–45. Also T. Poole," Tilting at windmills? Truth and illusion in The Political constitution" (2007) 70 *Modern Law Review* 250. Also consider I. Leigh, "Secrets of the political constitution" (1999) 62 *Modern Law Review* 298.

whose powers are fused. The term "fused" refers to the absence, strictly speaking, of the formal doctrine of separation of powers. In the UK while there is some doubt as to the extent to which, within fused powers, the doctrine of separation of powers may apply, it is claimed that in the exercise of legal powers distinctions are made between the different organs of state. The most distinctive feature of the constitution remains that the UK, unlike other European countries, does not have in a single document, a written constitution with overriding legal force and authority. It is necessary to explain what a constitution is intended to achieve and how the UK's constitution may best be defined and explained. Inevitably, given the historical nature of developments it is necessary to explain how the UK was formed. So much of present-day constitutional thinking and the way our legal culture has evolved is drawn from the past. So much of the future is dependent on the way public law has developed in terms of setting standards for administrators and addressing the question of how to regulate. Inevitably public law principles may enlarge the jurisdiction of the courts and public law concepts may begin to infiltrate areas of private law.[45]

Public law is dynamic and engages with many and various parts of our economy, and institutions engaging with various procedures, norms and systems of administration that engage the citizen with the state in all its various forms.

D: Constitutional Reform in its Historical Context

1-021 Tinkering with Britain's constitution is a fine art developed through centuries of incremental change. There has always been cultural resistance to changing the role and function of major institutions or the constitution itself. One simple reason for this is flexibility: elected governments come and go, but once elected, the government of the day is relatively free to govern with ". . . no institutional restraints on a legally sovereign legislature and a politically sovereign electorate".[46] The essence of political power is its legitimacy. The democratic will of the majority, exercised at a general election under the first-past-the-post electoral system, elects governments with a mandate to govern for up to five years largely free from restraints on their political decision-making or their legal powers to execute their policies.

1-022 Another reason for resisting change is that the common law is largely problem-centred. Unlike the civilian tradition concerned with the application of legal or constitutional principles, the common law rarely involves points of constitutional principle. Drawing on a mixture of past

---

45 See *Hoechst Marion Roussel v Kirin-Amgen Inc* unreported 21 March 2002 HL.
46 K. D. Ewing, "The Unbalanced Constitution" in *Sceptical Essays on Human Rights* (T. Campbell, K. D. Ewing and A. Tomkins (eds) (Oxford: Oxford University Press, 2001), p.104.

experience, case law or past precedent, pragmatic solutions to problems are often invented to fit the circumstances of the time. Much effort is given to making things work and ensuring where appropriate that the necessary repairs are made before any attempt to develop new structures. As McCrudden has observed:

> "A number of the principles which are said to describe, inform, and underpin the British constitution (majoritarian democracy, parliamentary supremacy, and constitutional conventions) may be seen as the embodiment of this tradition, concentrating as they do on 'the authority of experience and the continuity of practice' and ensuring the flexibility of the process by which decisions are made. In this tradition, authoritative constitutional structures *evolve*, they are seldom *made*."[47]

In terms of evolution it is clear that greater devolution to Scotland and a referendum on EU membership create a profound "constitutional moment" for the evaluation of the UK's constitutional arrangements. The politics of whether or not this will occur are not easy to predict or estimate.

The strength of the UK's constitution is that it has proved to be sufficiently flexible to accommodate major political differences through changes in the party in power. Political power, its loss and acquisition have led the way in shaping a modern Britain largely free from much judicial or legal restraint. Incremental constitutional change has occurred over centuries in tandem with Britain's economic development and changing role in the world. At the end of the nineteenth century Britain was a major industrial country with a large empire and equipped to legislate for many countries in the world. The grant of independence to the colonies developed the art of constitutional drafting, as many countries adopted the Westminster model of government in their constitutional arrangements. Gradually, after the Second World War, Britain began coming to terms with its new position in the world, without the British Empire and with the creation of the Commonwealth. The country has come under new influences, particularly since 1972 and its membership of the EU: perhaps the greatest change is the impact of the European civil law tradition and the EU on the UK's constitution.

Following the referendum in June 2016 and the decision to leave the EU, the UK will go through a period of uncertainty and economic volatility. The decision to invoke Article 50 TEU is likely to wait until October 2016 adding further uncertainty.

In the fundamental shift to accommodate Europe, with its civil law tradition, the way Britain is governed has changed. At the same time, the new "value for money" focus has brought modest but significant changes in the way government is able to govern. Such changes have been part of the general progression, an "organic change", rather than any revolutionary or

---

47 C. McCrudden, "Northern Ireland'" in J. Jowell and D. Oliver (eds), 3rd edn, *The Changing Constitution* (Oxford: Oxford University Press, 1994), p.325.

radical break with past tradition, but nonetheless with significant effects. One example is the development of various agencies to conduct the work of the Civil Service. Nearly 80 per cent of the Civil Service may be found in such agency arrangements. Yet the doctrine of ministerial responsibility remains virtually unchanged and must meet the demands of the increasingly complex relationship between civil servant and minister.

1-025 In the context of so many uncodified rules, understandings, norms, hard and soft law, legislation and case law, it is understandable to ask whether Britain has a constitution.[48] The question arises from the notable absence of a formal written constitution and the difficulties of clearly defining the powers of the executive and the roles of the legislature and Judiciary. The constitution may be described as unwritten, as opposed to written; flexible, as opposed to rigid; unitary, rather than federal; and institutional and practical, as opposed to theoretical and doctrinal. The contemporary monarchy maintains a largely symbolic role and continuity of tradition. Bagehot aptly described the monarch's formal powers as "the right to be consulted, the right to encourage, the right to warn".[49] The monarch retains the power to grant a dissolution of Parliament on the advice of the government.

1-026 The absence of a single codified or written constitution leaves the working out of the practicalities of the constitution in the system of laws, conventions and customs that are the hallmark of the medieval inheritance. A notable feature is the use of conventions—essential norms of political behaviour, difficult to categorise in any strictly legal or constitutional sense—that comprise the common practices and workings of government and that link the modern with the ancient, medieval constitution. A. V. Dicey's influence[50] since the nineteenth century has led constitutional lawyers to believe that conventions serve the purpose of examining past practices to determine future conduct. Unlike rules or laws such as statute law, conventions are not enforceable by the courts but often help explain the political workings of the constitution.

E: The essential characteristics of the United Kingdom's Constitution

1-027 The starting point for the study of public law is that unlike almost every country in the world the UK is unique in not having a codified or wholly written constitution. The absence of a codified

---

48 Neil MacCormick, "'Does the United Kingdom have a Constitution?': Reflections on *MacCormick v Lord Advocate*" 29 (1978) *Northern Ireland Legal Quarterly* 1. John Gardner, "Can there be a Written Constitution?" (2009) *Legal Research Paper Series Paper* No.17/2009.
49 Walter Bagehot, *The English Constitution* (London, 1867, reprinted and edited by G. Phillipson, (Sussex: Sussex Academic Press, 1997)), p.42.
50 See R. Cosgrove, *The Rule of Law: Albert Venn Dicey, Victorian Jurist* (London: Macmillan, 1980).

written constitution is the first obstacle to the study of public law. A draft of a written UK constitution published by the House of Commons, *Political and Constitutional Reform Committee* includes related documents suggesting how current constitutional arrangements may be best understood.[51] There is no special significance attached to the word constitutional and until quite recently no special pre-eminence was afforded to constitutional or administrative law. The Human Rights Act 1998 provides a statutory framework. Rights are now included as a characteristic of our constitutional arrangements. There are also many legislative enactments that spell out the relationship between the executive, Parliament and the Judiciary.[52]

1-028

The Human Rights Act 1998 incorporates most of the European Convention on Human Rights (ECHR) into domestic law. The ECHR was drafted in response to the Second World War and was heavily influenced by the English style of legislative drafting. The substance of the rights under the Convention is narrowly confined to legal rights written in the broad language of negative liberty or "freedom from unjustified interference". Rights included are to liberty and security (art.5), to a fair trial (art.6) and to no punishment without law (art.7). There is a right to life (art.2) and to freedom from torture (art.3), and a prohibition against slavery and forced labour (art.4). There are also freedoms associated with the individual in terms of religion, the right to privacy and the freedom of assembly (arts 8–12). Such rights have been narrowly interpreted without any formal consideration of their potential impact on issues of economic, social or political significance. The 1998 Act came about through sustained pressure from the Judiciary and academic writers. Despite the existence of many draft Bills of Rights (most notably those of Lord Lester),[53] the government delegated the drafting of the Human Rights Bill to the official Parliamentary draftsman. Its form was influenced by the requirements of drafting an official government bill, rather than a private member's one. Primacy is given to the sovereignty of Parliament, as the 1998 Act falls short of allowing the courts to hold that an Act of Parliament is unconstitutional or illegal. The most the courts may do is rule on incompatibility[54] between the 1998 Act and the legislation under review. It is then for Parliament, not the courts, to resolve any incompatibility. The courts are not bound by the jurisprudence of the Strasbourg Court of Human Rights but may give effect to those decisions.

1-029

Nevertheless it remains the case that unlike countries where there is a written constitution and the term "unconstitutional" carries with it a legal meaning which may imply enforcement or consideration by some higher authority or by the courts, British lawyers do not strictly speaking define "unconstitutional" in that legal sense. The term "unconstitutional" frequently appears in common usage and may, in a Parliamentary sense, imply the breach of a convention

---

51 House of Commons Political and Constitutional Reform Committee (2014) The text was prepared by Robert Backburn of King's College, London and Andrew Blick.
52 The Constitutional Reform Act 2005; and the Constitutional Reform and Governance Act 2010.
53 Lord Lester (Anthony Lester), a leading human rights lawyer in the UK, has pioneered a number of draft bills into the House of Lords. He was a member of the team who drafted *A Written Constitution for the UK* (London: Institute for Public Policy Research, 1989).
54 There is no UK equivalent of the US Supreme Court decision in *Roe v Wade* 410 U.S. 113 (1973).

or Parliamentary process, or failure to comply with the etiquette of the House of Commons. "Unconstitutional" may be contrasted with the term "illegal" which lawyers use to denote a judgment by a court on the lawfulness of a particular activity.

1-030 The common law has provided a rich source of law in the UK. This explains how and why the constitution developed in the way it has. The common law is composed of custom and tradition. The common law has many prerogative powers, and the long history of constitutional principles developed from the common law results in a system of public law that is ad hoc in its development. There is also legislation. In the past five years the volume and extent of legislation has continued to increase. Legislative complexity continues to provide a challenge for government and administrators in the interpretation and implementation of the law. There appears to be little respite in this trend.

1-031 The best-known examples of legislation are the Bill of Rights 1688 and Magna Carta 1215. The 800th anniversary of Magna Carta has just been celebrated and there has been considerable discussion over reasons for its influence and longevity. Modern examples include the Parliament Acts 1911 and 1949, the European Communities Act 1972, the various devolution Acts and the Human Rights Act 1998. The European Union Act 2011 has provided enhanced Parliamentary scrutiny over EU matters and referendum oversight of the UK's membership of the EU. On terrorism and counter-terrorist measures, the Protection of Freedoms Act 2012 is significant, as is giving enhanced powers to local government, the Localism Act 2011. There is a gradual Parliamentary awareness since[55] 1997 that certain legislation with constitutional importance should attract additional attention and receive the attention of the House of Commons by means of a Committee of the whole House.[56] This is a means of giving additional scrutiny and it is welcome recognition that legislation of a fundamental nature may alter the prevailing constitutional arrangements and is deserving of special attention such as post-legislative scrutiny. The use of referendum is another example of procedures for the acceptance of constitutionally significant legislation, for example, Scottish independence in 2014 or for membership of the EU[57] has been subject to public consultation. The House of Lords Select Committee on the Constitution has proposed that constitutional bills should be identified through written ministerial statement, including justification for the bill's status, that such bills should be cautious and proportional and that pre and post-legislative scrutiny should be available as well as the opportunity for full debate in both Houses of Parliament.[58]

1-032 Constitutional lawyers approach the question of where the constitution is to be found by pointing out that, whereas there is no written constitution in the formal sense, there are a large number of written documents, statutes, cases and unwritten rules and understandings, com-

---

55 This was the time of the introduction of the system of programming of bills.
56 House of Commons Library, *Standard Note: Timetabling of constitutional bills since 1997*, SN/PC/06371 (29 June 2012). There is a summary of constitutional change since 1911 in House of Commons Library, *Standard Note: Constitutional Change: timetable from 1911*, SN/PC/06256 (15 March 2012).
57 House of Lords Select Committee on the Constitution: 12th Report of Session 2009–10 *Referendums in the United Kingdom*, HL Paper 99.
58 A summary is provided in Jack Simson Caird, Robert Hazell and Dawn Oliver, *The Constitutional Standards of the House of Lords Select Committee on the Constitution* (University College London, January 2014).

monly called conventions, which comprise the Constitution of the UK. Constitutional lawyers look to an historical explanation of the development of constitutional law in the UK. This historical explanation of why the UK has developed its constitution in the way it has, does not fully address the question of why the UK uniquely among other European countries, did not enact its own written constitution in the sense explained above. This question becomes a recurring one throughout this textbook.

Some reasons for the lack of a written constitution may be advanced; such as historically there was no revolutionary break which necessitated the writing down of a completely new basis for the authority and legitimacy of government and law.[59] A reluctance to codify, a characteristic of the common law approach to legal problems, may be detected in the eighteenth and nineteenth centuries which may have been linked to the question of drafting a written constitution. Constitutional reform may have had little support as a political demand and consequently may not have been much considered. The English common law tradition encouraged a pragmatic approach to legal change and any constitutional amendment may have been accommodated through the Parliamentary process of statutory reform, rather than major constitutional revision. Characteristically as no great discontent or dissatisfaction may have been evidenced over the years, constitution-drafting was a low priority compared to economic, social and political reforms. A preference for tinkering rather than a complete rethink favoured leaving the UK's constitution to evolve. Finally, in the nineteenth century a sense of complacency mixed with a reverence for what appeared as ancient and historically consistent with medieval beginnings, left a sense of self-satisfaction with the distinctive attributes of the common law system which had progressed without a formal written constitution. At the beginning of the present century Parliamentary government was seen as a triumph of democracy over the despotism of absolute power. No single explanation seems satisfactory, however, and the UK's unwritten constitution remains as a legacy of the past which endures today. How far this will be the case remains uncertain as the referendum on EU membership and substantial devolution to Scotland will struggle to be accommodated within the UK's prevailing constitutional arrangements.

F: Summary and Conclusions

1-033

The evolving and changing public law of the UK arises from many recently-introduced fundamental constitutional reforms. There are many uncertainties in assessing future trends and directions. There is a strongly English focus on the UK's Constitution that inevitably arises

---

59   P. P. Craig, *Public Law and Democracy in the United Kingdom and the USA* (Oxford: Oxford University Press, 1990).

because of the devolved nations and increasing powers to each nation leaves questions about the UK as a whole.

In setting out the subject of study, account must be taken of the common law tradition and current influences from Europe and the EU. It is important to remember that the influence of the common law is shared with many jurisdictions in the world. It may be found even in countries that have adopted written constitutions after independence. The countries of the Commonwealth have adapted the common law system to their particular needs. Even countries with a civil law tradition of codified law find elements of the common law valuable in their analysis of legal problems and approaches to comparative law. One of the most important examples is to be found in the 1946 Japanese constitution, drafted after the Second World War and combining a Supreme Court with a Parliamentary system of government, Prime Minister and Cabinet.[60] The South African constitution is also a good example of drafting a constitution to fit the circumstances after the end of apartheid.[61] There is a growing interest and trend in developing a broader understanding for the study of comparative constitutions.[62]

1-034 Inevitably looking abroad provides a picture of the alternatives. It may be helpful in identifying the areas of study that have arisen from the presence of a written constitution in other countries, and in considering how the UK is the same or different.

1-035 An important innovation, in February 2001, was the appointment of a Select Committee of the House of Lords on the Constitution[63] "to examine the constitutional implications of all public bills coming before the House; and to keep under review the operation of the Constitution". Given the difficulties in defining the constitution, the House of Lords Select Committee on the Constitution proposed the following working definition describing the issues that fall within the constitution[64]

> "... the set of laws, rules and practices that create the basic institutions of the state, and its component and related parts, and stipulate the powers of those institutions and the relationship between the different institutions and between those institutions and the individual."

1-036 In summary the Committee identified "five basic tenets" of the UK's constitution. These include the following which may act as a guide to the principles that require to be addressed in any study of the constitution:

---

60 See C. Milhaupt, J. Mark Ramseyer, and Michael K. Young, *Japanese Law in Context* (Cambridge, MA: Harvard University Press, 2001), pp.2–17.
61 John F. McEldowney, "One-party dominance and democratic constitutionalism in South Africa" (2013) *Journal of South African Law* 269–91
62 Ran Hirschl, *Comparative Matters* (Oxford: Oxford University Press, 2014).
63 "Reviewing the Constitution; terms of reference and methods of working", First Report, Session 2001-02, HL Paper 11.
64 "Reviewing the Constitution; terms of reference and methods of working", para.20.

- the sovereignty of the Crown in Parliament;

- the Rule of Law, covering the rights of the individual;

- the Union State that permits autonomy within each nation;

- representative and accountable Government; and

- membership of the Commonwealth, the EU and other international organisations.

The work of the Committee has been transformative indicated by the publication of a study of all the Committee's reports in terms of setting constitutional standards for the working of the Constitution.[65]

The changing nature of the UK's constitution raises some tantalising questions about the future and requires careful consideration of the tensions and shifts in the balance of power. Fundamental reforms have been introduced in Britain that have the potential to change some of the underlying principles of the constitution. We need to develop a vocabulary for thinking about the constitution, to express what it is and the principles that underlie it. This is in part the motive for the work of the House of Commons Political and Constitutional Reform Committee on the codification of the UK's constitution. Thinking about the constitution means understanding how government controls and allocates powers and how citizens participate in the state. It also should prioritise different rules and recognise different values that contribute to the diversity of the constitutional history of the UK. Exploring the balance of power between individual rights and the authority of decision-makers may ultimately lead to the conclusion that a single document or written/codified constitution defining the different elements of power is appropriate for understanding the constitution. Equally significant is the development of administrative law and the setting of standards for judicial review through the courts exercising their supervisory jurisdiction over different types of bodies, agencies, local and central government and others under direct or indirect political control. As Oliver has noted[66]:

> "Indeed, whenever a person or body is in a position of power in relation to another, and in particular where a decision may affect the dignity, autonomy, respect, status and security of another, the question will arise whether such duties arise and what their content is."[67]

---

65 Jack Simson Caird, Robert Hazell and Dawn Oliver, *The Constitutional Standards of the House of Lords Select Committee on the Constitution* (The Constitution Unit, January 2014).
66 D. Oliver, "The Constitutional Standards of the House of Lords Select Committee on the Constitution", p.645.
67 See for example: Denis Baranger, "Parliamentary Law and Parliamentary Government in Britain" in Katja S Ziegler and Denis Baranger, Anthony Bradley, *Constitutionalism and the role of Parliaments* (Oxford:

Finally, Prosser's analysis of the economic constitution is a useful public law perspective that emphasises the interdependence of the market, the state and the delivery of public and private services. Managing the economy enables the government to make far reaching and significant decisions apply with different techniques and strategies that engage with constitutional norms as well as institutions. The coming years are likely to see the pre-eminence of economic management in the public law of this country.

1-038 The way forward is to recognise how public law derives its scope through the complex relationship between law and the social, political and economic context of the problem that the law is seeking to address. It is only possible to achieve a better understanding of the nature of law and the problems it is attempting to solve by recognising the boundaries of public law and the nature of political and legal power. Many UK constitutional lawyers look to Canada, Australia, New Zealand, the USA, Germany and France to find inspiration on how constitutional principles may influence and guide the UK's constitutional arrangements.[68] The UK's exit from the EU will need careful consideration in the coming years.

Further Reading

Introductory readings include:

Vernon Bogdanor, *The New British Constitution* (Oxford: Hart, 2009); Anthony King, *The British Constitution* (Oxford: Oxford University Press, 2007); Peter Leyland, *The Constitution of the United Kingdom* (Oxford: Hart, 2012); Robert Rogers and Rhodri Walters, *How Parliament Works*, 7th edn (London: Longman, 2015); Neil MacCormick, "Does the United Kingdom Have a Constitution?" (1978) 29 *Northern Ireland Legal Quarterly* 1–20; Martin Loughlin, *The British Constitution* (Oxford: Oxford University Press, 2013); *The Political and Constitutional Reform Committee of the House of Commons*, 14th Report; *Constitutional role of the judiciary if there was a codified Constitution*, 7th Report; *Consultation on A new Magna Carta*, (9 March 2015); and Conor Gearty, *Can Human Rights Survive?*, Hamlyn Lectures (Cambridge, Cambridge University Press, 2005).

For an historical dimension see:

W. Cornish, *Law and Society in England and Wales* 1750–1950 (London: Sweet & Maxwell, 1989); and A. V. Dicey, *Introduction to the Study of the Law of the Constitution* (London: Macmillan, 1885).

Studies of the Oxford Institute of European and Comparative Law, Hart, 2007), pp.15–46. Christoffer C. Eriksen, *The European Constitution, Welfare States and Democracy* (London: Routledge, 2013).
68   Alan Tomkins, *Our Republican Constitution* (2005).

For a theoretical perspective, see:
Martin Loughlin, *Sword and Scales* (Oxford: Hart Publishing, 2000).
A useful political science perspective may be found in:
Andrew Blick, *Beyond Magna Carta: A Constitution for the United Kingdom* (Oxford: Hart, 2015); Ian Budge, Ivor Crewe, David McKay and Ken Newton, *The New British Politics*, 2nd edn (Essex: Longman, 2001; Bill Jones, and Philip Norton, *Politics UK* (8th ed., Longman, Essex, 2014); Anthony King, *Who Governs Britain?* (Allen Lane, Pelican, 2015); Anthony King and Ivor Crewe, *The Blunders of Our Governments* 2nd edn (London: Oneworld, 2014); Alistair Clark, *Political Parties in the UK* (Basingstoke: Palgrave, 2012); Philip Norton, *Parliament in British Politics* 2nd edn (Basingstoke: Palgrave, 2013); and Peter Osborne, *The Triumph of the Political Class* (London: Simon and Schuster, 2007).

2

The Asymmetrical Constitution: The Structure of the United Kingdom

A: Introduction

In this chapter the main principles and sources which define the UK's Constitution are explained. We begin by first considering some of the historical developments which have helped shape our present arrangements in the Union Treaties involving England, Scotland, Wales and Ireland to form the United Kingdom of Great Britain and Northern Ireland. Having examined the historical development[1] of the UK, the introduction of devolution is explained and the government of Scotland, Wales, Northern Ireland and London are considered. The impact of legislation creating the Commonwealth is explained in the context of Parliamentary sovereignty. Also relevant to an understanding of sovereignty is membership of the EU. Accession into the European Community in 1972 ultimately challenged some of our traditional ideas about the UK's Constitution. The future of Europe is also important in determining our existing sources of law and the direction of change, especially during a period of debate of uncertainty over EU membership and financial instability within the Eurozone.[2] The UK's decision to withdraw from the EU will need careful consideration and re-calibration of public law in general including the future of the Union with Scotland.

2–001

---

1 J. W. F. Allison, *The English Historical Constitution* (Cambridge: Cambridge University Press, 2007).
2 House of Commons Library, *Reforming the EU: UK plans, proposals and prospects*, SN/1A/7138 (16 March 2015); House of Commons Foreign Affairs Committee, *The UK staff presence in the EU institutions*, Second Report, Session 2013–14, HC 219 (2 July 2013), p.3; House of Commons Library Briefing Paper, *The 1974–75 UK Renegotiation of EEC Membership and Referendum*, No.7253 (13 July 2015). See House of Commons Library, *Exiting the EU: UK reform proposals, legal impact and alternative to membership*, No.7214 (4 June 2015); House of Commons Briefing Paper, *Exiting the EU: impact in key UK policy areas*, No.7213 (4 June 2015); House of Commons Library, No.07212 *European Union Bill 2015/16* (3 June 2015); and House of Commons Library, *The EU referendum campaign*, No.7486 (27 January 2016).

B: The sources of constitutional law and the composition of the United Kingdom

2-002 The UK has been variously described as a unitary state. It is striking that there is no federal system for a population of nearly 64 million, in a country that is one of the most densely populated Member States in the EU. On the contrary the UK has a highly centralised system of government, a long tradition of local government and a variety of powers shared between each of the regions. There are also striking differences in the size, population and representation of each of the four nations. The House of Commons has 650 MPs. England with a population of 53.5 million has 533 seats, Scotland with a population of 5.3 million has 59 seats, Wales has a population of 3.1 million and has 40 seats and Northern Ireland has a population of 1.8 million has 18 seats. In the case of Scotland, England and Wales and Northern Ireland, each nation has its own distinct legal system and legal profession with its own system of courts. It is worth noting that tax receipts from each nation are roughly divided on the basis of 85.9 per cent England, 3.4 per cent per cent Wales, 8.6 per cent Scotland and 2.5 per cent Northern Ireland. The economic imbalance between each nation is most striking.

2-003 The United Kingdom Parliament and Crown is common to each. One unifying institution is the Supreme Court for the UK that acts as a final court of appeal for all the different jurisdictions, although not for criminal cases in Scotland. The introduction of devolution to Scotland, Wales and Northern Ireland has created a force in favour of allocating powers to regional communities. London, currently with a population of seven million, has a strong tradition of elected autonomy since the Metropolis Local Management Act 1855. In addition to the 32 elected London Borough Councils and the Corporation of London, there is a special form of devolution provided through a directly elected Mayor and a 25-member Assembly under the Greater London Authority Act 1999. It is no longer correct to see the UK as unitary; rather it may be described as a "union" state.

2-004 The recent referendum in 2014 on Scottish Independence rejected independence, but led to promises for increased powers to the Scottish Parliament[3] that have the potential to re-calibrate the nature of the UK, as similarly enhanced powers may be given to other nations such as England and large local authorities in the northern cities.[4] The Smith Commission and the inter-party proposals for Scotland's devolution are likely to radically change the distribution and allocation of resources in the UK.[5]

---

3   House of Commons Library, *Further devolution of powers to Scotland: devolved benefits and additional discretionary payments*, SN07107 (18 February 2015).
4   House of Commons Library, *Local government devolution: policy proposals*, SN 07065 (14 May 2015). See Iain McLean and Alistair McMillan, "The distribution of public expenditure across UK regions" (2003) 24(1) *Fiscal Studies* 45–71. See John McEldowney, "The Impact of Devolution on the UK Parliament" in A. Horne, G. Drewry and D. Oliver (eds), *Parliament and the Law* (Oxford: Hart, 2013), pp.197–219.
5   The Smith Commission's Welfare Proposals (21 January 2015); and HM Government, *The parties' publishd proposals on further devolution for Scotland*, Cm.8946 (October 2014).

THE SOURCES OF CONSTITUTIONAL LAW AND THE COMPOSITION OF THE UNITED KINGDOM

2-005

The union state has a unitary nature of the UK is under considerable strain from three sources. First, increasing powers to devolved nations, including large areas of fiscal responsibility has led to questions about the UK Parliament and in particular the fairness to English MPs. English MPs cannot vote on matters which have been devolved to other parts of the UK, but it is clear that Scottish, Welsh and Northern Ireland MPs can vote on these same matters when the UK Parliament is legislating solely for England. This is the so-called "West Lothian Question" and the Government's introduction in November 2015 of procedural rules for English Votes for English Laws has enormous constitutional significance.[6]

2-006

The second pressure is from the level of electoral support shown for the SNP at the last election, when the SNP secured 56 out of the 59 UK Parliamentary seats in Scotland. The rise of support for the SNP is likely to place further pressure on the UK Parliament to grant independence to Scotland. The third pressure arises from the referendum on EU membership that will be held some time in 2016/17. Voting preferences are different in each part of the UK. In England and Wales a majority of the voting electorate decided to leave the EU. A majority of voters in Scotland, Northern Ireland and London favored remaining in the EU.

England

2-007

It is possible to point to a number of fundamental statutes which created important legal principles in the early medieval relationship between the Crown, the courts and Parliament, such as the Magna Carta 1215.[7] The "echoes" of Magna Carta appear resilient to the passage of time and even inform current debates about the UK's Constitution and its future direction,[8] particularly the ideals of the rule of law and the propriety of Parliamentary procedures and practices over arbitrary unfettered powers. Previous history records that under William the Conqueror, England was a feudal state: all land was held of the King; the King's subjects owed allegiance; and law-making was in the power of the King. Early historical records show that Parliament had its early origin in the National or Great Council, representing advisers to the King. Parliament's growth in importance began in the thirteenth century and evolved slowly. In the late seventeenth and early eighteenth centuries, statutes such as the Bill of Rights 1689 and the Act of Settlement 1700 are recognisable as having created the institutions of government which have modern day significance. We have already mentioned that no revolution occurred in Britain which necessitated a complete severance from the past causing a major rethink of how government should govern. The fact that the Civil War led to the execution of

---

6 House of Commons Briefing Paper, *English votes for English laws*, No.7339 (December 2015).
7 Andrew Blick, *Beyond Magna Carta: a Constitution for the United Kingdom* (Oxford: Hart, 2015); and Anthony Arlidge and Igor Judge, *Magna Carta Uncovered* (Oxford: Hart, 2014).
8 The Political and Constitutional Reform Committee of the House of Commons, 14th Report, *Constitutional role of the judiciary if there was a codified Constitution*; 7th Report, *Consultation on A new Magna Carta* (9 March 2015).

Charles I and the experiment of republican government through Parliament, created change in the position of Parliament *vis-à-vis* the Crown. Continuity prevailed, however, in that the institutions of government survived albeit in a different form.

2–008 The Bill of Rights 1689 laid the foundations of the modern Constitution, because in England both the House of Lords and the last vestiges of Charles II's Parliament approved and thereby confirmed Parliament's, that is the House of Commons' authority. The grant of various freedoms contained in the Bill of Rights is accompanied by a sanction, that of "illegality". This term connotes both the statutory authority of the Bill of Rights and the interpretation of that authority when applied by the courts.

2–009 In Scotland, the Scottish Parliament enacted the Claim of Rights in 1689 following the English model with certain variations. In common with the English Bill of Rights, the use of proclamations to exercise powers was "declared illegal". Equally important in constitutional history is the Act of Settlement 1700. This complemented the Bill of Rights by enacting that the Church of England was to be established by law, ensuring the independence of the Judiciary and further regulating the King's authority, such as the power to grant pardons. No historical understanding of the development of the British Constitution in its present form would be complete without an explanation of the fact that the UK was formed through a series of legislative enactments. The Acts of Union with Wales, Scotland and Ireland helped to form a single entity. These Acts created the foundation of a legal entity that acknowledged the sovereignty of Parliament along with a cultural reticence to resist any interference in the maintenance of a unitary state. The enduring quality of the various Acts of Union remains a dominant influence today and may be seen in the various legislative competences of the different devolved powers under devolution discussed below. It is important to remember the extent to which local as opposed to central government was a dominant influence in early English legal history. The early office of Justice of the Peace, since Edward III, provided local justice in local courts. Local administration developed on an incremental basis and local justice provided a variety of regulatory and licensing powers. Much of administration and law was delivered at a local level supervised through central powers maintaining the unitary nature of the Constitution and the pre-eminent authority of Parliament.[9]

2–010 Current proposals are for devolution to be granted in the English regions, particularly large northern cities. In the case of London, Pt I of the Greater London Authority Act 1999 provides for a directly elected Mayor and a 25-member Assembly.[10] Specific statutory powers require the Mayor to develop, implement and revise strategies for transport, planning and development control. The Assembly is to review and scrutinise the Mayor's functions. The 1999 Act makes extensive provision for the carrying out of the Mayor's functions and includes detailed obligations in terms of the environment including a municipal waste management strategy, an air quality strategy, a noise strategy and a biodiversity action plan. The Greater London Authority Act 2007 conferred additional powers including a London Board within the Housing Corporation now part of the Homes and Communities Agency, additional planning

---

9 J. P. Dawson, *A History of Lay Judges* (Cambridge, MA: Harvard University Press, 1960), p.274.
10 White Paper, *A Mayor and Assembly for London*, Cm.3897 (1998).

powers for strategic developments, powers to appoint party political representatives to the Board of Transport for London and for non-binding confirmation hearings for selected senior posts namely the Chairs of the GLA functional bodies. In 2011, the Police Reform and Social Responsibility Act 2011 introduced Crime Commissioners for England and Wales, the London Mayor is the designated Crime Commissioner for London. This permits the London Assembly to scrutinise the Mayor's Office for Policing and Crime with the abolition of the Metropolitan Police Authority. The Public Bodies Act 2011 abolished the London Development Agency with some residual powers being given to the Greater London Authority. The Localism Act 2011 has expanded the London Mayor's powers including powers over land acquisition and social housing powers of the Homes and Communities Agency for London. There is now a London Environment Strategy to replace the previous statutory strategies. There are oversight powers given to the London Assembly to oversee or reject Mayoral strategies on the basis of a two-thirds majority.[11] The London Mayor has considerable input into the key areas such as transport, housing, policing, economic development and regeneration.

Wales

In the case of Wales, absorption with England may be said to owe its origins to the period of Edward I and the English domination of Wales by conquest.[12] One of the earliest statutory enactments was the Statute of Wales 1284 which applied to only part of what is defined today as modern Wales. It did, however, settle the independence of Wales by asserting the possession of the King of England over Llewellyn the Great's Principality of Wales, leaving the feudal territories of the Lords of the Marches unaffected. In 1471 a Council of Wales and the Marches was set up as an agency of the Privy Council and later in 1535 the Laws in Wales Act[13] was passed which stated that the "Lawes and Justice [were] to be ministered in Wales in like fourme as it is in this Realme". The result was an effective integration between England and Wales, with Wales divided into shires and hundreds comparable to the English equivalent. For a time, Wales was administered by a separate system of courts with specific representation for Wales in Parliament. However, the Council of Wales, which survived the early changes, had an expanded role to include some English border counties, but it was abolished in 1689. In 1830 Welsh circuits were absorbed into the English Court system and the judicial system of Wales was thereby assimilated into the English system.

Since 1964, there has been a Secretary of State for Wales, a position of responsibility in the Cabinet. The Welsh language is protected under the Welsh Language Act 1993. This Act provides for the appointment of a Board to encourage the use of the Welsh language in government and the courts. The introduction of devolution in 1998 has created a Welsh Assembly.

---

11 House of Commons Library, *The Greater London Authority*, Briefing Paper 05817 (13 May 2015).
12 John Davies, *A History of Wales* (Oxford: Oxford University Press, 1993).
13 27 Hen. 8 c.26.

Wales is a bilingual country with pride in its culture and language. The details of Welsh devolution are explained below.

Scotland

2–013 In the case of Scotland, there was a distinct entity we know today as Scotland, formed out of four kingdoms between the fifth and ninth centuries. Scotland stands apart from Wales and Northern Ireland as maintaining its own distinct independence.

2–014 The attempts by Henry VII to stabilise relations between England and Scotland through marriage of his daughter to Scotland's King James IV in 1503, came to little. Conquest was tried and failed by Henry VIII's union in 1544 and 1545, but in 1603 when Elizabeth I died, James VI of Scotland became James I of England signifying a personal, rather than a completely administrative or constitutional union. Administratively Scotland remained under a separate government from England. In 1707 the Treaty and Acts of Union formed the United Kingdom of Great Britain.[14] Turpin explains how this union was unitary rather than federal[15]:

2–015 In terms of these instruments the two Parliaments were superseded by a Parliament of Great Britain—"a new Parliament for a new State.[16]" This was to be a unitary, not a federal state; as K. C. Wheare observes[17] there was no model of federal government in existence which might have been urged against the unitary scheme then proposed and adopted. Scottish arguments for retention of the Scottish Parliament did not prevail.

2–016 The significance of these Acts of Parliament may be clearly appreciated in constitutional law and serve to show the scope and extent of legislative intervention. Through the Acts of Union, the UK was created as a legal entity. Similarly, the granting of independence to various colonies illustrates the authority of Parliament to confer independent status on particular countries, while appearing to exercise self-restraint over future legislative enactments. This self-denying aspect of Parliament's powers is an important convention for the intentions of a future Parliament. Strict constitutional theory forbids Parliament from binding its successors in legal terms. In practical terms Parliament may accept the political and economic limitations on its powers, without conceding any limit on its legal powers to legislate.

2–017 Thus, although the Acts of Union created the Parliament of the United Kingdom, English constitutional lawyers do not ascribe any significant status to those Acts, which are treated in the same way as any other Act of Parliament. We shall see that this assumption may be

---

14 See D. L. Keir, *The Constitutional History of Modern Britain 1485–1937* (London: Adam & Charles Black, 1938); S. B. Chrimes, *English Constitutional Ideas in the 15th Century* (London: Blackwell, 1966).
15 C. Turpin, *British Government and the Constitution*, 2nd edn (Cambridge: Cambridge University Press, 1990), pp.222–223. See A. V. Dicey and R. S. Rait, *Thoughts on the Union between England and Scotland* (London: Macmillan, 1920).
16 Scottish Law Commission, Memorandum No.32, 1975, p.16.
17 K.C. Wherea, Federal Government (4th edn, 1963) p.43

THE SOURCES OF CONSTITUTIONAL LAW AND THE COMPOSITION OF THE UNITED KINGDOM

questioned in the context of British membership of the European Community. Turpin has argued that an Act of Parliament is valid even if it may indirectly interfere with or ". . .violate fundamental provisions of the Union Legislation".[18] Some support for this view may be found in the decided cases, but the courts may appear equivocal on the issue. Some support for Turpin's view over the legal status of the Scottish Union may be found in the case of *MacCormick v Lord Advocate*.[19] In that case the Scottish courts were asked to consider the significance of the Act of Union. The Rector of Glasgow University in Scotland challenged the Queen's title as "Elizabeth the Second" on the grounds that this contravened art.1 of the Treaty of Union 1707.

2–018

The Royal Titles Act 1953 authorised the use of the numeral "II" and the challenge made by the Rector brought into issue the constitutional status of an Act of Parliament.[20] At first instance the justiciability of a challenge to the validity of an Act of Parliament was doubted and the challenge dismissed. On appeal to the First Division of the Inner House of Court of Session, Lord Cooper accepted the reasoning adopted in the lower court, but doubted if the 1953 Act had any bearing on the matter, as that Act had been enacted after the proclamation of the Queen as Elizabeth II. His opinion on the status of the Act of Union between Scotland and England is therefore *obiter dictum*, but nevertheless Lord Cooper questioned the English view of unlimited sovereignty of Parliament "which has no counterpart in Scottish Constitutional law".[21] Instead his view was emphatically that the Union Treaty did contain some fundamental and unalterable elements which made their status distinct and separate from any other Act of Parliament. However, in strict English constitutional theory Lord Cooper's view does not find favour. The English view is that there is no hierarchy of laws. No Scottish court has held a public Act of Parliament to be void since the Act of Union. When considering the Acts of Union Dicey admitted "the possibility of creating an absolutely sovereign Legislature which should yet be bound by unalterable laws"; but this is insufficient to create "unalterable statutes".

2–019

We shall return to consider the question of Parliamentary sovereignty in the following chapter, but it will become apparent that however attractive the notion of a fundamental law is in a constitutional sense, this has been resisted by English constitutional lawyers. Lord Cooper's opinion merely confirmed that a Scottish view of the British Constitution differs markedly from that of an English view! Equally it is clear that the creation of many of the constitutional principles especially the doctrine of the sovereignty of Parliament is the result of judicial decisions reached over the centuries. It is not always possible to rely on a consistent line of judicial precedent, but in some notable constitutional decisions Parliament emerged as the pre-eminent authority of sovereign power.[22]

---

18 C. Turpin *British Government and the Constitution*, 4th edn (London: Butterworths, 1999), p.241.
19 1953 S.C. 396; 1953 S.L.T. 255 Ct of Session.
20 See Colin Munro, *Studies in Constitutional Law*, 2nd edn (London: Butterworths, 1999).
21 Lord Guthrie in *MacCormick v Lord Advocate* 1953 S.C. 396.
22 Significant constitutional cases worthy of study: *The Case of Monopolies* (1602) 11 Co. Rep. 84b prohibited the King from dispensing with an Act of Parliament in matters of personal gain. Also see Bates case, *Att.-Gen. v Bates* (1606) 2 St. Tr. 371; *The Case of Prohibition del Roy* (1607) 12 Co. Rep. 63; and *The Case of Proclamations* (1610) 12 Co. Rep. 74 where the judges refused the King authority to create new offences by proclamation. In *R v Hampden* (1637) 3 St. Tr. 825, the courts by a majority upheld the King's power to levy money re the case of

Ireland

2-021 In the case of Ireland,[23] its early history was rooted in the law of the early Irish chiefs. The Brehon laws, as they were known, represent some of the earliest forms of law, contained in the form of law tracts which are complex in style and language and riddled with different forms of old and middle Irish. The administrations of England and Ireland before the Norman invasions of 1066 and 1171, shared a common characteristic namely that they were both regional. Ireland, unlike England, was relatively free from significant foreign intervention which allowed secular custom and native common law to take hold. England, from the eleventh century developed its own system of local courts, but under the influence of central administration and Royal power. Ireland, however, did not share the centralising effect of a single or unifying kingship. Instead, in Ireland, tribal loyalties formed the predominant influence and from the sixth to the eighth centuries there is documentary evidence of at least eight significant law tracts, the most notable being *Senchas Mar* or Patrick's law. One feature of these early laws was the division of the society into two groups, one free, the other unfree.

2-022 The English invasion of Ireland, carried out by Henry II, established an English administration in the area around Dublin known as the Pale, circa 1171. There had previously been attempts to establish an Irish Lord in Leinster in return for allegiance to Henry II as feudal Lord, but these efforts had limited success. Once conquest had secured influence, Henry II left the Irish Kings to continue to rule, but owing strict allegiance to Henry. The early records show that in 1226 a justiciar called De Mansio was appointed to act as the Royal representative in Ireland. The success of the English monarchy in Ireland was such that the English common law was gradually introduced.

2-023 The adoption of the common law in Ireland endured for many centuries to come. Under the English system of land law, tracts of land were granted and subinfeudation was widespread. Dublin was the administrative centre where the major Royal Courts carried out the King's justice under the King's Writ or Breve. Brehon laws, although referred to in records as late as 1558, were gradually superseded by the English common law. The assumption, often offered as an explanation for the continued preservation of Brehon law, is that Norman law was personal

---

Ship Money for funds to pay for ships to defend the realm under prerogative powers. Also useful to examine for constitutional purposes are *Thomas v Sorrell* (1674) Vaugh. 330; *Godden v Hales* (1686) 11 State Tr. 1166; and *The Seven Bishops' Case* (1688) 12 St. Tr. 371.

23 See J. McEldowney and P. O'Higgins, *The Common Law Tradition: Essays in Irish Legal History* (Dublin: Irish Academic Press, 1990); C. Palley, "The Evolution, Disintegration and Possible Reconstitution of the Northern Ireland Constitution" (1972) *Anglo-American Law Journal* 368; William Anson, "The Government of Ireland Bill and the Sovereignty of Parliament" (1886) 2 *Law Quarterly Review* 427; H. Calvert, *Constitutional Law in Northern Ireland: A Study in Regional Government* (Belfast: Stevens & Sons, 1968); and N. Mansergh, *The Government of Northern Ireland: A Study in Devolution* (London: Allen & Unwin, 1936).

THE SOURCES OF CONSTITUTIONAL LAW AND THE COMPOSITION OF THE UNITED KINGDOM

rather than territorial. Gradually Brehon law gave way to common law principles enforceable in the courts.

2-024 The common law taking root in Ireland eventually led to profound constitutional changes. Poynings Law 1494 provided that statutes in force in England had legal force in Ireland. The approval of the King in English Council was required for Irish bills. The existing Lord of Ireland became King of Ireland in 1541. Religious differences ensured that Ireland was governed according to English law but not that English law was accepted in Ireland. The Battle of the Boyne in 1690 assured Protestant ascendancy with the victory of William of Orange over James II.

2-025 The Act of Union[24] between England and Ireland was passed in 1800 and had the unusual characteristic of being enacted by both the English and Irish Parliaments. The latter succumbed to a degree of English influence and persuasion that tainted the propriety of the entire episode. The Act proclaimed that both pre- and post-Union legislation was subject to the "Parliament of the United Kingdom". It simultaneously ended the life of the Irish Parliament, united the Anglican Churches of England and Ireland and established the Union as "for ever after". Dicey[25] freely admitted that the Union was not "voluntary" and was, therefore, tainted with suspicion from its inception.

2-026 At the time of the Union, the majority of the population were Catholic tenants and excluded from the franchise and land ownership. After considerable pressure Catholic emancipation was granted in 1829 but this only served to make the Irish Land question a dominant issue for the remainder of the century. Protestant resistance and Orange Lodges feared the end to Protestant ascendancy and land ownership. The unsettled state of affairs in Ireland led to calls for constitutional reform, most notably Home Rule. Although a number of Home Rule bills were presented during the 1880s, these failed to find sufficient Parliamentary support. A failed uprising in Dublin in 1916 eventually advanced the cause of independence for Ireland.

2-027 In constitutional terms the Union endured until 1921–22 when the Irish Free State was formed. This necessitated a change to the Act of Union under subsequent legislation namely: the Irish Free State (Agreement) Act 1922; the Irish Free State Constitution Act 1922; and the Irish Free State (Consequential Provisions) Act 1922. While the Irish Free State became a dominion Northern Ireland, comprising six counties of the North East of Ireland, remained within the UK. The Government of Ireland Act 1920 provided for a separate Parliament and Government in Belfast but ultimate sovereignty resided within the competence of the UK Parliament. This form of devolved government under its terms of grant under the 1920 Act

---

24 Generally see Christopher Harvie, "Ideology and Home Rule" (1976) *English Historical Review* 91; James Bryce, "A. V. Dicey and Ireland 1880–1887" (1976) 91 *English Historical Review* 298–314; A. V. Dicey, "How is the Law to be enforced in Ireland?" (1881) 36 *Fortnightly Review* 539–552; J. F. McEldowney, "Dicey in Historical Perspective—A Review Essay'" in Patrick McAuslan and John F. McEldowney (eds), *Law, Legitimacy and the Constitution* (London: Sweet & Maxwell, 1985), pp.39–61.

25 A. V. Dicey, "Two Acts of Union—A Contrast" (1881) 30 *The Fortnightly Review* 168–78. Also see his views on the disestablishment of the Church of England: "The Church of England: The Legal Aspects of Disestablishment" (1890) 39 *The Fortnightly Review* 822–40; and see "The Defence of the Union" (1892) 61 *Contemporary Review* 314–331.

allowed the Northern Ireland Parliament, powers "to make laws for the peace order and good government of Northern Ireland". Northern Ireland became unique within the UK in having a written Constitution. Effectively the Northern Ireland Parliament was, within its own legislative competence, unrestrained by the sovereign power who had overriding legal powers under s.75 of the 1920 Act to govern Northern Ireland. A Constitutional Convention became established that the UK Parliament would not legislate on matters which were within the "transferred" powers of the Northern Ireland Parliament. Representation from Northern Ireland in the UK Parliament was set at 13 seats until 1948, and thereafter 12, until 1979 when the number was increased; it is currently set at 18 seats.

2-028 This experiment in devolved government was overshadowed by the early historical problem of Ireland's post-Union relationship with England. Catholics comprise about 40 per cent of its population and live under a nationalist identity that rejected the Union with England. Civil liberties, although theoretically protected under the 1920 Government of Ireland Act, were often ignored. From 1921–72 Northern Ireland was ruled by a single majority party, the Unionists, who dominated the Government of Northern Ireland. Religious and political differences were endemic and resulted in civil unrest. From 1968–72 attempts at constitutional reform by the Northern Ireland Government were too late to avert a constitutional crisis which resulted, in March 1972, with the arrival of British troops and the prorogation and eventual abolition of the Northern Ireland Parliament. The functions of the Parliament and Government of Northern Ireland were vested in the Secretary of State for Northern Ireland.

2-029 Direct rule was imposed from Westminster. The first period, from 1972–74, resulted in considerable Parliamentary time at Westminster being devoted to Northern Ireland's affairs. A new written Constitution for Northern Ireland in 1973 provided for a system of power-sharing, whereby the two communities in Northern Ireland might form a legislative assembly through proportional representation and an executive broadly representative of the community. The attempt to introduce power-sharing failed after a general strike of loyalist workers forced the resignation of a newly-formed power-sharing executive in 1974. "Interim" direct rule was resumed for a period of five years under the Northern Ireland Act 1974. A second attempt in 1982 to achieve a new form of power-sharing under the Northern Ireland Act 1982 failed and resulted in the return to direct rule. Currently Northern Ireland is governed by direct rule. Direct rule provides that the Government of Northern Ireland is the responsibility of a Secretary of State together with a Minister of State and up to four Parliamentary Under-Secretaries of State. The bulk of legislation for Northern Ireland is made through Orders in Council under the Northern Ireland Act 1974. Most Orders are subject to affirmative resolution of both Houses of Parliament but are not subject to amendment in debate. These procedures are heavily criticised for not allowing the same degree of debate and scrutiny as an ordinary bill.

2-030 Northern Ireland's formal written Constitution was created in order to achieve a greater consensus in its Government. Yet the status of its Constitution is formally that of an Act of Parliament. It may be modified, amended or repealed at a later date. Attempts to address the concerns of Unionists over the status of the Union with the UK may be seen in the various protections built into the constitutional status of Northern Ireland; for example, the Ireland Act 1949 simultaneously recognised the secession of Southern Ireland and its republican status while declaring that Northern Ireland would not cease to remain part of the "United Kingdom without the consent of the Parliament of Northern Ireland". After the abolition of the Northern Ireland Parliament in 1973, this guarantee was replaced by a new form of protection namely that Northern Ireland would not cease to remain part of the UK without "the consent of the majority of the people of Northern Ireland voting in a poll held for the purposes of this section". It is questionable whether such a "guarantee" constitutes a fundamental protection that would prevent amendment by a subsequent Act of Parliament. It is worthwhile examining this in more detail below as an example of the difficulty of "entrenching" any fundamental rule by Act of Parliament. However, there are special circumstances prevalent in Northern Ireland which must be taken into account. Section 1 of the Northern Ireland Act 1998 reiterates the protection set out under the 1973 Act that Northern Ireland will not cease to remain part of the UK without the consent of the majority. However, the Northern Ireland Act 1998 also repeals the Government of Ireland Act 1920. The implications of the repeal are that devolution under the 1998 Act is a new departure and that it is necessary to have a break with the past. It is open to debate whether the break with the past includes the idea of the entrenchment of the Union.[26]

2–031

The modern form of protecting the status of Northern Ireland owes its origins to art.1 of the Act of Union with England in 1800, which stated that the Kingdoms of Great Britain and Ireland shall "for ever after, be united in one kingdom". In common with Scottish and Welsh Acts of Union already noted above, might not the Union with Ireland appear to be a constituent treaty of such fundamental importance that its status absolves it from modification or repeal?

2–032

English lawyers addressed this issue in 1868 when the Irish Church Bill was debated in the House of Commons. The Bill set out to disestablish the Church of Ireland and thereby dissolve its union with the Church of England—a union guaranteed in the Act of Union 1800. An unsuccessful challenge to the validity of the Act was made in *Ex p. Canon Selwyn*.[27] The Irish Church Act 1869 disestablishing the Church of Ireland, was passed. Parliament may not legally bind future Parliaments. We have already seen how subsequent legislation has successfully amended, revised or changed the Act of Union including the devolution legislation under the Northern Ireland Act 1998.

2–033

Since 31 August 1994 and a cease-fire by the Irish Republican Army, attempts have continued to provide a peace process in Northern Ireland; the initiatives have involved constitutional innovation. The Northern Ireland (Entry to Negotiations, etc.) Act 1996 provided for elections in Northern Ireland to allow all-party negotiations. The decommissioning of arms has been the subject of a report under United States Senator George Mitchell on 22 January 1996 and the Northern Ireland Arms Decommissioning Act 1997 provides a statutory framework for arms decommissioning. The breakthrough came with an Agreement formed from multi-party negotiations. Known as the Belfast Agreement or the Good Friday Agreement,[28] it was signed on 10 April 1998. The Northern Ireland Act 1998 was passed granting devolution to Northern Ireland. Northern Ireland's form of devolution reflects its unique history and

---

26   Brigid Hadfield, "The Belfast Agreement, Sovereignty and the State of the Union" (1998) *Public Law* 599.
27   (1872) 36 *JP Journal* 54.
28   *The Agreement reached in multi-party negotiations*, Cm.4292 (1998).

the need for consensus-building as part of the peace process. The close interrelationship between the peace agreement and consensus-building through a devolved system of government is the major reason why devolution is important for the future of Northern Ireland. Thus devolution is only likely to succeed as long as the peace agreement holds; equally if a component of devolution fails, the peace process may be in jeopardy. In order to build a consensus, referenda on the Agreement were held in Northern Ireland and the Irish Republic in May 1998. In Northern Ireland there was a turnout of 80.98 per cent and 71.2 per cent approved the Agreement. In the Republic of Ireland, there was a turnout of 55.47 per cent and 94 per cent voted in favour. Elections for the Northern Ireland Assembly were held under the Northern Ireland (Elections) Act 1998 as part of the Northern Ireland Act 1998 and the requisite Order in Council was made to bring the new devolved Assembly into life. However, the new Assembly endured for no more than ten weeks following disagreement over the arms decommissioning arrangements. The Northern Ireland Act 2000 suspended the 1998 Act but the devolution Assembly was restored after further negotiations. The main details of devolution are more fully discussed below.

C: Devolution

2–034 The unitary nature of the UK emphasises the fact that there is no federal system and this underlines the unitary nature of the UK comprising England, Wales, Scotland and Northern Ireland. Since the introduction of devolution in 1998, there is a potential for the delegation of powers to lead to much more substantial delegation that might ultimately change the unitary nature of the state. It is first necessary to explain how devolution is defined and what is its significance? The term refers to the delegation of various central government powers to the regions, while retaining the sovereignty of the central legislature. Thus sovereignty is not divided between a federal legislature and a regional legislature. The focus of devolution is on the delegation of powers and the relationship between the regional body, and the central legislature and government. Devolution may be defined as a delegation or re-allocation of power from the centre to the regions. Another feature of devolution is the fact that the sovereign legislature is unaltered. Devolution may be suspended, abolished or redrafted at the discretion of the sovereign. In fact, there are many different forms of devolution. Before the 1998 devolution Acts for Scotland and Wales, there existed administrative devolution. The main experiment in devolved government comes from the period in Northern Ireland from 1920, under the Government of Ireland Act 1920, until 1973. Northern Ireland is a useful case study of devolved powers and as such provided a learning experience; the benefit of this is to be found in the 1998 devolution Acts.

Administrative devolution

Since the 1960s the arrangements for the government of Scotland and Wales evolved through decentralisation of a large range of administrative tasks. Gradually this resulted in "administrative devolution". In the case of Scotland, the Secretary of State for Scotland had five main departments with a wide range of statutory responsibilities and duties. The five departments were the Scottish Office; Agriculture, Environment and Fisheries Department; The Scottish Office Education and Industry Department; The Scottish Office Home Department and the Scottish Office Department of Health. There was also the Scottish Courts Administration, the department of the Registrar General for Scotland, the Scottish Record Office and the department of Registers for Scotland. The administration of the government of Scotland allowed the Secretary of State some freedom in the development of matters of particular significance for Scotland. Scotland has a legal system distinct from that of England and Wales. The Lord Advocate and the Solicitor-General for Scotland advise the Government on Scottish questions. Criminal justice, courts and prosecution matters under the Crown Office provide Scotland with its own distinct legal system.

In Wales the degree of administrative devolution was markedly less than for Scotland. There is a Secretary of State for Wales with sole responsibility in Wales for ministerial functions relating to a whole host of different areas such as health, education, personal social services, the environment, local government, the European Regional Development Fund and with oversight of economic and regional planning responsibilities for Wales.

In Northern Ireland following the introduction of direct rule in 1972, administrative devolution resulted in a hotchpotch of functions but without any locally elected Northern Ireland Assembly. What was intended as an interim arrangement of direct rule from 1972 became more permanent. The Secretary of State for Northern Ireland is the minister responsible for the government of Northern Ireland, and has a seat in the British Cabinet of the government in London. In addition, there are two Ministers of State with shared responsibilities for a number of key Northern Ireland departments such as the Departments of Agriculture, Economic Development, Education, Environment, Finance and Personnel, and Health and Social Services. The Northern Ireland Office became the United Kingdom Government Department for Northern Ireland.

Proposals for devolution in the 1970s

The idea of some form of legislative devolution for Scotland and Wales may be traced back to the 1960s. The arguments in favour of some form of devolved government rested on a number of trends that had become clear in the 1970s. The over-centralisation of governmental power in the UK and the growth of nationalism in Scotland and Wales put the issue of "legislative devolution" on the political agenda and the hiving-off of legislative and most likely fiscal powers to separate assemblies in Scotland and Wales. The experience of devolution in Northern Ireland was influential in considering the way forward to address the issues raised by devolution.

The Government of Ireland Act 1920 had provided devolution in Northern Ireland from 1920 until 1972. It formed the Constitution of Northern Ireland and established a Parliament for Northern Ireland with extensive legislative powers. There were powers transferred to the Northern Ireland Parliament and matters retained at Westminster. Overall the sovereignty of the UK Parliament remained intact and the Government of Ireland Act preserved the unity of the UK. Devolution offered a non-federal solution to the demands for greater local autonomy. The Northern Ireland experience also proved flexible. After events in 1972 culminating in the fall of the Northern Ireland Parliament after widespread civil unrest and street violence, the Northern Ireland Constitution Act 1973 was passed followed by a Northern Ireland Assembly Act 1973. Although the 1973 Act was overtaken by events in Northern Ireland both the 1973 Act and the Government of Ireland Act 1920 helped provide a model for some form of regional government in Scotland and Wales. The strength of the argument in favour of devolution and the rejection of federalism came from the analysis offered by the report of the Royal Commission on the Constitution, known as the Kilbrandon Report,[29] published in 1973. The Kilbrandon report identified dissatisfaction with the centralised Westminster model of government. The Report was greatly influenced by the Northern Ireland form of devolution introduced under the Government of Ireland Act 1920 which it regarded as having worked well in providing legislation particular to the needs of Northern Ireland. One strength of the system was the opportunity to judge whether UK Acts of Parliament ought to be applied in Northern Ireland after a period when the legislation was "tested" in England and Wales.

2–039 The UK Government's response to the Kilbrandon Report was to attempt to establish assemblies in Scotland and Wales. The Government ruled out devolution for England but undertook consideration of executive devolution to new English regional authorities. The matter of English devolution was finally dropped after the Government found a lack of consensus on the issue. In the case of Scotland and Wales, separate Scotland and Wales Acts passed in 1978 failed to receive the support of 40 per cent of the electorate necessary for the Acts to come into force. While a majority voted in Scotland in support of devolution, this only amounted to 32.9 per cent of the electorate and not the 40 per cent required. In Wales only 20.2 per cent of the vote favoured devolution representing 11.9 per cent of the electorate, well below the 40 per cent required. After the referendum results, devolution lapsed as a major issue for some time. It was conceded by some that the vote may have reflected what was on offer rather than a rejection of devolution in principle.

2–040 Pressure for some form of devolved government or outright independence has grown in recent years. Opposition parties unsuccessfully introduced a Devolution Bill in November 1987. The Campaign for a Scottish Assembly lobbied for devolution in the late 1980s. In July 1988, "A Claim of Right for Scotland" was launched and recommended a Constitutional Convention; its first meeting was held in Edinburgh on March 30, 1989. The left-of-centre Institute for Public Policy Research published its draft Constitution in 1991 which included a devolved assembly for Scotland, Wales and the English regions. More recently the Constitution Unit studied

---

29 *Report of Royal Commission on the Constitution* (Kilbrandon), Cmnd.5460-61 (1973); and *Memorandum of Dissent*, Cmnd.5732 (1974).

the question of devolution and considered a Scottish Parliament with legislative and tax-varying powers. Similar proposals were discussed for Wales. The election of the new Labour Government on 1 May 1997 firmly established constitutional reforms as a central element in the Government's agenda.

Devolution Acts of 1998 and their significance

In September 1997 referenda on devolution were held in Scotland and Wales. The result was that in Scotland 75 per cent of the voters were in favour of devolution, on a 60 per cent turnout. In Wales support for devolution was more marginal, and on a turnout of around 50 per cent the majority were in favour but by the narrowest of margins (0.6 per cent). The new Labour Government with a secure Parliamentary majority at Westminster could afford to be radical.

The Scotland Act 1998 created a new Scottish Parliament, elected for four years, with defined legislative powers to pass Acts (Sch.5 of the 1998 Act) and a limited tax-raising authority. There is a Scottish First Minister, and an appointment process for ministers nominated by the First Minister from members of the Scottish Parliament but requiring the agreement of that Parliament. The UK Parliament maintains overall legislative competence over matters relating to foreign affairs, including the EU, the Crown, defence, and economic and monetary matters. Over the first few years with a devolved Parliament, Scotland has developed a distinctive style and content in governing its own affairs.

The Government of Wales Act 1998 creates a Welsh Assembly, more limited in powers and scope than the Scottish Parliament. The Assembly is unable to legislate in terms of passing Acts, but may exercise the functions of the Secretary of State for Wales that have been transferred to the Assembly. This power includes subordinate legislative powers under Pt III of the Government of Wales Act 1998. There is a First Minister, and the Assembly operates cabinet-style committees for decision-making. It is possible that under political influence the powers of the Welsh Assembly could be increased beyond the modest powers it already has. Most notably unlike the Scottish Parliament, it does not have power to raise taxes. However, the Secretary of State for Wales may be forced to concede additional powers under pressure from the Welsh Assembly. This may not have been envisaged in the legislation, but, in practical terms, is how the Welsh form of devolution may result in more autonomy for Wales than originally planned. The Assembly, however, does not have powers to adopt primary legislation. As a result as Burrows has pointed out[30]:

> "In Wales there is the anomaly that an Assembly deriving its legitimacy from the will of the people demonstrated in elections lacks the power to carry out the functions associated elsewhere within the United Kingdom with such a body."

30 N. Burrows, *Devolution* (London: Sweet & Maxwell, 2000), p.186.

2-044 Finally, in the case of Northern Ireland, devolution is part of an ongoing peace process and as such has a number of unique qualities. There is an Assembly, elected for a four-year term, and a power-sharing executive unlike any other, with a requirement to address divisions between Nationalists and Unionists. There is a First Minister and a Deputy First Minister who must satisfy the requirements of a majority in the Assembly and a majority of both Unionists and Nationalist members of the Assembly. There is then a complex set of powers that may be devolved to the Assembly once it is up and running, with excepted matters listed in the Act as most likely never to be devolved. This leaves reserved matters which might be transferred under an Order in Council, and transferred matters that are devolved. The essence of devolution is that the constitutional order may create, but not impose, a system of government. As mentioned above, under the Northern Ireland Act 2000 devolution was suspended in May 2000 and then later restored, an indication of the fragility of the peace process underpinning devolution. It also underlines that legal sovereignty continues to reside in the Westminster Parliament.

D: Devolution in Scotland, Wales and Northern Ireland

General

2-045 Devolution also fits the Conservative Government's plan to revitalise regional government. While this is a step towards decentralisation, paradoxically it should not always be assumed that it will bring about any reduction in the centralising tendencies of government. Devolution does not prevent the UK Parliament from legislating on matters that fall under devolved powers. For example, in the 2000 and 2001 period, there were 14 bills passed by the UK Parliament on matters that fell within the legislative competence of the Scottish Parliament. Devolution provides mini-written constitutions for Wales and Scotland for the first time in the UK. There is an elected Mayor and Assembly for London, a limited form of devolution.

2-046 England is one of the nations that has only limited forms of devolution such as to London. The Greater London Authority and the London Mayor. Currently there are plans to have elected mayors and devolved powers to Manchester and other large cities.[31]

---

31 House of Commons Library, Briefing paper SN07029, *Devolution to local government in England* (20 May 2015).

Some common characteristics of devolution

2-047 Each of the four systems of devolution for Scotland, Wales, Northern Ireland and London has its own distinctiveness, but they share common characteristics, as devolution is evolving differently in each of the nations. The Wales's model of devolution to the National Assembly of Wales of being able to legislate where powers are conferred on it. In the case of Scotland and Northern Ireland powers are based on a reserved powers model where certain powers are reserved to Westminster while powers are conferred on the devolved nation. It is possible for reserved powers to be also devolved but this requires the consent of the Secretary of State and legislation. It is arguably that a reserved powers model might also be given to Wales.[32] This is the latest development in the draft Wales Bill 2015/16 being considered by the House of Commons.[33] It is highly likely that various tax raising powers will be devolved such as corporation tax, once this has occurred in other devolved arrangements.

2-048 Burrows[34] identifies common characteristics such as inclusiveness, diversity, sustainability, equal opportunity, modern working practices, flexibility and responsiveness, openness and accessibility. Devolution is very much a process rather than a single event. The future of devolution is linked to the generation of regional identity and local interest. The diversity of these influences makes it difficult to draw out common principles, but there are a number of influences that are common in the devolution of each region. The Westminster model of parliamentary government is shared in each form of devolution in Scotland, Wales and Northern Ireland. All three Executives have different powers and cabinet systems that are intended to reflect the differences, both subtle and practical in the way government operates in each of the regions. There are corresponding principles in each of the three devolved bodies for the regulation and registration of members' interests and powers for the attendance of witnesses and documents. There is also devolution in London. This is a distinct form of devolution because of the decision to have a directly elected Mayor separately elected from the London Assembly, the Greater London Authority, itself directly elected. It is planned that the London Mayor form of devolution is likely to be adopted in regions in the UK over the coming years.

2-049 Although the formulation of the sovereignty of the UK Parliament is expressed differently for each region, it is clear that sovereignty rests with the UK Parliament. In Scotland, and Northern Ireland, and now Wales each with their own law-making powers, sovereignty is retained by the UK Parliament over all matters including those matters that are devolved.

2-050 Funding arrangements follow a common arrangement that may be traced back to the period before devolution was introduced, and owe much to the arrangements introduced in the 1880s by the then Chancellor of the Exchequer. Building on the experience gathered

---

32 The Constitution Unit, *Delivering a Reserved Powers Model of Devolution for Wales* (London: The Constitution Unit, University College London, 2015).
33 House of Commons Library: Briefing Paper No.06641 *Electoral arrangements in Wales* (23 November 2015).
34 N. Burrows, *Devolution* (London: Sweet & Maxwell, 2000).

over the years' expenditure arrangements for Scotland, Wales and Northern Ireland were negotiated and brought within the overall remit of public expenditure controls. In the 1960s and 70s the rules developed further and in 1978 a non-statutory arrangement known as the Barnett formula was introduced for Scotland. The Barnett formula was further refined and developed even though it was intended to be a temporary arrangement. The formula determines the amount of additional changes to the expenditure of Scotland, Northern Ireland and Wales. The bulk of expenditure is outside the arrangement and large payments fall outside its remit. These are determined by block grant on an annual basis. There are also special circumstances that make the formula's application in Northern Ireland work differently.

2-051

The Barnett formula is intended to allow for an adjustment of any additional payments on the basis of an economic formula. The Barnett formula has three elements:

- the change in planned spending in departments in England;

- the extent to which there is comparability in the services carried out by each administrative department in the devolved administration when compared to the equivalent English departmental programme; and

- the population that is proportionate in each country.

The Barnett formula is part of the UK's central government's system of spending for government departments. The spending of all UK Government departments is divided between Departmental Expenditure Limits and Annually managed Expenditure budgets. This is used to set expenditure for overall budget purposes. The Barnett formula only applies to spending that is territorially identified and applies to Departmental Expenditure Limits.

2-052

Finance bills are not subject to the English Votes for English Laws (EVEL) arrangements. However, in discussing the proposals for EVEL it is clear that legislative changes that affect England only may have consequences for Government spending in England. This may have a knock-on effect in Scotland, Wales and Northern Ireland because of the way in which the Barnett formula for financial arrangements in the devolved nations operates. There may be annual changes in the block grants allocated to each of the four nations.[35] This is an important matter that exposes some weaknesses in the government's House of Commons Supply Procedures. One argument is that the Estimates procedures determine such matters rather than the legislation, but this is not commonly agreed by everyone.[36]

2-053

It is generally believed that if the formula is applied strictly then increases in expenditure in Scotland, Wales and Northern Ireland might be slower than the English equivalent. The

---

35 House of Commons Briefing Paper, *Devolution of financial powers to the Scottish Parliament; recent developments*, No.07077 (22 January 2016).
36 House of Commons Procedure Committee, *Proposed English Laws Standing Orders*, Oral evidence (8–9 September 2015).

Barnett formula is criticised for not assessing need, which may lead to distortions in its application. The Barnett formula is likely to remain in place for the foreseeable future.

The electoral arrangements for devolution share common characteristics. In Scotland, Wales and Northern Ireland, election is by way of proportional representation (PR). This was chosen to encourage multi-party government. PR may prevent any one group gaining a monopoly of power, and discourages adversarial politics found in the first-past-the-post system. Although PR is used in each region, there are differences:

The Electorate in Wales and Scotland

Voters have two votes. One vote is for a constituency elected by the first-past-the-post system. In Scotland there are 73 members of the Scottish Parliament. In Wales there are 40 members of the Welsh Assembly. The second vote is for the regions based on the constituency for the European Parliament. In Scotland there are eight regions with seven members in each, making 56 members in total. In Wales there are five regions each returning four members, making 20 members in total. The system of voting is adopted from the d'Hondt system of PR. Each elector votes for a particular party list.

The Electorate in Northern Ireland

Voters use the Single Transferable Vote system. Voters mark their preferences for their choice of candidate. There is a formula establishing the quota required to elect the number of representatives for the constituency. The constituency is based on the 18 constituencies used to vote for Westminster MPs representing Northern Ireland. There are six members returned for each of the 18 constituencies. This makes a total of 108 representatives for the Northern Ireland Assembly.

The Electorate in London

The Greater London Authority Act 1999 provides for different systems of voting for the London Mayor and for the 25-member Greater London Authority. The London Mayor is elected under the Supplemental Vote System, a form of PR. The Greater London Authority is elected under two systems. One system is for 14 constituency members elected from special constituencies on the first-past-the-post system. The other is for 11 members elected across London on a constituency list system using the Additional Member System.

Common to Scotland, Wales and Northern Ireland is the creation of a category of devolution issues. In general terms devolution issues such as the legal competence of the devolved body are the type of constitutional question that might arise. The scheme that has been adopted is that the lower courts in each of the three jurisdictions may refer devolution issues to the higher courts and ultimately the UK Supreme Court to be settled through judicial interpretation. The relevant Law Officers must be notified thereby providing an opportunity to make out a legal opinion.

2-059 There are wide powers given to the different Law Officers for this purpose. It is clear that this power expands considerably the role of the courts to set standards and give attention to the boundaries of the legislative competences of the devolution settlement in each of the three jurisdictions. Examples of where the boundaries may be set include areas reserved for the UK Parliament, breaches of European Community law or any incompatibility with Convention rights. It would appear in principle that it is possible for a devolution issue to be raised within any of the legal jurisdictions of the UK. This gives considerable scope for legal challenges beyond the territory of Scotland, Wales or Northern Ireland.[37] The question of what constitutes a devolution issue is also linked to the fact that all three devolved bodies are bound by the Human Rights Act 1998. Failure to apply the 1998 Act is itself a devolution issue. Legislation that is incompatible with the Human Rights Act 1998 is outside the legal competences of the devolved bodies. In Scotland s.29 of the Scotland Act 1998 applies and s.57 prohibits the Executive from making subordinate legislation that is incompatible with Convention rights. In Northern Ireland s.6 of the Northern Ireland Act 1998 is applicable. Section 24 also makes it incompatible for the Executive to make subordinate legislation that is incompatible with Convention rights. In Wales, s.107 makes a similar rule. There is a difference because the Welsh Assembly does not have equivalent legislative powers, thought these are likely to be granted in 2015. If secondary legislation is required by the UK Parliament for Wales that is incompatible with the Convention, then the secondary legislation may be permitted even if it is in breach of Convention rights. The reasoning is that because the UK Parliament is not bound to apply Convention rights in domestic law and it is within its powers to override the Human Rights Act 1998 by primary legislation then it is possible for Wales and England to undertake legal powers that are not permissible in Scotland and Northern Ireland. The UK Parliament might, however, enact legislation to override ss.6 and 24 of the Northern Ireland Act 1998 and ss.29 and 57 of the Scotland Act 1998.

2-060 At the May 2015 election, the Conservative manifesto included a promise to repeal the Human Rights Act 1998. This manifesto promise is being considered by the Government. In the case of Northern Ireland, there is a pre-existing Treaty agreement under the Anglo-Irish Treaty as part of the Belfast Agreement made in 1998, that the UK Government is obliged to "complete incorporation into Northern Ireland law of the European Convention on Human Rights with direct access to the courts and remedies for breach of the Convention".[38]

2-061 There is a further implication in making devolution issues include Convention rights.

When the UK Supreme Court was established in 2009, it inherited the transfer of Juridical Committee of the Privy Council's jurisdiction over devolution issues making the Supreme Court the final court of appeal on the powers of the devolved Parliaments and assemblies (with the exception of criminal law matters in Scotland). Issues to do with devolution have also been raised in the UK Supreme Court. A number of recent cases highlight

---

37 Aidan O'Neill, "Judicial Politics and the Judicial Committee: The Devolution Jurisprudence of the Privy Council" (2001) *Modern Law Review* 603.
38 Paragraph 2 of the "Rights, Safeguards and Equality of Opportunity", the Anglo-Irish Treaty.

the cultural distinctiveness of the Scottish legal system and the political sensitivities surrounding it. As we shall see, courts have generally upheld the powers of devolved bodies against challenge, except in relation to the primacy of EU law and interpretations of human rights, when the Supreme Court has on occasions overridden interpretations made by Scottish courts.

In *Axa General Insurance and others v The Lord Advocate*,[39] the lawfulness of an Act of the Scottish Parliament, the Damages (Asbestos-related Conditions) (Scotland) Act 2009, was challenged as to its compatibility with art.1 of Protocol 1 of the European Convention on Human Rights and its reasonableness in terms of the general judicial review jurisdiction of the Supreme Court, in particular on grounds of irrationality and arbitrariness. The claimants were insurance companies and their claim arose from their undertaking to indemnify employers against liability for negligence. The point of the Scottish Parliament's legislation was to include under Scots law liability for personal injury claims arising from various asbestos-related pleural plaques and related conditions.

2–062

The UK Supreme Court held that the claimants were entitled to make such a claim and that the courts had an overarching power to ensure that the 2009 Act was legitimate in its aims and proportionate in its response. The court took into account the political context of the legislation, including social policy and the public interest. It found that the legislation had a legitimate purpose and that the means to achieve its aims were reasonable and proportionate. The Court rejected the claimants' case and held that the legislation was compatible with the European Convention and did not offend any of the other grounds for judicial review on which the claimants relied.

2–063

The significance of the *Axa* decision is that the UK Supreme Court indicated that it has a residual jurisdiction to consider the legality of Acts of the Scottish Parliament. Lord Hope held that the approach to the question of the Supreme Court's review powers also applied to the other devolved institutions in Wales and Northern Ireland, but that it was significant that the Scottish Parliament is "a self-standing" democratically elected legislature. This sets an important benchmark for judicial review. Lord Hope cautioned that the courts "should intervene, if at all, only in the most exceptional circumstances".[40] His analysis is drawn not only from a comparative analysis of the sovereignty of the UK and Scottish Parliaments, but on the basis of the power of review itself: it constitutes an important oversight of the constitutional processes and checks and balances on the legislative programme of the Scottish Parliament and other devolved administration exercising legislative powers.

2–064

The Supreme Court has also considered the competence of the Northern Ireland Assembly[41] and the Welsh Assembly.[42] In the case of Welsh Assembly, the Supreme Court

---

39 [2011] UKSC 46; [2012] 1 A.C. 868 and [2011] CSIH 31; 2011 S.C. 662.
40 [2011] UKSC 46; [2012] 1 A.C. 868 at [49].
41 *Robinson v Secretary of State for Northern Ireland* [2002] UKHL 32; [2002] N.I. 390.
42 *Recovery of Medical Costs for Asbestos Diseases (Wales) Bill: reference by the Counsel General for Wales and the Association of British Insurers* [2015] UKSC 3; [2015] A.C. 1016. Also consider *Local Government Byelaws(Wales) Bill 2012—Reference by the Attorney General for England and Wales* [2012] UKSC 53; [2013] 1 A.C. 792.

held it lacked legislative competence in respect of a Medical Costs for Asbestos Diseases Bill as the Bill raised general fiscal competence which the Welsh Assembly lacked. In effect the Bill seeks to impose what are in effect new tortious or statutory duties on third parties to pay for the relevant NHS treatment.

E: Devolution in England

England[43]

2-065

We have already noted that there is no devolved legislature or executive for England. There is no House of Commons Select Committee for England and—unlike the position in Wales—no English Grand Committee.[44] There is no separate "voice" for England and its interests at Westminster—or in Whitehall.[45] There is no tier of elected regional government in England except in London.

London

2-066

The only formal form of devolution within England are the arrangements for London under the Greater London Authority Act 1999—and this does not involve the granting of any legislative power.[46] After a referendum under the Greater London Authority (Referendum) Act 1998 produced a large vote in favour, an office of elected Mayor and a 25-member London Assembly were created.[47] The first elections were held on 4 May 2000. The Mayor is elected by the Supplementary Vote System and the London Assembly by the Additional Member System. In 2005 a review was undertaken and the Greater London Authority Act 2007 was passed. This gave additional powers to the Mayor, including powers of appointment to some

---

43 See B. Hadfield "Devolution, Westminster and the English Question" [2005] *Public Law* 286; and "Devolution: A National Conversation?" in J. Jowell and D. Oliver (eds), *The Changing Constitution*, 7th edn (Oxford: Oxford University Press, 2011).
44 See discussion of Grand Committees below. The Welsh Grand Committee has been active since devolution. The Scottish Grand Committee has not been convened since about 2002.
45 See Report from the Institute for Public Policy Research, *The Dog that Finally Barked: England as an Emerging Political Community* (2012).
46 See HM Green Paper, *New Leadership for London* (1997).
47 For details see House of commons Library, The Greater London Authority SN/PC/05817 (24 January 2012). There are also a number of related documents SN/SC/1416 London Underground PPP SN/BT/1746.

public bodies in London: for instance, the appointment of Chairs or members or trustees of the London Regional Council, Arts Council, England, the appointment of senior members to various bodies such as Transport for London, the Mayor's Office for Policing and Crime, the London Fire and Emergency Planning Authority. The London Assembly was granted advisory confirmation powers over a small number of senior posts. Further legislative changes have followed under the Localism Act 2011,[48] the Police Reform and Social Responsibility Act 2011—which created the Mayor's Office for Policing and Crime—and the Public Bodies Act 2011.

The powers of the Greater London Authority are limited when compared with those of devolved bodies in Scotland, Wales and Northern Ireland. The Mayor holds almost all the executive powers[49] and is accountable to the London Assembly which has powers to amend the Mayor's annual budget. The Mayor has to produce a Spatial Development Strategy for London that covers many framework planning matters, though most planning is devolved to the London Borough level. The main executive agency, Transport for London, responsible for London Underground, is chaired by the Mayor. In addition, the Mayor is responsible for producing various strategic documents across a wide range of subject areas.[50] The Localism Act 2011 permits the operation of Mayoral Development Corporations for regeneration purposes. Financial powers include the operation of a supplementary levy of up to 2p in the pound under the Business Rate Supplements Act 2009 on all businesses.

English regions

There is no level of elected bodies with legislative or administrative power in England outside London apart from local authorities and from 2011 Police and Crime Commissioners under the Police Reform and Social Responsibility Act 2011. It was the policy of the Labour government in 2002 to create elected regional assemblies. A referendum was held in the North East region of England on the introduction of such an assembly, but on a turnout of 48 per cent only 22 per cent voted in favour, and the policy was dropped. Referenda were held in ten cities in May 2012 on the creation of new elected Mayors. Only one city, Bristol, voted in favour. There is evidently no appetite amongst the electorate in England for more elected bodies, despite the absence of a "voice" for England and its regions except in London.

The Cities and Local Government Devolution Act 2016 is intended to devolve "far reaching powers to regions covering transport and social care to large cities and in particular powers to

---

48 See Antonia Layard, "The Localism Act 2011: what is 'local' and how do we (legally) construct it?" (2012) *Environmental Law Review* 134.
49 See House of Commons Library, *Aviation: Mayor of London's proposals for a Thames estuary airport 2008*, SN6144 (25 July 2012).
50 On economic development, transport, culture, waste, air quality, ambient noise and biodiversity, climate change mitigation and energy, housing and health inequalities are amongst the strategic responsibilities.

Manchester". The main enabling legislation has a number of primary aims that form a template for this kind of devolution:

- an elected mayor for the combined authority with specified functions as well as chairing the authority;

- the Mayor may also hold the function of the Police and Crime Commissioner and these functions may be combined in a single election for the one post; and

- the intention is to further strengthen existing City Deals and Growth Deals by granting the additional powers to enable the elected Mayor to fulfil their functions including the tasks of combined authorities.

The likely outcome of this ambitious legislation is to provide the possibility of applying the model of the London Mayor outside London. Enabling legislation is being considered to ensure that devolved powers are granted to different regions on a similar model to the devolution granted to Scotland, Wales and Northern Ireland.[51] The Local Democracy, Economic Development and Construction Act 2009 is being supplemented by the Cities and Local Government Devolution Act 2016 provides the main structures for devolution with several areas in Tees Valley, Manchester, Liverpool, Greater Manchester, Sheffield and the North East. This is seen as a model of its kind that allows different kinds of local governance to be taken forward.

F: Devolution in Wales

The Government of Wales Acts 1998 and 2006

2–069

Devolution in Wales is distinctive from the other models of devolution used in Scotland and Northern Ireland. The Government of Wales Act 1998 provided for a 60-member National Assembly for Wales, elected under the same system as that used in Scotland—an Additional Member System. The National Assembly is the first bilingual legislative forum in the UK. It was granted delegated legislative powers, and the 1998 Act made no distinction between the Assembly and the government, which was formed from its members: it was a form of corporate governance.

---

51   House of Commons Library, Briefing Paper, *Combined authorities*, No.06649 (20 January 2016).

2–070 Transfers of functions were effected by Orders in Council approved by the UK Parliament under s.22 of the 1998 Act. The National Assembly for Wales (Transfer of Functions) Order 1999 provided for the devolution of power previously exercised by the Secretary of State for Wales to the Welsh Assembly. The transfers were categorised into 18 specified fields and later raised to 20 specified fields by Sch.5 to the Government of Wales Act 2006. None of them granted the Assembly primary legislative powers. Thus the National Assembly for Wales was confined to delegated legislative powers only within its specified fields of competences,[52] as compared with the devolution of "residual" powers to legislate on any matter except those reserved to the UK Parliament, to the Scottish Parliament under the Scotland Act 1998. There is lively discussion in Wales about whether the National Assembly for Wales, like the Scottish Parliament, should enjoy such residual powers. Significantly, financial autonomy through tax-raising powers was not included in the 1998 or 2006 Acts.[53]

2–071 Experience under the Government of Wales Act 1998 led to the separation of the Legislature and the executive. The creation of the First Minister for Wales and various ministers (there had been secretaries until then) began in earnest in 2000. The Welsh Assembly Government set up a Commission to consider the details of the Assembly's powers under Lord Ivor Richard. It reported in 2004.[54] The UK Government responded in its White Paper *Better Governance for Wales*.[55] The UK Parliament then passed the Government of Wales Act 2006 (the 2006 Act) which reformed the National Assembly for Wales and formalised the arrangements for a Welsh Assembly Government[56] consisting of a First Minister and up to 12 Welsh Ministers, all members of the Assembly.

2–072 The Assembly of 1998 had been granted power to make Assembly measures within the 20 specified fields subject to approval by the Queen in Council. The effect of an Assembly Measure was the same as that of an Act of Parliament. This procedure was superseded when Pt 4 of the 2006 Act came into force after a referendum in March 2011, and gave the Assembly primary legislative powers in its areas of competence.

2–073 It is possible under the 2006 legislation, as it was under the 1998 Government of Wales Act, for the Assembly to be given additional legislative powers in any of the 20 specified fields. This enhanced legislative power requires a referendum and an Order in Council approved by both Houses of Parliament. As of 2013 there has been one referendum (provision for which was

---

52 The specified fields of competences are agriculture, fisheries, forestry and rural development, ancient monuments and historic buildings, culture, economic development, education and training, environment, fire and rescue, and fire safety, sport and recreation, food, health and health services, highways and transport, housing and local government, public administration, the National assembly itself town and country planning, water and flood defence, tourism and the Welsh language.
53 There was subsequent discussion of this following the recommendations of the Holtham Commission, and the issue was actively considered by the Silk Commission. Both are discussed below. See also the announcement made by Danny Alexander on 24 October 2012 re: borrowing powers for the NAW. Written Answers: Hansard, Col.53WS (24 October 2012).
54 The Commission on the Powers and Electoral Arrangements of the National Assembly for Wales (Spring 2004).
55 CM.6582 (July 2005).
56 By s.45.

made in the 2006 Act), triggered by the Welsh Assembly on 3 March 2011, to consider whether the Assembly should have the power to legislate on all matters falling within the 20 specified fields. The result was approval, with 63 per cent in favour to 36 per cent against.[57] The consequence of the referendum was to bring into effect a new primary legislative procedure for the passing of "Acts" in the areas of Assembly competence.[58]

2–074

The Assembly has been active in developing its own approach to public policy and aspects of the law. Examples include the recommendation in October 2011 to reform the lawful defence of reasonable chastisement: legislation on this has not yet been forthcoming. There have been environmental protection measures such as the charging of 5p per customer for the use of plastic bags, similar to the position in the Irish Republic. Other new Welsh policies include a campaign against smoking in cars, options for the giving of consent to organ donation, and a pro-active health strategy, *Together for Health*. The First Minister supports a separate Welsh jurisdiction and this has generated a lively debate. Many of the issues raised by the Government and the Assembly, though controversial, reflect a significant desire to create distinctive Welsh policies.

2–075

In July 2012 the Attorney General referred to the Supreme Court—before Royal Assent had been given—the question whether the first bill passed by the Assembly since the 2011 referendum, the Local Government Byelaws (Wales) bill, was within its vires. The bill affected the function of the Secretary of State for Wales under s.236 of the Local Government Act 1972 in relation to by laws made without his consent, and this was not permitted by the Government of Wales Acts.[59] This was the first time that the Attorney General had used the power to refer any devolved Bill to the UK Supreme Court. The power of referral is also available in the devolution settlement Acts for Scotland and Northern Ireland and the case is significant for those devolved arrangements. The Supreme Court[60] was unanimous in holding that the Welsh Assembly had legislative competence to enact both ss.6 and 9 of the Bill. The contentious issue was s.9 of the Bill which the Secretary of State refused to approve because it had the potential to give Welsh Ministers powers to add to the schedule of byelaw enactments that would not require the Secretary of State's consent. The Supreme Court's interpretation does not broaden the Assembly's powers but clarifies the need for confirmation by the Secretary of State in the approval of byelaws. The case is important particularly because there are similar provisions for Scotland under s.33 of the Scotland Act 1998, and also for Northern Ireland.

---

57   House of Commons Library, *Referendum in Wales*, SN/PC/05897 (7 March 2011)
58   See Pt 4 of the 2006 Act. And see explanation of legislative powers on the Assembly website *http://www.assemblywales.org* [Accessed 31 March 2016]. For an update on recent developments See House of Commons Library Political developments in Wales to December 2012 SN/PC/06542 (31 January 2013).
59   See *http://www.bbc.co.uk/news/uk-walws-politics-19055404* [Accessed 31 March 2016].
60   Supreme Court Local Government byelaws (Wales) Bill 2012—Reference by the Attorney General for England and Wales [2012] UKSC 53; [2013] 1 A.C. 792.

The Silk Commission Review: Finance and Legislation

The UK Coalition Government decided in 2011 to institute a Calman-like process (see discussion of Scotland, above) for Wales. This led it to set up a Commission on Devolution in Wales, chaired by Paul Silk (hence the Silk Commission), the first Clerk to the Welsh Assembly.[61] The Commission's report will be in two parts: Pt 1 was published in the Autumn of 2012 on fiscal powers; and Pt 2 on devolved powers published in early 2014. The Wales Act 2014 was passed containing similar powers as the Scotland Act 2012, but it will require another referendum before it will come into force.

The background to fiscal powers for Wales is that the Independent Commission on Funding and Finance for Wales (the Holtham Commission) was established by the Welsh Assembly Government in 2008 to review the Assembly's funding and to consider the devolution to it of fiscal powers.[62] The Holtham Commission[63] was very critical of the Barnett formula which the UK Treasury applies to adjust the amount of public expenditure allocated to the constituent parts of the UK, and noted that "it lacked any objective justification and had survived for 30 years solely for reasons of political and administrative convenience".[64] The Commission recommended that the formula should be replaced by a new, needs-based formula; and that limited powers over certain taxes and borrowing should be included in the new arrangements.

This issue was further considered by the Silk Commission[65] in its first report, published in November 2012. The Silk Commission accepted that the Barnett formula required replacing, and also accepted Holtham's findings. The UK and Welsh Governments have agreed in principle that borrowing powers when agreed would mean an appropriate revenue stream being in place. The Silk report recommends that Welsh ministers should have powers and responsibilities for raising 25 per cent of their own budget. This would include borrowing and income tax-raising powers. The introduction of additional powers is subject to new legislation following a referendum in Wales. A variety of smaller taxes would also be included in the new financial arrangements devolved to the Welsh Assembly.[66]

The Silk Commission's second report on legislation has led to all-party discussion and

---

61 House of Lords Library Note, Debate on 19 July: Silk Commission on Devolution in Wales, LLN 2012/050 (12 July 2012). Submissions to the Silk Commission have been made available online.
62 The Holtham Commission was similar to the Calman Commission set up for Scotland which recommended that elements of taxing powers ought to be devolved, with reductions in the block grant from the UK Treasury and extended borrowing powers granted to the Scottish Parliament: these were implemented in the Scotland Act 2012, discussed above.
63 House of Commons, *Holtham Commission*, SN/EP/6288 (28 March 2012).
64 See Holtham Commission, *Independent Commission on Funding and Finance in Wales, First Report: Funding devolved government in Wales, Barnett and beyond* June (2009). See the Final Report *Fairness and accountability: a new funding settlement for Wales* (2010).
65 The Commission on Devolution in Wales, *Empowerment and Responsibility: Financial Powers to Strengthen Wales* (Chair Paul Silk) (2012).
66 Silk Commission, *Empowerment and Responsibility: Financial Powers to Strengthen Wales*, recommendations 2–10. The smaller taxes are the aggregates levy, stamp duty, landfill tax and air passenger duty for long haul

an agreement in November 2014 known as the St David's Day Agreement. The result will be a new reserved power model for Welsh devolution (this is the same approach in Scotland and Northern Ireland). Further devolved powers to enable the National Assembly of Wales to determine its own size, electoral arrangements and operational matters including the permanence of the Assembly and the withdrawal of the rights of the Secretary of State for Wales to take part in the proceedings of the Welsh Assembly.

The Draft Wales Bill 2015–16

2–080   The draft Wales Bill creates a reserved powers model of devolution, similar to Scotland, to the Welsh Assembly and makes changes to the electoral arrangements in Wales in line with commitments made in the St David's Day Agreement. There is also recognition that the Welsh Assembly and Government are permanent. Devolved powers will include the regulation and conduct of Welsh Assembly elections, the registration of voters and the calling of polls. An important Sch.1 will define reserved powers that covers the regulation of political parties, elections for the House of Commons, the European Parliament and Police and Crime Commissioners.

G: Devolution in Scotland

2–081   There is a long history to debates about Scottish devolution, including in the recommendations of the majority in the Royal Commission on the Constitution in 1973,[67] and those surrounding the Scotland Act 1978, which was never implemented because the required 40 per cent of the electorate did not vote in favour in a referendum (though a majority of those voting were in favour).[68] In the 1980s the campaign for devolution to Scotland was led by the Scottish Constitutional Convention which was formed in 1988.[69] The Scottish National Party was involved initially but withdrew early on as the constitutional options under consideration did not include independence. Membership of the Convention included 80 per cent of Scotland's MPs and MEPs, members from the Regional and Island Councils and most District Councils, and representative from the churches, business, industry, the unions and

---

flights. See Marc Weller, "A Foregone conclusion?" (2012) *New Law Journal* 1389; and C. Munro, "A Scottish divorce?" (2012) *New Law Journal* 1387.

67 Lord Crowther and later Lord Kilbrandon (Chair) *Royal Commission on the Constitution*, Cmnd. 5460 (1973).
68 The Act was repealed in 1979.
69 See its publications *Towards a Scottish Parliament* (1989); *Key Elements of Proposals for Scottish Parliament* (1990); and *Scotland's Parliament, Scotland's Right* (1995).

from the Labour Party and the Social and Liberal Democrats. The Conservative Party did not participate.

The Scotland Act 1998

The Scotland Act 1998 created a Scottish Parliament with 129 members, the first Parliament in Scotland since 1707. Elections to the Parliament are by a mixture of first-past-the-post for 73 constituency members and an Additional Member System for 56 regional list members. The Parliament chooses the First Minister, who then chooses the Cabinet. From the start it was clear that the electoral system might result in coalition or minority government. In 1999 and 2003 the elections in Scotland led to a coalition executive between Labour and the Liberal Democrats. The election in 2007 led to the formation of a minority Scottish National Party executive. The SNP won a majority in the 2011 election and rules since then as a single party majority government.[70]

The Scotland Act 1998 granted the Scottish Parliament "residual powers"[71] entitling it to legislate on all matters except those listed as reserved powers in Sch.4 and Sch.5: these remained under the control of the UK. The list of reserved powers includes the Crown, foreign affairs, including the EU, defence and macro-economic policy. Specific reservations were also made across a wide range of central government departments that included social security, immigration and nationality, misuse of drugs, energy and employment. The Scottish Parliament does not have power to legislate contrary to EU law or to the European Convention on Human Rights. Section 30(2) of the Scotland Act 1998 provides for the possibility of expanding the devolved responsibilities and altering the allocation of responsibilities between the UK and Scotland: it is this section that devolved power to the Scottish Executive to hold a referendum on Scottish independence in 2014 (see below).

The Scotland Act 1998 s.28, retains the sovereignty of the UK Parliament. However under the Sewel Convention—which is not part of the Act, but a Memorandum of Understanding between the UK Government and the Scottish executive—the UK Government undertook not to seek or support legislation in the UK Parliament on matters within Scotland's devolved competence without the prior consent of the Scottish Parliament, to be given by the passing of Legislative Consent Motions (which were also known as Sewel Motions). During the passage of the Scotland Act 2012 (see below) the UK Government reiterated the Sewel Convention and undertook not to legislate on devolved matters without the consent of the Scottish Parliament.[72]

---

70 The term "executive" was altered to "government" in the Scotland Act 2012.
71 These include agriculture and fisheries, the arts, education, the environment, health, home affairs, housing, law and justice, local government, planning, the police service, social work, sport and most areas covered by transport within Scotland.
72 Revised procedural rules were introduced in December 2005 governing the legislative consent process. See House of Commons Library: *The Sewel Convention* SN/PC/2084 (25 November 2005). The working of the Sewel

2-085 The Scottish Government resembles the UK Cabinet in some respects, in particular its reliance on ministerial and cabinet responsibility. The Committees of the Scottish Parliament differ from those at Westminster,[73] for instance in that there is no division between legislative and scrutiny committees. Unlike Wales and Northern Ireland, Scotland was given the power to set the Scottish Variable Rate (SVR) by the Scotland Act 1998, and this allowed the Scottish Parliament to raise or cut the basic rate of income tax by up to three pence in the pound. The power has not been exercised and will be repealed once the new Scottish Rate of Income Tax provided for in the Scotland Act 2012 comes into effect and this is expected to be in April 2016, though the Act does not specify any date. The implications of the change are significant. The basic and higher and additional rates of income tax will be set at 10 per cent points lower for Scottish taxpayers than for taxpayers than for taxpayers in the rest of the UK. This will leave the Scottish Parliament to decide the SVR—it might be set to be the same as the rest of the UK or higher or lower. However, the Scottish Parliament cannot set different rates for the upper and lower bands of income tax (there is a locking mechanism to prevent this).

2-086 The 2012 Act also discontinues two taxes—stamp duty and land and Building Transaction Tax for Scotland. There is the power to replace both taxes with new devolved taxes. In 2015, stamp duty was replaced with a land and Buildings Transaction Tax and landfill duty by the Scottish Landfill tax. New taxes may be introduced with the permission of HM Treasury. In order to preserve some integrity to the Barnett formula, the block grant for Scotland may be accordingly reduced. Scotland has created a new body, Revenue Scotland for the collection and administration of the Scottish Rate of Income Tax. The UK body HM Revenue and Customs has to work with the Scottish body.

The Scotland Act 2012

2-087 Pressure from Scotland for increases in the powers of the Scottish Parliament led to the setting up of the Calman Commission[74] in response to the SNP's proposals for independence and its increasing electoral success in Scotland. The Commission reported in 2009. It recommended that some powers of taxation ought to be devolved to Scotland with a subsequent reduction in the block grant from the UK, and that extended borrowing powers be granted to the Scottish Parliament. The UK Coalition Government formed in May 2010 decided to take forward many of the Calman recommendations. The Scotland Act 2012 made further adjustment to the list of reserved matters and those that have been devolved to Scotland.[75] The Act

---

Convention was considered by the Mckay Commission discussed below. For information about these motions see *http://www.gov.scot/About/Government/Sewel* [Accessed 31 March 2016].
73 See B. Dickson, "Devolution" in J. Jowell, D. Oliver and C. O'Cinneide, 8th edn, The Changing Constitution (Oxford: Oxford University Press), 2015 pp.249–79.
74 *The Calman Commission on Scottish Devolution*, Final Report (2009). See House of Commons: *Devolution of tax powers to the Scottish Parliament*, SN05984 (27 January 2012).
75 House of Commons, *Responsibility for reserved powers in Scotland*, SN/PC/06322 (2012). This note contains lists of reserved powers and the UK government departments responsible.

grants new powers to the Scottish Parliament to allow it to raise taxes by replacing part of the UK income tax with a new Scottish income tax, devolving stamp duty, land tax and landfill tax, and giving the Scottish Parliament new borrowing powers. The 2012 Act also clarifies the law in relation to the jurisdiction of the Supreme Court of the UK over criminal appeals, discussed below.

A significant difference between the Scottish Parliament and the UK Parliament is that the former, being a creature of statute, does not enjoy the inherent privileges of the two Houses of the UK Parliament but depends instead upon the provisions of the Scotland Acts of 1998 and 2016: in these respects the UK Parliament has greater autonomy because of Parliamentary privilege.

The Role of the Courts

Soon after the Scotland Act 1998 came into effect questions arose in litigation as to the nature and powers of the new Parliament. In *Whaley v Lord Watson of Invergowrie*[76] it was held by the Inner House of the Court of Session that the Scottish Parliament, being a creature of statute, does not enjoy the privilege of the UK Parliament to regulate its own proceedings (though by s.28(5) of the Act the validity of an Act of the Scottish Parliament is not affected by any invalidity in proceedings leading to the enactment).[77] Issues to do with devolution have also been raised in the UK Supreme Court. A number of recent cases highlight the cultural distinctiveness of the Scottish legal system and the political sensitivities surrounding it. As we shall see, courts have generally upheld the powers of devolved bodies against challenge, except in relation to the primacy of EU law and interpretations of human rights, when the Supreme Court has on occasions overridden interpretations made by Scottish courts.

The Scottish referendum and the Smith Commission Agreement

The outcome of the Scottish referendum in favour of maintaining the Union with England has far reaching consequences when the results became known in 2014. A Commission under Lord Smith was set up to take forward the promises made by the Government and agreed by all the major political parties. The Smith Commission Agreement made four undertakings. That fiscal devolution (outlined above) would be extended beyond the Scotland Act 2012; that welfare devolution would be further extended; that additional competencies would be given to the Scottish Parliament and the devolution arrangements would be established under a new UK statute. In terms of taxation all rates and bands of income tax earned

---

76   2000 S.C. 340; 2000 S.L.T. 475 Ct of Session.
77   See C. Munro, "Privilege at Holyrood" [2000] *Public Law* 347.

2-091

by Scottish taxpayers will be devolved. The UK will continue to have authority to set personal allowances, exemptions and the definition of income as well as taxes on savings and dividends. Outside these areas, the Scottish Parliament will have the main responsibility for income tax including the various bands of taxation. Air Passenger Duty and the Aggregates Levy are also devolved to Scotland. Up to 10 per cent of VAT raised in Scotland will be assigned to the Scottish Parliament. This is common in many federal systems and allows some autonomy but the overall level of VAT has to be set by the EU. It is estimated that about 60 per cent of the money spent by the Scottish Parliament spends will be directly from the Scottish Parliament. After the election of May 2015, the Government published the Scotland Bill 2015/16 implementing the main terms of the Smith Commission's recommendations (discussed below).

Welfare devolution is more complicated as there is a need for some degree of parity between the nations. The devolution of welfare is often subject to oversight by the UK authorities leaving the devolved system liable to be fined if they do not follow the same principles of welfare spending. This is the case in Northern Ireland and can be a source of conflict such as the recent decisions of the Northern Ireland Assembly to fail to implement austerity cuts. If policy-making in Scotland pulls away from the UK this will increase tensions between the different nations. The Smith Commission recommends that the Sewel Convention should be placed on a statutory basis and that devolution should be made permanent.[78]

The Scotland Bill 2015/16

2-092

The Scotland Bill 2015/16 extends further the powers of the Scottish Parliament related to the Smith Commission Agreement. This would mean that the Scottish Parliament would have powers to introduce new rates and bands of income tax above the UK personal allowance. This would apply to the same categories of income tax as the Scottish Rate of Income Tax set up under the Scotland Act 2012. This covers income from employment, pensions, taxable social security benefits and income from property. Reserved matters include Capital Gains Tax but this is subject to further discussion. VAT revenues are assigned to the Scottish Government's budget. Air passenger duty and Aggregates Levy are also devolved to the Scottish Government. There is some autonomy given to the Scottish Government to introduce its own air passenger duty. There is an ongoing debate about corporation tax and the argument that Scotland should be given full responsibility.

2-093

One interesting outcome is that adjustments will have to be made to the Barnett formula (the block grant) in the light of further devolution of taxes to Scotland. This will require careful negotiation.[79] This will require analysis of the Fiscal Framework for Scottish devolution and it is

---

78 See House of Commons Library Briefing Papers, *The Scotland Bill 2015–16*, No.07205 (4 June 2015).
79 House of Commons Library Briefing Papers, *Devolution of financial powers to the Scottish Parliament: recent developments*, No.07077 (1 March 2016).

likely to take some time to agree because of pressure from the SNP to have greater autonomy from the UK.

H: Devolution in Northern Ireland

Northern Ireland

Northern Ireland's constitutional status and history are closely intertwined.[80] This is reflected in the special circumstances of the need to provide arrangements for power-sharing between Nationalists and Unionists. The form of devolution in Northern Ireland is a reflection of the past but also a commitment to a power-sharing government for the future. The Government of Ireland Act 1920 was the first effort at a devolved government and Parliament within the UK, and the arrangements endured until 1972. From March 1972 to January 1974 devolution was suspended and then abolished, leading to a long period of "direct rule" from the UK which lasted until the implementation of the Northern Ireland Act 1998. During that period laws for Northern Ireland were made as UK Acts of Parliament passed at Westminster. The Belfast Agreement 1998 and the Northern Ireland Act 1998 were the results of agreement between the British and Irish Governments.

2–094

I: The Northern Ireland Act 1998

The Northern Ireland Act 1998 established an elected Assembly of 108 members, elected by Single Transferrable Vote (STV), and an executive. Northern Ireland, with a population of 1.8 million, has a disproportionately large Assembly when compared to the population sizes of Wales (3 million) and Scotland (5.1 million). This reflects the fact that the devolution arrangements are designed to address past sectarian problems there, as well as to provide a forum for passing and debating legislation. Sufficient representation from all parts of the community is required for its public legitimacy. The Assembly has an extensive list of devolved legislative

2–095

---

80 House of Commons Library, *Political Developments in Northern Ireland since October 2008*, SN/PC/05029 (23 March 2009).

powers,[81] which, since 2010, include justice and policing. Arrangements for allocating a minister for justice and policing are to be reviewed, with legislation to make permanent the transfer. Northern Ireland has no autonomous tax-raising powers. As in Scotland, Acts of the Northern Ireland Assembly must be compatible with EU law and the European Convention on Human Rights (ECHR).

2-096

The Northern Ireland Assembly's legislative programme has been relatively modest. By the end of the 2010–11 session 17 bills had received Royal Assent, with a further eight bills under scrutiny. In May 2011 the Executive announced that they had introduced a further 11 bills with four becoming law. There remains frustration at the slow pace of legislation.[82]

2-097

The Northern Ireland Government is composed of First and Deputy First Ministers and other Ministers: its composition must meet the need for "power sharing" between Nationalists and Unionists. Under the Northern Ireland Act 1998 Cabinet members are elected according to the d'Hondt system in order to secure the proportionate allocation of posts, with the exception of the Department of Justice.[83] There are also operational means to secure consensus within the Assembly: the 12 departmental ministries and statutory shadowing committees are all required to work on a strictly proportional basis. In effect this is a form of coalition "power sharing" government, between Nationalists and Unionists, with five different political parties representing different shades of opinion. The overarching framework prescribed by the Northern Ireland Act 1998 builds flexibility into the arrangements. However, overall the Assembly is weak as most parties are in the Government and hence there is no equivalent to the Opposition in the UK Parliament.

2-098

In August 2012, the Secretary of State for Northern Ireland launched a consultation document on measure to improve the operation of the Northern Ireland Assembly.[84] This includes the size of the Assembly, the length of Assembly terms, double jobbing by membership of different institutions and the development of an Opposition. The closing date for submissions was 23 October 2012: the results had not been published by February 2013.

2-099

In principle the UK procedures for committees and cabinet decision-making have been adopted for Northern Ireland, including conventions of Cabinet collective responsibility. However, these have not always been possible to apply in Northern Ireland's power-sharing executive. The provisions for election of Cabinet members do not require the parties to take up the places in the Cabinet they are entitled to, and yet the Northern Ireland Cabinet is

---

81 These include: agriculture, sea fisheries, forestry and rural development, culture and arts including leisure, language and diversity, education, employment and learning including higher and further education, enterprise, trade and investment, the environment, planning, pollution and local government, health, social services and public safety, including child protection mental health and hospitals, regional development, transport and social issues including housing and urban development.
82 *The Belfast Telegraph*, 7 November 2012.
83 See Northern Ireland Act 2009 Sch.1 s.4(3). The 2009 Act inserts a new Pt 1A into Sch.4A to the Northern Ireland Act 1998. Section 3C of Pt 1A excludes the policing and justice ministry from the D'Hondt system.
84 Northern Ireland Office, *Consultation Paper on Measure to Improve the Operation of the Northern Ireland Assembly* (August 2012).

required to be composed in proportion to the party strength in the Assembly. Almost all the main political parties are entitled to seats in the Executive. In March 2011, three Cabinet ministers failed to vote for the Budget in the Assembly. They had also voted against it at the relevant Cabinet meeting.[85] The Assembly could have passed a vote of censure on the Government, but chose not to do so, probably because elections in Northern Ireland were due on 5 May 2011. This leaves considerable doubts about the Assembly's willingness to hold the Executive to account.[86] Unionist pressure to unpick the power-sharing arrangements and return to a more Westminster-style model is developing. This is strongly resisted by Sinn Fein.

2-100

Devolution in Northern Ireland is inextricably linked to the ongoing peace agreement that underpins its continuation. The St Andrews Agreement (2006) provided the basis for its resumption in 2007. In December 2014 the Stormont House Agreement was reached and this has given rise to further financial powers being devolved. The Corporation Tax (Northern Ireland) Act 2015 grants corporation tax powers to the Northern Ireland Assembly.[87] Financial arrangements are likely to dominate relations with the UK as devolved regions will struggle for some degree of parity of treatment.[88]

J: Co-ordinating Devolution and the UK Parliament

We now turn to the implications of devolution for the UK Parliament. Currently the devolution Acts preserve the legislative supremacy of the UK Parliament: it retains the power to legislate on matters that have been devolved, and thus to override laws made by the devolved legislatures. However, the political reality is that its freedom to exercise that power is politically constrained by the existence of the devolved bodies, as the conventions about Legislative Consent Motions Sewel Convention (discussed below) confirm. The asymmetry of the devolution arrangements raises major issues for the UK Parliament, particularly the fact that there is no separate legislature for England or its regions and that laws passed for England by the UK Parliament may be voted on by MPs sitting for constituencies in Scotland, Wales or Northern Ireland.

2-101

---

85 *The Belfast Telegraph*, 10 March 2011.
86 House of Commons Library, *Political Developments in Northern Ireland January 2012–November 2012*, SN/PC/06477 (12 November 2012).
87 House of Commons Library, *Devolution of corporation tax to Northern Ireland*, SN7078 (12 February 2015).
88 Details of devolution are contained in House of Commons Library Briefing Paper, *Devolution of financial powers to the Scottish Parliament: recent developments*, No.07077 (13 November 2015).

The West Lothian question and English votes for English laws

2-102 The most challenging issue for the UK Parliament is the so-called West Lothian Question. Its origins lie in the 1880s in the debates on Home Rule for Ireland.[89] The question is whether it is right that MPs from areas where there is legislative devolution should be able to vote at Westminster on English domestic legislation. Tam Dalyell, MP for West Lothian, raised the question during discussions of devolution in the 1970s. Given the evolution of devolution today the question remains relevant. Some believe that it is largely unanswerable.[90]

2-103 The Coalition Government's *Programme for Government* of 2010 included a proposal to establish a Commission to Consider the West Lothian Question.[91] The Commission was established under Sir William McKay, Clerk of the House in the Commons from 1998–2002 "[T]o consider how the House of Commons might deal with legislation which affects only part of the UK, following the devolution of certain legislative powers to the Scottish Parliament, the Northern Ireland Assembly and the National Assembly for Wales".

2-104 The McKay Commission is not the first inquiry into the West Lothian Question. The House of Commons Procedure Committee reports of 1998–99 discussed the introduction of some form of 'in and out' legislative procedure for English legislation and recommended procedural changes to allow joint committees with the Scottish Parliament or the Welsh Assembly.[92] The Commons Justice Committee inquiry reported in May 2009, having taken evidence during sessions in 2007/08 and 2009/10.[93] The Committee pointed out that four-fifths of the population live in England but that the implications of devolution in Wales and Scotland had not been considered in relation to the way in which England was governed.

2-105 One "solution" to the English question that is mooted from time to time is that bills or clauses in bills that apply only to England, or only to England and Wales, ought to undergo a special procedure in the House of Commons: MPs sitting for constituencies in Scotland and Northern Ireland, and Wales if the matter does not affect Wales, ought to be restricted in their participation in the legislative process. This would raise a number of difficulties. It is difficult to single out provisions in bills that only affect England. Who should have responsibility for making these controversial decisions about participation of members in the legislative process in the House of Commons? Since the Autumn of 2015, there is a new EVEL

---

[89] There is an excellent discussion in John Kendle, *Ireland and the Federal Solution* (Montreal: McGill-Queen's University Press, 1989), pp.57–86. Roy Jenkins, *Gladstone* (London: MacMillan, 1989), pp.548–549.

[90] Professor Vernon Bogdanor, Evidence to the McKay Commission (June 2012). See also M. Russell and G. Lodge, "The Government of England by Westminster" in R. Hazell (ed), *The English Question* (Manchester: Manchester University Press, 2006); and Jim Gallagher, *IPPR, England and the Union How and why to Answer the West Lothian Question* (London: IPPR, April 2012).

[91] See Vernon Bogdanor, "The West Lothian Question" (2010) 63(1) *Parliamentary Affairs* 156–172.

[92] See Procedure Committee First Report, *The Procedural Consequences of Devolution*, HC 148; Second Report, HC 376; Fourth Report, HC 185; and First Special Report HC 814, all of same title (1998–99).

[93] Fifth Report *Devolution: A Decade on*, HC 529 (2008–09).

procedure. The Speaker of the House of Commons *certifies* that a Government bill in new clauses, amendments schedules or secondary legislation falls within the category of being subject to the new EVEL procedures. The assessment made by the Speaker may be made at the primary legislative stage, at second reading, after consideration on Report, after a new stage called reconsideration or on Commons consideration of any House of Lords amendment. The procedures are technically complicated because of the difficulties of determining whether or not a bill raises devolution issues. Certification takes place if in the Speaker's opinion two tests are passed. First, that the relevant bill, amendment, new clause, schedule motion or affirmative instrument must apply exclusively to England or to England and Wales and that must be within devolved legislative competence. The latter is likely to be open to challenge in the courts.[94]

2-106
If a bill is certified as an England-only bill (there are similar arrangements for England and Wales only bills) it will be debated at second reading and if agreed it will then go to either a public bill committee or the Legislative Grand Committee (England). The public bill committee will reflect the party share of seats in England, and include only members with seats in England. If there are no changes the bill goes to the Legislative Grand Committee. If there are changes, then agreement has to be reached on the basis of a Consent Motion in the appropriate Legislative Grand Committee. The Sewel Convention,[95] was an important aspect of the devolution settlement between the UK and Scotland, and is reflected in the Memorandum of Understanding between the UK Government and the Scottish Government (formerly Scottish Executive) and in Devolution Guidance Note 10. Nothing in the Scotland Act prevented the UK Parliament from legislating on matters which are within devolved competence: s.28(7) made that clear. However, during the passage of the Scotland Act, the UK Government announced that it "would expect a convention to be established that Westminster would not normally legislate with regard to devolved matters in Scotland without the consent of the Scottish Parliament". If, with the consent of the Scottish Parliament, Scottish Ministers agreed with the UK Government that a Westminster Bill should include provisions on devolved matters, Scottish Ministers would consider promoting a Legislative Consent Motion (formerly referred to as a "Sewel Motion" discussed below). To facilitate scrutiny of such proposals from the UK Government, the Scottish Executive advises the UK Parliament as early as possible of any bill that is likely to be subject to a Legislative Consent Motion and provides the relevant Committee with a detailed memorandum explaining the purpose and effect of any devolved provisions. The Committee will then be able to consider the proposal, taking evidence from interested parties if it considers that necessary, before making a recommendation to the full Parliament as to whether it should approve the Legislative Consent Motion. The Legislative Consent Motion procedure now extends to legislation affecting matters devolved to Northern Ireland (where they have not been used much as the Northern Ireland Assembly has passed few measures)

---

94 House of Commons Briefing Paper, *English votes for English laws*, No.7339 (2 December 2015).
95 See discussion in the Scotland section of this chapter. And see http://www.scotland.gov.uk/About/Government/Sewel/KeyFacts [Accessed 31 March 2016]; and House of Commons Library, *The Sewel Convention*, SN/PC/2084 (25 November 2005).

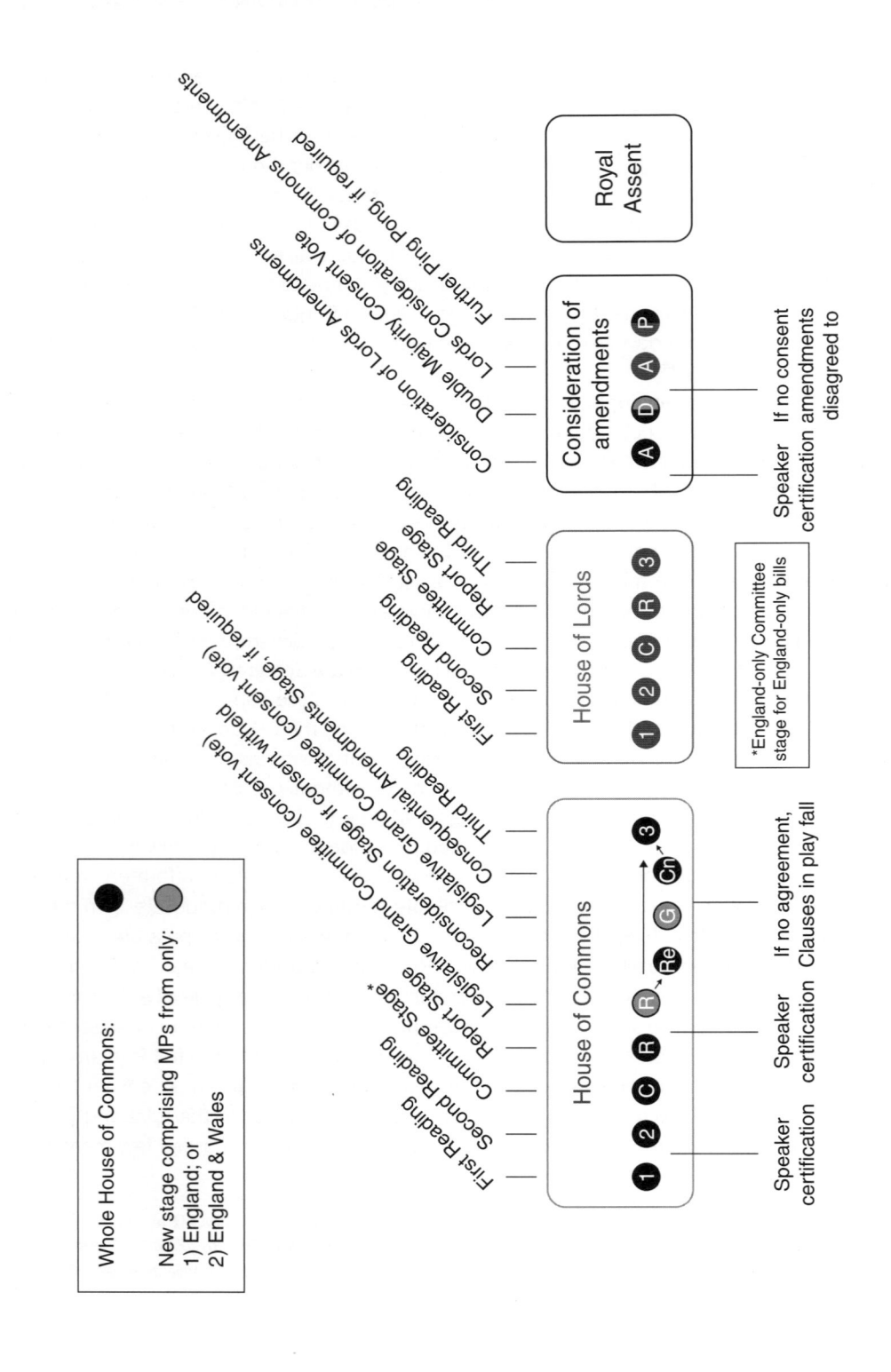

Legislative Process Flowchart

House of Commons

- First Reading (1)
- Second Reading (2)
- Committee Stage (C)
- Report Stage (R)
- Legislative Grand Committee (consent vote)
- Reconsideration Stage, if consent withheld
- Legislative Grand Committee (consequential consent vote)
- Third Reading (3)

Sub-flow: R → Re → G → Cn → 3

Speaker certification (First Reading area)

Speaker certification — Clauses in play fall (Report stage area): If no agreement

House of Lords

- First Reading (1)
- Second Reading (2)
- Committee Stage (C)
- Report Stage (R)
- Third Reading (3)

*England-only Committee stage for England-only bills

Consideration of amendments

- Consideration of Lords Amendments (A)
- Double Majority Consent Vote (D)
- Lords Consideration of Commons Amendments (A)
- Further Ping Pong, if required (P)

Speaker — If no consent certification amendments disagreed to

Royal Assent

Legend

- ● Whole House of Commons:
- ● New stage comprising MPs from only:
  1) England; or
  2) England & Wales

and to Wales.[96] From 2006–2011 they were part of the process by which Westminster passed primary legislation for Wales.

It is very difficult to estimate how many bills are likely to be subject to the EVEL procedures and even harder to know how effective the arrangements are likely to be when operating for a few years. The current Government has a majority of English MPs. A further difficulty would arise if the party or parties in government at Westminster relied for their majority in the House of Commons on MPs from the devolved territories: it could become politically impossible for laws to be passed for England if the Government was not entitled to call on its MPs in devolved areas to support its bills. A question might then arise as to whether a separate English Parliament—and government—should be established. This would produce a quasi-federal system in the UK, leaving the UK Parliament and government responsible for matters such as defence and foreign policy, fiscal policy and taxation, social security, etc. If changes to take account of the position of England were to be taken yet further and the UK Parliament's legislative powers were limited so that it could not legislate on matters within the legislative powers of devolved bodies in England, Scotland, Wales and Northern Ireland, the system would be truly federal.[97] Neither a quasi-federal nor a federal system would be workable. There would be a gross imbalance in power between England, which has some 90 per cent of the population of the UK, and Scotland, Wales and Northern Ireland, with much smaller populations. There is indeed no easy answer to the West Lothian and English Questions, though if Scotland were independent many of these particular sets of problems would disappear.[98] The bill then continues to second reading and committee stage as normal.[99] There is no proposal to amend the procedures in the House of Lords. (See Diagram 1, Outline of model—Bill starting in the House of Commons).

The use of Parliamentary procedure to amend the way a bill is debated and voted on is controversial and has attracted considerable debate. A preferable option would be to introduce primary legislation that settles arrangements that would have the benefit of debate and scrutiny. It is by no means clear that the Government's proposals have settled the matter. Even bills that appear only to affect England may have knock-on effects on other parts of the UK. For instance, bills that affect public expenditure in England (on introduction of private provision in the NHS in England, for instance) may result in changes to the allocation of public money to the devolved bodies by the Treasury under the Barnett formula: spending for the three devolved nations is based on Barnett and Barnett is set in relation to England.[100]

---

96 http://www.assemblywales.org/bus-home/research/bus-assembly-publications-monitoring-services/bus-lcm_monitor.htm [Accessed 31 March 2016].
97 Cabinet Office, *English Votes for English Laws: An Explanatory Guide to Proposals* (July 2015). Also see Cabinet Office, *English Votes for English Laws; Revised Proposed Changes to the Standing Orders of the House of Commons and Explanatory Memorandum* (July 2015).
98 House of Commons, 26 October 2015 Speaker's Statement on EVEL Implementation.
99 Cabinet Office, *English Votes for English Laws: An Explanatory Guide to Proposals* (July 2015). Also see Cabinet Office, *English Votes for English Laws; Revised Proposed Changes to the Standing Orders of the House of Commons and Explanatory Memorandum* (July 2015).
100 See House of Commons Library Research Paper 07/91 (December, 2007); and *Report of the House of Lords'*

2-109 A further difficulty would arise if the party or parties in government at Westminster relied for their majority in the House of Commons on MPs from the devolved territories: it could become politically impossible for laws to be passed for England if the Government was not entitled to call on its MPs in devolved areas to support its bills. A question might then arise as to whether a separate English Parliament—and government—should be established. This would produce a quasi-federal system in the UK, leaving the UK Parliament and government responsible for matters such as defence and foreign policy, fiscal policy and taxation, social security etc. If changes to take account of the position of England were to be taken yet further and the UK Parliament's legislative powers were limited so that it could not legislate on matters within the legislative powers of devolved bodies in England, Scotland, Wales and Northern Ireland, the system would be truly federal. Neither a quasi-federal nor a federal system would be workable. There would be a gross imbalance in power between England, which has some 90 per cent of the population of the UK, and Scotland, Wales and Northern Ireland, with much smaller populations. There is indeed no easy answer to the West Lothian and English Questions, though if Scotland were independent many of these particular sets of problems would disappear.

Legislative Consent Motions

2-110 The Sewel Convention,[101] was an important aspect of the devolution settlement between the UK and Scotland, and is reflected in the Memorandum of Understanding between the UK Government and the Scottish Government (formerly Scottish Executive) and in Devolution Guidance Note 10. Nothing in the Scotland Act prevented the UK Parliament from legislating on matters which are within devolved competence: s.28(7) made that clear. However during the passage of the Scotland Act, the UK Government announced that it "would expect a convention to be established that Westminster would not normally legislate with regard to devolved matters in Scotland without the consent of the Scottish Parliament". If, with the consent of the Scottish Parliament, Scottish Ministers agreed with the UK Government that a Westminster Bill should include provisions on devolved matters, Scottish Ministers would consider promoting a Legislative Consent Motion (formerly referred to as a "Sewel Motion"). To facilitate scrutiny of such proposals from the UK Government, the Scottish Executive advises the Parliament as early as possible of any bill that is likely to be subject to a Legislative Consent Motion and provides the relevant Committee with a detailed memorandum explaining the purpose and effect of any devolved provisions. The Committee will then be able to consider the proposal, taking evidence from interested parties if it considers that necessary, before making

---

Select Committee on the Barnett Formula, HL 139, 2008–09 (July 2009). Also see HM Government's response, Cm.7772 (December, 2009).

101 See discussion in the Scotland section of this chapter. And see http://www.scotland.gov.uk/About/Government/Sewel/KeyFacts [Accessed 31 March 2016]; and House of Commons Library, *The Sewel Convention*, SN/PC/2084 (25 November 2005).

a recommendation to the full Parliament as to whether it should approve the Legislative Consent Motion.

The Legislative Consent Motion procedure now extends to legislation affecting matters devolved to Northern Ireland (where they are not much used as the Northern Ireland has passed few measures) and to Wales.[102] From 2006–2011 they were part of the process by which Westminster passed primary legislation for Wales. These Motions normally relate only to certain specific provisions in Westminster bills, not to whole or even substantial parts of these bills.

Parliamentary Procedures and Select and Grand Committees[103]

There have long been House of Commons select committees for Scottish, Welsh and Northern Ireland Affairs. The remits of these committees extend to matters for which the Secretaries of State for these constituent parts of the UK are responsible and include relations with the devolved legislatures in Scotland and Wales (but not in Northern Ireland).[104] There are restrictions on the questions that can be asked in Parliament about devolved matters.[105] The devolved bodies themselves are not accountable to the Westminster Parliament and its select committees have been cautious about even appearing to inquire into the policies of devolved bodies. These select committees have inquired, however, into both general policy issues that are common to the various devolved arrangements and the constitutional settlements themselves: the distinction is not always easy to maintain, especially in the Welsh context where many of the devolved areas "overlap" with non-devolved areas.

By way of examples, matters reported on by the Welsh Affairs Committee in the 2012–13 Session have included *Broadband Services in Wales*,[106] and *Inward Investment in Wales*.[107] In the 2009–10 Session they published reports on *Wales and Whitehall*[108] and proposed Legislative Competence Orders relating to transport,[109] culture and other fields,[110] local government and others subjects.[111] The Committee's *Review of the LCO Process*[112] in 2009–10 is an example of

---

102 http://www.assemblywales.org/bus-home/research/bus-assembly-publications-monitoring-services/bus-lcm_monitor.htm [Accessed 31 March 2016].
103 See Ch.7 above.
104 See House of Commons Standing Order 152.
105 HM Cabinet Office, *Devolution Guidance Note 1*, paras 26–27 (November 2005). Questions may be raised of fact but these will normally be answered by the relevant devolved administration.
106 First Report, HC 580 (2012–13) (September 2012).
107 Second Report, HC 125 (2012–13) (June 2012).
108 Eleventh Report, HC 246 (2009–10).
109 HC 273 (2009–10). The Government Response was at HC 436.
110 HC 420 (2009–10).
111 HC 36 (2009–10).
112 Fifth Report, HC 155 (2009–10).

a Select Committee looking into as aspect of the devolution settlement itself: the Committee was generally positive about the operation of the LCO process and the performance of the Committee in dealing with orders promptly and developing expertise; they considered their joint working with the National Assembly through informal meetings with Assembly Committee members to aid "joined up scrutiny" in both Parliament and the Assembly; and they made recommendations for improvements, including greater openness and clarity.

2–113 The Scottish Affairs Committee's reports in the 2012–13 Session have included both matters of general policy—*A Robust Grid for 21st Century Scotland*,[113] and those to do with the devolution settlement itself: *The Referendum on Separation for Scotland: Terminating Trident—Days or Decades?*,[114] and *The Referendum on Separation for Scotland: Making the Process Legal*.[115]

2–114 The Northern Ireland Affairs Committee's Third Report of the Session 2010–12 was on *Fuel Laundering and Smuggling in Northern Ireland*[116] and its First Special Report of the 2012–13 Session was the *Government Response* to that report.[117] In each of these committees a dialogue between Parliament and the Government is conducted via the Government's response and the committees' evidence sessions and correspondence with the government department.

2–115 The general implications for the UK Parliament and the UK of devolution and of possible Scottish independence are clearly appropriate matters for inquiry and discussion in Parliament. The House of Lords has been particularly active in providing information and advice on these matters. For instance, the House of Lords Select Committee on Economic Affairs undertook an inquiry into the Economic Implications for the UK of Scottish Independence in June 2012 as a prelude to the referendum that was held in Autumn 2014.[118] The House of Lords Constitution Committee report on *Referendum on Scottish Independence*[119] explored the issues raised by the proposal for a referendum; and in its report on the *Scotland Bill*[120] that Committee commented that, while it did not consider that the Bill raised any issues of constitutional concern to which the attention of the House should be drawn, "we publish this report in order to assist the House in its deliberations on the Bill. We do so because of the clear constitutional importance of the Bill." They did however invite the Government to be clearer about the meaning of "cross-party consensus" when it indicated that it would wish to be satisfied that there was cross-party consensus if new amendments to the bill were proposed.[121]

2–116 There are also Scottish, Welsh and Northern Ireland Grand Committees consisting of all MPs[122] sitting for constituencies in those areas. They may meet away from

---

113 First Report, HC 499 (2010–12) (August 2012).
114 Fourth Report, HC 676 (2010–12) (October 2012).
115 Third Report, HC 542 (August 2012). See also the Committee's report, *The referendum on separation for Scotland: A Multi-option Question*, HC 543 (2012–13) (August 2012).
116 HC 1504 (2010–12).
117 HC 272 (June 2012).
118 House of Lords Economic Affairs Committee, *Call for Evidence* (11 June 2012).
119 HL 263 (2010–12) (February 2012).
120 17th Report (2010–12) (July 2011).
121 At para.30.
122 House of Lords Economic Affairs Committee, Call for Evidence (11 June 2012).

Westminster, for instance the Welsh Grand Committee met in Wrexham in October 2011. They inquire into and discuss matters of general interest, for instance the Welsh Grand Committee debated the Legislative Programme and the Budget in June 2012. However as of October 2012 the Northern Ireland Committee had not held a debate since the general election in May 2012. The Scottish Grand Committee has not been convened since about 2002.

There is, of course, no Secretary of State for England, and no Select Committee for English Affairs—there being no Secretary of State for England for a Select Committee to hold accountable—nor an English Grand Committee. Thirteen English regional select committees were established in the 2005 to 2010 Parliament. Some were more active than others, and several reports were published. However, opposition MPs would not serve on them, and the Standing Orders providing for them were not renewed after the 2010 election. There seems to be no appetite in the House of Commons for such committees.

The constitutional implications of UK devolution

It may be concluded that devolution has an organic quality. Self-reliance and a desire to be distinctive from the history of English influence are potent forces that will pull in the direction of greater independence. Nationalism may claim a stake in drawing together distinct and different groups as elected, subordinate bodies develop in confidence and legitimacy. These are potent forces that have the potential to develop in opposition to the centralising tendencies of the past. Substantial devolution to Scotland and also to the English regions raises doubt over the very existence of the Union itself. Scotland is moving inexorably towards a more substantial form of devolution than the other nations, with devolved and taxation powers that mean that 60 per cent of its money comes from its own resources. This marks a significant constitutional moment.

At the apex of the implications for devolution to Scotland, Wales, Northern Ireland and the English regions is the intergovernmental relations between the different governments in the UK. There is a *Memorandum of Understanding* but this is too weak an instrument in attempt to address the question of intergovernmental relations. As the Bingham Centre concluded in its analysis of the architecture of the union state this is far from satisfactory. The absence of any effective UK Parliamentary scrutiny or indeed relevant knowledge of the workings of the devolved nations raises serious issues for the UK Parliament. The remnants of the system of Scottish, Welsh and Northern Ireland's offices are hardly an adequate means to monitor and oversee the workings of different parts of the Union. The question remains how to provide adequate systems of accountability for the UK Parliament over administrations that are outside their control.

Devolution is raising difficult and challenging constitutional issues that suggest that the UK is at a constitutional cross-roads.[123] The Bingham Centre's Commission on devolution has

---

123 Bingham Centre for the Rule of Law, *A Constitutional Crossroads: Ways Forward for the United Kingdom* (May 2014).

suggested a form of Charter of Union to set out principles and procedures to ensure that there is a co-ordinated approach to devolution. There is potential for the UK to be placed under considerable strain that will make a new constitutional settlement almost inevitable. The form this will take is unclear but likely to include some form of federal state proscribed through a series of constitutional documents or ultimately a written constitution. Further uncertainty also arises because of the pending in/out EU referendum in 2016/17. Devolution is changing the nature of the UK and may lead to its ultimate fragmentation as the regions pull away from Westminster and the UK Parliament. This may result in an English Parliament alongside other devolved nations. The future of the UK is increasingly being decided away from London and the UK Parliament.

The Supreme Court and the Judicial Committee of the Privy Council

2-121   One of the most important implications of the UK's reputation and influence is that the common law provides remedies for injustice. Upholding the rule of law is seen by many as a means to guarantee rights and liberties. The legacy of the common law and its international reputation has in part been built upon by the creation of a Judicial Committee of the Privy Council under the Judicial Committee Act 1833. The extension of the jurisdiction of the Judicial Committee to any appeal to the Privy Council was provided by the Judicial Committee Act 1844 from any court within any British Colony or possession abroad.

2-122   The UK Supreme Court from October 2009 assumed the devolution jurisdiction of the Judicial Committee of the Privy Council on devolution issues. However, the Judicial Committee remains the highest court of appeal for many current and former Commonwealth countries, including overseas territories, Crown dependencies and military and sovereign base areas.

2-123   The jurisdiction of the Privy Council includes a limited appellate jurisdiction over the ecclesiastical courts of the Church of England, a legacy from the past. In recent times the scope of the work of the Judicial Committee has been expanded, initially through appeals granted by statute for a number of professional bodies and organisations such as under the Medical Act 983, the Dentists Act 1984, and the Osteopaths Act 1993.

The Commonwealth Charter

2-124   The Commonwealth is an opportunity for common ideals to be shared and followed. In March 2013, the Queen signed the Commonwealth Charter, containing common values and aspirations as well a long standing ideas about the role of the Commonwealth in a changing world. The Charter is broadly farmed with aspirations such as freedom from discrimination and rights. Enforcement procedures are weak but there is a Commonwealth Ministerial Action Group that provides a form of moral persuasion. There is much debate over whether this is effective and the question of agreeing compliance before the signing of the Charter as a means

Table 1 UK legislation implementing EU law 1993–2015

House of Commons Library
34,105 UK Acts and Statutory Instruments
4,514 related UK Acts and Statutory Instruments
Average: 13.2% of UK instruments are EU related

Sources: *House of Commons Library: EU obligations: UK Implementing legislation since 1993 SN/1A/7092* (29th January 2015).

of ensuring agreement was not pursued by the UK Government despite the recommendations from the Foreign Affairs Select Committee. Many Commonwealth Member States have poor records on rights regarding lesbian, gay, bisexual and transgender issues. There is scepticism that there will be any real improvement in the short term.[124]

2-125

The Commonwealth Heads of Government Meeting in November 2015, discussed issues of peace and security as well as migration and human rights. There was a general discussion about the rule of law and also human slavery and human trafficking. Concerns about climate change were also discussed in terms of encouraging sustainability.[125]

K: Europe and the Europeanisation of UK law

2-126

Continental influences on the common law extend from the development of the ECHR to membership of the EU. Human rights are examined more fully later in the book. The result is recognisable as a hybrid, namely that the English common law system is overlaid with civil law principles and influences while still retaining its main common law characteristics. The development of the Community into the EU signalled one of the considerable legal and constitutional achievements of the past 50 years but it has not been unproblematic or received magnanimity. The EU has had a significant impact on the UK's constitutional law, not least in providing a framework for many of the main economic and social frameworks that operate across Member States (See Table 1: UK legislation implementing EU law 1993–2015). The EU is a good exemplar of Tony Prosser's analysis of the "economic constitution" that forms such an important part of the UK's working constitutional arrangements.[126]

2-127

Joining the European Community in 1972 brought the UK into legal relations with a Community legal order which already possessed an independent legal personality and its own

---

124 House of Commons, Library Standard Note SN06611, *In brief: the Commonwealth Charter* (18 April 2013).
125 House of Lords, *In Focus Commonwealth Heads of Government Meeting (CHOSG) 27th to 29th November 2015*, Lif 2015/0057 (9 December 2015).
126 Tony Prosser, *The Economic Constitution* (Oxford: Oxford University Press, 2014).

institutions (See Table 3: Chronological Table of UK Membership of the EU 1973–2015). The original Community was the creation of three Treaty agreements: the Treaty of Paris 1951 setting up the European Coal and Steel Community; and two Treaties of Rome 1957 setting up the European Economic Community (EEC) and the European Atomic Energy Community. Only six countries formed the original membership which presently stands at 28. Seven institutions carry out the objectives and exercise the powers of the Community, namely the Commission, the Council, the European Parliament, the Court of Justice of the EU, the European Central Bank and the Court of Auditors. A fourth Treaty, the Treaty on European Union, was signed at Maastricht and ratified in 1993 under the European Communities (Amendment) Act 1993. The creation of citizenship of the EU is seen as a progression towards enjoying rights conferred by the Treaties as well as duties under them.

2–128 Since Maastricht, the EU has developed considerably both in size and design. The Treaty of Amsterdam which came into effect in 1999 and the Treaty of Nice signed on February 26, 2001 helped to enlarge the EU with the addition of ten new states from Eastern and Central Europe. The Treaty of Lisbon in 2007 was significant as it came about after failed attempts to create a Constitution for Europe in 2003 following the recommendations of the Constitutional Convention. The proposal for a Constitution was agreed by Member States, the UK retaining many opt outs, but two referenda in France and the Netherlands rejected the proposals. The Lisbon Treaty is currently the law that applies today in the EU. It is both a work of reform and consolidation. The latter is achieved by taking the Maastricht Treaty, the Treaty on European Union (TEU) signed in 1992, and the Treaty on the Functioning of the European Union (TFEU), originally the Rome Treaty 1957 the EC Treaty (TEC), and renumbering and in part rewriting the main articles. EC law and Community law are now EU law and there are reforms to the main EU institutions.

2–129 The 2008 financial crisis has placed the EU under great strain, most notably through the Greek crisis arising from large debts that are proving difficult to repay. Most Member States are struggling to recover from the crisis and many have experienced poor growth and high unemployment. Subsequent chapters in the book will touch on many of the main issues that arise from EU membership, notably sovereignty, but also the significant shifts in power from national government to the EU. Membership of the EU has resulted in competing tensions and strains between what Syrett calls "supernationalism and intergovermentalism".[127] This refers to tensions between goals set by the EU as distinct from the sovereign powers to Member States to make and create policies. Such tensions reflect profound differences in approach that reflect historical, political, constitutional and cultural differences that may be impossible to reconcile. The UK Government has made clear that reform of the EU is necessary and that a new relationship between the UK must be EU formed. The election of a Conservative Government in May 2015 and a promised in/out referendum in June 2016. UK negotiations on reform of the EU were concluded in February 2016.

---

127 See Keith Syrett, *The Foundations of Public Law*, 2nd edn (Palgrave Macmillan, 2014), p.247.

Table 3 Chronological Table of UK Membership of the EU 1973–2015

Year	Events
1973	UK joins the EEC
1975	UK referendum on EU membership
1977	UK's First Presidency
1979	European Monetary System created
1981	Greece joins the EU as part of enlargement
1984	UK budget rebate
1986	EU enlargements under UK presidency Spain and Portugal join
1987	Single European Act many unanimous decisions are replaced by Qualified Majority Voting
1990	UK joins the ERM to bring currency alignment between the pound and other EU currencies
1991	Maastricht Treaty signed with a time-line for Economic and Monetary Union
1992	UK leaves the ERM after a run on the pound
1993	Single Market established for the free movement of goods, capital, services and people
1997	Treaty of Amsterdam and the UK considers joining the Euro provided certain economic tests are met
1998	UK Presidency
1999	EU single currency introduced in 11 out of 15 EU member states- UK, Denmark, Sweden and Greece did not participate as Greece did not meet the criteria
2002	Euro coins and note issued
2003	Treaty of Nice to facilitate the entry of 10 new Member States from Eastern and Central Europe
2004	EU enlargement with 10 countries joining Poland, Hungary, Lith uania, Lativa, Estonia, Slovenia, Slovakia, Czech Republic , Malta and Cyprus. The EU has 25 countries with 456 million citizens
2005	UK Presidency
2007	EU enlargement and Treaty amendment bringing the EU up to 27 members The Treaty Establishing a Constitution for Europe is rejected after negative referendums in the Netherlands and France
2009	Lisbon Treaty came into force 1 December 2009. New posts include President of the European Council and a High Representative of the Union for Foreign and Security Policy and removed various intergovernmental pillars with the exception of foreign and defence policy
2010	Greek bailout because of severe economic problems
2011	European Union Act 2011 passed in the UK providing legislation and also a referendum in certain circumstances where UK transfers powers to the UK
2011	European Stability Mechanism agreed by 17 Member States and all Member states with the exception of the UK agree to a proposed " Fiscal Compact"

Table 3 (continued)

Year	Events
2012	The Fiscal Compact (Treaty on Stability, Coordination and Governance in the Economic and Monetary Union signed as an intergovernmental agreement but the UK and Czech Republic opt out
2013	The UK government made clear that a referendum will be held on UK membership of the EU
2015	Details of the referendum question and election manifesto of the newly elected Conservative Government

Source: House of Commons Library, *The UK in the European Union: In Brief* SN/1A/7060 (15 December 2014).

The European Commission

2-130 Up until 31 October 2014, the European Commission consisted of one national from each Member State, the President and the High Representative for Foreign Affairs. Since 2014, the Commission is to consist of the President and High Representative for Foreign Affairs, and membership that corresponds to two-thirds of Member States unless the European Council, through a unanimous vote, decides otherwise. Commissioners are pre-vetted and subject to approval by the EU Parliament. Their term of office is for five years.

2-131 The Commission is a form of "executive"—it represents the EU externally, initiates legislation and monitors Member States in their compliance with EU law and the Treaties. Powers granted to the Commission under art.17(1) of TEU include promoting the general interests of the Euston oversee the application of the Treaties and EU law, to manage and coordinate budgets and programmes; to achieve intergovernmental agreements and to take appropriate measures.

2-132 The Commission has a staff of nearly 25,000 and its working arrangements are to be found in various Directorates. The Commission may find itself being opposed by the policy of the Member States. In the UK an example arising from the financial crisis was the adoption by many Member States of state aid to assist and support the banking sector. The initial emergency having passed, the Commission adopted robust oversight of support for banks. In the UK the government re-capitalisation of the Royal Bank of Scotland of about £20 billion was not automatically agreed but it had to be justified and only after hard fought negotiations was it accepted. The Commission reserved the right to continue to oversee the arrangements or even intervene at a future date.[128]

2-133 The Commission may bring enforcement action against Member States and this may involve the European Court of Justice. A failure to implement Directives is one example where

---

128 Julia Black, "The Credit Crisis and the Constitution" in D. Oliver, T. Prosser and R. Rawlings (eds), *The Regulatory State: Constitutional Implications* (Oxford: Oxford University Press, 2010), pp.92–128.

action against the UK has been taken. On TV broadcasting and on business restructuring are two examples.[129] The UK Government's controls over British Airways Authority after privatisation were found to be illegal.[130] The Commission took action against the UK was a case[131] involving equal pay between men and women, a principle of the EEC Treaty under art.119. The outcome of the judgment delivered by the Court of Justice required the UK Government to introduce new legislation to give effect to the Equal Pay Directive. This involved amending the Equal Pay Act 1970 by the Equal Pay (Amendment) Regulations 1983 as the relevant statutory instrument.[132]

2–134

This is a good illustration of the interconnection between overall policy objectives contained in the EC Treaty and the force of law and interpretation by the Court of Justice. In the case of equal wages, the UK had not fully implemented the Equal Pay Directive. The UK had argued that art.1 of the Directive was silent on the point and therefore did not require the determination of equal pay by a job classification system. Further, it was argued that the worker could not insist on a comparative evaluation of different work.

2–135

The Commission may take action on what it regards as unacceptable state action in the subsidisation of industry. In July 1990 it took action to recover £44.4 million worth of concessions given to British Aerospace at the time of the acquisition of Rover cars. Eventually in May 1993 it recovered £57.6 million, the additional amount due because of lost interest calculated from August 1990.

2–136

One of the main challenges facing the Commission is that it appears to perform roles similar to National Governments but is in fact not held to account through any recognisable political process. In national elections, voters elect a national government rather than hold the national government to be accountable over the Commission. There are many initiatives to improve the Commission's standing and enable participation to flow from citizen to Member State to Commission.[133]

The Council of the European Union

2–137

The Council of the EU consists of the various ministers representing the Member States' governments (art.16(2) of TEU). The limit on membership is one from each Member State. Thus its membership varies according to the subject area under discussion and the jurisdiction of the minister concerned. The Council is an important link between Member States and the EU. Unlike the Commission, where national self-interest of Member States is subservient to Community interests, the Council represents the collective views of each Member State as part

---

129 See respectively, *Re Business Transfers: EC Commission v UK* (C-382/92) EU:C:1994:233; and *EC Commission v UK* (C-222/94) EU:C:1996:314.
130 Article 63 TEU, *EU Commission v UK* [2003] E.C.R. I-04641.
131 *Commission of the European Communities v UK* (C-61/81) EU:C:1996:314.
132 Equal Pay (Amendment) Regulations 1983 (SI 1983/1794).
133 See the discussion in *EU Democratic Legitimacy and National Parliaments* CEPS essay No.7 (25 November 2013).

of settling the objectives of the Treaties. Thus the Council is often engaged in bargaining and compromising national self-interest which is forged into Community policy. The Council may meet on its own initiative or that of the President of the Council. Meetings may be held under various subject headings, but there are various groupings determined by a qualified majority of Council members. The areas may vary according to the variety of issues that are important for the time.[134]

2-138 Foreign ministers meet as a General Council. There is a Presidency of the Council held in turn by each of the Member States for six months on a rotational basis. Increasing importance is given to the meeting of Heads of State and this is now recognised under art.2 of the Single European Act 1986.

2-139 The main role of the Council is contained in art.202 and is primarily a co-ordinating role and a deliberative function to consult with the Commission. The Council has the final say on most secondary legislation and this provides opportunity for the more powerful Member States. The Council may override Parliament's opposition to a measure on a unanimous vote, which is required to amend proposals made by the Commission. Voting by the Council may be by a unanimous, qualified majority or a simple majority vote. The latter is not usually used. The use of a unanimous vote procedure was common in the early life of the Treaties to safeguard the Treaty areas that might have been amended. As the Community has developed, the use of Qualified Majority Voting has become more prevalent. This is a sign of political maturity but also of the need for consensus-building to allow the Community to develop. The extension of Qualified Majority Voting since the Single European Act 1986 has enabled the EU to adapt and change rather rapidly and allowed large areas of internal market legislation to be undertaken. This has alarmed critics that there is insufficient oversight over the Council and that too much of its work is undertaken secretly with an excessive amount of confidentiality. Gradually there have been changes in the direction of greater openness. Article 15 TFEU provides for public access to the documents of the EU institutions and publication of draft legislative proposals.

2-140 Voting in the Council of Ministers is usually by qualified majority. There are some areas where unanimity is required, thus allowing a veto. Unanimity of the Council is required for laws affecting social policy and this includes areas such as the social protection of workers where their contracts of employment are terminated as well as representation of workers where there is a collective defence of the interests of workers. This is a politically sensitive area where there are financial constraints on Member States during a period of austerity. Voting weights accredited to countries has since 2014 been replaced by number of countries and their combined population.

---

134 There are a number of distinct areas, general affairs, foreign affairs, economic and financial affairs, justice and home affairs, employment, social policy, health and consumer affairs, competitiveness, transport, telecommunications and energy, agriculture and fisheries, environment, education, youth culture and sport.

The European Council

Since 1974 the European Council has been defined as the Heads of State or Government headed by the President of the Commission. Article 15 TEU defines its role as setting the general political directions and priorities of the EU. It meets twice every six months and its decisions are normally by consensus. Its recent role has been to address issued raised by the financial crisis—especially the question of the financial viability of Greece. In general terms the European Council has considerable influence over the EU, its direction and also in developing strategies for the financial well-being of the Member States. The European Council has been influential in establishing financial assistance to Greece and the conditions of loans and repayments.

The European Parliament

The Treaties establishing the EC envisaged an assembly or representative body to represent the people of the Community. The past 40 years has seen the role and function of the Parliament transformed. Since 1962 the European Parliament (arts 189–201, (arts 137–144 EC as amended)) became its designated name and the Single European Act 1986 refers to such a body. Members of the European (MEPs are often grouped together in terms of their political parties. Initially the UK adopted a first-past-the-post system to elect its MEPs (with the exception of Northern Ireland where PR is used). In 1999 the closed regional list system was used. The regional list system also corresponds to the electoral arrangements for the regional chambers in England, and also elections to the devolved institutions in Scotland and Wales. Elections to the Parliament are held once every five years.[135] The UK has 73 MEPs and in 2014 the EU Parliament has 751 members. It is envisaged that this might increase to 82 seats in 2024.

Occasionally a member of the national parliament may also be a "Euro MP" at the same time. There are concerns about the effectiveness of multi-membership in the hands of a single individual and steps are being considered to limit the number of bodies for which membership may be held simultaneously. There are also concerns about the low turnout at European elections in the UK. In 1999 the UK turnout was 24 per cent when the EU average turnout is 49.4 per cent. In 2014 the UK turnout was 35.6 per cent with an EU average of 42.6 per cent. The low turnout for elections is a problem that has not been fully addressed. It may be a sign of voter apathy or disillusionment with the institutions of the EU. It may also signal a disconnect between citizen voting and empowerment through the decisions made by the EU Parliament that are democratically accountable. There are strong signs of euro scepticism and this was in evidence in the UK with the rise of the UK Independence Party (UKIP) but it is also evident from discussions within the mainstream political parties. There is a growing sense of disillusionment and this is manifest in the promise of an in/out referendum on EU membership before 2017.

---

135 See Directorate General for Internal Policies, Constitutional Affairs, *The Electoral Reform of the European Parliament: Composition, Procedure and Legitimacy*, PE 510.02 (Brussels: 2015).

2-144 The European Parliament has developed incrementally. If the European Parliament are given greater powers and carry out its role as a substantive legislative body this would improve the accountability of the EU and provide a sound basis for its legitimacy. Currently it has budgetary, legislative and supervisory powers. Since the 1970s, the reform of the budgetary process has ensured that the EU Parliament has powers over adopting the annual budget with a power of veto over "non-compulsory expenditure" (economic and social spending). On legislative powers since the Single European Act 1986 has developed the potential to change fundamentally the European Parliament's role. There is a co-operation procedure with the Council requiring the Parliament to give an opinion and on a second reading stage, Parliament may approve, reject or amend the views contained in the legislation. Once agreed, the Act is formally the Council's measure and may be so adopted. The co-decision procedure under the Maastricht Treaty is also significant by giving the Parliament ultimate right to veto a legislative proposal by an absolute majority after two readings by the Council and the Parliament. The Parliament has also the right to veto the accessions of new Member States and assent with the Council to international agreements. The Amsterdam and Nice Treaties also extended co-decision-making and this has given much more incremental power to the European Parliament. After the Nice Treaty, the EU Parliament may take proceedings before the European Court of Justice to review the acts of the institutions. The Lisbon Treaty further encouraged co-decision-making and have created what is now termed the Ordinary Legislative Procedure to carry this out as the EU's default procedure and extended it to various areas such as Justice and home affairs, immigration, offences and penalties, police co-operation and trade and agriculture. This gives the EU Parliament equality with the Council. On budgetary matters, the EU Parliament and Council reviews expenditure together. A draft annual budget is prepared by the Commission and subject to approval by the Council and EU Parliament with a 42-day period to agree or receive amendments from the Council. A Conciliation Committee may be appointed and provides a forum for agreement. If this fails, then a new draft budget has to be submitted by the Council. On average the EU budget is around 2 per cent of the national budget of all the 28 Member States.

2-145 The fact that the Parliament's role is expanding is clear as it has sufficient standing to challenge acts of the Council or the Commission,[136] powers to set up a system of ombudsmen to investigate maladministration, and committees of inquiry[137] to review and investigate any allegations of misconduct. In 1999 following the Parliament's inquiry into allegations of abuse and fraud and corruption against the Commission, the Parliament's report[138] resulted in the resignation of the Commission. The Parliament's report into BSE ("Mad cow disease"), for example, is another high profile investigation. It is clear that there is considerable scope for altering the balance of powers between the Commission, the Council and the Parliament. It may be envisaged that there should be greater democratic accountability through an increase

---

136 *Roquette Freres SA v Council* (138/79).
137 General Report of the European Parliament, 1996.
138 *First Report on Allegations regarding Fraud, Mismanagement and Nepotism in the European Commission*, 15 March 1999. The second report followed on 10 September 1999.

in Parliamentary powers. Equally the more powers the Parliament is given, the more it must be accountable for its actions and decisions.[139]

The European Court of Justice

2-146 The European Court of Justice (ECJ) ensures that the interpretation and application of Treaty law is observed. It sits as a supreme authority on all questions of Community law. The Court is comprised of 28 judges, one each appointed from the Member States, appointed for a six-year renewable term. There is a President of the court appointed for a three-year renewable term. There are Advocates-General appointed by the Member States to act "with complete impartiality and independence, to make, in open court, reasoned submissions on cases brought before the Court of Justice". Sharing the same status, independence and security as the judges, the Advocates-General give a view of the case and although the court is not bound to accept their opinion, it often does so. The Court may sit as a five judge chamber or as a Grand Chamber of 13 judges.

2-147 Specific questions of EU law might be referred where relevant to the general issues in the case being heard before the national court. This is an important source of the court's jurisdiction under art.267. This includes a preliminary ruling where the matter it considers it necessary to enable it to give judgment. This includes cases where raises questions about the validity and interpretation of a matter of EU law.[140] There are circumstances when the national court may decide to make its own interpretation and where the public interest suggests that the matter was urgent and needed speedy resolution.[141]

2-148 There is also a General Court (originally known as Court of First Instance). There is the right of appeal on matters of law to the ECJ. The ECJ acts as an appeal court, a review court and a means to refer matters for consideration.

2-149 The Commission may take proceedings against Member States where the Member State has failed to comply with a Treaty obligation. This occurs after the Commission has made a ruling on the matter and has not complied then the case may be taken to the Court of Justice.

2-150 The ECJ may specifically empower national courts to take action over Directives that are not being properly enforced. On the application of Client Earth, a pressure group, the ECJ concluded that the UK Government should take timely action to meet NO2 air quality standards due to vehicle traffic. The 2008 Ambient Air Quality Directive imposes obligations on Member States to meet specific limits for air quality for certain substance such as nitrogen dioxide. The UK wished to postpone implementation of how it intended to meet the requirements of the Directive. This was refused by the ECJ and the UK Supreme Court has followed the analysis set

---

139 House of Commons Library, *The European Union: A Democratic Institution?*, Research Papers 14/25 (29 April 2014).
140 Lord Bingham in *R v International Stock Exchange Ex p. Else* [1993] Q.B. 534; [1993] 2 W.L.R. 70 CA (Civ Div).
141 See *OFT v Abbey National Plc* [2009] UKSC 34; and also *O'Brien v Department of Constitutional Affairs* [2010] UKSC 34 and [2013] UKSC 6; [2013] 1 W.L.R. 522.

by the European Court.[142] The UK courts may interpret EU law but also have some discretion over whether EU law is pertinent to the questions raised in any case. If the UK courts decide it is unnecessary to decide an EU point then this may be the interpretation the UK Supreme Court may prefer to take.[143]

The European Court of Auditors

2-151 The European Court of Auditors was established in 1977 after the Treaty amending Certain Financial Provisions of the Treaties 1975 came into force. After Maastricht the Court became recognised as a Community institution. It is based in Luxembourg. It is the guardian of the EU finances and operates as a collegiate body of 28 members, one each from each Member State. Appointments are renewable for a term of six years by the Council after consultation with the European Parliament. A President is elected from amongst the membership for a renewable three-year term. There is a Secretary General appointed for a renewable six-year term. The European Court of Auditors has five chambers with an elected Dean for a renewable two-year term. The full Court meets twice a month to discuss annual reports and also the EU budget. There are four chambers with responsibility for the audit of various areas of EU expenditure and revenue as well as a horizontal chamber that co-ordinates, evaluates and provides assurance and development.

2-152 The European Court of Auditors has a staff of over 900 and provides an important oversight of EU finances. There are 11 audit and administrative directives divided into over 50 units. The form of oversight is both *ex ante* through the process of consultation over legislative reform and *ex post* through the audit of the EU budget and its implementation.[144]

2-153 The European Court of Auditors have a challenging task to perform. The annual EU budget is unique from the budgeting arrangements of many Member States because it is based around the principle of budgetary equilibrium, namely that the running costs and expenditure should be paid out of revenue and not debt.[145] The bulk of EU expenditure is managed and audited at the national level subject to EU rules and binding obligations on Member States. There are clear obligations on Member States but shared responsibilities are absent between the European Court of Auditors and national audit authorities. There is a presumption of legality once finances have been spent and the Commission often provides guidance and evidence of good quality. In seeking to establish irregularity it is hard to rebut the presumption of legality unless there is clear evidence. There is a need for Commission audit systems to operate alongside Member States audit arrangements strengthened by the European Court of Auditors. There is also an absence of Member States sense of ownership of EU funds. In the

---

142 *R (ClientEarth) v Secretary of State for the Environment, Food and Rural Affairs*, CJEU Case C-04/13.
143 See the discussion in *R (G1) v Secretary of State for the Home Department* [2012] EWCA Civ 867; [2013] Q.B. 1008 and also *Pham v Secretary of State for the Home Department* [2015] UKSC 19; [2015] 1 W.L.R. 1591.
144 See Gabriele Cipriani, "The Responsibility for implementing the Community budget", CEPS Working Papers No.247 (2007). C. Harlow, *Accountability in the European Union* (New York: Oxford University Press, 2002).
145 Article 199 TEEC, now 310.1 TEFU.

late 2000s Finance Ministers in many Member States issued "national declarations" stating that finances were being applied legally and with regularity. This is not mandatory. The financial crisis in 2008 has led to tensions between Member States and the EU especially over the issue of ensuring a balanced budget. The desirability of balanced budgets in the aftermath of the financial crisis led to the adoption of the Fiscal Compact under art.3 of the Treaty on Stability, Coordination and Governance (TSCG) to attempt to ensure Member States balance their budgets.[146] In May 2014, the European Court of Auditors published a Special Report on the Establishment of the European Banking Authority. The report queried the ability of the Commission to exercise sufficient scrutiny of the new authority and it made a number of recommendations for improvements.[147]

The European Court of Auditors has powers under art.285 TFEU to carry out "external control" of all revenue and expenditure of EU institutions and agencies. As Barrueco[148] has pointed out it arguably needs more resources and powers to undertake this important role. This inhibits its ability to undertake a rigorous audit of budget implementation of the EU budget as well as the European Development Fund. However, the European Court of Auditors lacks power to initiate an infringement procedure and this power rests with the Commission. This only serves to highlight the problems for the European Court of Auditors when tackling problems caused by systemic financial weaknesses amongst Member States. There is also an absence of powers to monitor the Fiscal Compact and this will make the EU much weaker in its capacity to address issues of financial management at a period when the EU is facing new challenges. National audit institutions are needed to be more fully integrated into the overall audit of the EU.

L: Sovereignty and the United Kingdom Parliament

Sovereignty can be defined "as to where and with whom power" and authority reside.[149] The EU sits uneasily with the UK's understanding of sovereignty in the light of the Court of Justice of the EU asserting that EU law takes priority over national law. In that respect it is clear

---

146 John McEldowney, "Debt Limits in German Constitutional law—A UK Perspective" in Wolf-George Ringe and Peter M. Huber (eds), *Legal Challenges in the Global Financial Crisis: Bail-outs, the Euro and Regulation, Studies of the Oxford Institute of European and Comparative Law* (Oxford: Hart, 2014), pp.63–80.
147 European Court of Auditors, Special Report, "European Banking Supervision taking shape and its changing context", SR 05/2014 (14 May 2014).
148 Maria Luiz Sanchez Barrueco, "The Contribution of the European Court of Auditors to EU Financial Accountability in Times of Crisis" (2015) *Romanian Journal of European Affairs* 70–85.
149 House of Commons Library, *The European Union: A Democratic Institution?*, Research Papers 14/25 (29 April 2014).

that Dicey's analysis of parliamentary sovereignty faces a severe challenge. His formulation gave Parliament ultimate sovereignty with potentially unlimited power. Even Dicey accepted that in exercising such powers Parliament's democratic basis might mean limitations on how future powers were exercised. Nevertheless, Dicey held the view that, however theoretical was the power of Parliament, this had overarching effect even when confronting practical problems. Membership of the EU poses a severe test to UK sovereignty. As a result, the courts have adjusted their conceptual language and understanding to adapt to change. The UK's membership of the EU is without a written constitution, dependent on ss.2 and 3 of the European Communities Act 1972. EU law in the UK may be said to be derived from this Act. Section 2(4) permits EU law to be given priority to any UK legislation passed prior to 1973:

> "Any enactment passed or to be passed, other than one contained in this part of the Act, shall be construed and have effect subject to the . . . provisions of this section."

2–156
While s.2(1) provides for the direct applicability of Community law in the UK, and s.2(2) grants a general power for the future implementation of Community obligations by means of secondary legislation, there remains the question as to statutes passed after 1972 and the application of Community law. Where there may be inconsistencies or contradiction, Dicey's analysis would argue for the UK statute to be given priority by the courts over Community law.

2–157
A close reading of s.2(4) might suggest that in those terms Parliament in 1972 had given authority for priority to be given to Community law after 1972 and that even where there is conflict with a UK statute, Community law must prevail. Dicey's traditional view is that parliamentary sovereignty does not leave Parliament free to bind its successors. Priority for Community law is not consistent with parliamentary sovereignty because entrenchment of Community law is impossible.

2–158
Craig[150] suggests that two possibilities might be adopted by the courts to resolve the problem. One is to modify Dicey's doctrine and accept that Community law has priority as part of the UK's membership conditions. The second possibility is to adopt an interpretation that Parliament is presumed not to intend statutes to override Community law, so that it is assumed that statutes passed after 1972 are impliedly consistent with Community law.

2–159
Both possibilities have their respective merits. The second of Craig's options generally describes the direction the UK's courts have adopted until recently. The first requires consideration in the light of a recent House of Lords decision. The House of Lords referred to the European Court the issue of whether Community law was compatible with the Merchant Shipping Act 1988 in the *Factortame* case.[151] The 1988 Act had established a new register

---

150   Paul Craig, *Administrative Law*, 4th edn (London: Sweet & Maxwell, 1999). Also see P. Craig, "Britain in the European Union" in J. Jowell and D. Oliver (eds), *The Changing Constitution* (Oxford: Oxford University Press, 2000), p.61.
151   [1991] 1 A.C. 603; [1990] 3 W.L.R. 818 HL at [659]. Case C-213/89, EU:C:1990:257; [1991] 1 A.C. 603; [1990] 3 C.M.L.R. 375 HL.

of British fishing vessels to ensure that fishing quotas under the Common Fisheries Policy were exploited by vessels which were truly linked to the UK's fishing economy. The result of the Act was that a number of Spanish-owned British Companies could not be registered on the register of British fishing vessels. As a result, the Spanish fishermen sought a declaration that the 1988 Act was incompatible with the Community Treaty. The European Court and the Advocate-General gave their opinion that national courts must ensure compliance with EC law even where this might lead the national court not to apply an Act of Parliament. Lord Bridge[152] in the House of Lords responded to the European Court's ruling as follows:

> **"Under the terms of the Act of 1972 it has always been clear that it was the duty of a UK court, when delivering final judgment to override any rule of national law, found to be in conflict with any directly enforceable rule of Community law. . . . Thus there is nothing in any way novel in according supremacy to rules of Community law in those areas to which they apply and to insist that, in the protection of rights under Community law national courts must not be inhibited by rules of national law from granting interim relief in appropriate cases, is no more than a logical recognition of that supremacy."**

Factortame[153] is the clearest indication that EC membership is no longer compatible with Dicey's classical doctrine of Parliamentary sovereignty. The House of Lords has, in effect, abandoned Dicey's view in favour of a construction which indicates a willingness to apply Community law even where it may conflict with national law. The *Factortame* case also makes clear the compatibility of Community law and international law or customary law. Britain had unsuccessfully relied on the Article 5 provisions of the Geneva Convention to make its case. Thus a Member State of the EU cannot rely upon its rights even if granted under international treaty law to justify non-compliance with the rules of the Community.

2–160

The British courts in a number of cases have taken account of Community law. In the case of *Garden Cottage Foods v Milk Marketing Board*[154] a party injured by another's abuse of a dominant position, may be entitled to damages under art.86. Directly applicable rights and obligations created by the Community Treaty take precedence over national law as has been accepted in *Simmenthal*[155] and more recently in *Factortame*.[156] Equally significant is

2–161

---

152   Lord Eridge in *Factortame* [1991] 1 A.C. 603 at 659.
153   *R v Secretary of State for Transport Ex p. Factortame Ltd (No.2)* (C-213/89) EU:C:1990:257; [1991] 1 A.C. 603 HL.
154   [1984] A.C. 130; [1984] 3 W.L.R. 143 HL.
155   *Amministrazione v Simmenthal* (C-106/77) EU:C:1978:49; [1978] 3 C.M.L.R. 263; and *Emmott v Minister for Social Welfare* (C-208/90) EU:C:1991:333; [1993] I.C.R. 8.
156   [1991] 1 A.C. 603; (C-213/89) EU:C:1990:257; [1990] 3 C.M.L.R. 1.

the recognition by UK courts of the availability of damages in respect of liability for legislative breaches of Community law.[157] The acceptance by the courts of the *Francovich*[158] principle, whereby damages are available, broadens the range and scope of Community law. Inevitably this may lead to a rights agenda incorporated into the institutions of the UK.[159] This extends beyond the boundaries of public law to private law and the issues raised by commercial observance of the EU's competition rules. Thus the *Francovich* principle applies to all breaches of Community law whether committed by a Member State or other entity.[160] There is a further complication to EU membership and national sovereignty. EU law claims priority over international law obligations of the EU and its Member States.[161]

2-162 The European Act 2011 provides an additional layer of protection of UK sovereignty known as the "sovereignty clause" that contains in statutory form the common law understanding of UK sovereignty. It makes clear that EU law only applies on the basis of the UK's Parliamentary intention. The European Act 2011 is significant because it articulates the political understanding of sovereignty. It is also possible to see the European Act 2011 as simply a political statement rather than an enforceable statutory right. The Lisbon Treaty is also relevant as it provides two protocols that have provided national parliaments with a mechanism for objecting to Commission proposals in accordance with subsidiarity. It also guarantees a role for national parliaments under art.12 of the Treaty of European Union. This is known as a yellow or orange card procedures for objections. This early warning system is more a political reassurance rather than an effective legal instrument. The yellow card has only been used rarely and the orange card not all. The use of a red card scheme was originally suggested to veto unwanted EU proposals in 2013. The current proposals are that if a number of members states objected to draft legislation then there should be a power of veto.[162]

2-163 EU membership has helped influence the development of UK law. This is an evolutionary process. The UK Supreme Court in *Pham v Secretary of State for the Home Department*[163] discussed the question of proportionality and its application to the lawfulness of the Home Secretary's decision to strip an appellant of British citizenship (including EU citizenship) which would render the appellant stateless. The main issue in the case was whether proportionality was part of the common law and how much of EU law as required to decide the case. The Supreme Court was much concerned to show that the common law had become enmeshed in UK law as part of a judicial "toolbox" available to domestic courts. This is a sign of maturity in the development of judicial review in the UK and a degree of independent mindedness from relying on EU law.

---

157 *R v Secretary of State for the Home Department Ex p. Gallagher* [1996] 2 C.M.L.R. 951.
158 *Francovich v Italy* (C-6 and 9/90) EU:C:1991:428; [1992] I.R.D.L.R. 84.
159 *Bowden v South West Water Services* [1999] 3 C.M.L.R. 180; [1999] Eu. L.R. 573 CA (Civ Div).
160 *Crehan* (C-453/99) EU:C:2001:465; [2002] Q.B. 507.
161 See *Kadi v Council and Commission* [2008] ECR-I-06351 and *Germany v Council* [1998] ECR I-973.
162 House of Commons Library, *Parliamentary sovereignty and EU renegotiation*, CDP 0033 (2 February 2016).
163 [2015] UKSC 19; [2015] 1 W.L.R. 1591.

M: The Future Constitutional Arrangements in the UK: Some Conclusions

2-164

We have seen throughout this chapter how the UK's constitutional arrangements have undergone change and transformation. Is now the time for a rethink? The expansion of the EU to 28 members has enormous significance. Some favour adopting a federal States of Europe perspective with the necessary constitutional changes in both European and national institutions. The traditional doctrines of the UK's Constitution which help explain our present constitutional arrangements do not necessarily help us to understand the future of our existing institutions. EU policy influences our laws on competition policy, the free movement of goods, state aids, and the free movement of persons throughout the Community. Energy, the environment, agriculture and fisheries, transport, social security and sex discrimination have also been important areas in the development of EU law. National sovereignty is so bound up with these areas that Parliament's authority to legislate has become integrated with EU legislative policy. The application of EU law seems no longer dependent on Dicey's perception of where Parliament's power ultimately lies. Much will depend on the outcome of the referendum on EU membership in June 2016.

2-165

Is it time for a written Constitution? Dawn Oliver has pointed out finding the constitutional "moment"[164] is an important aspect of timing that offers the opportunity to determine the content and rationale of the Constitution. The UK may not have reached that point in time. The House of Commons, *Political and Constitutional Reform Committee*[165] has published an explanatory document, a Constitutional Code, that is non-statutory but provides an important guide to existing practices and procedures and identifies the various elements of the existing Constitution. There is also a draft Constitutional Consolidation Act. It is very detailed and contains a useful code of essential constitutional conventions. Placing constitutional conventions into a written form is also included. There is also a draft formulation of a written Constitution that sets out the basic law governing the UK including the relationship between the state and the citizen and elements of constitutional reform. This is pathbreaking as the various drafts take forward the IPPR constitution text prepared in 1991. The IPPR text had 129 articles and six schedules. In the aftermath of the Scottish referendum and proposed increased powers to Scotland, Wales and Northern Ireland as well as to the English regions, including changes to local government there may be a case for a written document. There are also profoundly important consequences in the role of the UK Supreme Court in respect of devolution issues.[166] Additionally, plans to amend/abolish the Human Rights Act

---

164 The phrase is from Dawn Oliver's in her paper "A new Magna Carta? Time for a 'constitutional moment'?".
165 House of Commons Political and Constitutional Reform Committee 2014/15.
166 In *Axa General Insurance v The Lord Advocate*, [2011] UKSC 46 and [2011] CSIH 31 the lawfulness of an Act of the Scottish Parliament, the Damages (Asbestos-related Conditions) (Scotland) Act 2009, was challenged as to its compatibility with art.1 of Protocol 1 of the European Convention on Human Rights and its reasonableness in terms of the general judicial review jurisdiction of the Supreme Court, in particular on grounds of irrationality

1998 will have major constitutional implications. Reform of the House of Lords in the direction of a wholly elected chamber will also profoundly change the nature of the Constitution.[167]

N: Summary and Conclusions

2–166 The constitutional history and sovereignty of the UK is defined by the creation of the various Acts of Union with Wales, Scotland and Ireland. Relations with the Commonwealth have helped delineate parliamentary and political power.

Membership of the EU is a major influence in formulating legal, economic and political decision-making. The EU is not static and membership provides a *process* for future development and an agenda for change. The UK's referendum and reform negotiations in February 2016 have to be assessed as to the outcome on the EU. The Syrian refugee crisis and economic and financial uncertainties remain serious issues.

2–167 Devolution is also the beginning of a *process* that continues to cede power from the centre to nations and localities. Enhanced powers to Scotland, Wales and Northern Ireland and the London Mayor and Assembly will inevitably place strains on the Union of the UK. Devolution to major cities will inevitably change the nature of central government and its powers.

2–168 The UK is made up of different nations that are drawn together in a centralised unitary state but are being taken in different directions in favour of the devolution of various powers.

Table 2 Legislation 2010–2014

Year	Number of Acts	Acts linked to EU	% of Acts	Acts that are exclusively EU
2010	41	12	29%	None
2011	62	25	40%	None
2012	48	23	48%	1 EU stability mechanism
2013	78	33	42%	2 Croatia entry
2014	30	13	43%	1 Data retention

and arbitrariness. The claimants were insurance companies and their claim arose from their undertaking to indemnify employers against liability for negligence. The point of the Scottish Parliament's legislation was to include under Scots law liability for personal injury claims arising from various asbestos-related pleural plaques and related conditions. The UK Supreme Court held that the claimants were entitled to make such a claim and that the courts had an overarching power to ensure that the 2009 Act was legitimate in its aims and proportionate in its response.

167 See Daniel J. Elazar, "Constitution Making: The Pre-Eminent Political Act" in Keith G. Banting and Richard Simeon (eds), *The Politics of Constitutional Change in Industrial Nations: redesigning the State* (London: Macmillan, 1985).

The future of the UK is uncertain as both centralising and devolution tendencies are reconciled. In the aftermath of the introduction of EVEL procedures there is an emerging English constitutional settlement that gives pre-eminence to England in the four nations. This may ultimately mean some form of federal system.[168]

Further Reading

For a theoretical perspective see:
Martin Loughlin, *Sword and Scales* (Oxford: Hart, 2000).
A useful political science perspective may be found in:
Ian Budge, Ivor Crewe, David McKay and Ken Newton, *The New British Politics*, 2nd edn (Essex: Longman, 2001); and Bill Jones, Denis Kavangah, Michael Moran and Philip Norton, *Politics UK*, 4th edn (Essex: Longman, 2001).
On devolution see:
N. Burrows, *Devolution* (London: Sweet & Maxwell, 2000); B. Dickson, "Devolution" in J. Jowell, D. Oliver and C. O'Cinneide, 8th edn, *The Changing Constitution* (Oxford: Oxford University Press), 2015 pp.249–79.
Aidan O'Neill, "Judicial Politics and the Judicial Committee: The Devolution Jurisprudence of the Privy Council" (2001) 64 *Modern Law Review* 603; and Bingham Centre for the Rule of Law, *A Constitutional Crossroads: Ways Forward for the United Kingdom* (May 2014).

---

168 C. McCrudden, "State architecture: subsidiarity, devolution, federalism" in M. Elliott and D. Feldman, The Cambridge Public Law (Cambridge: Cambridge University Press, 2015), pp.193–214.

3

Parliament

A: Introduction

Parliament occupies a central place in our constitutional arrangements. The late John Griffith[1] regarded parliamentary democracy as a flexible instrument judged, not by the theories of the Constitution, but by the way Parliament ensures the efficient use of government in the interests of the electorate. He was realistic about what was possible, as he felt Parliament should not be asked to do more than it can and no more than it is suited for. Recognising such limitations on parliamentary practice and theory gave rise to his views that political decisions should be taken by politicians and against any further judicialisation of the administrative process. It remains to be seen whether Parliament is capable of meeting an amazing challenge to address the needs of the twenty-first century while retaining many of the historical features of the eighteenth and nineteenth centuries. There are some innovations such as the development of public engagement strategies, including e-petitions and responses to public opinion through Westminster Hall debates.

3–001

The role of Parliament and its fundamental importance in the Constitution is considered in this chapter. Technically, Parliament consists of the Queen, the House of Commons which is a directly elected body and the House of Lords which is appointed but is currently being reformed. Reform of the House of Lords has been a recurring theme throughout the past

3–002

---

1   Graham Gee, "The political constitutionalism of J. A. G. Griffith" (2008) 28(1) *Legal Studies*, pp.20–45. Also T. Poole, "Tilting at windmills? Truth and illusion in The Political constitution" (2007) 70 *Modern Law Review* 250. Also consider I. Leigh, "Secrets of the political constitution" (1999) 62 *Modern Law Review* 298.
J. A. G. Griffith, "Judges in politics: England" [1968] *Government and Opposition* 485. The main work Griffith is probably most famous for is J. A. G. Griffith, *The Politics of the Judiciary*, 5th edn (London: Fontana, 1997).
J. A. G. Griffith, "The Place of parliament in the Legislative process" [1951] 14 *Modern Law Review* 279.
J. A. G. Griffith, "The Political Constitution" [1979] 42(1) *Modern Law Review* 1

century. The difficulty of reform is in achieving a balance between the continuity of the past, whereby patronage provided access to the Lords, and the changes needed to make the Lords a modern second chamber. It is broadly accepted that the role of the Lords is as a revising chamber, thus the pre-eminence of the Commons is unchallenged. The first stage of Lords' reform was achieved under the House of Lords Act 1999 which provided for 92 hereditary peers, 90 to be elected from among hereditary peers to sit temporarily in a transitional House of Lords. The elected hereditary peers signal the end of the hereditary peerage once the final composition of the House of Lords is settled. In January 2016 there were around 859 members of the House of Lords. This figure increases if some of the current members of the Supreme Court and those that are on leave of absence are included to around 880. It is expected that by the end of the current Parliament the number might rise to 900. The average age is 69.[2]

3-003 The UK's system of government in formal terms is described as a constitutional monarchy. Parliamentary government describes the fact that the Government's authority depends on the confidence of the House of Commons. By virtue of having no formal written constitution, government operates within the boundaries set by a variety of laws, conventions and understandings. In fact the UK's constitutional arrangements provide largely unfettered powers to the government of the day who are able through their majority in Parliament to exercise control over Parliament and its procedures relatively free from any restraint. The underlying traditions, customs and procedures and behaviour of the House of Commons is worth considering in terms of the style of debate and the way the Speaker of the House has to conduct business.[3]

3-004 As a result, the Government of the day may appear to enjoy unparalleled freedoms compared to countries with a written constitution. The source of government power may be traced to the relationship between government and Parliament. Government within the UK's constitutional arrangements is said to be limited and responsible. This means that the Government is accountable to Parliament and, through elections, representative. As explained in the previous chapter, the sovereignty of Parliament may become too easily the sovereignty of the House of Commons and this in turn the authority of the dominant political party. The political reality of power is that the government, having the majority of seats in the Commons, has the overall influence and authority over how decisions are to be taken. Political legitimacy flows from the authority of elections and the control of government business in the Commons allows the government to exert influence over Parliament itself. Lord Hailsham saw the danger[4] that "the sovereignty of the Commons has increasingly become, in practice the sovereignty of the government". There are few countries that have government able to exercise political power through legislation that is largely unfettered by the concerns of judicial challenge or institutional intervention. The point is summarised by Ewing[5]:

---

2   House of Lords Library Note, "Size of the House of Lords", LLN 2016/006 (29 January 2016).
3   House of Commons Library, *Background Paper: Traditions and Customs of the House*, SN/PC/06432 (3 October 2012).
4   Lord Hailsham, *Elective Dictatorship* (*The Listener Dimbleby lecture*) (London, 1976), pp.430–431.
5   Keith Ewing, "The Unbalanced Constitution" in T. Campbell, K. Ewing and A. Tomkins (eds), *Sceptical Essays on Human Rights* (Oxford: Oxford University Press, 2001), p.104.

> "British constitutional arrangements nevertheless provided the best means for social reform in the sense that there were no institutional restraints on a legally sovereign legislature and a politically sovereign electorate. And the best means also for social reform in the sense that the hierarchy of rights in the British constitution did not distinguish between rights according to their substance, but only according to their source. So unlike in other constitutional regimes, there was no priority in the British constitution for civil and political rights over social and economic rights."

An important feature of the government's day-to-day use of political power is the use of the party Whips in the system of whipping, which places pressure on MPs to vote according to party policy. This is an important mechanism in the hands of the government to force MPs on the government side to vote the government's bills into law. A similar system among the opposition parties has the effect of strengthening party solidarity in opposition to government policy. Party political power is therefore an important influence on the workings and practices of the House of Commons. An added dimension to government is the use and appointment of political advisors within government to project the government's message in the media. The art of government is rapidly becoming the task of media presentation. This represents a paradigm shift from a focus on Parliament and its procedures to the media and presentational skills. This shift may not endure beyond the life-time of one or more governments but it signals a remarkable reformulation of political power. In medieval times the general use of the term *parliament* meant "any meeting for speech or conference".[6] In that sense the institution of Parliament is linked to the popular idiom of the day—thus the media and presentation are given such importance.

In this chapter the focus is on the functions of Parliament, explaining its role in passing legislation, and in the debate and scrutiny of government. Separate consideration is given to the role of financial authority where the Commons exercises the "power of the purse" in voting for the taxation and spending of public money (See Ch.12). The role and possible reform of the House of Lords is considered. Finally, the privileges of Parliament are examined in the context of the rights and immunities of Members of Parliament and the work of the Committee on Standards in Public Life begun by Lord Nolan in 1994.

In recent years Parliament has struggled to set and enforce standards for its members. Lord Norton has noted that the public's perception about Parliament has been influenced by the televised coverage of Prime Minister's question time, the greater visibility of Parliament in terms of bad publicity and the generally poor reputation of MPs.[7]

Cash for questions and votes as well as expenses claims have diminished Parliament's standing with the public. The Select Committee of the House of Commons on Standards and Privileges

---

6   J. Griffith and M. Ryle, *Parliament* (London: Sweet & Maxwell, 1989), p.3.
7   P. Norton "Parliament: A New Assertiveness" in J. Jowell, D. Oliver and C.O'Cinneide (eds), *The Changing Constitution*, 8th edn (Oxford: Oxford University Press, 2015), pp.171–93.

was established in 1995 as a response to the setting up of a Standing Committee on Standards in Public Life chaired by Lord Nolan in October 1994 following newspaper allegations concerning MPs who may have accepted payment for putting down parliamentary questions. Allegations of corruption and sleaze have necessitated an investigatory role for the Committee rather than depending on the form of self-regulation that was acceptable in the past. The creation of a Parliamentary Commissioner for Standards, removable only by a resolution of the House, became necessary to maintain the register of MPs interests and to investigate any compliant made about an individual MP. In addition to these investigative powers, there are powers to oversee a Code of Conduct and to liaise with the Committee on Standards and Privileges in Misconduct Cases. After much soul-searching the House of Lords resisted attempts to impose any regulation over its own activities and in May 2009 followed the Commons example by appointing a Commissioner for Standards. The first Commissioner began his appointment in 2010. Both Commons and Lords Commissioners are non-statutory and appointed by resolution of their respective chamber. The damage to Parliament's reputation has not improved. Even in 2015 there have been concerns about MPs taking paid consultancy work, although no wrong doing is alleged.

3-009 Parliament has also struggled against the criticism that it is ineffective in scrutinising legislation and weak in ensuring that government is called to account. Steps to strengthen Parliament's role in both Houses for example are ongoing including a greater willingness to engage with citizens, including the annual youth parliament, in an attempt at greater transparency and relevance.

B: Parliament, Government and the Doctrine of the Separation of Powers

3-010 Parliament is Griffith and Ryle[8] explain the meaning of the term "Parliament" in its broadest sense "to refer to the House of Commons and the House of Lords, and the institution called the Executive or the Government." This explanation draws attention to the constitutional relationship between Parliament and government. The ability of government to control Parliament is a striking characteristic of the UK's constitutional arrangements and a sign of the strength of party politics. It is a recurring theme throughout this book. That such control may exist reflects the strength of political power over the institutions of the UK's Constitution. The recant experience of coalition government from 2010–2015 marked an important shift in the tradition of first past the post. Prior to the 2010 election there was the possibility of a hung parliament.[9]

---

8   P. Norton "Parliament: A New Assertiveness".
9   House of Lords Library Note, Debate on 20 January, *Coalition and Parliamentary Effect of Coalition Government*, LLN 2011/002 (17 January 2011).

PARLIAMENT, GOVERNMENT AND THE DOCTRINE OF THE SEPARATION OF POWERS

The use of pre-election guidance, the House of Commons Justice Committee considered how practices should be followed after general elections including the role of the Cabinet Manual,[10] the role of the Civil Service. It was generally accepted in the Coalition Agreement for Stability and Reform (May 2010) that there was no constitutional difference between a coalition government and a single party government. Working practices had to be modified to accommodate new arrangements of sharing power between two political parties. Significantly the Fixed-Term Parliaments Act 2011 established a five year fixed-term Parliament that helped cement relations between the Conservative and Liberal Democrats in holding together coalition government from 2010–2015. The Act is an important legacy from the Coalition that is set to shape future politics and influence the running of elections.

A dominant theme of this period in the UK's constitution in the aftermath of the 2008 financial crisis is austerity government and cuts in public spending. The flexible nature of the UK's constitutional arrangements proved remarkably adept at reformulating the contours of decision-making to accommodate both austerity planning and coalition government. It is striking at how easy it is for political decision-making to dominate when in many other constitutional arrangements discussion is usually elevated to constitutional debate and in many cases judicial approval.[11] It is also clear that political "tinkering" and adjustments here and there may change the delicate balance between exercising powers and being accountable for decisions.

3–011

Strictly speaking unlike most countries with a written constitution, the UK's constitutional arrangements do not operate under the formal requirements of the doctrine of the separation of powers. The US Constitution is often cited as a powerful example of separation of powers. The UK is not so easy to categorise. It is generally accepted that the separation of powers influences the UK constitutional order but does not determine it.

3–012

What is the separation of powers and how is it defined? The doctrine of the separation of powers is based on the theory that the separation of the legislative, executive and judicial functions provides the best means to restrain or prevent any abuse of governmental power. Originally the idea of separation of powers emanates from ancient Greece, and Aristotle believed in the ideals of government according to law. Associated with the ideals of accountable government was the perspective that more than one interest in government must be withheld from a single individual. This gave rise to the theory of mixed government, to avoid absolute power and to divide powers thus preventing any monopolistic tendencies. Writers such as Bolingbroke viewed the constitution as dependent on "balance" and in the eighteenth century government was limited by the idea of balance between the different organs of government, by ensuring that each part should work in balance with the other. In the seventeenth and eighteenth centuries the philosophy of Locke and Montesquieu[12] became influential. The philosophy was largely descrip-

3–013

---

10   Cabinet Office, Cabinet Manual (draft 24 February 2010) and the House of Commons Justice Committee, *Constitutional Processes following a general election*, HC 396 Session 2009–10 (March 2010).
11   See John McEldowney, "Debt Limits in German Constitutional law—A UK Perspective" in Wolf-George Ringe and Peter M. Huber (eds), *Legal Challenges in the Global Financial Crisis: Bail-outs, the Euro and Regulation, Studies of the Oxford Institute of European and Comparative Law* (Oxford: Hart Publications, 2014), pp.63–80.
12   John Locke, *Second Treatise of Civil Government* (1690); and Montesquieu, *The Spirit of Laws* (1748). See also

tive unlike its modern formulation which has become prescriptive of how government should govern. Munro[13] draws a sharp distinction between the doctrine as a "prescription" of what ought to be done and the description of how the constitution may exhibit certain characteristics. The separation of powers doctrine was adopted in countries with written constitutions, and as mentioned, most notably in America in the Federal Constitution of 1798. As a theory of government in the UK, it has been influential but not as an absolute and rigid rule. In essence the doctrine describes how power should be exercised rather than the realities of how power is enjoyed. As the Donoughmore Committee[14] commented, within the UK's constitutional arrangements "there is no such thing as the absolute separation of powers". Opposition to the theory of a separation of powers doctrine in England came from the view that a balanced constitution controlled by checks and balances affords the best protection against abuse. On this view all the different elements within the constitutional arrangements may be held in equilibrium. Reliance on a balanced constitution emerged in the context of the development of parliamentary democracy. The pre-eminence of political power, the organic nature of the constitution itself and the reliance on conventional rules defeated any demand for a separation of powers doctrine in the eighteenth and nineteenth centuries.

3-014
There was support for the theory of the separation of powers in the works of William Blackstone in his influential *Commentaries on the Laws of England*. Blackstone's influence did not succeed in elevating the separation of powers into a fundamental design for the constitution. In modern Britain the doctrine is deficient as an accurate description of present day constitutional arrangements. However, in modern times, the doctrine does retain important value as a description of how the different elements of our constitution might or should operate as independent from each other. This makes the value of the doctrine of the separation of powers an important element in the protection of the judiciary and its independence. As Lord Templeman explained in *M v Home Office*[15]:

> "...Parliament makes the law, the executive carry the law into effect and the judiciary enforce the law."

3-015
The question arises as to how the doctrine stands in relationship to the actual working constitution. The gradual application of the doctrine gave rise to a general acceptance of the value of judicial independence. Under the Constitutional Reform Act 2005, the Lord Chief Justice became head of the judiciary in England and Wales and in 2009 the Supreme Court became the appellate jurisdiction taking over that function from the House of Lords.

3-016
Undoubtedly judicial independence is being upheld but this may cause problems when judges are asked to undertake public inquiries that bring them into direct contact with party

---

T. R. S. Allan, *Law, Liberty and Justice* (Oxford: Oxford University Press, 1993), pp.48–64; and M. J. C. Vile, *Constitutionalism and the Separation of Powers* (Oxford: Clarendon Press, 1967).
13   C. R. Munro, *Studies in Constitutional Law*, 2nd edn (Oxford: Oxford University Press, 1999), p.303.
14   *Report of the Committee on Ministers' Powers*, Cmd.4060 (1932), pp.4–5.
15   *M v Home Office* [1994] 1 A.C. 377; [1993] 3 W.L.R. 433 HL.

political issues or the public media. Mr Justice Beatson has raised a query of whether or not judges should conduct such inquiries.[16] The recent Leveson Inquiry[17] into the media following examples of illegal "phone tapping" is a case in point as to whether or not this was a desirable role for a serving judge. Other examples such as the Hillsborough Inquiry into a football stadium disaster[18] and events in Northern Ireland relating to "Bloody Sunday"[19] are illustrative of the range of sensitive issues[20] that judges are expected to consider.

Also problematic is the Law Officers of the Crown, the Attorney General and Solicitor General are members of the government but are expected to give independent legal advice.

The role[21] of the Attorney General in the overall consent to prosecute certain criminal offences may be difficult and tinged with political, social and economic considerations. The decision of the independent Director of the Serious Fraud Office to drop his investigations of bribery charges against BAE Systems Plc was upheld by the House of Lords as perfectly lawful. Pressure to drop the case had come from Saudi Arabia and advice from diplomats, the foreign office and the Attorney General is well documented in the decision of their Lordships. It is clearly indicative of the problem of ensuring independence in a sensitive area in difficult cases where defining the public interest is often determined by a delicate balance of conflicting considerations.

The war in Iraq proved an example of where there was a vote in Parliament in 2003. The House of Commons voted by 412 to 149 to authorise the war had been proceeded by advice from the Attorney General on the legal basis for the war.[22] The Attorney General was forced to publish his advice[23] revealing how his opinion had been shaped by changing events and circumstances when it had proved impossible to obtain a new UN resolution. The ongoing Chilcot Inquiry into the war, established in June 2007, is expected to give further consideration to the role of legal advice and the challenges facing the Attorney General when his analysis may be crucial to the Government's policy making.[24]

Judicial independence, and the independence of Law Officers, is a cornerstone of democratic, responsible and accountable government. It is clear that in the absence of a written constitution in the UK means that there is no formal separation of powers. Legislative powers that may encroach on each of the three elements—judicial, executive and legislative is not unconstitutional. The way forward for the future might be a written constitution that ensures that separation of powers is observed and enforced.

---

16   J. Beatson, "Should judges conduct public inquiries?" (2005) 121 *Law Quarterly Review* 221.
17   *An inquiry into the Culture, Practices and Ethics of the Press*, HC 780 (2012–13), known as the Leveson Inquiry.
18   *The Hillsborough Stadium Disaster*, Cm 962 (1990), Lord Taylor.
19   *Report of the Bloody Sunday Inquiry*, HC 29-I-HC 29-X (2010–11), Lord Saville.
20   *Report of the Inquiry into the export of Defence Equipment and Dual-use Goods to Iraq and Related Prosecutions*, HC 115 (1995–96), Lord Scott.
21   *R (On the application of Corner House Research and others) v Director of Serious Fraud Office* [2008] UKHL 60; [2009] 1 A.C. 756.
22   HC deb 18 March 2003, Cols.760–911.
23   See P. Sands, *Lawless World* (London: Penguin 2005), pp.258–83.
24   House of Commons Library Briefing Papers, *Chilcot Inquiry*, SN 6215 (3 June 2015).

C: Parliament's Role

3-020 Walter Bagehot in *The English Constitution*[25] identified the role and function of Parliament to provide an expression of the will of the people, to provide information and to have an educative value. These roles are in addition to the functions of providing legislation and finance. A brief historical overview allows us to see all these roles emerge as part of the evolution of parliamentary democracy. Parliament's legal and political authority developed historically, and explains the close relationship between government and legislature as part of Parliament's evolution.

3-021 The early medieval meaning given to *Parliament* was that of "any meeting for speech or conference". In its law-making function Parliament shared judicial and legislative business. In the thirteenth century a common practice was to use parliamentary power to redress specific grievances contained in petitions presented to Parliament. Earlier kings asserted a wide power to redress grievances to individuals and a system of petitions was well established by 1280. Edward I was able to exploit the granting of petitions to extend his influence over even the most powerful of his subjects via the King's Council in his Parliament. Magna Carta (1215) is today regarded as a transformative document in legal history and a significant landmark in English constitutional history. Modern attribution to the values of Magna Carta such as freedom and liberty owe much to the influence of Sir Edward Coke,[26] a seventeenth-century Lawyer and Chief Justice during James I's reign, than to the actual text of the Magna Carta itself. The popularity of interpreting the Carta proved inspirational.[27] It is clear that Magna Carta served an important purpose of addressing the political and social problems of the time through an appeal to historical precedent and this rationale continues to be an enduring feature of the largely unwritten British Constitution, even to the present day.[28]

3-022 During the reign of Edward III (1327–77), the use of regular petitions being presented to the Commons was established. The Crown made law through parliamentary legislation as a means to expedite petitions in a similar way that Government Bills may be introduced in Parliament today.

3-023 During the fourteenth century Parliament gained influence through a variety of practices which assisted in the development of parliamentary power. Taxation required the consent of both Houses of Parliament and hence also required regular meetings. Parliaments, by the statutes of 1330 and 1362, were required to be held frequently. Although this was not always followed, Parliament began to meet regularly and developed a constitutional basis of "making law". By the end of the fifteenth century the institution of Parliament had replaced the Great Council of the King.

---

25 Walter Bagehot, *The English Constitution: Introduction by R. Crossman* (London: Fontana, 1963).
26 Sir Edward Coke (1552–1634). See Allen D. Boyer, *Sir Edward Cole and the Elizabeth Age* (Stanford: Stanford University press, 2003).
27 Faith Thompson, *Magna Carta: its Role in the making of the English Constitution, 1300–1639* (Minneapolis, MN: University of Minnesota Press, 1948). H. Butterfield, *The Englishman and his History* (Cambridge: Cambridge University Press, 1944).
28 See House of Lords, Library Note, *A Brief History of the Magna Carta*, LLN 2015/001 (29 January 2015).

3-024 In the seventeenth century, Parliament's powers grew in importance and influence as its constitutional status developed. The Petition of Right 1627 established that taxation was not to be levied without the consent of Parliament. In the seventeenth century, events of constitutional significance included: the English Civil War (1642–49); the defeat of the King and his execution; and the operation by Cromwell of a protectorate (1653). These events resembled a revolution. In 1661, however, the "convention Parliament of Lords and Commons" restored the monarchy by inviting Charles II to take the Throne. The restoration settlement legitimated the conventions developed by Parliament under Cromwell but also asserted the King's authority in Parliament under the Constitution. Parliament's authority ensured its continued supremacy. An uneasy settlement between King and Parliament led to the Bill of Rights 1688 which curtailed royal power under Parliament's authority. James II (1685–88) abdicated and fled, but constitutional change was accomplished by Parliament's acceptance of the Bill of Rights and, under William and Mary, by Royal Assent to Parliament's authority.

3-025 The term "Queen in Parliament" has the technical significance of the power to make laws vested in the Queen, Lords and Commons, and may be found in the enacting words of an Act of Parliament. In common usage "Parliament" is often used as a term to denote that authority.

3-026 The eighteenth and nineteenth centuries saw the continued development of Parliament's legislative activities. It had an important role in the life of the nation even though the franchise was narrow and unrepresentative of popular support, because few were allowed to vote. The Septennial Act 1715 provided for an election every seven years. During the eighteenth century the principal advisors of the King formed a cabinet and by convention were members of one or other House of Parliament. Support for policies was often obtained through corrupt practices and seldom through popularity. The offices of state, such as Prime Minister, emerged as royal influence replaced royal power. In more modern times monarchy has endured even after the abdication crisis in 1936 when Edward VIII abdicated the Throne.

3-027 The nineteenth century with the two major Reform Acts of 1832 and 1867 gave the franchise to a wider section of the population than ever before, and allowed all male urban householders to vote. Similarly, in 1880 county householders were granted the vote.

3-028 Parliament's legislative activities were greatly altered and change was brought about by various political, economic and social factors rather than constitutional reform. It is noteworthy that no general review of the Constitution occurred. Change was organic and often unpredictable. Constitutional arrangements preserved what was needed and discarded the unnecessary.

3-029 The style and content of legislation deserves mention. Up until the end of the nineteenth century, legislation was narrow in scope and covered matters of local and even temporary significance. Watson[29] observes that there was "a paucity of general statutes covering what we would term private law or mercantile law". Subjects covered included such matters as

---

29 A. Watson, *Failures of the Legal Imagination* (Philadelphia: University of Pennsylvania Press, 1988), pp.39–40; A. Watson, *Society and Legal Change* (Edinburgh: Scottish Academic Press, 1977); S. F. Milsom, *Historical Foundations of the English Common Law*, 2nd edn (London: Lexis Law Publishing, 1981); F. Pollock and F. W. Maitland, *The History of English Law* (Cambridge: Cambridge University Press, 1968); A. Watson, *The Evolution of Law* (Baltimore, MD: Johns Hopkins University Press, 1985); P. S. Atiyah and R. S. Summers, *Form*

divorce through Acts of Parliament, patents, and the incorporation of companies with limited liability. Rarely were general statutes passed and as codification was resisted in the common law tradition, there were only a few statutes which "consolidated" rather than codified the law, such as the Offences Against the Person Act 1861. Such statutes often expressed in statutory language the development by the judges of the main principles through the common law.

3-030 Dicey observed that Parliament had become the repository of all public power with Parliament overseeing a unitary state and legislating on particular issues no matter how local or specific. On this view Parliament exercised all public power. Craig refers to Dicey's analysis as "parliamentary monopoly": a belief that Parliament's legislative power in all matters was accompanied by the equally important view that the Commons could and should control the Executive. This has given rise to a strong tradition setting out "the order of things" which has been influential in the study of the Constitution.

3-031 The period of transformation from Parliament acting through legislation to deal with individual problems and grievances into a more collective action on social, economic and political problems may be said to have begun in the mid-nineteenth century. Precise dates are difficult to provide but it is generally agreed that between 1830 and 1850 central government expanded its functions to include railways, factories, poor law, public health and licensing. Legislation concerning these areas may be identified to indicate the growth in government activities and administration. Government policies were proactive in providing the impetus for change in society in the industrial and agrarian revolution of the period.

3-032 Simultaneous with the growth of central government activities, local and municipal government also changed. The Reform Act 1832 had broadened the franchise for central government. A Royal Commission reported on municipal corporations and their defects led to the Municipal Corporations Act 1835, which extended the franchise for local government. The result was that after 1835 the franchise included a wider range of people than before, bringing urban middle class interests into the activities of local government. Local government was further reformed, after the 1867 and 1884 central government franchise was expanded; the Local Government Act 1888 instituted a two-tier system of government in the metropolis.

3-033 Craig[30] points out that the local government system developed in the nineteenth century survived virtually unchanged until 1972:

> "The metropolis had a two-tier system with the London County Council at the top and metropolitan boroughs providing the second tier. County boroughs, the larger towns, were single purpose authorities. The counties were slightly more complex. The County Council was the main authority for the area. Beneath it existed three types of institution: non-County boroughs; urban districts; and rural districts.

---

and *Substance in Anglo-American Law* (Oxford: Clarendon, 1987); and M. Lobban, *The Common Law and English Jurisprudence 1760–1850* (Oxford: Clarendon, 1991).

30   P. Craig, *Administrative Law*, 2nd edn (London: Sweet & Maxwell, 1989), pp.34–51. J. B. Brebner, "Laissez-faire and State Intervention in nineteenth century Britain" (1948) 8 *Journal of Economic History* 61.

> The last of these could have parish councils within its area, thereby providing a third tier of authority."

3-034 Local government is a good example of the extensive legislative powers granted by Parliament to enable local authorities to expand their activities and diversify their interests.

3-035 Changes also occurred in parliamentary procedures for legislation, reflecting a change in the policies and directions of the government. Private bill procedures and Private Members' Bills gave way to Public General Acts of Parliament.

3-036 Craig notes two further trends in the centralisation of legislative power. The first is the use of standing committees of the whole House, which favoured discussion by the Government of policy in detail and helped expedite busy legislative programmes. Added to this was the increase in Cabinet committees to discuss and debate any legislative proposals, thus preparing the way for the safe passage of proposals knowing that agreement and party political support would most likely be given. The second is the growth of delegated legislation which considerably broadened the scope of government powers and ministerial discretion; this is discussed in more detail in Ch.10.

3-037 The growth of party politics is also significant in the development of Parliament's political authority. The extension of the franchise broadened Parliament's appeal and rooted its legitimacy in its responsiveness to the popular vote. This could easily detract from the power and authority of Parliament itself, if voting patterns were not focused on group activity and electoral manifestos. Electoral choices through elections replaced appointments through patronage, but patronage returned in a different guise as a means of operating party politics effectively.

3-038 The development of the parliamentary system of government is an important part of the discussion of administrative law. It also provides a perspective on the constitutional arrangements for the UK in its relations within the EU. Parliament's importance in financial matters is fully discussed in Ch.12. An important, but often overlooked aspect of Parliament is that the Parliamentary estate, formally under the management of the Clerk of Parliaments and under the House of Commons Commission Act 2015 under a newly created House of Commons Commission, is a complex and time-consuming administrative process. Achieving a modern and functional parliamentary democracy is partly a reflection of the culture and ambience of the buildings that are the public face of the debating chamber as well as the venue for the passage of legislation.[31] It is likely that the main Parliamentary buildings and debating chambers will have to be vacated, pending maintenance to the building and modernising of its existing infrastructure.

---

31 See the House of Commons Commission Act 2015 that provides details of how the Clerk and Chief Executive may manage the running of the Parliamentary estate.

D: Procedures and processes in enacting legislation

3-039 Both Houses of Parliament follow set procedures and rules. The parliamentary machinery of both Houses, through the Officials constitute an important element in ensuring that Parliament acts correctly in exercising its functions. The rules of procedure can be traced back to the fourteenth century; they have been progressively revised and updated in the light of experience and practice. One of the most important areas is in the procedures on legislation. A Select Committee on the Modernisation of the House of Commons established in 1997 gave attention to the way in which legislation is debated and scrutinised. Two reports are worthy of consideration and set the terms of various reforms in the conduct of legislation. Their first report in 1997 set the scene for a "more regular and systematic use of draft bills".[32] The Liaison Committee in 2000 made much the same analysis arguing that "better thought out and properly examined legislation will be out of all proportion to the modest expenditure involved".[33]

3-040 Recommendations by a special time-limited House of Commons Select Committee on Reform of the House of Commons in June 2010 chaired by Tony Wright included the setting up of a Backbench Business Committee responsible for the business of the House that was not ministerial led. The House of Commons in March 2010 had earlier agreed that a Backbench Business Committee should be constituted that would set an agenda for the working of the House on a weekly basis and Standing Orders of the House of Commons would accordingly be amended. This was a major transformation of how the House of Commons would act independently of the government of the day. Further recommendations included the election of Members to sit on the Business Committee.[34] The strengthening of departmental committees has been perceptively improved with the election of chairs of committees and the payment of an additional salary for the task of chair – a recommendation that had previously been adopted since 2003–04.

Pre-legislative scrutiny

3-041 The early publication of draft bills was experimented with in the 1990s. Special standing committees were used to add an additional layer of scrutiny and this also proved valuable. The practice slowly developed of the early publication of draft Government Bills and their

---

32 Select Committee on Modernisation of the House of Commons, *The Legislative Process,* HC 190, 23 July 1997 (1997–8), para.20.
33 Liaison Committee, *Shifting the Balance: Select Committees and the Executive*, HC 300, 3 March 2000 (1999– 2000); and Liaison Committee, *Shifting the Balance: Unfinished Business*, HC 321, 25 March 2001 (2000–01), para.37.
34 House of Commons Library, *The Backbench Business Committee*, Briefing Paper No.7225 (10 June 2015).

pre-legislative scrutiny through committee.[35] The government benefitted as well as Parliament as the procedure considerably improved the bill. Draft bills were routinely published and between 1997–2010, 76 bills were published in draft but only a few bills received pre-legislative scrutiny while others did not. The period from 2010–12 there were twelve bills published in draft-usually about four a year. This leaves many bills not subject to pre-legislative scrutiny. The choice of bills is very much a matter for the managers of the Government's legislative timetable. It is in the Government's interests to have their bills passed with little or no amendment and so avoid pre-legislative scrutiny. The adoption of public bill committees from 2006 has shown a significant improvement over the old standing committees and makes it possible for more bills to be considered for pre-legislative. One recent example is the Modern Slavery Act 2015 which was subject to pre-legislative scrutiny that involve setting up a special committee of both Houses to take evidence about the bill. The Committee provided an in depth report and assessment of the relevant bill and this provides a basis for discussion through the various stages of parliamentary debate. The result of the Committee's scrutiny gave better transparency and raised the subsequent parliamentary standard of debate as well as giving greater clarity on some of the technical policy issues. In the case of the Modern Slavery Act, the subsequent debate revealed large areas of disagreement between the Government and MPs. There were many amendments and revisions to the Act, including through the debates in the House of Lords some important changes relating to overseas domestic workers.[36]

Post-legislative scrutiny

Once legislation is enacted, it is far from clear how effective the new legislation has been or what lessons may be gained from the experience of its passing. In 2004, the House of Lords Constitution Committee[37] and later the Law Commission[38] recommended that post-legislative scrutiny should take place after three to five years initiated by the relevant sponsoring department. Since 2008, post-legislative scrutiny began, but few Acts have been scrutinised as part of post-legislative scrutiny. There are some examples such as the Gambling Act 2005, the Inquiries Act 2005, the Freedom of Information Act 2000, the Charities Act 2006, and the Mental Capacity Act 2005.[39] Once the post-legislative scrutiny reviews are undertaken they

3–042

---

35 House of Commons Library, *Pre-Legislative scrutiny under the Coalition Government*, SN/PC/5859 (4 June 2013); and also House of Commons Library, *Pre-Legislative scrutiny*, SN/PC/2822 (9 April 2010).
36 Generally, see House of Commons Library Note, *Human Trafficking: UK Responses*, SN/HA/4324 (13 January 2014). Home Office, *Regulatory Impact Assessment of ratification of the Council of European Convention on Action against Trafficking in Human beings* (6 October 2008); and also see the Home Affairs Committee, *The Trade in Human beings: Human Trafficking in the UK*, HC 23-1, 2008–09 (6 May 2009). See House of Commons Library, *Human trafficking: UK responses*, SN/HA/4324 (13 January 2014).
37 The House of Lords Constitution Committee, *Parliament and the Legislative Process*, HL 173-I, 2003–04 (29 October 2004).
38 Law Commission, *Post-Legislative Scrutiny*, Law.Com. 302, CM 6945 (October 2008).
39 House of Commons, *Post-Legislative Scrutiny*, SN/PC/05231 (23 May 2013).

are sent to the relevant select committee of the department concerned. The House of Lords have seized the initiative by setting up *ad hoc* committees for that purpose. It is estimated that between December 2008 and April 2010 seven post-legislative scrutiny memorandum were published.

3-043 The combination of pre-legislative scrutiny and post-legislative scrutiny offers much to enhance Parliament's role and gain public confidence in Parliament's role. Allocating resources and ensuring that both forms of scrutiny are adopted in a more systematic fashion than present would mark progress. Looking to the future, there is considerable potential for Parliament to adopt post-legislative scrutiny as a means of improving the quality of legislation and the public's perception of Parliament's role.

Forms of Legislation

3-044 Government Bills are presented on behalf of the sponsoring department by the relevant minister usually in the House of Commons. After the formal first reading the bill is printed and published in the prescribed form. Drafting the bill is usually undertaken by the Parliamentary draftsman. After first reading the second reading is taken when the House of Commons debates proposals. Opposition amendments may be taken but it is unusual for a Government bill to be defeated at second reading. The most notable example was the Shops Bill in 1986 to reform the law on Sunday opening of shops. After second reading the bill is referred to a public bill committee or in some circumstances to a committee of the whole House. On completion the bill is reported as amended to the whole House and further amendments may be proposed by ministers. The opposition may use the report stage to propose further amendments and have them debated. The choice of amendments for debate is at the discretion of the Speaker. After the Report stage the bill receives its third reading and only oral amendments may be made at this stage.

3-045 The procedures in outline above are time-consuming and subject to unpredictable delays and interruptions. Since 1997–98 the use of programming legislation has been adopted on an experimental basis. Programme orders set time-tables for the conclusion of various procedures of a bill. The Select Committee on the Reform of the House of Commons (Wright Committee) noted "serious concerns" with the handling of sufficient time at report stage of the public bill procedure. One reason was the large number of government amendments raised at report stage that crowded out the agenda. In fact the idea of programming legislation was to give some control to the allocation of time to undertake parliamentary business to strengthen scrutiny. Since 2004 programming has become an accepted norm in the transaction of Parliamentary business. The ambition of making time available for effective scrutiny has been somewhat frustrated as the Government of the day has been tempted to use programming to its own advantage in setting fixed end time for proceedings that may lessen the effectiveness of debate and discussion. The Procedure Committee, in its report in December 2013, recommended that when significant numbers of government amendments were tabled at report stage, the bill or significant parts of the bill should be recommitted to a public bill committee.[40] It also made an assortment of proposals to ensure adequate time at report stage for amendment and debate including a fixed time for third reading so that Members would indicate to the Speaker whether they wished to speak in the debate. These recommendations received luke warm responses from the government but it was accepted that there should be a deadline for tabling amendments three days before the day on which the debate is to take place.[41]

3-046

The Government may also use a "guillotine" procedure as a means of curtailing debate that provides for a limited number of days for debate and this may include when the bill is remitted to a Committee of the whole House on report. The guillotine motion is itself subject to the limitation of a three hour debate and then it is for the House of Commons Business Committee to proportion time for each part of the bill. Once the allotted time for discussion is reached the guillotine motion requires that the bill is voted on without any further debate.

3-047

The term legislation may be used in three senses. First, it refers to "Acts of Parliament". These are primary rules contained in government legislation and called "Public General Acts". Erskine May[42] defined such an Act as "a law affecting the whole public, one which belongs to the": generally today we would recognise such Acts as forming the bulk of government policy and as reflecting a major part of the legislative role of Parliament. Second, the term may refer to private Acts of Parliament. Erskine May[43] referred to such Acts as being "in the form of an Act of Parliament, some special rule affecting only a special section of the nation, what may be called *jus particulor*". Most legislation is in the form of Public Acts.

3-048

The vast majority of government legislation is to be found in legislation introduced into the House of Commons. However, it is possible for the government to introduce legislation in the Lords for tactical reasons. Two important examples of this are the Crime and Disorder Act 1998 and the Human Rights Act 1998. The former makes changes to the sentencing and criminal procedure in England and Wales and to the substantive criminal law in Scotland. The latter incorporates the bulk of the European Convention on Human Rights into domestic law. In addition to primary legislation, the legislative output of the Government also includes a vast number of statutory instruments which are loosely described by the phrase "delegated legislation". Generally, the average number of Public General Acts in any one year is 63; a corresponding assessment of the number of statutory instruments comes to over 6,000. Since 1900 the growth in legislation has been a remarkable feature of Parliament's activities. Griffith and Ryle conclude[44]: "In our opinion the growth of work and activity is the most noteworthy change in the functioning of the House of Commons in this century".

---

40   House of Commons Procedure Committee, *Programming* HC 767 2013–14 paras 5-7.
41   House of Commons Library, *Programming of Legislation – recent proposals* SN/PC/6877 (20th June 2014).
42   T. Erskine May, *Parliamentary Practice* (London: Lexis Legal Books, 1997). Also see D. Miers and A. Page, *Legislation*, 2nd edn (London: Sweet & Maxwell, 1990).
43   T. Erskine May, *Parliamentary Practice*.
44   J. Griffith and M. Ryle, *Parliament* (London: Sweet & Maxwell, 1989), pp.229, 312.

English Votes for English Laws

3-049 In October 22 2015 the House of Commons made changes to its Standing Orders to accommodate members from England, or England and Wales to give their consent to legislation that only affected England or England and Wales. The procedures will apply to all Government Bills and may be designated English Votes for English Laws (EVEL) procedures.[45] It is difficult to know how many bills will be brought under the EVEL procedures but the procedures are likely to enhance the distinction between England and the other devolved nations. The procedures under EVEL are important changes in the way legislation is passed.[46]

Private Members' Bills

3-050 Private Bills may be introduced by Members of Parliament and are usually termed "Private Members' Bills". Standing Order 14 (9), (10) and (11) provides that there should be 13 Fridays set aside for private bills. There are no programming rules applicable to such bills, but the procedures for their passage are similar to Public Acts of Parliament. There are primarily two methods or procedures which may be used. The first is a ballot of Members of Parliament held each session giving 20 Members the opportunity to introduce a private bill in the limited time available. Since 1972 the Government has allocated annually £200 towards drafting expenses but even this modest change has little impact. In 1982 Norman St. John Stevas MP successfully introduced his private Members' bill, Parliamentary Control of Expenditure (Reform bill). This bill was later adopted by the Government of the day in return for a number of changes which were duly made. The new revised bill successfully became law as the National Audit Act 1983. Nevertheless the experience was far from satisfactory, illustrating the dependence of the success of a private Members' bill on government assistance and drafting.

3-051 The second procedure is under "the Ten Minute Rule" this is under Standing Order 23. Members of Parliament unsuccessful in the ballot may set down a motion for leave to introduce a bill on Tuesdays and Wednesdays. Three weeks' notice is usually required and the majority of such bills have been allowed to lapse and are unsuccessful. It is estimated that only 10–12 Private Members' Bills become law each session. The ballot procedure is usually the best chance of a private Member's bill becoming law.

3-052 There is also a procedure under Standing Order 57 for special leave allowing a private Member to present a bill for its first reading after giving notice but without the leave of the House.

3-053 The number of Private Member's Bills since 1983–2014 is relatively small compared to Public Acts of Parliament. Their range and diversity of subject matter is one of their strengths representing an important link between constituents and Parliament. Environmental issues as

---

45   House of Commons Briefing Paper, *English votes for English laws*, No.7339 (2 December 2015)
46   See Chapter 2 on devolution.

well as disability protection and support for victims of crime are all within the assorted causes and issues raised by Private Bills.[47] The Lords also have an important role in engaging in taking forward technical amendments on the Law Commission (Lord Lloyd, 2008/09); the law of theft (Lord Goff in 1996/97); Gaming (Lord Allen in 1989/90); and on the sale of goods (Lord Rention in 1993/4).

Private Bills

Private Bills are legislation which affects specific groups or localities. They follow the same procedures as public Bills but there are additional requirements.[48] Private Bills are sometimes promoted by local authorities or other public bodies and were commonly used in the nineteenth century, but are not so common today. Private bill procedures are found in the Standing Orders of each House and have to use a small group of registered parliamentary agents. Promoters of the bill have to present a petition to Parliament on or before 27 November of each year and they have to bear the cost of drafting and employing the agents. The bill must be advertised in newspapers and official gazettes. Those who are specifically affected by the legislation may object and have the right to petition against the bill. Negotiating the details of the bill with those petitioners opposed is often essential to ensure that the bill stands a chance of success. This is expensive and the expense falls on the promoters of the bill. Examiners are appointed under Standing Orders to hear all sides. There is a Standing Orders Committee composed of 11 members in the House of Commons. The House of Lords equivalent committee has eight members. There are various mechanisms for objections but if there is a decision not to hear a petitioner than the matter may be referred to the House of Commons Court of Referees. The Court is composed of senior-back bench MPs and chaired by the Chairman of Ways and Means assisted by Speaker's Counsel.

3–054

In local authority matters many bills are about seeking specific statutory powers. In respect of the construction of roads, railways and waterways Transport and Works Act 1992 there is a special provision for that purpose, thus avoiding the need to make use of the Private bill procedure. Private Acts of Parliament were once an important device to promote specific interests—local authorities, railways, companies—and even to circumvent the existing law on planning matters. Since 1987 criticism of the use of private bill procedures in the planning system led to a recommendation[49] that private legislation should be available only as a last resort and not as an alternative to established statutory procedures. In fact, the increase in Public General Acts has reduced the quantity of private Bills.

3–055

---

47 House of Commons Library, *Successful Private Members' Bills since 1983–4*, SN/PC/04568 (17 June 2014).
48 House of Commons Library, *Private Bills in Parliament: House of Commons Background Paper*, SN/PC/06508 (7 January 2014).
49 *Report of the Joint Committee on Private Bill Procedure 1987–88*, HC 625; HL 97 (1988).

Hybrid Bills

3-056 The term legislation may also apply to a third category of bill known as a "Hybrid Bill". It is difficult to provide an exact definition of a Hybrid Bill. Erskine May[50] defines it as legislation which "affects a particular private interest in a manner different from the private interests of other persons or bodies of the same category or class". The term "Hybrid bill" is used because such a bill shares characteristics of both public and private bill procedures. The Speaker of the House of Commons and the House of Lords appoints a member of staff to be the Examiners of Petitions for Private Bills and this is usually the Clerk of Bills in the House of Commons and the Clerk of Private Bills in the House of Lords. Generally they apply to works of national importance that will outweigh private interests alone.[51] Since 1983 there have been 12 Hybrid Bills, the latest is the controversial HS2 high speed rail link. The Hybrid Bill procedure is similar to private Bills and the examiners of the bill have to be satisfied that the bill qualifies as hybrid. The hybrid procedures have had to be amended to ensure the adoption of the EU Directive on Environmental Impact Assessments. The House of Commons agreed to a new standing Order (Standing Order 224A) to ensure that the procedures of the House of Commons were fully compliant with the EU Directive. An additional change was the adoption of electronic deposit of documents relating to Hybrid Bills.

3-057 The High Speed Rail Link bill, currently before Parliament, was proposed by the Government in 2008–09. It has attracted cross political support from the main political parties. The scheme is to build a high speed rail link from London to Manchester and Leeds via Birmingham, the East Midlands, Sheffield and Crewe. This is the most recent Hybrid Bill, along with the environmental statement it is 50,000 pages and has attracted considerable public debate and discussion. The HS2 Action Alliance took judicial review against the decision of the Government to promote the link. One of the grounds for complaint related to questions about the adequacy of the consultation, specifically whether the use of a Hybrid Bill for the HS2 was compliant with the requirements of the EIA Directive. The Supreme Court accepted that the use of a Hybrid Bill procedure was a decision that was a matter for the national legislature rather than the ordinary process of development control. The Court was not persuaded that the Hybrid Bill process offered an inadequate process for scrutiny of the issues raised by the proposed rail link. Members of Parliament were perfectly able to scrutinise the proposals in the bill.[52]

3-058 It is planned that construction of HS2 should commence from 2026 so that it will be operational and completed by 2032.[53]

---

50 T. Erskine May, *Parliamentary Practice* (London: Lexis Legal Books, 1997).
51 House of Commons Library, *Hybrid Bills: House of Commons Background paper*, SN/PC/6736 (11 December 2013).
52 *R (on the application of HS2 Action Alliance Ltd) v Secretary of State for Transport* [2014] UKSC 3; [2014] 1 W.L.R. 32.
53 House of Commons Library, *High Speed Rail (London-West Midlands) Bill*, No.132 and I and 132-II, 2013–14 (22 April 2014).

Table of Hybrid Bills 1985–2013

Title	Date	Royal assent
Museum of London	7 November 1985	26 March 1986
Channel Tunnel	17 April 1986	23 July 1987
Norfolk and Suffolk Broads	18 November 1986	15 March 1988
Chevening Estate (Lords)	20 November 1986	15 May 1987
Dartford-Thurrock Crossing	1 April 1987	28 June 1988
Caldey Island	29 November 1989	1 November 1990
Agriculture and Forestry (Financial Provisions)	8 November 1990	25 July 1991
Severn Bridges	27 November 1990	13 February 1992
Cardiff Bay Barrage	4 November 1991	5 November 1993
Channel Tunnel Rail Link	23 November 1994	18 December 1996
Crossrail	22 February 2005	22 July 2008
High Speed Rail Link London-West Midlands	25 November 2013	

One caveat to introducing a private bill whether or not it is a Hybrid Bill, is Standing Order No.48 of the House of Commons, namely that the main object of such a bill may not create a charge on public funds, as this lies within the allocation of ministerial power only. In the case of a dispute over the exact procedure for a bill, the matter may be adjudicated by the Clerk of Public Bills and the Members concerned.

In constitutional terms there is no legal distinction between the authority of a private Act and a public general Act. The Courts are unwilling to allow a challenge to the validity of either a public or private Act as explained in 1974 in *Pickin v British Railways Board*.[54] This marks out the limits of judicial scrutiny under the UK's constitutional arrangements. This does not, however, prevent the Courts from taking account of EU law and whenever there is a conflict between a UK Act of Parliament and EU law, resolving the conflict in favour of the latter. This includes the *Factortame*[55] case illustrating the overriding of a UK Act of Parliament in subservience to EU law.

As we shall see in Ch.10, the growth in legislation has had an effect on the procedures, character and nature of the House of Commons, including the use of select committees. Backbench Members of Parliament have been given a greater role through the formation of the numerous select committees to expedite legislation.

Estimates of the volume of legislation are that on average Parliament produces around 11,000 pages of primary legislation and the same number of pages of statutory instruments annually. The actual number of Acts is declining but their length and complexity has increased.[56]

---

54 [1974] A.C. 765; [1974] 2 W.L.R. 208 HL.
55 [1991] 1 A.C. 603; [1990] 3 W.L.R. 818 HL; (C-213/89) EU:C:1990:257; [1990] 3 C.M.L.R. 375.
56 Full details are to be found in House of Lords, Library Note, *Volume of Legislation*, LLN 2013/008 (10 May 2013).

3-062

A distinctive feature of English law has been the formal structures and procedures adopted and an increasing use of statutory powers replacing many informal and conventional arrangements making the English common law less dependent on judge-made law and increasingly reliant on statutory interpretation. Atiyah and Summers identified the heavy reliance on statute law[57]:

> "...the English political-legal system relies more heavily than the American on statute law and less on case-law, and that, because statute law is more formal than case-law, this is one factor which makes English law more formal."

3-063

The authors conclude that to a large extent the wide use of legislation in the UK is a reflection of the constitutional arrangements present under the parliamentary system of government. The characteristics of the parliamentary system may be enumerated as follows: strong centralised political institutions; the English judiciary has a relatively weak role as compared with the centralised executive-legislative machinery; strong ministerial influence has a powerful control over the legislature; the UK parliamentary system combines executive and legislative powers; party political influence may strengthen cabinet government and this in turn strengthens the ministerial fiat; ministers are effectively in control of making most delegated legislation and it is uncommon for government-supported legislation not to be successfully passed through Parliament.

3-064

The growth in subordinated or delegated legislation continues today. Concern about delegated legislation led to the Donoughmore Committee on Ministers Powers in 1932 which recognised the problem of scrutiny over delegated legislation. Many of these problems remain. S. A. Walkland noted[58]:

> "Much of the suspicion of delegated legislation is aroused by the fact that civil servants are intimately associated with its procedures, and that the opportunities for participation in the process by representative and politically responsible members of the House of Commons are necessarily limited."

3-065

There are two areas where Parliament gives special attention to legislation. The first is EU legislation and the second is in the area of human rights. Special consideration is given to EU legislation; since 1972 the UK's accession into the EC has committed her to adopting a variety of

---

57 P. S. Atiyah and R. S. Summers, *Form and Substance in Anglo-American Law*, p.298. See N. J. Ornstein (ed), *The Role of the Legislature in Western Democracies* (Washington, D.C.: American Enterprise Institute for Public Policy Research, 1981).

58 S. A. Walkland, *The Legislative Process in Great Britain* (London: Allen & Unwin, 1968), pp.16–17. *Machinery of Government Committee*, Cd.9230 (1918); Hewart, *New Despotism* (London: Ernest Benn, 1929); *Report of the Committee on Ministers' Powers*, Cmd. 4060 (1932).

EC legislation. In 1972 both the House of Commons and the House of Lords provided new committees to scrutinise proposals for Community legislation and consider how best they might be adopted. The role of the UK Parliament with such legislation is to ensure that the domestic law is made consistent with EU law. Thus, the committee does not consider the substantive merits of legislative proposals or other EU documents. Its role does not include any formal input into the Community's own law-making processes. UK ministries participate in legislation through the Council of Ministers. The Treaty of Lisbon acceded to criticisms made that the EU is too distant and remote. It introduced the requirement that national Parliaments have to be consulted as part of the EU law-making process and the EU Commission may be required to consider proposing legislation when requested to do so by at least 1 million EU citizens. On the requirement of "subsidiarity" national Parliaments may object to legislative proposals. The role of the UK Parliament in EU matters has been refined by the European Union Act 2011 by providing that the UK Parliament has to approve through Act of Parliament *and* a referendum any amendment to the EU Treaties or any further extension of EU powers. There are also certain specified decisions that have to be approved by an Act of Parliament before they are confirmed by ministers.

3-066

It is noticeable that the remit of the House of Lords Scrutiny Committee over EU legislation is wider than the House of Commons Committee; the former's terms of reference allow for a limited inquiry into "the merits of community proposals". More time is devoted in the House of Lords Committee than in the Commons Committee and the Lords reports are generally accepted as authoritative and providing well-argued analysis. It is noteworthy that the Lords have taken the innovative step of setting up, on 8 February 2001, a Select Committee on the Constitution, chaired by Professor Lord Norton, a leading expert in this area.[59]

3-067

The second area where special attention is given is human rights. The Human Rights Act 1998 incorporates the main provisions of the European Convention on Human Rights. While the Act falls short of allowing the Courts to hold an Act of Parliament illegal or to strike down legislation, s.10 of the Act allows ministers to introduce remedial orders to amend any part of the legislation that is held by the Courts to be incompatible with the Human Rights Act. This is regarded as an extreme situation. In order to avoid any potential conflict between the Human Rights Act and legislation, s.19 of the 1998 Act provides that ministers are required to make a statement of compatibility accompanying the bill before the second reading of the bill. In cases where such a statement cannot be made then the minister in charge of the bill must indicate where the potential conflict or incompatibility with the Act may arise. There is a Joint Committee on Human Rights; this is a Select Committee of both Houses of Parliament established in February 2001. The government rejected the idea of a Human Rights Commission modelled on the Northern Ireland experience. Instead there is a Human Rights Advisor who provides the joint committee with advice on the implications of the Act. These arrangements complement the monitoring of the Human Rights Act undertaken by a special unit set up within the Lord Chancellor's department. Before the 1998 Act came into force in England and Wales in October 2001, resources were provided for government departments and Parliament to develop systems of administration to ensure that the law was compatible with the implications of the

---

59 *Reviewing the Constitution; terms of reference and methods of working*, First Report, HL 11 (2001–02).

new legislation. The landmark decision of *Pepper v Hart*[60] remains influential. This permits the Courts to read the debates in Parliament as reported in Hansard when interpreting legislation. In that regard s.3 of the Human Rights Act 1998 provides that "as far as it is possible to do so" primary and secondary legislation must be read and given effect so as to render the law compatible with the human rights requirements under the Act. This includes legislation enacted before and after the 1998 Act. In formal legal terms the Human Rights Act 1998 attempts to introduce a rights-based culture into the working of the Constitution while preserving the pre-eminence of the House of Commons? In so doing the Courts must take into account the jurisprudence of the European Court of Human Rights, and Courts along with other public authorities have a duty to conform to the European Convention on Human Rights itself. At the heart of this ambitious objective of bringing rights into the centre of decision-making is the need to interpret the Convention and assimilate Convention rights into the law. The plain meaning of statutes must be interpreted alongside the rights culture contained in the Human Rights Act. As Campbell[61] points out this has wider implications than simply giving effect to legal rules alone:

> "It will be necessary to hold onto a plain-meaning approach to the interpretation of statutes, and to openly acknowledge that interpreting the ECHR is a matter of moral reasoning in which Courts have no special expertise and in connection with which their decisions have no political legitimacy."

How this is likely to work out in the future is still uncertain. Amid uncertainty there is a degree of responsiveness to change.

E: Drafting and Interpreting Legislation

3-068 It is clear that in the drafting of legislation, human rights and EU law are taken into account. An important but often neglected subject is the question of how legislation is drafted. The existence of the Parliamentary Counsel Office is all too often ignored. The office came into existence in 1869 during Gladstone's first administration. Previously Acts of Parliament were drafted either by the judges or by practising lawyers or by Members of Parliament. The creation of the Parliamentary Counsel Office regularised the drafting of bills.

3-069 Parliamentary Counsel work out of the Parliamentary Counsel Office and are responsible for the drafting of the majority of Government Bills. Counsel are involved in advising

---

60 [1993] A.C. 593; [1992] 3 W.L.R. 1032 HL.
61 T. Campbell, "Incorporation through Interpretation" in T. Campbell, K. Ewing and A. Tomkins (eds), *Sceptical Essays on Human Rights* (Oxford: Oxford University Press, 2001), p.99.

government departments on aspects of Parliamentary procedure and in the drafting of amendments. The staff of the Office of Parliamentary Counsel in Whitehall, London comprise over 30 members headed by the First Parliamentary Counsel. The Finance Bill 1996 was subjected to external drafting through a contract awarded outside the Office of the Parliamentary Counsel. Such use of external drafting is an important development in terms of diversity. The Lord Chancellor is charged with the responsibility of codification and making suggestions for reform under the Law Commission Act 1965. This remit includes keeping the law under review. Reports are received from the Law Commission and the Lord Chancellor is required to consider these reports. An example of some controversy was the Public Order Act 1986, the result of recommendations made by the English Law Commission.

3-070

The Law Commission provides important input into the drafting of new legislation through its work on law reform and its duty to keep the statute book under review. It publishes consultation papers and its reports contain draft bills incorporating details of law reform proposals. There is a Common Law and Public Law team within the Law Commission engaged in an overview of public law matters.

3-071

The Law Commission Act 2009 provides new obligations on the Government of the day and for the setting up of a protocol between the Lord Chancellor and the Law Commission. The protocol is to ensure that there is a working relationship between the Lord Chancellor and the Law Commission and that ministers and their departments should work with the Lord Chancellor. The duty on the Lord Chancellor is to report annually to Parliament on the extent to which the Government has implemented Law Commission recommendations.[62]

3-072

There is also a special procedure for Law Commission bills that has existed since 1995 under Standing Order No.59. The procedure was refined further in 2008 by the introduction of a trial Law Commission procedure in the House of Lords in 2008. This has been used twice for the Perpetuities and Accumulations Act 2009 and the Third Parties (Rights Against Insurers) Act 2010.

3-073

Interpreting legislation is important and the ever present need to check bills as to their compatibility with the European Convention on Human Rights receives special attention. The addition of Explanatory Notes to Acts provides a much needed guide to understanding of the main elements of the legislation. This is a welcome development in an era where the complexity of legislation is an obstacle to understanding its significance. The House of Commons Library publishes useful and authoritative papers on legislative changes and issues of common interest.

3-074

Increasingly important in the techniques of drafting bills are the rules of statutory interpretation. It is more common than in the past for the Courts to look at reports of Parliamentary debates in *Hansard* as an aid to interpretation. The use of *Hansard* in certain circumstances as an aid to interpretation[63] has been approved by the House of Lords in *Pepper v Hart*.[64] The discussion and analysis contained in the reports of Parliamentary select committees is also very

---

62 House of Commons Library, *The Law Commission and Law Commission Bill Procedures*, SN/PC/7156 (27 March 2015).
63 Lord Lester, "*Pepper v Hart* Revisited" (1992) 15(1) *Statutory Law Review* (1994) 10. J. Steyn, "*Pepper v Hart*: a re-examination" (2001) 21 *Oxford Journal of Legal Studies* 59.
64 [1993] A.C. 593; [1992] 3 W.L.R. 1032 HL.

helpful. However, the availability of Parliamentary debates as an aid to interpretation should be distinguished from the bar on the Courts questioning the proceedings in Parliament. As Lord Browne-Wilkinson explained in *Prebble v Television New Zealand Ltd*[65]:

> "So far as the Courts are concerned they will not allow any challenge to be made to what is said or done within the walls of Parliament in performance of its legislative functions and protection of its established principles."

3-075 Lord Steyn in *Jackson v Attorney General*[66] has observed that the clear words in a statute have to be given priority over the preamble to the legislation. There is a marked reluctance from Lord Nicholls in *Wilson v First County Trust Ltd (No.2)*[67] to delve too deeply into the political and policy issues surrounding ministerial statements or various background documents. These are regarded as not determinative of the meaning of an Act of Parliament.[68] Reliance on a parliamentary select committee report when making a judicial decision is regarded as not permissible.[69] Indeed there are underlying issues about protecting parliamentary privilege that risks offending art.9 of the Bill of Rights that grants Parliament immunity.[70]

3-076 There are various aids in the interpretation of statutes. These consist of rules or presumptions about how words in a statute may be interpreted. Taken together they form what are called principles of statutory interpretation that are generally applied in English law. Different rules apply in the interpretation of European Community law. The continental style of drafting only sets out general broad principles. This leaves the exact details to be filled in by the judges, who are expected to promote the general legislative purpose of the law. Similarly, the Human Rights Act 1998 in the UK will bring its own style of interpretation as the law begins to be developed on a case by case basis.

3-077 In English law the principles of statutory interpretation consist of rules and presumptions and at the discretion of the judge may be applied when seeking to understand the meaning of a statute. The following are the main rules to aid interpretation.

(i) The Literal Rule

3-078 The literal rule refers to the method of interpretation of words in a statute by giving words their plain, ordinary or literal meaning. Courts attempt to find the parliamentary intention behind the statute. As an aid to interpretation the dictionary meaning of words may be used.

---

65 [1995] 1 A.C. 321; [1994] 3 W.L.R. 970 PC (NZ) at [323D].
66 *Jackson v Attorney General* [2005] UKHL 56; [2006] 1 A.C. 262 at [89].
67 *Wilson v First County Trust Limited (No.2)* [2003] UKHL 40; [2004] 1 A.C. 816 at [58]–[59].
68 A. Kavanagh, "Pepper v Hart and Matters of Constitutional principle" (2005) 121 *L.Q.R.* 98.
69 *Office of Government Commerce v Information Commissioner* [2008] EWHC 737 (Admin); [2010] Q.B. 98.
70 See *The Joint Committee in Parliamentary Privilege Report* (2013), p.316.

(ii) The Golden Rule

The golden rule when applied is used to modify the literal rule by seeking to avoid any absurdity. If the words used in legislation are ambiguous, the golden rule allows the court to avoid the absurdity and adopt a meaning that is suitable for the purpose intended rather than permit some absurd outcome. The application of the golden rule is at the discretion of the court. It may be used in preference to the literal rule. Where the Courts decide that public policy requires an interpretation beyond the literal interpretation of the words, the golden rule may ensure effect is given to public policy. In public law cases the golden rule is frequently used to understand the nature of the legislation.

(iii) The Mischief Rule

The mischief rule, otherwise referred to as the rule in *Heydon's Case*[71] allows the Courts to examine the law before the statute was made in order to ascertain the nature of the mischief which the statute was intended to remedy. The mischief rule allows the Courts some discretion in finding the construction of the statute that best applies to the facts of the case. In public law cases the mischief rule provides the Courts with the means to look behind the policy and objectives of the legislation.

(iv) The Ejusdem Generis Rule

In applying the rules of interpretation the court may read the statute as a whole to understand the overall context of the law. Normally the Courts give attention to the *ejusdem generis* rule, meaning that general words which follow particular words are limited in meaning to those of the particular words. The Courts may follow certain presumptions when interpreting a statute. Property rights or private rights are not implicitly interfered with unless there are very clear words. The individual's liberty is presumed not to be interfered with unless Parliament has provided clear words. Parliament is assumed not to have altered the common law unless the statute expressly makes this clear. There are also presumptions that for a criminal offence there must be proof of the requisite intention or guilty mind before the accused may be convicted. Statutes are generally presumed not to have retrospective effect. The Courts presume that crimes are not to be created by Parliament retrospectively because it would be oppressive or abhorrent to do so.[72]

---

[71] (1584) 3 Co. Rep. 7a.
[72] *R v Secretary of State for the Home Department Ex p. Leech* [1994] Q.B. 198; [1993] 4 All E.R. 539 CA (Civ Div) upholding the citizen's right to the free flow of communication between a solicitor and client.

(v) Human rights as an aid to interpretation

3-082 The question of statutory interpretation arises in the context of the Human Rights Act 1998. The point is explained by Sedley J in *R v Broadcasting Complaints Commission, Ex p. Barclay*,[73] that when Courts are considering the Convention and the Human Rights Act 1998 it might be relevant for the court to consider the clear Parliamentary intention. The European Convention on Human Rights might be used as a suitable interpretative guide.

> "Here the respective roles of Hansard and the Convention as aids to construction are likely to be complex and the court will not be assisted by a doctrinal ranking of one source above the other."

Interpreting rights and their compatibility with the Convention provides the Courts with a rich and illuminating jurisprudence that will deepen and enhance the common law.[74]

3-083 Lord Woolf[75] has suggested that a broad and purposive approach should be adopted when considering human rights and noted that this had been the way the Hong Kong Bill of Rights had been interpreted by the Courts. Lord Steyn[76] hoped that the way the Human Rights Act ought to be interpreted reflected "a disciplined approach" to the law. An indication of this discipline is that the Act should not be given retrospective effect.[77] Guidance on interpretation of the European Convention has proved difficult and contentious, especially in the light of the decisions of the Strasbourg based European Court of Human Rights. Section 2 of the Human Rights Act 1998 requires national Courts "to take account" of the case law of the European Court of Human Rights. This is not the same as being required to follow or to be bound by the case law. However, Lord Bingham in *R v Special Adjudicator Ex p. Ullah*[78] made clear that "a national court is under a duty such as imposed by s.2 should not without strong reason dilute or weaken the effect of the Strasbourg case law". This has given rise to some controversy especially when the Strasbourg jurisprudence is hotly debated by politicians in the UK.[79] In practical terms, the *Ullah* decision encourages UK Courts to keep pace with the Strasbourg jurisprudence and this acts as a minimum below which national Courts will not consider compatible with Convention rights under the European Convention of Human Rights.

---

73 (1997) 9 Admin. L.R. 265 at [272C]–[272D].
74 See A. Hutchinson, "Judges and Politics: An essay from Canada" (2004) 24 *Legal Studies* 275. Jeremy Waldron, *Law and Disagreements* (Oxford: Oxford University Press, 1999), pp.88–118. See Richard Stacey, "Democratic jurisprudence and judicial review: Waldron's contribution to political positivism" (2010) *Oxford Journal of Legal Studies* 749. See the discussion about Waldron's views in Mark Tushnet, "How different are Waldron's and Fallon's core cases for and against judicial review?" (2010) *Oxford Journal of legal Studies* 49.
75 *R v Director of Public Prosecutions Ex p. Kebilene* [2000] 2 A.C. 326; [1999] 3 W.L.R. 972 HL. Also see *R. Lambert* [2002] Q.B. 1112; [2001] 2 W.L.R. 211 CA.
76 [2000] 2 A.C. 326 at [371G].
77 *R v Secretary of State for the Environment Ex p. Challenger* [2001] Env. L.R. 12; [2000] H.R.L.R. 630 QBD.
78 *R v Special Adjudicator Ex p. Ullah* [2004] UKHL 26; [2004] 2 A.C. 323.
79 *Hirst v United Kingdom (No.2)* (2005) 42 E.H.R.R. 849 on the rights of prisoners to vote at elections.

Equally, national Courts may decide that the Strasbourg case law does not take account of the UK's position or has misunderstood the position in the UK. Increasingly UK Courts have found Convention rights to be part of domestic rights open to interpretation. In *Ambrose*,[80] Lord Kerr argued that the UK Courts are able to interpret rights and are able to exercise their own discretion even in areas where the Strasbourg Courts have not made any decision. Judicial opinion may differ on the question of interpretation as some judges may regard themselves bound by Strasbourg decisions.[81]

Adopting the principles[82] of *Pepper v Hart* it is important to remember that the use of *Hansard* is available in three circumstances set out by Lord Browne-Wilkinson as follows:

- the legislation is ambiguous, obscure or leads to an absurdity;

- the material relied upon consists of one or more statements by a minister or other promoter of the bill together with such other Parliamentary material as is necessary to understand such statements and their effect; and

- the statements relied upon are clear.

(vi) "Constitutional statutes" and their interpretation

Judicial interpretation of legislation has been fast developing especially in the recognition of the sovereignty of Parliament but also in recognising that there may be a number of "constitutional statutes" that should be accorded special significance. What is a "constitutional statute" and what significance might be accorded to such a statute? Lady Hale explained in the HS2 decision that in the absence of a written constitution, the UK had a number of "constitutional instruments":

> "They include Magna Carta, the Petition of Rights 1628, the Bill of Rights and (In Scotland, the Claim of Rights Act 1689, the Act of Settlement 1701 and the Act of Union 1707). The European Communities Act 1972, the Human Rights Act 1998 and the Constitutional Reform Act 2005 may now be added to this list."[83]

It is likely that the various devolution statutes may occupy special status in terms of constitutional fundamentals—especially as the Scotland bill 2015/16 may make Scottish

---

80 *Ambrose* [2011] UKSC 43; [2011] 1 W.L.R. 2435 at [128]–[129].
81 See Lord Rodger in *Secretary of State for the Home Department v AF* [2009] UKHL 28; [2010] 2 A.C. 269 at [98].
82 *Chief Adjudication Officer v Foster* [1993] A.C. 754; [1993] 2 W.L.R. 29.
83 *R (on the application of HS2 Action Alliance Ltd) v Secretary of State for Transport* [2014] UKSC 3; [2014] 1 W.L.R. 324 at [207].

devolution permanent. Such constitutional statutes, it is suggested create "principles as fundamental to the rule of law" that equates with a status that should be respected by the Courts. It is unclear as to how such fundamental principles will shape judicial discretion in the coming year.

European law has been particularly influential, especially in the role of the Courts after the Factortame decision that requires the Courts to give effect to EU law, even when it is incompatible with an Act of the UK Parliament.[84] In *R (Jackson) v Attorney General*[85] while upholding the Hunting Act 2004 as being properly enacted under the Parliament Act 1911 as amended by the Parliament Act 1949, the House of Lords raised the question of whether "the absolute nature" of Parliamentary sovereignty might be out of place in the modern UK. The comments were obiter dicta but gave rise to the suggestion that the Courts might refuse to apply an Act of Parliament that was in breach of fundamental constitutional principles. These observations were linked to the procedures and processes adopted under the Parliament Acts but this is indicative of the status given to the rule of law as fundamental to democratic government.[86] In *Thoburn v Sunderland City Council*[87] Laws LJ, suggested that the European Communities Act 1972 was a "constitutional statute", thus elevating its status to protection by the Courts if there was any attempt at repeal or amendment. Statutes which have the potential to affect the legal relationship between the citizen and the state or enlarge or diminish the scope of fundamental constitutional rights can only be amended or repealed by unambiguous words. The Courts have to balance the interests of democratically elected government accountable to Parliament and the fundamentals of the unwritten constitution. This does not guarantee that the values and moral principles will always be observed. The *HS2 case*[88] endorsed the approach in *Thorburn* and reaffirmed the role of the UK Courts in interpreting constitutional principles. Paul Craig[89] usefully categorises the approach as a form of "statutory construction". Accommodating different national law, EU law and approaches to human rights leaves Parliament to clearly and unambiguously state how any conflict over the interpretation of national law might be resolved. Dawn Oliver offers the suggestion that what is required is some form of comity between institutions and workability- "pragmatic principles established over centuries that the Courts will refrain from questioning the legal validity of Acts passed by the UK Parliament and that Members of the two Houses will respect the Courts and their decisions and will not undermine them and the rule of law".[90]

---

84 (C-213/89) EU:C:1990:257; [1990] 3 C.M.L.R. 1. *R v Secretary of State for Transport ex parte Factortame Ltd (No.2)* [1991] 1 A.C. 603; [1990] 3 W.L.R. 818 HL.
85 *R (Jackson) v Attorney General* [2005] EWCA Civ 126; [2005] Q.B. 579.
86 The debate on the 42 detention period in 2009/10 is a good example.
87 *Thoburn v Sunderland City Council* [2002] EWHC 195 (Admin); [2003] Q.B. 151.
88 R (on the application of HS2 Action Alliance Ltd.,) v Secretary of State for Transport [2014] UKSC 3; [2014] 1 W.L.R. 324.
89 Paul Craig, "Britain in Europe" in J. Jowell, D. Oliver and C. O'Cinneide (eds), *The Changing Constitution*, 8th edn (Oxford: Oxford University Press, 2015), p.121.
90 Dawn Oliver, "Parliament and the Courts" in A. Horne, G. Drewry and D. Oliver (eds), *Parliament and the Law* (Oxford: Hart, 2013), pp.309–37, 321.

The House of Lords Constitution Committee has suggested that a bill should be provided with a written statement why it may be of constitutional significance and the justification for its introduction.[91] This would provide clarity in how such statutes should be interpreted.

As already mentioned there is no hard and fast rule as to the rule of interpretation or presumption[92] the Courts may wish to follow. Courts exercise a discretion according to the context of the law and the facts of the case. Statutory interpretation is aided in the way the statute is drafted. The explanatory notes provided with Acts of Parliament also help to frame the main issues for debate and discussion. Finally, there are schedules to many modern Acts. There is an increasing tendency to use the schedules to contain more detail than is possible in the main part of the Act. This is to avoid the main part of the Act becoming unduly cluttered. This has the disadvantage that often reference must be made to the schedules of the Act to understand the main content of each of the sections.

3-088

F: The Deregulation Agenda

The acknowledged technical complexity of the law and the growth in legislation has seen a trend in favour of deregulation where it is shown that regulation may be unnecessary. Attempts to simplify legislation began with procedures first introduced under the Deregulation and Contracting Out Act 1994. This allowed for ministerial order by affirmative resolution to amend or repeal existing primary legislation.

3-089

There is a Better Regulation Framework (BRF) allowing each department to assess the nest cost to business and this assessment is validated by the Regulatory Policy Committee (RPC). The principle of "one in one out" applies to departments in an attempt to "cap" regulatory systems that may have simply increased burdens over a period of time.

3-090

The Regulatory Reform Act 2001 extends the powers of ministers under the 1984 Act with broad amending powers to primary legislation that can be introduced by order. The requirements are that the primary legislation is amended to reduce new burdens or increase an existing burden. The remit of the 2001 Act is sufficiently wide as to extend the powers available to ministers to include any person "in the carrying on of any activity". The width of the power extends to public bodies, charities and businesses. The use of the order procedure is intended to speed up the process of change and facilitate a more efficient use of departmental resources. This has implications for the work of the various committees of the House. The 2001 Act has been supplemented by the Legislative Reform Act 2006 allowing a Legislative Reform Order to reduce regulatory burdens and where necessary amend primary legislation. This is

3-091

---

91 House of Lords Constitution Committee, *The Process of Constitutional Change*, 15th Report, HL 177.
92 See *R v Secretary of State for the Environment, Transport and the Regions Ex p. Spath Holme* [2001] 2 A.C. 349; [2001] 2 W.L.R. 15 HL.

controversial because it contains a Henry VIII clause allowing secondary legislation to amend primary legislation. Equally controversial is the Public Bodies Act 2011 that empowered ministers, in the interests of savings to "cull" the number of public bodies or move their regulatory functions to the main government department. This eventually resulted in annual savings of £900 million, less than anticipated. The outcome did not live up to expectation as many public bodies survived in different forms and the public Administration Select Committee has been highly critical of the consistency of approach taken.[93]

Debate and scrutiny

3-092 Parliament's role is not confined to the passage of legislation. It performs a number of other functions—it informs, debates, scrutinises and approves. It is widely accepted that as the Commons has limited influence over the substance of legislation (since most governments can almost always ensure that their legislation becomes law), these other functions may be of questionable significance. Even though a government with a large working majority will nearly always ensure that its legislation is passed, the House of Commons provides, through its procedures and processes, legitimation for legislation. Debates, votes and censure are the life-blood of party politics and the House of Commons provides the opposition with a forum to censure the Government of the day. Opposition MPs may introduce bills, ask questions, introduce amendments, table motions and attend as members of select committees to oversee the activities of government departments.

3-093 Parliamentary select committees have existed for some time and have been appointed by both Houses of Parliament. The development of select committees has been piece-meal. The most prestigious is the House of Commons Public Accounts Committee (PAC) established in 1861 to ensure the financial scrutiny of government activities, and uniquely placed among the other select committees because the Comptroller and Auditor General may give evidence to this Committee, prepare reports and assist the Committee in its work. Once the Auditor General makes a report, there is an opportunity for the PAC to respond in the form of a report followed by the Treasury, on behalf of the Government department, setting out in a Treasury minute its own findings. Parliamentary scrutiny of government finance is a specialised area of activity, and one that emphasises Parliament's authority to approve expenditure. Public finance is examined in detail in Ch.12.

3-094 Since 1979 "new House of Commons select committees" were introduced in a reform of existing committee procedures intended to scrutinise the departments of government, covering all aspects of the departments' roles and adopting investigative techniques as a means of control based on inquisitorial techniques of oral and written evidence. Their main form of scrutiny is fact finding and they may make *recommendations* rather than exercise decision-making functions. The range of committees varies from the Commons to the Lords. Standing Orders

---

93 Public Administration Select Committee, *Who's Accountable? Relationships between Government and Arm's Length Bodies*, HC 110 (2014–15), para.78.

apply to various permanent committees of the House of Commons limited to the duration of the Parliament. Since 2010 there have been elected Chairs of Commons committees, rather than Chairs appointed by the Whips. Since 2003 committee Chairs were paid an additional salary on top of their House of Commons salary. The Liaison Committee made up of the Chairs of the various select committees has a pivotal role in keeping under review the working of the select committee system as a whole.[94] From July 2002, the Prime Minister agreed to appear before this committee, composed of the Chairs of the other select committees, and answer questions. The Liaison Committee offers form of regular review of select committees that is an ongoing process. The House of Lords committees are appointed on a sessional basis but often have continuous membership to ensure continuity beyond each session. It is possible for there to be joint membership of committees such as the Banking Standards Commission appointed in 2012 in the aftermath of banking scandals.

3-095
The number of select committees may change over time and are regulated by standing order. There is a departmental select committee for each government department that monitors policy, spending and administration. Normally each departmental committee has a minimum of 11 members. The government has usually 60 days to reply to their findings. The PAC and the Environmental Audit Committee have cross-departmental boundaries. There is a Backbench Business Committee that may schedule business and also may use Westminster Hall for non-government business.

3-096
The Liaison Committee has set out the aims and objectives of select committees including ten core tasks that include examining, strategy, policy, expenditure and performance, draft bills, delegated legislation, post-legislative scrutiny, European scrutiny, appointments, support for the House of Commons including Westminster Hall debates and public engagement.[95]

3-097
Technically, a select committee has power "to send for persons, papers and records", but this power is subject to practical restraints. The private citizen may choose to claim his right to silence, especially if there is a possibility of criminal proceedings pending. Although attendance may be made compulsory, replies to questions are largely left to the citizen's discretion.

3-098
In the case of civil servants, negotiation is required between the minister responsible for the department and the committee, if a civil servant is to be allowed to give evidence. Questions asked of civil servants by the committee are constrained by the embargo ministers may place on civil servants over matters of confidentiality, policy questions or the individual conduct of an official. The attendance of a particular civil servant, even though requested by the committee, is ultimately decided by ministers. In the *Westland* affair,[96] which raised issues relating to the leaking of a confidential letter of the Solicitor General, the Defence Committee was refused the

---

94 Examples of recent reports include: Liaison Committee, First Report (1999–2000, HC 300; 1999–2000 HC 748; and 2000–2001, HC 321).
95 Liaison Committee, Select Committee, *Effectiveness, Resources and Powers*, HC (2012–13), 697.
96 Michael Heseltine, then Secretary of State for Defence resigned over his allegation that he had been excluded from various Cabinet committees. See *The Observer*, 12 January 1986. Also see Marshall [1986] P.L. 184. Discussion of the affair may be found in the Defence Select Committee (1985–86, HC 519); Cm.9916 (1986) and Cm.9841 (1986).

attendance of five civil servants. The Westland company supplied helicopters to the Ministry of Defence and required re-organisation in the light of new market conditions. Rival financial packages from US and European companies caused intense debate within the Government and the Cabinet. The leaking of the confidential letter of the Solicitor General involved certain civil servants, allegedly acting under the direction of a Cabinet minister.[97]

3-099
Since then directions issued to civil servants, reminding them of their duty of loyalty to ministers and the government of the day, have raised doubts about the ability of select committees to penetrate the relationship between civil servants and ministers. In strict constitutional theory, this relationship supports the doctrine of ministerial responsibility whereby ministers, and not civil servants, are accountable directly to Parliament. *The Code of Practice on Access to Government Information* (1997) provides some guidance on when information may be withheld from select committees that would harm national security or defence or where information is provided in confidence. In 1998 the Foreign Affairs Select Committee was able to require the Government to debate its refusal to supply information on arms to Sierra Leone. In a rare example of its kind the Government conceded the release of confidential information but was able to defeat a motion of criticism over the government's conditions for the release of information.[98]

3-100
In addition to the new select committees there are a plethora of other committees of the House of Commons dealing with a variety of matters such as the Committee of Privileges, and the Select Committee on the Parliamentary Commissioner. In the House of Lords there are five major Lord select committees: the European Union Committee; the Science and Technology Committee; the Communications Committee; the Constitution Committee; and the Economic Affairs Committee.

3-101
The assessment of the impact of select committees on government behaviour is difficult and is considered in further detail in Ch.11. On the one hand, in favour of their role there is a fact-finding and information contribution, which undoubtedly exists, because of the select committee system. We know more and have more information about government as a result. On the other hand, there is a lack of success in bringing measurable differences in the way that government is conducted. Ministers and civil servants may, through careful briefing, actually second guess the committee's work. Often committees are *ex post facto* inquiries and they depend on the enthusiasm and skill of the individual MPs for their success. A lot may depend in the tenacity of the chairman and his skill in avoiding the division of opinion in the committee along party political lines. This system may be too random and haphazard to be relied upon. Ultimately political issues may intervene in the work of the select committees, as when back bench MPs attempt to use a select committee's findings in debates in the House of Commons to criticise or defend government policy. There is the added concern that strengthening select committees moves the locus of power away from the House of Commons to back-room committees. Reassurance on this point has come from the televising of proceedings of select committee hearings, which has done much to publicise their work and gain recognition for their important role. Finally, it may be conceded that select committees in this country look less

---

97 *Memorandum of Guidance for Officials Appearing before Select Committees*, Cm.78 (1987).
98 *Hansard*, HC Vol.315, col.865–959 (7 July 1998).

impressive than the US Congressional committees with which they are commonly compared. This seems an unfair comparison given the difference in the constitutional role of each.

Select committees have a further function, that is they provide a scrutiny over the financial affairs of the government. We have already discussed the PAC, but the role of each select committee includes within its remit scrutiny of departmental expenditures. Flegmann[99] and others have noted that only limited interest has been shown in the select committees' development of financial scrutiny over departments.

Parliamentary debate is often party political and adversarial in style whereas select committees are intended to be bi-partisan and inquisitorial. Craig observes[100]:

> "Select committees run counter to both of these tenets: they seek to strengthen the power of Parliament as against the executive, and to proceed by a more non-partisan approach."

The essence of committees, however, is that they are "committees of the whole House". Any weakening of that fundamental link might leave committees untrusted as an unrepresentative intrusion into government decision-taking and even a usurpation of parliamentary control. The tightrope existence between committees as "independent" scrutineers of government activities, and the application of party politics is difficult to explain. The further committees expand their independent scrutiny, the more tension may arise between their role and the government of the day. This may expose the constitutional limitations which surround their role.

G: Parliament—Fulfilling Public Expectations?

As noted above, modernisation of the House of Commons is a recurring theme of the past fifty years. Some landmarks of reform include the Hansard Society Commission Report *Making the Law* in 1993 is influential. The Hansard Society Report on *Strengthening Parliament* also calls for a greater role for select committees. The Liaison Committee[101] in 1999 made recommendations as to the composition and role of select committees. The Modernisation Committee in its report[102] of 12 February 2002 followed through with recommendations for

---

99 V. Flegman, "The Public Accounts Committee; A Successful Select Committee?", XXXIII Parliamentary Affairs (1980).
100 P. P. Craig, *Administrative Law*, 2nd edn (London: Sweet & Maxwell, 1989), pp.68–69.
101 (1999–2000, HC 300). For response see Cm.4737.
102 (2001–2002, HC 224-I and II).

reform. The use of Westminster Hall for debates and the use of more socially acceptable hours for sittings of the Commons and the Lords. The aim is to make Parliament more effective as well as to modernise its timetable.[103]

3-106 Parliamentary reform has followed two strands. The first is improving the role of select committees and the second is organising the activities of the Commons more efficiently through the timetabling of bills and the regulation of sitting times. The Hansard Commission Report, *Making the Law* in 1993 provided the basis for ideas for reform in the modernisation of the legislative process. Some ideas were readily accepted, such as in 1997 the use of explanatory notes to bills to replace the sketchy memorandum used previously. Also adopted is the use of special standing committees on bills and the adoption of the programming of bills has also proved influential.

3-107 Lord Norton has assessed how Parliament has possibly acquired a new assertiveness over government and this has great potential to improve the reputation of parliament.[104] This assessment is supported by the operation and use of pre- and post-legislative scrutiny but also because of the work of the select committees their work is being taken seriously by the government with importance in the overall scrutiny of legislation.[105]

Parliament and Public Engagement

3-108 Since 2011, the House of Commons has adopted proposals for a system of e-petitions including debates that are triggered by 100,000 signatures. The system is effective in gaining voter participation in the process. The majority of e-petitions fall under 1,000 signatures (97.7 per cent). By July 2013, there had been 21 petitions that reached 100,000 signatures. The importance of e-petitions is that the public are able to engage with Parliament and participate in the parliamentary process beyond writing to their MP or attending debates. There is also a Parliament TV service that broadcasts many of the main debates.[106] There is an active discussion on how best the public may engage with Parliament and improve the scrutiny of government through more direct access to information.[107]

Parliament, the Crown and prerogative

3-109 In a constitutional sense the Government's law-making powers are exercised by the Crown in Parliament. Today, legislation in its various forms is the most common source of the

---

103 Research Paper 02/41, *Modernisation of the House of Commons: Sitting Hours* (27 June 2002).
104 Philip Norton, " Parliament: A New Assertiveness" in J. Jowell, D. Oliver and C. O'Cinneide (eds), *The Changing Constitution*, 8th edn (Oxford: Oxford University Press, 2015), pp.171–93.
105 M. Benton and M. Russell, *Selective Influence: The Policy Impact of House of Commons Select Committees* (London: Constitution Unit, 2011).
106 House of Commons Library, *e-Petitions*, Briefing Paper No.064520 (20 October 2015).
107 House of Commons Liaison Committee, *Building public engagement: Options for developing select committee outreach. First Special Report of Session*, HC 470 (*2015–16*).

Government's legal powers. The powers of government may also exist by virtue of custom and derived from the common law. These provide the sources for the Crown's discretionary powers vested in the government of the day and known as the royal prerogative.

3-110

This is an area of law that is fast changing as statutory powers are gradually being used to replace prerogatives. This shift is ongoing as increasingly the prerogative is falling into disuses. Civil servants are employed by contract and not under the prerogative. The Fixed-Term Parliaments Act 2011 has replaced the prerogative surrounding the dissolution of government and the coalition government to 2010 is evidence of the Act working. Treaty making powers are subject to Parliamentary approval under the Constitutional Reform and Governance Act 2010.The use of military force has been put under intense public and parliamentary scrutiny that leaves the Government of the day with a working presumption that Parliament should be consulted, especially if war is to be undertaken.[108]

3-111

The significance of the royal prerogative as a source of governmental power is examined in detail in Ch.5 in the discussion of the powers and practices of government. It is sufficient here to mention how Parliament's legislative authority was established through limiting, by law, the authority of the Crown, but maintaining the continuity of the royal prerogative.

3-112

Munro[109] has defined the royal prerogative as "those attributes peculiar to the Crown which are derived from common law, not statute, and which still survive". In origin they appear based on custom and in the recognition given to them by the common law. The prerogative had an external use in waging war, but also a domestic application in royal patronage. Attempts to extend their scope in the fourteenth and fifteenth centuries were largely successful, even if resisted. A variety of royal powers were appended to the use of the prerogative, including the controversial one of levying different forms of taxation. Such powers were occasionally upheld by the Courts but the matter was never finally settled until the Bill of Rights 1688. By abolishing a number of prerogatives and amending others, the Crown's powers were curtailed but at the same time maintained.

3-113

Parliamentary control once asserted has remained intact; but as Munro[110] observes:

> "It is not surprising that modern governments have found it useful to retain such broad discretionary powers to act, which enable action to be taken without the necessity of prior parliamentary approval."

3-114

Gap-filling and residual powers are apt descriptions of how the prerogative may be perceived by modern government. Parliament moreover has condoned the use of the prerogative in this way and has sometimes replaced prerogative powers with statute.

3-115

Parliament has the power to regulate succession to the Throne as it thinks fit. Title to the Throne is determined under the Act of Settlement 1700 upholding the right of primogeni-

---

108 House of Lords Constitution Committee, *Waging War: Parliament's role and responsibility Follow up*, HL Paper 51 (2006–07), and HL Paper 236.
109 *See* C. R. Munro, *Studies in Constitutional Law*, 2nd edn (Oxford: Oxford University Press, 1999), p.256.
110 Munro, *Studies in Constitutional Law*, p.271.

ture; males are preferred over females. The right of succession to the Crown is restricted to Protestants. The Act of Settlement disqualifies Roman Catholics and those who marry Roman Catholics. The Sovereign must swear to uphold allegiance and maintain the Churches of England and Scotland. Proposals to amend the Act of Settlement and remove the discriminatory nature of the provisions were defeated in December 1999. The government is currently reviewing the Act of Settlement and it is likely that before long there will be changes proposed to the Act. There are also proposals to reform the law of treason. The Treason Felony Act 1848 provides a very broad definition that covers writing or overt acts that envisage or intend to deprive or depose the Queen from the throne. The punishment for treason was, until s.36 of the Crime and Disorder Act 1998, the death penalty. The 1998 Act has abolished the death penalty under s.1 of the Treason Act 1814 and made conviction for treason subject to life imprisonment.

3–116 Parliament has regulated succession to the Throne, as in 1936 under His Majesty's Declaration of Abdication Act 1936 permitting Edward VIII's brother to become King George VI. Parliament has also made special provision under the Regency Acts 1937–53 for the Sovereign's minority, incapacity or absence from the Realm. In recent years, public controversy has surrounded the role of the Monarchy. In common with almost all aspects of public life there are pressures to modernise the Monarchy and make it more accountable. The provision by Parliament of a Civil List of public money for the upkeep of the Royal Family has attracted attention to the role and function of the modern Monarchy. The Civil List Act 1952 provided that a sum of money was annually voted to the Monarch. This sum was amended by the Civil List Act 1972 increasing the sum allocated and requiring an annual report from the Royal Trustees on the current state of the royal finances. The Civil List Act 1975 built into the sum allocated a Treasury power to increase the sum to take account of inflation. In 1991 the Government agreed a ten-year arrangement whereby an annual sum for the Civil List, approximately £8 million, would be paid from the Consolidated Fund. The Sovereign Grant Act 2011 introduced a new financial system for the monarchy based on a formula linked to obligations on the Royal Household to keep proper accounts and are subject to annual audit by the Comptroller and Auditor General. The accounts are then submitted to Parliament. The Sovereign Grant is currently around £31 million but it may be adjusted to take account of the formula set by the legislation. Security measures for the protection of the Royal Family are separately accounted for and are not included in the Sovereign Grant.

3–117 The Queen's personal wealth and income is distinguished from official income and expenditure. Estimates of the Queen's personal wealth appear unreliable as private wealth is not officially disclosed to the public. Since 1992 the Queen undertook responsibility to make provision for certain members of the Royal Family out of her private wealth. With effect from 1993 the Queen undertook to pay income tax on her private income. This is a voluntary agreement as the Crown is not liable to pay taxes unless Parliament has expressly so provided. In 1999 the decommissioning of the Royal Yacht saved £12 million and further substantial savings are expected in travel costs. In 2002, the year of the Golden Jubilee, more detailed accounts of royal finances were made public. The death of the Queen Mother in

2002 encountered no taxation being payable on the passing of wealth from one sovereign to another within the Royal Family. The government contributes to the up keep of royal palaces and building with a grant of nearly £35 million. The popularity of the Monarchy endures with periods of criticism followed by intense popular acclaim. The future of the Monarchy is vested in the fulfilment of the function of Head of State and in relations with the Commonwealth.[111] How far the fickle nature of public opinion may be relied upon to maintain the existing status quo is anyone's guess but the personal standing of the current Monarch is high in public support and affection.

The Supreme Court in *R (Evans) v Attorney General*[112] dismissed an appeal against a Court of Appeal decision that the Attorney General was not entitled to issue a certificate under s.53 of the Freedom of Information Act 2000 overruling a decision made by the Upper Tribunal that communications between government departments and the Prince of Wales should be disclosed. This is a landmark decision supporting transparency and visibility in respect of a senior member of the Royal Family and ministers. It also represents an important role for the Courts in the oversight of the government.

H: The House of Lords

Historical developments outlined in the previous chapter explain how relations between the Commons and Lords were acrimonious. Even in the late-nineteenth century, the Lords attempted to assert its authority against the will of the elected and newly enfranchised House of Commons. The right to veto Money Bills was the main issue in 1860 when a measure for the repeal of paper duty was accepted in the Commons, but rejected by the Lords. Gladstone, as Chancellor of the Exchequer, had embarked on a major re-organisation of taxes, simplifying and clarifying their collection. According to Gladstone's Political Memorandum (26 May 1860), rejection by the Lords[113]:

> "amounted to the establishment of a revising power over the House of Commons in its most vital function long declared exclusively its own, and to a divided responsibility in fixing the revenue and charge of the country for the year."

The outcome of the Lords' rejection was for the Commons to pass a resolution containing the assertion of principle, namely that:

---

111 A. Marr, *Ruling Britannica* (London: Michael Joseph, 1995).
112 [2015] UKSC 21; [2015] A.C. 1787.
113 Quoted and discussed in John Morley, *Life of William Ewart Gladstone* (London: Macmillan, 1903), Vol.II, p.33.

> "in its own hands [the House of Commons] had the power to remit and impose taxes and that the right to frame Bills of supply in its own measure, manner and time is a right to be kept inviolable."

3-121 The solution came in the form of presenting a single bill to the Lords containing the various financial proposals, and thereby forcing the Lords to accept or reject the whole bill. This procedure did not prevent debate of the content of the bill, but it made rejection difficult.

3-122 The House of Lords opposed Gladstone's Church bill in 1869, but the bill was eventually passed. Irish Home Rule was similarly resisted in 1886 and 1893. Eventually the Commons acted to curtail the powers of the House of Lords by passing the Parliament Acts 1911 and 1949. This was achieved after some resistance from the Lords. In 1909 the Lords rejected the Finance Bill, but agreed to pass it on return of the Liberals after the election. After a second General Election in 1910, the passage of certain bills was achieved only when the Government threatened to swamp the Lords with newly created peers. The Lords finally agreed to pass the Parliament bill curtailing their powers.[114]

3-123 Both Parliament Acts are relevant to the powers of the House of Lords today. The 1911 Act achieved three major alterations in the law. The Lords' powers to veto or delay Money Bills were abolished. In the case of other public Bills, the Lords' absolute veto was abolished, and a power to delay legislation for two years was substituted. Finally, the life of Parliament was reduced from seven to five years.

3-124 The two-year period of delay still permitted the Lords an influence over the political policy of the government of the day. In certain circumstances this might become crucial and amount to an effective veto if the delay was timed to coincide with the period before a General Election.

3-125 Further reforms of the Lords were considered and resulted in the Parliament Act 1949. The results of the 1949 legislation may be outlined as follows. Together, the Parliament Acts 1911 and 1949, provide that bills may receive the Royal Assent if approved only by the Commons. This may occur either if the Lords fail within one month to pass a bill which has passed the Commons and been endorsed by the Speaker as a Money Bill, or where the Lords refuse in two successive sessions to pass a public bill other than a bill certified as a Money Bill. This last situation includes a bill to extend the maximum duration of Parliament beyond five years which has been passed by the Commons in those two sessions, provided that one year has elapsed between the date of the bill's second reading in the Commons, in the first of those sessions, and the date of its third reading in that House, in the second of those sessions. In many instances the Speaker's rulings on applying the Parliament Acts is important.

3-126 The definition of a Money Bill, as contained in the Acts (s.1 of the 1911 Act, as amended by the 1949 Act), and by the National Loans Act 1968, refers to a public bill which the Speaker certifies, and covers:

---

114 House of Commons Library Standard Note, *The Parliament Acts*, SN/PC/00675 (24 February 2014).

> "the important, repeal, remission, alteration or regulation of taxation; the imposition of charges on the Consolidated Fund or the National Loans Fund or on money provided by Parliament for the payment of debt or other financial purposes or the variation or repeal of such charges, supply, the appropriation, receipt custody, issue or audit of public accounts or the raising or guarantee or repayment of loans"."

A strict interpretation applies and rarely are certificates issued, even the Finance Bill presented annually does not often meet the above criteria.

The restrictions set out above on the Lords' powers seldom apply in practice and thus, the basic principle that "the Crown demands money, the Commons grant it, and the Lords assent to the grant" remains true today. The fact that the Speaker's certificate, once issued, is conclusive proof of the status of a bill, means that it may not be questioned in any court of law. The poll tax legislation, the Local Government Finance Bill 1988, did not qualify as a Money Bill. It was debated and amended in the Lords but passed after the Government defeated an amendment that the bill should take account of poll tax payers' incomes.

In fact, few bills have been introduced invoking the 1911 Act procedure. The examples often cited include the Government of Ireland Act 1914, the Welsh Church Act 1914 and the Parliament Act 1949 itself.

The War Crimes Act 1991 is also an example. In 1990–91 the War Crimes bill, retrospectively authorising prosecutions in Britain in respect of war crimes in Germany or German-occupied territory during the Second World War, resulted in sufficient controversy for the Government to invoke the Parliament Acts. The bill was passed after being twice defeated in the Lords but agreed in the Commons on a free vote. This example clearly illustrates the use of the Parliament Acts to ensure the ultimate authority of the Commons over the Lords. The European Elections Act 1999 and the Sexual Offences (Amendment) Act 2000 were passed following the procedure. The controversial Hunting Act 2004 was also enacted under the 1911 Act procedure.

Ironically there is a dispute over the question of whether the 1911 Act procedure was capable of allowing the change introduced by the 1949 Act. The principle objection to using the 1911 Act is that a power conferred for one purpose should not be used for another purpose. Given the fact that the 1949 Act consolidated and amended the 1911 Act this may be seen as a step in the direction originally taken by the 1911 Act and therefore the 1949 Act is consistent with the 1911 Act. In *R (Jackson) v Attorney General*[115] while upholding the Hunting Act 2004 as being properly enacted under the Parliament Act 1911 as amended by the Parliament Act 1949, the House of Lords confirmed that the Courts had jurisdiction to review the matter and affirmed that Parliament had intended to reform the powers of the House of Lords and restrict and limit their powers to amendment and delay rather than the power to veto. The 1911 Act permitted the House of Commons and the Queen to make laws irrespective of the House of Lords consent.

---

115   *R (Jackson) v Attorney General* [2005] EWCA Civ 126; [2005] Q.B. 579.

I: The Salisbury Convention: The House of Commons and House of Lords at work

3-132 Legislative conflict between both Houses of Parliament is not always resolved through the Parliament Acts. There is a Salisbury-Addison convention that means that the House of Lords should give a second reading to Government Bills which are linked to the Government's manifesto commitments. The scope and remit of the convention is the subject of some debate. In 2006, the Joint Committee on Conventions[116] was established and made recommendations on the working of the Salisbury convention. The Joint Committee noted that the convention had changed since 1999 and reform of the House of Lords that resulted in the end of the Conservative Party's majority over the other parties. There are some doubts as to what a "manifesto bill" is and the coverage of the Convention over bills that have constitutional significance. This is a critical question in terms of how the Lords are expected to behave over any election promise to abolish the Human Rights Act 1998 or leave the EU.[117] The value of the Convention may come in for some consideration in the current Parliament as the major political parties might contest its application and remit in an era of constitutional change such as the devolution settlement in Scotland.

3-133 Relations between the House of Commons and the House of Lords have become strained. On 26 October 2015 the House of Lords twice amended a motion, so as to decline to consider a statutory instrument, that would have implemented the Government's policy on tax credits. This has brought to the fore the question of the role of the House of Lords and perhaps its reform. The Government has set up a rapid review of the relationship between the two Houses chaired by a former Leader of the House of Lords, Lord Strathclyde.[118] The Strathclyde Review reported on 17 December 2015 and considered the understandings between the House of Lords and House of Commons. In addition to the Salisbury Convention where bills implementing manifesto commitments are not opposed in the House of Lords, there are other convention such as:

- the House of Lords does not usually object to secondary legislation;
- the House of Lords respects the financial privileges of the House of Commons; and
- governments should get their business in a "reasonable time".[119]

---

116 *Joint Committee on Conventions, Conventions of the UK Parliament*, HL Paper 265 (2005–6).
117 House of Lords Paper, *The Salisbury-Addison Convention LIF*, 2015/0002.
118 House of Commons Library, *Conventions on the relationship between the Commons and the Lords*, Briefing Paper No.5996 (4 November 2015).
119 House of Commons Library, *Conventions on the relationship between the Commons and the Lords*.

The Strathclyde Review suggested that the convention on statutory instruments was so flexible that it is "barely a convention at all". He recommended that the Lords powers over statutory instruments should be confined to a limited delay; that the Commons should be able to insist that a statutory instrument should be approved after a Lords defeat; that there might be a case for a Commons-only procedure. The implementation of the Strathclyde Review is a matter for debate.

J: Reforming the House of Lords?

Reform of the House of Lords[120] has proved an ongoing issue in contemporary constitutional law. A pattern emerges of a subject that is suddenly becomes important attracting media attention followed by a general period of inactivity. Contemporary issues include the size and composition of the House of Lords, retirement from the House of Lords is now possible under the House of Lords Reform Act 2014 but the appointment of new members remains controversial. The House of Lords defeated the Government on a vote on 26 October 2015 when it withheld agreement to the Government's controversial tax credit regulations. The Strathclyde Review undertook a review of the powers of the House of Lords power to withhold approval of a statutory instrument.[121]

3–134

Before 1999

Reform of the House of Lords proved to be a lengthy "work in progress". Attempts to reform the House of Lords have continued since 1949. Discussion of the aims and objectives of the Lords were included in a White Paper on House of Lords Reform[122] in 1968. The functions performed by the Lords may be summarised as follows:

3–135

- debate and discussion;

- the consideration of legislation including delegated legislation;

- the initiation of public legislation including both Government and Private Members' Bills;

- the revision of public Bills received from the Commons;

---
120 House of Commons Library, *House of Lords Reform*, No.CDP, 2016/0012 (13 January 2016).
121 *The Strathclyde Review: Secondary Legislation and the primacy of the House of Commons* (December 2015).
122 Cmnd.3799 (1968).

- the general scrutiny of Government and of private legislation;

- the work of select committees such as the Select Committee on the Constitution, the European Communities Select Committee and, finally; and

- in its judicial capacity as the Supreme Court of Appeal in domestic matters, excluding the law of the European Community.

3-136 Taken together, such functions contribute to the process of legislation and the general debate about government and its powers. The Lords were the first to allow radio and television to broadcast their debates. Generally, it is accepted that the quality and standard of debate is high. This is attributable partly to the fact that many of their Lordships hold or have held prominent positions in life, and partly to the individual expertise the Lords may bring to the discussion.

3-137 The fact that appointment to the Lords was appointed by patronage leads to the view that it does not have equal political legitimacy to the Commons. The limited role of revising legislation is one reason why the Lords is subservient to the Commons. Ultimately the Commons may overrule the Lords. Norton[123] offers the analysis that many of Parliament's functions may be formulated within six categories:

- legislative scrutiny;

- latent legitimisation;

- scrutiny and influence;

- tension release;

- support mobilisation; and

- providing the personnel of government.

Taking each of the six categories, their relevance to the House of Lords may be seen as follows.

3-138 Legislative scrutiny includes similar procedures in the Lords as in the Commons for the reading of bills, debate and scrutiny. It is said that the less crowded political agenda and the absence of party political divisions favours a more constructive role for the Lords in terms of scrutiny of the Executive, because of the greater influence of ideas and learned opinion from

---

123 P. Norton (ed), *Parliament in the 1980s* (Oxford: Oxford University Press, 1985). Also see D. R. Shell, "The House of Lords and the Thatcher Government", *Parliamentary Affairs* XXXVIII, pp.16–32; and Janet Morgan, *The House of Lords and the Labour Government 1964–1970* (Oxford: Clarendon, 1975).

eminent experts in their field. All this may seem to add up to a "constitutional safeguard" provided by the Lords.

Latent legitimisation is of more doubtful relevance to the Lords. The fact that it meets regularly and without interruption may provide a source of legitimacy; but the Commons undoubtedly is seen to offer legitimacy to government because it has claims to electoral support. In recent years the Lords has adopted a robust approach to the policies of the government of the day.

3–139

In addition to bills introduced into the Lords, the opportunity for revision comes in the form of amendments to bills. One estimate in the 1970s[124] was that:

3–140

> "...the number of amendments made has increased from an average per session of 511 under the 1964–5 Labour administration to 788 per session from 1970–74, 645 per session for 1976–79 and 1,061 per session in 1979–86."

The Lords may be said to fit into Norton's category of scrutiny and influence. In that connection, because the Lords are largely independent of party politics, they may have "a limited tension release function". Particular causes may be debated and pressure groups given a voice which may not be easily accommodated within the agenda of the House of Commons. This does not go so far as to provide "support mobilisation" in Norton's terminology, meaning popular support, because of the Lords' lack of political legitimacy.

3–141

After the House of Lords Act 1999

The new Labour Government in 1997 determined to tackle first the problem of composition. The House of Lords Act 1999 abolished hereditary peers but allowed for 92 to be retained comprising 90 elected from existing hereditary peers. The abolition of the hereditary element was a big step. It abolished the potential in-built Conservative majority and moves the House of Lords to the position of having only life members. The elected hereditary element in the transitional House is as much as has yet been achieved, but the past history of the House as a revising and debating chamber has been retained. It is clear that there is consensus over the House retaining only a revising role. There are no plans to increase its powers or change its function. There is a sense of renewal permeating the work of the revised House of Lords. There is also a growing self-confidence to speak out and criticise Government Bills and introduce amendments both on technical matters and on substantive points.

3–142

In March 1999 a Royal Commission[125] under the chairmanship of Lord Wakeham was set up with limited terms of reference to recommend reforms. The terms of reference were set in the context of maintaining the existing powers of the Lords as follows:

3–143

---

124 J. Griffith and M. Ryle, *Parliament* (London: Sweet & Maxwell, 1989), pp.490–491.
125 *A House for the Future*, Cm.4534, (January 2000).

> "Having regard to the need to maintain the position of the House of Commons as the pre-eminent chamber of Parliament and taking particular account of the constitutional settlement, including the newly devolved institutions, the impact of the Human Rights Act and developing relations with the EU:
> (a) To consider and make recommendations on the role and functions of a second chamber;
> (b) To make recommendations on the method or combination of methods of composition required to constitute a second chamber fit for that role and those functions;
> (c) To report by 31st December 1999."

3–144 The Wakeham Commission reported in January 2000 and made various proposals about the future of the Lords. Three characteristics were identified for the Lords:

- it should be authoritative, capable of holding the executive to account and scrutinising government;

- it should be sufficiently confident to use its powers and act effectively; and

- ideally it should be representative of British society as a whole.

3–145 The Wakeham Commission recommended lengthy terms of non-renewable membership of up to 15 years, salaries for members, and an independent Commission with the ultimate right to decide which party nominees are suitable for membership. Wakeham also recommended that there should be an elected element of up to 35 per cent of members and the continuation of appointed members. Thus he rejected making a straight choice between elected or appointed members by recommending a compromise. It was suggested that a regional list system might assist in ensuring local representation. The House of Lords at that time consisted of about 750 members including the 15 Law Lords and 26 Lords Spiritual. Wakeham recommended a smaller House composed of up to 550 members.

3–146 The Government published a White Paper on Lords reform.[126] While the main recommendations of the Wakeham Commission were accepted, it is clear that there are serious points of difference between the White Paper and Wakeham. The government appears to favour only 20 per cent elected members, and that the nominees of the party leaders should be put forward in consultation with the Appointments Commission but with the final say to the party leaders. Instead of the 15-year non-renewable terms proposed by Wakeham, the White Paper considers shorter renewable terms of five to ten years. The size of the House is to be capped at 600, and the present 750 will remain for the next ten years or so.

---

126 *The House of Lords—Completing the Reform*, Cm.5291 (November 2000).

3-147 Lords reform is a symptom of the dilemma that faces the constitution under modernisation. Legitimacy is best conferred through elections, and this is a strong argument for having a wholly elected House of Lords. The concern is that such a House might behave along party political lines and mirror the behaviour and activities of the Commons. Successive governments have sought to inhibit the Lords by pointing to its position of weakness—its lack of a satisfactory electoral mandate. Yet, in order to secure a more independent House of Lords, it is necessary to advance appointments through an independent and transparent system. Expertise thus appointed will allow the Lords to fulfil its role of scrutiny and advice separate from the pressure of party politics. This is an argument for preserving the appointed elements to the Lords. A compromise may result in an unsatisfactory outcome.[127] Members who are elected may appear to have a greater mandate than those members appointed because of their expertise. A two-tier House of Lords may gain neither authority nor self-confidence and certainly may never *represent* British society as a whole. Lords reform appears to have become more difficult than the government first realised. The government, sensing the problem of deadlock, has referred Lords reform to a joint committee of both Houses. This may provide a rare opportunity for Parliament to take the initiative. This is reminiscent of difficulties in 1911, 1949 and in the 1960s when all-party agreement was difficult to achieve.

3-148 It may be concluded that the Royal Commission on the Reform of the House of Lords found it difficult to determine a package of reforms that would command sufficient political support. The choices of a wholly elected or partially elected second chamber divides opinion and there is an implicit fear that an elected chamber might become a rival to the Commons. This may polarise political opinion and lead to a stalemate between the two Houses. The current nominated and appointed House has some support but a growing concern is the size of the House of Lords with some 847 members qualified to sit. Taken together with the House of Commons means that the UK has one of the largest Parliaments in the world. Current trends towards expansion of the House of Lords may make it hard for the physical accommodation in the House of Lords to cope with the number of members.

3-149 In 2007, the House of Commons voted for a wholly (80 per cent) elected chamber and this was followed by the House of Lords voting for an appointed chamber! The coalition government made a break through with a House of Lords Reform Bill in 2012. The bill envisaged that there would be a second chamber of 360 directly elected and 90 appointed members along with 12 Bishops and an indefinite number of ministerial members. Elected members, through a system of proportional representation would serve 15-year terms. Elections would be phased over that period with one third of seats put up for election every five years. The electoral system proposed would follow very broadly the system for European parliamentary elections with Great Britain divided up into ten regional constituencies and members elected from party lists. Northern Ireland would follow its own system of single transferable vote from a single constituency. Disappointedly the Government's bill failed after disagreements within the Coalition over more broadly based electoral reforms. The 2012 bill was probably one of the best chances for reform and this missed opportunity leaves reform in the category of "too difficult to handle".

---

127 *House of Lords Reform—the 2001 White Paper*, House of Commons Research Papers 02/002, (8 January 2002).

The Strathclyde Review (December 2015)

3-150 The Strathclyde Review[128] published in December 2015 considers the role of the House of Lords and the relationship between the Houses of Common and Lords.[129] The review arose after the House of Lords on 26 October 2015, passed two separate amendments to the Government's motions to approve statutory instruments to implement their policy on tax credits. The Government expressed concern about the decision of the House of Lords that raised questions about whether the House of Lords had acted within existing convention regarding statutory instruments and financial privilege. Lord Strathclyde's review recommended that the Lords' powers over statutory instruments should be limited to one of delay with the Commons being able to insist on a statutory instrument following a Lords' defeat. Also included in the recommendations was the possibility of a Commons-only procedure for statutory instruments. It is clear that there are profound implications for the future role of the House of Lords. The question of how to take forward reform is difficult as there are surrounding questions about the composition, role and functions of the House of Lords that also coincide with the size of the chamber. The options open to the Government are to consider the use of a Commons-only procedure for statutory instruments, that the Lords powers to consider statutory instruments should be limited to delay only, allowing the Commons to insist on the statutory instrument to be taken forward despite the Lords' defeat of a statutory instrument. There are also concerns about how relations between the Commons and Lords might best be improved.

Composition

3-151 The composition of the House of Lords reflects its historic past. After 1999 four categories of membership exist. First the Church of England, including the 26 Lords Spiritual comprising the Archbishops of Canterbury and York, plus the Bishops of London, Durham and Winchester together with 21 Senior Bishops of the Church of England. Other ecclesiastical groupings may be represented through nomination as Life Peers. The Roman Catholic Archbishop of Westminster is not included and only recently the Chief Rabbi, head of the Jewish faith, has been made a Life Peer. The second category of membership includes 90 elected hereditary peers. The Earl Marshal and Lord Great Chamberlain are retained making in total 92 hereditary peers. Thirdly there are 549 Life Peers appointed under the Life Peerages Act 1958. Since 2000 there is an Appointments Commission as an advisory body to oversee the appointment of peers and may eventually take over from the Prime Minister the function of nominating sufficient crossbench peers to fill vacancies. The trend is in favour of inviting nominations and obtaining greater transparency in the way appointments are made. Fourthly, the Appellate Jurisdiction Act 1876 (now

---

128 Lord Strathclyde, *The Strathclyde Review: Secondary legislation and the primacy of the House of Commons*, CM 9177 (17 December 2015).
129 House of Commons Library, Briefing Paper, *Conventions on the relationship between the Commons and the Lords*, No.5996 (7 January 2016).

repealed) allowed for Lords of Appeal in Ordinary to sit and vote in the House of Lords, even if they resigned or retired. The creation of the Supreme Court means that the House of Lords has ceased to exercise a judicial function and newly appointed Supreme Court judges are not eligible to sit in the House of Lords. This still leaves 20 members of the House of Lords eligible under the 1876 Act to sit and participate in the House of Lords. The House of Lords Reform Act 2014 provides that members of the House of Lords may resign and there is a new procedure for addressing the problem of inactive members that will ensure that at least some minimum attendance is expected. There is also an important restriction on a member of the House of Lords sitting as a member of the European Parliament. Conviction of a serious offence may result in disqualification from membership of the House of Lords. The House of Lords (Expulsion and Suspension) Act 2015 allows for a member of the Lords to be suspended or expelled.

3-152

The political composition of the House of Lords is often a sensitive issue if the government of the day desires to have its legislative programme speedily adopted.

Composition of the House of Lords in January 2016[130]

Party/Group	Life Peers	Hereditary Peers	Bishops (Lords Spiritual)	Total
Bishops	0	0	26	26
Conservative	201	49	0	250
Crossbench	147	31	0	178
Labour	209	4	0	213
Liberal	107	4	0	111
Non-affiliated	25	0	0	25
Others	16	1	0	17
Total	705	89	26	820

Select Committees

An active role for the Lords may be found in the business of the Lords select committees in areas of specialisation such as EC law and practice, where the Lords have established a good reputation for the authority of their reports.

3-153

The use of select committees in the House of Lords is noteworthy in its role as scrutineer of the Executive. Unlike the House of Commons, which has departmental select committees, the Lords has developed only three types of committee. Before 1970, these consisted of investigative committees on general matters, committees on public Bills, and public committees. Investigative committees covered a wide range of public affairs, but the practice of setting up such committees has gradually fallen into disuse.

3-154

Since 1970, the role of specific committees identified with particular bills was rarely used and there is a tendency to make use of investigative committees of the old style to cover a variety

3-155

---

130 House of Lords Library Note, *The Size of the House of Lords*, LLN 2016/006 (29 January 2016).

3-156

of ad hoc matters; examples include committees on unemployment (1979–82), overseas trade (1984–85), and on Private Members' Bills. These illustrate the variety and type of activities which come under scrutiny. In fact, life has been rekindled into the use of investigative committees as a form which adds stature to the Lords. Especially important in the public's perception of the House of Lords at work are the televised hearings of such committees.

In December 1972, the Lords set up an investigation into how best to carry out scrutiny of EC legislation. The result was the European Communities Committee, first appointed in 1974, and since then appointed every session. In addition, a number of sub-committees have been appointed to carry out a review in specialist areas of activity connected with the work of the main committee. The authority of the European Select Committee has been established, and it has been described as performing "an essential role" and making "a unique contribution to the process of European scrutiny by national Parliaments". Finally, the setting up of the Lords Select Committee on the Constitution appears a timely moment to take stock of current developments in constitutional matters in the UK. It is precisely this sort of role that the Lords excels in, standing back from party political in-fighting to take a broader look at developments to see the larger picture. The Constitution Unit at University College, London have undertaken research on the findings of the Constitution select committee and this provides a useful set of constitutional standards.[131]

K: Parliamentary Privileges

The nature of Privileges

3-157

In considering the function and role of Parliament, account must be taken of the individual Members of Parliament. The medieval history of the House of Commons and House of Lords is reflected in the retention of ancient privileges. As the title "the High Court of Parliament" reminds us, laws and customs of Parliament developed historically. Parliament was and still is a court. As the highest court in the land many of Parliament's procedures remain from its historical origins. Hood Phillips links parliamentary privileges with the royal prerogative as part of the common law. Parliamentary privileges are the rights that are[132] "recognised by the Courts and are deemed necessary to maintain the dignity and proper function of Parliament". In 1967 the House of Commons Report from the Committee of Privileges suggested that the term

---

131 Jack Simson Caird, Robert Hazell and Dawn Oliver, *The Constitutional Standards of the House of Lords Select Committee on the Constitution* (London: University College London, 2014).

132 T. Erskine May, *Parliamentary Practice* (London: Lexis Legal Books, 1997), p.70. May defined privileges as "the sum of peculiar rights enjoyed by each House collectively and by Members of each House individually".

"privileges" should be replaced by "rights and immunities". This suggestion appears attractive because it expresses more clearly the reality of the various "privileges" today.

The important privileges of the House of Commons, may be divided into two: first, freedom of speech and debate; and secondly, freedom from arrest.

In the case of freedom of speech this may be traced back to medieval times and is accepted by the Courts. The Bill of Rights 1688 asserted the freedom of speech of Members of Parliament by providing that "debates or proceedings in Parliament ought not to be impeached or queried in any court or place out of Parliament".

Freedom of speech is interpreted to mean that Members of Parliament are free from civil suits for defamation and are granted immunity in criminal law for words spoken in the course of parliamentary proceedings. Any threat of prosecution would itself be viewed as a contempt of the House. The House has its own internal rules and procedures and the office of the Speaker, on behalf of the House, can control debate within the House. Freedom of speech is, therefore, subject to adjudication by the House itself.

The term "proceedings in Parliament" is open to a variety of interpretations. Does the term refer only to debates as proceedings within the chamber? The Committee of Privileges in 1938 accepted that immunity applied to the asking of questions or the giving of notice of questions. However in 1957, a letter from a constituent to his Member of Parliament was held[133] not to be a proceeding in Parliament. An attempt to show a film about security matters in a committee room of the House of Commons that was banned by an interim injunction obtained by the Attorney-General, was considered not to be immune. The Speaker intervened to issue an order to ban the film, when a judge in chambers declined to issue an injunction applying to the Member of Parliament[134] or the House Committee.

The Supreme Court in *R v Chaytor*[135] distinguished between parliamentary proceedings that attracts privilege from matters that do not fall within the category of protection. The latter include claims for expenses or allowances that were not subject to such protection. The main protection is focused on freedom of speech for members to be free to speak their mind within the chamber. The rationale is that not everything done within the Houses of Parliament should attract privilege. Since 1958 it was accepted that correspondence between MPs and constituents did not attract privilege. Even the register of MPs interests is not deemed to be proceedings of Parliament, although this view is highly contested.[136]

The Chaytor case involved the trial of a number of MPs for alleged false accounting relating to their expenses claims. The Supreme Court undertook a general "scoping" exercise that canvassed an array of issues including the jurisdiction of the Courts over criminal law for conduct within the Houses of Parliament. Identifying the overlapping roles of Parliament and the Courts as well as the supervisory jurisdiction of the Courts requires a case by case analysis.

---

133 (1957/58, HC 227, HC 305), George Strauss MP.
134 See *Hansard*, HL Vol.575, col.52.
135 *R v Chaytor* [2010] UKSC 52; [2011] 1 A.C. 684; and also House of Commons Library, *Parliamentary privilege: current issues*, SN/PC/06390 (16 July 2015).
136 *Rost v Edwards* [1990] 2 Q.B. 460; [1990] 2 W.L.R. 1280 QBD.

3-164 Uncertainty may surround the operation of the immunities permitting free speech, but the procedure of referring doubtful or hotly disputed cases to the Committee of Privileges allows an important element of debate and discussion to take place. The strength of the system is therefore to be found in the autonomy of Parliament in these matters. On average at least a dozen cases appear to require the views of the Committee each year, which may or may not be adopted on report to the full House of Commons.

3-165 The Defamation Act 1996 provides the right for MPs and others to waive parliamentary privilege in order to pursue actions for defamation in the Courts. Section 13 of the 1996 Act provides that the protection of parliamentary privilege afforded by art.9 of the Bill of Rights 1688 might be waived. This important amendment was prompted by the case taken by Neil Hamilton, then an MP, who wished to pursue an action against the Guardian newspaper over allegations that he had received cash for asking parliamentary questions, an allegation he has strongly denied. In the course of legal proceedings the newspaper argued that it could not offer an adequate defence when it was unable to examine parliamentary proceedings in court.[137] Subsequently, Mr Hamilton withdrew his action but continued to claim his innocence. The Commons appointed Sir Gordon Downey to act as the first Parliamentary Commissioner for Standards to examine the conduct of MPs. The allegations against Mr Hamilton came under investigation. The calling of the General Election for 1 May 1997 took place before Sir Gordon could produce his final report. The definition of proceedings in Parliament may be considered by the Courts and cover matters relating to the reports of the Parliamentary Commissioner for Standards.[138] It was held in *Hamilton v Al Fayed*[139] that the Courts, in the words of Lord Woolf ". . .exercise a self-denying ordinance in relation to interfering with the proceedings of Parliament". It may be questioned as to whether this self-restraint will always endure.

3-166 There are important issues raised by the increasing use of the internet, televised parliament and the opening up of debates in Parliament to judicial scrutiny since *Pepper v Hart*. Section 13 of the Defamation Act 1996 opens up the use of proceedings in civil cases. An alternative is to repeal s.13 and provide the House with statutory authority to waive privilege on the basis of facts or on the merits of a particular case. The likelihood is that the question of privilege needs to be reconsidered in the light of s.3 of the Human Rights Act 1998. This means that art.9 of the Bill of Rights must now be read as compatible with Convention rights. Although Parliament is not regarded as behaving illegally if incompatible with Convention rights, it nevertheless needs to take account of Convention rights when resolving its historic privileges with rights under the Convention. The statutory protection provided under the Parliamentary Papers Act 1840 remains and this applies to the publication of papers printed by order of both Houses or under their authority. This protection was afforded to the Scott inquiry when it was published as a Parliamentary Paper.[140]

---

137 *Prebble v Television New Zealand* [1995] 1 A.C. 321; [1994] 3 W.L.R. 970 PC (NZ). A Privy Council discussion of what constitutes activity outside and inside Parliament. Also see *Rost v Edwards* [1990] 2 Q.B. 460; [1990] 2 W.L.R. 1280 QBD. For the Standing Orders see *Hansard*, Vol.265 HC, 610–12 (November 1995).
138 P. M. Leopold, "Free Speech in Parliament and the Courts" (1995) 15 *Legal Studies* 204.
139 [2001] 1 A.C. 395; [2000] 2 W.L.R. 609 HL.
140 The Rt Hon. Sir Richard Scott, The Vice-Chancellor, *Return to an Address of the Honourable House of Commons*

3-167 The second freedom claimed is that of arrest. This used to refer to arrest for civil cases, but this is of little effect as this procedure is rarely used today. Members of Parliament cannot claim immunity from criminal charges, arrest or imprisonment. It appears that arrest may even occur within the House itself, provided the House has given leave when it is a "sitting day".

3-168 It may be concluded that freedoms enjoyed by Members of Parliament may be greater than those itemised above as falling within the classification of the "proceedings of Parliament." Redlich in 1908 noted that[141]:

> "Parliamentary government as a system of law is intimately connected with parliamentary government as a political system determined by history and by national and social characteristics."

There are compelling arguments for the removal of this privilege and its abolition has been advocated for some time.[142]

3-169 The potential for conflict between Courts and Parliament involves a delicate balance of interests and setting realistic boundaries. In general, there is a degree of self-restraint that should guide MPs in their actions. In 2013, a joint committee on Privacy and Injunctions concluded that when court orders are used MPs should seek to justify the public interest and nullify their impact on Parliament. There is a form of comity emerging between the Courts and Parliament in ensuring a common approach.

Regulating financial and other interests

3-170 The disclosure of MPs' interests in the matters on which they may vote has become a matter of considerable importance. A House of Commons resolution on 25 May 1974 refers to the disclosure of "any relevant pecuniary interest or benefit." Members of Parliament from June 1975 are expected to register any such interest in a register of members' interests maintained by a senior clerk of the House who acts as Registrar. A Select Committee on Members' Interests may examine any matter arising from a failure to disclose an interest. The scope of the registration is all-embracing to include any pecuniary interest or benefit which a member may receive which should be included such as matters that

> "might be thought to affect his conduct as a member or influence his actions, speeches or vote in Parliament. Financial sponsorship,

---

dated February 1996. Report of the Inquiry into the Export of Defence Equipment and Dual-use Goods to Iraq and Related Prosecutions.
141 See J. Redlich, *The Procedure of the House of Commons* (London: Archibald Constable, 1908).
142 (1998–99, HL 43; 1998–89, HC 214).

> directorships, ownership of land, payments from clients, occupational or professional conduct or consultancies."

Registration of an interest does not absolve the member from stating in debate whenever he has a relevant interest in the matter. Sanctions against any member in default are rare and limited. In serious cases it may be regarded as a contempt. In 1990 John Browne MP failed to register his financial interests in a company. The Select Committee found the case proven and the House of Commons suspended[143] Browne for 20 days. Browne did not seek re-election in 1992. While this example illustrates the serious nature of a breach of the duty on members to disclose their interest, the policing of the register is left too often to the good faith of members. The influence of professional lobbyists is so all-embracing that the register and its operation should be re-examined in the light of modern practice.

3–171 Allegations of political corruption and sleaze have centred on the question of whether MPs have been willing to table questions in Parliament in return for financial rewards. The outcome was the setting up of the Nolan Committee under the chairmanship of Lord Nolan, a Law Lord. The Select Committee on Standards and Privileges was set up after the Nolan report recommended a Parliamentary Code of Conduct. The Committee on Standards in Public Life is a standing committee, first chaired by Lord Nolan. The Nolan Committee in their first report enunciated the seven principles of public life that are influential today:

- *selflessness*: holders of public office should act not solely in terms of the public interest but also in a way that avoids financial gain or other material benefits for themselves or their families;

- *integrity*: holders of public office should not put themselves in a position that permits others to exercise an outside influence on behalf of individuals or organisations that may seek to influence how they perform their public duty;

- *objectivity*: holders of public office should seek to make choices on merit and not on other criteria;

- *accountability*: holders of public office should hold themselves accountable for their decisions and their actions;

- *openness*: reasons for decisions should be given and information only restricted when the wider public interest demands such restrictions;

- *honesty*: holders of public office should declare any private interest relating to their public duties; and

---

143 *Hansard*, HC Vol.506, col.108 (1989–90); *Hansard*, HC, col.213.

- *leadership*: leadership should be provided by example, and these principles should be applied.

3-172 In addition to the Committee on Standards in Public Life, there is the Parliamentary Commissioner for Standards tasked to maintain the register of members' interests and to operate a Code of Conduct. This includes investigative powers to examine any complaint and report to the House, including powers to conduct an oral hearing as well as to undertake a review of written submissions. The Code of Conduct is generally seen as an example of self-regulation and was adopted by joint resolution. It was agreed in July 2001 that the House of Lords should similarly adopt a Code of Conduct and the Lords register their interests on the basis of the Code. The non-statutory basis for regulation of both Houses may not remain for long as growing public disquiet about the financial interests of MPs may require satisfaction.

3-173 The work of the Committee on Standards and Privileges has produced many reports and recommendations amounting to well over 100 reports. The majority of the reports related to mistakes, errors and abuse related to claims and allowances in respect of MPs and their work.

3-174 Despite great reluctance on the part of the Commons authorities the operation of the Freedom of Information Act 2000 has permitted the public to know more about MPs claims and allowances. In 2005 this led to prolonged litigation that eventually led to the Divisional Court upholding the Information Tribunal's ruling that information about MPs payments and claims could be justified in being made public to newspapers and the media.[144]

L: Summary and Conclusions

3-175 It may be concluded that modern parliamentary government in the UK has continued to develop, albeit alongside Parliament's medieval inheritance. Preserving the balance of the Constitution, whereby in Blackstone's analysis "the executive power should be a branch, though not the whole of the legislature" remains a perplexing and constant challenge to the institution of Parliament.

- the growth of party politics and the strengthening of cabinet decision-making altered the classical principles underlying Dicey's explanation of the Constitution, namely that Parliament could control the Executive;

- Parliamentary forms of control appear weak and ineffective while judicial influence and power has increased incrementally. The willingness of the Courts to oversee

---

144 *Corporate Officer of the House of Commons v Information Commissioner* [2008] EWHC 1084 (Admin); [2009] 3 All E. R. 403.

some parliamentary procedures and practices has intensified; Select committees have become more effective and have considerable potential to make government more accountable and provide greater transparency and information for the public. A new Education Centre on the parliamentary estate is an important step in making the public and young people more aware of the working of Parliament and its constitutional role; and

- reform of the House of Lords has failed to reach a political consensus while the size of the House of Lords continues to expand. The raid review of the House of Lords under Lord Strathclyde is likely to consider the powers of the House of Lords in the context of the relationship between Commons and Lords; The Strathclyde Review suggests clarifying the power of the House of Lords to defeat statutory instruments.

Further Reading

B. Dickson and P. Carmichael (eds), *The House of Lords: Its Parliamentary and Judicial Roles* (Oxford: Hart, 1999).

A. Horne, G. Drewry and D. Oliver (eds), *Parliament and the Law* (Oxford: Hart, 2013).

P. Norton "Parliament: A New Assertiveness" in J. Jowell, D. Oliver and C. O'Cinneide (eds), *The Changing Constitution*, 8th edn (Oxford: Oxford University Press, 2015).

Report of the Hansard Society Commission on Parliamentary Scrutiny, *The Challenge for Parliament: Making Government Accountable* (London: Hansard Society, Vacher Dod Publishing Ltd, 2001).

Royal Commission on Reform of the House of Lords, *A House for the Future*, Cm.4534 (London: Stationary Office, 2000).

P. Silk and Rhoderi Walters, *How Parliament Works*, 8th edn (London: Longman, 2015).

4

Government

A: Introduction

4–001 Government is carried out through Ministers of the Crown answerable to Parliament. Under the UK's constitutional arrangements, with the Queen as Head of State, government is carried on in her name as is fitting for a country with a constitutional Monarchy.

4–002 The system of government in the UK is often referred to as responsible government. In that sense there is a degree of self-limitation in how government may operate its legal authority. This is partly attributable to party politics but also to the theoretical possibility at least that the government may lose the confidence of the House of Commons. The government requires the authority of Parliament for the passage of legislation and the expenditure of money. Government in the UK is highly centralised and although local government is an elected tier below central government, its practical autonomy has been greatly eroded in recent times. Devolution since 1998 has introduced a new tier of government for London, Scotland, Wales and Northern Ireland with the prospect of further devolution in Scotland. Government in the UK must also take account of the changes in membership of the EU which currently comprises 28 Member States and 507.4 million people and is considered in detail in Ch.8. Many government decisions are made in co-operation with other Member States and are implemented more formally through European law.

4–003 Any consideration of the powers and role of government involves explaining how it is undertaken under an unwritten constitution. This is discussed in both this chapter and the next. In this chapter, first consideration is given to the prerogative powers of government which are a source of governmental power in addition to the extensive reliance on legislation already discussed in Ch.3. Secondly, the role of the Cabinet and Prime Minister and the administration of the government through the civil service is discussed. The institutions of government also include a wide variety of bodies connected with administrative decision-taking and these are discussed more fully in Ch.6.

4-004 Government is carried out according to the conventions of the Constitution and the rule of law, which prescribe how government ought to exercise power. Consideration is given to the importance of conventions and the rule of law in Ch.5.

B: Governing under the UK's Constitution

4-005 A legal perspective of Britain's constitutional arrangements may be said to be too narrowly defined and to focus only on a narrow legal and technical explanation of parliamentary sovereignty, which Dicey attributed in 1885 as Parliament's "right to make or unmake any law whatever". In the sense that Dicey ascribed such wide powers to Parliament, it might be asked whether the UK in fact possesses a constitution. Dicey also extracted an understanding of the institutions and principles of government.[1] Thomas Paine's analysis of the Rights of Man[2] which was influential in the drafting of the present American Constitution, noted the characteristics which defined a constitution.

> "A Constitution is not the act of a government, but of a people constituting a government, and a government without a constitution is power without right..."

4-006 Paine's analysis causes us to consider the question of where power and authority lie. Daintith and Page[3] summarise two elements: first the general neglect given to the question of who governs and how government works and secondly that in the absence of fundamental constitutional laws most commentators devote little attention to the powers and status of ministers and their importance.

> "The executive governs us; it comprises the individuals—mostly ministers and civil servants—who actually control, from day to day, the state's instruments of coercion, wealth and information. The idea that it might not be constitutionally important would seem too bizarre to mention, were it not for the fact that

---

1 Also see H. Cox, *The Institutions of English Government; being an Account of the Constitution, Power and Procedures of its Legislative, Judicial and Administrative Departments with Copious References to Ancient and Modern Authorities* (London: H. Sweet, 1863).
2 T. Paine, "Rights of Man" in *The Complete Works of Thomas Paine* (1791–92), pp.302–303. Also see the discussion in C. H. McIlwain, *Constitutionalism Ancient and Modern* (Ithaca, NY: Cornell University Press, 1947), pp.8–10; Rousseau, *Le Contrat Social* (1762).
3 T. Daintith and A. Page, *The Executive in the Constitution* (New York: Oxford University Press, 1999), p.2.

> the literature of constitutional law is remarkably reticent on the subject."

The relevance of this point has been noted by a number of political scientists. F. F. Ridley[4] argues that because of the width of government powers Britain "does not really have a constitution at all, merely a system of government, even if some parts of it are more important to our democratic order than others. . .". This statement pre-dates the Human Rights Act 1998 but it is a perceptive analysis of how the common law system of government may appear.

Ridley calls in aid the views of James Bryce in the latter part of the nineteenth century when he argued that

> ". . .there is no text to discriminate between constitutional and less than constitutional elements since labelling has no defined consequence, unlike countries where constitutions are a higher form of law."

The late John Griffith, a public lawyer, explained the political nature of power and government. Griffith considered the subject of Parliament and legislation[5] in his seminal articles.[6] Griffith's main argument[7] goes to the heart of governing and government and around his passions—constraints on "unbridled power", and identification with a communitarian view of political power while retaining an association with individual injustice. Griffith wrote from a particular perspective influenced in part by Laski,[8] Jennings[9] and Robson[10] and the Fabian tradition of the role of law. His anti-authoritarian stance was mixed with a scepticism that law might substitute for political choices".[11] The idea of confronting government power with

---

4   F. F. Ridley, "There is no British Constitution: A Dangerous Case of the Emperor's Clothes" (1981) 41 *Parliamentary Affairs* 340–345; Samuel H. Beer, *Modern British Politics*, 3rd edn (London: Faber & Faber, 1982); Max Beloff and Gillian Peele, *The Government of the U.K.: Political Authority in a Changing Society*, 2nd edn (London: Weidenfeld and Nicolson, 1985); Nevil Johnson, *In Search of the Constitution: Reflections on State and Society in Britain* (London: Methuen, 1977); *Introduction to Constitutions in Democratic Politics* in Vernon Bogdanor (ed), *Constitutions in democratic politics* (Aldershot: Gower, 1988); and J. M. Schaar, "Legitimacy in the Modern State" in William Connolly (ed), *Legitimacy and the State* (Oxford: Blackwell, 1984).
5   J. A. G. Griffith, "The Political Constitution" (1979) 42(1) *Modern Law Review* 1.
6   J. A. G. Griffith, "The Place of parliament in the Legislative process" [1951] 14 *Modern Law Review* 279.
7   R. Blackburn and A. Kennon (eds), with Sir Michael Wheeler-Booth, *Griffith and Ryle on Parliament, Functions, Practice and Procedures*, 2nd edn (London: Sweet and Maxwell, 2003).
8   Harold Laski (1893–1950) Political scientist, Professor at LSE from 1926. Philosophical construction themed on a modified Marxism. See H. Laski, *Authority in the Modern State* (London: Routledge, 1919) and later *Liberty in the Modern State* (George Allen & Unwin, 1930).
9   Ivor Jennings (1903–1965).
10 William Robson (1895–1980), Professor of Public Administration (1947–1962).
11 N. MacCormick, "Beyond the Sovereign State" (1993) 56 *Modern Law Review* 1, 11.

some superior rule of obligation is commonly accepted in written constitutions.[12] Equally there is no panacea to be found in a written constitution as the framers of the constitution may not accurately address the problems of where power and its abuse may be found. However written constitutions may settle the relationship between local and central government, the role of the courts and the separation of powers within the framework of the constitution. Ridley identifies four characteristics which he suggests are important and without which it is impossible to say a country has a constitution "in the current international sense of the word":

- the constitution establishes the system of government. This is taken to mean that the system of government depends on the constitution for its rules and is not independent from the constitution;

- the constitution sets the authority outside the order it establishes. The meaning intended is that the constitution should provide the legitimacy for law and the governmental system. Common to modern constitutions like the Japanese or Irish, there is some reference to "the people" in whom ultimate authority is derived for the constitution to gain legitimacy;

- the constitution is a form of law superior to other laws. This authority is partly due to the point made above, but also the principle of hierarchy admits the possibility of judicial review of ordinary legislation to test its constitutional validity; and

- the constitution is entrenched which thereby admits its general purpose, to limit the power of government; and because of its higher form of authority, this makes the constitution safe from political intervention. It is usual that only special procedures may be used to seek amendment and in such cases protection is afforded by requiring some form of popular consultation.

4–009 Ridley's analysis has some force when it is considered that in the absence of a written constitution in the UK, there is an omission in our present arrangements which fail to address Ridley's four characteristics. One answer might be that this is not surprising, as Ridley has in mind the formula for written constitutions which he is unfairly applying to our "unwritten arrangements". There remains, however, the question of what is fundamental in the UK's Constitution and how government might be made to conform to fundamental principles.

4–010 One answer is to consider how there may be what Daintith and Page[13] refer to as "external" and "internal" controls. External controls may be regulatory systems such as the courts or Parliament or through external contracts and financial controls. Internal systems may be found

---

12 M. Loughlin, *Public Law and Political Theory* (Oxford: Oxford University Press, 1992), pp.16–17. Loughlin notes the Diceyan legacy, namely that constitutional law is too formalistically defined by lawyers.
13 T. Daintith and A. Page, *The Executive in the Constitution* (Oxford: Oxford University Press, 1999), p.3.

through the institutions of government providing their own internal "checks and balances". Civil servants and ministers operate within important conventions, principles and understandings. Occasionally these procedures have a legal framework such as the processes and procedures used by government to account for public money. Often the procedures come in the form of minutes, letters, circulars and public statements. Inevitably there are restraints which are never made public but exist beneath the surface—personal promotion, professional standards and ultimately self-advancement all serve to provide standards in the machinery of government decision-taking.

In the aftermath of the 2008 financial crisis, there has been a growing awareness that a market economy interacts with the State in many ways that have important implications for governing and the government of the day. The most obvious overlap is in the management of the economy as a means of controlling the sovereign debt. There are many areas of economic management and regulation that reveal assorted rules and regulations that are used to govern the country. As mentioned in Ch.1, Tony Prosser defines and clarifies the importance of the "economic constitution", a term that conceptually sets the parameters of both enabling powers and controls on public power. This also defines "the plural constitution". The argument being that economic constitutions impose "substantive constraints on government lined to a particular vision of the limits of legitimate state action".[14]

4–011

Prosser also argues that economic management is a form of regulation that crosses" a wide range of different techniques and instruments "that may be used by the government to achieve its economic goals.[15] This is an important and too readily overlooked part of governing and government. Prosser's analysis provides a valuable understanding of the various layers of government activity and their connectivity to the visible actions of the government governing through Parliament and the civil service. It also provides both descriptive and normative analysis forming a useful "mapping" of the various layers of governing. The main point is that the connections between state institutions and non-state bodies or organisations provides a unique "road map" of the boundaries of government and non-governmental activities. This is recognition that there are working and practical forms of hard and soft law, national, European and International rules dovetail into the way political decisions are reached and constitutional powers are exercised. This takes us away from the traditional discussion of government to a broader conception of governing.[16] An example is the International Development (Official Development Assistance Target) Act 2015 that enables the UK to carry out a legal duty to meet a target for aid set in the legislation. The Act guarantees that ministers are under a discretion to exercise their powers in a particular way. Setting targets and creating economic regulations is an important development in the practices and procedures of how Britain is governed.[17] Setting a "tax lock" before the last general election was a Manifesto promise made by the Conservative Party. There was also a promise to legislate for running a "budget

---

14   Tony Prosser, *The Economic Constitution* (Oxford: Oxford University Press, 2015), p.241
15   Prosser, *The Economic Constitution*, p.4.
16   G. Anderson, "Beyond Constitutionalism Beyond the State" (2012) 39 *Journal of Law and Society* 359–83.
17   The Climate Change Act 2008 is another example of targets being set.

surplus" in "normal economic times" as a means of setting a legislative responsibility for future governments.[18]

4-012 None of these arrangements, however, will guarantee that government conforms to the acceptable and high standards which should reasonably be expected. Occasionally civil servants and ministers may be subject to scrutiny such as before a select committee or in a Parliamentary debate. Even here the ultimate sanction may not be found in resignation or judicial rebuke, but in the day-to-day political life of the nation. Newspapers and the news media have a contribution to make through investigative journalism in providing information and critical analysis of government activities.

4-013 Counterbalancing any checks and balances that this combination of factors may have is the secrecy which surrounds government in Britain. It begins with the need for collective Cabinet decision-taking and the anonymity of civil servants. Supported by both the civil and criminal law, Britain's secrecy laws have penetrated deeply inside the very culture of the machinery of government. Commercial confidentiality between government and business or industry in their contractual relationships also provides a reason for secrecy in many government activities. Recent attempts to provide open government through a newly enacted Freedom of Information Act 2000 have been tempered by the various exemptions in the Act. While the Act imposes a duty on public authorities and regional public authorities in England, Wales and Northern Ireland to respond to requests for information, the procedures are subject to a fee being payable and a long list of exemptions which are very broadly defined. Ironically, the Act may be more effective in terms of public authorities outside central government.

4-014 Finally, emphasis should be given to the ultimate check on government through elections which determine the fate of government policies. Political parties, individual politicians and pressure groups all promote the political agenda of the nation. In a constitutional sense political parties look to the electorate for a mandate to govern. Local as well as central government has to account to electoral choices determined by popular support.

4-015 The weakness about elections serving as a mainstay of fundamental principles is that the results are not necessarily representative of public opinion. There is a sizeable number, estimated in 1981 at 2.5 million, of eligible electors who are not registered to vote. In 2015 this estimate has reached a staggering 7.5 million.[19] The turnout at central government elections fluctuates around 65 per cent of the electorate. More significantly the British electoral system does not favour fairness between the number of votes cast at the election for one particular party and the number of seats held in Parliament by that party. The statistical returns of all the general elections since the franchise was reformed in the nineteenth century show how "the first past the post system" can distort electoral preferences. For example, at the general election in 1992, the Conservative and Labour parties respectively won 42 per cent and 34 per cent of the votes, each winning 336 and 271 seats. The Liberal Democrats won 18 per cent of the vote but only 20 seats. At the last election, May 2015, the Conservative Party won 36.1 per cent of the votes and 330 seats, Labour 30.4 per cent of the vote and 232 seats, UKIP 12.4 per cent

---

18   House of Commons Library Briefing paper, 07244 (3 July 2015) Background to the July 2015 Budget.
19   *The Guardian* 13 February 2015.

per cent of the vote and 56 seats, Liberal Democrats have 7.8 per cent of the vote and only eight seats.[20]

These results are used to support the claim that the current plurality system (as it is known) or two-party system discriminates against a third party or minority parties. More importantly, while the present electoral system may favour strong government, i.e. a government which holds a majority overall in the House of Commons, this may be at the expense of representative government. To the extent that this is true it may considerably weaken the case for relying on electoral choice as a mainstay of constitutional protection of fundamental principles. Daintith and Page also note a further weakness in the electoral mandate[21]:

4-016

> "'Democratic' control of the executive through the legislature may be a mixed blessing if the legislature's instincts are more populist or nationalistic than those of the executive, or if the legislature's key institutional values amount to no more than expediency and survival."

A further point is the time delay for the impact of policies to be fully understood or appreciated by the electorate. Government policies over a five-year term may fail to be effective and this limitation may curtail medium- or long-term planning.

4-017

The conclusion that can be drawn from the above analysis is that while there are many important and disparate elements containing fundamental principles in the working of the UK's Constitution, political scientists have been correct to point out that the Constitution does not fit easily within the ideas of constitutionalism resulting from the experience of modern written constitutions. It may seem surprising that British constitutional lawyers who have written many constitutions throughout the world should be reluctant to adopt a written constitution for Britain. Perhaps this distils the essence of constitutional law in the UK: systems of external and internal control are exercised within the limits of political power. Rules and procedures are exercised within an overall framework of legislative authority and statutory powers, and are no less the working constitution than the law is found in other countries with a written constitution.

4-018

C: Defining Central and Local Government

No special status is accorded to government within the UK's constitutional arrangements. The term "government" is not given a precise legal meaning and not accorded any special

4-019

---

20 House of Commons Library Briefing Paper, CBP 7 186, General Election 2015 (18 May 2015).
21 T. Daintith and A. Page, *The Executive in the Constitution* (Oxford: Oxford University Press, 1999), p.394.

pre-eminence. It may occasionally be found in a statute but rarely does the legal status or significance of government receive specific judicial evaluation. An example of reference to the word "minister" and the word "state" in the context of government may be found in the House of Commons Disqualification Act 1975 and in the Ministers of the Crown Act 1975. Both Acts contain technical rules applicable to government ministers, without explaining the powers, duties and responsibilities of ministers or the role of government.

4-020 Government may be defined in a variety of ways. Some definitions express the significance of the State, the way the State is governed, while other definitions may more generally refer to the executive powers enjoyed by the Cabinet and Prime Minister. Government carries out a wide range of activities with its own policies and ideas developed to administer public money or implement its election promises.

4-021 Government enjoys a wide range of powers of patronage and influence. Legal powers may be derived from statute, the prerogative or from the legal obligations arising from the European Community. External affairs such as foreign relations and signing treaties, or maintaining diplomatic relations, may be carried out through the Crown's prerogative in foreign affairs.

4-022 Government is also capable of forming contractual relations. Given the Government's vast economic power it can wield considerable influence as an economic contractor. Statutory authority is not normally required for the Crown to enter into contracts, though prior statutory authority is often necessary for the approval of expenditure. In the case of departments making contracts, this is achieved through the authority of a civil servant acting on behalf of the Crown and no statutory authority is needed. Increasingly central government has viewed itself as a commercial enterprise, freely entering into contracts, or as a regulator overseeing contract activities.

4-023 Government is amenable to the jurisdiction of the courts. Lord Templeman has observed[22]: "Parliament makes the law, the executive carry the law into effect and the judiciary enforce the law". A finding of contempt may be made against a government department or a Minister of the Crown. In *M v Home Office*, the House of Lords upheld a finding of contempt against a Minister of the Crown for not complying with an injunction. The injunction was granted ordering M to be returned to this country after the Home Office rejected his claim for asylum. Lord Templeman concluded[23]:

> "To enforce the law the courts have power to grant remedies including injunctions against a minister in his official capacity... For the purpose of enforcing the law against all persons and institutions, including ministers in their official capacity and in their personal capacity, the courts are armed with coercive powers exercisable in proceedings for contempt of court."

---

22 *M v Home Office* [1994] 1 A.C. 377; [1993] 3 W.L.R. 433 HL at [437].
23 *M v Home Office* [1994] 1 A.C. 377 at [437].

Lord Woolf in the House of Lords considered that it would rarely be justified to make use of injunctions against government departments in judicial review proceedings.

The generic term "government" requires further clarification. It is important to distinguish between central and local government. All the powers discussed above refer to central government. Local government has no special status under the UK's constitutional arrangements, even though it is elected and provides an enormous variety of services and activities for the community. Since the nineteenth century, local government has gained considerable statutory powers, which have been granted by central government enabling local government to carry out tasks and responsibilities in the provision of public health, education, planning, policing and other services.

Local government is perceived to be an agent of central government and carries out its tasks as a unique administrative agency. Each local authority has its own distinct legal personality. In law, local authority status as a body corporate gives it considerable financial autonomy within the framework of its legal powers. Local authority elections offer the local community an opportunity to participate in a different tier of government distinct from central government. Councillors, as local authority representatives, carry out their policies subject to the legal controls set by central government. Local government delivery of public services in the UK was influenced by the Conservative led Coalition Government's approach to competition and market economics. The Localism Act 2011 is a neat blend of the Coalition government's policies reinforced in the White Paper, *Open Public Services*, which is community based and focused on neighbourhood services. The Act brings together for England greater powers than those available in the devolved administrations in Scotland, Wales and Northern Ireland. This adds an important dynamic to the way government is delivered and the autonomy of each locality.[24] This may not always favour institutional local government as empowering local citizens but may create diffuse interests centred on their locality. The Coalition Government introduced wide ranging social reforms that impact on health, transport, water and waste as well as energy and social housing. The reforms set many burdens and responsibilities on local government and major changes in the financing and the methods of delivery of goods and services. The trend is in favour of market led solutions through the private sector rather than direct delivery of services by local authorities.

Compared to central government, local authorities do not operate as an emanation of the Crown. As statutory corporations, local authorities must act within their powers according to law. Local authorities do not all conform to a single model of government as central government may appear to. The role, function and organisation of local government is examined in more detail in Ch.13.

---

24 M. J Smith., "From Big Government to Big Society: Changing the State-Society balance" (2010) 639(4) *Parliamentary Affairs* 818–33; Peter Leyland, "Multi-layered Constitutional accountability" in N. Bamforth and P. Leyland (eds), *Accountability in the Contemporary Constitution* (Oxford; Oxford University Press, 2013), p.328;and M. Loughlin, *Legality and Locality: The Role of Law in Central-Local Government Relations* (Oxford:Clarendon, 1996); V. Lowndes, and L. Pratchett, "Local Government under the Coalition Government: Austerity, Localism and the 'Big Society'" (2012) *Local Government Studies* 38(1), 21–40; G. Mulgan, "Investing in Social Growth: Can the Big Society be more than a slogan?" *The Sunday Times*, 30 August 2010.

D: Crown and Prerogative

Definition and Review

4-028   In addition to the various forms of legislation outlined in the previous chapter on Parliament, an important source of governmental powers may arise from the use of prerogative powers. Various definitions are applied to the prerogative. Dicey defined the Royal prerogative[25] as "the residue of discretionary or arbitrary authority which at any given time is legally left in the hands of the Crown"; de Smith attributed to the Crown "inherent legal attributes" which belong to the Queen as a person, and to the institution called the Crown. The latter may be defined to include Her Majesty's Government or the State. Defining the prerogative in legal terms is always difficult. This is largely because of the complexities of its historical evolution and uncertainties about its present usage. Dicey's description of the prerogative as a "residue" of powers should be confined to powers or privileges that are unique to the Crown. A wider description of the prerogative meaning all the powers of the Crown that have their source in the common law is inaccurate. Powers or privileges enjoyed by private persons are not strictly speaking part of the prerogative. Some writers find it convenient to classify power under the prerogative as "personal" and distinguish this from "political" prerogatives. The former are exercised by the Queen as a person, the latter apply as Head of State. Personal prerogatives refer to the immunities and property rights of the Sovereign which survive today, such as a right not to be sued or prosecuted in the courts. Personal estates such as the Crown's Private Estates are vested in the Sovereign.

4-029   Political prerogatives are arrogated to the Crown whereby the Queen may act in her personal capacity, such as in the choice of the Prime Minister. Today the prerogative powers of the Crown are largely exercised by ministers responsible to Parliament who in theory act on behalf of the Crown. The Courts have recognised prerogative powers as early as the *Case of Proclamations*[26] (1610), but have from time to time restricted their scope and attempted to define their meaning.

4-030   The Royal prerogative is regarded as part of the common law powers of the Crown. It consists mainly of executive government powers such as the conduct of foreign affairs, the making of war and peace, the appointment of ministers, the dissolution of Parliament and the assent to Bills. The difficulty of exact legal definition may have prompted Dicey to define the prerogative in very broad terms[27]:

---

25 A. V. Dicey, *Law of the Constitution* (London and New York: Macmillan, 1889), p.424. Lord Reid in *Burmah Oil v Lord Advocate* [1965] A.C. 75; [1964] 2 W.L.R. 1231 HL at [99]. See also *Laker Airways Ltd v Department of Trade* [1977] Q.B. 643; [1977] 2 W.L.R. 234 CA (Civ Div).
26 (1610) 2 St. Tr. 723.
27 A. V. Dicey, *Law of the Constitution* (London and New York: Macmillan, 1889), p.424.

> "Every act which the executive government can lawfully do without the authority of the Act of Parliament is done in virtue of the prerogative..."

The difficulty of precise legal definition and the breadth of Dicey's vision of the extent of prerogative powers has not been helped by any clarity to be found in legal cases. The history of prerogative powers is the history of relations between the King and Parliament and the attempts by the courts to mediate.

The historical origins of the prerogative may be traced back to medieval times. The inherent powers of the King to govern the realm rested on the prerogative. Legal definitions appeared unhelpful as they may have attempted to expand or limit the powers of the King. Advice sought was usually influenced by the expected outcome in terms of defining the King's powers. Blackstone[28] identified the pre-eminence accorded to the prerogative in English law:

> "...[I]t signified in its etymology (from prae and rogo) something that is required or demanded before, or in preference to, all others."

Maitland[29] cautions us about the "often great uncertainty as to the exact limits of the royal prerogative". His suggestion that there is "no such doctrine as that a prerogative may cease to exist because it is not used", may not easily fit within modern representative government with extensive statutory powers.

Keir and Lawson[30] make the important distinction between the powers enjoyed by the King at common law and those powers conferred by statute. Statutes have restricted prerogative powers and in some cases statutes either repeal the prerogative completely or overlap with prerogative powers. An example where statutory authority has replaced prerogative powers are the powers of the sovereign to spend money or raise taxation prior to the seventeenth century. Such powers are today ceded to Parliament and statutory authority. Another example is the Crown Proceedings Act 1947 which abolished the Crown's absolute immunity from legal suit in contract and tort.

In adapting to changing circumstances the courts may be required to give further thought to long accepted principles. Until recently it was commonly assumed that injunctions were not available against the Crown. As already mentioned in *M v Home Office*[31] the House of Lords clarified the position regarding the availability of injunctions against the Crown. Lord Woolf, giving the views of the House, held that injunctions including interim injunctions were available against Ministers of the Crown. A minister could be personally liable for wrongs done by the minister when acting in an official capacity. The importance of the case lies in the clarification over the use of injunctions against the Crown. The current law lays emphasis on

---

28 Blackstone, Commentaries, Bk 1, p.239.
29 F. W. Maitland, *Constitutional History of England* (Cambridge: Cambridge University Press, 1908), p.418.
30 Keir and Lawson, *Cases in Constitutional Law* (Oxford: Clarendon Press, 1967), pp.72–80.
31 [1994] 1 A.C. 377; [1993] 3 All E.R. 537 HL.

the limited circumstances where it is considered appropriate to grant an injunction against the Crown.

4-036 How relevant is the prerogative to modern government when it is of such ancient origin? Present day prerogative powers may be found in: the Executive's power to conclude treaties with Sovereign States; the power to declare war; to provide for the security of the Realm; to grant pardons to convicted criminals or reprieve a sentence; to mint the currency; and to appoint Commissions by Royal Warrant. Some prerogative powers remain in the personal control of the Sovereign such as power to dismiss and appoint a Prime Minister and the power of dissolution of Parliament. The creation of the Coalition Government in 2010 led to the inclusion of many of the prerogatives in the *Cabinet Manual*. The responsibility of the Prime Minister at the time of resignation after an election to recommend to Her Majesty the person who is best able to command the confidence of the House of Commons is important. In the case of an inconclusive election result the incumbent Prime Minister is entitled to see if the current administration can form a new government allowed the then Prime Minister Mr Brown to see if another Labour led government could be formed in 2010. This proved impossible but the largest political party after the election in 2010, the Conservative Party was able to agree a coalition arrangement with the Liberal Democrats and form a government. The Fixed-Term Parliaments Act 2011 has important constitutional significance and it secured a five-year fixed term for the Coalition Government. The Act also removes the right of the Prime Minister to determine the date of the next election.

4-037 Undoubtedly the prerogative is a "residual" power as it can be removed, altered or amended by an Act of Parliament. No new prerogatives may be created but surprisingly old prerogatives have an "elastic quality" which allows their adaption into modern government. Lord Roskill in *Council of Civil Service Unions v Minister for the Civil Service*[32] considers that there are various prerogatives where the courts appear not to be able to review, such as the prerogative that applies to the "making of treaties, the defence of the realm, the prerogative of mercy, the grant of honours, the dissolution of Parliament and the appointment of ministers". These are evidently not amenable to judicial review because of their nature, and it should be noted that the list is not an exhaustive one. More recently the courts appear to have taken a different approach than Lord Roskill's. Arising from the application of the prerogative of mercy, it appears that the fairness of sentencing that fall under the exercise of the powers of remission of sentencing under the prerogative may be reviewed.[33] Similarly matters of defence are not wholly outside the power of judicial review, such as including the admission of gay people into the armed forces[34] and the use of an ordinance to remove island people to allow a US military base to be set up.[35] This change in emphasis is partly due to the nature of the rights agenda set by the Human Rights Act but also because increasingly the courts are invited to review all

---

32 [1985] A.C. 374; [1984] 3 W.L.R. 1174 HL at [418B]–[418C].
33 *R (Quinn) v Secretary of State for the Home Department* [2000] Prison L.R. 222; [2001] A.C.D. 45 QBD.
34 *R v Ministry of Defence Ex p. Smith* [1996] Q.B. 517; [1996] 2 W.L.R. 305 CA (Civ Div).
35 *R (Bancoult) v Secretary of State for the Foreign and Commonwealth Office* [2001] Q.B. 1067; [2001] 2 W.L.R. 1219 Div Ct.

public power whatever its source. It remains the case that there will always be a reluctance to review prerogative powers that underline government policy in the defence of the realm.

Some examples may be given of the use of the prerogative. A prerogative power was claimed as the basis for setting up a scheme for compensation payable to victims of violent crime. The Criminal Injuries Compensation Board has recently received statutory authority and recognition under the Criminal Justice Act 1988, s.108; but in 1964, it was set up by prerogative powers subject to express statutory approval by Parliament of the necessary government expenditure under the annual Appropriation Act.

In *Secretary of State for the Home Department Ex p. Fire Brigades Union*,[36] despite the existence of the statutory scheme under the Criminal Justice Act 1988, the Home Secretary attempted to introduce a tariff scheme under the prerogative. The tariff scheme was different from the statutory one and the Home Secretary purported to exercise powers under s.171 of the Criminal Justice Act 1988 which gave the Home Secretary discretion as to when to bring the statutory scheme into operation. It was accepted by Lord Browne-Wilkinson that the tariff scheme was inconsistent with the statutory scheme. In effect it might involve the winding up of the old Criminal Injuries Compensation Board and the creation of a new body, the Criminal Injuries Compensation Authority. The House of Lords by a majority held that such a tariff scheme introduced under the prerogative was unlawful. The tariff scheme under the prerogative was inconsistent with Parliamentary intent established under Pt VII of the Criminal Justice Act 1988. This case is important because it establishes the important relationship between statute and prerogative. Lord Browne-Wilkinson stated that[37] "the existence of legislation basically affects the mode in which such prerogative powers can be lawfully exercised". The case restored the validity of the scheme under the Criminal Injuries Compensation Board. As a result of the House of Lords decision, the Home Secretary introduced new legislation providing for the introduction of a new scheme of compensation under the Criminal Injuries Compensation Act 1995. In the final analysis the Government won the day but the entire episode illustrates the pre-eminence of statutory powers over the prerogative.

The civil service came under prerogative influence in the sense that the Crown has historically the power to appoint or dismiss its servants at pleasure. This power may be identified as a prerogative power. Gradually the civil service has been placed under statutory power under the Constitutional Reform and Governance Act 2010, another example of the movement in the direction of a statutory framework.

The prerogative power in the Crown to establish courts to administer the common law has fallen into disuse as new courts are created by statute. The Crown may pardon convicted prisoners. The Attorney General may enter a *nolle prosequi* in prosecutions on indictment. However, under s.23 of the Prosecution of Offences Act 1985, the Crown Prosecution Service has statutory powers to discontinue cases without the leave of the court.

---

36 [1995] 2 A.C. 513; [1995] 2 W.L.R. 464 HL.
37 See *Compensating Victims of Violent Crime. Changes to the Criminal Injuries Compensation Scheme* (Cm.2434 (December 1993).

4-042 The versatility of the prerogative is demonstrated by Turpin's[38] reference to orders in council such as the 1982 Order, as "prerogative legislation". This is an apt but perhaps misleading phrase. It is the case that during the two World Wars many prerogative orders in council were adopted without statutory authority. The Reprisals Orders in Council of 1915 and 1917, and more recently in 1982 the requisitioning of ships on account of the Falklands war, was achieved through the prerogative. The misleading part of the phrase is the word "legislation" when used alongside the word prerogative. This implies Parliamentary approval and scrutiny which may be misleading, because no such detailed scrutiny is undertaken. However, in the general sense legislation may mean the power to make rules for others. The prerogative may clearly fall within this meaning.

4-043 Prerogative powers that apply in relation to Parliament include the power to summon, to dissolve or to prorogue Parliament. The Royal Assent to Bills is also a prerogative power. Prerogative powers are not subject to the processes of scrutiny of the House of Commons, nor is it always clear when a prerogative power is being used. Such doubts can give rise to questions about the relationship between prerogative powers and statute. Wade suggests somewhat tentatively[39] that: "Prerogative powers may also, it seems, be atrophied by mere disuse".

4-044 As to the exact nature or remit of the prerogative Nourse LJ explained[40]:

> "It has not at any stage in our history been practicable to identify all the prerogative powers of the Crown. It is only by a process of piecemeal decision over a period of centuries that particular powers are seen to exist or not to exist, as the case may be. From time to time a need for more exact definition arises. The present need arose from a difference of view between the Secretary of State and a police authority over what is necessary to maintain public order, a phenomenon which has been observed only in recent times. There has probably never been a comparable occasion for investigating a prerogative of keeping the peace within the realm."

This sets the potential scope for future development of the prerogative to be largely discretionary, save for the fact that "no new prerogative" may be created.

4-045 Some doubts may be advanced as to the desirability of such a wide discretion. Does the Executive have a choice as to when *it* may rely on prerogative powers or require statute? Does the prerogative overlap with statute or co-exist with statutory authority? Conventional wisdom has drawn back from the creation of new prerogative powers to revive an existing statute or create new prerogatives. It is settled law that in the *Case of Proclamations*[41] the Crown has

---

38 Turpin, *British Government and the Constitution* (Cambridge: Cambridge University Press, 2011), p.382.
39 William Wade, *Constitutional Fundamentals* (London: Stevens and Sons, 1989), pp.58–64.
40 *R v Secretary of State for the Home Department Ex p. Northumbria Police Authority* [1989] Q.B. 26; [1988] 2 W.L.R. 590 CA (Civ Div).
41 (1610) 2 St. Tr. 723.

no prerogative to create new wrongs; but in *Malone v MPC*[42] Megarry VC accepted that the limited power to authorise telephone tapping under the prerogative was derived from the extension of the power to open articles sent through the post. Today such powers have a firmer statutory foundation under the Interception of Communications Act 1985. This followed the decision in *Malone* after a decision of the European Court of Human Rights[43] which held that the absence of legal controls over the circumstances in which phone tap warrants could be issued was incompatible with art.8 of the Convention.

4-046

It might be suggested that statutory authority is preferable to reliance on prerogative powers thus enabling debate and Parliamentary scrutiny to take place. This form of democratic check on the Executive provides a visible and public forum for discussion. In the *Council of Civil Service Unions v Minister for the Civil Service*[44] known as the *GCHQ Case*, in 1985, the House of Lords held that in legal principle the prerogative could be subject to judicial review in much the same way as an Act of Parliament or delegated legislation made under the Act. The Prime Minister relied on an Order in Council made under the prerogative to ban trade union membership by staff at the Government Communications Headquarters. Reliance on the Order in Council was claimed on the basis of national security. In the past prerogative powers had not always been amenable to judicial review, and *GCHQ* has settled the question of justiciability. However, the judges have shown reluctance to offer a fundamental reconsideration of how such review might operate. The wide discretion given to the Executive in their use of prerogative powers in the *Northumbria Police Authority* case may indicate a judicial willingness to support executive powers.

4-047

The supply of CS gas and baton rounds to the Northumbria Police Authority was open to the Home Secretary as a prerogative power "to supply equipment reasonably required by police forces to discharge their functions". The provision of equipment was authorised by the Police Act 1964 but also by the prerogative. Such a prerogative may be found in the Crown's right to prevent crime and maintain justice. This is an example of a prerogative being updated to the needs of modern society.

4-048

In *Secretary of State for the Home Department Ex p. Fire Brigades Union*[45] the House of Lords acknowledged the importance of statutory authority over the prerogative. The case concerned the attempt by the Home Secretary to introduce a tariff system of compensation under prerogative powers in preference to the system of compensation established under the Criminal Justice Act 1988. The House of Lords held that this was an abuse of prerogative powers and unlawful.

4-049

Prerogative powers may appear to sit uneasily with the legislative functions provided by a democratically elected Parliament. Nevertheless, the importance of the prerogative is undiminished. Consider, for example, the prerogative of mercy, one of the personal prerogatives of the Crown which is exercised theoretically by the Sovereign on advice of the Home Secretary.

---

42 [1979] Ch. 344; [1979] 2 W.L.R. 700 Ch D.
43 (1985) 7 E.H.R.R. 14 ECHR.
44 [1985] A.C. 374; [1984] 3 W.L.R. 1174 HL at [418B]–[418C].
45 [1995] 2 A.C. 513; [1995] 2 All E.R. 244 HL.

A pardon so granted may be free or conditional. It may be regarded as an essential power, a necessary part of the criminal process to remedy mistakes either at trials or appeal. At present such a power appears as a final determination made by the Home Secretary and to date the courts have been reluctant to provide review of how it is exercised. Arguments for and against such a review may be made but the question is, should such a power of pardon remain a prerogative and not a statutory power?

4-050 The preference for a legislative rather than a prerogative power is intended to regularise and bring up-to-date ancient practice and provide clarification of a vague and uncertain area of the law.

4-051 The courts have been willing to define the existence of the prerogative and its applicability. But in the *GCHQ Case*, the House of Lords were reluctant to extend judicial scrutiny to the question of whether prerogative powers should or should not be exercised. This potentially leaves a wide discretion as to whether statutory or prerogative powers should be used, which apparently does not fall within the remit of judicial scrutiny. However, in *R (Bancoult) v Foreign Secretary (No.2)*,[46] the House of Lords accepted that the prerogative power to make an Order in Council might be reviewed. An Order in Council had been made preventing displaced Chagos Islanders from returning home. The House of Lords upheld the Order on the grounds of security and cost factors. The case reveals that the courts are, at a minimum, willing to consider the basis of the use of prerogative powers, including an Order in Council. The Supreme Court in *R (on the application of Sandiford) v Secretary of State for Foreign and Commonwealth Affairs*[47] considered the circumstances of Mrs Sandiford, a British national in Bali, Indonesia, convicted of drug offences and awaiting execution by firing squad. Mrs Sandiford requested legal representation as part of consular assistance in such cases. The Supreme Court considered the Foreign Secretary's broad policy of not providing funding for legal representation under the exercise of prerogative powers. In fact, the Foreign Office considered the special circumstances of Mrs Sandiford's case including the question of her fair trial and had put Mrs Sandiford in touch with local lawyers but could not fund legal expenses. The Supreme Court rejected Mrs Sandiford's case but suggested that the Foreign Secretary should review the policy in the light if new information available in Mrs Sandiford's case.

4-052 The example of the *Northumbria* case[48] has shown the use of the prerogative to secure a particularly broad discretion to preserve the peace. Since the Second World War, legislation such as the Emergency Powers (Defence) Acts and various public order acts such as the consolidation in the Public Order Act 1986 and the Prevention of Terrorism (Temporary Provisions) Act 1984 on terrorism in the UK has shown the wide powers required for the maintenance of peace. But despite the width of these wide statutory powers, they do not preclude the future use of the prerogative.

4-053 An alternative perspective offers a more restrictive use of prerogative powers. On this perspective, if statutory powers exist which apply to the same activities as a prerogative power, the

---

46 [2008] UKHL 61; [2009] 1 A.C. 453.
47 [2014] UKSC 44; [2014] 1 W.L.R. 2697.
48 [1989] Q.B. 26; [1988] 2 W.L.R. 590 CA (Civ Div).

statutory powers should be used. In *Attorney General v De Keysers Royal Hotel Ltd*[49] the House of Lords preferred a statutory basis for possession of a London hotel for Staff Officers during the First World War, as opposed to the use of prerogative powers. Lord Moulton explained:

> "There can be no excuse for reverting to prerogative powers simpliciter—if indeed they even did exist in such a form as would cover the proposed acquisition, a matter which is far from clear in such a case as the present—when the legislative has given to the Crown statutory powers which are wider than anyone pretends that it possessed under the prerogative..."

In *Burmah Oil Co v Lord Advocate*,[50] the House of Lords accepted that the use of the prerogative did not prevent a claim for compensation even where the destruction of oil installations was required to prevent the enemy from using a valuable resource. After the decision of the House of Lords, the War Damage Act 1965 retroactively removed the subjects' rights to compensation.

4-054

Prerogative powers allow the Crown the power of incorporation, such as the incorporation of universities, professional societies and even the British Broadcasting Corporation. Additional powers required are usually statutory and the prerogative is confined to the power to hold property, enter contracts and engage in the terms of the activities contained in the Royal Charter. In most cases today, statutory authority is provided in the relevant legislation which is adapted to ensure the corporate entity has sufficient legal powers. Historically this "incorporation" of local authorities such as Parish, District and County Councils provided the early basis of local government.

4-055

E: The Prerogative in Foreign Affairs

Foreign relations often involve international agreements and are primarily conducted under prerogative powers. International agreements cover a wide range of activities contained in treaties, conventions, agreements, protocols or charters. While often binding in international law, their application as part of the UK's domestic law requires an Act of Parliament. While the Crown has no prerogative powers to enforce treaties as part of English law, the Crown possesses wide prerogative powers in foreign affairs where the Crown in an action for tort liability may plead the defence of "act of state" for acts performed abroad. This defence is strictly confined to acts done "abroad" and not within domestic jurisdiction.

4-056

---

49 [1920] A.C. 508 HL.
50 [1965] A.C. 75; [1964] 2 W.L.R. 1231 HL.

4-057

The term "act of state" is itself a complex expression which does not facilitate easy definition in constitutional law. Jackson and Leopold[51] define that the term act of state:

> "...is generally used for an act done by the Crown as a matter of policy in relation to another state, or in relation to an individual who is not within the allegiance to the Crown."

4-058

In *Laker Airways v Dept of Trade*[52] Lord Denning considered the use of the prerogative in connection with the designation of an airline. The Bermuda Agreement 1946, a Treaty between the US and the UK, stated that designated carriers would be able to obtain a foreign air-carrier permit from the US Civil Aeronautical Board which was subject to Presidential signature. On the part of the UK, the Civil Aviation Act 1971 permitted the Civil Aviation Authority (CAA) to issue an air transport licence to provide a designated carrier permission. The case arose when Laker Airlines, who had been granted a licence for its low-cost transatlantic air service, found that a change of government resulted in the Secretary of State issuing the CAA guidelines effectively withdrawing the licence designation from Laker. The Secretary of State claimed both statutory and prerogative powers. Lord Denning in an *obiter dicta* rejected the use of prerogative powers "to deprive the subject of a right conferred on him by statute". Once a licence had been granted under the 1971 Act, it could not be removed by prerogative powers.

4-059

Where an act of state is more directly relevant is where the Crown may use its authority to protect itself from action at the suit of a private individual. Here the courts may examine the facts to decide whether an act of state may be pleaded and whether done within the limits of the discretion. It has been held that a wrong committed by a Crown servant against a British citizen in a British territory has no defence of act of state. However, this view is not always accepted by the courts and each case would seem to depend on its own particular facts. Particularly confusing is the question of the definition of "British citizen" under the British Nationality Act 1981; does it mean the same as British subject, or those "who owe allegiance to the Crown"?

4-060

In defining the limits of the prerogative and its reviewability, the courts have broadened their review to the issuing of passports which are Crown property issued at the discretion of the Secretary of State. In *R v Secretary of State for Foreign and Commonwealth Affairs Ex p. Everett*[53] the Court of Appeal reviewed the Secretary of State's refusal to issue a passport under the prerogative. Taylor LJ explained that:

> "the grant or refusal of a passport is... a matter of administrative decision, affecting the rights of individuals and their freedom of

---

51 P. Jackson and P. Leopold, *O'Hood Phillips and Jackson: Constitutional and Administrative Law* (London: Sweet & Maxwell, 2001), p.321.
52 [1977] Q.B. 643; [1977] 2 W.L.R. 234 CA (Civ Div).
53 [1989] Q.B. 811; [1989] 2 W.L.R. 224 CA (Civ Div).

> travel. It raises issues which are just as justiciable as, for example, the issues arising in immigration cases."

4-061 This view rejected the argument that the issuing of passports fell within the category of foreign affairs involving executive functions and therefore outside the power of the courts to review. The Counter-Terrorism and Security Act 2015 provides a statutory basis for the removal and seizure of a passport from those suspected of terrorism as well as imposing temporary restrictions on travel. It also provides powers for the temporary exclusion of citizens from the UK.[54] It also places restriction son UK citizens and the retention of travel documents.

4-062 The prerogative in foreign affairs developed historically and continues to exist as an important "residuary" power of the Crown. The power to wage war and to make use of the armed forces are long standing traditional prerogatives. In the case of the armed forces, statutory regulation under the Armed Forces Act 2006 applies but the prerogative remains an important source of power.[55] The decision to deploy the armed forces in any armed conflict is a prerogative power exercised by the Prime Minister on behalf of the Crown. Decisions are reached in Cabinet with advice from the National Security Council and the Chief of the Defence Staff. It is rare for there to be a formal declaration of war and there are no legally enforceable obligation to obtain parliamentary approval or for that matter to keep Parliament informed.

Parliamentary pressure has been building to provide Parliament with a role. Since 2003 it has been common practice to allow Parliament to vote on military action. The practice began with the decision to take military action in Iraq. Parliament voted in favour by 412 to 149 votes. From the time of military action on 20 March 2003 until the end of combat operations on 1 May 2003 there were over nine ministerial statements and three written ministerial statements. Parliamentary oversight has become an important element of scrutiny. The practice of parliamentary debate and information has become well established. The Coalition government in 2011 accepted that in general Parliament should be informed prior to military action with the opportunity to debate, although in times of emergency this might not be possible. In practice there have been instances where troops were committed such as Helmand province in Afghanistan in 206 where there was no vote or debate. Military action in the Libyan campaign in Mali in early 2013 was not debated or voted on in Parliament. There was a debate and vote for action to be taken against the Assad regime in Syria in August 2013 and in action against the Islamic State (ISIS) in Iraq in September 2014. Significantly a Government motion to deploy troops in Syria in 2013 was defeated by 13 votes after debate. Although the Government could have continued to use the prerogative and taken military action, it accepted that it was bound by the Parliamentary vote. In November 2015, the Government managed to gain Parliamentary approval for action against ISIS/Daesh after a heated Parliamentary debate.[56]

---

54 House of Commons Library, *Deprivation of British Citizenship and withdrawal of passport facilities*, SN/HA/66820 (30 January 2015).
55 House of Commons Library, *Parliamentary Approval for Military Action*, Briefing Paper No.7166 (12 May 2015).
56 House of Commons Briefing Papers, *Iraq and Syria developments in 2015*, CBP 7261 (27 November 2015).

4-063 This leaves uncertainty over the precise role of Parliament and whether there is a convention that Parliamentary authority must be sought where there is a possibility of premeditated military action, or where military deployment has been made, or where retrospective approval might be given if military force is used in an emergency or where there are circumstances for Parliament to be recalled.[57] This is an area where clarity over Parliament's role is required.[58]

4-064 Some general conclusions might be made about the prerogative. Although the existence and precise limits of the prerogative are at times vague and unchartered, it is subject to judicial review and the remit of its use may be subject to judicial control. Many of the conventions, characteristic of the UK's Constitution, owe their origins to ancient prerogative powers. The principal convention, for example, is that the Queen shall exercise her formal legal powers only in accordance with the advice of ministers. The Fixed-Term Parliaments Act 2011 has removed the Sovereign's power of dissolution for a general election in order to provide a mandate for a particularly controversial government policy. The prerogative remains an important source of public power, although it is becoming increasingly subject to Parliamentary oversight and statutory replacement.

4-065 Total abolition of the prerogative and its replacement with statutory powers would, out of necessity, require codification of rules covering many of the areas it currently regulates. This may prove difficult and more challenging than might appear at first glance. Any codified arrangement would need to retain some degree of discretion in defining when prerogative powers may be used.

4-066 A major advantage is the inherent flexibility and versatility of the prerogative. For example the prerogative of mercy may remove "all pains, penalties and punishment". In foreign affairs, diplomatic relations and representation have their source in prerogative and not statutory powers. Democratic accountability is argued in favour of statutory powers over the prerogative because statutory authority is more visible, clearly defined and subject to the parliamentary process. It is also clear that prerogative powers when claimed to give sovereign immunity are subject to review. A detailed restriction on the immunities enjoyed by foreign governments is provided by the State Immunity Act 1978. It includes situations where civil actions may lie against foreign states that fall within the jurisdiction of the British courts. This covers commercial transactions and contracts, liability in tort, and patents. None of the provisions of the 1978 Act are intended to affect the immunities given to embassies and consular services of foreign diplomats under the Diplomatic Privileges Act 1964 and the Consular Relations Act 1968. A significant decision of the House of Lords on the limits and extent of sovereign immunity may be found in *R v Bow Street Magistrate Ex p. Pinochet (Nos 1 and 2)*, known as the *Pinochet case*.[59] The use of a claim of sovereign immunity to protect

---

57 See the Political and Constitutional Reform Committee, *Parliament's Role in Conflict Decisions*, HC 923 Session 2010–12. R. Joseph, *The War Prerogative* (Oxford: Oxford University Press, 2013). *The Governance of Britain: Constitutional Renewal*, Pts 1–3, CM 7342-I, Session 2007–08.
58 House of Lords Select Committee on the Constitution, *Waging War: Parliament's role and Responsibility*, HL Paper 236-I, Session 2005–06.
59 *R v Bow Street Magistrate Ex p. Pinochet (No.1)* [2000] 1 A.C. 61; [1998] 3 W.L.R. 1456 HL; also see *Pinochet (No.2)* [2000] 1 A.C. 119; [1999] 2 W.L.R. 272 HL.

General Pinochet from arrest and extradition was considered in detail by the House of Lords. The case against Pinochet was that, while Head of State in Chile, he had acted unlawfully in authorising torture and other illegal acts. The claim of sovereign immunity was held by a majority in the House of Lords to only afford protection to legal acts and not illegal ones. A distinction appears to have been drawn between the full immunity enjoyed by current and serving diplomats and Heads of State and the partial immunity enjoyed after service. The illegality complained about, the breach of human rights, fell under s.134 of the Criminal Justice Act 1988 which incorporated into British law the Convention on Torture. The application for extradition was made by Spain. General Pinochet is not a British citizen and the crimes alleged to have been committed were outside the UK. The majority in the House of Lords appear to construct the responsibilities of the courts in England and Wales as giving effect to international obligations on human rights. This is a trend that is noticeably moving the courts towards a universal jurisdiction over crimes committed under international law and the upholding of international human rights. The majority appear to have rejected the idea of upholding any protection afforded by sovereign immunity when human rights abuses were alleged against a former Head of State.[60]

F: The Crown and the Government

The Monarch as Head of State performs many ceremonial functions. The money to finance the Royal Family is separate from the expenses of maintaining the Government. Since George III's time, in return for the surrender to Parliament of the ancient hereditary revenues of the Crown and any income from Crown land, Parliament has made provision for the salaries and other expenses of the Royal Family. The Civil List Act 1952 provided for a fixed annual sum but the Civil List Act 1972 provided that the sum may be varied by Treasury Order. In 1975 the effects of inflation caused the Civil List Act 1975 to be passed allowing supplements to be paid. This remains the case today although from 1991 it was agreed that a fixed annual payment of about £8 million per annum would be made. The result, it was hoped, would avoid any need for incremental increases and would mean that Royal finances would fall into line with the principles of ordinary departmental expenditure. Increasingly the Royal Family is being treated like any other government department. Indeed, some expenses such as the Royal yacht before its decommissioning in 1999 were paid out of departmental expenses. In 1992 the Queen agreed to pay for certain members of the Royal Family out of her own funds. The Prince of Wales has never received any money from the Civil List as provision is made for income out of the Duchy of Cornwall. Also in 1992 the Queen agreed for the first time to pay income tax in respect of her private income.

4–067

---

60   Kriangsak Kittichaisaree, *International Criminal Law* (Oxford: Oxford University Press, 2001), pp.56–61.

4-068 The Sovereign Grant Act 2011 provides new financial arrangements for the Monarchy. This is a beneficial change in providing a single Sovereign Grant replacing previous sources of funding from 1 April 2012. It is set at around £38 million (2014–15) according to a formula under s.6 of the Act. Unlike previous arrangements, the Sovereign Grant is not specific to the current Monarch and is made in respect of official duties. It is subject to Parliamentary approval and scrutiny and will continue beyond the life-time of the current Monarch. The Monarchy also receives income from the Duchy of Lancaster and is subject to income tax and this funds the Privy Purse. It is currently around £13 million annually. The Queen has a private income from her personal investments and estimated to be around £330 million of investment income. There is also a proportion of funding from the profits of the Crown Estate. It is a managed property portfolio and is around £267 million surplus annually.[61]

4-069 While some favour abolition of the Monarchy claiming that it is unrepresentative or out of touch with ordinary people, the trend is more in favour of incremental modernisation. How to make the Monarchy compatible with a modern and vibrant democracy is less easy to achieve. Hereditary office appears inconsistent with elected and open competition. Today there is less tolerance of the ancient relics of the Constitution and it is generally accepted that the Monarchy's survival depends on the wish of the British people to maintain a Monarchy. This debate should not undervalue the importance of the Monarchy in the terms of Walter Bagehot's defined roles[62]: "the right to be consulted, the right to encourage and the right to warn". In these matters the Monarch is ruled by convention.

The personal powers of the Sovereign

4-070 Some of the personal powers of the Queen have been touched upon above. Three require some special mention. First the appointment of the Prime Minister, secondly the dismissal of ministers, and finally the dissolution of Parliament. In the case of the appointment of the Prime Minister, the Monarch's choice is governed by the convention that the person appointed must have the confidence of the House of Commons. The judgment as to who fulfils this criterion is usually straightforward: the party leader with the majority of seats is appointed as the Prime Minister. Where a party leader resigns or dies in office then the election of the leader falls to the rules of the political party in power. The resignation of Mrs Thatcher as Prime Minister in 1990 resulted in the Conservative Party's election of Mr Major as the leader of the Conservative Party, the party with the largest number of seats, and he therefore became Prime Minister.

4-071 The Fixed-Term Parliaments Act 2011 has settled one area of potential controversy surrounding the Monarch's powers to require a dissolution in the event of an unpopular government policy or proposal. Such a dissolution is only possible by consent of a special majority in the House of Commons. At the same time the Act provides for five-year fixed-term Parliaments

---

61 House of Commons, *Finances of the Monarchy*, SN/SG/00819 (11 September 2014).
62 Walter Bagehot, *The English Constitution* (London: Fontana, 1963), p.111.9.

and this remains the position until the Act is repealed or amended. In the event of the need for an earlier election, this is possible if the government loses a vote of no confidence or where the Government loses the support of two thirds of MPs.[63]

4–072

The second prerogative power relates to the dismissal of ministers. This is undertaken on the advice of the Prime Minister. This in turn must rest on the political reality of most government power, the ability to command the support of the political party in power. It is unlikely that today the Queen could exercise a personal choice over the dismissal of the Prime Minister or ministers. It is clear that the reality of public opinion must caution any interference with democratic choices made by the electorate.

4–073

Finally, there is the question of the prerogative of dissolution. The advice of the Prime Minister is normally accepted in these matters. A Cabinet decision is unnecessary before any request is made and it is accepted convention that the request for a dissolution should not be refused nor has one been refused over the past century.

4–074

The question of whether the Monarch's prerogative powers should be codified in a written constitution or provided for in a statute has been raised in several reform proposals and considered in the codified constitution prepared by the House of Commons Political and Constitutional Reform Committee.[64]

G: Cabinet and Prime Minister

Powers and functions

Executive powers in the UK are carried out by the Cabinet and Prime Minister. Crick, writing in 1964 commented[65]:

4–075

> "Of all Governments of countries with free political institutions, British government exhibits the greatest concentration of power and authority. Nowhere else is a Government normally so free to act decisively, so unfettered by formal restraints of constitutional law."

Crick's analysis appears equally valid in recent times. The Government enjoys considerable powers and rights over the citizen through a wide variety of sources. Statutory, prerogative

4–076

---

63   House of Commons Library Standard Note, *Fixed-Term Parliaments Act 2011*, SN/PC/6111 (16 October 2014).
64   See House of Commons Political and Constitutional Reform Committee, *Mapping the Path towards Codifying or Not Codifying the United Kingdom Constitution* (2014–15).
65   B. Crick, *The Reform of Parliament*, 2nd edn (London: Weidenfeld & Nicolson, 1968), p.16.

or EC Directives or Regulations may permit the Government or its agents to carry out different tasks and functions. Such extensive powers are said to be exercised according to the law. In this respect it may be noted that the courts' role in overseeing ministerial decision-taking becomes important when ministerial decisions are challenged in the courts. The function of judicial review in the oversight of government involves the broader question of how government is made accountable, and the different techniques both legal and political involved in the scrutiny of government.

4-077 The executive powers of government in the UK are exercised by or on behalf of ministers of the Crown who are members of the Cabinet. The Cabinet as an institution of government has its origins in the seventeenth and eighteenth centuries. No exact date for its beginning may be given as it evolved around confidential advisers to the Monarch. The Cabinet's independence from Royal influence was gradual and probably due to the incapacity of various Monarchs rather than a revolutionary break with tradition.[66]

4-078 Historical traces of the exact form the eighteenth-century Cabinet may have taken are obscure. References in 1740 as to the existence of the inner Cabinet bear similarities to the modern Cabinet system of today. As the role of domestic government expanded beyond the collection of finance, the regulation of the State became a shared enterprise not solely within Royal power. Various departments of State may be identified with specific responsibilities such as the Lords Commissioners of the Treasury. Hennessy[67] identifies the Privy Council as the model of how the earliest Cabinet took shape. Some writers are reluctant to link the modern Cabinet with any particular committee such as the Foreign Committee or Intelligence Committee of the Privy Council in the 1660s and 1670s.[68]

4-079 Blackstone[69] linked the Monarch with exclusive executive powers. Advice taken by the Monarch came from the Privy Council. Cornish notes[70]:

> "Queen Anne had held regular 'Cabinets' and the idea persisted, dividing at some stages into inner and outer works, but still contributing to a process in which the Monarch would play a decisive personal role. The Chief among these ministers, forerunner of the modern Prime Minister, remained so long as he kept the Royal confidence, though it was already part of that favour that he should also enjoy the support of the Commons on most issues."

---

66 The cabinet is fully discussed in: J. P. Mackintosh, *The British Cabinet* (London: Stevens and Sons, 1977); Ivor Jennings, *Cabinet Government* (Cambridge: Cambridge University Press, 1959); Patrick Gordon Walker, *The Cabinet* (London: Cape, 1972); and Douglas Wass, *Government and the Governed* (London: Routledge & Kegan Paul, 1984).
67 P. Hennessy, *Cabinet* (Oxford: Basil Blackwell, 1986), pp.100–103.
68 Jennings, *Cabinet Government*, p.86.
69 Blackstone, *Commentaries*, Bk I, Ch.6.
70 W. R. Cornish and G. de Clark, *Law and Society in England 1750–1950* (London: Sweet & Maxwell, 1989), pp.10–14.

4-080 Bagehot, writing of the English Constitution in 1867, identified the principal characteristics which linked the legislature and executive elements of the Constitution. He acknowledged "the efficient secret of the English Constitution" as the close union and complete fusion between the executive and legislative powers. The Prime Minister was at the head of the "efficient" part of the Constitution. Bagehot distinguished the "efficient" from the "dignified". The Queen was head of the "dignified" part of the Constitution. The "efficient" were the parts of the Constitution "by which it, in fact works and rules". The "dignified" parts were those which "executed and preserved the reverence of the population".

4-081 Bagehot's classification that the Cabinet and Prime Minister performed the "efficient" elements of the Constitution, endures today as a classic explanation of the theory of cabinet government[71]:

> "A Cabinet is a combining committee—a hyphen which joins, a buckle which fosters, the legislative part of the State to the executive part of the State. In its origin it belongs to the one, in its functions it belongs to the other."

4-082 Cabinet government has continued to develop, conforming to the theory of Bagehot's definition, but in recent times evolving modern characteristics. It is common practice under the Coalition Government for the Cabinet to meet away from London at various regional centres representing a change in past tradition and practice.[72]

4-083 Cabinet size and the allocation of seats within Cabinet does not conform to a rigid convention but, through the choice exercised by the Prime Minister of the day. Since the Second World War the size of the Cabinet has varied. The smallest modern Cabinet of 16 members was achieved by Churchill by excluding Ministers of Education and Agriculture and Fisheries. The recent experience of Cabinet Government suggests between 22 and 24 members. Mrs Thatcher's Cabinet had 22 members, Mr Wilson's 24, and Mr Blair had 23 members. The number of 22–23 appears settled. It is normal practice for all major departments of government to be placed under a Cabinet Minister and subject to Parliamentary scrutiny.

4-084 However, the House of Commons Disqualification Act 1975 and the Ministerial and other Salaries Act 1975 allow no more than 95 holders of ministerial office to sit and vote in the Commons. In addition, the Prime Minister may appoint between 20 and 30 Parliamentary private secretaries. Such appointments are largely held by supporters of the Government in the Commons. The pensions arrangements for ministers and senior office holders have been placed on a statutory basis under the Public Service Pensions Act 2013.and are subject to review by the Senior Salaries Review Body.[73]

---

71 Bagehot, *The English Constitution* (London: Chapman & Hall, 1867).
72 House of Commons Library, *A List of Cabinet Meetings held away from Downing Street*, SN 06601 (25 February 2014).
73 House of Commons Library, *Pensions of Ministers and Senior Office Holders*, SN 04586 (7 March 2014).

4-085 The working of the Cabinet, as distinct from its membership, has always been cloaked with secrecy. Gladstone, when Prime Minister, sent copies of Cabinet discussions to the Queen with personal notes and suggestions added. Glimpses of the Cabinet at work in recent times have emerged from the published diaries of ex-Cabinet Ministers, most notably Richard Crossman's Diaries.[74] Often such diaries reveal more about individual ministers than the exact functioning of the Cabinet, which remains secret. The 30-year rule allows the disclosure of Cabinet documents, but this is subject to "weeding" out those that remain sensitive or too confidential to be made available to the public. Some of the more confidential papers may be withheld for a longer period than the 30-year rule may provide. The confidentiality of Cabinet deliberations receives protection in a number of ways. Section 8(4) of the Parliamentary Commissioner Act 1967 protects the information that relates to the proceedings of the Cabinet. S.28 of the Data Protection Act 1998 provides exemptions for information from the data protection provisions of the Act if the minister's a member of the Cabinet. The Freedom of Information Act 2000 continues to work with the assumption that Cabinet papers are protected from disclosure. However, it is permissible for ministers when they leave office to be allowed to consult Cabinet papers in respect of an inquiry or query that relate to their time in office. This is subject to the consent of the serving Prime Minister and the opinion of the former Prime Minister. The question of confidentiality and its observance has arisen in the ongoing Chilcot inquiry set up as a Privy Counsellor inquiry into the conduct of the Iraq war.[75]

4-086 *The Haldane Report*[76] (1918) is one of the few reports that tackle the issue of what is the role and function of the Cabinet. Its description is a classic formulation of the theory and practice of cabinet government. The Cabinet's functions include the determination of policy to be submitted to Parliament, the control of the national Executive in accordance with policy presented by Parliament and "the continuous co-ordination and delineation of the activities of several Departments of State". A noticeable part of Haldane's description of the Cabinet function is the parliamentary aspect of the Cabinet's role, thus acknowledging Parliament's ultimate authority.

4-087 Since the *Haldane Report*, the Cabinet has continued to change reflecting the party political aspects of its development. In 1986, Peter Hennessy[77] published a confidential government memorandum which reveals how the modern Cabinet has developed. In *Questions on Procedure for ministers, A Guide for Cabinet Ministers* (1986, as amended in 1994) the business of the Cabinet is identified as:

> "(a) questions which engage the collective responsibility of the Government, either because they raise major issues of policy or because they are likely to occasion public comment or criticism;

---

74 *Attorney General v Jonathan Cape Ltd* [1976] Q.B. 752; [1975] 3 W.L.R. 606 QBD.
75 House of Commons Library, Briefing Paper SN6215, *The Chilcot Inquiry* (3 June 2015).
76 *Report of the Machinery of Government Committee*, Cd.9230 (1918).
77 Hennessy, *Cabinet* (1986), pp.8–13. Also published in *The New Statesman*, February 14, 18, 21 (1986).

> (b) questions on which there is an unresolved conflict of interest between departments."

The *Cabinet Manual* is an attempt to set out in a codified form many of the internal practices relating to the working of the Cabinet.[78] The benefits of the Cabinet *Manual* are that it may inform our understandings of the way decisions are made but it is not binding and it may grow in significance as a serious explanation of how powers are exercised. The need for amendment is important so that it is kept up-to-date but it should not be given the force of law or statutory authority. Parliament may not regard its existence as entirely beneficial as the Manual does not emanate from a Parliamentary committee.

4–088

In addition, financial proposals are submitted to the Cabinet and ministers may set out their views on general issues of policy before the Cabinet. Advice may be given by the Secretary to the Cabinet, as to the question of when matters which may be suitable for the discussion of the whole Cabinet may be raised. The Prime Minister's consent must be sought if an individual minister wishes to raise a matter at Cabinet.

4–089

A noticeable distinction is drawn between the individual work of ministers in departments and general policy issues to be put before Cabinet. Defining such a distinction is clearly problematic but leaves the setting of the tone, culture and overall policy of the Cabinet within the Prime Minister's ambit.

4–090

The evolution of the modern Cabinet through incremental change from the nineteenth century to the modern style of management, is a remarkable demonstration of the inherent flexibility in constitutional arrangements. Constitutional innovation may take place without any general reconsideration.

4–091

One innovation of modern cabinets has been the gradual increase in the Prime Minister's influence. Crossman[79] believed that the era of Prime Ministerial government was the reality of modern government. The outcome, he feared, was to relegate the Cabinet from the "efficient" to the "dignified" according to the Bagehot classification.

4–092

Examples cited of the so-called "decline" in the decision-making role of the Cabinet include the announcement that the first British A-bomb was tested without the Cabinet having made a formal decision on the matter, when the Atlee Government commissioned its development with only the Prime Minister and a number of close Cabinet colleagues consulted. The Prime Minister has regular meetings with the Queen and has an overall policy making role for the government.

4–093

In 1984 the decision of the Government to ban trade union membership at GCHQ Cheltenham was made by a small group of Cabinet Ministers rather than the Cabinet as a whole. In 1986 Mr Heseltine, the Secretary of State for Defence, complained and later resigned

---

78 See Andrew Blick and Lord Hennessy, *The Cabinet Manual and the Working of the British Constitution* (London: IPPR, 2011).
79 R. H. S. Crossman, *Diaries of a Cabinet Minister* (London: Henry Holt, 1976), 3 Vols. Also see Turpin, *British Government and the Constitution* (1990), pp.168–70; G. W. Jones, "Development of the Cabinet" in W. Thornhill (ed), *The Modernisation of British Government* (Oxford: Oxford University Press, 1975).

because the Cabinet had not discussed a key policy issue over the future of Westland Plc, a major defence supplier of helicopters. His resignation came at a Cabinet meeting, when it was decided that ministers' statements on the affair should first be submitted to the Cabinet Office for clearance as to their consistency with Government policy.[80]

4-094 In the final analysis, Westland may be seen as the assertion of Cabinet decision-making. However, in the initial stages the problem may have arisen because of the use of Cabinet committees, the restricted membership of each committee preventing a full debate of the issues before the full Cabinet. Mrs Thatcher's resignation in 1990 may have underlined the importance of Cabinet support, even when the Prime Minister appears popular and successful.

4-095 Committees of the Cabinet are of nineteenth century origin. Their use has evolved over time in an ad hoc way. Some committees are chaired by the Prime Minister, others by senior ministers. Some are referred to as standing committees which are permanent for the duration of the Prime Minister's period in office. Others are called ad hoc committees because they have specific and particular issues to exercise. One good example of this was known as the "Star Chamber", well known because it used to meet each autumn to reconcile the competing claims made by the various spending departments. Membership of the Star Chamber included the Chief Secretary to the Treasury and the Chancellor of the Exchequer. Since 1992 the Star Chamber has not met. Its current role is undertaken as part of the Comprehensive Spending Review which settles government expenditure over a three-year period and concludes its deliberations by July. There is a third category known as ministerial committees which are composed only of civil servants. The existence of such committees has been, until recently, kept within the inner workings of No.10 Downing Street. However, the committees and their operation are now more openly publicised and acknowledged. In 1999 it was discovered that there were well over 13 committees, 11 sub-committees and seven ministerial groups. The range of activities covered by such committees is comprehensive: Economic Affairs; Energy Policy; Public Services and Expenditure; Environment; Local Government; London; Home and Social Affairs; Women's Issues; Legislation; Constitutional Reform; Devolution; Northern Ireland; Intelligence Services; Food Safety; and Utility Regulation. The existence of a committee reflects the ebb and flow of government policy.

4-096 The Coalition Government adopted a number of committees including a National Security Committee covering international relations, defence, foreign policy and National Security. Also a Home Affairs Committee overseeing constitutional and political reform as well as immigration, health, education, schools and welfare. The Cabinet Office, *Guide to Making Legislation*[81] provides an explanation as to the role of policy making and the work of committees and its integration into the law making process.

4-097 Such committees have added to the debate on the question of Cabinet or Prime Ministerial government. Prime Minister's differ in style and temperament. One important means of oversight is the *Ministerial Code* 2010 that sets the principles of public life and the standards of behaviour expected of ministers and their departments, civil servants and the presentation of

---

80 Heseltine, Resignation statement, *The Times*, 10 January 1986.
81 Cabinet Office, *Guide to Making Legislation* London, (July 2014).

their policies. Controversies over the working practices and behaviour of political advisers have proved difficult to resolve and very few have led to investigation under the Code.[82]

The influence of the Prime Minister is seen as a key element in their functioning, appointment and operation. In theory, ministers have access to the full Cabinet should they require approval against the wishes of the committee but only where the committee chairman gives approval. Mrs Thatcher when Prime Minister continued the procedure of her predecessors by using committees to make key decisions. In 1980, the decision to replace Polaris with Trident was taken by an ad hoc committee with the Defence Secretary, Foreign Secretary, Chancellor of the Exchequer and Home Secretary present. The granting of independence to the Bank of England in 1997 through powers to set interest rates also appears as a decision undertaken without formal Cabinet discussion.

In addition to the above committees, there is conclusive evidence that Prime Ministers have developed the habit of summoning an "inner Cabinet" of key ministers. Clement Atlee, Chamberlain, Churchill, Eden and Wilson throughout their premierships made use of a small group of close friends or allies drawn from the Cabinet. In a constitutional sense the existence of such an inner Cabinet is not recognised in our formal constitutional arrangements. However, its existence is a political fact, reflecting the way in which Prime Ministers may wish to function. During periods of crisis such as the Falklands or Gulf Wars, small war cabinets exist containing key ministers relevant to the success of wartime operations.

The question arises as to whether such "inner cabinets" are consistent with Prime Ministerial government which may conform to a Presidential style or should be compared to collective decision-taking through cabinet government. The existence of the inner Cabinet and various committees of the Cabinet, such as the Defence and Overseas Policy Committee; the Economic Strategy Committee; the Legislation Committee; and a Home and Social Offices Committee is used as evidence to strengthen the view that Prime Ministerial influence is paramount.

Crossman wrote[83] in 1972 that Prime Ministerial government arose because the Prime Minister decides the membership of the Cabinet, sets the agenda of Cabinet discussion and organises Cabinet committees. An opposing view to Crossman is provided by Jones,[84] who doubts that the evidence against cabinet government is conclusive. Jones offers the analysis that trends in favour of Prime Ministerial government may just as easily be interpreted to show that the Cabinet's survival depends on effective delegation to cope with a growing bureaucracy in government. In recent years, Mrs Thatcher's style and method dominated the work of the Cabinet. Her years as Prime Minister seemed to support the view that "collective decision-making in Cabinet" had suffered a decline and a shift to a Presidential style.

---

82 House of Commons Library, *The Ministerial Code and the Independent Adviser on Ministers' Interests*, 03750 (12 May 2015).
83 Crossman, *Inside View* (London: Cape, 1972), pp.62–67.
84 G. W. Jones, "The Prime Minister's power" in *The British Prime Minister* A. King (ed), (London: Macmillan, 1985), p.216.

4-102 Mrs Thatcher came under the accusation that in all but name the style was Presidential rather than Prime Ministerial.[85] The same analysis is offered about Mr Blair. The reduction of Prime Minister's Questions Time (PMQs) to one occasion of 30 minutes each Wednesday in the week rather than the twice-weekly tradition of past Prime Ministers is viewed as an example of the shift in style.[86] Attendance at Heads of State in the EU or G8/G20 meetings has resulted in the Prime Minister not being able to attend PMQs. Gordon Brown attended 88.2 per cent while Mr Cameron attended 92.5 per cent of meetings.[87]

4-103 This is an indication of the setting of priorities away from Parliament. The use of political advisers and an active role for the Press Secretary to supplement a relatively small number of civil servants in the Prime Minister's Office is seen as further evidence of a shift in the direction of Presidential style. The small number of full Cabinet meetings and the delegation of policy to the various committees mentioned above suggest a shift in emphasis, if not in substance. The shift towards any Presidential style is vigorously denied by the Prime Minister. It is argued that it is a perception about modern government rather than any substantive change in the nature of cabinet government.

4-104 Another dimension to the debate is the party political nature of government's decision-taking. Prime Ministers are simultaneously leaders of their party. At a party political level, the choices exercised by the Prime Minister must ensure electoral success. The timing of the election and the decision to dissolve Parliament are at the discretion of the Prime Minister and choosing wrongly may have the penalty of losing the election and political power.

4-105 The ebb and flow of Prime Ministerial influence through Cabinet reshuffles and policy decision-making is often constrained by the realities of political life. In the case of Mrs Thatcher, the epitome of the shift to a Presidential-style Prime Minister, her demise as Prime Minister was the signal of ultimate Cabinet and therefore party control.[88]

4-106 It may be concluded that in recent years the shifts in style and management techniques between the Cabinet and Prime Minister do not necessarily signal institutional change in the role of the Cabinet. The Prime Minister remains primus inter pares with considerable powers to influence the Cabinet and ultimately the success or failure of the Government.

4-107 The Cabinet Office provides the Cabinet and Prime Minister with the administrative services necessary for the circulation of the Cabinet's agenda reports and recording the Cabinet's conclusion. It is headed by the Secretary to the Cabinet who serves as a Principal Private Secretary to the Prime Minister and is Head of the Civil Service. Contained within the Cabinet Office from 1970 to 1983 was the Cabinet "think-tank" as it was known or more precisely the Central Policy Review Staff (CPRS). The CPRS has the role to cross-departmental activities and take a long-term view of the policies and strategies to be recommended. It was staffed by non-civil servants and abolished by Mrs Thatcher in 1983. It was replaced by a Downing Street

---

85 M. Foley, "Presidential Politics in Britain" (1994) 6(3) *Talking Politics* 141.
86 B. Jones et al. (eds), *Politics UK*, 4th edn (London: Routledge, 1991), p.419.
87 House of Commons Library, *Attendance of the Prime Minister at Prime Minister's Questions (PMQs) since 1979*, SN/PC/04401 (15 December 2015).
88 B. Jones, "Thatcher and After" in Jones et al., *Politics UK*, pp.588–597.

Policy Unit which operates as part of the Prime Minister's Office. There is a communications and strategy section within No.10 to concentrate on media relations.

4–108

Also within the working of No.10, there are various political staff attached to the Prime Minister, including a Principal Private Secretary, press agent and various advisers. Political advisers have in recent years had an increasingly important role within government departments as well as within the Prime Minister's Office. Their role has increased under Mr Blair as Prime Minister. The image of the Prime Minister, in terms of media profile and in the international arena, has given rise to an increasing sense of Presidential powers. The implications of the terrorist attacks on 11 September 2001 and the use of an inner war cabinet to deal with the "war against terrorism" supports the view that for moments in the life-cycle of party politics, the Prime Minister is in charge rather than the Cabinet. It is difficult to predict whether this represents a paradigm shift in the relations between Cabinet and Prime Minister. Large Parliamentary majorities provide for differences in approach and both Mrs Thatcher and Mr Blair had successive majorities overall. In contrast Mr Major did not, and so adopted a more inclusive style of cabinet deliberation.

4–109

The House of Commons Political and Constitutional Reform Committee in 2014-15 published a report on the role and powers of the Prime Minister.[89] Part of the coalition agreement was the "principle of balance" including the allocation of Government business and responsibilities. The Conservative Prime Minister, Mr Cameron, made decisions in consultation with the Deputy Prime Minister, Mr Clegg (Liberal Democrat) and the need for such "agreement" percolated through cabinet committees and discussions. This reduced the "Presidential style" of governing to one of collaborative decision-making and overview of all decision-making processes between Prime Minister and Deputy Prime Minister. At the May election 2015, the electorate found favour with the Conservative Party and the Liberal Democratic's Party's share of the vote diminished significantly. The political lessons from coalition government may make such a coalition more difficult for the future.

Special advisers

4–110

The appointment of special advisers has become a feature of modern government. Technically, special advisers are often temporary civil servants, appointed by the Government of the day to assist ministers on matters that fall outside the political neutrality of civil servants.[90] Concerns expressed about their role and function have led to questions about their compatibility with serving civil servants, especially as many special advisers are appointed because of their political affiliation. Their appointment falls within the patronage of the government of the day but there are various Codes of Conduct that apply to their activities. The 2010 *Code of Conduct for Special Advisers* is a reflection of the Constitutional Reform

---

89 House of Commons Political and Constitutional Reform Committee, *Role and Powers of the Prime Minister*, HC 351 (2014–15).
90 House of Commons Library, Briefing Paper, 03813, *Special Advisers* (18 May 2015).

and Governance Act 2010. The Code requires special advisers to reveal gifts and hospitality received. The number of special advisers has varied over time. In 1995 there were only 34 but this has steadily increased and in November 2014, the number had reached 103 at a cost of £8.4 million.[91] This is the largest number in the history of modern government. It is also a reflection of the increasing role of political policy making as well as the search for specialist advice outside the normal range of civil servants. In 2003, the Committee on Standards in Public Life suggested that there should be a limit to the number of special advisers.[92] Controversy attaches to special advisers especially when their role is open to public censure and debate. In 2011 Mr Coulson, an adviser to the Prime Minister resigned amidst allegations about his former role as editor of the News of the World.[93] Mr Werrity, an adviser to Liam Fox, then the Defence Minister, resigned amidst concerns that Mr Werrity appeared to speak on behalf of the Government when he was associated with Dr Fox in some official capacity.[94] On 14 October 2011, Liam Fox also resigned, after an inquiry undertaken by the Cabinet Secretary was highly critical. Mr Adam Smith resigned in June 2012, as special adviser to the then Culture Secretary, Mr Jeremy Hunt, when it was revealed a that Mr Smith had sent a large number of emails to News International during a period when News International was bidding for BSkyB. Fiona Cunningham, special adviser to the Home Secretary, Thersea May resigned in 2014, when it was revealed that many leaks negative briefings about the then Education Secretary, Michael Gove, to *The Times*.[95] Setting clarity and standards in the respective roles of ministers and advisers is essential. The Code of Conduct for Special Advisers is one step. A more innovative possibility is to set up an Extended Ministerial Office.[96] This might provide a more direct and professional response to ministers in office. There is also the possibility of providing more training for special advisers and better standards and quality of delivery in terms of accountability systems.[97]

Collective and individual ministerial responsibility

4–111

Individual ministerial responsibility is the cornerstone of our constitutional arrangements. The responsibility arises from convention and is defined to mean that ministers are responsible, i.e. accountable, or answerable to Parliament. In modern times it has been interpreted to mean that ministers take responsibility for their departments and for the consequences of what has been decided as a matter of policy. Turpin has identified

---

91   House of Commons Library, *Special Advisers*.
92   Committee on Standards in Public Life, *Defining the Boundaries within the Executive: Ministers, Special Advisers and the Permanent Civil Service* (8 April 2003).
93   *Daily Telegraph*, 21 January 2011.
94   *BBC News*, 14 October 2011.
95   House of Commons Library, Briefing Paper 03813, *Special Advisers* (18 May 2015), p.12.
96   Mr Francis Maude, HC Deb (19 July 2013), c.18WS; and *Civil Service Reform Plan: One Year on*, Cabinet Office (July 2013).
97   The Constitution Unit, *Being A Special Adviser* (London: University College, London, 2014).

the meaning of responsibility and the question of how sanctions might apply to uphold responsibility.[98]

> "The obligations to answer, to submit to scrutiny, and to redress grievances may seem in practice to lack the support of any coercive rule or sanction. Undoubtedly these obligations are imperfect, resting as they do upon conventions, practices, and procedures which are liable to change and to be variously interpreted and applied, and which depend ultimately upon the political culture."

4–112

Ministerial responsibility has been acknowledged by the courts as a guiding principle of the Constitution. It provides constitutional principles as the basis for the Parliamentary scrutiny of the Executive. Ministers may appear before select committees to answer questions or before the whole House of Commons. It has been invoked as the basis of ministerial resignation, for example, Lord Carrington over the Falklands invasion by Argentina in 1982; and the resignation of Mr Leon Brittan in 1986, after he authorised the improper release of a confidential letter written by the Solicitor General to the Secretary of State for Defence.

4–113

In the classic case of resignation, that of Sir Thomas Dugdale in 1954 over the sale of land[99] in Devon compulsorily acquired during the War, resignation is seen not as an automatic or inevitable sanction, but as the basis of what the Prime Minister regards as the interests of the Government. The *Crichel Down* case is often referred to as supporting the convention of ministerial resignation for the acts of civil servants. Since 1984, official and private papers on the affair have cast doubts over whether the facts in 1954 support ministerial resignation over the alleged failure of civil servants to act correctly over the application of Commander Marten. It seems that the civil servants had not been negligent; rather, they acted according to the wishes of the minister.[100] In fact it may be argued that the Crichel Down example is atypical. Resignation is rarely used today for ministerial errors. It is unlikely that ministers would resign in similar circumstances today. The complexity of government and the difficult matter of linking ministerial policy with the complaint of failure have weakened the system of holding ministers to account. A single departmental budget may be worth several billions of pounds, and it is difficult to see how ministers may be able to exercise scrutiny over all the activities of their departments. Ministers are often in their job for a limited time and consequently have limited opportunities to discover whether or not their policy is working or is defective. In the Crichel Down affair ministerial resignations came about because of political embarrassment

---

98 C. Turpin, "Ministerial Responsibility: Myth or Reality?" in *The Changing Constitution*, J. Jowell and D. Oliver (eds), 2nd edn, (Oxford: Oxford University Press, 1989), pp.55–60. See D. Woodhouse, "Ministerial Responsibility in the 1990s: When Do Ministers Resign?" [1993] 46 *Parliamentary Affairs* 277.
99 *Report of the Public Inquiry into the Disposal of Land at Crichel Down*, Cmd.9176 (1954). See also I. F. Nicolson, *The Mystery of Crichel Down* (Oxford: Clarendon, 1986).
100 Nicolson, *The Mystery of Crichel Down*.

caused by revelations about ministerial impropriety in supervising the conduct of their respective departments.

4-114 Ministers may resign after appearing before select committees or the whole House of Commons to answer questions. For example, Mr Leon Brittan resigned in 1986, after it was alleged that he authorised the improper release of a confidential letter written by the Solicitor General to the Secretary of State for Defence. The resignation of Mr Brittan as Secretary of State for Trade and Industry typifies the modern approach to ministerial errors. Resignation appears to have been a means of protecting the government of the day from serious political damage and also a way for Mrs Thatcher, the then Prime Minister, to survive.

4-115 In theory, ministerial resignation might also follow from serious policy misjudgements, errors within a government department, or personal error arising from a minister's private life. Instances where some degree of fault is perceived to lie with the minister have been unusually numerous in the past 20 years. However, the fault is usually connected with the private life of the minister rather than an error of government policy. David Mellor in 1992 and Cecil Parkinson in 1985 resigned over sexual affairs, while Patrick Nicholls, Under-Secretary of State for the Environment, resigned in 1990 after being arrested for drunk-driving, and Tim Yeo resigned in 1994 for personal reasons during a period when public opinion became critical of the personal morality of ministers and members of Parliament. Ron Davies, the Secretary of State for Wales, resigned in 1998 because of his private life, as did Lord Caithness, Minister of State for Transport, in 1994. Two resignations in 1998, those of Peter Mandelson, the Minister without portfolio, and Geoffrey Robinson, Paymaster General, were due to an undeclared personal loan made by Robinson to Mandelson.

4-116 Ministerial responsibility came under scrutiny in 1992. This followed the collapse of the Matrix Churchill trial and led to the first modern, in-depth investigation of government decision-making, legal powers and administration, and the effectiveness of the Parliamentary process for holding government to account.

The Scott Report and ministerial responsibility

4-117 In November 1992, the trial of three former executives of the machine-tool manufacturer Matrix Churchill for the illegal export of arms to Iraq collapsed after a former minister, Alan Clark, gave testimony. He revealed that government departments had been aware of the nature of the equipment when export licences were granted. Despite this fact, four ministers had signed public interest immunity certificates intended to prevent confidential documents from being revealed to the defence at the trial. It was also revealed that one of the defendants had provided information to the Secret Service over a number of years. Signing the certificates also prevented full Parliamentary disclosure of the reality of government policy. Soon after the trial collapsed, and following public disquiet about the way it had been conducted, the Prime Minister set up an inquiry under Sir Richard Scott. Its aim was to find out the circumstances leading up to the trial and the role of government ministers.

4-118 The inquiry was not set up under the Tribunals of Inquiry (Evidence) Act 1921. Instead it was an independent inquiry entrusted to a single judge, on behalf of the Prime Minister, with its own procedures determined by the inquiry chairman, Sir Richard Scott, and put into practical operation by a team attached to the inquiry. The inquiry concerned the role of the Attorney General, thus preventing the Attorney General fulfilling his customary role of acting as legal adviser to the inquiry. Independent counsel was appointed[101] and carried out the role of investigator and adversarial ally to the chairman of the inquiry. As a result, the inquiry incorporated both inquisitorial and adversarial techniques. The inquiry lasted over three years.

4–119 The Scott Report into the "arms to Iraq" affair consists of five indexed volumes. Amounting to over 1,800 pages, it was published in February 1996 as a House of Commons paper. The conclusions reached in the Scott Report go to the heart of government accountability. Trade and its regulation fall under the provisions of the Import, Export and Customs Powers (Defence) Act 1939, passed on the outbreak of the Second World War. Until the Scott Report was published, this was a little-known but vital piece of legislation that had remained unrepealed and largely unnoticed. Successive governments enjoyed the benefits of the legislation without amending or reforming its basic provisions for fear that amending legislation would draw public attention to existing practice and lead to contentious debate. This fact alone drawn from the Scott Report confronts one of the basic assumptions made about parliamentary democracy—that when in doubt, the government of the day will seek parliamentary authority for its actions. Legislation should be updated to take account of changing circumstances, and keeping quiet about legislation that in modern times ought to have been revised is a serious flaw in the system of internal checks and balances.

4–120 In fact, the Scott Report leads to the conclusion that the operating assumption within the inner workings of government is that government has the necessary legal powers until specifically and categorically prohibited by legislation. This assumption or working practice is seriously called into question and challenged by the Scott Report. It is a fundamental weakness of existing systems of Parliamentary scrutiny that internal checks and balances very often fail to alert Parliament to the necessity for law reform.

4–121 More immediately, the facts leading up to the Matrix Churchill trial[102] in November 1992 that precipitated the Scott inquiry go back to the circumstances surrounding the outbreak of war between Iran and Iraq in 1980. The outbreak of war resulted in a speedy assurance from the government that no lethal weapons would be supplied through licensed sales to either side. This trade embargo was applied on the basis of the 1939 legislation, and a government statement made public the restrictions on sales to Iran and Iraq. Though ambiguously worded, these restrictions were added to by the government in 1981 with the view that every opportunity should be taken to exploit Iraq's potential as a promising purchaser of defence equipment, with the exception of lethal weapons interpreted in the narrowest sense.

4–122 In 1984 what became known as the Howe guidelines were promulgated and made public. The guidelines contained four restrictions, namely: that the consistent refusal to supply lethal weapons to either side should be maintained; that existing contracts and obligations should be fulfilled; that no new orders should be sanctioned for any defence equipment which might significantly

---
101 Presiley Baxendale QC.
102 See D. Leigh, *Betrayed: The Real Story of the Matrix Churchill Trial* (London: Bloomsbury, 1993).

enhance the capability of either side to the conflict; and that all applications for export licences for the supply of defence equipment to Iran or Iraq should be scrutinised with great care.

4-123 The Howe guidelines were certainly intended to tighten up and strengthen existing practice. However, they left considerable doubt as to the actual restrictions to be observed. The restriction on lethal weapons was vaguely expressed; the acceptance that defence equipment might be provided was equally unclear; and the juxtaposition of both concepts appeared contradictory. Defence equipment might indeed include lethal weapons, and lethal weapons might be required for defence purposes. Government policy as represented in the Howe guidelines appeared sufficiently ambiguous and flexible to provide very little difficulty in their observance. According to the Scott Report, up until August 1988 they appeared to be an accurate reflection of government policy.

4-124 The cessation of the Gulf war in 1988 brought to an end the apparent mischief that the Howe guidelines were intended to deal with. The signal given by the government, including Lord Howe himself, was that the end of the war and the ceasefire could allow economic opportunities to be exploited to the full.

4-125 It is clear, with the benefit of hindsight, that what was required was a full-scale review of the guidelines, the applicable law, and how arms sales are regulated. What occurred instead was incremental change through stealth, rather than a fundamental review. A more flexible approach over arms sales appeared to be necessary, and the government exploited the ambiguous guidelines to that end. A number of key government departments had responsibilities over arms sales.

4-126 The Foreign Office appeared reluctant to allow fundamental changes to the guidelines. The system of licensing required formal approval from the Department of Trade and Industry (DTI), which had overall responsibility for exports, and the DTI appeared willing to embrace a more open policy of trade. The Foreign Office attempted to keep the government advised of long-term strategies. Pressure from British companies intensified for a share in the arms trade and the economic opportunities of trade amidst intense competition from foreign companies. The Ministry of Defence broadly favoured a more market-based approach and supported the DTI in a more flexible interpretation of the Howe guidelines. The guidelines were subtly amended. The original 1984 Howe guidelines contained the following:

> "...we should not in future approve or sanction new orders for any defence equipment which in our view would significantly enhance the capability of either side to prolong or exacerbate the conflict..."[103]

The revised 1988 guidelines included:

> "...we should not in future approve new orders for any defence equipment which in our view would be of *direct and significant assistance to either country in the conduct of offensive operations in breach of the ceasefire*..." (author's emphasis).

---

103 *Hansard*, HC Vol.84, col.450w.

4-127　　Interpretation of the revised guidelines appeared to offer more flexibility than the original guidelines. Given the sensitive nature of the arms trade, the revised guidelines were not published or announced in Parliament. Incongruous though it sounds, it was naively believed by the government of the day that shifts in policy would probably be detected by the public at large, and so the revised guidelines would receive tacit public approval once they were operative. It was tacitly assumed that the government was prepared to withstand robust questioning on its policy both inside and outside Parliament. On the other hand, it was assumed that if the government made the guidelines public, then great public debate would arise, possibly resulting in political embarrassment. The Government might be forced into an unwelcome review of the entire arms licensing system. This had major implications for Britain's reputation abroad and might put at risk future arms sales.

4-128　　Scott considered that the guidelines on arms sales constituted a statement of policy and that revising the guidelines reflected a change in government policy. Government statements made in 1989 and 1990 about policy on arms exports[104] "consistently failed to discharge the obligations imposed by the constitutional principle of Ministerial responsibility".

4-129　　Sir Richard Scott also found that the Attorney General was at fault in not making clear to the court at the trial of the Matrix Churchill directors that Mr Heseltine, then President of the Board of Trade, was reluctant to agree to signing the certificate claiming public interest immunity.[105] A second criticism was that the Attorney General had mistakenly interpreted the law on public interest certificates when he claimed that ministers were bound to sign such certificates when requested to do so. Criticism was also made of a number of ministers for the reasons they gave for signing certificates.

4-130　　Aside from such criticisms, Sir Richard considers that ministers were, albeit perhaps mistakenly, engaged in acting in what they took to be the national, and therefore the public, interest. Ministers gained no direct benefits from the arms sales and had been influenced by the need to operate within the competitive conditions of the market. The information available to ministers at the time was less than the information available with the benefit of hindsight. Ministers and civil servants are to be judged by what they knew and believed then. At the heart of the ministerial defence on arms exports was the claim that ministers had applied the spirit of the guidelines out of necessity. In short, ministers could rely on their subjective assessment as a defence. They may now appear to have been mistaken but at the time they acted in good faith and with the public interest in mind. In effect, Parliamentary answers left Parliament and the public at best confused and at worst misled about the government's true policy on arms sales. The question of whether ministers were to blame for this state of affairs was a central issue of importance for the Scott Report. Scott approaches this issue with some degree of dexterity. He provides throughout the report an elaborate and detailed analysis of the facts and

---

104　See The Rt. Hon Sir Richard Scott, The Vice-Chancellor, *Return to an Address of the Honourable House of Commons dated 15th February 1996. Report of the Inquiry into the Export of Defence Equipment and Dual-use Goods to Iraq and related Prosecutions*, HC 115) (1996) (hereinafter the Scott Report), para.D4.63.

105　See John F. McEldowney, "The Scott Report: Inquiries, Parliamentary Accountability and Government Control in Britain" (1997) 4(4) *Democratization* 135–56.

evidence that justify the main conclusions reached in the report. In so doing he read, digested and had access to more secret information than possibly any other single individual in recent times. Far from being captivated by the ethos of secrecy, Scott adopts a stance highly critical of the conduct of government.

4–131 Scott provides detailed and systematic evidence about government indifference to Parliament and the public. Three ministers deliberately failed to inform Parliament about sales of arms to Iraq for fear of the public outcry that might result. On the sensitive issue of whether Parliament was misled, Scott found that, with regard to the policy on exports, Parliament and MPs were[106] "designedly led to believe that a stricter policy was applied than was the case". Scott does not accept that the Attorney General was not personally at fault. The department's attitude to disclosure of information was consistently grudging. The letters on exports to Iraq conveyed the idea that no military equipment had been sold to Iraq during the Gulf Conflict. This assertion could not truthfully be made.

4–132 Following its publication, the Scott Report was considered in debate in the House of Commons. No minister resigned, and by a majority of one, ministerial censure or resignation was avoided. The Scott Report provides an important summary of ministerial accountability where the focus is not on resignation but on the requirement to give information to Parliament. The Scott Report underlines the importance attached to information. It is expected that ministers should not knowingly mislead Parliament and that they should be as open as possible in the giving of information. However, the lack of any obligation on ministers to volunteer information when it is not specifically requested may result in their responsibility appearing too weak and inadequate if they are prepared to be economical in their answers. A more worrying legacy of the Scott Report is that ministers may be able to rely on a subjective defence. In other words ministers, when questioned, may be mistaken in their answers, but so long as they act in good faith and with the public interest in mind, they should not be held at fault. This leaves a remarkable void. Very often, only ministers will know whether their answers may mislead. Without an obligation to provide a full answer, full ministerial responsibility may remain elusive.

4–133 What is the long-term significance of the Scott Report? At the time there was much controversy over the procedures adopted by the inquiry. Criticism focused on the absence of the right to allow lawyers to cross-examine witnesses about information revealed during the day-to-day hearings at the inquiry.[107] Sir Richard came under intense public scrutiny. An inquiry headed by a single judge inevitably led to consideration of his personal views. The juristic techniques available to the inquiry, the careful collection of evidence, and the technical consideration of detailed Civil Service documents were often overlooked as the melodrama of the inquiry played out in public hearings and the media when the Attorney General, Mrs Thatcher and Mr Major gave evidence. The political debate captured the public's attention and distracted attention from the main issues.

4–134 The criticism that the inquiry had departed from the conventional wisdom of allowing cross-examination gained support from the authority of the six principles adopted by Lord

---

106 *Scott Report*, para.G117.
107 Lord Howe of Aberavon, "Procedure at the Scott Inquiry" [1996] *Public Law* 445.

Salmon in 1966 among criteria to guide future inquiries. Cross-examination is seen as one of the strengths of the oral tradition of advocacy at the Bar. This point was used to great effect as a means of criticising the report. However, Scott's rebuttal of any unfairness is equally cogent. The inquiry provided funds for legal advice and the large numbers of written submissions that were received made cross-examination impractical if the inquiry was to report within a reasonable time. The oral part was only a small fraction of the work of the inquiry. Scott's defence of the procedures adopted received support from the Council on Tribunals after the inquiry findings were made public.

4-135

A more serious matter raised by the holding of the inquiry is the propriety of an inquiry on behalf of the Prime Minister of the day about the government of the day rather than an inquiry on behalf of Parliament. Parliament appears to have divided along party political lines, favouring the government of the day. The facts and circumstances surrounding the Scott inquiry raised fundamental issues about Parliament and its role. What Scott had found was that Parliament had been unable to hold government to account in a satisfactory way. It had been misled, and had consistently failed to detect any alteration in government policy or, through the select committee system, exercise enough scrutiny to deter practices that were inconsistent with the original guidelines. Parliament also appeared weak and ineffectual when the Scott Report came to be debated. It had failed to set the agenda and felt honour-bound to vote on the Report, not according to any principles of Parliamentary etiquette, but on party political lines. The greatest irony is that, to protect the findings from legal proceedings, the Report was given the protection of Parliamentary privilege by being published as a report of the House of Commons.

4-136

Sir Richard's exhaustive inquiry allowed an outsider into the secret world of the Civil Service and the administration. As an outsider, was he qualified for the task in hand? Professor Martin Loughlin queries Scott's role and expertise[108]:

> **"Scott was obliged to examine a sphere of government decision-making, which generally remains secret, and his background in commercial law may not have been ideal training for the task. The conduct of foreign relations is an area in which 'ambiguity often seems the safest course'. . . From this perspective, reminded of the circuitous ways of foreign relations, Scott indeed may have been rather naive."**

4-137

Further criticism is that a judge caught up in the internal politics of party government is liable to become politicised as a result.[109] There is clearly a danger when judges are involved in public inquiries that inevitably lead to party political controversy.

4-138

This may explain why the Scott inquiry showed differences of opinion between government ministers and Sir Richard, reflecting differences in culture and attitude. On Sir Richard's part

---

108   Martin Loughlin, *Sword and Scales* (Oxford: Hart, 2000), p.43.
109   Rodney Brazier, "It *is* a Constitutional Issue: Fitness for Ministerial Office in the 1990s" [1994] *Public Law* 431.

4–139 there is the forensic role of law and lawyers applying prescriptive rules to facts and finding exemptions or exceptions. On the part of ministers there is a culture of secrecy, and an attitude that the role of law is one of enabling and facilitating the conduct of government policy—that unless an action is prohibited by law, it is permissible.

A more formidable issue is the fact that the Scott inquiry appeared to trespass on the role of Parliament itself and its internal functioning. While this may have been inadvertently undertaken, nevertheless the appearance is that the Scott inquiry roamed into the proceedings of Parliament strictly protected from outside inquiry under art.9 of the Bill of Rights. Article 9, respected by the courts, is followed in many leading cases. In the Privy Council case of *Prebble v Television New Zealand*[110] it was held, in an action which cited proceedings in Parliament, that if the action questioned Parliamentary proceedings then it would have to be stayed.[111] What constitutes proceedings of Parliament is an elastic concept. While the Register of Members' Interests does not,[112] it is clear that resolutions of the House, the reports from the committees of the House, and subsequent inquiries and reports do come within the category of proceedings.[113] According to Erskine May,[114] "everything that is said or done" within the precincts of the House forms part of the proceedings in Parliament. Patricia Leopold asks whether the Scott inquiry fell into this category, and concludes:

> "[I]n his report, Sir Richard severely criticised various aspect of parliamentary proceedings—the veracity of answers to parliamentary questions; a statement in the House of Commons by a minister; evidence to a select committee by a minister and a civil servant; and the choice of departmental witnesses for a select committee inquiry. But if Sir Richard had been debarred from making these criticisms, he would have been unable to do his job. However, the contrast is marked between the freedom he possessed as a one-man tribunal and the restrictions he would have had to observe as a judge in a court hearing. A Nelsonian blind eye has been turned to the problem. . ."[115]

4–140 It may be concluded that Sir Richard's report followed the trail to its logical conclusions. He exposed the weakness of government decision-making for which the government escaped the censure of resignation. He also exposed the fundamental weakness of Parliament itself, which Parliament has refrained from properly addressing.[116]

---

110   [1995] 1 A.C. 321; [1994] 3 W.L.R. 970 PC (NZ).
111   Also see *In Re Parliamentary Privilege Act 1770* [1958] A.C. 331; [1958] 2 W.L.R. 912 PC (UK).
112   *Rost v Edwards* [1990] 2 Q.B. 460; [1990] 2 W.L.R. 1280 QBD.
113   *Hamilton v Al Fayed (No.1)* [1999] 1 W.L.R. 1569; [1999] 3 All E.R. 317 CA (Civ Div).
114   Erskine May, *Parliamentary Practice* (Sir David Limon (ed), 22nd edn (London: Butterworths, 1997)).
115   Patricia Leopold, "The Application of the Civil and Criminal Law to Members of Parliament and Parliamentary Proceedings", in G. Drewry and D. Oliver (eds), *Law and Parliament* (London: Butterworths, 1998), pp.71–87.
116   Section 13 of the Defamation Act 1996 was passed to allow MPs to pursue legal claims for defamation where

Collective responsibility

4–141 Historically ministerial responsibility has been formulated to include the whole Ministry responsible for all official acts of the individual ministers. This carries the implication of collective responsibility when a minister is acting on behalf of the Government[117] as a whole. Undoubtedly collective responsibility means collective resignation, should there be a no confidence vote in the House of Commons in the government of the day. Such votes are rare. This leaves unanswered the precise formulation of collective responsibility, as inevitably different views within the Cabinet may lead to lack of unanimity over the precise nature of government policy.

4–142 Collective responsibility may have a different aspect other than explaining how the Cabinet is responsible to Parliament. It may explain the process which ties the Cabinet to confidentiality in its decision-making. Thus dissenting voices are silenced once a decision has been agreed in Cabinet.

4–143 The confidentiality aspect of Cabinet deliberations was acknowledged in the *Crossman diaries* case, *Attorney General v Jonathan Cape Ltd*[118] when the Attorney General attempted unsuccessfully to prevent the posthumous publication of Crossman's diaries compiled while he was a Cabinet Minister. The view of Lord Widgery CJ was that opinions by Cabinet ministers in the course of Cabinet discussions were protected by confidentiality, and in the public interest, publication could be prohibited by the courts. On the facts of the *Crossman* case a period of ten years had elapsed and it was considered unlikely that publication would damage the doctrine of joint Cabinet responsibility. Lord Widgery CJ rejected the view that the diaries should not be published because they disclosed advice given by senior civil servants.

4–144 The *Crossman* case should not be interpreted to mean that in every case publication of diaries would be accepted by the courts. Instead, the case lays the foundation for protecting Cabinet discussion on the basis of confidentiality and therefore the law of confidence. Thus, a claim that disclosure would not be in the public interest is usually sufficient to maintain confidentiality.

4–145 In 1976, after the *Crossman* case, Lord Radcliffe considered the publication of ministerial memoirs as Chairman of a Committee of Privy Counsellors on Ministerial Memoirs.[119] The Report identified working principles as to "the public interest" especially matters which in the international sphere might be detrimental to relations with other nations; or in the domestic sphere, information which would destroy the trust between ministers or between minister or advisers or private bodies.

4–146 Since publication of the *Crossman* diaries, the diaries of other ex-Cabinet Ministers, notably Barbara Castle and Tony Benn, have been successfully published in what might be regarded

---

the conduct of a person, in or in relation to proceedings in, Parliament is in issue. Immunity may be waived whereby the protection of parliamentary privilege prevented the courts from questioning what was said or done in Parliament.
117 *Falkland Islands Review*, Cmnd.8787 (1983).
118 [1976] Q.B. 752; [1975] 3 W.L.R. 606 QBD.
119 Cmnd.6386 (1976).

as against the spirit of the Radcliffe rules. Recent publications have also included diaries of ex-civil servants and advisers. Even the Former Head of MI5 has managed to have her diaries published albeit with reluctance on the part of the civil service and ministers. Retired Prime Ministers find a lucrative market among publishers willing to provide large cash advances for publication of diaries or reflections made during the period of office. Nevertheless, the confidentiality of the Cabinet has been used to prevent publication, by civil servants and others, of Cabinet discussion. The *Spycatcher* litigation[120] relating to the attempts by the British Government to prevent publication of the memoirs of Peter Wright who had been a scientific officer in counter-espionage from 1955–1973 ran the gauntlet of the use of injunctions and potential use of the criminal law. However, in the end it was found that as publication had taken place abroad it was impossible to make an injunction effective.[121] The global use of the internet and other facilities renders the enforcement of the law problematic.

4–147   The conclusion must be that stemming from the doctrine of collective cabinet responsibility, the secrecy of the system of government emanates from the principles of cabinet government. Mr Justice McCowan in *R v Ponting*[122] directed the jury that Clive Ponting, an Assistant Secretary of the Ministry of Defence, could not rely on his belief that the government deliberately misled Parliament over the sinking of the Argentine warship, the *General Belgrano*, during the Falklands war, in order to leak documents to Tam Dalyell MP, a critic of government policy. The Human Rights Act 1998 opens up possibilities that the courts may have to balance the right of the public to know, as against the interests of the government of the day to protect the state. The law is in somewhat of a state of flux. As rights are now available to ensure freedom of expression and open up the ethos of secrecy, government lawyers have become ingenious in attempting to frustrate memoirs in the Peter Wright tradition by seeking to use injunctions to seize assets or prevent any monetary benefit accruing from publication. In *Att.-Gen. v Blake*[123] the House of Lords refused to allow the government an injunction to seize the royalties of the former spy George Blake from the sale of his published memoirs. It was noted that Blake had not been convicted of an offence and that publication probably breached s.1 of the Official Secrets Act 1989. As there had been no conviction there was no statutory power to confiscate his assets. However, the majority of the Lords accepted that the former spy had a fiduciary duty which he breached and, had he been within the jurisdiction of the courts, they would have granted a permanent injunction against the memoirs. It was accepted that given the passage of time there was little in the book that was truly confidential but he was liable to provide an account of profits. This forms a separate form of action from the use of an injunction and opens up the possibility of acting as a deterrent to publication. Another possibility is that publication may breach copyright and this may further be used to restrict publication. At the heart of the government's anxiety is the prevention of embarrassing revelations but also the upholding of cabinet confidentiality.

---

120   *Attorney General v Guardian Newspapers Ltd (No.2)* [1990] 1 A.C. 109; [1988] 3 W.L.R. 776 HL.
121   *Attorney General v Guardian Newspapers Ltd (No.1)* [1987] 1 W.L.R. 1248; [1987] 3 All E.R. 316 HL.
122   [1985] Crim.L.R. 318 CCC.
123   [2001] 1 A.C. 268; [2000] 3 W.L.R. 625 HL.

4-148 The cases illustrate how government may be conceived as both a political entity and a constitutional institution. In that sense collective Cabinet decision-making is an effective means of allowing political debate and discussion to take place, while the inner workings of the Cabinet are protected from external scrutiny and accountability.[124] The Scott Report exposed the problems of working within the ethos of secrecy when using immunity certificates to restrict information available to the courts.

4-149 The traditional model of ministerial accountability remains problematical in the light of the experience of modern government. The size and complexity of departments and the role of the civil service and special advisers make it difficult to find a satisfactory solution that commands widespread support. The Public Administration Select Committee in 2007 noted the absence of "consensus, either among politicians or officials, about the way in which ministerial and civil service responsibilities are divided".[125]

4-150 One illustration is the absence of any ministerial resignation in the aftermath of major failures in the competition to run trains on the West Coast Main Line had to be cancelled after it was revealed that there were serious flaws in the bidding process. Three officials were suspended but the responsibility for the failure rested with ministers to ensure that the arrangements for bidding and competition were properly resourced and undertaken by suitably well skilled officials.[126]

H: The Civil Service

4-151 There are currently fewer than 450,000 civil servants and over 90 per cent of the civil service will be found in executive agencies. A brief overview of the role and function of the civil service is considered here. In Ch.11 executive agencies are explained and defined in some detail.

Definition

4-152 The Constitutional Reform and Governance Act 2010 has placed the civil service on a statutory basis and reformed its governance through the establishment of the Civil Service Commission. There is a Civil Service Code setting out the standards of behaviour of civil servants and the Commissioners uphold the system of appointments to the civil service and hear appeals from civil servants under the Code. The civil service is permanent and appointed on merit.

---

124 *Falkland Islands Review*, Cmnd.8787 (1983).
125 House of Commons Library, *Individual ministerial responsibility*, SN/PC/06467 (8 November 2012), HC 122 (2006–07).
126 *The Times*, 5 October 2012.

184 GOVERNMENT

Described[127] as "the ultimate monster to stop governments changing things,", the civil service provides the main administration for the activities of the government of the day. Civil servants may be defined in general terms as servants of the Crown employed in government departments. The Fulton Committee[128] in 1968 added certain exclusions:

> "servants of the Crown, other than holders of political or judicial officers, who are employed in a civil capacity and whose remuneration is paid wholly and directly out of monies voted by Parliament."

4–153 In most discussions about civil servants; the judiciary, Ministers of the Crown, the army, police, officials in local government or National Health Service, are excluded. Commonly-used terms to describe civil servants are: "public officials"; public servants; administrators; or Crown servants. The latter term has found acceptance in law, as describing the employment relationship and sometimes status of civil servants.

4–154 Civil servants are regulated by many different Acts of Parliament such as the Official Secrets Acts 1911 and 1989 and the Superannuation Act 1972. This is piecemeal legislation; none of the Acts clarifies the legal status, duties, obligations or rights of civil servants. In addition, there are numerous memoranda, such as instructions to civil servants when appearing before select committees or when acting under the Royal prerogative.

4–155 There has always been difficulty in precisely categorising the legal status of civil servants in their employment situation. Modern employment legislation has been applied to civil servants, granting rights in common with other employees regarding unfair dismissal. At common law, service as a civil servant was at the pleasure of the Crown. The exact basis of this rule is a mixture of constitutional law and public policy. The latter has always been difficult to estimate and predict. This is partly due to the fact that "there is in law no universally applicable definition of civil servant or civil service. The most important distinguishing characteristic is service on behalf of the Crown." There is difficulty in expressing a legal implication for such service.

4–156 In addition to the 1978 Employment Protection Consolidation Act, Pt V and s.138 on unfair dismissal, numerous other recent employment legislation also applies. The Equal Pay Act 1970, the Sex Discrimination Act 1975 and the Race Relations Act 1976, all apply to civil servants.

4–157 Pay and conditions of civil servants are negotiated through the Civil Service National Whitley Council, dating from 1919. National pay bargaining has gradually broken up and individual negotiations with trade unions are not uncommon. Employment conditions are likely to be further delegated to departments and agencies after the setting up of "Agencies under The Next Steps" in 1988. The Civil Service (Management of Functions) Act 1992 facilitates this system of delegation.

4–158 Some doubt has been expressed about whether there is a contractual relationship between the civil servant and the employer, the Crown. It seemed to be accepted in the *GCHQ*[129] case

---

127 Quoted in the preface in P. Hennessy, *Whitehall* (London: Secker & Warburg, 1989), p.xiii.
128 Cmnd.3638 (1968).
129 [1985] A.C. 374; [1984] 3 All E.R. 935 HL.

that a contractual relationship did not exist; or at any rate, in arguing for or against retraction of trade union membership, this issue of contract was not relied upon. This doubt has been resolved by the Constitutional Reform and Governance Act 2010.

Otton J considered the issue in *R v Civil Service Appeal Board Ex p. Cunningham*.[130] A prison officer, because of his status as a civil servant and constable, had forfeited his rights by not appearing before an industrial tribunal but had been given an assurance in the Civil Service Pay and Conditions of Service that he would not be "less favourably" treated as a result. Whether contractual rights existed was unclear. This matter of contract rights becomes important because of the present law on how an aggrieved citizen may seek remedies in the courts, through the procedure known as judicial review. Such a procedure must relate to public law matters, and normally disciplinary procedures of a purely domestic nature were not amenable to judicial review. A civil servant may have private contractual rights but also, as a public official, rights under the Civil Service Pay and Conditions of Service Code. Do such rights fall into the category of public law rights or are they entirely private law rights based on contract? The case law has not provided a clear answer to this question.

4-159

The Civil Service Appeal Board (CSAB), now replaced by the Civil Service Commission, to hear disciplinary action was the subject of judicial review. In *R v Civil Service Appeal Board Ex p. Bruce*,[131] Bruce, a civil servant, was an Inland Revenue employee who appealed to the CSAB against his dismissal. The Court of Appeal and the Divisional Court accepted that the CSAB was amenable to judicial review even though in that particular case an alternative remedy could have been sought. There was some doubt as to whether a contract might exist, as no intention to create legal relations existed. This point was obiter dictum and the *Bruce* case did not decide whether civil servants had contracts of employment. Earlier in *McClaren v Home Office*,[132] again *obiter dictum* Woolf LJ stated that "an employee of a public body is normally in the same position as other employees". The *McClaren* case concerned the appointment of prison officers, appointed under the Prison Act 1952 rather than the prerogative, so the case may be unhelpful when it is applied to civil servants normally appointed under the prerogative.

4-160

This uncertainty in the law is now addressed under the Constitutional Reform and Governance Act 2010 creating a statutory framework for all civil servants.

4-161

Role and function of the Civil Service

The convention of ministerial responsibility applies not only to the relationship between Ministers and the House of Commons but also to that between ministers and civil servants. The formulation of this principle may take a number of forms.

4-162

---

130 [1991] 4 All E.R. 310; [1992] I.C.R. 817 CA (Civ Div).
131 [1988] 3 All E.R. 686; [1988] I.C.R. 649 QBD.
132 [1990] I.C.R. 824; [1990] I.R.L.R. 338 CA (Civ Div).

4–163 First, civil servants owe a duty to ministers. Here there is no distinction between the Government of the day and the role of the civil service. The civil servant is answerable to the minister and through the minister, to Parliament.

4–164 Secondly, ministers do not normally reveal the role played by civil servants in formulating policy. Even when advice is problematic, rarely do ministers reveal the identity of civil servants.

4–165 Thirdly, civil servants may advise ministers on policy but in theory they are not called upon to act politically. The Civil Service Code makes clear that civil servants must carry out their duties "for the assistance of the administration as it is duly constituted for the time being, whatever its political complexion." Civil servants are expected to carry out their duties with "integrity and honesty" and "objectively and impartially".[133] Civil servants are also expected to standards of honest and financial integrity. The Civil Service Management Code 2015 provides standards and obligations that are integral to the contract of employment. The Bribery Act 2010 also applies to civil servants with criminal sanctions relating to financial relations and civil servants. Under increased public pressure, the Business Appointment Rules revised in 2013/14 provide rules for civil servants after retirement.

4–166 Linked to these objectives is the triennial review of departments at least once every three years. The Code also sets out circumstances for "whistle-blowers" but this is subject to some exceptions such as members of GCHQ or the security services.[134] The Public Disclosure Act 1998 which covers "whistle-blowers" and provides protection for private, public and voluntary sectors. The Act is confined to matters of malpractice and on the basis of that affords protection to the whistle blower. In order to qualify for protection there is a good faith requirement and a factual basis must be established for the basis of the whistle blower's belief to cover an external disclosure.

4–167 Criticism of the *Armstrong Guidelines* points to doubts over the effectiveness of such arrangements especially after the Westland affair. Differences between government ministers were being resolved by the disclosure of a confidential letter, between the Solicitor General and the then Secretary of State for Defence (Mr Heseltine), by the civil servants acting with the authority of the Secretary of State for Trade and Industry (Mr Britton). This disclosure broke the convention of strict confidentiality over the letters and advice of law officers. Civil servants did not seem able to prevent such disclosure and there may have been no option in the circumstances but to have complied with the instructions of the minister. Civil servants in this matter were prohibited from appearing before select committees or giving interviews to the press.

4–168 The appearance of civil servants before select committees is growing in importance. The Scott Report considered that civil servants should be able to appear before select committees unhindered by ministerial discretion. The Osmotherly Rules[135] (named after E. B. C. Osmotherly a Civil servant in 1977–78) provide guidance to civil servants and they are regularly updated to

---

133 House of Commons Library, *The Civil Service Code*, SN/PC/6699 (18 March 2015).
134 The Employment Relations Act 1999 provides employment rights to members of the security services subject to some limited exceptions.
135 House of Commons Library, *The Osmotherly Rules*, SN/PC/2671 (24 March 2015).

take account of changing circumstances. The rules have never been approved by Parliament but have become accepted as a guide for handling departmental queries before select committees. The most recent edition, 17 October 2014, includes responsibility of senior responsible owners of major projects to be called to select committees on the same principles as civil servants. The chain of responsibility remains unchanged namely that is through ministers, civil servants are called to give evidence. This is an important step forward as there is increasing importance given to the role of select committees. Calling named officials is possible under the general power to "send for persons, papers and records". Doubts exist as to the powers open to select committees to enforce this rule.

4–169

Ministers may claim to know what is in the best interests of the public as well as in the interests of the Government. Ministers are self-authorising over the publication of confidential information. Leaks may be authorised by a minister. Oddly, what appears to be a means of holding ministers to account, the doctrine of ministerial accountability, may allow a wide exercise of ministerial discretion.

I: Summary and Conclusions

4–170

- Prime Ministerial government has the appearance of a Presidential style despite the tradition of cabinet decision-making. The Presidential style of Prime Ministerial decision-making is often because the government of the day has an overall Parliamentary majority. It may also reflect media attention and the use of professional full-time media advisers;

- the civil service undertakes the conduct of government amid the glare of media attention and the appointment of political advisers to act as a link between government and the electorate;

- the exercise of prerogative powers is subject to review by the Courts;

- accountable and responsible government requires strengthening of select committees and the power of Parliament;

- the role and function of the modern civil service is undergoing considerable change. A useful contrast may be drawn between the Victorian legacy of the civil service and the modern tendency to transfer civil servant activities to Next Step agencies. The Constitutional Reform and Governance Act 2010 is a major step in clarifying the role, function and status of civil servants if considered alongside the Civil Service Code; and

- Ministers have increasingly sought advice from outside the civil service through the appointment of advisers sympathetic to the policies of the Government. This is a trend which was noticeable in the Wilson Government in 1974. The trend has continued and prompted a former retired civil servant to suggest that[136] "a large number of senior civil servants" might be replaced with politically appointed officials on contracts. Political neutrality, permanence, independence and professionalism are seen as advantages in the recruitment and ethos of public service. Such an ethos is under detailed scrutiny today. Diversity in its role, the modern civil service has to address the inclination of the government of the day to develop policy that is sold to the electorate in a media-friendly way.

Further Reading

A. C. L. Davies, "Beyond New Public Management: Problems of Accountability in the Modern Administrative State" in N. Bamforth and P. Leyland (eds), *Accountability in the Contemporary Constitution* (Oxford: Oxford University Press, 2013), pp.333–353.

T. Daintith and A. Page, *The Executive in the Constitution* (Oxford: Oxford University Press, 1999).

P. Riddell, *The updated guidance on the osmothery Rules* (London: Institute for Government, 20 October 2014).

Anthony King and Ivor Crew, *The Blunders of our Governments* (London: Oneworld Publishers, 2014).

---

136 John Hoskyns, "Whitehall and Westminster: An Outsider's View" (1983) 36 *Parliamentary Affairs*, 137–147.

5

The Rule of Law and Constitutional Conventions

A: Introduction

Constitutional conventions[1] are an important part of the UK's constitutional arrangements. Conventions may explain the common practices and workings of government and how the UK's unwritten Constitution accommodates change. This is especially important when the process of constitutional change today seems never ending and appears to have gathered further momentum since the financial crisis in 2008. We are entering a period of constitutional uncertainty as almost every part of the UKs constitutional arrangements has come under intense scrutiny and possible reform. Specific constitutional reforms often take their own direction without necessarily understanding or studying their significance or impact. A reminder that constitutional conventions and the rule of law are important is timely as many assumptions underlying their importance may be misunderstood or overlooked. Accountable and responsible government is only achievable through respect to the rule of law and constitutional conventions that underpin it.

The 800th anniversary of Magna Carta is also a timely reminder of the importance of law and the influence of the rule of law[2] that is built on principles of liberty and justice. Such "ancient liberties" provide a powerful underpinning of how the rule of law sets what Jowell refers to as "a principle of institutional morality that is inherent in any constitutional democracy".[3]

---

1 The most useful account may be found in G. Marshall, *Constitutional Conventions* (Oxford: Clarendon, 1984). See also Hood Phillips, *Constitutional and Administrative Law* (London: Sweet & Maxwell, 1987), Ch.6; and C. R. Munro, *Studies in Constitutional Law* (London: Butterworths, 1987).
2 Tom Bingham, *The Rule of Law* (London: Penguin, 2010).
3 J. Jowell, D. Oliver and C. O'Cinneide, *The Changing Constitution*, 8th edn (Oxford: Oxford University Press, 2015).

THE RULE OF LAW AND CONSTITUTIONAL CONVENTIONS

5-003 Dicey's influence has led constitutional lawyers to regard conventions as a means for past practices to be examined in order to determine future conduct. In that sense conventions appear to link the ancient, medieval Constitution with the modern and present-day Constitution. Conventions may provide some order to practices which are, by their nature, forms of political behaviour and therefore difficult to categorise in any strictly legal or constitutional sense. Conventions are usually descriptive of a particular practice.

5-004 Conventions have been likened to rules or laws in many of their characteristics, with the exception that conventions are not enforceable by the Courts. There is however some ambiguity about the meaning of enforceable, because the Courts acknowledge the existence of conventions as aids to interpretation.[4] Frequently, conventions may appear to be objective or neutral in the exposition of a rule or understanding. This may be misleading as conventions often contain value judgments prescribing how certain conduct of government or officials should take place. Conventions commonly recognise the political facts of life and help explain the political workings of the Constitution.

5-005 Conventions have grown historically as unwritten rules, and may adapt to the changing methods of modern government. That is their enduring quality. They are not the product of either judicial or legislative intervention, but rather of custom, usage, habit and common practice. The most formative period for their development was probably in the eighteenth and towards the end of the nineteenth century. Conventions have the shortcoming that they reflect the values of mid-Victorian Government, and perhaps fail to take account of modern party political realities. The growth in the complexity of the machinery of government may make accountability through conventions more of a myth than a reality. Many important practices are part of the internal working of government and it is difficult to give internal working practices special value or elevation to the status of convention.[5]

5-006 In this chapter the value and significance of conventions is examined. This is followed by an account of the influence of Dicey in defining and explaining the rule of law. The UK's constitutional arrangements provide that government is subject to law and may only exercise its powers according to law. The discussion on the rule of law leads into the question of the role of the Courts, preparatory to the discussion on administrative law in Ch.6.

---

4 See the *Crossman Diaries* case: *Attorney General v Jonathan Cape Ltd* [1976] Q.B. 752; [1975] 3 W.L.R. 606 QBD. Discussion of conventions may be found in *Ex p. Notts CC* [1988] A.C. 240. The Canadian Courts have discussed conventions. See *Reference Re Amendment of the Constitution of Canada* (1982) 125 D.L.R. (3d) 1.

5 C. Turpin, "Ministerial Responsibility: Myth or Reality?" in J. Jowell and D. Oliver (eds), *The Changing Constitution*, 2nd edn (Oxford: Oxford University Press, 1989), pp.55–57.

B: Conventions

Perhaps the most influential legal writer on the nature of conventions is A. V. Dicey who defined conventions[6] as "the rules which make up constitutional law" that made the UK distinctive. The use of the term "rules" is deliberate. In Dicey's definition he distinguished "laws" from "conventions". The former he defined as comprising, in the strictest sense, laws such as statute, judge-made law and common law doctrines which are enforceable by the Courts. The latter, conventions, are "understandings, habits and practices which are not enforced by the Courts but which regulate the conduct of members of the sovereign power". In 2011, the Cabinet issued a Cabinet Manual setting out many of the principles of the Constitution, following the example of the New Zealand Parliament.[7] The Cabinet Manual is entitled *A Guide to Laws, Conventions and Rules on the Operation of Government*. The Guide does not have the force of legislation but it is a useful source of current conventions and rules that apply to the UK Constitution. It is likely to require revision in the future as conventions and rules often change to adapt to circumstances. There is also a *Code of Constitutional Standards* based on the various reports of the House of Lords Select Committee on the Constitution published by the Constitution Unit, at University College, London.[8] The Code provides a useful synopsis of the main findings of the Select Committee that contain constitutional norms or principles. It is also illustrative of the importance of Committees and their role in holding government to account.

Dicey's emphasis on the "non-enforcement" of conventions by the Courts is suitably ambiguous to create controversy over whether in principle there is any real distinction between laws and conventions. Since not all laws are enforceable by the court, as some are enforceable by tribunals, and some through discretion bestowed upon ministers after inquiries, the distinction may seem a curious one today. Despite this reservation it is possible to see the usefulness of the distinction that laws are given effect to, or are recognised by, the Courts whereas conventions may not be recognised. A modern tendency is to adapt to changing times by placing conventional understandings within a statutory framework. The Constitutional Reform Act 2005 reforms the Lord Chancellor's role making clear the ministerial nature of the post and removing many of historical functions of the post.

Dicey's views about conventions appear to have been influenced[9] by John Austin

---

6   A. V. Dicey, *Law of the Constitution* (London and New York: Macmillan, 1889), Chs 14 and 15. Dicey tends to provide general principles in the early part of his text which he then re-capitulates later on as he reflects more deeply on their meaning. This may give rise to problems of interpretation (see pp.24, 28–32). Generally, see R. A. Cosgrove, *The Rule of Law, Albert Venn Dicey Victorian Jurist* (Chapel Hill: University of North Carolina Press, 1980), pp.87–90.
7   The Cabinet Office (2011).
8   Jack Simson Caird, Robert Hazell and Dawn Oliver, *The Constitutional Standards of the House of Lords Select Committee on the Constitution* (London: Constitution Unit, University College, London, 2014).
9   C. R. Munro, *Studies in Constitutional Law* (London : Butterworths, 1987), Ch.3, pp.35–52. Also Munro, "Laws and Conventions Distinguished" (1975) 91 *Law Quarterly Review* 218; and Munro, "Dicey on Constitutional Conventions" [1985] *Public Law* 637; J. Austin, *The Province of Jurisprudence Determined* (London : John Murray, 1832); and G. Marshall, *Constitutional Conventions* (Oxford: Clarendon, 1984).

(1790–1859), who distinguished non-legal rules from legal rules and believed in the general value of rules made for the guidance of man. Austin pioneered the analytical form of jurisprudence which was influential in Dicey's analysis of the Constitution. Conventions are regarded in Austin's analysis as part of "positive morality". But conventions do not appear to fit within Austin's definition of law as no clear sanction or enforcement accompanies any breach of a convention; they do however fit in with the idea of morality. Dicey followed this analysis when describing conventions as "the morality of the constitution".

5-010 However, taking a different perspective from Dicey, Jennings[10] doubted whether the distinction between laws and convention was of any "substance or nature". This might appear to place conventions in a diminished role in the Constitution. Perhaps Jennings doubted the validity of the distinction between laws and conventions to be determined by the Courts alone.

5-011 Jennings' views however would seem to ignore the working practices of most Courts who appear to follow Dicey's distinction that conventions may be recognised but not enforced. Rarely have the Courts in the UK used a convention as an enforceable rule. Some leading cases illustrate how the Courts are reluctant to treat conventions as enforceable. This does not prevent the Courts from recognising the existence of a convention and such acknowledgement may at times appear to be similar to enforcement.

5-012 In *Madzimbamuto v Lardner-Burke*,[11] the Privy Council had to consider a convention contained in a 1961 declaration that the Westminster Parliament was not to legislate for Southern Rhodesia. Lord Reid commented that the convention, although important, had no legal effect "in limiting the legal power of Parliament".

5-013 A similar convention of legislative self-restraint was said to have developed historically over Northern Ireland affairs. The Government of Ireland Act 1920, now repealed, provided for a Parliament for Northern Ireland. Over the years a practice developed, that in the House of Commons at Westminster ministerial responsibility excluded any discussion of Northern Ireland transferred matters, that is discussion of matters which were transferred to the competence of the Northern Ireland Parliament. Calvert explains[12]:

> "In this sense and in this sense only can these be said to be a convention, but its scope is somewhat limited. It is a convention only as to administrative practice. It does not inhibit legislation or discussion of a bill on a special motion. It operates only within the sphere of questions and other debates and only in relation to matters in respect of which there is, for the time being no ministerial responsibility at Westminster." .

---

10   I. Jennings, *The Law and the Constitution*, 5th edn (London: University of London Press, 1959).
11   [1969] 1 A.C. 645; [1968] 3 W.L.R. 1229 PC (Rhodesia).
12   H. Calvert, *Constitutional Law in Northern Ireland* (Belfast: Stevens & Sons, Northern Ireland Legal Quarterly, 1968), pp.103, 110.

Another example of where the Courts have recognised the existence of conventions, in *Attorney General v Jonathan Cape Ltd*.[13] Here the case involved the recognition of the important convention of collective ministerial responsibility. Richard Crossman, a Labour Minister from 1964–1970, had maintained a daily political diary with a view to publication after his death. Crossman died in 1974 and his executors published the diaries and also extracts from his diaries in the *Sunday Times*. The Attorney General argued that collective Cabinet responsibility provided a fundamental requirement of Cabinet secrecy which should be enforced through an injunction. Lord Widgery CJ concluded that a convention could not be enforced in that way if it was "an obligation founded in conscience only" but in general terms the Courts might be willing to enforce Cabinet confidences when "the improper publication of such information can be restrained by the court". Redress might therefore be available for a breach of a conventional rule.

Another example is provided in Canada. The British North American Act 1867 passed by the UK Parliament left Canada, after the Statute of Westminster 1931, an independent State but with little or no competence to amend the 1867 Act. Amendments had to be through the UK Parliament, usually at the request of the Canadian Parliament. In 1980 the Federal Canadian Government decided to end the power of the UK Parliament to legislate, and to incorporate the Charter of Rights as part of its independence. The question arose as to the legal powers of the UK Government when faced with a desire to change the existing status of the Canadian Constitution arising out of representations made from the Federal Government, when only two Canadian Provinces, Ontario and New Brunswick, agreed. The remaining Canadian Provinces objected to the Federal Government's terms.

The Federal Canadian Government claimed that the UK Parliament was bound to accede to its request. This raised the question of what the UK Parliament was required by convention to undertake under the Statute of Westminster 1931. Doubts were expressed as to the existence of such a convention and, if one existed, should it be enforced? The Foreign Affairs Committee in its report to the House of Commons 1980–81, concluded that there was no binding convention upon the UK Parliament to accede to the request of the Federal Canadian Government. The matter was put to the Supreme Court of Canada.[14] A majority decision concluded that there was no legal objection to the Federal Government position to petition the Queen for agreement without the consent of the Provinces, but "at least a substantial measure of provincial consent" was required, and as this was not present it was unconstitutional for the Federal Parliament to act. In the end nine Provinces (with the exception of Quebec) did agree and the Canadian Bill 1982 was passed. The Canadian example raised a great deal of discussion about how conventions arose, who decided on their importance and what role the court performed.

---

13   [1976] Q.B. 752; [1975] 3 W.L.R. 606 QBD. See also R. H. S. Crossman, Memoirs Diaries of a Cabinet Minister (London: Henry Holt, 1976), Vol.2.
14   *Reference Re Amendment of the Constitution of Canada* (1982) 125 D.L.R. (3d) 1. R. Munro, *Studies in Constitutional Law* (London: Butterworths, 1987), p.45; P. Hogg, *Constitutional Law of Canada* (Scarborough, Ontario: Carswell, 1997), p.795; and A. Heard, *Canadian Constitutional Conventions* (Oxford: Oxford University Press, 1991).

5-017 A recurring theme in most of the discussion is Dicey's distinction between laws and conventions and how this might be observed. Unlike common law rules made by judges, conventions are established by the institution of government. Conventional rules might conflict with formal legal rules and therefore are difficult to enforce. Perhaps the Courts' search for conventions, and judicial "recognition" of their existence is, as some writers concluded, "enforcing the convention"? Strictly speaking recognition does not mean enforcement in the same way as a statute or byelaw. The question of why conventions are obeyed is difficult to answer.

5-018 Conventions seem to arise in ordinary day usage and develop over a period of time culminating in their general recognition and acceptance. Once a convention is accepted and then followed, it becomes an acceptable form of good practice. Little is known about why conventions are actually obeyed. They do not normally imply any sanction for their breach and as Turpin has noted, they have a remarkable ability to survive and change[15]:

> "Conventions are always emerging, crystallizing and dissolving, and it is sometimes questionable whether a convention has been broken or has simply changed."

5-019 It is a mistake to confine the discussion of conventions merely to good political practices and thereby beyond constitutional significance. Although unwritten in form and unclear in existence, they offer important guidance over the behaviour of government.

5-020 Some significant constitutional conventions may be briefly mentioned. Dicey noted the importance of both ministerial and Cabinet responsibility. Individual ministerial responsibility may be distinguished from the collective responsibility of the government as a whole. The latter is highly unusual in modern times. The convention that a government that loses the confidence of the House of Commons must resign or advise dissolution has a significance in the constitutional history of the UK. Brazier[16] notes how such conventions have a certain vagueness and uncertainty about when they apply. When may a government be said to have lost the confidence of the House? How major or significant has a "policy" defeat to be before a principle of confidence is raised? Marshall's conclusion on these matters explains how old or even outmoded conventions may undergo change.

> "In the 1960's and 1970's, in any event, governments seem to have been following a new rule, according to which only votes specifically stated by the Government to be matters of confidence or votes of no confidence by the Opposition are allowed to count. Just conceivably one can imagine amongst recent Prime Ministers those who might have felt it their duties to soldier on in the general interest even in the face of such a vote."

---

15 C. C. Turpin, *British Government and the Constitution* (London: Weidenfeld and Nicolson, 1990), p.99.
16 R. Brazier, *Constitutional Texts* (Oxford: Oxford University Press, 1990), pp.345–389. Also see de Smith, *Constitutional and Administrative Law* (Harmondsworth: Penguin, 1989), pp.28–47.

5-021 The most important convention, which Dicey recognised, is collective responsibility of individual Ministers and of the Cabinet. As discussed in the previous chapter, individual ministerial responsibility is traditionally defined to mean that a minister is responsible for his private conduct and that of his department, including the acts of the civil servants in his department. This has at least four options. The most routine is to inform and explain policies and actions in the form of written or oral answers to Parliament or to Select Committees. Ministerial statements are a good example of this in every day practice. The second option is the use of apology. In cases where there are errors the use of apology has become commonplace. The House of Commons usually appears generous when an apology is made. Only in very serious cases will resignation be demanded. The third option is the promise to take action. A minister who is responsible may promise to take action and this may be deemed sufficient to meet a set of criticism or as a result of an inquiry. The Mid Staffordshire NHS Foundation Trust Inquiry under the chair of Robert Francis QC[17] made recommendations that had resulted in reforms to the Care Quality Commission, responsible for health care standards that avoided any further ministerial embarrassment. There is now "a duty of candour" on health care professionals as well as a number of new standards and patient focused responsibilities. The Home Secretary faced serious public criticism over delays in issuing passports in March 2013 and also concerns about the effectiveness of controls on immigrants. The UK Border Agency was scrapped and responsibility for issuing passports taken within the Home Office through the Passport Office coming within the remit of the Home Secretary.[18]

5-022 The third option is resignation. Increasingly as modern government is growing more complex and found in myriad agencies and organisations, it is difficult to trace responsibility and in a substantive way make the Executive accountable to Parliament. In contemporary times ministerial resignation because of a policy failure or mistake is rare. Resignation is more likely because of a personal indiscretion. There is some degree of responsibility for civil servant incompetence or negligence. One example is the ministerial resignation of Thomas Dugdale in 1954 following the Crichel Down inquiry which concluded that the Department of Agriculture had acted in an arbitrary manner. Various civil servants were criticised and the Minister, Thomas Dugdale, resigned. This resignation at the time was perceived to be a triumph over the bureaucracy of irresponsible civil servants. More recently, fresh evidence has suggested that ministerial resignation came about because of the government's embarrassment. As Peter Carrington, then joint Parliamentary Secretary, explained[19] in *Reflect on Things Past*, he and Dick Nuggent had offered their resignation to Churchill who agreed they should carry on. In such circumstances ministers may resign or retain office simply because the Prime Minister concedes it is in the government's interests.[20]

---

17 HC 947 (2013).
18 The Government Response to the Fourth Report from the Home Affairs Select Committee Session, HC 238 (2014–15); and *Her Majesty's Passport Office: delays in processing applications*, CM 8992 (December 2014).
19 P. Carrington, *Reflect on Things Past* (London: Collins, 1988); and P. Cosgrove, *Carrington: A Life and a Policy* (London : Dent, 1985), pp.55, 57.
20 House of Commons Research Paper, *Individual ministerial responsibility—issues and examples*, 04/31 (5 April 2004).

196 | **THE RULE OF LAW AND CONSTITUTIONAL CONVENTIONS**

5-023 Ministerial resignations since 1960 have appeared to arise from differences in policy over government collective decisions such as entering into the European Communities or disputes over government policy. An eclectic assortment of reasons may be offered to support the convention of resignation which meets the needs of the government of the day as much as any principle of accountability to Parliament. Nevertheless responsibility of ministers means that mistakes, blunders or the incompetence of ministers are issues which may be raised as matters for the debate and scrutiny of the House of Commons where resignation is rarely the sanction. Widespread criticism of the poll tax and the blunders in its introduction the inevitable unpopularity of the government led to the resignation of Mrs Thatcher when Cabinet colleagues felt unable to support her continuation in office.[21] Instead of outright resignation, which is very rare, criticism, rebuke or embarrassment may be the stimulus for ministers to improve. Overall the standing of the government of the day may decline when poor ministerial judgment is exposed to the glare of publicity. Constitutional conventions may give rise to greater political effects than have constitutional significance. This underlines the remarkable feature of the UK's unwritten Constitution which often leaves political judgment to determine the outcome of constitutional practices. To countries with a written constitution, this appears an unusual characteristic of the UK's Constitution where much political power resides and determines constitutional practice.[22]

5-024 Conventions have invariably attracted a wide spectrum of opinion from lawyers and political scientists. Why have conventions, and what purpose do they fulfil? Hood Phillips and other writers have remarked that conventions are really based on[23] "the wishes of the majority of the electors".

5-025 Examples supporting this view are: the conventions relating to the choice of government which is formed from the majority party in the Commons; the convention that the Queen should act on the advice of ministers; or the convention that the Queen will not refuse Royal Assent to a bill.

5-026 On more mundane matters such as a request by the Leader of the Opposition for the recall of Parliament during recess, the position is regulated by both convention and the Standing Orders of the House of Commons. Standing Order No.12 allows ministers to recall Parliament should the Speaker be satisfied by representations that[24] "the public interest does so require". In fact, convention seems to indicate that requests by Opposition MPs to recall Parliament in recent years have been invariably refused. Emergency recall has been rejected on four occasions in the past 20 years. However, since 1948 Parliament has been recalled 27 times: in 1950 to discuss military involvement in Korea; the Suez crisis in 1956;

---

21   See David Butler, Andrew Adonis and Tony Travers, *Failure in British Government: The Politics of the Poll Tax* (Oxford; Oxford University Press, 1994).
22   D. Oliver and R. Austin, "Political and Constitutional Aspects of the Westland Affair" (1987) 40 *Parliamentary Affairs* 20. Also see D. Woodhouse, *Ministers and Parliament* (Oxford: Clarendon Press, 1994).
23   Hood Phillips, *Constitutional and Administrative Law* (London: Sweet & Maxwell, 1987), p.119; and R. Brazier, "Choosing a Prime Minister" [1982] *Public Law* 395.
24   Standing Order of the House of Commons No.12 (1948).

and the Berlin crisis in 1961. More recently recall was granted over the Falklands invasion in 1982 and the Gulf war in 1990. A request for a recall in 1992 on the economy and the sending of British troops to Bosnia was refused. Parliament was recalled to debate the consequences of the terrorist attack in the US on 11 September 2001. On 24 September 2002, Parliament was recalled to discuss the potential use of weapons of mass destruction in Iraq. On 11 August 2011 Parliament discussed the problems of public disorder and the implications of problems in the global economy. Parliament was recalled on 29 August 2013 to debate the possibility of taking military action in Syria. The Government's motion was defeated by 272 votes for to 285 against.[25] In June 2016 Parliament was recalled because of the murder of the Labour MP Jo Cox.

Conventions as precedent for past practice may, in the examples shown, not provide much guidance as to future practice. The government may find it easy to make up its mind on the basis of the facts in each case.[26] Recently, the Strathclyde Review examined the relationship between the House of Commons and House of Lords. This involved considering a number of conventions: The Salisbury Convention that Bills implementing manifesto commitments of the Government are not opposed by the Lords at second reading and should not be objected to; that the Lords do not usually object to secondary legislation; and that the financial privileges of the House of Commons are respected and that Government should get their business undertaken in a reasonable time. The Strathclyde Review was triggered by the vote in the House of Lords on 26 October 2015 to reject a statutory instrument to implement the Government's policy on tax credits.[27] Doubts were expressed about the convention on statutory instruments and Lord Strathclyde concluded that the convention "is now so flexible it barely is a convention at all." This raises an important set of questions-how do conventions arise and how are they recognisable? Lord Norton helpfully explains that:

5-027

> "There is much misunderstanding of what constitutes a convention. They are non-legal rules that determine a consistent, indeed invariable pattern of behaviour."[28]

There is also an underlying morality at work. Conventions are a reflection of "right behaviour". Lord Norton is also doubtful about the creation of conventions simply through the words of the originator. The Salisbury Convention came from the words of Viscount Crambourne in 1945. The statement of Lord Sewel in 1998 became a convention and its status as a convention has come about because of the invariable practice of obtaining the consent of the Scottish Parliament when the UK Parliament is legislating on measure affecting Scotland.

---

25 House of Commons Library Standard Note, *Recall of Parliament*, SN/PC/01186 (30 August 2013).
26 See House of Commons Research Paper, *Individual ministerial responsibility—issues and examples*, 04/31 (5 April 2004).
27 House of Commons Library, *Conventions on the relationship between the Commons and the Lords*, Briefing Paper No.5996 (7 January 2016).
28 Lord Norton, *The Strathclyde recommendations are based on a false premise that there is a convention that the Lords does not reject statutory instruments*, The UCL Constitution Unit (Janauary 2016).

5-028 There is much ambiguity about whether there is a convention that if the House of Lords defeats a statutory instrument then there is a breach of any convention. The Joint Committee on Conventions in 2006 rejected this idea and as Lord Norton makes clear there is no invariable practice.

5-029 It is therefore concluded that there should be great care before deciding that a common practice has become an accepted convention and one that is invariably followed. An interesting example has arisen over Parliamentary approval for military action. Since 2003, there has been pressure for Parliament to be allowed a vote for any military action. The Labour Government proposed a resolution of the House to be passed giving Parliament the right to approve any "significant non-routine" deployments of the armed forces but without prejudice to national security or intelligence. The proposal was not implemented. In 2011, the Coalition government suggested that a convention has emerged in Parliament that before troops were committed to military operations, the House of Commons should have an opportunity of debate. This proposal was welcomed but there are doubts about whether there is a convention or not. From the initial Iraq vote in 2003 and March 2011, there had been no government vote or table motion on the use of British forces, including the commitment of British troops in Helmand in Afghanistan in 2006. The deployment of British military assets in Mali in early 2013 was also undertaken without any debate. However, in 2014 the deployment of British military assets was not debated for Mali. Later in 2014 there has been a vote and debate on the use of chemical weapons against civilians in Syria by the Assad regime and also UK responses to the actions of the Islamic State (ISIS) in Iraq in September 2014 when the Government was defeated. In November 2015 there was a return to the discussion and the Government won the debate. This may raise the possibility that it would be inconceivable for the deployment of armed forces to take place without prior Parliamentary approval. A Parliamentary resolution is different from a convention but there are arguments in favour of creating greater clarity over the existence of a convention or not. In the case of prior Parliamentary approval or debate before the commitment of military assets, there are widely different views on what such a convention may mean or whether such a convention exists.[29] If there is an invariably practice establishing such a convention it will require much more clarity and understanding as to what it may mean exactly.

5-030 Academic writers[30] and the Joint Committee on Conventions (2006)[31] have discussed the question of whether conventions might be formally codified. The House of Commons Political and Constitutional Reform Committee contained a codification of conventions in their draft Constitutional Code.[32]

---

29 House of Commons, *Parliamentary approval for military action*, Briefing Papers 7166 (12 May 2015).
30 Marshall has discussed codification as has Brazier in de Smith, *Constitutional and Administrative Law* (Harmondsworth: Penguin, 1989), p.46 and in new edition (1989), pp.34–37.
31 Joint Committee on Conventions, *Conventions of the UK Parliament*, HL Paper 265, HC 1212, 2005–06 (3 November 2006).
32 House of Commons, Political and Constitutional Reform Committee, *A New Magna Carta?*, 4th Report Session, HC 463 (2014–15).

5-031 It is suggested that the importance of conventions is such that they should be collected together into a single code which would attempt to be comprehensive. The attraction of such a code would be to end uncertainty and vagueness associated with knowing whether a particular convention exists or not. The disadvantage is that a code might lead to rigidity; once codified, would a convention lose its flexibility to change and so become fixed at one period in time? Are all conventions capable of enforcement by the Courts? This might invariably follow once a convention became written and adopted in a code. As already noted above, the *Ministerial Code* is an example of a form of codified working practices and understandings. This includes the presumption that the principles of collective responsibility apply to all Government ministers. Overall there is a duty to Parliament to account and to be held to account for policies, decisions and actions of their departments and agencies. The paramount importance is given to the "accurate and truthful information" to Parliament and there is an obligation to correct any inadvertent error or inadequate statement. Any minister knowingly misleading Parliament is expected to resign. Opennesss is also required, especially when questioned in Parliament and refusal to give information is limited to circumstances where it is not in the public interest that is consistent with statutory arrangements including the Freedom of Information Act 2000. Civil servants are accountable to ministers and the Ministerial Code refers to the Civil Service Code in terms of the accountability of civil servants and their duties. Civil servants are expected to be required by ministers to give evidence to Parliament and be as helpful as possible. The Public Interest Disclosure Act 1998 applies to civil servants (with the exception of the Security Service, the Secret Intelligence Service and the Government Communications Headquarters)[33] and there are many implications for civil servants when they are whistle-blowing.[34] The procedures and arrangements applicable to civil servants are explained in the Civil Service Code.[35] The Enterprise and Regulatory Reform Act 2013 makes the addition that any disclosure must be in the public interest. It is possible for whistle blowers[36] to disclose information to MPs.[37] There is an ever presence of "gagging clauses," particularly in the National Health Service where they are banned from 13 March 2013,[38] but also widely used in private contracts. One estimate is that up to 2011 "a total of £14.7 million of taxpayers' money was spent on compromise agreements, most of which included gagging clauses to silence whistleblowers".[39]

5-032 There is no direct accountability of civil servants to Parliament accountability comes through ministers. The role of Parliamentary Select Committees, particularly the public Accounts Committee in recent years has shown a robust approach to questioning senior civil servants that has provided civil servants with the unease that their evidence may be used to

---

33 The Police Reform Act 2002 applies the Public Interest Disclosure Act 1998 to the police from 1 April 2004.
34 House of Commons Library, *Public Interest Disclosure*, Standard Note SN/BT/248.
35 Civil Service Commission, *Whistleblowing and the Civil Service Code* (June 2011).
36 See *Parkins v Sodexho Ltd* [2011] U.K.E.A.T. 1239.
37 The Public Interest Disclosure (Prescribed Persons).
38 Section 43j of the Employment Rights Act 1996, and on 13 March 2013 the Health Secretary agreed that they should be banned in the National Health Service with immediate effect.
39 *The Daily Telegraph*, 26 March 2013. House of Commons Library Briefing Paper, *Whistleblowing and gagging clauses: the Public Interest Disclosure Act 1998*, No.00248 (27 March 2014).

hold ministers to account.[40] This does not necessarily lead to a more open and accountable scrutiny of ministers. The effectiveness of the UK Border Agency was never fully opened up to scrutiny and its inability to provide a good service was the subject of many denials,[41] until it was merged into the Home Office and made directly accountable to ministers as a result of strong public and media protest.

5-033 Breaching the code is potentially serious. Following the investigation by the Cabinet Secretary, Dr Liam Fox, then the Defence Secretary resigned in October 2011 over the way defence matters were being handled by his adviser Adam Werritty. No criminal offence was involved but there were questions about how the distinction between personal interest and government activities had become blurred.[42]

5-034 It is possible to summarise the subject matter of conventions as conventions arising in the exercise of prerogative powers, the workings of Cabinet, the proceedings in Parliament and relations between Lords and Commons, and finally, in relations between the UK and Commonwealth. This list is not exhaustive.

5-035 Conventions may be adopted into statute, such as the convention of the UK not legislating for a former dependent territory in the preamble and s.4 of the Statute of Westminster 1931.

5-036 The survival of conventions owes much to their general acceptance and the requirement of constitutional government with ultimate electoral accountability. When a convention is breached, the convention is usually sufficiently flexible to survive, even though there may be doubt as to its value once it is discovered that the convention was unable to prevent the breach in the first place. It is ultimately the electorate who will determine the government's worth if there are flagrant breaches of constitutional convention.[43] The Courts remain reluctant to enforce conventions. In 1981 Lord Diplock in *R v Inland Revenue Commissioners Ex p. National Federation of Self-Employed and Small Businesses Ltd*[44] made clear that while ministers were responsible to both Parliament and the Courts, there was an important distinction. This distinction he explained in terms of law and policy:

"They [Ministers] are accountable to Parliament for what they do so far as regards efficiency and policy; and of that Parliament is the only judge; they are responsible to a court of justice for the lawfulness of what they do and of that the court is the only judge."

5-037 Lord Diplock's distinction recognises the differences between Parliament's role to oversee conventions and the Courts' authority to determine what is lawful.

5-038 Some reflections may be offered on the value of conventions. Constitutional lawyers often face great difficulty when attempting to understand the different practices of government. Such practices do not easily conform to legal analysis and present problems of ordering, classifying and describing. Constitutional conventions provide a useful organising category, permitting the discussion of government behaviour and activities elevated to constitutional

---

40 Public Accounts Committee, *The Provision of the Out-of hours GP Service in Cornwall*, HC 471 (2013–14).
41 House of Commons, *Home Affairs Committee on the UK Borders Agency*, HC 792 (2012–13).
42 *The Guardian*, 14 October 2011.
43 N. Johnson, *In Search of the Constitution* (London : Methuen, 1977), pp.31–33.
44 [1982] A.C. 617; [1981] 2 W.L.R. 722 HL.

consideration rather than party politics. The attraction of a Cabinet Manual, the Ministerial Code and the Civil Service Code is to bundle miscellaneous working practices including conventions into a form of best practice underlines how the modern form of conventions is to set a moral tone hat influences the day-to-day pragmatism of political life. There are dangers that conventions may become too rigid and prescriptive. Loughlin warns that conventions may appear too neatly packaged and therefore may give a distorted analysis[45]:

> "It leads too easily to a false ascription of meaning to events and, by trying to generalise from the exceptional cases and ignoring the common case (in which resignation does not occur) has a distortive effect."

5-039

Taking Loughlin's caveat seriously, however, there is still value in studying and understanding conventions, although their limitations ought to be admitted. Conventions may appear descriptive, but in fact they are also normative and interpretative. Perhaps too great an expectation is placed on conventions to fill the gaps in the unwritten Constitution.

5-040

Johnson reflects that perhaps the place given to conventions within the UK's constitutional arrangements is misplaced and over-optimistic? This may arise from the changing nature of social life and the speed and variety of such change. Johnson notes[46] that:

> "there is no longer that degree of commitment to particular procedures, that respect for traditional values and habits, nor that breadth of agreement about how political authority should be exercised and for what purposes, which would justify the belief that convention alone is a sheet anchor on which we can rely for the protection of civil rights or for the survival of a particular form of government."

5-041

If in the past conventions appeared to offer predictability in the conduct of government activities, it is doubtful if this remains so today. In a general way this reflects on the workings of an unwritten constitution. Johnson warns that the qualities of flexibility and adaptability in the Constitution may become simply a means for executive power to increase.

Perhaps the most positive opinion about conventions is that of T. R. S. Allan who observes that conventions might provide[47] "a primary source of legal principle". Allan also argues that such principles might inform how the rule of law might develop. Indeed, the process of codification, both formal and informal, has greatly contributed to the creation of a constitutional rule book consisting of the Ministerial Code, the Cabinet Manual and the Civil Service Code. The House of Lords Constitution Committee's retrospective analysis of the Coalition government

5-042

---

45 M. Loughlin, *Public Law and Political Theory* (Oxford: Oxford University Press, 1992), p.53.
46 N. Johnson, *In Search of the Constitution*, n.30, p.33. Jeffrey Jowell, "The Rule of Law Today" in J. Jowell and D. Oliver (eds), *The Changing Constitution*, 3rd edn, Oxford: Oxford University Press, 1994), pp.58–62.
47 T. R. S. Allan, *Law, Liberty and Justice* (Oxford: Oxford University Press, 1993).

that lasted from 2010–2015 is an instructive illustration[48] of the ebb and flow of our constitutional arrangements to fit the political needs of the day.

C: The Rule of Law

5-043   The late Lord Bingham, in his important work on *The Rule of Law*[49] thoughtfully observed that the rule of law "remains an ideal, but an ideal worth striving for, in the interests of good government and peace, at home and in the world at large." This sets the tone for discussion of this important aspect of our Constitution.[50] The Constitutional Reform Act 2005 mentions the rule of law as an "existing constitutional principle" and there is a vibrant literature on its meaning and influence.[51] As noted already, Jeffrey Jowell suggests that the rule of law provides a form of "institutional morality" that is intrinsic to any constitutional democracy[52] and operates as a controlling influence on the government of the day. The House of Lords Select Committee on the Constitution identified retrospective legislation as a threat to the rule of law and warned that it should not be avoided whenever possible. In addition the rule of law requires clarity in the law and certainty as well as the avoidance of general warrants or unlimited financial penalties.[53] These guiding principles are important as over centralised Government in the UK within a unitary state may easily assume that its legal authority to take action accompanies the moral authority to do so. The rule of law is often in competition to the sovereignty of Parliament that is often under the influence of the Government. Governmental power is not confined by a written constitution or a domestically entrenched Bill of Rights. Government is said to be both accountable and responsible. Responsible government is carried out according to constitutional conventions, international obligations such as the European Convention on Human Rights, obligations through membership of the European Community and the rule of law. Great significance has been given to the rule of law within the UK's Constitution. Lord Sumption, has entered a note of caution, suggesting that the "lack of democratic legitimacy

---

48 House of Lords Constitution Committee, *Constitutional Implications of Coalition Government*, 5th Report (2014).
49 Lord Bingham, *The Rule of Law* (London: Allen Lane 2010), p.174.
50 There is also a worldwide discourse. See D. Marshall (ed), *The International Rule of Law Movement* (Cambridge, MA: Harvard University Press, 2014).
51 Brian Tamanaha, *On the Rule of Law: History Politics and Theory* (Cambridge and New York: Cambridge University Press, 2004); and Conor Gearty, *Can Human Rights Survive?* (London: Hamlyn Lectures, 2005), pp.103–104.
52 See J. Jowell, D. Oliver and C. O'Cinneide, *The Changing Constitution*, 8th edn (Oxford: Oxford University Press, 2015).
53 See Jack Simson Caird, Robert Hazell and Dawn Oliver, *The Constitutional Standards of the House of Lords Select Committee on the Constitution* (London, University College London, 2014), p.10.

is a potential problem about all judge-made law".[54] This caution may act as a restraint on the judiciary from making political decisions that are policy matters and best suited to the decision-making process of the Government. There are circumstances where the judges may regard their role as "implicitly" authorised by Parliament, such as the Human Rights Act 1998 which authorises the judges to consider the European Convention of Human Rights.

Constitutional lawyers continue to be influenced by Dicey's explanation of the rule of law contained in his *Introduction to the Law of the Constitution*. The term "rule of law" Dicey acknowledged was not originally his own but taken from the writings of William Hearn[55] (1826–88). Hearn, in fact, acknowledged that his understanding of the rule of law owed much to his analysis of the ideal of government, according to law, from the debates on English government in the seventeenth century. Hearn suggests that the rule of law is of ancient origin and may be found in the literature on the role of the State in society. One of the earliest writings on the ideal of the authority of the State acting according to pre-existing laws and not arbitrarily, may be found in Plato's Laws.

Similar ethical considerations apply in various writings in the twelfth and fourteenth centuries of how rulers or the State should apply the law and subordinate their authority to the law. In the thirteenth century in England, there was strong resistance to the idea that the King should be above the law. Considerable ambiguity surrounds the implications of Magna Carta (1215) when conceded by King John. Some of its chapters place the law of the land as paramount. By implication rather than expressly, the King's acceptance of Magna Carta was also acceptance of the principle of subservience to the law.[56] Sir John Fortescue (1394–1476), an English judge and early English authority on the rule of law, wrote that the King could not override the law as judges must decide according to law, even when commanded to do otherwise.

As mentioned above, Hearn's inspiration for his ideas on the rule of law lay in the constitutional conflicts of the seventeenth century. James I claimed royal authority over law despite much acknowledged advice to the contrary. The claim against such royal authority lay in its arbitrary nature and even though Monarchy was restored after the Civil Wars, royal authority was not. John Locke (1632–1704) articulated the principles which Hearn was later to rely on, namely that government should be exercised according to the law "promulgated and known to the people" as opposed to extraordinary powers dispensed through proclamation. It is noteworthy that Locke's clear analysis of how the governed should be governed, is less clear over how government itself should be subject to law. While accepting the ultimate authority of law, Locke conceded that discretion was a necessary element in rules and that the prerogative may be a required power for the ruler. Since it was impossible to make full provision for all problems, arguably, much discretion may be considered necessary.

Dicey's own reasoning about the existence of the rule of law depended in large part on the work of Blackstone, Coke and John Austin. In common with his views on conventions, it was

---

54 Lord Sumption, "The Limits of Law", 27th Sultan Azlan Shah Lecture, Kuala Lumpur (30 November 2013).
55 W. Hearn, *The Government of England, its Structure and Development* (London: 1867).
56 Bracton, *De legibus et consuetudinibus*. Fortescue, *De Natura legis naturae*, Bk.1 p.16. Coke in *Prohibitions Del Roy* (1607) 12 Co. Rep. 63.

Austin's analysis that had the greatest influence on Dicey, and in particular Austin's views on the ultimate omnipotence of Parliament. Dicey recognised the difficulty of resolving the operation of constitutional conventions and the compatibility of parliamentary sovereignty with the rule of law.

5-048 Parliamentary sovereignty had both a legal and a political dimension. Parliament was susceptible to change through the extension of the franchise and what Dicey perceived as "the working class vote". Dicey, somewhat grudgingly, accepted what he termed "the progress to democracy", but he admitted the potential for conflict between Parliament's sovereignty and reforming legislation which might radically alter the Union or challenge the fundamental characteristics of the Constitution. Dicey believed in the rule of law and the use of conventions as essential mechanisms against abuse, especially of discretionary power. Conventions recognised public "morality" which self-limited the power of Parliament.

5-049 In the absence of any formal doctrine of the separation of powers or a written constitution limiting the powers of the Executive within the State, the rule of law provided a convenient means to express concern over the uncontrolled powers of a newly enfranchised Parliament. Dicey feared the growth in incremental powers to the State—in particular, legislation which might interfere with individual liberty, particularly property rights.

5-050 The rule of law is susceptible to a number of different meanings often based on value judgments. In its broadest sense it may be viewed as a general political doctrine. The rule of law is both descriptive and prescriptive, characteristics it shares with conventions of the Constitution. Dicey found three meanings for the rule of law to be considered as part of the constitutional order of the UK.

5-051 First, Dicey insisted on the predominance of "ordinary law". Government power, especially when it affects the citizen, must be accompanied by observance of the correct legal rules and have the authority of law. Secondly, discretionary power however broadly based must not be abused or used in an unrestricted way to circumvent the legislative authority of Parliament. The Executive should be amenable to parliamentary control. Thirdly, Dicey believed that the enforcement of the principles of the rule of law was best achieved through the ordinary Courts and not as part of a written constitution or through the setting-up of a special system of Courts. Dicey assumed that civil liberties were best protected through the system of remedies which had developed historically through the Courts. Parliamentary sovereignty, which could at a whim destroy the delicate nature of the rule of law, was instead in Dicey's view intended to compliment and reinforce the rule of law. Concerns about the potential for the abuse of sovereignty were offset by Dicey's focus on the elected accountability of Parliament. Craig explains how Dicey attempted to reconcile the apparent contradiction that sovereignty might threaten the rule of law[57]:

> "The two main elements of Dicey's rule of law possesses both a descriptive and a normative content. In descriptive terms it was

---

57 P. Craig, *Public Law and Democracy in the United Kingdom and United States of America* (Oxford: Clarendon, 1990), p.21. Also see Harlow and Rawlings, *Law and Administration* (Cambridge: Cambridge University Press, 1984), pp.1–6, 15–19.

> assumed that the regular law predominated, that exercise of broad discretionary power was absent, and that all people were subject to the ordinary law of the realm. Public power resided with Parliament. In normative terms it was assumed that this was indeed a better system than that which existed in France, where special rules and a distinctive regime existed for public law matters."

Dicey's belief in the rule of law assumed fundamental importance in his understanding of the Constitution. A jaundiced view might be that Dicey hoped the rule of law might be a valuable tool in his attempt to argue against major political changes, to which he was personally opposed. Home Rule for Ireland, votes for women, and social legislation might be postponed if they offended the rule of law.

How might Dicey's vision of the rule of law apply today? A major misunderstanding in Dicey's belief in the rule of law was the scope of ministerial power and its delegation to a wide variety of other agents. Even in Dicey's time there was a miscellaneous number of administrative institutions outside the ordinary Courts; their existence was not fully appreciated by Dicey which greatly weakened the cogency of his arguments about the rule of law and the role of the Courts. The nature of the errors in Dicey's misconceptions are explained more fully in Ch.8. However, this should not detract from the eloquence of Dicey's views on the rule of law and the importance of Dicey's influence on the development of administrative law.

As remarkable as his description of the rule of law is, Dicey's analytical method, employed in the formulation of legal principles, also deserves mention. Dicey's method involved abstracting basic principles from legal materials. His style was to begin his text with generalised principles, discussed in more detail later in the work. At times the clarity of his original principles became obscured by the later discussion and contradictions may obscure the principle.

Dicey's critics have identified such weaknesses and some of Dicey's views have been revised and re-examined. The challenge mounted by his critics is to expose Dicey's analytical method and the political values upon which his theory rests. Both parliamentary sovereignty and the rule of law have been subjected to such criticism. Loughlin suggests that Dicey was mistaken in his perception of administrative power[58]:

> "In general public law should ensure that the legal framework within which government operated provided an effective and equitable structure for the implementation of the public good, as expressed in the positive functions of the State. From this perspective delegated legislation and administrative adjudication was not a symptom of despotic power but of the changing role of the state."

It may be concluded that Dicey's perception of the role of central government in 1885 was influenced by the centralising tendencies of government power and his belief that such powers

---
58   M. Loughlin, *Public Law and Political Theory* (Oxford: Oxford University Press, 1992), p.168.

could be adequately controlled. This depended on his view of the Courts enforcing the rule of law as a means of keeping in check the boundaries of parliamentary power. This raises the question of the role of the Courts in applying and upholding the rule of law. There is a perception that the common law offers a tradition of fundamental human rights or norms.

5-057 The Courts adopted different strategies depending on their perception of procedural rules, the nature and complexity of the law and remedies and the nature of the issues they were invited to consider, at the time. The emergence in the late seventeenth century of judicial review was largely free from doctrinal development, and reflected the changing nature of parliamentary power. Craig explains[59]:

> "On the one hand, the judiciary began to justify the exercise of jurisdictional control more specifically in terms of ensuring that the authority in question did not usurp or extend the area over which the legislature had granted it jurisdiction. The objective was to ensure that the agency did not assume authority to regulate behaviour or to legislate in areas outside those delegated to it by Parliament. On the other hand, the Courts become more aware, in form at least, of the legitimate limits to the exercise of their judicial power."

5-058 Craig's thesis is that the Courts often adopted conflicting directions and interpretations over the nature of legislative powers, the delegation of such powers to inferior bodies and the precise discretionary nature of their own judicial powers.[60] A number of cases may be cited in support of this view. A common theme is the question of whether the delegated body has competence to determine its own decisions. Accordingly, the power of appeal to a court of law is distinguished from a review. The former examines the correctness of the decision while the latter the legality.

5-059 This leaves the Courts with a less certain role in evaluating the activities of inferior bodies, and gives rise to a perception that the Courts' powers of review are limited to technical or procedural requirements as distinct from substantive review. Nevertheless, there are a number of legal cases where the Courts have sought to curtail the unfettered exercise of State power. In *Entick v Carrington*,[61] Lord Camden in the Court of Common Pleas examined the legal power of the Secretary of State to arrest John Entick, an alleged author of seditious writings, to seize his papers and books and use these as evidence. Entick successfully sued the officers and obtained damages when Lord Camden held that the warrant was illegal and void. The legal reasoning in the case depended on the absence of any legal authority supporting the legal claim that the warrants were lawful. The result was to leave the Courts with a power of review but subject to the legislative authority of Parliament. Statutes which expressly confer the rights of arrest or seizure may leave the Courts with a minimal role in finding any legal

---

59 P. Craig, *Public Law and Democracy in the United Kingdom and United States of America*, p.22.
60 See P. Craig, "Formal and sustantive conception of the Rule of Law" (1997) *Public Law* 467.
61 (1765) 19 St. Tr. 1030.

grounds to support the rights of the citizen beyond the narrow scope of the wording of the Act of Parliament.

There may be a number of limitations on the role of the Courts. The "intention of Parliament" is open to interpretation by the Courts. The Courts may be limited in the scope of their interpretation. Acts of Parliament cannot be held to be unconstitutional, severely limiting the extent of judicial intervention. Constraints on judicial activism in reviewing informal bodies often depend on the type of body, and their powers under review.

Implicit in our current unwritten constitutional arrangements is that there is no hierarchy of rights such that any one of them is more entrenched by the law than any other. This point is explained by Laws J in *R v Lord Chancellor Ex p. Witham*[62]:

> "The common law does not generally speak in the language of constitutional rights, for the good reason that in the absence of any sovereign text, a written constitution which is logically and legally prior to the power of legislature, executive and judiciary alike there is on the face of it no hierarchy of rights such that anyone of them is more entrenched by the law than any other. And if the concept of a constitutional right is to have any meaning, it must surely sound in the protection which the law affords to it. Where a written constitution guarantees a right there is no conceptual difficulty. The state authorities must give way to it save to the extent that the constitution allows them to deny it."

It may be fair to conclude that in the unwritten constitution where the common law accords legislative supremacy to Parliament, the existence of rights for the citizen may be difficult to imagine.[63]

Local government is not only an elected element of government but possesses wide statutory authority to carry out activities including the promotion of private bill legislation, the enforcement of criminal sanctions and the expenditure of public money. The Courts have held that a local authority acts unreasonably "if no reasonable public body" could have made a decision. The Wednesbury Corp was empowered to grant licences for Sunday entertainment subject to conditions which it thought fit. The condition—that no children under 15 be admitted to a cinema—was challenged as unreasonable and ultra vires; Lord Greene accepted that the Courts could not substitute its policy for that of the local authority—an inherent limit on the jurisdiction of the Courts. However, the Courts may intervene as to the legality of the decision on the basis of applying a test of reasonableness. Within the scope of unreasonableness, the Courts have a wide discretion as to the legality of the powers under review. In *Associated Picture*

---

62 [1998] Q.B. 575; [1997] 2 All E.R. 779 QBD at [783F]–[783J].
63 J. Jowell, "The Rule of Law Today" in J. Jowell, D. Oliver and C. O'Cinneide, *The Changing Constitution*, 8th edn (Oxford: Oxford University Press, 2015), pp.3–23. See T. R. S. Allan, *Constitutional Justice: A Liberal Theory of the Rule of Law* (Oxford: Oxford University Press, 2001).

Houses Ltd v Wednesbury Corp[64] Lord Greene acknowledged both the jurisdiction of review of the Courts and the jurisdiction of the decision-maker to make decisions.

5-064 A final dimension to the issue of the remit and scope of the rule of law arises with the Human Rights Act 1998. For the first time Convention rights may be enjoyed by citizens through interpretation of the European Convention by the Courts. This creates tensions between the traditional role of the judiciary to interpret and apply the rule of law within the boundaries of statutory enactment, and the significance of constitutional rights that must be given compatibility with our existing law. This shifts the analysis about the rule of law to a rights-based order seeking to locate and secure rights amidst a plethora of regulation and complex administrative machinery. Will rights endure? Are such rights sufficiently powerful to endure beyond the necessity of the moment or the emergency of war or civil unrest? Only time will tell. This is, after all, not only unchartered waters, but also a glimpse at real politics when judicial decisions will be seized upon as evidence of political judgment and morality rather than of technical law alone. Rights are likely to be seen as a means of holding to account and an opportunity to create challenges rather than providing a means to seek better government or administration. The pivotal role of the Courts depends on the sensitive exercise of discretion, and the hope is that the rule of law will ultimately mean not just justiciable rights but improvements in the policy implementation of decision-makers.[65] Underpinning rights are questions about how the common law development of the idea of the rule of law is likely to survive? Allan in his recent writing, *Constitutional Justice: Liberal Theory of the Rule of Law* has identified how the common law may take the high ground for the articulation of the ideas and conceptual framework that represents the reasoning of the common law embodying the ideals of justice. Rationality and justice operate under a common thread linking the medieval inheritance with the reality of the common law today. Thus the rule of law stands for principles that reflect fundamental values of society and these will endure beyond the life cycle of party politics or political whims. In his thought-provoking analysis the question may be asked as to whether seeing the Courts as the delivery system of such values as the rule of law, locates litigation with the protection of the value system. It is equally clear that governmental and non-governmental decision-makers, including business and commerce, through contract employment and a plethora of regulation impact on the day-to-day lives of many people. In so doing the value systems may very well locate rights and protection but they are also going to make-profit making decisions, and risk analysis may well prioritise market gain over any fundamental values. The Courts certainly have a part to play in developing the fundamental values in society but it may be peripheral and spasmodic rather than pivotal and predictable.

---

64 [1948] 1 K.B. 223; [1947] 2 All E.R. 680 CA.
65 See Martin Loughlin, "Rights, Democracy and Law" in T. Campbell, K. Ewing and A. Tomkins (eds), *Sceptical Essays on Human Rights* (Oxford: Oxford University Press, 2001).

D: Contemporary Debate on Judicial Discretion, the Rule of Law and the Sovereignty of Parliament

The question of the legitimacy of constitutional review by Courts is one of long standing in the English common law especially when the rule of law may be invoked as a means of holding government to account.[66] In the UK, pre-eminence is given to legal and parliamentary sovereignty and the role of the Courts is important, but generally stops short of overruling or confronting parliament. In recent times, since the UK's membership of the EU, the UK Courts are bound by the decisions of the European Court of Justice in Luxemburg which take precedence over a UK Act of Parliament.[67] EU law has also been influential more generally in setting precedence over national law and in many instances this has led to some rethinking of the law. It has also had an effect of bringing the common law and civil law systems closer together. Over the years the UK Courts developed principles and values to prevent any potentially abusive law making, including principles of proportionality as a ground for review. Dicey[68] writing in 1885, defined many of the judicial review principles and values in his explanation of the rule of law which contained a prohibition against any misuse of power. Collini has observed contrary to many of his critics in his historical context, Dicey did see the importance of judicial oversight and independence:

> "Furthermore, Dicey was at pains to insist that judges were still the chief upholders of English liberties: they are in truth, though not in name, invested with the means of hampering or supervising the whole administrative action of the government and of at once putting a veto upon any proceeding not authorised by the letter of the law."[69]

This has philosophical importance. It is accepted that the legitimate exercise of government powers has to promote basic values and that the rights of citizens require appropriate and fair procedures. There are two aspects to the role of constitutional review. The first is where judicial review is concerned with constitutional review, prevalent in jurisdictions with written

---

66 In the eighteenth century *Entick v Carrington* (1765) 19 St Tr. 1030 established principles that, in the absence of express statutory powers or judicial authority, the executive could not use a general warrant to achieve legal authority which the warrant in itself lacked.
67 See *Francovich v Italian Republic, Bonifaci v Italian Republic* (C-6 and 9/90) [1991] ECR I-5357; and *Factortame (No.2)* [1991] 1 A.C. 603; [1990] 3 W.L.R. 818 HL.
68 Albert Venn Dicey (1835–1922) English jurist and author of *Law and the Constitution* (1885).
69 S. Collini, *Public Moralists: Political Thought and Intellectual Life in Britain 1850–1930* (Oxford: Clarendon, 2011), p.295.

constitutions such as South Africa and the US. Courts are empowered to decline to apply legislation found not to be in conformity with the constitution. This is likely to be controversial since it is based on a pro-active role by the Courts and their interpretation of underlying rights-based values. The second form of judicial review applies to the decisions of the Executive or general administrative decision-making. This is less controversial than the first, but still raises issues about the scope of judicial power and the legitimacy of judicial review powers especially when applied to political decisions.

5–066 Democracy through the electoral mandate has to be reconciled with the need for judicial oversight. Jeremy Waldron[70] argues that respecting electoral wishes through a majority vote that allows citizen participation sets boundaries on judicial decision. In this context he argues that unelected judges should give way to majoritarian decision-making. The second form of judicial review is accepted by Waldron as a procedural form of ensuring that administrative decisions are in accordance with the rule of law. This stops short of merits or policy review for which there are democratic checks and balances. According to this view the adequacy or effectiveness of policy is ultimately a matter for electoral choice. Waldron is strongly opposed to unelected judges overriding electoral choices and so is opposed to the first aspect of constitutional review which has that potential.[71] Waldron also believes that rights are important and this suggests that such moral values should be embedded in good governance.[72] However, are there circumstances where such democratic rights might form the basis of an opposing perspective that entitles judges to offer constitutional review that, on occasions can override majoritarian decision-making? This question is the subject of much academic debate and is difficult to resolve.[73]

5–067 There is also an important distinction between procedure and substance. Testing substantive outcomes against a human rights standard also impacts on the procedures to be adopted and their role. There is considerable debate in the UK on the precise scope of review in terms of proportionality and human rights, since the Human Rights Act 1998. This is especially so when asked to adopt a judicial deference to administrative decision-makers.[74] The creation of a modern UK Supreme Court in 2009 and debates about a written constitution[75] have enlivened discussion about the role of the judiciary.[76] Some writers, notably T. R. S. Allan,[77] reject any idea

---

70 Jeremy Waldron, *Law and Disagreements* (Oxford: Oxford University Press, 1999), pp.88–118.
71 See Richard Stacey, "Democratic jurisprudence and judicial review: Waldron's contribution to political positivism" (2010) *Oxford Journal of Legal Studies* 749.
72 See the discussion about Waldron's views in Mark Tushnet, "How different are Waldron's and Fallon's core cases for and against judicial review?" (2010) *Oxford Journal of legal Studies* 49
73 See Richard Fallon Jnr. "The core of an Uneasy case for Judicial Review" (2008) 121 *Harvard Law Review* 693–736.
74 See Paul Craig, *Administrative Law*, 7th edn (London: Sweet and Maxwell, 2012), pp.628–636; and G. Huscroft "Constitutionalism from the Top Down" (2007) 45 *Osgoode Hall L. J.* 91.
75 John Gardner, *Can there be a written Constitution?*, Legal Research Papers Series, Paper No.17/2009, University of Oxford (May 2009).
76 Kate Malleson, "The evolving role of the Supreme Court" (2011) *Public Law* 754.
77 T. R. S. Allan, "Common Law reason and the Limits of Judicial Deference" in D. Dyzenhaus (ed), *The Unity of*

of deference, but accept some sphere of decision-making being protected from judicial review determined by the circumstances of the case and Parliament's role as the primary decision-maker. Jowell accepts that there are circumstances that are right for the court to defer to the legislature or the Executive on grounds of institutional competence. He argues, however, that this should not be done on the basis that the Courts are mistaken into believing that they lack constitutional competence. Jowell's distinction between institutional rather than constitutional competence is helpful. Institutional competence is about the capacity of the decision-maker to make the relevant decision. This engages with the court's structures and procedures and its capability to decide the matter in a better way than the body being reviewed. This approach offers a valuable analysis because almost invariably the form of accountability or review offered by the Courts is *ex post* and only rarely *ex ante*. The expertise of the Courts might be a limitation.[78] Jowell argues[79] that this is a better way to advance the scope of review rather than constitutional competence, which is about the authority of the body to determine the matter under consideration. The value of constitutional competence is the acceptance of individual rights that have to be considered in the context of majority rule. The Courts are there to delineate the boundaries of review based on this principle. Jowell is content to allow some recognition of the constitutional context but what matters most is the underlying values that should be upheld.

There is no definitive outcome in the debate as to where to place boundaries on the Courts and in many cases the issue is about the intensity of review rather than the absence of any judicial oversight. There is also a great deal of overlap and common agreement between opposing points of view. There are also many different perspectives on how best to define rights and values.[80] In some cases, these are more credible if provided by the relevant executive or administrative body. In other cases, a judicial dialogue about the scope, meaning and intent in their interpretation may make an essential contribution. There are a number of comments that can be usefully made about the arguments. First, the various opinions may be explained by differing perspectives on political power and concerns about the usurpation of democratic powers by the Courts. Waldron's analysis may be explicable by his New Zealand experience where, like the UK, constitutional arrangements do not envisage judicial review extending to the legality of Acts of Parliament or the merits of policy making. In contrast, constitutional review experienced in the US is considered to reflect a dynamic and reasonably well functioning liberal democracy.[81] Common to any differences of opinion are concerns about the judiciary

5–068

Public Law (Oxford: Hart, 2004), p.7; and T. R. S. Allan, "Human Rights and Judicial Review: A Critique of 'Due Deference'" [2006] *C.L.J.* 671.
78 See the useful discussion Jo Eric Khushai Murkens, "The quest for constitutionalism in UK public law discourse" (2009) *Oxford Journal of Legal Studies* 427.
79 J. Jowell, "Judicial Deference and Human Rights: A Question of Competence" in P. Craig and R. Rawlings (eds), *Law and Administration in Europe: Essays in Honour of Carol Harlow* (Oxford: Oxford University Press, 2003).
80 See R. Clayton, "Principles for Judicial Deference" [2006] *J.R.* 109; and also M. Hunt, "Sovereignty's Blight: Why Contemporary Public Law Needs the concept of 'Due deference'" in Bamforth and Leyland (eds), *Public Law in a Multi-layered Constitution* (Oxford: Hart, 2003).
81 Mark Tushnet, "How different are Waldron's and Fallon's core cases for and against judicial review?" (2010) *Oxford Journal of legal Studies* 49.

being seen as acting in an overtly political way. Second, there is no overall consensus and wider questions about the complexity of decision-making and the prioritises that should accompany good decisions that are not easily facilitated by legal principles or judicial oversight, that may be overlooked. Third, the assumption that underpin much of the discussion is that democratic accountability through political processes is effective. This is certainly premised on the assumption that majority rule commands respect. It is assumed that there are workable political parties and that elections will see regular changes in political power. The value of the UK discussion serves as a reminder of how important it is to respect the democratic process and as a common rationale for that respect some degree of judicial deference has to be accorded. Setting the balance and adjusting the level of judicial scrutiny is not an exact science. The determinative quality of any decision is not that the legislature has made a determination but that the intrinsic quality of the decision is consistent with fundamental values and principles. Setting the balance is also a matter of culture and determined by the role the judiciary may have in governance. A good example is the recent decision of the Supreme Court in *R (HS2 Action Alliance Ltd) v Secretary of State for Transport*[82] where the applicants argued that the adoption of a hybrid Bill procedure was not compatible with the requirements of the Environmental Impact Assessment Directive (Directive 2011/92/EU) requiring effective opportunities to participate in environmental decision-making procedures. The Government were pushing forward a plan to create a fast train link between the capital and Birmingham and the objectors to the proposed link claimed that there was a serious impact on the environment. The adoption of a hybrid Bill was subject to Government whipping procedures in the House of Commons, there would be inadequate time to debate the detailed and complex nature of environmental issues; and that the alternatives to the proposal would not be considered until the relevant elect committee after second reading. The Supreme Court held that the hybrid Bill procedure was an adequate safeguard of the interests of the parties.[83]

5-069
In the UK the contest between majoritarian democracy and respect for fundamental rights is marked. A number of examples serve to show how judicial power can be both expansive and also self-limiting depending on the nature of the task in hand. The suggestion is that judicial review is pragmatic and often influenced by the procedural rules and expectations placed upon the Courts by the legal profession in the choice of cases that are taken to court and form the basis for review.

5-070
In *R (Jackson) v Attorney General*[84] while upholding the Hunting Act 2004 as being properly enacted under the Parliament Act 1911 as amended by the Parliament Act 1949, the House of Lords raised the question of whether "the absolute nature" of Parliamentary sovereignty might be out of place in the modern UK. The comments were *obiter dicta* but gave rise to the suggestion that the Courts might refuse to apply an Act of Parliament that was in breach

---

82 *R (HS2 Action Alliance Ltd.,) and others v Secretary of State for Transport* [2014] UKSC 3; [2014] 1 W.L.R. 324.
83 The Supreme Court also rejected the view that the issues raised by the applicants should be referred to the European Court of Justice. Lord Reed made clear that where EU law is in direct conflict with UK domestic constitutional law, it was matter to be resolved by the UK Supreme Court.
84 *R (Jackson) v Attorney General* [2005] EWCA Civ 126; [2005] Q.B. 579.

of fundamental constitutional principles. These observations were linked to the procedures and processes adopted under the Parliament Acts but this is indicative of the status given to the rule of law as fundamental to democratic government.[85] In *Thoburn v Sunderland City Council*,[86] Laws LJ suggested that the European Communities Act 1972 was a "constitutional statute", thus elevating its status to protection by the Courts if there was any attempt at repeal or amendment. Statutes which have the potential to affect the legal relationship between the citizen and the State or enlarge or diminish the scope of fundamental constitutional rights can only be amended or repealed by unambiguous words. The Courts have to balance the interests of democratically elected government accountable to Parliament and the fundamentals of the unwritten constitution. This does not guarantee that the values and moral principles will always be observed.

In *R v Secretary of State for the Home Department ex parte Pierson*[87] it was held that the Home Secretary's very broad discretion in setting prisoners tariffs as the basis of a minimum sentence in parole cases could not be interpreted retrospectively because this offended the rule of law in the broadest way possible. This interpretation was primarily based around a presumption that the rule of law should be afforded primacy.

5-071

5-072

In the infamous *Corner* case,[88] involving serious allegations of corruption by BAE Systems, a major British company, the Director of the Serious Fraud Office decided to abandon the corruption investigation. Since the investigation was detailed and substantial the decision to bring it to an end was controversial. It emerged from the judicial review proceedings, that the decision to end the prosecution was based on advice from the British Ambassador amidst concerns that there was a public interest for no prosecution to be taken. The overriding concern of the Government was that if the prosecution went forward, there would be a threat to national security. It was claimed that British lives would be at stake. The Divisional Court held that the Director of the Serious Fraud Office had paid too little attention to the paramount importance of the rule of law. The House of Lords did not accept this view and took a narrower interpretation regarding the issues as standing outside the jurisdiction of the Courts. It was not a judicial function to encroach on the role of the Director when the national interest was involved. The case is helpful in providing a chronology of the process of consultation involving the Prime Minister, the Attorney General and also the Foreign Secretary. The information provided by the court case is also revealing of how legal advice is interpreted. The case is disappointing if it is expected that the Courts will penetrate the "veil of secrecy" offered by national security, but that moral doubts and uncertainties about the propriety of the decision are explained in the case.

5-073

The operation of self-restraint to accommodate the political climate and public opinion underlines many cases where Parliament has itself restrained government. The value of scrutiny where legislation is evaluated, subjected to public debate that relates to the underlying

---

85 The debate on the 42 detention period in 2009/10 is a good example.
86 *Thoburn v Sunderland City Council* [2002] EWHC 195 (Admin); [2003] Q.B. 151.
87 [1998] A.C. 539; [1997] 3 W.L.R. 492 HL.
88 *R (Corner House) v Director of the Serious Fraud Office* [2007] EWHC 311 (Admin); [2007] Env. L.R. 2.

rule of law culture. This has also been supplemented by the development of human rights in the UK under the Human Rights Act 1998, which sets important constraints on the exercise of legal powers. In the context of the UK the largely unwritten constitutional framework has located both liberty and legality as an intrinsic part of the exercise of political power. This may arguably be a deficient form of constitutional settlement. It is intended to underline party political choices through the electoral process. It is also inherently based on a majoritarian system whereby political power exercised by a majority mandate should also accommodate minority rights.

E: Summary and Conclusions

5-074
Dicey's belief in the rule of law paradoxically inhibited the Courts for many years from developing a coherent system of administrative law. His objection to the French *droit administratif* was more generally interpreted as an objection to administrative law, a view which Dicey later retracted.

5-075
Dicey also failed in his analysis of the rule of law to take account of the "body of special rights, prerogatives and immunities". Dicey considered that these no longer existed when in fact government powers include not only the statutory variety discussed above, but prerogative powers and common law rights. We have seen that the Courts have developed, in recent years, powers of review over the prerogative, but Dicey failed to appreciate the extent of government or State powers exercised through prerogative powers and therefore largely outside the controls implied in the rule of law.

5-076
Constitutional conventions are important guides to the "right behaviour" when it comes to the Constitution. The question of codification of conventions remains unresolved. Determining the existence of a convention is a matter of invariable practice rather than usual practice.

Further Reading

T. R. S. Allan, "The Rule of Law as the rule of reason: consent and constitutionalism" (1999) 115 *L.Q.R.* 221.

T. R. S. Allan, *Constitutional Justice: A Liberal Theory of the Rule of Law* (Oxford: Oxford University Press, 2001).

T. R. S. Allan, *The Sovereignty of Law: Freedom, Constitution and Common Law* (Oxford: Oxford University Press, 2013).
Tom Bingham, *The Rule of Law* (London: Penguin Books, 2010).
Mark Elliott and David Feldman (eds), *The Cambridge Companion to Public Law* (Cambridge: Cambridge University Press, 2015).
Anthony King and Ivor Crewe, *The Blunders of our Governments* (London: Oneworld, 2013).
G. Marshall, *Constitutional Conventions. The Rules and Forms of Political Accountability* (Oxford: Oxford University Press, 1984).

6

An Introduction to Administrative Law

In the preceding chapters the outline, structures and principles of the UK's Constitution have been examined, including the role of central government and the civil service. This chapter is intended to explain the development of administrative law: its nature, purpose and significance within the context of the UK's constitutional arrangements.

This chapter introduces the basic framework of administrative law in outline, including the impact of the procedures under the Human Rights Act 1998. In Pt III of the book, chapters will be found covering local government, judicial review, remedies and citizens' grievances in more detail. The explanation contained in this chapter is intended as useful background reading before the more advanced discussion undertaken in Pt III.

A: Introduction

Administrative law may be defined as the law relating to the control of government power including the detailed rules which govern the exercise of administrative decision-taking. It also takes account of the rules, procedures and laws that provide the legal basis for governing that enables the government to discharge its responsibilities to the citizen. This includes the requisite powers for the wide range of duties, obligations that ensure high standards of good administration and decision-making. At the outset it is important to note the wide variety of institutions and bodies are subject to administrative law: the Executive and central government; local authorities; tribunals; inquiries; fringe bodies or non-departmental bodies such as quangos; and even inferior courts. Each in their own distinctive way have a part to play in how the country is governed. Mapping the variety of Acts of Parliament; delegated powers and legislation; and rules and procedures involved is another way to define and categorise public law. The institutional design of public bodies is also relevant including the management of various economic instruments that interface with the private market as well as corporate organisations. The use of public contracts and the scope of contract in general has permeated public law to include regulatory agencies and the control of public powers. The EU is an important contributor providing a vast range of public powers that encroach on the regulation of the citizen as well as the State. Energy and environmental law are two good examples but many regulatory systems in place under the Bank of England to regulate banking are important as there is considerable provision of public money to support the banking system.[1]

6-004 Modern administrative law is intertwined with complex legislation and an ever increasing changing economic circumstances. Administrative law offers pressure groups an opportunity to challenge illegality. The Supreme Court, in an application by the pressure group, Client Earth, granted a declaration that the UK was in breach of its obligations under Directive 2008/50, the Air Quality Directive. This was particularly the case for Greater London where the target for Nitrous Oxide was not expected to be met until 2025, ten years after the expected date for meeting the target. The matter is pending consideration by the European Court of Justice but the case is indicative of the wide ranging nature of the review and oversight powers of the Supreme Court.[2]

6-005 A. V. Dicey was reluctant in his *Law of the Constitution* in 1885 to accept the idea of specialised and specific legal rules governing administrative decision-making. Nevertheless, English law has developed administrative law especially through the growth in case law over the last 30 years. Lord Diplock in *R v Inland Revenue Commissioners Ex p. National Federation of Self-Employed and Small Businesses Ltd*[3] regarded the development of English administrative law "as having been the greatest achievement of the English Courts in my judicial lifetime". Sir Stephen Sedley, a retired Lord Justice of Appeal with wide experience in the public law field, has explained how principles of judicial review "have waxed, waned, slumbered and woken, but in the long term matured in response to continuing change in society and polity which the law inhabits".[4]

6-006 Judicial review is also linked to accountability especially the form of democratic accountability that is an important aspect of Parliamentary control over ministers and policy making. Harlow and Rawlings usefully distinguish between the different approaches to administrative decisions characterised as "red light" and "green light" theories. Red light theorists place emphasis on law and legal rules providing a check on all forms of power, including legal rules to exercise control over political decisions. In contrast green light theorists prefer to emphasis democratic forms of accountability as setting priority on political forms of accountability.[5]

---

1   T. Prosser, *The Economic Constitution* (Oxford: Oxford University Press, 2015).
2   *R (ClientEarth) v Secretary of State for the Environment, Food and Rural Affairs* [2013] UKSC 25; [2013] 3 C.M.L.R. 29. House of Lords Library Note: Sustainable Development Goals, *Parliamentary Perspectives*, LLN 2015/028.. See also *R (on the application of O) v Secretary of State for International Development* [2014] EWHC 2371 (QB).
3   [1982] A.C. 617; [1981] 2 W.L.R. 722 HL.
4   S. Sedley, *Lions under the Throne: Essays on the History of English Public Law*, (Cambridge: Cambridge University Press, 2015), p.7.
5   C. Harlow and R. Rawlings, *Law and Administration*, 3rd edn (Cambridge: Cambridge University Press, 2009),

INTRODUCTION 219

6–007

Judges employ a wide variety of techniques when interpreting legislation and adjudicating disputes between the citizen and the State. Increasingly administrative law is examined in the context of the rule of law that gives rise to substantive principles. In *Ghaidan v Godin Mendoza*, Lady Hale noted that "power must not be exercised arbitrarily"[6] when the court held that gay partners were entitled to the same rights of inheritance as heterosexual partners. Lord Hope in the *R v DPP Ex p. Kebilene*,[7] when interpreting the Human Rights Act 1998, noted how the incorporation of the European Convention on Human Rights into domestic law will "subject the entire legal system to a fundamental process of review" and this might include reform of the judiciary. Recently, Jowell and others categorised "widespread acceptance that substantive principles of legality, certainty, equality and access to justice and rights are essential elements in any well-functioning constitutional democracy".[8] Jowell makes clear that "the practical implication of the rule of law has taken place primarily through judicial review of the actions of public officials".[9]

6–008

Account must be taken of changes that have been made to the procedures and rules that apply to administrative law as part of the general modernisation of procedures begun under the Woolf reforms to the civil justice system as a whole. The Civil Procedure Rules, specifically from 2 October 2000, known as CPR r.54.4 Judicial Review and various practice Directions and Pre-action Protocols apply. CPR r.54.4 also took account of the Bowman Report in 2000.[10] Previously the s.31(3) of the Supreme Court Act 1981 now renamed the Senior Courts Act 1981 under the Constitutional Reform Act 2005,[11] provides rules of standing and the procedures for judicial review. Placing administrative law under a specialised set of procedures and the Administrative Court, is intended to afford expertise as well as protection to public bodies. A judicial review jurisdiction has been conferred on the Upper Tribunal in respect of matters that fall under the tribunal system.

6–009

The term Administrative Law Court is used to describe the jurisdiction of the Divisional Court in matters of judicial review, with new case names and an amalgamated form of Practice Direction[12] intended to stream-line and modernise the system of review.[13] In addition to the creation of an Administrative Law Court, there are changes to the names of the various remedies, certiorari is a quashing order, prohibition is a prohibiting order, mandamus is a mandatory order.

---

    p.38; also see A. Tomkins, "In Defence of the Political Constitution" (2002) 22 *Oxford Journal of Legal Studies* 157; and M. Loughlin, *Public Law and Political Theory* (Oxford: Clarendon Press, 1992), pp.60–61.
6   *Ghaidan v Godin Mendoza* [2004] UKHL 30; [2004] 2 A.C. 557.
7   *R v DPP Ex p. Kebilene* [2000] 2 A.C. 326; [1999] 3 W.L.R. 972 HL at [375].
8   J. Jowell, D. Oliver and Colin O'Cinneide, *The Changing Constitution* 8th edn (Oxford: Oxford University Press, 2015), p.5
9   J. Jowell, "The Rule of Law" in J. Jowell, D. Oliver and Colin O'Cinneide (eds), *The Changing Constitution* 8th edn (Oxford: Oxford University Press, 2015), p.29.
10 The Bowman Report, *Review of the Crown Office List Lord Chancellor's Office* (2000). Also see N. Bamforth, "Reform of Public Law: Pragmatism or Principle?" (1995) 58 *Modern Law Review* 722.
11 Schedule 11(1) para.1of the Constitutional Reform Act 2005.
12 [2001] 1 W.L.R. 1001; [2001] C.P.L.R. 301 CA (Civ Div).
13 Michael Fordham, *Judicial Review Handbook*, 3rd edn (Oxford: Hart, 2001).

6-010 In this introductory chapter we examine the historical development of administrative law, the allocation of functions, the role of the courts and the function of tribunals and inquiries. There are noticeable underlying trends in the development of administrative law. First, as noted by Daintith,[14] "text-book writers have tended to see governmental power more as a threat to the individual than as the means of implementing public policy". The cause of this tendency is an emphasis on Parliamentary sovereignty, and the inspiration for the study of many of the rules of administrative law has been through the study of judicial review. This only represents one "mode" of government activity and usually one that is conflict-ridden and problematic. Thus, the temptation is for lawyers not to see administrative law not as a means to achieve good administrative decision-making, but as power which requires control either through legislation or the courts.

6-011 Secondly, an over-emphasis on case law may avoid consideration of the different techniques of decision-taking. Daintith identifies the Government's powers of bargaining and economic regulation as examples of how implementation of governmental policy may be achieved. This is a recurring theme which is returned to in Pt III. An understanding of administration as well as administrative law is necessary in the context of how government activities are carried out. Thirdly, there is a further dimension in the development of a rights focus to judicial interpretation under the Human Rights Act 1998. This is likely to encourage a litigious approach to problem-solving. In part this may question the adequacy of administrative law, developed before the 1998 Act came into force. It may be questioned whether the common law tests for legality or unreasonableness[15] are adequate to the standards of human rights.[16] The creation of an Administrative Law Court has the potential to provide conceptual coherence in the development of judicial review. The aspirational quality of rights should not be underestimated in encouraging greater attention to legal rules and their application than hitherto. Even if the courts decide to take a cautious and self-disciplined approach in interpreting the Human Rights Act, it is clear that an important turning point has been reached in the public law of this country.[17] It may in fact prove to strengthen the common law system of analysis and provide greater potential for judicial decision-making than at any time in its long history.

6-012 One of the important benefits of the new procedures is that procedurally claims begin through the ordinary court procedures for civil cases may be transferred, with the permission of the court, to a claim for judicial review. Conversely a claim for judicial review may be transferred into an ordinary claim under CPR Pt 30 and r.54.20.[18]

6-013 Judicial review is often controversial. It is sometimes seen as an interference, rather than as an aide to government policy making. Many view judicial review as an application

---

14   T. Daintith, "The Executive Power Today: Bargaining and Economic Control" in J. Jowell, D. Oliver and Colin O'Cinneide, The Changing Constitution 8th edn (Oxford: Oxford University Press, 2015), p.194.
15   J. Jowell and A. Lester, "Beyond Wednesbury: Substantive Principles of Administrative Law" (1987) *Public Law* 368.
16   P. Craig, "Ultra Vires and the Foundations of Judicial Review" (1998) 57 *Cambridge Law Journal* 63.
17   Sir J. Laws, "The Constitution: Morals and Rights" (1996) *Public Law* 622.
18   See the Senior Courts Act 1981 s.31(5) and CPR r.54.19.

of the theory of the rule of law to public bodies and an appropriate check on public power. Occasionally, politicians express irritation over its scope and potential for appearing to overturn or interfere with elected government and its democratic mandate.[19] Judicial review may also be the subject of conflict between judges and politicians.[20] It is certainly taken very seriously by civil servants and ministers. The pamphlet *The Judge Over Your Shoulder* [21] provides a collective common sense view of the rules, procedures and practices that ought to be followed when making good administrative decisions. It is also a means of protecting the civil service from judicial scrutiny, but it is in many positive ways a means of ensuring that a range of EU, human rights and common law principles are applied on a day to day basis.[22]

B: Administrative Law and Administration in its Historical Perspective

6-014

Administrative law may be examined from the perspective of the phenomenon of modern government possessing a vast array of State powers which may[23] affect the lives of the ordinary citizen, in both domestic and foreign affairs. A sharp contrast is obvious if the nineteenth century is compared to the present day: the size, shape and functions of government have greatly changed. Public expenditure in the 1870s represented less than ten per cent of the gross national product. Since the financial crisis in 2008, there is a budget deficit of over £75 billion, one of the largest since the Second World War.[24] The size and activities of the civil service, even with restraints and cutbacks, is larger today than in 1900. In 1900 there were 50,000 civil servants; by 1980 this had risen to 548,600. Outside central government there are some 600,000 local government officials, and 100,000 administering the Health Service.

---

19 See the analysis offered by Joshua Rozenberg, *Trial of Strength* (London: Richard Cohen, 1997).
20 David Howarth, "The politics of public law" in M. Elliott and D. Feldman (eds), *The Cambridge Public Law* (Cambridge: Cambridge University Press, 2015), pp.37–55.
21 *The Judge Over Your Shoulder*, 4th edn (2006) is one of many publications that remind civil servants that they must act legally and improve decision-making. House of Commons Library, *Judicial Review: A short guide to claims in the Administrative Court*, Research paper, 06/44 (28 September 2006).
22 Paul Craig, "Accountability and Judicial Review in the UK and EU: Central Precepts" in Nicholas Bamforth and Peter Leyland (eds), *Accountability in the Contemporary Constitution* (Oxford: Oxford University Press, 2013), pp.180–199.
23 D. L. Keir, *The Constitutional History of Modern Britain* (London: Black, 1938) provides a useful historical overview. Also see W. R. Cornish and G. Clark, *Law and Society in England 1250–1950* (London: Sweet & Maxwell, 1989).
24 House of Commons Briefing Paper, *Background to the July 2015 Budget*, 07244 (3 July 2015).

Similarly a rapid increase in the legal activities of the State[25] such as in the growth of legislation may also be recognised when compared to the period before and after 1900.[26]

6-015
Thus in 1900 Acts of Parliament covered 198 pages of the Statute Book; in 1935, 1515 pages; and in 1975, 2,800 pages. As for regulations these were comparatively few before the First World War: in 1947 Statutory Instruments covered 2,678 pages; in 1975, 8,442. In marked contrast, the volume of legislation in 2012 consisted of 20 Acts of Parliament with 1886 pages of legislation, each Act being on average 94 pages long. There were between 1983 and 2012 132 Acts of Parliament covering the Constitution, 36 Acts on Education, 37 Acts on Health, 110 Acts on Criminal Justice and 11 Acts on immigration. The number of Statutory Instruments (delegated legislation) in 2009 was 1420 with 11,414 pages.[27] As we shall see in contemporary times there is much greater and more detailed legislative interventions in the administrative process and in decision-making more generally.

6-016
Commensurate with the changes in government activities there have been changes in the habits, customs and expectations of citizens. Voting at elections before the Great Reform Act of 1832 was a mere 652,000 out of a population of 13.9 million. In 2015, under universal franchise there is an electorate of over 45 million with a turnout at general elections of around 65 per cent of the electorate. Party politics from the latter part of the nineteenth century dominate the exercise of political and therefore governmental powers.

6-017
What legacy remains from the formative period of administrative law in the nineteenth century? This question deserves close attention, as developments in the nineteenth century provide much of the explanation of how administrative law developed in England. Craig explains that[28]

> "the period between 1830 and 1850 witnessed a considerable expansion in the functions performed by central government. Reform in four main areas provides the basis for this expansion: factory legislation, the Poor Law, railways and public health."

6-018
These reforms were a result of the growing industrialisation in Britain. Administrative lawyers consider that administrative law developed on a pragmatic and often sporadic basis. There are a number of points to note. First, administrative law depended very largely on statutory intervention. In addition, regulation of many activities was carried on in an informal way sometimes using contract or through procedures avoiding the direct use of legal powers. Major

---

25 H. Parris, *Constitutional Bureaucracy* (London: George Allen & Unwin, 1969); D. Roberts, *Victorian Origins of the British Welfare State* (New Haven, CT: Yale University Press, 1960); W. Robson, *Justice and Administrative Law*; *The Dynamics of Victorian Business* (Roy Church (ed), 1980); and O. MacDonagh, *Early Victorian Government* (London: Weidenfeld and Nicolson, 1977).
26 *Justice/All Souls Review* 1981, paras.18–22 and cited in C. Harlow, *Law and Administration*, (London: Weidenfeld & Nicolson, 1984), pp.6–7.
27 House of Lords Library Note, *Volume of Legislation*, LLN 2013/008 (10 May 2013).
28 P. Craig, *Administrative Law*, 2nd edn (London: Sweet & Maxwell, 1989), p.45.

administrative developments were carried out through legislative initiatives or in certain cases, legislative acceptance of rules or existing arrangements.

Secondly, there was no single or coherent model which applied uniformly. Different forms of adjudication, fact-finding, decision-taking and policy making were used and made to fit particular circumstances. Debate focused on the nature of the growth in the legislative and judicial powers of the Executive. The categorisation of legal powers was a major preoccupation from the mid-nineteenth century until the 1930s and the setting up of the Donoughmore Committee on Ministers Powers.[29]

Thirdly, the courts' role in developing different techniques to overview administrative decision-taking was often marginal and limited by technicalities. One example of a legal technicality[30] is the difficulty of suing the Crown in tort, which remained problematic until the Crown Proceedings Act 1947. The Crown was allowed certain excepted privileges and this applied to central government ministries, thus precluding the courts' intervention. Crown servants could be sued individually for any wrong, but this did not offer an effective basis for establishing administrative law.

Fourthly, most State intervention through legislation directly interfered with private property rights and market forces. This is a legacy which remains today when courts are faced with the task of reconciling newly created public statutory rights of State interests with traditional private rights in contract and property law. In the nineteenth century, interpretation of statutory arrangements appeared unfamiliar and restrictive to judges instructed in the art of advocacy and in the technicalities of property law. An additional difficulty was the recognition of the different forms of State intervention with the growth in local government as a means of delivery of the many services needed for a locality.

Finally, the nature of legal rights changed remarkably during this period. Dicey described the nature of the change as a gradual shift from "individualism" to "collectivism". Developments in the growth of administration during the nineteenth century were greatly influenced by utilitarian ideology.

State intervention and legislation

The early development of state intervention provides important clues as to the regulatory techniques that were created. It also helps to explain the mixture of political, legal and social controls that took shape. The relationship between local and central government, the use of inspectorates and the role of the courts may be seen from the foundations set out in the middle part of the nineteenth century. MacDonagh[31] identifies the pattern for the growth

---

29 Cmd.4060 (1932).
30 *R v Commissioners of Income Tax* (1888) 21 Q.B.D. 313 CA; and G. E. Robinson, *Public Authorities and Legal Liability* (London: University of London Press, 1925). See G. S. Robertson, *Civil Proceedings by and against the Crown* (London: Stevens & Sons, 1908).
31 O. MacDonagh, *A Pattern of Government Growth: The Passenger Acts and their Enforcement 1800–1860* (Aldershot: Gregg Revivals, 1993).

in government activities in the nineteenth century. He believes it was based on a practical response borne out of identifying problems and suggesting solutions. Beginning with social problems and their amelioration, various legal responses were applied. General legal prohibition or regulation was attempted, followed by the creation of an administrative body charged with improving the efficiency of decision-taking. Gradually the newly formed administrative body adopted strategies to inform, persuade or encourage compliance with its directions. If necessary central government powers were used, and ultimately ministerial decision-taking might be adopted. Compliance techniques ranged from prosecutions to licensing strategies which might be used to achieve policy implementation and direct compliance. This called for further legislation in order to meet new problems or gaps in the law identified by the new administrative bodies. There was a cycle of formation, growth and demise of administrative bodies.

6-024 MacDonagh's analysis is not universally accepted. The main tenets of his analysis suggest that administrative developments depend on factual necessity rather than any ideological influences. Critics of MacDonagh argue that he failed to take sufficient account of such influences as Bentham's utilitarian principles. His main critic in this regard is Parris[32] who argues that nineteenth-century government must be seen as a function both of organic change and contemporary political and ideological thought, one of the main currents of which was Benthamism.

6-025 The debate between MacDonagh and Parris is largely unresolved. Their contribution to our understanding of administration in the nineteenth century is that pragmatic developments in administrative law may be due to the nature of changing administrative bodies. A number of influences may be involved in that development such as practical necessity, ideological belief and enthusiasm for change.

6-026 Cornish[33] explains how the boards system was transformed after 1832, when it developed some of its own independence: ". . .it was conceived as a way of conferring semi-autonomous authority for a particular function; this achieved a certain distinction from the immediately political."

6-027 In the creation of the Poor Law Commissioners after 1832, a wide variety of legal powers accompanied their role. Prosecutions, legal action through mandamus and an appointment power of local officers in workhouses were all combined in their functions. It is noticeable that the Poor Law Commissioners neatly linked central government with local government activities. Also noteworthy is that the granting of such powers was couched in general terms with the agreement of a Minister and Parliament in general rule-making. The Commissioners had the ability to make their own rules and regulations as part of their powers.

6-028 Experimentation was invariably involved in the choice of administrative body adopted for any particular activity. Cornish notes[34]:

---

32 H. Parris, *Government and the Railways in Nineteenth Century Britain* (London: Routledge, 1965).
33 W. R. Cornish and G. Clark, *Law and Society in England 1250–1950* (London: Sweet & Maxwell, 1989), pp.55– 58.
34 Cornish and Clark, *Law and Society in England 1250–1950*, p.58.

> "The Railway Department in the Board of Trade (1840) was to become a 'Board' (still departmental—1844) and a Commission (independent—1846) before being re-absorbed de facto (1849) and then de jure (1851) into the Board of Trade. Between the 1850s and 1906 those boards which constitutionally remained distinct from ministries were all important cases placed under some form of ministerial supervision."

Another model of administrative body was the inspectorates. Examples which came under the jurisdiction of the Home Office were factories, prisons, mining and burial inspectors. Inspectorates were fact-finders, investigators and adjudicators. They possessed limited powers to impose fines and prosecutions, but their role of serving notices and enforcing standards relied on voluntary compliance as much as coercive sanctions. Very often their activities involved some form of compromise because of hostility to the use of their powers and a reluctance to comply with the imposition of an external standard. The Factory Inspectors, in particular, adjusted their powers to meet opposition or objections. Inspectors had the status of magistrates, but the Home Office in 1844 directed inspectors not to use their enforcement jurisdiction by introducing a new Factories Act 1844 which constrained their powers.

Public Health was another area of administrative growth and an example of administrative decision-making which directly interfered with property rights. It is also illustrative of the use of private law techniques, such as actions in nuisance, combined with statutory powers. In administrative decision-making, findings from various reports and commissions of inquiry had confirmed the existence of disease and poverty amongst the poor. Health hazards were directly linked to urbanisation and industrialisation. Sanitary improvements were required and introduced on a piecemeal basis; first in 1848, then in 1872 and 1875 various Public Health Acts were passed giving legislative powers to various sanitary authorities to set standards and achieve improvements in living conditions.

Public health legislation directly interfered with property rights and substantially overlapped with the use of nuisance law in cases where an injury was caused by a neighbour's occupation of land. The role of the courts in applying and developing such remedies was largely a pragmatic one, taking each case on its own particular facts.

As industrialisation spread new processes and industry throughout the country, regulation of these activities was left to individual initiative in the first instance. By 1869, the judges had at last concluded that nuisance from noise, dirt and pollution from railways permitted an occupier of premises affected by the nuisance to seek legal redress.

Finally, another source of administrative growth was in the development of local government. Local corporations and parishes developed a myriad of legal powers to deliver many of the new responsibilities that gradually became entrusted to local authority control. A major source of income came through the raising of local taxes and rates. Slowly, incremental changes occurred to the various newly established administrative bodies, but eventually they were to come under local authority control. The Poor Law Commissioners shifted from a Board to a Tribunal of Appeal in 1847. In 1868 it could appoint district auditors, who in 1879 became civil servants on the creation of the Local Government Board.

Local authorities gained the administrative function of delivering what were termed "public goods". First the Municipal Corporations Act 1835 provided elected local authorities. From 1843–1929 local authorities gained responsibility for such "public goods", including water, gas, transport, education, housing and health services.

A distinctive feature of these developments was the acceptance of local political accountability through local elections and Parliament's willingness to encourage local legislation, to enable local authorities to carry out their tasks. Local authorities developed considerable legal powers through private Bill legislation.

Courts, lawyers and legal techniques

The growth in administrative bodies and their wide diversity broadened the scope of legal powers and raised questions about accountability and control. Arthurs[35] notes how a number of constraints were invoked to prevent abuses. Statutes or regulations often required ministerial approval for their implementation. Ministerial responsibility to Parliament constrained administrators from acting without recourse to political authority and observance of legal rules. Government Law Officers restrained and inhibited any internal decision-making since account had to be taken of their legal opinions.

Despite such constraints it is recognised that wide discretionary powers were enjoyed by many officials. Such powers[36] were often resented and, when in conflict with the landed interest or the new wealth industrialists, led to conflicts. Self-interest and protection led many administrative bodies to adopt codes of conduct and practice to ease the application of their rules.

A further consideration was the question of how best to supervise such administrative bodies. Many lawyers believed that this task was best performed by the ordinary courts. The preference for the use of the ordinary courts as opposed to the use of special administrative courts was reinforced by Dicey's scepticism of the benefits of *droit administratif*, the French system of specialised administrative courts. Dicey feared that the formation of administrative courts might encourage the encroachment on the private rights of citizens by governmental powers in the interests of the State, a hangover from the period of the Crown's extensive use of arbitrary powers. Dicey believed that the ordinary courts afforded the best protection against any incremental growth in the powers of government intervention.

Dicey's analysis has since been subject to criticism but his powerful influence has endured. de Smith described how Dicey's assumptions about the role of the courts may have misled English administrative lawyers into complacency after the nineteenth century[37]:

---

35 H. W. Arthurs, *"Without the Law": Administrative Justice and Legal Pluralism in 19th Century England* (Toronto: University of Toronto Press, 1985).
36 W. A. Robson, "The Report of the Committee on Administrative Powers" (1932) 3 *Political Quarterly* 346.
37 S. A. de Smith, *Judicial Review of Administrative Action*, 4th edn, (London: Stevens, 1980), p.7.

> "Representative and responsible Government was securely founded: political and administrative morality was unusually high; the administration of justice by the ordinary courts was even-handed and uncorrupt; the common law, itself pre-eminently pragmatic was tenacious but adaptable. Such an environment bred the assumption that England had little to learn from other countries in matters of public law. Moreover the absence of judicial review of the constitutionality of legislation conduced to a lack of informed interests amongst practising lawyers in the judicial problems of government. And the role assigned to constitutional and administrative law in legal education was conspicuously modest."

6-040 Throughout the period of growth in administrative bodies, it is noteworthy that the courts retained exclusive jurisdiction over the criminal law. Government had carefully circumvented any attack on the courts' powers in this area.

6-041 The fact that the courts had an unbroken historical past which could be traced back to the thirteenth century further encouraged the government to refrain from interfering with the role of the courts. To the extent that central government perceived the role of the courts, the question of judicial intervention depended on the nature of the body exercising powers. Limited immunity to the Crown preserved Crown activities from judicial supervision up until the Crown Proceedings Act 1947. Ministerial accountability to Parliament allowed discretion to be exercised and largely escape judicial scrutiny. Moreover, the growth in legislative powers enjoyed by Parliament as law-makers left the courts fewer facilities to exercise law-making powers of their own. The massive effort towards the enforcement of the new legislation was in the hands of an administrative bureaucracy and occasionally, local magistrates. The superior courts' role in enforcement declined in proportion to the spread of administrative decision-taking. Belief in the rule of law and the jurisdiction of the ordinary courts implied that ministers, officials and citizens were amenable to the same law. Moving to a new form of administrative law, supervision was seen as inconsistent with the supremacy of the law even as late as 1932. The Committee on Ministers' Powers found the proposal for such an Administrative Court inconsistent with the supervisory jurisdiction of the High Court and a threat to the rule of law. Such reservations over the development of administrative law have remained influential amongst lawyers in the UK until more recent times.

6-042 In addition to the role of the courts, other procedures are noteworthy. The various techniques of decision-making, adjudication, discretion, fact-finding and inquiries were supplemented by the development of statutory inquiries. Techniques of inquiry and investigation were commonplace in the work of the Royal Commission and even in some of the administrative tasks entrusted to Justices of the Peace, such as wage-bargaining in the eighteenth and early nineteenth centuries.

6-043 Statutory inquiries may be found in the 1801 Enclosure Act with ad hoc Commissions of Inquiry appointed. Some explanation may be advanced as to why such procedures were adopted. The use of private Bills or public Acts of Parliament did not always provide the necessary coverage of all the issues to be decided. Wade[38] attributes this fact as a reason for adopting inquiries outside Parliament. The procedures of Parliamentary committees, already existing inside Parliament and familiar in the passage of legislation, were conveniently adopted and employed.

6-044 Special law-making procedures were available through provisional orders. The provisional order procedure under an Act of Parliament granted powers to some statutory authorities to make a provisional order once an inquiry had been held and objections considered.

6-045 Special procedures were introduced applicable to enclosures to overcome the need for provisional orders. In 1845, the General Enclosure Act required publication of the enclosure scheme and a public meeting "to their objections". Similar procedures were permitted under the Local Government Acts 1858–1933 and various Public Health Acts 1848–1931. Eventually the need to make a provisional order was abandoned, allowing the order to take effect in the absence of any objections or opposition, as in the Statutory Orders (Special Procedure) Act 1945.

6-046 Another variation to provisional orders may be found in the Local Government Act 1894 whereby county councils could acquire land under a public inquiry procedure. The Council could make an order followed by a local inquiry if opposition to the order was made in a memorial to the Council.

6-047 The development of tribunals as a means of adjudication is also noteworthy. Railway companies were compelled in 1854 to afford "reasonable facilities and preferences" to particular traders, in an effort to prevent railways achieving a virtual monopoly. Complaints could be made to the Court of Common Pleas but this was unsatisfactory and in 1893 a tribunal of commissioners was appointed. Fifteen years later it was reformulated into a Railing and Canal Commission. Appointment was through the Home Secretary on the recommendation of the President of the Board of Trade. The Chancellor could nominate a High Court judge. The Commission adjudicated, found facts and achieved decisions on a judicial basis, having many of the formalities of a Court of Law.

6-048 Similar techniques[39] were employed in 1897 when workmen's compensation was payable. The use of tribunals developed an importance in the resolution of disputes over workmen's compensation. This has remained today.

6-049 Finally, a neglected but important element in nineteenth-century administration was the use of audit procedures as a check on financial arrangements. Central government audit combined judicial and administrative decision-making. The medieval Court of Exchequer responsible for carrying out the audit of public expenditure was identified by Holdsworth as analogous to "an administrative court". The decline of judicial scrutiny over public expenditure began in the sixteenth century when Parliament assumed responsibility for the power of appropriation. The nineteenth century saw the introduction of the modern office of Comptroller and Auditor General with responsibility given to the Public Accounts Committee

---

38   H. W. R. Wade, *Administrative Law*, 6th edn (Oxford: Oxford University Press, 1988).
39   The Exchequer and Audit Departments Act 1866.

to oversee public expenditure. Audit techniques included investigation, certification and reporting of accounts.

Local government audit may be traced to the fifteenth century with the records of a Commission for the hearing of the accounts of the collectors of money. Audit techniques included investigation, certification and where necessary the power "to charge" on the defaulters where sums were found improperly in their possession.

The development of the Poor Law in the sixteenth century and the consolidation of the Poor Relief Act 1601 provided safeguards in the form of audit undertaken by Justices of the Peace. In the eighteenth century the principles of modern audit procedure in local government evolved. The Poor Relief Act 1743 required church wardens and overseers to keep "a just, true and perfect account in writing fairly entered in a book or books. . .".

The requirements of signed and verified accounts were combined with the rights of rate payers to inspect accounts. Over a hundred years later the Poor Law Amendment Act 1844 introduced the office of District Auditor with powers to deal with illegality and misconduct. The techniques of certification were supplemented by powers to examine, audit and disallow accounts. In cases where misconduct was identified, legal remedies could be provided by the High Court. The role of the Justice of the Peace in these matters of audit was finally ended with the transfer of their functions to the District Auditor. As Jones notes[40]:

> "The audit remained judicial in nature; indeed, in comparison with the 1834 provision, the 1844 system was markedly more complete in its judicial character by virtue of the procedure for appeal to the High Court. It was also more effective in its precise statutory power to compel restitution and in its provisions for increasing the independence of the auditor."

Strengthening of the audit system was achieved by the District Auditors Act 1879, which provided for the payment of district auditors, partly out of central funds and partly from fees collected from the audited authorities. Adaptations of the principles of the audit system were continually made as changes were introduced to the system of local government.[41]

In terms of administration and law, the nineteenth-century legacy may be shortly stated: the assortment of different agencies, administrative bodies and the variety of institutions ranging from courts, inquiries, tribunals, inspectors, commissions and boards represent the "untidiness of the British Administrative System". The form and substance of judicial scrutiny offered by the courts as fact-finders, combined with adjudicatory and judicial functions, may be found replicated in the wide variety of bodies charged with regulating administrative bodies.

---

40 R. Jones, *Local Government Audit Law*, 2nd edn (London: HMSO, 1985). See Local Government Finance Act 1982, ss.19 and 20.
41 Today local government audit has been modernised under the Local Audit and Accountability Act 2014.

6-055 The role of the courts requires some additional consideration. Two distinctive roles were apparent. First, the courts[42] applied principles of law to the activities of the body under review. Historically, points of law could be raised on the record by the various prerogative writs, most notably certiorari for "error of law on the face of the record". Review in certain circumstances might also include mandamus, applied for by inspectors such as the mines inspectors, to compel the determination of charges made against mine owners and heard before magistrates.

6-056 Judicial decision-making established by the superior courts assisted in the development of the grounds for judicial review. Through the system of remedies, rights were gradually established. These included establishing procedures at hearings, rights of consultation and representation amongst the parties, knowing the case against the defendant and their right to an unbiased hearing.

6-057 Secondly, the courts had an extensive appeal jurisdiction. Since 1857 the Summary Proceedings Act provided an appeal by way of a case stated to the superior courts against errors of law by magistrates. Appeals through the use of the Factories Acts also permitted the courts a role in shaping standards for the performance of individual acts of the inspectors.

6-058 Taken together, both appeal and judicial review gave rise to an expectation that a greater role might be mapped out for the courts. This was slow in developing and only became more significant later in the present century. In the nineteenth century, Parliament created statutes with summary jurisdiction, such as the Summary Jurisdiction Act 1848, which made it impossible for the courts to correct errors of law except those which were within the technical question of jurisdiction. After the 1870s, the use of certiorari for errors of law on the face of record was rarely obtained. Various technical problems inhibited the development of judicial review by the courts, most notably Dicey's perspective that the existing "rule of law" was adequate to the tasks of the new administrative bodies, when it was clear that it was not.

6-059 Lawyers and courts, while providing useful procedures to oversee administrative decisions, did not necessarily benefit administrators. Lawyers gained influence through drafting laws, representation in Parliament, advising on the law and representing commercial and industrial interests. However, the superior courts were not actively engaged in regulating administrative decisions. Nor were lawyers developing legal principles to make administration effective. Once lawyers' techniques appeared unhelpful or unsatisfactory, they could be circumvented. Higher priority was given to the economic, political and social activities than to the vested interests of lawyers. Legal rules may not be taken as indicative of how administrative bodies make decisions. They may, however, act as legitimatising principles which allow administrative decision-making of a broad, discretionary kind to take place under a veneer of legality.

Allocation of functions

6-060 Modern administrative law remains influenced by the legacy of the past and the often bewildering development of various institutions, techniques and strategies to carry out administrative

---

42 Memoranda submitted by Government Depts. (HMSO, 6 Vols.) to the Franks Committee (1957).

decisions. It is important when reading early case law or interpreting statutory arrangements to place developments in their historical context.

In contemporary times it is convenient to attempt to classify administrative decision-taking in a way which may help identify the relevant legal powers, on whom the powers are granted and how those powers are exercised. Identifying these issues assists in clarifying the procedures and rules which govern the making of decisions, the methods of accountability and the role of the courts, if any.

6-061

It has already been observed how the volume of legislation, its detail and scope is remarkably different than in the past. From 1983–2012 the volume of legislation through Acts of Parliament has changed in terms of pages of legislation and the number of Acts of Parliament and Statutory Instruments. On average the UK has annually about 4,000 pages of legislation equally split between primary Acts of Parliament and Statutory Instruments. The subject matter is heavily weighted in favour of the Constitution, education, health, criminal justice and immigration—key sectors for public law scholarship.[43] It is also the case that many aspects of the legislative framework empower private and commercial organisations to deliver public services. Such cultural and legal changes are also reflected in changing judicial attitudes.

6-062

The classification of government institutions and various functions vested in those institutions is probably easier under a written constitution than under the arrangements in the UK. Under a written Constitution the citizen may be provided with legally enforceable rights. In the UK the citizen relies on the availability of remedies depending on the nature of the decision. The citizen may be affected by a decision-maker in different ways—such as whether there is an appeal procedure or whether review may be obtained through the courts or there is a tribunal. Decision-making itself involves broad discretion. Fact-finding and applying rules are discretionary elements in decision-making. Officials or administrators exercising their powers operate within a broad discretion in both the interpretation of rules and their application. Value judgments may be required as to the application of rules and how they are to be interpreted. Parliament may make the value judgments and embody policy decisions in precise rules in statutes. The degree of freedom of choice left to the decision-maker may vary according to the type of rule, the context and extent to which discretion may be exercised.

6-063

The definition of "discretion" is difficult. It is not a precise word with a clearly defined legal meaning and the context in which it is found may change its meaning. Discretion describes how value judgments, rules and procedures may be combined in the decision-maker.

6-064

In discussing the allocation of functions, consider first the form the relevant legal powers may take. These consist of first, primary legislation and delegated legislation; and second, there are prerogative powers, licences and contract.[44] An explanation of each is helpful within the context of administrative decision-making.

---

43   House of Lords Library Note, *Volume of Legislation*, LLN 2013/008.
44   J. Golding, "The Impact of Statutes on the Royal Prerogative" (1974) 48 *A.L.J.* 434.

C: Legislation, Guidance, Codes of Practice and Delegated Legislation

6-065 Parliament's law-making powers are exercised through Acts of Parliament which broadly provide the main policy and general details of the law. This leaves ministers, local authorities, corporations or other bodies to make rules, orders and regulations setting out in greater detail the technical and precise rules. Such delegated rules may take different forms and are known as delegated legislation.

6-066 The Queen in Council may make Statutory Orders in Council such as under the Emergency Powers Act 1920. Ministers and heads of government departments may make departmental rules or ministerial regulations under Act of Parliament. Similarly, local authorities may have wide powers to make regulations such as under the Local Government Act 1972. Various public bodies or even private bodies have been granted legal powers to carry out their activities. These may take the form of regulations, byelaws or orders. The courts also enjoy a variety of rule-making procedures such as the Rules of the Supreme Court under the Senior Courts Act 1981 (renamed and previously known as the Supreme Court Act 1981). There is a County Court Rule Committee, under the County Courts Act 1984, s.75 which make rules for the County Court. The introduction of changes to civil procedure following the Woolf reforms[45] is illustrative of various rule-making powers of the courts contained in the CPR.

6-067 Powers may be conferred to the Church of England under the Church of England (Assembly) Powers Act 1919, allowing measures in the form of delegated legislation to be enacted. Such measures may amend or repeal the whole or any part of any Act of Parliament. There are a multitude of Special Procedure Orders under the Statutory Orders (Special Procedure) Act 1945. A special joint committee of both Houses considers any objections and allows an opportunity for objections to a proposed order to be heard at a local inquiry. This procedure is particularly valuable for water, planning and various other statutory activities.

6-068 Delegated legislation might also loosely describe various codes of practice. These have legal effect because of the statutory provisions which permit their introduction. The Health and Safety at Work Act 1974 permits the Health and Safety Commission to approve a Health and Safety at Work Code which is issued under ss.16 and 17 of the Act. Guidance, codes, recommendations, directions and determinations describe the wide variety of types of delegated powers which operate in modern administrative law.

6-069 The rationale for delegated legislation is wide ranging. The Committee on Ministers' Powers 1932,[46] identified six reasons in favour of the "necessity for delegation", while admitting the need for safeguards and with the provision "that the statutory powers are exercised and the

---

45 Access to Justice (Final Report) 1996. See M. Zander, "The Government Plans on Civil Justice" (1998) 61 *Modern Law Review* 382.
46 Cmnd.4060 (1932).

statutory functions performed in the right way". The six reasons are: first, that pressure upon Parliamentary time is too great; secondly, the subject matter of modern legislation is technical; thirdly, it is difficult to include all the details in a single Act; fourthly, constant adaptation may take place without the necessity of amending legislation, thus flexibility is encouraged; fifthly, experimenting with new ideas is possible and lessons from past experience learnt; and sixthly, in a modern state, delegated legislation provides a convenient and speedy remedy when there may be either emergency or urgency in the matters covered by the legislation.

6-070

There is an ongoing and only partially successful deregulation agenda. The starting point was the Deregulation and Contracting Out Act 1994, supplemented by the considerably broader in scope Regulatory Reform Act 2001, intended to reduce the burdens on business and industry by reducing the level of government regulation of industry. The 1994 Act was used 48 times by April 2001 and involved the use of two powers contained in Pt 1 Ch.1 of the Act. First, there is a power to amend or repeal by ministerial order any primary legislation that is deemed to impose an unnecessary burden on business. Secondly, there are powers to improve enforcement procedures consistent with fairness and transparency. The unusual nature of the legislation is that it allows a Minister to use an order to suspend an Act of Parliament, a power previously seldom used in peacetime. This is usually referred to as a Henry VIII clause. Such a clause grants a wide power in the legislation that gives general discretion to a Minister including amendment powers without any additional primary legislation. There is a code of good enforcement practice introduced into the 1994 Act procedure for good practice in respect of the deregulation order.

6-071

The arrangements under the Regulatory Reform Act 2001 were similar to the 1994 Act. Regulatory reform orders follow the affirmative procedure route and have a specific mechanism for Parliamentary scrutiny in both Houses of Parliament. The Regulatory Reform Act extends the powers where an order may be made and allows minor changes to the draft order while it is being scrutinised. It also requires that any burdens under the Act must be proportionate to the benefits expected from them. Ministers must provide fuller information than under the 1994 Act to lay the basis for the order to be made and since January 2001 there was a Code of Practice on written consultation as to when an order may be made. This generic approach to the subject has proved not to be only as effective as the agenda for change driven by departments, and de-regulation often took less priority than the Government would have liked. A wholly new approach was required. The Deregulation Act 2015 is a detailed and comprehensive set of arrangements for the removal or reduction of burdens on businesses that are far more wide ranging than in the legislative history of the subject. Under an overall strategy of "cutting red-tape", the Act is the most serious attempt to achieve this purpose by "hollowing out" many activities regulated by the State.[47] The Act places a general desirability of promoting economic growth and repeals legislation that is of no longer of practical use.[48] There is within the Department of Business, Innovation and Skills, a newly established *Regulatory Policy Committee*, intended to provide an independent, external scrutiny of new regulatory and

---

47 These include: areas of business and commerce; companies and insolvency; transport; education and training; alcohol; sport and entertainment; administration of justice; public authorities; and legislative reforms.
48 The explanatory notes run to over 131 pages.

deregulatory proposals. Originally established in 2009 and 2012, the organisation has become an independent advisory non-departmental public body. It is also intended to improve the evidence base for regulation.

6-072 A form of delegated legislation which has become more popular in recent years is what Ganz[49] refers to as "quasi-legislation". Unlike Statutory Instruments or orders, the legal force of much "quasi-legislation" depends on the enabling Act of Parliament. Quasi-legislation may be defined to mean "codes of conduct, guidelines, circulars and a miscellany of rules". No one is quite sure of the extent and scope of quasi-legislation because it does not always conform to the clearest pattern of organisation. Some examples illustrate the meaning of the term. The Highway Code lays down general guidance and advice to motorists. Breach of any of its guidance does not make the offender subject to a criminal prosecution. However, it may be used in either civil or criminal proceedings as relevant to the consideration before the court. Equally there are other examples where it is not intended that powers exercised should form the basis of litigation but may provide general guidance to the public. The Food Standards Agency under the Food Standards Act 1999 provides powers for the new agency to issue reports and advise the public on standards in food. In exercising such widely defined powers the agency must under s.23 of the Act consider the costs and benefits of any exercise or non-exercise of its powers and the giving of advice or information. This must be undertaken within the general provisions of s.22, namely the publication of a statement of general objectives the agency intends to pursue and the general practice it intends to adopt.

6-073 The Police and Criminal Evidence Act 1984 (PACE) provides the police with various codes of conduct. Breach of any of the guidance in the code makes the police liable to disciplinary proceedings but not prosecution. Under the Utilities Act 2000 various codes of practice set out the conditions for Public Electricity Suppliers. These may be relevant in the determinations made by the regulator. Additionally, voluntary codes of practice have been agreed by the various electricity companies regarding their disconnection powers and rights of consumers. Such codes operate within the legal framework set by the Act and may form the framework for the regulator to implement policies.

6-074 As Ganz observed, one of the dangers inherent in quasi-legislation is that codes of practice may occupy a wider breadth of activity than originally intended by Parliament. One example is the Code of Practice on Picketing, which limited the number to six pickets. The enabling Act, the Employment Act 1980, did not include such a number but the practice of limiting the number of pickets to six has been accepted by the police and the courts.

6-075 Delegated legislation may be considered by the courts as to its legality, under the enabling legislation. Great care must be taken when ministerial circulars or advice are issued because such advice may pre-judge an individual case or a particular issue. Each case must be considered on its merits.

---

49 G. Ganz, *Quasi-Legislation: Recent Developments in Secondary Legislation* (London: Sweet & Maxwell, 1987).

D: Prerogative Powers, Licences and Contracts

The prerogative is an important source of governmental legal powers. In *Malone v Metropolitan Police Commissioner*[50] the Vice Chancellor, Sir Robert Megarry, recognised that the Home Secretary had a limited power to authorise telephone-tapping. This power was a residue of the power to open articles through the post, said to exist through the prerogative. Such powers have been made statutory under the Interception of Communications Act 1985, but the case is illustrative of the prerogative as a source of legal powers applied in modern circumstances.

6–076

In the *GCHQ* case, the House of Lords accepted the prerogative as the basis of legal powers to ban trade unions at the Government Communications Headquarters. The courts have expressed their willingness to review prerogative powers. Some doubts were expressed in the case as to the nature of the prerogative powers. The exact issue of the legal powers depended on seeing an order in Council as derived from the authority of the prerogative or under Act of Parliament.

6–077

This is a characteristic of prerogative powers. Their exact nature, scope and extent are often difficult to review or define. Occasionally this may give rise to difficulty when there are statutory powers which are incomplete or inadequate and the question arises as to whether the prerogative may supplement these powers.

6–078

In *R v Secretary of State for the Home Department Ex p. Northumbrian Police Authority*[51] the Court of Appeal was willing to supplement the Home Secretary's powers under the Police Act 1964 to permit the issuing of a circular providing plastic bullets and CS gas to local police forces. Relying on the prerogative power "to keep the peace", the Court of Appeal concluded that this entitled the Home Secretary to all that was "reasonably necessary to preserve the peace of the realm". This entitled the Home Secretary to rely on the prerogative powers even though the statutory arrangements appeared comprehensive and conclusive in the matter. The case has been heavily criticised but it represents an indication of how important it is to clarify the nature of legal powers.

6–079

The prerogative may be used when the Government of the day goes to war, even if the war is contested as not supported by international law. In *R (Gentle) v Prime Minister*,[52] a claim for an independent inquiry into the deaths of British soldiers in Iraq and the rights of the soldiers under art.2 of the European Convention on Human Rights, (the protection of the right to life), was rejected by the House of Lords. Their reasoning was that there is no duty for a country under art.2 that would give rise to rights that would ensure that a country could not go to war inconsistent with international law. This was a frustrating decision if the expectation is that the Human Rights Act 1998 would grant courts greater powers of review over the exercise of prerogative powers such as the decision to go to war.[53]

6–080

---

50 [1979] Ch. 344; [1979] 2 W.L.R. 700 Ch D.
51 [1989] Q.B. 26; [1988] 2 W.L.R. 590 CA (Civ Div).
52 [2008] UKHL 20; [2008] 1 A.C. 1356.
53 Also see *R (Abbasi) v Foreign Secretary* [2002] EWCA Civ 1598; [2003] U.K.H.R.R. 76 over the use of rights in the

6-081 Sources of legal powers are not restricted to legislation, quasi-legislation or prerogative powers. Increasingly public bodies rely on contracts or licences to establish the legal authority and powers necessary to carry out their activities. Such powers operate within a statutory framework but are undeniably private law powers.

6-082 In the case of gas, telecommunications, electricity and water, the newly privatised companies require licences issued by the Secretary of State to carry out their activities. Such licences, under the relevant legislation, provide criminal sanctions for anyone attempting to carry out specified activities without a licence. The licence conditions are detailed and technical. They contain legal powers, duties and conditions which must be performed.

6-083 The novelty of the use of licences in the newly privatised industries leaves the prospect of negotiation and modification a matter for political decision-making as well as legal powers. References to the Competition Commission are possible by any one of the new regulatory agencies set up to regulate utilities such as gas, electricity, water or telecommunications. The merger of gas and electricity regulation into a single regulator, OFGEM, is supplemented by the power of the new authority to modify licences following a Competition Commission reference. The statutory posts of the Directors-General of Electricity Supply and Gas Supply are merged into a single body called GEMA, the Gas and Electricity Markets Authority. Existing responsibility is shared between the Secretary of State and the regulators over how the industry is to be regulated and a division of powers for enforcing licences and their conditions is made. Such a framework requires careful consideration as to the exact nature of the legal powers, how they are to be exercised and by whom. Under the Utilities Act 2000 it is clear that economic regulation is combined with legal rules that are enforceable in the courts.

6-084 Monitoring the tariff charges of the various utilities also involves the legal powers of the regulators. Careful consideration of the economic and social aspects involved in the price formula is required, to balance the efficiency of the industry with consumer protection.

6-085 Contractual powers offer the most demanding and interesting use of legal powers in the allocation of functions of public bodies. As a source of power, there is usually some legislative authority permitting the use of contract. One example is the contractual powers of local authorities. Recent legislation such as the Local Government Act 1988 requires local authorities to subject to competitive tendering a number of services such as street-cleaning, vehicle maintenance, schools and welfare catering, refuse collection, and the management of sports and leisure facilities. The law requires that private companies be permitted to bid for the work involved. Setting performance standards and competitive tendering are included in the Local Government Act 1992. Such legal powers are intended to encourage contracts and competition and to increase the effectiveness of local authority powers.

6-086 Some doubts as to the legal powers to enter financial contracts arose in *Hazell v Hammersmith and Fulham*.[54] The local authority had invested substantial sums in various investments known as "interest rate swaps" in order to finance expenditure, during a period

---

detention of British citizens held in Guantanamo Bay, a US detention camp. The Court of Appeal held that the British Government is not under a positive duty to prevent any abuse of human rights.

54 [1990] 2 Q.B. 697; [1990] 2 W.L.R. 1038 CA (Civ Div).

when central government financial support to local authorities had diminished. In order to invest in such activities as interest rate swaps, the local authority relied on s.111(1) of the Local Government Act 1972, which empowered local authorities to borrow according to what was "calculated to facilitate or conducive or incidental to, the discharge of any of their functions". Doubts over the legality of such powers were raised by the District Auditor. The House of Lords held that the local authority borrowing powers under s.111(1) were curtailed by Sch.13 to the 1972 Act. It was concluded that the local authority had no contractual power to enter the swap market.

In *Credit Suisse v Allerdale BC*,[55] the Court of Appeal considered the operation of a local authority company and whether the establishment of the company was consistent with Sch.13 s.111 of the 1972 Act. The local authority wished to establish a leisure pool complex. The setting up of a company for such a purpose was regarded as a means of overcoming statutory borrowing restrictions. The company was formed and borrowed £6 million from Credit Suisse. The recession caused the company to fail and the bank claimed repayment of the loan. In considering the express and implied powers of the local authority, the Court of Appeal concluded that the local authority had no powers to set up a company for the purposes of borrowing the requisite finance for the various recreational activities favoured by the local authority. The Court of Appeal followed the approach in *Hazell v Hammersmith*. It acknowledged that local authorities were empowered under s.19(1) of the Local Government (Miscellaneous Provisions) Act 1976 to provide recreational facilities. Such authorisation, however, does not apply to borrowing. Thus the purported borrowing contract was ultra vires.

The method of statutory construction given by the Court of Appeal to the 1972 Act follows the pattern observed in previous decisions regarding local government. Unless there are clear words the courts will not imply any discretion or general assumptions concerning local authority powers. Indeed, the nature of ultra vires contracts are such that they cannot be enforced.

In another case, *Credit Suisse v Waltham Forest*[56] the same judges considered a claim against a local authority which had guaranteed a bank loan to a company. The Court of Appeal followed the *Allerdale* case and held that the borrowing was ultra vires.

Contractual powers may be the main source of legal powers for a particular activity. This may give rise to questions of the reviewability of the activities in question. In *R v Panel on Take-overs and Mergers Ex p. Datafin*,[57] the Take-overs Panel, a non-statutory body involved in regulating city take-overs and mergers, was provided with regulatory powers by contract. The courts regarded the takeover panel as an important element in the regulation of take-overs. The Government, together with the Bank of England, approved the appointment of the Chairman even though no statutory basis existed for the panel. The Court of Appeal regarded the "authority of the government" as sufficiently relevant to give the panel a public law dimension. In that way, the courts were prepared to offer judicial review of the panel's activities.

---

55 *Credit Suisse v Allerdale BC* [1997] Q.B. 306; [1996] 3 W.L.R. 894 CA (Civ Div).
56 *Credit Suisse v Waltham Forest* [1997] Q.B. 362; [1996] 3 W.L.R. 943 CA (Civ Div).
57 [1987] Q.B. 815; [1987] 2 W.L.R. 699 CA (Civ Div).

6-091 Contracts are likely to become an increasingly important source of legal powers. Daintith[58] explains how government has a number of powers available to carry on its activities. These powers divide into two: *imperium* and *dominium*. Under *imperium* the government may prohibit through legislation or promote through existing legal powers, various activities. Under *dominium* it might offer subsidies or purchasing agreements or licensing arrangements favouring one activity or another. The vast range of possibilities makes classification of the legal powers involved an important element in understanding how powers are allocated.

6-092 Techniques of contractual governance are increasingly important with the formulation of licences and "soft law" forms of governance. This is broadly defined and is widely used to engage in different ways of delivering public services. For example the system for licensing educational institutions to sponsor overseas students, outside the European Economic Area, relies on a point systems and licensing arrangements. New London College was licensed until December 2009 when the Secretary of State suspended its licence when it was found to be in breach of some of its duties. New London College sought to challenge the Secretary of State's decision. Many of the "rules" were contained in Sponsor Guidance but these were not laid before Parliament under s.3(2) of the Immigration Act 1971 as the rules related to requirements to enter or leave the UK and had to be satisfied by the migrant and the Supreme Court rejected the challenge. The Supreme Court accepted that there were various types of rules and guidance provide the basis for legal authority while not explicitly part of the legislation.[59]

E: Central and Local Government

6-093 Identical legal powers may be viewed differently depending on who exercises the power and how the power is exercised. There are a variety of factors relevant in the choice of decision-making bodies.

6-094 In the context of administrative decision-making, central government may be distinguished from local government even though both share the common feature of being directly elected. Local authorities represent local interests and are accountable to the local electorate. However, since the nineteenth century, the wide range of activities carried out by local authorities for housing, education, police and public health have required increasing statutory activity. Diversity in size and in politics have given local authorities a great deal of autonomy. However, local authority activities are not the only way to judge the role of local government. Viewed from the perspective of central government, local activities are carried out on behalf of central government policy making. The sovereignty of Parliament suggests that local

---

58 Daintith, T. Daintith, "The Executive Power Today: Bargaining and Economic Control" in J. Jowell, D. Oliver and Colin O'Cinneide, The Changing Constitution 8th edn (Oxford: Oxford University Press, 2015), p.194.

59 *R (New College London Ltd) v Secretary of State for the Home Department* [2013] UKSC 51; [2013] 1 W.L.R. 2358.

authorities' powers are allocated by central government. There is no independence or constitutional autonomy given to local authorities other than that presented by Acts of Parliament. Legal powers from Acts of Parliament give the government of the day authority to lay down policy and prescribe local authority activities. Legal powers may also be found through appeals by laws and circulars. The most decentralising is the Localism Act 2011 that provides more general empowerment to local authorities allowing local authorities to act as an ordinary individual and allowing innovative ways for local authorities to undertake activities. Combined authorities may be created through the membership of other local authorities in their area. The combined authority has takeover powers for example for an integrated transport authority and can receive statutory powers by order approved by Parliament

6–095

Many local authority activities, such as in the area of planning, leave the right of appeal to a Minister after a refusal of planning permission by a local authority. Byelaws made by a local authority require ministerial approval. Central government circulars may set policy guidance for local authorities.[60]

6–096

In the area of local authority finance, central government had extensive powers to place a legal "cap" on the amount of Community Charge which may be levied by the local authority. Ultimately, powers granted to local authorities may be removed by central government, such as the abolition of the Greater London Council and the Metropolitan counties, under the Local Government Act 1985. The successor to the Community Charge under s.1 of the Local Government Finance Act 1992 came into effect on 1 April 1993. The Secretary of State has powers under s.54 to determine the maximum budgetary requirement of each local authority and to place a "cap" on local authority expenditure.

6–097

Ministerial discretion provides extensive powers for central government decision-taking. Reserve powers are provided in many statutes allowing the Secretary of State authority to make decisions, delegate powers or allocate powers to other bodies. Central government powers operate within the framework of ministerial responsibility to Parliament; ministers alone may raise public expenditure through Act of Parliament. This power of taxation is exclusively controlled by the government of the day on the authority of Parliament.

6–098

Allocating functions between central and local government raises important issues about where political, legal and judicial powers ought to reside.

Types of agencies

6–099

In public law the names of particular institutions that are hived off from government follow no exact science. The civil service organised around the various departments of central government is undergoing radical change. On 1 April 1996 there were 494,292 permanent civil servants. Since 1988 the Next Steps initiative has been in operation intended to deliver better services within available resources. By 1 April 1996 there were 102 Next Steps agencies in the

---

60   Under the Education Act 1944, as amended. S. H. Bailey, "Central and Local Government and the Courts" [1983] *Public Law* 8.

Home Civil Service. In addition, there are agencies within HM Customs and Excise and the Inland Revenue. Taken together this amounts to 71 per cent of the civil service, approximately 350,126 permanent staff. Two years later there were 138 agencies over 76 per cent of the Civil Service. The powers and responsibilities of such agencies fall within the "Framework Documents" setting up the agency. Such agencies come within Treasury guidance and financial control. The increase in the number of agencies has required the re-writing of the Treasury Handbook on Government Accounting. In 1998 the White Paper *Modern Public Services*[61] advanced the idea of benchmarking or the setting of standards of best practice. The chief executive of the agency has responsibility for the day to day management and decision-making of the agency. In theory this leaves ministerial responsibility confined to the overall policy of the agency.

6-100
The Next Steps agencies need to be distinguished from other forms of agency established independently from the Next Steps arrangements. Such agencies may appear to share some similarities with the Next Steps type of agency. However, unlike Next Steps agencies these are usually set up under statute. For the purposes of convenience, they may be given the generic title of fringe organisations.

Fringe organisations and statutory bodies

6-101
The allocation of powers may be entrusted to various non-governmental organisations (quangos).[62] The House of Commons Public Administration Select Committee in its First Report 2014/15 recommended that "the government should establish a clear taxonomy of public bodies: constitutional bodies, independent public interest bodies, departmental sponsored bodies and executive agencies".[63]

Some have a statutory framework such as the Care Quality Commission that inspects health and social care services in England or Ofsted. Both examples illustrate the use of inspectorates as a functioning part of their respective roles. Many of their activities are directly related to carrying out statutory powers, but their remit outside government departments gives scope for a broader view of their activities. In 1993 the Cabinet Office listed four types of Non-Departmental Public Bodies (NDPs). Annual reports are published by the Cabinet Office providing statistical information and data. In common usage these bodies are often referred to as fringe organisations or quangos. Such bodies have a role in the process of national government but are not part of a department and operate at arm's length from ministers. The Public Bodies Act 2011 provided a mechanism for the reduction of the number of public bodies on a larger scale than ever before. The principle of "one in one out" applied as an attempt to place a constitutional "brake" on the creation of new agencies and bodies. The adoption of a "Henry VIII

---

61 Cm.4011.
62 See *The Civil Service Yearbook 2015* (London: HMSO, 2015).
63 House of Commons Public Administration Select Committee, *Who's accountable? Relationship between Government and arm's length bodies*, HC 110 (4 November 2014), p.3.

clause" namely that subordinate legislation was accepted to amend primary legislation made the Act controversial. Despite much public posture the outcome seems to have not lived up to expectations set by the Government. Gavin Drewry notes:

> "Nonetheless, the reform proved something of a damp squib, certainly if an official UK government list of some 500 NDBs (grouped round 24 ministerial department or offices) is anything to go by."[64]

6–102

Executive Agencies is a generic term to include quite a diverse range of organisations. They employ staff and have their own budget. Some may have the status of a public corporation. In 1979 there were 492 such bodies employing 217,000 staff and spending £6,150 million. In 1993 there were 358 employing 111,300 staff and spending £15,410 million. In 1996 there were 309 with expenditure of £21,420 million. In 2015 there are over 300 with an expenditure of £25,000 million.

The first type is an executive agency that are business units of a department accountable to ministers. They work within the policy framework of a department. The chief executive is responsible for day to day management. Their funding is often classified as "trading funds" and the examples are the Rural Payments Agency, the UK Space Agency and the Planning Inspectorate.

6–103

The second type are non-ministerial department. These organisations not have direct ministerial accountability but are independent from ministers. Examples include Ofsted, Food Standards Agency, Ordinance Survey and the UK Trade and Investment Agency.

6–104

The third type are a variety of administrative Non-Departmental Public Bodies (NDPB) that are part of central government but are not government departments. There are four basic models: The first is an executive NDPB that a variety of administrative, commercial, executive and regulatory functions. These are often of a technical nature such as the Health and Safety Executive, the Information Commissioner's Office or the Environment Agency. The second model is an advisory NDPB. Their main role is to provide advice such as the Veterinary Products Committee or the Social Security Advisory Committee. The third model is in the general category of Tribunal NDPB. These provide an independent form of scrutiny such as the Valuation Tribunal or the Traffic Commissioners. The fourth model is a form of Independent Monitoring Board, often with statutory powers such as within prisons or for the immigration removal centre and holding facility in England and Wales.

6–105

This is not an exhaustive list of fringe organisations. Privatisation of many nationalised industries has increased the range and scope of specialised statutory bodies. Mention has been made above to OFGEM that covers electricity and gas. In the case of railways, under the Railways Act 1993 there is the Office of Passenger Rail Franchising (OPRAF) and the Office of the Railway Regulator (ORR). Some regulatory agencies fall into different categories or are

---

64 See Gavin Drewry, "A Coalition Government in Westminster" in J. Jowell, D. Oliver and Colin O'Cinneide, *The Changing Constitution* 8th edn (Oxford: Oxford University Press, 2015), 194–221, p.209.
UK Cabinet Office, *Public Bodies* (2013).

6-106 simply unique examples of their kind. The Modern Slavery Act 2015 created an independent Anti-Slavery Commissioner located within the Home Office.

Baldwin and McCrudden have identified reasons for the creation of the wide variety of regulatory agencies. Hiving off government work may be more efficient and reduce the size of the civil service. Particular expertise is sought outside a government ministry. Independence from government may be required to develop the necessary experience and expertise. Delegation of rule-making functions may be required in order to facilitate giving technical detail. Constant up-dating and adjustment are more suited to such bodies than government departments. Interest groups, industry and policy formulation may be assisted through the creation of such agencies. Funding from outside government sources may be easier to achieve. Treasury interference or inter-departmental rivalries may be more easily resisted through the creation of regulatory agencies.

6-107 There are also a wide variety of functions discharged by such agencies. Baldwin and McCrudden[65] identify five different governmental functions present: first, the prevention of undesirable activities; secondly, the provision of techniques to the various parties to reach agreement or compromise; thirdly, the provision and allocation of various benefits such as particular services or ensuring good standards such as competitive and economical industries; fourthly, setting standards through legal mechanism; and finally, providing dispute facilities.

6-108 Decision-making bodies may be influenced by the need to provide some elements of adjudication in the decision-maker. Adjudication may be informal or formal. Informal adjudication may take place without lawyers and be confined to internal procedures. Formal methods of adjudication inevitably involve the use of the courts, tribunals or inquiries. Lawyers tend to become a dominant influence. Jowell[66] described this process as "judicialisation". The choice to be made is to consider the role of courts and the function of tribunals and inquiries.

F: Courts

The Judiciary and the Administration of Justice

6-109 Openness, integrity, impartiality and fairness are some of the characteristics necessary for a decision-maker to follow when adjudicating disputes. Courts appear to offer such characteristics. Although historically England had a large number of special local courts, these have now been displaced by a centrally organised system of courts: the High Court including

---

65 R. Baldwin and McCrudden, *Regulation and Public Law* (London: Weidenfeld and Nicolson, 1987).
66 J. Jowell, "Courts and Administration in Britain: Standard, Principles and Rights" (1988) *Israel Law Review* 409.

the Administrative Court, the Court of Appeal and, the House of Lords, but since 2009 the Supreme Court of the UK.

6–110 The courts gained independence in the seventeenth century and although proposed in the nineteenth century, a Minister of Justice covering judicial appointments, law reform and the legal profession, was never implemented. The jurisdiction of the High Court has developed as a place where the legality of acts and decisions of public bodies may be challenged.

6–111 It is the adjudicatory nature of the courts' role, with its implied independence and appearance of non-political decision-making, that makes the facility of the courts an important model for allocating powers. The value of the court may come from techniques for dealing with law and facts. An illustration of this valuable role is provided by the employment of High Court judges in chairing inquiries or investigations.

6–112 The Constitutional Reform Act 2005 introduced reforms to separate the judicial and legislative functions and separate the highest appellate Court from the legislature in the House of Lords by setting up of the Supreme Court of the UK before its establishment in 2009.

6–113 In England and Wales, the High Court exercises a civil jurisdiction. There are three divisions: Queen's Bench, Chancery and Family. On appeal there is the Court of Appeal, Civil Division. The Supreme Court comprises the High Court, the Court of Appeal and the Crown Court. Appeals lie to the House of Lords, now the UK Supreme Court, sitting as a court, from the Court of Appeal and in some instances direct from the High Court. There is a limited civil jurisdiction exercised by the county courts and by the magistrates' court.

6–114 Criminal jurisdiction is provided for summary offences before the magistrates' courts and in jury trials before the Crown Court. Criminal appeals may be taken to the Queen's Bench Divisional Court or to the High Court or to the Court of Appeal, Criminal Division. A further appeal on matters of law may lie to the House of Lords, now the Supreme Court.

6–115 Under the Appellate Jurisdiction Act 1876, the House of Lords when sitting as a court may be composed of up to 12 Lords of Appeal in Ordinary. Since the creation of the Supreme Court in October 2009 the 12 full time judges became Justice of the Supreme Court for the UK. Since 1966 the House of Lords, and now the Supreme Court, is not bound by its previous decisions though it does not depart from former decisions which it regards as normally binding.

6–116 In the UK, judicial appointments remain a matter for the Executive through the Queen on the advice of ministers. Unlike the US, there is no process of scrutiny and confirmation by Parliament. In the case of Supreme Court Judges, appointments are made by the Queen, on the advice of the Prime Minister.

6–117 The Supreme Court was established on 1 October 2009. New appointments to the Supreme Court are governed by the Constitutional Reform Act 2005 (as amended). Once a vacancy to the Supreme Court becomes available then there is an ad hoc Supreme Court Selection Commission consisting of five members, at least one of whom must be a member of the Supreme Court and one must be a lay member and three must be drawn from the Judicial Appointments Commission and the equivalent in Scotland and Northern Ireland. There are detailed rules on judicial appointments under the Supreme Court (Judicial Appointments) Regulations 2013 agreed by the President of the Court before Parliamentary approval can be given. One interesting development is that the Crime and Courts Act 2013 has amended the

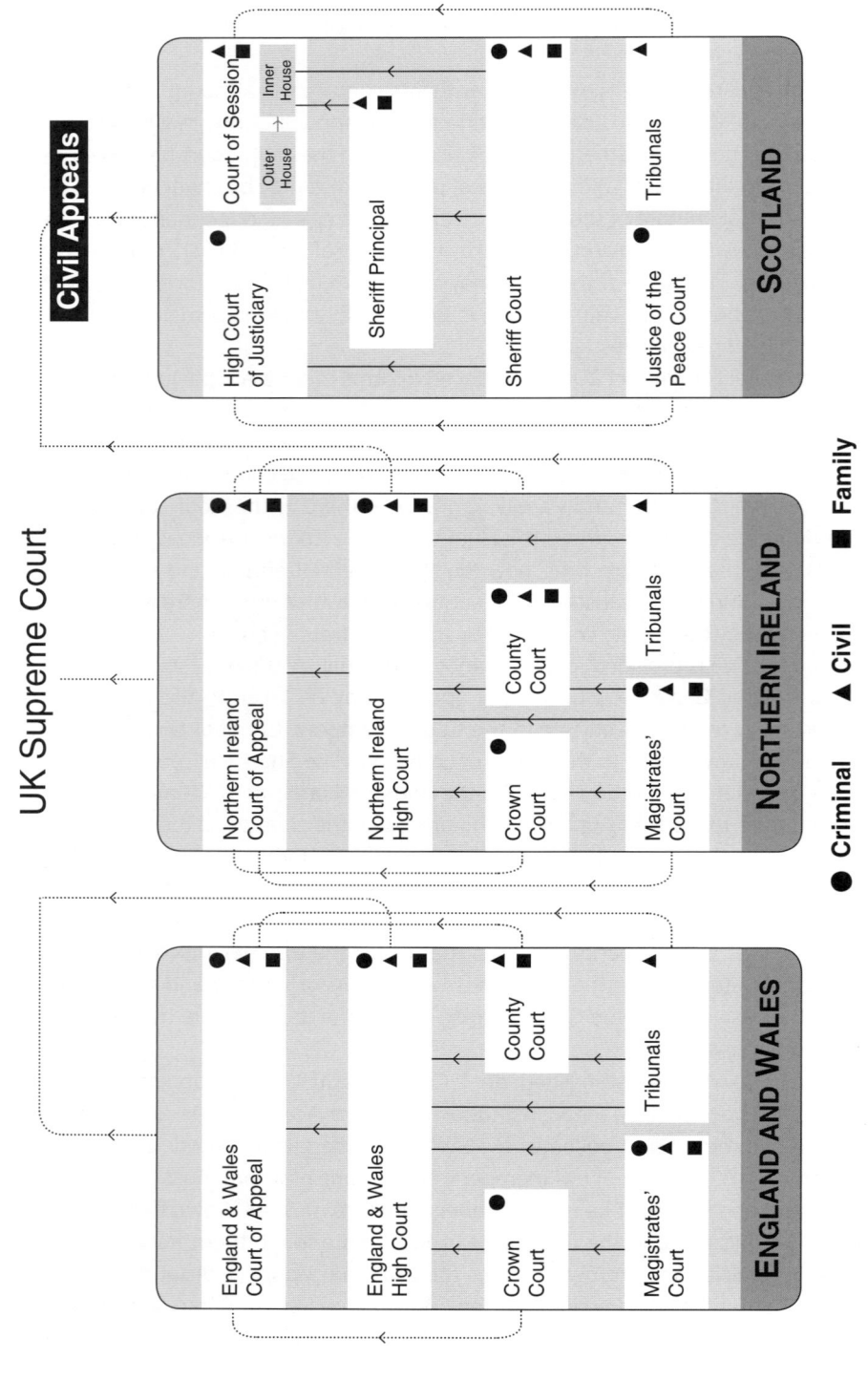

Figure 1 The Courts of Civil and Criminal Jurisdiction in England and Wales, The UK Supreme Court website at https://www.supremecourt.uk/docs/UKSC_StoryPanel_9_1100hx800w_v6.pdf

statutory framework of the Constitutional Reform Act 2005 and transferred from primary legislation into regulatory form the main substance of the arrangements.

6–118 Senior judicial positions such as the Heads of Divisions—Lord Chief Justice, Master of the Rolls, and President of the Family Division are appointments made by the Queen on the advice of the Prime Minister and Lord Chancellor. High Court judges, circuit judges and recorders are appointed by the Queen on the advice of the Lord Chancellor but the process of selection is made through the Judicial Appointments Commission formally set up in April 2006 under the Constitutional Reform Act 2005 (as amended).

The Courts and Legal Services Act 1990 changed the qualifications necessary for judicial appointments. Before 1990 judges of the High Court had to be barristers of at least ten years' standing. After the 1990 Act it is possible for solicitors with rights of audience in the High Court and for Circuit Court judges to be appointed. Appointment as a Lord Justice of Appeal to the Court of Appeal previously required standing as a barrister of at least 15 years or previous appointment as a High Court judge. After 1990 solicitors with rights of audience in the High Court are eligible and the 15 years has been reduced to ten years. Non-practising barristers may in certain circumstances be appointed High Court judges, where there is a particular specialism required.

6–119 Since 1994 appointments to the Circuit Court follow advertisement of the position available. In 1998 the principle of advertisement was extended to High Court appointments and the job description of magistrates. One of the tasks of the Lord Chancellor is to make an annual report to Parliament. An innovation in 2005 under the Constitutional Reform Act 2005 was the setting up of an independent Judicial Appointment Commission with the role to oversee, monitor and review appointments. It came into existence in April 2006. There is a lay chair and other appointments by regulations include serving judges. The majority must not be holders of judicial office. Since 2013 there are non-lawyers as well as legal practitioners who are not judges. The main disappointment for the view that the appointment process should be fully independent is that the process of appointment leaves the government of the day with the final say. The Constitutional Reform Act 2005 requires the Appointments Commission to have regard to "diversity" in the range of individuals available for selection.

6–120 There are few senior judges who are women and there is an under-representation on the judicial bench as a whole from the Black or Asian communities. As of September 2001, the Lord Chancellor's Department *Annual Report on Judicial Appointments* shows that out of the 12 Lords of Appeal there are no women. There is one woman head of Division and out of 35 Lord Justices of Appeal there are two women. In the High Court, there are eight women High Court Judges from a total of 105. On the Circuit Court only 47 Circuit Judges out of a total of 476 were women. In 2014 it was estimated that only 25 per cent of judges in England and Wales are women.[67] Currently 19 out of 108 High Court Judges and seven out of 35 Appeal Court Judges are women. The expectation is that in the future the judiciary will be composed of people from different ethnic and cultural backgrounds. This may prove hard to achieve. Only 10 per cent of QCs are women despite the number of women barristers

---

67 *The Guardian*, 9 October 2014.

being almost 50 per cent of the profession. Only 25 per cent of women are partners in large firms while the proportion of women in the solicitors profession is over 50 per cent. It is possible for two candidates of equal merit to be chosen on merit including the "purpose of increasing diversity". Only time will tell if the ambition of encouraging judicial diversity will be achieved.

6-121 The question of judicial appointment is particularly sensitive given the broad remit the judges have been given to their powers under the Human Rights Act 1998. One of the early cases on the Human Rights Act 1998 in Scotland was that the appointment of temporary sheriffs was an infringement of art.6 of the European Convention on Human Rights.[68] Section 3 of the Constitutional Reform Act 2003 has a legal duty to uphold the independence of the judiciary. Such independence[69] provides important safeguards. Judges must be free from political pressures when deciding cases. The terms and conditions of judicial appointments are therefore important in contributing to the independence of the judiciary. The Lord Chancellor has a duty to defend judicial independence and provide the necessary support to carry out their functions under s.3(6) of the Constitutional Reform Act 2005. There is an ambiguously worded "the need for the public interest in regard to matters relating to the judiciary or otherwise to the administration of justice to be properly represented in decisions affecting those matters". This may mean that the Lord Chancellor should pay attention to the "public interest" in protecting the independence of the judiciary. There is no explicit recognition of how this might be achieved.

6-122 The House of Lords Select Committee on the Constitution has recognised that the independence of the judiciary should not be undermined,[70] that the politicisation of the judicial appointments process should be avoided,[71] and that the roles of Parliament and the judiciary should not be conflated.[72] Linking the independence of the judiciary to the rule of law is helpful. The Constitutional Reform Act 2005 recognises that the Act does not adversely affect the "existing constitutional principle of the rule of law". Under s.5(1) there is a possibility that the Lord Chief Justice might make formal representation to Parliament about concerns relating to the judiciary or the administration of justice. This formal mechanism has not been used. However there have been circumstances where the Lord Chief Justice has warned about the use of a super-injunction being used to suppress Parliamentary debate or discussion.[73] On another occasion judicial views on legislation on legislation going through Parliament was the subject of a public lecture.[74]

---

68 *Starrs v Ruxton* 2000 J.C. 208; 2000 S.L.T. 42 and the subsequent legislation, Judicial Appointments etc. (Scotland) Act 2000.
69 See Robert Stevens, *The Independence of the Judiciary* (Oxford: Clarendon, 1993).
70 House of Lords Select Committee on the Constitution, *10th Report on Counter-Terrorism Bill: The Role of Ministers, Parliament and the Judiciary*, HL Paper 167 (2007–08), para.38.
71 House of Lords Select Committee on the Constitution, *10th Report on Counter-Terrorism Bill*, para.39.
72 House of Lords Select Committee on the Constitution, *2nd Report Crimes and Courts Bill*, HL Paper 17 (2014–15), para.6.
73 Judicial Communications Office, "Lord Justice's View on Super-injunctions", Press Release (20 October 2009).
74 Lord Chief Justice, Lord Judge, Mansion House Speech (14 July 2009).

6-123 Legislation that may include some form of ouster clause preventing or inhibiting judicial review may create conflict between the courts and the Executive. The House of Lords Select Committee on the Constitution has recommended that ouster clauses should be avoided.[75]

6-124 Public criticism of judges by politicians is not uncommon but ministerial censure of the judiciary is often resisted. There are exceptions. The Home Secretary in February 2013 accused "judges of making the UK more dangerous by ignoring rules aimed at deporting more foreign criminals".[76] In March 2013, Lord Neuberger, President of the Supreme Court criticised the Home Secretary for criticising judges, describing such criticism as "unhelpful and wrong".[77] Judges are also well aware that unpopular decisions may result in negative reaction to the judiciary and this could severely diminished judicial independence.

6-125 Judges have security of tenure. Judges of the High Court, Court of Appeal and Lords of Appeal hold office during good behaviour, subject to the power of removal by the Queen on an address presented to both Houses of Parliament.

6-126 Judicial appointments are made for life but since 1959 statutory retirement ages have been introduced: 72 for a circuit judge and 75 for a High Court judge. This was modified in 1993 when the Judicial Pensions and Retirement Act 1993 introduced a new retirement age of 70 which may be extended to 75. Since 1973 there are procedures for determining judicial incapacity and grounds of retirement.

6-127 Judicial salaries are charged permanently from the Consolidated Fund, relieving Parliament of the obligation of approving salaries every year. Salaries fall under the review procedure set up by the government for review by the advisory Review Body on Top Salaries. The Lord Chancellor with Prime Ministerial approval may increase salaries in line with the recommendations from the Review Body.

6-128 As noted above, the Lord Chancellor is concerned with all judicial appointments, including the magistracy, Circuit Court judges and High Court judges. The general administration of the Supreme Court is also his responsibility. The Rule Committee consisting of the Lord Chancellor and other judges, together with practising barristers and solicitors provides the Rules of the Supreme Court. The Lord Chancellor is also responsible for the allocation of business between the High Court and county courts.

6-129 The Law Commission has statutory responsibility to keep under systematic review the law including codification, simplification and where relevant modernisation of the law. There is a Judicial Studies Board and since coming into force its responsibilities include training on sentencing, criminal law, family law, civil matters and the Human Rights Act 1998.

6-130 The latter formed an impressive agenda for a sustained period of training for all members of the judiciary on the implications of the new Act. In the midst of considerable uncertainty, intensive preparations were made for the 1998 Act's coming into force in England and Wales and an extra £60 million allocated for legal aid and court costs. The judiciary at all levels

---

75 House of Lords Constitution Committee, *4th Report Justice and Security (Northern Ireland) Bill*, HL Paper 54 (2006–07), para.2.
76 *BBC News*, 17 February 2013.
77 *The Daily Telegraph*, 4 March 2013.

from magistrates' courts to the appeals courts have undergone intensive education and training programmes on the Act. A central issue is the extent of the application of Convention rights and the implications of a rights-based culture in English law. Courses organised by the Judicial Studies Board have explained the remit of the 1998 Act and how it might be interpreted. Similarly, administrators and civil servants have undergone training on the impact of the Act. The courts now have the difficult task of interpreting the proper procedures and merits of administrative decisions. While there were fears that the number of cases under the Act might overwhelm the court administration, a sensible case-by-case approach has been adopted. As Professor Anthony King has pointed out, there can be little doubt that[78] "...many of the changes in our traditional constitution are permanent and irreversible". It is an opportune moment to take stock of the direction a more rights-orientated public law will take us. There are some words of caution. While conceding, as everyone must, that human rights are intrinsic to our democratic system, there is room for consideration of the boundaries of judicial power as a custodian of rights. What degree of self-regulation should be exercised by judges when they are granted such overarching powers? How should decision makers be advised to achieve good decisions when individual rights may serve to inhibit risk-taking and long term strategies?

6-131 The Human Rights Act 1998 has certainly provided an important intersection between human rights and legal claims against the State that involve the judiciary in determining the legality of the State's actions. In many cases this is an exercise in judicial self-restraint as the democratic mandate of government decision-making has to be respected. Increasingly, the common law including public law is being influenced and shaped by the development of human rights and this is likely to continue for the foreseeable feature.[79] Judicial sensitivities are often ignored in the glare of publicity and news media hype.

6-132 Judges must exercise great care to ensure that a judge is not a party to a case and is free from any personal interest or bias in a case heard before him. The ordinary rules of natural justice apply. In the *Pinochet*[80] litigation, because of his status as chair of a trust set up by Amnesty International, Lord Hoffman had an interest in the proceedings and so should not have been a member of the panel that heard the case.

6-133 As mentioned judges are often required to preside over royal commissions or inquiries set up under the Tribunals of Inquiry (Evidence) Act 1921 and since 2005 under the Inquiries Act 2005. Ad hoc inquiries set up in the public interest are often chaired by a High Court judge. Judicial involvement in such a role is often accompanied by great publicity. The subject matter of many inquiries is often controversial and may indirectly involve judges in political issues of the day. Lord Widgery, then Lord Chief Justice, undertook an inquiry into events in Northern Ireland leading up to "Bloody Sunday". Lord Saville's report in 2010 re-examined the events in considerable detail. The involvement of senior judges in highly controversial issues

---

78 Anthony King, *Does the United Kingdom Still Have a Constitution?* (London: Sweet & Maxwell, 2001), p.90.
79 It is impossible to speculate on whether the Human Rights Act 1998 will be amended/repealed or replaced by a British Bill of Rights.
80 *R v Bow Street Magistrates Ex p. Pinochet (No.2)* [2000] 1 A.C. 119; [1999] 2 W.L.R. 272 HL.

has its dangers. The public may find it difficult to draw a distinction between the primary judicial function of judges and their role in inquiries set up by the government of the day.

6-134
In recent years the public and media attention on the procedures and outcome of the Scott inquiry[81] was particularly intense. There were a number of reasons for this heightened and at times almost hysterical attention given by the media to the inquiry. First, the nature of the inquiry itself and the undoubted public interest in its contents. Secondly, the public standing of the witnesses including the Attorney General; senior Government Ministers including the then serving Prime Minister Mr Major; and Mrs Thatcher, the previous Prime Minister. Thirdly, the nature of public cross-examination attracted media attention. The undoubted charisma of Sir Richard Scott and the appointment of a Counsel to the inquiry, Presiley Baxendale QC, all added a sense of drama to proceedings. Finally, the political parties seized on every opportunity afforded by the inquiry to embarrass Government Ministers about the potential findings of the inquiry. In the end the Government was able to use the charges laid by the opposition parties as a means to deflect criticism. This allowed media attention to diminish once any ministerial resignation was defeated in the House of Commons. All this served to illustrate the delicate nature of judicial independence, public scrutiny and media attention.

6-135
The Leveson Inquiry[82] into press freedom, chaired by the senior High Court Judge Sir Brian Leveson in 2012, is a good example of the central role judges may have in matters of media and public interest.[83] The Inquiry recommended that the press should be regulated by a new body established by the industry but independent and underpinned by a statutory framework. This was an attempt to provide a compromise between complete self-regulation and a system of tough statutory controls. The Government accepted the recommendations in part and have established a new regulatory body by royal charter with the power to fine up to £1 million.

6-136
Judges often have a difficult task in ensuring that they are perceived by the public as independent. The diversity of the tasks entrusted to judges by the government of the day only reinforces the importance of judicial independence. The public's *perception* of what it means to be independent proved highly influential in the selection of a judge to chair an independent inquiry into allegations of historic sexual abuse especially amongst politicians or figures who were or are prominent in British public life.[84] Eventually the Government appointed a New Zealand Judge, Justice Lowell Goddard as the inquiry Chair after the resignation of the first Chair Baroness Butler-Sloss and then the resignation of a second chair Fiona Woolf, a senior city lawyer. One of the main influences in setting up the inquiry has been the voice of child abuse survivors.

---

81   The Rt Hon. Sir Richard Scott, The Vice Chancellor, *Return to an Address of the Honourable House of Commons dated 15th February 1996. Report of the Inquiry into the Export of Defence Equipment and Dual-use Goods to Iraq and Related Prosecutions*, HC 115 (London: HMSO, 1996).
82   HC 779 (2012–13).
83   See the discussion of the *Leveson Report*, HC 779 (2012–13); and HL Paper 122 (2007–08).
84   House of Commons Library, *The Independent Inquiry into Child Sexual Abuse and background*, Briefing Paper No.07040 (25 September 2015).

6-137 Judges observe the convention that they must not become involved in party political activities. They must not engage in conduct which is likely to bring the judiciary into disrepute. Members of the government, and civil servants are constrained by convention not to criticise a judicial decision by attacking the competence or credibility of the judge. Similarly, MPs should exercise self-restraint in their criticism of judges. Michael Howard, is an example of a Conservative Home Secretary (1993–97) who publicly attacked named judges.[85] David Blunkett, a Labour Home Secretary in 2003, made clear that "he was personally fed up" with judges overturning decisions made by politicians and it was time "for judges to learn their place".[86] Parliamentary debate is expected to observe the sub judice rule when matters awaiting judicial decision are brought before the courts. At times this may seem an undue fetter on the freedom of the House of Commons to debate, but it is generally accepted as a necessary protection of the judiciary.[87]

6-138 Judges are protected at common law from any action for acts done or words spoken in their judicial capacity in a court of justice.[88] This protection appears extensive. It may even cover anything done or said however corrupt, oppressive or malicious. In recent years the protection afforded to superior court judges is increasingly applied to lower courts such as magistrates. The Courts and Legal Services Act 1990 provides that a magistrate will not be liable for any acts done within his jurisdiction nor for any acts outside his jurisdiction unless bad faith may be shown. Judicial incompetence which may result in a wrongful conviction does not render the judge liable in either civil or criminal law. Negligence or poor judgment does not result in disciplinary action. There is at least some extension of judicial immunity to the vast array of inferior tribunals where the duties involve judicial rather than administrative decisions. It may be questioned whether absolute judicial immunity outlined above is entirely defensible.

6-139 The immunity of advocates from actions for negligence has been re-examined by the House of Lords. In *Arthur J. S. Hall and Co (a firm) v Simmons*[89] the House of Lords rejected the argument that the administration of justice required that advocates should be protected. The immunity of the past appears to have no place in a modern society and for that reason immunity was removed for advocates in civil cases.

6-140 Finally, it is important to note that the courts have extensive powers in respect of contempt of court. Contempt of court allows the courts to punish conduct that threatens, obstructs or prejudices the administration of justice. The law has been amended in the Contempt of Court Act 1981. Civil contempt is the failure to obey the order of a superior court that has prescribed conduct for a party to a civil action. Criminal contempt may arise where there is conduct

---

85 See Lord Dyson MR, *The Third Annual BAILII Lecture: Criticising Judges: Fair Game or Off-Limits?* (27 November 2014); and J. Rosenberg, *Trial of Strength* (London: Richard Cohen, 1997), pp.5–6.
86 Lord Dyson gives this example in his annual lecture. The judge criticised was Collins J in his decision given in *R (Q) v Secretary of State for the Home Department* [2003] EWHC 195 (Admin); (2003) 100(15) L.S.G. 26. See generally A. Bradley, "Judicial Independence under attack" [2003] P.L. 397.
87 See *Hansard*, HC Vol.365 (1986–87), p.6, col.710 (13 July 1987).
88 A. Olowofoyeku, *Suing Judges* (Oxford: Clarendon, 1993); and *Sirros v Moore* [1975] Q.B. 118; [1974] 3 W.L.R. 459 CA (Civ Div).
89 [2002] 1 A.C. 615; [2000] 3 W.L.R. 543 HL.

calculated to interfere with proceedings which are in their nature criminal proceedings. However, both civil and criminal courts have jurisdiction over criminal contempt. Obedience to the orders of the court is required against litigants. In the case of the Crown or government departments, the courts may issue injunctions against officers of the court and the contempt jurisdiction of the courts extends to ministers. Contempt proceedings may be invoked for matters that are said to scandalise the court, or where there are threats made in the face of the court. Contempt proceedings may arise from publications that are held to prejudice the course of justice or other acts that interfere with the course of justice.

6–141

Securing judicial independence is a continuous process which at times involves judicial self-restraint and critical self-analysis. Judges are expected to be active members of society participating in discussion, and demonstrating that their independence does not mean isolation. Increased media scrutiny is likely to continue and require judges to observe the etiquette of careful judgment and thoughtful comment. Lord Dyson, The Master of the Rolls, has admitted that "the convention against criticism of judges' decisions has been eroded, even if it remains in place, albeit sometimes precariously, for Government Ministers. Uncertain and testing conditions therefore lie ahead".[90] Changes in culture and society, more generally, are responsible for the attitudes of the public to alter. Media attention and instant social network messaging are also contributory factors. The result is that judges have to be able to respond in a proportionate and well-reasoned way to public analysis and even criticism of their decisions. As Lord Dyson admits "judges must expect criticism and where appropriate they must offer a robust response".[91]

The development of judicial review

6–142

In the previous chapter, mention was made of Dicey's influential *Law of the Constitution* (1885), in which he suggested that the fundamental safeguard in the UK's Constitution against abuse of power was the doctrine of the rule of law. Rights, for example, to personal liberty or to hold public meetings arise "as the result of judicial decisions determining the rights of private persons in particular cases brought before the courts". The rule of law expresses the idea that the independence of the judiciary is part of a fundamental legal doctrine that government must be conducted according to law. Disputed cases require judicial decisions according to detailed rules in both substance and procedure.

6–143

The courts are uniquely placed to consider the relationship between the citizen and the State. The variety of roles that fall to the courts provides an opportunity for the courts to settle disputes. This includes the interpretation of statutes, reviewing discretion, sometimes adjudicating between different government departments, or in local and central relations and supervising regulatory agencies—all fall within the broad remit of the supervisory jurisdiction of the High Court. The principles of judicial review are drawn from a rich conceptual framework,

---

90   Lord Dyson MR, The Third Annual BAILII Lecture, *Criticising Judges: Fair Game or Off-Limits?*, p.27.
91   Lord Dyson MR, *Criticising Judges: fair Game or Off-Limits?*.

initially focused on interpreting the intention of Parliament and the doctrine of ultra vires. This has gradually given way to a broader approach based on ideas and influences drawn from the rule of law that are not entirely reliant on the intention of Parliament. We have already seen how Jowell encapsulates the rule of law approach very clearly:

> "In addition to the rule of law being recognised as what is called a "common law constitutional right", the practical implementation of the rule of law has taken place primarily through judicial review of the actions of public officials."[92]

6-144 Before 1977, litigants or "aggrieved citizens" as they are termed, had to choose which of a number of ancient prerogative writs was suited to their needs. These included habeas corpus, certiorari (a quashing order), prohibition (a prohibiting order) and mandamus (a mandatory order). Habeas corpus is still referred to as a writ; all the rest are now orders since the Administration of Justice (Miscellaneous Provisions) Acts 1933 and 1938. Such orders could not be "mixed" with other remedies such as declaration, damages or injunctions. Technical rules of standing (locus standi) applied to each remedy. Different grounds for seeking each remedy also applied. In the case of certiorari (a quashing order) and prohibition (a prohibiting order), the availability of the remedy depended on the body performing the function complained about.

6-145 Proposals to reform the procedures and the substantive law of remedies were made by the Law Commission in 1969, which recommended a comprehensive review of administrative law by a Royal Commission or body of comparable status. Although this advice was persuasively argued, it was rejected. In 1969 the Law Commission was instructed to study the law of remedies, which led to recommendations in 1977, contained in Order 53 and now s.31 of the Senior Courts Act 1981 (previously the Supreme Court Act 1981). These procedures, commonly known as Order 53, provide for the application for judicial review. Today the rules of procedure are to be found under the CPR Pt 54 Judicial Review, the Senior Courts Act 1981 and various practice Directions and Pre-action Protocols apply.[93]

6-146 In 1992–93, there had been an 18 per cent increase in the number of cases on current figures. The 1998 Human Rights Act is likely to increase the use of judicial review[94] and nearly 20 per cent of all judicial review cases raise a human rights issue. The most recent statistics take account of current trends and directions. Overall judicial review applications have increased from 2000 of around 4,238 annual applications to an annual high around 2013 of 15,594. The current year from 2014–2015 has seen a significant drop to only 4,062 applications. One

---

92 J. Jowell, The Rule of Law" in J. Jowell, D. Oliver and Colin O'Cinneide, *The Changing Constitution* 8th edn (Oxford: Oxford University Press, 2015), 13–37, p.29.
93 See House of Commons Library Briefing Paper, *Judicial Review: Government reforms in the 2010–15 Parliament*, No.6616 (4 June 2015). See *R (O) v Secretary of State for International Development* [2014] EWHC 2371.
94 *Practice Statement (Admin Ct: Administration of Justice)* [2002] 1 W.L.R. 810; [2002] 1 All E.R. 633 QBD. It is noted that from 2 October to 31 December 2001, some 19 per cent of judicial review cases raised an issue of human rights. In numerical terms judicial review receipts for 2001 showed an overall increase of 11 per cent on 2000.

reason is that the Upper Tribunal for Immigration and Asylum have taken over responsibility for the majority of civil immigration and asylum review cases from the Administrative Court.[95] Reductions in legal aid available for judicial review applications is also a reason for the steep decline in applications in recent months since 2014. Since 2013 there is a new fees structure for applications including fees when lodging requests for refusal of permission.[96]

6–147

An application for judicial review is made to the Administrative Court with the leave of the Court. The first stage is to request leave and if this is refused a second application may be made to a Judge in open court. All applications must be made to the Administrative Court, formerly the Divisional Court of the Queen's Bench Division.[97] Leave is based on the applicant showing grounds which the court considers to be of "sufficient interest". The first stage for leave must be made promptly and within three months of the grievance occurring. The Civil Procedure (Amendment No.4) Rule 2013 amended CPR Pts 52 and 54 into effect on 1 July 2013. The new rules provide that the claim for an application relating to a planning decision must be filed within six weeks of the date when the grounds became available. In the case of a procurement decision within 30 days. The aim is to ensure consistency with the Town and Country Planning Act 1990 (s.288) and the Public Contracts Regulations 2006.

6–148

At this first stage it is determined whether or not to proceed with the case. The new rules under the Civil Procedure (Amendment No.4) Rule 2013 amend CPR r.54.12 so that a refusal of permission and the application is without merit the applicant may not ask for an oral hearing. Once leave is granted, the second stage is a full hearing. Usually the first stage is on affidavit evidence and only one party, the applicant, is present. Remedies may be granted at the Court's discretion and remedies may be mixed; damages are available. The decision to grant a remedy is discretionary, depending on the nature of the body under review and the powers reviewed. Normally the application for judicial review is confined to "public law" matters, a term which is difficult to define and is often hard to reconcile with the various decisions made by the courts.[98]

6–149

Judicial review does not always afford the citizen redress. Parliament may entrust certain types of decision-making powers to ministers and not the courts. In *R v Secretary of State for Education and Science Ex p. Avon CC*,[99] the Court of Appeal reviewing the powers granted to the Minister of Education under the 1988 Education Reform Act, noted that:

> "Parliament did not entrust the making of that judgment, the Minister's approval for grant maintained status of a school to the Court but to the Minister who was answerable to Parliament."

---

95 Ministry of Justice, *Civil Justice Statistics Quarterly, England and Wales October to December 2014* (March, 2015).
96 Ministry of Justice, Judicial Review and Costs (updated), https://www.justice.gov.uk/courts/rcj-rolls-building/administrative-court/applying-for-judicial-review [Accessed 5 April 2016].
97 There is a High Court in London, but cases may be filed and heard in Birmingham, Cardiff, Leeds or Manchester.
98 See M. Sunkin, "What is Happening to Applications for Judicial Review?" (1987) 50 *Modern Law Review* 432; and Lee Bridges, George Mészáros and Maurice Sunkin, *Judicial Review in Perspective*, 2nd edn (London: Cavendish, 1995).
99 [1991] 1 Q.B. 558; [1991] 2 W.L.R. 702 CA (Civ Div).

6-150 The role of the courts may be limited or excluded in the allocation of functions by Parliament. In terms of subject matter, judicial review covers a wide range of activities. Sunkin[100] and research for the Public Law Project have identified the average case-load of applications for judicial review to consist of "immigration, housing, planning and licensing" cases. Education, homelessness and prisoners' rights are also fairly widely represented in applications. As already noted above there has been a significant rise in applications. In 1974 there were 1609, by 2000 this had risen to 4,250, and by 2011 the number was well in excess of 11,000.[101] Cuts in legal aid and increases in court fees are likely to have some longer-term effects on the availability and opportunity to make an application for judicial review.[102]

6-151 Historically, grounds for judicial review include review of a tribunal or official where there is an error of law. A description applied to review of such matters is "illegality". This ground has been considerably broadened in recent years to correct mistakes of law made by inferior bodies, where there was not necessarily any right of appeal. Even where there may be an overlap between an appeal and a review, the courts have a discretion to offer review. A second ground for review is where there is "irrationality". This is defined to mean, as Lord Diplock explained, where the decision[103]

> "... is so outrageous in its defiance of logic or of accepted moral standards that no sensible person who had applied his mind to the question to be decided could have arrived at it."

6-152 This ground affords the opportunity to review the exercise of statutory powers or discretion. The test of "reasonableness" leaves considerable judicial flexibility in how to apply for review which even extends to reviewing inferior courts such as the legal powers of magistrates.

6-153 The third ground for judicial review identified by Lord Diplock, is "procedural impropriety". On this ground the correct procedure has not been properly followed. A broader interpretation of procedural impropriety is where the rules of natural justice have been broken. There are two rules of natural justice. The first is to hear both sides of the case; giving an opportunity to hear each side is a fundamental part of the common law principles developed by the courts. The second is that no one should be a judge in his own cause. Decisions must be made in an unbiased way. An open mind and unprejudiced thinking before the case is presented, is required. Both rules of natural justice require fairness of decision makers and apply to a wide range of public bodies especially when required by the interests of the litigant. If there is a "legitimate expectation" or if rights are affected, then the courts have a discretion to apply such rules.

---

100 M. Sunkin, "The Judicial Review Case-load 1987–89" [1992] *Public Law* 490.
101 House of Commons Library Briefing Paper, *Judicial Review: Government reforms in the 2010–15 Parliament*, No.6616 (4 June 2015).
102 See as above.
103 *Council for Civil Service Unions v Minister for Civil Service* [1985] A.C. 374.

6-154   The application for judicial review may succeed if any of the grounds for review outlined above are proven to the court. The granting of a remedy and the ultimate success of the application is nevertheless discretionary.

6-155   Since December 2012, the Government launched a consultation process on reform of judicial review. The consultation concluded on 24 January 2014 but since then further reforms have been considered and a further consultation undertaken between September and November 2013. The outcome is the Criminal Justice and Courts Act that obtained Royal Assent in 12 February 2015. The Act sets limits on protective cost orders, greater transparency in the financial arrangements of applicants, and restrictions on judicial review where it is considered that the defendant's conduct may not have affected the outcome for the applicant. There are also powers to transfer planning cases to the Upper Tribunal.[104]

G: The Human Rights Act 1998

6-156   The Human Rights Act is examined in some detail in Ch.15. The experience of the Act has been the subject of intense debate as to whether or not the Act should be amended or repealed. A British Bill of Rights might be considered desirable. A brief outline of the main elements of the Act is relevant here. Suffice to mention that under s.3 of the Act "so far as it is possible to do so", primary and secondary legislation must be interpreted and enacted in a way that is compatible with Convention rights under the European Convention on Human Rights (ECHR). The Act falls short of allowing the courts to hold that an Act of Parliament is unconstitutional or illegal. The most the courts may do is rule on incompatibility[105] between the 1998 Act and the legislation under review. Since the Act came into force there have been three declarations of incompatibility.[106] It is then for Parliament, not the courts, to resolve any incompatibility. The courts are not *bound* by the jurisprudence of the Strasbourg Court of Human Rights but may give effect to those decisions. The impact of the Act is that under s.6 it is unlawful for a public authority to act in a way incompatible with Convention rights. Section 7 permits an individual to bring a claim under s.6 in an appropriate court or tribunal and to rely on a Convention right in any proceedings if a victim of the unlawful act. In a claim that a judicial Act infringes a Convention right, then s.9 of the Human Rights Act requires that proceedings should be brought by way of an appeal or judicial review. Remedies that are available include under s.8(4) payment of compensation or an order for damages.

---

104 House of Commons Library Briefing Paper, *Judicial Review: Government reforms in the 2010–15 Parliament*, No 6616 (4 June 2015).
105 There is no UK equivalent of the US Supreme Court decision in *Roe v Wade* 410 U.S. 113 (1973).
106 See *R (Alconbury Developments Ltd) v Secretary of State for the Environment, Transport and the Regions* [2001] UKHL 23; [2003] 2 A.C. 295 HL; *Wilson v First County Trust Ltd* [2001] EWCA Civ 633; [2001] 3 All E.R. 229; and *R (H) v North and East Region Mental Health Review Tribunal* [2001] EWCA Civ 415; [2001] 3 W.L.R. 512.

6–157 It will be for the courts to consider how to interpret the Convention rights under the Human Rights Act 1998. In *Alconbury*, the first case of its kind, the House of Lords considered how rights set out under art.6 of the ECHR may have an impact on how planning decisions are made. Article 6 provides that "...everyone is entitled to a fair and public hearing within a reasonable time by an *independent and impartial tribunal*..." (italics added). The case is examined in some detail in Ch.16 but it is sufficient here to explain that an applicant for planning permission has a right of appeal to the Secretary of State against any refusal or condition of planning permission. The planning system effectively gives the final say to the Secretary of State, an elected politician, who may include matters of policy as part of the overarching responsibility to ensure that policy issues are considered as part of the system. The Secretary of State's decision may be appealed to the High Court on the same basis as judicial review. The appeal is seen as confined to legal issues, and the courts do not consider the merits of the policy behind the decision. The Secretary of State is in theory responsible to Parliament for policy matters.

6–158 The House of Lords considered the full implications of human rights introduced under the 1998 Act for the planning system and concluded that the court should not have every aspect of planning law fall under the scope of review. To ensure that the relevant human rights procedures are followed, it was sufficient that there should be a review of the legality of the decision. It fell within the Secretary of State's remit, including policy matters, to determine appeals. Thus, while the House of Lords recognise the requirements of the Human Rights Act, this Act does not require judicial intervention in every aspect of the planning system, which is already susceptible to judicial review. This illustrates the court's sensible case-by-case approach.

6–159 It is also important to recognise that legal rights developed under the Human Rights Act 1998 have the potential to shift Britain's constitutional arrangements in a new direction. The Court of Appeal[107] in October 2001, in a series of significant judgments, outlined the significance of the Human Rights Act in terms of the powers of the courts to issue injunctions in matters of planning disputes. Issues of proportionality need to be considered by the courts before an injunction for threatened breaches of the law may be exercised under the discretionary powers of the courts. This is one example of the importance of the rights culture becoming an integral part of the judicial process.

6–160 Professor Ewing notes the danger of the unelected (judges) making important decisions over the elected (ministers):

> "We now have a constitutional system in which the output of the democratic process can avoid successful challenge and possible censure only if it can pass a test of democracy developed by a group of public officials who have escaped all forms of democratic scrutiny and accountability."[108]

---

107 *South Buckinghamshire DC v Porter (No.1)* [2001] EWCA Civ 1549; [2002] 1 W.L.R. 1359. See ENDS [Environmental Data Services] Report 323, p.57, *www.ends.co.uk/index.htm* [Accessed 5 April 2016].

108 K. Ewing, "The Unbalanced Constitution" in T. Campbell, K. Ewing and A. Tomkins (eds), *Sceptical Essays on Human Rights* (Oxford: Oxford University Press, 2001), pp.116–117.

The experience of the Human Rights Act 1998 is informative in terms of how rights may include the legality of the Government's decision-making in the aftermath of the financial crisis in 2008. In *R (Application of SRM Global Master Fund LP) v Treasury Commission*[109] (The Nationalisation of Northern Rock), claimants sought judicial review of the decision to nationalise Northern Rock. The standing of the claimants was that they were all share-holders of Northern Rock. Their complaint was that the valuation of Northern Rock at the date of nationalisation was unfair. Northern Rock was a going concern, although insolvent and that the conditions of the support provided by the Bank of England as the Lendor of Last Resort imposed high interest rates on Northern Rock for the monies provided by the Bank of England. This had the effect of making the valuation of the mortgage portfolio of Northern Bank unfairly benefit the Government through providing a profit for the Bank of England loans. The financial support provided by the Bank of England deprived shareholders of their profits and the provisions for compensation to existing shareholders was unfair. The case argued by the claimants was that through the economic device of loans and guarantees, the Bank of England secured for the taxpayers expropriation through nationalisation of Northern Rock but without adequate compensation to the Northern Rock shareholders. The case made out by the claimants was rejected. Stanley Burton LJ held that without Bank of England intervention, Northern Rock would have ceased trading. The Government through the Bank of England could have withdrawn support—there was no duty to provide financial support and no legitimate expectation to do so. There was no requirement to give such support and the compensation scheme for the shareholders had to accept Northern Rock's valuation based on the loans provided. The claim was dismissed. This illustrates the constraints on judicial discretion and review.[110]

6–161

The decision of the Supreme Court in the *HSE v Wolverhampton City Council*[111] considered the responsibilities of public authorities when deciding to exercise a discretionary power to achieve a public objective. The main question was whether or not costs to the public ought to be taken into consideration. The Supreme Court considered the responsibilities on public bodies and their application to the case in question. Planning permission for a block of four student residences had been applied for and granted. In the course of construction, the Health and Safety Executive (HSE), concerned about gas storage on site, applied for an order to revoke planning permission against Wolverhampton Local Authority. In refusing the application, the Council considered costs and came to the view that the if planning permission were revoked the cost of compensation that would be payable would be high and consequently refused the HSE's application. The HSE brought judicial review proceedings against the Council. The High Court refused that part of the claim. The Court of Appeal allowed the HSE appeal and held that the Council has to make its deci-

---

109 [2009] All E.R. (D) 139.
110 Dimitrios Kyritsis, "Constitutional Review in Representative Democracy" (2012) *Oxford Journal of Legal Studies* 32(2), pp.297–324.; and *R (Jackson) v Attorney General* [2005] EWCA Civ 126; [2005] Q.B. 579.
The debate on the 42 detention period in 2009/10 is a good example. *Thoburn v Sunderland City Council* [2002] EWHC 195 (Admin); [2003] Q.B. 151; *R (Corner House) v Director of the Serious Fraud Office* [2007] EWHC 311; and *R (Alconbury Developments Ltd) v Secretary of State for the Environment, Transport and the Regions* [2001] UKHL 23; [2001] 2 All E.R. 929 at p.980, [70].
111 *HSE v Wolverhampton CC* [2012] UKSC 34; [2012] 1 W.L.R. 2264.

sion in isolation from the economic circumstances of the decision. The Supreme Court adopted a different approach, and decided that a public authority was entitled to take into account the cost to the public purse. Section 97 required the authority to satisfy itself that revocation is expedient including consideration of the development plan and other "material considerations". As the payment of compensation is a relevant matter, the cost to the public purse has to be considered. In general principle, a public body has to take into account public spending.

6-162 Stephen Sedley makes a general observation about how the future of the common law is likely to be influenced by rights:

> "Whether or not a domestic rights instrument replaces the Human Rights Act, the common law has now developed the confidence to fill the spaces without requiring a prescriptive tabulation of rights. While the Supreme Court moves towards the concept of a special category of constitutional legislation, the courts have accepted that different rights enjoy differing degrees of fundamentality, starting with the right to life."[112]

Judicial review and human rights are set to become an area of intense debate in the years to come.

H: Tribunals and Inquiries

6-163 One of the distinctive parts of the early development of English administrative law is the existence of tribunals. The nineteenth century witnessed the growth[113] in various forms of adjudication. The Railway and Canal Commission, set up in 1888, was a good example of the use of a specialised tribunal, sharing some of the characteristics of a court but specialised in its findings and activities. The Railway and Canal Commission consisted of two members appointed by the Home Secretary, and a High Court judge nominated by the Lord Chancellor. The Commission was judicial in form and the proceedings resembled those of a court.

6-164 In the nineteenth century, the use of specialised commissions or tribunals was fairly common but not universal. Not all tribunals conformed to a single pattern. Often there were appeals to the courts. Even the county courts were used occasionally to undertake dispute settlement such as workers' compensation disputes.

---

112 S. Sedley, *Lions Under the Throne: Essays on the History of English Public Law* (Cambridge: Cambridge University Press, 2015), p.207.
113 W. A. Robson, "Administrative Justice and Injustice: A Commentary on the Franks Report" [1958] *Public Law* 12; and W. A. Robson, "Justice and Administrative Law reconsidered" (1979) 32 *Current Legal Problems* 107.

6–165 While the pattern of growth in adjudicating procedures was uneven, the necessity for adjudication became greater as the Welfare State took shape. State-contributed funds for unemployment benefit or sickness benefit to workers increased the scale of state expenditure and also the need for fair and reasonable procedures to solve disputes. The National Insurance Act 1911 provided state benefits and adjudication procedures over unemployment pay were deputed to Insurance Officers appointed by the Board of Trade. Appeals lay to a Court of Referees representing employers, employees and a chairman appointed by the Board of Trade. Often the procedures were cumbersome, complicated and bureaucratic with several levels of decision-making.

6–166 Both World Wars had significant consequences in shaping the role of government and responsibilities accepted by the State. State responsibility or involvement covered pensions payable to the disabled and dependants of the dead killed in action. A plethora of local tribunals assisted in the administration of appeals, known as the Pensions Appeal Tribunals.

6–167 Reconstruction of the inter-war economy saw the reorganisation of transport, both road and rail, and the streamlining of freight to assist in the regulation of trade and industry. Tribunals were commonplace as an effective way to administer such changes. The Second World War further increased the growth in government powers and the need for new tribunals. The reason was not seen as a reactive one, but proactive, as a means of increasing the availability of welfare services based on need. Tribunals could introduce new policies and new regulatory legislation.

6–168 Tribunals mirrored government activities, as the Franks Committee observed[114]:

> "The continuing extension of governmental activity and responsibility for the general well-being of the community has greatly multiplied the occasions on which an individual may be at issue with the administration or with another citizen or body, as to his rights and the post war years have seen a substantial growth in the importance and activities of tribunals."

6–169 The introduction of the modern Welfare State after the Second World War increased benefits payable by the State under the National Insurance Acts 1946 and 1948. Tribunals proliferated with the inherent dangers of increasing government powers. Warnings that the State was too powerful were not slow in coming. First in 1928 with W.A. Robson's *Justice and Administrative Law* which warned against the growth of judicial powers exercised by ministers and tribunals. A year later Lord Hewart CJ, author of *The New Despotism*, and who had held the offices of Attorney General and Solicitor General in the post-war Liberal Government, warned, for different political reasons to Robson, of the increase in civil service power and influence.

6–170 The concern over the use of the civil service in the machinery of tribunals was taken up by the Donoughmore[115] Committee on Ministers' Powers 1932. The Committee made

---

114 D. G. T. Williams, "Public Local Inquiries—Formal Administrative Adjudication" (1980) 29 *International and Comparative Law Quarterly* 701. Franks Committee, Cmnd.218 (1957).
115 Cmnd.4060 (1932).

recommendations in an attempt to find some rationalisation of the administrative system. Some tribunals were categorised as "specialised courts of law", others were called "ministerial tribunals". While recognising the value of each, the Committee recommended the use of the former rather than the latter, thus preserving the ad hoc development of the English tribunal system. The Committee left unresolved the value and the merits of tribunals as against courts.

6-171 The Second World War had incrementally increased the powers granted to ministers to operate the wartime emergency. Tribunals were required to cope with compensation claims for war damages, disability and bereaved persons. Arising out of the question of land acquisition, the Crichel Down affair caused the Government embarrassment. The outcome led to the setting up of a Committee of Administrative Tribunals and Inquiries under Sir Oliver Franks (the Franks Committee), only 25 years after the Donoughmore Committee.

6-172 The Franks Committee considered the Constitution and the workings of tribunals other than the ordinary courts of law, and examined the workings of such administrative procedures for holding inquiries by or on behalf of the Minister. This was the first occasion that the question of allocation was fairly grasped. The Committee examined the distinction between ministers' powers and tribunals. Franks concluded[116] that both decision-making ministers and tribunals should share characteristics of openness, fairness and impartiality. Tribunals were "not ordinary courts" and not appendages of government departments. Tribunals were set up for adjudication and were not part of the machinery of administration.

6-173 The outcome was the Tribunals and Inquiries Act 1958 which was later amended in 1966 and consolidated in the Tribunals and Inquiries Act 1971, and 1992. In May 2000 a Review of Tribunals was undertaken by Sir Andrew Legatt to provide a coherent structure for the organisation of the tribunal system. The complexity of much of the work of tribunals is due in part to the technical complexity of the law. This resulted in many changes to the tribunal system. The Tribunals, Courts and Enforcement Act 2007 followed. In outline the tribunal system was re-organised. The First-Tier Tribunal to make first instant decisions with the Upper Tribunal to hear appeals. The merger between courts and tribunals is recognised in the Constitutional Reform Act 2005 representing an important unitary form of procedure and assimilation in terms of status and those holding judicial office. The First-tier is organised into a system of chambers, each with their own specialisms and each headed by a judge as President. There are six divisions roughly corresponding to: the General Regulatory Division with an assortment of tribunals covering consumer credit, estate agent appeals, charity appeals, information disputes, driving standard agency appeals); the Social Entitlement Chamber that covers social security, child support, asylum support and criminal injury compensation; the Health, Education and Social Care Chamber covering mental health review, special educational needs and disability and care standards; the War Pensions and Armed Forces Compensation Chamber; the Tax Chamber covering income tax and VAT; and the Immigration and Asylum Chamber and the Property Chamber covering property, rent functions, leasehold valuation and agricultural lands.

---

116 *Franks Committee*, Cmnd.218 (1957).

6–174 Similar arrangements apply to the Upper Tribunal but with a smaller number of chambers comprising, Administrative Appeals Chamber, the Tax and Chancery Chamber, the Lands Chamber and the Immigration and Asylum Chamber. At the Upper Tribunal level, the President is a High Court judge. One significant feature of the arrangements is that the First-Tier Tribunal has power to review its own decisions and may refer the matter to the Upper Tribunal. In selected cases the Upper Tribunal may operate a judicial review functions closely similar to the Administrative Court.

6–175 In *R (Cart) v Upper Tribunal*,[117] the Supreme Court considered whether a refusal to leave to appeal by the First-Tier and Upper Tribunals was subject to judicial review. The Supreme Court gave a general analysis of the role of each Tribunal and concluded that the decisions of the Upper Tribunal were subject to judicial review. There are some qualifications based on the generality of the principle. These are that the appeal raises an important point of principle or law; that there is an additional compelling reason for the appeal to be heard. The principles that the rule of law applies and the courts have a general obligation to uphold the law. Since the decision the Civil Procedure (Amendment No.2) Rules 2012[118] were passed to ensure that the criteria in *Cart* are given general application.[119]

6–176 Appointments to both First-tier and Upper Tier tribunals are made by the Judicial Appointments Commission. Since 2007 responsibility for the system of staffing and Premises fell within Her Majesty's Courts and Tribunals Service, an executive agency situated within the Ministry of Justice.

6–177 Despite a long tradition of oversight through, first, the Council on Tribunals and later the Administrative Justice and Tribunals Council set up in 2007, the Government decided to abolish the Administrative Justice and Tribunals Council in 2013 under the Public Bodies Act 2011. This has left lacking any systematic overview of the system of tribunals and research into the operation of tribunals. This is a great pity, as the importance of the system of tribunals cannot be overestimated in their contribution to administrative justice.

6–178 The Franks Committee also included inquiries within its remit. It separated consideration of inquiries from tribunals but this separation is difficult to make in practice, and the legislation currently in force covers both tribunals and inquiries.

6–179 The purpose of inquiries, outlined by Franks,[120] is:

> **"To ensure that the interests of the citizens closely affected should be protected by the grant to them of a statutory right to be heard in support of their objections and to ensure that thereby the Minister should be better informed about the facts of the case."**

---

117 [2011] UKSC 28; [2012] 1 A.C. 663.
118 SI 2012/2208.
119 A similar decision was reached for Scotland in *Eba v Advoctae General for Scotland* [2011] UKSC 29; [2012] 1 A.C. 710.
120 *Franks Committee*, Cmnd.218 (1957).

6-180 The contrast between tribunals and inquiries is explained by Wade,[121] who offers a distinction between the respective roles of each. Wade argues that a tribunal "finds facts and decides the case by applying legal rules laid down by statute or regulation". An inquiry hears evidence, finds facts "but the person conducting it finally makes a recommendation to a Minister as to how the Minister should act in some question of policy".

6-181 However plain this distinction may appear, Parliament has experimented with many different procedures which share the characteristics of inquiries and those that share the characteristics of tribunals. Thus the distinction may not always be easy to find. Particularly prevalent in recent years has been the use of public local inquiries associated with housing, town and country planning, motorways and the compulsory acquisition of land. D. G. T. Williams has found no fewer than 105 statutory provisions incorporating mandatory inquiries. Public local inquiries can be seen as large in scale, expensive in outlay and slow in reaching conclusions when major issues are at stake for example, the third London Airport, the Sizewell B inquiry into nuclear power generation, and a variety of large inquiries on motorway planning. Many of the issues at such inquiries have required intervention by the courts to review the procedures at the inquiries, admissibility of evidence and fairness in cross-examination of witnesses. There is also the ultimate question of whether the Minister ought to accept the decision of the inquiry if there are errors in the conduct of the inquiry.

6-182 The Inquiries Act 2005 provides a new legal framework for holding inquiries and repealed the 1921 Act. The new Act gives ministerial powers and discretion in a manner that was not possible before. The appointment of an inquiry is discretionary when "particular events" have caused or may cause public concern The Minister appoints the chair of the inquiry, and may agree, amend or suggest terms of reference after consultation with the chair. If a judge is to be appointed to serve the inquiry, there are consultation requirements with the Lord Chief Justice in England, the Lord President of the Court of Session in Scotland and the Supreme Court President if a Supreme Court Justice is appointed. Since 2005 there have been a number of inquiries held under the Act, most notably the Mid Staffordshire NHS Foundation Trust Inquiry under the chair of Robert Francis QC[122] and the Leveson Inquiry into the Culture and Ethics of the Press chaired by Lord Justice Leveson.[123]

6-183 Both inquiries and tribunals provide for the citizen's consultation and participation in the decision-making process. This may be seen as supplementary to the decision of ministers and the role of Parliament. There are plans to modernise the planning system.[124] In particular the government is actively considering plans to revise the way large public inquiries may be used, preferring instead to use a new Parliamentary inquiry for major projects rather than the long-drawn-out process, delay and expense of an inquiry.

---

121 H. W. R. Wade, *Administrative Law*, 6th edn (Oxford: Oxford University Press, 1988).
122 HC 947 (2013).
123 HC 375-I (2013–14) and HC 780-I (2012–13).
124 Planning Green Paper, *Delivering a Fundamental Change December, 2001 and New Parliamentary Procedures for processing major infrastructure projects* (December 2001). 323 Ends Report 39–40 (December 2001).

I: Summary and Conclusions

6-184 Modernisation of the administration of justice has resulted in the creation of an Administrative Law Court, the streamlining of procedures for judicial review and the development of good administration. Specialist tribunals are merged into the court system. The spirit of the age of constitutional reform and changes to the system of judicial review are in part judge-led, as well as judge-designed. An increase in judicial power has been accomplished through innovative ideas and thinking about the development of judicial review and its application to the ordinary citizen. The transformation of judicial power has also involved assimilation of many European elements into UK law, including the enactment of the Human Rights Act 1998, incorporating most of the ECHR. While there is an increasing trend in terms of judicialisation of many aspects of public power, albeit under the doctrine of Parliamentary sovereignty, there are also signs that the UK is entering unchartered constitutional territory. Certainly in matters concerning the EU, the judiciary,[125] and not the UK Parliament, has the final say. There is the potential recognised by lord Steyn in the Jackson case that if Parliament were to attack "fundamental constitutional standards or processes" the courts might have to react.[126]

6-185 It may be concluded that, at the apex of constitutional power, judges now command the heights, controlling how power—generally defined—is allocated, reviewed and assessed. It is tempting to see the judicial role increasing further to fill the void left by perceptions in any weakening of Parliamentary authority. Judicial review is interlinked to judicial independence that underpins the rule of law. Inevitably judges may often be found at the centre of politically contentious issues that may challenges the legality of power. This may impose constraints on the Executive and in the case of abuse of power may act as a deterrent against abuse. It may also bring judges into the public forum of media attention and debate.

Further Reading

P. Craig, *Administrative Law*, 7th edn (London: Sweet & Maxwell, 2012).
C. Harlow and R. Rawlings, *Law and Administration*, 3rd edn (Cambridge: Cambridge University Press, 2009).
J. Jowell, D. Oliver and C. O'Cinneide (eds), *The Changing Constitution*, 8th edn (Oxford: Oxford University Press, 2015).

---

125 *R v Secretary of State for Transport Ex p. Factortame (No.2)* [1991] 1 A.C. 603; [1990] 3 W.L.R. 818 HL.
126 *R (Jackson) v Attorney General* [2005] UKHL 56; [2006] 1 A.C. 262.

A. Le Sueur (ed), *Building the UK's New Supreme Court: National and Comparative Perspectives* (Oxford: Oxford University Press, 2004).
P. Leyland, *The Constitution of the United Kingdom*, 2nd edn (Oxford: Hart, 2012).
S. Sedley, *Lions Under the Throne: Essays on the History of English Public Law* (Cambridge: Cambridge University Press, 2015).
K. Syrett, *The Foundations of Public Law* 2nd edn (London: Palgrave, 2014).

Part II

Public Law, Politics, Ideas and Influences

Part II consists of three chapters. In Ch.7, the electoral system is discussed in terms of representative government. The question of political influences on the institutions of government is examined linked to the overall theme of accountable government. Chapter 8 provides an explanation of the ideas and influences which continue to influence and inform public law scholarship in the UK. Chapter 9 explains the European dimension to the UK's constitutional arrangements with membership of the EU.

II–001

7

The Electorate, Politics and the Constitution

A: Introduction

Representative democracy is one of the most important measurements to judge the success of an electoral system.[1] In the UK the trust that resides in Parliament to hold government to account also gives rise to the idea that citizens have a right to participate in the electoral process for the selection of members of the House of Commons. The bi-cameral, two chamber system of Parliamentary government provides the House of Lords and the House of Commons with each a role in passing legislation and in debate and holding government to account. The House of Commons is wholly elected and this is manifest in its authority and dominance over the unelected House of Lords.[2]

There are many changes to the electoral system for European, local and parliamentary elections and the introduction of diversity in the electoral systems used; financial controls over party political funding; and improvements to the administration of elections through the creation of a new Electoral Commission. The development of regional government, through systems of devolution to Scotland, Wales, and Northern Ireland and the introduction of mayoral elections for London, has introduced different proportional systems of elections into the UK. The traditional, "winner takes all", First Past the Post (FPP) system remains for Parliamentary elections and local elections in England and Wales and Scotland. Elections to the European Parliament are conducted on the basis of a regional list system. The additional member system is used for the Scottish Parliament and Welsh Assembly, and the London Assembly. A supplementary vote system is used for the London mayoral election, and Northern Ireland operates a Single Transferable Vote (STV) system for all elections with the exception of elections to the

7–001

7–002

---

1 Robert Blackburn, *The Electoral System in Britain* (London: Macmillan, St Martin's Press, 1995).
2 A detailed account is provided in The House of Commons Library, *General Election* 2015, Briefing Paper CBP7186 (28 July 2015).

268 THE ELECTORATE, POLITICS AND THE CONSTITUTION

7-003 UK Parliament from Northern Ireland. The plethora of new voting systems only serves to show the striking anomaly which is the FPP system for the British general election to Westminster. In time this is likely to be amended, though in what way is less than certain.

It is also clear that referendums have an important role in the transition to new constitutional structures. An important aspect of democratic government is the growing use of referendums. The referendum on 23 June 2016 resulted in a decision to leave the UK (51.9%) as opposed to remain (48.9%). The European Union Referendum Act 2015 was passed to pave the way for the referendum.[3] The procedures including financial controls and expenditure are set out in the enabling legislation.

7-004 In addition to the formal and institutional changes noted above, a shift has occurred in the traditional balance of powers between elected and non-elected elements of the constitution. First, there is general dissatisfaction with the standards of politics and the public perception about the poor standing of the political parties is shown by the low turnout at elections: at the general election in 2001, turnout was disappointingly low at only 59.4 per cent, but elections in 2005, 2010 and 2015 the turnout was around 65 per cent. Yet the UK today has more systems of election and more opportunities for electoral choices than ever in its history. Despite, or perhaps because of this mismatch between the opportunities for citizen participation and voter satisfaction with the result, there is an ever-increasing quest for an accurate assessment of the political mood of the nation. Finally, in 1999 the abolition of the hereditary principle for membership of the House of Lords resulted in 92 hereditary members, 90 members, being elected from the list of the soon to be abolished hereditary peers. The future reform and likely composition of the House of Lords is unclear at present, but rests on the question of what percentage of the Lords should continue to be appointed and what percentage elected. The failure of the House of Lords Reform Bill 2012 to be passed is likely to postpone reform of the House of Lords for some time to come and for the foreseeable future.

B: What are Electoral Systems Intended to Achieve?

7-005 The concepts of citizenship and participation depend on an effective electoral system. As Blackburn[4] has observed:

> "The crucial democratic link between politicians and people—or government and the governed—is the electoral system. The quality of that electoral system itself determines the quality of our democracy."

---

3 House of Commons Briefing Paper, *The EU referendum campaign*, No.7486 (27 January 2016).
4 House of Commons Briefing Paper, *The EU referendum campaign*, p.1.

7-006 Yet oddly for many commentators in the UK, supreme authority has never resided in the people.[5] Over the past few decades great attention has been given to the question of whether the current electoral system in the UK lives up to these high ideals. No one can doubt that the debate on electoral reform is an important element in any healthy democracy. However, the future of electoral reform is difficult to predict following the referendum held on 5 May 2011 on whether the system of elections for MPs to the House of Commons should be changed to an alternative vote system replacing FPP resulted in a clear 68 per cent no and only 32 per cent. Over 6 million voters voted in favour of change while 13 million voted against with a small turnout of only 41.9 per cent. Many reasons for voter "apathy" might be given, perhaps a certain inertia or even indifference about the need for reform. The timing of the referendum may not have been best for the pro-reformers as the Conservative Party could argue for the current status quo of the simplicity of FPP, even though their coalition partners, the Liberal Democrats were in favour. It will take some time for reform to gain momentum once more.

7-007 The UK is described as having representative and responsible government within a parliamentary democracy. The nature of that democracy depends on the electoral system. The relative political stability of the UK is attributed to the electoral system and the development of strong political parties. The fact that a government is able to command a strong majority sets the remit on how government governs and their attitude to party political power and Parliament itself.

7-008 It must be remembered that the modern system of parliamentary elections gradually evolved from the nineteenth century. Progress towards universal adult franchise and the elimination of election corruption was gradual. The development of the present electoral system is due more to pragmatism than the adoption of a theoretical ideal system. No pretence is made that present arrangements are ideal, rather that they produce strong government and therefore are seen to leave choice with the electorate.

7-009 Elected government raises questions about accountability, the representative nature of government and the powers of government in the House of Commons. Also important are the growth and influence of political parties and the use of the electoral manifesto and public opinion when considering how the policies of government are made. Increasingly relevant are the influences of pressure groups, the media and the press on government policy making.

7-010 Constitutional lawyers are particularly concerned with the question of how parliamentary accountability and sovereignty are compatible; this raises one of the most difficult issues under the UK's constitutional arrangements. Johnson, writing[6] in 1975, fears that over the years there has been "a retreat from constitutional ways of thinking in Britain". This makes it more difficult to set limits on the powers of government and uncertainty arises as to the principles which govern many of "the institutions and practices, political habits and modes of behaviour".

7-011 In recent times criticism of the electoral system has focused on two issues. First, what may be termed "institutional" criticism summarised by Ganz[7] to mean

---

5   See C. Turpin, *British Government and the Constitution*, 3rd edn (London: Butterworths, 1995), p.417.
6   N. Johnson, *In Search of the Constitution* (London: Methuen, 1977), pp.vii–viii. See Table 1, p.69.
7   G. Ganz, *Understanding Public Law*, 3rd edn (London: Fontana, 1994), p.4.

> "that the elected part of Parliament, namely the House of Commons, having achieved supremacy over the unelected parts, namely the Queen and the House of Lords have summoned its sovereignty to the government which controls it through the party machine."

7-012 This represents a profound challenge to the idea of elected and accountable democratic government. Secondly, criticism is made that the UK's electoral system of "first past the post" has a discriminatory effect against minority parties. The UK and recently Italy, stand out from other European countries in adopting a FPP system of elections for central government. This is said to favour strong government with a decisive majority. In fact, coalition governments were not uncommon before the Second World War when governments were formed on a multi-party arrangement. Election results, since the Second World War, show a marked disparity between votes cast and seats gained in the House of Commons. Turpin notes that a party can be put in power with far less than a majority of votes and may govern without having to accommodate its policies to the interests of a majority of voters represented by the other parties in Parliament. Such alleged unfairness in the voting system has resulted in calls for reform of the current electoral system for central government, and the introduction of some form of proportional representation. The question of further progress largely depends on the judgment of the major political parties and the government of the day.

7-013 The Coalition Government 2005–2010 created a document of 30 pages *Programme for Government* that attempted to address the combined party manifestos of both Conservative and Liberal Democrat partners. The Fixed-Term Parliaments Act 2011 became a constitutional framework that ensured that whatever differences might arise, the coalition had a major incentive to survive the full five years, for fear that the party that triggered an election before that time might not receive electoral support. Under the framework of Coalition government many working arrangements grew and certainly raised concerns about the way major issues on Scottish independence, the EU and human rights were handled.

C: Parliamentary Democracy, Origins, Ideas and Influences

7-014 Different meanings are accorded to the idea of democracy. In countries with written constitutions, it is customary to locate the sources of power, the authority of the constitution and the basis of law as resting on the people.[8] This is an aspiration, even an ideal that may be

---

8   See the United States Constitution, and the Japanese Constitution drafted on the American model in 1946.

unattainable given the reality of how power is in fact exercised. Such constitutional idealism places individual rights at the centre of the values which are sought to be protected. This creates a constitutional tradition where the political and legal institutions are made to conform to set values and rights. In such a tradition the protection of minorities or diverse groups is made an aspiration as part of the creation of a stable and diverse community. Such a tradition of constitutional idealism is illustrated in countries such as the US which offer individual rights and constitutional protections as part of their constitutional arrangements. Even countries with one party states may offer constitutional arrangements which appear to give democratic authority to the people as a means of providing some form of legitimacy for government.

In the UK, history and tradition have contributed to a different political tradition than the constitutional idealism discussed above. Solutions are worked out according to experience and institutions are expected to operate flexibly and develop as a response to experience and the needs of the time. The UK's tradition developed historically and the principles which have influenced its development, such as parliamentary sovereignty, conventions and majority government, are a reflection of that political development.

7–015

The evolution of parliamentary democracy and the ideals of democracy fit uneasily within the doctrine of parliamentary sovereignty. This is better understood when two different meanings of sovereignty are compared. First, legal sovereignty, as outlined in earlier chapters, is far removed from the people, as it is vested to the Crown in Parliament. A government with an overall majority is freer than in most other democratic countries to introduce its own legislative programmes with the likelihood of their passage into law. As in theory Parliament is free "to make or unmake any law", this provides considerable scope for government to exercise public power.

7–016

Secondly, there is political sovereignty. Political sovereignty emphasises the elected nature and authority of government. Political scientists[9] find it helpful to understand that the legitimacy of government depends on its elected and representative nature. Constitutional lawyers have been greatly influenced by Dicey's attempts to reconcile parliamentary sovereignty with popular franchise.

7–017

Dicey, parliamentary sovereignty and popular democracy

Reforms in the electoral franchise in 1832 and 1867 gradually moved the UK towards a popular franchise. Existing governmental institutions survived but were subtly changed. Effectively the House of Commons became the centre of political power and determined the composition of the government. There was no fixed idea of democratic government and no theoretical model to which political and legal institutions were expected to conform. Instead parliamentary democracy gradually evolved.

7–018

---

9   Ben Syed, "Electoral Systems and Party Funding" in J. Jowell and D. Oliver (eds), *The Changing Constitution*, 4th edn (Oxford: Oxford University Press, 2000), p.293.

7-019 Dicey's vision of constitutional and administrative law in the UK, and how any extension of the franchise might be accommodated within existing frameworks and institutions, is relevant in understanding how parliamentary sovereignty and popular franchise challenged the established order. Dicey recognised the importance of legal sovereignty but conveniently distinguished legal from political sovereignty. In his essay[10] "Democracy in England in 1880", Dicey outlined his belief that "English democracy depended on love of order, the spirit of ordinary morality as the guide to public life and of constitutional morality" and in Dicey's view secured the sovereignty of the people. The clear implication was that political power must be tempered by obedience to the norms of the Constitution—a view advanced out of fear that popular franchise posed a threat to the natural order maintained under the Constitution.

7-020 Dicey's attempt to reconcile his vision of democracy with his description of the main constitutional doctrines in the Constitution was fundamentally challenged both by his contemporaries and recent writers. His thesis rested on two premises: first, that the power of Parliament could be used to control government because "the will of the nation" was represented in the House of Commons; secondly, that democracy could be "self-correcting" namely, the flexibility inherent in an unwritten constitution allowed change but preserved the sovereignty of Parliament and the rule of law.

7-021 The challenge to Dicey's views came from contemporary writers of the period and succeeded in convincing Dicey of some errors in his views, which received a belated acknowledgement from Dicey in his later writing. However, this did not cause any major re-think of the propositions Dicey advanced. Dicey's attempted reconciliation of the rule of law and sovereignty of Parliament revealed further weaknesses in his own analysis. Irish Home Rule in the late nineteenth century was influential in Dicey's thinking.

7-022 A number of conclusions may be deduced from Dicey's formulation of constitutional principles with the experience of democratic, elected and popular government. First, when the rule of law is challenged by Parliament, it is parliamentary sovereignty which remains supreme. Craig observes[11]:

> "If the majority within Parliament does enact legislation which is detrimental to minority interests, no sanctions can be expected from the Common law. When representative democracy proves incapable of aligning the interests of the elected representatives with the nation as a whole, so that some are constitutionally disadvantaged, the oppressed can but hope for a shift in their political fortune."

7-023 Secondly, the "advance in democracy" whereby the franchise was broadened, hastened the development of party politics. Votes were won rather than bought. The Executive demanded

---

10 A.V. Dicey, 13 June 1880, *Nation*; and J. F. McEldowney, "Dicey in Historical Perspective—A Review Essay" in Patrick McAuslan and John F. McEldowney (eds), *Law, Legitimacy and the Constitution* (London: Sweet & Maxwell, 1985), pp.47–60.
11 P. Craig, "Dicey, Unitary, Self-Correcting Democracy" (1990) 106 *Law Quarterly Review* 105–143.

more control over the activities of the Commons as Cabinet Committees proliferated; delegated legislation increased in range and extent and gradually power moved from the Commons to the Executive. These developments put strain on Dicey's vision of the ideal Constitution to the extent that it may be questioned whether it destroyed the vision entirely. In Dicey's later writings contained in his lectures[12] on the relation between law and public opinion in England during the nineteenth century, Dicey refined and broadened his understanding of democracy as including either a social condition or a form of government. The former he drew from de Tocqueville, that democracy created "a state of things under which there exists a general equality of rights and a similarity of conditions of thoughts, of sentiments and of ideals". The latter, influenced by Austin, he defined in its "older sense" to mean "a form of government; namely a constitution under which sovereign power is possessed by the numerical majority of the male citizens".

7-024

Dicey found the referendum mechanism a useful tool to counterbalance the tendency to party politics in government which he feared contributed to the decline of Parliament's prestige. A referendum also emphasised the role of the people as part of the political sovereignty of the nation. Dicey's vision of the unity of the UK provides a link between elections to Parliament and, through the House of Commons, the authority of the government of the day. That vision is an uncomplicated vision of a single unitary state wherein change could easily be accommodated through the politics of the day, while guarded against by the morality of the Constitution through the supremacy of the law. Conventions of the Constitution provided "a modern code" but undoubtedly it distracted the balance implicit in Dicey's "self-correcting" vision of the Constitution.

7-025

Contemporary writers such as Bagehot[13] realised that parliamentary democracy did not always entail the "election of just and moderate men". Legislation might distort and change the fundamentals of the Constitution. Instead of representative democracy, policies became party political dominated by a single leader controlling a Cabinet government. Belatedly, Dicey recognised this threat in the form of home rule in Ireland and in the passage of administrative legislation granting wide discretion, largely unsupervised, to administrators.

7-026

Craig[14] concludes how Dicey's influence has endured despite much criticism and weakness in his analysis:

> "The realisation that political and social developments had undermined many of the premises upon which Dicey has built his constitutional doctrine was never truly appreciated by the immediate successors to Dicey in the field of constitutional scholarship. They were content to draw upon Dicey's conclusions without ever evaluating the reasoning through which those conclusions were reached."

---

12   A.V. Dicey, *Lectures on the Relation between Law and Public Opinion in England during the Nineteenth Century* (1908) (London: Macmillan, 1963).
13   W. Bagehot, (R. S. Crossman (ed)), *The English Constitution* (1867) (London: Kegan Paul & Co, 1891).
14   P. Craig, "Dicey, Unitary, Self-Correcting Democracy" (1990) 106 *Law Quarterly Review* 105–143.

7-027

By the end of the nineteenth century, parliamentary democracy brought with it the recognition that party discipline might curtail the independence of individual MPs; that debate in the House of Commons may be curtailed by procedures which favoured the Executive; and that the Cabinet rather than the House of Commons exercised real political power. This leaves unresolved the question raised by Turpin that "if the people were acknowledged in constitutional theory as the source of political authority debates on these matters would be conducted in different terms". In a similar way Keir writing about parliamentary democracy for the period 1867–1937 identified the[15] "distinctive characteristics" within the UK's constitutional arrangements which may influence future developments[16]:

> "In the modern state, an extended executive able to make, enforce, and interpret law, has come into being under imperfect parliamentary and judicial control. The principles of the separation of powers have been violated. Considerations of 'policy and government' as they would have been called in the seventeenth century, have been accorded a larger place in the constitution than they have held for two hundred years."

7-028

The life cycle of politics means that political power is constantly shifting, while the institutions of government are often remarkably static. Pre-eminence given to elected government in the UK system leaves the potential for conflict between elected and unelected elements of government. This leaves unelected judges often having to give due deference to political policy making.

7-029

One of the remarkable features of the UK's political system is the two-party system. Government and a single "official opposition" is mainly a reflection of the electoral system and has a physical manifestation in the architectural design and shape of the House of Commons. Thus adversarial politics are encouraged and seen as part of the political culture of the country. The failure of smaller parties to make any inroads into the power of the Conservative or Labour Party is also a feature of the existing state of the political parties. The major parties seem remarkably agile at providing a broad range of options to favour the widest possible appeal. In fact, as Colley has observed[17]

> "...since 1885 the Conservatives have been the single dominant party for 85 years. By contrast, in only 18 of these 107 years has a single party other than the Conservatives had a clear Commons majority. In other words, the one party dominance that characterised British politics so often in the 18th and 19th centuries has become if anything still more pronounced in this century."

---

15 D. Keir, *Constitutional History of Modern Britain* (London: Black, 1938), p.520.
16 Keir, *Constitutional History of Modern Britain*, p.520.
17 Linda Colley, "The Illusion of a Two-Party State", *The Independent*, 28 October 1992.

Parliamentary franchise 1832–1948

The Representation of the People Act 1832, known as the Great Reform Act, represents the starting point for modern elected government. The 1832 Act was intended to broaden the franchise and introduce a more fair and representative system of elections. Keir described the reforms as introducing[18]

> "organic changes which reflected the increasing ascendancy of the radical thought stimulated by Bentham and reinforced by the democratic impulse received from the doctrine of the French revolution."

The Act maintained the influence of property rights, but property other than land fulfilled the qualification necessary to be included within the franchise. Old boroughs were abolished, and the population shift to the towns was for the first time represented in the franchise. New boroughs were created and this process of reform applied throughout the country. The 40-shilling freeholder was retained but an additional residence qualification was added. New qualifications in terms of copyholders, leaseholders and tenants at will with rent not less than £50, were included.

In counties, tenants at will were retained and this preserved and continued the landlord's influence. An entirely new qualification, that of the £10 occupier, was created. The outcome of these reforms was to increase the electorate by 50 per cent, adding 217,000 to the electoral total of those qualified to vote.

The significance of the 1832 Act was remarkable. In previous chapters we have noted how, in constitutional terms, incremental change accompanied organic growth. Reform of the electorate introduced by the 1832 Act resulted in a marked shift in political power and influence from the unelected to the elected. This change only became noticeable gradually. In the case of patronage and royal influence the decline in royal power over the Cabinet had been gradual. In 1834 after royal attempts to influence the appointment of the Prime Minister and ministers through the selection of Sir Robert Peel, Peel failed to obtain a majority at a general election and royal influence was rejected.

The 1832 Act also introduced a new procedure for registration of voters. This began a process of law reform which proved significant in shaping the modern law.

In 1867 the Representation of the People Act introduced the vote for many urban workers and extended new categories of eligible voters in boroughs to include lodgers and certain occupations. Even after 1867, the electorate was entirely male and this principle had been upheld by the courts. A further extension of the franchise was achieved under the 1884 Representation of the People Act which, by extending the franchise to certain householders in counties, enfranchised agricultural workers.

It is difficult to estimate the effects of both the 1867 Act and the 1884 Representation of the People Act as many qualified voters may have failed to register. It is estimated that apparently only 60 per cent of adult males were on the register before 1914.

---

18 Keir, *Constitutional History of Modern Britain*, p.595.

7-037 In 1918 a considerable achievement was made in introducing universal adult male suffrage, by sweeping away the old complex property qualification. Instead of property, there was a residence qualification, requiring living in the constituency or adjoining constituency six months before a qualifying date. There was also a business and university qualification. This shift from property to residence as the basis of the qualification significantly broadened the franchise. For the first time a limited franchise for women over 30 was granted and, in 1928, for women over 21.

7-038 In 1945 the Representation of the People Act joined the local government franchise to that of central government. Three years later the business and university franchise was removed thus introducing the principle of "one man one vote". The 1948 Representation of the People Act also provided that only one member of Parliament should be returned for each constituency. The modern system of popular vote or universal franchise had been achieved.

D: The Electorate

7-039 The Representation of the People Act 2000 has reformed and consolidated the registration of voters for both parliamentary and local elections. In addition, there have been changes on party political funding and the administration of the electoral system introduced by the political parties, Elections and Referendums Act 2000. The potential impact of art.3 of the European Convention on Human Rights on free elections, and art.10 on the freedom of expression has to be taken into account in electoral law under the Human Rights Act 1998. Since 1948 a number of changes in the franchise have been made in the direction of further extending the principle of universal franchise. First, the voting age was lowered from 21 to 18 in 1969 under the Representation of the People Act 1969. The age period for entitlement to be on the electoral register is based on whether the citizen reaches 18 during the period of the register. As soon as the citizen reaches 18, he or she may vote. Secondly, for the first time under the 1969 Act, merchant seamen may register as if they were resident at a home address or hostel. Thirdly, the Representation of the People Act 1985 introduced overseas voting. Any British citizen resident overseas, provided their residence in the UK was within the preceding five years, is entitled to vote.[19] Fourthly, the Representation of the People Act 2000 provides changes to the system of registration and introduces flexibility to the electoral register by allowing names to be added or deleted. It is possible for an elector to become registered during the year, replacing the concept of a fixed electoral register. In order to be qualified as an elector, s.1 of the Representation of the People Act 1983 stipulates that:

---

19   Representation of the People Act 1985, ss.1–3. See s.59 of the Representation of the People Act 1993.

- you must be registered on the register of parliamentary electors for the constituency and you are only entitled to vote once in any parliamentary constituency and you cannot vote in more than one constituency; and

- electors must be 18 years or above on the date of the poll, be either a Commonwealth citizen or a citizen of the Republic of Ireland and not be subject to any legal incapacity to vote.

7-040

The Representation of the People Act 1983 provided, under s.5 criteria to judge the circumstances for a person to be in residence. The Representation of the People Act 2000 adds to the criteria. The courts have taken a broad and purposive interpretation under art.3 of the Convention in *Hipperstone v Newbury Electoral Officer*.[20] This permitted protestors at Greenham Common to claim that their makeshift temporary accommodation used while making their protest was sufficient to allow them to register as voters.

7-041

The Representation of the People Act 2000 makes more generous provision to qualify as a voter:

- service voters, on making a service declaration may be qualified to register in the normal way or as an overseas voter;

- overseas voters on making an overseas elector's declaration may be qualified;

- mental patients may be registered provided they fulfil the requirement of residence in their mental institution;

- prisoners remanded in custody may be eligible to vote subject to the requirements of residence;

- remand prisoners and patients in mental hospitals may be registered;

- homeless people provided there is an available address for night or day will be eligible to become registered; and

- postal votes are available to any eligible voter. This makes postal voting a viable option for many people who in the past were unable to qualify. At the 2001 election it is estimated that 1.4 million used a postal vote, an increase from 738,614 postal votes issued in 1997. In 2010 over 15 per cent of the electorate had a postal vote and the figures for May 2015 suggest a further increase.

---

20 [1985] Q.B. 1060; [1985] 3 W.L.R. 61 CA (Civ Div).

7-042 Disqualification includes aliens, minors under 18, peers and hereditary peers no longer able to sit in the House of Lords, convicted persons detained in penal institutions, and those disqualified for five years because of a corrupt practice.

7-043 The Coalition government took forward further changes to the electoral arrangements aimed to reduce fraud and move from household registration to individual registration. The Northern Ireland Assembly already has a system of individual registration under the Electoral Fraud (Northern Ireland) Act 2002. The Electoral Registration and Administration Act 2013 maintains the annual updating and renewal of the electoral register in the area of registration. Reserve powers are provided for the relevant minister to abolish this requirement, presumably pending the introduction of an individual registration scheme rather than on the basis of the current system of household registration. The registration officer is give a wider discretion to include a person in the relevant registration area to apply for registration. There are also civil penalties that may be imposed by registration officers for a breach of the registration procedures. The new register prepared under the Act was first used in the May election 2015[21] but this is still on the basis of household registration. Maintaining and updating the register is funded through up to £9.8 million of public money. One particular concern is the registration of young people and students. The Electoral Commission provides research and analysis of the voting registration system. It is expected that individual registration will be actively taken forward from the summer of 2015.

The Electoral Registration and Administration Act 2013 and individual registration

7-044 Individual voter registration is set to take up from the previous registration system based on the register prepared for the end of December 2015. The introduction of the new arrangements is being monitored by the Electoral Commission with a system of regular reporting on registration. There are concerns that some voters may not be registered under the new system especially students and part-time workers or causal workers moving from job to job. The progress to move to the new arrangements may end up with fewer registrations. The December 2015 electoral register will be used as part of the Boundary Commission's review of electoral boundaries for the next election.[22]

Constituency boundaries

7-045 Since 1911, s.7 of the Parliament Act 1911 has required the maximum duration of Parliament to be five years. The Fixed-Term Parliaments Act 2011 introduced five-year fixed-term Parliaments. The number of constituencies is divided up between the different parts of the UK.

---

21   House of Commons Library, *Individual Electoral Registration*, SN/PC/06764 (3 February 2015).
22   House of Commons Library, *Individual Electoral Registration*.

Constituency size is roughly 60,000 people though there are variations on this. The drawing up of constituency boundaries, a key feature of the reformed electoral arrangements since 1832, is one of the most controversial issues of electoral practice. Electoral boundaries have a critical influence on determining electoral results.

Since 1944, for central government there are four permanent and independent Boundary Commissions for England, Scotland, Wales and Northern Ireland. This system is to be changed by the creation of an Electoral Commission set out below. The Speaker is chairman of each Commission with a deputy chairman appointed from the High Court. Reports from the Boundary Commission are laid before the House of Commons by the Secretary of State together with a draft Order in Council to give effect to the Commissions' recommendations. The draft order must be approved by resolution of each House before the final order is approved by the Queen in Council. This process is not without problems. In 1969 the then Labour Government was in receipt of the Commissions' recommendations in April. No action was taken until June, notwithstanding the obligation to take action "as soon as may be" possible to lay a resolution before the House of Commons. When the resolutions were laid, no attendant Orders in Council accompanied the proposals. A Bill intended to implement the proposals and providing the Home Secretary with immunity because of any breach of duty was introduced. The Bill did not pass the House of Lords.

Mandamus was sought by an elector, Mr McWhirter,[23] to compel the Home Secretary to lay a draft Order in Council in accordance with the 1949 and 1958 Acts. The Home Secretary duly agreed to comply and the mandamus application was withdrawn. In the event a Bill was introduced with a positive recommendation by the Government to reject it. The Government used its majority and in that event the Bill was rejected. The Government had made use of its majority to influence the outcome, when the spirit of the arrangements was intended to prevent direct political intervention by the government of the day. The ensuing election had to be fought on the old 1954 boundaries and not the new ones. After 1970 when the Conservative Government was returned the new boundaries were implemented.

The controversial nature of the drawing up of the boundaries was recognised when Parliament set up the Boundary Commission[24] with rules contained in the 1949 and 1958 Acts. The events outlined above showed how a cynical use of power could frustrate Parliament's intentions.

There is no exact science in drawing up constituency boundaries, and predicting the outcome of any proposed changes is often difficult. An attempt to set out legislative rules for the line drawing of constituency boundaries was made in 1986. The Parliamentary Constituencies Act 1986 consolidated previous legislation, and in Sch.2 contains rules for the redistribution of seats. The Parliamentary Voting System and Constituencies Act 2011 amended the Parliamentary Constituencies Act 1986 be introducing regular Boundary Commission reviews every five years rather than past practice of between eight to twelve years. The Act also introduced a new set of principles to attempt to secure greater equality between the distribution

---

23   *R v Home Secretary Ex p. McWhirter* (1969) 119 N.L.J. 926; Times, October 21, 1969 Div Ct.
24   *R v Boundary Commission for England Ex p. Foot* [1983] Q.B. 600; [1983] 2 W.L.R. 458 CA (Civ Div) at [603].

of seats in constituencies. Numerical equality is viewed as preferable to geographical location which might favour the Conservative Party over Labour. Implementation of the new principles was delayed by the Liberal Democrats while in coalition passing the Electoral Registration and Administration Act 2013 which amended the Parliamentary Voting System and Constituencies Act 2011, and this resulted in the May 2015 elections being fought under the old boundaries and not the new principles. The new principles will not be part of a boundary review until 2018.

7-051
Currently there are 650 seats, Wales has 40, Northern Ireland, 18 and Scotland 59 seats.[25]

7-052
The rules are complex and difficult to interpret. Broadly they are as follows: r.1 sets the number of seats for each of the four parts of the UK; r.2 requires that only one member may be retained for each constituency; r.3 applies to the city of London only; rr.4–6 set out how boundaries are to be drawn for each constituency; and r.7 provides for any variation or departure from the rules set out in rr.4–6, but there is considerable scope for interpretation of each of the rules.

Rawlings has pointed out that[26]

> "the Commission will clearly be well advised not to allow an excessive growth in Welsh and Scottish constituencies given that the seat minimum set out in rule 1 even if not exceeded, still incorporate a substantial measure of over-representation."

7-053
Such imbalance may appear odd in a modern electoral system, but this is a reflection of the historical development of electoral rules. Northern Ireland received additional seats after the demise of the system of self-government with its own elected Parliament under the Government of Ireland Act 1920. The introduction of devolution in 1998 has not resulted in any re-adjustment. However, in the future it is clear that adjustments to the seats accorded to the four geographical regions may have to be made after the introduction of devolution in Northern Ireland, Scotland and Wales.

7-054
Interpretation of rr.4 and 5 involves how the boundaries of each seat should be determined. Rule 4 provides principles for local government boundaries. Rule 5 provides the objective for the drawing up of the boundaries, namely the achievement of equal-sized constituencies in numerical numbers of electors.

7-055
Reconciliation of rr.4 and 5 is controversial and was the basis of an important challenge in the courts by the Labour Party in 1983. Some explanation of each rule is required.

7-056
Rule 4 involves the Commission determining an electoral boundary for each constituency taking account of local government boundaries. Since 1976 the changes in population growth and in the movement from inner cities to outlying regions caused distortion in the sizes of constituency electorates. This resulted in disparity between constituencies, with nearly 30 per cent

---

25 House of Commons Library Briefing Paper, *General Election 2015*, CBP7186 (18 May 2015).
26 See H. F. Rawlings, *Law and the Electoral Process* (London: Sweet & Maxwell, 1988), pp.24–72.

over quota in one example of the proposed constituencies of Hornsey & Wood Green and nearly 15 per cent under quota in Hendon South.

7–057 Rule 5 involves the Commission setting an electoral quota taking account "as far as is practicable" of the geographical limits set for the local government boundaries. The application of this principle of equal constituencies, in terms of number of electors, was rendered almost impossible by the requirements of the local government boundaries set out in r.4.

7–058 In 1982 the Commission completed its review and made proposals to correct imbalances between constituencies taking account of the demographic changes mentioned above. A number of constituencies were removed from the Greater London Council area. In order to keep within the physical limitations of r.5, great distortion arose in the constituency size in terms of the number of voters represented. The two examples of Hornsey & Wood Green, and Hendon South showed the disparity. Criticism was made that the Commission's proposals violated the principle of one vote having equal value in every constituency.

7–059 The Labour Party believed the proposals were unfavourable to their electoral prospects. Before the Boundary Commission Report was brought before Parliament, and to avoid exclusion from judicial review by the courts once the Report was approved, the Labour Party through its then leader, Mr Foot, sought the remedies of prohibition and injunction against the Boundary Commission. Their contention was based on two arguments:

(1) that the Commission had failed to give proper weight to r.5 containing the principle of equal representation between constituencies; and

(2) the Commission was failing in its duty to propose constituencies which crossed county and London Borough boundaries. The point of this argument was to insist that the Commission ought to give primacy to r.5 in practice.

7–060 Unsuccessful in the Divisional Court, the applicants appealed to the Court of Appeal. Sir John Donaldson first asserted the correctness of the courts' powers to check whether ministers or local authorities or other bodies including the Commission had exercised their powers according to law—"the courts can and will interfere in the defence of the ordinary citizen". He went on to conclude[27] as between rr.4 and 5:

> **"The requirement of electoral equality (Rule 5) is, subject to the second limb of Rule 5, subservient to the requirements that constituencies shall not cross county or London Borough boundaries."**

---

27   R v Boundary Commission for England Ex p. Foot [1983] Q.B. 600; [1983] 2 W.L.R. 458 CA (Civ Div) at [603].

7-061 The second limb of r.5 authorises departure from r.4 only where[28] "it is desirable to avoid an excessive disparity between the electorate of any constituency and the electoral quota". However, in the argument advanced by the Labour Party it was claimed that the Commission had exercised their discretion wrongly. The Court of Appeal concluded that the Commission had exercised such a discretion but it was exercised on sufficient grounds. Any objection based on this argument was rejected by the court.

7-062 The Court of Appeal upheld the Commission's proposals and rejected the application, leave was later refused to the House of Lords.

7-063 One effect of the courts' interpretation is the primacy and respect for local government boundaries (r.4) over equal representation between constituencies (r.5). However, the Court of Appeal entered a caveat in certain circumstances where disparity between electoral boundaries might be unacceptable[29]

> "the theoretical possibility that in a given instance the disparity between the electorate of a proposed constituency and the electoral quota might be so grotesquely large as to make it obvious in the figures that no reasonable commission which had paid any attention at all to rule 5 could possibly have made such a proposal."

7-064 Leaving open the possibility of reviewing any disparity in the electoral quota which is "grotesquely large" for the future, must cause the Boundary Commission difficulty for the years ahead in the balance needed between rr.4 and 5. In fact up until the *Foot* case the courts have shown remarkable consistency in self-restraint in this area. This is shown in the judgment of Oliver LJ in the *Foot* case arguing that judicial intervention is inappropriate in boundary disputes. For the future it might be advisable to reconsider the formula "as near the electoral quota as possible" and substitute precise guidelines to the Boundary Commission in terms of the percentage of divergence which is permissible.

7-065 Such criticisms are not shared by all commentators. As MPs are said to be constituency trained, they will not favour cross-boundary constituency work which may entail two or more local authorities. Departure from local boundaries adds to the Boundary Commission's task and complexity. Perhaps the most difficult problem at the heart of the matter is how to preserve community participation in electoral activities, when shifts in population change the nature of the community. However, popularity of voting has not been inhibited by boundary changes. Electoral turnout at central government elections is well over 70 per cent of the electorate so it may be asked, do electoral boundaries really matter? The answer depends largely on party politics. It is rather difficult to find any precise constitutional basis for any objection to the electoral system. There is a sense of constitutional propriety, meaning that government may lose its political authority if it does not pay sufficient attention

---

28 *R v Boundary Commission for England Ex p. Foot* [1983] Q.B. 600 at [603].
29 *R v Boundary Commission for England Ex p. Foot* [1983] Q.B. 600 at [603].

to the electorate.[30] In theory government is said to be representative, even if in practice the Commission appears to need to be given greater priority to achieve equality between constituencies.

The Electoral Commission

The creation of an independent body to oversee the regulation of elections and electoral administration has been advocated by a number of reports.[31] The details of the new Electoral Commission are contained in Pt 1 of the Political Parties, Elections and Referendums Act 2000. The new Electoral Commission was set up in October 2000. There is a Boundary Commission with separate Boundary Commissions for England, Scotland and Northern Ireland. The Secretary of State will no longer be able to modify the Commission's recommendations regarding constituency boundaries. Recommendations are expected to be laid before Parliament by draft Order in Council. The main functions of the Electoral Commission are:

7–066

- to oversee regulation of the political process such as spending arrangements and the preparation of an annual report on all elections;

- reviewing and reporting on election law and related matters, referendums, distribution of seats at parliamentary elections, boundary changes, and the registration of political parties;

- to be consulted on any reforms on electoral law; and

- to keep the public informed of electoral systems and the method of elections for the different tiers of government and for Europe.

The status of the Electoral Commission is comparable to the National Audit Office. Appointments to the Commission are formally made by the Queen, but by approval of the Speaker of the House. There is scope for party political representation with the establishment of a Parliamentary Parties Panel to provide input into the deliberations of the Commission. The Electoral Commission will consist of between five and nine office holders but they must not have had any connection with a political party ten years prior to their appointment.

7–067

---

30   See R. Blackburn, *The Electoral System in Britain* (London: Macmillan, 1995).
31   The *Jenkins Commission*, Cm.4090 (1998) and the *Neill Committee*, Cm.4057.

E: Election Campaign and Finance

Registration

7-068 Regulation of the conduct of elections is provided for by a number of statutes. The Representation of the People Acts 1983 and 1985 apply to election campaigns, election expenditure and the conduct of elections. The Political Parties, Elections and Referendums Act 2000 is the current law. Underpinning the new system of regulation is a requirement that political parties should be registered, building on the principles set out in the Registration of Political Parties Act 1998. If the candidate is not a member of a political party, then they must describe themselves as independent. There is also a requirement that each political party must register a treasurer responsible for compliance with Pts III and IV of the 2000 Act. It is expected that each political party should have a campaign manager and if one is not appointed then the treasurer is responsible. Nomination papers must be submitted to a returning officer signed by the proposer and seconder, and containing eight other electors. A system of deposits is used; these are forfeited if the candidate fails to obtain one-twentieth of the votes cast. The deposit is usually set at £500. Proposals to increase this amount have received a mixed reaction. In addition, each candidate must make an election return including any details of donations of £50 or more. Candidates are entitled to make use of public rooms for election meetings. Selecting a candidate to represent a political party is an important part of the work of the constituency party. In *Jephson v Labour Party*[32] an industrial tribunal found that a women-only shortlist proposed by the Labour Party breached the Sex Discrimination Act 1975. This had the potential of restraining the selection of candidates through some form of positive discrimination. The Sex Discrimination (Election Candidates) Act 2002 provides a change retrospectively to the Sex Discrimination Act 1975 and removes the application of the 1975 Act to the measures adopted by political parties to reduce inequality in the numbers of men and women selected as candidates. The new arrangements apply to registered political parties and apply to elections held in Northern Ireland as well as Scotland and Wales but rune out by 2030 unless renewed by Parliament.

7-069 The Equality Act 2010 allows political parties more generally to take steps to promote candidates of under-represented groups within the political party. Discrimination is otherwise unlawful.

Election expenses and accounting requirements

7-070 A long-standing controversial issue, and one of considerable importance in the winning of elections, is the question of election expenditure. Since the end of the nineteenth century, the

---

32 [1996] I.R.L.R. 116.

Corrupt and Illegal Practices Prevention Act 1883 established a limit on election expenses for each candidate.[33] Major political parties are able to spend large sums. It is estimated that in the 2005 election the major parties spent £42.3 million. In 2010, this was £31.1 million, £ 16.7 million by the Conservatives, £8 million by Labour and £4.8 million by the Liberal Democrats. Electoral spending for 2015 is expected to be in line with 2010. Pts III and IV of the Political Parties, Elections and Referendums Act 2000 imposes new duties on political parties with legal controls on the regulation of donations and campaign expenditure.[34] The Political Parties, Elections and Referendum Act 2000 provides a raft of measures aimed to achieve greater accountability and transparency over the election expenses:

- duties are imposed on the treasurer of a political party. These duties vary according to the amount of expenditure. Accounts have to be prepared using a set formula approved by the Electoral Commission where expenditure is greater than £250,000 or less than £5,000. Above £250,000 accounts must be audited. Wide powers are given to the Electoral Commission to monitor these arrangements; and

- controls on Donations to Registered Parties are contained in Pt IV of the Political Parties, Elections and Referendums Act 2000. The most fundamental change is that, following the Neill Committee's recommendation[35] anonymous and foreign donations are banned. The identity of donors must be known and donation is widely defined to cover gifts of money, property or sponsorship of services at less than commercial rate. Donations below £200 may be disregarded and political parties are required to make quarterly returns of donations received in excess of £5,000 from individual donors in any one year. The Electoral Commission prepares a register of all donations. All donations to a political party in excess of £7,500 and £1,500 locally must be reported to the Electoral Commission on a quarterly basis. In 2006 controversy over individual donations to Labour and Conservative parties brought to the fore the question of funding political parties. All the names and details of the donors are published on the Electoral Commission website. There are rules as to who is qualified to be a donor that broadly speaking excludes foreign donors. This has proved more complex as it is possible to be resident overseas and registered on the electoral roll in the UK. The Political Parties and Elections Act 2009 provides additional rules prohibiting donations and loans from persons not resident in the UK for income tax purposes.

There are special provisions for Northern Ireland taking account of the impracticality of banning foreign funding.

7–071

---

33 The present limit for each candidate is approximately £3,648 plus an additional 4.1p for every registered voter in a County constitution or 3.1p in a Borough constituency.
34 House of Commons Library, *Political party funding: sources and regulations*, SN/PC/71217 (16 March 2015).
35 *5th Report from the Committee on Standards in Public Life* (October 1998).

- controls on campaign expenditure are in place for the first time, setting a limit on the ability of the political parties to spend in relation to election campaigns. There is a limit of £30,000 to be spent in any one constituency up to a maximum limit of £810,000 in England, £120,000 in Scotland and £60,000 in Wales for UK Parliamentary elections. In practical terms this means that the limit for the party that fights every seat in each constituency is over £19 million. There is defined a "relevant time" for the calculation of election expenditure and for general elections it is a period of one year before the poll. The definition of campaign expenditure is generously defined to include market research, opinion polls and rallies, transport and the provision of facilities to engage in electioneering. Sch.9 of the Act makes similar provision for European elections and elections to the Scottish Parliament and Welsh Assembly. There are also controls on the involvement of third parties covering individuals or groups. This includes expenses by third parties or groups in connection with election material and in any way promoting or procuring the election of a registered party. Limits are placed on what is termed "controlled expenditure"; and

- controls on political donations and expenditure by companies are also applicable. Sections 139–140 of the Political Parties, Elections and Referendums Act 2000 provide for the first time that shareholders must give approval before making a donation to a political party. This brings the position of company donations into line with an earlier change in the law applying to trade unions. Trade union contributions are covered by the Trade Union Act 1984. Political funds may only be established and maintained after balloted approval has been obtained from the membership within the last ten years. Funds for political objects are affected and the term "political objects" is defined in the 1984 Act as to "relate to activity designed to secure and maintain a candidate in elected office". It is possible that once approved under the 1984 Act, the individual trade union member may opt out of the donation. The means to exercise this right must not cause discrimination among trade union members.

The rules settled under the 2000 Act have left the issue of state funding of political parties unresolved. It is unlikely that state funding will be provided in the foreseeable future because of cuts in public spending to meet the current deficit.

Elections and the Media

7-072 Unlike the USA, in the UK expenditure on TV is precluded, although the parties are entitled to purchase advertising in the press. Advertising on TV or radio in the UK is banned.

7-073 Section 333 of the Communications Act 2003 provides that Ofcom, the main telecommunications regulator for the UK regulates election broadcasting with powers to make rules and regulations including the frequency and timing of Party Political Broadcasts. The BBC and ITC, the Independent Television Commission (the predecessor of the IBA for independent TV), may provide Party Election Broadcasts. Supplementary coverage is provided in news and current affairs programmes, interviews with candidates and general discussion programmes. Both the BBC and ITC seek to establish impartiality in the conduct of election broadcasts and news reports.

7–074

The general test of entitlement to a single electoral broadcast is based on the number of candidates fielded at the election, around 50, though the question of the allocation of broadcast time between the main parties is more difficult to ascertain. One view is that it is based on the allocation of seats in the House of Commons at the dissolution of Parliament before the election. Another view is that the allocation should be based not only on seats won but also on votes obtained.

7–075

The election in May 2015 proved particularly controversial following a consultation on the composition of the list of major political parties in January to February 2015. It was then determined that broadcasters had to offer one broadcast to the parties on the list. The surprising omission was the Green Party, which was unsuccessfully challenged by the party. Ofcom's consultation was important[36] as it revealed some of the difficulties, that might arise, if Britain's main political parties receive only fragmentary support in Scotland and Wales. Section 93 of the Representation of the People Act 1983 requires that each broadcasting authority must have a code of practice. Set piece US style presentation between Government and the Opposition parties is also an area of political conflict. At the May 2015 election the Prime Minister only agreed to one such "debate" and each participant agreed to strict rules of engagement that were agreed before the broadcast took place.

7–076

A number of legal challenges to the criteria for inclusion in Party Political Broadcasts have been made in the past. The Communist Party unsuccessfully challenged the BBC in its allocation of broadcasts. It was argued that the BBC assisted the candidates who were permitted broadcasts and that such expenditure for TV programmes should count against each individual candidate's election expenses. Section 9(4) of the Representation of the People Act 1969 as amended by s.75(1)(c) permits broadcasting authorities to present to the electorate party figures who happen to be candidates, without incurring the problem of each candidate's expenditure maximum for elections.[37]

7–077

The fact that allocation decisions over election broadcasting are amenable to judicial review provides an important safeguard. However, many issues are unresolved. The time schedules of programmes, the content of interviews, and the perspective of the interviewer may all contribute to give one party more favourable exposure than another. The major political parties engage in monitoring television programmes and make claims of political bias whenever appropriate. Claims are made by the smaller parties that the present arrangements favour the two larger parties. Little may be expected to change, as the present arrangements are unlikely to be reformed if they continue to favour the larger parties. One change is that s.144 of the Political Parties, Elections and Referendums Act 2000 provides that each

---

36 A detailed analysis is provided in House of Commons Library, *Political Broadcasts*, SN/PC/03354 (17 March 2015).
37 *Grieve v Douglas-Home* 1965 S.C. 315; 1965 S.L.T. 186 Court for Trial of Election Petitions .

broadcasting authority must adopt a code of practice on local election broadcasting during an election period. The Human Rights Act 1998 introduces the dimension of fairness in the exercise of freedom of expression, for example, under art.10. In *Bowman v UK*[38] an election rule under s.75 of the Representation of the People Act 1983 making it an offence for someone other than a candidate to spend more than £5 on campaigns to elect a candidate, effectively prevented an anti-abortion worker from campaigning at an election. The European Court held this was a violation of art.10. Care must therefore be exercised in assessing the impact of regulating elections to avoid an unfair or discriminatory practice.

7-078 Newspapers also have a dominant role in the election campaigns of the various political parties. Supervising newspaper coverage is equally problematic. Unlike the BBC and ITC which claim impartiality, newspapers are free to be partisan. The Press Council is the body charged with the self-regulation of the newspaper industry. This raises the question of whether there is the need for privacy laws to protect public figures from an intrusive invasion of their personal and private lives. Politicians accept the glare of publicity as a necessary part of their profession, but recent complaints about press behaviour have raised the issue of whether private and personal affairs of public figures should be kept from public scrutiny in the press.

7-079 Many complaints and criticisms are made of press coverage[39] during elections. The fact that newspapers legally support one political party as against another may lead to gross distortions in the news and unfairness to the other parties. Generally, it is accepted that newspapers favourable to the Conservatives outnumber those favourable to Labour. Equally clear is that minority parties may not be represented by the large national newspapers.

7-080 Support for each party brings large-scale donations. In the case of the Conservatives, almost 30 per cent comes from company donations. In the case of the Labour Party, almost 55 per cent comes from trade union donations with a political levy. Donations have fallen as trade union membership has diminished.

7-081 The 1976 Committee on Financial Aid to Political Parties recommended annual grants should be payable from the Exchequer funds to the central organisations of the parties. There is a strong case for state support for political parties especially amidst public concerns about donations. State funding would remove this necessity from political parties and this might change the culture of party finances. In 2004 the Electoral Commission rejected state funding. Sir Hayden Phillips a retired civil servant made an effort to secure all party support for state funding and this proved impossible. The austerity crisis since 2008 makes any likelihood of state funding a remote possibility.

7-082 Individual donations once free from much controversy or legal controls are now made more transparently as all the main political parties have agreed to make public donations. In the past the conditions which may attach to such contributions were hidden from public scrutiny and the implication of this might well be serious if the information regarding conditions was made public. A particularly sensitive question is the suggestion that there might be a link

---

38 (1998) 26 E.H.R.R. 1; 4 B.H.R.C. 25 ECHR.
39 *R v Broadcasting Complaints Commission Ex p. Owen* [1985] Q.B. 1153; [1985] 2 W.L.R. 1025 Div Ct; and H. F. Rawlings, *Law and the Electoral Process* (London: Sweet & Maxwell, 1988), p.207.

between political donations by individuals or companies and the granting of personal honours by the Monarch on the advice of the Prime Minister.

Party politics is the lifeblood of the working Constitution. Political rivalry occupies a central feature of the competition for electoral victory. Fairness ought to be a prominent feature in how parties are funded and how they carry out their activities. Financial advantage to the two larger parties may effectively deprive smaller parties of a fair opportunity to put their case to the electorate.[40]

"Purdah" at central and local elections and referendums

One of the most important aspects of the election system is that the period immediately before central or local government elections or referendums is subject to restrictions on the activity of civil servants.[41] This period is known as "purdah." In the case of elections, purdah is regulated by the Civil Service Code and Civil Service Management Code. In the case of the 2015 general election, the first to be held under the Fixed-Term Parliaments Act 2011, the government announced purdah on the day of the dissolution of Parliament on 30 March 2015 and the period extended until the election was held on 7 May 2015. There is a Code of Recommended Practice on Local Authority Publicity under s.4 of the Local Government Act 1986. Purdah leading up to a referendum is governed by s.125 of the Political Parties, Elections and Referendums Act 2000. Section 125 provides for restrictions on the publication of promotional material by central and local government. The intention is to avoid the machinery of government from being involved in the day to day electoral campaign of the government. This includes the printing, distribution or dissemination of literature setting out government policy at the expense of taxpayers. The referendum in 2011 on the adoption of the alternative vote system to replace FPP was held under the arrangements set by s.125. This included clear instructions to civil servants to act impartially and to avoid announcements, ministerial visits and other activities that may have had an impact on the referendum campaign.

This section is likely to prove controversial when interpreted for a proposed referendum on EU membership. The European Union Referendum Act 2015 provides that restrictions under s.125 do not apply to the referendum on EU membership to be held before 2017. The reason for this "opt out" of s.125 is that there are concerns that the interpretation of s.125 might inhibit the Government's ability "to conduct ordinary day to day EU business".[42] Perhaps more fundamental is the Government's ability to provide an explanation to the public on matters raised by the referendum debate during the course of the run up to the referendum. This is an important

---

40 See H. F. Rawlings, *Law and the Electoral Process* (London: Sweet & Maxwell, 1988), p.207. See Trade Union Act 1913, s.3(1)(b); *Report of the Committee on Financial Aid to Political Parties*, Cmnd.6601 (1976); C. Munro, "Elections and Expenditure" [1976] *Public Law* 300; and *Conservative and Unionist Central Office v Burrell* [1982] 1 W.L.R. 522; [1982] 2 All E.R. 1 CA (Civ Div).
41 House of Commons Library, *"Purdah" before elections and Referenda*, Briefing Paper 05262 (16 July 2015).
42 HC Deb, cc.233–234 (16 June 2015).

point that needs to be addressed before the referendum takes place. An EU referendum is likely to hinge on technical issues about sovereignty and rights that require debate within the political boundaries of those that are in favour of membership and those against.

7–086 The arrangements for the forthcoming European referendum are the subject of a detailed ongoing inquiry undertaken by the Public Administration and Constitutional Affairs Select Committee, due to report before 2017.

7–087 The Scottish independence referendum was regulated under the Scottish Independence Referendum Act 2013. Each jurisdiction-Wales, Scotland and Northern Ireland have their own sets of rules, broadly similar to England's for elections to their devolved administrations.

Europe

7–088 In 1979, direct elections to the European Assembly, now called the European Parliament, were first held. Prolonged negotiations had taken place within the Community to settle the question of the allocation of seats in each Member State. Once the allocation of seats was carried out, each Member State was left to introduce the necessary domestic election law and machinery. In the UK responsibility rested on the Boundary Commission to draw up Assembly boundaries. In Northern Ireland arrangements in place before 1979 had introduced a system of elections for the Northern Ireland Assembly and these arrangements were sufficiently flexible to accommodate European Assembly elections. The arrangement of the electoral system in Northern Ireland was changed to meet the needs of the minority Catholic population by the use of proportional representation rather than the FPP system.

7–089 The European Assembly Elections Act 1978, as amended, provides the main legal framework for elections. The European Parliamentary Elections Act 1999 amends the law and replaces the system of FPP with a regional list system for Scotland, Wales and England. In Northern Ireland the STV system is used. At the Edinburgh summit in December 1992, it was agreed to increase representation to reflect German unification. The European Parliamentary Elections Act 1993 increases the number of representatives for the UK to be elected to the European Parliament. There are 87 seats for the UK. Representation for Scotland and Northern Ireland remains unchanged. The 1993 Act sets up a European Parliamentary Constituencies Committees for each of England and Wales. The work of the Committee is in drawing up constituency boundaries for European Parliamentary Constituencies. Draft recommendations approved by the Secretary of State have to be laid before Parliament for approval. The UK has 73 seats in the 751 member European Parliament with an expected increase in 2024 of 82 seats.[43]

7–090 Doubts about the legality of adopting the British electoral system were raised in Scotland in a court case[44] taken by the Social Democratic Party/Liberal Alliance, that the FPP system was discriminatory, and was in conflict with the spirit of art.138 of the Treaty, which implied equality

---

43 Director General for Internal Policies, *Policy Department Citizen's rights and Constitutional Affairs: The Electoral Reform of the European Parliament: Composition, procedure and legitimacy* (2015), p.12.
44 *Prince v Secretary of State for Scotland* [1984] 1 C.M.L.R. 723; [1985] S.L.T. 74 Ct of Session.

of voting procedures throughout the Community. The UK is alone among other Member States in not having an electoral system based on some form of proportional representation. The Scottish Court refused the application, as inter alia it was doubtful if enforceable rights were created under art.138. There were additional procedural objections to making a reference under art.177 which were not in the applicant's favour owing to problems with how the pleadings were drafted.

This leaves unresolved the question of whether the UK's electoral system is a fair one and ultimately, the question of whether, in the period of debate after the drawing up of the Maastricht Treaty, the UK's electoral system is sufficiently representative. Voter turnout at European Parliament elections was 32.6 per cent in 1979 and 1984, 36.2 per cent in 1989 and 1994. This is relatively low when compared to central government elections. The trend has continued to remain low as in 2009 it was 34.7 per cent, and in 2014, turnout was 34.19 per cent.

F: Manifesto, Mandate and Pressure Groups

Manifesto and mandate

Political parties aspire to become the government. The relationship between the electoral process which influences the selection of the government and the policies of the government once elected, is one of intense and continuous debate. Governments are free to depart from any electoral promise but they do so at the expense of their own popularity. The question of allowing the electorate some influence over the functioning of the government of the day is not easy to address. By-elections caused by the death, illness or retirement of MPs, give an opportunity for the popularity of the Government's policies to be judged by the electorate. Normally a by-election is held within three months of the vacancy occurring. However successful opposition parties may be in winning by-elections, it is difficult to regard such results as accurate predictions of the outcome of a general election or of government popularity. Opinion polls may help gauge public opinion but are not always reliable.

The electorate may exercise some influence over the government of the day through the implications of the electoral policies contained in the party manifesto. Is there a mandate to govern? The idea of electoral mandates has its appeal. It stresses the principle of representative government and that an MP is somehow a "delegate" of the people. However popular this view may appear, it does not accord with historical precedent. Turpin notes the resolution in 1947 of the House of Commons that members of the House of Commons are not delegates[45]

---

45   C. Turpin, *British Government and the Constitution*, 3rd edn (London: Butterworths, 1995), pp.535–539. *Hansard*, HC Vol.440, col.365 (15 July 1947), quoted in Turpin, p.535.

> "...the duty of member being to his constituents, and to the country as a whole rather than to any particular section thereof."

7-094 The independence of MPs is a zealous guarantee of an individual's right to vote according to conscience but the reality of political power seems oddly inconsistent with individual MPs voting according to free will. Party government is the modern form of government and MPs are expected to conform.

7-095 A more realistic view of the practical role attributed to the MP's function is provided by Griffith and Ryle[46]:

> "When a voter at a general election, in that hiatus between Parliaments, puts his cross against the name of a candidate, he is (most often) consciously performing two functions: seeking to return a particular person to the House of Commons as Member for that Constituency; and seeking to return to power as the Government of the country a group of individuals of the same party as that particular person. The voter votes for a representative and a Government."

7-096 Griffith and Ryle's analysis places emphasis on representation as well as government. Not all MPs can be involved in government even if their own party wins the election. The role an MP may adopt may involve membership of a select committee or one of the many backbench committees formed to promote the interests of particular causes. The Conservative Party "1922 Committee" is a good example of the function such a committee may perform. It may warn and criticise. It provides a conduit for party workers in constituencies to make their views known to the government of the day when the Conservative Party is in power. As a critic of the government, an MP must be prepared to both maintain the government in power and scrutinise its activities.

7-097 From the perspective of the MP, the idea of government possessing a mandate seems strangely inconsistent with his own role and function. From the perspective of the political party, an electoral mandate or manifesto promise may control party members, focus the activities of MPs, and help unite the party. From the perspective of the electorate, the manifesto may appear to clarify the policies of each political party and thereby allow choice of support.

7-098 There are important lessons emerging from the experience of coalition government 2010–2015.[47] The use of a 30-page document *Programme for Government*, providing an official guide to governing and containing the main election promises of the coalition partners set new

---

46 Griffith and Ryle, *Parliament: Functions, Practice and Proceedings* (London: Sweet & Maxwell, 1989), p.69.
47 Richard Rawling, "A Coalition Government in Westminster" in J. Jowell, D.Oliver and C. O'Cinneide (eds), *The Changing Constitution* (Oxford: Oxford University Press, 2015), 194– 222. P. Norton, *The British Polity* 5th edn (London: Longman, 2011). House of Lords Constitution Committee, *Constitutional Implications of Coalition Government*, HL 130 (2013–14)

terms of reference for governing the UK. There was also a four-page *Agreement for Stability and Reform* laying out the basis for parties operating within the government. The importance of close co-operation between Prime Minister and Deputy also proved important and ensured that governing was relatively cohesive. The context for governing was also assisted by the *Ministerial Code* and the *Cabinet Manual*—both documents that assigned an appropriate level of rule-making and consultation to ministers and civil servants. Future political scientists will find the system of coalition government an interesting subject to research as it highlighted the need for collective responsibility and the use of constitutional conventions. The Fixed-Term Parliaments Act 2011 should not be overlooked as coalition government had to operate within a predetermined five-year Parliament.

The courts may take account of the manifesto in elections. This occurred in *Bromley*[48] the House of Lords considered the now defunct Greater London Council's manifesto promise to reduce fares on public transport in London. Lord Diplock was clear that the manifesto did not provide a local authority with a mandatory requirement to carry out policies. Members of a local authority must not "treat themselves as irrevocably bound to carry out pre-announced policies" in election manifestos.

7–099

However, this view is not always consistently followed. In *Tameside*,[49] Lord Wilberforce regarded the electoral policy of the Conservative local authority to retain grammar schools as one which "bound" the authority to carry out its task.

7–100

The current view of the courts is more likely to follow the direction set by Bromley. In terms of central and local government relations the view of Lord Templeman in *Nottingham CC v Secretary of State for the Environment*[50] is similar to the strict "allocation of power" analysis made out by Lord Diplock in *Bromley*. The analysis is based on the theory that legal powers should be exercised not according to their political agenda but according to law. The role of the courts is confined to determining the law and not the politics or policy of the law. Policy may only be questioned in Parliament and not the courts[51]:

7–101

> "Where Parliament has legislated that the action to be taken by the Secretary of State must, before it is taken be approved by the House of Commons, it is no part of the judge's role to declare that the action proposed is unfair, unless it constitutes an abuse of power the sense of which I have explained; for Parliament has enacted that one of its Houses is responsible. Judicial review is a great weapon in the hands of the judges; but the judges must observe the constitutional limits set by our parliamentary system on their exercise of this beneficent power."

---

48   *Bromley LBC v Greater London Council* [1983] 1 A.C. 768; [1982] 2 W.L.R. 92 HL.
49   *Secretary of State for Education and Science v Tameside Metropolitan Borough Council* [1977] A.C. 1014; [1976] 3 W.L.R. 641 HL.
50   *Nottinghamshire CC v Secretary of State for the Environment* [1986] A.C. 240; [1986] 2 W.L.R. 1 HL at [255].
51   [1986] A.C. 240, Lord Scarman at [250]–[251].

7-102 The distinction between review according to law and review as to policy may be difficult to make, but the implications are clear: party politics set certain boundaries for the courts in determining the extent of their review powers. An example of policy dispute between a local authority and the relevant minister is found in *R v Secretary of State for Education and Science Ex p. Avon C*. Ralf Gibson LJ explained[52]:

> "...The application was misconceived in so far as it asked the court to intervene in what was analysed, a dispute as to educational policies between Avon [the local authority] and the minister..."

7-103 In a concurring judgment Nicholls LJ commented:

> "Given the notice of the subject matter of the decision, it was difficult to see how the Council's challenge on the ground of 'irrationality' could ever get off the ground."

7-104 Both judgments stressed how inappropriate it was to review the minister's decision in such circumstances.

7-105 The courts assume that policy questions are under the doctrine of ministerial responsibility, a matter for parliamentary discussion and debate. The formulation of party policy through the manifesto gives electors an opportunity to see the shape of their Government's policies. Rarely are such manifesto promises seen as an enforceable mandate in the legal sense, against party policy changes or shifts in government policy.

7-106 In the *Wheeler*[53] case, the Administrative Court refused to order a referendum when it was argued that the Labour Party in their manifesto promised a referendum on the Lisbon Treaty. Manifesto promises are not legally enforceable but part of the politics of governing.

7-107 The influence of party manifestos has perceptibly increased since 1979. The government of the day's adoption of more radical policies such as privatisation and reforms in education, the health service and local government highlights the importance of the manifesto in government policy. Careful drafting of manifesto promises is seen as an important political expedient. The calculating of "keeping pledges" is a way to continue keeping faith with the electorate.

7-108 It is equally clear that the courts will adopt a robust view when confronting corruption. Lord Scott explained in the House of Lords decision of *Porter v Magill*[54] how political corruption might take a variety of forms:

---

52 *The Independent*, May 25, 1990, CA; (1990) 49 L.G.R. 498.
53 *R (Wheeler) v Office of Prime Minister and Secretary of State for Foreign and Commonwealth Affairs* [2008] EWHC 1409 (Admin); [2008] A.C.D. 70.
54 [2001] UKHL 67; [2002] 2 A.C. 357, p.515 at [132]. See Anti-Terrorism, Crime and Security Act 2001 containing tougher laws on corruption.

> "Gerrymandering, the manipulation of constituency boundaries for party political advantage, is a clear form of political corruption. So, too would be any misuse of municipal powers, intended for use in the general public interest but used instead for party political advantage."

The case concerned allegations made by Mr Magill, the District Auditor for Westminster City Council, against three officers and three councillors, that through wilful misconduct they had jointly and severally lost £31 million to the Council. The Council operated a housing policy that was alleged to favour voters more likely to vote Conservative. Council-owned residential properties were being sold in such a way as to enhance the political chances of the Conservative Party at election time. The House of Lords held that it was unlawful to dispose of property for the purpose of promoting the electoral advantage of any party represented on the Council.

Pressure groups

Pressure groups are an important part of the political life of Britain. Broadly defined by Grant[55] as "groups that seek to influence public policy", this definition recognises such characteristics as a defined membership, with stated objectives in terms of public policy and paid staff. Pressure groups may create their own social movement, and self-interest in promoting their cause. The question is to what extent pressure groups contribute to democracy.

The first point to note is that pressure groups are not a modern phenomenon. Patricia Hollis has written that pressure groups in the nineteenth century came from two groupings, those that lobby for an interest and those that adopt a crusade for a cause. The lobby of a vested interest may be seen as "within" the establishment, the crusade for a cause may be perceived as coming from outside the establishment and thus distinct from vested interest.

In the nineteenth century, after the 1832 Reform Act, Parliament became increasingly responsive to public opinion. Claiming to speak for public opinion gave pressure groups a legitimacy. Hollis concludes that pressure groups significantly contributed to the life of the nation.[56]

> "Nineteenth-century pressure from without did have some effect on legislation; it had a marked effect on class harmony and social tranquillity; and both enlarged the realm of government and the breadth and base of government."

---

55 Wyn Grant, *Pressure Groups, Politics and Democracy in Britain* (Hemel Hempstead: Philip Allan, 1989), p.3; and C. Harlow and R. Rawlings, *Pressure Through Law* (London: Routledge, 1992).
56 P. Hollis, *Pressure from Without* (London: Edward Arnold, 1974), p.ix.

7-113 Hollis makes a number of further observations, namely that pressure groups depend on "a sense of political pluralism". Their purpose is to provide an alternative means to express political ideas. There is a belief that this alternative strengthens the existing political institutions and the political health of society. There is also a sense that pressure groups may exert greater flexibility into existing political institutions and therefore provide an important channel of action or alternative political strategy.

7-114 In modern times there are a number of distinctive pressure groups which are easily identifiable and have well-known campaigners prominent among their membership. Groups such as Greenpeace (an environmental group) and Campaign for Nuclear Disarmament (CND, a group campaigning for no nuclear weapons) fit into the category of protest groups and are good examples of their kind. Also important but not seen as protest groups, are the various bodies representing "sectional" interests such as the Law Society, Bar Council, British Medical Association and the like. Grant notes that business alone has over 1,800 associations representing their interests. Added to these are groups such as the Confederation of British Industry (CBI) and the various trade unions, which all contribute to the activities of persuasion and representation of their interests. Particularly useful by way of analysis are the various farmers' unions representing the agricultural sector. These have been successful in representing their interests in the government's attitude to the Common Agricultural Policy of the EU.

7-115 The argument in favour rests on a number of assumptions. First, there "is more to democracy than an occasional vote"; pressure groups engage in "participatory democracy". Secondly, pressure groups are specialised to the particular issues and therefore provide more effective opposition than the main opposition party. This permits minority parties or views to be better represented.

7-116 Criticism of pressure groups casts doubts on their effectiveness as agents of democracy. Brittan has argued that because of the entrenched nature of the various "industrial, economic and political interest groups"[57] this will limit what may be achieved by any form of economic management, new or old, attempted by the government of the day.

7-117 Brittan's argument is that democracy should not be seen as[58] "an unprincipled auction to satisfy rival organised groups who can never in the long run be appeased because their demands are mutually incompatible".

7-118 There is value in Brittan's observations, not least because of the unreliable nature of any accountability over the activities of pressure groups. Grant warns of the damages of allowing pressure groups too much influence. In the competition for public opinion, there is no guarantee that pressure groups will not eventually run into political issues and as a consequence either misunderstand or misrepresent the issues. This is often the point of criticism raised by government ministers or the main political parties. In that sense pressure groups may be held in check by political parties and their policies.

7-119 Grant concludes with a useful analysis of pressure group activities and results[59]:

---

57 S. Brittan, "The Economic Contradictions of Democracy" (1975) *British Journal of Political Science* 5, pp.129–159.
58 Brittan, "The Economic Contradictions of Democracy".
59 Wyn Grant, Pressure Groups, *Politics and Democracy in Britain* (Hemel Hempstead: Philip Allan, 1989), p.163.

"Pressure group power is limited: it is based on the ability to persuade and to influence, rather than to take decisions or, with certain exceptions, to veto them."

The contribution of pressure groups is an eclectic one. Through their activities the government of the day may be influenced and their contributions may improve the quality of policy making and decision-taking. However, there are dangers. Inside groups may achieve unwarranted influence and unduly tip the balance against a more open style of government. Within political parties, pressure groups may operate largely undetected and provide a counterbalance to the public debate outside.

In the final analysis pressure groups may be seen as an inevitable result of the close bargaining of party politics. Not everyone may join in and the temptation is to split off and join a group representing only one's interests. Taken to extreme levels, the damages of pressure group activity should be recognised; but pressure groups perform a valuable task of ensuring that the distance between government and the governed does not become too great.

G: Electoral Reform

The UK, until changes introduced in Italy in 1993, was unique among other Member States of the EU in adopting for central and local government elections the "first past the post" or "plurality" system. Northern Ireland has had its own separate electoral system with proportional representation on the STV system for local government elections since 1973, as well as for elections to the Northern Ireland Assembly. Since the introduction of devolution the UK has the experience of a number of electoral systems. This is a remarkable change undertaken in a short period of time. Voting systems are complex and there is no single formula which translates votes into seats.

First Past the Post

Characteristics:

- used for Parliamentary and Local Government elections in England, Wales and Scotland; and

- one constituency for each member to be elected and each elector has only one vote. The most votes wins. Losing votes are not counted in terms of seats.

Criticism of the UK's present electoral arrangement has come from the smaller parties, who point to the electoral results of past general elections to show that their share of the popular vote is not reflected in terms of the number of seats obtained in the House of Commons. The disproportion of votes to seats is also clear when it is recognised that rarely does the winning party which forms the government, with a majority of seats, win with more than 50 per cent of the total vote. Thus the Conservatives in 1983 with 42.4 per cent of the vote, in 1987 with 42.3 per cent of the vote, and in 1992 with 41.86 per cent had the majority of seats to form a government. Turpin draws attention to the "strikingly demonstrated disproportionality" which may result[60]

> "In each of the two 1974 elections the Liberals with over 18 per cent of the total vote, won only 2 per cent of the seats, and it was observed that more than ten times as many votes were needed to elect a Liberal M.P., as to elect a Labour or Conservative M.P."

7-125 In 1983, election statistics show that the Liberal/SDP alliance received 25.4 per cent of the vote and only 23 seats, while Labour received 27.6 per cent of the vote but 209 seats. The pattern of disproportion has continued in the 1987, 1992, 1997 and 2001 elections. The elections in 2005 and 2010 continued this trend. The election in 2015 was a major shift in the Liberal/SDP alliance with only eight seats and 7.9 per cent of the vote. As one of the coalition partners, coalition government resulted in a dramatic reduction in the party's electoral support. The UK Independent Party (UKIP), one of the smaller political parties in the UK, received 3.9 million votes and one seat only. In contrast the Conservatives had 11.3 million votes and 329 seats and formed the Government with a working majority. More remarkable is that in Scotland, the Scottish Nationalist Party (SNP) had four per cent of the UK vote and 56 seats at Westminster.

7-126 A noticeable feature of FPP is that what may appear to be slim margins between the parties may produce winning outcomes. Compared to the 2010 election, the Conservatives gained 35 seats but lost one, a net change of winning 24 seats. Labour gained 22 seats and lost 48, a net change of losing 26 seats. The Liberal Democrats lost 49 seats and the Scottish National Party gained 50 seats. The Conservatives have an overall majority of 11 seats in the House of Commons not including the Speaker.[61]

7-127 From time to time a Speaker's Conference on electoral law may be convened to secure all party support for any reform proposals. The conference is usually in private and proceedings are not usually published. Recommendations, if any, are not binding on the Government.

7-128 The conclusion drawn by many critics is that the "first past the post system" does discriminate unfairly against smaller parties. Conversely it favours the two major parties.

7-129 Proposals for reform have come from the Liberal Democrats, the Institute of Public Policy Research, and the Hansard Society Commission on electoral reform. Of the two major parties, the Labour Party's review under a Commission chaired by the late, Lord Jenkins[62] favoured an

---

60 C. Turpin, *British Government and the Constitution*, 3rd edn (London: Butterworths, 1995), p.440.
61 The House of Commons Library, *General Election 2015*, Briefing Paper CBP7186 (28 July 2015).
62 Lord Jenkins, *The Report of the Independent Commission on the Voting System* (London: HMSO, 1998).

alternative vote system with some modification. The referendum defeat for electoral reform in 2011 leaves electoral reform a matter for the future. The pressure for change of a number of years ago seems to have diminished after the referendum results.

The aims and objectives of the electoral system

In considering the question of electoral reform it is important to identify the aims and objectives of any electoral system. A number of different expectations may be said to arise from the electoral system. These are: that the result produces a legislature reflecting the main trends and views of the electorate; that the government is able to act according to the wishes of the majority of the electorate; that government is strong and stable; and that the representatives chosen by the electorate are sufficiently competent to perform their task of governing and legislating.

Many of these expectations will not be met, or an electoral system cannot be agreed to that will deliver conflicting aims and objectives, in any single electoral system. Representativeness, good government and electoral choice may be claimed by a variety of different electoral systems. It is often difficult to anticipate in advance the effect of a particular system in terms of the electoral outcome. Thus competing demands are made, often partisan and inclined to favour one system as against another, without much evidence to judge or make conclusions as to the most suitable system.

Bogdanor has argued that the UK's electoral system is no longer justifiable. This view points to the "adversarial" nature of British politics and the arrangement of a two-party system. The FPP plurality system has favoured strong majority government. This means the electorate make a clear decisive choice and that the electoral system discourages coalition government or compromise politics. Bogdanor[63] points out that election results in Britain do not necessarily reflect the pressure of popular support for or against policies among the electorate. Distortions in the seats gained through the votes cast means that the electorate who do not vote for a winning candidate have little chance to have their votes counted and their opinion is not represented in the overall outcome of the election.

Bogdanor identifies particular groups such as women and minorities within the UK as being disadvantaged by the present arrangements. Co-operation between the political parties is handicapped, consensus is difficult to attain and compromise is shunned. However, it may be pointed out that for a lengthy period since the Second World War the electoral system has permitted strong and responsible government. Radical changes in policy, for example privatisation of the nationalised industries introduced since 1979, would have been more difficult to accommodate under any other electoral system. Thus change and continuity, the hallmark of the UK's unwritten Constitution, may be combined and strengthened under the present electoral arrangements. Nevertheless, criticism of the electoral system has been strengthened by the argument that since 1979, the Government has abandoned consensus policies in favour of

---

63 V. Bogdanor, *The People and the Party System* (Cambridge: Cambridge University Press, 1981), p.205.

strong non-consultative government. Critics of Mrs Thatcher attribute the cause of her "style and intent of government" to the electoral success of a large-seat majority.

7-134 The suggestion is made that some form of proportional representation is to be preferred. How far does present dissatisfaction go in terms of popular demand for reform? Stuart Weir[64] has completed empirical research into this question. He concludes that

> "The survey showed that dissatisfaction with the governing system was at 63 per cent, as high in 1991, as in the crisis torn mid-1970s. Most voters agreed that government power is too centralised (60 per cent to 18 per cent) that rights are too easily changed (54 per cent to 22 per cent) and that Parliament does not have enough control over government (50 per cent to 23 per cent)."

7-135 If these findings are borne out by subsequent research then they indicate that there is both popular and intellectual demand for reform of the UK's electoral system. However, if reform is required what reforms might be adopted?

7-136 There is a great lack of clarity, not only in the form of any new arrangements, but also in their expected results. This is hardly surprising given the complex task of devising a new electoral system.

H: Single Transferable Vote

7-137 Characteristics:

- In use in elections in Northern Ireland and the Republic of Ireland. In Northern Ireland it applies to the Northern Assembly, the European Parliament and local government.

- Voters are entitled to as many votes as candidates. Preferences are allowed and each voter may state their preference. Election is based on there being a quota and once a candidate reaches the quota they are elected. The candidate with the lowest number of first preferences drops out. The surplus votes are re-allocated to the second preference candidate until the seats allocated for the constituency are filled.

7-138 The STV system is currently in use in Northern Ireland and in the Republic of Ireland. This system is based on redrawing existing constituencies into larger multi-member

---

64 Stuart Weir, "Waiting for Change: Public Opinion and Electoral Reform" (1992) 63 *Political Quarterly* 197 at p.216.

constituencies. This would create five member constituencies based on the electoral quota of about 3 million voters. Voting on the ballot paper is undertaken by indicating an order of preference for each candidate. Winning an election according to this system requires setting an "electoral quota." Broadly this means setting a proportion of votes expressed as a percentage which must be achieved before a member is returned for that constituency. Depending on the number of seats for each constituency the successful candidate will require 16.6 per cent of the vote whereas in a two-member constituency 33.3 per cent of the vote is required. Once a candidate passes the electoral quota, the candidate wins. Passing the electoral quota is determined by the returning officer counting the number of first preference votes. It is possible that often a candidate will achieve a sufficient number of first preference votes. On this basis the number of seats will determine the number of winning candidates. Once a sufficient number of first preference votes are achieved, the returning officer counts all the second preferences recorded by the voters who gave first preference votes. In this way no votes are wasted. Once the second preference votes are counted, the returning officer transfers a proportion of the preferences given to each candidate. This may permit another candidate to achieve the electoral quota or better. The process is continued permitting all the candidates who reach the electoral quota to be elected.

In theory the advantage of such a system is to provide a coincidence between the distribution of votes among parties and the distribution of seats. Variables in such a system will depend on the size of constituencies determined by the number of voters and the number of seats in each constituency. It is assumed that the smaller the number of constituencies, the greater the degree of representativeness possible. If the entire country were treated as a single constituency this would amount to the minimum distortion. Only in Israel and the Netherlands does this arrangement operate.

Regional List System

Characteristics:

- In use in elections for the European Parliament.

- Electors vote for a party list of candidates and the emphasis is on the party rather than the candidate. Seats are allocated in the basis of a proportion of the vote won by the political party.

An alternative to STV is the list system, popular in Western Europe. Votes are cast for parties, seats are distributed according to the parties' proportion of their share of the votes. Candidates are thus elected on the allocation of votes in the order of preference. Modification of these arrangements is usually introduced by a "cut-off point" being applied. If a party fails to reach this barrier it will not be qualified to receive any seats.

Additional Member System

7-142 Characteristics:

- In use for the Scottish Parliament, Welsh Assembly and Greater London Authority.

- Voters have two votes: one vote is used to elect a constituency member, the other vote is used to vote for the political party.

- Constituency votes are counted on the basis of FPP.

- Party vote is counted on the basis of a fair share of seats based on a distribution of votes. The total number of seats won by the party is intended to reflect the votes cast for the party.

7-143 The first use of the additional member system was in the election of the Scottish Parliament, Welsh Assembly and Greater London Authority.

Supplementary Vote

7-144 Characteristics:

- In use for the election of the London Mayor.

- Voters have a first and second preference, the aim being to achieve a vote that records for the winner more than 50 per cent of the votes cast. Failing this the candidate with the highest percentage of first votes goes through to a second round, the aim being that the winning candidate secures 50 per cent of the vote.

7-145 The first use of the supplementary vote system resulted in Ken Livingstone being elected London Mayor. The system is suitable for the election of an individual.

Alternative Vote

7-146 Characteristics:

- Proposed by the Jenkins Commission for Parliamentary elections to the House of Commons.

- Voters have two votes. One vote might be recorded using the alternative vote system for an MP for an individual constituency, the second vote might be used to vote for either a party or a candidate. The first vote would result in roughly 80 to 85 per cent of MPs elected. The second vote would fill the remaining seats.

- One person is elected on the basis of a majority. Voters have more than one preference. The winner is the candidate with the majority of first preferences. In the event that there is no outright winner, the candidate with the lowest number of first preferences drops out, second preference votes are then re-distributed.

The Jenkins Report made a number of recommendations for electoral reform. The key point is the adoption of a variant of the alternative vote system. Seyd explains[65]:

> "The Jenkins Commission recommended a variant of AV—AV Top Up—which combined the Alternative Vote in single member constituencies (80–85 per cent of the total) with small top up areas with members elected from lists (15–20 per cent of the total). The inclusion of top ups was intended to ensure that the system was more proportional than straight AV."

The complexity of different proportional voting systems is clear. One distinguishing feature is that voters are given a choice between political parties rather than for candidates.

Proportional representation has many advocates. Critics point to the fear that a government elected under such a system may not have a worthy overall majority. Weak government, proliferation of small parties and a constant need to go to the electorate are seen as characteristics of the proportional representation systems in countries such as Italy, Holland and Israel. Critics further argue that there is a high likelihood of a hung Parliament. Coalition between the parties is inevitable and there is a greater likelihood for the need for coalition government.

Proportional representation does pose major questions in terms of many of the constitutional conventions, the role of political parties and ultimately how Parliament might function. This is not always appreciated. Membership of the Cabinet is currently *de facto*, restricted to the government of the day. Inclusion of opposition-nominated MPs and members of smaller parties might change the nature and role of the Cabinet. Cabinet secrecy and collective decisions might be more difficult to achieve. MPs would be freer from the importance of strict party discipline and the power of the whips which might change the relationship between MP and party.

Many of these changes might be seen as beneficial but undoubtedly they may flow from proportional representation. David Butler concludes[66]:

---

65 Ben Syed, "Electoral Systems and Party Funding" in J. Jowell and D. Oliver (eds), *The Changing Constitution* (Oxford: Oxford University Press, 2000), p.318.
66 D. Butler, "Electoral Reform" in J. Jowell and D. Oliver (eds), *The Changing Constitution* (Oxford: Oxford University Press, 2000), p.383.

> "In these and many other matters the rules of the game of British politics would be transformed if appeals to the people no longer produced single party parliamentary majorities. A change in voting procedures would have fundamental consequences. Electoral systems are not matters of technical detail. They lie at the very heart of a nation's arrangements."

7-152 The future likelihood of electoral reform is difficult to assess for Parliamentary or local government elections. The Government is not committed to the introduction of proportional representation in the foreseeable future and it is suspected that opposition parties are unsure of the exact effects of its introduction, although the Liberal Democrats are most enthusiastic about its introduction. The debate is likely to continue. The winning party under the first past the post system has a vested interest to perpetuate the existing FPP system.

I: Referendums

7-153 Referendums have an important role in any well-functioning democracy. Dicey in the late nineteenth century was an eventual convert to the value of a referendum.[67] His main ground for seeing the value of the referendum was that it avoided the "evils" of the party system and the conflict between political parties. Dicey regarded party political conflicts as an impediment to the consensus necessary for the effective working of the political system. In the aftermath of the Irish Home Rule debate in 1886 and in 1894 when a new Home Rule Bill was introduced for Ireland, Dicey supported a referendum as a device to avoid "extreme" legislation. At the time the influential National Review held a symposium on the merits of the referendum. Dicey believed its role on matters of fundamental constitutional importance was invaluable. There were few converts to this idea. On the whole, the value of a referendum was not seen in terms of a generally applicable principle, but it was conceded that on some matters of constitutional importance, a referendum might have a role. This view did not hold sway in the debates on the Parliament Act 1911. Then the opposition were unsuccessful in the demand for a referendum to affirm the changes in the role of the House of Lords.

7-154 In contemporary times in the Northern Ireland (Border Poll) Act 1972, referendum was approved to allow the electors of Northern Ireland to vote on whether Northern Ireland should remain part of the UK or join with the Irish Republic. There was also express provision in the Northern Ireland Constitution Act 1973 for holding a referendum on the status of Northern Ireland. We have seen the use of referendum in the adoption of devolution.

---

67 See Richard Cosgrove, *The Rule of Law Albert Venn Dicey, Victorian Jurist* (London: Macmillan, 1980), pp.105–110.

7-155 The decision to join the European Community in 1972 was taken without a referendum. However, the political controversy about joining has remained a sensitive issue in British politics. The Referendum Act 1975 was seen as an attempt to avoid internal party political disagreements and allowed the electorate to vote on 5 June 1975 on the question of whether the UK should stay in the European Community. The majority, 67.2 per cent, voted for staying in the Community out of an electoral turnout of 65 per cent. The referendum has not settled the question of membership of the European Community. The signing of the Maastricht Treaty was accompanied by demands for a referendum, although a Bill proposing this course of action failed in the House of Commons. The 1997 general election campaign saw the renewed efforts of the Referendum Party, formed in 1994, to have a referendum to consider membership of the Community. The Referendum Party failed to attract significant electoral support.

7-156 The use of referendums was at the centre of the debate on devolution in 1978. Both the Scotland Act 1978 and the Wales Act 1978 allowed for a referendum on the matter of devolution. The test of agreement was a threshold requirement of 40 per cent of the electorate. If this failed to be achieved, then both the 1978 Acts had to be repealed. While a majority of those that voted in Scotland favoured devolution, this amounted to only 32.9 per cent of the electorate. Devolution failed to be implemented in Scotland. In Wales only 20.2 per cent were in favour, representing only 11.9 per cent of the electorate. Devolution also failed to be implemented in Wales. The referendum may have tested the wishes of the electorate on the form of devolution on offer rather than on the principle of devolution per se. The limitations of the referendum are found in the way the question is posed and on the timing of the referendum. These matters may be influential with the electorate. Referendums are not necessarily a good barometer of public opinion; rather they may provide politicians with a way forward when party political loyalties are divided. In all the examples mentioned above the referendum has not proved conclusive.

7-157 However, having gained from the lessons of 1978, the government adopted a different and altogether more straightforward approach to devolution in 1997. In September 1997 referendums were held in Scotland and Wales. The result was that in Scotland 75 per cent of the voters were in favour, on a 60 per cent turnout. In Wales support for devolution was more marginal, and on a turnout of around 50 per cent the majority were in favour but by the narrowest of margins (0.6 per cent). The new Labour Government with a secure Parliamentary majority at Westminster could afford to be radical.

7-158 The first UK wide referendum since 1975 (on European Community membership) was held on 5 May 2011 on whether the system of elections for MPs to the House of Commons should be changed. The result was decisive with 68 per cent no and only 32 per cent in favour of replacing the FPP system with an alternative vote system instead. Referendums were used, with limited success in 1978 but more successfully in 1997, for devolution to Scotland and Wales. A referendum on both sides of the border in the Republic of Ireland and Northern Ireland confirmed the peace process in 1998 for Northern Ireland. A referendum was promised for entry into the single European currency, at a time when the economic conditions are considered to be appropriate. The promise did not need to be kept and events since 2008 and the Greek crisis in 2014/15 has made the UK's membership of the euro very unlikely.

The Referendum on Scottish independence in 2014 was confined to Scotland and resulted in a majority in favour of the continuation of the Union. The turnout was very high at 84.59 per cent, the "No" vote against independence was 55.30 per cent and the "Yes" vote 44.70 per cent. There is a UK referendum planned to take place before the end of 2017 on EU membership. There are various controls over party spending in national referendum campaigns set at £5 million for each of the largest political parties under Pt VII of the Political Parties, Elections and Referendums Act 2000.

7–159 The Localism Act 2011 provides a framework for referendum to be held by local authorities in terms of setting up elected Mayors. This is an important development that may advance the creation of "mega-city" authorities in Manchester or the surrounding areas.

7–160 The European Union Act 2011 provides for a referendum when the Government wishes to make further amendments to an EU Treaty or when there are proposals for any extension of the powers of the EU institutions that may impinge on UK sovereignty. Unusually the Act provides for an Act of Parliament and a referendum. The referendum is used to ratify the Act of Parliament and in effect gives the electorate an opportunity to agree or not with the Act of Parliament that includes the relevant Treaty changes. In these circumstances the referendum is not advisory but a requirement before the Act of Parliament may be given effect.

7–161 There are some limitations in the use of the referendum mechanism as seen with the devolution issue in 1978; determining the ground rules for holding a referendum is itself controversial. The initiative lies with the government of the day and the outcome of the referendum may be unduly influenced by the way the question is drafted and the rules relating to how the electorate's choice may be counted. There is also a question of how fully informed the electorate may be in determining the choices represented in the referendum. The way information is presented may provide a biased account. The media and advertising may distort the values of the arguments presented by different groups.

7–162 In principle there is great merit in the use of the referendum. The idea behind the referendum may appear to be an attractive one, namely that it appeals to the authority of the electorate rather than relying on political choices decided in Parliament. This may be misleading. The nature of the UK's current constitutional arrangements are that the referendum may disguise where real political power and authority actually reside.

J: Summary and Conclusions

7–163 In the 1970s and 1980s, election results favoured one or other of the two major parties. In 2010 the election of a Conservative led coalition government broke the mould in British politics. The election of May 2015 resulted in a Conservative majority government. It is unclear if this will mean a return to two-party politics in Britain. Elections provide the basis for the British voters' confidence primarily in either of the two main political parties. This may change over the next decades as political debate many change according to circumstances. Although the dogma of the parties may sharply differ, there is striking similarity in the accretion of political power to the Prime Minister of the day under both Conservative and Labour administrations. It is equally clear that despite the long history of voting for either of the two major parties to form the government, voter apathy and dissatisfaction is today more apparent than ever. As Professor Anthony King shrewdly observes,

> "...at all ten general elections held between 1931 and 1970 the Conservative and Labour parties have always won more than 85% of the popular vote and frequently more than 90%. Nothing like that has happened since. At the seven general elections held between February 1974 and May 1997, the two main parties never won as much as 85% of the vote, and on five of the seven occasions their combined share of the vote fell to 75% or less."[68]

Perhaps more worryingly is that the two major parties, Conservative and Labour have been largely rejected by voters in Scotland. The rise of the SNP with 56 out of the 59 MPs at Westminster is likely to further complicate the question of English votes for English laws. Not since the Irish Home Rule debate at the end of the nineteenth century[69] is the question of the future of the union within the UK open to debate as the SNP promise another referendum on Scottish independence.

Voter apathy and political inertia are some of the major challenges facing political parties and the future of the electoral system. Some progress has been made in the modernisation of the British electoral system. The challenge remains as to how to reform the electoral system for Parliamentary and local elections.

Further Reading

R. Blackburn, *The Electoral System in Britain* (London: Macmillan, 1995).
Alexandra Kelso, *Parliamentary reform at Westminster* (Manchester: Manchester University Press, 2009).
P. Norton, *The British Polity*, 5th edn (London: Longman, 2011).
House of Lords Constitution Committee, *Constitutional Implications of Coalition Government*, HL 130 (2013–14).

---

68 Anthony King, *Does the United Kingdom Still Have a Constitution?* (London: Sweet & Maxwell, 2001), p.61.
69 John Kendle, *Ireland and the Federal Solution: the debate over the United Kingdom Constitution 1870–1920* (Montreal: McGill-Queen's University Press, 1989).

Thomas Quinn, *Electing and Ejecting Party Leaders in Britain* (London: Palgrave Macmillan, 2015).

Richard Rawling, "A Coalition Government in Westminster" in J. Jowell, D. Oliver and C. O'Cinneide (eds), *The Changing Constitution* (Oxford: Oxford University Press, 2015), pp.194–222.

General Election Results 1945–2015

Year	Party	Votes per cent	Seats per cent
1945	Labour	47.7	61.4
	Conservative	39.7	32.8
	Liberal	9.0	1.9
	Others*	3.6	3.9
1950	Labour	46.1	50.4
	Conservative	43.4	47.4
	Liberal	9.1	1.4
	Others	1.3	0.5
1951	Labour	48.8	47.2
	Conservative	48.0	51.3
	Liberal	2.5	0.9
	Others	0.7	0.5
1955	Labour	46.4	44.0
	Conservative	49.7	54.8
	Liberal	2.7	0.9
	Others	1.2	0.3
1959	Labour	43.8	40.9
	Conservative	49.4	57.9
	Liberal	5.9	0.9
	Others	0.9	0.2
1964	Labour	44.1	50.3
	Conservative	43.4	48.3
	Liberal	11.2	1.4
	Others	1.3	0.0
1966	Labour	48.0	57.8
	Conservative	41.9	40.1
	Liberal	8.5	1.9
	Others	1.5	0.1
1970	Labour	43.1	45.7
	Conservative	46.4	52.4

Year	Party	Votes per cent	Seats per cent
	Liberal	7.5	0.9
	Others	3.0	1.0
1974 (Feb)	Labour	37.2	47.4
	Conservative	37.9	46.8
	Liberal	19.3	2.2
	Others	5.6	3.6
1974 (Oct)	Labour	39.2	50.2
	Conservative	35.8	43.6
	Liberal	18.3	2.0
	Others	7.7	4.1
1979	Labour	36.9	42.4
	Conservative	43.9	53.4
	Liberal	13.8	1.7
	Others	5.4	2.5
1983	Labour	27.6	32.2
	Conservative	42.4	61.1
	Liberal/SDP	25.4	3.5
	Others	4.6	3.2
1987	Labour	30.8	35.2
	Conservative	42.3	57.8
	Liberal/SDP	22.6	3.4
	Others	4.3	3.6
1992	Labour	34.4	41.6
	Conservative	41.9	51.6
	Liberal Dem.	17.8	3.1
	Others	5.9	3.7
1997	Labour	43.2	63.4
	Conservative	30.7	25.0
	Liberal Dem.	16.8	7.0
	Others	9.3	4.6
2001	Labour	40.7	62.5
	Conservative	31.7	25.2
	Liberal Dem.	18.3	7.9
	Others*	9.3	4.4

* Others include Green Party, Plaid Cymru, SNP, N.Irish Parties, Independent Labour, Commonwealth, Independents, etc.

Year	Party	Votes per cent	Seats per cent
2005	Labour	35.2	55.0
	Conservative	32.4	30.7
	Liberal Dem.	22.0	9.6
	Others	10.4	4.7
2010	Labour	39.8	29.0
	Conservative	47.2	36.1
	Liberal Dem.	8.8	23.0
	Others	4.2	11.9
2015	Labour	35.7	30.4
	Conservative	50.9	36.9
	Liberal Dem.	1.2	7.9
	Others	12.2	24.8

Year	Number of Seats	Electorate Size	Electorate Turnout
1945	640	33,240,391	72.8
1950	625	34,412,255	83.9
1951	625	34,919,331	82.6
1955	630	34,852,179	76.8
1959	630	35,397,304	78.7
1964	630	35,894,054	77.1
1966	630	35,957,245	75.8
1970	630	39,342,013	72.0
1974 (Feb)	635	39,753,863	78.8
1974 (Oct)	635	40,072,970	72.8
1979	635	41,095,649	76.0
1983	650	42,192,099	72.7
1987	650	43,180,753	75.3
1992	651	43,249,721	77.7
1997	659	44,863,488	71.5
2001	659	44,403,238	59.4
2005	646	44,180,243	61.4
2010	659	45,597461	65.1
2015	659	46,425,386	66.1

Source: *British Governments and Elections Since 1945* (London, 2015).

8

Public Law and Legal Thought

A: Introduction

Public lawyers face a daunting task when it comes to thinking, assessing and evaluating the UK's constitutional and administrative law. Complex and detailed, the UK's Constitution along with the varieties of rights, duties and powers associated with government and governing in the UK is embedded in strong traditions and institutions that are undergoing seemingly endless changes and fluctuations.[1] A long unitary tradition of a single sovereign Parliament is fast becoming a decentralised and localised system of government with increasing devolved powers to the four nations. It is clear that the direction of change points to some form of quasi-federal if not outright federal constitution. The ebb and flow of change is also catalysed by much greater political intervention in the day to day governance of the nation. The economic regulation of state intervention is wide ranging from setting standards in schools and education to the National Health Service and the interrelationship between the provision of public funding to the regulation of banks, utilities and the delivery of wide ranging social and economic policies.[2] The UK Constitution has not always delivered a degree of institutional coherence that fits with models of accountability and theories of the state.

8–001

There are widely demarcated differences in approach between a focus on institutions and government to a normative assessment of values and rights. Even here it matters a great deal if the emphasis is on legislation, statutes and rules of interpretation as well as judicial decisions in terms of dicta and the various standards set for the performance of public duties and responsibilities.

8–002

---

1 Stefan Collini, Richard Whitmore and Brian Young (eds), *Economic Policy, and Society British Intellectual History 1750–1950* (Cambridge: Cambridge University Press, 2000).
2 See T. Prosser, *The Economic Constitution* (Oxford: Oxford University Press, 2014).

8-003 This chapter is an attempt to outline some current discussion and debate about public law. Whether, as Loughlin believes, there is a crisis in "public law thought" may be open to conjecture, but there is certainly a sustained and important debate concerning the nature of public law, the value of a theoretical approach to the subject and its future development. Alternatively, Allan has argued,[3] that the common law represents a superior form of constitutionalism, placing the rule of law at the apex of political power, and that the common law approach to public law can be compared to the view of public law from the civil law perspective. It is hoped that the brief introduction to legal thought in this chapter will facilitate the analysis and inquiry undertaken in the remainder of this textbook. What are the aims and objectives of public law? Is public law a distinctive subject? What are its boundaries? How do public lawyers differ in their approach to problems or disputes from private lawyers? Discussion of these questions is essential to understanding the value and nature of public law.

B: Contemporary Issues and Debates

8-004 It is important to set public law in the current context of austerity cuts and large government borrowings that determine many of the political dimensions of the exercise of public power. Defining the size of the state, the role and function of government at all levels- central, local, devolved and European is also a highly contested part of the party political system. Resolving the final constitutional settlement in the next decade will be both challenging and unpredictable.

8-005 Conceptually, UK public law is difficult to define. Stefan Collini has noted that

> "to study French political theory is to study lawyers. To study modern German political theory is equally to study lawyers. The same could not be said of England, however, and perhaps as a result our English political science has hitherto no great method."[4]

8-006 Van Caenegem[5] reminds us that "the concept of public law is itself somewhat problematic". He describes how continental jurisprudence developed a system of public law distinguished as a separate field of study from private law. In marked contrast, England, he observed, did not conform to such a separation or distinction[6]:

---

3 T. R. S. Allan, *Constitutional Justice: A Liberal Theory of the Rule of Law* (Oxford: Oxford University Press, 2001).
4 S. Collini, *Public Moralists* (Oxford: Clarendon, 2006), p.250.
5 R. C. Van Caenegem, *An Historical Introduction to Western Constitutional Law* (Cambridge: Cambridge University Press, 1995), p.1.
6 Van Caenegem, *An Historical Introduction to Western Constitutional Law*, p.3.

> "Until the nineteenth century, and even beyond, English doctrine proudly maintained that, unlike the continent, England knew no separate public law or public-law courts; the traditional common law assumed that the law was indivisible in the sense that the same body of rules applied to the government and its agents as well as to private citizens."

John Gardner[7] queries whether the UK has a constitution and if so can there be a written constitution? In his analysis Gardner locates one of the major question of our time "the straightforward moral and political debates about what judges do when they interpret" and the inevitable consequences of how meanings are changed, re-interpreted and become the case law of the country.

The absence of a separate public law jurisprudence in England did not inhibit the growth of a common law inheritance, as outlined in the preceding chapters, through the contributions of various writers and their ideas, influential in the development of the UK's constitutional arrangements. An approach that considers the historical constitution[8] and the significance of the Diceyan doctrine of parliamentary sovereignty serves to emphases the distinctiveness of the English Constitution. As Allison has pointed out the historical constitution has managed to encourage continuity and change, including its adaptability to European Law[9] and this should not be overlooked in terms of understanding from a comparative perspective the historical development of English law.

This chapter is intended to examine the major, legal and philosophical thinking, influential in the development of public law.

English public lawyers have traditionally focused mainly on Albert Venn Dicey (1835–1922) and his contemporaries that remain influential and their importance endures in understanding current constitutional arrangements, if only to see how ideas have been changed or have moved on. and his critics. Today there is a vast literature on contemporary legal thought and its influence on public law, a reflection of a growing interest in thinking about public law. One perception is that public law may become dominant when thinking about legal principles particularly in the growth of a public law contract or in contractual relations in public administration.[10] There is a growth in public-private partnerships and the introduction of many commercial ideas into government, for example resource accounting and budgeting with its roots in company accounts and market valuation. Borrowing from the private sector and the creation of a purchaser-provider relationship provides the beginnings of a new legal framework in the

---

7   John Gardner, *Can there be a written Constitution?*, University of Oxford Legal Research Paper Series Paper, No.17/2009 (May 2009).
8   J. W. F. Allison, *The English Historical Constitution* (Cambridge: Cambridge University Press, 2007).
9   Allison, *The English Historical Constitution*.
10 See M. Freedland, "Government by Contract and Public Law" [1994] *Public Law* 86. See also T. R. S. Allan, "Pragmatism and Theory in Public Law" (1988) 104 *Law Quarterly Review* 422; T. R. S. Allan, "Constitutional Rights and Common Law" (1991) 11 *Oxford Journal of Legal Studies* 453; and T. R. S. Allan, *Law, Liberty and Justice* (Oxford: Clarendon, 1993).

public sector.[11] There is a view that a "public law of contract" is discernible from the analysis of legal principles that apply to government by contract.[12]

8-011 Interest in the theoretical underpinnings of public law includes Harlow and Rawlings distinction between "red light" and "green light" theories of how to interpret administrative law. The red light theory is premised on a minimal exercise of state power and strong opposition to expanding the state or the accretion of state power through large central or local government interventions into the ordinary lives of the citizen. The interference in rights—primarily property rights—is opposed. Dicey recognised that the rule of law might operate within the confines of preventing abuse of power and checking on illegality. Its modern proponents see judicial review as a form of common law constitutionalism that allows the courts to adjudicate between the citizen and the state but not necessarily to overstep their role into the political domain. Leyland argues[13] that under "red light" theory the courts may act as "checks and balances" and rebuff arbitrary power. Craig observes how law may perform an important function of control as a form of self-correcting democracy.[14]

8-012 In contrast the "green light" theory is liberal and more communitarian and focused on a social democratic model where law enables the delivery of social welfare and justice. Underpinning the green light analysis is the belief that through Parliament, the democratic will of elected politicians should be implemented. This recognises that legal principles are often located in a political constitution, the primacy of which must need to be recognised by the courts by paying deference to the politics of legal rules and the policies that underline them. There is considerable support for the green light theory from scholars in the tradition of Griffith[15] and Robson.[16] The nature of state powers brings also the necessity for systems of accountability and control. This can be achieved through the adoption of ministerial accountability and the development of adequate systems of accountability—often without necessarily relying on the courts or judicial oversight but mainly relying on the citizen and the political nature of the exercise of public powers. The use of tribunals for example was seen as a powerful mechanism of accountability that contained both legal and lay elements. Harlow and Rawlings have always been modest about any claims for green or red light theories representing a definitive answer on how to analyse public power and the growth of the administrative state. There is much value in the understandings green and red light theory, however, the arguments from both perspectives are invaluable insights into the debate about the functions of judicial review.

8-013 Craig[17] provides the view of how constitutional and administrative law are inter-related. He also explains how the background of political theory assists in understanding both how society

---

11 I. Harden, *The Contracting State* (Buckingham: Open University Press, 1992).
12 A. C. L. Davies, *Accountability: A Public Law Analysis of Government by Contract* (Oxford: Oxford University Press, 2001).
13 P. Leyland, *The Constitution of the UK* (Oxford: Hart, 2012), pp.205–7.
14 P. Craig, "Dicey: Unitary, Self-correcting, Democracy and Public Law" (1991) 106 *Law Quarterly Review* 105.
15 J. Griffith, *The Politics of the Judiciary*, 5th edn (London: Fontana, 1997).
16 W. Robson, *Justice and Administrative Law*, 3rd edn (London: Stevens, 1951).
17 P. Craig, *Public Law and Democracy in the United Kingdom and the United States of America* (Oxford: Clarendon, 1990). Also see H. Arthurs, *Without the Law* (Toronto: University of Toronto Press, 1985).

and law have developed, and how the contribution of different commentators on the UK's constitutional arrangements can be assessed. Loughlin[18] discusses the connection between public law and politics. He explores the development of ideas and influences in public law, specifically addressing an inquiry into the nature and distinctiveness of public law. In his work *Sword and Scales*,[19] he considers changes in our perception about both law and politics and recognises the ascendancy of rights that permeate our understanding of relationships within society:

> "In modern times, however, politics has undergone a radical shift in perspective. Rather than being concerned with the rights of citizens and the duties of subjects, it is scarcely an exaggeration to suggest that modern politics is primarily concerned with the rights of citizens and the obligations of government. Alongside this shift in perspective, we also see a transformation in our understanding of law. Both the conceptions of law as a set of customary practices of governance and of law as the command of the sovereign are able to be accommodated within the traditional approach to politics. With the inversion of political perspective, however, we see a revolution in our understanding of law. Once treated as a code based on duties, law now presents itself as being founded on rights."

8–014

The Human Rights Act 1998 has generated an unprecedented literature on aspects of human rights and how this may impact on the law,[20] particularly administrative law. Defining the scope of human rights law is difficult and the traditional boundaries between private and public law may not be helpful in attempting to understand the range and scope of rights and their impact on the citizen. Public law has become an important forum to probe the boundaries between law, theory and politics.[21] The latter may underpin many of the moral considerations that underline public law principles. A rights-based approach is linked to the rule of law and this has encapsulated many debates about what the rule of law means and how this might be viewed in contemporary discussion.[22] Jowell succinctly explains:

> "Although the rule of law is not the only requirement of a constitutional democracy, it is of great practical significance in promoting fair decisions, restraining the abuse of power, encouraging investment and in furthering empowerment and respect for equal human dignity."[23]

---

18   M. Loughlin, *Public Law and Political Theory* (Clarendon Press: Oxford, 1992),
19   M. Loughlin, *Sword and Scales* (Oxford: Hart, 2000), pp.232–234; and T. R. S. Allan, *Law, Liberty and Justice* (Oxford: Oxford University Press, 2001).
20   T. R. S. Allan, *Constitutional Justice, A Liberal Theory of the Rule of Law* (Oxford: Oxford University Press, 2001).
21   John Griffith, "The Brave New World of Sir John Laws" (2000) 63 *M.L.R.* 159.
22   J. Jowell, "The Rule of Law" in J. Jowell, D. Oliver and C. O'Cinneide (eds), *The Changing Constitution*, 8th edn (Oxford: Oxford University Press, 2015), pp.22–23.
23   Jowell, "The Rule of Law", p.14.

8-015 Craig[24] recognises various elements in a "rights based vision of public law": the formal including the need for legal authority to be authorised, transparent and fair; the substantive that the law should encapsulate and enforce moral rights underpinned by an appropriate theory of justice; and that the rule of law should include values of accountability and participation including procedures and practices that are appropriate. Many public lawyers[25] have contributed to a rights-based vision of public law that with variations and differences in interpretation advance common values and principles that engage with judicial review and assist in bringing government to account. Judicial review also assists in providing standards—high values and principles, including legality in decision-making.

8-016 A "rights based" vision of public law shared by many public lawyers is also the subject of intense criticism and debate. Craig analyses the criticism from public law scholars such as Thomas Poole[26] who criticises the views of public lawyers who are attracted to a common law constitutionalism. Poole's main argument is that participation in adjudication is limited and that the main focus ought to be on legitimacy and the all too apparent fallibility of government. His main thesis is that judicial review does not fit the vision of public law advanced by the rights-based approach. In reply Craig considers that Poole's arguments are at the very least contestable, especially as there is a wide divergence amongst public lawyers as to precisely what a rights-based approach involves. It is clear that rival theories are by their nature often contestable but their value is to widen and deepen the nature of public law scholarship.[27] Public law is set to attract a wide range of theorists setting out to analyse the role of law and the state. Economics is increasingly important in identifying regulatory bodies and setting standards in public life.

C: The Common Law Tradition

8-017 Constitutional and administrative law evolved historically, mainly from tradition and the general development of the common law. The common law tradition is the subject of specialist works of legal history such as Milsom's *Historical Foundations of the English Common Law*.[28] Such accounts are instructive in the insights they provide on the role of lawyers in the development

---

24 Paul Craig, *Administrative Law*, 7th edn (London: Sweet and Maxwell, 2012), pp.20–25.
25 Paul Craig, "Political Constitutionalism and the Judicial Role: A Response" (2011) 9 *I-CON* 112; and A Tomkins, "The Role of the Courts in the Political Constitution" (2010) 60 *U.T.L.J.* 1.
26 Thomas Poole, "Legitimacy, Rights and Judicial Review" (2005) 25 *Oxford Journal of Legal Studies* 697; Thomas Poole, "Back to the Future?: Unearthing the Theory of Common law Constitutionalism" (2003) 23 *Oxford Journal of Legal Studies* 453; and Thomas Poole, "Questioning Common Law Constitutionalism" (2005) 25 *Legal Studies* 142.
27 A. Tomkins, *Our Republican Constitution* (London: Hart, 2005).
28 2nd edn (London: Butterworths, 1980).

of the common law, particularly in terms of the adoption of legal techniques and methods of analysis. However, rarely are substantive issues of constitutional and administrative law made distinctive. Legal skills are explained and analysed but the emphasis in such works is on the development of the common law in terms of courts and procedures, property law, including both land law and equity, contract, and occasionally the criminal law. Legal methods and techniques developed in the area of property relations are relevant to understanding the traditions of the common law. As English law did not develop a separate jurisdiction over matters of constitutional and administrative law, however, the same common law techniques are helpful in understanding the role of the State and its relationship with the citizen.

General assumptions about the nature of law informed the mind of common lawyers. One such assumption was that law is perceived as having universal application. No special status is awarded to the State or to the Constitution and disputes between the citizen and the State are not seen as peculiar or different. Thus, English law failed to recognise any intrinsic differences between disputes arising out of the law of contract between two private citizens and contractual disputes where the contract is between the citizen and the State.

8–018

The fact that today courts make a distinction between public and private law has come about in the context where English law in the past failed to draw any such distinction. The absence of any special group of rules or analysis associated with public law in its early development creates difficulties in defining public law and delineating its boundaries with private law. The question of what is the distinctiveness of public law, assuming that it is possible to identify such, is not readily answered.

8–019

However, despite such difficulties it is possible to identify some of the characteristics found in the common law tradition which are important in understanding public law. Atiyah and Summers[29] identified formal reasoning and pragmatism as major influences in English law.

8–020

Formal reasoning contains a number of influences which relate to how law is perceived and developed. Interestingly, both contract and property law provide the most useful analysis and examples of formal reasoning. How might formal reasoning be explained? First, rules are recognised as legally authoritative, that is by their context or status, their validity is accepted. Formal reasoning may place emphasis on certain requirements such as a seal, or registration of title, a signature of a witness or the requirements of writing. Technical correctness is a hallmark of the precision associated with formality and the idea that problems may be reduced to a study of the rules alone.

8–021

Secondly, formal reasoning places weight on the value of coherence. That the law is a unified body of law lies at the heart of the judges relying on previous decisions and on the

8–022

---

29 Useful background reading may be found in M. A. Eisenberg, *The Nature of Common Law* (Cambridge, MA: Harvard University Press, 1988); P. S. Atiyah and R. S. Summers, *Form and Substance in Anglo-American Law* (Oxford: Clarendon, 1987); S. F. C. Milsom, "Reason in the Development of the Common Law" in *Studies in the History of the Common Law* (London: Hambledon, 1985); and D. Sugarman, "Legal Theory, the Common Law Mind and the Making of the Textbook Tradition" in W. Twining (ed), *Legal Theory and Common Law* (London: Blackwell, 1986), pp.26–61. There is an excellent explanation of the role of the textbook in P. Birks, *Introduction to the Law of Restitution* (Oxford: Clarendon, 1992), pp.1–3.

authority of the particular court. The creation of legal principles through points of law or legal doctrine further supports the view that law is internally coherent. The influence of stare decisis makes clear the distinction between judgments which are binding and those that are merely persuasive. As law reporting developed, the tradition of authoritative decision-making in the higher courts on points of legal technicalities influenced the lower courts in their decisions. Assumptions underlying this unified operation of law is that law provides protection to the individual and that reverence, universality and respect are provided by the legal process.

8-023
Pragmatism[30] is not inconsistent with formalism and when combined, seems influential in helping to develop legal principles. How formalism and pragmatism may be combined is illustrated in the example of administrative law. Writing in the second edition of his work on *Judicial Review of Administrative Action*, de Smith observed that as English law originally failed to admit the existence of administrative law, its existence today has been influenced by pragmatic development. His analysis is equally valid if applied to the whole enterprise of public law as he explained[31]:

> "...in place of integrated coherence we have an asymmetrical hotch potch, developed pragmatically by legislation and judicial decisions in particular contexts, blending fitfully with private law and magisterial law, alternately blurred and jagged in its outlines, still partly secreted in the interstices of medieval forms of action".

8-024
De Smith found that administrative law lacked clear principles and noted that the "dearth of coherent principles of administrative law" is an example of looking for formalism in the quest for certainty, clarity and reason through principle. De Smith's explanation that administrative courts were opposed to the traditions of the English common law in the seventeenth century, is compelling. Suspicion was commonly held that any encroachment by a specialised court in the sphere of public law might re-kindle the arbitrary powers of the discredited court of Star Chamber and the prerogative courts in medieval times.

8-025
The void left by no separate administrative law court was rapidly filled by ad hoc developments. The strongly held view was that the ordinary courts may control the Executive and its agents in much the same way as any other legal dispute might be resolved by the courts.

8-026
Pragmatism and formalism encapsulate the essential qualities of the common law. How influential have such characteristics been in shaping public law? Some writers link the formalism, explained above, to "the common law frame of mind". This seeks "to dig deep" to find coherent and unified rules amid the irrational, the chaotic or the exceptional. Generalisations are drawn to create principles with the appearance of objectivity and coherence. Such techniques of analysis are familiar to lawyers and are applied to find great principles or define legal

---

30 See Brian Simpson, "The Common Law and Legal Theory" in W. Twining (ed), *Legal Theory and Common Law* (London: Blackwell, 1986), pp.8–25. Stare decisis in its modern meaning binds courts to agreed legal principles. In historical terms the common law tradition had developed based on customary rules rather than formal law.
31 S. A. de Smith, *Judicial Review of Administrative Action*, 2nd edn (London: Stevens, 1973), p.4.

issues and are particularly suited to case law analysis. Lawyers make use of judicial decisions and seek to explain their relevance as a coherent set of rules available to be applied to a new set of problems or facts. The mastery of techniques of case law analysis depends, whenever relevant, on drawing distinctions, recognising exceptions and if necessary special circumstances in order to categorise and create a coherent set of legal rules.

8-027

Like any model of analysis, it may be readily adapted for different purposes. Applied to judicial decisions by lawyers it is also applied by academic lawyers in their textbooks. The influence of the "common law mind" is seen particularly in the development of legal education in the mid-nineteenth century.

8-028

English law in the public law area developed a system of remedies rather than rights. Remedies may be traced to the development of legal actions in the early history of the common law. The inheritance of the medieval Constitution focused on Parliament's powers and their development, to supersede the King's powers to make law and influence affairs of State through patronage. Once Parliament's authority was resolved the question of rights was regarded as a residual matter.

8-029

The judges, responsive to the need to develop legal rules, attempted to interpret the needs and problems of society through flexible solutions applied in individual cases. Much of the development of English law depended on the ability of the law to grant a suitable remedy in an individual case. While remedies may have offered solutions to practical problems, often these were constructed in narrowly defined ways and limited by procedure and form. No codified set of statutes or codified doctrine existed.

8-030

The English common law was particularly influenced by the practitioner's concerns. This may explain how its survival and the haphazard nature of its development was achieved. The common law was remarkably anti-theoretical in its approach. Notions of policy, justice and legal doctrine found in the common law were determined by procedure and form rather than through reasoned or theoretical principles. From an impartial view the law had to find an appropriate remedy to solve the case.

8-031

Opposition to codification also marked out the English common law tradition as distinctive. This was particularly striking in the case of the criminal law in the nineteenth century. Bentham's *Principles of Penal Law* set out basic principles of law, both in theory and in substance, and contained a draft criminal code. Generally, codification was not proceeded with even after Brougham, as Lord Chancellor, appointed Criminal Law Commissioners to consider consolidation of existing common law principles and statutes into one coherent set of rules. Continental systems[32] of law more easily adopted codified systems of law influenced by the French *Code Napoleon* and the Roman law tradition found in the *Corpus Juris Civilis*. In part this may be a reflection of the differing political developments in England compared with European

---

32 In contrast in Germany, Anton Thibaut (1772–1840) a Law professor, Heidelberg, argued in his essay "On the Necessity for a General Civil Code for Germany". Reservations about the universal nature of such a code were made by Friedrich Carl Von Savigny (1779–1861). R. C. Van Caenegem, *Judges, Legislators and Professors: Chapters in European Legal History* (Cambridge: Cambridge University Press, 1987). I. Loveland, *Constitutional law*, 2nd edn (London: Butterworths, 2001).

countries. But evaluation is difficult because the common law rarely articulated explanations of its own developments in contrast to scholars proposing and formulating codes.

8-032 Another distinctive feature of the common law tradition bearing on the development of public law is the development of statute law. Parliament's role as a regular source of legal change was bound up with the theory of the sovereignty of Parliament. The eighteenth-century Constitution emphasised a balance between the Executive and Parliament freely admitting that parliamentary power might become governmental power. The nineteenth-century Constitution with an extended franchise made Parliament a major source of law through legislation.

8-033 Statutory law was an important source of formal reasoning that maintained the sovereignty of Parliament. As Atiyah and Summers note[33]:

> "England has a long tradition of narrow, detailed drafting; the English draftsman has always (or at any rate for at least two centuries) tried to produce language which is capable of neutral, non-purposive interpretation. An English statute has traditionally been drafted in such detail that it can be said to be a catalogue of rules."

8-034 The strong orientation in favour of hard and fast rules contained in the mass of technical statutory law reflects the traditions of English government, based on a single winning party with strong political objectives presented in legislative form and passed by Parliament. There is an equally strong tradition of skilled parliamentary drafting carried out by professional lawyers, with skills developed through the experience of permanent officials over a period of time. Most of this expertise remains confined to the resources of government departments.

8-035 The traditions of parliamentary sovereignty are therefore reinforced by the absence of any judicial power to review the legality of Acts of Parliament and until recently in the context of European Community law, this tradition remains strong. While public lawyers in the UK require the skills of reading cases and interpreting judicial decisions, equal and perhaps more important are the interpretative skills over complex, technical and precisely drafted statutes. Public law in the UK is to be found more in a statutory form than in the decisions of decided cases by judges.

8-036 Statutory developments have been so extensive that, it will be appreciated, this has added to the diffuse nature of the subject. Specialisms developed in public law where statutory developments have been extensive include such subjects as local government, housing, planning law, immigration and the environment. The specialist nature of these subject areas make any generalisations of legal principle difficult. Moreover, any generalisations that attempt to explain the context where government activity takes place, such as housing, immigration or social security law, invariably become entangled in a mass of technical and complex rules that add further difficulty to understanding the nature of public law in the UK.

8-037 A similar problem arises in the examination of principles of judicial review. Judicial review of administrative decisions lacks any detailed code of general principles. Any attempt to formulate such a code is frustrated by the pragmatic and often sporadic nature of judicial review.

---

33   P. S. Atiyah and R. S. Summers, *Form and Substance in Anglo-American Law* (Oxford: Clarendon, 1987), p.323.

Arguably, legal principles derived from a small number of legal cases are limited in their general application.

The eclectic and diffuse nature of public law, the absence of clearly defined principles and the historical legacy of an unwritten constitution have affected the development of public law. Public lawyers engage in a certain amount of gap-filling. This means finding solutions from past experiences which do not always fit the challenges posed by new problems. Hence the attention given to conventions, understandings or practices which explain the working of the Constitution, but which may in reality be little more than the political habits of the government of the day. The attraction of accomplishing legal changes relatively easily within an unwritten constitution compared to a written constitution may be misleading. Equally important is the possibility at least that the flexibility of an unwritten constitution may be adapted to the needs of government anxious to extend public power potentially unlimited or uncontrolled by any constitutional brake or device.

8-038

The main characteristics of the UK's common law tradition may be briefly summarised. The unitary and centralised nature of the State, the formality and pragmatism of English law, the continuity offered by an unwritten constitution have their origins in the historical influences of the past and notably in the last century. As McCrudden observed[34]:

8-039

> **"An important theme running through British thought concentrates on history and tradition when evaluating the processes by which political and legal decisions are made. Problems are solved, in this empiricist tradition, on the basis of experience. Solutions are what works and what lasts. Institutions should therefore operate flexibly, learn from the past and develop to suit the conditions of their time. This is the essence of the common law tradition."**

D: The Historical Legacy

The question arises as to the influences public law has experienced throughout its development. Arguably, the content of public law which is found in statutes, common law principles, conventions, rules and institutions may only be understood in the broader context of the ideas and influences which a society experiences. Most contemporary legal writers would accept that it is impossible to understand administrative law as a distinct subject without recognising the close interrelationship with the constitutional arrangements within which administrative law must operate.

8-040

There is no complete congruence between legal theory or the ideas of political scientists

8-041

---

34 C. McCrudden, "Northern Ireland and the British Constitution" in J. Jowell and D. Oliver (eds), *The Changing Constitution*, 2nd edn (Oxford: Oxford University Press, 1989), p.298; and 3rd edn (1994), pp.323–379.

or philosophers and public law. Differing assumptions about the role of the State, the exercise of power and the role of law itself make any informed discussion of legal theory and public law difficult to achieve. A further caveat is that traditionally lawyers have reacted against broadening the nature of their inquiry beyond the confines of legally enforceable rights and the study of purely technical legal rules. This is a reflection of an approach confined to the study of court orientated rules. However, the nature of public law is such that many issues are not justiciable before the courts and depend not on legally enforceable rights, but on an understanding of the nature of law and political power under democratic and accountable government.

8-042 The task of assessing the influence of legal thinking on public law may be facilitated by the division of the discussion into two parts: first, consideration of the historical influences and second, an introduction to contemporary discourse on public law. It is not possible to account for the development of all political theory in the nineteenth century. A selection is necessary of the influences confined to explaining some of the main developments in public law.

8-043 The eighteenth-century enlightenment is a convenient starting point to begin to trace the influences of legal thinking, theory and philosophy on public law. The UK had established, without revolution, effective change by the end of the seventeenth century, contained in the Bill of Rights (1689), the Act of Settlement (1701) and the Act of Union (1707). Taken to be the framework of modern constitutional arrangements, the shape, function and operating practices of the Constitution remained to be defined and clarified.

8-044 In the field of constitutional law, Montesquieu's (1689–1755) influence was one of the most remarkable.[35] Influential in the idea that institutions of the State both political and legal might be criticised, he advanced the view that law was linked to the needs of society. His studies in England from 1729–31, and particularly the influence of the writings of John Locke (1632–1704) led him to believe that natural law rights could be determined through constitutional law, the liberty of the individual. Montesquieu found attractive the liberalism of the English Constitution and promoted the value of the UK's constitutional arrangements in Europe.

8-045 Montesquieu's influence became known in terms of social contract theory which linked the civil state, the laws and constitutions to the general state of society. Montesquieu helped promote belief in the doctrine of separation of powers setting out how government ought to carry out its legislative, executive and judicial functions, each working independently. Undoubtedly these ideas became influential as to how government was perceived to act within a framework contained in the eighteenth-century Constitution. Building on Locke's thesis of the sovereignty or supremacy of Parliament, Montesquieu identified the various functions of government such as the legislative, executive and judicial. Believing in "checks and balances", Montesquieu also identified the necessary balance between the different elements of government to achieve some degree of self-regulation. Approaches to marketization of the state and government by consent are also sketched out in Locke's writing but are often not fully worked up into a grand political theory or mature statement, provide instead an important mapping exercise in setting out the parameters of legal, constitutional and political power. As Jeremy Waldron notes:

---

35 Montesquieu, *L'Esprit des Lois* (1748); *Defense de l'Esprit des Lois* (1750).

> "Locke did not develop a complete or watertight theory of politics: but he developed a profound and convincing political philosophy—by which I mean a foundation in thought for approaching and reflecting upon the real problems of right, equality, objectivity and power in politics."[36]

The quest for order in society[37] is a familiar theme amongst constitutional writing in the eighteenth century. This theme was developed in the writings of William Blackstone (1723–80) in his *Commentaries on the Laws of England*. Blackstone asserted the sovereignty of Parliament but this did not prevent him from accepting some natural law ideas as a means of achieving enforcement. Natural law concepts formed part of various social contract theories in an attempt to reconcile Parliament's legislative supremacy and individual justice. At times, there emerges in Blackstone's writing an explanation of constitutional "rights". These are asserted as part of the general protection afforded to the citizen under the law. Arguably such statements appear idealistic rather than practical and there is no acknowledgement of the difficulty of attempting to put their meaning into practice. We shall see below the importance of Blackstone in the development of the science of law.

Nevertheless, natural law concepts were significant for many eighteenth-century legal writers because a law of nature conveniently fitted the natural reasoning of the period. Certainly in European legal philosophy, natural law concepts helped form international law, and provide a strong tradition for a debate over the role of law in society. Both Montesquieu and Blackstone contributed to the discussion of natural law concepts in England. Blackstone's formal presentation of the law and formidable understanding of legal principles helped make the influence of his Commentaries extend beyond a small legal audience, to become part of "the literature of England". In the English courts, during the period when codification took root in Germany and France, principles of English law became solidified. The question arises as to what were the influences at work in the decisions of the courts during the seventeenth and eighteenth centuries?

Developments in public law included some early seventeenth-century cases that laid the foundations of natural justice and standards of reasonableness as principles of the common law. The explanation for such judicial creativity came from the separate development of "natural rights" from natural law. Political writers in the eighteenth century influenced by Locke's explanation of and justification for the English revolution, developed more sophisticated understandings of rights being created through legal rules. Legal writers such as Coke (1552–1634) had linked property to rights and both Locke and Coke contributed to the views on the rule of law and natural rights which were later influential amongst French writers prior to the French Revolution. Locke's thinking on the rule of law had an important influence on

---

36   Jeremy Waldron, "John Locke" in David Boucher and Paul Kelly, *Political Thinkers*, 2nd edn (Oxford: Oxford University Press, 2009), pp.207–223.
37   See *The letter from Dicey to Leo Maxse*, 25 September 1909. Quoted in Richard Cosgrove, *The Rule of Law: Albert Venn Dicey, Victorian Jurist* (London: Macmillan, 1980), p.62.

Blackstone, whose analysis of the royal prerogative included the view that the Crown should not enjoy any immunity from civil liability by virtue of the nature of the prerogative.

8-049 Judicial developments in the eighteenth century were about the relationship between law, the State and moral authority. One of the leading eighteenth-century cases of *Entick v Carrington* (1765)[38] applied, in a practical way, the principle of individual rights as a protection against the implementation of a general warrant of arrest against John Wilkes which the courts declared illegal.

8-050 It will be apparent that a number of themes, recognisable from the discussion in Pt I of the textbook, emerge from the eighteenth-century writings on legal theory and political thought. These include the doctrine of the separation of powers, the rule of law and natural rights. Such constitutional principles become relevant in understanding the English Constitution. Particularly important was the influence of the doctrine of separation of powers as a protection against abuse and tyranny. By the end of the eighteenth century the role of the courts in developing common law principles had become articulated in disputes between the King and the judges over taxation and in the legality of arrest, search and seizure. The focus on principles of the common good were identified as an objective of law and good government. These principles became more fully developed at the beginning of the nineteenth century as pertinent to the questions raised about the increasing use of legislation.

E: The Science of Law

8-051 Attempts to systemise English law came from two directions. One approach, influenced by Blackstone, attempted to add continental ideas about rights to the reasoning implied in the common law. The other approach dominated by Jeremy Bentham (1748–1832) aimed to provide a codification of principles. While different directions may be detected in both approaches, there was common ground. The methodology of science and the reasoning of statistical study were influential in the writings of both Blackstone and Bentham. This ensured that scientific methodology was integral to the analytical methodology and the legal reasoning employed in the development of the common law.

8-052 Blackstone encouraged the idea that English law was "a science which distinguished the criterion of right and wrong".[39] His attempts to reconcile the historical development of the common law with a flexible but rule-bound system gave rise to an analytical method. This

---

38 *Entick v Carrington* (1765) 19 St. Tr. 1030.
39 See J. A. G. Griffiths, "The Political Constitution" (1979) 42 *Modern Law Review* 1; and *The Politics of the Judiciary* (London: Fontana, 1991). Echoes of Jennings' view are apparent in Loughlin's thesis. See Jennings, *The Law and the Constitution* (London: University of London Press, 1959), p.300: "The process of explanation is the function of constitutional law (or jurisprudence) or of that part of political science which is concerned with the actual

proved to be very influential especially when later adopted by Dicey in his analysis of the English Constitution. The essential of Blackstone's legacy found that English law could be understood from a deductive system of reasoning incorporating natural law principles. This required a mathematical approach to law through a deductive method of analysis. It favoured the formality of legal rules and the formal reduction to specific points of the resolution of any dispute.

8–053

It is not surprising to find that at the end of the eighteenth century many lawyers had become empiricists at a time when scientific discovery and science attracted the attention of the age. Whether this was coincidence or not is difficult to determine. What was remarkable was that lawyers found that through detailed empirical investigation, law was treated as practical and relevant rather than theoretical and abstract. The law on pleading was a clear example of the view that the legal system was a functioning set of rules that provided the tools for the practitioner to fashion remedies for the client. Writers considered "the science of pleading" rooted in the belief that the precision of rules would give rise to the revelation of truth. The system of writs accentuated the idea that correct procedure gave rise to an accurate record and this laid the foundations of law.

8–054

On a broader analysis empirical methodology lay at the root of deciding cases. The development of case law followed from the efforts to systematise. The idea that English law could be found in decided cases rested on the development of a reliable and comprehensive system of law reports. The system of stare decisis and the doctrine of precedent rested on judicial reasoning being applied by analogy to cases with similar facts. Technical and formal rules applied in an analytical and scientific way rooted the common law to the empiricist tradition and the logic of the judges.

8–055

Within this tradition lay considerable self-doubt and disenchantment. The desire for a clearly defined set of rules for judges to apply prompted many English lawyers to examine the value of the civil law as a source of principles and jurisprudence. Generally, there was considerable reluctance to reconcile the common law with the civil law system in all its forms.

8–056

Bentham's disillusionment with the common law identified in his later writings came from the inadequacy of the procedural rules, the absence of clear principles and the lack of comprehensiveness. His pursuit of universal codification of English law proved a lifetime work which ultimately ended in frustration. There is evidence to show that in determine the contents of codes and their application, Bentham shared the techniques implied in the scientific method as a means to determine concepts and ideas. Lobban explains[40]:

> "An Introduction [to the Principles of Morals and legislation] was perceived by Bentham to be a 'metaphysical' work, standing in relation to the substantive law as a treatise of pure mathematics stood to natural philosophy."

workings of institutes; the process of justification belongs to political theory (or the philosophy of law) or to that part of political science which relates to the theory of institutes".

40   M. Lobban, *The Common Law and English Jurisprudence 1760–1850* (Oxford: Clarendon Press, 1991), p.155.

8-057 Bentham's codification project was ultimately rejected despite many attempts through numerous Royal Commissions and law reform initiatives. Bentham had sought to devise a science of principles derived from the immutable laws of human nature. In his principles of utility may be found the science of law reform. Diagnosing a wide range of social reforms from prisons to the workhouse, from education to the courts and from the substantive criminal law to a codified constitution, Bentham's ambitious aim was that through codification a legislative solution to the problems of society may be found.

8-058 The measurement of law against some standard or criterion was the dominant theme in Bentham's pioneering work, *A Fragment of Government*, (1776) followed by his *Introduction to the Principles of Morals and Legislation* (1789). Bentham's[41] task, to develop a science of human action, began with a search for fundamental meaning in defining legal terms. His initial inquiry disputed the basic assumptions underlying Blackstone's *Commentaries* that all law was to be accepted without questioning its utility. Bentham questioned not only how law might be defined but what law should be. Bentham divided law into two categories: the first, that of the legislator, he described as "authoritative law"; and the second, law that was unauthoritative. By this means he questioned the quality of law according to his theory of utility, namely the greatest happiness principle. This became an important theme developed at great length in his book *A Fragment of Government*. Bentham's influence became apparent in the impact of his ideas on how legislation was to be appraised by lawyers in the nineteenth century. Bentham insisted that legislation should encourage the general good and to that end linguistic analysis might be called in aid of statutory interpretation. Weak laws might be avoided by an accurate analysis of legal terminology and an understanding "of the art of legislation".

8-059 Bentham's influence was wide ranging. His philosophy was read by a wide range of interested disciplines beyond law. In particular, he was influential in fostering the idea that law might create improvements if subjected to an analytical approach and careful appraisal. The full importance of Bentham's work became clear in the nineteenth century as Bentham's legislative principles became influential. One explanation of Bentham's influence was the interpretation given to Bentham's writing by John Austin (1790–1859). Austin's lectures on jurisprudence were first published in *The Province of Jurisprudence Determined* (1832) which were later amended and expanded by a number of editors after his death. In terms of thinking about issues of public law, Austin's influence was probably the most significant in the nineteenth century, partly because his lectures appeared in the style of a textbook and in the absence of a major rival, Austin's views dominated jurisprudence.

---

41 P. Schofield, "Jeremy Bentham and Nineteenth Century English Jurisprudence" (1991) 12 *Journal of Legal History* 1, pp.58–88. Also see S. Collini, D. Winch and J. Burrow, *That Noble Science of Politics: A Study in Nineteenth Century Intellectual History* (Cambridge: Cambridge University Press, 1983); J. M. Burns and H. L. A. Hart (eds), *A Comment on the Commentaries and A Fragment on Government* (London: Athlone Press, 1977); J. Dinwiddy, "Early Nineteenth Century Reactions to Benthamism", Transactions of the Royal Historical Society XXXIV (1984), pp.47–69; and J. Bowring (ed), *The Works of Jeremy Bentham*, 11 Vols (London: William Tait, 1843). See C. W. Everett (ed), *The Limits of Jurisprudence Defined* (New York: Columbia University Press, 1945).

8-060 Comparing Austin to Bentham is difficult, but it is generally accepted that Austin's view of law was narrower than Bentham's. It is also suggested that had Bentham published in his lifetime his work *Of Laws in General*, this might have established Bentham's pre-eminence over Austin. The narrowness of Austin's analysis is due to the distinction he drew between the analysis of legal terms and reform of the law. Bentham conveniently drew both together, while Austin's desire to strictly interpret the law came from his definition of law to be "a command supported with a sanction".

8-061 The essential clarity of the conception of law helped later writers, such as Dicey, to distinguish laws from conventions. Austin, along with Bentham, promised an analytical form of jurisprudence. Laws could be considered by jurists through defining their meaning and explaining their terms. Austin was less concerned than Bentham with considering what laws ought to consist of. Nonetheless both were influential in the development of public law in the nineteenth century.

8-062 Both Austin and Bentham belonged to the analytical school of jurisprudence. The analytical jurists classified, defined and expressed laws freed from any normative analysis. An equally significant influence in nineteenth-century jurisprudence came from the historical school of jurisprudence. The historical school disputed that all law might be resolved as a command of a sovereign and insisted that custom, history, and opinion might be important sources of law. In contrast to the analytical school, the historical school, founded by Savigny (1779–1861) and influenced by Maine's (1822–88) *Ancient Law* (1861) and *Early Law and Custom* (1883), examined the relationship between law and morality. This inquiry questioned how existing practices and institutions reflected moral ideas and influences.

8-063 Both analytical and historical[42] schools came under various attempts to combine the strengths of each at different times throughout the nineteenth century but with limited success. Taken generally there emerged a "science of jurisprudence", as an attempt to combine the virtues of both analytical and historical schools. Methodology became an important means to bridge the differences between each of the philosophical schools of thought.

8-064 The science of law united both analytical and historical schools in the study of legislation. Denis Caulfield Heron (1825–1881) in his work, *An Introduction to the History of Jurisprudence*[43] wrote how legislation was a "compromise between history and philosophy". The influence of codification in Europe encouraged consideration of law as a means of setting standards. While codification itself was rejected in England, the search for some reasonable standard to judge law united the historical method of the historical school with the analytical style and method of the analytical school.

8-065 In the nineteenth century the development of public law came under similar influences as other areas of knowledge. Generally, it was commonly assumed that law could be regarded in the same way as other disciplines. In particular the science of law influenced how writers such as Dicey came to consider Parliament's role in developing legislation. Public law was influenced by the popularity of law reform. Law reform became a major catalyst for change

---

42 J. M. Kelly, *A Short History of Western Legal Theory* (Oxford: Clarendon, 1992), pp.312–325.
43 D. C. Heron, *An Introduction to the History of Jurisprudence* (London: J. W. Parker & Son, 1860).

and in the late nineteenth century became the forum for debate as to precisely the extent of Parliament's role.[44] The Reform Acts of 1832 and 1867 by extending the franchise, considerably broadened the franchise and the scope for change through an extended scope for Parliament's legislative authority.

8-066
As a result, English law resisted the attempt to provide a single jurisprudence of rights and remedies. The jurisprudence of Blackstone, Bentham, Austin and Dicey allowed lawyers to conceive law through an analytical jurisprudence rooted in an empirical tradition bearing many characteristics of scientific proof. Strict procedural rules determined the precise point of dispute for deliberation by the court. Judges attempted to discover through deductive reasoning the resolution of the dispute from the material facts presented by the litigants in each case. So much lay outside the control of any single system of rule. The litigant determined the cases that came to court and the facts each case presented. The judges responded to the challenge in a haphazard way drawing on a wide range of sources and ideas to find solutions. The jury added to the lack of predictability of outcome. The common law built on the reasoning common to "ordinary men" and the rules of procedure that guided the discourse set the agenda for judges. The absence of a systemised English law and a coherent theoretical underpinning of the principles of law underlines the importance of the analytical method used in the common law.

8-067
Schofield noted[45] that the science of law had two parts, "the first an analysis and a classification of the general principles which are to be found in advanced systems of law, and the second the discovery of the origin and growth of legal notions". Public law was greatly influenced by both the methods of analysis and the search for principles in the growth and development of the common law tradition.

F: Dicey and his Contemporaries

8-068
The emergence of an influential group of academic lawyers in the late nineteenth century must be set against a background of neglect in legal education. The 1846 Select Committee on legal education described[46] "the lamentable state of legal education" and criticised the teaching of

---

44 Denis Caulfield Heron (1825–1881), Professor of Jurisprudence and Political Economy, Queen's College, Galway, 1849–1859, QC 1860, MP for Tipperary 1868–74, Third Sergeant-at-Law 1880, Vice-President, Social Inquiry and Statistical Society of Ireland (1871–81). T. Porter, *The Rise of Statistical Thinking 1820–1900* (Princeton, NJ: Princeton University Press, 1986); and John A. Hannigan, *Environmental Sociology* (London: Routledge, 1995). See Martin Loughlin, "The Pathways of Public Law Scholarship" in *Frontiers of Legal Scholarship* (London: John Wiley, 1996), pp.163–188.
45 Philip Schofield, "Jeremy Bentham and Nineteenth Century English Jurisprudence" (1991) 12 *Journal of Legal History* 1, pp.58–88.
46 J. H. Baker, "University College and Legal Education 1826–1976" (1977) 30 *Current Legal Problems*, pp.1–13. See D. Sugarman in W. L. Twining (ed), *Legal Theory and the Common Law* (London: Blackwell, 1986), Ch.3.

law in the universities of Oxford and Cambridge. Practical training in articles or pupillage was not well regulated or examined. Only gradually did change occur, first in 1852, with the establishment of the Council of Legal Education to regulate education of Bar students. Then in 1877, the Law Society succeeded in establishing solicitors' qualifying examinations and eventually in 1903, a School of Law in London.

The Royal Commission Report, in 1856, continued demands for reform and the preference that universities should concentrate on the theoretical and philosophical study of law, leaving the teaching of practical law to the profession.[47]

The creation of new courses and posts in Oxford and Cambridge in the latter half of the nineteenth century brought a new intellectual influence. The question was how to establish a role for academic lawyers which numbered Maine (1822–88); Whewell, Professor of International Law in Cambridge (1887); Bryce (1838–1922), Regius Professor of Civil Law at Oxford (1870–93); Anson (1843–1914), Warden of All Souls, Oxford (1899–1914); Holland (1835–1926), Chichele Professor of International Law and Diplomacy, Oxford (1874–1910); and Dicey (1835–1922), Vinerian Professor of Law, Oxford (1882–1909).

The answer came from analytical jurisprudence; so influential in shaping legislation, it also influenced academic law.[48] Academic lawyers faced two pressures: one from within university education where academic respectability required a body of expertise and coherence; the other came from the legal profession which required understanding of legal principle, and practical explanation. As already mentioned above, academic lawyers found that legal textbooks offered a suitable solution. This permitted an exposition of the law as a coherent whole, together with an analysis of legal doctrine consistent with the tasks of legal education and scholarship. In the field of public law, Dicey's writings came to dominate.

It has already been noted that Dicey's lectures at Oxford came to be published in 1885 in his *Introduction to the Law of the Constitution*. Influenced by the analytical school of thought, Dicey carefully set out the legal principles which guided the student of the Constitution. Originality of thought was not claimed, but by identifying the guiding principles which underpinned the unwritten constitution he created a legal textbook for lawyers devoid of much historical explanation.

Dicey's contribution to public law and his enduring influence may be examined in two respects. First, Dicey's method of analysis and its significance when interpreting the law of the Constitution. Secondly, Dicey's explanation of the Constitution, especially his description of the legislative sovereignty of Parliament, the rule of law and the role of constitutional conventions, may be noted as to its significance for the study of public law. Throughout this textbook various references may be found to the explanation of basic principles provided by Dicey. Even though his ideas remain controversial, they are nevertheless influential. Interpreting Dicey's writing is not easy, particularly as he appears to write for different audiences involving different styles of

---

47 Philip Schofield, "Jeremy Bentham and Nineteenth Century English Jurisprudence" (1991) 12 *Journal of Legal History* 1, pp.58–88.
48 Henry Maine, *Ancient Law: its Connection with the Early History of Society and its Relation to Modern Ideas* (London: J. Murray, 1920).

argument and presentation. His text book, *Law of the Constitution*, has resulted in Dicey being regarded as "the high priest of constitutional theory".[49] Here Dicey's approach was "analytical, formalist, scientifically mechanical, descriptive and positivist".[50] The book was also dogmatic in setting out "blackletter" texts that carried with them a carefully nuanced approach to infallibility.[51] Greatly influenced by John Austin (1790–1859),[52] Dicey valued legal rules and an authoritative presentation of legal argument, similar to a mathematician presenting mathematical data. The claim of an objective and "forensic account of the law" was at the centre of his endeavour, his greatest appeal was to lawyers and judges by tackling constitutional issues from a legal perspective. Dicey's reputation came from the book, its general acceptance in teaching, and in receiving widespread recognition as a distinctive contribution in the method of text book writing.[53]

8-074

Formulating unwritten constitutional rules and conventions into a form of a written code was also part of his intention and was consistent with the style of his presentation. Beneath the mask of professorial impartiality lay many normative judgments. This had inherent dangers, not least that the rules formulated in the text might not be accurate or even a true assessment of how government worked or ought to work. It is not surprising that Dicey's misinterpretation of the French system of administrative law should be sharply criticised and lead eventually to his later admission[54] that he had misunderstood the French system.[55] This has led to him misunderstanding the potential dangers from the development of administrative law in England. However, the damage had already been done, and it took nearly a century for English lawyers to fully accept that administrative law was a positive development as a check on administrative decisions, while remaining consistent with the common law.[56] A further admission by Dicey on the value of re-formulating legal rules into codes and digests came in 1896 when he wrote to Bryce:

> "I have grown sceptical as to the merit of 'digests' of the modern kind as a method of reproducing statements of law. They involve immense waste of space and I think a good deal of repetition and lead to an affection of precision in the use of terms, which in the

---

49   M. Loughlin, *Public Law and Political Theory* (Oxford: Clarendon Press, 1992), p.140.
50   Mark D Walters, "Dicey on Writing the Law of the Constitution" (2012) *Oxford Journal of Legal Studies* 21–49, p.22.
51   A. V. Dicey, *Conflict of Laws* (London: Stevens & Sons, 1949)
52   John Austin, *Lectures on Jurisprudence* (London: 1863). Austin was Professor of Jurisprudence in 1826 in the newly formed University of London. He was one of the analytical school of jurisprudence.
53   See C. Elton, "Review of *Law of the Constitution*" (1886) 726 *The Academy* 229; A. W. B. Simpson, "The Rise and Fall of the Legal Treatise: Legal Principles and the forms of Legal Literature" (1981) 48 *University of Chicago L. Rev.* 632.
54   A. V. Dicey, "The Development of Administrative Law in England" (1915) *Law Quarterly Review* 148–153.
55   I. Jennings, *The Law and the Constitution*, 5th edn (London: University of London Press, 1959) and Harry Arthurs, "Rethinking Administrative Law" (1979) 17 *Osgoode Hall Law Journal* 1–45.
56   H. Arthurs, Without the Law (Toronto: University of Toronto Press, 1985).

> present condition of English legal terminology is and must be an affectation rather than a reality."[57]

Despite this scepticism Dicey continued to write textbooks including new editions of his *Law of the Constitution*.[58] The appeal to legal rules and formalistic legal principles is hard to reconcile with Dicey's political stance on matters that were the subject of Parliamentary law reform such as his opposition to votes for women, the recognition and value of trade unions and the growth of the welfare state. Dicey was a complicated person, not least when it came to his strongly held political views on Home Rule, a subject above all others that attracted his attention. As Mark Walters concluded Dicey advocated "albeit anonymously, an integrated form of jurisprudence that combined descriptive, historical and normative elements together".[59] Viewed from that perspective it is possible to see the combination of legal exposition and political tract at its most powerful and influential.

8-075

Dicey's analytical method of inquiry favoured abstracting basic principles from legal material and subjecting constitutional law to scientific study. Dicey presented a vision of constitutional law corresponding to the earlier influences of Blackstone, Bagehot and Montesquieu. The English Constitution when subjected to Dicey's analysis appears as a triumph of achievement. Dicey's formulation of principles have the hallmark of a codified constitution providing uniformity, and formality through the application of Dicey's analytical method. Dicey's achievement was to provide the required exposition, conceptualisation and systematisation of constitutional law in the UK. In short, Dicey's *Law of the Constitution* filled a gap without encroaching upon law reform or the codification movement.

8-076

The enduring qualities of Dicey's analysis are reflected in his formulation of constitutional principles. It is useful to draw together the main elements in Dicey's thinking which remain influential today. It is readily apparent that Dicey borrowed many of his ideas from the various schools of jurisprudence mentioned above. Here we are concerned with general principles only; the details of many of these principles are discussed in the appropriate part of the textbook.

8-077

Dicey's vision of constitutional and administrative law begins with his analysis of sovereignty, both political and legal. Dicey acknowledged that Parliament could "make or unmake any law" but accepted that political and legal sovereignty could be distinguished. Political sovereignty placed certain influence with the majority of the electorate but this was to be entirely self-adjusting. Craig noted[60]:

8-078

---

57 A. V. Dicey to Oliver Wendall Holmes (19 April 1896), Holmes Jr. Papers HOLLIS 601674, Box 42–8, Harvard Law Library Special Collections.
58 Dicey also wrote two editions of his text book on A. V. Dicey *Conflict of Laws* (London: Stevens & Sons, 1949).
59 Mark D. Walters, "Dicey on Writing *The Law of the Constitution*" (2012) *Oxford Journal of Legal Studies* 21–49, p.40.
60 P. Craig, *Public Law and Democracy in the United Kingdom and the United States of America* (Oxford: Clarendon, 1990), pp.15–16. Also see D. Sugarman, "The Legal Boundaries of Liberty: Dicey, Liberalism and Legal Science" (1983) 46 *Modern Law Review* 102–111.

> "The absence of constitutional review and the Diceyan conception of sovereignty are therefore firmly embedded within a conception of self-correcting majoritarian democracy."

8-079 Dicey's idealism led him to believe that a unitary state embodying elected government might reinforce the rule of law. Paradoxically, the rule of law which later commentators considered the weak element in Dicey's analysis, came to reinforce sovereignty. The assumption is that the Commons might control the government. Dicey's style of analysis at first appears descriptive. His focus on principles and analytical style appears to offer a neutral perspective of the Constitution. Beneath the level of general description there are strong elements of value judgment. Dicey assumed that the English model of the Constitution was a better model than France or Germany or Switzerland, whose Constitutions Dicey had studied in great detail.

8-080 Dicey's rule of law adopted ideas from William Hearn (1826–1888) in his work *The Government of England, its Structure and its Development* (London: Longmans, 1867); and his understanding of conventions came from Edward Freeman (1823–1892) in his work *Growth of the English Constitution* (London: Macmillan, 1877). The essentials of Dicey's analysis are as follows: the rule of law depended on the absence of broad discretionary power and that all public power resided with Parliament. The courts' power to review legislation was inappropriate when Parliament's role was to keep government under scrutiny. Judicial review did not require a separate or distinct system of courts when the Commons might control the Executive and the direction of all governmental power was through Parliament.

8-081 Such assumptions lie behind Dicey's vision of judicial intervention being limited only to legislative intention. Even when the development of judicial scrutiny began in areas where the legislature had jurisdiction, Dicey was reluctant to envisage the courts developing beyond a narrow and defined remit, namely to ensure that the authority or power was exercised within its jurisdiction.

8-082 Conventions come under the same tension as the rule of law when threatened by the sovereignty of Parliament. Dicey's reconciliation of conventions to a "modern code of constitutional morality" and thereby representative democracy, linked the power of Parliament to that of democracy. Government was believed to be representative.

8-083 However, democracy was narrowly defined as confined to male citizens. The dangers of popular opinion when it called for trade union reform, Home Rule for Ireland or votes for women were seen as threats to the single unitary model of the Constitution. Dicey's later writing reflected his concerns about the break-up of the constituent parts of the UK through any federal constitutional arrangement.

8-084 To summarise, Dicey's skill at linking the historical roots of the common law tradition to constitutional change in the nineteenth century gave coherence to his vision of constitutional law. Adept at combining the influences of both the analytical and historical schools of jurisprudence, Dicey's work on the Constitution became influential. This was due to the combination of Dicey's analytical and expository style and the effect of providing in a codified form, a set of principles to guide discussion of constitutional law. Dicey had recognised a gap in textbook writing in constitutional law and by skilful analysis he provided a legacy for future generations of lawyers. Eight editions of the work were published during Dicey's lifetime. None were given substantial revision, though his last edition in 1914 received a revised introduction. By that time the shortcomings in Dicey's analysis had been noted and recognised.

8–085

The growth in delegated powers and in party government extended beyond any of Dicey's ideas of representative government. The ability of the Commons to control the Executive was doubted. Dicey also doubted whether the rule of law could survive given the combination of party politics and weak parliamentary control. The growth in legislation, and especially the debate over Irish Home Rule, had pointed to a growing tension between Dicey's model of the ideal constitution formulated in 1885 and the reality of the Constitution in 1914.

8–086

Such acknowledged defects in Dicey's vision of the constitution, apparent even to Dicey himself, did not lessen the importance of the Law of the Constitution. Paradoxically, the more defective the work was shown to be, the more influence it seemed to hold over lawyers and public law.

8–087

The most glaring weakness in Dicey's analysis was his failure to recognise the development of administrative law and his misunderstanding of French *droit administratif* which he erroneously saw as equivalent to tyranny and something alien and continental. English traditions were seen as superior to French traditions and the character of English law and its institutions influenced Dicey's vision of English administrative law.[61] In 1915 Dicey belatedly recognised administrative law as a branch of English public law. In so doing Dicey identified a role for the courts in overseeing the exercise of powers by government departments. Relying on cases such as *Local Government Board v Arlidge* and the *Board of Education v Rice*, Dicey believed that the courts offered greater guarantees of the rule of law than ministerial responsibility.

> "But any man who will look plain facts in the face will see in a moment that ministerial liability to the censure not in fact by Parliament, not even by the House of Commons, but by the party majority who keep the Government in office, is a very feeble guarantee indeed against the action which evades the authority of the law courts."

8–088

Despite his earlier reservations about judicial review, Dicey gave the impression that the courts might provide the best protection of liberties within existing constitutional arrangements.[62] Dicey's death in 1922 left unanswered in any detail whether this revision of his earlier views might have altered the fundamental principles of the constitution he explained in 1885. Dicey's contemporaries at Oxford—Bryce, Pollock, Holland and Anson—also wrote textbooks setting out principles in a coherent and lawyerly fashion. However, it is Dicey, alone amongst his contemporaries, whose influence became the most significant.

---

61 A. V. Dicey, "The Development of Administrative Law in England" (1915) 31 *Law Quarterly Review* 148. See F. H. Lawson, 'Dicey Revisited', (1959) *Political Quarterly* 109–126.
62 H. Arthurs, *Without the Law* (Toronto: University of Toronto Press, 1985); and H. Arthurs, "Rethinking Administrative Law" (1979) *Osgoode Hall Law Journal* 1–45.

G: Public Law and Political Change

8-089 Over one hundred years have passed since publication of the *Law of the Constitution*. During this period public law has continued to be influenced by Dicey's work. No less an influence came from writers challenging Dicey's vision of the Constitution.

8-090 Criticisms of administrative bureaucracy and inefficiencies at the expense of individual freedom were made in the late 1920s and throughout the period leading to the Second World War. William Robson[63] was influential in re-considering the Dicey model of the Constitution which he complained lacked an adequate administrative law to meet the demands of an extensive administrative State. A source of major concern was the "acquisition of legislative and judicial functions by the Executive".

8-091 Shortcomings in the system of tribunals, then in existence, were pointed out. Other writers criticised Dicey's analysis that administrative law was foreign or alien to English law. Particularly forthright in pointing out the errors in Dicey's analysis and understanding of French administrative law, Jennings asserted that administrative law had a valuable role in a country with a highly developed sense of political organisation. Jennings also disputed Dicey's analysis of sovereignty and questioned the value of individual rights contained in the rule of law as outlined by Dicey. In general Jennings favoured a broader, more sociological approach to public law. Dicey had analysed public law in terms of applying private law concepts and principles to government, sovereignty and the State. Jennings adopted a different approach, preferring to develop public law concepts in terms of duties, powers and responsibilities by adopting a "sociological method".

8-092 Jennings defined the role of the lawyer interested in the Constitution as different from the practitioner[64]:

> "The sociological process is simply to examine the facts, including the ideas of any given society. A jurist or a constitutional lawyer, unlike the practising lawyer is not concerned with the set of ideas possessed by lawyers alone, but with the ideas of people generally."

8-093 Broadening the debate as to the relationship between the nature of law and the State brought more influences in the development of public law. The most formidable was the work of Harold Laski[65] (1893–1950), whose influence on the theory of the State called into question assumptions behind the liberal State and the exercise of political power. Laski was greatly

---

63 W. A. Robson, *Justice and Administrative Law* (London: Stevens & Sons, 1951). Also see W. A. Robson, "The Report of the Committee on Ministers' Powers" (1932) 3 *Political Quarterly* 346.
64 I. Jennings, *The Law and the Constitution* (London: University of London Press, 1959). See Jennings, "The Report on Ministers' Powers" (1932) 10 *Public Administration* 333; and Jennings, "In praise of Dicey 1885–1935" (1935) 13 *Public Administration* 123.
65 H. Laski, *Studies in the Problem of Sovereignty* (New Haven, CT: Yale University Press, 1917); *Authority in the Modern State* (London: Routledge, 1919); "The Growth of Administrative Discretion" (1923) 1 *Journal of Public*

influenced by American jurists such as Holmes and Pound. By rejecting high theory, he argued for practical, common-sense and realistic assessments to be made of the reasoning behind judicial decisions and an exposition of assumptions which lay behind the value judgments contained in policy decisions.

Laski also questioned the single, unitary view of the State favoured by Dicey. Far removed from Dicey's idealism of the perfection he found in the Constitution, Laski sought justification for the consequences of government power and linked economic and social power to legal authority. Developing these ideas caused Laski to challenge the liberal theory of the State with the result that his sociological approach found support in the writings of Jennings and Robson.

Variations in Laski's reasoning, especially in his later works, have echoes of the influences of pragmatism which may also be found in other writers of the period. No single, coherent theme may be identified from amongst all of Dicey's critics but the debate about the nature of public law had changed remarkably from Dicey's influence. The period 1928–1932 marked an intense debate about public law.

Robson's influential *Justice and Administrative Law* was published in 1928. A year later the Lord Chief Justice, Lord Hewart, had published *The New Despotism*,[66] and a year after came F. J. Port's *Administrative Law*.[67] Hewart's warning of "administrative lawlessness" feared that government had become too powerful and, in common with Dicey's fears voiced in 1915, Hewart feared that the rule of law might become meaningless. All these influences came to the fore when in 1929 the Donoughmore Committee was set up inquiring into Ministers' powers, the use of delegated legislation and judicial decision-making. The Report was published in 1932 and Laski was included amongst the membership of the Committee. Hewart's *New Despotism* claimed that the power of government had expanded[68]:

> **"The official is anonymous, he is not bound by any course of procedure nor by any rules of evidence, nor is he obliged to give any reasons for his decision. . . The exercise of arbitrary power is neither law nor justice, administrative or at all."**

English administrative law with its distinctive use of administrative tribunals and inquiries was ill co-ordinated and lacked rationality.

Despite such strictures little was achieved by the Donoughmore Committee in terms of unifying the hotchpotch of administrative tribunals into a coherent whole. After Donoughmore, tribunals grew in an uncontrolled and bureaucratic way with specialised and complex rules accompanying their development.

Administration 92; *Report of the Committee on Ministers' Powers*, Cmd.4060 (1932); Annex of *Studies in the Problem of Sovereignty*; and "Judicial Review of Social Policy in England" (1926) 39 *Harvard Law Review* 839.

66 G. Hewart, *New Despotism* (London: Ernest Benn, 1929), pp.43–44.
67 F. J. Port, *Administrative Law* (London: Longmans, 1930).
68 Hewart, *New Despotism*, pp.43–44.

8-099   The rejection of Robson and Laski's analysis which favoured an independent tribunal system may be attributed to *droit administratif* and Dicey's objections. The Committee feared that setting up a uniform and independent tribunal system amounted to a rival form of administrative law to the ordinary courts and especially so if judicial review was excluded. While Dicey's influence still inhibited the growth of administrative law, it was only after the Second World War that the opportunity to break with the past arose. The Franks Committee in 1957, set up after the Crichel Down affair, reported in favour of creating a proper system of tribunals with clearly defined objectives and procedures under the Council of Tribunals. In effect this abandoned Dicey's opposition to such a system.

8-100   Recognition that administrative law had a proper place in English law came slowly. In 1964 Lord Reid observed,[69] "We do not have a developed system of administrative law—perhaps because until fairly recently we did not need it." Thereafter doubts about the existence and need for administrative law slowly dispelled. What remained, however, was a fundamental debate about the role of the courts in the future development of administrative law.

8-101   Dicey's rule of law asserted that the ordinary law should be supreme and that the ordinary courts should act as the cornerstone of the rule of law. Expanding the role of the courts through increased judicial intervention as the means of developing administrative law seemed to many to be supporting Dicey's rule of law. Under this view administrative law came to mean only judicial review. Remedies available to the litigant were narrowly and often procedurally defined and restricted to issues which to the courts appeared similar to settling contract or tort liability disputes in the private sector. This comparison of administrative law to actions in the private sector is useful when understanding how judicial review in the early development of administrative law remained restricted and constrained by narrow and technical concerns.

8-102   While Laski, Robson and Jennings had set a new agenda for the development of public law, judicial attitudes seemed to reflect Dicey's influence. One reason lay in the historical development of remedies and the narrow confines of statutory intention in terms only of legislative intent. The courts were presented with individual rights and specific remedies with the requirements of a specific locus standi rather than any broader inquiry into how powers were exercised. No conceptual framework for administrative law was put in place once administrative law became an established part of English law.

8-103   Another reason may be gleaned from the nature of Dicey's inheritance bequeathed to lawyers. With hindsight Dicey's original principles seem untenable given the nature of political and economic changes since 1885. Later writers had successfully shown contradictions in Dicey's principles and even Dicey's later revisions failed to support his original premise. Despite these flaws and rather like a many-headed hydra, Dicey's influence was not confined to his written text but his vision of constitutional arrangements triumphed over past practices and early history. Errors or flaws in Dicey's principles seemed to have been overlooked or distinguished as if they represented old precedents, which allowed Dicey's vision to continue and *Law of the*

---

69 *Ridge v Baldwin* [1964] A.C. 40; [1963] 2 W.L.R. 935 HL. See H. W. R. Wade, *Administrative Law* (Oxford: Clarendon, 1988); "Law, Opinion and Administration" (1962) 78 *Law Quarterly Review* 188; and *Constitutional Fundamentals* (London: Stevens and Sons, 1980).

Constitution to remain a significant textbook for the study of constitutional and administrative law. Dicey's analytical method, which owes much to the empirical tradition in law, has also remained influential in the style of public law scholarship.

Robson and Laski invigorated the study of public law by broadening the terms of inquiry into the nature of power and how power is exercised by the State. Economic, social and political issues became relevant in understanding public law. Further advances in understanding public law came from the influence of philosophy on law, which underwent a remarkable transformation under the influence of H. L. A. Hart.

8–104

Dicey, following Austin and Bentham, defined law as the command of a sovereign. After the Second World War jurisprudence became influenced by linguistic analysis from the writing of Wittgenstein and Gilbert Ryle.[70] The Oxford lawyer and philosopher H. L. A. Hart[71] questioned the Austin view of sovereignty and law, pointing out inadequacies in the understanding "of all law as a command". This contributed further to the discourse on public law by bringing questions of morality and explicit notions of adjudication in seeking to explain why laws are obeyed. Distinguishing legal from moral rules, Hart argued, depends on how society views the status of a particular rule.

The diversity of the influences in the development of public law includes contributions from political science, international studies and sociology. The blurring of subject categories as well as legal categories further complicates the question of whether public law is a distinctive subject. Daintith observes that a noticeable trend in writing about public law[72] "is the prevailing descriptive and eclectic mode of writing about the UK's Constitution and public law". The various influences currently at work in public law scholarship may be noted as follows.

8–105

H: Public Law in the Twenty-First Century

Contemporary public lawyers have contributed to defining public law and setting its boundaries. David Feldman and Mark Elliott have pointed out there is a contest over the nature and functions of public law.[73] Perceptions and analysis of public law have also changed, reflecting the ebb and flow of political and social life, but also global influences including those from countries with new constitutions. There are a number of dimensions to the debate, including

8–106

---

70 Kelly, *A Short History of Western Theory* (Oxford: Clarendon, 1992), pp.403–447.
71 H. L. A. Hart, *The Concept of Law* (Oxford: Clarendon: 1961); and "Definition and Theory in Jurisprudence" (1954) 70 *Law Quarterly Review* 37. See also J. Raz, *The Morality of Freedom* (Oxford: Clarendon, 1986).
72 T. Daintith, "Political Programmes and the Content of the Constitution" in W. Finnie, C. M. G. Himsworth and N. Walker (eds), *Edinburgh Essays in Public Law* (Edinburgh: Edinburgh University Press, 1991), pp.41–55.
H. D. Laswell and N. S. MacDougal, "Legal Education and Public Policy" (1943) 52 *Yale Law Journal* 203.
73 Mark Elliott and David Feldman, *The Cambridge Companion to Public Law* (Cambridge: Cambridge University Press, 2015).

competing ideas about the proper function of government and the state. Is there a minimal state simply to protect citizens and defend them from external threats? Does the state have to deliver public services, limiting freedom of property for the public good? Public law may be both the means to limit the state as well as provide the mechanisms of delivery. Jeremy Waldron cautions against the over use of public law techniques and judicial review that may limit the legitimacy of democratic government in making choices that determine the future development of the state. This may set boundaries on the extent of public law challenges but it should certainly not be interpreted to set limitations on the importance of the rule of law. It opens up the question as to how far Constitutional Courts or Supreme Courts can act to control arbitrary government. The potential for public law to impede elected government also throws into question the political nature of law. The late John Griffith, at the London School of Economics, argued that "any underlying norms were political not legal".[74] Martin Loughlin, for example, argues that law is often used to "legitimate the results of politics".[75] Aside from political considerations, the law is often used in a coercive sense in upholding the rights of the state to apply sanctions. Sir John Laws seeks to reconcile both legal and moral issues that surround legal sanctions upheld by public law principles.[76]

8-107
There is also an emerging consensus that public law has gained its own distinctiveness and has its own recognisable values and principles. That said there is as Feldman admits important boundaries to be recognised:

> "Drawing the boundary is the job of the legal rules regarding justiciability and legal accountability. By comparison, the boundary between "public law" and non-public law" is softer. We should not expect that the primacy of the public interest in 'public law' will allow us to fashion rules and principles of 'public law' which can avoid the need to take the public interest of government into account in the 'private law' of tort, contract or trusts. Public law is therefore not as distinct from non-public law as it is from public non-law; but that does not mean that it is not distinctive."[77]

8-108
Different approaches are evident from public law scholars setting different priorities for their work. Tony Prosser identifies the importance of the economic constitution, the role of regulation and the understanding of various forms of soft and hard public law. Setting the boundaries of public law is made more complex by the contractual state operated through government contracts.

---

74 J. A. G. Griffith, "The Political Constitution" (1979) 42 *Modern Law Review* 1; and J. F. McEldowney, "J. A. G. Griffith: Parliament and Legislation" (2014) *Public Law* 85–99.
75 M. Loughlin, *The Idea of Public Law* (Oxford: Oxford University Press, 2003), pp.33–52.
76 Sir John Laws, *The Common Law Constitution* (Cambridge: Cambridge University Press, 2014).
77 Mark Elliott and David Feldman, *The Cambridge Companion to Public Law* (Cambridge: Cambridge University Press, 2015), p.36.

8-109 Sir John Laws has recognised that there is a balancing of rights-based morality that is individualistic but must accommodate the practical working and morality of government. Trevor Allan has shown how the common law has created a powerful constitutionalism as an interpretative aid to a better understanding of public law.[78]

Stephen Sedley, usefully summarises how public law may make a difference through the development of the rule of law:

> "What is signals today is a shared ideal that individuals and society should not be subject to the whim of the powerful and that their rights and obligations should be determined by laws made by an elected legislature which respects fundamental rights, administered without discrimination by independent and competent judges and enforced by an uncorrupted executive."[79]

8-110 Many of these aspirations and ideas come together in the attention given to human rights.

I: Human Rights and Public Law

8-111 Human rights has become a cause in itself.[80] It generates optimism and specialism amongst some public lawyers. It certainly provides a focus for debate and it has the potential to join together many disciplines, including philosophy and law. Perhaps the most important is an understanding of how power may be taken from vested interest and distributed amongst ordinary people. The pathway of human rights is also a representation of struggle and conflict. Mapping human rights is a means of mapping human struggles through "agitation, protest and destabilisation".[81] There is an idealistic element that is able to captivate many people. At a more practical level, Stephen Sedley defines the aspirations and ambition attributed to human rights which "represent a claim on the state which every individual can make".[82] He admits that "there is nothing in principle or in practice which confines human rights to the sphere of public law". This is potentially path breaking as Sedley recognises that the constitutional environment in recent years has introduced "a culture of human rights" with public

---

78　T. R. S. Allan, *The Sovereignty of Law: Freedom, Constitution and Common Law* (Oxford: Oxford University Press, 2013).
79　Stephen Sedley, *Lions under the Throne* (Cambridge: Cambridge University Press, 2015), p.280.
80　Costas Douzinas and Conor Gearty, *The Meaning of Rights* (Cambridge: Cambridge University Press, 2014).
81　C. Gearty, "Human rights: the necessary quest for foundations" in Costas Douzinas and Conor Gearty, *The Meaning of Rights* (Cambridge: Cambridge University Press, 2014), 21-39, p.37.
82　Sedley, *Lions under the Throne*, p.193 and the analysis that follows in Ch.10.

law is at its heart. Such a cultural change may well mark a significant departure from the past. One reason for this possibility comes from the Human Rights Act 1998, which for the first time allows British citizens to use domestic courts to enforce Convention rights. British law is entering a period of considerable uncertainty as the transition to a rights-based culture is undertaken through cases decided by the judges. This has the potential to alter the dynamics of the common law as increasingly common law ideas become homogenised into a coherent whole with rights a central part. This proposition that human rights are intertwined with the common law and not wholly dependent on statute is likely to be contested. The debate as to whether or not the Human Rights Act 1998 should be repealed and or replaced by a British Bill of Rights is indicative of the difficult process the UK is going through as age-old constitutional assumptions are held up for inspection. It is possible that many institutions and practices will be found wanting. Sedley's optimistic hopes are that the rule of law is egalitarian and that it might ultimately minimise injustice in the world.

8-112 At the same time it is clear that as Professor Anthony King has pointed out that[83] "...many of the changes in our traditional constitution are permanent and irreversible". It is an opportune moment to take stock of the direction a more rights-orientated public law will take us. There are some words of caution.

8-113 While conceding, as everyone must, that human rights are intrinsic to our democratic system, there is room for consideration of the boundaries of judicial power as a custodian of rights. What degree of self-regulation should be exercised by judges when they are granted such overarching powers? How should decision-makers be advised to achieve good decisions when individual rights may serve to inhibit risk-taking and the development of long-term strategies? Human rights may also end up challenging cultural assumptions or vested interests. For example the rights of prisoners to vote[84] is highly contested by many members of the public as well as the current government. This is a good example of rights, public and political opinion not being in tandem with a resultant crisis of legitimacy between the state, government and courts.[85] It is also indicative of the scope and context of the political issues that often surround contested rights.

8-114 There is also the opportunity for judicial creativity, particularly over the development of a right to privacy in the UK. In *Kaye v Robertson*[86] the Court of Appeal denied that there is a right to privacy in English law. This view was upheld by the House of Lords in *R v Brown*.[87] Lord Hoffman commented that the common law did not recognise such a right and that Parliament was reluctant to introduce one. In court decisions after the introduction of the Human Rights Act 1998, the courts have gone to great lengths to create such a right. In *Douglas*

---

83 Anthony King, *Does the United Kingdom Still Have a Constitution?* (London: Sweet & Maxwell: 2001), p.90.
84 See *Hirst v UK (No.2)* [2005] ECHR 681; (2006) 42 E.H.R.R. 41, [2001] EWHC Admin 239; [2001] H.R.L.R. 3, also *Scoppola v Italy (No.3)* [2012] ECHR 86.
85 House of Commons, *Prisoners' Voting Rights*, Standard Note SN/PC/01764 (11 February 2015).
86 [1991] F.S.R. 62; Times, March 21, 1990 CA (Civ Div).
87 [1996] A.C. 543; [1996] 1 All E.R. 545 HL.

v Hello Ltd,[88] the courts acknowledged the possibility of an arguable right to privacy. This decision has the potential[89] of developing into a full right of privacy even though in the past, the judges had been reluctant to do so. The House of Lords in *Campbell v MGN Ltd*, acknowledged that a newspaper could publish information about the drug addiction of a celebrity, but this stopped short of disclosing all the details of the treatments she was receiving. This conclusion was reinforced by the Press Complaints Commission Code of Practice, applicable to newspaper and news media. Lord Nicholls was clear in showing that the "duty of confidence" had changed to a question of the boundaries set by a person's private and public life.[90] This is an example of how the Human Rights Act may provide judges with new perspectives and allow the common law to be supplemented by a "rights" jurisprudence. Ofcom, responsible for the Broadcasting Code, has recognised that privacy should be considered in terms of balancing the rights of broadcasters and individual rights. In *Murray v Big Pictures (UK) Ltd*,[91] the child of J. K. Rowling succeed in claiming that his right to privacy should be protected when undercover journalists photographed him in a public place when his parents were not present.

There are other examples of how rights from a European perspective may infiltrate into English institutions and the legal system—even when there are misunderstandings over UK law. In *Hill v Chief Constable of West Yorkshire*,[92] the claimant Mrs Hill was the mother of the last victim of a serial murderer who had murdered 13 young women between 1975 and 1980 in West Yorkshire. Mrs Hill claimed that the police made a number of mistakes that would not have been made by a competent police force exercising reasonable care. Her claim for negligence was rejected by the House of Lords. Lord Keith accepted that there was a general duty on the police to enforce the law but this did not carry a private law duty towards individual members of the public. His analysis contained additional observations on the liability of the police in terms of the public interest and the need to protect police resources and engaged with policy making and police discretion. He observed that the Court of Appeal were right to consider that the police were subject to an "immunity" similar to legal professional immunity.[93] The idea of police "immunity" gave rise to misunderstanding in the Strasbourg Court. In *Osman v United Kingdom*[94] the claimants, Mr and Mrs Osman, were the son and wife of a man who had been shot and killed by a Mr Paget-Lewis. The claimants alleged negligence, on the part of a consultant psychiatrist and the Commissioner of the Metropolitan Police, that resulted in suffering loss and damage. The allegations arose from the alleged failure of the police to apprehend Mr Paget-Lewis prior to shootings that he was involved in. The facts of the case involve events leading up to the tragic death of the man who was shot and killed by Mr Paget-Lewis, a school teacher who had become infatuated with the son while teaching him. The events leading

8–115

---

88 [2001] Q.B. 967; [2001] 2 All E.R. 289 CA (Civ Div).
89 See *Earl Spencer v UK* (1998) 25 E.H.R.R. CD 105 before the 1998 Act came into force.
90 *Campbell v MGN Ltd* (No.2) [2005] UKHL 61; [2005] 1 WLR 3394.
91 [2008] EWCA Civ 446; [2009] Ch 481.
92 [1989] A.C. 53; [1988] 2 W.L.R. 1049 HL.
93 *Rondel v Worsley* [1969] 1 A.C. 191; [1967] 1 W.L.R. 142 HL—immunity was granted to a barrister in respect of negligent claims for the conduct of proceedings in court.
94 [1999] 1 F.L.R. 193; (2000) 29 E.H.R.R. 245 ECHR.

up to this tragedy began with various incidents reported to the police alleged to have been caused by the actions of Paget-Lewis. Despite the fact that the Local Education Authority had arranged for a psychiatric assessment of Paget-Lewis and despite evidence of the increasing use of harassment against the Osmans, there appeared to be insufficient evidence to warrant a prosecution. After a short period away from the school, Paget-Lewis returned and took part in a number of killings. He killed the father of the boy, Mr Osman, injured the son, wounded a teacher in the school and also killed the teacher's son. The applicants, Mrs Osman and her son, alleged that the police were negligent in failing to arrest Paget-Lewis earlier and to take steps to prevent any harm to the Osmans. In English law the existing case law on liability against the police rested on the operation of an immunity[95] in the public interest. This immunity might be rebutted in circumstances where it could be shown that there was some form of a "relationship of proximity" between the police and the applicants. The police claimed this immunity and unsuccessfully applied to the first instant court to have the case dismissed as having no reasonable cause of action. The police appealed to the Court of Appeal. The appeal was successful in the Court of Appeal applying the case of *Hill v Chief Constable of West Yorkshire*[96] and holding that there was not a sufficient proximity, thus upholding police immunity. Though one of the Appeal Court judges, McGowan LJ took the view that there was a possible proximate relationship. The House of Lords refused leave to appeal. The applicants, the Osmans took their case to the European Court of Human Rights. It was argued that arts 2, 6 and 8 of the Convention applied. Article 2 provides an obligation on the authorities to take steps to safeguard citizens within their jurisdiction. The European Court held that art.2 was not breached. However, under art.6 the applicants argued that they were entitled to have the full matter of their case considered and not dismissed on the basis of a procedural rule or of no case to answer on the basis of the "immunity" set out in the *Hill* decision. The application of art.6 required that the Osmans were entitled to a full determination of their case on its merits and a full assessment of whether or not they fell within the proximity test. The European Court of Human Rights found that art.6 had been breached. The Court awarded damages of £10,000 to each applicant and a sum of £30,000 in costs. Their art.6 rights had been insufficiently protected by the courts. In considering the case the European Court of Human Rights ruled that the Court of Appeal in England when considering the Osmans' case had breached art.6. However, this perspective on English law was widely criticised and in *Z v United Kingdom*,[97] the Grand Chamber of the Strasbourg accepted that the reasoning in *Osman* was due to a misunderstanding and that English law was not incompatible with art.6.

8–116 If convention rights have an impact on the law of tort, it is quite likely that depending on the scope of rights, the law of contract may be similarly treated. McKendrick[98] suggests that the impact may be significant. Consider the situation where, because of an illegal contract unenforceable by the courts, the party concerned argues that Convention rights require

---

95 *Hill v Chief Constable of West Yorkshire* [1989] A.C. 53; [1988] 2 W.L.R. 1049 HL.
96 *Hill v Chief Constable of West Yorkshire* [1989] A.C. 53; [1988] 2 W.L.R. 1049 HL.
97 *Z v United Kingdom* (2001) 34 EHRR 97.
98 E. McKendrick, *Contract Law* (London: Macmillan, 2000), p.15.

some remedy. It is equally the case that the role of human rights and the role of contracts within the public sector are changing the shape of how government governs. Since *Osman* and the European Court of Human Rights re-interpretation of the decision,[99] the UK courts have considered the duties of the police and the central part of the *Hill* decision which would undoubtedly be decided in the same way[100] today without the expression of any so called "police immunity". There have been cases where a police force is liable in negligence for failing to take proper care for the protection of a police officer against a criminal attack. The cases were decided more on the basis of an employment contract than on negligence.[101] There are also cases where the emergency services have been treated in similar ways to the police and claims in negligence have been successfully made.[102] The liability of public authorities is an important area of law.[103] In *Michael and others v Chief Constable of South Wales Police*[104] the Supreme Court considered a claim for negligence against a police force whose response to an emergency call failed to prioritise the caller's concern that she (Ms Michael) might be killed. During the emergency call a scream was heard and later Ms Michael was found dead, the victim of a brutal attack. The children of the deceased claimed damages that Ms Michael's art.2 rights (the right to life) had been breached. The Supreme Court held (by a majority, the leading judgment from Lord Toulson) that in general English law does not impose liability on a defendant for injury caused by a third party. Exceptions may arise where there is someone in close proximity to the defendant failed to take adequate care and the defendant was in a position of control over the third party. If the defendant assumes responsibility to safeguard the claimant, there might be liability based on the law of tort.[105] The majority in *Michael* concluded that the police had no liability and the call handler had not represented to the caller any guarantee of assistance, there was insufficient proximity in the relationship between the police and Ms Michael. A strong dissent was given by Lord Kerr who relied on a broader test of proximity favoured by the majority. He reasoned that "if the police had not negligently downgraded the urgency of Ms Michael's call, on the facts as they are known at present, it is probable that she would still be alive".[106] The absence of a duty in circumstances defined by the majority is a welcome development as it allows the courts to consider each case on its facts and the public policy considerations involving police liability.

The Human Rights Act also creates the question of the range and scope of rights. The potential for the Act to have a "horizontal" effect arises because under s.6 of the Act, the

8–117

---

99 *Z v UK*, application No.29392/95, 10 May 2001 and *TP and KM v UK*, application No.28945/95, 10 May 2001.
100 See *Brooks v Commissioner of Police of the Metropolis* [2005] UKHL 24; [2005] 1 W.L.R. 1495 HL and *Van Colle v Chief Constable of the Hertfordshire Police and Smith v Chief Constable of Sussex Police* [2009] A.C. 225.
101 See *Costello v Chief Constable of Northumbria* [1999] 1 All E.R. 550; [1999] I.C.R. 752 CA (Civ Div), *Mullaney v Chief Constable of the West Midlands* [2001] EWCA Civ 700; [2001] Po. L.R. 150.
102 *Kent v Griffiths* [2001] Q.B. 36; [2000] 2 W.L.R. 1158 CA (Civ Div).
103 E. McKendrick, "Negligence and Human Rights: Re-considering Osman" in D. Friedmann and D. Barak-Erez (ed), *Human Rights in Private Law* (Oxford: Hart, 2001), p.331.
104 [2015] UKSC 2; [2015] A.C. 1732.
105 *Hedley Byrne v Heller Partner Ltd* [1964] A.C. 465; [1963] 3 W.L.R. 101 HL.
106 *Michael (FC) v Chief Constable of South Wales Police* [2015] UKSC 2; [2015] A.C. 1732, p.51 at [181].

courts are public authorities and have a duty to make decisions that are compatible with the Convention.[107]

8-118 Mapping the future impact of rights that are integrated into the English common law is the subject of controversy and differing perspectives. As previous chapters have shown there are a number of discernible trends. Linking past thinking with the current vogue for a pre-eminence of human rights in legal disputes may cause a substantial re-think about the boundaries of public law and political decision-making. Trust, the axiom of ministerial responsibility, is likely to be displaced by a more juridical formulation. Political power wrestles for primacy over other forms of governance including the managing of resources and spending decisions on all forms of public money. There is a preference for judicial power to be seldom heard and rarely seen. Alternative systems of decision-making including professional organisations and bodies are expected to conform to the political norms set by the government of the day. Evidenced based policy making appears threatened when set against political policy choices. Media debates may drown out alternative analysis or even expert opinions.[108]

8-119 The role of ancient institutions, the reverential style of past generations and respect for dignity and status are being replaced by a modernisation process that appears to know no boundaries. Public power, however exercised, is to be made more accountable and subject to regulatory structures and rules. This increases the role and variety of legal work for lawyers and puts legality at the centre of the decision-making process. A modern UK Supreme Court is accompanied by demands for a representative bench.[109] Change and modernisation are working together to provide the need for greater use of comparative analysis and an evaluation of the shift from political power and its systems of control to judicial power and the processes of judicial accountability.

8-120 In *Ghaidan*[110] the different treatment of a same sex couple was compared to a heterosexual couple in respect of a tenancy agreement when one of the partner's died. Although Parliament had reformed the law for heterosexual unmarried couples, the rights of homosexual couples had not been addressed in the legislation. Section 3(1) of the Human Rights Act 1998 was used to construe the legislation so that it would be read as compatible with the human rights of the homosexual couple. The wording of the legislation or indeed the precise intention of the legislation did not suggest that homosexual rights should be protected. A more holistic approach was adopted to consider inconsistency and even if this meant having to "read" into the legislation the possible way the legislation might be interpreted. The House of Lords were prepared to accept that the tenancy agreement should allow a surviving member of a same sex couple to enjoy the tenancy rights that are the same as a heterosexual couple. The *Ghaidan* case set new parameters for judicial interpretation providing a purposive approach to

---

107 M. Hunt, "The Horizontal Effect of the Human Rights Act" [1998] *Public Law* 423; and another perspective: Buxton LJ, "The Human Rights Act and Private Law" (2000) 116 *Law Quarterly Review* 48.
108 Consider the role of the Institute for Fiscal Studies or the Independent Office of Budgetary Responsibility.
109 K. Ewing, "The Unbalanced Constitution" in T. Campbell, K. Ewing and A. Tomkins (eds), *Sceptical Essays on Human Rights* (Oxford: Oxford University Press, 2001), p.117.
110 *Ghaidan v Godin-Madoza* [2004] UKHL 30; [2004] 2 A.C. 557.

rights that allow judges to take rights forward within the confines of Parliament's legislative intention. It might be suggested that *Ghaidan* is taking matters too far and crosses the line between judicial interpretation and judicial legislation. This is a rare example. In *Hounslow LBC v Powell*,[111] Lord Hope sensitively made the point that Parliament has the right to enact legislation and not judges. An indication that judges are sensitive of their powers is that the number of declarations of incompatibility issued by the courts has been only 29 (up until March 2015) with 20 finalised and only nine to be decided upon.[112] The Joint Select Committee on Human Rights regularly monitors the operation of the Human Rights Act 1998 and regularly reports to Parliament.

J: Summary and Conclusions

8–121

Contemporary writing on constitutional and administrative law has reflected the fast-developing specialisms[113] which may conveniently fit within the broadest definition of public law. These include planning law, environmental law, housing law and welfare law. In addition, there is a growing interest in cross-boundary disciplinary study. Regulation and how the public sector is subject to economic indices and rules provide important insights into the development of public law. Such subjects receive separate treatment in specialised texts but the nature of the subject matter raises questions about government powers, administrative decision-taking and the role of the courts. Generalisations made from the study of such specialisms about public law require careful elucidation.

8–122

Also noticeable is the trend to develop expertise within public law itself. Subjects include privatisation, regulation, EU law, local and central government, and public finance. Public law issues are therefore increasingly perceived as involving not only the courts but a range of institutions and bodies, some with quasi-governmental functions. Another significant influence on the development of public law is the increasingly relevant writings undertaken by political scientists. A good example is N. Johnson's *In Search of the Constitution*, which critically examines the existing constitutional arrangements in the UK in 1975 and is worth consulting for its perception of the systemic weaknesses in the UK's constitutional arrangements.[114]

---

111 [2011] UKSC 8; [2011] 2 A.C. 186.
112 Declarations of Incompatibility made by UK Courts Parliament (11 March 2015), *http://www.publications.parliament.uk/pa/jt201415/jtselect/jtrights/130/13006.htm* [Accessed 6 April 2016]. Joint Human Rights Committee 7th Report on Human Rights (11 March 2015), para.4.3.
113 T. Daintith, "Political Programmes and the Content of the Constitution" in W. Finnie, C. M. G. Himsworth and N. Walker (eds), *Edinburgh Essays in Public Law* (Edinburgh: Edinburgh University Press, 1991), pp.41–55; and J. Mitchell, "The Causes and Effects of the Absence of a System of Public Law in the United Kingdom" [1965] *Public Law* 95.
114 N. Johnson, *In Search of the Constitution* (London: Methuen, 1980), p.viii.

8-123 Two areas in particular may be mentioned as coming under intense scrutiny as part of the socio-legal approach and analysis of public law issues. First, is the subject of non-judicial means of dispute resolution between citizens and administration. Attention is given to tribunals, inquiries, ombudsmen and MPs as part of the dispute procedures involved in grievance machinery. Empirical research, case studies and theoretical analysis are often combined in research projects covering a wide range of institutions.

8-124 Secondly, and related to the first, regulation of the newly privatised utilities has set a new direction for public lawyers. Hybrid powers involving statutory authorities, licences, contracts and Company Act company agreements, provide the main means for carrying out many of the main activities in the provision of telecommunications, water, gas and electricity. Research into these fields involves economists, political scientists and lawyers.

8-125 The "descriptive and eclectic" mode of writing about public law has also extended to a more radical critique of the UK's constitutional arrangements. Public lawyers have become increasingly aware of the political origins and nature of the changes in society as reflected in the legislation passed as a result of the policies of the government of the day. As a result, a large body of literature attempts to set the boundaries of public law within the framework of theoretical debate. Attempts to provide new criteria or norms to evaluate the "legitimacy" of government action or principle to direct critical analysis of government decision-taking have not been wholly successful. However, frustrated such attempts have been, there is merit in setting out to improve the analysis of values and techniques intended to provide for more open and accountable government.

8-126 As part of this development of more theoretical-based studies there is a growing unease about the futility of the operation. Loughlin's expectation that legal theory helps us to render explicit the styles of public law thinking is somewhat blunted by the difficulty of finding a suitable vocabulary to provide public lawyers with an appropriate agenda for the future. There is in fact a veritable hotchpotch of theories and ideas competing for influence in setting public law on a clear direction for the future. Loughlin summarises his vision for the future[115]:

> "In confronting these important issues concerning the relationship between government and law, the functional logic of modern law must be accepted. This means that any contribution which public law may provide to the development of effective and accountable structures of government should be based on a sociological orientation.[116] Studies need to be rooted in a socially constructed field and, from that perspective, should investigate the interplay of cognitive and normative considerations. The normative structure of law should be recognised. But unlike the normatist approach, the question of laws' normative structure is itself an object of inquiry."

---

115 M. Loughlin, *Public Law and Political Theory* (Oxford: Clarendon Press, 1992), p.262.
116 T. Daintith, "Political Programmes and the Content of the Constitution" in W. Finnie, C. M. G. Himsworth and N. Walker (eds), *Edinburgh Essays in Public* Law (Edinburgh: Edinburgh University Press, 1991), pp.41–55.

Other writers have sensed the need for new directions but have been reluctant to set out an agenda for the future. This is not surprising as the post economic crisis since 2008 has reshaped many aspects of public law thought in terms of defining the state and the role of the citizen within state power.

The breadth of the inquiry presently undertaken by public lawyers is formidable. As Daintith has observed, "the conscientious search for a structure of constitutional obligation might well show that we possess no reliable rules over large areas of public life".

The focus of public law scholarship extends from the legal to the non-legal. Because many of the informal rules or understandings which guide public institutions are important, the task in hand extends beyond the ordinary remit of legal training. Political science, history, sociology and economics have a relevance to the future direction of public law within the UK even if that relevance requires justification and explanation to fit each task under review.

Further Reading

J. W. F. Allison, *The English Historical Constitution* (Cambridge: Cambridge University Press, 2007).

T. R. S. Allan, *Constitutional Justice: A Liberal Theory of the Rule of Law* (Oxford University Press, 2001).

T. R. S. Allan, "The Constitutional foundations of judicial review: conceptual conundrum or interpretive enquiry" [2002] *CLJ* 87.

D. Boucher and P. Kelly (eds), *Political Thinkers*, 2nd edn (Oxford: Oxford University Press, 2009).

Stefan Collini, Richard Whitmore and Brian Young (eds), *Economic Policy, and Society British Intellectual History 1750–1950* (Cambridge: Cambridge University Press, 2000).

S. Collini, "Discipline History and Intellectual history reflections on the historiography of the Social Sciences in Britain and France" (1988) *Revue de synthés* IV3–4(109), pp.387–99.

P. Craig, "Public Law, Political Theory and Legal Theory" [2000] *Public Law* 211.

P. Craig, "Competing Models of Judicial Review" (1999) *Public Law* 428.

M. Elliott and D. Feldman (eds), *The Cambridge Companion to Public Law* (Cambridge: Cambridge University Press, 2015).

I. Hampsher-Monk, *A History of Modern Political Thought* (Oxford: Blackwell, 1992).

C. Harlow and R. Rawlings, *Law and Administration*, 3rd edn (Cambridge Law in Context, 2009).

J. Jowell, D. Oliver and C. O'Cinneide (eds), *The Changing Constitution*, 8th edn (Oxford: Oxford University Press, 2015).

M. Loughlin, *Foundations of Public Law* (Oxford: Oxford University Press, 2010).

Janet McLean, *Searching for the State in British Legal Thought* (Cambridge: Cambridge Studies in Constitutional Law 2012).

D. Oliver, "The Underlying Values of Public and Private Law" in M. Taggart (ed), *The Province of Administrative Law* (Oxford: Hart, 1997).

S. Sedley, *Lions under the Throne* (Cambridge: Cambridge University Press, 2015).

M. B. Taggart, "The Nature and Functions of the State" in P. Cane and M. Tushnet (eds), (Oxford: Oxford University Press, 2003).

9

The European Union

A: Introduction

The UK's membership of the EU continues to be controversial and is likely to remain so for the foreseeable future. The EU provides the setting for many important constitutional issues and is a source of law as well as an influence on the delivery of many policies associated with social and economic developments. The EU comprises 28 Member States. The majority of the Member States, after satisfying certain economic criteria and the maintenance of sound financial management have created a common currency, the Euro, and agreed fixed exchange rates. Seventeen out of the 28 Member States are members of the Euro, the UK is not a member. The Euro has led to the development of a central European Bank in Frankfurt and the introduction of a new Exchange Rate Mechanism.[1] Concerns exist that the Euro members will take the EU in a different direction, isolating the non-Euro members.

9–001

A referendum on EU membership held on 23 June 2016 set the time-scale for debating UK membership. The referendum question was "Should the United Kingdom remain a member of the European Union or leave the European Union?".[2] The referendum outcome on a turnout of 71% is that 51.9% wished to leave, while 48.9% wished to stay. Scotland, Northern Ireland and London wished to remain, while England and Wales wished to leave.

9–002

The decision and timing as to when to activate Article 50 is proving to be difficult amidst a leadership election for a new Conservative leader to replace Mr Cameron who will resign as PM in the Autumn.

---

1 See Peter Huber and Wolf-Georg Ringe, *Legal Challenges in the Global Financial Crisis Oxford Institute of European and Comparative Law* (Oxford: Hart, 2014).
2 House of Commons Library, *The EU Referendum Campaign*, Briefing Paper No.7486 (27 January 2016).

9-003 UK reform negotiations agreed the following with the Council of Ministers[3] in February 2016:[4]

Economic governance

9-004
- The Eurozone countries should not discriminate against non-Eurozone countries;
- the EU Central Bank will have authority over credit institutions in Eurozone members and those that have voluntarily adopted the EU's prudential supervision;
- emergency measures will not result in non-Eurozone countries; and
- respect for rights and competencies of non-Eurozone States.

Competitiveness

9-005
- Competition should be the main driving force of the EU and increased efforts are required to increase competitiveness;
- the EU institutions and Member States will take active steps to reduce regulatory burdens and costs especially on SMEs;
- unnecessary regulation will be reduced and repeal of red tape regulations will be advanced;
- the EU Commission will carry out an annual review and intensify efforts to simplify regulations and reduce regulatory burdens; and
- measures inconsistent with subsidiarity will be repealed.

Sovereignty

9-006
- The UK is not committed to further political integration;
- references to the "ever closer union" in the EU Treaties should not be seen as an aim

---

[3] See David Cameron, "The EU is not working and we will change it", *The Telegraph*, 15 March 2014.
[4] House of Commons Library, *Reforming the EU: UK plans, proposals and prospects*, SN/1A/7138 (16 March 2015).

of political integration. It was agreed that the UK would be recognised as not engaged in any further political integration;

- national parliaments will have a greater opportunity to record their opinions and these must be respected especially in areas of subsidiarity and proportionality; and

- if a number of national parliaments (55 per cent) object through a "red card" principle, then Member States will discontinue the consideration of draft legislation.

Social benefits and free movement

- Freedom of movement and non-discrimination will be respected;

- some social security systems of certain Member States have proved to be more attractive than others;

- it is legitimate that EU and National measures might be introduced to avoid or limit flows of workers from Member States where there are negative effects for the States of origin and the States of destination;

- there may be "exceptional magnitude" that might trigger an alert and a mechanism to restrict the flow of restrict "in work" benefits. A one-off emergency brake of seven years was agreed; and

- Member States may have discretion to index the export of child benefits to a Member State, other than where the worker resides to the standard of living in the state where the child resides; The arrangements to start in 2020 and apply to new arrivals into the UK.

The UK government has developed an idea that there should be some form of "red card" to veto unwanted EU proposals. This was first raised as a possibility in 2013. It was re-discussed in November 2015 and it has emerged as a potential means of allowing sufficient number of national parliaments to group together to stop unwanted legislation. The idea builds on the Lisbon Treaty of an early warning mechanism or orange and yellow cards that has the potential to give national parliaments a greater say over the activities of the EU. The yellow card has rarely been used and the orange card has not been used at all.

In the meantime, there is an inevitable sense of separation between Britain and the EU particularly in terms of the UK personnel in the staff of EU institutions. The House of Commons Foreign Affairs Committee noted that

> "We were seriously concerned to learn that the number of UK nationals on the staff of the European Commission as fallen by 24% in

> seven years, and now stands at 4.6% of the total. This compares to 9.7% for France which has almost the same share of the EU's population."[5]

9-010 Since the UK joined the EU, the UK's government EU machinery has evolved to ensure that EU policy interests are considered as part of its ability to undertake European business[6] through a specialist Cabinet Office European Secretariat.

9-011 The Lisbon Treaty 2007 is the latest in a long series of evolving changes to the EU. Its origins came from the failure to have the European Constitution drawn up in 2003 ratified after the Treaty was signed by all the Member States. This is a symptom of the often contested nature of the EU, its institutions and design. The Constitutional Treaty required a referendum to be ratified and in June 2005. A referendum was held in France and the Netherlands and the result was a rejection of the proposals in the Treaty.

9-012 The implications and reforms introduced by the Treaty of Lisbon are considered in this chapter. The aim of this chapter is to examine European influences on the UK's system of public law taking account of how membership of the EU has affected our constitutional arrangements, including sovereignty, the economy and our relationship with EU institutions.

B: Evolving Europe

9-013 It is relevant to give some details of the pathway the UK's membership of the EU has taken. In 1 January 1973, when the European Communities Act 1972 took effect and the UK became a member of the European Community.[7] The UK's membership of the Community, however, is not static. Membership is part of an ongoing process. Change within the Community and the creation of a new European legal order. Intense political debate and controversy very often

---

5 House of Commons Foreign Affairs Committee, *The UK staff presence in the EU institutions Second Report*, 14 HC 219, Session 2013–14 (2 July 2013), p.3.
6 Details are provided in House of Commons Library, *How the UK Government deals with EU Business*, Standard Note, SN/1A/6323 (12 May 2012).
7 Before the creation of the European Union, the term European Community and its abbreviation (EC) referred to the three distinct communities, namely the European Coal and Steel Community, the European Economic Community, and the European Atomic Energy Community, and as a result it is common to refer to the EC. Finally, a fourth was added by the Treaty on European Union has created a European Union (EU) wider than the Economic Community. Currently EC membership comprises: the UK; France; Germany; Italy; Ireland; Denmark; The Netherlands; Belgium; Luxembourg; Portugal; Greece; Spain; Austria; Finland; and Sweden. In Ch.1, the structures of the EC have been shortly outlined. A more comprehensive analysis is provided in P. J. G. Kapteyn, P. Verloren Van Themaat, Laurence Gormley (eds), *Introduction to the Law of the European Communities* (Dordrecht: Kluwer, 1990).

accompany discussion of the future direction of the Community (see Diagram 1, at the end of this chapter). The UK is an important, albeit at times reluctant part of the single market, a major economic and social unit which has as its objective, benefits for the economies of the Member States. The development of a true single market among Member States is the ambition of the Single European Act, signed by all Member States in 1986. Slowly this ambition is being realised. Membership of the Community has raised significant implications for the UK's existing constitutional arrangements. Many of these issues, such as the impact of membership on the UK's sovereignty, are being addressed. There are also noticeable cultural changes, difficult to assess and quantify when it is remembered how new directions and influences may come into national law from European ideas and influences. Milsom[8] reminds us that the development of a system of law into a legal system is a rare occurrence:

> "It has happened twice only that the customs of European peoples were worked up into intellectual systems of law; and much of the world today is governed by laws derived from the one or the other."

The apparent fusion of the civil and common law systems within the integration of European law gives rise to a new understanding of what is a legal system.

Membership of the European Union

The UK's membership[9] of the EU has undergone significant change from the time the UK joined the European Community and new policies and objectives have marked the development of the EU.[10] The original treaty arrangements envisaged four areas where economic freedoms within a common market might be established. These include goods, persons, services and capital. An important area of policy concerned with fundamental principle is the development of a Common Agricultural Policy which has proved controversial and difficult.

Additional areas of substantive Community law include provisions covering competition and harmonisation of laws, social policy, research, technological development and environmental policy. Provisions covering commercial policy are intended to facilitate major political, economic and institutional reform.

In 1986, reforms towards a single market among Member States were introduced through the Single European Act 1986. The 1986 Act was intended to remove any remaining barriers as obstacles to a single internal market. The form of the 1986 Act was a Treaty which was later ratified into UK domestic law by legislation.

The main objective of the 1986 Act was to achieve a single internal market by the end of 1992. Community competence is therefore extended into a wide variety of new areas including

---
8   S. F. C. Milsom, *Historical Foundations of the Common Law*, 2nd edn (London: Butterworths, 1981), p.1.
9   Josephine Steiner, *Textbook on EEC Law*, 7th edn (London: Blackstone, 2000).
10 Gordon Slynn, *Introducing a European Legal Order* (Hamlyn Lecture, 1992), pp.41–62.

environment, energy, regional policy, and a common commercial policy. A significant part of these reforms are institutional and procedural in terms of giving more potential for the European Parliament to exert some influence in certain areas of Community law.

9-019 Equally important is the establishment of a new European marketing system leading to harmonisation of economic and monetary policy. Since 1969, the development of Economic and Monetary Union has been advocated. Ten years later the European Monetary System (EMS) came into operation with all Member States including the UK and also latterly Greece, Spain and Portugal joining after they became members of the Community.

9-020 Four elements were included[11] in the EMS; membership entitles Member States to participate in but not necessarily join each of the elements of the EMS. The four elements are: the Exchange Rate Mechanism, which obliges members to maintain exchange rates within certain limits; the European Currency Unit, which calculates the value of Community currencies pending the development of the Euro (this role has been superseded by the introduction of the Euro and the establishment of a central bank); the European Monetary Co-operation Fund, which regulates the issues of the ECU (European Currency Unit) throughout the Community; and to allow short-term credit facilities among Member States.

9-021 The UK agreed to enter the Exchange Rate Mechanism. This was intended to enable the UK to plan implementation, on an incremental basis, of the next two stages. However, events during September 1992 resulted in an unexpected and dramatic change when the UK was forced to leave the ERM as the pound came under severe pressure from the financial markets. Similar factors caused other Member States to leave the ERM.

9-022 At the heart of the debate on the EMU was the question of the role of the European System of Central Banks. It appears that for some time there was some reluctance in the UK to vest control in the European Central Bank away from the Bank of England[12]: The UK's possible entry into the Euro is unlikely given the experience of Greece and the financial crisis since 2008. Many Eurozone countries are struggling to find economic growth and there is concern that large financial debts will continue to hamper economic developments.

C: Evaluating Membership of the European Union

9-023 An evaluation of EU membership is being actively undertaken and the government has undertaken detailed and substantial reviews of all the key areas where the EU can be said to impact

---

11 Bank of England, *Economic and Monetary Union: An Evolutionary Approach* (December 1989); and *Economic Progress Report* (Treasury, 1989).
12 Bank of England, *Economic and Monetary Union* (December 1989).

on the UK. It is hard to analyse competing claims made for and against membership as the premise on which membership is based may be altered by any reform proposals agreed by the EU as the basis for negotiation. There are also conflicting interpretations of the economic data. It is clear that the EU is the UK's most important trading partner and in 2014, the EU accounted for 45 per cent of UK goods and services exports worth £227 billion and also 53 per cent of UK imports of £288 billion. UK exports have declined in recent years. The arguments about membership may depend on answering the question of whether the UK benefits from being a member of a large trading block or whether the UK would be able to negotiate better trade deals on its own?

9-024

It is generally agreed that UK withdrawal would most likely have the greatest impact on foreign direct investment, immigration and the labour market and the UK's contribution to the EU Budget. UK contributions to the EU Budget are around one per cent of total public expenditure amounting to 0.5 per cent of GDP, an estimated £9.8 billion. The UK is a net contributor, but there are areas where it receives significant support from the European Regional Development Fund and the European Social Fund. This is often supported by matched funding or support from the private sector. Leaving the EU would leave the UK having to make up any shortfall and create a likely policy vacuum.[13] The EU Budget spent by the EU is also a source of political controversy. In fact expenditure for 2014–2020 is €960 billion, around one per cent of EU Gross National Income.[14]

9-025

Opinion is divided as to whether or not Treaty reform is needed. It is clear that any Treaty amendment under art.48 of the Treaty of European Union will take a long time, not least because it will require agreement between all 28 EU Member States. Examples of the changes that might be required include amendment of the EU free movement Directive 2004/38 and regulations such as 492/2011. This would require qualified majority support of at least 55 per cent of the Member States representing 65 per cent of the EU population. Further and more substantive changes are envisaged and require a wide ranging review of Treaty changes to make reform a possibility.[15]

D: The European Union Institutions and Structures

9-026

One remarkable fact is emerging that the UK's presence in the various EU institutions has been steadily declining. The House of Commons Foreign Affairs Committee has already noted

---

13 House of Commons Library, *Exiting the EU: impact in key UK policy areas*, Briefing Paper No.07213 (4 June 2015).
14 House of Commons Library, *EU Budget 2014–20*, Briefing Paper, No.06455 (31 July 2015).
15 House of Commons Library, *Reforming the EU: UK plans, proposals and prospects*, SN/1A/7138 (16 March 2015), p.22.

that decline in UK nationals being members of the European Commission. The same problem applies to the UK's membership of other important EU institutions:

> "In the increasingly-powerful European Parliament, the UK's share of administrator-grade staff has fallen from 6.2% to 5.8% since 2010 (while France's has risen from 7.55 to 8.6%); and in the General Secretariat of the Council of the EU, the UK's share of administrator-grade staff fell from 4.8% to 4.3% over the same period while France's fell from 7.7% to 6.9%."[16]

9-027 The Treaty of EU recognises seven EU institutions: the European Council; the Commission; the Council; the European Parliament; the Court of Justice; and the European Central Bank and the Court of Auditors. It is necessary to outline in more detail the role and function of the various institutions of the EU since the Treaty of Lisbon has come into force.[17]

Council and Commission

9-028 The Council comprises the political representatives of the Member States. It is the policy making and coordinating institution for the EU and has a pivotal role in the legislative process. The legislative role is significant because it must approve Commission initiatives. In its legislative role, the Council has shared responsibility with the European Parliament. Council representation is through elected ministers from the members states who work within the ten configurations that allows the Council to undertake its role. The team areas are the result of historic development and cover: general affairs, foreign affairs, economic and financial affairs, justice and home affairs, employment, social policy, health and consumer affairs, competitiveness, transport, telecommunications and energy, agriculture and fisheries, environment and education, youth culture and sport. The Council's business may be conducted at two levels, the legislative part which is open to the public and the non-legislative part that is private and not open to public access.

9-029 Council decision-making is undertaken by qualified majority unless there is a specific exception set out in the Treaties. There is a formula for qualified majority based on votes and on a percentage of the EU population. Each Member State is entitled to a number of votes based on its population size. France, Germany, Italy and the UK have each 29 out of a total of 352 votes. The significance of population has gradually become the accepted practice for undertaking voting procedures. From 1 November 2014, qualified majority is achieved through a criteria based on percentage of the population. A draft decision must be supported by at least 55 per cent of the Member States (16 states under the current 28 member EU), representing at

---

16 House of Commons Foreign Affairs Committee, *The UK staff presence in the EU institutions*, Second Report Session 2013–14, HC 219 (2 July 2013), p. 3.
17 House of Lords Library, *Note The European Union*, LLN 2014/015 (23 April 2014).

least 65 per cent of the population. Where the Council does not act on a Commission proposal, the qualified majority threshold is 72 per cent of Member States (21 states under the current 28 member EU), representing at least 65 per cent of the EU population.[18]

9-030

The adoption of Qualified Majority Voting is intended to avoid the operation of a veto which might arise if unanimous voting was required. The future of the EU is largely dependent on the economic influence and support of the larger Member States, particularly Germany. Attempts to make the Council more transparent have only been partly successful in achieving this outcome. The arguments in favour of transparency are important as public confidence in the institutions of the EU is under severe strain.

9-031

Council decision especially under the Committee of Permanent Representatives (COREPER) and various working groups remain private and not open to public scrutiny. COREPER operates at two levels. COREPER I is composed of heads of each EU Member State's permanent team in Brussels and COREPER II is composed of the deputy heads. This level of confidentiality is seen to create a persuasive sense of secrecy which adds to the question of the legitimacy of the EU's institutions. Very often formal votes are not taken and this adds to the sense that decisions are being made "behind closed doors".

9-032

A significant change in the Lisbon Treaty is the use of the co-decision procedure with the Commission. This involves up to three readings of a Commission proposal and co-legislative powers for the European Parliament and Council. The co-decision procedure has increased since the Treaty of Lisbon. It applies to 85 legal areas compared to 44 previously and it has gained considerable momentum. The role of the Council seems to have gained exponentially since the financial crisis and the need for pre-emptive action.

9-033

The EU Council is at the highest-level of decision-making and may adopt conclusions on the Multiannual Financial Framework. The Treaty of Lisbon formalised the Multiannual Financial Framework (MFF) and established the MFF as a Council regulation covering a period of at least five years. This is the critical mechanism for the means of negotiating the revenue needed to meet expenditure.[19]

The Commission

The EU Commission is a collegiate body that is composed of one Commissioner for each Member State. Membership of the Commission consists of 28 members, who must be nationals of an EU Member State. There is also a President of the Commission. There is a staff of 23,000 organised between various directorate-generals or services. There is a directorate general with powers to set policy and set agendas within their field of competences. Commissioners are nominated by Member States and are usually drawn from former politicians with some experience in government. The aim of national governments is to ensure that the Commission

9-034

---

18 House of Commons Library, *The European Union: a democratic institution?*, Research Paper, 14/25 (29 April 2014).
19 House of Commons Library, *EU Budget 2014–20*, Briefing Paper, 06455 (31 July 2015).

reflects the balance of European political interests. Members of the Commission serve a term of four years in office, enjoy various privileges and immunities to ensure that their duties are carried out unimpeded. Commissioners are appointed by the Council by a qualified majority vote and with the consent of the European Parliament. The independence of the Commission is important and, although commissioners are drawn from Member States, they must not be seen to act in a partisan way.

9-035 The Commission acts as an independent body, is headed by a President and is the "watchdog" of the Community. The Commission proposes and initiates legislation and monitors compliance by Member States of the EU law, and the Treaties. The Commission represents the EU externally.

9-036 The Commission has a President, six Vice-Presidents and each member of the Commission has a personal staff, namely his cabinet, and Chefs de Cabinet who meet regularly to discuss the role and objectives of Commission policy. Collaboration between the Council and the Commission is required. The President of the Commission is nominated by the European Council and subject to a vote of consent of the European Parliament.

9-037 Powers granted to the Commission and the Council permit the taking of decisions which become legally binding on Member States and individuals within the Community. The formulation of such powers gives the initiative to the Council, on a proposal from the Commission and after consultation with the European Parliament, to take appropriate legal measures. In theory there is great scope for the broadening of such powers under art.235 based on the doctrine of "implied power", namely that filling a gap in express powers may fit within the generally granted power if it is implied or necessary. There are doubts as to the precise scope and requirements for such powers. The Commission acts as an "overseer" of the interests of the Community and art.5 obliges it to take appropriate measures to ensure "fulfilment of the obligations" from the Treaty. Extensive investigative powers are granted to the Commission which require Member States and even individuals to provide information allowing the Commission to carry out its task. The Commission, since 2014, has embarked in developing its policies within the areas of Economic and Monetary Union, sustainable and inclusive growth, justice and security and also in developing external relations.

9-038 A number of specific policy areas fall within the jurisdiction of the Commission such as the competition policy of the Community and the implementation of the Common Agricultural Policy. This delegates to specific commissioners wide ranging powers and activities.

The European Council

9-039 The European Council was set up in 1949 in Strasbourg and has its own institutions and pre-dates the setting up of the European Union. It is an intergovernmental body of 47 members that aims to guarantee the "dignity of the nations and citizens of Europe by enforcing respect for our fundamental values: democracy, human rights and the rule of law". These aspirations have formed the European Convention on Human Rights that forms the requirements of art.6 of the Treaty of Lisbon. The Treaty of Lisbon ensured that the European Council became an

EU institution. This ensures that twice yearly the various heads of government of the Member States will attend a "summit" meeting to decide the EU's general policy direction and its priorities. These are matters left unresolved at the Council of European Union meetings. The European Council does not have legislative functions or powers to formulate new laws.[20]

9-040

The European Council has a full-time President and a foreign secretary known as the High Representative of the Union for Foreign Affairs and Security Policy. Selection of both positions are by the European Council through a qualified majority. The President serves for two and a half years and is renewable once. The High Representative may serve for up to five years.

The European Parliament

Directly elected since 1979, the Parliament was originally perceived as having an advisory role. It has gained substantive powers since the 1970s, particularly with respect to the EU's annual budget. It also has legislative and supervisory powers. Today it has 767 MEPs directly elected from the 28 Member States. Larger Member States have a greater share of the seats. The UK has 73 members, France 74 and Germany 99. In the Great Britain, the election system is based on the regional list system, the country being divided into 11 electoral regions for that purpose. Increasingly important are the political groups and the lobbying that is carried out. There are 17 standing committees with a specialist focus and an elected chair.

9-041

The European Parliament has gained through various Treaty changes substantive legislative powers. In 1986, the Single European Act gave the Parliament the right to a second reading of legislation. There is a "cooperation procedure" whereby the Council could only approve a previously rejected proposal by unanimous vote rather than by a qualified majority. The European Parliament has the right to veto the accession of new Member States and assent with the Council to international agreements. The Maastricht Treaty also gave the European Parliament the right to veto a legislative proposal by an absolute majority after two readings of the proposal by the Council and the European Parliament. The Amsterdam and Nice Treaties gave the European Parliament, the right to institute proceedings before the European Court of Justice to review acts of the institutions.

9-042

The Treaty of Lisbon acknowledged under art.14(1) that the European Parliament and the Council should have co-equal status in budgetary and legislative matters. The co-decision procedure was renamed the Ordinary Legislative Procedure. The European Parliament's role was extended to various areas such as immigration, offences and penalties, police co-operation, some aspects of trade union and agricultural policy.

9-043

The European Parliament may assist in the scrutiny of the Commission, who are required to give answers to questions raised by the Parliament. The Council sends reports to the Parliament and three times every year Parliament provides a review of the Council's activities. The European Parliament may pass a motion of censure against the Commission.

9-044

---

20 Details of the importance of the Treaty of Lisbon are set out in the House of Commons Library, Implementing the Lisbon Treaty SN/IA/5331 (8 February 2010)

9-045

In terms of future developments in the EU it is likely that the Parliament will perform an increasingly important role. The European Parliament holds a number of characteristics which make its existence difficult to reconcile with the traditional idea of a democratically elected and accountable UK Parliament. There is no equivalent ministerial responsibility. It appears too remote and not directly answerable to the mandate of electors because it remains too diffuse and lacking in identity that separates it from other EU institutions. Yet it remains the only directly and therefore democratic element in the EU institutional framework. Its expansion of its powers suggest that it may be self-seeking—gathering more powers for its own purposes and expanding the EU Budget and the EU's remit. Voter turnout of only around 43 per cent in EU Parliamentary elections suggests that its image and legitimacy have serious shortcomings that need to be addressed.[21]

9-046

The role of the European Parliament remains distinctive, however. For example, it can refer matters to the Court of Justice if the Council or the Commission infringe Community rules. Article 232 (ex.175) provides the Parliament and other institutions with the power to bring actions to establish if there is an infringement of a Treaty obligation. Article 193 (ex.38c) provides the Parliament with the power to set up a Committee of inquiry to review or investigate any matter of maladministration in the implementation of Community law. The establishment of a European Ombudsman appointed by the Parliament allows it to receive reports and inquire into maladministration. Article 192 (ex.138b) provides Parliament with a power to request the Commission to make appropriate proposals that are necessary for the implementation of Treaty obligations. Together with art.251 (ex.189b), the Parliament has the right of co-decision with the Council on certain limited and defined areas, in essence a veto power that may apply to areas such as health, and consumer affairs. Parliament may also ask questions and the Commission is required to reply. Parliament is consulted on an advisory basis at the pre-legislative stage to ensure that deliberations are complete. EU citizens can petition the Parliament and this form of direct involvement is likely to be an important aspect of its future development.

The Court of Justice of the European Union

9-047

The Court of Justice, commonly called the European Court, ensures that the Treaty and its obligations are interpreted.[22] There are 28 judges appointed with the agreement of the Member States. The number of judges may be expanded to meet the growth in the number of Member States. A wide range of matters comes within its remit ranging from social and economic to constitutional and administrative law. The jurisprudence of the Court is influenced by the civil law tradition. The Court can sit in chambers of up to five judges or as a Grand Chamber of 13 judges.

---

21 Generally See Paul Craig, " Britain in the European Union" in J. Jowell, D. Oliver and C. O'Cinneide (eds),*The Changing Constitution*, 8th edn (Oxford: Oxford University Press, 2015).

22 Court of First Instance, *Reflections on the Future Development of the Community Judicial System, by the Court of First Instance of the European Community* (1991) 16(3) *European Law Review* 175–189.

Overall the ECJ's workload has increased. This has been noted by Slynn[23]:

> "Not far short of 400 new cases have been arriving at the Court each year, though in 1990/91 the number was down to 355. Allowing for 200 judgments and, on average, 130 withdrawals or summary dismissals, the backlog can only increase, and by September 1991, the 'stock' of cases before the Court and the Court of First Instance amounted to 782, of which 614 were before the Court."

The Court of Justice of the European Union, consists of three courts, the Court of Justice (ECJ), the General Court (formerly known as the Court of First Instance) and the Civil Service Tribunal. The latter was created in 2004 and has jurisdiction to hear and determine at first instance disputes between the EU and its staff, it has a workload of around 120 cases per annum. All three courts provide a rich and varied jurisprudence that has guided the legal system of the EU and informed the substantive law of the Member States on EU matters.

Delays can amount to over 24 months, commensurate with the scope and range of the Court's activities which are broader and more linked to the economic, political and social issues than would be commonly found in English judicial decisions.

Article 230 (ex.173) EC provides that the European Court of Justice may review all measures adopted by the institutions and consider their intended consequences and effect. Standing is given to Member States, the Council and the Commission and, since the Treaty of Amsterdam, a limited standing has been given to the Court of Auditors.

TFEU art.252 places a duty on the Advocates General to make reasoned submission of the cases brought to the Court. This is an important mechanism to ensure that the legal issues are properly addressed and the Court is well informed of the issues. The opinions of Advocate General may also become a useful guide on the direction and approach the Court may take, although the Court may not choose to follow this advice.

E: The Jurisprudence of the European Court

The jurisprudence of the ECJ has significant effects on the UK's constitutional and administrative law and legal system. There are many ways whereby a case may be taken to the ECJ. The Commission may decide to initiate proceedings against a Member State for failure to comply with a Treaty obligations. This allows the Commission to issue an opinion and set out reasons for the case being taken to the ECJ. The Member State may wish to comply but if this does not happen then the Commission may take a case to the ECJ.

---

23   Gordon Slynn, *Introducing a European Legal Order* (Hamlyn Lecture, 1992), pp.136–137.

9-054 A case may be taken by one Member State against another. In such circumstances the case must be referred to the Commission for a reasoned opinion. If the Commission finds that a state is in breach of a duty, then it must take measures to ensure compliance. It is also possible for a Member State to challenge the legality of an EU measure through proceedings in the Court. A good example is the Working Time Directive (93/104), a challenge made by the UK government that the EU Council was exceeding its powers.[24]

9-055 The jurisdiction of the European Court is provided under art.267 (previously art.234 (ex.177)), which permits the European Court to give preliminary rulings on Community law. A preliminary ruling may be requested by the courts of the Member States.

9-056 At first guidelines as to when to refer cases to the European Court were provided for the UK's courts in *Bulmer v Bollinger*,[25] and although criticised, they provide the general approach adopted by the UK's courts. In deciding whether to refer to the European Court, Lord Denning explained that: (i) the decision must be necessary; (ii) the decision must be conclusive of the case, and if necessary; and (iii) the Court has to exercise its discretion to determine all the circumstances and consideration given to matters such as the delay involved, difficulty of the issues, the expense involved and the burden on the Court. The main area of dispute arising from Lord Denning's three categories was the issue of "conclusive". On a narrow interpretation this might inhibit an English judge from referring a matter if there was doubt as to the suitability of the European Court resolving the dispute before it with sufficient clarity. On a broad interpretation, as EU law is part of domestic law it might be considered that any domestic court of the Member State of the EU is entitled to receive the opinion of the European Court. Lord Denning explained that the facts should first be established by the English courts before a reference might be made. He added that if the law was clear then it was unnecessary to refer the matter to the European Court. This point is also open to question, as some argue that it is perfectly acceptable to receive an interpretation of a clear point of law just as it is for an unclear one. Article 234 (ex.177) permits a preliminary reference made by "any court or tribunal".

9-057 In *R v International Stock Exchange Ex p. Else*[26] Lord Bingham made the crucial point that referral of cases involving any "doubts" over the interpretation of EU law was a discretion left with the national court. Lord Bingham's approach is to be preferred as it sets the elements of interpretation as shared between Member States and the ECJ.

9-058 Another possibility, is where there can never be an appeal. This applies in the case of the Supreme Court, because it is the final appellate court within the UK where the Supreme Court might be bound to refer such a question to the Court. But the procedure applies to decisions where there are no further domestic remedies available. There is therefore an important

---

24 See *UK v EU Council* (C-84/94) EU:C:1996:431; [1996] 3 C.M.L.R. 671 and also see *Gibson v East Riding Council* [2000] 3 C.M.L.R. 329; [2000] I.C.R. 890 CA (Civ Div).
25 [1974] Ch. 401; [1974] 3 W.L.R. 202 CA (Civ Div). Also see *R v Henn* [1981] A.C. 850; (1980) 71 Cr. App. R. 44 HL; and *R v Plymouth Justice Ex p. Rogers* [1982] Q.B. 863; [1982] 3 W.L.R. 1 QBD. See J. McEldowney, "*Pigs Marketing Board for Northern Ireland v Redmond*" [1980] *Northern Ireland Legal Quarterly* 165–172, Case 83/78: EU:C:1978:214; [1979] 1 C.M.L.R. 177. See [1997] E.C. 1 ECJ.
26 [1993] Q.B. 534; [1993] 2 W.L.R. 70 CA (Civ Div).

role originally given to the House of Lords (now the UK Supreme Court). In *Chiron Corp v Murex Diagnostics Ltd*,[27] it is regarded as the court against which there is no judicial remedy. Reference to the European Court will be made where the question is required for the decision in the case. If there is already case law on the matter or where the Court of Justice has already resolved the issue, then no reference is required.

9-059
In addition to preliminary rulings it is possible for references to be made directly by the House of Lords, now the Supreme Court. In such cases the requirements are that the principles in dispute, or raising matters of Community law, should be set out in the reference. This invariably involves the formulation of specific questions to be taken before the European Court.

9-060
In England the first reference arising for the House of Lords was a case in 1981, *R v Henn*[28] which raised the question of whether importing obscene or indecent articles, which was a criminal offence in the UK, amounted to a restriction of imports within art.30 and whether this was justifiable under art.30. The European Court accepted the judgment in terms of art.36 relating to "public morality, public policy or public security".

9-061
References to the European Court may be made by the Employment Appeal Tribunal, the High Court and by the Magistrates' Court. Criminal law matters often raise issues of EU law. Increasingly the interpretation of Community law forms part of the law of the UK. Courts and tribunals are adopting a positive approach towards the interpretation of Community law and there is general satisfaction that the UK courts are showing such a positive view.[29]

9-062
In Northern Ireland the first reference made by the Magistrates' Court concerned the prosecution of Redmond, a pig dealer, under the Northern Ireland Movement of Pigs Regulations 1972, enforced by the Pigs Marketing Board, which was set up under a scheme requiring local pig producers to sell to the Board, bacon produced by pigs in Northern Ireland.[30]

9-063
The European Court determined that the prosecution was inconsistent with Community law and the Board's powers unlawfully interfered with the Community market in pig meat. A similar fate awaited other marketing boards, but the reference illustrated the flexibility of the European Court's procedures. In marked contrast to the formality of English procedure, the European Court greatly assisted the magistrates in the formulation of the issues involving Community law raised in the case. This raises the question of how Community law takes effect in the UK. The Community legal order consists of Regulations, Articles, Directives and decisions and how each takes effect in the UK requires explanation.

9-064
The importance of making reference to the court may have diminished as national courts at the level of the Member States are increasingly able to make their own determination of EU law. The UK Supreme Court acknowledged in *OFT v Abbey National plc* that there a referral to

---

27 [1995] All E.R. (E.C.) 88; [1995] F.S.R. 309 CA (Civ Div).
28 [1981] A.C. 850.
29 *Sixth Annual Report to the European Parliament on Commission Monitoring of the Application of Community Law*, COM (89)411 final, Appendix pp.31–34.
30 See J. McEldowney, *"Pigs Marketing Board for Northern Ireland v Redmond"* [1980] *Northern Ireland Legal Quarterly* 165–172, Case 83/78: EU:C:1978:214; [1979] 1 C.M.L.R. 177. See [1997] E.C. 1 ECJ.

the ECJ was not required as the parties did not show any enthusiasm for a referral and it was a matter that needed to be resolved in the public interest without further delay.[31]

9-065 Lord Bridge in *Factortame*[32] declared:

> "It has always been clear that it was the duty of a United Kingdom Court, when delivering final judgment, to override any rule of national law found to be in conflict with any directly enforceable rule of Community law."

9-066 In *O'Brien v Department of Constitutional Affairs*,[33] the Supreme Court reflected on the appropriate interpretation of the Directive on part-time workers when applied to part-time judges and decided to ask for the guidance of the ECJ over matters of interpretation.

9-067 In *Pham v Secretary of State for the Home Department*[34] the UK Supreme Court should willingness to decide matters relevant to the UK without necessarily raising EU issues where it was thought that EU law would make no difference to the decision in the case.[35] This is an important step in terms of developing the common law while taking account of EU decisions as part of domestic law.

9-068 An important issue that has dominated UK public law is national and parliamentary sovereignty. Concentration on unelected elements of the European institutions has left the UK with the sense that the UK's national elected Parliament has become subservient to unelected EU institutions, most notably the EU Commission. The gradual erosion of a Member State veto in the Council of Ministers and cases such as *Factortame* contribute to the collective sense of sovereignty ebbing away. The European Union Act 2011 contains a definition of sovereignty being retained by the UK Parliament. This is the so called "sovereignty clause" and it is connected with the use of a referendum to oversee any future adjustment by the UK Parliament of a Treaty, law or legislation without prior approval. However, such apparent "entrenchment" is more a political gesture than a legal reality as the EU Act 2011 may be repealed at some future date.

9-069 The question of the sovereignty of national parliaments is also part of EU law. Article 12 of the TEU provides a strengthening of the role of national parliaments and the mechanisms of early warning through orange and yellow card procedures that gives national parliaments more power. As far back as 2013, the UK suggested that a "red card" system might be adopted to exercise a veto over any unwanted EU proposals. In February 2016, this proposal has become a real possibility in the negotiations between the EU and UK on UK membership.

---

31 [2009] UKSC 6; [2010] 1 A.C. 696. There are also cases showing similar reluctance such as *McCall v Poulton* [2008] UKSC 6; [2010] 1 A.C. 696.
32 *Factortame (No.1)* [1990] 2 A.C. 85; [1989] 2 W.L.R. 997 HL; *Factortame (No.2)* [1991] 1 A.C. 603; [1990] 3 W.L.R. 818 HL at [658]–[659]. See *Van Gend en Loos v Nederlandse Administratie der Belastingen* (26/62) EU:C:1963:1; C.M.L.R. 105.
33 [2009] UKSC 6; [2010] 1 A.C. 696.
34 [2015] UKSC 19; [2015] 1 W.L.R. 1591.
35 See *R (G1) v Secretary of State for the Home Department* [2012] EWCA Civ 867; [2013] Q.B. 1008.

This would depend on a percentage of national Parliament's commonly agreeing to object to an EU proposal.[36]

F: Sources of European Union Law

As explained above the European Court provides an important source of Community law. This raises the question of the concept of "direct effect" and its meaning as to the "rights or obligations" which are enforceable rights by individuals or Member States within the Community. The answer may depend on the interpretation of "direct effect". Ambiguously worded, the term can be found in international law as well as Community law. In international law the term refers to national courts applying at the suit of individuals rights and obligations.

9-070

In addition to the sources of Community law provided by the European Court's jurisprudence there are rules, regulations and laws arising under the various Treaties. Regulations under art.249 (ex.189), as amended by the TEU are directly applicable but little further guidance is provided other than the fact that they bind Member States in their entirety without further implementation. Occasionally regulations may be drafted in a conditional or provisional mode, requiring further action for their implementation, but generally they apply with immediate effect. This means that they may create individual rights enforceable before national courts.

9-071

Articles of the Treaty are said to have internal effect in the Member States of the Community. However, doubts exist as to when all Articles of the Treaty would be so treated. Over time the European Court has held many of the Articles of the Treaty to be directly applicable. Directives are described under art.249 (ex.189) as being "directly applicable". It was once thought that only regulations might have "direct effect" as distinct from "direct applicability". The latter term was interpreted to mean that direct effect was not given. However, in a number of decisions[37] the European Court took the view that some Directives might have "direct effect".

9-072

While not all Directives might be said to have "direct effect", in the *Marshall Case*[38] it was decided that Directives might be relied upon by individuals within Member States against any part of the "state". The question of direct effect depends on the subject matter and whether the wording is "unconditional and sufficiently precise". Not every national court has accepted the view that Directives may have direct effect. Not all Directives before the courts may fall into

9-073

---

36 House of Commons Library: *Parliamentary sovereignty and EU renegotiation*, CDP-0033 (2 February 2016).
37 *Grad v Finanzamt Traunstein* (9/70) EU:C:1970:78; [1971] C.M.L.R. 1. *Van Duyn v Home Office* (41/74) EU:C:1974:133; [1975] Ch. 358. Also see *Johnston v The Chief Constable of the Royal Ulster Constabulary* (222/84) EU:C:1986:206; [1986] 3 C.M.L.R. 240.
38 *Marshall v Southampton and South West Hampshire AHA (Teaching)* (152/84) EU:C:1986:84; [1986] 1 C.M.L.R. 688.

the category of direct application because of a further ambiguity caused by the concept of the "state". This term is not precisely defined but may be generally used to mean a public body or agency of the State. It is difficult to put this characteristic of such bodies into categories which give rise to general principles of universal application.

9-074 A broad interpretation was adopted by the House of Lords in *Foster v British Gas*[39] as to a body "which has been made responsible pursuant to a measure adopted by the State for providing a public service under the control of the state". Such a body might be granted "special powers" which differentiate it from any individual. On such an interpretation the State could be all-embracing as to include any entity which had legal powers over individuals and this might cover a Company Act company. On such an interpretation, noticeably broader than in other areas of law, the House of Lords held that the then British Gas Corporation under the Gas Act 1972, then a nationalised industry, fell within the definition.

9-075 A further possibility over direct effect has been mooted by the European Court which is to allow a Directive to have an application in domestic law indirectly, as a means to interpret national law as part of Community law.[40] The possibilities of interpretation make this area of law subject to intense discussion and debate. Particularly so, since many of the Community's most significant social and economic policies are enacted into legislative form through the means of Directives.

9-076 An important dimension arises from the *Francovich*[41] principles where a failure by the Member State to implement Community law or comply with their obligations under Community law might provide the individual citizen with a remedy in damages. This might include damages for example for failure to implement a Directive.

9-077 The UK courts have always faced a formidable challenge in developing their interpretative skills to overcome the difficulties mentioned above. Not least is the difficulty that even if a Directive is held to be directly applicable, thereby conferring on an individual various rights against the State, there is not always an available remedy in domestic law open to the court. This leaves a considerable gap in the jurisprudence of the ECJ in the development of the principle that there is a strong obligation on Member States to enforce Directives through domestic courts.[42]

9-078 Finally, there are decisions of the Community which are binding under art.249 (ex.189). This is largely unproblematic as the decision is addressed to a specific issue or problem and may be made to an individual or Member State. The assumption is made that because the decision is made to address an individual or Member State it should be integrated and enforced as a binding rule.

---

39 (C-188/89) EU:C:1990:313; [1990] 3 All E.R. 897 at [922].
40 Known as the Von Colson principle (14/83) EU:C:1984:153. See Grainne de Burca, "Giving effect to European Community Directives" 1992 *Modern Law Review* 215; and Steiner "Coming to terms with EEC Directives" (1990) 106 *Law Quarterly Review* 144.
41 See *Francovich v Italian Republic* (C-6/90 and C-9/90) EU:C:1991:428; [1993] 2 C.M.L.R. 66; N. Gravells, "Disapplying an Act of Parliament pending a Preliminary Ruling: Constitutional Enormity or Community Law Right?" [1989] *P.L.* 568; Barav (1989) 26 C.M.L. Rev. 369; and Churchill (1989) 14 *European Law Rev.* 470.
42 N. O'Loan, "UK Implementation of the Services Directive 92/50" (1994) 3 *Public Procurement Law Review* 60; and the Public Service Contracts Regulations 1993 (SI 1993/3228).

In the early years of the Community, the European Court rejected the idea that fundamental rights might be protected directly by the Court's interpretation of Community law. Instead reliance was placed on national courts and constitutions developing their own jurisprudence of fundamental rights. However, in subsequent years and more recently is the question of the activities of the European Court in interpreting and discussing Community law[43] requiring national courts to accept the status of Community law. The question of compatibility between the law of the Member State and Community law has been reviewed in a protracted series of cases arising from the *Factortame* litigation.[44]

The facts of *Factortame* are as follows. In 1988 the Divisional Court requested a preliminary ruling under art.177 from the European Court to determine the compatibility of the Merchant Shipping Act 1988 and the provisions of the Community Treaty. The 1988 Act and subsequent regulations required shipping vessels previously registered under a nineteenth-century statute to re-register with new conditions to prevent Spanish fishing vessels entering the register and thereby gaining access to British fishing areas which are under Community quota regulation. Registration was thereby conditional on a nationality requirement. Spanish fishing vessel owners sought to challenge the legality of the 1988 Act in terms of the Community law and sought an interim injunction by way of judicial review.

A secondary issue in the *Factortame*[45] case arose in connection with the grant of interim relief. The Court of Appeal set aside an interim injunction granted by the Divisional Court pending the outcome of the European Court. The House of Lords upheld the Court of Appeal's decision, because it reasoned that English courts could not grant an interim injunction against the Crown. However, this question of whether Community law obliged national courts to grant interim protection of Community rights was also referred to the European Court. Pending the outcome of the decision, the European Court gave interim relief and the UK government introduced an Order in Council amending the relevant s.14 of the 1988 Act.

The ruling of the European Court examined two issues: first, the issue of sovereignty, the validity of a UK statute and subordinate legislation as against Community law; and secondly, the issue of interim relief in the form of injunctions against the Crown.

On the first question of sovereignty, the European Court reasoned that Community law prevailed over UK law even if the result meant abrogation of the 1988 Act. Because of the extent to which the 1988 Act offended against Community law, it was inapplicable and ineffective. This outcome asserts the right of the European Court to disapply national legislation. On the second question, on the availability of interim relief against the Crown, it would appear that interim

---

43 UK's Sunday Trading laws—trading on Sunday. See *Torfaen BC v B&Q Plc* (145/88) EU:C:1989:593; [1990] 1 C.M.L.R. 337. On disablement benefits under the UK's Social Security Act 1975 see *Thomas v Adjudication Officer* [1991] 2 Q.B. 164; [1991] 2 W.L.R. 886 CA (Civ Div).
44 See *R v Employment Secretary, Ex p. EOC* [1995] 1 A.C. 1; [1994] 2 W.L.R. 409 HL.
45 See *Francovich v Italian Republic* (C-6/90 and C-9/90) EU:C:1991:428; [1993] 2 C.M.L.R. 66; N. Gravells, "Disapplying an Act of Parliament pending a Preliminary Ruling: Constitutional Enormity or Community Law Right?" [1989] *P.L.* 568; Barav (1989) 26 C.M.L. Rev. 369; and Churchill, (1989) 14 E.L. Rev. 470.

9-084 relief must be available to give full effect to Community law. It appears that injunctions and interim injunctions are available against the Crown when an issue of Community law arises.[46]

The *Factortame* decision supports those who view the European Communities as creating a new era for the jurisprudence of the UK This much is acknowledged by the House of Lords and it appears not to be confined to cases involving the application of Community law. In the *GCHQ* case, Lord Diplock accepted the concept of proportionality as part of English Administrative Law, which suggests[47] borrowing from the French system of administrative law. More recently Lord Goff[48] discussed the concept of Leichtfertigkeit, or recklessness, in German law in his discussion of the English law on recklessness. The development of human rights jurisprudence and the influence of the EU is set to continue to find relevance in the UK's domestic law and institutions.

9-085 There are general principles of EU law to be found under art.220 (ex.164) as a means of interpretation and since the TEU this includes for example human rights under art.6(f).

G: The European Court of Auditors

9-086 The European Court of Auditors,[49] established under the 1975 Treaty amending Certain Financial Provisions of the Treaties became, under art.4 of the Maastricht Treaty, an institution of the Community. Its importance continues since the Treaty of Lisbon that named it the European Court of Auditors. The European Court of Auditors is a collegiate body of 28 members, with one from each Member State. The Court is based in Luxembourg and it has important functions for ensuring that the finances of the Community are properly accounted for. Each Member State is entitled to one member of the Court appointed by the Council of Ministers and in consultation with the European Parliament for a renewable period of six years. Members of the Court must act in a non-partisan way. There is an elected President from among the members, appointed for a renewable term of three years. There are five chambers with an elected Dean for each Chamber. Each Chamber provides two areas of responsibility that includes the adoption of special reports, specific annual reports and opinions as well as annual reports on the EU Budget and the European Development Funds for adoption by the Court as a whole. Meetings of the full 28-member Court occur twice a month and this is the process for adoption of the general

---

46 See *M v Home Office* [1992] Q.B. 270; [1993] 3 W.L.R. 433. The House of Lords held that the courts had jurisdiction to issue injunctions against officers of the Crown.
47 [1985] A.C. 374; [1984] 3 W.L.R. 1174 HL. See Sophie Boyron, "Proportionality in English Administrative Law: A Faulty Translation?" (1992) 12 *Oxford Journal of Legal Studies* 237–264.
48 *R v Reid* [1992] 1 W.L.R. 793; [1992] 3 All E.R. 673 HL at [689].
49 D. O'Keefe, "The Court of Auditors" in D. Curtin and T. Heukels (eds), *Institutional Dynamics of European Integration* (Dordrecht: Kluwer, 1994).

budget of the EU and the European Development Funds. The European Court of Auditors has a staff of over 900 and operates under 11 audit and administrative directorates. Translators and administrative specialists combine to ensure publications are in the 23 official EU languages.

9-087

The activities of the Court centre around the task of examining the accounts of all revenue and expenditure of the various EU bodies and of the finances of the EU. This covers the general budget of the EU. The Court also monitors the work of DGXX, the Directorate that is concerned with Financial Control within the Community. Audit arrangements include both internal and external audits. There is also an important initiative over the past five years to combat fraud within the Community. The Court must liaise with the audit arrangements and procedures in Member States. Once EU funds are transferred to Member States the scrutiny of EU money falls under the budget arrangements of the Member States. This means that 28 separate budget systems have to be considered by DGXX and also by the Court.

9-088

Various strategies for the improvement of the accountability of the Community budget in Member States may be considered such as the Commission's Anti-Fraud Strategy and Work Programme. There is a Unit for the Co-ordination of Fraud Prevention with extensive legal powers. There are further additional measures to consider in order to achieve sound financial management of the Community that emerge from the UK budgetary system. Many of the main suggestions are usefully summarised in a Treasury Report.[50] The main principles that may be considered that emerge from an analysis of the report are as follows:

- use of targeting according to risk of fraud;

- setting precise goals and targets in the anti-fraud action programme of the Commission;

- enhanced co-ordination of anti-fraud measures;

- fraud-proofing new legislative proposals;

- periodic review of all budgetary operations;

- all Community expenditure should be subject to principles of sound public finance; and

- prior appraisal should precede the commitment of Community money in order to assess whether economic benefits are in keeping with the resources deployed.

9-089

Emphasis is placed on budgetary controls and discipline. Also since 1996, there are frequent use of spot checks to prevent and deter fraud.[51] The 2013 Annual Report[52] records that

---

50   HM Treasury, *European Community Finances*, Cm.2824 (April 1995), p.14, para.50.
51   Regulation 2185/96.
52   European Court of Auditors 2013 Annual Report, ECA/14/49 (5 November 2014)

the EU's financial accounts are generally regarded to be "reliable" and are a fair representation of the financial position of the EU. This has been the case since 2007. One troubling aspect of the accounts is the "error rate" recorded as 4.7 per cent which has been consistently above the two per cent threshold of acceptability. This means that it is estimated that 4.7 per cent of EU money should not have been paid out from the EU Budget. There is a question of how such errors occur and how might they be prevented in the future? The strong possibility that such errors are illegal, the result of fraud or breaches of the rules. The EU Commission may seek repayment of the funds from Member States but this is usually because of incorrect expenditure rather than the detection of fraud or illegality. Concerns arise that perhaps projects are not being properly managed or their objectives are not being met.

9-090 In 1999, problems of corruption found in the operation of the Commission after a report on mismanagement and sleaze, which led to the resignation of the Commission in 1999, there are more robust arrangements to scrutinise expenditure. This led to the creation of a European Anti-Fraud Office[53] with extensive investigative powers. The aim is to provide extensive preventative arrangements against fraud as well as creating a culture where fraud is unacceptable. The European Court of Auditors reports any fraud or irregularities to the European Anti-Fraud Office where there are legal powers to address any findings made by the European Court of Auditors. It is highly likely that increased public pressure will be exerted in the coming years to ensure that the European Court of Auditors continues to exercise vigilance over EU finances.

H: Europeanisation and the Creation of a European Public Law

9-091 The constitutional and political complications of the TEU[54] have caused the UK to consider once more the question of its own parliamentary sovereignty. While it is doubtful if the Treaty fundamentally alters the UK's constitutional relationship with the Community since this was established in the Single European Act, it is less clear what effects the Treaty may have on political decision-making.[55]

9-092 In evidence to the House of Commons Select Committee on Foreign Affairs it was argued that greater political power may be transferred from the Government in the UK to the Community. This may be due to economic and social factors as much as to the Treaty. However,

---

53 Commission Decision 1999/352. Also see [1999] OJ L136; and Council Decision 1999/394, [1999] OJ L149.
54 Second Report of the Foreign Affairs Select Committee, *Europe after Maastricht, Minutes of Evidence*, Vol.II, HC 223-ii (1991/92).
55 T. Koopmans, "European Public Law: Reality and Prospect" [1991] *P.L.* 53–63.

it is likely to rekindle a debate about the nature of political power in the UK. In evidence to the Commons Foreign Affairs Committee, Paul Taylor explained that:

> "For political reasons, however, members of the executive who are opposed to the development of closer relations with the Community would like it to be believed that the legislation is equally a victim—to conjure up a common enemy is to strengthen an alliance."

9–093

Political and constitutional issues are easily intertwined but it is clear that national governments of Member States in the Council of Ministers may veto proposed legislation of which they disapprove. Member States may continue to pursue their own policies within the Community and subsidiarity permits regional differences to be retained.[56]

9–094

Sovereignty, whether political or legal, is not the only issue raised by the proposals for a EU. Harlow[57] has raised the question of how the Community as a common market has created its own internal political system of "pressure group politics and its attendant professions of lobbyist and public relations expert". Her view is that the Community's origins as a transnational organisation has produced "the 'wheeler/dealer' style of Brussels politics" borrowed from the world of diplomacy and the influence of American-style business with its forms of professional lobbyists and interest group politics. There is a need for further research on the question of how decision-making is transparent within the EU.

9–095

This gives rise to questions about how far "open" government and, among decision-makers, accountability may be found within the Community? The answers may not easily be found in any institutional changes nor in the policy formulations involved in EU. Harlow argues that the UK's parliamentary system may provide a valuable contribution to how a more open and democratic community may evolve.

I: The European Convention on Human Rights and Fundamental Freedoms and European Union Law

9–096

Human rights provide an example of the importance of wider European influences and are not confined simply to membership of the Community. In 1949 European States, including

---

56 C. Harlow, "A Community of Interests? Making the Most of European Law" (1992) 55 *M.L.R.* 331–350.
Justin Greenwood, *Representing Interests in the European Union* (London: Macmillan, 1997).
57 Greenwood, *Representing Interests in the European Union*, p.344.

the 28 currently existing members of the Community, founded an international organisation known as the Council of Europe. This was an attempt to form a "unified" Europe and address the problem of human rights. The outcome was a Treaty known as the European Convention on Human Rights (ECHR). Further, it was hoped that such an organisation might act as a "watchdog" against human rights atrocities and, through Community action, as a deterrent preventing further atrocities from taking place. This primary function of the Council of Europe has gone into abeyance, leaving the ECHR as a means to raise legal issues in the Member States of the co-signatories. Out of the 25 Member States, 23 formed an agreement and put into force, in 1952, the ECHR. The main objectives of the Convention are to secure civil and political rights. Other social rights are protected under a separate arrangement known as the European Social Charter signed in 1961. A number of important decisions made by the European Court of Human Rights under the ECHR concern Northern Ireland[58] and the question of interrogation techniques and methods. The Court held that such techniques did not constitute a "practice of ill-treatment", but held that certain techniques disclosed "torture" and other "inhuman treatment".

9-097 Many of the techniques continued to be used after the judgment of the Court, nevertheless new procedures were introduced for the interrogation of suspects. Public opinion was greatly influenced by the significance of the findings.

9-098 The existence of the ECHR helps to establish a "new legal order" as part of the desire to deal with domestic problems on a European rather than a State basis. However, there are problems in integrating the ECHR with the EU.

9-099 Almost as a parallel development to the ECHR, the Treaty of Maastricht and, following on from that, the Treaty of Amsterdam have created a new art.6(2) of the Social Chapter of the original Treaty of Rome, to provide employment rights and social security rights. The incoming Labour government adopted the Social Charter as part of the substantive law of the UK by the Treaty of Amsterdam in 1997. The Amsterdam Treaty further extended the jurisdiction of the Court of Justice of the EU to include justice and home affairs. A whole raft of issues covering social, environmental and consumer protection are integrated into Community policy-making covering aspects of discrimination including sex, racial or ethnic origin.

9-100 In December 2000, a new EU Charter of Fundamental Rights, including social rights and civil and political rights, was agreed and adopted at Nice in December 2000. This is a detailed document containing 54 articles and covered various freedoms and values of human dignity, freedom, equality and solidarity. The Charter is an amalgam of the Council of Europe's Social Charter, the Charter of the Community on the Fundamental Social Rights of Workers of 1989. In certain parts of the UK, there is considerable controversy about making the European Court of Justice at Luxembourg responsible for interpreting human rights in addition to the Strasbourg Court of Human Rights under the ECHR. The UK negotiated along with Poland, Protocol 30 stating that the Charter does not extend the ability of the European Court of Justice to find that any provision in domestic law is inconsistent with the terms of the Charter. It is also suggested that the Protocol might apply to domestic courts. Doubts exist, however,

---

58   *Ireland v UK*, European Court H.R. Series A, Vol.25 (January 18, 1978), 2 E.H.R.R. 25.

as to whether Protocol 30 is effective in what it is seeking to achieve.[59] In December 2011, the European Court of Justice ruled that the UK Protocol does not "intend to exempt" the UK from the obligations to comply with the Charter.[60]

9–101

There are divergent views as to where the balance of competence should be drawn between the EU and Member States.[61] This is a matter that will need to be clarified in the near future.

9–102

The development of the Convention and the jurisprudence of the European Court of Human Rights throughout many of the Member States has increased awareness of human rights. In the past the EU has been slightly ambivalent about how far it should pursue a rights focus as part of the obligations of Member States. The drawing up of a new Charter is a promising development but it comes at a time when the work of the European Court of Human Rights is at an all-time high with an enlargement of its membership and an increase in its workload. The obvious concern is that the EU may not develop in parallel but as a rival. This might seem incongruous, but the creation of rights within the EU Treaties will inevitably lead to a need for some form of synergy of ideas and processes with the ECHR. This might even include the possibility of merging the Strasbourg and Luxembourg courts in a unified jurisdiction, but this idea is some way off the main agenda for reform at the moment.

J: Conclusions and Summary

Undoubtedly the EU exercises a major influence on the UK since the UK joined in 1972, including its constitutional and administrative law[62] as well as its economy and way of life. The Euro crisis has largely defined the EU over the past five years. The subject of democratic legitimacy is at the forefront of how the EU is evaluated. Meeting the Euro crisis has raised some concerns that decision-making is too authoritarian and not sufficiently inclusive. The problem is that the 28-member EU has to take into account the 17 Eurozone States. This has the unfortunate consequence of reinforcing the perception that the more powerful Member States such as Germany have the final say over the smaller Eurozone states such as Greece. There has also been an increase in the influence of the European Central Bank in order to support and maintain the Euro in a period of economic volatility. There is a clearly emerging two-tier form to the EU—the

9–103

---

59 House of Commons Library, *Effects of the EU Charter of Rights in the UK*, SN/1A/6765 (17 March 2014); and *Ab v Home Department* (7 November 2013).
60 High Court Decision, *NS v Home Secretary* (21 December 2011); and *Rugby Football Union v Consolidated Information Services Ltd* (C-411/10 and C-493/10) EU:C:2011:865; [2011] UKSC 55.
61 See the discussion in the House of Commons Library, *Effects of the EU Charter of Rights in the UK*, Standard note, No.6765 (17 March 2014).
62 House of Commons Library, *EU Treaty change: the parliamentary process of bills*, Briefing Paper, 03341 (11 June 2015). Provides a good overview of the subject taking account of UK bills linked to the ratification of EU Treaty amendments.

17-member Eurozone and the non-Eurozone states within an overall 28-member state. There is also an alarming gap in the financial measures needed to address the economic crisis and the legal and constitutional framework for implementation and control. Austerity measures have influenced how many view the EU especially the "top-down" system of command and control used to accommodate austerity controls. This leaves many citizens' quite bewildered at the absence of direct democratic accountability over decisions that have a serious impact on their lives. Attempts to improve the EU under the Treaty of Lisbon by giving more powers to the Parliament have not proved successful in encouraging voter turnout or participation.[63]

9-104 Evaluating the UK's membership of the EU is a major political debating point leading up to the referendum on EU membership. There is a long history of UK doubts and uncertainties surrounding EU membership. In 1974–75 the then Labour government promised a renegotiation and referendum on EU membership and after negotiation over the Community's regional policy, budgetary corrections and agreed market access to New Zealand dairy products, a referendum was held in June 1975 with 67 per cent voting in favour of staying on a turnout of 64 per cent.[64] In 1984, at Fountainbleau, the UK negotiated a rebate on the high proportion it contributed to the EU Budget that was then spent on the Common Agricultural Policy. This has achieved substantial savings and further revisions in 1994, 2000, and 2007. In 2013 this was estimated to be €4.1 billion, an increase to the 2012 rebate of €3.7 billion.

9-105 In terms of Treaty amendments, the UK has also a history of negotiating opt outs. The Treaty of Amsterdam in 1999 contained an opt out in the form of a protocol that excluded it from all measures concerning asylum, immigration and visas and agreement over further opt outs on a case by case basis. The Treaty of Lisbon was ratified by the UK. It included the EU Charter encompassing widely drawn rights and the ECHR. The UK negotiated an "opt out" under Protocol 30.

9-106 Negotiating the terms of EU membership[65] also includes an assessment of whether or not to exit the EU.[66] A *YouGov* poll in February 2015 suggested that 45 per cent of the electorate would remain while 35 per cent might want to leave the EU.[67] Diagram 2, at the end of this chapter, sets out the instances of a referendum[68] being held in the EU and it shows how notoriously unpredictable referendum results can be.[69]

9-107 The development of a European public law is a question of future strategy and direction. This will continue to evolve even if the UK were at one extreme to exit the EU. UK membership has always been intrinsically partially consensual and partly conflicted.[70] Many of the EU

---

63 House of Commons Library, *The European Union: a democratic institution?*, Research Paper, 14/25 (29 April 2014).
64 House of Commons Library, *The 1974–75 UK Renegotiation of EEC Membership and Referendum*, Briefing Paper, No.7253 (13 July 2015).
65 See House of Commons Library, *Exiting the EU: UK reform proposals, legal impact and alternative to membership*, No.7214 (4 June 2015).
66 House of Commons Briefing Paper, *Exiting the EU: impact in key UK policy areas*, No.7213 (4 June 2015).
67 House of Commons Library, *European Union Bill 2015/16*, Briefing Paper, No.07212 (3 June 2015).
68 This is the question approved by the Electoral Commission.
69 *The Economist*, 17 October 2015. Special Report, The Reluctant European.
70 Przemyslaw Bishop, *Conflicts between Community and National Laws: An Analysis of the British Approach*, Sussex European Institute Working Paper No.66 (June 2003) provides a good analysis of the main issues..

influences on the UK's domestic legal system have already been noted and are likely to continue, albeit under different circumstances, even if the UK leaves EU membership. A growing jurisprudence exists in the European Court of Justice and in the UK's adaptation of EU law. Principles of French or German law may be found, explained and examined in English courts' decisions at the highest levels. Influences such as the ECHR are also relevant and important. Koopmans[71] has written that common influences may be detectable even amid differences between Member States. Citizens are more litigious[72] and perhaps more likely to challenge authority in some European countries than in others. While different Member States have adopted Directives of the Community in distinct ways, the European Court receives an overview of the activities of all the Member States. His conclusion is that despite differences,[73] "we are bound to come to one European system. The integration process cannot be discontinued". The forthcoming decade is likely to be the test of how far this aspiration might be realised.

The UK Referendum in June 2016, to leave the EU raises questions as to what "leave" may mean? The answer is unclear as different elements in the current relationship with the EU might be worth maintaining, such as membership of the single market. It remains to be seen what will be negotiated once, and when, Article 50 is activated. Effectively there will be two years to conclude negotiations.

Further Reading

G. Anthony, *UK Public Law and European Law: The Dynamics of Legal Integration* (Oxford: Hart, 2001).

Paul Craig, "Britain in the European Union" in J.Jowell, D. Oliver and Colm O'Cinneide (eds),*The Changing Constitution*, 8th edn (Oxford: Oxford University Press, 2015).

Paul Craig, "The European Union Act 2011: Locks, Limits and Legality" (2011) 48 *C.M.L. Rev.* 1881.

P. Craig and G. De Burca, *EU Law, Text, Cases and Materials*, 6th edn (Oxford: Oxford University Press, 2015).

D. Feldman, *Civil Liberties and Human Rights in England and Wales* (Oxford University Press, Oxford, 2002).

J. R. Gordley and A. T. Von Meheren, *The Civil Law System: An Introduction to the Comparative Study of Law*, 2nd edn (Boston: Little, Brown, 1977).

K. P. E. Lasok, *Law and Institutions of the European Union*, 7th edn (London: Butterworths, 2001).

---

71 T. Koopmans, "European Public Law: Reality and Prospect" [1991] *P.L.* 53–63.
72 *Johnston v Chief Constable of the RUC* (222/84) EU:C:1986:206; [1986] 3 C.M.L.R. 240.
73 Koopmans, "European Public Law: Reality and Prospect", p.63.

Diagram 1: Key Treaties 1990–2015

Date	Treaty	
7 February 1992	TEU	Maastricht
October 1997	Treaty of Amsterdam	
11 December 2000	Treaty of Nice	
18 June 2004	Treaty Establishing a Constitution for Europe	Not ratified
December 2007	Treaty of Lisbon	Reorganised the Treaty arrangements including the Treaty of Rome

Diagram 2: Referendums on Europe

Country	Date	Subject	Outcome
Denmark	June 1992	Maastricht Treaty	50.7 against (revised later)
Ireland	June 1992	Maastricht Treaty	68.7 in favour
France	September 1992	Maastricht Treaty	51.1 in favour
Switzerland	December 1992	EEA membership	50.3 against (talks followed for ten years)
Denmark	September 2000	Euro membership	53.2 against but shadows the Euro
Ireland	June 2001	Treaty of Nice	53.9 against but reversed later
Sweden	September 2003	Euro membership	56.1 against
Spain	February 2005	Eur. Constitution	76.7 in favour
France	May 2005	Eur. Constitution	54.9 against
Netherlands	June 2005	Eur. Constitution	61.5 against
Luxembourg	July 2005	Eur. Constitution	56.5 in favour
Ireland	June 2008	Treaty of Lisbon	53.2 against but reversed year later
Greece	July 2015	EU, ECB and IMF bailouts	63.1 per cent rejected the proposals

Sources: *The Economist*, 17 October 2015, House of Lords Library LIF/2015/0018. In Focus, Greek Referendum on EU, ECB and IMF Bailout proposals.

Part III

Government, Regulation and Accountability

The preceding chapters in Pts I and II have been primarily concerned with providing an introductory framework of the constitutional and administrative law of the UK, including the ideas and influences which have shaped its development. Part III of the textbook comprises an examination in more detail of some of the increasingly specialist areas of public law in the UK. Chapters 10–12 are intended to explain, respectively, how present day government operates within the parliamentary system of accountability, how the civil service is managed and how public finance is scrutinised. Chapter 13 comprises an analysis of local government and its relationship with central government. Chapter 14 outlines some of the regulatory arrangements after privatisation of the major utilities.

10

Government and Accountability

A: Introduction

In previous chapters the roles of government and Parliament have been discussed in outline. In this chapter it is intended to explain how in theory and in practice government may be made accountable. As Bamforth and Leyland have outlined the term "accountability" has become "more frequently used" than perhaps any other in the analysis and discussion of public law in the UK.[1]

10–001

Accountability takes many forms. A wide variety of techniques and institutions are involved in the scrutiny of government, including the work of parliamentary select committees and courts. The system of government is essentially one of party government and the political process may exert influences on the style of government and public affairs. Also relevant in how government may be held to account for its actions, is the work of the various audit bodies such as the National Audit Office, accountable for both local and central government audit arrangements. Reference to the role of public finance may be found in more detail in Ch.12.

10–002

How government may formulate its policies and how it carries out the tasks of government may place strain on existing constitutional arrangements. In recent years an increasing trend towards centralisation of government powers has coincided with a period of government with a large working parliamentary majority. The size of the government's parliamentary majority may affect the ability of Parliament to scrutinise effectively the Executive. Worldwide, the experience of governments with a large parliamentary majority raises questions about the effectiveness of constitutional arrangements to hold government to account. There is a tendency

10–003

---

1 N. Bamforth and P. Leyland, "Introduction: Accountability in the Contemporary Constitution" in N. Bamforth and P. Leyland, *Accountability in the Contemporary Constitution* (Oxford: Oxford University Press, 2013), pp.1–14.

even for elected or popular governments to behave in an authoritarian way.[2] The strength of opposition parties is often the determining factor in establishing how effectively a government is scrutinised.

10-004 The traditional form of elected government is being slowly transformed by various regulatory styles of government.[3] These have a multiple purpose. One is to deliver through economic management various aspects of governing that are relevant to society. This includes elements of substantive justice which may operate as a form of distributive justice. Public services are often delivered by state actors that cover publicly entities such as the National Health Service. Education and policing are also good examples. Prosser identifies an institutional map of governance that goes beyond the traditional contours of centralised government and extends into different agencies, institutions and organisations. His analysis points to the question of "how the network of institutions for scrutiny and accountability has succeeded in fulfilling the need for constitutional legitimacy and scrutiny which Parliament cannot meet".[4]

B: Accountability Defined

10-005 To be accountable[5] is to give reasons and explanations for actions or decisions taken. The characteristic of medieval accountability was the direct responsibility of the individual servant to the King.[6] The idea of accountability may be traced back to the earliest form of organised government. Normanton has pointed out how accountability has[7] "an historical connection between administrative secrecy and the hierarchical state". Such a connection may arise where the State is a hierarchy and all accountability is to the head. Accountability as a means of authorisation control may promote secrecy[8]:

---

2   See T. J. Pempel (ed), *Uncommon Democracies: The One-Party Dominant Regimes* (Ithaca, NY: Cornell University Press, 1990); Arend Lijphart, *Democracies: Patterns of Majoritarian and Consensus Government in Twenty One Countries* (New Haven, CT: Yale University Press, 1984); Jean Blondel, "Party Systems and patterns of Government in Western democracies" (1968) *Canadian Journal of Political Science* 1(2), pp.180–203; Dennis P. Patterson, "The Strategy of Dominant Political Parties: Electoral Institutions and Election outcomes in Africa" (2011) *American Political Science Association*; and Hanna Lerner, *Making Constitutions in Deeply Divided Societies* (Cambridge: Cambridge University Press, 2012).
3   See the discussion in C. Scott, "Regulatory Governance and the Challenge of Constitutionalism" in D. Oliver, T. Prosser and R. Rawlings (eds), *The Regulatory State* (Oxford: Oxford University Press, 2010), pp.15–34.
4   T. Prosser, *The Economic Constitution* (Oxford: Oxford University Press, 2014), p.19.
5   See 1st Report of the Public Service Select Committee, *Ministerial Accountability and Responsibility*, HC 234 (1996–97).
6   E. Normanton, *The Accountability and Audit of Governments* (Manchester: Manchester University Press, 1966), p.2.
7   Normanton, *The Accountability and Audit of Governments*, p.4.
8   Normanton, *The Accountability and Audit of Governments*.

> "The ruler must learn what his servants have been doing, so that he can promote or punish; private persons need know nothing of the secrets and errors of administration, and within unitary states they are rarely allowed to do so. Government is an authoritarian mystery."

The link between secrecy and accountability has not entirely ended with medieval government. Present day government may be described as responsible government, but this does not always give rise to open or adequate accountability. One explanation is that accountability may be both internal and external. Internal accountability relates to internal guidance within government departments based on rules of conduct that are not statutory, and some may not be widely published. A good example is the use of Treasury Solicitor's Guidance or Treasury Memorandum as a means of checking on government expenditure and accounts. Internal accountability may prove effective, but it is often hidden from external scrutiny and to some extent this may perpetuate secrecy as the nature of internal review involves confidential and sensitive information.[9]

External accountability relates to the idea that Ministers are "responsible" or "answerable" to Parliament. This covers such matters as appearing before select committees or answering parliamentary questions. Information provided through parliamentary debate and media coverage contributes to the functions of holding Ministers to account and also controlling government. Advice tendered to civil servants as to their duties and responsibilities in attending before select committees, sets out lines of responsibility between civil servants and Ministers. However, such advice, if invoked, might be considered restrictive of more open government.

It is also possible to see accountability linked to economic regulation. Tony Prosser[10] has usefully identified two economic models of regulation—regulation as infringement of private autonomy and regulation as a collaborative exercise. In its simplest form the former is favoured by giving regulator greater independence and autonomy to make and implement decisions. Its aims are to maximise economic efficiency whilst leaving elected governments to set policy and implements overall strategy. The latter emphasises systems of political oversight and accountability often described as "governments in miniature". It is clear that whilst the validity of Prosser's two economic models of regulation is not in doubt, in fact there is more convergence between Prosser's two models than is perhaps fully appreciated. It is argued that increasing regulator independence, favoured by the EU, may put in danger the systems of accountability that are essential for legitimacy as well as effective regulation that sit under various political policy making processes. There is a slowly emerging literature in Britain that is addressing the twin aims of legitimacy and accountability.

Accountability also involves legal redress. The appeal to courts or tribunals or the establishment of an inquiry with investigative powers with the right to examine evidence and establish

---

9   See T. Daintith and A. Page, *The Executive in the Constitution* (Oxford: Oxford University Press, 1999).
10 T. Prosser, "Regulation and Social Solidarity" (2006) 33 *Journal of Law and Society* 364–87.

facts provides an external assessment of government actions. As part of the fact-finding process a court, tribunal or inquiry may seek to establish reasons or justifications for action taken. The giving of reasons becomes an important element for establishing the grounds for decision making. This is aimed at remedying citizens' grievances but it also assists in improving the quality of administration. Well reasoned and considered decisions with recourse to advice and consultation are the hallmark of good government. Judicial decisions appear to be in sympathy with those aims. In *Rowling v Takaro Properties Ltd*[11] the Privy Council considered how Ministers may be liable under a duty of care, in an action for negligence arising out of their public duties as Ministers. Considering whether such a duty may be imposed was a question of "an intensely pragmatic character". In *Lonhro v Tebbit*[12] the Court of Appeal accepted this point and affirmed the role of the court to consider the issue. In *M v Home Office*[13] the House of Lords held that the contempt jurisdiction of the courts extended to Ministers of the Crown.

10-010 There are also various forms of accountability involved in achieving better administration. In addition to the courts these involve various audits carried out by the Comptroller and Auditor General and the National Audit Office.[14] There are various ombudsmen, namely the Commissioner for Local Administration in the case of local authorities, or the Parliamentary Commissioner for Administration in the case of central government. Ombudsmen perform important investigative functions.

10-011 Responsible government also implies parliamentary control as Turpin has noted[15]:

> "The notion of 'responsible government' implies both acceptance of responsibility for things done and 'responsiveness' to influence, persuasion, and pressure for modifications of policy. Activist parliamentarians of our day aim to 'redress the balance' of the constitution in favour of Parliament by strengthening both control and responsibility of the executive, without making a fine discrimination between these concepts."

10-012 There have been further attempts to clarify different forms of accountability. Sir Robin Butler, when Head of the Civil Service, made a distinction between "the duty to give an account" and "the obligation to accept responsibility". This formulation can be found in the booklet produced as guidance to ministers known as *Questions of Procedures for Ministers*. This document has no legal status but it sets out current thinking on such matters. The question arises as to how the distinction made by Sir Robin Butler works in practice. The answer may be

---

11 [1988] A.C. 473; [1988] 1 All E.R. 163 PC (NZ) at [172].
12 [1992] 4 All E.R. 280; [1992] B.C.C. 779 CA (Civ Div).
13 *M v Home Office* [1992] Q.B. 270; [1994] 1 A.C. 377 CA (Civ Div).
14 The NAO has also assumed responsibility for the oversight of the audit of local authorities since the abolition of the Audit Commission. See House of Commons Library, *Local Audit in England*, Briefing Paper, No.07240 (24 June 2015).
15 Turpin, "Ministerial Responsibility: Myth or Reality" in J. Jowell and D. Oliver (eds), *The Changing Constitution* (Oxford: Oxford University Press, 1989) (2nd edn, 1994), p.56.

found in considering the findings of the Scott Inquiry.[16] Clearly Sir Richard Scott accepted the basis of the distinction but then reaches a number of conclusions that find difficulty in drawing any clear line between the duty to give an account and the obligation to accept responsibility. If the findings of the Scott inquiry are closely examined, it is apparent that the following conclusions are reached. Sir Richard Scott considered that the guidelines on arms sales, known as the Howe Guidelines, were conceived as a statement of policy and that as a result of revising the guidelines this reflected the actuality that policy had been changed. Government statements made in 1989 and 1990 about policy on arms exports "consistently failed to discharge the obligations imposed by the constitutional principle of Ministerial responsibility".[17]

10–013

As outlined in Ch.4, Sir Richard Scott also found that the Attorney General was at fault in not making clear to the court at the trial of the Matrix Churchill directors that Mr Heseltine, then President of the Board of Trade, was reluctant to agree signing the certificate claiming public interest immunity.[18] A second criticism was that the Attorney General had mistakenly interpreted the law on public interest certificates when he claimed that Ministers were bound to sign such certificates when requested to do so. Criticism was also made of a number of Ministers for the reasons they gave for signing public interest immunity certificates.[19]

10–014

It is clear that Sir Richard considers that Ministers were, albeit perhaps mistakenly, engaged in acting in what they took to be the national and therefore the public interest. Ministers gained no direct benefits from the arms sales and had been influenced by the need to operate within the competitive conditions of the market. The information available to Ministers at the time was less than the information which is now available with the benefit of hindsight. As outlined in Ch.4 above Ministers and civil servants are to be judged by what they then knew and on the basis of what they believed at that time. At the heart of the ministerial defence on arms exports was the claim that Ministers had applied the spirit of the guidelines of necessity. In short, Ministers could rely on their subjective defence. They may now appear to have been mistaken but at the time they acted in good faith and with the public interest in mind.

10–015

While Scott reserves strongest criticism for the failure of Ministers in not publishing the revised guidelines and giving Parliament the opportunity to debate them, but stops short of laying blame having found faults in the conduct of government. Could Scott have come to conclusions on the same evidence that would have forced ministerial resignation?

10–016

There are thus several important implications to be drawn from Scott's findings on government wrongdoing. Ministers might consider that they have obtained the best "get out" clause possible from ministerial blameworthiness, that their view of events may be accepted as the best judge of establishing the limits of their own responsibility. After all it was a Minister, Mr Alan Clark, who precipitated the discovery that the guidelines had been revised from his

---

16 The Scott Report: The Rt Hon. Sir Richard Scott, The Vice-Chancellor, *Return to an Address of the Honourable House of Commons dated 15th February 1996. Report of the Inquiry into the Export of Defence Equipment and Dual-use Goods to Iraq and Related Prosecutions*, HC 115 (1996) (London: HMSO, 1996).
17 *Scott Report*, D4.63.
18 See the *Scott Report*, G13.69–72.
19 See the *Scott Report*, G54, 67, 106, 117, 125.

frank disclosure at the "arms to Iraq" trial that the guidelines were regularly bypassed. The Scott report carefully finds blame to be attached to the actions of several Ministers but the question of fault-finding and ultimate resignation is left to the political arena. If there are shortcomings on blame it is Parliament that must act not tribunals of inquiry. For the future it would appear that a Freedom of Information Act might be the only effective way to police ministerial integrity in these matters.

10–017
The publication of the Civil Service Code[20] and its regular updates appears to confirm the existing orthodoxy.[21] One way forward is proposed by Diane Woodhouse[22]:

> "Moving into the twenty-first century, the convention of ministerial responsibility can be defined loosely as requiring, first, information rather than resignation; secondly, ministerial 'accountability' for everything but 'responsibility' for only some things; thirdly, civil servant 'responsibility' for some things but 'accountability' only when this suits ministerial interests."

10–018
The added dimension to parliamentary control is political accountability to the electorate. This raises questions about how party politics influence government.

C: The Scott Report and Parliament

10–019
The Scott inquiry raises a serious question about the propriety of an inquiry on behalf of the Prime Minister of the day about the government of the day rather than an inquiry on behalf of Parliament. It was inevitable that Parliament would divide along party political lines, favouring the government of the day. In the media battle over presenting the findings of the inquiry the main findings of the Scott inquiry appear to have been overlooked. The Scott inquiry had found that Parliament was unable to hold government to account in any satisfactory way. Parliament had been misled, and had consistently failed to detect any alteration in government policy or, through the select committee system, exercise enough scrutiny to deter practices that were inconsistent with the original guidelines. It is clear that Parliament also appeared weak and ineffectual when the Scott report came to be debated. Parliament had failed to set the agenda and felt honour bound to vote on the report, not according to any principles of parliamentary etiquette, but on party political lines. Both opposition and government used the report to claim political advantage. The greatest irony is that, to protect the findings from legal proceedings,

---

20   *Hansard*, HC (February 12, 1997), cols.273–293.
21   *Hansard*, HL (9 January 1996); Written Answers 21 (1 January 1996).
22   Diane Woodhouse "Ministerial Responsibility: Something Old, Something New" [1997] *Public Law* 262.

the report was given the protection of parliamentary privilege by being published as a report of the House of Commons. Sir Richard's exhaustive inquiry allowed an outsider into the secret world of the civil service and the administration. As an outsider, was he qualified for the task in hand? Professor Martin Loughlin queries Scott's role and expertise[23] and questions whether a single judge sitting independently without any expert assessors appreciated the realities of government decision making and the dilemma of ministerial discretion. Sir Richard is probably the first independent person to have had complete access to the secret world of the civil service and their relations with ministers. There is also a further concern that a judge caught up in the internal politics of party government is liable to become politicised as a result.[24] There is clearly a danger when judges are involved in public inquiries that inevitably lead to party political controversy.

10–020

The different style and culture involved in decision making between the judicial, ministerial and administrative may explain why the Scott inquiry showed differences of opinion between government ministers and Sir Richard, reflecting differences in culture and attitude. On Sir Richard's part there is the forensic role of law and lawyers applying prescriptive rules to facts and finding exemptions or exceptions. On the part of ministers there is a culture of secrecy, and an attitude that the role of law is one of enabling and facilitating the conduct of government policy that unless an action is prohibited by law, it is permissible.

10–021

There are also questions raising constitutional issues surrounding the fact that the Scott inquiry appeared to trespass on the role of Parliament itself and its internal functioning. The concern is that Sir Richard may have inadvertently trespassed into the proceedings of Parliament strictly protected under art.9 of the Bill of Rights from outside inquiry. As already discussed in Ch.4, art.9, is followed in many leading cases and is applied in the Privy Council case of *Prebble v Television New Zealand*.[25] It was held, that in an action which cited proceedings in Parliament, if the action questioned parliamentary proceedings then it would have to be stayed.[26] It is not always exactly clear what constitutes proceedings of Parliament. The concept is an elastic and flexible one. The Register of Members' Interests is not,[27] it is clear that resolutions of the House, the reports from the committees of the House, and subsequent inquiries and reports do come within the category of proceedings.[28] Erskine May,[29] notes that "everything that is said or done" within the precincts of the House forms part of the proceedings in Parliament. Patricia Leopold queries whether the Scott inquiry fell into the category that would exclude him from inquiring into the "proceedings in Parliament". Leopold concludes that it was necessary for Sir Richard to make the inquiries that he undertook otherwise:

---

23   Martin Loughlin, *Sword and Scales* (Oxford: Hart, 2000), p.43.
24   Rodney Brazier, "It *is* a Constitutional Issue: Fitness for Ministerial Office in the 1990s" [1994] *Public Law* 431.
25   [1995] 1 A.C. 321; [1994] 3 W.L.R. 970 PC (NZ).
26   Also see *In Re Parliamentary Privilege Act 1770* [1958] A.C. 331; [1958] 2 W.L.R. 912 PC (UK).
27   *Rost v Edwards* [1990] 2 Q.B. 460; [1990] 2 W.L.R. 1280 QBD.
28   *Hamilton v Al Fayed* [1999] 1 W.L.R. 1569; [1999] 3 All E.R. 317 CA (Civ Div).
29   Erskine May, Sir David Limon (ed), *Parliamentary Practice*, 22nd edn (London: Butterworths, 1997).

> "...But if Sir Richard had been debarred from making these criticisms, he would have been unable to do his job. However, the contrast is marked between the freedom he possessed as a one-man tribunal and the restrictions he would have had to observe as a judge in a court hearing. A Nelsonian blind eye has been turned to the problem."[30]

10-022 The delicate question of the remit of Sir Richard's inquiry and parliamentary proceedings does not appear to have been addressed in setting up the inquiry. Sir Richard exposed the weakness of government decision making for which the government escaped the censure of resignation. He also exposed the fundamental weakness of Parliament itself, which Parliament has refrained from properly addressing.[31]

D: The Party System

10-023 Political parties engage in policy formulation and in setting the agenda for the period they hope to occupy government. In the case of the Conservative Party, policies are determined through a variety of advisers through the co-ordination of the Conservative Research Department. Included are the Institute of Economic Affairs, the Centre for Policy Studies founded in 1974 by Sir Keith Joseph, and the Adam Smith Institute. The annual party conference rarely sets the scene for the formulation of policy, rather it acts as a fulcrum of support for the party leadership. Historically, a key feature of the procedure for the selection of the Leader of the Conservative Party was the role of the influential backbench 1922 Committee whose chairman, not the chairman of the Conservative Party, was responsible for the conduct of all ballots. The timetable for election was within 28 days of the opening of the new session of Parliament. The process of election was by a secret ballot system amongst all the elected MPs holding the party whip and who were members of the Conservative Party. The elected candidate who becomes Leader of the Party and, if the party is the government of the day, the Prime Minister, was the one candidate who

> "...both receives an overall majority of the votes of those entitled to vote and (ii) receives 15 per cent. more of the votes of those entitled to vote than any other candidate."

---

30 Patricia Leopold, "The Application of the Civil and Criminal Law to Members of Parliament and Parliamentary Proceedings" in G. Drewry and D. Oliver (eds), *Law and Parliament* (London: Butterworths, 1998), Ch.5, pp.71-87.
31 Section 13 of the Defamation Act 1996 was passed to allow MPs to pursue legal claims for defamation where the conduct of a person in or in relation to proceedings in Parliament is in issue. Immunity may be waived whereby the protection of parliamentary privilege prevented the courts from questioning what was said or done in Parliament.

The second ballot was more straightforward with the winner declared on the basis of an outright majority.

Descriptions of the election of Mr Heath in 1965, following the resignation of Sir Alex Douglas Home, show how the victory of Mr Heath over other candidates came through careful electioneering, well-managed campaigns and well-focused appeals to backbench loyalties. The leadership election of Mrs Thatcher in 1975 showed similar tactics in winning loyalty from backbench MPs. Clearly party leaders who then become Prime Minister have the reality of party support as the basis of exercising power.

On 19 November 1990, the premature resignation of Mrs Thatcher as Prime Minister reinforced the power of party politics and underlined the collective force of cabinet government. Nigel Lawson in his memoirs[32] explains the consequences of the Prime Minister's political unpopularity:

> "It was unprecedented: yet there were good reasons why no fewer than 45 per cent of her parliamentary colleagues felt unable to support their leader of the previous fifteen years and more in the first ballot and amongst the 55 per cent who did there were many, particularly amongst her ministerial colleagues, who had allowed their loyalty to get the better of their judgment in the first ballot but would not have done so in the second. Those reasons essentially boiled down to one: the conviction that Margaret had become an electoral liability and that the Conservative Party could win the coming general election only under a new leader."

Nicholas Ridley[33] attributed Mrs Thatcher's failure to gain sufficient votes in the first ballot to win the leadership to bad tactics. The first error was the timing of the election to coincide with a period when the Prime Minister had to be out of the country whilst attending a conference in Paris. Secondly, there was a clear mistake in deciding "to appoint a weak campaign team".

The team contained five ex-Cabinet Ministers who Ridley believes did "not know large numbers of MPs". The team merely canvassed opinion and did not seek to persuade. This example underlines the point already noted of the careful relationship required between the political party and the leadership.

The election of the leader of the Conservative Party following the defeat of Mr John Major at the General Election on 1 May 1997 highlighted the problems of the lack of input into the constituency party. The election of Mr William Hague took three ballots, although the canvass of constituency support was in favour of Mr Kenneth Clarke. The constituency associations were not part of the ballot which was confined to Conservative MPs. Following the defeat of the Conservative Party in the 2001 election, Mr Hague resigned the leadership. The election of

---

32 Nigel Lawson, *The View From No.11* (London: Bantam, 1992), pp.1000–1001.
33 Nicholas Ridley, *My Style of Government* (London: Hutchinson, 1991), pp.241–242.

10-029 a new leader followed new rules drawn up in 1998 and used for the first time, whereby the parliamentary party had a pivotal role effectively replacing the domination of the 1922 Committee. Conservative MPs determine from a list of those who wish to stand the names of two candidates to go forward to a second ballot. In 2001, at the first stage the ballot reduced the field from five candidates that stood to two candidates. The two names are then subject to election by the whole party membership on the basis of one member, one vote. In 2001, a final ballot took place making Mr Iain Duncan Smith the Leader of the Party.

10-030 There was a turnout of 79 per cent of party members and Mr Duncan Smith received 60 per cent of the vote. In the event in October 2002, Mr Duncan Smith proved to be unpopular with the party and MPs. Lacking support amongst Conservative MPs, a ballot was held and by 90 votes to 75 he was voted out of the leadership. Michael Howard was the only candidate to succeed him and he was elected unopposed without a ballot. This made it possible to elect a new leader without the long drawn out process of ballots. The election of 2005 proved a third consecutive defeat for the Conservatives and Michael Howard resigned as leader. David Cameron was elected to succeed him and on a ballot of the party membership he won 67.6 per cent of the votes. Changes in the party organisation followed with members having a role in the election process involving ballots. A national membership was created with a centrally held list of members. The election of a leader is a mixture of MPs and members. MPs may trigger the election of a leader with a ballot to reduce the field to two candidates. The final ballot is with the Conservative Party members participating on the basis of one member one vote. This is a radical departure from past practice.[34]

In the case of the Labour Party, unlike the Conservative Party, the formulation of policy is partly carried out through the party conference. Thus, "direction and control" of the work of the party is in theory left to the conference. This body provides a wide canvass for Labour Party support. The trade unions and other affiliated groups comprise about 90 per cent of the conference votes. There is a National Executive Committee elected by the party conference which sets out the main developments and direction of policy. There are various sub-committees which carry out the actual work of devising policy. The manifesto is jointly arrived at by the National Executive Committee and the leadership of the parliamentary party comprising the party leader, deputy leader and shadow cabinet, if out of government. Advice to the Labour Party comes from a wide variety of sources including the Adam Smith Institute, the Institute for Public Policy Research and various trade union-funded advisers.

10-031 Attempts to shift control from the parliamentary party leadership to the National Executive Committee have been unsuccessful. Given the fact that the Labour Party had been unsuccessful in gaining office in the General Elections from 1978–1992, the Labour Parliamentary Party has resisted attempts to have the annual conference impose control over its policy. In fact, centralising tendencies within the party have adopted a more directed approach to policy than hitherto. This has resulted in policy initiatives largely controlled by the party leadership. The election victory in May 1997 confirmed strict party discipline as an element in election success. Similarly, the victory in 2001 continued the tradition of strong party discipline.

---

34 Philip Norton, *The British Polity* (London: Longman, 2011), pp.130–142.

10-032 Two successive election defeats, 2010 and 2015 have created a question of electoral credibility that has left the Labour Party in some difficulty.[35] The Labour Party commissioned a review in 2013 of the Party's electoral rules. Since 2014, Labour Party members elect a leader from candidates who have been nominated by at least 15 per cent of all Labour MPs with each party member receiving one vote only with votes of equal weight.[36] The election of Jeremy Corbyn as Labour Leader on 12 September marked a departure from previous leaders.[37] The recruitment of new members allowed the inclusion of affiliated members and allowed participation from "grass root" supporters that gave a voice to a wider spectrum of opinion than in the past.[38] This may leave a dilemma for the party in the form of a populist leader with grass roots support but with little support from amongst Labour MPs. It remains to be seen how inevitable political tensions may be resolved.[39] There is also an underlying tension between the role of MPs and their constituency party. Do MPs have a mandate as representatives of the constituency party? Do MPs have the freedom to make decisions on the merits of a particular issue even if this is in conflict with the general views of their constituency party? Resolving both questions is likely to take some time for many MPs over the coming months.

10-033 The above procedure with its weighting in favour of, respectively, affiliated labour organisations, the Constituency Labour Party and the Parliamentary Labour Party, makes the question of the manifesto a difficult issue in the development of the policies of any future Labour Government. Attempts by the National Executive Committee to mandate the Parliamentary Labour Party with an election manifesto drawn up by the National Executive Committee would leave any future Labour Government with little discretion over their policies. This would pose a serious question about the propriety of a future Labour Government being bound by the National Executive Committee, a body that is not responsible for the implementation of any policies. One tactic has been to have annual elections to the National Executive Committee and this has given the party leadership greater influence.

10-034 The Liberal Democratic Party, from 1988, has had a Federal Party for matters of policy common to England, Scotland and Wales. For specific matters within each of the regions, there is a state party for each region. The Federal Party determines issues which overlap with policies decided in each of the regions. There is a Federal Policy Committee, responsible for research and development. Ultimate authority is found to rest within the Federal Conference, which has representatives from the local party. Election of party leader is by the system of a Single Transferable Vote (STV) and by secret ballot. Nominations must be supported by 200 members and the nominee must be a member of the Parliamentary Party in the House of Commons.

10-035 The internal organisation of political parties may well have repercussions on the government's treatment of various issues and in the organisation of the government itself. Accountability of the government of the day to political parties emphasises the nature of

---

35 Thomas Quinn, *Electing and Ejecting Party Leaders in Britain* (London: Palgrave Macmillan, 2015).
36 *Labour Party Rule Book* (2015).
37 The current rules are to be found in the *Labour Party Rule Book* (2015).
38 House of Commons Library, *Leadership Elections: Labour Party*, Briefing Paper, 03938 (23 September 2015).
39 Philip Norton, *The British Polity* (London: Longman: 2011), pp.143–156.

party government. Thus it is likely that the policies created through the political process will also have an effect on the institutions of government itself.[40] In that way different forms of accountability are continually evolving. For example, impeachment of Ministers preceded the development of political accountability to Parliament. The fact that one form of accountability gives way to some new idea is recognised by Marshall who identifies a number of elements in the continuous development of constitutional practice. Marshall identifies "removability", "answerability" and resignation as elements in this process.

10-036
Accountability involves the principles of cabinet and individual responsibility to Parliament, the role of Parliament may be examined from this perspective.

E: The Role of Parliament

10-037
Parliament provides the framework for government accountability but it also provides the government with the means to carry out its policies through legislation. Parliament's relationship with the Executive is always changing. Televised proceedings of the House of Lords began in 1985 and the House of Commons in 1989. This has provided greater media attention and publicity than ever before. A positive effect is to bring Parliamentary proceedings into social media and televised committee hearings have proved interesting and informative. The set piece of Prime Ministers Questions (PMQs) has proved controversial revealing strong exchanges and often an adversarial and confrontational style that appears to be counterproductive receiving a generally unfavourable public reception. Media attention has also focused on "cash for questions" and a general scandal about MPs expenses and salaries.[41] The reputation of Parliament has suffered a great deal. Attempts to restore Parliament's reputation have proved challenging. Self-regulation of members is gradually being replaced by greater reliance on independent bodies such as the Independent Parliamentary Standards Authority (IPSA) under the Parliamentary Standards Act 2009.[42] The period from 2010–2015 experienced a Conservative led Coalition Government and this has been followed in 2015 by a Conservative majority government. A recurrent concern is that the legislature has become too dominated by the Executive. Some commentators have attributed Parliament's role[43] to merely one of influencing policy. Whilst others believe that there is little need to refer to Parliament when the vast

---

40　Geoffrey Marshall, "The Evolving Practice of Parliamentary Accountability: Writing Down the Rules" (1991) *Parliamentary Affairs* 460–469.
41　Robert Winnett and Gordon Rayner, *No Expenses Spared* (London: Corgi Books, 2010).
42　There are separate arrangements for Scotland (the Scottish Parliamentary Corporate Body) and Wales (the National Assembly for Wales Remuneration Board).
43　P. Norton, "Independence, Scrutiny and Rationalisation: a Decade of Changes in the House of Commons" in L. Robins (ed), *Political Institutions in Britain: Development and Change* (London: Longman, 1986), pp.58–86.

majority of government work is accepted into law. As we shall see, strengthening Parliament has been a major theme of recent efforts intended to make Parliament more effective. The House of Commons has gained additional powers that has the potential to challenge the Government.[44]

10-038

The increase in the volume of legislation passing through Parliament illustrates the problems of modern government. New legislation is complex and detailed, often amending previous Acts of Parliament and seeking to meet every contingency. The problem of increasing governmental powers gives rise to increasing administrative bureaucracy. Reid noted[45]:

> "In 1913 there were 38 new statutes occupying only 301 pages. In 1956, there were 59 new statutes occupying 1,016 pages. In 1988, 55 statutes were passed and in 1989, 46 statutes in 2,489 large pages. Those statutes cover primary legislation."

10-039

In addition, in the last decade it is estimated that over 7,000 Orders in Council had been made through which Ministers may be given power to issue rules, and on an annual basis around 1,000 statutory instruments are issued. Most primary legislation emanates from central government whilst local authority and public corporation byelaws, departmental rules and regulations or decisions, add to the increase in legal powers and the breadth of their distribution.

10-040

Parliamentary accountability offers a wide variety of forms of control over government. One form is in the scrutiny of legislation, another is through the work of the new departmentally-related select committees, and a third is through parliamentary debate and ministerial responsibility.

Scrutiny and passage of legislation

Parliament's role in the scrutiny of primary legislation involves debate at the various stages of the Bill. Scrutiny of legislation provides a good example of both procedural rules and debate used as a means of scrutiny. The first reading is purely formal: the title of the Bill is approved.

10-041

The second reading may be referred to a Second Reading Committee which is a standing committee, nominated for the consideration of the Bill referred to it. It is intended to save time allowing a number of non-controversial bills to proceed through the House of Commons with the minimum of time spent in debate in the Chamber of the House. The procedure is open to objection by at least 20 members of the House.[46] After second reading, the Bill goes to one of the standing committees unless the House disagrees. It is possible for some parts of the Bill

10-042

---

44 P. Norton, "Parliament: A New Assertiveness?" in J. Jowell, D. Oliver and C. O'Cinneide, (eds), *The Changing Constitution* (Oxford: Oxford University Press, 2015), pp.171–193.
45 William K. Reid, "Changing Notions of Public Accountability" (1992) *Public Administration* 8–87.
46 See Lord Renton, "Modern Acts of Parliament" in *The House Magazine*, 11 February 1991, p.14.

to be examined by the standing committee whilst the remainder is examined by a committee of the entire House. The procedure in committee can be painstaking and involve consideration line by line of each clause of the Bill.

10-043 Once through the committee stage the Bill, if amended, is reported to the House. There then follows the third reading. At this stage the debate is confined to general principles only and verbal amendments may be moved. Once carried by vote, the Bill is then sent to the House of Lords for consideration. There the procedure generally follows that of the Commons. After the Lords, the Bill is returned. It is then subject to assent by the Commons including any amendments introduced by the Lords.

10-044 Parliamentary scrutiny of delegated legislation is less uniform when compared to primary legislation. There is no requirement to comply with a single standard procedure. The explanation for the lack of standardisation in procedure lies in the fact that delegated powers are exercised by a very wide variety of bodies and fall within specialised rules according to the nature of the powers involved.

10-045 The procedures which may be invoked, according to the nature of the regulations or orders to be enacted, are as follows. The first procedure is that of laying the delegated legislation or instrument before Parliament. Invariably this procedure applies to statutory instruments but the requirement of laying does not apply to all such instruments, even those that fall within the Statutory Instruments Act 1946.

10-046 Statutory instruments may take effect immediately but are subject to annulment by Order in Council of either House. Section 5 of the 1946 Act prescribes a period of 40 days before laying where an instrument subject to a negative resolution may be annulled. Excluded from the time period are days when Parliament is dissolved, prorogued or adjourned. Statutory instruments may be laid in draft before Parliament and made subject to a resolution that no further proceedings need be taken.

10-047 Statutory instruments may be subject to affirmative parliamentary procedure. These may be laid before Parliament either in draft or completed form, but do not take effect until approved. This requires government time, as normally a Minister must present the instrument and there are no amendments possible. Occasionally an instrument may be laid to have immediate effect but will cease to have this effect unless approved by resolution within a prescribed time period. There are, in uncommon examples, procedures for laying instruments and Parliament is only to be informed of the action to be taken, thus leaving Ministers in control. There is also a lack of clarity over the precise legal requirements of laying instruments. One view is that in the cases of instruments subject to negative resolution and possibly those requiring positive resolution, the requirement is directory and not mandatory. This leaves uncertain a key issue of requiring appropriate sanctions over the government in the exercise of parliamentary control.

10-048 The second procedure involved in the parliamentary supervision of delegated legislation is the use of scrutinising committees. The Select Committee on Statutory Instruments usually meets with a Lords Committee to form a Joint Committee. Its role and function is to bring some improvement to the form and content of statutory instruments. A small number of instruments gave rise to a referral to the House. The terms of reference of the Joint Committee were agreed in 1973 and include consideration of any instrument to decide whether special attention of the House needs to be drawn to any matter coming within any one of eight categories. These are as follows: does the instrument impose any charge on the public revenues or any fee to a public authority for services or a licence?; does the instrument made in pursuance of an Act of Parliament exclude challenge by the courts?; does the instrument have retrospective effect in circumstances where the parent Act does not confer any such authority?; has there been any unjustifiable delay in the publication of the instruments or in the laying procedure before Parliament?; are there unjustifiable delays in informing the Speaker in the case of instruments in operation because of a matter of urgency and before Parliament was informed?; are there doubts as to the legality of the instrument?; is the drafting in order and not defective?; and could the wording or construction of the instrument require additional explanation?

10–049

An important innovation since 1973 has been the power to refer instruments to a Standing Committee on Statutory Instruments to question their merits. However, it appears that the referral is limited as each committee meets only once, is limited to one and a half hours of debate, and cannot reject an instrument or secure a debate in the Commons. The Committee may take evidence only from government officials or HMSO. Some commentators claim that the main benefit of the standing committee is that the government has made use of its role to save time on the floor of the House. In 1989–90, the *Select Committee on Procedure*[47] received evidence recommending that: debate in the House of Commons on instruments subject to affirmative resolution should not proceed until the Committee reported on the instrument; the remit of the Committee should extend to include Northern Ireland instruments requiring negative resolution; the Committee should be free to take evidence from any source; and that codes of practice should be more regularly open to scrutiny. Finally, greater regard should be taken of the Committee by other departmental committees.

10–050

An additional check on the procedures for statutory instruments is the requirement of publicity. First in 1893 under the Rules Publication Act, and now under the Statutory Instruments Act 1946, there are specific requirements for the printing and publication of statutory instruments, i.e. that "they should be printed and sold as soon as possible".

10–051

The use of statutory instruments extends from rules relating to national insurance contributions, welfare benefits and employment protection procedures affecting the everyday lives of many people. Normally security and taxation matters are outside the remit of statutory instruments, with the exception of Northern Ireland since 1972 where direct rule has been carried out through the use of statutory instruments. This leaves many major issues largely under-debated in the House of Commons and therefore not subject to the normal scrutiny of parliamentary debate.

Pre- and post-legislative scrutiny

10–052

The use of specialist evidence finding committees, has become a feature of the scrutiny of bills. Special standing committees were used for this purpose and their use is accepted to

---

47   See *Commission on the Legislative Process* (Hansard Society, 1992).

produce a high quality of scrutiny. Since 1997 the use of pre-legislative scrutiny has greatly improved the possibility of greater and more in-depth scrutiny of legislation. Draft bills are published to allow informed debate and discussion. In the 2010 Parliament, 35 draft bills were given additional scrutiny by being published in advance allowing committees more opportunity to debate their content.[48] A recent example is the Modern Slavery Act 2015 which illustrates the importance of changes to the Bill that have greatly improved the final Act.[49] It is also illustrative of the time that pre-legislative scrutiny procedure takes, especially in the collection of additional expert evidence. The Modern Slavery Bill was first announced on 25 August 2013. Then pre-legislative scrutiny began when the draft Bill was published on 16 December 2014. The Joint Committee published its report on 8 April 2015 and the Bill was passed just before the election in May 2015. The Joint Committee on Pre-Legislative Scrutiny was chaired by Frank Field MP and his committee took painstaking attention over the legislative drafting of the final version. The result of the Committee's scrutiny is intended to give better transparency to the Bill and raise the subsequent parliamentary standard of debate as well as give greater clarity on some of the technical policy issues. In the case of the Modern Slavery Act, the subsequent debate revealed large areas of disagreement between the Government and MPs. There were many amendments and revisions to the Act, including through the debates in the House of Lords some important changes relating to overseas domestic workers.[50] Between 2010 and 2012, the Coalition Government published 12 bills in draft and there is an undoubted case for the trend in favour of pre-legislative scrutiny to be encouraged.

10–053   Since 2008, post-legislative scrutiny has been used to review Acts of Parliament once they have been enacted for five years in order to assess whether or not they have achieved their intended objectives. The Inquiries Act 2005 and the Mental Capacity Act 2005 are two examples of the operation of post-legislative scrutiny. Post-legislative scrutiny was also undertaken for the Pensions Act 2007. This Act had far-reaching impact on pensions and resulted in a re-organisation of the existing pension system.[51] Post-legislative scrutiny also took place over the Freedom of Information Act 2000.[52] The operation of post-legislative scrutiny has the potential to make Parliament more deliberative and expert in its approach to legislation.[53] By January 2013 there had been 58 Memorandums and detailed consideration of post-legislative scrutiny discussed in the House of Lords. Post-legislative scrutiny is an important technique of assessment and is likely to be productive of improvements in legislative drafting and policy making.

---

48   House of Commons Library, *Pre-Legislative Scrutiny under the Coalition Government 2010–15*, Briefing Paper, 05859 (13 August 2015).
49   House of Commons Library, *Human Trafficking: UK responses*, SN/HA/4324 (13 January 2014), p.9.
50   See John F. McEldowney, "A UK Perspective on Human Trafficking: Aspects of the Modern Slavery Act 2015", Vatican, Rome, Pontifical College of Social Sciences (April 2015).
     House of Commons Library, *Human Trafficking: UK responses*, SN/HA/4324 (13 January 2014), p.9.
51   Department for Work and Pensions, *Post-Legislative Scrutiny of the Pensions Act 2007*, Cm 9001 (January 2015).
52   HC 96 (2012–13).
53   House of Commons library: Post-Legislative Scrutiny SN/PC/05232 (23 May 2015).

Select committees

10–054

One of the main functions of the House of Commons is to scrutinise the policies of the government of the day. Accountability may therefore be achieved through a number of select committees which carry out this task. Such committees are normally appointed under the permanent Standing Orders of the House. Committees have a long history that may be traced back almost 400 years. Following consideration of the committees in use in the House of Commons, reforms were introduced and adopted in 1979. The "new" select committees, as they are often referred to, are directly related to the departments they oversee. As Philip Norton has observed, the 1979 reforms were "the most significant".[54] Select committees allow greater and more detailed scrutiny, greater specialisation, the calling of independent evidence and a greater ability to form an independent view from the government of the day. The initiative for the formation of the new select committees owed much to the then leader of the House, Norman St John Stevas, who pledged support from the government in the operation of the new committee system.[55]

10–055

In theory the new select committees are independent from party politics. However, in practice the nomination for the selection of backbench MPs to serve on a committee through the Committee of Selection had been undertaken through intense party political activity. The whips were consulted as to who to appoint and this became a means of influence over the membership. The system of using whips has been changed from 2010 in respect of chairs of committees. In 2008–09 amongst the recommendations of the Committee on Reform of the House, chaired by the Tony Wright MP and contained in *Rebuilding the House* were a number intended to strengthen the chairs of select committees. It favoured the selection of chairs being elected by the House and that members of the Committee should be elected by their respective parliamentary parties. Another important recommendation was the appointment of a Backbench Business Committee to allocate backbench business independent of the government of the day. These recommendations were approved in 2010. Currently elections of chairs of committees are carried out by secret ballot on an alternative vote system. This marked a considerable break with the dominance of party whips. MPs are enabled to operate much more independently and also make use of the media to good advantage. There are several examples of this including the Treasury Committee (Andrew Tyrie MP), the Home Affairs Committee (Keith Vaz MP), the Culture Media and Sport Committee (John Whittingdale MP), the Public Accounts Committee (Margaret Hodge MP).

10–056

Membership of the select committee endures for the lifetime of the Parliament. The chairmanship of committees is shared between the opposition and the government. The procedure allows each committee to elect its own chairman but the party of the chairman has been agreed beforehand. The powers of the committees are to send for papers, persons and records. In their

---

54 Philip Norton, "Parliament: A New Assertiveness?" in J. Jowell, D. Oliver and C. O'Cinneide, (eds), *The Changing Constitution* (Oxford: Oxford University Press, 2015), 171–193, p.174
55 P. Giddings, "What has been achieved?" in G. Drewry (ed), *The New Select Committees: A Study of the 1979 Reforms*, 2nd edn (Oxford: Oxford University Press, 1995).

work the committees are department-led. One innovation was the setting up of a Parliamentary Commission on Banking Standards as a ten-member Joint Committee with the Commons and Lords. The Committee broke new ground by exploring expertise together from specialist panels on a wide range of subjects related to the banking crisis in 2008. The final report, *Changing Banking for Good*,[56] was more authoritative than would have been possible if the Commission had not had access to specialist information. The Government found that the recommendations of the Commission were worthy of acceptance and agreed to implement them.[57]

10–057 In 2006 the introduction of Public Bill committees to replace standing committees was a welcome development. This provides a system of taking oral and written evidence (with the exception of bills that come from the House of Lords) on the proposals in the Bill. This has the benefit of ensuring that more information and analysis is available. None of this deters the government from its success in having bills passed and the amendments approved are usually government amendments.[58] The tendency is to allow the government to use the procedure to make adjustments and changes that might have been desired in the original Bill but because of speed or departmental timing were not included. As a committee is appointed afresh for each Bill this leaves a lot to be desired in terms of continuity. It may make strategic planning rather difficult.

10–058 Select committees have a role in overseeing some aspects of public expenditure, but the main work in this area is delegated to the Public Accounts Committee, a specialist scrutiny committee. The view put forward by *Ryle*[59] is that there is a case for expanding the role of departmental select committees into the questions of choices over public expenditure plans. This expanded role might also lead to a greater contribution to the various debates on finance bills and detailed tax proposals. This idea is further considered below in the recommendations put forward by the Hansard Commission.

10–059 The advantages of the new select committees include better information for Members of Parliament, and this informs the quality of scrutiny offered in the Commons debate. Public understanding and knowledge is thereby increased in the work of the select committee. The examination of witnesses, especially since the most topical issues when examined by the committee are televised, has increased the public awareness of the work of the committees. This gives expert witnesses and pressure groups an opportunity to be heard. The fact that reports are not normally aired in the House of Commons suggests that the government may not face the full extent of the pressure generated by the Reports of the Select Committee.

10–060 A central question in the role of the committees in providing scrutiny of government policies is the attendance of witnesses before the committees. Gavin Drewry[60] has identified that

---

56 Select Committee on Reform of the House of Commons, *Rebuilding the House*, Session 2008–09, HC 1117. And the full report: CM 8661.
57 *The Government's Response to the Parliamentary Commission on Banking Standards*, CM 8661 (July 2013), p.5.
58 Louise Thompson, "More of the Same or a Period of Change? The impact of Bill Committee in the 21st century House of Commons" (2013) 66(3) *Parliamentary Affairs* 477.
59 Select Committee on Procedure, *Memorandum by Michael Ryle on The Select Committee System*, HC 19-II (1989–90).
60 *Memorandum from Gavin Drewry, Reform of the Select Committee System*, submitted on behalf of the Study of Parliament Group, Select Committee on Procedure, HC 19-II (1989–90).

there are instances "where select committees have faced difficulties in summoning witnesses and compelling disclosure of documents". Some instances of these difficulties may be noted. In 1984, the Government declined to allow the Director of the Government Communications Headquarters (GCHQ) to give evidence to the Select Committee on Employment.[61] In the notable Westland Affair, in 1986, officials of the Department of Trade and Industry were refused permission to give evidence to the Defence Committee, although the Head of the Civil Service appeared and gave answers to specified questions.

10–061

The attendance of witnesses has raised questions about whether the right to silence or the protection against self-incrimination might apply. This is a difficult area as the giving of evidence may lead to controversy. One of the most difficult issues is the Iraq war and the and the existence of weapons of mass destruction. Lord Hutton conducted an inquiry into the tragic death of Dr David Kelly, a key civil servant and scientific expert. The aftermath of the death of Dr David Kelly and later the publication of the Hutton Report[62] (2004) into the circumstances surrounding Dr Kelly's death, caused the Liaison Committee on 16 October 2013 to consider the role of committees when receiving evidence from civil servants. Dr Kelly had attended the Foreign Affairs Committee in 15 July 2003. The BBC journalist Andrew Gilligen had suggested that the evidence might not be as strong as the Government had insisted. Dr Kelly's subsequent attendance at the Foreign Affairs select committee was authorised by the then Secretary of State for Defence but only on condition that Dr Kelly's evidence related to the story raised by Andrew Gilligan and not on the wider issue of the use of weapons of mass destruction and the Iraq war. In the event cross-examination of Dr Kelly was more wide ranging.

The Osmotherly Rules provide guidance on the role of civil servants and other government officials appearing before select committees.[63] The rules are regularly updated. The most recent version is produced in October 2014 in a document entitled *Giving Evidence to Select Committees—Guidance for Civil Servants*. The giving of evidence to committees is one of the mechanisms for the application of the constitutional doctrine of ministerial responsibility. Committees operate under the general powers of Parliament to call any individuals to give evidence. What exactly does this power cover? On 17 October 2014, a new edition of the Osmotherly Rules was published giving general guidance on the attendance of civil servants before select committees. As well as applying to civil servants, the rules now apply to "Senior Responsible Owners" of the government's major projects. The width of this term is welcome since it makes the organisers of major projects directly accountable to Parliament for the implementation of their project.[64]

10–062

---

61 *First Report from the Employment Committee*, HC 238 (1983–84), paras 6–7.
62 HC 247 (2003–04). Lord Hutton [2006] *Public Law* 807. D. Runciman (ed), *Hutton and Butler: Lifting the lid on the workings of power* (Oxford: Oxford University Press, 2004).
63 The Osmotherly Rules are named after a civil servant W. B. C. Osmotherly, the first rules may be dated back to 1977/78 but a draft was in existence in the early 1970s. House of Commons, Standard Note, *The Osmotherly Rules*, SN/PC/2671 (24 March 2015)
64 Peter Riddell, "The updated guidance on the Osmotherly Rules" (2014), http://www.instituteforgovernment.org.uk/blog/9228/the-updated-guidance-on-the-osmotherly-rules/ [Accessed 7 April 2016].

10-063 Ambiguity remains over how much accountability may be gleaned from the rules in general. Civil servants gave evidence, not on their own behalf, but on behalf of ministers. This is an important contribution to ministerial responsibility rather than an opportunity to explore personal views or judgments on matters of government policy. Personal views given in evidence might effectively undermine the impartiality of civil servants. One important group of civil servants, accounting officers are accountable to Parliament for the stewardship of the department's resources and this has major policy implications for the government of the day.

10-064 The current rules retain the right of ministers to refuse to allow a particular named civil servant to appear before the Committee. The minister may suggest an alternative name. Formally the Committee may compel the attendance of a civil servant but in practice this is rarely insisted upon.

10-065 Select committees have general powers "to send for persons, papers and records". Information may be received in confidence and departments may be consulted before the release of any sensitive information. Information provided to committees are covered by Parliamentary privilege. Responses to committee findings should be given by departments within a two month period. Occasionally the government may decline to respond or may take time to respond. The House of Lords Constitution Committee experienced a ten month delay in response to one of their reports.[65]

10-066 The question arises as to how successful the new select committees are in the scrutiny of government and, perhaps as important, how success may be measured. In the past opinions have been divided. In the early history of select committees, George Jones argued[66] that the committees have failed to fulfil their terms of reference and therefore they are not worth pursuing. The opposing view appeared from much of the evidence received by the Select Committee on Procedure, which was generally praiseworthy of the performance of the committees and only minor adjustments are recommended.

10-067 The Institute for Government has recently assessed the role and working of *Select Committees under Scrutiny*.[67] This assessment is positive. Select Committees "are progressing and improving". One criticism is that the committees do not evaluate their own progress and the committee system generally lacks the capacity to assess what has been achieved and what remains to be achieved. One major improvement is the election of chairs of committees by MPs that provides a sense of legitimacy that was lacking in the past. Concerns exist over the problem of resources and the growing diversity of practice amongst committees. Diversity may be a good development but it can also create unintended consequences in terms of rivalry and competition for scarce resources. Backbenchers hold the key role in determining how effective scrutiny becomes. As always they may be conflicted by their own party allegiances as well as personal ambitions. The benefits of committee inquiries into government cover such areas as: improvements in the government's evidence base for policy making; providing better analysis of the available evidence and in the setting of priorities; delivering more openness in providing

---

65   HL Debate (12 January 2015), c.656.
66   G. W. Jones, "Send the Watchdogs Packing", *The Times*, 4 November 1989.
67   Hannah White, *Select Committees under Scrutiny* (London: Institute for Government, 2015).

a forum for explanation and evidence; and learning by providing evidence of past mistakes and how to avoid them for the future. Processes and procedures are thereby improved and the views of civil society more generally may be assessed as committees operate across a wide range of witnesses and groups. Finally, it is arguable that committee may also enhance democracy more generally through openness and transparency.

10–068

Philip Norton, in evidence to the Committee on Procedure provides a comprehensive evaluation of committees and suggests that "select committees are now the essential agents for such scrutiny of Parliament in subjecting government to informed, detailed and continuous scrutiny". The latter point is perhaps one of the most essential elements in any system of accountability. Continuous scrutiny allows past experience to be supplemented and applied. Norton notes how techniques of questioning and cross-examination of Ministers have improved and how[68]

> "there is sufficient evidence to demonstrate changes in public policy, changes that would not have taken place but for the recommendations of the committees."

10–069

Norton also draws attention to the value for money offered by the select committee system which has meagre resources and financial assistance. The key to the success or failure of the committee system appears to be the development of the political will to make the system effective. Norton identifies some shortcomings such as: limited interest by members in committee reports; limited time and resources; absence of career development in the select committee structure; finally, attention to set debates in the Chamber of the House of Commons does not give the attention to committees that they deserve. Additional pressure on the select committee system can come from government through the need to pass large volumes of legislation and from the career demands and self-interests of the backbench MPs who serve on the committees. It may be concluded that whilst the new committees have not radically altered the relationship between Parliament and the Executive, they have provided information and knowledge about the internal workings of government. There is also the contribution made by the committees in keeping a clear focus on the work of backbench MPs. The decision by the Prime Minister to appear before the Liaison Committee is a step in the direction of giving select committees a greater role.

In 2010 the creation of a Backbench Business Committee was agreed. In common with all committees, members are elected but this is done on a sessional basis only. This provides an opportunity for allocating backbench business on 35 days each session with 27 of them on the floor of the House of Commons. E-petitions are also possible from members of the public. Once a threshold of 100,000 signatures is reached, then debates can be tabled. The Business Committee has the opportunity to debate matters that are not necessarily agreeable to the government of the day. This has given public opinion an opportunity for airing in ways that would not have been possible in the past.

---

68   P. Norton, *Memorandum to the Select Committee on Procedure*, HC 19–11(1989–90), p.139.

F: Parliamentary reform: The way forward?

10-070 Whilst successive governments have shown an apparent lack of interest in the effectiveness of parliamentary procedures, a recently published Hansard Society Commission Report[69] sets out an analysis of current weaknesses together with recommendations to improve the effectiveness of Parliament. The report in 2001, *The Challenge for Parliament: Making Government Accountable*, raises the central question of how effectively Westminster scrutinises the Executive. In the Commission's view, Parliament "has been left behind by far-reaching changes to the Constitution, government and society in the past two decades". The Commission undertook an analysis of the various procedures and mechanisms used by the Commons and Lords in their pursuit of accountability debates, ministerial statements, select committees and inquiries, and the work of the ombudsman and the National Audit Office. Also included are the role of the courts and the work of inspectors and regulators. The report provides both an authoritative account of problems in filling the "serious gaps and weaknesses" identified in the system of accountability, and a "vision" of how a reformed Parliament might work. In doing this, the Commission adopts seven principles for reform, summarised below and remain working principles for the future of parliamentary reform. These include various principles:

- *Parliament at the apex*:[70] Under this principle, Parliament is seen as providing a framework for the different bodies and functions developed to ensure accountability of the Executive;

- *Parliament must develop a culture of scrutiny*:[71] This principle is aimed at strengthening the culture of politicians, changing attitudes and beliefs to ensure scrutiny and accountability of the Executive: Committees should play a more influential role within Parliament;[72]

- *the Chamber should remain central to accountability*:[73] Financial scrutiny should be central to accountability;[74]

- *the House of Lords should complement the Commons*:[75] The role of the Lords, whatever

---

69 Report of the Hansard Society Commission on Parliamentary Scrutiny, *The Challenge for Parliament: Making Government Accountable* (2001). Hereinafter the *Hansard Commission*, http://www.hansardsociety.org.uk/wp-content/uploads/2012/10/The-Challenge-for-Parliament-Making-Government-Accountable-2001.pdf [Accessed 7 April 2016].
70 *Hansard Commission*, p.107.
71 *Hansard Commission*, p.107.
72 *Hansard Commission*, p.107.
73 *Hansard Commission*, p.109.
74 *Hansard Commission*, p.110.
75 *Hansard Commission*, p.xii.

its position after any further reforms, is seen as complementary to the Commons. Close co-operation and co-ordination between the two Houses is required in an effort to provide support for greater scrutiny; and

- *Parliament must communicate more effectively with the public.*[76]

10–071

The influential Institute for Government in their report Parliamentary Scrutiny of Government [77] has considered that the importance of evaluation of the impact of parliamentary scrutiny needs to be undertaken in a clear and systematic way. Arguably, it is only by evaluation will the test of effectiveness by analysed and judged. It is also necessary to understand different perspectives from the viewpoint of stakeholders, MPs. Ministers and civil servants. The evaluation of scrutiny is an essential aspect of improving government and governance, as John Griffith pointed out many years ago.[78] The Institute for Government is also practical focused, believing that case studies and examples are likely to provide a useful basis for analysis. Setting standards for scrutiny is also essential in terms of justifying public expenditure and costs.

Parliamentary debate and ministerial responsibility

10–072

Accountability for the actions and policy of the government of the day involves public debate in the media and in Parliament. The question arises as to how effective parliamentary debate may be in changing the opinion of the government or in forming a separate policy agenda from the government of the day. The answer may depend on the size of the parliamentary majority enjoyed by the government. There are only a small number of examples where the outcome of a speech made in a debate has been influential for the course of legislation. The Immigration Rules under the Immigration Act 1971[79] resulted in a government defeat because of speeches made by several Conservative MPs and the failure of the Foreign Secretary to give concessions. In 1986 the Shops Bill was lost in a second reading despite the government's overall majority. Speeches made by many Conservative MPs resulted in the unprecedented loss in modern

---

76 *Hansard Commission*, p.xiii.
77 Hannah White, *Parliamentary Scrutiny of Government* (London: Institute for Government, 2015).
78 Graham Gee, "The political constitutionalism of J. A. G. Griffith" (2008) *Legal Studies* 28(1), pp.20–45. Also T. Poole, "Tilting at windmills? Truth and illusion in The Political Constitution" (2007) 70 *Modern Law Review* 250. Also consider I. Leigh, "Secrets of the Political Constitution" (1999) 62 *Modern Law Review* 298.
J. A. G. Griffith, "Judges in politics: England" [1968] *Government and Opposition* 485. The work Griffith is probably most famous for is J. A. G. Griffith, *The Politics of the Judiciary*, 5th edn (London: Fontana, 1997).
J. A. G. Griffith, "The Place of parliament in the Legislative process" [1951] 14 *Modern Law Review* 279.
J. A. G. Griffith, "The Political Constitution" [1979] 42(1) *Modern Law Review* 1; R. Blackburn and A. Kennon, (eds), with Sir Michael Wheeler-Booth, *Griffith and Ryle on Parliament, Functions, Practice and Procedures*, 2nd edn (London: Sweet and Maxwell, 2003).
79 Immigration (leave to Enter and Remain) Regulations Order 2000 (SI 2000/1161).

times of a government Bill after second reading. The paucity of such examples serve to show that Parliamentary debate may have limitations in terms of accountability over government policy.

10-073 Political opinion and support for the government in office requires that the government must take account of its political standing. In constitutional terms, a government that loses the confidence of the House of Commons must either resign or advise dissolution. For example, in 1924, under Ramsay Macdonald, and in 1979 under James Callaghan, the Government was defeated in a confidence motion and advised dissolution. Similarly, the classic formulation of ministerial responsibility attributes to the entire Ministry responsibility for all official acts performed by individual Ministers. Turpin concludes that accountability of government through ministerial responsibility[80]

> "...depends upon procedure and custom, upon intangible understandings and traditions, and upon political circumstances and the government's need for the co-operation of opposition and backbenchers. Ministerial responsibility, both collective and individual, in large part involves conflicts of interests between the government on the one hand and Parliament and the public on the other."

10-074 Brazier,[81] writing in 1990, records that since 1960, there have been 24 ministerial resignations on grounds of collective responsibility. In the case of individual responsibility there have been 12. It is not uncommon for Ministers to resign because of private and personal matters. Whilst Ministers are responsible for their private conduct, the conduct of their department and acts of their civil servants, this does not always give rise to resignation. The resignation of Mr Stephen Byers, the Transport Secretary, came about because of internal conflict over policy and the role of advisers in his department. Resignation was not an inevitable outcome, but resulted from a general sense of lack of control and command over his department. History is rich in examples where resignation does not follow when there has been a perceived ministerial failing. Since the 1990s, the number of resignations has diminished. The Coalition Government may have made it more difficult as the desire to provide coherent policy making for the five years of the lifetime of the Parliament might have contributed to the diminution in resignations as party politics dominated.[82] There was also a need to balance Conservative and Liberal ministers in the coalition arrangements. The last major resignation came on 14 October 2001 when Dr Liam Fox, then Defence Secretary, resigned over an alleged breach of the Ministerial Code and the failure to operate the Code when it came to the role of his adviser.[83]

---

80 C. Turpin, "Ministerial Responsibility: Myth or Reality?" in J. Jowell and D. Oliver (eds), *The Changing Constitution* (Oxford: Oxford University Press, 1989), p.85.
81 R. Brazier, *Constitutional Texts* (Oxford: Oxford University Press, 1990), pp.359–360.
82 A. Flinders, "The Enduring centrality of Individual Ministerial responsibility within the British Constitution" (2000) 6 *Journal of Legislative Studies* 73.
83 House of Commons Library Standard Note: Lobbying SN/PC/04633 (25 January 2012).

10–075 In 1982, the then Home Secretary Mr Whitelaw did not resign even though a breach in security allowed an intruder into the Queen's private bedroom. A year later, in 1983, the then Secretary of State for Northern Ireland, Mr Prior, did not resign because of a break-out at the Maze prison in Northern Ireland owing to security lapses. The Hennessey Report into the escape of prisoners concluded that there were no policy mistakes responsible.

10–076 The question of ministerial resignation has as much to do with damage limitation by the Prime Minister of the day as with accountability to Parliament. In that sense the Prime Minister's judgment of what may be acceptable to the House of Commons for the survival of the government may depend on parliamentary debate. A reasonably wide latitude appears to be given to Ministers given the pressure of work many endure. In 1971–72, the collapse of the Vehicle and General Insurance Company did not lead to ministerial resignation. There was criticism of civil servants and the acceptance that Ministers may experience a steady turnover of appointments and departments, and that the actual percentage of matters within departments which are referred to Ministers for personal attention is very small. In the case of the Vehicle and General collapse in 1971, less than one per cent of the department workload was referred to the Minister; and there had been since 1964, six different Ministers appointed.[84] In the debate, following the inquiry into the collapse of the insurance company, the Home Secretary explained[85]:

> "In my own department we get 1 1/2 million letters a year, any one of which may lead to disaster. It is no minimising of the responsibility of Ministers to Parliament to say that a Minister cannot be blamed for a mistake made if he did not make it himself and if he has not failed to ensure that that sort of mistake ought not to be made."

10–077 One example is the dismissal of Derek Lewis as Head of the Prison Service following the report by Sir John Learmont into prison escapes from Parkhurst.[86] The then Home Secretary Michael Howard refused to resign, drawing on the distinction between operational and policy matters; he claimed that as the Home Secretary was responsible for policy and no policy had been found to be at fault, he was entitled to rely on this fact and not resign. On this fine distinction, the question of responsibility is confined to the duty to be accountable. Thus it may be argued that ministerial responsibility for the acts of civil servants appears to be non-existent.

10–078 Ministerial responsibility is susceptible to the ebb and flow of political debate. What may appear settled may, on reflection, seem less clear. For example, the resignation of Thomas Dugdale, over the sale of land at Crichel Down in 1954, was attributed to criticism of his civil servants' behaviour. With the benefit of hindsight and access to official papers it

---

84 *Hansard*, HC Debates Vol.831, col.419 (16 February 1972). See *Report of the Tribunal of Inquiry into the Cessation of Trading of the Vehicle and General Insurance Co*, HC 133 (1971–72); and HL 80 (1972) (15 February 1972).
85 *Hansard*, HC Debates, Vol.836, col.33 (1 May 1972). C. Turpin, "Ministerial Responsibility" in J. Jowell and D. Oliver (eds), *The Changing Constitution* (Oxford: Oxford University Press, 1994).
86 *Hansard*, HC Vol.264, cols.502–506 (18 November 1995).

appears that the civil servants who were blamed were the victims of ministerial indecision and policy changes. Resignation came from backbench pressure and the Prime Minister's political judgment.[87] Ministerial responsibility that leads to resignation may ultimately depend on public opinion and political judgment.[88]

G: Government and the Crown

Ministers and public interest immunity

10-079 Accountability, it has been noted from the foregoing discussion, may also be linked to secrecy. As Birkinshaw some years ago noted,[89] in historical terms Parliament saw secrecy for its proceedings "as a necessary protection against the Crown's absolutist tendencies". The struggle for information became the centre of the desire for control. This legacy remains. So does the status of the Crown. A great deal of secrecy and mystique still surrounds the Crown, both as to the personal wealth and fortune of members of the Royal family and also as to the relationship and role of the Monarch with the government of the day.

10-080 Ministers are chosen by the Prime Minister but appointed by the Queen; in constitutional theory they are servants of the Crown. Major public powers remain vested in the Crown or in Ministers who act as servants of the Crown. Civil servants under ministerial direction remain servants of the Crown. The creation of modern government has not dispensed with the various common law powers, privileges and immunities that were ascribed to royal power but today they are exercised by the government of the day with few powers remaining personal to the Queen.

10-081 In the appointment of Prime Minister, the convention of whether the person to be appointed commands the confidence of the House of Commons is left to the Queen and her advisers. Normally the leader of the largest party is selected, but in making a choice the Queen may face difficult judgments when there is no overall majority party and the choice of person is less obvious.

10-082 In the dismissal of Ministers, the Queen's prerogative is exercisable by convention, on the advice of the Prime Minister, but the retention of this prerogative maintains the role of the Crown in constitutional matters.[90] Finally in the dissolution of Parliament the normal

---

87 P. Carrington, *Reflect on Things Past* (London: Collins, 1988), pp.90–93.
88 House of Commons Library, *Individual Ministerial Responsibility*, SN/PC/06467 (8 November 2012).
89 P. Birkinshaw, *Freedom of Information* (London: Butterworths, 1988), p.63.
90 See The Petitions of Right Act 1860, repealed by the Crown Proceedings Act 1947.

convention is that in the exercise of the prerogative of dissolution, the Queen acts on the advice of the Prime Minister.

The Crown's exercise of powers does not readily conform to the normal arrangements for accountability. The Crown has traditionally enjoyed certain Crown privileges. Before the Crown Proceedings Act 1947, claims against the Crown for breach of contract were brought through Petition of Right, thus providing that the Home Secretary's agreement had to be sought before proceedings could begin. In addition, in constitutional law, the presumption of statutory construction is that the Crown is not bound by an Act of Parliament. This does not prevent the Crown from benefiting from statutory powers. The Crown Proceedings Act 1947 permits claims formerly made by Petition of Right to be made and enforceable through ordinary civil proceedings instituted in county courts. This does not affect the taking of proceedings against the Queen in her own personal capacity, which remain by way of Petition of Right.

10-083

The Crown retains certain privileges which may be beneficial to the government of the day in the exercise of Crown powers. The remedies of injunction and specific performance were traditionally not available against the Crown. Crown Servants may be sued personally for civil wrongs committed by them even when they are acting in their official capacity at the time. The House of Lords held in *M v Home Office*[91] that the courts could issue injunctions against Crown officers in judicial review proceedings. Ministers are amenable to the contempt jurisdiction of the courts. The use of prerogative powers is amenable to judicial scrutiny by way of judicial review, but prerogative powers give considerable powers to the government of the day in addition to any statutory authority. In the exercise of Executive powers to allocate licences, approve appointments to public office, engage in contracts, undertake research and development and provide loans and subsidies, the carrying out of government is by nature confidential and often removed from direct accountability. It is in the nature of government that some of its most important activities are free from direct parliamentary scrutiny or control.

10-084

Crown immunity or public interest immunity as it is more commonly called, provides the government of the day with an important claim in the event of legal proceedings. Crown privilege or immunity[92] may be claimed as the basis for the non-disclosure of documents which are confidential. The Crown may argue that to disclose such documents in legal proceedings may be "injurious to the public interest". Most of the authorities on Crown immunity involve civil proceedings rather than criminal prosecutions.

10-085

In the House of Lords in 1942 in *Duncan v Cammell Laird & Co Ltd*,[93] the basis of such a claim was made clear: Crown privilege may be claimed in respect of two alternative grounds. First that the disclosure of the contents of a particular document would injure the public

10-086

---

91 [1994] 1 A.C. 377; [1993] 3 W.L.R. 433 HL.
92 The terminology currently used by the courts is public interest immunity. This term is preferred over Crown Privilege. See *Rogers v Secretary of State for Home Department* [1973] A.C. 388; [1972] 3 W.L.R. 279 HL. See *Alfred Crompton Amusement Machines Ltd v Customs and Excise Commissioners (No.2)* [1974] A.C. 405; [1973] 3 W.L.R. 268 HL.
93 [1942] A.C. 624; [1942] 1 All E.R. 587 HL. In *Glasgow Corp v Central Land Board* 1956 S.C. (H.L.) 1; 1956 S.L.T. 41 HL, the House of Lords held that *Duncan v Cammell Laird* did not apply in Scotland.

interest such as endangering national security or prejudicing diplomatic relations with other countries. Secondly, that the document comes within a certain category, or "class" of document which by its nature should be withheld to ensure the proper working of the public service. In the first ground the Crown had to satisfy the court of the nature of the contents of the particular document. In the second ground, the category of documents that fitted the particular class of documents for which immunity was sought, was very broad. In seeking to find a balance between freedom of information and protection of the state, the class of documents was reviewed. A statement made by a Minister in the proper form could claim immunity and establish within which of the two categories the document came. The *Duncan* case concerned a civil action undertaken by the widow of one of the sailors drowned when the submarine Thetis sank whilst undergoing sea trials. In order to pursue her action in negligence, the plaintiff claimed from the Ministry of Defence documents such as the plans of the submarine. The effect of the *Duncan* case considerably restricted the official documents allowed to be admitted in evidence in legal proceedings, giving the Crown a wider discretion to withhold documents than had previously been accepted.

10-087 Under s.28 of the Crown Proceedings Act 1947 the courts may make an order for discovery of documents or require the Crown to answer interrogatories. However, this power did not affect an existing rule of law that the Crown may refuse to disclose any documents or answer any questions on the ground that this would be injurious to the public interest.

10-088 In 1968 the House of Lords considered the law in *Conway v Rimmer*,[94] which concerned a number of documents being withheld in a civil action undertaken by a probationary police constable. The Secretary of State objected on the grounds that the reports fell into classes of documents where disclosure would not be in the public interest. The reports related to the conduct of individual officers and investigation into particular crimes. In reaching a conclusion on these matters the House of Lords rejected the approach in *Duncan* as restrictive in admitting documents, preferring instead to assert a judicial power to consider and decide on whether the documents should be excluded. Lord Reid distinguishing *Duncan* asserted the judicial role "to hold the balance between the public interest, as expressed by a Minister, to withhold certain documents or other evidence and the public interest in ensuring the proper administration of justice".

10-089 The House of Lords also accepted the need to give the greatest weight to the Minister's opinions. However, the question arises as to whether the courts will always be prepared to exercise their judgment by balancing the interests of the Minister against the interests of disclosure. It appears that certain classes of documents ought never to be disclosed. For example Lord Widgery in *Attorney General v Jonathan Cape Ltd*[95] claimed that "no court will compel the production of cabinet papers in the course of discovery in an action". Thus routine or less sensitive documents may be more likely to be admitted in evidence than higher grade or more secret documents.

10-090 Following *Conway*, the House of Lords have further considered how to strike the balance of interests between competing claims of the Minister and the need to disclose information. In

---

94 [1968] A.C. 910; [1968] 2 W.L.R. 998 HL.
95 [1976] Q.B. 752; [1975] 3 W.L.R. 606 QBD.

Burmah Oil Co Ltd v Bank of England,[96] the Chief Secretary to the Treasury signed a certificate that the production of documents would be "injurious to the public interest." The documents related to negotiations between the Bank of England, Burmah Oil and the Government over the purchase by the Bank of England of stock in British Petroleum (BP) owned by Burmah at a specific price per unit of stock. Within a year the value of the stock had doubled and Burmah brought an action against the Bank of England with regard to the sale on the ground that it was unreasonable and unconscionable. The sale took place at a time when Burmah experienced financial difficulties and the Government insisted that they could not share in any profit from the resale of the BP shares by the Bank of England. It had originally been intended that some profit in any sale of the shares might be shared between the Bank and Burmah.

The House of Lords concluded that on judicial inspection of the documents they did not contain material which was necessary for a fair consideration of the case. The case establishes a number of points.

10-091

First, no class of document is entirely excluded from the process of balancing the different interests between the Minister and the need to disclose information. Secondly, that the courts had a power of inspection of documents. This includes deciding the category or class of document to which the documents may belong, whether disclosure is necessary for a fair trial of the issues in the case and whether the balance of interests criteria, outlined above, has been satisfied to permit disclosure. In these matters it is not always clear at what stage inspection is used. It is not always the case that the court will order inspection. When inspection is required, is it fair to both parties that the judge should examine documents which one of the parties has not seen?

10-092

The third point to emerge in *Burmah Oil* is that the courts are unwilling to grant immunity from disclosure simply because the documents contain matters of "candour", though it may be regarded as a factor which might be useful in deciding on the balance of interests criteria. The courts are sensitive to arguments in favour of more open government that may lead to a fishing expedition for information. Speculative claims are unlikely to gain favour with the judges.

10-093

When public interest immunity is pleaded the other party faces a difficult task to persuade the judge to admit the documents in question. What standard of case must be made out? In the *Burmah Oil* case the judges differed in their choice of criteria to be satisfied before disclosure is granted. Some judges preferred a real likelihood, others, reasonable probability; and Lord Wilberforce who dissented, suggested that a positive case must be shown before the documents would be admitted. What must be shown is that the documents must be necessary for "fairly disposing the case".

10-094

There are various matters relevant to deciding how the balance of interests is to be calculated. In *D v National Society for the Prevention of Cruelty to Children*,[97] D's application to have NSPCC documents admitted was refused because of the nature of the NSPCC; its voluntary status, statutory powers and the receipt of information on a confidential basis, required

10-095

---

96   [1980] A.C. 1090; [1979] 3 W.L.R. 722 HL.
97   [1978] A.C. 171; [1977] 2 W.L.R. 201 HL.

immunity. In *R v Chief Constable Ex p. Wiley*[98] the House of Lords held that public interest immunity in police complaints proceedings did not extend to the use in civil proceedings of information generated through the complaint proceedings. Public interest immunity did not in a general way extend to the use of the documents or information contained in the police files. All relevant documents ought to be capable of disclosure unless it might cause substantial harm.

10-096
In *Halford v Sharples*[99] a claim was made by Alison Halford, then Assistant Chief Constable of Merseyside, that her promotion within the police was blocked because of sex discrimination. In support of her claim she wished to have access to confidential files but one was refused by the Court of Appeal. The reasoning that there was an overwhelming public interest in maintaining the integrity of police complaints and disciplinary files prevented disclosure of the files to Alison Halford but it also prevented the Chief Constable from relying on information on the files. An important element in the reasoning in this case came from reliance on an earlier Court of Appeal case, *Makanjoula v Commissioner of Police for the Metropolis*.[100] In *Makanjoula*, statements that had been given to the police by witnesses were withheld from the court, even when the witnesses might have given their consent. Bingham LJ said[101]:

> "Where a litigant asserts that documents are immune from production or disclosure on public interest grounds he is not (if the claim is well founded) claiming a right but observing a duty. Public interest immunity is not a trump card vouchsafed to certain privileged players to play when and as they wish. It is an exclusionary rule, imposed on parties in certain circumstances even where it is to their disadvantage."

10-097
Interpretation of "observing a duty" in the judgment of Bingham LJ in *Makanjoula* became the central issue in the recent *Matrix Churchill* case. Criminal prosecutions taken against certain directors of Matrix Churchill by Customs and Excise, over allegations that the company had broken trade sanctions in the sales of weapons to Iraq, resulted in public interest immunity being claimed by Ministers over confidential documents relating to the government's policy on arms sales. The Ministers concerned claimed that they had "a duty" to sign the certificates and were advised to do so by the Attorney General. One Minister, Michael Heseltine, only signed the certificate after he was instructed that he was under a clear duty to do so.

10-098
Some support for this view that Ministers are under a duty to sign public interest immunity certificates, is taken from what was said by Bingham LJ in *Makanjoula*. However, a further reading of the judgment of Bingham LJ reveals further clarification on whether there is a duty in all cases to assert an immunity claim. Bingham LJ added[102]:

---

98 [1995] 1 A.C. 274; [1994] 3 W.L.R. 433 HL.
99 [1992] 1 W.L.R. 736; [1992] 3 All E.R. 624 CA (Civ Div).
100 [1992] 3 All E.R. 617 CA (Civ Div).
101 [1992] 3 All E.R. 617 at [623].
102 [1992] 3 All E.R. 617 at [623G]–[623H].

> "This does not mean that in any case where a party holds a document in a class prima facie immune he is bound to persist in an assertion of immunity even where it is held that, on any weighing of the public interest, in withholding the document against the public interest in disclosure for the purpose of furthering the administration of justice, there is a clear balance in favour of the latter."

There is a division of opinion over the interpretation of the judgment of Bingham LJ In the *Matrix Churchill* case Ministers claimed that at the time the certificates were signed they had no choice but to sign the certificates. Some legal opinion takes the view that there is no obligation or duty on Ministers to make a claim. Ministers are free to authorise disclosure to the public of confidential documents and by analogy are free to decide whether to sign certificates or not.

The better view is that Ministers have a discretion as to whether to claim public interest immunity or not. They are not bound to sign a certificate even where there is a *prima facie* case that the documents may belong to a class where public interest immunity may be sought. The courts decide "where the balance of public interest lies" in such cases.

Since the Matrix Churchill trial, the House of Lords have now accepted in *Ex p. Wiley*[103] a number of propositions about public interest immunity. The view that there is a class of documents which may guarantee exclusion from disclosure is no longer tenable. This view has been made clear by the Lord Chancellor and the Attorney General in changes that have been announced to the administration of public interest immunity certificates.[104] Furthermore it is considered that in criminal cases the scales of justice have to be more keenly balanced to protect the accused. The House of Lords in *Ex p. Wiley* also rejects the proposition that there is a duty on Ministers to sign public interest immunity certificates. From the above discussion, it may be concluded that the Attorney General's interpretation is unsound in principle and wrong in its potential effects on the accused.

A further consideration is whether there is any distinction between civil and criminal cases. In a criminal trial, accused persons may be convicted notwithstanding that there is evidence showing their innocence. This appears inconsistent with the public interest. In criminal litigation the courts have been concerned about the balance of interests and the protection of the accused when public interest immunity is claimed by the prosecution. In *R v Governor of Brixton Prison Ex p. Osman*[105] Lord Justice Mann accepted that public interest immunity may be claimed in criminal proceedings but he noted ". . .that the application of the public immunity doctrine in criminal proceedings will involve a different balancing of interest to that in civil proceedings". Relying on a number of authorities including *Marks v Beyfus*,[106] Lord Justice Mann noted that the privilege of public interest immunity

---

103 *R v Chief Constable of the West Midlands Ex p. Wiley* [1995] 1 A.C. 274; [1994] 3 W.L.R. 433 HL at [423].
104 *Hansard*, HL Vol.576, col.1507, and *Hansard*, HC Vol.287, col.949 (18 December 1996).
105 [1991] 1 W.L.R. 281; [1992] 1 All E.R. 108 Div Ct.
106 (1890) 25 Q.B.D. 494 CA.

> "cannot prevail if the evidence is necessary for the prevention of a miscarriage of justice. No balance is called for. If admission is necessary to prevent miscarriage of justice, balance does not arise."[107]

10-103 The courts have not always been consistent in their approach. In *R v Lewes Justices Ex p. Home Secretary*[108] concerning criminal libel, the House of Lords upheld a claim for Crown privilege in respect of police documents relied upon by the Gaming Board. An applicant had been unsuccessful in applying to the Gaming Board for a licence for a Bingo Club. He alleged that the police had sent the Gaming Board a libellous letter and for this reason he had been unsuccessful in his application. Lord Reid reasoned that much of the information came from a letter from the police based on information from sources that must be protected. The nature of the information may disclose the source and this required protection. This case is open to a narrow interpretation. Although the House of Lords upheld the claim made on public interest immunity to prevent disclosure of documents, the case may be said to have raised special facts. Lord Reid noted that the documents were not intended to deprive the applicant of any legal right. The only reason the documents came into existence was because the applicant "is asking for a privilege and is submitting his character and reputation to scrutiny". It is significant that Lord Reid upheld the important principle that should be observed in public interest immunity cases namely that the "course of justice should not be impeded by the withholding of evidence".

10-104 In *Ward*[109] the Court of Appeal observed that there were requirements laid upon the prosecution if they wished to claim public interest immunity. First, notice must be given to the defence if the prosecution wished to rely on immunity and that the prosecution are applying to the court for a ruling. Secondly, the defence must be given some idea of the category of information involved. Thirdly, the defence must be given the opportunity to make representations. Lord Justice Glidewell made clear that it was for the court to make the ultimate decision as to whether evidence is to be disclosed. This does not prevent the Crown Prosecution Service deciding in exceptional cases to volunteer information without obtaining a court order.

10-105 The courts have generally been sensitive in criminal prosecutions to prevent the claim of public interest immunity from interfering with the rights of the accused. Lord Justice Mann in *Ex p. Osman (No.1)*[110] noted that: "it may be that prosecutions are not initiated where material is not to be exposed, or it may be that the force of the balance is recognised by prosecuting authorities and the immunity is never claimed". In *Neilson v Laugharne*[111] Lord Justice Oliver

---

107 [1992] 1 All E.R. 108 at [118A]–[118B].
108 [1973] A.C. 388; [1972] 3 W.L.R. 279 HL.
109 *R v Ward* [1993] 1 W.L.R. 619; [1993] 2 All E.R. 577 CA (Civ Div). Also see *R v Davis* [1993] 1 W.L.R. 613; [1993] 2 All E.R. 643 CA (Civ Div).
110 [1992] 1 All E.R. 108 at [116].
111 [1981] Q.B. 736; [1981] 2 W.L.R. 537 CA (Civ Div) at [839H]. See Adam Tomkins, "Public Interest Immunity after Matrix Churchill" [1993] *P.L.* 650.

said: "If public policy prevents disclosure, it prevents it, in my judgment, in all legal circumstances except to establish innocence in criminal proceeding".

In the *Matrix Churchill* case, which involved a criminal prosecution, the trial judge allowed the documents to be admitted in the case and this, together with evidence from a former Minister, led to the failure of the prosecution case. The furore caused by the case in Parliament and the broader implications that Ministers may have misled Parliament led to the setting up of an inquiry under Lord Justice Scott. The higher appellate courts had until *Ex p. Wiley*[112] been mainly concerned with civil proceedings. The use of public interest immunity certificates in criminal cases has given rise to a clear difference of opinion on the part of the Government's legal advisers and the Scott report on this issue. Sir Richard Scott recommended that class claims should no longer be used in criminal litigation and seldom used in civil litigation.[113] However in the Government's response,[114] the view of government advisers remained as follows:

10–106

> "The understanding of those advising Government was and is that the general principles of PII [Public Interest Immunity] apply in the same way in criminal proceedings as they do in civil proceedings. In each case both class and contents claims can properly be advanced; and in each case the public interest in non-disclosure falls to be balanced (at the material time, by the court) against the public interest in disclosure for the purposes of the administration of justice. The balance is much more likely to come down in favour of disclosure in criminal proceedings, and procedural differences exist, but the general principles are the same."

However, in *Ex p. Wiley* Lord Templeman explained[115]:

10–107

> "Prosecution authorities know which documents are relevant to the prosecution but they cannot know for certain which documents will be relevant to the defence... In order to avoid criticism and a miscarriage of justice one way or the other, the police authorities now feel obliged to disclose documents of doubtful relevance and materiality."

---

112   *R v Chief Constable of the West Midlands Ex p. Wiley* [1995] 1 A.C. 274; [1994] 3 W.L.R. 433 HL.
113   *The Scott Report*, Vol.III, para.G18.86 at [1525].
114   *Government's Response*, para.3.1, p.14.
115   *R v Chief Constable of the West Midlands Ex p. Wiley* [1995] 1 A.C. 274; [1994] 3 W.L.R. 433 HL at [423]. See T. R. S. Allan, "Public Interest Immunity and Ministers' Responsibilities" (1993) *Criminal Law Review* 660; A. W. Bradley, "Justice, Good Government and Public Interest Immunity" (1992) *Public Law* 514; and G. Ganz, "Matrix Churchill and Public Interest Immunity" (1993) 56 *Modern Law Review* 564.

10-108 In the light of these differences, criminal cases involving PII claims have to be considered in a different context than cases where civil issues are resolved.

10-109 The Criminal Procedure and Investigations Act 1996 contains a Code of Practice which lays down the basis for documents relevant to the investigation to become available to the defence. The 1996 Act does not make substantive changes to the case law on PII. The Act strengthens the view put forward by Scott that in criminal cases the issue of disclosure of information is whether it might be of relevance to the defence. The Act introduces the requirement of defence disclosure. Paradoxically the Act will limit the role of the judge as there will be few occasions when the judge will have to rule on disclosure because the Act will require disclosure of most material.

10-110 In summary the following appears to be the current law. There is a strong presumption that ministers are expected to apply a "balancing of interests test". PII Certificates cover a wide range of issues. Their use covers sensitive information such as the protection of the disclosure of information related to international relations, the prevention and detection of crime. There is no exhaustive catalogue of their use. The main issue is the operation of judicial discretion in respect of sensitive matters. The advantage of their use from the defendant's perspective is that they are part of the normal procedures of the court. This means that their scope is quite limited as the judge is only able to consider the evidence before the court rather than a broader review of the case file. The disadvantage from the viewpoint of the state is that their limited role might not be sufficiently restrictive of evidence that can be made public. There are very rare circumstances that will stop a trial of the issues. This may cause concern to government lawyers when there are substantial damage claims against the government.

10-111 The likelihood that such claims will fall under the use of Special Advocates in matters of national security known as Closed Material Procedures (CMP) in civil or criminal proceedings. Special Advocates were first used in hearings involving national security deportation cases and have been extended to their use in criminal proceedings and in other cases where sensitive national security issues are raised. The Government's *Justice and Security Green Paper* (CM 8194, October, 2011) and the resultant Justice and Security Act 2013, has proved highly controversial, Pt 2 permitting the extension of CMP in civil proceedings. Striking the balance in the interests of justice between human rights, national security and the rule of law has proved difficult for the Government of the day.[116]

---

116 David Anderson QC, *A Question of Trust: Report of the Investigatory Powers Review* (June 2015). See House of Lords Library, *Reports into Investigatory Powers*, LLN 2015/018 (8 July 2015). The case of *R (Mohamed) v Secretary of State for Foreign and Commonwealth Affairs* is illustrative of the complexity of the issues involved. The facts of the case begin in 2008 when Binyan Mohamed, a UK resident, was detained in the US and held in custody at Guantanamo Bay. He sought judicial review against the Foreign Secretary arising from his claim for disclosure of information that he alleged showed the details and conditions of his arrest he claimed was in the possession of the UK government. His allegations of torture included the time of his arrest in Pakistan in 2002 and subsequent detention. He was then taken to Morocco and Afghanistan before his transfer to Guantanamo in 2004. His main claim was also based on the allegation that those who tortured him received questions and materials from British intelligence officers. Mr Mohamed claimed disclosure of information,

H: Government and Secrecy

10–112 The ethos of secrecy is an intrinsic part of government. Whilst cabinet government requires and maintains the confidence of the House of Commons, its deliberations and decisions are bound together through collective cabinet responsibility. This is intended to ensure confidentiality of decision making as much as responsibility.

10–113 Many of the rules of the cabinet are confidential. Ministers are not expected to divulge the existence of cabinet committees, or the membership of the committees or the rules under which the committees operate. Such confidentiality appears to favour Prime Ministerial influence, the exchange of information on a need-to-know basis within government, and the protection of the civil servants in giving advice. Confidentiality is also required in the contractual and financial relations undertaken by the government of the day. For example in January 1985 a leak of information on the Government's policy on foreign exchange rates resulted in a story in the *Sunday Times*.[117] Nigel Lawson, then Chancellor of the Exchequer, recalls in his memoirs[118] how the leak came from Bernard Ingham, then Press Secretary to the Prime Minister. The leak cost the government a great deal of upheaval in the exchange markets and confidence in the City. This is an illustration of the need for confidentiality within government and this example also underlines the influence of the press and media over the government's economic policies.

10–114 The ethos of secrecy in government is maintained through the use of various restraints on free access to information. The most formidable are the various legal restraints such as s.2 of the Official Secrets Act 1911. The breadth of this section was illustrated in 1984 by the prosecution of Sarah Tisdell, a civil service clerk convicted for leaking the Government's plans for policing and keeping order at Greenham Common, the base intended to receive Cruise Missiles. Clive Ponting, a senior civil servant, was prosecuted under this section for leaking documents relating to the sinking of the Argentinian Warship The General Belgrano during the Falklands War. Although the jury was instructed that Ponting had no defence because he claimed that he owed a duty to Parliament to provide information, the jury, to his surprise, acquitted.

10–115 In addition to s.2, there are a variety of devices such as "D" notices, available to indicate to the press and media that publication may not be within the law. An official committee of press and broadcasting representatives known as the Defence, Press and Broadcasting Committee acts as a scrutineer of the system.

10–116 Conventions that Ministers do not reveal the inner workings of government remain. However, since the *Crossman Diary* case,[119] which permitted the posthumous publication of Richard Crossman's diaries, a number of former cabinet Ministers have published their diaries, even when the diaries were made contemporaneously with their official duties.

---

which he believed showed that he was tortured, to assist his defence in his trial before a US military commission.
117   *Sunday Times*, 6 January 1985.
118   N. Lawson, *The View from No.11*. (London: Bantam Press, 1992), pp.1–469.
119   *Attorney General v Jonathan Cape Ltd* [1976] Q.B. 752; [1975] 3 W.L.R. 606 QBD.

10-117 Actions for breach of confidence may also be involved to protect official secrets such as in the litigation arising out of the Spycatcher book.[120] This book contained the memoirs of Peter Wright, a former member of MI5, revealing details of the inner workings and operations of the security services.

10-118 The question arises as to the compatibility of open government with confidentiality. This question is considered in more detail in Ch.20, but it is apparent that the UK does not benefit from any general presumption in favour of access to official information. This gives rise to the question of how effective government accountability may be within the restrictions imposed on information. The ethos of secrecy pervades the culture of how government conducts its business. Limitations on the flow of information available to the public restricts the opportunities for the critical analysis of government policy. This may have a detrimental effect on how effective government and its related agencies may be in making policy decisions. The decision to release more information on Treasury forecasting of the economy in September 1992 was made in an effort to gain greater credibility for government ministers in managing the economy. This is a good illustration of the obvious benefits to be gained by making more information available allowing more informed judgments. The use of the National Audit Office to check on government and Treasury forecasting is an example of transparency.

10-119 Gradually through public and media pressure, advances are being made to create greater openness in government. A step in the direction of greater openness came in 1993 with publication of the White Paper on Open Government[121] and a proposed relaxation of the laws prohibiting disclosure of information. There is a *Code of Practice on Access to Government Information*[122] issued in 1994 and revised in 1997. This Code sets out how a complaint may be made and how there are five commitments to open government. These are: to supply the facts and analysis with major policy decisions; to open up internal guidelines about departments' dealings with the public; to supply reasons for administrative decisions; to provide information under the Citizen's Charter about public services; and to respond to requests for information. A formal request may be made for information with a guarantee of a reply within 20 working days. Citizens should be able to clarify information and check its accuracy. For example, the Data Protection Act 1984 requires that information must be obtained and processed fairly and lawfully, it must be held only for specific purposes and not used or disclosed in any way incompatible with those purposes. The Data Protection Registrar set up under the Act along with the Data Protection Tribunal, oversees the regulation of information used and classified under the 1984 Act.

10-120 Citizens may view access to more information as a means of redressing grievances but also there is the greater opportunity to participate in government decision making. Government consultation through White Papers, Royal Commissions, and committees of inquiry, all contribute to the provision of more information as well as to the general level of government accountability.

---

120 *Attorney General v Guardian Newspapers Ltd (No.2)* [1990] 1 A.C. 109; [1988] 3 W.L.R. 776 HL.
121 Cm.2290 (1993).
122 Cabinet Office, Whitehall, London.

Some steps in the direction of greater accountability have taken place. The new select committees discussed above have made an important contribution in this area. In 1977 the then Head of the Civil Service issued what has become known as "the Croham" Directive, namely that background material on policy matters should be published unless ministers specifically object. This system has declined in use since 1979 but it is illustrative of how important initiatives may be taken.

Clearly the Human Rights Act 1998 is likely to have an impact on how access to information is considered by the courts. Article 8 of the Convention provides respect for family life and the home. The right to receive information is to be found under art.10(1) but this has not given rise to a substantive right to know. The boundaries of the protections and rights under a rights-based focus have to be considered in the context of providing from public bodies access to official information.

At the same time there are obvious limitations on a general policy on openness. Private citizens may wish to have some degree of privacy protection. Commercial organisations may wish to have copyrights and patents protected and government as a major contractor may be inhibited from open access. Setting the boundaries is not easy. The Freedom of Information Act 2000, which applies to England and Wales but not Scotland, where separate arrangements are being considered, is an attempt to provide some general principles such as a general right of access to information but subject to general limitations and exceptions. However, it is not currently in force. It will be phased in, first with central government in November 2000 and then later the entire Act will be in force by July 2005. The Act builds on previous attempts at greater transparency especially with the Data Protection Act 1998, Access to Medical Reports Act 1988 and the Environmental Information Regulations 1992.[123] Critics see the Act as a disappointment because of the extensive exceptions and exemptions. However, as Feldman explains[124]:

> "All one can say in favour of the Act is that it represents a small and extremely tentative first step towards making real openness in government the norm."

Section 1 of the Act provides a general right of access to information held by public authorities. The definition of a public authority includes central government departments, local government including health authorities and maintained schools. There are a variety of other bodies including the British Council who are included. In terms of positive rights, the citizen is provided with the right to information because there is a duty on public authorities to respond to a request for information. The request must be in writing and, within 20 working days, once confirmed that the information is with the public authority there is a right to access to the information. A fee may be payable and there appears no obligation to become proactive in tracing

---

123 Environmental Information Regulations (SI 1992/3240).
124 D. Feldman, *Civil Liberties and Human Rights in England and Wales*, 2nd edn (Oxford: Oxford University Press, 2002), p.786.

the information or investigating whether the information is in fact in the possession of the public authority. The exemption categories are all-embracing. Section 14 provides grounds for refusing the request if it is regarded as vexatious or would be too expensive to provide. There is a raft of exclusions including where the information is available through other means. Some of the main areas where information does not have to be disclosed are if the information would:

- be prejudicial to defence or the capability of the security or armed forces;
- be prejudicial to the interests of relations with other countries;
- be prejudicial to the economic interests of the country;
- infringe the privileges of Parliament; and
- be prejudicial to the audit functions of public authorities discharging their functions.

10-125 It is difficult to qualify the term "prejudicial" and how this might be interpreted by the courts. Information does not have to be disclosed if it is likely to be actionable and a breach of confidence or prejudicial to commercial interests, or would be subject to legal professional privilege.

10-126 The Act also has an enforcement procedure. The Data Protection Commissioner is renamed under s.18 as the Information Commissioner. The Data Protection Tribunal is renamed the Information Tribunal.

10-027 The Freedom of Information Act has created a cultural shift in the way information is handled. The Government continues to resist transparency leading to a number of cases. This may be for understandable reasons such as preserving the confidentiality of the Attorney General. The main issue is the compatibility with the public interest. The convention that the Attorney General's advice to ministers was not given sufficient weight by the Information Tribunal was considered in *HM Treasury v Information Commissioner*. The Attorney General's role was upheld as deserving of consideration in terms of Parliament's intention was to ensure under s.35(1)(c) of the Act to be considered as exempted from disclosure.

I: Summary and Conclusions

10-128 Philip Norton[125] asks whether Parliament may have a new assertiveness in its scrutiny of Government. Certainly there are changes in the way committees work and an increasing role

---

125 P. Norton, "Parliament: A New Assertiveness?" in J. Jowell, D. Oliver and C. O'Cinneide, eds., *The Changing Constitution* (Oxford: Oxford University Press, 2015), pp.171–193.

for backbench MPs. Parliamentary reform is often full of expectation but delivers less than expected. Reforms have usually focused on the House of Commons, its procedures and practices. There is little assessment by Parliament itself of whether or not scrutiny is effective or how to evaluate the scrutiny that is provided. Reform of the House of Lords is related to its composition rather than how well it scrutinises the Executive. Engagement with the public is increasing especially with e-petitions.

10–129

Access to more information and knowledge of government strategy is an important element in the ideals of democratic government. We live in an information age. The political life of the nation is focused on presentation to the media and the management of information. Good government depends on access to information, informed public debate and reasoned analysis. There are some positive signs that public information has been improved. The Freedom of Information Act 2000 provides a development in favour of open government and access to information. It may, however, fall short of the expectation of making government accountable through greater transparency. There is also a welcome trend in favour of the informal codification of various parts of our constitutional arrangements including *The Ministerial Code*, October 2015 is an important codification of working practices.[126]

10–130

Accountability has become increasingly important in recent years yet the term is elusive and often ill defined. Increasingly it is used as a means of holding to account through a variety of political, legal and cultural pressures a widely defined group of decision makers. Achieving systems of accountability is seen as a means of achieving good government and decision making. Public lawyers often inspect the contemporary Constitution through the lens of Parliament in its institutional role of holding government to account. As Prosser has wisely observed "these multi-level structures of accountability are of value in producing countervailing views and sources of information. However, once more there is only limited co-ordination between them; pluralism means a fragmented rather than a networked constitution".[127] This leaves a lot to be desired and a sense of disappointment that the government can fall short in the quality of its policy making and the values of good governance.[128]

10–131

As the influential Institute for Government[129] points out the UKs constitutional and institutional arrangements are subject to subtle pressures that provide a complex pattern of change. The Constitution adapts and is adept at taking effective action when required. Yet the Westminster model remains an overpowering influence over how party politics dictates policy choices, determines what is effective and defines the public interest. The recent historical dominance of two parties may ultimately give way to a form of multi-party politics and increasingly fluid party allegiances. The long term influence of these developments on the UK's Constitution is far from clear. The UK's decision to leave the EU will have a serious impact on

---

126 Cabinet Office, *Ministerial Code* (October 2015).
127 T. Prosser, *The Economic Constitution* (Oxford: Oxford University Press, 2014), p.251.
128 Anthony King and Ivor Crewe, *The Blunders of our Governments* (London: Oneworld Books, 2014).
129 Miguel Coelho, Vigyan Ratnoo and Sebastian Dellepiane, *Political Economy of Policy Failure and Institutional Reform* (London: Institute for Government, 2014).

the effectiveness of the working of government and its institutions as the UK enters a period of economic and political uncertainty.

Further Reading

Anthony King and Ivor Crewe, *The Blunders of our Governments* (London: Oneworld Books, 2014).

N. Bamforth and P. Leyland, "Introduction: Accountability in the Contemporary Constitution" in N. Bamforth and P. Leyland, *Accountability in the Contemporary Constitution* (Oxford: Oxford University Press, 2013), pp.1–14.

T. Daintith and A. Page, *The Executive in the Constitution* (Oxford: Oxford University Press, 1999).

A. C. L. Davies, "Beyond New Public Management: Problems of Accountability in the Modern Administrative State" in N. Bamforth and P. Leyland, *Accountability in the Contemporary Constitution* (Oxford: Oxford University Press, 2013), pp.333–353.

E. Fisher, "The European Union in the Age of Accountability" (2004) 23 *O.J.L.S.* 495.

Hansard Society, *Report of the Hansard Society Commission on Parliamentary Scrutiny: The Challenge for Parliament—Making Government Accountable* (London: Hansard Society, Vacher Dod Publishing Ltd, 2001).

P. Norton, *Parliament in British Politics* (London: Longman, 2013).

D. Oliver and G. Drewry, *Public Service Reform: issues of Accountability and Public Law* (London: Pinter, 1996).

T. Prosser, *The Economic Constitution* (Oxford: Oxford University Press, 2014).

C. Scott, "Accountability in the Regulatory State" (2000) 27 *Journal of Law and Society* 38.

11

Beyond New Public Management and the State

A: Introduction

11–001

The modern civil service has remained remarkably resilient although under intensive reform and changes in its working practices. It has traditionally operated under public service principles that are distinct from private or political interests. In 1976 the number of civil servants had reached a high point of 751,000, but by 1979 it had fallen to 732,000 civil servants. There was a further decline in numbers; in 1989 the number dropped to 570,000 and 450,000 by 2000. In 2014, the number of civil servants was around 401,890 and at 31 March 2015, 405,570. One of the largest departments is the Department of Work and Pensions with one fifth of civil servants employed in the department or its agencies.[1] On 31 March 2015,16 per cent of civil servants were in the Ministry of Justice, 15 per cent in HMRC and 14 per cent in the Ministry of defence[2]. Overall roughly 54 per cent of civil servants are female but at the higher levels of the civil service, there are more men than women. Only 10 per cent of all civil servants volunteering an ethnic origin were from an ethnic minority. The civil service in age profile is getting older. The proportion of civil servants over 40 in 1991 was 44 per cent and in 2015 the proportion is 69 per cent. Civil servants are predominantly male, in 2011 34 per cent of the senior civil service were women and only 5 per cent from ethnic minorities.[3] There is a striking pay differential between public and private sectors. Only 1,076 civil servants have an annual salary greater than £100,000 and only 11 civil servants earned more than £200,000. The average salary was £24,980. Comparable responsibilities in the private sector are more likely to have higher remuneration. One factor to be considered might be the enhanced pension arrangements of

---

1 House of Commons Library, *Civil Service Statistics*, Standard Note, SN/SG/2224 (5 November 2014); and also House of Commons Library, *Public Service Reform*, SN/PC/06011 (11 August 2011).
2 House of Commons Library Briefing Paper, *Civil Service Statistics*, No.2224 (9 November 2015).
3 Bill Jones and Philip Norton, *Politics UK* (London: Routledge, 2014), p.395.

civil servants where most are on non-contributory schemes. There are also regional variations in salaries.[4]

11-002 Substantial cuts in the size of the civil service came under the Conservative led Coalition government and these are expected to continue under the Conservative government elected in May 2015. Predicting the future size of the civil service is difficult with planned cuts of funding of 30 per cent to be implemented by 2020.

11-003 The civil service has continued to evolve and adapt to change by redefining its role and objectives. The Fulton Report in 1969, which examined the lack of effective management in the civil service gave rise to concerns about its future direction and role. Demands for greater efficiency and effectiveness in the civil service has become a recurrent theme in the relations between the government and the civil service. Senior civil servants advise ministers on major policy issues, take many policy decisions, implement and co-ordinate complex administrative schemes and manage large departments. Yet the civil service remains politically neutral and largely evidenced based in its advice and policy making. Such tasks require not only high administrative skills, but also managerial ability. Perceived deficiencies in the structures and management techniques within the civil service have resulted sometimes in a struggle to maintain the past traditions of public service ethos especially in an era of austerity and with the pressure on jobs, pensions and conditions of service. The remarkable growth in special advisers, appointed by the government of the day, has also shaped the relationship between ministers and the civil service. As Rawlings has pointed out the shift towards market-led solutions and the business model of performance management has been influential in creating an "age of managerialism"[5] that is influential in policy making.

11-004 Another recurrent issue within the civil service has been recognition that long-term or strategic planning was absent from the system of Cabinet government. Civil servants recognised that seldom was the impact of government policies fully reviewed, discussed and considered in the light of future policies, by the Cabinet.

11-005 In this chapter the changing role of the civil service will be discussed. These include a major shift from government as providing services to the government's role in ensuring the purchase of services from various specialist providers, some in the private sector and some in the public sector.[6] The continued use of various agencies is important in terms of changing the "culture" of the civil service and opening it up to different influences. Nevertheless the "Whitehall mandarin" beloved of the media remains an enduring icon. The operation of agencies has resulted in the creation of a large number of arm's length public bodies that reside in the various agencies that form the bulk of civil service activities. These remain, at least in theory, situated within existing structures of parliamentary accountability and ministerial control. The

---

4   House of Commons Library Briefing Paper, *Civil Service Statistics*, No.2224 (9 November 2015), pp.8–12.
5   R. Rawlings, "A Coalition Government in Westminster" in J. Jowell, D. Oliver, and C. O'Cinneide (eds), *The Changing Constitution* (Oxford: Oxford University Press, 2015), pp.194–221.
6   A. C. L Davies, "Beyond New Public Management: Problems of Accountability in the Modern Administrative State" in N. Bamforth and P. Leyland, *Accountability in the Contemporary Constitution* (Oxford: Oxford University Press, 2013), pp.333–353.

creation of many agencies has challenged some of the principles of the civil service established since the Northcote-Trevelyan Report in 1853 which may be taken to be the beginning of the modern development of the civil service. Since Fulton, the aims, objectives and management of the civil service have undergone intense scrutiny. The steps taken to introduce management techniques into the civil service will be examined below and the setting up of the various agencies, by hiving off department activities, is explained in terms of the constitutional implications for parliamentary accountability. Such fundamental changes to the civil service have raised questions about its future direction and development. Questions about Agency status have raised issues about the criteria used to measure their success and the value of agencies in the efficiency of service provision. Overall issues of accountability arise because of the complex delivery systems of different organisations, contracts and procedures are holding those to account through the traditional system of ministerial accountability. In this context, accountability may be to consumers whether they be regarded as citizens or customers or to Parliament and ministers. Here accountability may mean as Dawn Oliver explains: a legal, political, social or moral duty on the part of the *accounter* to explain and justify his or her action or inaction to particular bodies demanding explanations".[7]

11–006

The civil service, its organisation and status provide an important dimension on how government governs. The Constitutional Reform and Governance Act 2010 has created a statutory basis for the civil service together with the *Civil Service Code* that provides a set of ethical standards and principles on how the civil service operates. This is not an exhaustive list but it provides a useful framework for understanding the contractual relationship between the civil servant and employer.

B: Civil Service: Evolution, Change and the Managing of Government

11–007

Since the nineteenth century, the civil service has been the focus of attempts to reform its role and function. Prior to Mrs Thatcher becoming Prime Minister in 1979, the civil service had largely withstood major reforms to its organisation and management. These comprise Plowden in 1961, Fulton in 1968 and reforms under Mr Heath in 1970 in hiving off departments. Two efficiency reviews in 2004, the Gershon Review[8] and the Lyons Review[9] underpinned the

---

7   D. Oliver, "Accountability and the Foundations of British Democracy—The Public Interest and Public Service Principles" in N. Bamforth and P. Leyland, *Accountability in the Contemporary Constitution* (Oxford: Oxford University Press, 2013), pp.289–308.
8   HM Treasury, *Releasing resources to the front line* (July 2004).
9   HM Treasury, *Well Placed to Deliver?—Shaping the Pattern of Government Services* (March 2004).

Blair Government's ambition to reduce public service manpower and decentralise government outside London.

11-008
The path way of civil service reform that has transformed public administration into a market based business that is at the core of the development of new public management has become entrenched into the operation and working of the civil service has its origins as far back as the 1960s. In 1961 the Plowden Report[10] on the public expenditure process introduced the Public Expenditure Survey (PES) which was aimed at changing the financial procedures involved in planning government strategy. This involved "regular surveys" of public expenditure as a whole over a period of years ahead. Decisions "should be taken in the light of those surveys". The creation of a continuous programme of the spending objectives for the medium term was intended to allow bilateral discussions in Cabinet at the beginning of the autumn. It also encouraged civil service efficiency within a framework directed by ministers. In reaching policy decisions within departments the civil service was expected to be more cost effective and better informed of the economic advice tendered to ministers. However, the civil service proved resistant to any fundamental changes and the PES ran into major economic problems during periods of inflation and itself came under considerable change.

11-009
In 1968, the Fulton Report[11] on the civil service made recommendations for major changes. When it reported, the civil service had grown to 20 times the size of the civil service in 1854. Arguably the increase in size reflected larger departments and a greater workload with an increasingly complex system of government. Both its size and the variety of work expected from civil servants confirmed the need to reconsider how the civil service was managed. Particularly important throughout the last two decades has been the need to improve strategic planning and management of resources.

11-010
The period to the end of 1982 saw the first results of 133 Rayner Scrutinies intended to make the civil service more effective and when Sir Derek Rayner relinquished the post, his successor, Sir Robin Ibbs, continued the process begun by Rayner.[12]

11-011
The foundations for change, having been established in the late 1970s have been continued. Repackaging, rebranding and using various changes in vocabulary, the civil service has come under a "new public management" ethos that has continued throughout the period of successive Labour and Conservative government's including up to 2015, the Conservative-led Coalition with a comparison between public sector and business management techniques reveals that different management roles are preferred by different layers of management. Top management in the private sector deals with strategy, policy in new opportunities and even areas of uncertainty where a surprise change in the business environment may threaten existing arrangements. In public sector management little adaptation and learning are built into the processes and no clear differentiation is made between layers of management.

---

10   Plowden Report, *The Control of Public Expenditure*, Cmnd.1432 (1961).
11   *Fulton Report*, Cmnd.3638 (1968).
12   Les Metcalfe and Sue Richards, *Improving Public Management*, 2nd edn (London: Sage, 1990), p.10.

C: Management Techniques: New Public Management and beyond

11-012 The Rayner efficiency studies encouraged the development of management techniques in the civil service. Since 1980 further changes introduced into the civil service have continued the development of new structures and organisation in the civil service. The changes in the 1980s have laid the foundations of a new public management strategy (NPM). The argument in favour is that wasteful and ineffective public sector might be transformed into a more effective and efficient deliverer of services under the influence of the private sector. Government would thereby be transformed from deliverer of public services to the purchaser of services from the private and public sectors.[13]

11-013 The advocates of NPM also stressed that the Government would be better able to manage resources if the true costs of services were fully known and appropriately budgeted. The adoption of NPM has further benefits. Direct accountability of public service providers to users, customers and citizens provides a different form of accountability than the traditional form of ministerial responsibility to Parliament. Critics are not so convinced. Dividing up different forms of accountability may not lead to results that overall improve accountability. The electorate and Parliament may struggle to identify who is at fault and whether blame should attach to Government, contractor or even the consumer for a failure to be vigilant. More importantly it may not be possible to have sufficient information to identify who is at fault and whether any one is to blame.

11-014 NPM is productive of an underlying market based designed system of delivery that lend weight to the private sector and often marginalises the role of government. Since the Conservative led Coalition Government was elected in 2010–2015, the role of NPM has continued. NPM techniques encourage opportunities for entrepreneurial and consumer choices to prioritise the delivery of public services. Perhaps more importantly NPM techniques may also reduce costs and contribute to budget cuts overall and achieve more with less. As A. C. L Davies observes:

> "The proponents of NPM often present contracting out as a way of achieving this (achieving more with less), because the government can set out its objectives and leave to potential bidders the task of developing innovative ways of meeting those objectives at a lower cost."[14]

---

13   Institute for Government, *Making and Breaking Whitehall Departments* (London: Institute for Government, 2013).
14   A. C. L Davies, "Beyond New Public Management: Problems of Accountability in the Modern Administrative State" in N. Bamforth and P. Leyland, *Accountability in the Contemporary Constitution* (Oxford: Oxford University Press, 2013), 333–353, p.339.

The critics of NPM argue that contractors may cut corners and make savings and are not easy to hold to account when profit may determine the outcome rather than the standards of delivery or service.

11-015 NPM is likely to remain a prominent part of government's ambition to deliver public services. Its use has been recognised by past Labour and Conservative governments.

11-016 NPM is only one aspect of how the civil service is being managed. There remains the traditional question of the relationship between ministers and civil servants. This raises the potential for civil servants owing a duty to the government of the day rather than directly to Parliament. Some examples in the 1980s include the Maze prison breakout in 1983, the Clive Ponting trial in 1985 and the Westland affair in 1985–86, which brought greater attention to the role of civil servants than ever before. In the Maze prison breakout, civil servants were found at fault for a major failure in security at the Maze prison for which the Governor was held responsible. No minister resigned because the escape was not attributed to any failure of policy but the Governor of the Maze did resign.

11-017 In the case of Clive Ponting, a civil servant was prosecuted under the Official Secrets Act for releasing the text of a memorandum on the sinking of the *Belgrano* during the Falklands War. Although acquitted by a jury, the trial judge stated that civil servants owed a duty to ministers as "the government of the day" rather than Parliament. In 1985–86 Mr Leon Britton, then Secretary of State for Trade and Industry, resigned after he authorised civil servants to take the improper action of releasing a confidential letter written by the Solicitor General to the Secretary of State for Defence.[15]

11-018 The civil servants involved in the examples mentioned above received greater publicity about their role in the conduct of government than ever before. The later litigation on the *Spycatcher* book containing the memoirs of Peter Wright, a former MI5 officer and the evidence in Australia from the then Head of the civil service, Lord Armstrong, maintained at a high level, public interest in the civil service.[16] The civil service has continued to enjoy greater publicity than at any time in their history.

D: The Development of Agencies

11-019 Creating a more managerial and business-oriented ethos within the civil service is an ongoing work in progress. The senior civil service, comprising no more than 20,000 people are likely to come from a wider diversity of backgrounds than in the past and bring a broader, open minded

---

15 G. Marshall, "Cabinet Government and the Westland Affair" [1986] *P.L.* 184; D. Oliver and R. Austin, "Political and Constitutional Aspects of the Westland Affair" (1987) 40 *Parliamentary Affairs* 20; Hennessy Report, *Report of an Inquiry by H.M. Chief Inspector of Prisons into the Security Arrangements at H.M. Prison Maze*, HC 203 (1983–84).
16 *Attorney General v Guardian Newspapers Ltd (No.2)* [1990] 1 A.C. 109; [1988] 3 W.L.R. 776 HL.

approach to business and managerialism. The background to the development of the Next Steps Initiative involving the use of agencies to deliver departmental responsibilities began after Robin Ibbs succeeded Derek Rayner as Head of the Efficiency Unit in 1983. While anxious to maintain the momentum set by Rayner, Ibbs shared the same drive for greater efficiency inside the management structure set within the civil service. The main question was how to assess Financial Management Information (FMI) and how might initiatives to remedy any problems with the FMI system be introduced.

11-020

The period from 1983–1986 was dominated by the attempt to implement FMI. In theory FMI, by delegating executive responsibility to managerial decision-makers at a local level, gave more budgeting control to individual civil servants, who would become largely autonomous and removed from the direct oversight of ministerial control. Civil servants, at least in the potential given to them to set and manage their own policy, seemed remarkably freed from the tight hierarchical control favoured within the traditional civil service. No major structural reforms had been introduced to implement the major changes such delegation may produce and not surprisingly difficulties were experienced in the full implementation of FMI.

A new initiative, in the form of a scrutiny report, begun in 1986 by Sir Robin Ibbs was published in 1988. The report from the Efficiency Unit, *Improving Management in Government: The Next Steps* suggested—to the surprise at least of Nigel Lawson, then Chancellor of the Exchequer—that executive functions of government should be hived off into separate executive agencies to be run like businesses by chief executives.

11-021

Setting objectives, however well formulated, did not guarantee their success, and Ibbs went one step further than before. The Next Steps scrutiny team in their report recommended that agencies should be established to carry out some of the executive functions of government. Departments could set the general policy and resources, but agencies should be developed to carry out the tasks allocated.

11-022

The Next Steps agencies, as they were referred to, were to be set up but as Nigel Lawson noted this left unresolved two major questions[17]:

11-023

> "It was clear that Ibbs had not addressed the two principal problems involved in a change of this kind, however sensible the concept may have been. The first was the question of Parliamentary accountability. Members of Parliament would not take kindly to the idea of a Minister being able to shrug off a constituent's complaint as being nothing to do with him since the wrong suffered by the constituent had been inflicted by an autonomous agency, whose head was, according to the original Ibbs blueprint, effectively accountable to no-one."

The second problem identified by Lawson was that of maintaining effective financial control over the agencies' expenditure. Resolution of this problem came through an agreement

11-024

---

17   Nigel Lawson, *The View from No. 11*, (London: Corgi, 1993), pp.390–392.

11-025 reached with the Treasury and the appointment of Peter Kemp as manager of the Next Steps project with the status of Second Permanent Secretary.

11-026 On the question of accountability[18] the creation of Next Steps agencies gave rise to fundamental questions about the relationship between the agencies, the civil service and the role of ministers.

In February 1988 a small cohesive Next Steps Unit was set up under Peter Kemp in the Office of the Minister for the Civil Service. By 1991 it was estimated that over 50 executive agencies, comprising 200,000 civil servants had been set up. Currently over 80 per cent of the civil service are in such agencies and these are likely to grow and extend. Various agencies with many varied objectives and aims exist, often with clusters of agencies dedicated around a central department. The Prison Service, the Courts Service and the Tribunals service fall under the responsibility of the Ministry of Justice. Their size and range of expertise are widely varied. Some other executive agencies were created with Her Majesty's Stationery Office (one of the largest), the Central Office of Information, the Land Registry and the Passport Office.

11-027 The Vehicle Inspectorate was one of the first agencies, responsible to the Department of Transport for heavy goods vehicles and licensees of garages. The model adopted became the standard practice. Responsibility for the day-to-day operations of each agency were delegated to an Agency Chief Executive. The Agency Chief Executive is responsible for management within a framework of policy objectives and resources set by the responsible minister in consultation with the Treasury.

Managing the Civil Service in an area of change also has to confront the stereotype as explained by Gillian Peele[19]:

> **"The bias at the higher levels towards graduates of Oxford and Cambridge has not, however, been the only concern about the civil service's composition. It was clear from the Cassells Report of 1983 that although almost half of the civil service were women, they formed a much higher proportion of the junior grades than of the senior one ... The evidence on recent developments with respect to the role of women in the civil service is somewhat mixed. By 1994 very few of the top 38 posts at permanent secretary rank were held by women..."**

11-028 The proportion of women in the civil service is changing, but only very gradually. In 2014, 53 per cent of the civil service were women and 10 per cent from ethnic minorities. Placing women in the most senior positions within the civil service is a challenge for the future of the civil service.

---

18 *The Next Steps Initiative*, (London: HMSO, 1988); Cm.1761 (1991); and *The Government's reply to the Seventh Report from the Treasury and Civil Service Committee*, HC 496 (1990–91).

19 Gillian Peele, *Governing the United Kingdom*, 3rd edn (London: Blackwell, 1995), p.137.

11-029   The innovatory nature of the agency arrangements has given rise to a number of initial problems. Prior to the grant of agency status, a business plan and corporate identity requires careful consideration. The term Chief Executive carries high expectations of managerial control and business initiative. However, in public sector activities these may appear illusory because detailed financial control may still rest with the Treasury. Thus it took some time before bonus payments based on group and not individual initiative were accepted. This required protracted negotiation in the Vehicle Inspectorate before it was agreed. Chief executives are generally drawn from the civil service and this may continue old interests and pressures in the new guise of agency status. Similarities with business appear inapplicable when it is recognised that ultimately financial failure is not a sanction.

11-030   The experience of Agency status is sometimes mixed. Passport administration when transferred to the Passport Agency appeared to be sensible and logical. The Home Office could release a specified activity that might be an attractive area for agency status. The issuing of passports might be seen as standing outside any party political issues and be devoid of any controversial issues. The Home Office assumed that this was an area devoid of much attention. Nothing prepared the Home Office for the problems of delivery systems working effectively and manpower issues that overtook the managements structures that were then in place. The tasks required needed more ministerial attention and in the end this resulted in the Passport Agency being moved back into the Home Office.[20]

11-031   It is therefore no exaggeration to claim that[21] Agencies under "Next Steps are radically altering the organisation of the Civil Service". It will also require careful scrutiny to determine if any of the desired changes in the management of civil service activities is actually achieved through agency status.

11-032   Research work by Elizabeth Mellon into the working of a number of executive agencies have suggested criteria for evaluating an Agency. Three methods of evaluation may be adopted. First, an examination of performance measures from inside and outside the organisation may determine whether available resources have delivered services more efficiently and effectively. In this assessment an examination of cutting costs, and the performance criteria set out in the originating framework documents may be helpful. Secondly, to test the extent to which control has been given to members of staff inside agencies, which may assist in determining how leadership and responsibility within the agency may have changed. Thirdly, the introduction of the concept of "customers" within the civil service may allow feedback from customers, and responsiveness to customer needs may be quantified and tested.

11-033   Useful as such criteria may be, there are doubts as to whether agency status in itself may produce significant change to the operating practices of civil servants.

---

20   Anthony King and Ivor Crewe, *The Blunders of our Government* (London: Oneworld, 2014), p.292.
21   Elizabeth Mellon, Memorandum, Appendix 1 in *Evidence to the Treasury and Civil Service Committee Seventh Report, The Next Steps Initiative*, HC 496 (1990–91).

E: Agencies, Accountability and Control

11-034 Agency status has raised questions regarding accountability and control. How do agencies fit into the structure of constitutional oversight offered by select committees, ministerial responsibility and the existing status of the civil service? The answer to these questions has been raised, not only within the civil service and the government, but also in Parliament. At the forefront of discussion is the Parliamentary Select Committee on the Treasury and Civil Service. Reports since 1987–88 have both monitored and contributed to the information available on the role of agencies. It is now accepted that agencies have a bi-partisan approach from the political parties, and that the Committee itself has a role in monitoring arrangements on an annual basis. The Government has continued to provide assistance to the Committee on the subject of agencies.

11-035 In their Fourth Report 1990/91, the Select Committee on the Treasury and Civil Service noted that while agency status increased, the core departments in central government should continue to exercise "general responsibility for the oversight of the Civil Service".

11-036 In allocating agency status, the Chief Executive is required to manage the agency effectively[22] "to achieve the ends dictated by the Minister responsible". The Chief Executive is a civil servant in formal terms. The Chief Executive may appear before select committees responsible directly for the work as head of an agency. Thus the Chief Executive appears to give evidence to select committees like any other civil servant on the minister's behalf. While this preserves the constitutional continuity between agency and civil service, Select Committees have voiced concern that in effect chief executives are not like any other civil servant because their responsibility as chief executives, laid down in framework documents differs from ordinary delegated authority given to the civil service by ministers.

11-037 The Child Support Act 1991 introduced a new system of child benefits and the legislation had been introduced rather rapidly after a White Paper was published with little opportunity for a time-scale for implementation. The delivery of the new arrangements was entrusted to the new established Child Support Agency. The Agency had less than a year to recruit 5000 staff, appoint senior staff including the Chief Executive. The tasks facing the Agency included the collection of over £530 million in maintenance payments and handling over one million cases. In fact, within one year the case load increased to 2.5 million cases. There were high expectations that the new Agency would be cost effective and this would lead to real savings. The tasks proved more complex than first estimated. The Agency received bad publicity amidst the mounting crisis and complexity of tackling so many claimants. Its named was soon dubbed to "the Complete Shambles Agency". There were complaints made to MPs and the Parliamentary Commissioner for Administration (the Ombudsman) made findings showing that frequently the Child Support assessment was in error and that maladministration was found in many examples.[23] In December 1993 over 150,000 cases

---

22 Cm.1263 (1990), p.3; *Hansard*, HC Vol.186, cols.270–2W.
23 *The Guardian*, 19 January 1995. *Parliamentary Commissioner for Administration, Investigations of Complaints Against the Child Support Agency*, HC (1994–95), p.135.

were re-opened and reassessed in the light of administrative problems. Subsequently a new Agency chair was employed and an additional 700 staff employed.[24] Delay and various back-logged material were addressed and the overall policy had to be reassessed. This led to the Child Support Act 1995 being passed introducing new policy arrangements that avoided the collection of maintenance payments. The National Audit Office was highly critical of the conduct of the Agency and the failure of the delivery of benefits to many children.[25] There was a large back log of cases that built up and many assessments were later shown to be wrong. A new Government took office and changed some of the policy including new legislation under the Child Support Act 2000. Despite some fundamental changes to the way the scheme worked, it did not radically alter the underlying problems. Over ambitious targets proved difficult to meet with the available resources and time-scales. Perhaps flawed policy making, an underestimate of the complex tasks entrusted to the Agency and an overestimate of the likely cost savings led to successive problems that reveal serious shortcomings. In 2006, the National Audit Office[26] refused to sign off the accounts of the Agency. Matters came to a head when an independent Report under Sir David Henshaw recommended a new approach and the eventual abolition of the Agency and the removal of the Government from regulating child maintenance.[27]

11-038
Parliamentary accountability for agencies appears to continue to rest on the minister who is responsible to Parliament. Accountability also follows from this, through scrutiny by select committee, and individual MPs may ask parliamentary questions about areas within ministerial control.

11-039
Parliamentary questions[28] and procedures have proved difficult for agencies to fit into existing practices. Ministers normally reply to questions by promising to write to the MP When a parliamentary answer states that an executive agency will write, the letters written are to be sent to the Department of the Library, House of Commons. However, on detailed financial policy where the Agency Chief Executive is responsible, ministers may have little scope for reply. Inconsistency of approach between different agencies and departments may arise. One recommendation is that all replies from chief executives should be included in the Official Report. In this way access to all replies either from ministers or chief executives would conform to a common method.

11-040
The formulation of how Next Steps agencies fit within the conventional arrangements for ministerial responsibility has sometimes struggled but in general the main principles are familiar ones drawing an important distinction between operational and policy matters. Chief executives may answer for operational or day-to-day decisions, while ministers retain responsibility

---

24 House of Commons Library, *The Operation of the Child Support Agency 94/20* (31 January 1994).
25 See the discussion of the Public Accounts Committee, *Child Support Agency: Client Funds and Accounts*, HB 196–97 (1997–98), p.313.
26 See *The Guardian*, 28 April 2011 and also Anthony King and Ivor Crewe, *The Blunders of our Government* (London: Oneworld, 2014), p.93.
27 Sir David Henshaw, *Report to the Secretary of State for Work and Pensions, Recovering Child Support: Routes to Responsibility*, CM 6894 (London: HMSO, 2006), pp.1–5.
28 Third Report of the Select Committee on Procedure, *Parliamentary Questions*, HC 178 (1990–91), para.125.

for policy matters. Even when ministers may interfere in operational matters, unless there are clear policy issues at stake, chief executives shoulder the burden of responsibility.

11-041
The experience of the Rural Payments Agency in delivering a new system of single farm payments is an example of the complexity of government, often under the intense pressure of timetables it has little control over. Changes in the EU's Common Agricultural Policy (CAP) in the late 1990s included the replacement of past subsidies by a single payment system. Agriculture is a devolved matter and each of the four nations opted for different ways of introducing the reform. The Scottish and Welsh governments opted for a simple historical based approach to the calculation of payments. Northern Ireland applied at a more complex combination of historical use related to each hectare of land. In England, the most complicated option was chosen relating to an historical approach combined with a calculation of each hectare of land with the addition of a "tapering" arrangement marking a shift from historic use to present day operations on the land. The relevant government department, the Department for Environment, Food and Rural Affairs (Defra) agreed that the Rural Payments Agency should be given the responsibility of implementation of the new scheme. The reforms were not phased in, but introduced as a single package announced in February 2004 and due to start from 1 January 2005. Payments were expected to be made in tranches beginning on 1 December 2005 and the last on 30 June 2006. The task proved more complicated and difficult than planned. The target of payments of 96 per cent by May 2006 was not met and the EU set target of June 2006 looked likely to be missed with the potential for a large fine. Payments made were not properly calculated and often overpayments were made because of computer errors. The National Audit Office identified many overpayments with an overall estimate of £ 5.4 million, there were also many underpayments.[29] The Rural Payments Agency struggled to meet the demands of the new system and the performance of the Agency was poorly rated. In addition fines were paid to the European Commission because of the breaches by the UK. Many poorer farmers were hit badly, leading to insolvency of some. The National Audit Office calculated that in the autumn of 2006 farmers were paying £18 million to £22.4 million in overdraft interest.[30] The explanation for the problems seemed to be the complexity of the scheme, poor IT systems and lack of ministerial oversight over the Rural Payments Agency. The Agency had been in the middle of re-organising its own management system and over dependency on IT left the delivery vulnerable. As King and Crewe observed:

> "Neither Defra nor the Rural Payments Agency, nor individual managers within either of those organisations, effectively "owned" delivery of the scheme. Indeed, almost everyone involved agreed that no one really understood the scheme in its entirety (always assuming that it was capable of being understood)."[31]

---

29 National Audit Office, *Defra and Rural Payments Agency: Delays in Administering the 2005 Single Payments Scheme in England*, HC 1631 (London: HMSO, 2006), p.5.
30 National Audit Office, *A Second Progress update on the Administration of the Single Payment Scheme by the Rural Payments Agency*, HC 880 (London: HMSO, 2009), pp.1, 5.
31 A. King and I. Crewe, *The Blunders of our Governments* (London: Oneworld, 2014), p.181.

11-042 The Agency sacked its Chief Executive amidst the fiasco. The dual problems of Agency status resulting in its isolation from ministers and the complexity of the scheme became clear with the delivery of the scheme almost impossible to achieve in the time available.[32]

11-043 Undoubtedly one of the benefits attributable to agency status has been a growth in publications concerning the function of the agencies. Detailed accounts, future plans, corporate strategy, reviews of activities over the past financial year, objectives and key performance targets have all been included in a mass of agency annual reports. One criticism raises questions about the variety and lack of standardisation in the way such reports are produced, and the details of information they contain. Such inconsistency may give rise to confusion. Generally, publications from agencies have been welcomed as providing additional information to Parliament.

11-044 A key factor in determining control over agencies is the question of budget management and financial scrutiny. The Chief Executive of an agency is appointed an Accountancy Officer or Agency Accounting Officer and is therefore accountable to the Committee of Public Accounts for the financial budgets of the agency. The Treasury has issued a note of guidance setting out the obligation for annual reports and accounts. This accountability through the publication of annual reports and accounts is also provided by the work of the National Audit Office.

11-045 The financial arrangements for agencies fall under direct vote, that is supply financed by the relevant government department or under trading fund arrangements. Supply financed agencies cover a wide spectrum of activities. Some agencies rely entirely on voted expenditure to cover only operating and capital requirements while some agencies may cover all their costs. Supply financed agencies are cash limited in the normal departmental appropriation accounts. In such cases the departmental Accounting Officer remains accountable for all payments to the agency for votes for which he accounts.

11-046 In the case of trading fund agencies, the Treasury has published a guide to the Establishment and Operation of Trading Funds.[33] This guide sets out the criteria for the use of trading funds for

> "certain kinds of operations within Government, particularly those where the outputs of the organisation are financed from related receipts and the demand for output fluctuates, for which cash control based on inputs can inhibit effective management."

11-047 Trading funds therefore provide agencies with greater flexibility than the normal restrictions implied in vote finance. In particular, the financing framework covers all operating costs, receipts, capital expenditure, borrowing and cash flow. Compared to voted expenditure, trading funds have standing authority to meet outgoings from receipts and do not require

---

32 House of Commons, Public Accounts Committee, *A Progress Update in Resolving the Difficulties in Administering the Single Payment Scheme in England*, HC 285 (2007–08), p. 3 and Evidence 23, Q 200 (2 July 2007).

33 Appendix 10, Memorandum submitted by HM Treasury, *Guide to the Establishment and Operation of Trading Funds*, 7th Report of the Treasury and Civil Service Committee, The Next Steps Initiative; HC 496 (1990–91), p.123.

advance approval by Parliament of income and expenditure. Such a fund may borrow and create reserves, thus maintaining a higher degree of flexibility than voted expenditure which may have difficulty meeting unexpected demands.

11-048 Agencies set up under the trading fund arrangements fall under the detailed requirements of the Government Trading Act 1990, which amends the Government Trading Funds Act 1973. The 1990 Act broadened the statutory criteria for setting up such funds. This necessitates removal from the normal parliamentary supply controls of the fund's expenditure and receipts. Before setting up such a fund parliamentary approval by affirmative Order is required, setting overall limits on borrowing.

11-049 The statutory tests are as follows. First, operations to be financed by a trading fund must already be carried out by a government department. Secondly, revenues of the fund must primarily consist of receipts "in respect of goods or services provided". This means that funds arise from payment for goods, services rendered and not through block grants or taxation. Finally, the funds must be established in the interests of "improved management, efficiency and effectiveness".

11-050 The enabling powers under both the 1973 and 1990 Acts are supplemented under s.2 of the 1973 Act, which provides administrative suitability for each fund to be worked out with the Treasury and the sponsoring government department responsible. Trading funds are therefore more likely to provide greater flexibility for agencies than voted accounts.

11-051 Accountability is driven through both the internal structures and accounting practices of each Agency as well as external information to parliamentary select committees and published reports. The Assets Recovery Agency is an example of an Agency with a well-considered purpose, but still finding difficulty coping with the growing nature of the problem, it is tasked to address.[34] The Agency was set up to extract the proceeds of criminal activities from the criminals responsible. Set up in 2003, the Agency closed in 2007 amidst problems of justifying the money spent on the Agency and the sums recovered. The Proceeds of Crime Act 2002 established the Agency with various powers of confiscation. The aims of the Agency included financial investigations and theft or money laundering. The other aims included disrupting organised criminal networks. Setting up the new Agency was undertaken with some speed which left inadequate time to prepare for the tasks allocated to the Agency. The Home Office, the department responsible, had not prepared a business plan, leaving the management of the Agency without a clear agenda. The tasks allocated to the Agency proved demanding and difficult. Cases took longer than expected to resolve and criminals often used legal strategies to challenge the work of asset recovery. The National Audit Office found that the Agency had failed to meet its targets prior to becoming self-financing.[35] In January 2007, the Government announced that the Agency was being merged within the Serious Organised Crime Agency. Many reasons can be advanced for the problems with the Agency. Certainly insufficient time was spent in setting up the Agency, and it was abolished too quickly. A pilot study would have revealed many of the problems and the time-scale needed for evaluation of success. The

---

34 House of Commons Public Accounts Committee, Assets Recovery Agency, HC 391 (2006–07); also the Cabinet Office Performance and Innovation Unit, *Recovering the Proceeds of* Crime (23 February 2003).
35 National Audit Office, Assets Recovery Agency HC 253 (2006–07) (21 February 2007).

Agency was improving with the experience it had developed from its early case load. Policy making might also have been improved in terms of setting practical targets and the passing of the legislation had not been accompanied by a rigorous analysis of what was required.

F: Civil Servants and Ministers

The Armstrong Memorandum in 1985 asserted that the duty of the individual civil servant is "first and foremost" to the Minister of the Crown.[36] The Civil Service Code (1996) was further revised in 1999 and takes account of the Official Secrets Act 1989, the role of civil service in their relationship with ministers and in giving evidence before select committees. The Code contains the requirement that civil servants should not deceive or knowingly mislead Parliament or the public. This has given rise to questions concerning the procedures to be adopted in the event of a dispute between a civil servant and a minister. While the legal position is clear that civil servants do not owe any direct duty to Parliament but absolute loyalty to ministers, there is concern that the public interest does not always coincide with the law. In effect civil servants may find that they are covering up for ministerial mistakes or bad policy decisions. This raises questions about the role of Parliament in its holding of civil servants to account. No satisfactory solution to this question appears given the convention of ministerial responsibility.

11–052

Further reforms have followed. The Constitutional Reform and Governance Act 2010 provides a statutory basis for the civil service, replacing past convention and practice. Civil servants are appointed on merit in fair and open competition, with the exception of certain appointments such as special advisers and short term appointments. The Civil Service Code (revised in October 2015) is a valuable document emanating from the Constitutional Reform and Governance Act 2010. The Code makes explicit the nature of the contract between the civil servant and employer. Civil servants are expected to carry out their role "diligently and with dedication and a commitment to the Civil Service". The core values of the civil service are "integrity, honesty, objectivity and impartiality". There are assorted obligations such as carrying out their duties with truthfulness and openness. Policy making is expected to be "evidenced based and assessed solely on the merits of the case". Civil servants are expected to serve the Government of differing political persuasions and to do so impartially.

11–053

The Civil Service Code provides a procedure for civil servants to raise any grievance or concerns if they are being asked to act in a way that is contradictory of the Code or inconsistent with the principles of the civil service. There is a Civil Service Commission to oversee the Code and ensure that any unlawful activities are reported to the police or the authorities. Political objectivity is a key underlining principle of the civil service.

11–054

---

36   Sir Robert Armstrong, *The Duties and Responsibilities of Civil Servants in Relation to Ministers: Note by the Head of the Home Civil Service*, HC Official Report, Vol.74 (1985).

11-055 The Civil Service Code provides rules governing the financial interest of civil servants. These rules are enforced by the Prime Minister and are there to ensure that civil servants are not able to profit improperly from their public position. The disclosure of interests include shareholding, directorships that might be incompatible with their official status. There are strict rules about dealing with any departmental related activities involving a civil servant having financial gain or advantage. There are strict rules about receiving gifts or hospitality. Breach of the Code can result in contractual implications as well as criminal prosecution. The Bribery Act 2010 also applies to civil servants and provides from criminal sanctions in appropriate cases of financial misconduct. The propensity for public services to become contracted out to private sector businesses led to the Business Appointment Rules (revised in 2011) relating to companies or commercial organisations when bidding with civil servants and government departments in any commercial activities. There is an independent body, the Advisory Committee on Business Appointments appointed by the Prime Minister to oversee this important area of interaction between private organisations and civil servants.

11-056 Civil servants are strictly prohibited from standing for election to the House of Commons. Linked to this prohibition, there are rather vague but nevertheless important restrictions on the political activities of civil servants. The Civil Service Management Code suggests that such restrictions are based on the kind of political activities and also the grade and seniority of the civil servant. The senior civil service are unable to participate in national political activities and are barred from expressing views in public on matters of national political controversy. There are arrangements for less senior civil servants to take leave and engage in national politics but such leave may be refused where civil servants are employed in sensitive areas or where the questions over impartiality of civil servants may arise. Sensitive posts are those related to providing close advice to ministers or where there are sensitive policy issues at stake. At the lowest level of grades within the civil service such as industrial and non-office grades then there is freedom to engage in all political activities at national and local levels. However, they are expected not to wear uniforms or act when on duty in political activities. The Civil Service Code provides important procedures and regulations.

G: Formulating Systems of Accountability

11-057 The Treasury and Civil Service Select Committee[37] has received detailed evidence on the question of accountability of Next Steps agencies chief executives. One view was that the Chief Executive for an agency might have some form of parallel responsibility to that of the minister and thus fit into a separate category of direct accountability to Parliament from the minister.

---

37 Minutes of Evidence taken before the Treasury and Civil Service Select Committee, HC 27 (1993–94) (23 November 1993).

This view was rejected as inconsistent with the doctrine of ministerial accountability. The example of Derek Lewis, the former Director-General of the Prison Service, who resigned following the Report by Sir John Learmont inquiring into prison escapes from Parkhurst.[38] The then Home Secretary Michael Howard refused to resign, drawing on the distinction between operational and policy matters. He claimed that as the Home Secretary was responsible for policy and no policy had been found to be at fault, he was entitled to rely on this fact and not resign. The Lewis case shows how difficult it would be to "force" agency chief executives to hold ministers to account. In the case of the Next Steps agency there is greater transparency between administrators and policy-makers, and ministers and chief executives. The relationship between ministers and chief executives is contained in the framework documents subject to review every three years. The "quasi-contractual nature" of that relationship may give rise to questions of adequate decision-making and accountability for any policy or management mistakes giving rise to claims in negligence.

11-058 One of the most difficult areas is civil servants contact with lobbyists. Lobbyists are a fact of business and political life. They are also an important avenue for democracy to flourish in terms of bringing to attention the views of interest groups and businesses. Inevitably as the public private divide becomes more blurred, there may be contact between civil servants and lobbyists that is hard to regulate. Before 1998 there was little regulation of lobbying. The Nolan Committee promulgated standards of public life and how to ensure honesty and probity. The Civil Service Code supports this approach and the Committee on Standards in Public Life oversees the standards on which Parliament and ministers should behave when lobbied. The Bribery Act 2010 provides criminal sanctions for illegal payments, gifts or hospitality. Meetings between civil servants and lobbyists are regularly recorded and records kept and there is a strong case for such records to be made public.[39] Civil servants have to act in an even handed way and meetings between different lobbyists need to be fairly conducted. Meeting one side in favour of a particular policy would also mean meeting the opposing point of view.

11-059 The relationship between ministers and civil servants is often overshadowed by the appointment of special advisers. This is a category of adviser that are temporary civil servants employed to assist ministers in a wide range of matters that would not be appropriately addressed by permanent civil servants. Advice from special advisers is usually characterised as more politically focused than would be expected from civil servants. Special advisers are bound by the Civil Service Code but excluding sections 1 and 5 relating to impartiality and objectivity.[40] The Ministerial Code 2015 limits the number of special advisers to two for each minister. In 2014 there were a total of 103 special advisers.[41] The amount of public money in payment for special advisers in 2013–14 is £8.4 million.

---

38 *Hansard*, HC Vol.264, cols.502–506 (18 November 1995).
39 HC 36 (2008–09).
40 See House of Commons Library Briefing Paper, *Special Advisers*, No.03813 (2 November 2015).
41 Committee on Standards in Public life, Defining the Boundaries within the Executive: *Ministers, Special Advisers and the Permanent Civil Service* (8 April 2003), p.50.

11-060 The 2010–15 Parliament highlighted some examples of special advisers becoming involved in high profile incidents. The former editor of the *News of the World* resigned in January 2011 as an adviser to the Prime Minister following allegations about his former role as editor. In 2011 attention focused on Mr Werrity, a friend of the Defence Secretary, Mr Fox, who described himself as an adviser to Dr Fox and gave the impression that he spoke for the UK government. After an investigation by the Cabinet Secretary, Mr Fox resigned on 14 October 2011.[42] In June 2012, Adam Smith resigned as special adviser to the Culture Secretary after it was revealed to the Leveson Inquiry that Mr Smith had exchanged 500 emails, text messages and phone conversations with *News International* during the period that Mr Hunt was considering News Corporation's bid for control of BskyB. In 2014, Fiona Cunningham resigned as special adviser to the Home Secretary after it was revealed that she had been the source of negative briefing to *The Times* regarding the Education Secretary. There had been an ongoing dispute between the two ministers.

11-061 There are several documents applicable to special advisers[43] and on 15 October 2015, a revised *Code of Conduct for Special Advisers* was published. Special advisers are expected to serve the government as a whole, and the Prime Minister and not just the government minister. There are changes that separate the political life of the special adviser with the role of advising ministers. In any parliamentary election, where the special adviser is standing, the role of the special adviser should be identified. The 2015 Code includes the role that special advisers may convey to officials (civil servants) the instructions views and priorities of the minister as well as any priorities set by ministers, more generally. There is always the potential for conflict between civil servants, special advisers and ministers.[44] This is inevitable when policy making is informed by political debate as well as evidenced based policy.

11-062 The growth and importance in special advisers is probably an inevitable consequence of the complexity of modern government. It may be seen as a preferable development to the outright appointment of the civil service by ministers, that would change the nature of the civil service.

H: BSE—a Case Study of Crisis Management, Policy Making and Problem Solving

11-063 The relationship between civil servants, advisers and ministers often comes under detailed scrutiny during a period of crisis. Invariably, complex and technical issues surround policy

---

42 *BBC News*, 14 October 2011.
43 Cabinet Office, *The Code of Conduct for Special Advisers* (October 2015); Cabinet Office, *The Model Contract for Special Advisers* (October 2015); Cabinet Office, *The Civil Service Code* (November 2010); Cabinet Office, *The Ministerial Code* (October 2015); and the Civil Service Order in Council 1995.
44 Bernard Jenkin, *Civil Service World* (22 October 2015).

making and decision taking. Two examples serve to show the problems of tackling policy under intense political controversy and media attention. The first is the foot and mouth epidemic and the second is the bovine spongiform encephalopathy (BSE) crisis. The first example showed how managing a crisis in the absence of an up-to-date emergency plan tests resources to their limits with the result that panic and confusion took over and policy was not proactive but reactive. Decisions when to order a cull of cattle and make use of the Army were taken often too late and with poor direction. In the second case, the BSE crisis in Britain over the past decade highlights the important link between scientific research, regulation and government decision-making. It serves to illustrate the dilemma faced when regulatory decisions to protect the environment, agriculture and human health must be based on uncertain scientific knowledge. It also starkly demonstrates the economic cost and the possible human cost of regulatory inaction owing to scientific uncertainty.

In 1999 the roles of the main institutional actors in the crisis, including the Ministry of Agriculture, Fisheries and Food (MAFF), the scientific community, government research scientists and ministers were the subject of an independent inquiry chaired by Lord Phillips, a senior judge.[45] The remit for the Inquiry was to establish and review the history of the BSE epidemic (a prion disease of cattle) and variant Creutzfeldt-Jakob Disease (vCJD, the human form of the disease). The Inquiry was also to establish what action had been taken in response to the BSE epidemic and present recommendations for the future. A number of key findings were made by the Inquiry that raised questions over both the scientific advice and the role of decision-makers in developing a suitable regulatory regime in response to BSE. The aim of the Inquiry was not to apportion fault but to understand the nature of advice given and the lessons to be learnt.

The Phillips Inquiry found that BSE was not caused by scrapie in sheep, but was probably the result of a chance appearance of a new spongiform encephalopathy in a single animal during the 1970s. The original hypothesis made by a senior government vet, that BSE was the result of cattle being fed scrapie-infected meat and bone meal, was based on the best available information at the time. It was not, however, subsequently questioned by scientists even though there was increasing evidence that this may not be the case. The assessment that BSE was very unlikely to jump the species barrier and cause disease in humans was largely based on this assumption. The Phillips Inquiry's assessment of scientific evidence found that an exceptionally small dose of infective material, potentially as little as a gram, is needed for the transmission of BSE between animals. Evidence for this was found relatively early in the BSE epidemic but was largely overlooked by scientists, even though it had large implications in terms of the potential for transmission and the epidemiology of BSE.

Phillips also found that senior government scientists including the Chief Medical Officer continued to inform the public that BSE could not pass the species barrier and was not transmissible to humans as late in the epidemic as 1990. This was despite growing evidence and concern that this may not be the case and came after the discovery of an infected cat. It was

---

45 *The BSE Inquiry. The Inquiry into BSE and variant CJD in the United Kingdom* (London: HMSO, 1999). Archived at http://webarchive.nationalarchives.gov.uk/20060715141954/bseinquiry.gov.uk/ [Accessed 11 April 2016].

never indicated that reassurances that beef was safe to eat were based on the fact that the most infective material was removed from the meat carcasses.

11-067   The Southwood Report[46] was the subject of criticism in arriving at conclusions that were claimed to be unfounded and unwarranted. A further criticism of the Southwood Report is that information was considered to be, on occasions, poorly communicated in the Report. In particular, the statement that:

> "From the present evidence, it is likely that cattle will prove a 'dead-end host' for the disease agent and most unlikely that BSE will have any implications for human health. Nevertheless, if our assessment of these likelihoods are incorrect, the implications would be extremely serious."

11-068   The Phillips Inquiry also made a number of findings that went to the nature of the response by the MAFF and Government ministers to the BSE crisis. Firstly, there was an atmosphere of secrecy and a lack of openness on the part of Government departments. This affected not only the information available to the public but the ability of government departments to work together. Indeed, in general throughout the crisis, Government departments failed to communicate and work together. The BSE epidemic and the potential spread of a spongiform encephalopathy to humans were problems that fell within the remit of several departments including the Department of Health, MAFF and, once large scale slaughter and disposal of carcasses began, the Department of Environment, Transport and the Regions. A lack of co-operation between departments reduced the speed and effectiveness of the Government's response to the BSE epidemic. For example, although by late 1987 MAFF officials were concerned about the prospect of meat from diseased cattle entering the human food chain, they did not pass on their concerns to the Department of Health. Similarly, the Department of Health was not informed as to MAFF's concerns about the incorporation of cattle products in medicines. It is noteworthy that the lesson of communication and co-operation between departments appears still not to be learnt. In the recent foot and mouth epidemic MAFF did not initially discuss with the Environment Agency the environmental risks associated with mass incineration or burial of animal carcasses; nor have all the mass burial sites used by MAFF for disposal of carcasses been authorised, as required by the 1998 groundwater regulations, by the Environment Agency.[47]

11-069   The Phillips Inquiry also found that there were excessive delays in Government departments acting on clear scientific advice. For example, nearly three years elapsed between the Spongiform Encephalopathy Advisory Committee (SEAC)[48] advising that schools should be warned of the risks associated with dissecting bovine eyeballs and schools actually being warned.

---

46   Department of Health, *Report of the Working Party on BSE* (The Southwood Report) (London: Department of Health, 1989).
47   See "Confusion reigns over foot and mouth burial sites" in *The Ends Report*, No.320, p.9.
48   The SEAC was established in 1990 as a standing committee reporting to MAFF and the Department of Health on spongiform encephalopathy.

11-070 The Phillips Inquiry found that research indicating that BSE was a new disease was withheld by MAFF. For example, the Chief Veterinary Officer refused permission for research work undertaken on BSE to be submitted to a scientific journal. Such non-submission could, of course, be for a number of reasons, e.g. a poorly prepared article or poor data, but given the serious nature of the BSE epidemic it would seem essential to address any such faults speedily and release material for publication. Withholding research information had a number of consequences. First there was a lack of accurate information in the public domain; and second the dissemination of scientific information to the broader scientific community was inhibited. Any impediment to the communication of scientific data to as wide a scientific community as possible would inevitably slow understanding of the risks posed by BSE.

11-071 It was found that measures to halt the spread of BSE and limit any potential transmission to humans were inadequate and misconceived. In part this probably arose because of the nature of BSE and the large uncertainties with regard to the risks posed to humans by the disease. The Inquiry Report puts this dilemma in the following terms: "At the heart of the BSE story lie questions of how to handle hazard—a known hazard to cattle and an unknown hazard to humans".

11-072 Finally, the Phillip's Inquiry found that the public was generally insufficiently informed about BSE and any risks to humans associated with the disease in cows. There was a marked lack of openness and transparency in the availability of information to the public. In the early stages this may have arisen to avoid perhaps unwarranted public concern affecting both home and export markets for an economically important industry. It may have become perpetuated by the uncertainties remaining unresolved, while balanced against a large and highly evident economic cost of full disclosure of information.[49]

11-073 The BSE crisis highlights some of the challenges facing modern government. A previously unseen risk that has unpredictable consequences and outcomes challenged the decision-making functions of both ministers and civil servants. Ministers, while relying on expert specialist advice, appeared to delegate the key decisions to experts, without recognising that the public interest required sound political and economic judgements to be made—most importantly to inform the public of the full facts. Failure to engage in an open debate about risk left the public losing confidence in ministers and in the process of government. Parliament also appears to have been left on the side-lines while centre stage was given to media attention and hype.

I: Beyond New Public Management and the Future

11-074 As Gavin Drewry has pointed out:

---

49 I am grateful to Sharron McEldowney for the details of the above case study.

> "Public administration has been displaced—at least in part—by a 'new public management' (NPM) which rejects bureaucratic methods and structures in favour of market-based and business-like regimes of public service."[50]

11-075 This may be regarded as a global phenomenon or, as Hughes[51] refers to it, "a new global paradigm". This new paradigm for public management sharply contrasts with the early foundations of the modern civil service. The Northcote-Trevelyan Report and reforms of 1853 set the standard for the service to be built on public trust and stewardship of public funds. Replacing the earlier form, based on patronage and appointment on favour, the new civil service after the Northcote-Trevelyan reforms was characterised by political neutrality, appointment on merit, and permanence, and was generally admired and respected. The establishment in 1969 of the Civil Service College and an internal code of discipline further enhanced its reputation. Rarely was the criminal law required, except in the case of some well-publicised breaches of the Official Secrets Act 1911, 1920–1939 later amended in 1989. The Freedom of Information Act 2000, has the potential to provide more open government.

11-076 Changes have also introduced in the management of the civil service. As mentioned above the Next Steps initiative provided a change in structure and organisation. The unitary structure of the past was replaced by the use of agencies—an idea that appears to have been considered many years previously, in the Fulton Report[52] of 1968. However, it was not until 1979 that a substantial reconsideration of the organisation of the civil service was undertaken.

11-077 At the heart of the organisational reforms is the separation between the policy functions of the civil service (undertaken by about 20,000 civil servants working in close collaboration with ministers) and the delivery of services. The latter is undertaken by agencies that operate at arm's length from government or the policy making side of the civil service. The distinction between policy making, for which ministers are in theory accountable to Parliament, and operational decisions, which are undertaken by civil servants in agencies and for which ministers appear not to be directly accountable, was ironically in vogue when the nationalised industries were in public ownership. The distinction, such as it is, forms one of the main boundaries between those situations that call for ministerial resignation and those in which the fault is seen as lying with civil servants. An example is the distinction between the role of the Home Office and of the police. The former sets guidelines, while the latter is free to interpret and implement guidelines depending on operational needs.

11-078 Executive Agencies have proliferated. Gavin Drewry estimates:

> "By 1st April 1997 there were 110 agencies in the Home Civil Service, plus Customs and Excise, Inland Revenue, the Crown Prosecution

---

50 Gavin Drewry, "The New Public Management" in J. Jowell and D. Oliver (eds), *The Changing Constitution*, 4th edn (Oxford: Oxford University Press, 2004), pp.168–189.
51 O. Hughes, *Public Management and Administration*, 2nd edn (London: Macmillan, 1998), quoted in Drewry.
52 Fulton Report, *The Civil Service*, Cmnd.3638 (1968).

> Service, and the Serious Fraud Office, operating on next steps lines: these bodies covered nearly 77 per cent of the civil service—364,163 permanent staff."[53]

11-079 The latest figures for 2013, indicate that there are 175 agencies covering a wide range of government departments and activities.[54]

11-080 Each executive agency is headed by a Chief Executive whose role is equivalent to that of the head of a medium-sized company, with performance targets for the delivery of their services and budget responsibility in many cases as trading funds. The transformation of the civil service into agencies has had profound implications for the culture of the civil service and the system of accountability and control. Civil service culture fits under the traditional—and some would argue, malleable—concept of ministerial responsibility, while accountability and control fall under the scrutiny of the National Audit Office and the various select committees of the House of Commons.

11-081 The future direction for public services was outlined in the March 1999 White Paper of the Blair Government, *Modernising Government*.[55] The aim is for government to fulfil a more strategic role, to be more forward-thinking and to make the users of public services the focus of strategy and reforms. Instruments to ensure the implementation of this strategy include: the development of best practice; the use of close targets and monitoring; the adoption of best value on an economic and financial evaluation, across all aspects of public service; and the integration of stronger business principles into the working of government.

11-082 The original NPM idea was that the state was to become the purchaser of public services maintaining a monitoring and supervisory role. This is moving into various forms of contracting out including even the purchasing of services. Contracting procurement services sets a new level for NPM that leaves the government with a further reduction in the role of government-government "steers" but does not "row". This has further implications for the future of government oversight as well as parliamentary systems of accountability. The original concept of NPM was that government might engage in specialist areas outside the mainstream of civil service "know how". However, the use of small specialist units contracted for particular areas of expertise may create a silo mentality that is counter productive of good administration and becomes difficult to hold to account. There is also a question of pooling resources and this may also be used to save money but it might also fail to become sufficiently accountable.

11-083 As A. C. L Davies[56] has pointed out one of the largest use of NPM techniques is in the creation of an internal market in the National Health Service. Originally involving Primary Care

---

53 Gavin Drewry, "The New Public Management" in J. Jowell and D. Oliver (eds), *The Changing Constitution*, 4th edn (Oxford: Oxford University Press, 2004), p.177.
54 Cabinet Office, *Public Bodies 2013* (19 December 2013), https://www.gov.uk/government/publications/public-bodies-2013 [Accessed 11 April 2016].
55 *Modernising Government*, Cm.4310 (1999).
56 A. C. L Davies, "Beyond New Public Management: Problems of Accountability in the Modern Administrative

Trusts (PCTs) engaging management consultants, under the Health and Social Care Act 2012, PCTs have been abolished and since 2013, the purchasing role has been subsumed by the Clinical Commissioning Groups (CCGs), largely in the hands of General Practitioners (GPs). GPs were chosen because of their close proximity to patients and knowledge of the patients' needs. Commissioning is not within their general area of competence and this has necessitated, in many cases, employing expertise from the private sector. It will be hard to recognise what part of the CCG's statutory responsibilities are being performed by the system of management instituted under the new arrangements and how much by the CCGs. While CCGs retain overall statutory responsibility, the lines of control and accountability are complex and difficult to interrogate.

11-084 The form of NPM that involves commissioning and procurement marks a new stage in the development of managing public services. There are similar issues at stake in the role of local government and the creation of new powers under the Localism Act 2011.

11-085 Equally important, is a public perception of increasing prime ministerial power, and concern about an increasingly presidential style, at a time when devolution to the regions and the fragmentation of the party system is at its keenest. This increase in prime ministerial power has not been matched by a commensurate change in the scrutiny functions of Parliament. In fact, the converse appears to be the case. Parliament and its structures appear weakened, and parliamentary accountability appears diminished in value. As already noted, at the same time that there appears to be a diminution in parliamentary accountability there is an increase in the powers of the courts, not least through the development of judicial review, the Human Rights Act 1998, and the Equality Act 2010. Leaving the EU, is likely to have a major impact on the management of government and the arrangements for the protection of individual liberty.

J: Summary and Conclusions

11-086 The Civil service continues to undergo change as it reflects the social and economic circumstances of the society. Managerialism and a more business-focused outlook are distinguishing features of the modern civil service. Yet this is often contested and it may not be enduring. A number of important changes brought about by the previous Labour government, were carried on by the Conservative led Coalition from 2010–15. The White Paper *Modernising Government*[57] called for more joined up government; consolidated the ideas of the citizen as a regulator as well as a consumer of goods and services. This is perceived as introducing greater flexibility in working with the private and public sectors to develop "joined up" government. It includes initiatives to avoid "borrowing to spend", in favour of policies of prudent resource allocation,

---

State" in N. Bamforth and P. Leyland (eds), *Accountability in the Contemporary Constitution* (Oxford: Oxford University Press, 2013), pp.333–353 and 341–345.

57 Davies, "Beyond New Public Management: Problems of Accountability in the Modern Administrative State".

low inflation and low unemployment. There is also a remarkable centralisation of the Cabinet Office, with greater use of advisers and others appointed to guide the government in its policy making. Although technically civil servants, the advisers are political appointees and have not been recruited on the basis of an open system of appointment.

In management terms the civil service as a public sector institution is going through a creative time, developing new ideas on public management. However, two *caveats* require consideration. First, public management is not necessarily best described as a business because of the added dimension of accountability. Pressures for accountability need to be accommodated within public sector management techniques. As Metcalfe and Richards point out:

> "Pouring new managerial wine into old accountability bottles may have explosive consequences. Part of the future agenda of public management will be designing accountability systems."

The second caveat is that government itself, by hiving off activities to agencies, remains subject to the question of how best to develop for the future. This may pose the most demanding challenge for the civil service especially as past experience has through administrative change that has been gradual, piecemeal and incremental.

The role of the senior civil servant in advising ministers retains civil service power and influence. Ministers often seek the support of outside advisers to provide political and specialist support in carrying out their policies. It has been argued that identifying civil servants, often named to the public, with particular government policies impairs the political neutrality of civil servants[58]:

> "Individual senior civil servants are already associated with particular government policies. The present government's recent appointments at senior levels of the civil service acknowledge and reflect this political reality by the selection of civil servants committed to the formulation and effective implementation of specific policies consistent with the general framework of government policy. Civil servants have become, in a sense, political advocates, capable of arguing the case for and implementing different sets of policies depending upon the political complexion of the government of the day."

One effect of agencies in the civil service is to allow greater scrutiny to be given to civil service activities as an indirect result of establishing new agencies. In this new environment, civil service secrecy and confidentiality comes increasingly under threat. Annual reports from agencies provide much more information than previously available from within government

---

58 L. Metcalfe and S. Richards, *Improving Public Management* 2nd edn (London: Sage, 1990), p.236.

departments. The business of government and the management of administration are now closely combined with results that are still to be fully determined.

11-091 NPM has an important role in engaging private and public sectors. Government as a purchaser of services may also create access to specialist advice and expertise, largely outside the traditional experience of the civil service. Government can rely on contractual arrangements as well as the traditional forms of parliamentary accountability.

11-092 NPM has developed into a new form allowing procurement and, potentially, purchasing to be contracted out to the private sector. In theory there is a distinction between procurement and purchasing but this is hard to achieve in practice. Contracting out the procurement element is a risk business as it is often claimed that the civil service does not have sufficient expertise—but surely this would also make it difficult to know whether the procurement purchased from the private provider has worked satisfactorily. Accountability systems may not be able to cope with the new form of NPM and certainly may be late in finding any inadequacies. It remains to be seen how effective the new form of NPM will be and to what extent it will become more widespread. The NHS is one of the areas where the new form of NPM has been adopted. The success or failure of the new arrangements are likely to have major consequences for the delivery of public services and the future role of the civil service.

Further Reading

Gavin Drewry, "The New Public Management" in J. Jowell and D. Oliver (eds), *The Changing Constitution*, 6th edn (Oxford: Oxford University Press, 2007), pp.185–205.

A. C. L Davies, "Beyond New Public Management: Problems of Accountability in the Modern Administrative State" in N. Bamforth and P. Leyland, *Accountability in the Contemporary Constitution* (Oxford: Oxford University Press, 2013), pp.333–353.

O. Hughes, *Public Management and Administration*, 3rd edn (London: Macmillan, 2003).

P. Leopold, "Standards of conduct in Public Life" in J. Jowell and D. Oliver (eds), *The Changing Constitution* 7th edn (Oxford: Oxford University Press, 2011).

D. Oliver, "Accountability and the Foundations of British Democracy—The Public Interest and Public Service Principles" in N. Bamforth and P. Leyland, *Accountability in the Contemporary Constitution* (Oxford: Oxford University Press, 2013), pp.289–308.

House of Commons Library, *Public Service Reform*, Standard Note, SN/PC.06011 (11 August 2011).

12

Public Finance

A: Introduction

Prosser's[1] analysis is that the scrutiny and control of public expenditure[2] is one of the most important areas of public law. Austerity budgeting and public spending cuts have to be accommodated within existing institutional arrangements. The processes and procedures are multi-leveled and technically complex. The financial crisis and political influences often dominate the technical rules of financial reporting and control, with significant constitutional ramifications and potential for tensions between party political controls and parliamentary accountability. The unprecedented growth in public spending of the 2000s, the financial crisis[3] and support for the main clearing banks since 2008, aggressive use of quantitative easing that currently stands at over £375 billion (about 14 per cent of annual nominal GDP) all necessitated[4] the Treasury's Spending Review 2010. This involves a planned overall 40 per cent cut across public spending that is set to continue to 2018, when it is hoped the

12–001

---

1   T. Prosser, *The Economic Constitution* (Oxford: Oxford University Press, 2014), p.110.
2   For a more detailed account including the issues raised in this chapter See J. F. McEldowney, "Public Expenditure and the Control of Public Finance" in J. Jowell, D. Oliver and C. O'Cinneide (eds), *The Changing Constitution* (Oxford: Oxford University Press, 2015), pp.350–377.
3   A budget deficit of 11.1 per cent of GDP set tough challenges for effective public expenditure controls. Public sector net borrowing of around £60 billion is set to remain at 7.05 of GDP with a forecasted reduction of borrowing not expected until 2018/19 depending on favourable economic conditions and on a broadly optimistic assessment public sector net debt is projected to be 76 per cent of national income.
4   Michael A. S. Joyce and Marco Spaltro, *Quantitative easing and bank lending: a panel data approach*, Bank of England, Working Paper No.504 (August 2014); Julia Black, *Managing the Financial Crisis—The Constitutional Dimension*, LSE Working Papers (12/2010); and "The Credit Crisis and the Constitution", in D. Oliver, T. Prosser and R. Rawlings (eds), *The Regulatory State: Constitutional Implications* (Oxford: Oxford University Press, 2010); and J. F. McEldowney, "Debt Limits in German Constitutional Law—a UK perspective" in Wolf-Georg Ringe and Peter M Huber (eds), *Legal Challenges in the Global Financial Crisis* (Oxford: Hart, 2014), pp.63–78.

economy will begin to make a surplus. Quantitative easing has continued since, and is a sign of the vulnerability of economic growth and volatility of financial markets.[5] Uncertainties about the UK's continued EU membership and the outcome of further financial powers to devolved administrations are also likely to overshadow the functioning of public expenditure controls for the foreseeable future, and may raise doubts over the reduction of the financial deficit.[6] Overall, in common with many developed economies, the UK has suffered a major decline in GDP per capita as the financial crisis weakened the economy. The post-financial crisis has also thrown up some interesting comparisons. The UK's influential Institute for Fiscal Studies estimated that "by 2011, German GDP per capita was already 2.2 per cent above its pre-crisis peak". In contrast, by 2013, France and the UK had regained less than half their lost output".[7] There is an emerging "economic constitution", a phrase defined by Prosser,[8] that defines values legal, social and theoretical issues associated with democratic politics and the means used to regulate different aspects of the Constitution in the general areas of utility regulation.

12-002 Public finance refers to the government's requirements in relation to raising and spending money. The House of Commons performs the important function of authorising public expenditure and taxation. In the management of the economy, government exercises wide powers through economic policy, and controls through its influence on the economy and the Bank of England. Money supply, interest rates and the economic policy of the government of the day are often linked to the various international financial institutions such as the International Monetary Fund and the World Bank. EU expenditure is also monitored by the European Court of Auditors.

12-003 The purpose of this chapter is to examine the main procedures and institutions used to manage, control and hold to account public expenditure. The main focus is on the UK's central government, although increasing devolution to Scotland will have importance in planning overall expenditure totals as more financial powers of taxation and spending are devolved to Scotland. The starting point is to provide an introductory outline of first, the sources of government revenue and second, the structures for the control and planning of public expenditure.

---

5   John Wanna, Lotte Jensen and Jouke de Vries, *Controlling Public Expenditure* (Northhampton, MA: Edward Elgar, 2003); and Alex Brazier and Vidya Ram, *The Fiscal Maze* (London: Hansard Society, 2006).
6   R. Bacon and C. Hope, *Conundrum: Why Every Government Gets things Wrong—And What we can do about it* (London: Biteback Publishing, 2013).
7   Antoine Bozio, Carl Emmerson, Andreas Peichl and Gemma Tetlow, "European Public Finance and the Great Recession: France, Germany, Ireland, Italy, Spain and the United Kingdom Compared" (2015) *Fiscal Studies* 36(4) 405–430.
8   T. Prosser, *The Economic Constitution* (Oxford: Oxford University Press, 2015).

B: The System of Planning and Financial Control

12-004

The development of a system of financial control has evolved over centuries on an ad hoc basis. The procedures for financial control are complex with numerous changes and additions added as need arises. In recent years the pace of change has quickened and the Treasury provides a number of manuals containing detailed accounts of the main financial rules and procedures for government departments.[9] Part of the reason for such complexity lies in the nature and diversity of the assortment of rules. Many rules are developed as constitutional conventions or customs. Some are to be found in primary legislation. Most are contained in codes and memorandums addressed to the system of internal checks and balances that are intended to ensure that financial probity and propriety is observed. In the absence of express statutory authority, the legality of many of the rules rests on the prerogative powers of the Crown. Filling the gaps in this way has provided a time-honoured contribution to the diversity of the British Constitution. In fact, the area of public finance provides an opportunity to examine regulation that is applied as internal rules and practices within government itself and through external rules and systems of accountability.

12-005

The authoritative source for parliamentary practice is Erskine May's *Treatise on the Law, Privileges, Proceedings and Usage of Parliament* which has undergone revision through a number of editions. Additional rules and codes are to be found through Treasury guidance developed over the years and in *Government Accounting*, a regularly updated guide to the procedures and rules that apply to financial control.

Public revenue

12-006

Government raises taxes in order to finance public spending. Public expenditure[10] is forecast for 2015/16 to be £673 billion. Government revenue is forecast to be £673 billion and the deficit, the difference between what the government receives in revenue and what it spends is £70 billion.[11] The scale of the figures may be difficult to appreciate. In 2013/14 public spending in the UK overall as a whole per head of the population was £8,936 but this is an average that fluctuates and is different in the devolved parts of the UK.[12]

---

9   There are a variety of documents available from the Treasury on the work of the Accounting Officer, including the Cabinet Office *Best Practice Handbook*. See HM Treasury, *Managing Public Money* (October 2015), para.iii.
10 House of Commons Library, *Public Expenditure by country and region*, Briefing Paper No.04033 (19 May 2015) provides a useful breakdown of information.
11 House of Commons Library, *The budget deficit: a short guide*, Briefing Paper No.06167 (13 July 2015). Details of the economy and its performance are to be found in the Institute for Fiscal Studies, *Green Budget* (London: IFS, 2015).
12 England expenditure is £8,678 (three per cent below the national average); Scotland, £10,275 (15 per cent

12-007 Taxation takes many forms and must be authorised by Act of Parliament. An annual Finance Act sets the limits of the amount payable each year. The courts have been vigilant in ensuring that legal authority has been correctly granted. In *Bowles v Bank of England*,[13] Bowles was successful in suing the Bank of England for a declaration that income tax could not be deducted by virtue of a budget resolution alone and until such tax had been imposed by Act of Parliament, he was not required to pay it. The case led to the Provisional Collection of Taxes Act 1968 which gives statutory force for a limited time to resolutions of the House of Commons varying taxation levels and soon to be made part of the Finance Act.[14]

12-008 In 1975, in *Congreve v Home Office*[15] the Court of Appeal held that it was unlawful for the Home Office to make use of its revocation powers under the Wireless Telegraphy Act 1949, to revoke the TV licence to prevent licence holders benefiting from an overlapping licence purchased to avoid an increase in the licence fee. Congreve and about 20,000 other licence holders had purchased a second licence while their existing licence was still valid, in anticipation of an increase in the licence fee. Lord Denning claimed that the Bill of Rights 1689 had been infringed as a levying of money without grant of Parliament. There is some doubt on this interpretation. Congreve had sought avoidance of a tax through the purchase of a second licence, clearly not intended by the Wireless Telegraphy Act. However, the case illustrates how the judges will adapt statutory interpretation to uphold the principle of authorisation.

12-009 In *Woolwich Building Society v Inland Revenue Commissioner (No.2)*,[16] the House of Lords considered the general principle that money paid to a public authority pursuant to an ultra vires demand should be repayable as of right. The case arose out of an Inland Revenue demand for tax from the Woolwich Building Society, which was later declared by the courts to have no lawful basis. It was accepted that the money paid to the Revenue was not paid under any mistake of law on the part of the tax payer; but the Woolwich Building Society had no express statutory right to repayment of the money. The House of Lords held that money pursuant to an ultra vires demand was prima facie repayable as a common law right of the subject. Lord Goff considered how far the principle might[17]

> "... extend to embrace cases in which the tax or other levy has been wrongly exacted by a public authority not because the demand was

---

above the national average); Wales, £9,924 (11 per cent above the national average); and Northern Ireland £10,961 (23 per cent above national average). The national average is defined as the UK average. See House of Commons Library, *Public Expenditure by country and region*, Briefing Paper No.04033 (19 May 2015) provides a useful breakdown of information.

13 [1913] 1 Ch. 57 Ch D. Also see *British Oxygen v Board of Trade* [1971] A.C. 610; [1969] 2 W.L.R. 892 HL; *Burmah Oil v Bank of England* [1980] A.C. 1090; [1979] 3 W.L.R. 722 HL.
14 See House of Commons Library Research Paper, *Budget 2014: Background Briefing*, SNEP, 06828 (14 March 2014) contains details of the 2014 Budget and economic forecasts for the economy.
15 [1976] Q.B. 629; [1976] 2 W.L.R. 291 CA (Civ Div).
16 [1993] A.C. 70; [1992] 3 All E.R. 737 HL.
17 [1992] 3 All E.R. 737 at [764D–764E]. (See also Lord Slynn at [783], for example). See J. Beatson, "Restitution of Taxes, Levies and Other Imposts: Defining the Extent of the Woolwich Principle" [1993] *L.Q.R.* 401.

> ultra vires but for other reasons, for example because the authority has misconstrued a relevant statute or regulation."

Lord Goff's views, although obiter dicta emphasise the vigour with which the courts may review the taxation powers of the revenue. In the *Woolwich* case the payment of tax amounted to almost £57 million with interest and dividends, an illustration of the role of the courts in revenue matters with an indirect effect on expenditure totals. The government has estimated that the total cost of repaying composite rate tax to all building societies which had overpaid amounted to £250 million.[18]

The annual cycle of raising and spending money continues the tradition of established constitutional practice. The government, in the name of the Crown demands money, the Commons grant it and the Lords give assent. Central government has the important long-term role of managing the economy. The government receives direct taxes levied on income or capital and indirect taxes levied on spending. The Inland Revenue under the authority, direction and control of the Treasury, collects direct taxes and Her Majesty's Customs and Excise are responsible for collecting customs duties on goods entering the European Community and most excise duties. They also collect Value Added Tax (VAT). There is an increase in the use of indirect taxation varying from petrol duties to airport taxes. In addition to taxation, the government may borrow money to finance its expenditure. This may be achieved through borrowing from the International Monetary Fund or World Bank. The government may also obtain receipts from the sale of assets. For example, receipts from privatisation sales have netted HM Treasury a sizeable amount of money Roughly £67 billion has been raised from privatisations since 1972–2014.[19]

All public revenue is paid into the Consolidated Fund. In addition, the National Loans Acts 1968–73 and extended by the Government Trading Act 1990, established a National Loans Fund as the central government account for all government borrowing and most domestic lending operations. Loans from the Fund require statutory authority.

The Treasury, planning and financial control

The Treasury[20] is the main department under the Chancellor of the Exchequer responsible for the management of the economy. The 1918 Haldane Report[21] identified a number of functions that describe the modern Treasury. In addition to the management of the economy, the

---

18   Beatson, "Restitution of Taxes, Levies and Other Imposts: Defining the Extent of the Woolwich Principle", p.428. Beatson also notes the effect of the decision in *Pepper v Hart* [1993] Q.B. 278; [1992] 3 W.L.R. 916 CA (Civ Div) on the taxation of benefits in kind which may lead to £30 million in refunds of tax.
19   House of Commons Library, *Privatisation*, Research Paper 14/61 (20 November 2014).
20   An excellent account of the Treasury may be found in Henry Roseveare, *The Treasury* (London: Penguin, 1969); and M. Wright, *Treasury Control of the Civil Service 1854–1974* (Oxford: Clarendon, 1969).
21   Cd.9230 (1918).

Treasury, with the authority of Parliament, imposes and regulates taxation, arranges funds to meet day-to-day demands for public services and manages and controls the national debt. Finally, in the control of public expenditure the Treasury supervises and prepares the supply estimates.

12-014 The Treasury combines the work of a government department with the role of exercising internal financial control over government departments. Control is usually a *priori* because the Treasury prepares, monitors, audits, and authorises under parliamentary authority, the expenditure of money. The rules relating to public finance have a miscellany of sources. The Treasury produces a large loose-leaf guide to *Government Accounting* which is regularly updated with amendments. Conventions, practices and statutory arrangements are noted and described. In addition, and dating back to 1934, with a revision in 1977, there is a *Treasury Handbook: Supply and other Financial Procedures of the House of Commons*. This is a foundation document for the *Government Accounting* manual.

12-015 The development of resource accounting and resource budgeting under the Government Resources and Accounts Act 2000, fully operational since 2003–04, is intended to gauge public expenditure more accurately than previously. Whole Government Accounts include accounts of bodies within central government,[22] trading funds and public corporations including NHS Trusts and Foundation Trusts.

The July 2007 green paper *The Governance of Britain*[23] set the steps to simplify financial reporting to Parliament. The aim was to align the different bases on which financial information was reported to Parliament and ensure continuity between different formats. This builds on the principles laid before Parliament since 1998 in the Treasury's Code for Fiscal Stability, comprising transparency, stability, responsibility, and fairness and efficiency in the formulation of fiscal policy.[24] The Alignment (Clear Line of Sight Project) undertaken by the Treasury engages with the aims of greater transparency. The Fiscal Responsibility Act 2010 strengthened the Code and has been repealed and replaced by the Budget Responsibility and National Audit Act 2011. It created the new Office for Budget Responsibility and also modernised the governance arrangements for the National Audit Office. Under s.1 of the 2011 Act, there is the *Charter for Budget Responsibility* (HM Treasury, 2011). This is a detailed formulation and implementation of fiscal policy and policy for the management of the national debt. Financial control is supported by the document, HM Treasury, *Improving spending control* (April 2012). There is an annual Financial Statement and Budget Report containing the details of the Government's policy. The Coalition Government has adopted two fiscal rules to constrain government spending and borrowing as follows:

- fiscal mandate: the structural current budget must be forecast to be in balance or in surplus at the end of the five-year Parliament; and

---

22 This also includes local authority accounts that are linked to trading funds and central government accounts.
23 Green paper, *The Governance of Britain*, Cm.7170 (July 2007), also see the earlier white paper, *Modernising Government*, Cm.4310 (March 1999).
24 HM Treasury, *Improving Spending Control* (April 2012).

- the supplementary target states that public sector net debt as a share of national income should be falling by a fixed date of 2015/16.

It is also expected that the Treasury should make regular progress reports to Parliament to ensure that the strategy to provide reductions in borrowing and for sound finances in the relevant Economic and Fiscal Strategy Reports and Pre-Budget reports is observed.

12-016

The Act provides Parliament with the power to vote on the government's medium-term fiscal plans including proposed borrowing and debt totals. The Coalition Government formed in 2010 is expected to meet the borrowing expectations in the Act.[25] The Office for Budgetary Responsibility[26] was set up when the Coalition Government took office after the election in May 2010. The Budget Responsibility and National Audit Act 2011 provides that the OBR's role is to make independent budget forecasts for public finances and the economy. It is unclear how far the OBR can rely on departmental and Treasury information while retaining its independence. The nature of any parliamentary scrutiny is also uncertain if the Coalition Government succeeds in its ambition to continue fixed-term five-year Parliaments for the future. This is likely to require organisational changes in the conduct of the business of the House related to the length of the Parliament.[27]

12-017

The Chancellor of the Exchequer presents the annual budget, containing a financial statement and review of taxation levels, to the House of Commons in the spring of each year. For a brief period from 1993–1996, the government adopted a "unified budget" covering both the government's tax plans[28] for the coming year *and* the government's spending plans for the next three years. In July 1997 the Labour government reverted to spring budgets with a Pre-Budget Report announced in the autumn of each year. In May 2010 there was an emergency budget after the Coalition Government took office, accompanied by a detailed breakdown of departmental spending.

12-018

The timetable for the financial year from April to March coincides with the announcements of taxation and spending plans. In addition to the oral Budget statement to the House of Commons the Financial Statement and Budget Report contains an analysis of financial strategy and proposed plans and developments.[29] Treasury control of the purse will be at its most intense with the implementation of the Spending Review 2010 under the system of Whole Government Accounts.

12-019

---

25 House of Commons Library, *Budget 2014: Background Briefing*, Research Paper, SNEP-06828 (14 March 2014).
26 See House of Commons, *Government borrowing, debt and debt interest payments: historical statistics and forecasts*, Standard Note, SN/EP/5745 (23 July 2014). HM Treasury, *Consolidated Budgeting Guidance from 2012–13* (March 2012).
27 House of Commons Library, *The Office for Budget Responsibility*, Research Papers, SN/EP/5657 (24 June 2014).
28 Tax Law Review Committee, *Making Tax Law*, TLRC Discussion Paper No.3 (2003) advocating simplification of the tax system and reviewing parliamentary scrutiny of tax legislation.
29 House of Commons Library, *The Budget and the annual Finance Bill*, Research Paper, SNB13 (5 December 2013). Also See House of Commons Library, *LIBOR, Public Inquiries and FCA disciplinary* powers, Research Paper, SN/BT/6376 (29 July 2014).

12-020 The Treasury[30] was the central department responsible for regulating financial institutions as part of a Tripartite Agreement between the Treasury, the Bank of England, and the Financial Services Authority under the revised Memorandum of Understanding 2002. The Tripartite arrangements ended in April 2013 when the Bank of England received new responsibilities as supervisor of the UK's financial infrastructure under the Financial Services (Banking Reform) Act 2013.[31]

12-021 The Treasury may act as a guide to departments in terms of advice and consultation. In preparing legislation, departments are required to keep the Treasury informed of any proposals for legislation with a financial implication. Consultation is expected at an early stage and the amendments to Bills should be included if they affect the financial arrangements. This represents a major influence over how departments consider spending public money.

12-022 The key official within departments, who exercises considerable responsibilities for public finance, is the Accounting Officer. The Accounting Officer is appointed by the Treasury and their responsibilities are contained in a detailed Memorandum which they each receive on appointment. Accounting Officers are in effect expected to combine their task of ensuring a high standard of financial management in their department with the duty to serve their minister. An Accounting Officer is appointed for every vote account in compliance with s.22 of the Exchequer and Audit Departments Act 1866, and s.4(6) of the Government Trading Funds Act 1973 and the Government Trading Act 1990 provide for the appointment of a Departmental Accounting Officer by the Treasury for Trading Accounts. The Accounting Officer is given responsibility for signing accounts and appearing as the principal witness on behalf of the department before the Committee of Public Accounts (PAC).

The Accounting Officer

12-023 The Accounting Officer has the crucial role of ensuring that Treasury approval is obtained for expenditure and that funds are applied to the extent and for the purposes authorised by Parliament. The internal network of Treasury control over expenditure depends on his exercise of authority. He is a powerful ally to both Government, Treasury and the PAC in controlling expenditure and ensuring propriety. He provides the link between internal control and the external audit carried out by the Comptroller and Auditor General (C & AG) and the Public Accounts Committee, while maintaining his independent status. Each government department has an Accounting Officer[32] appointed by the Treasury under the Government Resources and Accounts Act 2000, and directly responsible to the House of Commons for the authorisation and control of departmental expenditure. If the permanent head of a department is appointed as an Accounting Officer, he is known as the Principal

---

30 The Treasury has considerable powers to freeze assets of individuals under the Crime and Security Act 2001.
31 See Bank of England, Prudential Regulation Authority, *Consultation Paper Strengthening Accountability in banking: a new regulatory framework for individuals*, FCA CACP14/13/PRACP14/14 (July 2014).
32 See the Treasury guidance, *Managing Public Money* (updated annually), Ch.3.

Accounting Officer and in large departments is supported by a Principal Finance Officer and the Principal Establishment Officer. Chief executives of agencies established under the Next Steps initiative may be designated Agency Accounting Officers. Accounting Officers appointed by the Treasury may be assigned to distinct revenue and expenditure arrangements involving public funds. Accounting Officers are obliged to undertake two functions: to ensure that resources in their department deliver departmental objectives 'in the most economic, efficient and effective way' taking account of regularity and propriety; and to ensure that there is adequate internal audit conforming to the *Government Internal Audit Manual* and under the current version of *Managing Public Money*, Ch.3 (a guidance manual for public accounting).[33]

12-024

Ministers may be held to account in matters of public expenditure by the Departmental Accounting Officer[34] answerable to Parliament through various committees of the House of Commons. Specifically, Accounting Officers may be asked to defend the performance of their wider responsibilities for the economy, efficiency, and effectiveness of departmental expenditure before the Public Accounts Committee (PAC).[35] There is a presumption that the Accounting Officer will maintain, even in the face of ministerial resistance, the standards of strict financial propriety and regularity as well as "prudent and economical administration, efficiency and effectiveness". The *Pergau Dam*[36] affair of 1995 showed how Treasury procedures operated when the minister overruled the Permanent Secretary of the Overseas Development Administration acting as Accounting Officer, who had reservations about the economy and efficiency of the grant in aid to Malaysia for the construction of a dam. Guidance for resolving disputes is contained in *Managing Public Money*, as is the "template" for the use of what are termed "Dear Accounting Officer Letters".[37] This is illustrative of a weakness in Treasury procedures that are ultimately answerable to ministers who may, under certain circumstance, override the decision of Accounting Officers. As far as it is known, however, the Pergau Dam case is a rare exception to the normal expectation that reservations expressed by Accounting Officers should be acted upon.

12-025

Reliance on the Treasury to oversee financial controls is gaining in importance. Increases in Treasury statutory powers under the Banking Act 2009, ss.74 and 75, which enabled the Treasury to make regulations relating to the fiscal consequences of any banking stabilization powers, led to expressions of concern by the House of Lords Delegated Powers and Regulatory Reform Committee that the Treasury's powers lacked sufficient parliamentary scrutiny.[38] The

---

33 There are a variety of documents available from the Treasury on the work of the Accounting Officer, including Cabinet Office, *Best Practice Handbook*.
34 See HM Treasury, *Managing Public Money* (October 2007), para.iii,
35 See for example Department for Education, NAO, *Communications with component auditors* (August 2014).
36 *R v Secretary of State for Foreign Affairs Ex p. World Development Movement Ltd* [1995] 1 W.L.R. 386; [1995] 1 All E.R. 611 Div Ct (*Pergau Dam*). See F. White, I. Harden and K. Donnelly, "Audit, Accounting Officers and Accountability: the Pergau Dam Affair" [1994] *Pub L.* 526–34.
37 HM Treasury, *Dear Accounting Officer (DAO) letters* (26 June 2014).
38 House of Lords, *Delegated Powers and Regulatory Reform Committee Session 2008–09*, HL 12 (2009), paras 3–4.

454 PUBLIC FINANCE

12-026 retrospective nature of the powers was also criticised by the House of Lords Constitution Committee.[39] Despite the concerns the Treasury's powers remained in the Banking Act 2009.

Ministers overruled the Accounting Officer on the choice of new trains to replace existing rolling stock on Northern Rail.[40] Funding the charity Keeping Kids Company (formerly Kids Company) by the Cabinet Office and other government departments amounting to over £43 million in government grants was the subject of differences of opinion between senior civil servants and ministers. Ministers overruled senior civil servants. In August 2015, Kids Company closed and filed for insolvency. There are ongoing parliamentary inquiries about the funding arrangements.[41]

12-027 There are important responsibilities to ensure that appropriate advice is tendered to ministers "on all matters of financial propriety and regularity and more broadly as to all considerations of prudent and economical administration, efficiency and effectiveness". Thus where the Accounting Officer is unhappy with a course of action, he is free to draw the attention of the minister to his advice. If overruled then "he should ensure that both his advice and the overruling of it are apparent clearly from the papers".[42] Controversy surrounding the payment of any money by the Treasury may be raised by the PAC, or the C & AG may inquire into accounts.

C: Planning and Controlling Public Expenditure

12-028 The Treasury's annual Public Expenditure Survey (PES) is the central factor in planning and controlling public expenditure. Since 1963, following the Plowden Report[43] which recommended that decisions on public expenditure should be taken "in the light of surveys of public expenditure as a whole over a period of years, and in relation to prospective resources", there has been an annual survey published as the Public Expenditure White Paper. This sets out the aims and objectives of all government spending for the forthcoming three financial years for central government departments and local government. The Public Expenditure White Paper published in the 1980s contained two volumes. Volume I contained an outline of the general spending policies of the Government and merged in 1988–89 in an expanded version of the Autumn Statement. A supplement containing the statistical information of the aggregate of departmental spending is published along with the Autumn Statement in an Autumn

---

39 House of Lords, *Select Committee on the Constitution Banking Bill*, 3rd Report, Session 2008–09, HL 19 (2009), and 11th report, HL 97.
40 *Public Finance* 27 February 2015.
41 NAO, *Investigation: the government's funding of Kids Company*, HC 556, Session 2015–16 (29 October 2015).
42 *Government Accounting Amendment* 4/1992, para.6.1.5.13. Amendment 7/1997 (3/97).
43 Plowden Report, Cmnd.1432 (1961).

Statement Statistical Supplement. Volume II, which had covered individual departments, has been replaced by a series of separate papers published by departments in 1988–89. A further refinement in 1991–92 has been the publication of departmental reports. The Public Expenditure White Paper has now effectively been replaced by the Autumn Statement Statistical Supplement and Departmental Reports.

12-029

The planning of public expenditure sets the agenda between differing departmental demands for money. There is a Comprehensive Spending Review setting out the winners and losers over a three-year period on government planning. Since 1979 the Government developed the objectives of limiting the amount of money supply in the economy and cutting public spending and taxation. Greater efficiencies were required and the Government, as we have already noted in the previous chapter, adopted a wide range of techniques within government departments such as the Rayner Efficiency Studies (1979), the Financial Management Initiative (FMI) (1983) and the Next Steps (1988) to achieve this. Such strategies are designed to reduce cost, improve the economy and efficiency of government, avoid waste and provide greater value for money. Accountancy techniques and business practices have been adopted as principles of government policy replacing the traditional Whitehall model in the organisation and management of government departments.

12-030

Following withdrawal from the Exchange Rate Mechanism in September 1992, the Government's Autumn Statement introduced a number of changes to the system of public expenditure control through the introduction of a New Control Total. This replaces the planning total and differs from it by excluding the main elements of cyclical social security and privatisation proceeds; it includes local authority self-financed expenditure. Cyclical social security expenditure is excluded as recognition of the fact that this element of spending is very difficult to control. Privatisation proceeds are excluded at a time when proceeds have fallen to less than three per cent of the planning total, but they were included in the planning total when proceeds were high and expanding. The inclusion of local government self-financed expenditure reflects the significance of an important area of public finance currently estimated to be £1.4 billion. The intention of the New Control Total is to insulate the planning process from fluctuations in the cycle of economic growth and for the government to have a more accurate assessment of expenditure plans. This, it is hoped, will lend greater stability to the planning process over the long term—a persistent criticism made about the old planning total was that it failed in its objectives of long-term planning.

12-031

The Treasury also performs an important policy function in terms of economic forecasts, the state of the economy and the prospects for inflation, unemployment and growth. Criticism has been made of the accuracy of the Treasury forecasts and the failure to identify in the late 1980s and in the 1990s the increase in credit and housing inflation. The Treasury, possibly because of its dual role as both a government department and as an important constitutional control over government expenditure, is itself more scrutinised than most other departments of government. It retains its power and influence and expertly manages confidential and, from an economic perspective, sensitive information. Since 1997, the sensitive issue of setting interest rates belongs to the newly independent Bank of England described below.

The Bank of England

12-032 The Bank of England, the UK's central Bank, acts as a banker to the government, and with the other major banks is a member of the clearing system. Since 1997[44] the Bank of England has had operational responsibility for the setting of interest rates to meet the government's inflation target. The Bank of England Act 1998 provides a statutory framework for the Bank's role. Under s.4, there is a requirement of annual reports to the Chancellor of the Exchequer, which must be laid before Parliament. There is a Monetary Policy Committee of the Bank that meets on a monthly basis and sets interest rates. This removed interest rates from the political objectives of the government of the day. Membership of the Monetary Policy Committee is subject to confirmation hearings by the Treasury Select Committee who may question the proposed appointee.[45] The Bank of England and Financial Service Bill 2015/16 proposes changes to the procedures of the Committee from eight to six meetings per year and alterations to the publishing arrangements providing information and data.[46] There would be a requirement to publish the minutes of the meetings as soon as is reasonably practical after the meetings are held.

12-033 The Treasury Select Committee holds regular sessions on policy with the Bank of England including regular hearings with the Monetary Policy Committee and the newly created Financial Policy Committee, with statutory responsibility for maintaining financial stability of the UK economy. The Chancellor of the Exchequer provides broad policy parameters for the Bank. The UK's decision not to enter the euro in 1998 is one example[47] of the powerful influence of Gordon Brown when Chancellor under Tony Blair's Premiership.[48] Accountability for the new arrangements is through a report to the Treasury Committee and to the House of Commons. The Bank issues a Quarterly Inflation Report, a Quarterly Bulletin containing research and analysis, and an annual report and account of its activities. The Bank also publishes the Financial Stability Report containing informed debate about financial stability. In extreme economic circumstances the government retains the right to override the Bank, but subject to ratification by the House of Commons.

12-034 The Bank of England's *Framework for Monetary Policy*[49] has twin objectives: to deliver price stability through the government's inflation target; and to support the government's

---

44 *Hansard*, HC, col.508 (20 May 1997).
45 *Hansard*, HC 520 (1999–2000). The Treasury Committee's views are not binding on the Treasury, and only in one instance was the nominee challenged by the committee.
46 House of Lords Library Note, Bank of England and Financial Services Bill (HL) HL Bill 65 of 2015/16 LLN 2015/037 (22 October 2015).
47 R. Ware, *EMU: The Constitutional Implications*, House of Commons Research Paper 98/78 (27 July 1998).
48 For a full account, see A. Rawnsley, *The End of the Party* (London: Viking, 2010), pp.188–97.
49 The accounts held in the Bank of England on the government's behalf are the Consolidated Fund and the National Loans Fund. Also held are the accounts of the Inland Revenue and Customs and Excise (the Revenue Departments), the National Debt Commissioners, and the Paymaster General. There are detailed internal rules for the various financial transactions carried out by central government departments including the use of credit cards, debit cards, and the handling of receipts and payments. The Monetary Policy Committee comprises four external members appointed by the government, the Governor of the Bank of England, two Deputy Governors, and two other senior officials of the Bank. Meetings are attended by a non-voting Treasury representative.

economic policy. The Bank's performance over the past years has been subject to public debate[50] especially since the banking crisis.[51] The setting of interest rates by the Bank and removed from overt political manipulation by the government of the day resulted in economic stability and low inflation prior to the financial crisis from 2008.[52] The UK economy is also scrutinised by external organisations such as the International Monetary Fund (IMF) and the Organisation for Economic Co-operation and Development (OECD),[53] providing the Bank with comparative analysis in making decisions about the UK economy.[54] The Bank's performance is regularly monitored by what was the House of Lords Select Committee on the Monetary Policy Committee of the Bank of England, now the House of Lords Economic Affairs Committee.

The financial crisis led to substantial criticism[55] of the Tripartite arrangements of banking regulation. Banking failures led to the whole or partial nationalization of four major banks and two Building Societies and the injection of capital sums into the banking sector amounting to nearly £117 billion by the end of December 2009. After the formation of the Coalition Government in May 2010 there followed the unexpected abolition of the FSA, and the return of financial regulatory powers to the Bank of England. The transfer of many of the functions of the FSA to the Bank of England has resulted in a new system of financial regulation under the Financial Services Act 2012 comprising the following: the Financial Policy Committee, responsible for macro-prudential regulation and testing the resilience of the financial system of the UK economy; the Prudential Regulation Authority (PRA), an independent subsidiary of the Bank of England responsible for micro-prudential regulation of financial institutions and assessing balance sheet risk and the regulation of around 1700 financial firms,[56] and the Financial Conduct Authority (PCA) responsible for the conduct of business and markets regulation. The latter will supervise firms in the UK providing financial products and services in the

12-035

The decision is frequently made by majority vote: see Bank of England Act 1998, Pt I. See Bank of England, *Framework for Monetary Policy* (21 October 1999).

50 HM Treasury, E. Balls and G. O'Donnell (eds), *Reforming Britain's Economic and Financial Policy: Towards Greater Economic Stability* (2002).

51 John F. McEldowney, "Managing Financial Risk: The Precautionary Principle and Protecting the Public Interest in the UK", in J. R. Labrosse, R. Olivares-Caminal and D. Singh (eds), *Risk and the Banking Crisis* (2011);
J. F. McEldowney, "Defining the Public Interest: Public Law Perspectives on Regulating the Financial Crisis", in J. R. Labrosse, R. Olivares-Caminal and D. Singh (eds), *Financial Crisis Management and Bank Resolution* (New York: Informa Law, 2009), pp.103–32.

52 Members of the Eurozone are subject to the Resolution of the European Council on the Stability and Growth Pact [1997] OJ C236/1.

53 OECD, *OECD Economic Surveys: United Kingdom* (2005). There are also IMF country reports.

54 The Bank has a useful working paper series that provides authoritative analysis of the economy.

55 FSA, *The Turner Review: A regulatory response to the global banking crisis* (March 2009).

56 The Prudential Regulation Authority is required to promote the safety and soundness of firms and also to ensure that policyholders are protected. See House of Commons Library Research Papers, *The Independent Commission on Banking: The Vickers Report*, SN/BT/6171 (30 December 2013). House of Commons Library Research Papers, *Banking executives' remuneration in the UK*, SN/BT/6204 (13 January 2013). HL Paper 27-II (19 June 2013).

UK and to international customers.[57] The new arrangements give a pivotal role to the Bank of England and seek to adopt a preventative stance to avoid and prevent another financial crisis. The Bank of England and Financial Service Bill (HL) 2015–16 is intended to end the subsidiary status of the PRA and brings the PRA into the Bank of England that would exercise regulatory functions under a new Prudential Regulation Committee (PRC). It is hoped that the new arrangements would give the Bank of England clarity in its authority.

12-036 The Bank of England is undergoing a major evaluation of its role and functioning. There is a significant new Bill before Parliament, the Bank of England and Financial Services Bill 2015/16. The aim is to improve the accountability and governance of the Bank of England. This includes amending the membership of the Monetary Policy Committee and also introducing new auditing information sharing requirements upon the Bank giving the Treasury and the National Audit Office greater oversight powers. There are also proposals to introduce new powers and duties requiring the Bank to disclose information to the Treasury regarding the action taken to address failures in banks or other financial institutions.[58]

The Private Finance Initiative

12-037 Private financing[59] for public projects is intended to shift the burden that falls on the public purse onto the private sector.[60] In 2012/13 the public sector spent a total of £230 billion on procurement of goods and services[61] and there is a target of procuring 25 per cent of goods and service from small and medium enterprises. All private financing is under intense review. The principle underlying private finance is that it may lead to better executed projects, provide close co-operation between private and public sectors, avoid government deficits, and bridge the gap between public spending and revenue income. The Private Finance Initiative (PFI) was launched in 1992. There have been a variety of PFI projects in the NHS, roads, prisons, tunnels, light railway systems, major equipment, and office accommodation.[62] PFI

---

57 See House of Commons Library Research Papers, *LIBOR, Public Inquiries and FCA disciplinary powers*, SN/BT/6376 (29 July 2014).

58 House of Lords Library Note, *Bank of England and Financial Services Bill HL Bill 65 of 2015–16*, LLN 2015/037 (22 October 2015).

59 See Economic and Fiscal Strategy Report 1998, *Stability and Investment for the Long-term*, Cm.3978 (June 1998). Until 1989 private capital could be advanced for the public sector only in strict accordance with the Ryrie rules, Treasury enforced restrictions on private sector involvement in public projects. See Memorandum by David Heald, "Private Finance in the UK Public Sector: Escaping from the Dilemmas of the Ryrie Rules", Treasury and Civil Service Select Committee, HC 508-1 (1992–93); M. Freedland, "Public Law and Private Finance—Placing the Private Finance Initiative in a Public Law Frame" [1998] *Pub L.* 288. See *PFI: Strengthening long-term partnerships* (2006).

60 See Grahame Allen, *The Private Finance Initiative (PFI), Research Paper 03/79* (21 October 2003).

61 House of Commons, Public Procurement, Research Paper, SN/EP/6029 (31 January 2014).

62 For details, see *Hansard*, HC, col.998 (12 November 1992); *Private Finance*, Treasury Release 20/93 (17 February 1993); NAO, *PFI Contract for the New Dartford and Gravesham Hospital*, HC 423 (1998–99); NAO, *Examining the Value for Money of Deals under the Private Finance Initiative*, HC 739 (1998–99); NAO, *PFI: The First Four Design,*

developed the twin objectives of encouraging value for money in public sector expenditure and placing the financial risks on the private sector. Arising out of PFI arrangements is the Public Private Partnerships Programme (PPP), introduced by the Labour government in 1997 and intended to encourage rationalization and upgrading of local authority property, to improve value for money, to encourage the use of joint ventures, and to remove unnecessary obstacles to partnership. It is also a means of "off balance sheet" financing, a mechanism to help meet public spending targets. Risk taking is shared with the private sector but usually at a higher cost than traditional procurement. The Treasury is the key regulator in terms of assessing risk and ensuring standards of delivery and that cost-overrun risks are met by the private sector.

PFI has grown in scale since its introduction in 1992 and it is estimated to be nearly 17 per cent of total public sector capital investment.[63] The NAO[64] noted that by 2013–14 there were at least 684 operational PFI projects with a total value of over £151 billion over 20 different sectors (this figure relates to England only as PFI is a devolved matter).[65] This means that the operation of PFI is one of the largest programmes in the world.[66] Assessing the value of PFI projects is controversial.[67] The NAO estimates savings from correctly managed operational PFI contracts of £1.6 billion. This is an aspirational total and while there is evidence of some £1,372 million savings this is a short fall over what is expected. Criticism of PFI is longstanding and the lack of transparency over complex and technical details has added to the controversy surrounding many schemes. Accounting systems within the PFI are also complicated.[68] PFI arrangements provide capital assets to be recorded as off balance sheet accounts for the public sector and it appears that this might be common practice amongst private contractors. A further concern is that parliamentary scrutiny of PFI is *ad hoc*, and too narrowly focused on issues of impropriety. PFI gained a bad reputation over the failure of the London Underground Metronet PPP in June 2007, where large sums of public money were guaranteed. This was a £17 billion modernisation programme for the London Underground to run 30 years that was at the centre of considerable political and management controversy.[69] Large losses accrued as

12-038

Build, Finance and Operate Road Contracts, HC 476 (1997–98); NAO, *PFI Contract to Complete and Operate A74(M) M74 Motorway in Scotland*, HC 356 (1998–99); and NAO, *PFI Contracts for Bridgend and Fazakerley Prisons*, HC 253 (1997–98). See NAO, *Examining the Value for Money of Deals under the Private Finance Initiative*, HC 739 (1998–99).

63 The law relating to public procurement covers EU Treaty Principles including Directives 2011/0438(COD). Public Utilities 2011/0439 (COD), Public Procurement Concessions 2011/0437 (COD).
64 National Audit Office, *Managing the relationship to secure a successful partnership in PFI projects*, HC 375 (2001–02). See *National Audit Office Annual Report 2006*.
65 National Audit Office, *Savings from operational PFI contracts* (23 November 2013)
66 D. McKenzie, *PFI in the UK and PP in Europe* (2009), *Public Private Finance Yearbook* (2008).
67 HM Treasury, *PFI: Strengthening Long-Term Partnerships* (March 2006).
68 There are two systems of accounting relevant to PFI – government financial reporting based on a modified Generally Accepted Accounting Practice in the UK or UKGAAP (since 2009–10 IFRS), and the national accounts (European System of Accounts or ESA and supplemented since 2004 by Eurostat Guidance).
69 See *R (Transport for London) v London Regional Transport*, 30 July 2001, unreported, a failed attempt by the then London Mayor Ken Livingstone to have the contract stopped by the courts.

12-039 weekly cash flow deficits failed to be met because of major shortfalls in revenue. The result was that Metronet went into administration and its business was transferred to two nominee companies of Transport for London[70] under long-term arrangements agreed with the Treasury. Lessons were learnt to the effect that too little regulation and public sector techniques to cap public money sat uneasily with market-led competitive contracts entered into by the main companies.

The case for any PFI is likely to need stricter risk assessment than in the past to avoid failures. Large and complex projects seem ill-suited to PFI arrangements. It may however prove to be necessary to risk continuing PFI strategies in the midst of public spending cuts. A newly created Infrastructure Financing Unit allows the Treasury should monitor each project and take steps to ensure adequate finance. This includes looking at different ways to finance projects. Current estimates are that between £500 million and £1 billion of higher costs are contractually binding within existing PFI projects and are difficult to reduce.[71]

12-040 The attraction of such long-term contracts are that they are resistant to the vagaries of elections or political changes in government and parliamentary oversight is often too late to be effective. The NAO has suggested a more robust form of economic modeling should be used and gathering data by departments on performance of particular contracts has not always been consistent or transparency.[72]

D: Devolution and Funding of the Scottish Parliament, National Assembly for Wales and the Northern Ireland Assembly

12-041 The creation of the Scottish Parliament, National Assembly for Wales, and Northern Ireland Assembly requires consideration of the financial relationship between the UK's financial system of control and the devolved administrations.[73] The general principles are contained in *A Statement of Funding Policy* issued by the Treasury. These are: that responsibility for overall fiscal policy, and in the drawing up of budgets and public expenditure allocation is retained

---

70 The local government body responsible for the management of the transport system in London including the implementation of the transport strategy under a Management Board appointed by the Mayor of London.
71 NAO Report of the Comptroller and Auditor General, *HM Treasury: Financing PFI Projects in the credit crisis and the Treasury's response*, HC 287, Session 2010–11 (27 July 2010), p.12.
72 NAO, *Review of the VFM assessment process for PFI* (October 2013).
73 House of Commons, *Public expenditure by country and region*, Research Paper, SN/EP/4033 (29 July 2014). Also See Alan Trench and Guy Lodge, *IPPR, Devo More and Welfare: Devolving Benefits and Policy for a Stronger Union* (London: Institute for Public Policy Research, 2014).

within the UK's Treasury; that the UK government funding of devolution will normally be determined through departmental spending reviews; and that devolved administrations will make decisions for programs within the overall totals.

The UK Parliament will vote the relevant provision for the devolved administration by means of a grant. At the devolved level additional elements of the budget will come from locally financed expenditure, funds from the European Commission, and borrowing undertaken by local authorities. In the case of Scotland, additional funds may arise from tax raising powers under devolution through the Scottish Variable Rate of Income Tax (though these powers have not as yet been exercised) and also through non-domestic rates. These arrangements have given the Scottish Parliament and committees an opportunity to scrutinise the spending plans and priorities of the Scottish Executive. There is a three-stage process from April to June (Year 1) and September to December (Year 1) and January to February (Year 2). There are some striking innovations such as the Finance Committee that oversees the consultation process within Parliament and an annual evaluation report allowing strategic planning throughout each year of the spending review period. The Executive submits a provisional expenditure plan (an annual evaluation report) and this is considered by the Scottish Parliament, along with a report of the Finance Committee. The Executive prepares a draft budget in September including spending plans for the following financial year. Based on comments made and information received, it is possible for the Finance Committee to make out an alternative budget, but within spending limits set by the Executive. In December, the Finance Committee prepares a report which is debated in plenary session and this allows amendments to be made to the Executive's spending plans. There is an annual Budget and accompanying Bill presented in January by the Executive. This provides parliamentary authority for spending in the coming financial year. Once the Bill is introduced it is given a speedy passage as only members of the Executive are able to move amendments. The advantages of this system are that there is more transparency than is the case with the UK Parliament and an opportunity for fuller debate and reflection on spending plans; and that counter-proposals may be made through the Finance Committee.

12-042

It is clear that in respect of devolution, the UK government retains a number of techniques of overall financial control.[74] These include the right to make adjustments to the budgets to devolved administrations, and the assumption that devolved administrations will carry any additional or unforeseen financial burdens. The UK government retains responsibilities for the receipt and disbursement of funds from the EU.

12-043

It is generally assumed that any changes in the budgets or financial arrangements for devolved administrations funded from the UK's tax revenues or by borrowing will depend on the spending plans of the comparable departments of the UK. The requirement of apparent 'parity' is achieved in general through the Barnett Formula.[75] This is to be considered in

12-044

---

74 Schedule 5 of the Scotland Act 1998 list reserved matters to the UK Parliament to include economic matters such as the currency, financial and monetary policy and Financial Service Regulation. See Iain McLean and Alistair McMillan, "The distribution of public expenditure across UK regions" (2003) 24(1) *Fiscal Studies* 45–71.
75 The Barnett Formula was first adopted in the 1978 PES under Joel Barnett, then Chief Secretary to the Treasury.

the annual Estimates, though the precise mechanism for undertaking this has yet to be fully determined.

12-045 The Barnett Formula determines changes to expenditure within the assigned budgets of the devolved administrations. Under the Formula, Scotland, Wales, and Northern Ireland receive a population-based proportion of changes in planned spending on comparable UK government services in England, England and Wales or Great Britain as appropriate.[76] The formula works on the principle that changes to the planned spending of departments of the UK government are calculated and applied against a comparability percentage and against each country's population as a proportion of the UK's population. The Barnett Formula is under scrutiny and is unlikely to survive changes to the devolution settlements in Wales and Scotland. The Welsh Assembly undertook an Independent Review chaired by an economist Gerald Holtham, and the Holtham Commission has recommended that the formula be replaced.[77] The Silk Commission has taken matters further, recommending that the Barnett Formula should be replaced and that Welsh ministers should have powers and responsibilities for raising 25 per cent of its own budget, including borrowing and income tax raising powers[78] and taken forward in the Wales Bill 2015[79] but subject to a referendum. Northern Ireland is considering its options in the light of decisions about the Barnett Formula in general.[80]

12-046 In the case of Scotland, the Calman Commission[81] has undertaken similar studies arguing for greater transparency in funding arrangements between the UK and Scotland with a needs assessment introduced across the UK as part of the formula. The Scotland Act 2012, will not

---

Scotland's Parliament, Cm.3658; Scotland Act 1998; and *Serving Scotland's Needs: Department of the Secretary of State for Scotland and the Forestry Commission: The Government's Expenditure Plans for 1999–2002*, Cm.4215 (March 1999). *A Voice for Wales*, Cm. 3718; Government of Wales Act 1998; and *The Government's Expenditure Plans 1999–2002*, Departmental Report by the Welsh Office, Cm.4216 (March 1999). Belfast Agreement, 10 April 1998; Northern Ireland Act 1998; and *Northern Ireland Expenditure Plans and Priorities—The Government's Expenditure Plans 1999–2002*, Cm.4217 (March 1999). HM Treasury, *Funding the Scottish Parliament, National Assembly for Wales and Northern Ireland Assembly* (31 March 1999). In Scotland, Northern Ireland and Wales, local authorities may borrow within set limits to fund their capital expenditure. There are some exceptions to the Barnett Formula, as where various categories of expenditure are the sole responsibility of the devolved administration. HM Treasury, *Funding the Scottish Parliament, National Assembly for Wales and Northern Ireland's Assembly* (31 March 1999), para.3.3.

76 See House of Lords, *Select Committee on the Barnett Formula*, 1st Report Session 2008–09, HL 139 (17 July 2009).

77 Calman Commission, *Independent Commission for Funding and Finance for Wales* (2009). Holtham Commission, *Replacing Barnett with a needs-based formula* (June 2009).

78 Commission on Devolution in Wales (Chair Paul Silk), *Empowerment and Responsibility: Financial Powers to Strengthen Wales* (November 2012). See John McEldowney, "The Impact of Devolution on the UK Parliament" in A. Horne, G. Drewry and D. Oliver (eds), *Parliament and the Law* (Oxford: Hart, 2013), pp.197–219.

79 HM Government, *Wales Bill: Financial Empowerment and Accountability*, Cm.8388 (March 2014). House of Lords Library Notes, *Wales Bill (HL Bill 34 of 2014–15)*. The Bill provides a structure for the devolution of stamp duty.

80 Northern Ireland Assembly, *Funding the United Kingdom Devolved Administrations*, Paper 82/10 (20 June 2010).

81 Commission on Scottish Devolution, *Serving Scotland Better: Scotland and the United Kingdom in the 21st Century Final Report* (The Calman Commission) (June 2009).

come into force until 2016 and contains additional revenue powers and also new borrowing powers. The Scottish Parliament may reduce the UK rate of income tax by 10p in every pound and may add additional taxation as it deems necessary.[82] The Scottish Referendum[83] result in September 2014 was in favour of the retention of the Union. There was an understanding given by all three main political parties that substantial devolved powers on taxation, borrowing and on tax receipts would be forthcoming in new legislation[84] to be presented to Parliament before the next election in May 2015.[85] At the same time and unexpectedly the Prime Minister announced that devolution to Wales, Northern Ireland and possibly to the English regions would be considered along with Scotland. It will be remembered that the McKay Commission[86] recommended setting up a constitutional convention to consider the implications of devolution on the UK. On the West Lothian question, the Commission had expressed some sympathy with the underlying principle that decisions that affected one part of the UK should be taken by the consent of the majority of the electorate for that part of the UK but dismissed the idea of an English Parliament for English matters. The position of the UK centralised system of expenditure controls is likely to have to be reconsidered with the potential for substantial devolution of taxation and expenditure powers in the wake of the Scottish referendum. The two new devolution Bills, the draft Wales Bill 2015/16 and the draft Scotland Bill 2015/16, are likely to have implications for adjusting the Barnett Formula and system of block grant.

There is already an Auditor General for Scotland, and his office scrutinises the departments that fall under the Scottish Executive, NHS trusts and health boards, further education colleges, Scottish Water, and various government agencies.[87] There is an Auditor General for Wales with a Wales Audit Office, replacing the Audit Commission and the NAO in Wales since 2005.[88]

---

82 House of Commons Library, *Devolution of tax powers to the Scottish Parliament*, Research Paper, Standard Note 5984 (17 July 2013).
83 House of Commons Library, *Impact on the UK of Scottish independence: social security and tax credits*, Research Papers, SN06957 (7 August 2014).
84 The timetable is a Command Paper by 31 October 2014, a White Paper by 30 November with a consultation process and a draft Bill by 25 January 2015 with second reading by 7 May 2014.
85 House of Commons Library Research Papers, *Scotland: Devolution Proposals*, SN/PC/06987 (23 September 2014). Also see The House of Lords Library, *Referendum on Scottish Independence*, LLN/2014/020 (2014).
86 Mckay Commission: *Report of the Commission on the consequences of devolution for the House of Commons* (March 2013).
87 This amounts to about 200 public accounts. There are: 25 Scottish Executive departments; 23 NHS boards and trusts; 32 councils; 40 police; fire and other bodies; 39 further education colleges; and 37 non-departmental public bodies.
88 In the cases of Scotland and Wales, both Auditor Generals exercise similar functions to their English equivalent (see below). However, unlike England, both Auditor Generals are able to scrutinise local and central government. This encourages an interconnected approach to auditing the public sector. Taken together, accountability falls on the devolved administration, with the UK Treasury operating under the system of financial control.

E: Parliament and the Control of Public Expenditure

12–048 Parliamentary control of expenditure rests on principles and procedures known as the "supply procedure" which may be briefly outlined as follows: The Executive requests Parliament for funds to meet the expenditure by government departments and related bodies. This request comes in the form of supply estimates. Most of the money required to finance the services of government departments is covered by supply estimates.[89] Once the supply estimates are approved by the House of Commons they form the basis of the statutory authority for the appropriation of funds. This allows the Treasury to authorise funds out of the Consolidated Fund Act through the authority of the Appropriation Act. Significantly, in respect of formal supply resolutions approved by the House of Commons there is a formal requirement for legislative authority. Issues of money from the Consolidated Fund are authorised by the Consolidated Fund Act. Authority for the appropriation of money for the various purposes contained in the Estimates is granted in the annual Appropriation Act.

12–049 "Parliamentary control of the purse" is a basic principle of the Constitution that has evolved since before the Bill of Rights 1689.[90] The authority of the Commons over these matters is based on its powers over expenditure and taxation.[91] *Managing Public Money*, the Treasury's Code of expenditure rules, stipulates the protection afforded by the constitutional principle of the requirement of statutory authorisation for the expenditure of public funds and for the raising of finance through taxation. The nature of the protection rests on three principles, namely that propriety and regularity require parliamentary approval for departmental activities and services; that the Treasury may exercise delegated approval for departmental expenditure subject to ultimate parliamentary authority; and finally, that parliamentary authority, while at times dependent on Treasury support for much of its control mechanisms, is nevertheless paramount.

12–050 The requirement of statutory authority instituted by Gladstone in the mid-nineteenth century created a "circle of control" based on an annual cycle of revenue and expenditure. The management of public revenue is carried out by the Crown. Strong party controls over the members of the House of Commons and the general influence of ministers where the government has a majority in the House of Commons reduce the House of Commons' powers of control in practice to the right to criticise.

12–051 The Constitutional Reform and Governance Act 2010, introduced by the previous government, takes forward the Line of Sight (Alignment) Project, instituted since 1997, to bring

---

89 Certain specific activities subject to certain criteria may be financed by a trading fund under the Government Trading Act 1973.
90 Bill of Rights 1689, art.4 requires parliamentary authority for the raising of taxation. See G. Reid, *The Politics of Financial Control* (London: Hutchinson & Co, 1966); M. Wright, Treasury Control of the Civil Service 1854–1974 (Oxford: Clarendon, 1969); and D. W. Limon and W. R. McKay (eds), *Erskine May: Parliamentary Practice*, 22nd edn (London: Butterworths, 1997), p.732 (23rd edn, 2004).
91 See Parliament Acts 1911 and 1949.

transparency to financial reporting to Parliament.[92] The inclusion of the public spending element of non-departmental bodies into financial reporting is an aid to transparency. The enhancement potential for Parliament is dependent on MPs being willing to include public finance in their scrutiny functions.

12-052

The centrality of government rather than backbench control over expenditure decisions is evidenced in Standing Orders of the House of Commons nos 46 and 47, which provide the Crown with the initiative and sole responsibility for expenditure. Private members, including the opposition, are unable to propose increased charges on public funds or initiate legislation involving expenditure out of public funds without a financial resolution. The initiative is with the government as the Commons may not impose conditions on the grants authorised or the resources applied for without the demand by the government.

12-053

An Appropriation Act satisfies the requirement for statutory authority through the supply procedure of the House of Commons on an annual basis by means of the Consolidated Fund Acts and by an Appropriation Act. Revenue collection is largely undertaken through HM Revenue and Customs, and as part of the Budget and Public Finance Directorate of the Treasury.

Supply procedures and the Consolidated Fund

12-054

The supply procedures required to enable the House of Commons to vote supply and provide the government with funds from the Consolidated Fund, are technical and formal.[93] Little substantial scrutiny[94] is involved in such procedures.[95] The policy objectives on which the money is spent are not determined by the Commons but by the government of the day. Policy objectives, however, underline the constitutional authority of Parliament and the internal controls exercised by the Treasury. It must be emphasised that presentation of the main estimates to Parliament does not provide sufficient authority for expenditure. Statutory authority in the Appropriation Act is required. The system is complicated by the fact that in any one parliamentary session Parliament is asked to authorise not only estimates for the current year but also Votes on Account for future years and any excesses from the previous year.

12-055

Supply estimates provide the House of Commons with the information needed to provide the government with funds from the Consolidated Fund. Votes on Account and the

---

92 Since 1997 this is subject to the NAO auditing the forecasts to ensure that Treasury assumptions are made transparent, though the system of making forecasts is not open to such scrutiny. See Fabrizio Balassone and Daniele Franco, "Public investment, the stability Pact and the 'golden rule'" (2000) 21(2) *Fiscal Studies* 207–9.
93 House of Commons Library, *House of Commons Budget Debates and Finance Bills Parliamentary Information List*, Research Paper, SN/PC/02271 (10 July 2014).
94 William MacKay and Charles W. Johnson, *Parliament and Congress* (Oxford: Oxford University Press, 2010), pp.254–61.
95 HM Treasury *Supply Estimates: a guidance manual* London: HM Treasury 2011. The Procedure Committee is currently considering the reform of the Estimates. See Edward Leigh and John Pugh, *Options to Improve Parliamentary Scrutiny of Government Expenditure House of Commons Library*, 2010.

Consolidated Fund Act must be approved by the date of the budget. Estimates of departmental expenditure are drawn up and must be approved by resolutions of the Commons for the necessary release of funds from the Consolidated Fund. The Treasury publishes a single volume entitled *Central Government Main Estimates* containing one estimate for each department. The estimates provide the major part—over 70 per cent—of annual public expenditure. The Treasury persuaded Parliament in 2001 to replace cash-based Appropriation Accounts with Simplified Estimates and Departmental Resource Accounts.[96]

12-056 An annual Appropriation Act, which is normally not subject to any debate, is enacted by July/August each year, authorising the Bank of England to make payments to government from the Consolidated Fund. The Appropriation Act gives statutory authority for the distribution of money between votes, but this often follows the spending of some of the money, which needs only the Consolidated Fund Act (giving a total figure) for approval. The estimates must conform to Treasury format and approval and must not be altered unless Treasury authority has been granted.[97] There are two Appropriation Acts in each parliamentary session, one in March for the previous financial year, the other in July for the current main estimates.[98] The audit carried out by the Comptroller and Auditor General (C & AG) discussed below is focused on the estimates which, when divided into heads of expenditure, appear as "votes".

12-057 Departments work on the supply estimates in the summer or early autumn of each financial year. On or about the time of the budget each year, the estimates are published. If a department's needs exceed the estimates, then a "supplementary" may be passed subject to Treasury and parliamentary approval. The Standing Orders of the Commons provide the government with three opportunities to introduce supplementary estimates, with the benefit of a guillotine procedure ensuring their speedy passage. Supplementaries may be presented in June, in November, and in February. At other times of the year estimates may be submitted but without the benefit of the accelerated "guillotine" procedure. In 2004 the government introduced a change that gives select committees up to 14 days to consider supplementary estimates. The direction of reform has largely been focused on financial scrutiny by select committees, rather than by individual members of Parliament.

12-058 The Treasury takes very seriously the requirement for statutory authority for authorisation of public expenditure which "must be and can only be given year by year by means of votes and the Appropriation Act".[99] A minister, "when exercising functions which may involve the

---

96 HM Treasury, *Central Government Supply Estimates 2002–3 for the year ending 31st March 2003: Main Supply Estimates*, HC 795 (2001–02).
97 See HM Treasury, *Managing Resources—Full Implementation of Resources Accounting and Budgeting* (April 2001).
98 The reform was the result of the work of the Liaison Committee, the PAC, The Treasury Committee, and the Procedure Committee. See Procedure Committee, *Estimates and Appropriation Procedure*, HC 393 (2003–04).
99 Details of the rules relating to supply may be found in *Supply Procedure, Government Accounting* (2000, rev.) The Appropriation Act begins life as the Consolidated Fund (Appropriation) Bill. Estimate day debates may take place in July and at the time of the Appropriation Act; in November–December for the winter supplementary estimates followed by any debates and a Consolidated Fund Act; and in February–March for the spring supplementary estimates, followed by any debates on the Consolidated Fund Act. HM Treasury, *Supply*

expenditure of money may only do what he does if Parliament votes him the money".[100] Since 1982, there have been three specific days to consider the Estimates. The Commons may only reduce the estimates, but even this is unlikely if the government of the day has an overall majority. In modern times the Commons has not rejected an estimate and the scrutiny function appears a limited one.

12-059

Over the years the presentation of the Estimates has become more readable. Today they contain economic information and are cross-referenced to the Departmental Report. Since an agreement in March 1995 between the PAC, the government, and the Treasury Committee to introduce a simplified format of the Estimates with effect from 1996–67, the estimates are published in a single volume divided into three parts and linked to overall government planning. There is a new requirement on departments to produce an Estimate Memorandum to their parliamentary select committee at the same time as Main or Supplementary Estimates are presented. Improvements in the presentation of financial reporting have been in place since 2009. Amendments to the Provisional Collection of Taxes Act 1968, that allow the government to collect taxes, have resulted in a resolution being given the same statutory effect since the Budget report in 2011. This change in procedure is partly as a result of the introduction of Fixed-Term Parliaments in 2011 of five years to allow for the carry-over of business at the end of the session.[101] There are limits to the duration of the resolution of seven months to allow time for the relevant Finance Bill to be given legal effect. The experience in 2012 and 2013 has been subject to criticism[102] as not giving sufficient time for scrutiny especially when Finance Bills are over 600 pages long and only allotted two days for debate and there are delays between stages of the Bill's passage through Parliament.

12-060

The Treasury's annual PES[103] is the central factor in planning and controlling public expenditure. Inside the Treasury the Budget and Public Finances Directorate sets the agenda between different departmental demands for money. The Central Expenditure Policy group referees the bids between spending departments and reports through the Chief Secretary to the Treasury to the Cabinet in July on the likely outcome in expenditure totals. Between the end of the PES round in October and the Autumn Statement in November, winners and losers in the expenditure debate have to be settled. The Code for Fiscal Stability since 1998 (referred to

---

and other Financial Procedure of the House of Commons (1977), paras 47–49, now largely updated by *Supply Procedure, Government Accounting*. The PAC considered in 1932 the question whether the Appropriation Act is sufficient authority for the expenditure, whether there is or is not specific statutory authority for the service concerned. The Treasury accepted that provided the government of the day undertakes to ask Parliament for authorisation, services under the Appropriation Act would come within the PAC Concordat. However, in the first instance, it is preferable to seek specific statutory authority. The Estimates indicate where proposed expenditure is to be met by the Appropriation Act as the sole authority.

100 HM Treasury, *Supply and other Financial Procedure of the House of*, paras 47–49.
101 The Fixed-Term Parliaments Act 2011.
102 Treasury Committee Budget 2013, HC 1063 (2012) (20 April 2013), Treasury Committee *Fourth Special report of Session 2012–13*, HC 1076 (26 March 2013).
103 It is over 40 years since the Plowden Report recommended that decisions on public expenditure should be taken "in the light of surveys of public expenditure as a whole over a period of years, and in relation to prospective resources".

earlier) provided an emphasis on principles of fiscal management such as transparency, stability, responsibility, fairness and efficiency.

12–061
In September 1992, after the UK's withdrawal from the Exchange Rate Mechanism,[104] the government's Autumn Statement introduced changes to the system of public expenditure control through the introduction of a New Control Total. This replaced the planning total and excludes the main elements of cyclical social security expenditure and any privatisation proceeds. It includes local authority self-financed expenditure. Totals for the control of public expenditure include both local and central government expenditure. Refinements have been made, such as, in 1998, the introduction of Total Managed Expenditure (TME) comprising the total of public sector current expenditure and public sector net investment. All expenditure under TME facilitates better management under Treasury scrutiny. In 1998 the introduction of a Comprehensive Spending Review (CSR) allowed departments to take a more radical look at across-the-board expenditure and resist the temptation to see expenditure planning only in terms of an annual review. It also allowed comparison between Departmental Expenditure Limits which set firm three-year spending limits (the limits for departmental spending within the public expenditure total) and Actually Managed Expenditure which covers items which are reviewed and set on an annual basis (the actual expenditure undertaken by the department).

12–062
PES continues to provide a politically expedient outcome which achieves consensus from ministers. PES underlines the Treasury's pre-eminence and the role of the Chief Secretary in the development of ministerial policy. PES supported by the CSR, and the *Code of Fiscal Stability* has the potential to transform the setting of public expenditure totals through greater transparency and openness in the planning process.

The Treasury and departmental controls over public expenditure

12–063
The Bank of England's independence in respect of interest rates marked a shift from prime ministerial influence to direct Treasury control and through the Chancellor of the Exchequer limited oversight through the Chancellor's relationship with the Bank of England's Monetary Policy Committee. This shift is most marked in recent years and is well documented in accounts on the role of the Chancellor of the Exchequer.[105] The various rules that set out apparent controls on the discretion of the Treasury and Chancellor, such as fiscal rules that determine the amount of borrowing relative to the size of the economy, are Treasury-made rules. The

---

104 The Exchange Rate Mechanism was established to prepare the way for the introduction of the single European currency (Euro) and revised in 1999 to take account of the setting up of the Euro.

105 Robert Peston, *Brown's Britain* (London: Short Books, 2004), pp.76–7; and A. Rawnsley, *The End of the Party* (London: Viking, 2010), n.20, p.65. The importance of removing unnecessary burdens is highlighted in the Hampton Review, *Reducing Administrative Burdens* (2005). The perception of increasing Treasury influence is apparent from the reconstruction of the old building into a newly designed set of offices for the 1,050 staff. The offices were designed by Norman Foster and opened in 2002. The Treasury has undoubtedly gained from its newly found self-esteem

Treasury is effectively empowered to self-regulate,[106] and through improvements in the economic instruments to manage the economy.

The pre-eminence afforded to the Treasury through PES is complementary to the overall role of the Treasury in managing and controlling public expenditure. Under the Banking Act 2009, the Treasury may make regulations over the use of stabilization powers for the banking sector.[107] It exercises internal and less visible systems of control as well as external and more visible techniques. Treasury control is much improved through the adoption of a variety of *a priori* techniques. It prepares, monitors, audits, and authorises under parliamentary scrutiny according to set rules and procedures. The relevant conventions, practices, and statutory arrangements are codified in various manuals. The most detailed is *Managing Public Money*. Dating back to 1934, with a revision in 1977, there is also a *Treasury Handbook: Supply and other Financial Procedures of the House of Commons*. The *Code of Fiscal Stability* is important because of its statutory authority and amendments are made through affirmation by the House of Commons. In addition, the Treasury has a *Handbook on Regularity and Propriety*. The *Financial Reporting Manual 2009–10* sets out all the technical accounting and disclosure requirements for the annual report and accounts.

12-064

In preparing legislation, departments are required to keep the Treasury informed of any proposal with a financial implication. Consultation is expected at an early stage and the amendments to Bills should be included if they affect the financial arrangements. This represents a major influence over how departments consider spending public money. Since the late 1990s the Treasury has adopted a more strategic role with reorganisation and regular contact with spending departments through annual spending reviews and targets setting inputs and outputs.

12-065

Treasury control may be exercised within government departments through the Accounting Officer (discussed above) appointed by the Treasury, whose responsibilities are contained in detailed memorandum. Accounting Officers are in effect expected to combine their task of ensuring a high standard of financial management in their departments with their duty to serve their ministers. The Accounting Officer is given responsibility for signing accounts, and ensuring Treasury sanction is obtained for expenditure authorised by Parliament and appearing as the principal witness on behalf of the department before the PAC.

12-066

There is a specialized manual for government Internal Audit. This contains the basic standards for the Treasury's internal audit representing good practice. An internal audit is an independent appraisal within a department as a service to management in measuring and evaluating standards within the department. Through the system of internal audit, the Accounting Officer may be assisted in his task. Internal audit is not however seen as a

12-067

---

106 There is also the quality of the civil service and a list of distinguished outsiders including in the recent past Shriti Vadera from UBS, Nick Stern from the World Bank, and John Kingman from BP. Currently, Edward Leigh MP and John Pugh MP have been asked to advise on accountability mechanisms.
107 See House of Commons, *The Centre of Government—No.10, The Cabinet and HM Treasury,* Research Paper, 05/92 (21 December 2005); C. Thain "Treasury Rules OK? The Further Evolution of a British Institution" (2004) 6(1) *British Journal of Politics and International Relations* 123.

substitute for line management; it is a means to ensure that appraisal within a department is properly carried out. It is usual practice to carry out such appraisal by the appointment of a unit charged with responsibility to the Accounting Officer. As the Accounting Officer is usually the permanent head of the department this "reflects the view that finance and policy cannot be considered separately". Thus good management is the key to his function. He must ensure compliance with parliamentary requirements in the control of public expenditure. In his role he is to avoid waste and extravagance and to seek economy, efficiency, and effectiveness in the use of all the resources made available to the department. However, the Accounting Officer is also expressly concerned with *policy*. He has responsibility to advise ministers on all "matters of financial propriety and regularity", more broadly as to all "considerations of prudent and economical administration, efficiency and effectiveness" and to ensure that departmental expenditure is justified to the PAC. In matters where a minister may disagree, he is free to set out his own advice and the overruling of it by the minister. He is free to point out to ministers the possibility of potential criticism by the PAC of ministerial decisions.[108]

12-068
This in effect was the procedure followed in the *Pergau Dam* affair, discussed above. Procedures exist for an Accounting Officer to notify the C & AG should his advice be overruled.

12-069
The adoption of resource accounting under the Government Resources and Accounts Act 2000 is consistent with a more managerial approach to budgeting to match more closely resources used to meet departmental objectives[109] and the introduction of Whole of Government Accounts consistent within the UK. Generally the Accepted Practice regime[110] is to provide a more complete financial analysis alongside the Alignment ("Clear Line of Sight") Project to ensure effective financial reporting.

F: Resource Accounting

12-070
The 1995 NAO Report[111] usefully defined resource accounting as involving two elements:

- a set of accruals-based techniques for accounting and reporting on the expenditure of UK central government; and

---

108 *Supply Procedure, Government Accounting*, above, n.36, and amendment 4/05, s.4.1.2, para.15.
109 The Government Resources and Accounts Act 2000 amends the Exchequer and Audit Departments Acts 1866 and 1921.
110 D. A. Heald and G. Georgiou, "Consolidation principles and practices for the UK government sector" (2000) 30 *Accounting and Business Research* 153. HM Treasury, *Whole of Government Accounts progress to December 2000*, Memorandum to the Committee of Public Accounts and the Treasury Select Committee (unpublished).
111 NAO Report, *Resource Accounting and Budgeting in Government*, HC 123 (1994–95), para.10.

- a framework for analysing expenditure by departmental objectives, related to outputs wherever possible.

Capital spending is made to account wholly in the year in which the capital purchase or disposal is made. In contrast it is argued that accruals accounting makes up for these deficiencies. The NAO Report summarises the main benefits of accruals accounting over the existing cash accounting system:

- accruals accounting records expenditure and income in the accounting period to which they relate;

- accruals accounting spreads the cost of capital items across their useful lives;

- accruals accounting provides a detailed snapshot of the assets, liabilities and net worth of an organisation at a given moment of time and through a balance sheet provides a better picture of the true cost of departments' activities; and

- accruals accounting is intended to increase information and detailed inventories of departmental holdings, deployment and stewardship of assets.

12-071

Resource accounting based on an accruals accounting system is intended to match more closely the resources used to departmental objectives. The outputs of departmental activities can then be used to measure departmental achievements. It is intended that departments will in future provide a schedule showing the true cost of resources consumed and a schedule measuring output performance against each main objective. Introducing such a system has depended on the adoption of the UK *Generally Accepted Accounting Practice*[112] supplemented by specific requirements developed for departmental accounts. The Government Resources and Accounts Act 2000 sets out the necessary statutory authority for the principles of resources accounting. The Treasury provides useful templates as to how accounts should be prepared and how these might be analysed.

12-072

G: The Contingencies Fund

There is a Contingencies Fund which may be used to finance urgent expenditure. In practical terms it is an example of a lacuna in Commons control over expenditure is the Contingencies

12-073

---

112 This is defined as the accounting standards required of the Companies Act 1985 and the accounting standards set by the Accounting Standards Board.

Fund which may be used to finance urgent expenditure. The Fund is a reserve fund intended to meet unforeseen items of expenditure and where advances that are made are regarded as "exceptional". In technical terms it is used "to meet payments for urgent services in anticipation of parliamentary provisions for those services becoming available". Total advances outstanding from the Fund should not exceed two per cent of the previous year's total estimates provision.[113] Money withdrawn from the Fund must be repaid. The Treasury may authorise payment out of the Fund subject to the limit of two per cent set under the Contingencies Fund Act 1974. The instructions contained in *Managing Public Money* and *Supply Estimates: A Guidance Manual* provide that the criterion is not convenience, but urgency in the public interest. If the amount of money involved, or the potentially contentious nature of the proposal is such as to create difficulty in justifying anticipation of parliamentary approval, it may be necessary to present a Supplementary Estimate, outside the normal timetable, to be followed by a special Consolidated Fund Bill.

12-074 The Contingencies Fund is unusual in that the main scrutiny of the government's use of the Fund largely depends on effective Treasury rather than parliamentary control. Legislation giving authority for the expenditure involved must be introduced at the earliest possible time and ought never to be postponed. Guidance issued in 1992 makes clear that the government of the day must be prepared "to take the responsibility of assuming that legislation being considered by parliament will pass into law".[114]

12-075 The Contingencies Fund has been used for a variety of purposes and recently for the funding of the London Olympics in 2012.[115] Historically, this includes relief of national disasters, the manufacture of the first atomic bomb, victory celebrations, and in time of war for financing urgent supplies. It funded the Pergau Dam project following the decision of the Divisional Court declaring the aid to be *ultra vires*.[116] In 2008–09 advances from the Fund to the Department of Transport amounted to £1.5 billion plus £0.6 billion to the Ministry of Defence for normal departmental spending. Significantly, the Contingencies Fund was used to support the making of payments in the banking crisis through the use of a Supplementary Estimate of over £42 billion for the banks recapitalization.[117] No amendment or debate occurred in the grant of this request though generally the financial crisis was the occasion for many questions and debates more generally. Concern about the use of the Contingencies Fund is focused on the question of parliamentary accountability. The total expenditure from the Fund is considerable, but there are no clear statutory conditions for expenditure from the Fund. Reliance is placed on the system of internal Treasury control and audit[118] by the C & AG. No select committee directly monitors the use of the Fund and there are no satisfactory means to inquire into the

---

113 See *The Contingencies Fund Account 2009–10*, HC 373 (22 July 2010).
114 See J. McEldowney "The Contingencies Fund and the Parliamentary Scrutiny of Public Finance" [1988] *Pub L.* 232–45.
115 NAO, *London 2012 Olympic Games and Paralympic Games—Post Games Review*, HC 794, Session 2012–13 (2 December 2012).
116 See discussion below.
117 *Hansard*, HC, vol.482, col.952 (2007–08).
118 See *Contingencies Fund 2004–05*, HC 755 (3 March 2006).

policy behind the government's use of the Fund prior to the Fund being used. Any *ex post facto* inquiry faces a corresponding difficulty as the money has already been spent. The fact that the money is to be repaid seems hardly an adequate safeguard when questions arise about the purpose for which the Fund has been used.

Doubts about the legality of the existence of the Fund in the past have given way to greater risk analysis of the use of the Fund and tighter Treasury oversight. Parliament has, in effect, through inactivity allowed an exception in the form of the Contingencies Fund to the principle that Parliament should vote money before expenditure is incurred. There is also tacit acceptance that Treasury control may be more effective in this instance than parliamentary scrutiny, especially as such internal controls include robust systems of risk assessment.

12-076

H: The Committee of Public Accounts (PAC), Select Committees and the Comptroller and Auditor General (C & AG) and Audit

Once expenditure is settled the question of scrutiny and audit arises. Since 1861 the PAC acts on behalf of Parliament to examine and report on accounts and the regularity and propriety of expenditure, which are matters usually covered by the C & AG's certification audit. In more recent times value for money audit (VFM) examinations have become a major part of the work of the PAC. In that regard the PAC works with the assistance of the C & AG. The PAC has proposed changes to Standing Order No.148 which will enable it to appoint specialist advisers, a facility available to other committees. The constitutional importance of the PAC is beyond question and linked to efficiency in government. There is a case for a systematic rather than random follow up by the PAC of how its recommendations have been treated by the government. The PAC produces about 50 reports a year. Its 12th Report in 2010 on *Maintaining financial stability across the United Kingdom's banking system*[119] provided an analysis of the banking crisis. It has undertaken reviews into the Her Majesty's Revenue and Customs (HMRC) and the way in which tax disputes with large corporations have been resolved and the closeness of the relationship between accountancy firms and HMRC.[120] It

12-077

---

119 Public Accounts Committee Reports, *12th Report on Maintaining financial stability across the United Kingdom's banking system*, HC 190 (9 February 2010).
120 Public Accounts Committee, *HM Revenue and Customs 2010–11 Tax Disputes*, HC 138 (2010–12); and *Tax avoidance: The Role of large Accountancy Firms*, HC 870 (2012–13). Generally see R. Bacon and C. Hope, *Conundrum: Why Every Government Gets things Wrong—And What we can do about it* (London: Biteback Publishing, 2013).

has raised concerns about the adoption of smart meters to ensure consumers obtain cost savings.[121] The PAC has become more effective by linking its work into the work of other committees in a more coordinated way than in the past and drawing general lessons from its inquiries.[122] Evidence to the PAC is usually from senior civil servants and officials leaving ministerial policy making largely unchecked and raising sensitivities amongst civil servants that the manner of PAC questioning is directed to holding officials, rather than ministers to account.[123]

12-078 The PAC's authority and remit[124] differ from those of other select committees in two ways. First is the non-party political approach it adopts to its task and the fact that it is chaired by a senior opposition MP and has no more than 15 members. Secondly, its inquiries are almost all audit-based and it receives expert assistance from the C & AG through the work of the NAO. In the case of VFM examinations, its reports to Parliament carry considerable weight. In November 2009 the PAC was critical of the Treasury's indemnity of £28 billion to the Bank of England and a further emergency liquidity assurance of £60 billion to the Royal Bank of Scotland and the Halifax Bank of Scotland (HBOS).[125] Parliament had not received any prior notification before the indemnity had been agreed by the Treasury. Recent concerns about the use of long-term contracts for public services involving public money beyond the lifetime of the current Parliament have been raised.

12-079 Select committees generally exercise *ex post facto* control over public expenditure. The Treasury Committee has been particularly active in developing strategies to obtain more information on public expenditure and its more effective control. In the recent financial crisis involving banking regulation, the Treasury Committee led the way. It undertook 41 evidence sessions and published nine reports relating to the crisis between 2007 and 2009 and has remained active in scrutiny.[126] It is accepted that much of the work of committees is by its nature retrospective review.

12-080 The Scrutiny Unit established in November 2002 in the Committee Office of the House of Commons provides select committees of the House of Commons and joint committees of the two Houses with advice on expenditure matters but also on the impact of draft Bills. The Scrutiny Unit undertakes research as well as policy impact. It also publishes a Review of

---

121 PAC, *Preparation for the roll-out of smart meters*, 63rd Report (2014).
122 See Public Accounts Committee Reports, *63rd Report on Delivering high quality services for all*, HC 1530 (2006).
123 See Public Accounts Committee Reports, *The Dismantled National Programme for IT in the NHS*, HC 294 (2013–4); *High Speed 2: A Review of the Early Programme Preparation*, HC 478 (2013–14); *The National Offender Management Information System*, HC 292 (2008–09); and *Tax Avoidance–Google*, HC 112 (2013–14). One of the more controversial is: House of Commons Public Accounts Committee, *High Speed 2: A Review of Early Programmes Preparation*, HC 478 (2013–14).
124 See Public Accounts Committee Reports on the poor quality of higher education, HC 283 (2000–01); and on the C & AG's Reports, *The Millenium Dome*, HC 936 (1999–2000) and HC 989-I (2000–01).
125 PAC Report, *Maintaining Financial Stability Across the UK Banking System*, 12th Report, HC 190 (2001–10), para.11.
126 Julia Black, *Managing the Financial Crisis—The Constitutional Dimension*, LSE Working Papers (12/2010), n.1, p.31.

Departmental Annual Reports, and provides training and support on Impact Assessments. It assists in the Treasury's Alignment Project set up in July 2007 to ensure that financial reporting and accounts are consistent and transparent.[127]

This provides a detailed and in-depth overview of how departments are performing in terms of Treasury guidance and output measurements. The primary function of the C & AG since the Exchequer and Audit Act 1866 has been the requirement to examine accounts on behalf of the House of Commons. The National Audit Act 1983 recognized the constitutional implications of this requirement, made the C & AG an Officer of the House of Commons, and provided for his appointment. As head of the NAO, which was created under the 1983 Act and replaced the Exchequer and Audit Department, the C & AG is independent from both politics and political influence of the government of the day. This independence allows the C & AG to qualify financial accounts when he is not satisfied with the financial arrangements. In November 2002 this occurred over the Strategic Rail Authority sponsored by the Department of Transport[128] until it was agreed that Network Rail should be consolidated. The NAO's activities[129] cover benchmarking, quality control, developing efficient and effective monitoring systems, and engaging in annual reporting functions over departmental spending involving the audit of more than 600 accounts covering over £800 billion of public expenditure.[130] It is unable to comment on policy. Its annual net working resources are approximately £76 million with outsourcing costs of nearly 20 per cent and employing 900 staff. The remit of the NAO was established under the 1983 Act, which has been criticised for failing to give the C & AG the right to trace "all public money". The NAO has also undertaken a significant monitoring of the financial management of the EU.[131] Excluded from the jurisdiction of the NAO in National Audit Act 1983 Sch.4 is the audit of the remaining nationalized industries and other public authorities. Local authorities are separately audited by the about to be abolished Audit Commission which is itself subject to audit by the NAO. Increasingly, the NAO is called upon by the Executive as an "accountability adviser of choice" especially in areas of government policy implementation including through regulatory bodies.[132] Julia Black[133] detects a sense of confusion as to who the NAO acts for and to whom it is accountable, especially when used by the Cabinet Office and Treasury. Greater

12-081

---

127 See HM Treasury, *Alignment (Clear Line of Sight) Second Parliamentary Memorandum* (2009–10).
128 Eleventh Report of the Public Accounts Commission, Session 2001–02, HC 1251 (2002).
129 There is a Public Audit Forum providing a discussion for the audit agencies; the NAO; the Northern Ireland Audit Office; the Audit Commission for Local Authorities; and the National Health Service in England and Wales and Audit Scotland.
130 National Audit Office, *Corporate Plan 2003–4 to 2005–6* (2005) contains details of the bodies audited.
131 See Report by the Comptroller and Auditor General, *Financial Management of the European Union: A Progress Report*, HC 529 (2003–04).
132 NAO, *Reorganising Central Government*, HC 452, Session 2009–10 (2010). Also see NAO, *Ofcom: The Effectiveness of Converged Regulation*, HC 490, Session 2010–11 (2010).
133 Julia Black, "Calling Regulators to Account: Challenges, Capacities and Prospects" in N. Bamforth and P. Leyland (eds), *Accountability in the Contemporary Constitution* (Oxford: Oxford University Press, 2013), 354–388, p.381.

12-082 clarity about the NAO might be needed to ensure that there is no further blurring of the lines of responsibility.[134] More welcome is the use of the NAO by committees of both Houses of Parliament.

The NAO is funded out of moneys provided by Parliament but one-fifth of the NAO's budget comes from audit fees, including international clients. The NAO acts on behalf of Parliament and is subject to oversight by the Parliamentary Public Accounts Commission. The corporate governance arrangements of the NAO considered following John Tiner's report in February 2008, the 14th Report of the Public Accounts Commission.[135] The recommendations included limiting the length of term of the C & AG, the terms and conditions of service and remuneration. Also included were recommendations about the role of the NAO and its relationship with the C & AG. Following the Tiner review, the Public Accounts Commission considered the next steps to be taken and published a response on 4 March 2008.[136] Its response was also considered by the NAO and further consultations took place before the clauses[137] in the Constitutional Reform and Governance Bill were agreed by the government but were omitted in the final legislation.[138] The Budget Responsibility and National Audit Act 2011 separated the C & AG as an independent officer of Parliament from the NAO, with the NAO receiving a new corporate status, providing resources to the C & AG who will be its Chief Executive but under an independent Board.[139]

12-083 Significantly, following the Gershon Review in 2004, the NAO has undertaken regular reviews of efficiency savings across government. Its current strategy, is estimated to help make savings of £35 billion planned over the coming year in terms of the administrative costs of running government departments.[140]

12-084 The Local Audit and Accountability Act 2014 has extended the role of the NAO to include local public bodies. These include, fire authorities, police and crime commissioners, clinical commissioning groups for the NHS and NHS Trusts. Local audit, formerly undertaken through the Audit Commission has now been replaced by NAO supervision.[141]

---

134 NAO, *Performance of Ofgem: NAO, A Review of Economic Regulators' Regulatory Impact Statements for the House of Lords Select Committee on Regulators* (London: NAO, 2007) cited by Black, "Calling Regulators to Account: Challenges, Capacities and Prospects" as an example of confusion over role and function.
135 HC 328 (2007–08).
136 Public Accounts Commission, 16th Report, HC 1027 (2007–08), para.16.
137 HC 1027 (2007–08).
138 See House of Commons Library, *Constitutional Reform and Governance Bill*, Research Paper, 09/73 (6 October 2009). These include: the term of office of the C & AG with a new maximum of ten years; the remuneration package to be linked to a comparable office of similar status and include some restrictions on employment after leaving office. There is a new corporate entity for governance granted to the NAO and its relationship with the C & AG—the C & AG is through the Chief Executive. The C & AG is not an employee of the NAO. This is intended to provide a strategic approach to the NAO and how it operates
139 Remuneration, terms of conditions of the C & AG and limitations on powers to require efficiency and cost-effectiveness in the exercise of his responsibilities. There are similar powers for Wales.
140 Public Accounts Committee, *Progress with value for money savings and lessons for cost reduction programs*, HC 439-I (11 September 2010).
141 House of Commons Library, *Local Audit in England*, Briefing No.07240 (24 June 2015).

Certification audit

12-085 The NAO[142] undertakes two forms of auditing, Certification Audit and VFM Audit. In the case of certification audit, the C & AG carries out on behalf of the House of Commons the audit and certification of all government departments and a wide range of public sector bodies. These include appropriation accounts of departments. The C & AG provides an audit certificate which states his opinion as to whether either: (a) the "account properly presents" the expenditure and receipts of the vote and payments of the organisation; or (b) the account presents a "true and fair view" where accounts are prepared on an income and expenditure basis.

12-086 This form of audit is "department-led", that is, focused on departments. Increasingly, the style of the audit seeks to ensure "regularity and propriety" with the addition that the custodians of public money have stewardship responsibilities. The link between the Treasury and the NAO is through the Departmental Accounting Officer and is one of partnership but based on independent actors with specific responsibilities. The C & AG may seek an explanation from the department concerned if he is dissatisfied with any aspect of the accounts and may qualify his certificate with his reservations. The primary focus of such an audit is to assess whether accounts are accurate or whether they may mislead someone relying on them. They must present a "true and fair view", must be "properly presented", and in the case of agencies must follow the format of Treasury accounts. In particular, if there is expenditure which requires Treasury authority which has not been given, the matter is reported through a draft report in the first instance to the Accounting Officer and then to the PAC and Parliament.

12-087 Normally, the audit work involved in certification audit is confined to the proper presentation of receipts and expenditure. In common with most of the auditing work of the NAO it is scrutiny *ex post facto* with the implication that any past errors may provide lessons for the future. This is open to the criticism that an *a priori* examination might offer a means of avoiding mistakes and therefore save public money.[143] The NAO has claimed that in 2005–06, its work resulted in £555 million in savings as a result of auditing over 500 accounts covering £800 billion in expenditure.

Value for money examinations

12-088 VFM examinations are potentially more far-reaching as a means of audit. The National Audit Act 1983 s.6 provides a statutory basis for VFM examinations at the discretion of the C & AG. Included within this jurisdiction are government departments and other public bodies where the C & AG has statutory rights of inspection or where he is the statutory auditor. VFM audit is not extended to any of the nationalized industries.[144] The 1983 Act placed VFM examinations on a statutory basis and over 60 reports are produced on an annual basis. However, the Act

---

142 Tom Ling, *The NAO and Parliamentary Scrutiny, a new audit for new times*, CfP Policy Paper Series (2005).
143 Public Accounts Committee, *Managing Risks to Improve Public Services*, HC 444 (2004–05).
144 *Government Accounting* (1989), para.7.1.20, revised in 2003.

makes an important proviso that VFM examination shall not be construed as entitling the C & AG to question the merits of the policy objectives of the department or body concerned.[145]

12-089 Evaluating efficiency and effectiveness has been a common theme in recent years in the development of government policy objectives.[146] The NAO is ambitious in developing VFM examinations through their efforts to identify and prevent waste. It has become commonplace that government borrows techniques, methods, and objectives from business or commerce. How to measure efficiency and effectiveness is the key issue, and evaluation may be as difficult as setting the objectives in the first place.

12-090 In 1981 the Treasury and Civil Service Committee in its *Report on Efficiency and Effectiveness*[147] set out some criteria for evaluating efficiency and effectiveness. The criteria include clarifying the intention of the programme, setting *objectives* which are quantified as targets. Objectives can be assessed in terms of *output*. An *efficient* programme is one where the target is achieved with the least use of resources and instruments for change. An *effective* programme is one where the intention of the programme is being achieved. This means that the intention is contained in operational objectives that are set as defined targets. Thus the output of the programme is equal to the target set. In this way an effective and efficient programme may be evaluated.

12-091 The NAO has developed VFM strategies[148] that emphasise the avoidance of waste, the setting of clearly defined policy objectives, and obtaining good value for the taxpayer. There is a duty on government departments to consider the NAO's reports and the PAC recommendations, and to provide replies to the House of Commons on matters raised in the reports. There is a strong parliamentary link with the PAC following up the recommendations made by the NAO.[149] This is consistent with the Gershon Report that argued strongly for making efficiency savings to redistribute funds for better use. The government's claim was that £4.7 billion savings might be so identified[150] but there is a considerable risk that a reduction in the quality of services might result if over-ambitious targets have to be met. There is the need for a cost–benefit analysis to be used to assess the amount of savings as against the quality of services.

12-092 VFM examinations seem to be a blend of conventional auditing skills with management consulting techniques. In the former they benefit from a degree of independence and

---

145 See C. Beauchamp, "National Audit Office: Its Role in Privatization" (1990) *Public Money and Management* 55–8, 57. For examples, see National Audit Office, *The Work of the Directors of Telecommunications, Gas Supply, Water Service and Electricity Supply*, HC 645, Session 1995–96 (1996). Compare the approach to the early comments made to the Fourth Report of the Public Accounts Committee (4 November 1988).
146 See a critical analysis by the NAO over selling the National Air Traffic Control System, HC 1096 (2001–02).
147 Treasury and Civil Service Committee, *Efficiency and Effectiveness in the Civil Service*, HC 236. See also Cabinet Office Efficiency Unit, *Helping Managers Manage* (1984).
148 National Audit Office, *Helping the Nation Spend Wisely Annual Report* (1999) 13. See National Audit Office, *A Framework for Value for Money Audits*, Cmnd 9755; Treasury Minute on the First Four Reports from the Committee of Public Accounts Session 1985/86, paras 21–3; Cmd.8413, para.87; A. Hopwood, "Accounting and the Pursuit of Efficiency", in A. Hopwood and C. Tomkins, *Issues in Public Sector Accounting* (Deddington: Philip Allan, 1984); and J. Sizer, *An Insight into Management Accounting* (London: Pitman, 1979).
149 Public Accounts Committee, *Achieving Value for Money in the Delivery of Public Services*, HC 742 (2005–06).
150 National Audit Office, *Progress in Improving Government Efficiency*, HC 802 (2005–06).

objectivity and the ascertaining of facts through the skills of an auditor. The latter draws on the analytical skills of the management consultant. In comparison with ordinary certification auditing VFM takes the opportunity to understand the effects of policy and whether those effects relate to the intention behind the policy. The NAO's experience of VFM studies has been growing since 1983.[151] In 2005–06 the NAO provided Parliament with 61 major reports on VFM, representing a substantial part of the NAO's work.[152] In 2009–10 the NAO undertook 90 reports on VFM.

Particularly difficult is the distinction between the implementation of policy, a legitimate concern of VFM, and the merits of policy which we have already noted is outside the jurisdiction of the NAO. A criticism leveled at all public sector VFM examinations is that the emphasis on economic criteria does not take account of political choices and policy making or whether the merits of the policy, outside the remit of the NAO, impacted on the efficiency of decision making. Given its present remit, it is clearly impossible for the NAO to move to assess the merits of policy even where this may be indicated by their examination. The *ex post facto* nature of VFM has the benefit of hindsight but this may make it difficult to evaluate all the pressures experienced by a sponsoring department.[153] The NAO published a critical analysis of the banking crisis and the problems caused by the failure of Northern Rock.[154]

12–093

Perversely, the very transparency encouraged by audit systems may inhibit initiative and creative risk taking in favour of a cautious approach over-reliant on audit advice. Placing trust in the audit process itself may be a worthy goal and achieves better control over-expenditure but it may encourage heavy reliance on monitoring techniques instead of a more fundamental assessment of priorities. The political agenda may also become heavily dependent on the audit trail to provide legitimacy and public confidence for policies. This may obscure the setting of priorities and lead to the adoption of short-term as opposed to long-term goals.

12–094

The independent status of the C & AG means that heavy reliance is placed on co-operation between the departments, their Accounting Officers, and the NAO.[155] This is indicative of the delicate balance between gaining access to information through co-operation and maintaining an independence.[156] Although the NAO has achieved international status as a public sector

12–095

---

151 See J. McEldowney, "Audit Cultures and Risk Aversion in Public Authorities: An Agenda for Public Lawyers" in R. Baldwin (ed), *Law and Uncertainty Risks and Legal Processes* (London: Kluwer Law International, 1997), pp.185–210.
152 National Audit Office, *Annual Report 2006*.
153 F. White and K. Hollingsworth, *Audit, Accountability and Government* (Oxford: Clarendon, 1999).
154 National Audit Office, *The Financial Services Authority: A review under section 12 of the Financial Services and Markets Act 2000*, HC 500, Session 2006–07 (27 April 2007) 49 noted that from 2001–02 there were an average of 200 cases each year dealing with money laundering and other breaches of the financial standards. In *The Financial Services Authority: A review under section 12 of the Financial Services and Markets Act 2000*, para.4.63, 17 cases involving financial penalties totaling £17.4 million, £14 million of which was for one market protection case and £505,00 related specifically to financial crime.
155 See the proposals contained in the Budget Responsibility and 2010 National Audit Bill (HL) to modernise the work of the NAO and its governance arrangements.
156 Memorandum from Michael Power, Professor of Accounting, London School of Economics, HM Treasury Select Committee Evidence 173, p.174.

audit office of high reputation and quality, criticisms remain of its capacity to operate proactive or preventative strategies to ensure effective public spending.

I: The Courts

12-096 The courts have, since the sixteenth century, accepted Parliament's role in the matter of financial control. There is limited opportunity for judicial oversight in matters of expenditure. Public finance issues that arise before the courts involve issues of taxation – the supply side. Central government cases include *Auckland Harbour Board* v *The King*,[157] in which Viscount Haldane noted that payments out of the Consolidated Fund without parliamentary authority were illegal. In *Woolwich Building Society* v *Inland Revenue Commissioner (No.2)*[158] the House of Lords articulated the general principle that money paid to a public body pursuant to an *ultra vires* demand for tax should be repayable as of right. The *Woolwich* case arose out of an Inland Revenue demand for tax from the Woolwich Building Society. The demand was later declared by the courts to have no legal basis. It was accepted that although the money paid to the Revenue was not paid under any mistake of law on the part of the taxpayer, the Woolwich Building Society had no express statutory right to repayment of the money. The House of Lords held that money paid pursuant to an *ultra vires* demand was *prima facie* repayable as a common law right of the subject. In the *Woolwich* case the payment of tax amounted to almost £57 million with interest and dividends, an illustration of the role of the courts in revenue matters which can have a substantial indirect effect on expenditure totals. The government has estimated that the total cost of repaying composite rate tax to all building societies which had overpaid amounted to £250 million. There is also the prospect of challenges due to the Human Rights Act 1998.[159] A challenge from "tax-paying pacifists"[160] seeking to adopt the jurisprudence of the European Court of Human Rights on European Convention on Human

---

157 [1925] A.C. 318 PC (NZ) at [326].
158 [1993] A.C. 70; [1992] 3 W.L.R. 366 HL at [764D]–[764E] (see also Lord Slynn at [783E]–[783G]); J. Beatson, "Restitution of Taxes, Levies and Other Imposts: Defining the Extent of the Woolwich Principle" [1993] 109 *Law Quarterly Review* 401. *Pepper* v *Hart* [1993] Q.B. 278; [1993] 1 All E.R. 86 CA (Civ Div) on the taxation of benefits in kind which may lead to £30 million in refundable taxes. In *Metzger* v *Department of Health and Social Security* [1977] 3 All E.R. 444 Ch D, the duty of the Secretary of State for Social Services to carry out reviews of the rates of pension payable under the Social Security Act 1975 was considered and the cost of uprating pension benefits ascertained. The impact on public expenditure would have been large if the court had decided to grant a declaration. In the event it refused to do so.
159 *R (Wilkinson) v IRC* [2005] UKHL 30; [2005] 1 W.L.R. 1718 and *R (Morgan Grenfell) v Special Commissioner* [2002] UKHL 21; [2002] S.T.C. 786.
160 *R (on the application of) Boughton v Her Majesty's Treasury (The Peace Tax Seven Case)* [2005] EWHC 1914 (Admin) and [2006] EWCA Civ 504.

Rights (ECHR) art.9 (freedom of thought and conscience) to challenge the use of taxation for military purposes was rejected by the Court of Appeal. This does not rule out the use of ECHR Art.9 arguments in the future, depending on how far the Strasbourg court is willing to develop its jurisprudence on human rights into this area.[161]

It is accepted that the role of the courts generally in decisions on taxation and public expenditure[162] has been slight, but there is scope for future development, especially in expenditure related to health care and social service delivery. In *R (W) v Birmingham City Council*[163] a restriction by the Health Authority to only fund social care for critical needs was declared illegal.[164] However, the Supreme Court in *McDonald*[165] was reluctant to interfere with policy decisions on how best to allocate funds for the care of a patient with severe mobility problems who claimed for a night time care assistant rather than the use of incontinence pads, the cheaper option. The case is illustrative of the dilemma and challenges facing public authorities under austerity budgeting and is indicative of the Supreme Court's reluctance to overturn policy based public expenditure decisions.[166] In *Pergau Dam*[167] (see above), the applicant, an international pressure group, challenged the legality of aid granted by the Secretary of State for Foreign Affairs to fund the construction of the Pergau Dam in Malaysia. The pressure group relied on information obtained through an NAO Report and information gleaned from

---

161 See *R (Wilkinson) v IRC* [2005] UKHL 30.
162 In 1975, in [1976] Q.B. 629; [1976] 2 W.L.R. 291 CA (Civ Div), the Court of Appeal held that it was unlawful for the Home Office to make use of its revocation powers under the Wireless Telegraphy Act 1949, to revoke TV licences to prevent licence holders benefiting from an overlapping licence purchased to avoid an increase in the licence fee. Congreve and about 20,000 other licence holders had purchased a second licence, while their existing licence was still valid in anticipation of an increase in the licence fee. Lord Denning claimed that the Bill of Rights 1689 had been infringed as a levying of money without grant of Parliament. There is some doubt on this interpretation as Congreve had sought avoidance of a tax through the purchase of a second licence, clearly not intended by the Wireless Telegraphy Act 1949. However, the case illustrates how the judges will use statutory interpretation to uphold the principle of authorisation. In *Bowles v Bank of England* [1913] 1 Ch. 57 Ch D, Bowles was successful in suing the Bank of England for declarations that income tax could not be deducted by virtue of a budget resolution alone, and until such tax had been imposed by Act of Parliament he was not required to pay it. The case provided the background for what is now the Provisional Collection of Taxes Act 1968 which gives statutory force for a limited time to resolutions of the House of Commons varying taxation levels pending the enactment in the Finance Act.
163 [2011] EWHC 1147 (Admin); [2011] Eq. L.R. 721.
164 In *R (D) v Worcestershire County Council* [2013] EWHC 2490 (Admin); [2013] B.L.G.R. 741, the High Court rejected a claim for disability payment in the context of severe cuts in the local authority budget. See "Harsh but Fair?" (2013) *New Law Journal* 13.
165 *R (McDonald) v Royal Borough of Kensington and Chelsea* [2011] UKSC 33; [2011] 4 All E.R. 881—The Equality and Human Rights Commission, *Close to Home—An inquiry into older people and human rights in home care* (23 November 2011), http://www.equalityhumanrights.com/legal-and-policy/our-legal-work/inquiries-and-assessments/inquiry-home-care-older-people/download-inquiry-report [Accessed 11 April 2016], pp.90–91 was critical of the decision.
166 *R (KM) v Cambridgeshire County Council* [2012] UKSC 23; [2012] 3 All E.R. 1218 adopted a similar approach in the scrutiny of local authority powers but a reluctance to overturn policy based expenditure decisions.
167 Above at [7]. See I. Harden, F. White and K. Hollingsworth, "Value for Money and Administrative Law" [1996] *Pub L.* 661, p.674.

debates and evidence taken by the PAC and the Foreign Affairs Committee. The NAO and the PAC assumed the legality of the aid but criticised aspects of its value for money. However, it was revealed in various correspondences that the Accounting Officer had serious reservations about the project.

12-098 Despite such Accounting Officer reservations written ministerial instructions were given to proceed with the financial aid. The Pergau project was funded, purportedly under Overseas Development and Co-operation Act 1980 s.1. The Divisional Court held that the provision of aid was *ultra vires* the 1980 Act. As a result of this decision, the C & AG qualified his opinion of the aid on the basis of irregularity. Despite this finding and the decision of the Divisional Court, the government found the necessary additional aid required to finance the dam from a repayable charge on the Contingency Fund. Eventually the money was found from the Reserve Fund. Questions of legality may also be raised when value for money is questioned or the use of public funds is thought not to be proportionate.

J: Summary and Conclusions

12-099 The scrutiny and approval of public expenditure provides an important constitutional check on government spending. Since the introduction of resource accounting and the adoption of the Alignment Project in relationship to estimates and planning expenditure there is potential for greater scrutiny. Parliament has potential to make financial scrutiny more robust and to make changes to government spending plans. One rare example is the recent defeat of the government's proposed cuts in Tax Credits,[168] but that is an exception rather than the normal practice. The National Audit Office emerges has an important role in financial scrutiny that provides Parliament and the PAC with important oversight. Recent improvements in financial information through the Constitutional Reform and Governance Act 2010 and the strengthening in the systems of accounting and auditing open up clear potential for greater parliamentary oversight.[169] The Budget Responsibility and National Audit Act 2011 created the new Office for Budgetary Responsibility and modernisation of the governance arrangements for the National Audit Office.[170] These have the potential for significant improvements in parliamentary oversight and in contributing to strengthening accountability over government.

12-100 However, the financial crisis and the balance of influence between parliamentary control and government spending has shifted markedly to the government's advantage. This is partly because of the need for rapid public spending cuts and partly because the systems of

---

168 House of Commons Library, Briefing Paper, No.CBP/7300 (15 October 2015).
169 Mark Sandford, *External Scrutiny: The Voice in the Crowded Room*, CfPs Policy Paper Series (2002).
170 The Fiscal responsibility Act 2010 was repealed.

accountability are the main means of delivering and controlling public spending. The Office for Budget Responsibility since May 2010 has provided an independent assessment of the public finances is an attempt to provide transparency[171] and has provided an important source of financial information at a time when living standards have declined most markedly leading to inequality,[172] especially amongst young people in the UK.

12-101
The government's expenditure objectives are more visible and transparent than before but, being driven by large fiscal deficits, parliamentary accountability is likely to be weak. Evaluation of the case for cuts and the proportion of savings, the role of accountability systems, has given way to a government-centred agenda for change that priorities spending leaving little room for parliamentary control.

12-102
Strengthening parliamentary scrutiny largely depends on the House of Commons in general or individual MPs regarding financial control as relevant in their overall role in the scrutiny of government. The PAC has been notable in adopting a robust questioning the value for money in public expenditure, mainly driven by the approach of the current Chair.

12-103
The financial crisis has also revealed the limited extent of *ex post* select committee scrutiny; despite the fact that the crisis had a major impact on institutions that control and regulate public finance, little could be done at the time. An unfortunate aspect of the Banking Act 2009 was the restricted role it gives to Parliament's role: the Bank of England was given real powers to implement stabilization options that were not subject to parliamentary control[173]; and the Treasury was granted even wider regulatory powers without the need for prior parliamentary approval. The work of the Treasury Select Committee, however, in actively reporting on aspects of the financial crisis[174] has proved important and the Lords Select Committee on the Constitution has also been vigilant.[175]

12-104
The work of financial scrutiny has permeated many of the departmental select committees which have begun to adopt public expenditure as a subject for scrutiny[176] aided

---

171 National Audit Office, *HM Treasury: Examination of the Forecasts prepared by the interim Office for Budget responsibility for the emergency Budget 2010*, Session 2010–11, HC 142 (22 June 2010).
172 Institute for Fiscal Studies, *Living Standards, Poverty and Inequality in the UK: 2014* (London: IFS, 2014).
173 See Banking Act 2009, ss.5, 10 and 74. Section 74 gave the Treasury Henry VIII-type powers to make regulations to cover stabilization measures.
174 HC Treasury Select Committee, *Too important to fail—too important to ignore*, 9th Report Session, HC 261-1 (2009–10), p. 3. Summary, HC Treasury Select Committee, *Banking Crisis: Dealing with the Failure of UK Banks*, Session, HC 416 (2008–09), paras 203–29. House of Commons Library, *Big Society Bank/Big Society Capital*, Research Paper, SN/BT/5876 (13 June 2014). Treasury Select Committee, *Reporting Contingent Liabilities to Parliament*, Session 2009–10, HC 181. Treasury and Civil Service Committee, *The Regulation of Financial Services in the UK*, 6th Report, HC 332-I (1994–95).
175 HL Select Committee on the Constitution Banking Bill, Session 2008–09, HL 19, and HL 97. Also See Jack Simson Caird, Robert Hazell and Dawn Oliver, *The Constitutional Standards of the House of Lords Select Committee on the Constitution*, UCL Constitution Unit (January 2014).
176 See Education and Skills Committee, *Public Expenditure on Education and Skills*, HC (2004–05); HC 168, The Home Affairs Committee, HC (2004–05); HC 280, the Northern Ireland Affairs Committee (2004–05); and Northern Ireland Departments' 2002–03 Resource Accounts, HC 173.

by the establishment in 2002 of the Scrutiny Unit.[177] This also aids select committees in pre-legislative scrutiny. However, audit systems have a remarkable tendency to centralise control.

12–105 Constitutional lawyers have accepted that controls over public expenditure lie at the heart of Parliament's control over government. The plethora of controls such as internal Treasury rules and procedures, audit systems, parliamentary reports, and management systems are fashioned to serve the dual purpose of the economic needs of the government of the day, and the interests of Parliament. Inside the system of financial control, the internal workings of government can be detected, often less visible and transparent than the workings of the external systems of parliamentary accountability in select committees and in the role of the courts. Financial control systems share many characteristics familiar in the development of the common law—continuity and certainty in developing rules with the potential for incremental change. But, equally incrementally, financial controls appear to have developed many of the qualities of a codified system—written manuals containing fundamental principles that have been improved, updated, and strengthened containing many years' experience. It is possible to see financial controls as a model of what can be achieved with systemic change over 40 years through the appropriate combination of external expertise in the form of the NAO and the internal scrutiny performed by select committees. Treasury dominance in its influence over public expenditure is most marked especially in borrowing and debt arrangements. The partial or whole nationalization of four major banks represents a major stake in terms of public finances. This is a systemic weakness at the heart of public expenditure control, namely that gaps left by parliamentary inertia are readily filled by executive controls driven by Treasury influence. The government's pre-eminence in the rules of procedure that allows it the initiative in public expenditure severely weakens the ability of individual MPs to play a role in financial matters. A modest reform that permits expenditure increases (within the remit of offsetting costs elsewhere) to MPs would make a substantial change. It would allow a greater emphasis to be given in parliamentary debate to the policies and decisions that inform, manage, and control public expenditure. At a time when audit systems are strengthened, Parliament's relevance faces further decline. The weaknesses and inertia in parliamentary control appear to reflect a decline in the standard and quality of our democracy today.[178] The influential *Institute for Fiscal Studies* concluded that Public sector net debt is likely to dominate and constrain future government policy for planned public expenditure for future generations.[179] This fact alone should encourage MPs to take a greater interest in ensuring that public money is well spent. Prosser sees the system of financial control linked to the economic constitution", through multiple means of accountability which have the potential to be mutually reinforcing.[180] Leaving the EU is likely to place considerable pressure on the "economic constitution" with long-term implications for the UK economy.

---

177 Scrutiny Unit set up under the late Robin Cook, then Leader of the House of Commons.
178 O. Gay and B. Winetrobe, *Parliamentary Audit: the Audit committee in Comparative Context* (2003).
179 IFS, *The IFS Green Budget 2014* (London: IFS 2014), p.22.
180 T. Prosser, *The Economic Constitution* (Oxford: Oxford University Press, 2014), p.253.

Further Reading

R. Bacon and C. Hope, *Conundrum: Why Every Government Gets things Wrong—And What we can do about it* (London: Biteback Publishing, 2013).

E. Balls and G. O'Donnell (eds), *Reforming Britain's Economic and Financial Policy: Towards Greater Economic Stability* (2002).

A. Brazier and V Ram, The Fiscal Maze (2006).

O. Gay, and B. Winetrobe, *Parliamentary Audit: The Audit Committee in Comparative Context, Report to the Audit Committee of the Scottish Parliament* (2003).

Terence Daintith and Alan Page, *The Executive in the Constitution* (Oxford: Oxford University Press, 2000).

Hansard Society, Commission on Parliamentary Scrutiny, *The Challenge for Parliament: Making Government Accountable* (2001).

Edward Leigh and John Pugh, Options to Improve Parliamentary Scrutiny of Government Expenditure House of Commons Library, 2010.

William MacKay and Charles W. Johnson, *Parliament and Congress* (Oxford: Oxford University Press, 2010).

Lord Sharman of Redlynch, *Holding to Account: The Review of Audit and Accountability for Central Government* (2001).

C. Thain, C. and M. Wright, *The Treasury and Whitehall: The Planning and Control of Public Expenditure 1976–1993* (Oxford: Oxford University Press, 1995).

T. Erskine May, *Parliamentary Practice*, 22nd edn (London: Butterworths, 1997).

Paul Silk and Rhoderi Walters, *How Parliament Works*, 4th edn (London: Longman, 1999).

Colin Thain and Maurice Wright, *The Treasury and Whitehall* (Oxford: Clarendon, 1995).

HM Treasury, *Resource Accounting Manual* (London: HMSO, 2000).

HM Treasury, *Government Accounting: A Guide on Accounting and Financial Procedures for the Use of Government* (London: HMSO, with supplements from 1989–2002).

HM Treasury, *Supply Estimates* (London: HMSO).

HM Treasury, *Regularity and Propriety* (London: HMSO, 1997).

HM Treasury, *Code for Fiscal Stability* (London: HMSO, 1998).

Fidelma White and Kathryn Hollingsworth, *Audit, Accountability and Government* (Oxford: Oxford University Press, 1999).

13

Local Government

A: Introduction

The UK's unitary state gives no special constitutional status or protection to local government. Local government is a directly elected institution with a variety of statutory powers provided by Parliament that allows local government political choices and legitimacy that is distinct from central government. The increasing importance of devolution to Scotland, Wales and Northern Ireland and London, has resulted in a multi-layered constitution. This has important significance for local government as the Government plans to allow a major decentralisation of powers to elected mayors and greater financial autonomy to local authorities. This is likely to have a marked impact on the future of local government with the potential to change the nature of central government as local authorities will have widely different ways of delivering public services in their communities.[1]

The Coalition government from 2010–15 pursued a policy of localism, providing local authorities with considerable more powers under the Localism Act 2011. The election of Police Commissioners and the promise of directly elected mayors in specific local authority regions are trends in the direction of delegating powers to a local level. In 2012 and 2013, 28 city regions signed up to city deals whereby enhanced legal and financial powers are provided on transport, business rates and adult education. More recently, agreement has been reached to devolve powers to Greater Manchester, South Yorkshire, the North East and Tees Valley. Liverpool and West Midlands have been added to the list of devolved regions. In the case of Greater Manchester Combined Authority there is agreement to establish a new Mayor of Greater Manchester. The Cities and Local Government Devolution Act 2016 contains legislative proposals to bring all these proposals into effect. Combined authorities may be set up under a legal structure with or without an elected mayor under the Local Democracy, Economic

---

1 House of Lords, *Devolution to City Regions in England*, LIF 2015/0053 (24 November 2015).

Development and Construction Act 2009. The operation of combined authorities is when two or more local authorities may agree to share their functions. Additional powers may be provided through an order made by the Secretary of State. The development of devolution deals is an ongoing strategy that is likely to gain additional momentum under the proposed Devolution Bill.[2]

13–003 Despite all these developments, a remarkable feature of Parliamentary power has been its centralisation in the hands of successive governments. This gives central government ultimate legal authority over local government. The absence of any formal protection to local government makes local authorities vulnerable to political change and variable policies.[3] In the absence of any federal system offering local government an entrenched protection, local government can be amended or modified at the whim of central government. Similarly, newly devolved government to Wales, Scotland and Northern Ireland is subject to Parliamentary authority. In strict constitutional theory devolution may be retracted, modified, suspended or amended. As noted in earlier chapters in the book, the term asymmetrical seems appropriate to describe current arrangements since devolution. Centralised and ultimate sovereignty continues to rest with the UK Parliament, with subordinate law-making powers delegated to Scotland, Wales, Northern Ireland and the London Mayor. Local government has only the powers that have been conferred on it by Parliament. Local government continues to deliver diverse public services and in the UK as a whole provides a means for decision-making that is different from central government. Locally elected authorities provide citizens with a large range of services with a degree of local autonomy. Local authority activities are wide-ranging across a range of public services from the police, public health to education and street cleaning. Superficially, local government may appear uncomplicated. In fact, because of the political nature of changes in the way local government is financed and its role and function being determined by the life cycle of party politics, the law and regulation of local authorities is unduly complex and technical. It deserves a more coherent treatment and a major simplification of the law is long overdue. The UK operates under a multi-layered constitution, asymmetrical but with increasing decentralisation of power to local government.[4] Despite the fact that the UK has acceded to the European Charter of Local Self-Government 1985 this has not given rise to any enhanced status to local authorities.

13–004 Elected local authorities have wide statutory powers including powers of local taxation. They also receive large financial support from central government, roughly 60 per cent of their expenditure. As an administrative agency, local government appears similar to other agencies with statutory powers and duties. In law, local authorities are statutory corporations. They are subject to judicial review, and accountable for their expenditure to Auditors under the

---

2 House of Commons Library, *Combined Authorities*, Briefing Paper, 06649 (20 January 2016).
3 S. H. Bailey, and M. Elliott, "Taking Local Government Seriously: Democracy, Autonomy and the Constitution" [2009] *C.L.J.* 436; and C. Bevan, "The Localism Act 2011: The Hollow Housing Law Revolution" (2014) 77(6) *Modern Law Review* 964–82.
4 Ian Leigh, "The Changing Nature of the Local State" in J. Jowell, D. Oliver, and C. O'Cinneide (eds), *The Changing Constitution* (Oxford: Oxford University Press, 2015), pp.279–304.

National Audit Office.[5] Local government is also accountable to the Commissioner for Local Administration, with similar functions to the Parliamentary Commissioner for Administration. Local authorities may develop their own politics and policies within the legal powers they possess. Because of their elected nature, local authorities are accountable to their electorate for their policies and spending plans. This form of electoral accountability may give rise to political and ideological differences with central government. Conflicts between the centre and local authorities are not easily reconciled, and this has often increased the centralising tendencies of the legislation passed for local government. The role of the courts in interpreting the powers, duties and responsibilities has given rise to important interpretations of the grounds and role of judicial review.

This chapter is intended, first, to explain the role and function of local authorities in a period of change and modernisation. The account is limited to England and Wales, as Scotland has its own system of law applicable to local government, and Northern Ireland's arrangements are distinctive to that region. Second, to explain relations between local and central government set challenges for the courts and judicial review. Finally, to consider the longer term trend for local government as part of the development of policy on localism consistent with devolution. Centralised controls remain as local government has in theory the potential to develop and gain more autonomy over its own affairs.

13–005

B: Transforming Local Government in an Era of Change

Local government has undergone a number of transformational changes. These are considered as follows in terms of distinct historical periods of development.

13–006

Phase One: 1979–1997

Local government has come under intense change and increased scrutiny often in conflicting directions depending on the political ideology of the government of the day. The first phase under the Conservative Government of Mrs Thatcher in 1979 sought to reduce local authority expenditure and bring tighter controls over public services provided by local authorities. At that time there were many conflicts between local and central government over local government finance, and the role and functions of local authorities. A number of disputes involving financial

13–007

---

5   The Audit Commission was abolished from 1 April 2015 and its role transferred to the National Audit Office under the Local Audit and Accountability Act 2014.

issues led to litigation. A significant increase in the number of applications *for* judicial review—roughly one third are disputes involving local authorities—illustrated how the judicial element in resolving the conflict took on its own momentum. This includes cases taken against a local authority as well as local authorities seeking judicial redress against central government or other agencies including other local authorities. The Conservative Government appeared to see the elected element of the local authority as less important than the legal powers used to hold local government to account. There were attempts to give the citizen greater opportunities to challenge local authority decisions. The Committee of Inquiry in 1986 under the Chairmanship of David Widdicombe (hereinafter the Widdicombe Report),[6] recommended that the right of objection to accounts should be extended to all ratepayers and that greater publicity should be given to the auditors' reports. The latter recommendation became law under the Local Government Finance (Publicity for Auditors Reports) Act 1991. As a result, changes took place in the way local authorities are expected to manage their own affairs, including their control of their financial arrangements. Traditionally local authorities have employed the necessary staff to carry out the services for which they are responsible. This includes, for example, social service staff, teachers, and refuse collection. The Local Government Act 1988 required local authorities to subject a number of services such as street cleaning, vehicle maintenance, schools and welfare catering, refuse collection and the management of sports and leisure facilities to competition. Competition has set new management challenges and has had profound effects on the way local authorities manage themselves. The law requires that private companies must be permitted to bid for the work involved and this element of competition within public service provision sets new directions for the future of local authorities. The Local Government Act has been amended by the Local Government Act 2000 removing the requirement on compulsory competitive tendering.

13–008 In May 1991, the Secretary of State for the Environment instigated a review of local government and following this a number of consultative documents were published. The outcome was the Local Government Act 1992 that includes changes to introduce performance standards for local authorities and increased powers for competitive tendering in line with the provisions in the Citizen's Charter.[7] These developments were in line with the idea of constraining local government's expenditure plans and making local government more responsive to the market.

13–009 Perceptible changes are evident in the role of local authorities as a result of these developments. First, there is a tendency towards centralisation of powers and policy decision-making. Secondly, there is a challenge to the effectiveness of local authorities being accountable to their own electorate. Current government thinking questions the efficiency of local government elections as an adequate means of accountability over local government. Since 1979 the bipartisan approach of the major political parties to local authority decision-making has been abandoned. Local authorities are perceived as "instruments of social welfare" and therefore seen as acting in opposition to the policies of central government. Thirdly, there is a tendency to envisage local authorities developing management styles more consistent with regulating local authority activities rather than delivering the services. Fourthly, there is a perceptible shift

---

6   Widdicombe Report, Cm.9797 (1986).
7   *Citizen's Charter*, Cm.1599 (1991).

in the variety and type of legislation which local authorities are required to follow. The Victorian style of legislation, containing broadly drafted wide discretion with enabling powers, has continued in modern times supplemented with complex, technical and precisely formulated provisions which require enforcement. Legal rules have replaced broad discretion. Detailed regulations, codes of practice and rules proliferate. The courts are expected to enforce such rules even if they may be in conflict with policy objectives of the duly elected local authority.[8]

Phase two: 1997–2002

The new Labour Government in 1997 embarked on an ambitious programme of modernisation and reform. The White Paper *Modern Local Government—in Touch with the People*[9] provides the long-term goal of the government to provide a new sense of community leadership. There followed two major statutory reforms. The Local Government Act 1999 repeals the compulsory competitive tendering arrangements, which is outlined below in more detail. A second part of the 1999 Act is the introduction of a new "best value" concept. Detailed regulations followed outlining how the concept was to be implemented. Over the past two years, local authorities have been expected to develop a Performance Plan for the local authority implementing best value. Best value reviews are conducted to ensure that performance targets are reached and the management of the local authority is up to standard.

The system of best value review has the following component parts[10]:

- identifying the current position of the service looking at performance and the market;

- determining the scope of the review to ensure that all aspects are covered and addressing priorities;

- consultation and comparison with customers and other providers;

- challenging the service and demonstrating it is competitive so that a gap analysis may be undertaken; and

- development of an action plan to ensure continuous improvement.

It is clear that all local authorities must meet the best value requirements of the legislation. This is a vague concept defined in the DETR paper as[11] "...about the cost and quality of services that meet the aspirations of the people". Local authorities must meet the centrally set

13–010

13–011

13–012

---
8   See *Report of the Committee of Enquiry into Local Government Finance*, Cmnd.6453 (1976) (The Layfield Report)/
9   Cm.4014 (1998).
10 *Warwick District Council Best Value Performance Plan 2002–03*.
11 DETR, *Best Value in Housing Framework* (1999), paras 1.3, 2.4.

performance indicators established by central government. They must publish an annual performance target and publish how they meet the standards of performance. Fundamental reviews must take place and this represents a further extension of regulation, command and control.

13-013
There are also detailed powers under the 1999 Act dealing with the capping powers over local government council tax. These are powers exercised by central government "to cap" or restrict the increases in council tax levied by local authorities. In theory the 1999 Act might mean a relaxation of the capping powers which are considered to be an excessive use of central government discretion since they were first introduced in 1992 when the council tax was introduced. In fact, on closer examination it is clear that the 1999 Act retains the power of the Secretary of State to cap the local authority's council tax. In s.30 Sch.1 there are powers to identify local authorities that are thought to be spending excessively. The Secretary of State is free to categorise a local authority and warn the relevant authority to take measures to prevent excessive spending. Once warned then there are extensive powers for calculating the amount of expenditure that is excessive and the Secretary of State may then nominate the authority for action to be taken. This may take the form of setting a sum for the authority's annual budget and for the incoming financial year setting targets to be met. In extreme circumstances where there is evidence of serious mismanagement it would be possible for central government to bring in their own management team to take over the management of the local authority. In July 2002, Hull City Council received criticism from an Inspector's report that may have led to central government operating its powers.[12]

13-014
In addition to the introduction of best value there is also a new management agenda contained in the Local Government Act 2000. The question of the governance of local authorities has not received much attention since the Widdicombe Committee last inquired into the business of local government in 1986. The aim of local authorities performing their role for the community is being strengthened by the idea that by April 2002 all local authorities are expected to introduce a new management structure. The idea is to introduce some form of democratic renewal as set out in the White Paper, *Strong Local Leadership: Quality Public Services*.[13] There is no single prescribed model. Local authorities are expected to choose the model that is agreed through consultation with the local community. There are various models on offer. One model is to be found in the London elected mayoral system. This is becoming increasingly popular with central government. Another model might be to set up a cabinet form of executive decision-making and variations on this theme might be employed. In total there are three models on offer as follows:

- mayor and cabinet with a directly elected mayor;

- a mayor and council manager executive, the mayor being directly elected and the authority appointed by the council as a council manager; and

- a leader and cabinet as an executive.

---

12 *Local Government Chronicle*, 25 July 2002. Civil servants were sent into to take over the powers of the city.
13 Cm.5237 (December 2001).

Local authorities have not adopted the mayoral model, though the emerging trends are difficult to predict. Only one electoral mayor other than London is proposed by referendum at Watford; only 13 authorities have held mayor referendums and only seven voted in favour. In May 2002 local elections were held; seven mayoral elections were held, five referendums were held on mayoral elections.[14] By 2006, the then Labour Government admitted disappointment as only 12 local authorities had by then adopted an elected mayor model. Since 2012 onwards, proposals have been made for conurbation or metro mayors. This has proven to be popular in the Greater Manchester Combined Authority. There are 16 elected mayors by Summer 2015.

Pt II of the Local Government Act 2000 provides that there should be improvements in the management and efficiency of local authorities. Each local authority should have a management committee appointed to take decisions on behalf of the authority. The management committee is composed of between five and nine leading councillors. Pt III of the Act makes changes to the audit arrangements and in particular removes the power of surcharge. Auditors will be able to seek advisory notices rather than a prohibition order as in the past.

Many of the new arrangements, such as the new management structures, are taking effect and it is too soon to evaluate them as the transitional arrangements are being put into place. The policy underlining the changes, however, is that a responsive and community-managed local authority will be more democratic. Despite this optimism that changes will be successful there is much local voter apathy and a belief that while local consultation may be improved, public service delivery is beyond the capacity and the structure of local authorities.

Phase three: The era of Localism under the Localism Act 2011 and decentralisation strategies

The most significant departure from the previous policy of successive governments from the 1980s of setting restraints on local authorities is the Localism Act 2011. The Act provides more general empowerment to local authorities than in the past allowing local authorities to act as an ordinary individual and allowing innovative ways for local authorities to undertake activities. Introducing an element of creativity into local authorities has the potential to invigorate them and develop their potential. Combined authorities may be created through the joining with other local authorities in their area. The combined authority has takeover powers for example for an integrated transport authority and can receive statutory powers by order approved by Parliament.

The Act has enabling powers to allow the transfer of public functions from central government to local government. This also includes the transfer from agencies and other quangos to local government to improve local accountability or promote economic growth. This empowerment in favour of local government establishes an important and potentially far reaching change in central local relations. The Act goes further by requiring local authorities to consider expressions of interest from voluntary or community bodies, charities or even parish councils,

---

14   House of Commons Library, *Briefing Paper Directly Elected mayors*, No.05000 (12 May 2015).

employees and local workers in providing services on behalf of the local authority. This is an important element in the new legislation and is consistent with the so-called "Big Society" idea that is intended to release community led public spirited and to some extent voluntary and unpaid work from citizens. The Act requires local authorities to maintain community assets and if they come up for sale to consider bids and proposals from community groups if they want to bid in the open market.

The Influence of the "Big Society"

13-019 David Cameron initiated the "Big Society" policy in May 2010. Its underlying belief is that ""big government" has failed and there is a need for a stronger civic society. Philosophically, the Big Society promotes "liberty" that stands between the tough individualism of Thatcherism and the traditional paternalism of the role of the state. Its aim is to advance the cause of the local community and a mutualism centred on community groups in an effort to reinvent urban democracy. It is reminiscent of Tony Blair's Third Way, the "Big Society" has three important themes: first, opening up public services through voluntary organisations, charities and social enterprises, including employee-owned co-operatives; secondly, encouraging social action and enabling the citizen to participate in society; and thirdly, community empowerment including giving local councils and neighbourhoods more powers to make local decisions and shape their communities. Partly this is a response to failures in big government and the over-centralised state, partly linked to reforming public services and building stronger communities and encourage responsibilities with powers from the state being made available to local communities. Benefits include providing support for voluntary groups and charities, mitigating the severity of the financial cuts, supporting diversity in society and reducing the size of the state. Examples include a National Citizen Service programme open to all 15–17 year olds to encourage personal development as well as a Big Society Capital Bank to make it easier for charities and social enterprises to access capital. Planned increase in voluntary work and charitable activities to encourage local community initiatives are in evidence. Various community based initiatives receive government funding and support through the Big Society Network and also Lottery Funding, Cabinet Office Grants and various charitable donations. Examples abound across many of the public service delivery sectors. In education and sports, social services and help for the elderly, the voluntary sector has been encouraged through many initiatives to provide support for their local communities, such as food banks, clothes and shelters for homeless. In essence the collaboration with civil society is expected to advance local decisions with individual influence. Volunteering and civic responsibility go together. The Localism Act 2011 introduces a wide variety of community rights. There is the right to bid for community assets supported by a £250 million Community Asset Fund to raise local money to finance community assets. To date there are1,500 assets of community value listed, the right to challenge local authority decisions and the right to build for the community are included. Neighbourhood planning with communities given a say in development are also supported by £23million fund. The community right to reclaim land that is underused or pre-owned by public bodies is also included. Local citizens are invited to use the Sustainable

Communities Act 2007 for changes to improve their local areas. Community action includes the Big Lottery's £190 million to encourage local community initiatives. Doubts remain about the longevity of the Big Society agenda beyond the next election or of its sustainability thereafter. Despite such Big Society voluntary initiatives, the private sector retains its dominance over many local services that used to be exclusively public.

C: Local Authorities, Organisation and Structure

The movement in favour of unitary local government authorities has gathered momentum. The re-drawing of local government took considerable time to implement. The Local Government (Wales) Act 1994 and the Local Government etc (Scotland) Act 1994 provided for unitary authorities in Wales and Scotland replacing the dual authority system inherited and re-organised in the 1970s.

13–020

- *Scotland*: 32 unitary authorities; and

- *Wales*: 22 unitary authorities.

There has been no equivalent legislation to introduce unitary authorities for every local authority in England. As a result, there are the following local authorities:

13–021

England

- 47 unitary authorities;

- 34 county councils; and

- 238 district councils.

London

- 32 London Boroughs; and

- one Greater London Authority and one elected mayor under devolution arrangements.

13-022 Under the Local Government Act 1992, the Local Government Commission for England was established with the task of undertaking a review of local government areas. Matters of such party political sensitivity exposed the ground rules of the Commission, given in the form of guidance, to a great deal of controversy. Matters of s.13(6) of the 1992 Act that should guide the Commission included preference to be given to "natural communities" and that account should be taken of peoples" preferences. However, the government insisted in its revised guidance issued in 1993 that the aim of having a unitary system of local authority should be considered. In R v Secretary of State for the Environment Ex p. Lancashire C[15] the guidance that sought to give undue weight to the Government's preference for unitary authorities was unlawful.

13-023 The approach taken thereafter was to consider the introduction of unitary authorities on a consultation basis. This process, begun in 1992, has proved more time-consuming and complex than was first envisaged. In addition, periodic electoral review is undertaken to rectify electoral imbalances in a local authority area. The Commission completed its review in early 1995. In the end, 50 all-purpose unitary authorities were proposed. Since March 1996 over 30 local authorities have been considered and the results of these deliberations will be forthcoming in the form of further consultation papers. The preference for an overwhelming number of unitary local authorities appears to have been held in check.

The modern functions of local authorities

13-024 Organisational and structural changes have also opened up a discussion as to the functions of local government. The position of local government within the UK's multi-layered constitutional arrangements has been the subject of much debate and political adjustment. The role and function of local authorities was examined in the Widdicombe Report (1986). The main characteristics of the modern local authority were identified. These include its diversity, the opportunities given for local democracy, the responsiveness to local needs through the delivery of services and finally its contribution to the national political system through its diversity of politics.

13-025 Diversity comes about through the geographical size and management style in different local authorities. The size of local authorities varies throughout the country and this includes the geographical areas covered, the size of population (from as few as 25,000 to over 1.5 million), and the amount of local authority expenditure which varies considerably from one authority to another. The Widdicombe Report drew attention to the difficult question of the role of local authorities. There remains intense debate as to how local authorities with such diversity in politics, size, finance and policy priorities may best develop relations with central government. In 1976 the Layfield Report[16] on local government finance identified two opposing views of local authority activities which were relevant to the Widdicombe inquiry.

---

15   [1994] 4 All E.R. 165; 93 L.G.R. 29 QBD.
16   *Report of the Committee of Enquiry into Local Government Finance*, Cmnd.6453 (1976) (The Layfield Report).

13-026 The "centralist" view is that local authorities act as agents for central government. As custodians of the interests of the local community they mitigate the dangers of remoteness and bureaucratic organisation which would occur if government were entirely centralised. On this view emphasis is placed not on the elected element in local authority activities, but on the sovereignty of Parliament to direct local authorities to carry out activities on behalf of central government policy-making. On this view local authorities are less free to develop their own distinctive policies which may conflict with central government's general direction and policy-making.

13-027 The opposing view is the "localist" view, that local authorities are decentralised with real political authority and power in respect of the functions which can appropriately be performed at the local level. On this view emphasis is placed on the statutory duties local authorities are expected and, in many cases, required to perform. Local authorities are entitled to develop their own strategies and are free to promote their own distinctive policies even if these might conflict with the policy of the government of the day.

13-028 The Widdicombe Report found this dichotomy of views unhelpful in the sense that the true constitutional status of local authorities was that they derived all their powers, not as autonomous entities with an entrenched constitutional status, but from Parliament. The view of central government and the tendency towards centralism in the past policies of central government left local authorities no option but to accept "as a fact of life" the reality of central government's legal authority. Today the debate remains just as intense and crosses party political lines. Those who favour reducing the power of the state desire a streamlined and slim local authority component. Those that favour public service delivery see local authorities as part of the delivery system, providing for the community a responsive public service.

13-029 There are many instances where the traditional functions of local authorities are being changed.[17] The introduction of elected Police Commissioners and the development of Academy status for many schools are examples of the transfer of many powers and duties away from the traditional local authority role. Plans to further develop autonomy for communities outside the traditional local authority role. The Localism Act 2011 provides the potential for greater autonomy than ever in the recent history of local government.

13-030 Local authorities possess some widely drawn statutory powers in addition to many specific statutory duties. A few examples illustrate how local authorities may be provided with wide statutory powers. Any local authority may exercise under s.111 of the Local Government Act 1972 general powers "to do anything which is calculated to facilitate or is conducive or incidental to, the discharge of any of their functions". Such powers, especially if used to raise money by borrowing or lending money, must also conform to detailed rules regulating these activities. Section 137 of the Local Government Act 1972 is a general power to incur expenditure subject to an annual financial limit. Such a power is intended to be used where there is no other statutory power available. More recently, the Local Government and Housing Act 1989 provides local authorities with a general power to promote economic development and considerable flexibility in carrying out their plans. Regulations assist in setting the limits of the permitted

---

17   T. Byrne, *Local Government in Britain*, 7th edn, revised (London: Penguin, 2000).

activities which may fall within their powers. The Local Government (Amendment) Act 1993 extends local authority powers to make grants to ethnic minorities by extending their powers under s.11 of the Local Government Act 1966. There are general powers under s.2 of the Local Government Act 2000 for the promotion of the economic, social and environmental wellbeing of the area. This is more broadly drafted than s.137 of the Local Government Act 1972 meaning that the benefit does not have to be commensurate with the expenditure.

The Cities and Local Government Devolution Act 2016

13-031   The policy of devolving legal and financial powers to local authorities is set out in the proposals in the new Cities and Local Government Devolution Act 2016. The policy direction in favour of local government has come from an economic strategy to reduce the size of central government departments and reduce spending in order to address the current deficit. The Act is consistent with past attempts to devolve power but there is growing support for this form of devolution demonstrated by the various city deals entered into between central and local government. This marks a new era in local autonomy and identifies local partnerships as a way of taking matters forward to the next stage of more intensive devolution. It is almost inevitable that once the idea of devolution begins to take shape it should become more popular. This may also be a reaction to the party political arrangements at the level of central government. The creation of metro-cities or large combined authorities is also an important aspect of the proposals. It is also symptomatic of a growing recognition that many local authorities offer strong leadership and have good experience of local engagement with corporate organisations. Various bids and suggestions for devolved powers will be negotiated over the coming years.[18]

Elections

13-032   The Local Government Act 1972 provides arrangements for the return of local councillors for each electoral area, that is at county, district or parish level. Electoral areas are designated according to the different levels of local government. There is a Local Government Boundary Commission, established under the 1972 Act for the purposes of keeping under review the "electoral arrangements" of the principal authorities. The Commission may also determine the number of councillors that may be returned for each constituency. The aim in carrying out both functions is the same, namely to provide arrangements "in the interests of effective and convenient local government".

13-033   Pt II of the Local Government Act 1992 establishes a Local Government Commission. One of its tasks is to take over the responsibilities of the Local Government Boundary Commission for England in the conduct of periodic reviews of electoral arrangements. Directions or guidance

---

18 House of Commons, *Cities and Local Government Devolution Bill 2015–16*, Briefing Paper, HL, No.CBP07322 (8 October 2015).

may be given to the Commission by the Secretary of State. The setting up of the Commission is intended to review matters concerning elections, boundaries and the structure of local government without recourse to a Royal Commission or similar inquiry. Three advantages are claimed from a unitary system of local government. First, a unitary system might promote local democracy by increasing the accountability of local authority communities; secondly, a unitary system might reduce bureaucracy and administrative costs inherent in the duplication of central management at county and district level; and thirdly, a unitary system offers the opportunity for improved co-ordination and cost-effectiveness in the delivery of local government services.

Under the 1972 Local Government Act the structure of local authorities is as follows. In the case of the county councils the area is divided into electoral divisions, with one council member returned for each division. Elections must be held every four years with each member retiring simultaneously.

In the case of the Shire district councils, the area is divided into electoral wards with three members normally returned for each ward. All the members of the council retire simultaneously, but it is possible to opt for a system of election based on one third of the council retiring at a time. Voting takes place only in those wards where a member is retiring. In wards where there are only one or two members returned, it is not possible to vote every year.

In the case of the metropolitan district councils, the electoral area is divided into wards with three members for each ward. One third of the members stand for election and elections are commonly held in three years out of four. On the principle that a member retires in each ward at each election, the entire electorate has the opportunity to vote.

In the case of the Parish or Community Council, any number of councillors may be elected. There is no maximum number for the size of the Parish Council, but the minimum is set at five. There are requirements under the Representation of the People Act 1983 that each District Council or London Borough Council must appoint an electoral officer. Responsibility falls on the electoral registration officer to prepare and publish each year an electoral register for both parliamentary and local government elections.

The electoral qualification for local government is similar to central government. However, disqualification is more widely drawn. Tenure of any office of profit at the disposal of a local authority or any of its committees is a disqualification for office as a councillor. Also bankruptcy, surcharge by the auditor or conviction for corrupt or illegal practices and incurring imprisonment within five years of an election is also a disqualification.

The electoral registration officer must also publish notice of the election, receive nominations and co-ordinate the arrangements for polling day. Turnout at local government elections is usually significantly less than at elections for central government—on average 40–50 per cent, compared to 75 per cent at a general election. In the elections held in May 2002, the turnout was 34.4 per cent. There are about 23,000 councillors in Britain. They appear to be untypical of the cross-section of the community. Byrne[19] notes how many are older than the age of 54, predominantly male, a large majority are owner-occupiers, white

---

19   T. Byrne, *Local Government in Britain*, 7th edn (London: Penguin, 2000), pp.196–199.

collar in occupation and most were well educated, to A level or above. Also a high proportion were among the better paid.

D: Change and Structure in Local Government

Structure and organisation

13-040 Unlike central government with a clearly defined executive, up until the Local Government Act 2000 there was no clearly defined concept of providing through different models some form of executive branch for local government. It will be for local authorities to opt for one of the models identified above. However, unlike central government there is no equivalent of ministerial responsibility, leaving a gap in the arrangements for accountability which in the past had been filled by the development of a separate Audit Commission from 1982–2015 when the Audit Commission was abolished. There is also a local government ombudsman. It will be interesting to speculate whether an elected mayor will embrace a prime ministerial or presidential style of leadership where this model of governance is adopted. This is likely to be only in a minority of local authorities The development of an executive element is likely to be the most popular and under this model the question of decision-making and accountability is evolving.

13-041 Local government may be described as combining an elected element, namely the councillors, and an administrative staff comprising, at the most senior level, professional officers. The council chairman is annually elected; decisions are taken by resolutions of the council or through officials acting with delegated authority. The council usually works through a large number of committees. Standing orders and minutes are kept of the conduct of meetings and under the Public Bodies (Admission to Meetings) Act 1960 members of the public are normally admitted.[20] The Chairman has power to exclude the public in cases of disorderly conduct[21] and meetings may be kept confidential and closed to the public where the nature of business or public interest requires.

13-042 Following the Widdicombe Committee report legislation was introduced to bring greater openness into the conduct of local authority business. The Local Government (Access to Information) Act 1985 requires councils to give public notice of meetings, make available certain relevant documents and make the agenda, minutes and relevant reports public. The main caveat is that they do not have to be disclosed if confidential information relating to

---

20 See *R v Liverpool City Council Ex p. Liverpool Taxi Fleet Operators Association* [1975] 1 W.L.R. 701; [1975] 1 All E.R. 379 QBD, which discusses the rights of the public to attend meetings.
21 *R v Brent HA Ex p. Francis* [1985] Q.B. 869; [1984] 3 W.L.R. 1317 QBD.

government departments or the like is disclosed. Reports and background papers are open to inspection by members of the public for four years in the case of any background papers and six years for other papers.

Excluded from open access are matters relating to personal information about members of staff in connection with employment and this restriction includes access to information regarding wages and the payment of benefits.

The Widdicombe Committee paid particular attention to the role of the principal officer of a local authority and the committee structure of local authority decision-making. The aim of the Widdicombe Committee was to strengthen the system of democratic accountability. For example, *R v Waltham Forest LBC Ex p. Baxter*[22] illustrated how leading councillors and local political activists met and later attended meetings of the council. The link between ideology and local authority decision-making seemed complete. This link was criticised by the courts.

The Local Government and Housing Act 1989 provides important changes to the organisation and management of committees ensuring that representation on committees and sub-committees comprises various political groups. There are provisions to prevent officers from serving on more than one local authority and for the non-voting of non-elected and appointed members of committees. Some provision is made for the appointment of political advisers. The changes introduced in 1989 were less than those recommended by the Widdicombe Report.

Competitive tendering for local authority services

The history of competitive tendering and its reform under the new Labour Government may be outlined as follows: the shift in focus from local authorities in the 1980s as[23] "providers of services" to local authorities as "enablers and regulators" is well illustrated by the introduction of competitive tendering. For a period up until 2000, Britain was the only European country in which competitive tendering for certain local authority services was compulsory. The British experience probably represented the most systematic and comprehensive experience of compulsory tendering. The stages adopted in the use of competitive tendering began in the National Health Service prior to 1988 and introduced catering, domestic and laundry services to competitive tendering. Individual health authorities extended various support services such as porters and ground maintenance to competitive tendering. In various central government departments such as the Ministry of Defence and also in the civil service competitive tendering has been extensively used.

In 1980, the Local Government Planning and Land Act 1980 (Pt III) required certain local authority construction and maintenance work to be made subject to competitive tendering.

---

22 [1988] Q.B. 419; [1988] 2 W.L.R. 257 CA (Civ Div).
23 *Municipal Review* (April, 1989), p.9. See Byrne, T. Byrne, *Local Government in Britain*, 7th edn (London: Penguin, 2000), Chs 9 and 10. Also see *The New Local Authorities: Management and Structure* (The Bains Report) (London: HMSO, 1972).

13-048 Highways and building work were included. Traditionally for such work local authorities operated their own Direct Labour Organisations (DLO). After 1980 DLOs could continue to carry out their work but on the basis of winning a competitive contract not on an automatic basis.

In 1985 the Government issued a White Paper: Competition in the Provision of Local Authority Service[24] (February 1985) which argued for an extension of competitive tendering to a wider range of activities such as catering, refuse collection, building, cleaning schools, welfare catering and sporting and leisure activities. The Local Government Act 1988 required local authorities to provide competition for the above services. DLOs are permitted to bid for contracts but are not given any preferential treatment. Services subject to contract bids were expected to be subject to competition at six month intervals between 1 August 1989 and 1 January 1992. The extension of competition into local authority activities is set to continue. Parallel legislation such as the Education Reform Act 1988 and the Local Government and Housing Act 1989 continued to introduce competitive elements into education and local authority companies.

Private finance initiative projects

13-049 The Government has taken steps to encourage private finance to be invested in public sector activities. Since November 1992 the Private Finance Initiative (PFI) allows private finance to be used for public sector capital activities including buildings, computer technology, know-how and new management systems. The most notable examples of PFI are in the Channel Tunnel Rail Link and other new construction projects. HM Treasury have insisted that their criteria for a PFI project is that "the genuine risk" is transferred to the private sector and the project represents value for money when public sector finance is involved. The idea behind the PFI strategy is that of a public-private partnership allowing some degree of contracting out where public services are contracted from the private sector. PFI has the potential to transform the problems of long-term capital under-funding in local government. In the context of local authorities PFI requires careful supervision because of the restrictive nature of local authority powers. PFI has been used extensively throughout the country for about 450 major projects such as new hospital buildings, roads, prisons, education and Northern Line Trains. The supervision of each project is vested in a central government department.

Central-local government relations

13-050 As outlined above, relations between local and central government have proved controversial, especially when there may be ideological differences about role and function. Central government has sought greater accountability over the provision of public services, especially with

---

24 See Audit Commission, *Competitiveness and Contracting Out of Local Authorities Services* (London: HMSO, 1987).

Local Authority Finance

13-051 Local government finance is highly complex and the complexity has not diminished in recent years. As already noted, local authority spending is at least 60 per cent of public spending. The vast amount of expenditure is taken up with education, housing and personal social services.

13-052 The structures of local government's financial arrangements are complex and have undergone considerable change. In outline the following description is an attempt to explain the main features of the system, from the old system of rating valuation to the new system of community charge, in operation until 1 April 1993, and afterwards its replacement by the Council Tax.[25]

13-053 Historically local authorities were given wide discretion and a degree of self-regulation over the financial arrangements and accounting practices in use in local government. Local authority expenditure is divided between revenue and capital. Revenue expenditure refers to short-term matters such as salaries and office supplies and is funded out of current income; capital expenditure refers to longer term spending such as buildings and is funded from borrowing. The latter has caused central government to restrict and control the extent of local government borrowing in order to control public spending as part of its long-term policy.

13-054 Local authority finance is often complicated and beset by technical and detailed legal rules. Current expenditure is funded from three main sources of income: charges made by local government for services, etc.; central government grants; and, up until 1990, rates. Of the three, the main sources of local authority income came from rates (now replaced by the Council Tax) and grants from central government.

13-055 Rates were based on a property valuation and were levied on both domestic and business occupancy. Their origin may be traced to the earliest development of local authorities. In the Vagabonds Act 1535, churchwardens were responsible for the administration of the poor through relief charged upon each parish. The Poor Relief Act 1597 recognised the growing scale of the amount of relief and introduced a general system of local rating. Compulsory rating, enforced through distress and sale of chattels for non-payment, was accompanied by a system of audit, later through a district auditor under the Poor Law Amendment Act 1866, and proper accounting introduced by the Poor Relief Act 1601. Consolidation of enforcement procedures was further provided in the General Rates Act 1967. The basis of the rating system depended on regular valuation of property values. Property values, which set the basis of the rating system, had not been revalued since April 1973 in England, and any re-valuation was seen as problematic, which prompted the Government to consider changes in the rating system of local government finance.

---

25 C. M. G. Himsworth, "Poll Tax Capping and Judicial Review" [1991] *Public Law* 76–92. Also see C. M. G. Himsworth and N. C. Walker, "After Rates? The Community Charge in Scotland" [1987] *Public Law* 586.

13-056 A further complication arose when local authorities increased the amount of revenue from the rates by sharply increasing rate levels. By 1974 this had caused a "crisis in local government finance which led to the setting up of the Layfield Committee[26] into local government finance which reported after two years of deliberations in 1976".

13-057 An additional complication to the rating system was the need for major financial support from central government through a Rate Support Grant under the Local Government Act 1966 and later amended by the Local Government, Planning and Land Act 1980 Pt VI. In the mid-1970s the extent of central government grants received by local authorities exceeded the amount raised by rates. Over 60 per cent of local authority funding came through central government grant, an indication of the dependency of local authorities on central government. The form of grant, the Rate Support Grant (RSG), was as a block grant which left local authorities free to determine how spending priorities could be identified within their statutory duties imposed on local authorities. Local authorities could increase the level of their rates to take account of their expenditure.

13-058 Central government desired to impose a new financial discipline on local authorities and imposed a revision of the RSG system on each local authority. The revision was set out according to the assessment of each local authority spending conducted by central government under the Local Government, Planning and Land Act 1980. Included under the 1980 Act were controls on local government capital expenditure in an effort to reduce local government expenditure and curtail the freedom of local authorities to depart from the financial policies of central government.

13-059 The theory behind the 1980 Act was that differences in local authority spending habits might be identified and controls applied to the more prolific spending authorities. Further refinements to the 1980 Act were provided by the Local Government Finance Act 1982 by setting spending targets and penalties on local authorities. The 1982 Act introduced the Audit Commission to improve the financial management of local authorities. The 1982 Act also abolished supplementary rates.

13-060 Local authority ingenuity contrived to avoid the effects of central government's initiatives at control. Setting targets for local authority spending did not prove effective and in 1984 the Rates Act included powers to the Secretary of State to control the making of rates and the issuing of precepts. This introduced the concept of "rate capping" whereby the Secretary of State could determine the rates of "over-spending" authorities and limit their rate levels. This led to further "creative accounting" by local authorities. Central government found the making of regulations and their enforcement a complex and expensive game of "cat and mouse" between local and central government.

13-061 The abolition of the Greater London Council and the six Metropolitan Counties took place in 1985 as a further attempt to curtail the more irritating excesses of local government. However, these changes and the adaptation of the rates system to bring it within central government control failed to address the central issue of how to provide a satisfactory system for the finance of local government.

---

26 *Reports of the Layfield Committee*, Cmnd.6453 (1976).

13-062 The Layfield Committee in 1976 in reviewing local government rating, had noted the difficulty of re-valuation of property based on notional rental values. The Layfield Committee recommended that re-valuation should take place on the basis of property sale price. The system of rating remained unchanged, although the government in its election manifestos from 1979 promised to introduce reforms to the rating system. The Department of Environment published in December 1981 a Green Paper entitled *Alternatives to Domestic Rates* which examined the three options possible for reform: a local sales tax a local income tax; and a Poll Tax. There were, however, considerable doubts about the desirability and cost of the Poll Tax, not least from the then Chancellor of the Exchequer Nigel Lawson who "was unequivocal" in his opposition to the Poll Tax, and who noted that the Poll Tax was chosen as the best option for the reform of local government finance. Nigel Lawson in his memoirs stated[27]:

> "The Poll Tax was then given fresh momentum by the removal of Patrick Jenkin as Environment Secretary in the first week of September 1985 and his replacement by Kenneth Baker, who as Minister of State in charge of local government was part-author of the original proposal."

13-063 Dissatisfaction with the rating system resulted in its abolition and replacement with the Community Charge, commonly called the Poll Tax, under the Local Government Finance Act 1988 and the Local Government and Housing Act 1989. The responsibilities of local authorities included the conduct of a canvass of properties in their areas, allocating between chargepayers the various categories of charge such as the personal or collective community charge, maintaining a register and a public extract, imposing penalties and demanding payments.

13-064 The introduction of the Community Charge was intended to remove the need for the complex rate-capping procedures and the acrimonious relations between local and central government. The tax was essentially on each of the electors in each local authority. All adults were expected to pay the tax and it was first implemented in Scotland in 1989 in advance of England and Wales. Originally in 1988 the charge was estimated at £200 per capita, but by 1990 when the tax came to be implemented the average tax was around £400. The business rates remained unaffected by the introduction of the Community Charge.

13-065 Complications in the implementation of the charge added to the general dissatisfaction over the tax. Non-payment of the tax, difficulty of enforcing court orders against defaulters and massive administrative costs of keeping the register up to date made the tax difficult and cumbersome to collect. Anomalies arose in the way the charge was calculated leading to larger than expected charges. Some Conservative local authorities, considered to be well run and managed, found charges over 30 per cent greater than had been expected. In others the cost was up to 36 per cent greater. As a result, the Secretary of State was forced to use his charge capping powers with a formula, which proved controversial, to limit the amount of the charge on certain local authorities. In 1990, 21 local authorities were charge-capped. Extra

---

27   Nigel Lawson, *The View from No. 11* (London: Corgi Press, 1992), pp.561–585.

assistance from the Treasury only served to reinforce the earlier doubts about the efficacy of the Community Charge. Invariably the Government's popularity diminished which may have contributed to the leadership crisis leading to the resignation of Mrs Thatcher.

13-066 The dissatisfaction with the Community Charge caused the Government to reconsider once more the basis of taxation for local government. A Council Tax took effect from 1 April 1993 under the Local Government Finance Act 1992, involving an element of property valuation in the setting of the charge. Ironically this has required the valuation of the entire housing stock in order to implement the changes introduced by the new tax. The tax is based on the banded capital value of domestic property, with discounts for the number and status of the adults who are resident in the property. There are provisions for people on low incomes. There is a Valuation Office Agency responsible for the valuation of domestic property for the Council Tax.

13-067 The current law is to be found in the Local Government Finance Act 1992. The Council Tax may best be described as "a hybrid". It is not wholly a property tax but in part bears some resemblance to the Community Charge as it has some elements of "a household tax", because of the use of rebates depending on the income of the occupier. The property element comes from the fact that the Council Tax is based on a valuation of property in which the person lives on 1 April 1991. There are eight property bands with different limits in England, Scotland and Wales to take account of differentials in the property market. In theory the higher band tax payer will pay about three times as much as the lower band payer. The household element comes from a rebate scheme based on income. This element is intended to mitigate the poverty of the household in cases of small or no income. Thus the household will be unaffected by the tax set by the Council if the means of the occupants of the property are such that there is a reduction in tax. There are, in addition, certain groups specifically exempted.

E: Judicial Oversight and Local Authority Activities

13-068 Local authorities are subject to the rules of administrative law in the same way as any other administrative decision-maker that has statutory powers. In fact, some of the most important principles of administrative law emerged in cases involving local authorities. In *Associated Picture Houses Ltd v Wednesbury Corp*[28] the courts tested the condition of a licence, restricting children under 15 to admission to Sunday performances in a cinema, according to whether the condition was unreasonable or not. In upholding the condition of the local authority as legal the courts established a test of reasonableness which has been influential in the development

---

28   [1948] 1 K.B. 223; [1947] 2 All E.R. 680 CA.

of administrative law. The test is known as *Wednesbury* unreasonableness when the authority has come to a conclusion "so unreasonable that no reasonable authority could ever have come to it". Judicial review of discretionary powers exercised by local authorities involves ensuring that the purpose, policy and objectives of a statute should not be frustrated in the exercise of statutory powers. Irrelevant considerations should not be taken when making decisions. Ignoring facts or errors of law or fact, may give rise to a ground for challenge.[29]

13-069

Judicial review may be seen as an important means to check on the legality of local authority activities. It also provides for the resolution of disputes between the parties especially in the resolution of disputes between central and local government.[30] Sunkin[31] has estimated that "approximately 20 per cent were challenges to decisions of other local authorities". A sizeable proportion of the applications for judicial review involve the local authority in areas such as homeless persons, education disputes, matters involving planning and the environment, and the internal affairs of local authorities.

13-070

Local authorities have also a role in representing the public interest and a limited role in seeking to protect rights narrower but analogous with the Attorney-General's role. Section 222 of the Local Government Act 1972 contains legal powers for the "promotion and protection of the interests of the inhabitants of their area." A local authority is competent to take proceedings in its own name without the consent of the Attorney-General. Proceedings by local authorities have included action against illegal trading under the Shops Act 1950, the control of noise pollution and trading in breach of controls over sex shops.[32] The constitutional importance of judicial review is underlined by the authors of the study as follows[33]:

> **"There are lessons to be drawn here about the constitutional significance of judicial review. Judicial review is often depicted as a weapon in the hands of the citizen against the over-mighty powers of central government, and it has certainly performed this role in a number of recent high profile cases. Our data suggests, however, that over the past decade it has been used more often as a weapon to further limit the autonomy of local government rather than as a constraint on the power of the central state."**

Public lawyers interested in local government will consider that the recent Court of Appeal decision in *Credit Suisse v Allerdale BC*[34] is significant. Allerdale local authority engaged in a

13-071

---

29 *Secretary of State for Education and Science v Tameside MBC* [1977] A.C. 1014; [1976] 3 W.L.R. 641 HL.
30 [1977] A.C. 1014.
31 M. Sunkin, "The Judicial Review Case-load 1987–89" [1991] *Public Law* 490 at [498].
32 See *Solihull MBC v Maxfern Ltd* [1977] 1 W.L.R. 127; [1977] 2 All E.R. 177 Ch D. Also B. Hough "Local Authorities as Guardians of the Public Interest" [1992] *Public Law* 130.
33 Hough "Local Authorities as Guardians of the Public Interest", pp.193–194.
34 [1997] Q.B. 306; [1996] 3 W.L.R. 894 CA (Civ Div).

joint venture through a number of companies set up by the local authority, technically known as "local government influenced companies", to build and operate a leisure complex. A time-share scheme was envisaged as the best means to operate the complex. Credit Suisse, a leading international banking institution, provided substantial loans repayable over a fixed period. The District Auditor queried the legality of the local authority joint venture companies, the local authority involvement and the investment of Credit Suisse. This arose when the ability of the local authority companies to repay the loans came into doubt. The case involved legal consideration of the powers and duties of the local authority and its relationship to Credit Suisse. The Court of Appeal held that the arrangements with the joint venture companies was ultra vires the powers of the local authority.

13-072 The Court of Appeal has therefore adopted a highly restrictive approach in the interpretation of local government powers. The result of the case left Credit Suisse largely exposed to debts and liabilities that arise from the ultra vires transaction. This will seriously inhibit local government joint ventures with the private sector.

13-073 Local authorities possess wide statutory enforcement powers which may give rise to litigation. In *Kirklees MBC v Wickes Building Supplies Ltd*,[35] the local authority sought an interlocutory injunction under s.222 of the Local Government Act 1972 restraining a DIY shop from trading contrary to s.47 of the Shops Act 1950. Criminal prosecutions under the Shops Act 1950 had little deterrent effect with large stores prepared to pay fines as a "tax" on Sunday opening. The use of an injunction by the local authority was an attempt to enforce the law when criminal prosecutions were ineffective. The use of injunctions is a common practice for local authorities in a range of circumstances where the criminal law may be of dubious value in terms of its effectiveness. In such cases the question arises as to the making of a cross-undertaking in damages. In the *Kirklees* case the local authority declined, most likely because such an undertaking might result in large liabilities for the local authority should the case be finally resolved in favour of the shops. Lord Goff in the House of Lords accepted that a local authority could be treated in the same way as the Crown and not be required to give an undertaking in damages.

13-074 Occasionally major issues of policy are raised involving the precise nature and role of the local authority. In *Bromley LBC v GLC*[36] the House of Lords held unlawful the subsidy of the now defunct GLC to the London Transport Executive. The majority group in the GLC had regarded themselves bound by an election manifesto and had accordingly fettered their discretion unreasonably. The subsidy supported a reduction in fares of 25 per cent and this was regarded by the House of Lords as an improper exercise of discretion. The majority in the House of Lords also held that local authorities owed a general fiduciary duty to their rate payers.

13-075 Local authorities are statutory corporations. They may enter contracts and freely negotiate commercial arrangements. Local authorities are subject to their own statutory powers and the ultra vires rule. This rule means that a local authority should not act outside its statutory

---

35 [1993] A.C. 227; [1992] 3 W.L.R. 170 HL.
36 [1983] 1 A.C. 768; [1982] 2 W.L.R. 92 HL.

powers. Each local authority has its own legal personality[37] and may make use of Private Bill legislation to enhance its powers. Private Bills are a regular means for local authority powers to be extended—though it is doubtful if a local authority can sue for libel in respect of its governing or administrative reputation. However a local authority or[38] "any corporation, whether trading or non-trading, which can show that it has a corporate reputation (as distinct from that of its members) which is capable of being damaged by a defamatory statement, can sue in libel to protect that reputation, in the same way as can a natural person, although there will of course be certain types of statement which cannot defame an artificial person".

13-076

Loughlin[39] has reviewed the increase in the use of legal rules settling disputes over the functions, structures and financial arrangements of local government. One area which illustrates this phenomenon are disputes over local government finance, particularly over the rate support system under the rating system replaced by the Community Charge and later the Council Tax.

13-077

The Secretary of State was obliged to follow complex rules to set the amount of RSG available for the year. A report had to be prepared and laid before the House of Commons before the individual local authority grant could be determined. Disputes on the policy which informed the Secretary of State's view of the aggregation rules gave use to court cases challenging the application of the rules. In one such case however, *R v Secretary of State for the Environment Ex p. Nottinghamshire C*[40] the House of Lords showed reluctance to interfere in the discretion of the Secretary of State who was making a "political judgment". Only in exceptional cases would judicial review be available and only if the Secretary of State had failed to consult or ignored matters expressly listed in the legislation. Local authorities have continued to seek to exploit ambiguities, "loopholes" or uncertainties in the law in order to increase the revenue available to their needs. Often Labour-controlled authorities have spearheaded the manipulation of financial rules to meet expenditure programmes. The court's willingness to declare some of the more speculative local authorities schemes as unlawful may be seen in *Stockdale v Haringey LBC*.[41] The Court of Appeal struck out as unlawful the use of Haringey LBC's loans fund to maintain its expenditure programmes.

13-078

Local authorities have continually resorted to new techniques to find additional revenue and as these techniques are put in place, so central government rules are introduced to attempt to control prolific spending by local authorities through "innovative financing". Central government's frustrations were not helped by the additional complexity of the rules and the excessive legalism of their application. The growth in litigation and the need for expensive legal opinions before decisions could be reached contributed to the decision to replace local authority rates with first the Community Charge and then the Council Tax.

---

37   Per Balcombe LJ in *Derbyshire C v Times Newspapers* [1992] Q.B. 770; [1992] 3 W.L.R. 28 CA (Civ Div) at [75].
38   [1992] Q.B. 770.
39   M. Loughlin, "Innovative Financing in Local Government: The Limits of Legal Instrumentalism" Pts I and II [1990] *Public Law* 372–407 and [1991] *Public Law* 568–599.
40   [1986] A.C. 240; [1986] 2 W.L.R. 1 HL.
41   88 L.G.R. 7; [1989] R.A. 107 CA (Civ Div).

Controls over local government expenditure

13-079 A particularly difficult area was the power of central government to "rate cap" local authorities for excessive spending. The "rate cap" was a fiscal device used by central government to prevent an individual local authority from increasing its revenue by increasing the rates charged to inhabitants within its area. This was a bitterly contested power under the Rates Act 1984 which it was hoped the introduction of the Community Charge would end. In theory the Community Charge was a per capita tax, allowing a substantial level of autonomy to local authorities. Local authorities with large expenditure totals would charge their inhabitants more than local authorities with lower expenditure requirements. Central government labelled local authorities who were high spenders as wasteful. It was expected that such local authorities would be electorally unpopular as inhabitants would suffer higher Poll Tax Bills. Potentially the Poll Tax had the political significance of giving electoral advantage to the Conservatives rather than the Labour-controlled local authority. Labour-controlled authorities were alleged to need to spend large amounts of public money to provide their services.

13-080 The introduction of the Community Charge, first in Scotland, then in England, required the Government to introduce "charge capping powers". These were similar to the rate-capping powers abolished with the rates. They were proved necessary because the Government undertook a review of the appropriate level of total standard spending of all local authorities which resulted in an allocation of the appropriate spending needed for each individual local authority. The result of that exercise showed that a number of local authorities' Community Charge Bills exceeded the expectations of the central government based on their predictions and calculation of the requirements for each local authority.

13-081 In *Hammersmith and Fulham LBC v Secretary of State for the Environment*[42] the House of Lords considered the legality and the operation of the Poll Tax capping rules. Two arguments were made by Hammersmith and Fulham against the Secretary of State's decision to cap the local authority Poll Tax charge. First, that the Secretary of State should satisfy himself that the authority's budget was excessive; and secondly the Secretary of State should consider whether the authority's budget should be designated as requiring the application of the Poll Tax cap. Both arguments were rejected by Lord Bridge. In upholding the legality of the Secretary of State's powers the House of Lords left the subjective judgment of the Secretary of State intact. The judicial viewpoint was that there was no objective criterion which could be used to determine excessive expenditure. No "procedural impropriety" could be found in the Secretary of State's decision. As a result, separate and therefore different levels of expenditure applied in different local authorities. In applying this criterion, the Secretary of State admitted that differences based on political considerations might apply. This gave rise to inconsistencies in the level of the "cap" with the political implication that Labour-controlled local authorities were not fairly treated. However, the courts were unwilling to offer any review of the criteria. The House of Lords concluded that the Secretary of State was the best judge of the differences and was free to set his own principles. There was no obligation to set out the reasons behind the principles.

---

42   [1991] 1 A.C. 521; [1990] 3 W.L.R. 898 HL.

The *Hammersmith and Fulham* decision raises important questions about the use of judicial review. The local authority perspective is that the role of the courts is to act as a fetter on the potentially unrestrained powers of central government. Statutory interpretation should be sufficiently creative to allow the courts an opportunity to intervene. From the courts' perspective, however, there is difficulty in finding suitable and acceptable standards which may be used to adjudicate between central and local government. Courts have found this area of the law to be complex. Especially so when the doctrine of ministerial responsibility applies in the case of central government Ministers who are accountable to Parliament.

The complexity of the legal rules, the vagueness of standards of judicial review and the political nature of local authority decision-making, give the courts wide discretion when reviewing the powers of local authorities. The courts are in a sensitive area of having to adjudicate between central and local government over matters involving the fundamental role of local authorities.

Local authority speculation in the swaps market highlights another dimension to judicial review. In *Hazell v Hammersmith and Fulham LBC*,[43] Hammersmith had invested substantial sums in the swaps market in order to find investment income to finance expenditure. The basic principle of the swaps market is that a borrower at a fixed interest rate contracts with a third party to pay or receive the difference between his interest liability and what it would have been at a variable interest. Many local authorities became active in this lucrative market. Hammersmith had gained up to £37 million in interest premiums by the end of 1989. But with the rise in interest rates on local authority borrowings and the loss of confidence in the stock market, it was estimated that Hammersmith might lose between £74 million and £186 million. A large number of other local authorities had similarly invested. The precise legality of the investments was open to doubt.

The local authority relied on s.111(1) of the Local Government Act 1972 which empowered local authorities certain borrowing powers: "calculated to facilitate, or conducive or incidental to, the discharge of any of their functions". The local government auditor challenged the legality of local authority investment in the swaps market as being unlawful. This court case initiated by the auditor was opposed by the banks and financial institutions who wished to show the transactions were lawful.

If the transactions were held to be unlawful, the banks would have to bear the burden of the debts because local authority liability could not extend to transactions which were potentially void because of their illegality. In a curiosity of the case, the local authorities who at first argued for the lawfulness of the transactions found that their best interests would be served if the transactions were declared void. This would leave the local authority free of the bulk of any debt liability.

The House of Lords concluded that Hammersmith's swap transactions were ultra vires. Their reasoning relied on the statutory interpretation of s.111(1). Particular emphasis was placed on Pt 1 to Sch.13 of the 1972 Act[44] which limited the general powers of borrowing given to local

---

43 [1990] 2 W.L.R. 1038; [1991] 2 W.L.R. 372.
44 This section should be read alongside Sch.13 which limits s.111(1): The terms of Sch.13 are such that Lord

authorities under s.111(1). Lord Templeman concluded that the Schedule was "inconsistent with any incidental power to enter into swaps transactions".

13-088 The case had far reaching effects. Local authority debts arising out of the swaps market were generally taken up by banks and financial institutions through protracted litigation in an attempt to unravel the nature of many individual swaps transactions. Currently, uncertainty arises as to the liability of financial advisers and lawyers advising local authorities to enter the swap market.

13-089 Loughlin[45] criticises the courts. He argues that in reaching their decisions the Lords adopted a "strict constructionist line" and were affected by their perceptions both of the nature of the swaps market and the reasons for local authority investment in it. This raises the question of how suitable the courts may be in developing "a managerial role" over local authorities. Loughlin questions whether the courts have sufficiently developed techniques to interpret complex regulatory and financial issues. There is also the question of the adjudicative functions performed by courts and their suitability in enforcing legal rules of such complexity involving financial management.

13-090 In this regard the characteristics of legislation affecting local authorities in the 1980s deserve mention. Loughlin describes this as "a new style of legislation", namely precise directive powers setting out a comprehensive regulatory structure. Such legislation gives the courts little opportunity not to apply the exact wording and letter of the law to local authorities. Courts are, in effect, required to exercise a regulatory role over local authorities.

13-091 Against this criticism there is the counterbalancing argument that the courts are effectively the only fair way to determine what the law is. In the decision of the auditor to seek a judicial remedy lies the question of whether the legal rules were correctly applied by the local authority. Ultimately such legal issues require the courts to clarify the law however inconvenient or overridden with policy issues.

13-092 The question of the management of local government sets new challenges for the courts. The traditional value of the courts in developing procedural redress on the basis of *Wednesbury* unreasonableness or where local authority councillors may be surcharged as in *Roberts v Hopwood*[46] is only a starting point. Courts are increasingly required to develop their legal

---

Templeman (at p.387) stated: "Schedule 13 establishes a comprehensive code which defines and limits the powers of a local authority with regard to its borrowing. The Schedule is in my view inconsistent with any incidental power to enter into swaps transactions." "1. Without prejudice to section III above—(a) a principal council may borrow money for the purpose of lending money to another authority. . . (b) a local authority. . . may borrow money for any other purpose of class of purpose approved for the purposes of this sub-paragraph by the Secretary of State and in accordance with any conditions subject to which the approval is given. . ." "However this general power is negatived by the provision of para.7 and is subject to regulation 7. (1). Where expenditure incurred by a local authority for any purpose is defrayed by borrowing, the local authority shall. . . debit the account from which that expenditure would otherwise fall to be defrayed with a sum equivalent to an instalment of principal and interest combined such that if paid annually it would secure the payment of interest at the due rate on the outstanding principal together with the repayment of the principal not later than the end of the fixed period [of the loan]."

45 Loughlin, [1991] *Public Law* 568–599. Also see N. Deakin, "Local Government; Some recent change and future Prospects" [1991] *Parliamentary Affairs* 493–504.
46 *Roberts v Hopwood* [1925] A.C. 578 HL; and *Pickwell v Camden LBC* [1983] Q.B. 962; [1983] 2 W.L.R. 583 QBD.

techniques of review and are required to make more exacting judgment on the regulation of decision-making in local authorities. This raises questions about how best local authorities may be managed.

13-093

The role of the courts is often problematic. Increasingly called upon to enforce legal controls over local authority activities, the complexities of financial management, social, economic and political issues expose the inadequacies of many legal techniques of analysis. Invariably courts offer ex post facto review, limited to highly technical and procedural problems which may not fit the management requirements which the law adopts when used as a regulating mechanism. How to best interpret legislative powers in the context of local authorities has given rise to quite strict interpretation.[47] Techniques of statutory construction in use by the ordinary courts pose the question raised by Loughlin. Do the courts possess "the cognitive conceptual and material resources" to enable them to perform the functions expected?

13-094

The challenge for the future development of judicial review is reminiscent of the challenge identified in 1947 by William Robson which then formed the development of administrative law. Robson explained that administrative law had to respond[48]

> "to the creation of new types of offences against the community, the growth of a new conception of social rights, an enhanced solicitude for the common good and a lessening of that belief in the divinity of extreme individualistic rights which was evinced in the early 19th century."

13-095

Today the courts face a growing belief in the market as a regulator, the preference for individual choice, and sceptism about the ability of local government to manage and deliver services as part of their statutory responsibility.

F: Audit and Accountability

13-096

For many years the Audit Commission established under Pt III of the Local Government Finance Act 1982 was responsible for the audit of local authorities in England and Wales. The Audit Commission built on the established system of local authority audit with its modern origins in the late nineteenth century. However, the earliest origins of auditing may be traced back to the fifteenth century. District Auditors for each local authority are appointed by the Audit Commission. Auditors may be either officers of the Commission or appointed private firms of accountants. The status of the Commission rested on its professionalism and statutory powers.

---

47   See *R (MK) v Barking and Dagenham LB Council* [2013] EWHC 3486 (Admin).
48   W. A. Robson, *Justice and Administrative Law* (London: Stevens & Sons, 1947), p.31.

It was not directly responsible to any Minister but makes annual reports to Parliament. The Commission was itself subject to audit by the National Audit Office. As Radford has pointed out that the Audit Commission was appointed[49]

> "with the twin objectives of emphasising the independence of the audit process and greater value for money in local authority spending, the government being of the view that 'improving public sector efficiency is still in large measure a matter of improving scrutiny, monitoring and management within the context of existing institutions'."

13-097

Auditors appointed by the Audit Commission had to ensure in the word of Lord Sumner in *Roberts v Hopwood* that[50]

> "The purpose of the whole audit is to ensure wise and prudent administration and to recover for the council's funds money that should not have been taken out of them."

13-098

In 1983 the House of Lords in *Bromley LBC v GLC*[51] established that local authorities had a fiduciary duty to their ratepayers. Lord Diplock noted that such a duty was "not to spend money thriftlessly" but make full use of the financial resources available. In the context of establishing good guidance for local authorities, the Commission has followed this principle and has attempted to apply it to the development of strategies for the future of local authorities.

13-099

The Audit Commission also advised on the legality of local authority investments or financial plans. This is an important task and, as discussed above, illustrates the watchdog function the Commission performed in the example of *Hazell v Hammersmith*[52] which was initiated by the District Auditor. In giving advice, the Audit Commission is primarily addressing the Auditors under its control, although this does not preclude the advice becoming widely known to the local authority.

13-100

The most controversial investigation carried out by the District Auditor is into the policy of Council house sales undertaken by Westminster City Council. The auditor's report makes allegations of political bias and illegality in the operation of the right-to-buy scheme for Council housing. The House of Lords have upheld the auditor's report in *Porter v Magill*.[53] The case concerned allegations made by Mr Magill, the District Auditor for Westminster City Council, against three officers and three councillors that through wilful misconduct they had jointly and severally lost £31 million to the Council. The Council operated a housing policy that was

---

49   Mike Radford, "Auditing for Change: Local Government and the Audit Commission" [1991] *M.L.R.* 144.
50   [1925] A.C. 578 HL.
51   [1983] 1 A.C. 768; [1982] 2 W.L.R. 92 HL.
52   [1992] 2 A.C. 1; [1991] 2 W.L.R. 372 HL.
53   [2001] UKHL 67; [2002] 2 A.C. 35.

alleged to favour voters more likely to vote Conservative. Council owned residential properties were being sold in such a way as to enhance the political chances of the Conservative party at election time. The House of Lords held that it was unlawful to dispose of property for the purpose of promoting the electoral advantage of any party represented on the Council. The power to levy a surcharge has been abolished by Pt V of the Local Government Act 2000.

13-101 An equally controversial and difficult area in the giving of legal advice was cross-boundary competitive tendering, where the Commission has considered such arrangements as of dubious legality on the basis that local authorities have no legal powers to enter into municipal trading for a profit.[54] The Audit Commission combined two functions, watching and checking accounts and warning of future problems ahead. In this proactive role the Commission sought to influence local authorities into providing greater efficiency and effectiveness as good value for money.

13-102 The Audit Commission was abolished from 1 April 2014. Local public bodies, including local authorities, Police and Crime Commissioners and Clinical Commissioning Groups (the arrangements for commissioning under the National Health Service) are all required to appoint auditors under the Local Audit and Accountability Act 2014. The National Audit Office will have oversight of the new arrangements and specifically value for money studies. The role of the National Audit Office is likely to have importance in ensuring continuity over the entire audit process.[55] It remains to be seen whether or not the new arrangements will provide the level and detail of oversight previously provided by the Audit Commission.

G: Summary and Conclusions

13-103 Local government is undergoing immense changes during a difficult financial period. Local authorities have been heavily affected by the impact of the financial cuts—around 40 per cent in real terms on public spending totals across both central and local government. The influential Institute for Fiscal Studies in February 2015 predicted that mid to long-term growth was likely to be patchy and remain stubbornly weak. Council taxes are generally frozen but the signs are that central government is willing to allow local authorities to raise their own revenue to pay for their own locally delivered services. However, in many instances the local authority is as a deliverer of funding through central government budgets for which it has no autonomy or control. There are also many instances where experimentation in techniques, such as the election of Police Crime Commissions and the setting up of independent schools such as Free Schools or Academy Schools has brought their traditional role under attack. In theory the

---

54 Report of the Audit Commission, *"Cross Boundary Tendering: Local Authorities doing work for One Another"*, Audit Commission Technical Release 23/90 (London, 1990).
55 House of Commons Briefing Papers, *Local Audit in England*, No.07240 (24 June 2015).

Localism Act 2011 has given the illusion of many new powers and certainly the potential to raise new funds through local taxes but it is unclear if any such powers will make a significant difference. It should always be remembered that local government has little constitutional protection in the UK. Central government is all powerful and can set new powers and agendas, limit or increase funding which may consequently leave unwelcome uncertainty. These are major limitations on local government and their powers but also a recognition that local government may achieve the much needed improvement in business confidence and create a new stimulus to the economy. Compared to many other European countries, the UK's unitary system gives very little constitutional protection to local authorities. Central government retains considerable control and financial powers over local authorities. UK local authorities have a wide range of functions and statutory powers including responsibilities for education and schools, social services especially children's services and adult social care. There are strong economic arguments in favour of strengthening rather than diminishing local government and refashioning the local/central relationship including the reduction of central government powers to intervene on local government issues. Local government, under the influence of New Public Management strategies, has experienced outsourcing and privatisation agendas, including public-private partnerships, often involving hybridised relationships between the private sector and local authorities. Some critics[56] see this as a retreat from centralising controls in favour of a re-municipalisation of local authorities, perhaps strengthening local government and providing a re-invigorated public sector ethos. The Localism Act 2011 is often cited as a step towards giving local decision-making priority and dispersing power from central government bureaucracy to local people and their communities. The political rhetoric of local community and the "Big Society" is high in the dynamics of a power shift from central government to people living in local communities. Localism meaning decentralisation is in vogue, although the reliance of local government on central government controls over their finance remains. Recent proposals under the Cities and Local Government Devolution Bill 2016 for devolution to local government may mark a new era of local government autonomy but without any increase in public funding or any additional tax raising powers. Public sector cuts are pre-eminent, minimising local authority duties owed to local communities will lead to wide divergences in the design and implementation of local authority duties and a less coherent policy over key sectors such as energy, housing and health.

13-104   Revitalising the local economy and developing around large cities what are known as "metro areas" was the policy of the Coalition Government. Decentralisation may also prove popular in the North of England and opens up the potential for a new relationship between local and central government through the influence of local income tax, independently funded activities and assigned revenue giving autonomy to local authorities.

13-105   Local government is likely to come under increasing pressure to gain autonomy and deliver public services through local funding. Liberating local authority from central government controls is likely to take some time and it is not clear that this direction will be pursued as a

---

56 Hellmut Wollmann, "Public service in European Countries between Public/Municipal and private Sector Provision—and reverse?" (June 2013), unpublished paper.

consistent policy by central government. As Ian Leigh[57] has pointed out, there is a certain "ambivalence" in central government's attitudes. Local government is simultaneously being empowered with more financial and legal powers and at the same time often constrained by central government removing more activities from their remit such as a role in education. There is another aspect to devolution to local authorities and that is the impact this will have on the future of central government. Working out the relationship between local and central government remains a highly technical but ultimately political decision.

Further Reading

S. H. Bailey, *Cross on Principles of Local Government Law*, 3rd edn (London: Sweet & Maxwell, 2004).

T. Byrne, *Local Government in Britain*, 7th edn (London: Penguin, 2000).

I. Leigh, "The Changing nature of Local and Regional Democracy" in J. Jowell and D. Oliver (eds) *The Changing Constitution*, 7th edn (Oxford: Oxford University Press, 2011) and also 8th edn (2015).

M. Varney, "Local government in England: Localism delivered" in C. Panara, and M. Varney, *Local Government in Europe* (London: Routledge, 2012).

---

57 I. Leigh, "The Changing nature of Local and Regional Democracy" in J. Jowell and D. Oliver (eds) *The Changing Constitution*, 7th edn (Oxford: Oxford University Press, 2011), p.302.

14

Privatisation and Regulation

A: Introduction

Privatisation policies have continued to evolve since the 1980s. The term privatisation is the transfer from the public sector to the private sector the ownership and responsibility of a company.[1] As privatisation developed, the policy began to become an important economic strategy of successive governments. The major nationalised utility industries have been transformed into Company Act Companies. New regulatory agencies and a legal framework to regulate the utilities have been put in place. A wide range of statutory powers, contracts, licences and conditions provide the main legal mechanisms which govern the relationship between regulator, the company and the consumer.[2] Largely discretionary, but also of great importance to the future of each industry is the role of the relevant Secretary of State and the complex legal powers that are devoted to the relationship between the regulator and the Secretary of State. Regulating the privatised utilities has proved to be more complex and detailed than at first predicted. The initial single regulator model has rapidly given way to a Commission model, combining a broader range of expertise and oversight. The legislative framework of the original privatisation arrangements has had to be amended to take account of problems as they occurred. The result is a complex hotchpotch of legislation, regulation, rules, guidance, codes and licences, far removed from the consolidation and simplification that it was hoped might result after privatisation. This is a good example of many elements of "soft law" that form an important part of the post-privatisation arrangements. In addition to privatisation there are various "contracting out" arrangements for public sector services. There is also a temptation to

14–001

---

1 House of Commons Library, *Privatisation*, Research Paper, 14/61 (20 November 2014).
2 Thomas Perroud, *La fonction contentieuse des autorités de régulation en France et au Royaume-Uni*, PhD thesis in co-tutorship of the University of Warwick School of Law and the University Paris 1 Panthéon-Sorbonne School of Law (Paris: Dalloz, 2013).

see privatisation as setting the boundaries of public law. Public law regulates public law activities and not private law matters. However, many privatisations engage with regulatory bodies[3] whose role and functions are the concern of public law.[4] The regulatory role of independent regulatory regulatory bodies has become a major area of discussion for public lawyers and political scientists.[5] This has resulted in a broadly-themed literature on accountability.[6]

14-002 There have been a number of stages in the strategy to regulate the privatisation of public corporations that had been under state ownership after nationalisation in the 1940s and 50s. Regulation has a long history in the UK and it was required throughout the period of nationalisation. It was often at arm's length with the operational decisions being taken by the industry itself. A series of White Papers in the 1960s and 70s attempted to provide some transparency in the control of the nationalised industries. The first stage of privatisation began in the 1980s and 90s with the adoption of a privatisation strategy intended to remove Government from the business economics of the different industries. This period is concerned with the transfer of the nationalised companies into Company Act Companies with as wide as possible shareholding.

14-003 The enabling legislation also had a number of features: the setting up of individual regulators for the main utilities; the creation of licences and pricing arrangements; the development of a regulation strategy including the challenge of replacing the past ethos of "self-regulation" with greater competition; the liaison between individual regulators and the Monopolies and Mergers Commission (MMC), now replaced by the Competition Commission under the Competition Act 1998, over competition policy; and protection of the interests of consumers and the creation of rather weak but vocal consumer groups to represent consumers. The regulatory agencies that emerged from the early legislation include the Office of Telecommunications (Oftel), the Office of Gas Supply (Ofgas), the Office of Electricity Regulation (OFFER), the Office of Water Services (Ofwat) and the Office of the Rail Regulator (ORR). The second stage in the regulation of the privatised utilities has come about more recently. In order to align UK competition policy more closely with the EU, the Competition Act 1998 replaces the MMC with the Competition Commission and relevant to co-ordinating the competition policy in the utility sector is the cross-utility panel. Replacing the single regulators for gas and electricity is the merger of Ofgas and OFFER into Ofgem under the Utilities Act 2000. The Office of Communications Act 2002 provides for the establishment of Ofcom to replace five regulators: the Office of Telecommunications (Oftel); the Independent Television Commission;

---

3 T. Prosser, "Regulation and Social Solidarity" (2006) 33 *Journal of Law and Society* 364–87. See the discussion in C. Scott, "Regulatory Governance and the Challenge of Constitutionalism" in D. Oliver, T. Prosser and R. Rawlings (eds), *The Regulatory State* (Oxford: Oxford University Press, 2010), pp.15–34.
4 A. C. L Davies, "Public law and privatisation" in M. Elliott and D. Feldman (eds), *The Cambridge Public Law* (Cambridge: Cambridge University Press, 2015), pp.172–192.
5 Julia Black, "Calling Regulators to Account: Challenges, Capacities and Prospects" in N. Bamforth and P. Leyland (eds), *Accountability in the Contemporary Constitution* (Oxford: Oxford University Press, 2013), pp.354–388.
6 See: T. Prosser, " Regulation and Legitimacy" in J. Jowell, D.Oliver and C.O'Cinneide (eds), *The Changing Constitution* (Oxford: Oxford University Press, 2015) pp.329–349.

the Broadcasting Standards Commission; the Radio Authority; and the Radio-communications Agency.

Some privatisations have not followed the model outlined above. For example, air traffic control was created in 1996 into a company, National Air Services. The Transport Act 2000 provided for the sale of up to 51 per cent of the shares (now owned by the major airlines) with the Government retaining a golden share.

This chapter is focused mainly on the major utilities and how utility regulation has developed since nationalisation. Regulation provides public lawyers with an important dimension to the development of public administration. In contrast to other countries, most notably the US, regulation is done in the main without recourse to the courts. This reluctance to use courts is intended to provide regulators within the boundaries of their legal powers quite wide discretion over policy and its implementation. There are issues about accountability and how the traditional vehicle for accountability such as ministerial accountability to Parliament may appear ill-suited to the problems that arise from regulating the privatised utilities. The early stages of the development of Ofgas, OFFER and Oftel were highly personalised; the individual regulator provided the lead and set the relationship between regulation and the industry. The new structure underpinning Ofgem is that the personality of the regulator is less important and that the procedural rules for regulation become more transparent and are more objective in their application. The focus of regulation has also shifted. In the early stage it was mainly concerned with creating effective Company Act Companies with shareholders well rewarded through high dividends. The fact that many privatised utilities remained as monopolies gave rise to problems over competition policy. One attempt to tackle this problem was the introduction of additional regulatory powers under the Competition and Service (Utilities) Act 1992. However, a more fundamental rethink took place in the Utilities Act 2000 with a new emphasis being given to the protection of consumer interests and the promotion of efficient competition. Making both these objectives compatible with one another is going to prove to be difficult.

B: Nationalisation Policy and Structures

The model adopted for most nationalised industries followed the Morrisonian[7] model named after Herbert Morrison whose ideas were the most influential. Thus the public corporation was the chosen form with statutory powers to provide services for the newly nationalised industries. Such arrangements were heavily influenced by ideology[8]:

---

7   H. Morrison, *Socialisation of Transport* (London: Constable & Co, 1933).
8   R. Molyneux and D. Thompson, "Nationalised Industry Performance: Still Third Rate?" (1987) 18 *Fiscal Studies* (1987), p.48.

> "The public corporation must not be a capitalist business . . . It must have a different atmosphere at its board table from that of a shareholders meeting; the board and its officers must regard themselves as high custodians of the public interest."

14-007 A number of influences could be directed by ministers upon the nationalised industry. Such influences included the power of appointment to the boards of nationalised industries, the issuing of general directions as to policy, and specific ministerial approval over financial planning. Also included were ideas about encouraging the buying of British goods, an emphasis on the direction of returns on profits which could be ploughed back into the industry and overall policy objectives on employment conditions such as wage bargaining. The theory of ministerial supervision could in practice allow ministers to "run the industry". Critics of the nationalised industries feared that such intervention might interfere with the efficiency of the industry itself.

14-008 Nationalisation however did not come about as a coherent and well-considered plan. Initially corporations were given little guidance on the policies they were to follow. There was general uncertainty as to the precise role such industries should play in the economy, and confusion over the extent to which government influence should dictate managerial decisions. In general, it was considered sufficient to appoint prudent managers to allow the industries to run themselves. The major issue was whether the nationalised industries required more direct intervention. The answer to this question was slow in coming.

14-009 The government of the day located the running of the nationalised industries as an important part of the general economy. Three government White Papers[9] in 1961, 1967 and 1978 set out policy considerations which were influential. The 1961 White Paper set out financial targets to be achieved, specified as a rate of return on assets set by ministers. The formula used was crudely expressed; each nationalised industry was required to manage their affairs with the requirement of taking one year with notice to be sufficient to meet all items chargeable to revenue account. Thus "targets" were set for the industry to pay its way. Within this framework the industries were remarkably free to develop their own management strategies.

C: Privatisation Policy and Objectives

14-010 Privatisation shared with nationalisation strong ideological reasons for its introduction. As Craig noted[10]:

---

9 *Financial and Economic Obligations of the Nationalised Industries*, Cmnd.1337 (1961); *Nationalised Industries: A Review of Economic and Financial Objectives*, Cmnd.3437 (1967); and *The Nationalised Industries*, Cmnd.7131 (1978).

10 J. Craig, "Putting privatisation into practice: the case of Zambia Consolidated Copper Mines Limited" (2001) 39(3) *Journal of Modern African Studies* 389–410.

> "The reasons for privatisation are, like those for nationalisation, eclectic. They include the following; improving efficiency, reducing government involvement in decision-making of industry, ordinary share ownership, encouraging share ownership by employees, alleviating problems of public sector pay determinate, reducing the public sector borrowing requirement and the enhancement of economic freedom."

The success of privatisation also extended to many other countries and has become a global phenomenon of the late-twentieth and early-twenty-first centuries, raising important questions about oversight and accountability.[11]

Driven by strong ideological beliefs that the nationalised industries required dramatic reconstruction, the Government also desired to widen share ownership. Privatisation began with a crucial distinction between smaller privatised companies and larger activities. For example, smaller companies such as Amersham International, Jaguar, Sealink and British Aerospace operate within a competitive framework and pose little concern to the constitutional lawyer as to how their activities may be regulated. The Government's initial forays into implementing its privatisation policy were based on identifying these smaller activities which were privatised as the first phase of the Government's policy. In contrast the larger privatisations such as British Telecom in 1984, British Gas in 1985, and electricity in 1989 required a regulatory framework which attempts to deal with the larger market to which the newly privatised industry belongs. The popularity of wider share ownership, the removal of large companies dependent in the past on government support into the private sector has resulted in privatisation strategies being continued under the new Labour Government elected in 1997. Mention has been made of the Private Finance Initiative in previous chapters and this has involved private public partnerships. Contracting out strategies have been in operation in local and central government and within the National Health Service. There is also the popularity of management buy-outs such as may be found in the examples of parts of British Coal and in the National Freight Corporation. The Government has sold some of its remaining shareholdings and added new privatisations to its list. Since the first privatisation, remaining shares have been sold in British Telecom and in the electricity industry there has been the sell-off of British Nuclear Fuels. New privatisations include: British Coal under the British Coal Act 1993 and the Coal Industry Act 1994; British Rail under the Railways Act 1993 and amended by the Transport Act 2000; and HM Stationery Office.

The relative success of many privatisations has drawn worldwide attention to the UK's experience of privatisation. Attention has focused on regulation and regulatory techniques.

---

11   M. Bovens, "Analysing and Assessing Public Accountability: A Conceptual Model", European Governance Papers, EUROGOV, EUI (2006). See Martino Maggetti, "Legitimacy and Accountability of Independent Regulatory Agencies: A Critical Review", Centre for Comparative and International Studies, University of Zurich (2010); C. Ménard, M. Ghertman (eds), *Regulation, deregulation, reregulation institutional perspectives. Advances in new institutional analysis* (Cheltenham: Edward Elgar, 2009).

D: Regulation Structures and Techniques

14-014 The characteristics[12] of the British approach to legal regulation have a long history and have evolved gradually on a case by case basis. It is useful to place the newly created regulatory bodies in the context of the approach to regulation adopted in the UK. Historically the regulation and scrutiny of industry in Britain developed from the nineteenth century. Legal powers were first granted through Private Acts of Parliament in return for statutory responsibilities assumed by the industries—the railways and the electricity companies are two good examples. Also relevant is the experience of the early Poor Law Commission in 1834, which struck a balance between central and local government. This early form of government regulation permitted commissioners to determine the qualification and duties of local poor law guardians and they, in turn, appointed paid officers to administer relief, subject to the Poor Law Commission. The establishment of boards, which acted in a quasi-ministerial manner combined administrative decision-taking and both non-political or semi-independent status. A number of examples such as railways and the factories inspectorate, illustrate the experiment of placing certain activities beyond the direct reach of political intervention. Eventually these activities succumbed to ministerial control but attempts at combining or isolating ministerial intervention with regulation were made. In the example of the railways, the Railway Department in the Board of Trade in 1840 was a department board in 1844, a Commission in 1846 before absorption into the Board of Trade in 1851.

14-015 A wide variety of powers were enjoyed by such regulators; invariably, a statutory framework would set the general shape and scope of the individual board or inspectorate. Additionally, codes of practice, circulars, directions, rules, regulations were all included as part of that legal framework. Occasionally a feature of regulation involved enforcement procedures through adjudication processes which invariably might involve a fine or criminal sanction. For example, the early factory inspectorate under the Factories Act 1934 had the status of a magistrate with corresponding legal powers. Inevitably claims of partisanship and bias were made against individuals in carrying out their duties and activities. One of the characteristics of the nineteenth century was a remarkable degree of detail and openness in the reports published by the various boards, departments and agencies. This characteristic gradually diminished as the nationalisation process took place in the post-Second World War period which was characterised by secrecy and lack of information on the actual performance of each industry.

The Role of the Courts

14-016 Overviewing the activities of boards, inspectors and Ministries, the courts had a limited but important role. Various devices such as Crown immunity up until 1947 were used to prevent law suits in the case of torts and the amenability to judicial review depended to some extent on

---

12 See R. Baldwin and C. McCrudden, *Regulation and Public Law* (London: Weidenfeld and Nicolson, 1987); and W. R. Cornish and G. de Clark, *Law and Society in England 1850–1950* (London: Sweet & Maxwell, 1989).

the remedy sought. In the case of mandamus, for example a Crown servant could not be compelled to perform a duty solely owed to the Crown. A wide array of legal powers were available. For example, the Poor Law Commission were advised to keep within the rules of natural justice and when they acted all their members had to be present. The courts were unpredictable in their application of the rules of natural justice. Technical distinctions were the hallmark of this area of the law. At one time the courts appeared to apply distinctions based on the classification of the bureaucratic function as "judicial", "quasi-judicial", "legislative" or "administrative". In 1964 the House of Lords adopted a more permissive approach in the landmark case of *Ridge v Baldwin*[13] and thereby abolished the technical distinctions which inhibited the development of judicial review.

14-017

In summary, the characteristics of regulation such as judicial scrutiny, adjudication of disputes and ministerial accountability were all in place during the lifetime of nationalisation. No coherent system existed to oversee and monitor the system of regulation, as development was ad hoc and pragmatic. The legal controls that there were, seldom became the subject of litigation. Few lawyers were involved apart from internal law advisers over the Company Act provisions and the requirements of the specific statutory authority of each of the nationalised industries. The paucity of legal cases is an example of where the role of the court is limited by the nature of the regulatory structure. Challenges to the regulator's role are reluctantly taken by the courts.[14] There is a tacit assumption that within the boundaries of legality the regulator has a broad discretion.[15] Although judicial review is available even when a matter of private law is involved the courts may intervene.

14-018

In the unreported decision of the divisional court *R v Director General of Gas Supply Ex p. Smith*,[16] Pill J applied the rules of national justice to the investigative powers of the Director General of Gas Supply in his role in determining whether British Gas was justified in using its disconnection powers where it suspected an offence was committed. Relying on the main legal authorities such as *O'Reilly v Mackman*[17] the courts have developed the potential for intervention to review the decision of regulators or ministers where it is thought unreasonable, procedurally inconvenient or on some grounds of unfairness. The danger of the courts substituting its view for that of the designated authority who have been given that authority by Parliament was recognised by Lord Justice Watkins in *R v Secretary of State for Trade and Industry Ex p. Lonrho*.[18] The boundary of the courts" jurisdiction would seem to be that the courts should not "arrogate to themselves executive or administrative decisions". Interpretation of this phrase is difficult to predict and open to narrow or broad interpretations.[19]

---

13 [1964] A.C. 40; [1963] 2 W.L.R. 935 HL.
14 *R v Independent Television Commission Ex p. TSW Broadcasting Ltd* [1996] E.M.L.R. 318 Div Ct.
15 See *Mercury Communications v DG of Telecommunications* [1996] 1 W.L.R. 48; [1996] 1 All E.R. 575 HL.
16 CO/1398/88. See J. McEldowney "Theft and meter tampering and the gas and electricity utilities" (Autumn 1991) *Utilities Law Review* 122–126. Also see *R v British Coal Corporation and the Secretary of State for Trade Ex p. Vardy* [1993] 1 C.M.L.R. 721; [1993] I.R.L.R. 104 Div Ct.
17 [1983] 2 A.C. 237; [1982] 3 W.L.R. 1096 HL.
18 [1989] 1 W.L.R. 525; [1989] 2 All E.R. 609 HL.
19 *R v Panel on Takeovers and Mergers Ex p. Datafin Plc* [1987] Q.B. 815; [1987] 2 W.L.R. 699 CA (Civ Div).

14-019

EU law is also influential. In *Foster v British Gas Plc*,[20] the European Court interpreted a dispute concerning the implementation of an EC Directive 76/207 (9 February 1976) on equal treatment for men and women as regards access to employment working conditions and promotion. The case has implications for anybody that engages in supply services such as privatised industries, quangos and civil servants. Under the principle of the *Marshall case*,[21] if the British Gas Corporation were a public body then the corporation were in breach of the Directive. British Gas Plc as successors would have to accept liability for the unfair dismissal. More important was the question of how Community law is applied by the national courts as EC Directives cannot be directly applied by national courts and tribunals, but where a private individual has a complaint against a state body a Directive will be directly enforceable. The judgment of the European Court has left to the national courts their ideas of public service and the application of criteria laid down by the courts. This leaves a degree of uncertainty for the future as to the precise nature of the criteria and the likely result. There is confusion in the courts as to how directly and indirectly effective Directives may be applied.

E: Regulating and Privatising the Utilities

British Telecom

14-020

The privatisation of British Telecom in 1984 and the Telecommunications Act 1984 were the first major reforms of a public utility industry which had been from 1912 until 1981 a State-owned monopoly. In 1981 the first stage, prior to privatisation, took place when legislation, the British Telecommunications Act 1981, separated telecommunications from postal services thereby establishing British Telecom as a public corporation. The 1981 stage relaxed the restrictions of supply of customers' equipment and allowed licensing of other telecommunications systems. The 1984 Telecommunications Act created a Director General of Telecommunications (DGT) with regulatory powers based on guidelines as to how the DGT is expected to perform his duties. The hallmark of this particular privatisation was the need to find a suitable competitor for British Telecom. The Government effectively promoted the creation of a competitive rival, Mercury, which is the only competitor licensed to date to compete with British Telecom. The experience of nationalisation may be seen in the power under the 1984 Act to refer, for

---

20 *Foster v British Gas* (C-188/89) EU:C:1990:313; [1990] 2 C.M.L.R. 833.
21 *Marshall v Southampton and South West Hampshire AHA (No.1)* (C-152/84) EU:C:1986:84; [1986] 1 C.M.L.R. 688. R. Nobles, "Application of E.C. Law to Supply Services" (1990) *Utilities Law Review* 127–129; B. Fitzpatrick, "Direct Effect of Directives" (1991) *Utilities Law Review* 34–38.

example, British Telecom to the MMC and the matter is one which operates against the public interest.

14-021
The legal structure of the 1984 Act is significant because it provided a model for future privatisation. The characteristics of the 1984 Act are the use of an independent regulator (Oftel) appointed by the Secretary of State (s.1 of the 1984 Act), and that the operators of telecommunications systems must possess a licence granted by the Director General of Oftel and the Secretary of State. There is a power to refer matters to the MMC to decide if the matter referred is in the public interest. The Director General of Fair Trading has powers to supervise and investigate any possible anti-competitive practices or abuses of market power. Included in the regulation is a price formula designed "to cap" the prices charged to consumers for services. Privatisation of water (Ofwat) and electricity (OFFER) followed similar principles.

14-022
Another characteristic is the requirement to build a pricing structure into the regulatory arrangements. The form of price regulation was based centred around the Retail Price Index minus three per cent. The success of the pricing mechanism to be judged on the efficiency of the industry. Pricing mechanisms proved to be no substitute for healthy competition as a means of controlling prices and protecting consumers.

14-023
The creation of the Director General of Telecommunications as a means to secure effective competition, economy, efficiency and growth and development of the telecommunications business in the UK both nationally and international depends on the effectiveness of the regulatory system. In embryo it was a first step in developing regulatory experience over the newly privatised industry. At the time, criticism of the 1984 Act focused on three matters: first, the legislation failed to provide any requirement that adequate information is available to the DGT; secondly, there was concern that the resources of the DGT may not be adequate to maintain supervision of the organisation; and thirdly, that the DGT and Office of Telecommunications (Oftel) may be perceived as too closely linked with the industry. Thus their independence and impartiality might be questioned if they were perceived as too protective of the industry.

14-024
The Government's strategy for privatisation also addressed the question of the value of the market as a regulator of the newly privatised activity. Rather than simply privatise a monopoly, some liberalisation was attempted both before and after privatisation. This policy required legal powers to regulate the market. In the case of telecommunications, competition between Mercury and BT was created when Mercury was set up to provide an element of competition. The duopoly that resulted has itself been subject to criticism and review. Oftel has been concerned with the terms of Mercury's network connection with BT. After delays and intervention by the courts, Oftel ruled that the two networks should have full interconnection charges based on BT's costs and a time-scale was set for the implementation of connection arrangements. This applied to both national and international calls. In March 1991, the long-awaited White Paper[22] on the duopoly review was published. Its main conclusion, that all applications for new licences to provide new telecommunications systems would be considered, and this would

---

22 *Competition and Choice: Telecommunications Policy for the 1990s*, Cm.1461 (1991).

include both national and international services. This may be seen as broadening the possibilities for competition beyond the original framework of the 1984 Act.

14-025

The 1984 telecommunications regulatory structure was perceived to be weak. Additional powers have been introduced under the Competition and Services (Utilities) Act 1992 intended to set a uniform standard of regulation for the utilities, and in the case of telecommunications, gas and water, greater competition. Thus the 1992 Act introduces additional powers for the Director of Telecommunications to set standards for levels of performance, provide greater information to the Director on the working of the industry, to determine disputes between the customer and the industry, and to make provisions relating to consumer protection such as disconnection charges. Many of these proposals arose from the Citizen's Charter initiative.[23]

The Office of Communications Act 2002

14-026

The various regulatory bodies covering telecommunications, television and radio are to be merged into a single regulator Ofcom under the Office of Communications Act 2002. The five bodies covered by Ofcom are: the Office of Telecommunications (Oftel); the Independent Television Commission; the Broadcasting Standards Commission; the Radio Authority; and Radio-communications Agency. This followed the removal of telecommunications from the original Utilities Bill in 2000. Oftel was a pioneering regulator, as it was the first established under the privatisation legislation. As such it was expected to create the necessary competition in the communications market and ultimately it was hoped that this would be the best form of regulation of the industry. The Office of Communications Act 2002 contains seven sections and establishes Ofcom and provides general duties. The Act also provides for the management of Ofcom and its organisation and finance. A further step was taken in the Communications Act 2003. This was a liberalising Act, intended to life restrictions on ownership of the UK broadcasting licences by firms or individuals outside the European Economic Area and allowing ownership of several Channel 3 licences.[24] Ofcom is an important example of evolving regulatory experience and developing new systems of transparency and impact assessments including a consumer panel. As Prosser has explained, Ofcom has consulted extensively on a range of key issues such as public service broadcasting and telecommunications markets.[25]

---

23 *Citizen's Charter*, Cm.1599 (1991). On telecommunications see NAO, *The Office of Telecommunications: Licence Compliance and Consumer Protection*, HC 529 (London: HMSO, 1993); NAO, *The Sale of the Second Tranche of Shares in British Telecommunications Plc*, HC 568 (London: HMSO, 1993). See Scott [1993] *Utilities Law Review* 183.

24 T. Prosser, "The Office of Communications" in T. Prosser, *The Regulatory Enterprise* (Oxford: Oxford University Press, 2010), pp.153–175.

25 T. Prosser, "Regulation and Legitimacy" in J. Jowell, D. Oliver and C. O'Cinneide (eds), *The Changing Constitution* (Oxford: Oxford University Press, 2015), 329–349, p.347.

Energy and natural resources utilities

In the 1980s and 1990s, energy and natural resource utilities were regulated as single regulators before the Utilities Act 2000. The evolution of utility regulation is one of the most important developments in the UK's experience of regulation.

Gas

The privatisation of the gas industry faced similar regulatory problems as identified in the case of telecommunications. In 1985 the Government decided to privatise British Gas and the question of how competition and efficiency might be achieved was given serious consideration but with limited and disappointing results.

The nationalisation of the British gas industry in 1948 and its centralisation in 1962 had created a single industry centralised under a public corporation responsible for the activities of 12 area boards who were autonomous over the manufacture and supply of gas. Sole rights to purchase gas from producers had been granted to the corporation in 1982 and pricing had been characteristically low with a resultant lack of investment. This lack of investment has been attributed to poor policy direction by the government of the day.

Privatisation was undertaken by the Gas Act 1986 which followed the model set by telecommunications in 1984. A regulatory structure was set up under a Director General of supply (Ofgas) and an Ofgas office. The newly created Company, British Gas, did not have any competition and unlike BT and Mercury none was created by the 1986 Act for the Gas Industry. No attempt was made to restructure the industry in the 1986 Act. The 12 regional boards could have become gas companies with a company to control the distribution system. The strong ideological belief that the timetable of the Government's privatisation strategy should not be altered or slowed down meant that restructuring of the gas industry was avoided.

It is clear that the Gas Act 1986 in practical effect insulated British Gas from competition. As no new competitor was created it was difficult not to see the monopoly of British Gas as virtually impregnable by any new entrant to the market.

Finally, the 1986 Act provided a complex formula for pricing supervised by the Director General of Gas Supply (DGGS) and Ofgas. Legal powers similar to Oftel were provided to Ofgas to promote efficiency to gas suppliers and users. The DGGS might impose conditions upon the grant of authorisation to a public gas supplier and there is a possibility of a referral to the MMC to specify any modification to the authorisation. Compliance powers granted to the DGGS and investigative powers over conditions granted in the authorisation were all part of the regulatory framework.

The powers of the regulator were considerably less than the powers possessed by British Gas. For example, under the 1986 Act it was impossible for the DGGS to alter the legal structure of the gas industry. Some doubts existed, at the time, as to the powers of the DGGS to provide transparency of pricing and in opening up the transmission system through supplies to third parties.

14-034 In the case of gas, the Director General had powers to promote competition within the contract market, i.e. over 25,000 therms per annum, but lacked a general duty to promote competition overall. In contrast the Director General of Electricity has such powers which are widely drawn but not easily interpreted with a precise and clear meaning. Gas privatisation had resulted in a virtual monopoly for British Gas; unlike the telecommunications industry with Mercury, no competitors were established at the time of privatisation. British Gas was in a strong market position post-privatisation with the resultant effect that the regulator (Ofgas) became a surrogate competitor in its attempts to regulate the gas industry effectively. A major threat to any monopolistic conduct is the use of the Fair Trading Act 1973 (Sch.8) in requiring the MMC to consider whether such conduct militates against the public interest. A wide range of remedial action is available including adjusting contracts, the formation or winding-up of a company and consideration of the division of the business "by the sale of any part of the undertaking or assets or otherwise. . .".

14-035 In the early stages of the newly privatised life of British Gas, it was apparent that a number of grounds for dissatisfaction existed. These included: individual prices were unclear and companies had difficulty estimating future gas costs; a wide variation in prices was experienced between customers with the same or similar levels of requirement; tendering for contracts lasted for only three-month periods at a time, and future gas costs were difficult to estimate, given the lack of transparency in pricing; British Gas was reluctant to quote prices for interruptible supplies and required in many cases the installation of dual-fired equipment which was costly; British Gas were also unwilling to offer supply to certain types of companies which would close down when supplies were interrupted.

14-036 Such complaints were reviewed by the MMC after Ofgas made a reference on the basis of there being a monopoly enjoyed by British Gas. The MMC upheld this view of a monopoly and concluded that greater competition was required. An additional finding was that the only effective means of remedying adverse consequences flowing from the monopoly status of British Gas was direct gas to gas competition. A long list of recommendations relating to the pricing and tendering of gas, third party access to the gas transmission system operated by British Gas, and transparency in the system of gas schedules were also made by the MMC.

14-037 Inevitably the MMC findings in 1988 required a reorganisation of the gas market and provided the regulator with increased powers in terms of enhancing his status and in securing compliance with his objectives. Ultimately the Secretary of State's wide powers under Sch.9 to the Fair Trading Act provide a threat hanging over the industry should the monopolistic practices be continued. As a result, British Gas in February 1990 entered into a number of undertakings which included: not to purchase more than 90 per cent of gas on offer; not to require the inclusion of contract terms which could frustrate that objective; to provide common carriage quotations within a four-week period. In addition, price schedules were introduced for firm and interruptible contract customers to prevent British Gas from blocking market entry by a strategy of discriminatory pricing.

14-038 In July 1991 the effectiveness of the remedies applied by British Gas after the MMC Report (1985) was referred to the Office of Fair Trading (OFT) for consideration. The result of that review was published in October 1991 and concluded that although British Gas had complied with its undertakings, nevertheless the dominance of British Gas in the market had remained. British Gas, because of its size and market dominance was able to assert its influence. Thus it could cross-subsidise, act in a predatory manner on pipeline competition and set price levels in the indemnities market that a competitor could not match. All these factors led the OFT to conclude that the behaviour of British Gas should lead to a fundamental reconsideration of the market position of British Gas. In 1993 the MMC published two reports on Gas. Some conclusions may be reached from a reading of the reports. First that competition had been attempted in the gas industry before privatisation but with very limited success. The Oil and Gas (Enterprise) Act 1982 initiated competition in gas supply by allowing competing gas suppliers access to British Gas's pipelines. In fact, no agreement was ever reached. The 1986 Gas Act as outlined above, preserved the de facto monopoly of British Gas. Even though the 1986 Act gave freedom of competition to suppliers of large industrial and commercial customers above 25,000 therms, this did not remove the monopoly position of British Gas. In 1995 a new Gas Act was passed that gave additional powers to the regulator to allow for a more radical restructuring of British Gas to provide additional competition for suppliers to domestic customers and for access to the gas pipeline. This new structure had the following features:

(a) the setting up of Trans Co, British Gas's transportation and storage business with assets inclusive of about £17.4 billion;

(b) from March 1995 separation of Trans Co from British Gas; and

(c) the Gas Act 1995 came into force on 1 March 1995.

14-039 The 1995 Act sets up a new structure for the licensing of gas supply. The main features of the 1995 Act are that access is now available to the pipeline owned by British Gas for any licensed supplier. There are licences for the following:

(a) Public Gas Transporter (PGT) for firms that operate a pipeline system and contract with gas shippers;

(b) gas shipper licences for licence holders who contract to provide a public gas transporter to be conveyed through the pipeline of the PGT; and

(c) gas supplier licences for companies that sell at the meter gas which has been delivered through pipelines by a shipper. This includes supply to domestic customers.

14-040 The introduction of licensed suppliers into the domestic market is a gradual one. The above analysis of the British Gas example points to inherent structural problems in the way British Gas was privatised. Splitting up the distribution side from the production of gas supply might have avoided the problems of monopoly mentioned above. The model for such a restructuring may be seen in the Electricity Act 1989 (discussed below) where the transmission grid was separated from the production and distribution system.

14-041
Additional powers have been granted to the Director of Gas Supply under the Competition and Service (Utilities) Act 1992. These include the powers to set standards, improve the procedures for complaints by customers and set regulations to determine disputes over the accuracy of bills. An increase in competition in the gas market is intended by reducing the gas monopoly threshold of 15,000 therms to a lower amount or to abolition of the threshold altogether. These changes are the result of the introduction of proposals contained in the Citizen's Charter.

14-042
The Citizen's Charter Report on an annual basis sets out the achievements of the Charter.[26] In the Report there is a list of a wide range of achievements including setting up codes of practice, setting standards for dealing with complaints and arranging for payments for failure to meet standards. For example, in 1994 British Gas paid a total of £2,439,272 in compensation. The bulk of this went to a single domestic user. The public electricity suppliers in 1994 paid £115,000 and the water companies paid £267,900.

14-043
In addition to the Citizen's Charter the government has embarked on new procedures to simplify existing regulations and unnecessary rules. The Deregulation and Contracting Out Act 1994 provides that amending orders, called deregulation orders, may be introduced to amend delegated legislation or where necessary primary legislation. This procedure is a novel way to lift the burden of unnecessary regulation from industry.

14-044
The British Gas example also shows the flexibility inherent in the legal mechanisms used to regulate the industry. The legal basis for referral to the MMC and the resultant modification of the authorisation allowed gradual changes to be introduced. The existing legal framework is also sufficiently flexible to realise the creation of a separate gas transmission subsidiary company. This could be achieved by British Gas voluntarily adopting the recommendations of the OFT. In the event of non-compliance, the regulatory structure is sufficiently flexible to hold the threat of referral to the MMC. The combination of regulatory supervision by Ofgas, overview by the OFT and MMC combines wide legal powers with oversight by the relevant Secretary of State.

Electricity

14-045
The experience gained from gas and telecommunications privatisations proved to be insufficient to meet the challenge posed by electricity privatisation. The Government's proposals to privatise the Electricity Supply Industry (ESI) faced a sterner test because the electricity industry was the largest of the UK's nationalised industries in terms of turnover and capital employed.

14-046
Electricity privatisation also posed some of the most complex legal problems. Electricity is a natural monopoly, involves the use of fuels as diverse as solar power and nuclear energy, and is a heavy polluter of the environment. Under nationalisation the generation, supply and transmission of electricity were integrated by the 1957 Electricity Act. The Central Electricity

---

26 *Citizen's Charter Improving Service*, Cm.2970 (September 1995).

Generating Board (CEGB) was put in charge of both generation and transmission. A national grid was created with 12 area boards for distribution purposes. These purposes were left to the autonomy of the boards particularly in respect of financial matters. Consumers' interests in England and Wales were represented by 13 district organisations. There were 12 Area Electricity Consultative Councils, one for each area board and an Electricity Consumers' Council.

The privatisation strategy adopted by the Government was contained in the White Paper *Privatising Electricity*[27] which set out six objectives to be followed, namely: the needs of customers should be considered an important part of the industry; competition is an essential guarantee of customers' interests; regulation was required to promote competition, oversee prices and protect customers' interests; security and safety should be maintained; customers should be given new rights; and share ownership should include those who work for the company.

In the case of electricity privatisation, the experience of both British Gas and Telecommunications suggested that a different model should be adopted to provide increased competition as part of the legal structure for the newly privatised industry. The ESI is a key industry in the energy field—especially in promoting energy efficiency and addressing environmental concerns.

Despite objections to the White Paper proposals and the belated recognition that the nuclear power side of generation was too much of a high risk in terms of economic cost (partly owing to decommissioning costs), the Government pushed ahead with the existing proposals. In October 1989 and after the Electricity Act 1989 had been passed for the privatisation of the industry, the Government reluctantly removed the nuclear side of the industry from privatisation and it will remain in Government control. A separate company called Nuclear Power was set up under Government ownership. A nuclear levy, known as the non-fossil fuel levy acts as a subsidy to nuclear electricity, and is payable by all users of electricity.

The Electricity Act 1989 adopted a combination of licensing, contractual and statutory powers to regulate and operate the newly created structure under the post-privatisation arrangements. Licensing is a power which combines the work of both Secretary of State and the Director. Wider reserve powers are given to the Secretary of State in the case of electricity than in gas or telecommunications. Such reserve powers given to the Secretary of State (s.96) are for preserving the security of electricity supply, the maintenance and the security of buildings or installations used for the purposes connected with the generation, transmission or supply of electricity. The Secretary of State may set the percentage of electricity required from non-fossil fuel after consultation with the Director General of Electricity and suppliers; such order is subject only to negative resolution in the procedure of laying the order before Parliament.

The Director General of Electricity with the consent of the Secretary of State and after consulting public electricity suppliers and affected individuals may set individual and overall standards of performance. The Director General of Electricity was required to publish information which is expedient to provide information for customers of public electricity supplies.

This wide range of statutory powers is also reinforced by licensing conditions such as the avoidance of cross-subsidisation and the separation of accounts between different businesses.

---

27   Cm.322 (1988).

14-053 The 1989 Act follows the pattern in the privatisation of British Gas which allows the DGES a discretion to make a reference to the MMC. But the Secretary of State for Energy can direct the MMC not to proceed with the reference. Once a report is prepared the Secretary of State may prohibit publication of "any matter" if it appears to him that it would be against the public or commercial interest of "any person".

14-054 The Secretary of State possesses wide powers to keep a register of information on licences, modifications and the like. Effectively placing the Secretary of State as the ESI's licensing authority, the 1989 Act allows intervention in the work of the DGES as a regulator that challenges any sense of independence or freedom from political influence which the DGES may want to develop. While the DGES has a duty to review the "carrying on" of electricity generation, transmission and supply, the Secretary of State may give the DGES directions as to the priorities or matters which form the DGES's remit.

14-055 The Secretary of State's powers extend to the day-to-day operations of the ESI. The constitution of generating stations and the consents required may be supervised by the Secretary of State, under s.36 of the Act. The use of fuel stocks, and the requirement that electricity is available from non-fossil fuel sources are all part of the wide powers possessed by the Secretary of State.

14-056 The management functions of the person operating the generating station could be directed by the Secretary of State as well as the "specified objectives" which may be given to the National Grid Company to operate the transmission system. It is clear that the legal powers contained in the 1989 Act provide the Secretary of State with the means to take over the operational management of the industry. Finally, wide emergency powers are included in Pt III of the 1989 Act which provide the Secretary of State with extensive powers to give directions to the industry. The term "civil emergency" is widely defined in subjective terms in s.96 of the 1989 Act. It includes any national disaster or other emergency which in the opinion of the Secretary of State is against the interest of national security or commercial interests. The power to give directions does not contain any requirement of laying the direction before Parliament. The 1989 Act provides the Secretary of State unparalleled powers in the history of the ESI to intervene in the day-to-day running of the industry. Electricity privatisation provided more extensive regulatory powers than previous privatisations. The few changes introduced by the Competition and Service (Utilities) Act 1992 include standards of performance, complaints and disputes, the level of achievement of each public electricity supplier, and the power for the Director to make determinations regarding the accuracy of bills.

The Utilities Act 2000

14-057 Reports on the various utilities pointed out the strengths and weaknesses of the arrangements.[28] The Utilities Act 2000 reflected the ideas contained in the DTI Green Paper *A Fair Deal for*

---

28 See National Audit Office, *The Work of the Directors General of Telecommunications, Gas Supply, Water Services and Electricity Supply*, HC 645 (1995–96).

Consumers: Modernising the Framework for Utility Regulation.[29] The Act achieves four aims and objectives as follows:

- the merger of Ofgas and OFFER into a single regulatory body (Ofgem);
- to provide for a fair deal and greater consumer protection than in the past;
- to meet more widely defined social and environmental objectives; and
- to provide and implement more transparent trading arrangements.

In order to meet these new objectives there are a number of changes to the licensing regime for electricity. The 14 PES licences and second-tier licences are to be abolished and there will be a single-tier licence. The separation of supply and distribution will result in the distribution business being sold off to companies under the Companies Act. Distribution licences are likely to remain but subject to tighter control and supervision. There are also powers to standardise licence conditions and provide a more coherent framework for modification. The aim is to provide some stability and consistency to allow licence holders to develop their future strategic plans.

The new Utilities Act 2000 also brings additional regulatory controls over electricity companies in the following areas:

- the powers to introduce efficiency standards of performance on both suppliers and distributors;
- a requirement to meet greater transparency through the disclosure of directors' pay and remuneration in terms of meeting performance standards;
- a requirement on suppliers to have a certain percentage of electricity to come from renewable supply; and
- a power to raise a cross-subsidy to meet the needs of various identifiable groups.

The Utilities Act 2000 introduces a revision of the Gas Act 1986 in favour of consumers. A specific requirement is to ensure that the disabled, or the chronically sick and those who are pensioners or live on low incomes in rural areas are given protection. The consumers' interests are to be somehow reconciled with different categories of consumer and at the same time fit within the general duties of the regulator and the Secretary of State to promote efficiency and economy in the use of gas. The licensing scheme under the Gas Act 1995 and the Electricity Act 1989 are brought into alignment by the Utilities Act 2000. The Competition Commission

---

29   DTI (March 1998).

appears to have the final say on whether to modify licence conditions, replacing the previously held Ofgas power of referral.

Water

14-061
The privatisation of water also proved a greater problem than gas or telecommunications. Water privatisation had to address one of the most complex[30] legal arrangements for water services. In the case of water, ten public water authorities and 29 private water companies comprised the water industry before privatisation. The Water Act 1989 had to address the problem of not only the new structure under privatisation but the question of merger and investment in the water industry, which also included major health and environmental issues. In the run up to privatisation, concern among the water authorities was expressed because of the fear of predatory takeovers by French water companies.

14-062
Privatisation was carried out under the Water Act 1989 which created a new public body, the National Rivers Authorities (NRA) now subsumed under the Environment Agency under the Environment Act 1995 with the rights and liabilities of the existing water authorities divided between the NRA and successor companies. The 29 statutory water companies are retained as water undertakers for their areas. The successor companies inherit the responsibilities of sewerage and water subject to the terms of the instruments of appointment. The various commercial companies as water and sewerage undertakers have received powers under the Water Industry Act 1991. The duty to maintain and develop an efficient and economical water supply and sewerage system falls under ss.37 and 94 of the 1991 Act. The supply of water for domestic purposes must be wholesome and of adequate quality. There is a Water Services Office with a Director General of Water Services.

14-063
NRA, within the Environment Agency, has responsibilities for the control of river and coastal water pollution, water resource management, land drainage, fisheries, navigation and flood defence. A major feature of the legislation is a complex pricing formula, detailed environmental protection arrangements, and a new regulatory body under the Director General of Water Services. The latter is required in effect to balance the protection of the consumer from monopoly exploitation and the efficient running of the utility.

14-064
The Water Act 1989 (s.230(3)) gives the MMC, now the Competition Commission, power to consider whether any proposed merger might prejudice the Director General of Water Services' ability to regulate the industry and whether the proposed merger was against the public interest.

14-065
A merger must fulfil the requirements that:

(a) either it must not reduce the number of companies under independent control; or

(b) the merger must achieve some other benefit of greater significance.

---

30 See R. MacRory, *The Water Act 1989*, Current Law Statutes (1989); and I. Byatt, "The Office of Water Services: Structure and Policy" [1990] *Utilities Law Review* 85–90.

The latter may be achieved by a substantial benefit to customers. Nevertheless, a large number of the existing water companies had received French investment before the Act was in force, thus the regulatory protection appeared too late to be effective.

The Water Act 1989, however, broadly follows some of the legal characteristics of the post-privatisation arrangements of the other main utilities. The main regulatory instrument is the licence which contains a regulatory mechanism which "caps" the price companies may charge their customers. The annual increase is restricted to the "RPI plus an additional factor K allocated to the companies on an individual basis for each of the next 10 years". This is designed according to Director General of Water, Ian Byatt "to off-set the significant investment programmes which have been necessary to achieve the higher standards which we all seek".

In the case of water, reference to the MMC may be made by the Secretary of State for Trade and Industry following advice from the OFT. The water companies may appeal to the MMC if they wish to contest the action of the Director General of Water Services in respect of determining the "K" factor in the price cap, amendments to their licences and accounting guidelines.

The actual management of the industry is, subject to the legal framework identified above, left to the individual water companies to develop. Within Ofwat's remit is a periodic review every ten years of the company, investment programme, management plan, efficiency standards and the regulatory regime in general.

Additional powers and responsibilities were added under the Competition and Services (Utilities) Act 1992. Section 39 of the 1992 Act makes changes to the mergers procedures, under the Water Industry Act 1991, as to the matters which the MMC must take into account, such as the number of companies in separate ownership, in considering water mergers referred to the MMC. In addition, the 1992 Act provides the giving of greater information on research, consumer views and an improved complaints system for customers as part of the proposals contained in the Citizen's Charter. Clearly the water privatisation plans present yet another example of problems in terms of efficiency and accountability. The present statutory formulation would seem to do little to achieve competition between the different parts of the industry.

The Water Act 2014

The water industry in England and Wales has been privatised and regulated as limited monopolies since 1989. Privatisation arrangements gave rise to very limited competition options for the consumer. Customers are unable to choose their water supplier and there is no competitive market. The Cave Review[31] recommendations were that there should be greater competition in the sector including access to upstream and retail activities. The aims of greater competition

---

31 Martin Cave, *Independent Review of Competition and Innovation in Water Markets* (April 2009). See House of Commons Library, Increasing competition in the water industry in England and Wales, No.CBP 7259 (17 July 2015).

are to encourage lower prices and opportunities for better pricing as well as alternatives in waste disposal services. The aim is to reduce water costs by using water more efficiently. The Government's White Paper[32] took account of the Cave Review and the result is the Water Act 2014.

14-072 The Water Act 2014 breaks new ground for the water industry by reforming the market in water. This is to be achieved through enabling all businesses in England and public sector customers to switch their water and sewerage suppliers. There are also rules and procedures for cross-border arrangements with Scotland. Opportunities are provided for new businesses to provide new sources for water and sewerage. The aim is to develop a national water supply network and thereby ensure that water companies may buy and sell water between themselves. Owners of small-scale water storage systems are able to sell excess water to the public. There are also provisions for new water or sewerage companies and developers to connect new building developments to the water mains and sewerage systems. These are very ambitious plans and it remains to be seen whether or not competition will flourish. There are complex arrangements for switching suppliers and creating a vibrant market that is competitive and efficient. Oversight of the new arrangements will also depend on the activities and enthusiasm of Ofwat, the industry regulator. The regulator is also provided with additional pricing powers through price control review. The omission of appropriate arrangements for competition in the original privatisation arrangements are being remedied within the existing water industry. It remains to be seen how effective the new arrangements are likely to be. Domestic water consumers will not be able to make use of the new legislation until April 2017. Even then it will require extensive monitoring by Ofwat to ensure that the water companies are working efficiently. There are regular five year price control reviews that ensure that water companies operate effectively. One aspect that will have to be fully worked out is measures to prevent hidden cross-subsidies or exploitation of one sector of the market by another. Estimates of savings are hard to calculate but additional competition might result in long term savings over a 30-year period.

14-073 Innovation of a cross-border English-Scottish market will take some time. In theory it will enable suppliers to co-operate across the border between Scotland and England. The effectiveness of the regulator[33] will also have to be closely monitored as the new framework for water services is implemented.[34]

---

32   Defra, *Water Life*, Cm.8230 (December 2011).
33   The role of Ofwat was considered in a review carried out by David Gray in July 2011 (http://webarchive.nationalarchives.gov.uk/20130822084033/http://www.defra.gov.uk/environment/quality/water/industry [Accessed 12 April 2016]). It was accepted that regulation had worked reasonably well and achieved stability in investment and forward planning. There were additional findings, however, that considered there were too many burdens on the water companies and priority should be given to reducing costs and introducing cultural changes within the companies. It was also felt there is a need for greater co-operation between the various agencies including Ofwat, the Environment Agency and the Drinking Water Inspectorate, which should engage more effectively with companies and other stakeholders.
34   S. Weatherill (ed), *Better Regulation* (Oxford: Hart, 2007).

F: The Broader Regulatory Structure: Learning from Experience

In addition to the regulatory agencies put in place post-privatisation, mention should also be made of the various "quasi-governmental agencies" or non-departmental public bodies. There is a wide range and a large number of such bodies ranging from the Gaming Board, the Advisory Conciliation and Arbitration Service, Health and Safety at Work, Civil Aviation Authority, the OFT, the Competition Commission, to the Environment Agency. Their diversity and size is reflected in their ad hoc development.

Innovatory procedures and specialisms give rise to new agencies such as the Human Fertilisation and Embryology Authority under the Human Fertilisation and Embryology Act 1990. Regulating professional standards of various occupations may require statutory interventions. The Osteopaths Act 1993 establishes a new body known as the General Osteopathic Council. This Council will regulate the professional education and conduct of around 2,000 persons in the UK in the delivery of osteopathic treatment. The Care Quality In the UK, the regulation of the National Health Service (NHS) has seen reforms to the Care Quality Commission (CQC) to ensure its effectiveness and address failures in elderly care, including private care homes.[35] New legislative arrangements since the Health and Social Care Act 2012 include a broader range of powers and duties that cover all aspects of the NHS including regulating local NHS services, general practitioners, social care including elderly care. The Care Act 2014 provides stronger regulatory responsibilities than in the past.

The reasons for creating such agencies and the likelihood that they will continue to be favoured as a means of exercising administrative powers are varied. Studies undertaken as to why fringe bodies are created have identified a number of reasons.[36] Fringe organisations may protect certain activities from direct political intervention. As they are outside the departmental system of government they may provide access to expertise and greater independence in decision-making. They may permit and encourage new initiatives away from the restrictions of both civil service and ministerial direction. Fringe organisations appear to lessen the grip of a single bureaucracy and allow greater diversity in decision-making. All the advantages claimed for such bodies make them attractive to successive governments as a means of spreading patronage in the appointment and selection of the management of such bodies.

Fringe organisations give rise to questions about accountability[37] and patronage as well as concerns about their effectiveness. Accountability may vary with the organisation

---

35 T. Prosser, *The Regulatory Challenge* (Oxford: Oxford University Press, 2010), pp.111–135. See the House of Commons Standard Note, Health and Social Care, Safety and Quality Bill 2014, SN 07011 (5 January 2015).
36 D. C. Hague, W. J. M. Mackenzie and A. Barker (eds), *Public Policy and Private Interests: The Institutions of Compromise* (London: Macmillan, 1975).
37 See *Laker Airways Ltd v Department of Trade* [1977] Q.B. 643; [1977] 2 W.L.R. 234 CA (Civ Div). This case provides a good case study of the complexity in the legal arrangements which provide for the giving of directions and guidance to the Civil Aviation Authority (CAA) under the Civil Aviation Act 1971. The Court of Appeal held that

concerned. It may be to a Minister or to a select committee of Parliament. Occasionally there is accountability to the courts, although the exact outcome of judicial review may depend on the statutory arrangements setting out the relationship between ministers and the agency.

14-078 Regulatory bodies require systems of regulation that address risk and its assessment. There are two aspects in particular, the number and range of regulatory bodies and the form risk evaluation might take and both aspects are open to political influences. Since the election of a Coalition Government in 2010 the UK, is undergoing a serious transformation of its regulatory system. There is a serious attempt to cut "red tape" and complex rules. As a result of the financial crisis there are major public sector cuts. Some 50 per cent of the 900 regulatory bodies or quangos (most of them, however, not being involved directly in regulation in a narrower sense) are being abolished or merged linked to de-regulation and the reduction in regulatory burdens. There is also a serious look at the regulatory use of civil law sanctions rather than criminal fines This follows from the Macrory Review,[38] which looked at the role of sanctions and the functioning of criminal sanctions in regulations. The Macrory Review accepted that the existing use of criminal sanctions for regulatory offences could be supplemented by the use of civil sanctions. He accepted that a punitive regulation system was necessary rather than reliance on simple moral persuasion or good behaviour. He recommended an extension of the range and variety of penalties available to regulators and the principle that a regulators' own sanctioning powers should be used rather than recourse to the formalised use of the criminal courts.

14-079 The implementation of many of the Macrory Review's recommendations is to be found in the Regulatory Enforcement and Sanctions Act 2008. This underlines the shift beyond the criminal courts to regulator based systems of sanctions and enforcement. The Act underlines the five principles of regulation set out in the Hampton Report prior to the Macrory Review namely that enforcement action should be transparent, accountable, proportionate, consistent and targeted.

14-080 The impact of the Hampton and Macrory Reports is important in mapping the future direction for regulation in the UK.[39] The Hampton Report reinforces and encourages a targeted approach to regulation that requires all regulators to perform risk assessments and to adopt an effective, efficient and proportionate response while avoiding unnecessary burdens on business. The underlying philosophy is that financial information should only be sought when required. Intervention should be targeted and not invasive or detrimental to market conditions.

---

the Secretary of State's guidance was ultra vires because it appeared that the policy guidance given to the CAA contradicted the precise objectives set out in the 1971 Act. It was unclear how the contradiction was made out. The effect of the decision was to permit Mr Laker to run his Skytrain service to the USA. Subsequently Laker Airlines went bankrupt; the Civil Aviation legislation was amended by the Civil Aviation Act 1982.

38 R. Macrory, *Regulatory Justice: Sanctioning in a post-Hampton World: A Consultation Document* (London: Cabinet Office, May 2006); and *Regulatory Justice: Making Sanctions Effective* (London: Cabinet Office, November 2006).

39 See Generally the FSA, *The Turner Review: A regulatory response to the global banking crisis* (March 2009).

14-081
The UK approach to regulatory agencies is indicative of changing economic and political attitudes. It is also linked to the inherent flexibility to be found in the UK's constitutional arrangements—parliamentary procedures and accountability through select committees and the doctrine of ministerial responsibility. In the UK the relationship between regulator and systems of accountability must be considered within the political context of policy making. Regulator independence and autonomy is nevertheless achieved through scrutiny and accountability to Parliament and ministers indicative of regulator as enterprise. The result is considerable flexibility and ambiguity in terms of how regulatory agencies are treated and this is a weakness in the present constitutional arrangements that deserves further attention for the future.

G: Summary and Conclusions

14-082
Privatisation has provided public lawyers with new challenges in extending their knowledge of regulation into areas of contract and licensing, which involve private law techniques in drafting and understanding legal rules.[40] Privatisation has formed an important element in economic policy making during the 1990s. This remains an important legacy that in different forms selling off state assets and delivering public services through different forms and structures has become important. Privatisation underpins the overarching theme that many aspects of public powers are not to be found exclusively in public bodies alone but in a myriad of different ways that government may use to allow different ways to get things done. Prosser[41] is correct to see how different aspects of the economic constitution reveal much about how power is exercised that deliver a wide range of public services. As Prosser explains, the UK's constitution is highly plural and this transcends any distinction between the political and legal constitution.

14-083
The British experience of regulation began in an ad hoc manner—there is no coherent policy making to achieve a consistent approach among regulators, combining accountability with performance indicators. The Utilities Act 2000, created a new system of regulatory Commission and this is proving to be a highly flexible means of engaging with policy making while ensuring effective regulation.

14-084
Privatisation has provided an important agenda for developing innovative and creative legislation concerning the regulation and the day-to-day running of the newly privatised enterprises. It is a phenomenon of global significance.[42] The UK has led the way in developing

---

40 Julia Black, *Calling Regulators to Account: Challenges, Capacities and Prospects*, LSE Working Papers, 15/2012; G. Marcou, "Régulation et service public. Les enseignements du droit comparé" in: G. Marcou and F. Moderne (eds), *Droit de la régulation, service public et intégration régionale*, Tome 1: *Comparaisons et commentaires* (Paris: L'Harmattan coll. Logiques juridiques, 2006), pp.11–63.
41 T. Prosser, *The Economic Constitution* (Cambridge: Cambridge University Press, 2015), pp.252–253.
42 T. Prosser, *The Regulatory Enterprise: Government Regulation and Legitimacy* (Oxford: Oxford University

strategies and innovation. The UK model has been used throughout Europe, North America and Japan and also among developing and newly-industrialised countries.[43]

14-085 There is also the question of the precise techniques available to public lawyers when regulating privatised industries and seeking to achieve a balance of interests between consumers, the market, the industry, and the role of government. A number of issues arise. First, reliance on the use of licences and contracts has involved legal drafting in the technical side of formally operating the industry. Complex and detailed licences have required skilled interpretation and careful drafting. In the case of utilities in general they run to many hundreds of pages and provide in formal, legal language the mechanisms of running the industry. Secondly, the outcome of increasing complexity in the regulation and supervision of the private utility companies provides work for many of the leading London firms of solicitors with an ever-demanding appetite for well trained and educated lawyers. The combination of contract and licences has stretched the demands on public lawyers to understand legal regulation in a broader context than before.

14-086 Developing a coherent system of regulation has proved to be more difficult than first assumed. The 2008 financial crisis highlighted major flaws in the regulation of financial services especially in the assessment of risk and taking preventative action in the public interest. The UK model of regulation of privatised industries has struggled to find a place within the parliamentary system of control. The theory of ministerial responsibility remains the cornerstone of systems of constitutional accountability. The absence of any workable alternative makes it difficult to come up with a coherent system of effective control. Efforts since 2010 to reduce the number of regulatory agencies have not been entirely effective. Although there are general powers vested in ministers to take overall control, this has also proved more challenging than first assumed. Finding principles and coherence in the operation of systems of complaints, appeals and the system of hearings needs attention. Universal service as a concept is emerging as an important element in public service delivery. The creation of the Competition Appeal Tribunal for adjudicating and policing competition policy provides one overarching system for competition policy.

14-087 Privatisation is likely to remain an important element in economic policy but the size and range of privatisations is limited as the size of the state ownership has diminished considerably. Public law struggles to accommodate a sufficiently robust system of accountability. Regulatory systems are part of the architectural landscape of the constitution. Eventually the diverse and differentiated forms of accountability will become more coherent. Finding suitable parliamentary systems of control will require considerable effort.[44]

Press, 2010). R. Mulgan, "Accountability—an Ever Expanding Concept" (2000) 78(3) *Public Administration* 555– 573.

43 See Istvan Pogany, "Privatisation and Regulatory Change in Hungary" in M. Moran and T. Prosser (ed), *Privatization and Regulatory Change in Europe* (Maidenhead: Open University Press, 1994). Also see Jacques Pelkmans and Norbert Wagner, *Privatization and Deregulation in Asean and EC* (Institute of Southeast Asia Studies, 1990); and L. Gray Cowan, *Privatization in the Developing World* (New York, West Port, CT, London: Prager, 1990).

44 Julia Black, "Calling Regulators to Account: Challenges, Capacities and Prospects" in N. Bamforth and

Further Reading

Cosmo Graham, *Regulating Public Utilities* (Oxford: Hart, 2000).

House of Commons Library, *Privatisation*, Research Paper, 14/61 (20 November 2014).

House of Lords Select Committee on the Constitution, Regulators, *UK Economic Regulators*, 1st Report, Session 2006–07, HL 189-I (London, 2007).

R. Macrory, *Regulatory Justice: Sanctioning in a post-Hampton World: A Consultation Document* (London: Cabinet Office, May,= 2006).

R. Macrory, *Regulatory Justice: Making Sanctions Effective* (London: Cabinet Office, November 2006).

T. Prosser, *Law and the Regulators* (Oxford: Clarendon Press, 1997).

T. Prosser, *The Regulatory Enterprise: Government Regulation and Legitimacy* (Oxford: Oxford University Press, 2010).

T. Prosser, "Regulation and Legitimacy" in J. Jowell, D. Oliver and C. O'Cinneide (eds), *The Changing Constitution* (Oxford: Oxford University Press, 2015), pp.329–350.

T. Prosser, *The Economic Constitution* (Cambridge: Cambridge University Press, 2015).

D. Vogel, *National Style of Regulation* (London: Cornell Press, 1986).

P. Leyland (eds), *Accountability in the Contemporary Constitution* (Oxford: Oxford University Press, 2013), pp.354–388.

Part IV

Citizens' Grievances, Human Rights and Civil Liberties

Chapters 15–18 take account of the development of civil liberties and human rights in the UK. Chapter 15 is an analysis of how citizens' grievances are considered. The chapter covers the various mechanisms in use other than the courts. This includes tribunals, inquiries and the ombudsman system. Informal mechanisms are also discussed. Chapter 16 explains the impact of the Human Rights Act 1998 and Chs 17–18 are concerned with judicial review and obtaining remedies through judicial review in the Administrative Law Court. The role of the rule of law may be found in a wide variety of ways in which public law may seek to protect the individual as a way of ensuring that legal protection is available to the aggrieved and that legality should accompany the exercise of administrative discretion.[1]

---

1 P. Craig, "Political Constitutionalism and Judicial Review" in Christopher Forsyth et al., *Effective Judicial Review* (Oxford: Oxford University Press, 2010), pp.19–42; S. Collini, *Public Moralists: Political Thought and Intellectual Life in Britain 1850–1930* (Oxford: Clarendon, 2011), p.295; and Jeremy Waldron, *Law and Disagreements* (Oxford: Oxford University Press, 1999), pp.88–118. See Richard Stacey, "Democratic jurisprudence and judicial review: Waldron's contribution to political positivism" (2010) *Oxford Journal of Legal Studies* 749. See the discussion about Waldron's views in Mark Tushnet, "How different are Waldron's and Fallon's core cases for and against judicial review?" (2010) *Oxford Journal of legal Studies* 49.

15

Citizens' Grievances

A: Introduction

15-001

The purpose of this chapter is to consider the opportunities for the citizen either individually or collectively to make complaints about public bodies and seek redress. The focus of the chapter is on the means to resolve disputes other than recourse to the courts. The courts and judicial review are examined in detail in subsequent chapters. It is likely that attitudes to complaints will change as the importance of human rights and the opportunities the Human Rights Act 1998 provides for citizens to enforce their rights begins to take effect. The Act has undoubtedly created a rights-based legal culture whereby legal powers will be subjected to rigorous scrutiny as to the potential for challenge. Significant though this will be, the traditional use of tackling citizens' grievances should not be overlooked. This chapter is focused on the complaints industry outside the use of review in the Administrative Law Court. There are many recent significant political developments that are likely to have implications for the citizen, and how rights are likely to be regarded in the future. This includes the potential repeal of the Human Rights Act 1998 and its subsequent replacement by a new British Bill of Rights. There are also important developments in the Protection of Freedoms Act 2012 and the passage of the Modern Slavery Act 2015, the establishment of the first Modern Slavery Commissioner with powers to regulate and protect victims through measures to address all forms of human trafficking and slavery. There are also controversial proposals for the retention of communications data under the Investigatory Powers Bill 2015/16.

15-002

Generally administrative law is regarded as the means to hold the administration accountable. Responsible government is also accountable government. As far back as the 1980s, the Canadian Law Reform Commission's Report recognised the various elements at work in public administration and this was constantly changing to produce and applies rules which, even though they are not legislation, nonetheless govern the activities of administrators[1]:

> "Control of administrative action is a function that can be shared among many institutions or types of decision-makers. Law and bodies entrusted with law application and creation are primary candidates for organising control. However a plurality of independent modes, bodies and procedural regimes that reflect the diverse nature of the control function, is called for. For instance, legal control can address jurisdiction only, or questions of law; control through an appeal can reach facts and the merits of a decision. Non-legal control bears not upon the legality of a decision, but upon its regularity, expediency or financial soundness. A legal dispute may involve several parties, or simply an individual and a decision-maker. This we call a contentious procedure. It implies adversaries which is treated by following a trial-type procedure. The suitability of that model for all legal controls is questionable."

15-003 Both "hard" and "soft" law is available to address citizens' grievances. Informal and formal means of obtaining redress are possible. The vast array of grievance mechanisms include adversarial as well as inquisitorial methods. This may involve some form of investigatory function, for example under the jurisdiction of the ombudsman. Inquisitorial procedures are seen in the work of inquiries such as the Scott inquiry or in the general approach taken in tribunal hearings. Grievance mechanisms such as adjudication or mediation are supposed to be adopted as a pre-action to judicial review applications and more generally in civil procedures.

15-004 There are also a wide range of formal investigative powers entrusted to specific bodies to deal with citizens' complaints. Such bodies have "specialist grievance" procedures for dealing with complaints arising out of particular areas of activity. Some examples are as follows. Complaints related to the various public utilities such as gas, water, electricity, and telecommunications may be made to the relevant regulatory body. Statutory arrangements under the Utilities Act 2000 have improved access and transparency. In the case of data protection set up under the Data Protection Act 1984, replaced by the Data Protection Act 1998, a complaint may be made to the Data Protection Registrar. The 1998 Act has been amended by the Freedom of Information Act 2000 and the Data Protection Commissioner has been given greater powers and re-named the Information Commissioner. Complaints about the police may be made to the Police Complaints Authority which has a duty to supervise the complaint, and it may invite an officer from a constabulary other than the one under investigation to carry

---

1 *Towards a Modern Federal Administrative Law* (Law Reform Commission of Canada, 1987), p.23. Also see Working Paper 51, *Policy Implementation, Compliance and Administrative Law* (Law Reform Commission of Canada, 1986).

out an investigation into the complaint.² In reality there is a complaints industry offering a formula for handling public sector complaints ranging from education to health. There are a wide variety of techniques available for handling complaints from independent investigation to internal responses or the use of an ombudsman system.

The chapter is focused on alternatives to the courts and the importance of informal and internal means to redress disputes involving the administration. This includes the use of tribunals, inquiries and ombudsmen. The Justice-All Souls review as long ago as 1988, recognised the problem that there is no single institution within the UK³ "to keep under constant review all the procedures and institutions whereby the individual may challenge administrative action". There is a need for different forms of dispute or grievance resolution to be brought into a coherent and well organised system where the citizen may access all forms of grievance resolution through a single point.

15–005

The referendum decision to leave the European Union is likely to have major constitutional repercussions for the approach to citizens' rights. It is likely to take considerable time before the full implications of leaving the EU are worked out in full.

B: Informal Mechanisms of Complaint and MPs

An aggrieved citizen may find that the first avenue of redress concerning a public body is to make a formal complaint to the body concerned. In fact the citizen may find that the help of their constituency MP is a necessary first step in making any complaint because of the complexity of complaining. Many MPs feel that they play a significant role in "troubleshooting" on behalf of their constituents. The use of emails and e-petitions has provided a new mechanism for members of the public to access Parliament and engage with their MP. The proposal for e-petitions arise from the period of coalition government from 2010 to May 2015. This has provided the forum of Westminster Hall for a debate on issue raised by e-petition⁴. A tax on sugary drinks on Westminster Hall was held on Monday 30 November 2015. The threshold is over 100,000 electors.⁵

15–006

MPs may also take advantage of various contacts they may have on select committees, within government departments and among Cabinet Ministers. If a letter from an MP fails to

15–007

---

2   Established under the Police Act 1984 and amended by the Police Act 1996 and Police (Conduct) Regulations; SI 1999/730.
3   Justice-All Souls Review, *Administrative Justice: Some Necessary Reforms* (Oxford, 1988), Ch.4, pp.75–84.
4   House of Commons Library, Debate Pack, *Debate on an e-petition on a tax on surgery drinks*, CDP 2015/0109 (25 November 2015).
5   House of Commons Library, Briefing Paper No.06450 (20 October 2015).

provoke a satisfactory response then an MP may raise the issue in a parliamentary question or during a debate in the House of Commons or during a half-hour adjournment debate.

15-008 An MP may make use of an Early Day Motion, as a means to raise a complaint from a constituent. This acts as an accurate "notice board" for any grievances raised by MPs especially when there is a common cause of complaint affecting many constituents or involving several constituencies. If the matter is very contentious the debate may be accompanied by the collection of a large number of signatures supporting the debate. Topics included in Early Day Motions are very broad and through debate, grievances may be aired on a regular basis during each parliamentary session[6].

15-009 Enthusiasm for the MP system as a form of redress should be tempered by the problem that many citizens may not know their MP, may fail to understand the role of an MP, and may not have confidence in the MP's abilities to remedy any grievance. Disputes may fall outside the remit of the MP when there are legal proceedings imminent or where the matter may be more properly dealt with by an alternative means of redress. Various studies have suggested that the work of MPs and the reputation of Parliament may not be at the highest given the expenses scandal and questions about remuneration arrangements.[7] The inadequacy of the MP as an effective watchdog was partly acknowledged in the setting up of the central government Parliamentary Commissioner for Administration. This should not detract from the worthwhile advice given by MP's to their constituents. Today MPs are bound by the *Code of Conduct for Members of Parliament* and also a *Guide to the rules relating to the conduct of Members*.[8]

15-010 In terms of informal means to redress grievances, there are a wide number of pressure groups or trade unions who may act as a watchdog for the citizen. There are various local Citizens Advice Bureaus, mostly staffed with volunteers who provide information and advice on access to both formal and informal means to redress grievances. Law Centres may provide legal advice and may specialise on specific problem areas which require specialist advice such as housing and immigration problems. Sometimes the matter complained about involves some form of consumer redress such as a housing problem which may fit in the category of a private law problem between the landlord and tenant or, if there is a public body involved, local authority and tenant. The hybrid nature of such problems makes a knowledge of both public and private law essential.

15-011 Citizens' grievances in the public law arena may benefit from newspaper or media coverage to force officials to take account of the citizen's grievance. This may involve "in depth" investigative journalism or simply drawing attention to the nature of the disputes. Most newspapers have a reader's column where complaints are aired.

There are some important developments in open government under the Code of Practice on Access to Government Information, revised 1997, and the Freedom of Information Act 2000 is also relevant in providing access to information. From 1 January 2005 citizens were given the right to make requests for information under the Freedom of Information Act 2000. The Act is

---

6 House of Commons Library, *Members and constituency etiquette* Briefing Paper, 02028 (29 September 2015).
7 There is a wide ranging discussion of the role of Members of Parliament in Philip Norton, "The House of Commons under pressure" in Bill Jones and Philip Norton, *Politics UK*, 8th edn (London: Routledge, 2013), pp.328–340.
8 House of Commons publications on the Parliamentary website.

wide ranging and applies to all information held by public bodies. There are strict timetables for compliance of 20 working days of receipt of the request. There is an appeal structure including the First-Tier Tribunal (Information Rights). Cabinet ministers or a Law Officer may issue a conclusive certificate or ministerial veto against a decision or enforcement notice.[9] There is an Information Commissioner with an investigative and enforcement role. This includes overriding a public authority's application of an exemption test, including an exemption made in the public interest. These powers have been enhanced by the Coroners and Justice Act 2009.

There are Environmental Information Regulations 2004 for environmental information claims and Privacy and Electronic Communications (EC Directive) Regulations 2003. There is a memorandum of understanding between the Information commissioner and government departments.

15–012

C: Tribunals and Inquiries

Tribunals

In considering alternatives to the courts in the adjudication of disputes, importance must be given to the work of tribunals. Tribunals were commonly in use in the nineteenth century and this remained the case up until 2009 when tribunals were subsumed into the courts system. Tribunals helped to perform a wide variety of functions and provided a variety of specialist ways of helping to redress citizen's grievances. The coming into force of the Human Rights Act 1998 also required that the way tribunals operated had to take account of the requirements under Article 6 of the Convention to a fair trial and public hearing in terms of the procedures and processes in use in a tribunal.

15–013

The Franks Committee[10] in 1957 recommended the creation of the Council of Tribunals to keep under review the working and the constitution of tribunals. The work of the Council closely monitored the development of the system of administrative tribunals "to provide some consistent principles" to guide the work of tribunals. Since the Tribunal and Inquiries Act 1958 following the recommendations of the Franks Committee, the number of tribunals which fell within the jurisdiction of the Council on Tribunals, at one time exceeded a total of 83. The Leggatt Review[11] estimated that the total number of tribunals may be more than their estimate of 137. Franks regarded tribunals as part of the machinery provided by Parliament for the purposes of adjudication rather than as part of the machinery of the administration. A wide variety of bodies and institutions rely on the work of tribunals.

15–014

---

9   House of Commons Library, *Freedom of Information*, Briefing Paper, No.02950 (28 May 2015).
10 *Report of the Committee on Administrative Tribunals and Enquiries*, Cmnd.218 (1957).
11 Sir Andrew Leggatt, *Tribunals for Users One System, One Service: Report of the Review of Tribunals* (March 2001).

15-015

The Report by Sir Andrew Leggatt into the *Review of Tribunals*[12] made a number of recommendations in an attempt to bring coherence to the system of tribunals and to provide coherence between one part of the civil justice system, the courts and the system of tribunals. The courts came under the Woolf reforms while the latter had not. As Sir Andrew noted[13]:

> "The last 50 years have brought an accelerating accumulation of tribunals as bodies whose function it is to decide disputes that would otherwise go to the courts. Together they form the largest part of the civil justice system in England and Wales, hearing about one million cases each year. That number of cases alone makes their work of great importance to our society, since more of us bring a case before a tribunal than go to any other part of the justice system. Their collective impact is immense."

15-016

It is the variety and diversity of tribunals and their different uses that is also striking. Various disciplinary bodies can take the form of a tribunal. For example: the General Dental Council; the Central Council for Nursing, Midwifery and Health Visiting;[14] the General Medical Council; and the Architects Registration Council for the UK exercise a variety of disciplinary powers within a statutory framework. Licensing also forms an important function of the work of tribunals such as the Civil Aviation Authority, or the Consumer Credit Licensing Hearings. As Hendry has noted[15]:

> ". . . a multiplicity of tribunals each operating within the bounds of a confined jurisdiction and each directed toward disposing of claims and arguments arising out of a particular statutory scheme."

15-017

The Legal Profession in England and Wales is regulated by a number of organisations and bodies under the overarching supervision by the Legal Services Board. Each has their own distinct regulatory culture and system for handling complaints and discipline. The Bar Standards Board (BSB) and the Solicitors Regulation Authority regulate respectively Barristers and solicitors. In addition there are other regulatory (SRA) bodies for different aspects of the legal profession[16] including the Council for Licensed Conveyances.

15-018

Some areas of tribunal activity have come under particular scrutiny by the courts, partly because of the nature of the work involved. For example, the Prison Board of Visitors with its

---

12 Leggatt, *Tribunals for Users One System, One Service: Report of the Review of Tribunals*.
13 Leggatt, *Tribunals for Users One System, One Service: Report of the Review of Tribunals,* para.1.1.
14 Dentists Act 1984 s.27.
15 K. H. Hendry, "The Tasks of Tribunals: Some Thoughts" (1982) 1 *Civil Justice Quarterly* 253.
16 There is the Costs Lawyers Standards Board; the Intellectual Property Regulation Board; ILEX Professional Standards; and the Master of the Faculties (the Faculty Office). Each represent a smaller but important part of the legal profession.

origins in the Prison Act 1898 appears to have developed into a tribunal in all but name when performing a wide adjudicative function on charges of offences under the Prison Act 1952 and amendments. The disciplinary function can be vast as over 81,000 disciplinary offences were punished in the year 1989. Such disciplinary proceedings are subject to judicial review by the courts. There is concern that legal representation should be available at such hearings as the powers of the Board of Visitors have been compared to the jurisdiction of the magistrates' courts. In *R v Board of Visitors of HM Prison, the Maze, Ex p. Hone*,[17] Lord Goff noted the observations made on behalf of the appellant:

> "A hearing before a board of visitors is a sophisticated hearing. In particular, he [counsel for the appellant] submitted there is an oral hearing; a formal plea is entered; cross-examination is allowed and witnesses are called; the onus and standard of proof are the same as in a criminal trial; free legal aid is available; punishments are imposed; a plea in mitigation can be entered, and the board has greater powers of punishment than those exercised by magistrates' courts."

15-019

The House of Lords rejected the submission that those appearing before the Prison Board had a right to legal representation by a lawyer. The courts have consistently upheld the principle that the rules of natural justice apply to the Board of Prison Visitors in making their adjudications. It may be expected that the Human Rights Act 1998 will have implications in the way decision-making is reached in terms of art.6 (right to a fair hearing) under the Convention. Article 8 of the Convention applies to the correspondence of prisoners[18] including interviews with journalists.

15-020

Tribunals are often compared to courts and may appear to perform the work of departments in adjudications. However, the Franks Report was clear[19]: "tribunals . . . are not ordinary courts, but neither are they appendages of Government Departments . . .".

15-021

Defining the role and objectives of tribunals presents formidable problems given the great diversity of their work and the lack of uniformity in their functions. All tribunals which deal with disputes between the citizen and the government are concerned with administrative power and how it may properly be exercised. The Justice-All Souls review noted[20]:

> ". . . that the true role of the courts is restricted to a review of legality and the judges are not concerned with the merits in the sense of the rightness (or wrongness) of the decision. Tribunals on the other hand, are given a different role. Very commonly they are concerned

---

17 [1988] A.C. 379; [1988] 2 W.L.R. 177 HL; *Hone v Maze Prison Visitors* [1988] A.C. 379; [1988] 2 W.L.R. 177 HL.
18 *R v Secretary of State for the Home Department Ex p. Simms* [2000] 2 A.C. 115; [1999] 3 W.L.R. 328 HL.
19 Franks, *Report of the Committee on Administrative Tribunals and Enquiries*, Cmnd.218 (1957), para.40.
20 *Justice-All Souls Review*, p.212.

> with the merits of the decision and typically they will be given the task of deciding, as between citizen and the state, whether an official has dealt correctly with a claim or application."

15-022 Tribunals may also exercise similar decision-making functions as Ministers. Franks expressed a preference for tribunals over the largely discretionary powers of Ministers and preferred courts over tribunals. In the allocation of functions, it appears quite difficult to decide the advantages of one over the other. However, it is possible to set out some of the reasons for creating independent statutory tribunals.

15-023 The main reasons and by implication the advantages claimed for a system of tribunals are the following. Tribunals provide access to expert and specialist knowledge of complex areas of law and practice. The forum of a tribunal allows a wider degree of expertise than would normally be possible with the courts. In addition, tribunals are claimed to provide cheap, reasonably speedy and efficient means for the resolution of disputes. The procedures may claim to be less formal than courts though as pointed out above, some tribunals appear to have inherited procedures almost identical to the courts. Another claimed advantage is that tribunals are not bound by very complex and legalistic rules of evidence and the decisions reached at tribunals may cover more widely developed considerations than the courts.

15-024 This raises the broader question of whether tribunals may offer a distinctive system of adjudication that is not orientated to the adversarial process in the way that the courts are. Lord Denning in *R v National Insurance Commissioner Ex p. Viscusi*[21] suggested that tribunals were "more in the nature of an inquiry before an investigating body charged with the task of finding out what happened".

The Leggatt Review of the Tribunal System

15-025 The Leggatt Review on tribunals was published on 16 August 2001 and comprised a number of important recommendations covering the reform of the tribunal system resulting in a single tier system replacing the multiplicity of over 70 tribunals. The main recommendations included the development of rules for tribunals to follow a coherent and integrated system offering a tribunal service. The intention was for the tribunal rules to be consistent with the Civil Justice Review[22] introduced for the first time for civil cases and later applied to criminal and administrative courts. The Leggatt Review envisaged the division of tribunals into various headings, education, employment, finance and revenue, health and care, immigration and asylum, property, land and valuation, social security, pensions and criminal injury compensation, transport

---

21 [1974] 1 W.L.R. 646; [1974] 2 All E.R. 724 CA (Civ Div).
22 Lord Woolf's Civil Justice Review see the Civil Procedure Act 1997 and the Civil Procedure Rules. T. Cornford and M. Sunkin, "The Bowman Report, Access and Recent Reforms of the Judicial Review Procedure" [2011] *Public Law* 11. J. Sorabji, *English Civil Justice after the Woolf and Jackson Reforms: A Critical Analysis* (Cambridge: Cambridge University Press, 2014).

and aspects of trade, competition, patents and copyright. Leggatt proposed the creation of a general tribunal and a first tier of tribunal decisions.

The Tribunals Court and Enforcement Act 2007

The Act creates two general tribunals. The First-Tier Tribunal making first instance decisions and a second-tier Upper Tribunal to hear appeals. There is also a senior President of Tribunals. The integration of tribunals and courts is accompanied by the Constitutional Reform Act 2005 that guarantees judicial independence. The role of the Senior President is important in providing an overarching view of the case load and administration of the tribunal system. The composition of tribunals is a combination of legally qualified members with non-legal members covering the expertise of the subject area. In September 2013 the first-tier tribunal comprised six divisions including:
The General Regulatory Chamber covering a wide range of areas such as consumer credit, estate agent appeals, charity appeals, information disputes and driving standards agency appeals. The second area covers the Social Entitlement Chamber that includes social security, child support, asylum support and criminal injuries compensation. The third area is the Health, Education and Social Care Chamber covering mental health review, special education needs and disability and care standards. The fourth area is The War Pensions and Armed Forces Compensation Chamber. The fifth are is the Tax Chamber covering income tax, VAT and duties. The sixth area is the Immigration and Asylum Chamber and the seventh is the Property Chamber including residential property, rent functions, leasehold valuation and agricultural lands. One of the major changes is to create a single system of administration under the general Courts and Tribunals Service. The First-Tier Tribunal may review its own decisions in many cases saving the need for an appeal or re-hearing. The right to appeal to the Upper Tribunal is based on a point of law only.

The Upper Tribunal has a smaller number of chambers. These include: the Administrative Appeals Chamber; The Tax and Chancery Chamber; the Lands Chamber; and the Immigration and Asylum Chamber. Each tribunal has a President—a High Court Judge—and each Chamber may hear appeals from one or more chambers of the First-Tier Tribunal. A novel innovation is that the Upper Tribunal may, in specified cases, act as an administrative court and have limited powers of judicial review. Certain cases may also be transferred from the Administrative Court to the Upper Tribunal and this may also apply to cases transferred from the Upper Tribunal to the Administrative Court. There is a right of appeal with leave to the Court of Appeal.[23] This innovation is intended to provide integration between the tribunal system and the courts. Members of Tribunals share the designation of judge and receive an enhanced respect for their status and role. Appointments are made by the Judicial Appointments Commission. Eligibility is intended to bring together the wide diversity of potential applicants.

---

23 The equivalent is available in Scotland ss.13–14 of the Tribunals Courts and Enforcement Act 2007.

15-028 The question of whether a refusal of leave to appeal by both First-tier and Upper Tribunal is itself subject to judicial review by the Administrative Court arose in the case of *R (Cart) v Upper Tribunal*[24] and *Elba v Advocate General for Scotland*[25]. The Supreme Court clarified the arrangements for judicial review by the Administrative Court. The most important point is that the Upper Tribunal's decisions are themselves subject to judicial review. However, this review power should be used sparingly and only in cases where there is a "compelling reason". There are various public policy reasons for restricting judicial review. This was recognised and that the criteria for making appeals to the Court of Appeal and also appeals from the Upper Tribunal to the Court of Appeal was clarified by the Supreme Court. The strict criteria recognise that there is an important point of practice or principle that require an appeal to be considered; That there is some compelling reason for the appeal to be heard. The overarching importance of upholding the rule of law and ensuring that the courts have sufficient resources to manage the most significant cases. Another consideration is that the time limit for judicial review was amended to only 16 days after the date on which the Upper Tribunal's decision was sent to the applicant. There is no right to an oral hearing on reconsideration of refusal on the papers.[26] Another aspect of the case of *Elba* is the willingness of the Supreme Court to see that there should be alignment between the systems in Scotland and in England. The Supreme Court accepted that the Scottish Courts could correct an error even if it was within the jurisdiction of the tribunal. The importance of bringing together the different cultures and working practices of the different tribunals is one of the responsibilities of the Tribunal Procedure Committee chaired by a Court of Appeal judge.

15-029 The new arrangements are intended to set controls over the future creation of tribunals. Increasingly there is evidence of the Upper Tribunal setting guidance in the form of precedent for first-tier tribunals.[27] There is also a question of cost and expenses. Tribunals are more cost effective and their general informality in many cases gives them a clear advantage in terms of costs over the formal system of courts. It is not unlikely that the courts will fall under the influence of tribunals and this may include a more informal style. The administration of courts and tribunals under the Courts and Tribunals Service means that the working relationship between courts and tribunals will be more likely to be closer and more integrated than in the past. Despite the creation of the new system, there are some tribunals that are outside the current arrangements. These include the Investigatory Powers Tribunal under the Regulation of Investigatory Powers Act 2000 and the specialised Competition Appeal Tribunal under the Enterprise Act 2002. The Terrorism Act 2000 created the Proscribed Organisations Appeal Commission.

15-030 Cuts in funding legal aid have seriously reduced the number of cases heard by tribunals. There is also the matter of fees for employment tribunals from February 2013.[28] The average of

---

24 [2011] UKSC 28; [2012] 1 A.C. 663.
25 [2011] UKSC 29; (2011) S.L.T. 768.
26 Rule 54.7A(3) and (8).
27 See *Sinclair Gardens Investments (Kensington) Ltd, v Ray* [2015] EWCA Civ 124; [2015] P.L.S.C. 343.
28 House of Commons Library, *Employment tribunals fees*, Briefing Paper, No.7081 (15 September 2015).

single cases fell by 67 per cent between October 2013 and June 2015. The average of multiple cases fell by 69 per cent during the same period.

The Administrative Justice and Tribunals Council was created soon after the implementation of the Leggatt reforms. Its general aim was to keep under review the working of the administrative justice system. This included the working of specified tribunals and the statutory inquiries. The aim was to ensure that the system might be efficient and contribute to the good administration that is long regarded as one of the aims of the administrative justice system. The Council was abolished on 19 August 2013 when the Public Bodies Act 2011 was implemented.

The abolition of the Council was the subject of critical comment.[29] The new Leggatt reforms to tribunals will take some time to assess and analyse. Clearly the new tribunal system is fully compliant with art.6(1) of the ECHR but there are over arching questions about whether administrative justice will improve overall. There needs to be a feedback loop between the work of tribunals and the system of administration. The importance of judicial independence is an integral part of the system but many of the tribunals are linked to economic matters that are certainly subject to political and social changes in government policy-making.

There is also a question of expertise and specialism. Are these attributes seen as important today? There is an emerging tension between self-interest and expertise and a strong emphasis on democratic accountability and legitimacy. At times the debate between legal experts and political considerations is not easy to reconcile—especially when the costs of justice are seen as coming under the austerity arrangements put in place since the financial crisis of 2008.

D: Inquiries

Aggrieved citizens may find that the forum which allows their viewpoint or objections to be most clearly expressed and openly considered is through the use of inquiries. Compared to tribunals, where there is a need to adjudicate disputes between the citizen and the state, inquiries developed historically as an alternative to the Private Bill procedure where proposals for powers by government in matters involving public authority were investigated through parliamentary committees. Inquiries, developed from different considerations than the tribunal system. Wade notes[30]:

> "The typical tribunal finds facts and decides the case by applying legal rules laid down by statute or regulation. The typical inquiry

---

29 The House of Lords Secondary Legislation Scrutiny Committee, 2nd report, HL 8 (2013–14) and 7th Report of the Secondary Legislation Scrutiny Committee, HL 36 (2013–14).
30 Wade, *Administrative Law*, 6th edn (Oxford: Oxford University Press, 1988), p.900.

> hears evidence and finds facts, but the person conducting it finally makes a recommendation to a minister as to how the minister should act on some question of policy, e.g., whether he should grant planning permission for some development scheme."

15-035 In essence inquiries allow the citizen the right to a hearing before an important administrative decision may be made. This means that inquiries allow more public participation than would otherwise be possible especially in the planning law area where there is controversy over the location of an airport, a power station or a major motorway.

15-036 Traditionally inquiries are limited to an investigative role, usually through the provision of evidential material to allow a Minister to reach an ultimate decision. Rarely do they make the actual decision. Inquiries have developed in an ad hoc way. As a valuable technique in administrative law, the basic elements of independent investigation, presentation of evidence and the making of recommendations allow for great flexibility. Inquiries also have the potential to cross the boundary between public law and private law issues. For example, the Department of Trade enjoy wide powers to appoint inspectors to investigate companies which include, under s.177(1) of the Financial Services Act 1986, the power to appoint inspectors if it appears to the Secretary of State that there is a breach of the Company Securities (Insider Dealing) Act 1985.

15-037 Inquiries into accidents may be set up under various statutory powers. Section 466 of the Merchant Shipping Act 1894 gives powers to hold an inquiry into a collision of a ship at sea;[31] there are various statutory powers to hold inquiries into railway accidents, gas explosions, or nuclear installations. The normal formulation of the terms of reference of such inquiries includes questions of why did the accident occur, and what lessons may be gained from past mistakes? In some instances, the basis of the inquiry may give rise to criminal prosecutions or disciplinary procedures.

15-038 Civil liability may therefore be largely dependent on the outcome of an accident inquiry and this raises questions about the confidentiality of evidence and the rights of witnesses who give evidence and afterwards find that criminal prosecutions are taken. In that respect account needs to be taken of the possibility, now accepted but at one time doubted, that in English criminal law a corporation could be convicted of manslaughter. In P&O European Ferries Ltd, Turner J held that an indictment for manslaughter might lie against P&O Ferries after the Zeebrugge disaster.[32] The evidence which may form the basis of any criminal prosecution may come from the evidence obtained as part of the findings of the inquiry into the disaster. The Sheen Report[33] found that from the Board of Directors: "through the managers of the marine department down to the Junior Superintendents' fault could be established". The conclusion reached in the report was that "from top to bottom the body corporate was infected with the disease of sloppiness".

---

31 The Report was carried out by Sheen J, with assessors and published in July 1987. Also see J. McEldowney, "Public Inquiry into the Piper Alpha Disaster" [1991] *Utilities Law Review* 2.
32 *R v Coroner for Kent Ex p. Spooner* (1987) 3 B.C.C. 636; (1989) 88 Cr. App. R. 10 QBD.
33 See McEldowney, "Public Inquiry into the Piper Alpha Disaster".

15–039 Inquiries may also have an important role in establishing facts arising from social problems such as child abuse. Such inquiries may come under s.26 of the Child Care Act 1980 or inquiries undertaken by review panels appointed by local authorities or local agencies. The standing of the person appointed to hold the inquiry and the nature of the recommendation may prove influential with the government of the day even though there is no obligation to accept any of the recommendations made in the report prepared by the inquiry. Not everyone favours the inquiry as an investigative technique in such cases. In 1981 the Annual General Meeting of the British Association of Social Workers rejected the use of committees of inquiry in such cases. Dissatisfaction of the Association has focused on the showpiece nature of the inquiry and the feeling that those under investigation are perceived by the media as "on trial".

15–040 The principles identified by Franks that ought to apply to inquiries such as openness, fairness and impartiality, have been recognised in the Tribunals and Inquiries Acts 1958 and in s.11 of the 1971 Act and their consolidation in the Tribunals and Inquiries Act 1992. This legislation permits the Lord Chancellor to make various procedural rules for the conduct of inquiries. An example of these rules may be found in the Town and Country Planning (Inquiries Procedure) Rules 1988.[34] In drawing up such rules the Council on Tribunals may be consulted; such rules are advisory only.

15–041 In addition to the above procedures there are a miscellaneous number of statutory provisions which permit the holding of inquiries. Formal powers for the investigation of improper official behaviour of officials in 1921 were enacted under the Tribunals of Inquiry (Evidence) Act 1921. The 1921 Act is sparingly used for such matters of "urgent public importance". It has been estimated that these powers have only been used in fewer than 20 occasions in the past. There are also a variety of non-statutory inquiries where it is desired to carry out an investigation and a statutory inquiry is not required. The best known example of this is the Crichel Down inquiry,[35] and the Stansted inquiry into the location of London's third airport. Inquiries may be set up where there are public concerns about the role of Ministers. In 1963 Lord Denning's inquiry into the Profumo affair was set up informally and had no statutory powers. The Salmon Commission later recommended that such inquiries should not normally be used in matters of such public concern. Perhaps the most controversial and intrusive into the internal working of government is the Scott inquiry. The inquiry was established after the collapse of the trial of three former executives of the machine tool company Matrix Churchill charged with deception in obtaining export licences led to the setting up of an inquiry chaired by Scott LJ. At the trial the prosecution had alleged that the intended use of the machine tools supplied to Iraq was for weapons. The defence claimed that the government was fully aware of the use of the machine tools which had been subject to a licence application. Evidence given by Alan Clark, the former Minister of State at the Department of Trade and Industry confirmed that there was no deception as the Government were aware of the intended use of the machine tools. The judge quashed public interest immunity certificates served by the

---

34 Town and Country Planning (Inquiry Procedure) Rules 1988 (SI 1988/944).
35 *Report of the Public Inquiry into the Disposal of Land at Crichel Down*, Cmnd.9176 (1954). See Ch.3 for a fuller discussion.

prosecution to prevent disclosure of intelligence information. The documents released at the trial revealed how high level departmental and ministerial contact had taken place over the licence application. Controversy surrounds the use of public interest immunity certificates and the role of government Ministers in signing the certificates. Also of significance is the question of the legal advice tendered by the Attorney General that Ministers were under a duty to sign the certificates. The role of Customs and Excise in bringing the prosecutions is also questioned.

15–042 The terms of reference of the Scott inquiry were announced by the Prime Minister[36] "to examine and report on decisions taken by the prosecuting authority and those signing public interest immunity certificates in *R v Henderson* and any other similar cases that he considers relevant to the inquiry; and to make recommendations". The Chairman of the inquiry appointed an independent counsel to the inquiry who in practice took the main burden of asking questions of witnesses. The inquiry has heard evidence in public and the evidence is available from the Public Records Office.

15–043 The Scott inquiry was not set up under the Tribunals and Inquiry (Evidence) Act 1921 and thus it did not have statutory powers to subpoena witnesses. The Prime Minister gave assurances that civil servants and Ministers would be required to give evidence. Former Ministers accepted invitations to attend including Lady Thatcher, the former Prime Minister. John Major also gave evidence as serving Prime Minister. Witnesses had been given immunity from prosecution for their evidence given at the inquiry.

15–044 As an ad hoc inquiry with no express statutory powers, this gave Sir Richard Scott the freedom to determine the procedures to be adopted at the inquiry itself. The procedures adopted at the Scott inquiry proved as controversial as the subject of the inquiry itself. The starting point is to consider the six cardinal principles adopted by Lord Salmon as guidance for inquiries laid down by the Royal Commission 1966 under the chairmanship of Lord Salmon.[37] The six Salmon principles are as follows:

(1) before any person becomes involved in an inquiry, the tribunal must be satisfied that there are circumstances which affect him and which the tribunal proposes to investigate;

(2) before any person who is involved in an inquiry is called as a witness he should be informed of any allegations which are made against him and the substance of the evidence in support of them;

(3) he should be given an adequate opportunity of preparing his case and of being advised by legal advisers; his legal expenses should normally be met out of public funds;

---

36 *Hansard*, HC Vol.214, col.74 (16 November 1992). *R v Henderson* unreported November 1992. Also see D. Leigh, *Betrayed: The Real Story of the Matrix Churchill Trial* (London: Bloomsbury, 1993).
37 Cmnd.3121 (1966).

(4) he should have the opportunity of being examined by his own solicitor or counsel and of stating his case in public at the inquiry;

(5) any material witnesses he wishes to be called at the inquiry should, if reasonably practicable be heard; and

(6) he should have the opportunity of testing by cross-examination conducted by his own solicitor or counsel any evidence which may affect him.

It is important to remember that the six principles, outlined above, are not rules of law but guidance which might be followed. The Salmon principles were intended to provide the basis for Tribunals operating under the Tribunals of Inquiry (Evidence) Act 1921. While many commentators see the principles as a matter of fundamental fairness,[38] the Scott inquiry was free to depart from them. The approach taken by Scott was to acknowledge that as far as possible the principles should be applied and followed. However, the nature of the Scott inquiry required both adversarial and inquisitorial techniques. In the end the procedures that were adopted of necessity reflected the inquisitorial approach taken by the inquiry. Scott rapidly discovered that if the inquiry adopted all of the six Salmon principles it might take a considerable time to complete. The principle that caused most controversy relates to the question of cross-examination and legal representation at the inquiry. In the past, notable inquiries such as Crom-Johnson LJ into the Crown Agents affair took considerable time and were subject to extensive delay. Cross-examination by lawyers at the inquiry was held largely responsible for that delay.

The question of whether Scott was correct in adopting an inquisitorial approach remains highly debated. Criticism focused on the argument that the inquisitive nature of the procedures was inappropriate when conducted in public hearings, left witnesses unprotected and put due process in jeopardy. Scott's response to such criticisms, notably from Lord Howe,[39] was to point to the increasingly large amount of written submissions received throughout the entire period of the inquiry, the fact that oral proceedings were only a small fraction of the inquiry's work and that witnesses were granted legal advice at considerable cost to the taxpayer though admittedly not cross-examination. This last point, the absence of cross-examination rights remains a contentious issue. In its recent consideration of the Scott procedures, the Council on Tribunals broadly favoured the Scott approach whenever inquisitorial procedures were involved. There remain some lurking doubts that perhaps the procedures were in some way defective because the key element of cross-examination by lawyers was absent. There was also the sheer scale of the work generated by the inquiry. Lord Howe makes the following observations[40]:

> "My own case may be seen as a useful illustration. Unrepresented as I was until very near the end (only my closing submissions were

---

38 Lord Howe, "Procedure at the Scott Inquiry" [1996] *Public Law* 445–460.
39 Lord Howe, "Procedure at the Scott Inquiry".
40 Lord Howe, "Procedure at the Scott Inquiry".

> prepared by counsel and solicitors rather than myself), I struggled to keep abreast of the mountains of transcripts that filled the months before and after I gave evidence, and over the years during which I was obliged to comment on several distinct batches of preliminary conclusions. I estimate that I spent at least 30 unrewarding (and unrewarded) days, testifying to or preparing the increasingly prolix questionnaires, which they had to inflict upon others as well as themselves. By contrast with this prolonged ordeal, Lord Justice Edmund Davis's Aberfan report was published within nine months of the disaster. So too was Lord Justice Bingham's Report on the collapse of BCCI."

15-047 Following on from Lord Howe's strong reservations about the Scott inquiry procedures, the Council on Tribunals considered the way forward. In general terms the key objectives of an inquiry are effectiveness, fairness, speed and economy. No single constitution or model set of rules are possible to achieve these goals. However, the Council did recommend "that inquiry reports of any length should provide for an executive summary of the findings and recommendations".[41]

15-048 Controversial inquiries have been held under the Tribunals of Inquiry (Evidence) Act 1921 such as the Lord Saville inquiry into events surrounding the deaths of 13 people and injury of a similar number in Northern Ireland during Sunday 30 January 1972. The inquiry began taking evidence in March 2000. The hearings from the main witnesses were completed by February 2004. Over 2,500 people were interviewed and 922 were asked to give oral evidence. The report was published in June 2010 and it contained ten volumes with over 5,000 pages. The entire cost of the inquiry was £192 million, one of the most expensive in history. The high cost and time-scale has been seen as a turning point in the history of such inquires.[42]

15-049 More commonly used are powers under the compulsory acquisitions of land legislation to hold a public local inquiry. The Acquisition of Land Act 1981 provides an opportunity for objectors to make their case heard in the case of the compulsory purchase of land. However, the role of the inquiry is not confined to this objective alone, as the effect of such inquiries is to provide administrators with a sense of the public interest. The courts have upheld this view of the inquiry as a means of providing authorisation for the use of land for public use. In this sense the inquiry procedure legitimates and informs government decision-making in addition to providing the citizen with a means of redress.

---

41 *Advice to the Lord Chancellor on the procedural issues arising in the conduct of public inquiries set up by Ministers Council on Tribunals* (July 1996).
42 See Louis Blom Cooper, "What went wrong on Bloody Sunday: a critique of the Saville Inquiry" (2010) *Public Law* 61–78. There are various examples of inquiries including the Dunblane School Inquiry (March 1996); the Child Abuse in North Wales Inquiry (June 1996); the Saville Inquiry (June 1998); and the Harold Shipman Inquiry (23 January 2001).

15-050 Planning appeals require that the Secretary of State should allow the appellant and the local planning authority an opportunity of putting their case. Invariably, though not necessarily, this may mean holding an inquiry under powers granted to the Secretary of State under the Local Government Act 1972 to direct that a local inquiry should be held. Planning appeals arise when planning permission has been refused or is granted subject to conditions. Public local inquiries have recognisable characteristics. They are held in the locality where the proposed schemes are situated. The inspector is normally appointed by the Minister with the relevant statutory authority. Currently the Department of the Environment has a corps of nearly 400 inspectors responsible for over 3,000 inquiries each year. The subject matter of the inquiry relates to the objections to the proposed scheme received by the Minister from private parties or local authorities. The purpose of the inquiry is to provide the relevant Minister with the necessary information to allow the Minister to consider the scheme in light of the public benefit to be derived from the scheme if implemented. Weighing up all the material factors is greatly assisted by the inquiry process. However, this does not preclude taking other matters into consideration, including the policy of the government, advice from experts or departmental considerations.

15-051 A particularly controversial area of planning are highways inquiries into large motorway projects. Detailed rules exist as to the conduct of these inquiries and efforts are made to improve the information available to objectors.

15-052 Distinct from planning appeals the planning system adopts inquiries as a means to allow public participation in the planning process. Local plan inquiries allow objectors to raise issues surrounding the publication of local plans or structure plans prepared under Pt II of the Town and Country Planning Act 1971. The Town and Country Planning (Costs of Inquiries etc.) Act 1995 authorises the Secretary of State to recover from local planning authorities the costs borne by the Secretary of State in relation to the appointment of inspectors to hold local public inquiries. The 1995 Act provides express powers for the defrayment of such expenses.

15-053 The inquiry procedure is a key issue for planning and administrative lawyers. Inquiries may resemble a court where the trial of the issues involves the presentation of the appellant's case after the inspector makes introductory comments. The appellant has a right of final reply, and often the legal representation at inquiries ensures that the proceedings are formal and may appear over-legalistic. The adversarial nature of the proceedings is characterised by the cross-examination of witnesses who may be experts in their field. Witnesses who give evidence are protected from actions for defamation because they enjoy absolute privilege. However, the inspector has the right to intervene, ask questions, and re-examine witnesses. The extent that an inspector adopts an inquisitorial style may be due to the style and personality of the inspector. An inquiry may attract news media and unlike a court does not have contempt powers, thus the issues tested at an inquiry may well be simultaneously examined in the media. The inspector is at a disadvantage compared to the courts in controlling outbursts of anger or strong feelings among the participants. The Planning Inquiries (Attendance of Public) Act 1976 provides that in principle oral evidence should be given in public and that documentary evidence should be open to inspection.

15-054 Inquiries may be seen as a safety valve for the views of the community and local opinion is often organised to put their case. In theory, at the discretion of the inspector, anyone may attend an inquiry, while certain groups are entitled to appear such as the National Park Committee where the land is situated in a National Park. However, the giving of evidence is left to the discretion of the inspector.

15–055 The nature of the discretion exercised by the inquiry inspector is subject to statutory rules such as the Town and Country Planning (Inquiries Procedure) Rules 1988.[43] Evidence may be taken on oath and may require the attendance of persons and documents. A timetable for the inquiry may be drawn up with a pre-inquiry meeting to ensure that the inquiry is held efficiently and expeditiously. This allows the Secretary of State to serve notice of the issues which are likely to be relevant and to be considered. The date fixed for the inquiry must be within eight weeks of the conclusion of a pre-inquiry meeting and not later than 22 weeks after the date of notification of the holding of an inquiry. The 1988 rules also allow the Secretary of State an influence in the appointment of assessors and to indicate the weight to be attached to their opinion.

15–056 After the inquiry is held and the inspector's report is made to the Secretary of State, r.16(4) provides the basis for the resolution of any disagreement between the inspector's report and the Secretary of State. Generally, the Secretary of State is free, provided the procedures are correctly followed and due weight is attached to the inspector's findings, to make his own conclusion. Then the Secretary of State must notify all the parties to the inquiry of his decision and his reasons under r.16(5) of the 1988 rules. The applicant may make further representations within 21 days, and if necessary the Secretary of State may re-open the inquiry.

15–057 The courts have exercised vigilance over the conduct of inquiries, the findings of fact made by the inspector and the observance of natural justice throughout the inquiry proceedings. It would also be possible to argue that the Human Rights Act 1998 has importance in ensuring that the procedures of the inquiry are fair and that human rights are protected.

15–058 The Franks Committee envisaged that inquiries would be informal, accessible and open. Legal representation gives rise to the question about legal aid and advice. Legal advice and assistance but not legal aid is normally available at inquiries on the same basis as tribunals. Section 250 of the Local Government Act 1972 empowers the award of costs in connection with statutory public inquiries. There is little guidance in the section as to how this power may be exercised. There is considerable debate about how this wide discretion may be exercised; though restrictive in the present exercise of this discretion, some argue that the rules should be permissive to permit the speedier resolution of matters when one party delays or acts inefficiently. Examples of where it may be used include where one party refuses to discuss the matter or provide information or has been unable to support their decision by the necessary evidence.

15–059 In contrast to the use of inquiries at a local level, inquiries into large-scale developments place greater stress and strain on the system of inquiries. The model of the public local inquiry seems ill-suited to dealing with these major issues. For example, the inquiry concerned with the Greater London Development Plan in 1970 took 240 days. The inquiry into the Sizewell B

---
43 SI 1988/944.

Power Station[44] lasted 340 days. In the case of the Third London Airport inquiry chaired by Lord Roskill, a non-statutory inquiry was set up with 11 Commissioners with both investigative and adjudicative powers. These procedures offered an alternative to a planning application with a site chosen and a public local inquiry focused on the suitability of the site. Instead a more wide ranging investigation could be undertaken reviewing a whole range of possibilities and hearing local evidence about the site in anticipation of any decision. The inquiry was able to carry out its own evaluation of air patterns and regional transport planning. Evaluating all this information and any objections provided an invaluable source of information for the Secretary of State.

However, as Grant has observed[45]:

> "But the crucial question which in fact subsequently determined that action taken by the government, was excluded from the Commission's terms of reference. It was the question of the need for the airport at all."

This suggests that there are serious weaknesses in such a format of inquiry if the main issue does not come under the terms of reference of the inquiry. There are more serious questions raised.

The final stage in the long running saga of a third London airport has been reached quite recently. Yet another public inquiry was held, looking into the more modest proposal that there should be a new Terminal 5 for Heathrow. The inquiry lasted four years with an estimated cost of £84 million. Its recommendation that there should be a new Terminal 5 was finally approved by the Secretary of State in November 2001. The long delays, large expense and the complexity of the inquiry format has led to concerns about the efficiency of the system of inquiries.

However as to the procedures, public participation is an important goal of the inquiry system and the use of large inquiries gives opportunities for the public to object, hear evidence and find out more information on complex issues. At the same time as the Roskill inquiry, the government introduced procedures for a Planning Inquiry Commission in the Town and Country Planning Act 1968. The arrangements consist of a two-stage process. The first stage is analogous to a Royal Commission and consists of a general investigation and only at the second stage do objections come to be considered. The Planning Inquiry Commission procedure has not been implemented, partly because it was considered unfair that having taken part in the first stage, to hear objections in the second stage might not appear to offer objectors a fair hearing. The Sizewell B inquiry, already mentioned above, was carried out under the Electric Lighting Act 1909 into the Central Electricity Generating Board's (CEGB) proposal to build a nuclear generating station at Sizewell, Suffolk. The investigation examined the

---

44 T. O'Riordan, R. Kemp and M. Purdue, *Sizewell B: An Anatomy of the Inquiry* (Basingstoke: Macmillan, 1988). The inquiry was chaired by Sir Frank Layfield.
45 M. Grant, *Urban Planning Law* (London: Sweet & Maxwell, 1982), p.603.

merits of different types of nuclear generating stations, and assessed the British-designed steam-generated heavy-water reactors compared to the more popular American-designed Pressurised Water Reactor (PWR). The decision to recommend the building of the PWR followed after the Layfield inquiry. The Sizewell B inquiry was the longest public inquiry ever held; surprisingly the full costs of nuclear electricity only became apparent when the Government later embarked on its electricity privatisation scheme. As Nigel Lawson, for a time Energy Secretary, noted in his memoirs[46]:

> "It turned out that for years the CEGB, wittingly or unwittingly, had been making a deceptive case in favour of the economics of nuclear power that had taken in even Frank Layfield and was not finally exposed until the government was in the final stages of the privatisation of the industry in 1989, and a detailed prospectus had to be drafted."

15-064
The scale of the deception appears staggering, as the CEGB had in 1989 estimated decommissioning costs at £3.7 billion whereas in 1990 the costs were estimated to be in excess of £15 billion. The virtues of the inquiry had quickly turned into shortcomings as ministerial suspicion over the true cost of decommissioning were not satisfied until the Layfield inquiry was completed and then the decision to go ahead with the building of Sizewell B was taken without the matter being given a satisfactory analysis.

15-065
Such shortcomings in the inquiry system may be because the ultimate decision depends on political and ministerial discretion which is outside the control of any inquiry. Inquiries may be regarded as providing important techniques in the administrative system of decision-making. O'Riordan has identified some procedural techniques in use at the Layfield inquiry. The investigative nature of the proceedings was supported by the appointment of a counsel to the inquiry. This enabled evidence to be sifted on behalf of the inspector and its presentation made more ordered. There was also a pre-inquiry stage to allow for the strategic planning of the inquiry. Since Sizewell, a Code of Practice has been published containing details of how a pre-inquiry meeting is to be held, should the Secretary of State require one.

15-066
The use of inquiries, albeit with some of the shortcomings mentioned above, is seen as an important element in allowing public participation in the administrative process. The findings of inquiries do not have to be followed as in the Vale of Belvoir inquiry where the Energy Secretary rejected the inspector's report. Doubts about inquiries have focused on the delay, expense and the postponement of decisions because of the need to consult and the requirements of inquiries. Frustration over the inquiry process may have led the government to support a hybrid Bill which became the Channel Tunnel Act 1987, to allow the building of the Channel Tunnel construction project between Britain and France. No inquiry was therefore necessary and the tunnel could be constructed without delays in the planning process. This

---

46   N. Lawson, *The View from No.11* (London: Corgi, 1992).

procedure, although criticised, was speedier and more efficient than the procedures under a public inquiry but at the expense of public participation.

Current government thinking is to be found in the Planning Green Paper *Planning: Delivering a Fundamental Change*[47] considered major changes to the planning system alongside a consultation paper on the new procedure for major projects. There has been considerable debate about how to address the many delays and shortcomings of the system of planning. In May 2015 two new initiatives have been taken. The Energy Bill 2015/16 to expedite the grant of permission from wind farms above 50 megawatts. The Housing and Planning Bill 2015/16 to promote starter homes, and allowing major housing schemes to fall under the Planning Act 2008 and thereby provide access to a simpler planning development consent regime. There are also powers for the Secretary of State to intervene in cases where it is thought the planning arrangements are too slow. The new Bills are expected to make planning decisions simpler and speedier. In the case of "brown field sites" there are powers for the granting of automatic planning permission for housing. These measures are intended to address shortfalls in house building in Britain.[48]

The Inquiries Act 2005

The Tribunals of Inquiry(Evidence) Act 1921 provided the basis for various inquiries up until 2005 when it was repealed under the Inquiries Act 2005. The Act provides an entirely new framework for inquiries, while retaining the right of the Government to appoint a non-statutory inquiry. There are wide ranging powers for ministers to appoint an inquiry where there is a particular set of events or cause for public concern. The inquiry is not there to determine civil or criminal liability. The appointment of the chair, terms of reference are a matter for the minister and report to Parliament. Ministers are given wide discretion. In the appointment of a judge to chair the inquiry, even though there should be consultation with the president of the court concerned, the minister is free to make the appointment if the judge is willing and the relevant president of the court is reluctant. The minister may suspend an inquiry and may bring the matter to a conclusion.

The Act also sets out procedures and processes to be followed by the Chair of the Inquiry. It is also possible to convert a non-statutory procedure into an inquiry under the Act. The Act eliminates the need for Parliament to approve an inquiry and the discretion of ministers over the inquiry is enhanced by the legislation. One of the most prominent example of an inquiry held into the Mid-Staffordshire NHS Foundation Trust chaired by Robert Francis QC.[49] There is also the Leveson Inquiry into the Culture, Practices and Ethics of the Press.[50]

---

47   HMSO, 12 December 2001.
48   House of Commons Library, *Planning Reform Proposals*, Briefing Paper, No.06418 (30 November 2015).
49   HC 780-I (2012–13), House of Commons Library, *The Francis Report*, SN/SP/6690 (2 December 2013).
50   HC 375-I (2013–14)

The Chilcot Inquiry

15-070

In June 2009, it was announced that a Privy Counsellor inquiry commissioned by the Prime Minister would examine the run up to the initiation and conduct of the Iraq war. The inquiry was not undertaken under the Inquires Act 2005, but as an ad hoc inquiry under terms of reference agreed with the Prime Minister.[51] The inquiry as yet to report and evidence on national security issues was taken in private. The inquiry has been delayed in publishing its final report. The inquiry held its final round of public hearings between 18 January and 2 February 2011. It is expected that the report will be published in July 2016. The complexity of the subject matter and its sensitivity has made the inquiry one of the most controversial in recent years. The total cost of the inquiry from its establishment on 15 June 2009 until 31 March 2014 was £9,016,500.

The Independent Inquiry into Child Sexual Abuse (Lowell Goddard)

15-071

On 4 February, the Home Secretary announced the setting up of a statutory inquiry into child sexual abuse to be led by the New Zealand Judge Lowell Goddard. This is likely to be a difficult inquiry as it covers complex and sensitive issues that take the inquiry into the inner workings of the major institutions in Britain. The inquiry is also very ambitious and it is hoped that it will be concluded by 2020.[52] This is an early estimate and it may prove to be difficult to keep to. Exemptions under the Official Secrets Act 1989 have been granted. The inquiry will act under the Inquiries Act 2005 and take evidence from witnesses as well as making findings that may amount to evidence for criminal or civil wrongs. The inquiry, however, is unable to make findings of criminal or civil liability on its own.

Inspectorates

15-072

Finally, in the general context of tribunals and inquiries an additional technique adopted in administrative law for the examination of a complaint is through the use of inspection powers. Inspectorates have a history extending back into the nineteenth century such as the development of factory inspectors. A modern example is the use of inspectors to provide information on prisons through the report of the HM Chief Inspector of Prisons, or since 1987, the formation of HM Inspectorate of Pollution which, although independent from government, incorporates the industrial Air Pollution Inspectorate and the Radiochemical and Hazardous Waste Inspectorate from the Department of the Environment. Powers granted to the HM Inspectorate of Pollution under the Environmental Protection Act 1990 (now under the Environment Agency)

---

51 House of Commons Library, *Chilcot Inquiry*, Briefing Paper, SN6215 (3 June 2015).
52 House of Commons Library, *The Independent Inquiry into Child Sexual Abuse and Background*, Briefing Paper, No.07040 (25 September 2015).

are comprehensive, including the power to make examinations and investigations, take samples, test articles and substances found on premises and require information. Inspection along with licensing powers may provide greater sanctions for the enforcement of standards than the traditional role of fact-finding and distributing blame from the use of an inquiry.

E: Ombudsmen: Local and Central

Central Government

The system for citizens' complaints about the administration was considered in 1961 in an influential report by *Justice*.[53] Many complaints do not warrant the full-scale use of an inquiry, or indeed give rise to an action in the courts. The expense, uncertainty and the difficulty in always establishing facts may leave the ordinary citizen aggrieved and without a satisfactory remedy. An illustration of the deficiency in the system for citizens' grievances came in the *Crichel Down* case, which highlighted the difficulty of finding a suitable means of redress. Even the use of Members of Parliament may be unsatisfactory as a means of investigating and finding the facts needed to establish redress. *Crichel Down* also illustrated the sheer impossibility in many cases of establishing the exact nature of the mistake or the basis for the policy where the decision is politically sensitive and where access to information is impossible for the ordinary citizen.

15-073

The 1961 Justice report recommended the introduction of the Scandinavian idea of an officer or commissioner with investigative powers known as an ombudsman. The technique depends on the receipt of a complaint by the ombudsman who may enter government departments and inspect correspondence, discuss matters with officials and ascertain what has taken place and why.

15-074

The Parliamentary Commissioner Act 1967 established a Parliamentary Commissioner for Administration or ombudsman. Soon after, further commissioners were established including a Commissioner for Local Government, discussed below. The exact nature and jurisdiction of the ombudsman for central government may be considered. Dame Julie Mellor is the current Ombudsman and she provides a detailed annual report of her activities.

15-075

The Parliamentary Commissioner for Administration (PCA) must be considered, not as a replacement of the parliamentary system and ministerial accountability, but as a supplement. Thus, the PCA receives complaints through MPs and appears before the House of Commons Select Committee on the Parliamentary Commissioner. The Chairman of that Select Committee may be consulted on the appointment of the PCA who holds office under the

15-076

---

53   A Report by Justice, *The Citizen and the Administration* (London: Stevens, 1961).

Crown. The PCA holds office during good behaviour, but he may be removed by the Crown following addresses by both Houses of Parliament. The PCA is an ex officio member of the Council on Tribunals. The PCA is assisted by a staff of about 90, appointed with the approval of the Civil Service Department. Unlike the Comptroller and Auditor General, the PCA is not an officer of the House of Commons.

15-077 The PCA is likened to an agency of Parliament; the holders of the office to date have been lawyers or ex-civil servants. The appointment of a civil servant carries the advantage of someone who may understand the system from within, but the disadvantage of being perceived as too close to the body that is being investigated. The appointment of a lawyer has the advantage of bringing independent legal analysis and techniques to bear on the complainant's case and the disadvantage of an over-formalistic and legalistic approach to complaints.

15-078 The 1967 Act gave the PCA jurisdiction over central government departments. There is a list, contained in Sch.2 to the Act, which sets out the various departments and bodies which fall within the PCA's jurisdiction. It is noteworthy that Ministers fall within the PCA's jurisdiction. Government departments include the Home Office, the Treasury, Department of Transport and Environment, Ministry of Defence, and the Foreign Office etc. This list did not include various governmental quangos but in 1987, under the Parliamentary and Health Service Commissioners Act 1987, over 50 such bodies were included within the PCA's jurisdiction. These additions include the Arts Council, the various research councils and tourist boards. The list may be amended by Order in Council. But there are restrictions on the scope of such an Order in Council. An entry to the schedule may be inserted provided it relates to a government department whose functions are exercised by the Crown, or if it relates to a body established by a Minister, and all or some of its members are appointed by the Crown and at least half the revenue is provided by Parliament. Excluded are bodies which act in a predominantly commercial manner or a corporation carrying on an industrial undertaking under public ownership.

15-079 Complaints have been rejected as not falling within the jurisdiction of the PCA such as against the Parole Board, local authorities, the courts, the police and nationalised industries. There is a Sch.3 list of excluded matters outside the PCA's remit of investigation. Exclusions included in the list cover matters of foreign affairs, the commencement or conduct of civil or criminal proceedings and the prerogative of mercy. Contractual and commercial relations and personnel matters are excluded as are the grant or award of honours, awards, privileges or charters. Despite criticism of the exclusion of government contractual matters from the remit of the PCA, the Government has maintained opposition to their inclusion. The main argument for their inclusion rests on the absence of practical remedies or adequate ways to investigate an individual's grievance as opposed to the departmental scrutiny offered by the National Audit Office.

15-080 The hospital service was excluded under the 1967 Act from the jurisdiction of the PCA mainly because it was organised by local authorities. Separate provision was made under the National Health Service Reorganisation Act 1973 for the appointment of Health Service Commissioners. Direct access is allowed for complaints to the Service Commissioners whose office is held by the PCA. The complaint must be made by the person aggrieved or in certain circumstance where he is unable to make a complaint, by a member of the same family or representative appointed for the purpose. Health Service Commissioners may investigate any alleged failure in a service provided by the authority, or a failure in a service provided on its behalf or other action it may have taken. The complainant must show that injustice or hardship resulted from any alleged failure in the service taken by the authority or taken on its behalf. In respect of any other action taken by the authority, maladministration must be shown. The precise meaning of this term is discussed below.

15-081

Finally, the National Health Service Commissioner reports to the Secretary of State, rather than to Parliament as is the case with the PCA. The Health Service Commissioners Act 1993 is a consolidation of the law relating to the Health Service Commissioners. The Act is intended to facilitate consultation between the Health Service Commissioners and other Commissioners including the Local Commissioners for Administration. The Health Service Commissioners remain empowered to examine complaints made directly to them. Complaints that may be considered are those that relate to maladministration, failure in the provision of a service to be provided by a health service body. The complaints may relate to delays in admission to hospital, a failure to indicate that patients may refuse to be examined in front of medical students and inadequate or illegible medical notes. However, there remains no jurisdiction to investigate matters solely from the exercise of clinical judgment.

15-082

The Health Service Commissioners (Amendment) Act 2000, which began life as a Private Member's Bill, extends the jurisdiction of the Health Service Commissioners to investigate complaints against doctors, and other health service providers. The list includes pharmacists, dentists, and ophthalmic surgeons. A loophole is closed by the Act which in the past allowed doctors and other health care workers to avoid investigation after they retired from the National Health Service.

15-083

Provided the body to be investigated falls within the PCA's jurisdiction then an investigation may be undertaken but it is assumed that the investigation may only concern the administrative functions of the department. This appears to exclude the department's legislative role, although the interpretation of legislation falls within the remit of an administrative function. Also excluded might be any judicial function of a department, as tribunals and courts are outside the jurisdiction of the PCA. However, after considerable debate s.110 of the Courts and Legal Services Act 1990 provides that administrative functions undertaken by staff of courts or tribunals appointed by the Lord Chancellor, shall be deemed to fall within the remit of the Lord Chancellor's department and therefore fall within the jurisdiction of the PCA. Remaining outside the PCA's jurisdiction will be action taken under the direction or authority of a person acting in a judicial capacity.

15-084

The PCA is not a substitute for legal action in the courts, or the remedies available through a tribunal. Where the complainant has a right of appeal or remedy in law it is not normal for the PCA to investigate. However, a proviso to the 1967 Act in s.5(2) may permit an investigation if the PCA is satisfied that in the particular circumstances it is not reasonable to expect the right or remedy to be investigated or invoked. It is possible therefore to see the PCA as an alternative to the courts but it may be the case that an overlapping jurisdiction is required. In *Congreve v*

Home Office[54] a complaint to the PCA was accompanied by legal redress through the courts which eventually was granted by the Court of Appeal in the matter of overlapping television licences. This appears an unusual case as the PCA may have doubted, until the Court of Appeal decision was made, that the complainant had a legal remedy and had this been clear in the first instance may not have felt able to offer an investigation.

15-085
In the leading case, *R v Inland Revenue Commissioners Ex p. National Federation of Self-Employed and Small Businesses Ltd*,[55] on the rules of standing in administrative law, the House of Lords considered the boundaries between maladministration and legality. Lord Roskill considered "that there was an important boundary between administration whether good or bad which is lawful and what is unlawful performance of a statutory duty". Injustices caused by maladministration fell within the remit of the Ombudsman while illegality and its consequences fell within the review power of the courts. It is possible to have a complaint that raises both issues about legality and maladministration. As the courts are the most suitable means for redress the Ombudsman may decline to investigate. Most likely the question of whether to accept jurisdiction is for the Ombudsman's discretion.

15-086
A complainant must have "sustained injustice in consequence of maladministration". The term maladministration is not defined in the 1967 Act but in the debate on the second reading of the 1967 Bill, Richard Crossman explained that maladministration[56] "might include bias, neglect, inattention, delay, incompetence, ineptitude, perversity, turpitude, arbitrariness and so on." The word injustice was used in the legislation in preference to "loss or damage" which might be construed with legal overtones too restrictive to the spirit of the legislation.

15-087
The PCA is not entitled to question the merits of the policy of a "decision taken without maladministration" under s.12(3) of the 1967 Act. This is a difficult section to interpret, and at one time was given a restrictive meaning that the quality of discretionary decisions could not be questioned even when it was shown that they contained bias or perversity. However, after prompting from the Select Committee, the PCA was willing to criticise decisions which were bad on their merits.

15-088
Studies of the meaning given to the term maladministration have indicated that drawing any useful distinction between merits and maladministration is pointless. The lack of merits is surely grounds for maladministration? Reform proposals made in 1977 by Justice said that[57] "maladministration" might be replaced by "unreasonable, unjust, or oppressive action" by government departments. This proposal was rejected[58] by the Select Committee on the PCA and later in 1988 the Justice-All Souls report declined to make any recommendation for change.

15-089
Complaints received by the PCA each year are on average approximately 700, though there was a significant increase in 1991 bringing the total for that year to over 800. The procedure of referring the complaint through a Member of Parliament, a requirement of the current

---

54   [1976] Q.B. 629; [1976] 2 W.L.R. 291 CA (Civ Div).
55   [1982] A.C. 617; [1981] 2 W.L.R. 722 HL at [663C]–[663E].
56   *Hansard* HC Debates, Ser.5, 734 col.42.
57   HC 350 (1967–68), para.36. G. Marshall, "Maladministration" [1973] *P.L.* 32.
58   *Review of Access and Jurisdiction*, HC 615 (1977–78).

law, has been subject to much debate and criticism. In theory the addition of this requirement keeps in place the principle of ministerial responsibility to Parliament by linking the investigation of complaints to the role of the MP The number of MPs who refer complaints each year stands at around 400. The PCA receives just as many direct complaints as from MPs. In practice the complainant may be referred back to his or her MP by the PCA and the complaint is then correctly made through the MP Nevertheless the use of the MP filter is seen as a curtailment in the role of the PCA and perhaps the office is unduly inhibited from developing its full potential. On the other hand the concern is that the removal of the MP filter might cause the PCA's workload to expand to an unacceptably high level. The removal of the MP filter is recommended in a recent Cabinet Office Review of the ombudsman discussed below.

15-090
The debate on access raises fundamental questions about the role of the PCA. The procedures adopted by the PCA are investigative and targeted on individual case files and this is costly and time-consuming. Presently it is estimated that the average time taken by the PCA is over 15 months to complete an investigation. Is such an investigative system capable of handling very large numbers of complaints? How far could an expanded role be met by the necessary expertise and resources? Only when both these questions are satisfactorily answered will the role of the PCA be adequately considered.

15-091
There is no rule that the complainant must be a British citizen but there is under s.6(4) of the 1967 Act a requirement of residence. There is also a time limit. Section 6(3) provides that the PCA must be informed of the complaint within 12 months from the date when the citizen had notice of the matter complained of. Special circumstance may permit an extension of time.

15-092
The PCA in carrying out its investigation may hold formal hearings and allow legal representation in the course of the investigation. Section 8 of the 1967 Act allows access to official documents and papers and the PCA's powers are analogous to those of the High Court. A limitation is provided under s.8(4) which permits the issuing of a certificate of immunity in respect of Cabinet papers issued by the Secretary to the Cabinet.

15-093
The remedies available to the PCA are first under s.10 of the 1967 Act to make a report which is normally sent to the MP who raised the complaint. A copy of the report is sent to the principal officer of the department concerned. An annual report is prepared by the PCA and laid before Parliament. That report details the PCA's activities for the year. In detailing his findings, departments are subject to scrutiny by Parliament and this provides a major source of the PCA's influence. Departments may conform to his recommendations under threat of an adverse report. Under s.10(3) of the 1967 Act, the PCA may lay a special report before Parliament giving details of the complaint, attempts to resolve it and the outcome. Secondly, the PCA operates through negotiation and conciliation. There are no formal powers to enforce the PCA's decision. Thus a department in the legal sense cannot be compelled to pay money, to take action or to refrain from a particular practice. However departments may make administrative changes as a result of the findings of the PCA; the Driving and Vehicle Licensing Centre introduced changes to deal with delays for applicants for driving licences.[59]

---

59 See Gregory, "The Select Committee on the Parliamentary Commissioner for Administration 1967–80" [1982] P.L. 49–88.

15-094 The co-operation necessary for the PCA to gain access and a working relationship with the department concerned may make it difficult to give the PCA sanctions with an enforcement power. The PCA depends on negotiation and following the exposure of maladministration it is hoped will give rise to a remedy. The PCA has succeeded in gaining financial settlements for the citizen in a variety of tax cases where repayment was made by the department concerned. In the *Sachsenhausen* case the PCA criticised decisions made by Ministers not to allow compensation to be payable to the victims of Nazi atrocities applying the rules laid down by the then Foreign secretary R. A. Butler, that compensation was only payable to those detained in concentration camps or equivalent conditions.[60] This led to compensation payable as a result of the PCA's intervention. The Barlow Clowes Affair investigation in 1988 conducted by the Ombudsman did lead "99 per cent of investors to receive at least 85 per cent of their capital" and came about through the findings of the PCA's investigation.

15-095 However, there are grounds for concern that perhaps such examples reflect an increasing problem of finding maladministration. In the first few years after 1967 only 10 per cent of cases investigated resulted in such a finding being made. In the 1970s this increased to about 30 per cent and in the 1980s, 40 per cent. In the mid-1980s about 75 complaints annually are found to show maladministration. The main departments concerned are Social Security and the Inland Revenue.

15-096 An important development in the PCA's role is the growth in recent years of case studies containing advice on administrative practices. Potentially this may create the most significant contribution of the Ombudsman system. Through this means the individual complainant receives the benefit of the PCA's interpretation of the rules, and the existence of principles within government departments. This provides a blend of external scrutiny and internal review; fact-finding through investigation combined with administrative guidance.

15-097 The attraction of using the PCA for the citizen is that the costs are borne by the PCA, not by the complainant, and the investigative role of the PCA may be crucial where there are no other remedies available for redress. An assessment of the effectiveness of the PCA is a mixed one. While the PCA has shortcomings there are sufficient successes to suggest that the PCA has made a worthwhile contribution in providing citizens redress where before none existed. Recently the Prime Minister is said to have blocked the release of information agreed by the Ombudsman in a case concerning the deputy Prime Minister after a complaint was made to the Ombudsman when a citizen was refused information on how many conflicts of interest had been disclosed by ministers. The information was released from many government departments with the exception of Mr Prescott's.[61]

15-098 The techniques of the PCA have proved valuable and have been copied in a wide variety of areas in the private sector including insurance, newspapers, building societies and banking.

---

60 The PCA was influential in obtaining changes to the 1974 and 1975 Finance Acts for the repayment of interest for delayed tax repayments.
Third Report of the Parliamentary Commissioner (1967–68). The report was debated 5 February 1968; *Hansard*, HC Vol.5, col.108.
61 *The Guardian*, 27 July 2002.

A more difficult question is the value of the investigative techniques employed by the PCA. As a contrast to the adversarial style of courts, are the PCA's inquisitorial powers more effective in finding facts and evaluating behaviour? Has the PCA encouraged good administration and affected the existing culture within government departments?

15-099

The PCA is susceptible to judicial review[62] and must comply with the Human Rights Act 1998. However, the courts are reluctant to intervene when the PCA acts in accordance with his own discretion whether to initiate, continue or discontinue an investigation (s.5(5) of the 1967 Act) or decide the procedures to be adopted in any investigation (s.7(2) of the 1967 Act).

15-100

The Ombudsman's role in investigations has proved very helpful in discovering facts and finding evidence that would be difficult to obtain other than through an investigative role. The shortcoming that there are no formal enforcement powers other than publicity and moral sanction is often seen as a major defect. It is clear that the Ombudsman's findings may be scrutinised by judicial review. This has emerged in the many issues surrounding the information given to members of a final salary pension scheme after the scheme collapsed. The Court of Appeal concluded that the findings of the Ombudsman were not binding on the Department of Work and Pensions but there had to be cogent reasons to set aside or reject the findings made by the Ombudsman relating to the facts.[63] The government's reasons for rejecting the findings of the Ombudsman in the Equitable Life Scandal lacked cogency and reasoning and could be put aside.[64] The Equitable Life case regarding pensions and investments to large numbers of policy holders[65] where investors were given a guaranteed annuity rate. The rate was set at a level that later proved to be over generous and by the end of the 1980s as economic conditions changed, the amount to be paid was unsustainable. There were two ombudsmen reports that finally concluded that there had been maladministration[66]. Sir John Chadwick was invited to set up a scheme and he recommended handling each policy holder on a case-by-case basis. There was considerable delay in having the recommendations for compensation to be implemented and complexity in understanding the scheme. Eventually the Government agreed that there would be a compensation scheme of £1.4 billion and the terms and conditions of the scheme proved to be complex.[67] The scheme ended in December 2015 and it is expected that payments will be made by this date. The scheme was created under the Equitable Life (Payments) Act 2010. The Equitable Life case highlighted the strengths and weaknesses of the arrangements. Delays and complexity inevitably troubled the entire affair. Undoubtedly without the Ombudsman's involvement compensation was unlikely to be paid. In 2014/15, the

---

62   R v Parliamentary Comr Ex p. Dyer [1994] 1 W.L.R. 621; [1994] 1 All E.R. 375 Div Ct. N. Marsh, "The Extent and Depth of Judicial Review of the Decisions of the Parliamentary Commissioner for Administration" (1994) Public Law 347–50.
63   R (Bradley) v Work and Pensions Secretary [2008] EWCA Civ 36; [2009] Q.B. 114.
64   R (Equitable Members Action Group) v HM Treasury [2009] EWHC 2495 (Admin); (2009) 159 N.L.J. 1514.
65   See the full details of the scheme in House of Commons Library, Briefing Paper, Equitable Life Compensation Scheme Number 5971 (5 November 2015).
66   House of Commons Library, Equitable Life Payments Bill, Research Paper, 10/53 (13 August 2013).
67   House of Commons Library, Equitable Life Compensation Scheme, Briefing Paper, No.5971 (5 November 2015).

Ombudsman received 29,000 complaints, assessed in depth on 6,815 cases and investigated or resolved 5,058 cases. The average length of time for investigation is 117 days.

Local Commissioners for Administration

15-101 Redress of citizens' grievances in local government is provided by the appointment of Local Commissioners for Administration under the Local Government Act 1974 following the influential Justice report in 1969 on the creation of a local government ombudsman. There are three Local Commissioners for Administration for England and one for Wales under two separate Commissions, one for England and the other for Wales. The Local Government Commissioner (LGC) does not act under the same constitutional relationship as the PCA does for central government, who is acting through ministerial responsibility and complaints through the complainant's MP.

15-102 The jurisdiction of the LGC is similar to the 1967 Act and the PCA, and the powers of investigation are the same as the PCA. The LGC may investigate complaints where a member of the public has "sustained injustice in consequence of maladministration." The number of complaints has steadily increased over the years. In 1983–84 there were approximately 3,000 complaints, but in 1990–91 the number had increased to over 9,000. Originally there was a councillor filter equivalent to the MP filter for the PCA discussed above. The Widdicombe Report[68] recommended and the Government accepted the desirability of allowing direct access and this was granted under the Local Government Act 1988. In terms of jurisdiction, in common with the PCA the LGC may not inquire into contractual or commercial matters. The Widdicombe Committee recommended reform to allow these areas to be investigated but this was not implemented by the Government. The Widdicombe Report also favoured the LGC to be given powers to initiate investigations on their own behalf but this was also rejected. The Government was concerned that if such powers were given the LGC might have problems in their relations with local authorities. However, under procedures introduced by the Local Government and Housing Act 1989, the LGC may issue codes of practice on good administrative procedures for local authorities. In particular, s.31 of the 1989 Act allows the Secretary of State to publish a code to be laid and approved by a resolution of each House of Parliament.

15-103 Maladministration is interpreted by the LGC in a similar way to the PCA. In *R v Local Commissioner for Administration for the North and East Area of England Ex p. Bradford Metropolitan City Council*,[69] Lord Denning considered that the LGC is concerned in matters of maladministration, with the manner in which decisions are reached and the manner in which they may or may not be implemented. The nature, quality and reasonableness of the decision are not part of the LGC remit. The subject matter of investigations conducted by the LGC covers a wide cross-section of local authority activities; housing, planning and education comprise a large proportion of the case load of the LGC. Section 266–269 and Sch.16 to the

---

68 Cm.9797 (1986).
69 [1979] Q.B. 287; [1979] 2 W.L.R. 1 CA (Civ Div).

1993 Education Act extend the LGC's remit to appeal committees in grant-maintained schools. Complaints are made within 12 months from the day the complainant has notice of the matter complained of, although there is a discretion to investigate complaints out of time.

A Commission may not investigate a complaint which affects all or nearly all of the inhabitants of a local authority. Complaints about public passenger transport and the internal management of local authority schools are also excluded from this jurisdiction.

The remedies offered by the LGC comprise, first, a report of the investigation showing maladministration is made available for public inspection for three weeks. If the local authority fails to take account of the report, the LGC may make a further report. Secondly, the LGC having made a report and attempted to persuade the local authority to comply with the terms of the report, the local authority is, under s.26 of the Local Government and Housing Act 1989, under a duty to consider the LGC's report and must within three months respond to it. A further report may be made by the LGC and if the local authority does not take satisfactory action, the report may be published in a local newspaper with the local authority's reasons for not implementing the report.

The LGC is unable to take any further action to enforce its report. Unlike the PCA who has recourse to the House of Commons, there is no satisfactory equivalent for the LGC, although under s.5 of the Local Government and Housing Act 1989, a local authority must appoint a monitoring officer to report on findings of maladministration.

Despite strong advice to the Widdicombe Committee in favour of giving the LGC power to seek judicial review, this was not favoured by the Committee in its report. Instead the Widdicombe Report recommended that following an adverse report in favour of the complainant, the complainant should be able to go to the County Court for a remedy.

Compared to the now abolished Audit Commission, the LGC has less proactive powers to seek enforcement for its findings. This may indicate that the role of the LGC is a more difficult one, as the experience of non-enforcement of the LGC reports by some local authorities may indicate. Legal powers to enforce the LGC findings may be counterproductive and give rise to disputes between local authorities and the LGC in the courts.

The possibility for judicial review of the LGC's findings was envisaged when the 1974 Act was debated in the House of Commons. A number of challenges to the jurisdiction of the LGC have resulted in judicial scrutiny, of the powers of the LGC. These decisions have focused on the role of the LGC. The first is *R v Local Commissioner for Administration for the South Ex p. Eastleigh BC*[70] After a complaint to the LGC from a householder that Eastleigh BC failed to properly inspect sewers in accordance with the Building Regulations 1976,[71] the LGC found maladministration and that the householder had suffered maladministration. However, the LGC accepted that even if the inspection of the sewers had been carried out diligently it was unclear that the defects would have been spotted. Consequently, Eastleigh should pay only part of the costs of any remedial action. Eastleigh BC sought judicial review. Lord Donaldson in the Court of Appeal reinforced the earlier observations of Lord Denning[72] when he distinguished between the merits

---

70 [1988] Q.B. 855; [1988] 3 W.L.R. 113 CA (Civ Div).
71 Now see Town and Country Planning (General Permitted Development) Order 1995 (SI 1995/418).
72 [1979] Q.B. 287; [1979] 2 W.L.R. 1 CA (Civ Div).

or reasonableness of a decision of a local authority and the means adopted by the local authority. The Court of Appeal accepted the legality of the LGC's report but granted Eastleigh BC a declaration on the basis that the LGC's report did not justify his findings.

15–110 Lord Donaldson considered judicial review of the LGC's reports as unusual and "unlikely to succeed". Soon after *Eastleigh*, Woolf LJ in the High Court found that a report made in 1986 by the LGC in *R v Commissioner for Local Administration Ex p. Croydon LBC*[73] was ultra vires. The case arose out of an unsuccessful appeal by parents against the decision of Croydon LBC as to the school their daughter should attend. The appeal was heard by the Education Appeal Committee established by Croydon. The LGC investigated a complaint by the parents about the outcome of the appeal. The LGC found maladministration in the way the Appeal Committee gave weight to Croydon's policy on education. The Council sought judicial review of the LGC's investigation. In holding that the LGC acted ultra vires, several grounds for review were considered. First, that the possibility of legal action by the parents should have been considered by the LGC throughout his investigation, and this might have resulted in the LGC declining jurisdiction in the matter. Secondly, the Appeal Committee had evaluated the evidence and based its decision on the merits of the case. The LGC had no grounds for finding maladministration in such circumstances.

15–111 One of the difficult issues raised in the case is the suitability of using the courts compared to the LGC. Woolf LJ concluded that the courts were more appropriate in cases such as the *Croydon* case where the issues demanded an understanding of the relevant law and legal obligations. The preference for using the courts for legal disputes is important in clarifying the jurisdiction of the LGC, even though it is unclear where the boundaries may be set.

15–112 There have been other cases. In *R v Lambeth BC Ex p. Crookes*[74] it was considered that a complaint of maladministration might be made before a challenge involving procedural irregularity. This fits with the idea that judicial review should be the mechanism of last resort as explained in *R v Hammersmith and Fulham LBC Ex p. Burkett*.[75] Maladministration will rarely provide the grounds for judicial review as a form of redress. However, this does not preclude judicial review being used nor should the availability of judicial review prevent a complaint of maladministration.[76] One possible solution is for the LGC or the PCA to refer matters to the High Court when legal issues arise in the course of their investigation.

15–113 The *Croydon* case firmly establishes the principle that the LGC's reports are subject to judicial review. In both cases of *Eastleigh* and *Croydon* the courts appear to deal with the review of the LGC's powers rather than reviewing the exercise of the LGC's discretion. However in *Ex p. Dyer* in the Divisional Court, Simon Brown LJ concluded that judicial review is available to review the LGC's discretion. This result may not be entirely satisfactory. The threat of judicial review, however rare, may inhibit the working of the LGC when confronted by local authorities

---

73 [1989] 1 All E.R. 1033; 87 L.G.R. 221 QBD.
74 (1997) 29 H.L.R. 28; [1996] C.O.D. 398 QBD.
75 [2001] Env. L.R. 684.
76 *R v Local Commissioner for Administration in North and North East England Ex p. Liverpool City Council* [2001] 1 All E.R. 462; (2000) 2 L.G.L.R. 603 CA (Civ Div); and *R v Local Commissioner for Administration Ex p. H* (1999) 1 L.G.L.R. 932; [1999] C.O.D. 382 QBD.

prepared to use the courts to challenge the LGC's decisions. This may have the unfortunate consequence of damaging the standing and investigative functions of the LGC and the citizen may be less certain of having a grievance remedied. The likelihood of many cases being challenged in the courts is small; nevertheless, the LGC must take account of the possibility of judicial review when writing their reports.

An assessment of the value of the LGC has been conducted in a number of studies with favourable results. The quality and scope of investigations are of a high standard. The investigations are based on individual complaints and the extent to which local authorities can learn from the various case studies of individual complaints. The question arises as to whether the reports of the LGCs may lead to better administration within local authorities. There is a question of co-ordinating complaints mechanisms within local authorities. The Widdicombe Committee heard evidence of the extensive system of internal complaints procedures within local authorities. Is there a case for greater co-ordination of the work of the LGC with the internal system of complaints resolution within local authorities? Under the Localism Act 2011 there is a Housing Ombudsman and this is a good example of the ombudsman principle being developed in a flexible and proactive way.

The European Ombudsman

The European Parliament may appoint an Ombudsman under EC art.195 (ex.art.138(e)) to receive complaints of instances of maladministration against the activities of the Community institutions or bodies. The European Ombudsman was established in July 1995 and has an establishment of 16 including five legal officers. Although based in Strasbourg there is an office in Brussels from February 1997. Since its inception there have been over 1,000 complaints. There have been a large number arising out of the French nuclear tests in the Pacific. The limitations on the remit of the European Ombudsman are that his jurisdiction does not extend to allegations against national governments of the Member States. However, it is possible for him to initiate complaints himself and he may gain the co-operation of Community institutions in pursuing his investigations. The Ombudsman may act on his own initiative or may receive complaints directly through an MEP. The remit is confined to maladministration of Community institutions and there are formal Rules of Procedure that govern how he may carry out his tasks. The Ombudsman may be dismissed by the Court of Justice at the request of the European Parliament.

Reforming the Ombudsman System

A review of the role and organisation of the central and local government system together with the Health Service Commissioner was carried out by the Cabinet Office[77] as part of the

---

77   P. Collcutt and M. Hourihan, *Review of the Public Sector Ombudsman in England* (London: Cabinet Office, 2000).

Modernising Government[78] strategy. Its findings called for a more coherent and fused system of ombudsmen. Recommendations include removing the MP filter for the central government ombudsmen, re-modelling the ombudsman system to take account of the changes in the way government is conducted and improvements in streamlining the legislation. A single commission involving all three ombudsmen might be more focused with a coherent set of priorities and working practices. Greater emphasis is recommended to be given to the process of informal adjudication and a less confrontational style in favour of a more conciliatory approach. The idea of setting up partnerships with a community-based focus on the Community Legal Service and the Community Health Councils is aimed at providing citizens with a more holistic approach to complaints. The organisation of the Commission should also reflect more community-based representation. The outcome is intended to align the ombudsman system with the new public management style of governance. One interesting idea is that the proposed new Commission might be able to refer a matter raising an issue of law to the courts for legal consideration.

15-117 The Law Commission in 2010 published a report on the administrative justice and reforms to the public sector ombudsman system. The proposals include repeal of the MPs filter for the Parliamentary Ombudsman and giving a wider discretion of ombudsmen to deal with complaints which might give a remedy in the courts, including powers to the Administrative Court to stay judicial review proceedings to allow investigation by the Ombudsman if thought to be appropriate. It might also be possible to allow the Ombudsman to refer a matter of law to the Administrative Court in appropriate cases.[79]

F: Summary and Conclusions

15-118 The plethora of systems for dealing with citizens' complaints has developed on an ad hoc basis. The principles of providing alternatives to the courts is at the heart of the system of informal and formal grievance procedures. The compelling idea is that the courts are not always suitable for dealing with citizens' grievances and the diversity of the system of tribunals is an example of how valuable the alternatives appear to be. The merger of tribunals and courts brings greater uniformity in handling cases. The economic crisis and public sector cuts has resulted in major reductions in legal aid and in the funding of the system of courts. Finding alternatives to the courts today has an important economic dimension and is broadly in line with finding cost effective ways of delivering justice. Political choices overshadow the way in which rights and grievances are settled. The relationship between the Human Rights Act 1998 and the European Convention on Human Rights is particularly contested as is the way in which rights

---

78 *Modernising Government*, Cm.4310 (1999).
79 Law Commission, *Administrative Redress: Public Bodies and the Citizen 2010*, Law Commission 322, HC 116 (2010–12).

and grievances are treated within British culture.[80] Grievances and their effective resolution is an important test of how a democracy functions. There are also important benefits in ensuring that appropriate checks and balances are a part of good administration. Finding a common thread to bring together all the ombudsman systems is a highly desirable but elusive goal. The Ombudsman system provides important benefits for public administration. This is one of the areas where informality and proactive investigation may have benefits over formal, legalistic and court focused systems that are expensive and depend on legal expertise.

Further Reading

K. D. Ewing and C. A. Gearty, *The Struggle for Civil Liberties: Political Freedom and the Rule of Law in Britain, 1914–1945* (Oxford: Oxford University Press, 2000).

D. Feldman (ed), *Law in Politics, Politics in Law* (Oxford: Hart, 2013).

C. Harlow and R. Rawlings, *Law and Administration*, 2nd edn (London: Butterworths, 1997).

M. Loughlin, *Public Law and Political Theory* (Oxford: Clarendon, 1992).

C. O'Cinneide, "Human Rights and the UK Constitution" in D. Oliver, J. Jowell and C. O'Cinneide, *The Changing Constitution* (Oxford: Oxford University Press, 2015), pp.67–103.

---

80 The example of the rights of all prisoners to vote at elections is a good example of how rights can be highly contested. House of Commons Library, *Prisoners' Voting Rights*, Standard Note, SN/PC/01764 (11 February 2015).

16

Human Rights and Civil Liberties

A: Introduction

The subject of this chapter is the citizen and civil liberties. For many centuries, the protection of civil liberties in the UK formed "a patchwork" rather than a coherent code of rights. Freedoms were perceived in terms of remedies enforceable through the courts. Rights were intended as a specific protection granted to a minority or as a response to a specific set of problems or to remedy an injustice. There was also a perception that civil liberties were better protected through the development of institutions rather than the enforcement of written fundamental rights. It was widely believed that institutions under parliamentary authority, including Parliament, would provide adequate protection. It was assumed that the courts, through the development of remedies for individual cases, were more likely to protect the liberty of the citizen than reliance on written documents that might become worthless if not supported by the institutions of the Constitution. In a broader sense there is acknowledgment that "political and social pressures" may be more effective in protecting liberty than purely legal rights. Many of these perceptions remain today, including concerns that by enacting the Human Rights Act 1998 judges are placed in the unenviable position of having the final say as to whether or not rights have been infringed. Criticism of the Human Rights Act 1998 has been the subject of review and the newly elected Conservative Government has proposed to amend/replace the Human Rights Act 1998 with a British Bill of Rights, subject to consultation to be concluded by the middle of 2016. There is considerable uncertainty over the outcome of the current debate and consultation. The political nature of rights and their protection is underscored by the nature of the debate.

16-001

The Labour Government fulfilled its manifesto promise by enacting the Human Rights Act 1998 which came into force in October 2000 in England and Wales, a far reaching major constitutional change. The Act makes Convention rights under the European Convention on Human Rights available to citizens in the UK.

16-002

16-003

The Human Rights Act 1998 creates opportunities for the development of a new culture of rights in the UK at an important stage in the development of constitutional change and reform. Debates about human rights are truly global in scale[1] and significance. The decision to leave the European Union is likely to have major constitutional implications in the area of human rights and fundamental freedoms.

B: The Human Rights Act 1998

The method of incorporation of the European Convention on Human Rights

16-004

The UK was the first Government among the member countries of the Council of Europe to ratify the European Convention on Human Rights (ECHR) in 1951. The Convention was itself drafted with the aid of British lawyers and it adopts an English style of drafting commonly found among legal draftsmen of the time. As a result, many of the Articles are broadly defined in terms of freedoms that are for the most part negatively expressed. In 1966 the Government accepted the right of individual petition under the European Convention. In the past the reluctance to embrace full integration of the Convention into domestic law came from a profound belief that Parliament and the rule of law would secure the protection of rights unaided by the Convention. In the past successive governments were consistent in their scepticism about rights, fearing that to incorporate the Convention would transfer to the courts overarching powers that would usurp Parliament's authority. The tide in favour of incorporating the Convention turned gradually and perceptibly. The House of Lords Select Committee on a Bill of Rights in 1978 recommended in favour of incorporation.[2] A year earlier the Standing Advisory Commission on Human Rights recommended a Bill of Rights for Northern Ireland. Support for a Bill of Rights has emerged from a variety of different groups and prominent individuals, particularly senior members of the judiciary.[3]

---

1 Foreign and Commonwealth Office Annual Report, *Human Rights*, Cm.5211 (September 2001).
2 *Legislation on Human Rights with Particular Reference to the European Convention: A Discussion Document* (London: HMSO, 1976). See Lester et al., *A British Bill of Rights*, Constitution Paper No.1 (London: Institute of Public Policy Research, 1990), pp.16–18. *Report of the House of Lords Select Committee on a Bill of Rights* (1978).
3 Scarman, *English Law—the New Dimension* (London: Stevens & Sons Ltd, 1974); Sir John Laws, "Is the High Court the Guardian of Fundamental Constitutional Rights" (1993) *Public Law* 63; Sir John Laws, "Judicial Remedies and the Constitution" (1994) 57 *Modern Law Review* 213; Sir S. Sedley, "The Sound of Silence: Constitutional Lawyers without a Constitution" (1994) 110 *Law Quarterly Review* 270; Lord Taylor, Richard Dimbleby Lecture, *The Judiciary in the Nineties* (BBC Education, 1992); Sir H. Woolf, *Protection of the Public—A New Challenge* (London: Stevens, 1992); Sir H. Woolf, "Judicial review: A possible programme for reform" (1992)

16–005

The Human Rights Act 1998 came into force on 2 October 2000 in England and Wales. The Act requires courts to apply most[4] of the ECHR as Convention rights within the legal system. The period leading up to the Act coming into force provided an opportunity for preparation. In an unprecedented way judicial training was undertaken at all levels of the legal system. Public authorities undertook a review of procedures and practices to ensure compliance with the Act.

16–006

Section 3 of the Act provides that the courts will be required to uphold Convention rights unless the legislation is so clearly incompatible with the Convention that it is impossible to do so. This means that when interpreting primary or secondary legislation it must be read in a way that "so far as it is possible to do so" it is compatible with Convention rights. Section 4 of the Act provides that when s.3 has been applied if it is the case that the provision is incompatible with a Convention right, then the superior courts have a power to make a declaration of incompatibility. In so doing the Human Rights Act 1998 is consistent with the traditions of parliamentary sovereignty and there are no powers under the Act to strike down legislation for incompatibility. It was hoped that the formulation of the Act in this way would avoid the implications of the European Communities Act 1972 and the impact of the *Factortame*[5] decision. Section 10 of the Human Rights Act is consistent in attempting to uphold parliamentary sovereignty through the powers of amendment where there has been a holding that a provision is incompatible. The relevant minister is given powers under s.10 of the Act to amend the legislation that the courts have considered is incompatible by remedial order. There is no mandatory legal requirement to introduce a remedial order. Schedule 2 to the Act provides that a remedial order may only be made if there are "compelling" reasons. There is a special fast track procedure laid down for remedial orders involving a timetable for the order to be laid in draft before Parliament for 60 days. The Draft Order must include an approved explanatory statement by the Commons and Lords. Only in an urgent case can the requirement of the draft be waived and this is subject to approval by joint resolution of both Commons and Lords.

16–007

Bills prepared after the Human Rights Act has come into force will be compatible with the Act. Section 19 of the Act provides that the relevant minister should provide a statement of compatibility before the second reading of the Bill. In the event that this is not possible then a statement to this effect is also possible under s.19. Parliament is free to enact legislation where the implications are that there is incompatibility. The Human Rights Act is not entrenched and so it may be amended by subsequent legislation. In common with there being no mandatory requirement to introduce a remedial order, there remains scope for ministers and Parliament to have the final say. While there is a mandatory duty on the courts to give effect to Convention rights, as far as it is practicable, the jurisprudence of the European Court of Human Rights at

---

Public Law 221; Sir K. Schiemann, "Locus Standi" (1990) *Public Law* 342; and Lord Scarman, "The Development of Administrative Law: Obstacles and Opportunities" (1990) *Public Law* 490.

4 Article 13 of the Convention which guarantees anyone an effective remedy does not apply under the Human Rights Act 1998.

5 [1990] 2 A.C. 85; [1989] 2 W.L.R. 997 HL.

Strasbourg is highly authoritative, but it is not judicially binding.[6] It might be possible to depart from a Strasbourg decision but this is likely to be unusual. Interpreting s.2 of the Act has proved to be controversial. Lord Bingham in *R (Ullah) v Special Adjudicator*[7] made an important point that while the Convention was not strictly binding on UK domestic courts, it was expected that "in the absence of some special circumstances" to follow any clear and constant jurisprudence of the Strasbourg Court. The *Ullah* principle, as it became known became, readily adopted in the sense that alignment with the Strasbourg court's decision is expected and that the meaning of the Convention should be undertaken in a similar way without national courts having the opportunity to reinterpret the Convention. This may be interpreted as "keeping pace" with the Convention and its interpretation by the Strasbourg Court. Judicial interpretation invariably involves a margin of appreciation of the domestic legal culture. In some cases the opportunity to follow the Strasbourg jurisprudence has resulted in decisions that attract considerable publicity. In *N v Home Secretary*, the deportation of an AIDS sufferer was held to be a breach of art.3 rights as there were no medications available in the country of deportation.[8]

16-008
One of the most controversial areas has been the question of whether to grant the right to vote to all prisoners, as voting rights are restricted to remand prisoners.[9] This issue has been the subject of protracted public debate and continues to overshadow the political debate about human rights. In 2001, three convicted prisoners challenged the decision of the Electoral Registration Officer not to register the three prisoners to vote. The High Court dismissed their application and argued that it was a matter for Parliament and not the courts.[10] However, on 20 March 2004, the European Court of Human Rights (Strasbourg) accepted the argument that the UK's ban on prisoners' voting rights breached art.3 of Protocol 1 of the ECHR. The UK Government appealed the decision to the Grand Chamber and the Grand Chamber by a majority of 12 to 5 held that there had been a violation of human rights. The UK Government strongly opposed the decision. It agreed to bring forward limited legislation to allow prisoners with a custodial sentence of less than four years to vote at elections. The timetable for the passage of legislation was not pre-determined. A backbench motion was proposed and debated in the House of Commons soon after on 10 February 2011. It was agreed by a majority of 234 to 22 to continue the ban.

16-009
There are other decisions of the Grand Chamber and applicable to the UK, all of them are consistent with granting votes to prisoners.[11] The UK Government agreed to bring forward new legislation and on 22 November 2012, a new draft Bill was published the Voting Eligibility (Prisoners) Bill 2012. This was subject to pre-legislative scrutiny, which resulted in a recommendation that the Government should introduce legislation to allow all prisoners serving

---

6   See House of Commons Library, *UK cases at the European Court of Human Rights since 1975*, Briefing Paper, No.05611 (23 December 2015)
7   [2004] UKHL 26; [2004] 2 A.C. 323 HL.
8   [2005] UKHL 31; [2005] 2 A.C. 296.
9   House of Commons Library, *Prisoners' Voting rights*, Standard Note, SN/PC/01764 (11 February 2015).
10 *Hirst v HM Attorney General* [2001] EWHC Admin 239; [2001] H.R.L.R. 39.
11 *Scoppola v Italy (No.3)* [2013] 1 Costs L.O. 62; (2013) 56 E.H.R.R. 19.

sentences of 12 months or less to vote in all UK Parliamentary, local and European elections. The Government have only made a brief response but there is no legislation pending. The UK Supreme Court has accepted that the blanket ban is incompatible with EU Law. It refused, however, to make any "declaration of incompatibility" with the Human Rights Act 1998.

Parliament and the Human Rights Act

The Human Rights Act 1998 provides extensive powers to the courts to consider human rights. These powers stop short of allowing the courts to scrutinise legislation. The courts cannot hold legislation as unlawful or unconstitutional or set aside an Act of the UK Parliament. The Human Rights Act 1998 protects parliamentary sovereignty and the most a court can do is to grant a declaration of incompatibility. This is where it is not possible to construe the legislation in a way that is consistent with Convention rights. The declaration is not binding on the parties and does not affect the validity or operation of primary legislation. The declaration of incompatibility is an important innovation in the Human Rights Act 1998. Since the Act came into force on 2 October 2000, the UK courts have made 29 declarations of incompatibility, of which 20 have become final. This number is likely to be reduced as in the period 2010/15 only three declarations were made. The use of the declaration of incompatibility is declining remarkably.[12] The three recent examples included the High Court decision[13] that the Safeguarding Vulnerable Groups Act 2006 was incompatible with the right to a fair hearing and respect for private life for the safeguarding of vulnerable groups. The Government passed the Protection of Freedoms Act 2012 to amend the 2006 Act. The second example was the legal framework for the disclosure of convictions and cautions under the Police Act 1997 and the Rehabilitation of Offenders Act 1974 (Exceptions) Order 1975. The Court of Appeal held that this was incompatible with art.8, the protection of private life.[14] The Supreme Court upheld the Court of Appeal decision.[15] The Government amended the Order to take account of the findings.[16]

The third example related to the retrospective use of fast track legislation and the Jobseekers (Back to Work Schemes) Act 2013. The Act reversed an earlier Court of Appeal decision that held that the various regulations were illegal and outside the powers of the primary legislation. The Government appealed to the Supreme Court and the judgment of the Supreme Court was pending when the[17] fast track legislation was passed. The High Court declared that the fast track legislation was illegal as it was incompatible with the right of access to the courts

---

12 House of Commons, Human Rights Joint Committee (11 March 2015).
13 *Royal College of Nursing v Secretary of State for the Home Department* [2010] EWHC 2761 (Admin); [2011] P.T.S.R. 1193.
14 *R (T, JB and AW) v Chief Constable of Greater Manchester, Secretary of State for the Home Department and Secretary of State for Justice* [2013] EWCA Civ 25; [2013] 1 W.L.R. 2515 .
15 [2013] EWCA Civ 25.
16 The Rehabilitation of Offenders Act 1974 (Exceptions) Order 1975 (Amendment) (England and Wales) Order 2013.
17 *R (Reilly) v Secretary of State for Work and Pensions* [2013] UKSC 68; [2014] A.C. 453 .

in art.6(1) of the Convention.[18] The Government appealed the decision of the High Court to the Court of Appeal which upheld the decision of the High Court. The declaration of incompatibility remains to be finalised.

16-011 There is another important aspect of the Human Rights Act and that is parliamentary scrutiny. This is an important part of the democratic process, aimed to ensure that as far as it is practicable legislation passed by the UK Parliament should be compatible with human rights. Parliamentary oversight is provided through the Joint Committee on Human Rights set up since February 2001.[19] The Joint Committee is a watch-dog monitoring and informing debates on Bills and more generally of the implications and importance of human rights. Generally, this has empowered Parliament to take a more robust interest into how human rights are protected and the implications of Bills and their amendment. In particular areas of concern such as terrorism[20] the committee has been particularly active and critical of any attempts to dilute human rights.[21]

The scope of the Human Rights Act 1998

16-012 Section 6 of the Human Rights Act 1998 stipulates that it is unlawful for a public authority to act in a way that is incompatible with a Convention right. The term public authority is ambiguous and this opens up the question of whether the Human Rights Act applies in litigation between private parties or to a dispute outside the confines of public law. This question has been put in terms of whether the Act is intended to have vertical or horizontal effect. The wider horizontal effect is favoured by Professor Sir William Wade.[22] On the other hand the narrower vertical effect is supported by arguing that the Act is intended to bring public authorities under Convention rights and that such rights have rarely if ever been applied to situations involving private rights alone. Indeed, the terms vertical and horizontal may be unhelpful and fail to address the question of the scope of the Act. This is a question of great debate[23] and will ultimately depend upon the courts. A public authority is defined by the Act to include a court or tribunal. In private litigation it could be argued that the court or tribunal as a public body is itself required to apply the Convention. This interpretation considerably

---

18 *R (Reilly) v Secretary of State for Work and Pensions* [2014] EWHC 2182 (Admin); [2015] Q.B. 573.
19 Murray Hunt, "The Joint Committee on Human Rights" in A. Horne, G. Drewry and D. Oliver (eds), *Parliament and the Law* (Oxford: Hart, 2013), pp.223–250.
20 See A. Zuckerman, "Closed Material Procedure—Denial of Natural Justice: *Al Rawi v Security Service*" (2011) 30 C.J.Q. 345.
21 See House of Commons Library, *Special Advocates and Closed Material Procedures*, SN/HA/6285 (25 June 2012). The proscribed Organisations Appeal Commission; the Employment Tribunal in cases involving national security; control order cases under the Prevention of Terrorism Act 2005; financial restriction proceedings under the Counter-Terrorism Act 2008; and the Sentence Review Commission and Parole Commission in Northern Ireland. *A v Secretary of State for the Home Department* [2004] UKHL 56; [2005] 2 A.C. 68.
22 Sir William Wade, "Human Rights and the Judiciary" (1998) *European Human Rights Law Review* 520.
23 Buxton LJ, "The Human Rights Act and Private law" (2000) 116 *L.Q.R.* 48.

broadens the potential scope of the application of Convention rights under the Human Rights Act. Lord Justice Sedley considered how the common law might be interpreted in discussing the scope of any potential law on privacy when applying the Human Rights Act in *Douglas v Hello! Ltd*.[24] In *Venables v News Group Newspapers*,[25] it was noted that the court as a public authority was obliged to act in a way that is compatible with Convention rights when adjudicating a common law cause of action. The court upheld the concept of a right to privacy,[26] particularly when it came to a breach of the Press Complaints Commission when broken by the press in a deliberate manner.

A public authority is not liable in legal proceedings if it can be shown that there is a statutory requirement upon it to act in the way it has. It would therefore be open to the court to consider the statutory requirement as to whether it may be made compatible or to issue a declaration of incompatibility. Proceedings for a person who claims a human rights infringement or breach of the Convention may be by way of appeal or judicial review. Section 7 provides that proceedings should be brought within one year. The person must satisfy the "victim" test for the purposes of art.34 of the Convention. This is the same test of standing that applies before the European Court of Human Rights. It is generally agreed that the "victim" test is narrower and more restrictive than the more liberal rules of standing in the UK that a claimant has to overcome for judicial review.[27] Pressure groups appear precluded from taking proceedings under the victim test but they would not be precluded by the rules of standing for judicial review.

Section 8 of the Human Rights Act provides a general remedial discretion to a court or tribunal which finds that a public authority has acted unlawfully under s.6. The Act does not create any new powers; the remedial discretion is one the court or tribunal must act on according to law. Damages may be awarded but consistent with the jurisprudence of the ECHR.

Territorial scope and the theatre of war

The scope of the application of the Human Rights Act has become an area of political controversy. As the Act is based on an international treaty, the question of whether liability arises to the State for events that occur outside the State. The House of Lords in *Al-Skeini*[28] considered the events leading up to the deaths of a number of Iraqi civilians killed by British troops. One civilian was in a British military prison while the other deaths were as a result of encounters with British troops around Basra. Interpreting the Convention, the House of Lords held that there

---

24 [2001] Q.B. 967; [2001] 2 W.L.R. 992 CA (Civ Div) at [129].
25 [2001] Fam. 430; [2001] 2 W.L.R. 1038 Fam Div.
26 Article 10(2).
27 See Ch.18. Mark Elliott, "The Human Rights Act 1998 and the Standard of Substantive Review" [2001] *Cambridge Law Journal* 301. See *DG of Fair Trading v Proprietary Association of Great Britain* [2001] UKHR 429, [2001] All ER (D) 372.
28 *Al-Skeini v Defence Secretary* [2007] UKHL 26; [2008] 1 A.C. 153.

was no requirement for an investigation and this fell within the discretion of the UK authorities. Having failed in the House of Lords, the applicants applied to the Strasbourg Court and invited consideration of the Convention in circumstances of the case. It was argued that the UK had assumed authority and therefore responsibility for the maintenance of security in the region of South East Iraq. This was sufficient to provide a link between the responsibility of the State, the UK, and the deceased. This required the UK authorities to institute an investigation.[29]

16-016 In another case, this time involving the internment of the accused for three years by British force in Iraq, the Grand Chamber at Strasburg considered the case after the House of Lords rejected the attempt by the applicants to have the internment arrangements reviewed as a violation of art.5 of the ECHR. The House of Lords in *Al-Jedda*[30] accepted that the UK had become the occupying force, not under a UN mandate as claimed, but as under the responsibility of the State. However, the House of Lords held that the art.5 rights of the applicants were displaced by the UN Security Council Resolution that imposed a duty to intern the applicant and this took priority over art.5 rights. The Strasbourg Court[31] accepted that the UK was the authority that exercised control over the area. On the question of the UN Security Resolution there is a presumption in favour of operating within the requirements of the Convention to avoid any conflict of obligations. In the absence of any explicit recognition of detention without trial, the protections under art.5 applied. Subsequent case law before the UK Supreme Court, notably *R (Smith) v Defence Secretary*[32] showed the reluctance on the part of the UK courts to order the investigation of the death of a soldier who died of heat stroke while serving in Iraq. Attitudes since then have changed and in *Smith v Ministry of Defence*, the Supreme Court acknowledged the Strasbourg Courts decisions in *Al-Skeini* and accepted that compatibility with the Convention would include extending art.1 protection and specifically art.2 rights to members of the armed forces while serving abroad.[33] The scope of the Convention has been generally accepted and its importance acknowledged in the preparation of legal advice by the Government.[34]

16-017 The application of the Convention has also been used in cases involving the detention, interrogation of terrorist suspects. The Anti terrorism, Crime and Security Act 2001 addressed many security issues, but specifically the perceived threat that foreign Islamic extremists were the major threat to the UK's security. Traditional approaches to the threat from foreign nationals include criminal prosecution or deportation of suspects to their country of origin. Detention without trial after the Northern Ireland experience had proved controversial and ineffective and this was also possible but not the most favoured option. Criminal prosecutions faced the problem that evidence would be subject to judicial scrutiny and if held in open court would

---

29 *Al-Skeini v UK* [2011] ECHR 1093; (2011) 53 E.H.R.R. 18.
30 *R (Al –Jedda) v Defence Secretary* [2007] UKHL 58; [2008] 1 A.C. 332.
31 *Al-Jedda v UK* [2011] ECHR 1093.
32 [2010] UKSC 29; [2011] 1 A.C. 1.
33 [2013] UKSC 41; [2014] A.C. 52.
34 House of Commons Library, *ISIS/Daesh: The Military response in Iraq and Syria*, Briefing Paper, No.06995 (3 December 2015).

expose the security services to public scrutiny. Additional problems about the truthfulness of evidence arise if the evidence is not corroborated. Allegation of torture or oppressive interrogation might make evidence inadmissible. Deportation of suspects also faced legal problems as the risks of deportation related to concerns that suspects, once repatriated would face torture in their own countries. The ECHR specifically prohibits torture or ill-treatment and as a matter of international law prohibits deportation where there is a risk of torture.

16-018

Part 4 of the 2001 Act allowed the Executive to imprison suspected terrorists who could not be deported. The suspicion required under the Act fell short of beyond a reasonable doubt needed for a criminal trial and rested largely on security service evidence based on only reasonable belief and not tested by the use of the normal criminal courts. Suspects as detainees have the right to appeal to a special tribunal, the Special Immigration Appeals Commission. However this is a limited right as suspects are not entitled to know the evidence against them or the reasons for the detention. Specially security vetted lawyers known as a Special Advocate are allowed to represent detainees.

16-019

The legislation was severely criticised and the subject of legal challenges. The famous *Belmarsh case*[35] in 2004, considered the human rights implications of the legislation. The House of Lords held that s.23 of the 2001 Act was incompatible with arts 5 and 14 ECHR and this resulted in a declaration of incompatibility being issued. The Government responded by introducing the Prevention of Terrorism Act 2005 which was also subject to strong parliamentary scrutiny and amendments. The objection made in the *Belmarsh* decision was that non-nationals were being treated less favourably than nationals. The aims of the 2005 Act were to introduce derogating and non-derogating control orders irrespective of the nationality of the suspects concerned. The aim is to attempt to achieve sufficient elements of compatibility with art.5 in order to ensure that the legislation is not impugned by the courts.

16-020

The House of Lords has had the opportunity to consider many aspects of the 2005 Act. In general, the judges concluded that the control order regime was compatible with art.5. However, there are a large number of reservations made about the arrangements on the 2005 Act that raised issues about the compatibility with art.6, the right to a fair trial. The House of Lords[36] concluded that that the person under the control order should be given sufficient information about the allegations to allow the issues raised to be adequately addressed by their legal representative. In the case of open material, ie not secret in itself, the requirements of a fair trial would not be satisfied by general assertion rather than by specific allegations. This gives rise to a specific set of problems when the State seeks to withhold certain sensitive information. The results of judicial concerns about the use of control orders under the 2005 Act led to the Act's repeal.

---

35   *A v Secretary of State for the Home Department* [2004] UKHL 56; [2005] 2 A.C. 68.
36   A. Kavanagh, "Judging the Judges under the Human Rights Act: Deterrence, Disillusionment and the 'War on terror'" [2009] *P.L.* 287. Also See A. Kavanagh, "Special Advocates, Control Orders and the Right to a Fair Trial" (2010) 73 *M.L.R.* 836; and M. Garrod, "Deportation of Suspected Terrorists with "Real Risk of Torture: The House of Lords Decision in Abu Qatada" (2010) *M.L.R.* 631.

The Human Rights Act and public bodies

16-021 As noted above, ss.6 and 7 of the Human Rights Act 1998 makes it unlawful for public authorities to act in a way that is incompatible with Convention rights unless primary legislation permits no other course of action. The precise application of the Human Rights Act to public bodies is open to considerable debate. Section 6 (3)(b) and (5) applies to acts of persons other than public authorities, where those acts are done in exercise of "functions of a public nature", but not if the "nature of the act" is private. There is no express definition of a public authority or body or indeed what a private body may include. This makes it difficult to be certain as to the remit of the legislation. There is a further complexity namely the distinction between a public or private body that is relevant in determining whether a case is suitable for judicial review. Some guidance may be drawn from the case law on judicial review but this is not helpful as the Human Rights Act relies on the jurisprudence of the Strasbourg court. There are two cases that give some guidance on how the UK courts approach the distinction between public and private bodies.

16-022 In *Aston Canlow and Wilmcote with Billesley Parochial Church Council v Wallbank*,[37] a case involving the question of lay rectors being liable for the costs of repairs to their Parish Church (known as chancel repairs). Chancel repairs are of medieval origin and their liability derives from the privatisation of Church Lands after the reformation. The Chancel Repairs Act 1932 gave the Parochial Church the right to bring court action if the lay rector failed to repair the chancel. The costs of repairs had become substantial and in order to defray costs the Church authorities were keen to spread the costs amongst the parishioners through the local Parochial Parish Council. The claim by the Church authorities, namely the Church of England, a public body was objected to and the argument made to resist the demands for payment was that the costs infringed the Convention rights (Private Property Protocol 1 art.1). The disputed amount was in excess of £95,000 but this proved to be a small estimate. The House of Lords held that the Parochial Parish Council was not a core public authority and that the Parochial Parish Church was not a hybrid authority. This resulted in the Wallbanks' having to pay a repair of £186,986 plus VAT and costs amounting to over £250,000 and an additional amount of £200,000 in legal fees, a considerable sum. It is possible to take out insurance for such repairs and the Law Commission in 2006 suggested that the chancel repair liability should be abolished.[38]

16-023 The main principle in determining whether a body was public or not was that cases had to be decided very much on a case-by-case basis. The reasoning in the Wallbanks' case is one where the private law matters relating to the repairs and the undertaking of chancel repairs is of long standing and this consideration influenced the decision making of the House of Lords. The case is complicated by the fact that the Church of England is an established Church, the

---

37 *Aston Canlow and Wilmcote with Billesley Parochial Church Council v Wallbank* [2003] UKHL 37; [2004] 1 A.C. 546.
38 See The Land Registration Act 2002 in force from 24 September 2003. After 2013, chancel repair liability will only bind new owners of registered land if it is protected by an entry in the register.

Queen is the Head of State and Head of the Church of England and this is recognised by the State. There is, however, great reluctance to see the Church of England as being treated as a public authority and perhaps opening up the possibility of many cases against the Church. It is also possible to see the case as reflecting the possibility that for some purposes an organisation may be treated as a public body and for other purposes it is treated as a private body.[39]

The nature of what is a public body also arose in the case of *YL v Birmingham City Council*.[40] This is an important decision on the approach taken by the courts when there are overlapping functions involving private charitable and voluntary organisations. The case of YL concerned a patient (YL) in a nursing home run by Southern Cross a large private company with expertise in running private care homes. YL was asked to leave the home under a 28-day notice to quit after disagreements with her family. The family claimed that the private care home had breached the art.8 rights of the patient. The House of Lords focused on the nature of the private company and the contract with the residents of the home. Considerations included the funding of the company and the statutory arrangements surrounding the care of elderly patients. A distinction was drawn between a core public authority and a hybrid authority. The latter was only bound by s.6 of the Human Rights Act 1998 in relation to acts which were not private in nature. The majority, Lord Scott included, held that the Human Rights Act did not apply to private homes. However the funding and relationship between the patient and the private home is often complicated. Private homes are often the recipient of large amounts of public funding through social service payments and also in respect of statutory responsibilities. Private care homes are also subject to regulation by the Care Quality Commission. Lord Bingham (dissenting) noted the various matters that might be considered when construing a public function such as the role and responsibility of the State, the subject matter of the dispute, the question of the public interest, and the question of whether there are penalties or not for the performance of the function. The listing of factors is an important approach but this may leave uncertainty as to the designation of public functions.

16–024

There was considerable concern raised by the House of Lords decision and the resultant parliamentary debate brought forward legislation, s.145 of the Health and Social Care Act 2008, providing that private nursing homes are to be treated as public authorities for the purposes of the Human Rights Act. This might not be sufficient as there are many aspects of elderly care that may not come within the terms of s.145. In *R (Weaver) v London and Quadrant Housing Trust*[41] it was held that the termination of a tenancy by the Trust set up to deliver social housing supported by public funding was covered by the Human Rights Act. It was accepted that there were many "hybrid authorities" making the consideration of contractual relations only one part of the deliberation in a case.

16–025

Concerns were expressed during the passage of the Act about the extension of the Act to the mass media and to religious groups. Section 12 accords the media special protections, most notably in warning if an injunction is likely to be made, but also the court is expected to

16–026

---
39 House of Commons Library, *Chancel Repair Liability*, Standard Note, SN/PC/04535 (29 November 2007).
40 *YL v Birmingham City Council* [2007] UKHL 27; [2008] 1 A.C. 95.
41 [2009] EWCA Civ 587; [2009] 4 All E.R. 865.

give particular attention to the balance between personal protection and privacy. Section 13 of the Act provides that the court must take account of religious freedoms and when applying Convention rights give effect to that freedom. The Church of England appears uniquely to qualify as a public authority and may fall within the protection of s.13. However, as we have seen in the *Aston Canlow* case this was not the interpretation adopted by the House of Lords in respect of chancel repairs. It is doubtful if religious buildings, not belonging to the Church of England, are in a similar position. The way the Act is to be interpreted will largely determine its scope and importance. As noted in previous chapters the courts have taken a cautious, restrictive interpretation preparing the way on a case-by-case basis to develop Convention rights into the existing public law culture.

Interpreting the Human Rights Act 1998 and policy considerations

16-027 In *R v Lambert*[42] it was held that the Human Rights Act did not have retrospective effect. There has been significant progress in determining the full impact of art.6 (right to a fair trial) in cases involving the use of temporary sheriffs in Scotland,[43] and in procedures for Mental Health Tribunals.[44]

16-028 Significantly, an applicant for planning permission has a right of appeal to the Secretary of State against any refusal or condition of planning permission. The Secretary of State is part of the planning process and hears appeals on the main issues of planning applications. When considering such appeals, the Secretary of State may bring broader government policy to bear. This effectively gives the Secretary of State the ultimate decision over planning policy and its implementation. There are no express rights for third parties and no right of appeal against a grant of planning permission. The Secretary of State's decision may be appealed to the High Court on the same basis of judicial review. Such an appeal is confined to legal issues; the courts do not intervene on the grounds of fact or policy.

16-029 In the *Alconbury Case* the High Court first examined the application of art.6 to the Secretary of State's powers. art.6 requires that ". . .everyone is entitled to a fair and public hearing within a reasonable time by an independent and impartial tribunal. . .". Specifically at issue were the Secretary of State's powers to "call in" an application for consideration either on his or her own initiative or on the initiative of the planning inspectorate. The number of call in powers is very small compared to the number of planning applications.[45] The High Court concluded that the Secretary of State's powers were inconsistent with art.6. It was reasoned that the Secretary of

---

42 [2001] UKHL 37; [2001] 3 W.L.R. 206.
43 *Starrs v Procurator-Fiscal (Linlithgow)* 2000 J.C. 208; 2000 S.L.T. 42 High Ct of Justiciary.
44 *R (H) v Mental Health Tribunal, North and East London Region* [2001] EWCA Civ 415; [2002] Q.B. 1 and *R (C) v Mental Health Review Tribunal* [2001] EWCA Civ 1110; [2002] 1 W.L.R. 176.
45 Richard Macrory estimates that there are about 130 call-ins out of some 500,000 applications and only 100 recovered cases out of 13,000 appeals.

State acted as both a policy-maker and a decision-maker. Judicial review was an inadequate protection because the courts had limited powers of intervention and there was not a full appeal on the merits. The House of Lords considered the full implications of civil rights and the planning system. It was held:

- that disputes involving planning matters such as compulsory purchase orders and the determination of planning conditions did involve rights protected by the Convention;

- that the House of Lords reviewed many cases determined under the Convention where ministers take decisions and are answerable to Parliament. However, art.6 does not require the court to have full jurisdiction over every aspect of the powers of those making decisions on planning matters. Lord Hoffman reasoned that the jurisdiction of the courts was one that related to a full jurisdiction to deal with the case as the nature of the decision requires;

- that it was not appropriate nor required that the court should have every aspect of planning law fall under the review; it was sufficient that there should be a review of the legality of the decision and of the relevant procedures followed; and

- that the extent to which judicial review had been expanded over recent years was sufficient to provide the necessary protection for the individual.[46]

16-030

The decision of the House of Lords marks a significant development in how rights may be attached to our existing system of planning and environmental protection. The Lords recognise the development of a rights-based culture, but the area of policy and its implementation appears to fall under parliamentary accountability.

16-031

A number of important outcomes follow from the case. First, the development of a new system of planning appeals be it a tribunal or a court may be undertaken, but not at the insistence of the courts. Secondly, rights impact on the way decisions are reached, the factual basis of the decision, and the legal principles that apply. Rights and ethics are to be found not simply through a formalistic application of rules but also through the development of policy. The *Alconbury Case* underlines the role that a rights-based analysis may play in the future development of environmental law.

16-032

After *Alconbury* it might be concluded that the courts are likely to adopt a relatively restrictive interpretation of the Human Rights Act at least in terms of attempting to integrate rights into the national legal culture. A similarly restrictive approach has been taken in *R (Vetterlein) v Hampshire C*.[47] In a judicial review in the administrative court, a challenge under art.8 (protecting the right to home and family life) was rejected. The facts concerned local taxpayers whose claim was that a proposed incinerator was a threat to the enjoyment of their home. The

---

46 Text of a Public Lecture delivered in New Zealand in the Summer of 2001.
47 [2001] EWHC Admin 560; [2002] Env. L.R. 8.

decision reinforces the need to show a strong connection between the harm complained of and the protection offered by art.8.

16–033 Article 8 was invoked in *Marcic v Thames Water Utilities Ltd*.[48] The case involved the protection that should be afforded to householders in areas prone to repeated flooding from nearby streams. The statutory water authority was aware of the potential for flooding but had not listed the remedial works as an immediate priority. The homeowner had carried out substantial preventative measures funded out of his own resources. It was common ground that major works were required before the threat of flooding could be prevented. In fact, as the problem of flooding is so common throughout the country, it was very unlikely that the statutory water authority would carry out any work. It was estimated that the total cost of such projects was £1,000 million.

16–034 The issue in the case taken by the homeowner was whether a suitable remedy was available. Under the common law, the principle of the law of nuisance, the rule in *Rylands v Fletcher*, and negligence afforded some limited protection against pollution. However, the statute the Water Industry Act 1991—authorising the sewerage arrangements for the area did not provide for any direct form of compensation. Instead there is under s.18 a duty, enforceable only through an order by the Secretary of State or the Director of Water Services. A breach of the order might give rise under s.22 to an action by someone who has suffered loss or damage as a result. As no order had been made, this left the complainant with potentially no remedy. The Human Rights Act 1998 might provide a solution. This gap in the statutory provision might be filled by the use of art.6 (fair procedure) and art.8. The case is on appeal but the first-instance decision was in favour of the homeowners. The court held that s.18 arrangements did not prevent the use of the various actions in common law and that the human rights implications gave the court the discretion to consider the question of why the statutory water authority had not carried out remedial work. Investigation of the merits system used by water companies in determining the allocation of their resources and their system of establishing priorities provides an important role for the courts in their scrutiny of policy and the circumstances where priorities are to be set. The case is illustrative of the potential provided by a human rights view of legal concepts. The individual with rights is regarded differently from a complainant with remedies.

16–035 This difference is also highlighted in the case recently decided by the European Court of Human Rights, *Hatton v UK*[49] 2 October 2001. The issue in the case was the noise implications of night flights over Heathrow. Since 1962 late night flights were banned between 23.30 and 06.00. In 1993 a quota system was introduced, and in 1998 a consultation paper on noise pollution was published by the Government. The applicants argued that the levels of noise and the recurrent use of night flights interfered with their rights under art.8 of the Convention. The argument in favour of night flights and used to justify their continuation was that it was in the interests of the economy to allow such flights to occur. The Court reviewed the policy behind the restrictions set up in 1993, the working of the quota system, and the measure adopted to

---

48 [2002] EWCA Civ 64; [2002] 2 All E.R. 55.
49 Application 36022/97, ECtHR, 2 October 2001.

limit the noise of aircraft flights. By a majority of five to two the Court considered that art.8 had been breached. Significantly, the case points to a review and evaluation by the courts of the processes at work in the determination of policy, and economic arguments, including competing claims, are also evaluated. For example, the complainants might be free to move house or accept that living in the vicinity of an airport carries with it the likelihood of aircraft noise. The *Hatton* case, like *Marcic*, resolves a common approach to human rights and the environment.

Finally, the Court of Appeal has recently considered the significance of the Human Rights Act in terms of the discretion exercised by the courts when considering whether or not to issue injunctions for breaches of planning control. The use of an injunction is a powerful remedy for the enforcement of the law. Section 187B of the Town and Country Planning Act 1990 empowers a local authority "where it considers it necessary or expedient" to apply for an injunction. The breach of an injunction carries with it the sanction that a breach may amount to a contempt of court with severe penalties such as imprisonment or a fine. In four cases, *South Bucks DC v Porter*; *Chichester v Searle*; *Wrexham v Berry*; and *Herstmere BC v Harty*,[50] the Court of Appeal considered whether the grant of injunctions in the lower courts was compatible with art.8(1) of the Human Rights Act 1998. The question of an individual's rights under art.8 ". . .to respect for his private and family life, his home. . ." was relevant when an injunction was granted to preserve the environment. The Court had to balance individual rights under art.8 with the local authority's desire, on behalf of the community as a whole, to protect the environment. In considering the appropriateness of issuing an injunction, was the court required to consider the full merits of the planning dispute or the much narrower question of whether the law had been breached? The question of the full planning merits of any dispute was a matter for the planning authorities. However, if the grant of an injunction interfered, as it almost invariably would, with individual rights under art.8, how far did the court have to consider the merits of the planning case before granting an injunction? The Court of Appeal reasoned that rights were now a relevant matter for consideration when deciding whether or not to award an injunction.

16-036

Proportionality requires that the injunction should be appropriate and necessary for the objectives to be achieved. In deciding the four cases, the Court of Appeal remitted three for reconsideration by the lower courts, holding that the lower courts had been too inclined in their approach in favour of issuing an injunction. In the fourth case (*Harty*) the Court of Appeal had adopted the correct test and the use of the injunction was upheld.

16-037

The broader rights-based approach adopted by the Court of Appeal is indicative of the changing culture of rights that pervades judicial thinking. The case law set out above has a number of distinctive attributes:

16-038

- the courts are limiting their own overt intervention in the political processes of decision making, and the application of the principle of proportionality allows the judges the discretion to maintain this approach;

---

50   12 October 2001. [2001] EWCA Civ 1549; [2002] 1 All E.R. 425.

- legal rules and conventional practices appear to require that rights should be assimilated within the operating discretion and principles that guide decision-makers; and

- the courts are likely to develop this area of the law on the pragmatic techniques of common law reasoning, case by case.

16–039
There are instances where the courts have to accept the policy implications of highly political choices. One important example is the decision in *R (SRM Global Master Fund LP) v Treasury Commission*[51] that arose over the nationalisation of Northern Rock. The claimants sought judicial review of the decision to nationalise Northern Rock in terms of its value and the compensation payable. The standing of the claimants was that they were all shareholders of Northern Rock. Their complaint was that the valuation of Northern Rock at the date of nationalisation was unfair. Northern Rock was a going concern, although insolvent and that the conditions of the support provided by the Bank of England as the Lender of Last Resort imposed high interest rates on Northern Rock for the monies provided by the Bank of England. This had the effect of making the valuation of the mortgage portfolio of Northern Bank unfairly benefit the Government through providing a profit for the Bank of England loans. The financial support provided by the Bank of England deprived shareholders of their profits and the provisions for compensation to existing shareholders was unfair. The case argued by the claimants was that through the economic device of loans and guarantees, the Bank of England secured for the taxpayers' expropriation through nationalisation of Northern Rock but without adequate compensation to the Northern Rock shareholders. The case made out by the claimants was rejected. Stanley Burton LJ held that without Bank of England intervention Northern Rock would have ceased trading. The Government through the Bank of England could have withdrawn support—there was no duty to provide financial support and no legitimate expectation to do so. There was no requirement to give such support and the compensation scheme for the shareholders had to accept Northern Rock's valuation based on the loans provided. The claim was dismissed. This illustrates the constraints on judicial discretion and review.[52]

16–040
The decision of the Supreme Court in the *HSE v Wolverhampton City Council*[53] considered the responsibilities of public authorities when deciding to exercise a discretionary power to achieve a public objective. The main question was whether or not costs to the public ought to be taken into consideration. The Supreme Court considered the responsibilities on public bodies and their application to the case in question. Planning permission for a block of four

---

51 [2009] EWCA Civ 788; [2010] B.C.C. 558.
52 Dimitrios Kyritsis, "Constitutional Review in Representative Democracy" (2012) 32(2) *Oxford Journal of Legal Studies* 297–324. *R (Jackson) v Attorney General* [2005] EWCA Civ 126; [2005] Q.B. 579.
The debate on the 42 detention period in 2009/10 is a good example. *Thoburn v Sunderland City Council* [2002] EWHC 195 (Admin); [2003] Q.B. 151; *R (Corner House) v Director of the Serious Fraud Office* [2008] EWHC 246 (Admin); [2008] C.P. Rep. 20; and *R (Alconbury Developments Ltd) v Secretary of State for the Environment, Transport and the Regions* [2001] UKHL 23; [2003] 2 A.C. 295, p.980 at [70].
53 *HSE v Wolverhampton CC* [2012] UKSC 34; [2012] 1 W.L.R. 2264.

student residences had been applied for and granted. In the course of construction, the Health and Safety Executive (HSE), concerned about gas storage on site, applied for an order to revoke planning permission against Wolverhampton Local Authority. In refusing the application, the Council considered costs and came to the view that the if planning permission were revoked the cost of compensation that would be payable would be high and consequently refused the HSE's application. The HSE brought judicial review proceedings against the Council. The High Court refused that part of the claim. The Court of Appeal allowed the HSE appeal and held that the Council has to make its decision in isolation from the economic circumstances of the decision. The Supreme Court adopted a different approach, and decided that a public authority was entitled to take into account the cost to the public purse. Section 97 required the authority to satisfy itself that revocation is expedient including consideration of the development plan and other "material considerations". As the payment of compensation is a relevant matter, the cost to the public purse has to be considered. In general principle, a public body has to take into account public spending.

C: The European Convention on Human Rights

16-041

The jurisprudence of the ECHR is highly authoritative[54] in the interpretation courts must give to Convention rights under the Human Rights Act 1998. The content of the ECHR specifies basic rights and liberties agreed in the early 1950s. The ECHR was signed at Rome in 1950, ratified by the UK in 1951 and came into force in the states that ratified the Convention in 1953. The ECHR is an international treaty and has the force of international law.[55] Read in that light, the ECHR appears enthusiastic and idealistic representing expectations about rights that may not always result in practical realities given high unemployment or economic depression. Nevertheless, such rights provide a rich jurisprudence arising from the ECHR. The First Protocol covers art.1 which provides for the citizen the peaceful enjoyment of his possessions and arts 2 and 3 respectively provide the right to education and to take part in free elections. Convention rights are broadly expressed and cover in consecutive order: the right to life (art.2); freedom from torture or degrading treatment, or punishment (art.3); freedom from slavery or forced labour (art.4); the right to liberty and security of the person (art.5); the right to a fair trial (art.6); the prohibition of retrospective laws (art.7); the right to respect for family life, home and correspondence (art.8); freedom of thought and religion (art.9); freedom of expression (art.10) and freedom to join a trade union and to engage in peaceful assembly (art.11); and finally the

---

54 See House of Commons Library, *UK Cases at the European Court of Human Rights since 1975*, Briefing Paper, No.05611 (23 December 2015).
55 See C. Gearty, "The European Court of Human rights and the Protection of Civil Liberties" [1993] *Cambridge Law Journal* 89.

16-042 right to marry and found a family (art.12). The ECHR omits general economic and social rights which may cause political controversy.

There are specific provisions permitting the derogation from such provisions at times of emergency such as in Northern Ireland or following the September 11 attacks on New York and Washington. It is not possible to derogate from freedom from torture, or inhuman or degrading treatment (art.3), or from slavery (art.4) and on retroactive criminal offences (art.7). In time of war or grave public emergency a state may under art.15 derogate from the right to life but this only applies to lawful acts of war.

16-043 In addition to the main articles of the ECHR, there are a number of protocols signed by the Member States which allow Member States to enter a reservation. For example under the Education acts in force in the UK there is a reservation to art.2 of the First Protocol to the Convention as to the right to education. This stipulates so far as it is "compatible with the provision of efficient instruction and training and the avoidance of unreasonable public expenditure". Many of the rights are qualified by provisos or exceptions and are subject to judicial interpretation.

16-044 The procedures are complex and time-consuming. To some extent, the ECHR is a victim of its own success as the world's most important human rights court. The time factor has now become quite acute. It is estimated that it may take over six years from commencing proceedings to completion of the case after it has been considered by the Court. The popularity of individual petitions has led to a backlog of over 2,500 applications. This may lead to abuse being uncorrected and the delay in hearing cases may cause remedies to be too delayed to be effective.

16-045 A case may be taken by one State party as against another under art.24 or in the case of the UK since 1966, at the petition of an individual against his own State under art.25. In 1998 the pre-existing institutions of the European Commission of Human Rights and the European Court of Human Rights were superseded by a new full-time European Court of Human Rights. All applications go directly to the Court and the right of individual petition became mandatory for all Member States since 1998.

16-046 The question of whether the petition is admissible depends on the exhaustion of domestic remedies the petition must be presented within six months of the particular decision and any petition which is ill-founded or an abuse of the rights of the petitioner will be rejected. The petition must not under art.27 be incompatible with the ECHR and must raise a violation as a matter of law.

16-047 Blackburn has estimated[56] that "the total number of judgments of the Court in its entire history to 1998 was 903; yet in the first nine months of 1999 alone the figure was 108". The evidence is that the number of registered applications is increasing. Blackburn has found that on 26 June 1999 there were[57] "10,000 registered applications and more than 47,000 provisional files, as well as around 700 letters and more than 200 overseas phone calls per day".

---

56   R. Blackburn "Current Developments, Assessment and Prospects" in R. Blackburn and J. Polakiewicz (eds), *Fundamental Rights in Europe* (Oxford: Oxford University Press, 2001), p.77.
57   Blackburn "Current Developments, Assessment and Prospects".

16-048　The Court of Justice at Strasbourg is composed of 41 judges. The force of international law and inter-state relations means that in practice Member States do tend to follow the findings of the Court. Changes introduced in the UK as a result of decisions of the Court include the Contempt of Court Act 1981, the Interception of Communications Act 1985 and in Northern Ireland, the Homosexual Offences (Northern Ireland) Order 1982.[58]

16-049　There have been a number of cases taken against the UK alleging a breach of the ECHR. In over a dozen cases the Court has ruled against the UK Government.

16-050　The first case against the UK from an individual petition was *Golder*[59] where a former prisoner claimed under art.8 the right to privacy for his private correspondence and under art.6, a fair hearing. Golder had been refused access to a solicitor under the Prison Rules and denied the opportunity to bring an action against a Police officer. The Court held that the Prison Rules were inconsistent with the ECHR and later this resulted in a change in the Prison Rules. The Court has also held that the censorship by the prison authorities of prisoners' correspondence was in breach of art.8 in *Silver v UK*[60] and that there was a lack of an effective remedy under national law. The procedures for the hearing of charges made against prisoners by the Prison Boards of Visitors was found to be in breach of art.6 relating to the right to a fair trial in *Campbell and Fell v UK*.[61]

16-051　The use of birching in the Isle of Man was held in *Tyrer*[62] to be a degrading punishment under art.3. Since 1976 when the UK's declaration under art.25 was renewed, the Isle of Man was excluded from individual petitions although under art.63 the ECHR may still apply to the Isle of Man. The UK has brought the *Tyrer* judgment to the attention of the Isle of Man authorities thus satisfying the UK's obligations under the judgment but no law preventing judicial corporal punishment of juveniles has been enacted.

16-052　The Court has considered the use of corporal punishment in schools in the cases of *Campbell and Cosans*.[63] While the Court could not find any breach of art.3 on inhuman and degrading treatment, they were prepared to hold that there was a breach of art.2 of the First Protocol, which requires the State to "respect the rights of parents to ensure such education and teaching in conformity with their own religious and philosophical convictions". Since 1986, corporal punishment in state schools has been abolished in England, Wales and Scotland. This applies to publicly-funded pupils of independent schools but not to the independent schools sector as a whole.

16-053　Individual rights such as under art.8, the right to privacy and family life, have been the subject of individual petition. In *Dudgeon*[64] the Court held that various laws in Northern Ireland making homosexual practices illegal[65] between consenting males was a breach of his privacy

---

58　Homosexual Offences (Northern Ireland) Order (SI 1982/1536).
59　*Golder v UK* (1975) 1 E.H.R.R. 524 ECHR.
60　(1983) 5 E.H.R.R. 347 ECHR.
61　(1985) 7 E.H.R.R. 165 ECHR.
62　*Tyrer v UK* (1978) 2 E.H.R.R. 1 ECHR.
63　(1982) 4 E.H.R.R. 293 ECHR. See *Teare v O'Callaghan* (1982) 4 E.H.R.R. 232. The Isle of Man High Court quashed the decision of Magistrates over corporal punishment in line with the ECHR.
64　*Dudgeon v UK* (1981) 4 E.H.R.R. 149 ECHR. See Homosexual Offences (Northern Ireland) Order 1982.
65　Homosexual Offences (Northern Ireland) Order (SI 1982/1536).

and the law in Northern Ireland was subsequently changed to fall into line with the decision of the Court. The *Dudgeon* case has been applied by the courts in their interpretation of the law in the Irish Republic.

16-054 In *Gaskin v UK*[66] the release of confidential records for the period the applicant was in care were refused. The Court accepted that this refusal was a breach of art.8 because there was inadequate provision for an independent review of what should or should not be disclosed.

16-055 The Court has also considered the law of contempt in *Sunday Times v UK*.[67] This case arose out of the House of Lords decision in *Attorney General v Times Newspapers Ltd*[68] over the legality of the *Sunday Times* publication of articles relating to the drug thalidomide. The Commission had held by a majority that the injunction granted by the House of Lords against the *Sunday Times* was in breach of art.10, the right to freedom of information. The Court ruled by a majority of 11 votes to 9 that the injunction was inconsistent with the ECHR. This was the first time that the Court had to consider consistency between a common law rule of contempt of Court and the ECHR. The difference in approach in the case taken by the House of Lords and the Court of Justice represents a marked contrast in the jurisprudence of each. While the House of Lords attempted to balance the differing interests between the parties, the Court of Justice focused on the application of freedom of expression to the issues raised in the case.

16-056 The Court has not refrained from considering the question of pornography in the context of freedom of expression under art.20. In *Handyside*[69] the Court considered the legality of the English courts order to destroy copies of the *Little Red Schoolbook* under the Obscene Publications Act. The book, aimed at children, contained explicit sexual information which had led to the conviction of the applicant under the Obscene Publications Act. The Court held that the conviction was not a breach of art.10, on freedom of speech.

16-057 The procedure for the release of mental patients under s.66(3) of the Mental Health Act 1959 was held to be a breach of art.5 of the ECHR in *X v UK*.[70] The case was notable because the Court had viewed habeas corpus available in the English courts as not a sufficient remedy. Recourse to the Mental Health Review Tribunal was also regarded as inadequate because the tribunal had powers only to make a recommendation. The Mental Health (Amendment) Act 1982 brought English law into line with the judgment of the Court.

16-058 The Court considered the provisions of the Trade Union and Labour Relations Act 1974 and their compatibility with art.11 of the ECHR in the *Young James and Webster cases*.[71] Three British Rail employees refused to become members of a closed shop agreement entered into by British Rail and the Unions in 1975. The closed shop agreement was held to violate the freedom of association protected under art.11. Since the case was decided, the law relating to trade unions has been substantially altered. In the case of the Government Communications

---

66 (1989) 12 E.H.R.R. 36 ECHR.
67 (1979) 2 E.H.R.R. 245 ECHR.
68 [1974] A.C. 273; [1973] 3 All E.R. 54 HL.
69 *Handyside v UK* (1976) 1 E.H.R.R. 737 ECHR.
70 (1981) 4 E.H.R.R. 188 ECHR.
71 [1982] E.C.C. 264; (1982) 4 E.H.R.R. 38 ECHR.

Headquarters where 7,000 civil servants were deprived of their rights to join a trade union, the Commission ruled the application inadmissible.[72]

16-059

In *Malone v UK*,[73] telephone tapping was held by the Court to be a violation of art.8 on the right to privacy. Since then the law has been changed to take account of the Court's decision which revealed how the regulation of telephone tapping was carried out through administrative guidance rather than a statutory basis.

16-060

In *McCann, Farrell and Savage v UK*[74] the shooting of IRA suspects in Gibraltar was not disproportionate to the aim of defending life and protecting property from unlawful violence. However, it was accepted by a majority of 10 to 9 that the killing of the IRA members breached the victims' art.2 rights to life. The majority held that the inefficient organisation of the undercover operation made their deaths likely, though avoidable. However, the compensation that was payable was only confined to the costs of the applicants.

16-061

Aside from the use of the individual petition procedure it is possible for action to be taken by another State against the UK. The first such case was the *Republic of Ireland v UK*.[75] In 1971, Ireland lodged complaints with the Commission alleging that there had been a failure by the security forces to protect life under art.2 over deaths which arose in Londonderry in 1972, that detained suspects were subject to treatment which amounted to torture, inhuman and degrading treatment contrary to art.3, and that internment without trial violated arts 5 and 6, and in its operation it violated art.14. Finally, the allegation was made that the UK Government had failed to honour the rights and freedoms contained in art.1 of the ECHR.

16-062

The Court upheld complaints relating to interrogation methods as a breach of art.3. In addition, the Court rejected discrimination contrary to arts 4 and 5 by accepting that the focus of internment was justifiable against Republican terrorists because of the level of violence from that element in the community. As a result of the Court's decision, the UK Government sought to incorporate the substance of art.3 into the domestic law in Northern Ireland and enacted s.5 of the Northern Ireland (Emergency Provisions) Act 1987 which allows the courts in Northern Ireland to exclude evidence where there is *prima facie* evidence that the accused was subject to "torture, to inhuman or degrading treatment, or to any violence or threat of violence".

16-063

Northern Ireland has continued to prove a problem for the UK's emergency laws and their compatibility with the ECHR. A wide variety of individual applications have been received by the Commission. McCrudden notes[76]:

> "A wide variety of issues has been raised, ranging from allegations of breach of fair trial protections, to torture, from interference with

---

72 See *Council for Civil Service Unions v Minister for the Civil Service* [1985] A.C. 374; (1988) 10 E.H.R.R. 269; (1985) 7 E.H.R.R. 14.
73 (1984) 7 E.H.R.R. 14 ECHR.
74 Application 1894/91 (1991) ECHR.
75 (1978) 2 E.H.R.R. 25 ECHR. K. Boyle and H. Hannum, "Ireland in Strasbourg" (1976) *Irish Jurist* 243.
76 C. McCrudden, "Northern Ireland and the British Constitution" in J. Jowell and D. Oliver (eds), *The Changing Constitution*, 2nd edn (Oxford: Oxford University Press, 1989), pp.320–321.

> correspondence, to internment, from arrest and detention under the PTA [Prevention of Terrorism Act] to the law on reasonable force, from discrimination to the voting system."

16-064 In *Brogan*[77] the Court considered art.5 which protects the freedom of the person in respect of arrests, questioning and detention for up to seven days under the Prevention of Terrorism (Temporary Provisions) Act 1984. The question of the length of detention was considered by the Court. While accepting the availability of habeas corpus as a remedy, the Court considered that in respect of applicants detained for more than five days the ECHR had been infringed. For applicants detained for up to four or five days, the Court regarded their detention as not an infringement of the ECHR. The outcome of the *Brogan* decision proved difficult for the UK Government and the operational decisions of the Police in Northern Ireland. Taking such matters as general security into account, the UK Government decided to derogate under art.15 from its obligations under the ECHR. The requirements under art.5 that the accused should be charged "promptly" resulted in the Court holding that art.5 was infringed by the Prevention of Terrorism (Temporary provisions) Act 1984.

16-065 It is clear that the experience of the ECHR provides an insight into the jurisprudence of the courts. It remains an intriguing question as to the future direction that is likely to be taken given the potential for community rights to be assimilated into the ECHR. An early indication is to be found in *R v Human Fertilisation and Embryology Authority Ex p. Blood*.[78] The Court of Appeal held that the widow could seek medical treatment under arts 59 and 60 of the EC Treaty which gave her directly enforceable rights. The facts of the case arose when the widow had requested sperm samples to be taken from her seriously ill husband who was in a coma so that at a later date the sperm could be used by her in treatment by artificial insemination. The husband was unable to give consent and later died. The Embryology Authority in the UK refused to allow the treatment to be carried out as they claimed it infringed the 1990 Human Fertilisation and Embryology Act.

Citizens' rights and citizenship

16-066 Citizens' rights may involve consideration of some of the freedoms identified under the ECHR such as the freedom of expression, the right to privacy, the freedom of religion and freedom from racial discrimination or the freedom of movement involving immigration and deportation. The citizen's freedom of expression also raises questions of censorship and obscenity. In outline the various laws that regulate and seek to control obscenity may be considered.

16-067 We have already seen that in *Handyside*, discussed above, the ECHR permits restraints on freedom of expression on the grounds of morality under art.10(2). Attempts to regulate

---

77 *Brogan v UK* (1989) 11 E.H.R.R. 117; Times, November 3 ECHR.
78 [1999] Fam. 151; [1997] 2 W.L.R. 806 CA (Civ Div).

and control obscene publications since the eighteenth century moved the jurisdiction over obscene materials from the ecclesiastical to the common law courts. At common law, an offence punishable by the common law courts was the publication of obscene material. It was an offence to publish a book that tended to corrupt public morals and was against the King's peace. The Obscene Publications Act 1959 creates the statutory offence of publishing an obscene matter. The test of obscene is "if taken as a whole, such as to tend to deprave and corrupt persons who are likely, having regard to all relevant circumstances, to read, see or hear the matter contained or embodied in it". The question of what is obscene is subject to judicial interpretation[79] and originated in the common law. The issue of what is obscene is a matter for the jury properly instructed on the law. The legal meaning of obscene must be distinguished from the meaning given to the word by the ordinary layman. In the *Oz case*[80] the judge left the jury with the impression that obscene could be equated with repulsive, lewd, or filthy material. The crucial question is not only whether a publication fulfils any of these conditions but whether it "has a tendency to deprave and corrupt". An article which is so filthy that causes revulsion may paradoxically not "deprave and corrupt". The conviction was quashed because the judge failed to make clear to the jury the requirement that the article must deprave and corrupt while making clear it may have been lewd. It is possible that an article may be deemed obscene if it had a tendency to deprave and corrupt but was not lewd.

16–068

The use of the Obscene Publications Act 1959 in not confined to sexual activities. The publication of *Cain's Book* which highlighted the favourable effects of drug-taking fell within the scope of "deprave and corrupt". Smith and Hogan note[81]:

> **"The difficulty about extending the notion of obscenity beyond sexual morality is that it is not now apparent where the law is to stop. It seems obvious that an article with a tendency to induce violence is now obscene, and if taking drugs is depravity, why not drinking, or, if evidence of its harmful effects accumulates, smoking?"**

16–069

The scope of the 1959 Act also applies to a wide range of literature where readers may engage in their own sexual fantasies without involving any overt sexual activity of any kind. It is possible that an article may be deemed obscene even when directed only to persons already depraved.

16–070

The Obscene Publications Act 1959 as amended by s.1(2) of the Obscene Publications Act 1964 also makes it an offence to publish an article for gain or not. The terms "publication for gain" shall mean "any publication with a view to gain, whether the gain is to accrue by way of consideration for the publication or any other way".

---

79 See *Smith and Hogan's Criminal Law*, 4th edn (Oxford: Oxford University Press, 1992), p.730.
80 *R v Oz* [1972] 1 Q.B. 509; [1972] 2 W.L.R. 823 CA (Civ Div).
81 *Smith and Hogan*, p.731. *R v Anderson* and *R v Oz* [1972] 1 Q.B. 304; [1971] 3 W.L.R. 939 CA. *Calder (John) Publications Ltd v Powell* [1965] 1 Q.B. 509; [1965] 2 W.L.R. 138 Div Ct.

16-071 Despite the scope of the legislation, the 1959 and 1964 Acts preserve the common law of conspiracy to corrupt public morals or outrage public decency. Scope for this offence is considerable given the vague nature of the crime of conspiracy and the potential for overlap with the Obscene Publications Acts. Assurances have been given that the use of conspiracy charges will not be used to circumvent the protections available under the Obscene Publications Acts. Such protections under the Obscene Publications Acts include the following. The defendant had not examined the article and had no reasonable cause to suspect that it was obscene and that publication of it would be an offence under s.2 of the Acts. There is also a defence of public good. Once the jury have determined that the article or book is obscene, the defendant may show that publication of the article in question "is in the interests of science, literature, art or learning, or of other objects of general concern".

16-072 There is considerable debate as to the application of the Obscene Publications Acts to works of literature or art. The line to be drawn between what is acceptable and what is not is based not on the intention of the author, but whether the article or book is obscene. The article or book "must be taken as a whole" and considered by the jury after direction by the judge. Very often the jury may find the judge's direction influential as to the outcome of the case.

16-073 The Obscene Publications Act 1857 provided that on summary procedure obscene articles may be forfeited. Section 3 of the Obscene Publications Act 1959 provides that on an oath made before a magistrate a warrant may be issued authorising search and seizure of goods which may be obscene and are intended to be published for gain. The owner may appear and present his case as to why the offending article should not be forfeited with a right of appeal to the Crown Court. This may give rise to inconsistencies between different attitudes among different magistrates. There is no national or uniform standard, although the advice of the Police and the Director of Public Prosecutions may be taken when considering whether to forfeit articles.

16-074 There are a range of offences connected with posting indecent or obscene material. The test is objective, namely offending against recognised standards of propriety, and includes sending unsolicited matter describing human sexual techniques. It is possible to interpret indecent and obscene in this context to extend beyond the sexual area. Section 49 of the Customs and Excise Management Act 1979 permits customs officers to seize and destroy "indecent or obscene books" and other articles imported into the UK. The test is whether an article offends current standards of propriety.

16-075 Reform of the Obscene Publications Acts has been recommended by the Williams[82] Committee in 1979. A clear distinction should be drawn between material which should be prohibited and denied access to by anyone who wishes to see it. Restricted material should be available to those who wished to see it but not available to the general public. The Committee stressed the need to protect young people and therefore restrict the material that is available.

---

82 Cmnd.7772 (1979). *DPP v Whyte* [1972] A.C. 849; [1972] 3 W.L.R. 410 HL. See *Knuller v DPP* [1973] A.C. 435; [1972] 3 W.L.R. 143 HL. See *Hansard*, HC Vol.695, col.1212 (3 June 1964); *Hansard*, HC Vol.698, cols.315–316 (7 July 1864); Post Office Act 1953 s.11; *Stanley* [1965] 2 Q.B. 327; [1965] 2 W.L.R. 917 CA; and the Unsolicited Goods and Services Act 1971 s.4.

The Williams Committee would effectively remove the categorisation of obscene, indecent or violent in favour of a clearer distinction based on access to material.

Protecting the public from obscene material also extends to videos[83] and the cinema. The Cinemas Act 1985 provides for the licensing of premises for film exhibitions. There is a British Board of Film Censors, founded in 1912 and given statutory powers to act on behalf of local authorities in setting standards and the censorship of films. The Board, renamed the British Board of Film Classification, has led to an age group category awarded to every film and the extension of this system to videos was made in 1984 under the Video Recordings Act 1984 and amended by the Video Recordings Act 1993. Videos are controlled as to the content and the classification of the material. In 1988 the enforcement of the 1984 Act was vested in the Weights and Measures Authorities at local level. Local authorities are responsible for licensing sex establishments in their locality under the Local Government (Miscellaneous Provisions) Act 1982. Indecent photographs of children under 16 are prohibited under the Protection of Children Act 1978.

Under the Theatres Act 1968 it is an offence to present or direct the performance of a play which is obscene. The term obscene is taken from the Obscene Publications Act 1959 which applies. This means that if taken as a whole the work's effect was such as to deprave and corrupt persons in all the circumstances likely to attend it.

D: Religion and Race

The freedom of religion involves the freedom to practice religion, freedom of discrimination between religions and equal treatment of different religions. In the UK, older laws failed to grant religious toleration but many disabilities have now been removed within the framework of a State-recognised established Church. The question of religious belief and the legal recognition of a religion may arise in connection with charitable status with the Charity Commissioners and under the Places of Worship Registration Act 1855 for purposes of celebrating marriages, taxation arrangements and charitable status.

Various fringe religious groups or factions have attempted and sometimes succeeded in securing charitable status. The law may find it difficult to categorise such groups and to distinguish religious cults from a recognised religion. The value judgments inherent in such a distinction are difficult to make.[84]

---

83 Video Recordings Act 1984.
84 Lord Chancellor (Tenure of Office and Discharge of Ecclesiastical Functions) Act 1974 allowing the Office of Lord Chancellor to be held by a Roman Catholic. *Re South Place Ethical Society: Barralet v Attorney General* [1980] 1 W.L.R. 1565; [1980] 3 All E.R. 918 Ch D. See *Ex p. Segerdal* [1970] 2 Q.B. 697; [1970] 3 W.L.R. 479 CA (Civ Div). For example, the Unification Church known as the "Moonies" which has charitable status but has

16-080 The existence of an established religion, the Church of England, has ensured through successive statutes that the Sovereign is "the Supreme Governor of the Realm in all spiritual and ecclesiastical causes as well as temporal". It is therefore required that the Sovereign is a member of the Church of England and marriage to a Roman Catholic is grounds for disqualification.

16-081 A major issue is the teaching of religion in schools, compulsory under the National Curriculum under s.2(1)(a) and (8) of the Education Reform Act 1988; and the designation of religious schools. Recognition of religious affiliation is contained in ss.6 and 7 of the Education Reform Act 1988. Schools may be divided into county and voluntary schools. In the case of county schools under s.9(1) of the Education Act 1944, county schools are state schools owned and maintained by local education authorities. Maintained schools as they are commonly referred to, are required to have a daily act of worship under s.7(1) of the Education Reform Act 1988, "wholly or mainly of a broadly Christian character". Exemptions to reflect a particular form of worship may be obtained. Generally the law permits a child's religion and education to be matters for parents until the age of discretion.[85]

16-082 Voluntary schools are either controlled, aided, or special agreement schools, each with their own specialised sets of rules. Most of the voluntary schools have a religious affiliation such as Church of England, Roman Catholic, Methodist or Jewish. The daily act of worship will therefore be denominational. There are powers under s.13 of the Education Act 1980 to approve schools within the voluntary status such as Muslim Schools. This is a delicate issue. The freedom of Muslims to participate in their own schools has to be balanced against the need to have a racially balanced education system free from sectarian differences which may be exacerbated by the separation of education on the basis of religion. A voluntary-aided school may adopt a religious admission policy by giving account to s.6(3)(a) of the Education Act 1980. This applies where the school is over-subscribed. The House of Lords ruled that the parental wishes of some parents could be defeated on the basis of the School's own admission policy. In effect this may protect the religious preferences of some parents at the expense of others. The parents of two girls one a Hindu, the other a Muslim were unsuccessful in their application to enter a Roman Catholic School which favoured Roman Catholic and other Christian girls as part of the school's admission policy.[86]

16-083 The protection of the Christian religion is acknowledged in the law of blasphemy and in various statutes protecting Sunday. Acceptance of religious belief is also recognised in laws which exempt Sikhs from wearing crash helmets on motorcycles and on construction sites.[87] Such arrangements are minor exceptions to the general assumptions that the law is mainly concerned with the Christian or Jewish religions. There is a duty to protect freedom of speech within universities under s.43(2) of the Education (No.2) Act 1986. There are related codes of

---

caused questions to be raised about its activities and suitability, see *Hansard*, HC Vol.926, cols.1597–1598 (23 February 1977).
85   *Ex p. Choudhury* [1991] 1 Q.B. 429; [1990] 3 W.L.R. 986 QBD.
86   House of Commons Library Briefing Paper, *Religious Education in Schools (England)*, No.07167 (4 January 2016).
87   Motorcycle Crash helmets (Religious Exemption) Act 1976 and s.1 of the Employment Act 1988.

practices and under s.202 of the Education Reform Act 1988 provides for academic freedom within universities. Balancing the various freedoms is not easy when there may be competing claims. The duty to protect against radicalism is also part of a policy of preventing the radicalisation of students while studying extremism on campus. In November 2005 the Universities UK issued a code of guidance entitled *Promoting Good Campus Relations: Dealing with Hate crimes and Tolerance*. There are growing signs of radicalisation and this is seen as a serious issue for public authorities. The Counter-Terrorism and Security Act 2015 places on a statutory basis a strategy known as Prevent, to ensure that institutions are aware of and take steps to address radicalisation.

Human rights and euthanasia

Euthanasia has largely been opposed by religious groups and this opposition has been upheld by the courts. The question of the use of pain-killing drugs by doctors raises religious and ethical issues. In *R v Adams*[88] Devlin J expressed a traditional but not exclusively Christian position that doctors should not prescribe drugs which would shorten life. In *Airedale NHS Trust v Bland*,[89] the House of Lords was still opposed to euthanasia but held that in the case of an insensate patient with no hope of recovery when it was known that stopping medical treatment would result in death, there was no criminal act provided it was in the patient's best interests not to prolong his life. The courts would provide guidance in the form of a declaratory judgment to doctors in cases of withholding life-prolonging treatment. A minority of judges considered that it was important that Parliament should consider the moral, social and legal issues involved in such cases. In *Pretty v United Kingdom*,[90] the European Court of Human Rights (ECtHR) rejected the applicant suffering from an incurable degenerative illness who was appealing against the refusal of the Director of Public Prosecutions to grant her husband immunity from prosecution if he assisted in her suicide. Her claim on the basis of arts 2, 3, 8, 9 and 14 of the Convention was unanimously rejected. The ECtHR has consistently upheld the obligation of the State to protect life. There have been a number of significant UK cases associated with the right to life in the context of assisted dying, most notably that of *R (Pretty) v Director of Public Prosecutions*[91] rejecting the opportunity to judicially approve assisted dying. Recently this case has been followed by another UK Supreme Court decision in *Nicklinson*.[92] Mr Nicklinson had a catastrophic stroke that had left him for over none years paralysed and unable to move, save for his head and eyes for over nine years. He was unable to self-administer any lethal drug but wanted another person to do this, although he was prepared to use a contraption that would allow the self-administration of the drug. The Supreme Court in *Nicklinson* took

16–084

---

88 [1957] Crim. L.R. 365.
89 [1993] A.C. 789; [1993] 2 W.L.R. 316 HL.
90 [2002] E.C.H.R. 423; [2002] All E.R. (D) 286 ECHR.
91 *R (Pretty) v DPP* [2002] All E.R. (D) 286; (2002) 35 E.H.R.R. 1 ECHR.
92 *R (Nicklinson) v Ministry of Justice and DPP* [2013] EWCA Civ 961; (2014) UKSC 38.

account of the previous case law and considered revised guidance that had been issued by the Director of Public Prosecutions on assisted suicide after the controversy of previous cases and public concern that the existing guidance was unclear. The Supreme Court rejected by a majority of seven to two, the idea advanced by Mr Nicklinson that the current law on assisted suicide was incompatible with art.8. The Supreme Court held that the State had a margin of appreciation and this left the law as a matter for Parliament to reform rather than for the courts to rule as incompatible with art.8. The Supreme Court also upheld the role of the Director of Public Prosecutions in terms of the exercise of discretion to prosecute and also to set criteria for a case-by-case consideration of the facts. This decision draws attention to the nature of art.8 rights as not being absolute but being qualified leaving the State some room for interference with the rights of the individual that are "necessary in a democratic society". All the Supreme Court Justices were aware of the sensitive nature of the case and by its nature the need for protecting vulnerable citizens. An absolute prohibition on assisted suicide is arguably justified to protect such vulnerable people but the current arrangements for decisions on prosecution are open and transparent involving consideration of all the facts by independent lawyers and judges. The majority accepted the overall jurisdiction of the courts on such matters but equally accepted the limitations set by the nature of assisted suicide that would require parliamentary discussion and resolution. Lord Neuberger urged that Parliament should look at the existing law and come to a conclusion. Underpinning much of the analysis are concerns about moral values, the sanctity of life and the protection of the vulnerable. This leaves open the future possibility that a court may have to consider the matter once again and in certain circumstances may grant a declaration of incompatibility.

16-085 The *Nicklinson case* is indicative of the dialogue that is opening up between the prosecution authorities, the government, Parliament and also medical and legal experts. This is unprecedented but it is inevitable once assisted dying and human rights are brought together when considering the role of art.8. This has had a good effect in bringing to the fore questions that had been dormant for some time as to who should decide when to end the life of a terminally ill patient or a patient with limited quality of life. The test of the quality of life is highly subjective as often the quality of life is hard to measure if confined to narrow criteria or judged on the basis of finance as a form of cost benefit. The legal debate has some limitations. It is clearly difficult to come to a conclusion as the issues pose moral judgments about life and death and the medical implications of deciding whether or not to assist dying.

16-086 The ink was hardly dry on the Supreme Court decision when Lord Joffe introduced his fourth Bill on Assisted Dying in the House of Lords. The Bill[93] was relatively short composed of 13 sections and provided circumstances for a terminally ill patient to lawfully request assistance in the ending of their life. The request had to be by the individual and not by a third party. The Bill set conditions for an assessment of the medical condition of the patient by two independent medical practitioners and there is a period of 14 days for "cooling off". There is no duty to assist on any medical practitioner and there were various codes of practice that may help to

---

93 The Assisted Dying No.2 Bill 2015. See House of Commons Briefing Paper, *The Assisted Dying (No.2) Bill 2015*, No.7292 (4 September 2015).

settle the intention of the patient. There were also clearly defined crimes that apply to deception or wilfully concealing or providing misleading information. The Bill set a limited period of life set at ten years where it would be renewed after careful review. Underpinning the Bill were questions of eligibility of the patient, assessing their capacity to make a decision and the ability to monitor and scrutinise the operation of the law. The Bill represented a seismic shift in the role of medical practitioners traditionally seen to alleviate suffering and looking after patient care and their needs to one of taking active steps to end a patient's life. This was and remains a sensitive question at a time when medical practitioners, hospitals and care homes are under intense pressure and public criticism over the standards of National Health Care. There is a heightened state of public concern about hospitals, avoidable deaths, and the delivery of elderly care in private care homes.[94] Regulating medical standards and practice has been radically changed with the creation of the Care Quality Commission and additional powers to inspect, audit and assess medical care. Litigation over health standards following complaints from patients is increasingly common.

16–087

The sensitive issues that the Bill relied on were the certification process and the determination of a large number of factual questions including the fitness of the patient to make such a decision. Many doctors will not wish to be involved in assisted dying and decline to participate. This would leave relatively few doctors engaged with this responsibility, and leave patients in some difficulty in seeking to find a doctor, unfamiliar with their case history but involved in making a critical decision about their lives. The Bill was defeated in the Autumn of 2015 but many issues remain to be considered, though it is unlikely that the issue of assisted dying will be discussed in Parliament in the short term.

16–088

The issues raised in the Bill remain important. There is a question of whether the medical profession ought to be given the main responsibilities in any scheme for assisted dying. An alternative might be to provide access to the courts and review by a judge. There are many examples where the courts have had to consider the termination of death involving turning of life support systems or in matters of forced feeding or the withdrawal of certain kinds of medical treatment. The application of a "do not resuscitate" direction is also subject to judicial scrutiny.

16–089

There is also a question of how to certify the basis of any personal decision for assistant dying. The patient has to be of sound mind, the declaration must be voluntary and the patient has to show that implications of the decision are fully understood. Patients that come within the procedures are not subject to an inquest after their death but there may be circumstances where a request for an inquest should be considered and the reasons given as to why it should take place.

---

94 See Michael Hill, *Social Policy in the Modern World: A comparative Text* (London: Blackwell, 2006), Ch.12, "Ageing Societies";*With Respect to Old Age: Long Term Care—Rights and Responsibilities* (1 March 1999); a Report by the Royal Commission on Long Term Care (Cm 4192-1); *Learning from Bristol: The Report of the Public Enquiry into Children's Heart Surgery at the Bristol Royal Infirmary 1984–1995 (Chair: Professor Ian Kennedy)*, Cm.5207 (18 July 2001); and Robert Francis QC, Final Report (6 February 2013). The House of Commons Health Committee, *2013 Accountability Hearing with the Care Quality Commission*, 6th report of Session 2012–13, HC 761 (22 January 2014).

Freedom of religion and the criminal law

16–090 Freedom of religious belief may be considered in the context of the criminal law. In *Blaue*[95] the victim of a stabbing was a member of the Jehovah's Witnesses. She was told that unless she received a blood transfusion, which was the recommended standard medical treatment, she would die. She refused the treatment on religious grounds and her assailant was found guilty of her manslaughter. Lawton LJ recognised that the religious belief of the victim, whether reasonable or not, had to be accepted as part of the principle that the defendant had to take the victim as he found her. The victim in legal terms was defined to include physical attributes such as an "egg shell skull", and also the religious beliefs of the victim.

16–091 However, in *R v Senior*[96] in the case of a child in need of medical treatment, it was held that to withhold medical treatment from the child on the grounds of religious belief was manslaughter. Religious belief may be expressly recognised in a statute such as s.4 of the Abortion Act 1967 which recognises religious belief not to participate in an abortion on the ground of conscientious objection.

16–092 Religious discrimination is expressly prohibited in Northern Ireland, on the grounds of employment, education and the provision of services to the public. Similar provisions do not apply in other parts of the UK.

16–093 Freedom from racial discrimination is an example of piecemeal reform to meet particular problems. Since the 1950s and 60s the number of immigrants from India, Pakistan and the West Indies seeking employment in the UK focused attention on the multi-racial and multi-ethnic nature of the UK. Three Acts of Parliament have been extended to cover race relations while immigration policy has been tightened and reviewed. The current legislation is the Race Relations Act 1976 which strengthens and extends legislation passed in 1965 and 1968. The first attempt at legislation in 1965 made it illegal to discriminate against a person on the grounds of race in certain places of public access such as hotels, restaurants, theatres, sports grounds, places of entertainment, pubs and dance halls, and under s.5, in the disposal of tenancies and also in the creation of the offence of racial discrimination. The difficulty of proving intent to stir up racial hatred made this part of the Act largely ineffective. The Act created a new conciliatory procedure operated by the Race Relations Board (RRB) which made an annual report to Parliament. Failure to achieve a satisfactory settlement of a dispute might result in action by the Attorney General who could take action in the High Court or County Court through an injunction.

16–094 Following criticism of the 1965 Act, the Race Relations Act 1968 was enacted. The Act allowed the RRB to take cases to court rather than having to rely on the Attorney General. The Act also extended the application of the law to a wider range of activities such as goods, facilities and services, employment, housing and advertisements. The Act also extended to the Crown. Interpretation of the Act by the courts gave rise to a number of difficulties. Certain private social or political clubs which operated a bar on the basis of race were held to escape

---

95 [1975] 1 W.L.R. 1411; [1975] 3 All E.R. 446 CA.
96 [1899] 1 Q.B. 283 Crown Cases Reserved.

the provisions of the legislation. Discrimination against a person on the grounds of a person's nationality as distinct from national origins was not contrary to the Act. The RRB could take action on its own initiative to investigate suspected cases of discrimination. Working on informal techniques of compromise the RRB could attempt to find a solution. The 1968 Act had failed to be effective and after a White Paper, a new Act was passed in 1976. Building on the experience of the previous legislation, the 1976 Act set out to remedy some of the shortcomings mentioned above.

16-095 The 1976 Act extended the scope of the 1968 Act to cover partnerships and clubs, contract workers and discrimination on the grounds of nationality rather than national origins. Direct and indirect discrimination and discriminatory practices such as victimisation are also included within the scope of the Act. Such practices are illegal if they fall within employment, education, goods and services, housing, clubs or advertisements.[97]

16-096 The definition of discrimination remains the same, namely a person discriminates if on racial grounds he treats another less favourably than he treats or would treat other persons. It is an offence to incite, instruct or induce someone to act in a discriminatory way. The courts appear to have developed a relatively simple test; would the complainant have received the same treatment from the defendant but for his or her racial background?

16-097 The 1976 Act allows direct access to the individual who feels that there is a grievance. Assistance is then given by the Commission for Racial Equality (CRE) which replaced the RRB and the Community Relations Commission. The CRE may give advice or assistance and if necessary instigate proceedings in the County Court by seeking an injunction. It has considerable powers to require the furnishing of information and the production of documents and if necessary seek court orders to enforce the production of documents. The CRE is appointed by the Home Secretary and it makes an annual report to the Home Secretary which is laid before Parliament. It has 15 members and is independent from government.

16-098 Discrimination is unlawful in employment except where there is a particular racial group where this is a specified qualification for a specific job such as the theatre. Employment in a private household is not included under the Act.

16-099 In the case of employment where there are allegations of discrimination, the complainant must complain to an industrial tribunal. The burden lies on the complainant, and if successful the complainant may achieve compensation, or reversal of the policy or act of discrimination. Enforcement in the field of employment depends on the victim of discrimination complaining to an industrial tribunal with an appeal on a point of law to the Employment Appeal Tribunal.

16-100 As a result of the difficulty of proving intention under the 1965 Act for the offence of inciting racial hatred, the 1976 Act replaced the requirement of intention with an objective test. The defendant, if his conduct was judged to stir up racial hatred, was guilty of the offence irrespective of whether he intended to do so or not. Further refinement to the law was achieved under Pt III of the Public Order Act 1986 which added seven further offences to the offence of stirring up racial hatred. In the field of racial discrimination some advocate a different approach than that outlined in the 1976 Act. Positive discrimination or reverse discrimination

---

97 *Racial Discrimination*, Cmnd.6234 (1975).

is intended to encourage affirmative action to provide positive steps to redress any racial discrimination in society. For example, in employment or education, one possibility is to allocate places on the basis of race or ethnic origin thus ensuring that there is a fair balance to the opportunities available to ethnic groups. The definition of discrimination under s.1 of the Race Relations Act makes affirmative action illegal. There are some exceptions such as ss.35–38 which may permit a particular group to be granted education, training and special needs. Introduction into the UK of a full programme of affirmative action requires careful consideration and research.

16–101 Following the findings of racism by the Macpherson Report into the death of Stephen Lawrence, the Race Relations (Amendment) Act 2000 applies to the police. The effect of the Act is to broaden the impact of the previous acts and make it a requirement that there is a public duty on all public authorities to eliminate unlawful discrimination and this includes direct or indirect discrimination or victimisation. The act makes Chief Officers of Police vicariously liable for acts of racial discrimination by Police officers under their direction and control. The exemption for national security found in the Race Relations Act 1976 is amended to make it compatible with the Convention. The Act blurs any distinction between public and private as it brings within its scope public functions carried out by private sector organisations. The Racial and Religious Hatred Act 2006 make provisions for offences involving the stirring up of hatred against anyone on racial or religious grounds. The Act amends the Public Order Act 1986 by creating new grounds for an offence in England and Wales. The definition is broad in order to include a wide range of religious groups and is not confined to Christian religions. The offences cover hatred against a group where the hatred is not based on religious belief of the group but the fact that the group do not share the particular religious beliefs of the perpetrator.[98]

E: Work

16–102 The UK enacted specific laws to oppose sex discrimination. There are two statutes relevant to sex discrimination, first the Equal Pay Act 1970 and secondly the Sex Discrimination Act 1975. The Equal Pay Act is intended to provide women with equal pay when undertaking equal work, or where a job evaluation scheme has been carried out and the work is rated as equivalent to a man's work. In the case of a collective bargain agreement between employer and trade union that provides different rates for men and women, the collective agreement may be referred to an Industrial Arbitration Board for the removal of any clause which is unfair or discriminatory.

16–103 Women who believe that they are not getting equal pay may refer their claim to an industrial tribunal. The onus of proof is that she has to show that her work is similar to that of a man's.

---

98 House of Commons Library, *The Racial and Religious Hatred Act 2006*, Standard Note, SN/PC/03768 (2006).

Once this element of proof has been discharged the onus is then on the employer to show that there are material differences between the man's work and the woman's work. Compensation is payable of up to two years' arrears of pay. The Equal Pay Act has also a more general application to a woman's terms and conditions of employment including sickness pay and holiday bonuses. For example Lloyds' Bank Ltd operated a pension scheme which in *Worringham and Humphreys v Lloyds" Bank Ltd (No.2)*[99] was held by the European Court of Justice to be a violation of art.19. Male employees over 25 were expected to contribute five per cent of their salary to the pension fund while female employees of the same age were not required to make any contribution. The male employees over 55 received extra salary to compensate them and if they left before 55 they received a full refund.

The Sex Discrimination Act 1975 bears similarity to the scope of the provisions of the Race Relations Act 1976. In the case of sex discrimination, Pt II of the 1975 Act prohibits discrimination in employment and applies to the arrangements for the terms and conditions of employment, access to training, promotion and benefits and to dismissal. This includes job advertisements and includes that a refusal or deliberate omission to offer employment because of a person's sex is unlawful.

16-104

There are a number of exceptions to the Act such as employment in private households, and genuine examples where the job may only be performed by someone of a certain sex. The Equal Opportunities Commission has powers to bring proceedings in the County Court and extensive powers to carry out formal investigations into employers' policies and practices. In cases where it establishes that there is discrimination or contravention of the equal pay provisions, it may issue a non-discrimination notice. Codes of Practice may be issued or inquiries may be carried out into a specific complaint provided the Commission is satisfied that there has been a breach of the statute before embarking on the inquiry.

16-105

The Disability Rights Commission Act 1999 set up a Commission to replace the National Disability Council established under the Disability Discrimination Act 1995. The Commission is a non-departmental body with the majority of its members disabled. The Commission has similar functions to the Equal Opportunities Commission and may take formal investigations and issue non-discrimination notices, provide assistance in relation to agreements and facilitate the resolution of disputes.

16-106

There are also important whistleblowing rights under the Public Interest Disclosure Act 1998.[100] The Act protects workers to disclose information about malpractice at their workplace or former workplace. There are various conditions attached to the right to make any disclosure of information. The conditions are important because they provide workers with protection from suffering any detriment as a result of made any disclosure. There is a public interest test under the Enterprise and Regulatory Reform Act 2013 relating to the failure or failing to comply with any legal obligation.[101]

---

99 [1982] 1 W.L.R. 841; [1982] 3 All E.R. 373 CA (Civ Div).
100 House of Commons, *Whistleblowing and gagging clauses*, Briefing Paper, No.CBP 7442 (4 January 2016).
101 See *Parkins v Sodexho Ltd* [2001] UKEAT 1239. There are also legal amendments contained in the Small Business, Enterprise and Employment Act 2015.

F: Immigration, Citizenship and Extradition

Citizenship and the right of abode

16-107 The Treaty on European Union provides for the first time in the context of the Community, the formulation of rights for the Citizen of the EU. The first of the rights pertaining to European citizenship conferred by the new Treaty is the right to move and reside freely throughout the territory of the Member States. The concept of citizenship is an important one for the bestowal of rights and the ascertainment of responsibilities. Race relations in the UK are not exclusively determined by the Race Relations Acts. In fact an important aspect of immigration policy has been the question of the rights of immigrants to enter and remain within the UK. Restrictions may be imposed on British subjects.

16-108 At common law a British subject was synonymous with allegiance to the Crown within His Majesty's dominions. Aliens owed a temporary allegiance. Historical reasons influenced the categorisation of British subjects to be defined as including the UK and Colonies. The status of British subject became the basis of citizenship and this was recognised under the British Nationality Act 1948. Historical reasons also combined with economic factors to influence restrictions on the freedom of Commonwealth citizens to enter and live in the UK. For example, after a period of growth in emigration from India, Pakistan and the West Indies in the 1950s, there followed a period of restriction, first under the Commonwealth Immigrants Act 1962 and secondly, under the Immigration Act 1971. Thus holding citizenship does not qualify one for living within the UK.

16-109 A major change in the law took place under the British Nationality Act 1981 which came into force in 1983. At the end of 1982 anyone who was a citizen of the UK and Colonies under the 1971 Act and had the right to abode in the UK became a British citizen.[102] Those that did not have a right of abode but had some connection with a British dependent territory became British dependent territories citizens. Those who did not qualify as either British citizens or British dependent territories citizens become British overseas citizens. So although the 1981 Act introduces the requirement of citizenship as the basis of immigration control, the concept of citizenship is defined to include all those who had the right of abode prior to the 1981 Act. The right to abode is specified in detailed provisions of the 1981 Act.

16-110 From 1983 onwards birth in the UK ceased to be a qualification for British citizenship. At the time of birth, if either parent is either a British citizen or ordinarily resident, i.e. "settled" in the UK, then British citizenship is acquired. A minor who is adopted becomes a British citizen if the order is made by a UK court and either adoptive parent is a British citizen on the date of

---

102 If a parent subsequently becomes a citizen or is ordinarily resident here while the child is still a minor the child is a citizen of the UK. A child adopted through a UK court order becomes a British citizen if the adopter is a British citizen.

the Order of adoption. In other cases those born in the UK acquire British citizenship through registration if they have spent the first ten years of their life in the UK. British citizenship may be gained through a system of naturalisation.[103] The Home Secretary has a discretion to naturalise certain categories of applicant but there is no appeal against his refusal. Those married to a British citizen or with a five years' residence in the UK may be included as naturalised citizens.

16-111

The question raised under the Immigration Act 1971 and the British Nationality Act 1981, in force since 1983, together with a variety of immigration rules and regulations is whether a person has a right of abode in the UK. This question will determine whether the person is subject to immigration control. Those who are subject to control, that is they do not have the right to abode, can be classified as those who are expected to be permitted to enter and remain and those that have no such expectation. Determination of such a category depends on the application of immigration rules under s.3(2) of the Immigration Act 1971. This section provides that either House of Parliament may disapprove of a statement of rules within 40 days of such resolution. Section 39(2) of the 1981 Act provides that all British citizens have a right of abode. Commonwealth citizens before 1981 have a right of abode satisfied on the production of a certificate of entitlement. The right of abode also extends to citizens of the European Community. Two countries where immigration have proved problematic are the Falkland Islands and Hong Kong. First is the case of the Falklands. After the Falklands War the Government passed the British Nationality (Falkland Islands) Act 1983. Those born in the Falklands to parents who were settled there have become British citizens. Second is the case of Hong Kong where the potential for large-scale immigration into the UK has increased after the period of British rule and the handing over of the colony to China. The Hong Kong Act 1985 provides a unique category of "British Nationals (Overseas)" after July 1997. This category carries no rights to UK residence. However a small category of Hong Kong citizens have been granted British citizenship with entry rights intended to encourage them to remain in Hong Kong with the knowledge that they may leave Hong Kong and live in the UK as an assurance against unfavourable treatment by the Chinese.

16-112

Further changes to the status and registration of British citizens comes from The British Overseas Territories Act 2002. This Act follows discussion and consultation with the fourteen British Overseas Territories[104] resulting in a White Paper in March 1999. The fourteen British Overseas Territories include: Anguilla; Bermuda; the British Antarctic Territory; the British Indian Ocean Territory; the British Virgin Islands; the Cayman Islands; the Falkland Islands; Gibraltar; Montserrat; the Pitcairn Islands; St Helena and Dependencies; South Georgia and the South Sandwich Islands; the Sovereign Base Areas of Akrotiri and Dhekelia in Cyprus; and the Turks and Caicos Islands. The aim of the Act is to give British citizenship with the right of abode to the British Dependant Territories on the same basis as granted to the Falkland Islands in 1983.

---

103 British Nationality Act 1981 s.6 and Sch.1.
104 *Partnership for Progress and Prosperity: Britain and the Overseas Territories*, Cm.4264 (March 1999).

Immigration rules and procedures

16–113 Administration of the immigration rules represents an important example of administrative discretion. This is an area of great political controversy and it is the subject of much legislative change. Sections 1 and 2 of the Immigration Act 1971 provides that all persons who have a right to abode are free to come and go. Section 3(2) of the 1971 Act provides for immigration rules and procedures to regulate entry into the UK and providing powers for immigration officials to ensure that the requirements of the immigrations rules are fulfilled. A person who fails to meet the requirements of the rules or does not have the right of abode may be refused leave. The immigration rules are in effect given the force of law and may form the basis of a legal challenge in the High Court on the basis that the rules have been incorrectly interpreted or applied. The question of judicial review is related to the question of whether there are available alternative remedies. The immigration rules are also supplemented by instructions issued from time to time by the Home Office.

16–114 Nationals of the European Community once free to enter are free from any restrictions on employment or occupation and no work permit is required for prospective workers. Community nationals and their families enjoy generous rights within Member States subject to refusal on the grounds of personal unacceptability such as public security or public health. Citizens of the Republic of Ireland are part of a Common Travel Area permitting immigration-free travel within the specified area but subject to the provisions applying to emergency powers. New legislation passed in 1987, the Immigration (Carriers' Liability) Act 1987, makes it a criminal offence for the owner of a ship, aircraft or a carrier to allow any person who requires leave to enter the UK to arrive in the UK without any necessary passport and visa. The provisions of the 1987 Act make it difficult for asylum seekers as claims for asylum are made on arrival in the country of destination, and not prior to departure. Carriers may in certain circumstances have the penalty under the 1987 Act waived in cases where asylum is granted.

Asylum

16–115 This is one of the most complex and sensitive areas of the law. It is estimated[105] that in 1999 there were "71,160 applications for that year and 102,870 claims outstanding overall the highest number ever recorded". Asylum seekers appear to be on the increase, hence the sense of urgency for every new enactment. There are a plethora of rules and regulations and several major statutory requirements. The Immigration Rules 1994, the Asylum and Immigration Appeals Act 1993, and the Asylum and Immigration Act 1996 amended by the Immigration and Asylum Act 1999 provide a comprehensive range of powers for asylum seekers. There are special considerations that apply where a person seeking entry claims asylum. Asylum may refer to political refugees, that is those "owing to a well-founded fear of being prosecuted for reasons of race, religion, nationality, membership of a particular group or political opinion". Making a

---

105 D. Stevens, "The Immigration and Asylum Act 1999: A Missed Opportunity?" [2001] *M.L.R.* 413.

judgment as to the presence of any of these factors in any particular case requires the discretion of the Secretary of State. Factors which may be considered are facts and information which the Secretary of State is aware of, even if such factors are unknown to the applicant. The question is whether there is "a real likelihood" of persecution which may be based on "substantial grounds" or a "serious possibility" of persecution. The House of Lords upheld the decision of the Secretary of State to refuse the asylum applications of the six applicants who were Tamils from Sri Lanka, but on appeal to the adjudicator the Tamils were successful on the basis of the findings of the adjudicator made from the evidence before him.[106]

16–116 The Asylum and Immigration Appeals Act 1993 was intended to accelerate the process of immigration control to cope with the growth in the numbers of asylum seekers and problems of blatant abuse. The rights of appeal of asylum seekers are also covered in the Act. New measures include powers under s.3 to undertake fingerprinting together with arrest powers granted to immigration officers. Section 8 of the 1993 Act provides a right of appeal in cases where a claim for asylum has been refused. This is subject to the terms of the Asylum and Immigration Act 1996 and the Immigration and Asylum Act 1999 discussed below. In certain cases, the Secretary of State may certify that in his opinion the asylum seeker's claim is without foundation. Special time-limits will apply in such cases. If the special adjudicator agrees with the Secretary of State's assessment there can be no further appeal to the Immigration Appeal Tribunal. Section 9 provides for a right of appeal on a point of law to the Court of Appeal or in Scotland, the Court of Sessions, from a final determination of the Immigration Appeal Tribunal. The introduction of an appeal represents an important improvement, as hitherto an application for judicial review was the only way in which decisions of the Tribunals could be challenged. The right of appeal does not preclude judicial review. However, the 1993 Act does remove long-established rights of appeal from would be visitors and certain categories of students and their dependants. This means that judicial review may become overburdened with applications from visitors or certain categories of students deprived of the right of appeal under the Act. In addition to the above, the 1993 Act introduces changes to the Immigration Rules dated 5 July 1993. Member States are comparatively free to provide their own restrictive arrangements. At the time of adoption of the Single European Act, Member States adopted a General Declaration retaining the power of the Member States as regards the control of immigration from Third World countries and attempting to control the illicit traffic in drugs and the illegal market in antiques and art. There is also a Dublin Convention signed in June 1990 for asylum seekers suggesting a common approach to restricting asylum seekers throughout the Community, though it is doubtful if once asylum is granted by one Member State there is any free movement within the Community between Member States.

16–117 The Immigration Rules 1994 have been added to by the Asylum Appeals (Procedure) Rules 1996 and the Asylum and Immigration Act 1996. Further changes are made by the Immigration and Asylum Act 1999 explained below. The 1996 Act considerably strengthened the existing law. The 1996 Act has three aims, namely: to deal with any bogus claims for asylum expeditiously; to combat immigration racketeering through stronger powers, new offences and

---

106 See *R v Secretary of State for the Home Department Ex p. Sivakumaran* [1988] A.C. 958; [1988] 1 All E.R. 193 HL.

higher penalties; and finally, to reduce the economic incentives which attract people to come to Britain in breach of the law.

16-118 The Act achieves these aims in several ways as follows. It excludes cases from appeals to the Immigration and Appeals Tribunal and substitutes appeals to a special adjudicator. There is a system of certification by the Secretary of State. The special adjudicator may conclude that the appellant does have a well-founded fear of prosecution and allow appeal against removal; or dismiss the appeal on the grounds that the special adjudicator is not satisfied that the appellant has a well-grounded fear of persecution at the date of the hearing. In the latter case the special adjudicator is free to accept or reject the certificate of the Secretary of State. Under these procedures there is no longer the possibility of making a reference back to the Secretary of State. There are changes to the law on removal to "safe third countries" certified as such by the Secretary of State. There is an appeal to a special adjudicator in such cases. There are new immigration offences of obtaining leave by deception under s.4 of the 1996 Act and assisting asylum claimants to obtain leave by deception. There are increased penalties and additional powers of arrest and search under s.7 of the 1996 Act. There is a draconian rule under s.9 that a person subject to immigration control is not eligible for a council tenancy, introduced after a number of cases struck down the attempt to impose this rule by statutory instrument. There are also provisions covering social security and child benefit.

16-119 The Immigration and Asylum Act 1999 makes the Home Office administratively responsible for providing support and accommodation for asylum seekers pending determination of their application. There is a new Home Office Agency, the National Asylum Support Service, and the Act provides a new system of appeals. The Act also allows new grounds for removal to Member States of the EU or to other safe third countries. Extensive powers are granted to use new technology to record and process asylum seekers. There are additional powers for the running of detention centres and new offences for carriers of illegal immigrants and for setting up "sham marriages". There is a new offence under s.4 of the Immigration and Asylum Act 1999 that pertains to an asylum claimant who remains in Britain, having gained asylum on the basis of a bogus claim. In these circumstances the asylum claimant continues to commit an offence while being in the country. Powers of detention include detaining vehicles and restrictions on only qualified persons under s.84 of the 1999 Act that may give immigration advice or offer immigration services. Section 22 of the 1999 Act amends s.8 of the Asylum and Immigration Act 1996 which made it an offence for an employer to employ an illegal immigrant. The new powers under s.22 of the 1999 Act allow the Secretary of State to issue a code of practice setting out the steps employers are expected to take to meet their requirements under the Act.

16-120 The 1999 Act creates a reform and consolidation of the appeal system. The claims for asylum fall under new rules the Immigration and Asylum Appeals (Procedure) Rules 2000.[107] There is a new Human Rights Appeal procedure under s.65, namely that the authority has breached the asylum seeker's human rights. There is also under ss.74–78, the introduction of a single-tier appeal for consolidation of the grounds of appeal that would include the notice of additional grounds served on a person appealing a decision.

---

107 Immigration and Asylum Appeals (Procedure) Rules (SI 2000/2333).

Refugee or humanitarian protection

16-121 There are specific rules for UK refugee families to be joined in the UK by their immediate family members. The EU Dublin III Regulations apply and have created a framework for such families. Priority is given to family unity and this takes precedence over any other considerations. The House of Commons Library provide a useful set of documents setting out the details of the rules and their application.[108]

The Immigration Bill 2015–16

16-122 The Government proposes to establish a Director of Labour Market Enforcement tackling illegal workers. Details in the new Bill include rules about immigrants' access to residential accommodation and powers to restrict illegal renting. Changes in appeal rights under the Immigration Act 2014 are proposed to remove immigrants who wish to make a claim arising out of human rights considerations. New civil penalties are proposed against transport carriers. There are also related immigration skills such as fluency in English and fees on employers who wish to sponsor non-EEA nationals.[109]

Deportation

16-123 Deportation of all who are not British citizens is regulated under the Immigration Act 1971 as amended by the British Nationality Act 1981 and the Immigration Act 1988 and the Immigration Rules 1990. Schedule 14 to the Immigration and Asylum Act 1999 makes further amendments. Anyone who is not a British citizen, with certain specified exceptions, is subject to deportation. There are generally four grounds: first, if the Home Secretary deems it "conducive to the public good"; secondly, on the recommendation by a court on conviction of a person over 17 for an offence which is punishable by imprisonment; thirdly, where a person breaks any entry conditions or overstays the period of entry permitted by the immigration officer; and fourthly, he or she is the infant child or wife of a person against whom a deportation order is made.

16-124 The Immigration Act 2014 enhances the powers for the deportation of persons illegally in the UK along with additional enforcement powers. Part 2 of the Act amends rights of appeal and limits the appeal rights where there has been a human rights or asylum or humanitarian claim. In considering art.8 rights the court or tribunal must also have regard to the public interest and this has to be respected. The Act also creates new regulatory powers over migrants' access to services. This includes detailed provisions for migrants with time-limited access and students to contribute to the NHS. There are investigative powers to consider sham marriages

---

108 House of Commons Library, *The UK's refugee family reunion rules: striking the right Balance?*, Briefing Paper, No.07511 (19 February 2016).
109 House of Commons, *Immigration Bill 2015–16*, Briefing Paper, No.07304 (6 October 2015).

and also regulatory powers over advice givers. General restrictions apply to anyone who is unlawfully in the UK in terms of driving licences and civil penalties against employers for failing to take care in their responsibilities.

G: Personal Freedom and Police powers

16-125 The maintenance of law and order and the protection of the citizen through the detection and prevention of crime is an important aspect of the State. The citizen's personal liberty and freedom are often provided in rules of evidence and the right to a fair trial. Minimum safeguards are provided for the arrest, detention and trial of an accused on criminal charges. For example, there may be the requirement that there should within a reasonable period of time be a trial before a court and a fair hearing. There is a right not to be held incommunicado and a relative or friend is entitled to be requested to be informed of the arrest. There is also under s.58 of PACE the right to consult a solicitor privately at any time. The rules of evidence at a criminal trial entitle a person accused to know the evidence against him; entitlement to some form of legal representation is also required as is assistance in the form of legal aid in the preparation of his case. The Human Rights Act 1998 and Convention rights provides an important set of overarching requirements as to how personal freedoms are to be treated by the courts in the future. There is also an important role vested in the Crown Prosecution Service (CPS) responsible for criminal prosecutions. Between 2004 and 2007 statutory charging arrangements vested all but the most minor offences with the CPS. From 2012–2015, a new system of transferring the responsibility to the Police for many offences was part of a pilot scheme. This has been extended and gives the Police a wider discretion than in the past.[110]

16-126 The well-known "right to silence" of the suspect or accused is today governed by the Criminal Justice and Public Order Act 1994. This permits a court or jury to draw such inferences as appear proper" from the failure of the accused to give evidence at his or her trial or without good cause to answer any question. The right to a fair trial is contained in art.6 of the ECHR.

16-127 The law relating to the powers of arrest, questioning of suspects and their rights is untidy and unduly complicated. In practical terms the scope of the citizen's freedom is often dependent on the exercise of Police powers and in individual cases how the Police officer exercises his discretion. The courts have not always followed a consistent approach of how to determine the exact scope of Police powers. Judicial intervention has therefore been sporadic. Setting the delicate balance between protecting the suspect and allowing the Police sufficient powers

---

110 Prosecution of Offences Act 1985; and the Prosecution of Offences Act 1985 (Specified Proceedings) Order 1999. See Home Office, *police Powers to prosecute strengthened* (23 October 2012). House of Commons Library, *Charging decisions and Police-led prosecutions*, SN/HA/06840 (5 March 2014).

to undertake their duties is difficult. The Royal Commission on Criminal Procedure,[111] set up in 1977, reported in 1981. The outcome of the Royal Commission's deliberations is the Police and Criminal Evidence Act 1984 intended to transform many of the common law principles into a single coherent statute. At the same time, the Prosecution of Offences Act 1985 created the CPS headed by the Director of Public Prosecutions, organised on the basis of 31 areas, each headed by a Chief Crown Prosecutor covering at least one or two Police forces for that area. The power of the private citizen to prosecute is retained but the bulk of prosecutions are taken by the CPS and the CPS may take over any private prosecution when it is regarded as in the public interest.

16–128

A further Royal Commission was set up[112] and its main recommendations are found in the Criminal Justice and Public Order Act 1994, and the Criminal Procedure and Investigations Act 1996. There are additional powers under the Crime and Disorder Act 1998 and the Criminal Justice and Police Act 2001. The Regulation and Investigatory Powers Act 2000 provides the Police with surveillance powers. These powers are discussed in Ch.20 on secrecy.

16–129

The Police and Criminal Evidence Act 1984, hereinafter referred to as PACE, generally extended Police powers on the basis of additional statutory powers but introduced a number of requirements in the form of codes of practice made by the Home Secretary under s.66 of PACE and intended to act as safeguards for the accused. These safeguards include that those under the exercise of Police powers should be informed of the reasons for the exercise of those powers, that reasons be recorded contemporaneously, that senior officers should undertake a review of the use of powers, and that various codes of conduct and practices should be set up to administer the exercise of Police powers. There are also extensive provisions under s.58 which confer rights on suspects, such as access to legal advice at Police stations.

16–130

The arrangements under PACE have been extended to Northern Ireland and research into the operation of arrangements under PACE has been undertaken. Questions concerning the efficacy of the safeguards under PACE have been raised.

Arrest

The Police have no general powers to detain suspects for questioning unless they are arrested. Unlawful detention and arrest may amount to false imprisonment which may be actionable as well as a criminal offence. The exercise of arrest powers involves an element of compulsion, and requires that the person arrested is informed that he is under arrest. In effecting an arrest no more physical force must be used than is reasonably required. Unreasonable use of force becomes an actionable assault. The person arrested must be made aware of the fact of his arrest as soon as it is practicable, except where the arrest is by a private citizen and the ground of arrest is obvious. There are stop-and-search powers available under a number

16–131

---

111   Cmnd.8092.
112   See A. Sanders, "Constructing the Case for the Prosecution" (1987) 14 *Journal of Law and Society* 229. The Royal Commission on Criminal Justice, Cm.2263 (1993), chaired by Lord Runciman.

of statutes. Under s.23 of the Misuse of Drugs Act 1971 a constable may search and detain a suspect who he has reasonable grounds to believe to be in unlawful possession of a controlled drug. Section 163 of the Road Traffic Act 1988 provides that a uniformed constable may require a driver of a motor vehicle or a cyclist to stop. Additional powers exist to require the production of insurance or motor licence. Powers of arrest under PACE fall into two categories: either with a warrant or without a warrant. Arrest without warrant is provided under s.24. The Royal Commission on Criminal Procedure envisaged that the Police should be able to arrest an individual without a warrant if the crime suspected was an imprisonable offence rather than a fine. An additional safeguard was that arrest should be linked to one that is necessary. Necessary conditions may be found in the general arrest conditions in PACE. This is intended to be the main power for arrest without warrant. Any member of the public may arrest, without warrant, anyone who is in the act of committing an arrestable offence or where there are reasonable grounds for suspecting the committing of an arrestable offence. In addition, a constable may arrest, without warrant: anyone whom he has reasonable grounds for suspecting of having committed an arrestable offence, even though no such crime has been committed; and anyone who is about to commit an arrestable offence or he has reasonable grounds to believe is about to commit such a crime. A constable, with reasonable grounds, may arrest any person whom he suspects is committing or has committed or attempted an offence which is not an arrestable offence, provided that service of the summons is impracticable or inappropriate because certain general arrest conditions are satisfied.

16-132 The question of what is an arrestable offence is clarified in s.24, such as murder, treason, and other crimes imprisonable for five years or more. However, there are a number of offences which do not fit this category, such as offences relating to crimes against property and sexual offences, which are also made arrestable even though they may not carry prison sentences of five years or more. In fact, Sch.2 to PACE contains numerous provisions retained under s.26 of PACE and granting the power to arrest without warrant. Various inchoate offences such as conspiring, or attempting to commit or incite or procure the commission of any arrestable offence is also arrestable. The common law power to arrest for breach of the peace is also included.[113] It is important that the Police should inform the defendant of the fact and reasons for their arrest. This should be undertaken as promptly as possible but even if there are time delays provided the reasons for arrest and the fact of arrest are properly explained this is necessary for the arrest to be made lawful.[114]

16-133 It may be concluded that the Police have very wide powers to arrest without a warrant. Section 24(3) grants a power of arrest "where an offence has been committed" and where the Police constable may arrest anyone who is guilty of the offence. The "necessity" to arrest is an important element in how arrest powers should be used.[115] This is an important qualification

---

113 For example, the Street Offences Act 1959 s.7(3); and the Immigration Act 1971 s.1(3). Since PACE there have been additions to the list such as: the Sporting Events (Control of Alcohol etc.) Act 1985; and the Public Order Act 1986 s.3(6).
114 See *Lewis v Chief Constable of South Wales* [1991] 1 All E.R. 206; Independent, October 24, 1990 CA (Civ Div).
115 See *Hayes v Chief Constable of Merseyside police* [2011] EWCA Civ 911; [2012] 1 W.L.R. 517.

that should apply to any use of s.24 of PACE.[116] The courts may decide that the question of whether the powers are necessary or not may determine whether the arrest is legal or not.

16-134 The requirements of arrest procedures are to be informed of the arrest and of the ground of arrest. In *Abbassy v Metropolitan police Commissioner*,[117] a civil case, the Court of Appeal accepted that an arrest for "unlawful possession" was sufficient as a reason to arrest for theft. Even when the arrest is unlawful initially, if the Police failed to inform the suspect of the ground of arrest, the Police may make a lawful arrest once they comply with this requirement. Arrest with a warrant as provided by statute, empowers the justice to either issue a summons requiring that person to appear before a magistrates' court or to issue a warrant to arrest the person to appear before the court. A warrant is obtained from a magistrate after information is made in writing and substantiated on oath. An arrest warrant may be executed through the use of reasonable force to enter and search premises. A warrant protects the Police from liability for the search.

16-135 Aside from the powers of arrest, PACE provides powers of detention after arrest and before charge. Prior to PACE there was considerable doubt as to the legality of detention powers. Once the Police decide that there is sufficient evidence to charge a person, he must be charged otherwise he must be released. PACE leaves considerable latitude to the Police as to how this power may be interpreted. Section 30 of the Criminal Justice Act 2003 provides that an arrested person should be brought to the Police station as soon as possible after arrest, and s.30(1) provides an exception if the arrested person is granted bail by a Police officer at any time before arriving at a Police station on the basis of a form of street bail.

16-136 It is possible for detainees to be kept up to 24 hours without being released or charged (s.41). This is possible of extension to 36 hours on the permission of an officer of the rank of superintendent or where the offence is indictable (s.42). The period of 36 hours may be extended by warrant of further detention up to 36 hours, if a magistrates' court provided the extension is needed to secure or preserve evidence by questioning the detainee. There is a whole raft of forensic and related evidence that might be collected under ss.61 and 62 of PACE.

16-137 The maximum permitted period of detention is 96 hours but there is a vague expression as a rider to this such as "a person must normally be brought before a magistrates' court as soon as practicable". The time limit is taken from the moment the person arrives at the Police station. This leaves the Police time to interrogate before arrival at the Police station. In *Parchment*[118] although the Police may have broken various rules in their interrogation of a suspect if carried out at the Police station, because the interrogation was carried out in the period before arrival at the Police station, the court held that the Police had not acted illegally.

16-138 Safeguards are provided under various codes of practice which require that certain powers may be exercised only by senior officers or a designated custody officer, defined as

---

116 *Lord Hannifield v Essex Chief Constable* [2013] EWHC 243 (QB); [2013] 1 W.L.R. 3632
117 [1990] 1 W.L.R. 385; [1990] 1 All E.R. 193 CA (Civ Div).
118 [1989] Crim. L.R. 290.

being independent from the investigation. The custody officer has various responsibilities under PACE including informing suspects of their rights, keeping detailed custody records, authorising and releasing from detention and deciding whether suspects should be charged or not. Considerable variation appears to exist in how the rules are interpreted and the practices of different Police stations throughout the country.

Search and seizure

16-139 Powers of search and seizure are often provided on the basis of a valid arrest. Following an arrest, a Police constable has the power to search a suspect to determine whether he may present a danger to himself or others or has evidence relating to suspected offences or has anything which might assist his escape. Section 1 of PACE and additions provided by ss.139 and 140 of the Criminal Justice Act 1988 provide powers to stop-and-search for any offensive weapon, stolen goods or for equipment used in offences such as a burglary. Extensive stop-and-search powers are also available under the Misuse of Drugs Act 1971 as well as a plethora of other legislative enactments. Powers exercised under PACE must comply with a code of practice. The suspect must be informed of the grounds for the search and that such "reasonable grounds" must be made out before and not after the stop-and-search powers are exercised. It is accepted that such stop-and-search powers are controversial and require tact, forbearance and understanding on the part of the Police when exercising their powers in multi-ethnical or multi-racial societies.

16-140 Searching premises and seizing goods may arise under search warrant powers under ss.8 and 9 of PACE. At common law the Police had no general power to obtain warrants, and warrants could not be generally authorising of Police powers to search and seize goods. Such restrictions have been largely removed by Pt II of PACE which consists of general powers to enter premises and search after an arrest, a general power of seizure, and general powers of entry. In addition, a number of statutes provide quite specific powers for the Police to search premises, for example in the areas of theft or drugs-related crimes.

16-141 Search without a warrant may arise following an arrest (s.32 of PACE) or, ancillary to arrest powers, there is a power to search premises and finally, the power to search without a warrant the home of the arrested person (s.18 of PACE). In *McLeod v UK*, the Police forcibly entered the complainant's home on the basis that entry was required to prevent a breach of the peace. There had been a dispute over the property of the complainant's former husband. The complainant argued that her art.8 rights to the enjoyment of her private property had been violated. The UK courts held that this was a lawful use of force to enter the premises. However, the ECtHR upheld the arguments made by the complainant and that the use of such powers could not be justified.[119]

---

119 *McLeod v MPC* [1994] 4 All E.R. 553; Independent, February 21, 1994 CA (Civ Div).

Interrogation of suspects

16-142 A large part of the safeguards to be found in PACE for the interrogation of suspects in custody depend on the actions of the custody officer. The arrival of the suspect at the Police station under arrest or when he is arrested results in the custody officer informing the suspect of: his right to have someone informed of his arrest; the right to consult privately with a solicitor; and the availability of free legal advice. There are detailed rules for the detention of suspects, including the conditions of cells and rooms. A search of the suspect may be carried out and any property may be retained by the custody officer. The right to consult a solicitor is stated in categorical terms under s.58(1) of PACE "to consult a solicitor privately at any time"; however, the remaining subsections provide a number of caveats restricting this right. These allow for consultation to be "as soon as practicable". An officer of or above the rank of superintendent may delay access where the suspect is suspected of a serious arrestable offence and where the officer believes that one of four situations may arise: interference with or harm to evidence connected with a serious arrestable offence; interference with or physical injury to other persons; alerting other persons suspected of having committed such an offence but who have not been arrested for it; and the hindering of the recovery of any property obtained as a result of such an offence.

16-143 While access to legal advice may only be delayed for up to 36 hours, the scope of the delay provisions is sufficiently wide to enable the Police to restrict the suspect's rights to consult a solicitor. Further, the term "serious arrestable offence" is sufficiently broad to encourage this category to be expanded and come within the terms of the delay power. The extent of Police discretion relies on judicial supervision by the courts. In *Samuel*, the defendant's request to see a solicitor was denied, and the Police found incriminating evidence in various searches of his house. He was kept in the Police station overnight and after an in-depth interrogation he later confessed to the offences of burglary; after he was charged, his solicitor's attempts to interview him were frustrated by the Police. The Court of Appeal was critical of the Police handling of the case and held that a suspect should always be able to see a solicitor after being charged. The confession obtained by the Police was excluded by the Court and the defendant's conviction quashed.

16-144 Some qualification to the principles in *Samuel*[120] came in *Alladice*.[121] The Court of Appeal accepted that a confession obtained by the Police after refusal of access to a solicitor did not render the confession inadmissible. These cases illustrate some of the difficulties of oversight by the courts. Attempting to balance the interests of the Police with those of the accused in the face of statutory provisions which are capable of wide and diffuse interpretation is difficult. Since *Alladice* the Divisional Court in *Robinson*[122] accepted that a solicitor's clerk may be refused access if the Police believe that the clerk is unsuitable to give advice based on the capacity of the clerk in the view of the Police to perform that function.

---

120 *R v Samuel* [1988] Q.B. 615; [1988] 2 W.L.R. 92 CA.
121 *R v Alladice* (1988) 87 Cr. App. R. 380; [1988] Crim. L.R. 608 CA.
122 (1989) 139 N.L.J. 186.

16-145 An important element in Police practice is the requirement that the person arrested and charged must be brought before a magistrates' court. Release on bail may be granted by a custody sergeant following the arrest without warrant; or by the magistrate or by a High Court judge. Conditions of bail may include the accused being asked to enter his own recognisance to keep the peace. A general power remains, that magistrates may make it a condition of bail that the accused does not breach the peace and such bail conditions are open to rigorous enforcement by the courts. The practice of setting particularly restrictive bail conditions on striking miners in 1984 came to be regarded as "usual conditions". This power led to the criticism that the courts were exercising a system of group justice. There appears to be no direct appeal against such orders of the court and the restrictions imposed as bail conditions may be used to inhibit political agitation.

16-146 The outcome of the interrogation process is often a statement which has some damaging effect on the accused. This may be through the provision of information which may assist the Police in the gathering of intelligence or the obtaining of additional evidence. In fact, the possibility exists that the Police may find it convenient to use such information to create a factual basis for the conclusions they may wish a court to reach. PACE covers the admission of confession evidence under ss.50–60 and 76–78 of the 1984 Act and the various codes of practice. There is a revised Code of Practice C (1995) for interviewing suspects. The courts have a general discretion at common law and under s.78 of PACE to exclude evidence, generally to ensure that the accused was not induced to incriminate himself by deception. Section 78 has been used to exclude identification evidence in breach of the code of practice, and to exclude the evidence of previous convictions of persons other than the accused. However, it is unclear the extent to which this power may be used to exclude illegally obtained evidence.

16-147 Section 76 covers the admissibility of confessions where the confession may have been obtained

> "by oppression of the person who made it, in consequence of anything said or done which was likely in the circumstances existing at the time, to render unreliable any confession which might be made by him in consequence thereof."

16-148 Oppression is defined under s.76(8) of PACE as including "torture, inhuman or degrading treatment and the use or threat of violence". Lord Lane in *Fulling*[123] explained that the word should be given its ordinary meaning such as the

> "exercise of authority or power in a burdensome, harsh, or wrongful manner; unjust or cruel treatment of subjects, inferiors etc. the imposition of unreasonable or unjust burdens."

---

123 *R v Fulling* [1987] Q.B. 426; [1987] 2 All E.R. 65 CA.

16-149 Oppression is not satisfied merely by breaches of the law or the codes of practice under PACE, which do not necessarily amount to oppression. Unreliability of a confession is used more often than the claim of oppression. Breaches of PACE, improperly conducted interviews, and improper inducement may lead to exclusion on the basis that the confession is unreliable.

16-150 The right of the suspect to be silent in the face of Police interrogation is a central principle of English law and is of long standing. The right to silence provides that no person may be required to give information to the Police in the course of a criminal prosecution. This means that the suspect may decline to answer questions during interrogation. It also means that a person charged with a criminal offence cannot be required to give evidence in court at any stage of the trial. In the past no adverse inferences may be drawn from an accused's silence at an interview or failure to give evidence in court. In recent years the future of the right to silence has been the subject of intense debate, resulting in its removal in 1994. Sections 34–39 of the Criminal Justice and Public Order Act 1994 allows a court or jury to draw inferences from an accused's silence.

16-151 Following the discovery of a number of miscarriages of justice in the *Confait*; *Birmingham Six*; and *Guildford Four* cases,[124] concern about Police practices and the trial of criminal cases has led to discussion of the adversarial system at a criminal trial. Recent research has pointed to the inadequacy of accountability over the Police and questioned the effectiveness of the adversarial system of trial. Even more worrying is the conclusion that "internal, legalistic reforms would leave untouched the class, gender and race biases of the system". The search for a suitable reform of the system of criminal justice is problematic. The same researchers conclude that the desire for greater accountability has little meaning as it is directed at providing after the fact explanations which can be simply self-serving to the Police to construct the facts to meet the criteria of accountability. The research concludes[125]:

> "Accountability, if it is to have any relevance to Police-work practices, must be both prospective and able to penetrate the control networks which the Police utilize to perpetuate Police values and ideologies and screen out external inspection mechanisms."

Accountability of the police

16-152 Under the Police Reform and Social Responsibility Act 2011 major changes have been introduced to the system of policing. In 2012, local Police Authorities were abolished after the creation of directly elected Police and Crime Commissioners (PCC). The Police are organised at a local level into 43 Police areas for England and Wales, each with a PCC. The intention is to provide a direct form of community accountability through the elected PCC over polic-

---
124 See M. McConville, A. Sanders and R. Leng, *The Case for the Prosecution* (London: Routledge, 1991).
125 McConville, Sanders and Leng, *The Case for the Prosecution*, pp.207–208.

ing. PCCs have had a range of statutory responsibilities transferred from the local Police Authorities.[126] This includes a statutory duty to "secure the maintenance of the Police force" for their area with an overall responsibility to ensure that the "Police force is efficient and effective". In addition the Police Reform and Social Responsibility Act 2011 imposes duties on the PCC to hold the Chief Constable to account for the way in which the Chief Constable's duties are carried out. This includes the implementation of the PCC's crime and Police plan, the incorporation of the Home Secretary's strategic policing requirements and the effectiveness of engagement with the local community. The PCC's overall responsibility to produce a local policing plan is one that has to be considered collaboratively with local authorities and criminal justice agencies. Perhaps more importantly is the power of the PCC to appoint the Chief Constable as well as powers to require resignation or suspension. In London arrangements are different as the (Elected) Mayor's Office for Policing and Crime was established to replace the Metropolitan police Authority. The Head of the Metropolitan Police is appointed by the Queen on the advice of the Home Secretary. Requirements for the Head of the Metropolitan Police to resign or be suspended may only occur with the Home Secretary's consent. There are various policing functions conducted by the London Assembly through the Police and crime panels.

16–153
The role of the Home Secretary is also an important element in Police policy making and strategic planning while retaining the character of local Police forces. Traditionally the Home Secretary had a duty to determine "strategic priorities" for policing in all areas of the country. The Police Reform and Social Responsibility Act 2011 has introduced a new duty on the Home Secretary to issue a policing document—the strategic policing requirement. This is a pivotal document as it contains details of "national threats" and the necessary capabilities to address such threats. Account has to be taken by the PCCs of the document, the resources needed and priorities set by the Government of the day. In addition there are a broad range of issues relating to the conditions of service of Police forces and the powers of the Home Secretary to regulate many aspects of Police administration and equipment. Overseeing the new arrangements are powers granted to Her Majesty's Inspectors of Constabulary to report to the Home Secretary.[127]

16–154
The overall accountability of the Police is complicated by the multi-level system of Police governance and the considerable divergence of practices between different Police forces. The House of Commons Home Affairs Select Committee is the main overseer of the Home Office and related Police matters. Inquiries undertaken by the Select Committee are important including recently the way in which the Police brief the press on policing matters.[128] Overall accountability for the legality of police action is often dependant on the role of the courts to scrutinise Police powers.[129]

---

126 House of Commons Library, *police and Crime Commissioner Elections 2012*, Research Paper, 12/73 (29 November 2012)
127 House of Commons Library, *police Funding*, Briefing Paper, CBP7279 (17 August 2015).
128 HC 234-1 (2013–14).
129 See *Hill v Chief Constable of West Yorkshire* [1989] A.C. 53; [1988] 2 W.L.R. 1049 HL.

Complaints against the police

16-155 The citizen may seek redress against the Police through an application for judicial review or as a collateral matter raised in the defence of a criminal charge, or seek to show that the police acted unlawfully. In the event of the acquittal of criminal charges because of evidence which shows Police doing wrong, this may result in civil action against the Police; the most common basis for such action is for assault or wrongful arrest. It is not uncommon to bring an action in damages against the Chief Constables who may be vicariously liable for the unlawful actions of officers under their command.[130]

16-156 There are extensive provisions contained in s.49 of the Police Act 1964 and ss.83–100 and 105 of PACE originally establishing a Police Complaints Authority (PCA) under Pt IV of the Police Act 1996. The regulations for complaints procedures were provided under the police (Complaints) (General) Regulations 1985. The PCA did not prove as effective as many hoped. An Independent Complaints Commission (IPCC), appointed by the Home Secretary was established under the police Reform Act 2002. A number of disciplinary offences such as abuse of authority, neglect of duty or using unnecessary violence are available against Police officers. Informal resolution of complaint is favoured. The process of complaining involves the Chief Constable deciding whether it should be formally investigated. The IPCC supervises the complaint and may appoint an officer from another force to investigate the complaint. The IPCC report goes to the Chief Constable who may decide to refer the report to the Director of Public Prosecutions (DPP) with a view to prosecution. The IPCC has the power to direct the Chief Constable to refer its report to the DPP. Disciplinary charges may be taken against the Police officer involved. In such cases a fair hearing must be given to the officers concerned.

16-157 The IPCC has an overall duty to record deaths and serious injuries in Police custody. Its independence is underpinned by the requirements to ensure that the arrangements are "efficient and effective and contain a manifest and appropriate degree of independence". There are additional powers granted under the Police Reform and Social Responsibility Act 2011. Appeals may be made to the IPCC against a decision of an appropriate police Authority or PCC. The IPCC may refer the matter directly to the DPP who may decide whether or not to take action. The IPCC has not found it easy to reconcile many conflicting issues that arise over policing.[131]

16-158 Criticism of the system of complaints is that the system relies too heavily on the Police to investigate complaints against themselves. The PCA is concerned with delays in action being taken by the Police and the tendency to retire officers early on ill health where there may be a case for disciplinary action. The rise in the number of civil actions against the Police may test public confidence in the ability of the PCA to act efficiently.

---

130 *Webb v Chief Constable of Merseyside police* [2000] Q.B. 427; [2000] 2 W.L.R. 546 CA (Civ Div) and also *Costello v Chief Constable of Derbyshire* [2001] EWCA Civ 381; [2001] 1 W.L.R. 1437. There are also provisions under s.57 of the Criminal Justice and Police Act 2001.

131 IPCC, *Statutory Guidance to the police Service on the Handling of Complaints* (2013).

16-159 Statements used in Police disciplinary hearings are the subject of public interest immunity. This may prevent disclosure of information in civil or criminal proceedings. Documents generated under the Police complaints procedures under s.49 of the Police Act 1964, now Pt IV of the Police Act 1996, are similarly regarded. Grievance procedures available through an application before an industrial tribunal on the grounds of racial and sexual victimisation may be treated differently. The Police officer complained of sexual discrimination. In determining the case the Employment Appeal Tribunal distinguished grievance procedures for Police officers from disciplinary proceedings. While in the former, the applicant was entitled to receive documents, in the latter she was not.

16-160 The Police have a pivotal role in the personal freedoms of the citizen. The accountability of the Police becomes a significant factor in protecting citizens' rights. More effective accountability may be found, not through greater political control as advocated by some writers, but through effective complaints procedures, and a wider discussion of Police practice and culture. The UK's constitutional arrangements for the protection of civil liberties provides prohibitions and restrictions as well as freedoms and rights. Civil liberties are said to be facing a crisis; not readily cured by the enactment of a Bill of Rights, nor easily amenable to any particular legislative reform. In the life cycle of political and constitutional affairs it may be that the most important protection afforded to civil liberties is that the political culture and institutions are continually questioned as to their efficacy in providing the citizen with an adequate enjoyment of civil liberties.

Reform proposals and work in progress

16-161 The Government is considering major changes to the Police complaints system in England and Wales. A Home Office Review that there was an absence of public confidence as well as distrust from the Police and in the current system. The proposals include giving more authority to the directly elected PCC to determine how complaints are handled at a local level. There is also active consideration to changes in the PCC, though there is uncertainty the form such changes might take. The idea might be to use an ombudsman style body that would allow the PCC to undertake its own fully independent investigations and determine a wider range of possible remedies than are available at present.[132]

H: Summary and Conclusions

16-162 The Human Rights Act 1998 provides citizens with Convention rights as part of domestic law. The UK courts must also "as far as it is possible" give importance to the Convention

---

132 House of Commons Library, *Police Complaints Reform in 2016*, Briefing Paper, No.7493 (3 February 2016).

when attempting to interpret and make compatible both primary and secondary legislation. Inevitably this will lead to fundamental changes in the way rights are approached and, as will be outlined in Chs 17 and 18, in the development of judicial review. Human rights are significant in the way constitutional and administrative law is likely to develop in this country. The culture of public law has undergone change and that includes the variety of institutions and agencies that public law embraces with the far reaching potential of trickling rights into areas of private law; or at the very least suggesting that the boundaries that may separate public and private law are not robust enough to withstand the influence of rights. The courts will continue to have to grapple with the delicate balance between intervention and agency autonomy or ministerial policy. The intrinsic and enduring quality of the common law is its ability to adapt to change. Problem-focused and responsive to needs, the common law has customised solutions to fit new circumstances. Undoubtedly, human rights and their protection is under intense political scrutiny amidst questions about the UK's membership of the EU. The relationship between the ECHR and the UK courts is particularly open to political debate and scrutiny. There is considerable uncertainty as to the future of rights in the UK. The UK's decision to leave the EU will have considerable implications for human rights in the UK.

Further Reading

Tom Bingham, *The Rule of Law* (London: Penguin, 2011).
R. Blackburn and J. Polakiewicz, *Fundamental Rights In Europe* (Oxford: Oxford University Press, 2001).
K. Ewing, "A Theory of Democratic Adjudication: Towards a Representative, Accountable and Independent Judiciary" (2000) 38 *Alberta Law Review* 708.
K. Ewing and C. Gearty, *The Struggle for Civil Liberties* (Oxford: Oxford University Press, 2000).
H. Fenwick, *Civil Liberties and Human Rights*, 5th edn (London: Cavendish, 2015).
C. O'Cinneide, "Human Rights and the UK Constitution" in D. Oliver, J. Jowell and C. O'Cinneide (eds), *The Changing Constitution*, 8th edn (Oxford: Oxford University Press, 2015), pp.67–103.
Stephen Sedley, *Ashes and Sparks* (Cambridge: Cambridge University Press, 2011).
J. Waldron, "A Rights-Based Critique of Constitutional Rights" (1993) 13 *Oxford Journal of Legal Studies* 18.

17
Judicial Review

A: Introduction

The focus of this chapter is on judicial review,[1] where an aggrieved citizen may seek redress against a public authority through the courts. Judicial review may also arise where there are inter-governmental disputes. This is where, for example, disputes arise between different government departments or between local and central government. This list is not exhaustive as administrative decisions cover a variety of powers and duties that are susceptible to judicial review. The role of the courts must be understood in the context of the administrative process itself. This may set boundaries on the availability of judicial review. For example, judicial review does not normally extend to the policy and merits of decisions taken by elected Ministers. Rarely does judicial review consider the financial viability or even the effectiveness of policy making. Evidenced-based policy making is rarely tested in the courts. In such cases the conventional constitutional wisdom is that the political merits of decisions are accountable to Parliament and the political process, rather than the courts. Drawing the fine distinction between legal and political accountability is a difficult judgment that judges are called upon to make.[2]

17–001

We have already seen[3] the wide range of institutions and procedures for the resolution of grievances other than the courts. These alternatives range from informal mechanisms to tribunals, inquiries and ombudsmen. In this chapter the primary concern is the means the courts may use to hold the exercise of powers by authorities to account. Public authorities

17–002

---

1 House of Commons, *Judicial Review: A short Guide to Claims in the Administrative Court*, Research Paper, 06/44 (28 September 2006).
2 House of Commons, *Judicial Review: Government Reforms in the 2010–15 Parliament*, Briefing Paper, No.6616 (4 June 2015).
3 See Ch.15.

and bodies enjoy a vast array of statutory powers supplemented by a bewildering assortment of administrative rules such as licences, codes of practice, guidelines, regulations and contractual conditions. Public bodies are provided with a plethora of administrative powers. Their status and the context of the problem that they are called upon to address determines the allocation of powers and the systems of accountability that apply. The past two decades has witnessed an expansion in the variety and types of public bodies and agencies that have been created.

17-003
Traditionally, courts offer a form of external check on the legality of administrative powers. The courts may determine the nature of legal powers and how powers may be exercised. The focus is usually directed at resolving a dispute between the individual and the administration. In the UK, traditionally the litigant seeks a remedy in order to create rights. The Human Rights Act 1998 has added a dimension of rights and the litigant is able to rely on Convention rights to enforce remedies. The transition of a rights-based emphasis into the legal culture of the country[4] is ongoing and will require some "self-restraint" on the part of the judiciary.[5]

17-004
At first impression judicial review may appear limited, confined to a formal, technical and narrowly focused form of accountability. Too often this may appear negative in form, setting out what may or may not be done within the law. Thus judicial review may appear pragmatic and unsystematic. Normally courts offer *ex post facto* rather than *a priori* review, limited to remedies for wrongful actions rather than providing a prescription for the future conduct of administration. As a result, it is difficult through the case law developed by the courts to develop principles of good administration.

17-005
Undoubtedly, the impact of judicial rules over the long term may encourage a better understanding of keeping within the law.[6] There is also greater awareness today of the availability of judicial review, and the existence of pressure groups engaged in litigation has gained media and public attention. Judicial review has continued to expand during the 1990s. This is marked by a perceptible growth in judicial self-confidence in their role, and increased visibility in a number of headline cases[7] that have attracted public comment and media attention. The judges have exposed new areas of governmental power to judicial review.

17-006
Judicial review is not confined to the needs of the individual citizen. Government bodies may engage in judicial review as a means of establishing the basis of their relationship with the citizen, or with another public body. In the chapter on local government, it was noted how relations between local and central government were considered by the courts. Intra-governmental disputes between local and central government may be the basis of judicial review as much as the individual citizen seeking redress.

---

4   Lord Irvine, "The UK Supreme Court: The Modest Underworker of Strasbourg" *The Clifford Chance Lecture* (25 January 2012).
5   *R (Lichniak) v Secretary of State for the Home Department* [2001] EWHC Admin 294; [2002] Q.B. 296.
6   The pamphlet *The Judge Over Your Shoulder* has had a number of editions warning civil servants to act within the law.
7   On the work of pressure groups see, for example *R v Secretary of State for Foreign Affairs Ex p. World Development Movement Ltd* [1995] 1 W.L.R. 386; [1995] 1 All E.R. 611 Div Ct; and *R v Inspectorate of Pollution Ex p. Greenpeace Ltd (No.2)* [1994] 1 W.L.R. 570; [1994] 4 All E.R. 321 CA (Civ Div).

Judicial review must also be considered within the overall constitutional context of accountability of public bodies. There remains the broader question about the role of the courts in reviewing administrative action. Controlling administrative decisions is further complicated if the forms of political accountability appear weak and the role of the courts appears to be expanding. Are the courts able to respond to an expanded role in carrying out their functions? Such a role might lead to greater scrutiny of the judiciary and may bring judges more closely within the agenda of political debate.

B: The Classification of Administrative Decision-making

The starting point is to determine the exact nature of the administrative decision. Working out the classification of different types of decisions The making of administrative decisions affects the lives of many citizens. In the context of the body making a decision, it is necessary to consider the various ways decision-making may be classified. A discretion whether or not to make a decision or pursue a course of action may be classified as a power to make the appropriate decision, whereas an obligation to take action may be classified as a duty to act or make a decision. There is a working presumption that provided the action is not prohibited by law, there is freedom to do anything. Determining what falls within the law involves careful consideration of the nature of the body making the decision, the nature of the legal powers involved, and the question of whether the correct procedures have been applied. The answer to these questions generally involves statutory interpretation as many legal powers have a statutory basis. In previous chapters, we have noted how many governmental powers are derived from the prerogative which are reviewable by the courts. Contract or licences may also form the basis of legal powers. Disputes may involve civil action in tort or contract rather than judicial review. The courts may be confronted with a hybrid of powers, some statutory, contractual or prerogative.

Powers and duties provided by statute are open to interpretation by the courts. The courts' role in interpreting statutory enactments depends on resolving ambiguities through the interpretation of the meaning of words in the statute and giving account to parliamentary intention. There are differences in the style of drafting statutory provisions. The Victorian style was to encapsulate the common law position within a statutory framework. Modern statutory drafting may be more technical and detailed with narrowly defined powers and duties leaving little room for any creative statutory interpretation by the judges. There is also a judicial role in "filling in gaps", or seeking to give effect to Parliament's intentions through techniques of statutory interpretation. Government White Papers and official reports may be useful in construing parliamentary intention.

17-010 The House of Lords accepted in *Pepper (Inspector of Taxes) v Hart*[8] that the rule prohibiting courts from reading parliamentary material as an aid to statutory construction should be relaxed. Where the legislation was ambiguous or obscure or the literal meaning led to an absurdity then it might be helpful to examine the relevant parliamentary materials, subject to questions regarding parliamentary privilege. This might include statements by a Minister or other promoter of the Bill which led to the enactment of the legislation, and other material which might be necessary to understand such statements provided the statements were clear. However, the relaxation of the rule is confined to Ministers or promoters of the Bill which might exclude full parliamentary debates. Lord Browne-Wilkinson explained how the courts in construing statutory instruments had regard to the statements made by Ministers who may have initiated the debate on regulations.[9] Expanding this principle to primary legislation would enable the courts to understand the nature of the issues raised by the legislation.

17-011 Earlier cases had accepted that the courts might consider *Hansard* in ascertaining whether a statutory power had been used for an improper purpose. The House of Lords in *R v Secretary of State for the Home Department Ex p. Brind*[10] attached importance to what the Minister had said in Parliament as an aid to interpretation. Indeed, in general matters of statutory interpretation beyond the ministerial remit, the courts may be called upon to draw a line between political and legal material that has to be interpreted by a regulatory agency. In *R v Radio Authority Ex p. Bull*,[11] the Court of Appeal examined the decision of the Radio Authority to regard Amnesty International's campaign for human rights as mainly of a political nature. Under s.92(2)(a)(i) of the Broadcasting Act 1990, advertising of a political nature was banned from the radio. Interpretation of the political nature of human rights and the restrictions imposed by the 1990 Act required the Court of Appeal to make a careful value judgment of Amnesty's campaign, even though Lord Woolf accepted that such a campaign was "commendable".

17-012 The House of Lords relaxation of the rules regarding statutory interpretation is probably acceptance of practices that have been developing over the last 30 years. Does this make it more likely for the courts to question the merits of a decision? Traditionally, the courts have refrained from overtly considering the merits of the case and judicial review may fall short of substituting judicial decision-making for that of the decision-maker entrusted by Parliament. The limits of judicial review were acknowledged by Watkins LJ in *R v Secretary of State for Trade and Industry Ex p. Lonrho*[12] when he suggested that the courts' role would not take on the responsibility of making "executive or administrative decisions". The dangers of an excessively interventionist approach by the courts were pointed out by Lord Scarman in *Nottingham C v Secretary of State for the Environment*[13]:

---

8   [1993] A.C. 593; [1993] 1 All E.R. 42 HL.
9   *Pickstone v Freemans Plc* [1989] A.C. 66; [1988] 2 All E.R. 803 HL.
10 [1991] 1 A.C. 696; [1991] 2 W.L.R. 588 HL.
11 *The Times Law Reports*, 21 January 1997.
12 [1989] 1 W.L.R. 525; [1989] 2 All E.R. 609 HL.
13 [1986] A.C. 240; [1986] 2 W.L.R. 1 HL at [250]–[251].

> "Judicial review is a great weapon in the hands of the judges; but the judges must observe the constitutional limits set by our parliamentary system upon the exercise of this beneficent power."

The courts in the UK cannot review the legality of a UK Act of Parliament in matters of strictly domestic law that does not involve matters of European Community law. Section 2 of the Human Rights Act 1998 provides the power for courts when considering cases that raise issues of interpretation of a Convention right, to take into account judgments, decisions or advisory opinions of the European Court of Human Rights. They are not bound by the decisions but they must interpret them. Legislation may not be struck down by the UK's courts for incompatibility with Convention rights. The most the courts may do is to make a declaration of incompatibility under s.4(2) of the Act.

Statutory appeals

The citizen may have available a right of appeal. Appeals provide the courts with an opportunity to rule on the legality of particular decisions and are as important as judicial review when considering the role of the courts and the procedures open to the citizen. Unlike judicial review which developed from common law origins, appeals are statutory in origin. The statutory formulation includes express provision usually setting out the grounds for appeal and the appellate jurisdiction of the courts. It is difficult to generalise any principles involved in appeals provided by statute. Parliamentary developments in creating appeals have been on a case by case basis depending on the nature of the issues expected to be raised on appeal. The Franks Committee noted[14] "the desirability of some form of appeal", but there is no universal principle setting out a minimum standard of when an appeal should be provided, nor the scope of an appeal once conferred by statute.

The existence of an appeal procedure raises the question of whether, under an appeal procedure, the legality of action may be challenged. The Law Commission has noted that many judicial review applications were initiated as desperate and ill-disguised attempts to appeal against the decision in question. Conversely, appeals may be widely interpreted to include matters that could be reviewed. Occasionally the courts have accepted a wider remit to the appeal system even where it may overlap with the application for judicial review. An appeal against the decision of the district auditor under the Local Government Finance Act 1982 raised questions of the legality and fairness of the auditor's decision. Such matters, the Court of Appeal acknowledged, could also be the subject of an application for judicial review. In *Lloyd v McMahon*,[15] the Court of Appeal was content to allow the appeal in that instance, to include issues of the legality of the auditor's decision. In the House of Lords, Lord Bridge accepted the

---

14 Cmnd.218 (1957).
15 [1987] A.C. 625; [1987] 2 W.L.R. 821 HL.

overlapping jurisdiction of an application for judicial review and appeals under the 1982 Act, but preferred the wider grounds of an appeal to raise the legality of the auditor's report.

17-016

In *Foster v Chief Adjudication Officer*,[16] the House of Lords allowed a social security claimant an appeal to a tribunal when a benefit claim was rejected but based on consideration of whether the regulations were ultra vires. The Commissioners were given jurisdiction to consider the question of vires, thus indicating a trend in favour of plaintiffs raising, through private law claims in ordinary civil proceedings, issues of legality.

17-017

Appeals are not normally provided against discretionary decisions involving Ministers or policy matters involving the allocation of resources or the implementation of Cabinet decisions. The absence of an appeal structure may be due to the political nature of the policy where the appropriate forum is in Parliament. However, this may not be a satisfactory reason to cover all cases where there is no appeal. In Ch.15, criticisms made by the Council on Tribunals of the lack of a proper appeals system following the replacement of supplementary benefit payments by payments from the social fund made by social fund officers under the Social Security Act 1986, were noted. The absence of an appeal procedure was perceived as creating unfairness. The Council on Tribunals view judicial review as an inappropriate means of appeal from tribunal decisions. For example, instead of judicial review of immigration cases the Council on Tribunals (now abolished) favoured the introduction of an appeal on a point of law from the Immigration Appeal Tribunal, under the Asylum and Immigration Appeals Act 1993 as amended by the Asylum and Immigration Act 1996 and the Immigration and Asylum Act 1999.

17-018

Statutory appeals may be used as an alternative to an application for judicial review which is subject to a three-month time limit whereas some appeals are restricted to six weeks. For example, the Acquisition of Land Act 1981 forbids any challenge to a compulsory purchase order other than under its s.23 appeal procedure to the High Court on matters of law.

17-019

Appeals may consist of an appeal on questions of fact or on the merits of a decision. Usually the right of appeal is confined to "persons aggrieved". The grounds of appeal may vary according to the content of the statute. Lack of evidence and the failure to give adequate reasons, may amount to an error of law which may be considered on appeal. A decision may be reversed on appeal to the courts on a point of law. The leading case of *Edwards v Bairstow*[17] concluded that a decision of the Inland Revenue Commissioners might be reversed by the courts where the facts did not justify the inference or conclusion of the Commissioners. In such instances the courts are willing to consider issues of fact giving rise to questions of law when no reasonable interpretation would support the finding of facts disputed in an appeal.

17-020

There is, at present, no satisfactory arrangement for standardising the grounds for an appeal, the availability of an appeal or the way appeals are considered by the courts. Woolf LJ, as he then was, has suggested[18] that a more coherent appeals system might replace the present random and chaotic system.

---

16   [1993] A.C. 754; [1993] 1 All E.R. 705 HL.
17   [1956] A.C. 14; [1955] 3 W.L.R. 410 HL.
18   H. Woolf, "A Hotchpotch of Appeals—The Need for a Blender" (1988) 7 *Civil Justice Quarterly* 44.

The application for judicial review: public and private Law

17-021 The availability of judicial review allows a decision or action to be challenged in the courts on the basis of remedies available in public law. This means that the grounds for challenge depend on rules developed by the courts as grounds for review in public law. The distinction between public law and private law becomes important when considering the procedures known as the application for judicial review. In Ch.6, judicial review was examined in outline. Recent changes to the procedures for the application for judicial review since 2000, include CPR Pt 54 *Judicial Review* and various practice directions and protocols.[19] This system replaced Order 53, but the terminology of Order 53 is relevant in the cases decided before 2000. The Administrative Court, formerly the Divisional Court of the Queen's Bench Division, has the jurisdiction to hear applications for judicial review. The Crown Office is responsible for the administration of applications for judicial review. There are also changes to the terminology used. Applicants for judicial review are now referred to as claimants and the system of remedies to be discussed in Ch.18 has been renamed; certiorari is a quashing order, prohibition, a prohibiting order and mandamus, a mandatory order.

17-022 Since 2013 there are over 50 judges nominated to sit in the Administrative Court. Additional resources are available from the use of Deputy High Court Judges.

The average time for an application for permission to apply for judicial review was eight weeks and the average time waiting for a substantive determination was 20 weeks (from lodging to decision). In expedited cases hearings were held within a few weeks. There is a procedure for urgent cases to be dealt with set out in the practice statement.[20] In keeping with the approach to civil justice, there is a *Pre-Action Protocol*[21] requiring that after 4 March 2002 all claims for judicial review must fall under the arrangements in the *Protocol*. The *Protocol* sets out a code of good practice that should be followed when making a claim for judicial review. The Protocol has now been subsumed into the case management system for civil cases and this includes arrangements for Alternative Dispute Resolution (ADR). It is possible, though not always desirable for litigants in person to make an application for judicial review. Increasingly this is happening as the availability of legal aid for judicial review has been reduced.

17-023 It is necessary to consider in greater detail, how the courts have developed an exclusive jurisdiction for the application of judicial review for public law matters. So, for example, after some uncertainty it is clear that decisions by the Jockey Club, a non-governmental body are not capable of being challenged through judicial review.[22] This is central to an understanding of the position of the litigant who wishes to obtain remedies in public law. The claim for exclusivity

---

19 *Practice Statement (Admin Ct: Administration of Justice)* [2002] 1 W.L.R. 810; [2002] 1 All E.R. 633 QBD.
20 [2002] 1 W.L.R. 810 at [635].
21 [2002] All E.R (D) Feb.
22 *R (Mullins) v Appeal Board of the Jockey Club (No.1)* [2005] EWHC 2197 (Admin); [2006] L.L.R. 151. Details of the case law are set out in *R v Disciplinary Committee of the Jockey Club Ex p. Aga Khan* [1993] 1 W.L.R. 909; [1993] 2 All E.R. 853 CA (Civ Div).

is partly justified by the claim that it is premised on the specialism of the Administrative Court. Feldman astutely points out that the growing case load over the past few years has resulted in a lessening of the specialist nature of the Administrative Court:

> "The need to cope with a growing caseload means that most judges hearing cases in the Administrative Court are no longer specialists, the Administrative Court now deals with a good number of tort claims, particularly in relation to cases concerning detention of prisoners, immigration detainees and people affected by the military action in Iraq and Afghanistan, so the procedures are having to be adapted in order to do justice between the parties."[23]

17-024 The most significant sign of judicial self-confidence at work, however, is the way procedural reforms have modernised judicial review with implications for the substantive law as well as the long standing nature of the common law tradition of "judge-made law". As will be demonstrated, most of the reforms are the work of judges operating within the shadow of Parliament with the tacit understanding that they are to be trusted in their creative role. The current procedures for application for judicial review can be traced back to the work of the Law Commission. In 1969, the government rejected proposals from the Law Commission[24] for a Royal Commission on administrative law, agreeing only to a study of the existing law of remedies for the judicial control of administrative action. As a result, the opportunity was lost to conduct a review of the entire system of administrative law. The Law Commission made recommendations on the law of remedies,[25] and it was left to the Rules Committee of the Supreme Court to implement modest proposals for reforms in the application for judicial review, under Order 53 of the Rules of the Supreme Court. This reform received statutory modification in s.31 of the Supreme Court Act 1981. The Supreme Court Act 1981 has been renamed as the Senior Courts Act 1981.

17-025 Section 31 of the Senior Courts Act 1981 and Order 53 streamlined the procedures for obtaining remedies. The procedure has been streamlined under the Pre-Action Protocol arrangements under the Civil Procedure Rules, consistent with the Woolf reforms on civil justice. There is a two-stage process and the claim begins with filing documents such as official letters or replies. There is the hope that maybe some informal settlement might be reached that would avoid litigation. The defendant has up to 21 days to respond and set out whether or not they contest the claim. Notice is also given to third parties. The granting of permission is decided by a single judge on the papers, usually without a hearing. It is possible for a short hearing to be held in the circumstances of the case. Hearings are held in the case of interim

---

23 D. Feldman, "The distinctiveness of public law" in M. Elliott and D. Feldman (eds), *Public Law* (Cambridge: Cambridge University Press, 2015), pp.17–36.
24 The Law Commission was established by statute in 1965 to review the law and recommend codification. See Cmnd.4059 (1969).
25 Law Commission Report, No.73 (1976).

relief. Permission may be granted with conditions attached. If refused or granted there is an application process for a hearing to renew the application. If withheld, then there is the possibility of an appeal to the Court of Appeal. This process is used as a "filter", a means of excluding cases. Claims for judicial review have to be made "promptly" and this requirement is also linked to the filter and acts as a means of preventing the courts from being flooded out with applications.

17-026

The requirement of taking a judicial review "promptly" has been modified by s.84(2) of the Criminal Justice and Courts Act 2015 amends s.31 (3C–3F) of the Senior Courts Act 1981 by inserting a new section. Permission must be refused if it appears to the High Court to be highly likely that the outcome for the applicant would not have been substantially different. The "highly likely" to succeed test is acceptable to be applied if it is appropriate to do so for reasons of exceptional public interest. Interpretation of this new requirement will be important in terms of the future development of "meritorious" applications for judicial review.

17-027

Promptness is predicated on the assumption that the case can be prepared and organised. The court may extend time if there is a good reason to do so and in the case of urgent matters adjustments may be made. The requirement of promptness is analysed in the *Uniplex* case, a decision of the European Court of Justice. In *Uniplex (UK) Ltd v NHS Business Services*,[26] the Court considered the principles of certainty and the requirements of access to justice. This is an important question of setting the standards of justice and access to the courts linked to upholding the rule of law. In EU matters the Court was clear that the question of promptness should not be applied in claims asserting EU law involving rights. Adapting human rights jurisprudence into EU law is not always easy and is very much a work in progress that will require to be worked out on a case by case basis.

17-028

The question of whether or not the test of promptness is compatible with art.6 was upheld by the Strasbourg Court of Human Rights.[27] In *Pham v Secretary of State for the Home Department*,[28] the UK Supreme Court considered an asylum case involving making an order depriving an individual of his British citizenship under s.40(2) of the British Nationality Act 1981. The appeal against the Special Immigration Tribunal involved interpreting EU law as well as the human rights of the citizen. Here there was a difference in the test of proportionality under EU law and the law relating to human rights. The Supreme Court were reluctant to resolve any difference between EU law and human rights. The judges were reluctant to take the issue of EU law as central to the case. Lord Sumption considered that it was potentially unfair to have different standards applied to two aspects of the application, Member State withdrawal of citizenship involving EU law and the withdrawal of British citizenship under UK law. Under s.31(6) of the Senior Courts Act 1981, the court may refuse an application for may refuse relief on the grounds that "such relief is likely to cause substantial hardship or prejudice the rights of, any person or would be detrimental to good administration". The courts have a wide discretion as to the range of relief that may be given. An applicant is able to seek any one or more of

---

26 (C-406/08) EU:C:2010:45; [2010] C.M.L.R. 47.
27 *R (Berky) v Newport City Council* [2012] EWCA Civ 38; [2012] 4 Costs L.R. 633.
28 *Pham v Secretary of State for the Home Department* [2015] UKSC 19; [2015] 1 W.L.R. 1591.

five remedies: mandamus; certiorari; prohibition; declaration; or injunction. At the same time, interlocutory procedures such as discovery and interrogatories are theoretically available. In addition, the court may award damages if claimed by the applicant and if they could have been awarded in an action at the same time. The inclusion of declaration and injunction alongside the prerogative orders of mandamus, certiorari and prohibition was innovatory. For the first time traditionally private law remedies, that is remedies also available by ordinary writ, might be obtained alongside the traditional public law remedies of the prerogative orders of mandamus, certiorari and prohibition, under a single application for judicial review. The introduction of a uniform system made it easier to apply for judicial review. There are about 50 judges assigned to the Administrative Court.

17-029 The "exclusive nature of the application for judicial review" was expressed by Lord Diplock in the House of Lords in *O'Reilly v Mackman*.[29] Lord Diplock made the distinction between public and private law and considered that it was an abuse of the process of the court to use an ordinary action for a public law matter when it should have been taken under the application for judicial review. The House of Lords considered the actions brought by writ in the case of four plaintiffs who were prisoners in Hull Prison charged with various disciplinary offences arising out of riots in December 1976 and in 1979. The plaintiff claimed that the Board of Visitors, in the exercise of their disciplinary functions, had breached the rules of natural justice. Lord Diplock held that the prisoners' challenge to the legality of the Board's decisions could not be made by ordinary writ but should have been made through the application for judicial review under Order 53, amended by s.31 of the Supreme Court Act 1981, now CPR Pt 54.

17-030 The reasoning in the case rested on the assumption that the prisoners' legitimate expectation of the rules of natural justice rested in public law, not private law. Lord Diplock established a general rule that an applicant seeking to establish rights recognised in public law was required to make use of the Order 53 procedure. His reasoning for this rule rested on a number of assumptions. First, Order 53 contains certain safeguards, such as the requirement of standing, the use of affidavits at the first stage in the application, and the time limit of three months which sets a restriction on the period. These safeguards permit a legal challenge to be mounted. Secondly, Order 53 provides a speedy resolution of the issues. In theory, these procedures offer, in the public interest, safeguards to public bodies and third parties.

17-031 The question of distinguishing between public and private law came to be considered in a number of cases following *O'Reilly v Mackman*. In *Cocks v Thanet*,[30] the House of Lords considered whether a declaration and injunction sought by the plaintiff, Cocks, in the county court, claiming that a local authority had breached its duty under the Housing (Homeless Persons) Act 1977, should have been brought under the Order 53 procedure for judicial review. The House of Lords, in a decision given on the same day as *O'Reilly v Mackman*, concluded that the issues raised by the plaintiff were public law matters. The local authority had a duty to inquire if the plaintiff might be made homeless and whether he was legally entitled to temporary or permanent accommodation. Such public law rights needed to be determined before any private

---

29 [1983] 2 A.C. 237; [1982] 3 W.L.R. 1096 HL.
30 [1983] 2 A.C. 286; [1982] 3 W.L.R. 1121 HL.

rights such as the plaintiff may have could be established. Ironically, once the local authority established that the plaintiff was entitled to be housed, then private law rights existed. The court appeared to classify the decision-making function of the local authority as a public law matter when concerned with the question of whether the criteria in the 1977 Act were satisfied. Once the criteria were satisfied by the applicant and the local authority acted in its executive capacity in considering the rights of the applicant, this gave rise to an action in private law.

In *Davy v Spelthorne BC*,[31] the plaintiff owned premises used to make pre-cast concrete. The plaintiff entered an agreement with the local planning authority not to appeal to the Secretary of State against an enforcement notice in respect of the use of the premises on condition that the authority would not seek to enforce the notice for three years. Two years after the notice was served and the time for an appeal had lapsed, the plaintiff brought an action in the Chancery division, claiming that the agreement was ultra vires, and also claiming damages in respect of negligent advice given to him by the local authority. The local authority applied to strike out the proceedings on the basis of the rule in *O'Reilly v Mackman*. The Court of Appeal followed *O'Reilly v Mackman* and struck out the plaintiff's claim for an injunction restraining the local authority from implementing the enforcement notice and an order that the enforcement notice should be set aside. However, the claim in damages could stand as a private law matter as it was based on a common law duty of care. The local authority appealed to the House of Lords on the basis that the claim for damages should also be struck out.

The argument that the claim for damages was linked to the exercise of a statutory duty, and therefore a public law matter, was considered alongside the opposing argument that the plaintiff's common law rights had been infringed. The House of Lords decided that no public law issues were involved in the plaintiff's claim for damages for negligence. In reaching the decision in *Davy*, the House of Lords distinguished the decision in *Cocks*. In *Cocks*, the challenge depended on public law rights under the 1977 Act being declared before any private law rights existed. In *Davy*, public law rights were not being exercised by the plaintiff, although the failure of the local authority to enforce the notice may have been a breach of its discretion. The plaintiff was claiming damages for negligent advice on the part of the local authority that resulted in his losing the opportunity to appeal the enforcement order. Thus, because the plaintiff did not seek to impugn the enforcement order it did not give rise to public law rights, and it was not an abuse of process to proceed in negligence against the local authority.

Does the approach of the House of Lords in *Davy* show some relaxation of the rule in *O'Reilly v Mackman*? The most difficult analyses relate to cases raising a combination of public and private law issues. The decision in *Davy* shows the reluctance of the courts to interfere with the award of damages in an action in negligence by imposing Order 53 procedures on ordinary litigation. A similar approach appears evident in *Roy v Kensington and Chelsea and Westminster Family Practitioner Committee*.[32] In *Roy*, a general medical practitioner engaged in private consultancy work in addition to his National Health duties was considered by the Family Practitioner Committee to have spent too little time on his National Health duties, and his

---
31   [1984] A.C. 262; [1983] 3 W.L.R. 742 HL.
32   [1992] 1 A.C. 624; [1992] 1 All E.R. 705 HL.

remuneration was accordingly reduced by 20 per cent. Roy brought an action against the decision of the Committee, and the Committee applied to strike the action out because it breached the exclusivity rule in *O'Reilly v Mackman*. The House of Lords refused to strike out the claim. Lord Bridge explained that the case involved the litigant asserting his rights in private law. Lord Lowry agreed but considered that it was possible to distinguish two different approaches in the interpretation of *O'Reilly v Mackman*:

> "The 'broad approach' was that the 'rule in *O'Reilly v Mackman*' did not apply generally against bringing actions to vindicate private rights in all circumstances in which those actions involved a challenge to a public law act or decision, but that it merely required the aggrieved person to proceed by judicial review only when private law rights were not at stake. The 'narrow approach' assumed that the rule applied generally to all proceedings in which public law acts or decisions were challenged, subject to some exceptions when private law rights were involved."

17–035 Choosing between these approaches is not always possible, and Lord Lowry acknowledged that it might be preferable for the matters to be heard rather than conduct an analysis over procedure.

17–036 Difficulty in choosing how to apply the rule in *O'Reilly v Mackman* arises because in many cases litigants have "a bundle of rights".[33] In *Roy* these included "his private law rights against the committee, arising from the statute and regulations and including the very important private law right to be paid for the work he has done".[34] Since *O'Reilly v Mackman*, the courts have developed a more flexible approach.

17–037 A welcome signal that the House of Lords is prepared to adopt a flexible approach to *O'Reilly* may be found in *Mercury Communications Ltd v Director General of Telecommunications*.[35] Lord Slynn delivered the unanimous view of the House. The case arose, not through Order 53 procedures, but in the Queen's Bench Division (Commercial Court) by originating summons seeking a declaration. The issue arose out of a licensing dispute between Mercury and British Telecommunications and the Director General of Telecommunications under the Telecommunications Act 1984. Both the respondents, Mercury and British Telecommunications, claimed that the Director General had misconstrued the licence and therefore raised matters of public law which should not properly fall under the originating summons procedure but instead should be taken under Order 53. The Director General sought to enforce the licence under the originating summons as raising enforceable licence matters that came within the jurisdiction of the summons. The question that required consideration was whether a public law matter was involved; if this was the case, then the matter would have to be taken under

---

33   [1992] 1 A.C. 624 at [725H].
34   [1992] 1 A.C. 624.
35   [1996] 1 W.L.R. 48; [1996] 1 All E.R. 575 HL.

Order 53 through new proceedings for judicial review. The difficulty with this question is the lack of a clear definition or distinction between public law and private law in English law.

A further difficulty in deciding between private and public law arises from some general exceptions to the rule established in *O'Reilly v Mackman*. Lord Diplock, while accepting that the application of the rule was to be determined case by case, envisaged two possible exceptions. First, where the parties agreed to use the ordinary writ procedure or summons to obtain a declaration or injunction, they might waive the rule in *O'Reilly v Mackman* and proceed with their case. Second, an exception to *O'Reilly v Mackman* might arise where the challenge is collateral, that is, when an issue of public law arises in the course of some other claim involving private law.

The exact nature of the collateral exception has been considered in a number of subsequent decisions. In *Wandsworth LBC v Winder*,[36] Wandsworth Borough Council was the landlord of a flat occupied by Winder. Winder had a contractual right to occupy the flat on standard conditions, including the condition that the rent would be paid. The local authority, using its statutory powers under the Housing Act 1957, increased the rent charged. Winder refused to pay the whole increase but continued to pay rent and only such increase as appeared reasonable to him. The local authority took proceedings in the county court for arrears of rent. The question of a collateral issue arose when Winder sought to defend his refusal to pay the rent increases by arguing that the increases were ultra vires and void. He counterclaimed for a declaration that the only rent payable was the old rent. In the House of Lords, the authority argued that Winder's counter-claim should only be by way of judicial review. In fact, Winder had applied for judicial review, but it had been refused because he was outside the time limit of three months. Did Winder's counter-claim come within the collateral exception to the rule in *O'Reilly v Mackman*? Lord Fraser in the House of Lords distinguished *Cocks* and *O'Reilly v Mackman*. *Winder* was distinctive from both cases and was based on private law rights, based on contract. Winder had not initiated litigation, but merely sought to defend the legal action taken against him. Lord Fraser considered that Winder's case did not fall into Lord Diplock's exception of a collateral matter to the rule in *O'Reilly v Mackman*. The House of Lords found in Winder's favour and allowed the *ultra vires* question to be considered even though it was not under the Order 53 procedure. In the event, Winder's defence later proved unsuccessful.

In a number of cases the courts have sought to distinguish *Winder*, adopting a case by case approach in settling on whether to allow ordinary civil actions to raise matters of public law. In delineating between public and private law for the purposes of the rule in *O'Reilly v Mackman*, clear principles are hard to determine. The nature of the body must be considered alongside the activities the body performs.

O'Reilly v Mackman has provided a new direction for administrative law, but the distinction between public and private law, and the question of whether a claim should be brought by ordinary action or by way of judicial review, causes litigants to bear enormous costs, as noted by Lord Saville in *British Steel v HM Commissioners of Customs and Excise*:

---

36   [1985] A.C. 461; [1984] 3 W.L.R. 1254 HL.

> "[T]he cost of this litigation, borne privately or through taxation, must be immense, with often the lawyers the only people to gain. Such litigation brings the law and our legal system into disrepute; and to my mind correctly so. It reinforces the view held by the ordinary person that the law and our legal system are slow, expensive and unsatisfactory. In this day and age it is surely possible to devise procedures which avoid this form of satellite litigation, while safeguarding both the private rights of individuals and companies and the position and responsibilities of public authorities."[37]

17-042 The public/private distinction[38] is an example of the problem of incremental development case by case. In practical terms there are limits to the judicial power to self-regulate this area of law. No satisfactory solution will be forthcoming until the legislature defines the concept of public law and codifies administrative law as a whole.[39] In fact, the nature of administrative law invites a broader question as to who should ultimately decide matters of public policy—politicians or lawyers? The demarcation between the merits of the decision, not generally reviewable by the courts, and the legality of the decision itself poses one of the most difficult issues for the courts.

17-043 What guidance may be provided in delineating public from private? The courts have adopted a case by case approach in settling on whether to allow ordinary civil actions to raise matters of public law. In delineating between public and private law for the purposes of the rule in *O'Reilly v Mackman*, clear principles are hard to determine. The nature of the body must be considered alongside the activities the body performs. In the case of Walsh, who was employed by the East Berkshire Health Authority, even though the regulations of his employment were statutory, he was refused leave to challenge his dismissal through judicial review. The Court of Appeal in *R v East Berkshire Health Authority Ex p. Walsh*[40] decided that mere employment by a public authority does not make the matter one of public law and therefore justiciable. Similarly, if the decision-maker is mistakenly bound by a policy or previous practice may likewise be regarded as justiciable. This permits a court to consider if the case is suitable or not or where it might be inconvenient or inappropriate for judicial review to apply. It is noticeable, however that there are areas where the courts seem unwilling to offer review. In *Ex p. Puhlofer*,[41] the House of Lords restricted access to judicial review to cases under the Housing (Homeless Persons) Act 1977. Similarly, in *Ex p. Swati*[42] the discretion to refuse leave

---

37   [1997] 2 All E.R. 366 CA (Civ Div) at [379].
38   See *Boddington v British Transport Police* [1999] 2 A.C. 143; [1998] 2 W.L.R. 639 HL allowing the legality of the criminal law to be considered in criminal proceedings.
39   See *Steed v Secretary of State for the Home Department* [2000] 1 W.L.R. 1169; [2000] 3 All E.R. 226 HL.
40   [1985] Q.B. 152; [1984] 3 W.L.R. 818 CA (Civ Div). Also see *R v Lord Chancellors Dept. Ex p. Nangle* [1992] 1 All E.R. 897; [1991] I.C.R. 743 QBD.
41   [1986] A.C. 484; [1986] 2 W.L.R. 259 HL; *Ex p. Benwell* [1985] Q.B. 554. See *Ex p. Dew* [1987] 1 W.L.R. 881; [1987] 2 All E.R. 1049 QBD.
42   [1986] 1 W.L.R. 477; [1986] 1 All E.R. 717 CA (Civ Div).

is operated when there are alternative remedies. In immigration cases there is adjudication by the Immigration Appeal Tribunal and appeal to the courts from that Tribunal under the Asylum and Immigration Appeals Act 1993.

In *Doyle v Northumbria Probation Committee*,[43] which posed the question of raising matters of public law as a defence in a civil action by writ, the facts concerned probation officers who took action for breach of contract against their employers, a probation authority, a body corporate with statutory powers. The dispute raised matters of contract and the matter came to court within the time limit set for an action in contract, namely six years. The defence argued that the case raised a fundamental question about the legal powers of the probation authority that should have been raised by judicial review. Henry J considered that the plaintiff's claim was entirely based on private law rights and to decide otherwise left the plaintiffs out of time for judicial review. He concluded that there were three operating principles from the legal authorities.[44] First, for cases which fall within the *O'Reilly v Mackman* rule, the courts must "be astute" to see that there is no evasion of the protections afforded by Order 53 in cases which are unmeritorious. Secondly, there is no "overriding objection" to public law issues being litigated in writ actions. Thirdly, that in principle, Order 53 should not be used for the litigation of private law claims. A further qualification important to note is that where the parties agree, this will permit an ordinary action to raise matters of public law.

Drawing together some conclusions from the case law is difficult. Some examples serve to show how judicial decision-making is influenced very much on the facts of each case, the nature of the dispute involved and the application of the three operating principles noted by Henry J, in the *Doyle* case. In *Gillick*[45] an ordinary action challenging the health authority's guidance to medical practitioners on contraceptive advice was permitted to proceed even though an application for judicial review was possible. In *Ex p. Noble*[46] a deputy police surgeon sought to challenge his dismissal by way of judicial review and this was dismissed on the grounds that a private action was more appropriate. Similarly this line of reasoning was applied in *McLaren v Home Office*[47] that an ordinary writ was appropriate for a declaration of a prison officer's employment conditions.

The exact nature of the distinction between public and private law is problematic and leaves the need for law reform to be greater than perhaps in 1969 when a Royal Commission was proposed but rejected. However, in 1988 an unofficial Royal Commission namely the Justice-All Souls Review Committee[48] recommended reform of the rule in *O'Reilly v Mackman* and that the House of Lords should reconsider their decision. The report criticised the imprecision of the term "public law" and suggested that Parliament might wish to consider the

---

43 [1991] 1 W.L.R. 1340; [1991] 4 All E.R. 294 QBD.
44 See the discussion in *Gillick v West Norfolk and Wisbech AHA* [1986] A.C. 112; [1985] 3 W.L.R. 830 HL.
45 [1986] A.C. 112.
46 *R v Derbyshire C Ex p. Noble* [1990] I.C.R. 808; [1990] I.R.L.R. 332 CA (Civ Div).
47 [1990] I.C.R. 824; [1990] I.R.L.R. 338 CA (Civ Div).
48 Justice Report, *Administrative Justice: Some Necessary Reforms* (Oxford: Oxford University Press, 1988).

circumstances where an applicant might be obliged to use Order 53 and be barred from proceeding by action or originating summons.

17–047
As matters stand the procedural rules under Order 53 are to be used by litigants who think that they have mainly a public law matter. If it later appears that this was the wrong procedure then Order 53, r.9(5) permits matters to continue as if the procedure had been by ordinary writ. This is only permitted if the applicant has sought an injunction, declaration or damages. However, a litigant who commences an ordinary writ and then raises public law matters may only do so if the court exercises a discretion to proceed as if the issue had been raised by Order 53. That discretion is rarely exercised and would only be exercised if it would not be unfair to the respondent and where the court would be prepared to waive the safeguards included in the Order 53 procedure.

17–048
It may be concluded that on the basis of procedural rules the distinction between public and private law is important to litigants. The signs are that the courts are beginning to recognise the problems in making such a distinction in cases, as in *Roy*, where the litigant has a "parcel of rights". Careful consideration is required of the question as to whether any great disadvantage seems to come from allowing the ordinary writ procedure to raise some matters of public law. However, great uncertainty surrounds the principles as to when the courts regard such cases as acceptable. One possible way forward is to consider clarifying the protections afforded under Order 53 to public bodies and consider extending these to the ordinary writ procedure.

17–049
Lord Woolf, writing extra-judicially in 1999, expressed the optimism that technical difficulties relating to the choice of the wrong procedure will be a problem of the past.[49] Lord Steyn in *Boddington v British Transport Police*[50] reiterated the view that the primary focus of *O'Reilly v Mackman*

> "is situations in which an individual's sole aim was to challenge a public law act or decision. It does not apply in a civil case when an individual seeks to establish private law rights which cannot be determined without an examination of the validity of a public law decision. Nor does it apply where a defendant in a civil case simply seeks to defend himself by questioning the validity of a public law decision."

17–050
While the courts have shown some consistency in their flexible interpretation of the exclusivity principle, it should not be assumed that the law is straightforward. A clear case of a private law claim should be begun promptly by the private law procedure. Similarly, a case involving public law should be begun by judicial review and a borderline or unclear case should sensibly begin with the judicial review claim.

---

49 Lord Woolf, "Judicial Review—The Tensions between the Executive and the Judiciary" (1998) 114 *L.Q.R.* 579.
50 [1999] 2 A.C. 143; [1998] 2 W.L.R. 639 HL at [172G]–[172H].

Judicial review: overall policy and trends

17–051

The austerity crisis has drawn attention to the amount of public money used to support the system of judicial review. This is highly politicised and raises questions of how much public money should be spent as well as the availability of judicial review. In December 2012, the Coalition Government launched a consultation process on reform of judicial review that continued until 24 January 2013, *Judicial Review: proposals for reform*. This was followed by an additional consultation from September 2013 until November 2013 *Judicial Review: Proposals for Further Reform*.

17–052

There are mixed motives behind the consultations and the Coalition Government's desire for reform. At one level it is to save money and prevent useless cases from being taken by filtering out through the procedures for review. The aim is to reduce time, money and simplify procedures including shorter time limits to take cases, restrictions on the right to an oral renewal of an application where a judge has refused permission in a prior judicial process or where the claim is judged to be unmeritorious. There are proposals to limit the right to appeal to the Court of Appeal and changes in the rules relating to costs and also standing rules to prevent the taxpayer having to pay for unmeritorious cases.

17–053

The number of judicial review applications varies in any one year but the average[51] is around 12,000 applications lodged with the Administrative Court. The bulk of applications in 2013 are related to immigration and asylum cases. Only a small number of application, roughly 1,500 cases are granted permission to proceed to a full hearing. Many cases are not proceeded with and nearly 50 per cent of cases were refused permission meaning that the judge was not convinced that there was an arguable case. Settlements are common and may represent a potential for changing the way in which judicial review is undertaken. There are also suggestions that some form of ADR might be the best way forward. This is a largely unchartered area but ADR would offer a way to resolve disputes in a highly cost effective way. The Pre-Action Protocol for judicial review applications includes the instruction that the parties should consider ADR as it may offer a more suitable procedure than proceeding to litigation. The number of judicial review applications has fallen in the last two years due to reductions in legal aid.

17–054

Judicial review claims that are proceeded with do not inevitably lead to the Government losing their case. Only a small number are cases where the courts find against the government. This may not ease concern that judicial review is a "threat" to the smooth working of government or may be used by opponents of the government to cause embarrassment and delays in implementing policies. Pressure groups may justify the use of judicial review as a means to test the legality of government decisions and raise public awareness. An important part of judicial review is to check on the legality of the government of the day as a means of upholding the rule of law.

Steps taken to reduce the workload of the Administrative Courts are ongoing. The

---

51   See House of Commons Library, *Judicial Review: Government reforms*, SN/HA/6616 (14 February 2013). Also see the Judicial Statistics regularly published by the Ministry of Justice and the courts on a monthly basis. These are then revised on an annual basis. See Ministry of Justice, *Revision of Judicial Review Figures* (2013).

bulk of cases involving immigration judicial review have been moved to the Upper Tribunal (Immigration and Asylum) Chamber under s.23 of the Crime and Courts Act 2013. This is partly in response to delays in having cases heard but also the increase in the work load that made the Administrative Court less efficient than it should have been.

17–055 In planning cases the Government reduced the time limit from three months to six weeks and in procurement cases to 30 days. In cases without any merit the right to an oral hearing was removed and the fees were increased to £215 for oral renewals. These changes attracted criticism that they would reduce the accessibility of judicial review. The Government has gone further and decided to create within the High Court a specialist Planning Court to deal with judicial review and statutory appeals relating to nationally Significant Infrastructure Projects and other planning matters.

17–056 The perception that judicial review in planning matters has created "unacceptable delays" in the case of key infrastructure developments and housing projects. We have already seen that the requirement of taking a judicial review "promptly" has been modified by s.84(2) of the Criminal Justice and Courts Act 2015 amends s.31 (3C–3F) of the Senior Courts Act 1981 by inserting a new section. Permission must be refused if it appears to the High Court to be highly likely that the outcome for the applicant would not have been substantially different. The "highly likely" to succeed test is acceptable to be applied if it is appropriate to do so for reasons of exceptional public interest. It will remain to be seen whether or not the new arrangements will have any major impact on the role of judicial review and the number of applications.

17–057 Judicial review is particularly vulnerable because of high costs and expenses. The complexity of legal analysis and argument makes it difficult to take cases as litigants in person. In most cases judicial review is dependent on legal aid and this has in the past been generously provided. The Coalition Government in 2013 announced restrictions on the availability of judicial review especially in certain prison cases or for applicants "lacking a clear connection with the UK". Legal costs are normally borne by the losing party which also enters a note of caution when taking cases. There is no absolute right to any remedy even if the application proves to be meritorious and successful. Remedies are only discretionary and may be refused and this creates a further hurdle to any application. Attempts to remove guaranteed legal aid for judicial review set out in the Civil Legal Aid (Remuneration) (Amendment) (No.3) Regulations 2014 that came into force in April 2014 was challenged as to its legality. The High Court held that this was illegal as there was no rational link between the regulations and the aim claimed by the Government to only bring cases that were likely to succeed.[52]

17–058 One positive development has been the regionalisation of Administrative Courts with hearing centres in Cardiff, Leeds, Manchester, Birmingham and Bristol. This is to take away the London and South East-centred approach to administrative cases.

---

52 (2015) *New Law Journal* 5 (6 March 2015).

Grounds for review

17-059

The various principles of judicial review give considerable discretion to the courts in flexibly interpreting and applying the grounds for review.[53] Increasingly influenced by rights under the European Convention and also EU law, the courts have created a rich jurisprudence to build judicial review. There is a great deal of pragmatism and some uncertainty as to the future direction and interpretation in judicial review.[54]

17-060

Deciding the procedural route to take action in the courts depends on the nature of the dispute and the grounds for complaint. It is also necessary for the grounds for review applied by the superior courts to be considered. It is significant that there has not been any consolidation into statutory form of the different grounds available for review. This area has been left to develop on a case by case basis, sometimes exposing judicial differences of opinion.[55] Lord Diplock acknowledged the achievements of the courts in developing judicial review in the landmark decision in the *Council of Civil Service Unions v Minister for Civil Service*[56] when he suggested that "the English law relating to judicial control of administrative action has been developed upon a case by case basis which has virtually transformed it over the last three decades". In the same speech Lord Diplock referred to the grounds for judicial review as consisting of three "heads" upon which administrative law is subject to control. These have been considered in outline in Ch.6 and are as follows: "illegality", meaning the decision-maker must understand the law and give effect to it; "irrationality", by which a decision which is unreasonable or so outrageous in its defiance of logic or of accepted moral standards that "no sensible person who applied his mind to the question to be decided could have arrived at it"; and finally there is "procedural impropriety", by which there is a failure to observe basic rules of natural justice or to fail to act with procedural fairness towards the person who will be affected by the decision. A further possibility, that of proportionality was also mentioned. Here the courts have to balance the appropriateness of the various objectives set out in law, the adverse effects which its decision may have on the rights, the liberties or interests of the persons and purposes it pursues. Proportionality, while recognised fully in French, German and EC law has only become understood in its "application in English Administrative law in recent years" although it is a concept which has historical roots in much earlier cases. The above developments must be understood in the context of the absence of any codified system of administrative law.

17-061

The grounds for review may now be considered in further detail bearing in mind that Lord Diplock's classification is not exhaustive. Increasingly important are the European Convention on Human Rights and the influence of EU law.

---

53 Lord Carnwath in *Kennedy v Information Commissioner* [2014] UKSC 20; [2015] A.C. 455.
54 Also see *Mandalia v Home Secretary* [2015] UKSC 59; [2015] 1 W.L.R. 4546 on the application of policy making by decision-makers.
55 *R (Bancoult) v Foreign Secretary (No.2)* [2008] UKHL 61; [2009] 1 A.C. 453.
56 [1985] A.C. 374; [1984] 3 W.L.R. 1174 HL.

Ultra vires and excess of jurisdiction

17-062 Lord Diplock's classification of illegality comprises a number of categories. Some categories may overlap and the classification is not exhaustive. As a general principle public bodies are expected to act within their legal powers. When a power is vested in a public body and the public body acts in excess of that power, its acts are invalid and ultra vires. The task of the courts, through judicial review is to consider the legal powers of public bodies at common law, statute or under the royal prerogative[57] and determine whether the public body has acted within its powers. Determining whether or not a public body is within its powers depends on statutory interpretation. The breadth of the powers contained in the statute will influence the courts' powers to intervene. Even broadly drafted powers are not immune to review. In *Hazell v Hammersmith*,[58] as noted in the chapters on local government and in the work of the Audit Commission, the House of Lords found that swap transactions were not authorised under Sch.13 to the Local Government Act 1972. This was notwithstanding a broadly drafted power contained in s.111 of the 1972 Act, namely that a local authority ". . .shall have power to do anything (whether or not involving the expenditure, borrowing or lending of money or the acquisition or disposal of any property or rights) which is calculated to facilitate, or is conducive or incidental, to the discharge of any of their functions".

17-063 The House of Lords viewed the swap transactions as speculative and therefore outside the remit of local authority powers. The extensive nature of s.111 has been increasingly narrowed by the courts in an attempt to keep local authorities within their legal powers. On the same approach to the interpretation of local government powers following the House of Lords in *Hazel* is the Court of Appeal in *Credit Suisse v Allerdale BC*.[59] Allerdale local authority engaged in a joint venture through a number of companies set up by the local authority, technically known as "local government influenced companies", to build and operate a leisure complex. A time-share scheme was envisaged as the best means to operate the complex. Credit Suisse, a leading international banking institution, provided substantial loans repayable over a fixed period. The district auditor queried the legality of the local authority joint venture companies, the local authority involvement and the investment of Credit Suisse. This arose when the ability of the local authority companies to repay the loans came into doubt. The case involved legal consideration of the powers and duties of the local authority and its relationship to Credit Suisse. The Court of Appeal held that the arrangements with the joint venture companies were ultra vires the powers of the local authority. The result of the case left Credit Suisse largely exposed to debts and liabilities that arose from the ultra vires transaction. This will seriously inhibit local government joint ventures with the private sector.

17-064 Powers granted for one purpose cannot be assumed to provide powers for another purpose, even if closely related. In *Attorney General v Fulham Corp*[60] Fulham Corporation had

---

57 *R v Wandsworth LBC Ex p. Beckwith* [1996] 1 W.L.R. 60; [1996] 1 All E.R. 129 HL.
58 [1992] 2 A.C. 1; [1991] 2 W.L.R. 372 HL.
59 [1997] Q.B. 306; [1996] 4 All E.R. 129 CA (Civ Div).
60 [1921] 1 Ch. 440 Ch D.

statutory powers under the Baths and Wash-houses Acts 1846–78 to establish baths and wash-houses. The question arose as to whether facilities for washing and drying clothes which included the operation of drying equipment by employees of the corporation, came within the powers of the legislation. The court held that the statutory powers only permitted the carrying out of clothes washing by customers themselves, and did not extend to operating a laundry service.

The review of statutory powers also extends to their exercise by Ministers. The Court of Appeal in *Laker Airways* held that the Secretary of State had acted ultra vires.[61] Guidance under the Civil Aviation Act 1971, subsequently amended, to the Civil Aviation Authority to the effect that British Airways should be the sole carrier on the Stansted to New York route, resulted in Laker Airways having their licence withdrawn. The guidance had been approved by both Houses of Parliament. The Court of Appeal regarded the guidance as effectively a directive power. The guidance was also contrary to the objectives given to the Civil Aviation Authority. Also the guidance was intended to explain and amplify the meaning of the objectives and not to replace them. The Court of Appeal considered that Laker Airways should be entitled to fly the New York route.

17–065

Local government provides another example of the power of the courts to review statutory powers. The courts may appear quite innovative in construing statutes when local authority powers are involved. In *Bromley*,[62] the House of Lords was asked to consider the "fair fares" policy of the GLC (now abolished). "Ordinary business principles" were applied to the reduction of fares and as the policy did not operate on those principles the proposed reduction in fares was ultra vires. Although the GLC had powers to make grants "for any purpose" to the London Transport Executive (LTE) the grant involving a supplementary rate was quashed because the purposes for which it was intended were ultra vires. There was "a fiduciary duty" on the GLC as a local authority, and the fares policy failed to live up to that standard which was owed to ratepayers. The Courts had to balance the GLC's duty owed to ratepayers against its wider power to provide reasonable transport facilities for transport users. The fact that a "fair fares" policy had been a manifesto condition in the election of the ruling party in the GLC was not relevant to the courts' powers of review, as such a condition was "not binding" on the local authority.

17–066

The application of any legal principles in this area of the law is always difficult. The courts may construe the statute as providing incidental powers within the jurisdiction of the body concerned provided the act is not expressly forbidden. In *Attorney General v Crayford UDC*,[63] the general powers of management of local authority housing under s.111(1) of the Housing Act 1957 were considered by the court in respect of a local authority decision to issue insurance policies to its tenants. Did such a scheme fall within "prudent management" by the local authority of its housing? The court held that the scheme was within the local authority's powers. The question of whether the scheme was ultra vires or not depended on whether it

17–067

---

61   [1977] Q.B. 643; [1977] 2 W.L.R. 234 CA (Civ Div).
62   [1983] 1 A.C. 768; [1982] 2 W.L.R. 92 HL.
63   [1962] Ch. 575; [1962] 2 All E.R. 147 CA.

"may fairly be regarded as incidental to, or consequential upon" the powers granted to the authority under the 1957 Act.

17-068 A public authority must direct itself according to law and must not purport to exercise powers it does not have nor the powers that someone else may have. Statutes invariably provide that powers may only be exercised by a specific body or person or that the powers must operate within certain safeguards which must be obeyed. The ultra vires doctrine will apply where the delegation of powers is improper. Effectively the courts wish to ensure that discretion is properly exercised, free from pressure and unfettered in its application.

17-069 Some examples serve to illustrate the courts' review of the exercise of the delegation of discretion. In *Ex p. Brunyate*,[64] the Court held that a local education authority may not use its powers to dismiss and appoint governors as a means of changing the educational policy of the Education Act 1944. The Court of Appeal in *R v Monopolies and Mergers Commission Ex p. Argyll Group Plc*[65] noted that the Monopolies and Mergers Commission, rather than its chairman should have decided whether to proceed with a reference made to it by the Secretary of State in the case of a takeover bid. The fact that the delegation of power to the chairman was ultra vires did not prevent the court from refusing to quash the chairman's decision.

17-070 In *R v Waltham Forest LBC Ex p. Waltham Forest Ratepayers Action Group*,[66] the courts struck down a decision of Waltham Forest councillors which was based on instructions from a pressure group known as the Local Government Group.

17-071 Over-reliance on rules, exercising a discretion when fettered by contract or pre-existing rules have all been regarded by the courts as examples of a failure to exercise discretionary powers correctly. Some latitude may be given to the correct delegation of ministerial powers to officials.[67] In *Carltona*,[68] a wartime case arose when a factory owner challenged the Commissioners of Works over the exercise of requisition powers granted by statute. In fact, the Commissioners never met and their powers were carried out by officials acting on their behalf. The Court of Appeal broadly interpreted delegation and upheld the legality of the procedures. Some official self-restraint must be taken not to extend the *Carltona* principle too broadly. In *Ex p. Oladehinde*[69] the House of Lords upheld the lawfulness of the Home Secretary's common practice to delegate to senior officials, namely immigration officers, his powers under the Immigration Act 1971 to serve notices of deportation. In such instances of delegation, the House of Lords noted that care should be taken not to widen the delegation of powers unduly. Some caution must be exercised to establish that the officials are sufficiently senior and that they possess the necessary experience to carry out the statutory duties under the 1971 Act. The

---

64 *R v Inner London Education Authority Ex p. Brunyate* [1989] 1 W.L.R. 542; [1989] 2 All E.R. 417 HL.
65 [1986] 1 W.L.R. 763; [1986] 2 All E.R. 257 CA (Civ Div).
66 *Ex p. Baxter* [1988] Q.B. 419; [1987] 3 All E.R. 671 CA (Civ Div).
67 *Lavender (H) & Son Ltd v Minister of Housing and Local Government* [1970] 1 W.L.R. 1231; [1970] 3 All E.R. 871 QBD. See *Local Government Board v Arlidge* [1915] A.C. 120 HL.
68 *Carltona v Commissioners of Works* [1943] 2 All E.R. 560 CA.
69 *R v Secretary of State for the Home Department Ex p. Oladehinde* [1991] 1 A.C. 254; [1990] 3 W.L.R. 797 HL.

Carltona principle is applied to central government departments and the devolution of functions to civil servants.

17-072

In local government s.101 of the Local Government Act 1972 permits the delegation of wide powers to officials to carry out specific functions of the local authority. The nature of any delegated power must be given close scrutiny. If the power rests with an officer who may consult with members of the council, it is wrong for the powers to be actually exercised by the councillor rather than the officer.

17-073

A discretion which is mistakenly bound by a policy or previous practice may likewise be regarded as an abuse of discretion and subject to possible review by the courts. In *Bromley*,[70] discussed above, the local authority mistakenly felt bound by its election manifesto. The House of Lords held that this was an abuse of power. A contract to bind a public body and its successors to exercise its powers in a particular way is likely to be declared void by the courts.[71] In such cases the courts will consider the nature of the powers being exercised. A commercial body that enters a commercial undertaking not to increase its statutory charges was considered to be making an acceptable exercise of power by virtue of its status as a commercial undertaking.

17-074

The exercise of discretionary powers may be influenced by the doctrine of estoppel. Estoppel has been developed as part of private law; it is relevant in public law as creating narrow and strictly defined exceptions to the strict application of the doctrine of ultra vires. The basis of estoppel was succinctly explained by Wade as[72]

> "a person who by some statement or representation of fact causes another to act to his detriment in reliance on the truth of it is not allowed to deny it later, even though it is wrong."

17-075

In private law, particularly in the law of contract, estoppel may prevent the enforcement of contractual rights where there was some undertaking not to enforce those rights in law. In the area of public law estoppel may arise where a citizen may be misled by advice from an official or public body and suffer detriment. However, as a general principle estoppel cannot be used to give a public body powers which it would otherwise not have. In *Maritime Electric Co*,[73] an electricity authority misread a customer's electricity meter and consequently undercharged the customer for two years. The authority had a statutory duty to collect the full amount and could not use the doctrine of estoppel to accept the lesser amount because it lacked the statutory powers to do so.

17-076

The question arises as to whether there are situations where the courts might be willing to enforce an ultra vires decision. Estoppel might assist an applicant when relying on advice. In *Western Fish Products*,[74] where the power to make a decision was incorrectly delegated but

---

70   [1983] 1 A.C. 768; [1982] 2 W.L.R. 92 HL.
71   *Ayr Harbour Trustees v Oswald* (1883) L.R. 8 App. Cas. 623.
72   H. W. R. Wade and C. F. Forsyth, *Administrative Law* (Oxford: Oxford University Press, 1988), p.261.
73   *Maritime Electric Co v General Dairies Ltd* [1937] A.C. 610; [1937] 1 All E.R. 748 PC (Canada).
74   *Western Fish Products Ltd v Penwith DC* [1981] 2 All E.R. 204; 77 L.G.R. 185 CA (Civ Div).

where the plaintiff assumed it to be correctly delegated, then provided the courts are satisfied about the nature of the incorrect assumption, the plaintiff may in certain circumstances rely on the estoppel principle as an exception to what would otherwise be an ultra vires decision. The Court of Appeal asserted that estoppel could not prevent a statutory body from exercising its discretion or performing its duty.

17-077 Considerable difficulty surrounds defining the nature of the assumption made by the plaintiff that might be sufficient to satisfy the estoppel principle in public law cases. Two possibilities emerge from the *Western Fish Products* decision. First, estoppel may only operate when it reasonably appears to the plaintiff that the authority to make a decision has been correctly delegated to the relevant officer or body and where "there is some evidence" justifying the plaintiff in believing that the officer or body was binding the authority. Secondly, depending on the construction of the statute, Megaw LJ explained that estoppel may arise where there is a procedural requirement in the statute waived by the statutory body in the exercise of its powers. For example, ". . .if a planning authority waives a procedural requirement relating to any application made to it for the exercise of its statutory powers, it may be estopped from relying on lack of formality".

17-078 In an earlier case, that of *Robertson v Minister of Pensions*,[75] where a citizen relied to his detriment on an assurance he was given that he was entitled to a military pension by someone who had no power to make the assurance, Denning J advanced a wide interpretation that the plaintiff is entitled to rely upon a government department "having the authority which it assumes. He does not know and cannot be expected to know, the limits of that authority".

17-079 However this wide interpretation was rejected in *Western Fish Products* and also by the House of Lords in *Howell v Falmouth Boat Construction Co Ltd*,[76] which considered that Denning's interpretation of the estoppel principle did not seem consistent with the principle that legal authority cannot be delegated.

17-080 Estoppel may arise when a change of policy occurs and the result is to the detriment of the plaintiff. For example, in *Lever Finance*[77] a planning officer, when asked by Lever Finance as to whether fresh planning permission was required in respect of their decision to alter the original plans of a housing scheme, concluded that no fresh application was required. Lever Finance began construction but after neighbours objected they were then advised that planning permission was required. Lever Finance applied for planning permission which was then refused. The Court of Appeal accepted that the planning officer had followed common practice, that Lever Finance relied on the planning officer's advice, and therefore the planning officer had authority to bind the council.

17-081 There has been criticism of the approach in *Lever Finance*. In *Western Fish Products Ltd*, the Court of Appeal restricted the use of estoppel in planning matters as estoppel could not prevent a statutory body from exercising its discretion or duty.

---

75   [1949] 1 K.B. 227; [1948] 2 All E.R. 767 KBD.
76   [1951] A.C. 837; [1951] 2 All E.R. 278 HL.
77   *Lever Finance Ltd v Westminster (City) LBC* [1971] 1 Q.B. 222; [1970] 3 W.L.R. 732 CA (Civ Div).

The law relating to estoppel in public law is unsatisfactory. This may be due to the difficulty of importing estoppel's private law characteristics into public law and of reconciling the principles of estoppel with the overriding obligations found in statutes. Even creative interpretations of statutory duties, discretions and procedural rules may result in hard cases where there is no legal remedy.

One solution favoured by Wade[78] in seeking to find compatibility between the application of the ultra vires doctrine and fairness to the plaintiff, is to compensate the plaintiff when the law must be enforced but injustice results. Compensation provides the means of ensuring fairness while retaining the doctrine of ultra vires. However, compensation has been found to be equally difficult to apply in public law.

Instead of adhering to the strict application of the doctrine of ultra vires, consider whether balancing the different interests between the parties might provide a more acceptable solution? This approach provides a more fundamental evaluation of the true function of ultra vires. Thus a decision taken by a public body might be enforceable even if it were ultra vires where the injury to the plaintiff was such that the public interest would not be served by enforcing the decision. Invariably such an approach invites considerable judicial discretion in setting the principles to be applied in such cases. Also it might be considered inappropriate to reconsider the doctrine of ultra vires in this way as the doctrine performs an important function of keeping a check on the discretion of public bodies.

The ultra vires doctrine may apply where there are certain procedural requirements contained in the statute. Procedural requirements or conditions may be imposed before specific statutory powers may be exercised. Procedural requirements may be merely discretionary or mandatory. The latter is likely to lead to a decision being quashed. In certain examples it may be helpful to classify the type of error or mistake made by the public body. Some are minor and may not affect the jurisdiction of the body making the decision. The courts' powers of supervision are usually intended to allow public bodies to make decisions within their jurisdiction. Thus in finding on the merits of a case the public body should be allowed to make mistakes that are not so fundamental that the jurisdiction of the body is impugned. Defining whether a mistake goes to jurisdiction or not is largely dependent on the role of the courts and the nature of the procedural rules.

In *Anisminic*,[79] the UK Government received payment from the Egyptian Government of a sum of money intended to compensate for loss of British property sequestered. The Foreign Compensation Commission, on behalf of the UK Government, had the task of determining claims made against the money available. An Order in Council set out the conditions required before any payments could be made. The Commission concluded that Anisminic had not made out its case. The Commission's interpretation of the Order in Council required that Anisminic should be British and a "successor in title". Anisminic could fulfil the former but not the latter condition and challenged the Commission's interpretation of the Order in Council in the courts despite the ouster clause contained in s.4(4) of the Foreign Compensation Act 1950, namely

---

78 Wade, *Administrative Law*, p.385.
79 *Anisminic Ltd v Foreign Compensation Commission* [1969] 2 A.C. 147; [1969] 2 W.L.R. 163 HL.

that the Commission's determination "should not be questioned in any court of law". The House of Lords concluded that the Commission had erred in law in holding that Anisminic should be a "successor in title". The ouster clause was held not to protect "purported" determinations, only real determinations.

17-087
The question arises as to the nature of the error that is regarded as a jurisdictional error and therefore open to review by the courts. Are all errors jurisdictional? In *Anisminic*, the Foreign Compensation Commission had correctly interpreted its powers to consider Anisminic's application and inquire into the facts of the application. If the Commission had considered matters extraneous to its powers its determination would have been a nullity. Lord Roskill considered:

> "There are many cases where although the tribunal had jurisdiction to enter on the inquiry, it has done or failed to do something in the course of the inquiry which is of such a nature that its decision is a nullity."

17-088
Lord Reid identified those errors which may be considered as going to jurisdiction. These are: acting in bad faith; making decisions without the requisite powers; breaching the requirements of natural justice; failing to take into account relevant considerations; or taking into account irrelevant considerations. The list is not exhaustive, but it is based on the assumption that there is a distinction between those errors which do and those that do not go to jurisdiction.

17-089
The courts have considered the nature of such a distinction. In *Pearlman v Keepers and Governors of Harrow School*,[80] Lord Denning explained that any such distinction between errors which are jurisdictional and those that are not are so fine that the distinction may be discarded. Pearlman was a tenant who had installed central heating. He applied to the county court for a declaration that it constituted a "structural alteration" of the premises. The county court decided that it did not and Pearlman sought certiorari to quash this decision in the High Court, notwithstanding the fact that the county court decision was by statute "final and conclusive".

17-090
Lord Denning's attempts to render obsolete the distinction between errors within jurisdiction and those that were outside jurisdiction was rejected in the Privy Council case of *South East Asia Fire Bricks*[81] by Lord Fraser. Lord Diplock in *O'Reilly v Mackman*[82] believed that there was still an important distinction to be drawn between those bodies where error of law within jurisdiction remained relevant and bodies where it had become an unnecessary distinction. Inferior courts fell within the category of review such as tribunals and administrative agencies, while the ordinary courts such as the County Court in *Pearlman* were entitled to rely on

---

80 [1979] Q.B. 56; [1978] 3 W.L.R. 736 CA (Civ Div). See *Williams v Bedwelty Justices* [1997] A.C. 225; [1996] 3 W.L.R. 361 HL.
81 *South East Asia Firebricks Sdn. Bhd. v Non-Metallic Mineral Products* [1981] A.C. 363; [1980] 3 W.L.R. 31 PC (Malaysia).
82 [1983] 2 A.C. 237; [1982] 3 W.L.R. 1096 HL. Lord Diplock drew a distinction between different bodies such as commissions and tribunals on the one hand and courts on the other. The former were open to review while the latter could rely on the principle of errors which are within jurisdiction as free from review.

the distinction between errors within jurisdiction which are not reviewable and errors outside jurisdiction which are subject to review.[83]

17–091

It may be concluded that such a distinction between errors that are within jurisdiction and those that are not, is necessary to safeguard the decision-maker and allow freedom to make the decision freed from over-rigid intervention by the courts. The courts are in turn allowed some discretion in setting the limits of their own jurisdiction. The most recent trend is in favour of removing any distinction between errors that are and those that are not jurisdictional ones. This is the approach of the court in *Palacegate Properties Ltd v Camden LBC*[84] suggesting that it was unnecessary to find a distinction between the different types of jurisdictional error.

C: Abuse of Discretion

17–092

Discretion exercised by a public body must not be exercised wrongly. Abuse of discretion may arise where the power has been exercised for a purpose not intended or expressed in the statute when the powers were conferred. The use of powers for improper purposes may result in the powers being declared ultra vires by the courts. For example, compulsory purchase powers should not be used for an ulterior or improper purpose. In *Sydney Municipal Council v Campbell*[85] compulsory purchase powers "to carry out improvements in remodelling any portion of the city" under the Sydney Corporation Amendment Act 1905 could not be used to secure a benefit of an increase in land values.

17–093

In construing a statute, the courts may look at the "policy and objects" of the statute in order to consider whether the motivation for a decision and its outcome are within the powers conferred by Parliament. In *Padfield*,[86] mandamus was granted by the House of Lords in favour of milk producers who had complained that the differential element, based on geographical areas, in the price fixed for their milk purchased by the Milk Marketing Board was too low. The Agricultural Marketing Act 1958 provided two methods of grievance resolution, arbitration and procedures under s.19 involving the setting-up of a committee of investigation. The first was accepted as unsuitable for the type of complaint. The second, the Minister declined to do. Padfield sought an order of mandamus. The House of Lords concluded that the Minister had misunderstood his powers and therefore frustrated the purpose of the Act. The terms of the Minister's powers to refer the matter to a committee of investigation were if the Minister "in any case so directs". Lord Reid noted that this showed that the Minister had some discretion, but such a discretion must be in accordance with the intention of the statute. The courts,

---

83   *R v Greater Manchester Coroner Ex p. Tal* [1985] Q.B. 67; [1984] 3 W.L.R. 643 QBD.
84   (2001) 3 L.G.L.R. 18; (2001) 82 P. & C.R. 17 Div Ct.
85   [1925] A.C. 338 PC (Aus).
86   [1968] A.C. 997; [1968] 2 W.L.R. 924 HL.

in considering whether discretion has been exercised reasonably, may consider reasons for the decision or in the absence of reasons, may infer whether the decision is a reasonable one or not.

17-094 In the event, after the House of Lords decision in *Padfield*, the Minister was compelled under the Agricultural Marketing Act 1958 to set up an inquiry in the form of a committee of investigation. This was duly convened and reported in favour of the complainants but the Minister's ultimate discretion allowed him to take no action.

17-095 In the exercise of discretion, it is possible to take into account irrelevant considerations or fail to take account of relevant considerations. Abuse of discretion on these grounds may occur for the most altruistic reasons but may not conform to the relevant statutory requirements. In *Roberts v Hopwood Poplar BC*,[87] the Borough Council introduced a "minimum wage" for its employees. The power to set wages under s.62 of the Metropolis Management Act 1855 contained the power to pay "such salaries and wages as . . . [the council] may think fit". This conferred a broad discretion on the local authority but the district auditor questioned the validity of the setting of a minimum wage and accordingly surcharged the local councillors. The House of Lords noted that the national average wage for similar workers was substantially less than the minimum wage set by the Council. The rationale for the minimum wage was based on an election mandate which the councillors felt bound to follow. However, the payment of the minimum wage was made without due regard for the interests of the ratepayers. The House of Lords viewed the minimum wage payments as amounting in effect to gifts to the workers which was an improper purpose and not intended by the legislation. The Council had not taken account of the wages paid to other workers and the result was that the minimum wage was unlawful. The House of Lords reached its conclusion by balancing the interests of the ratepayers with the statutory powers exercised by the local authority as to what is reasonable and a proper exercise of discretion.

17-096 A similar approach is evident in the *Bromley*[88] decision. The House of Lords held that the "fair fares" policy of the Greater London Council was ultra vires on the basis that the decision had not taken account of the fiduciary duty owed by the council to the ratepayers. In balancing the different interests of ratepayers, transport users and the duties of the local authority, the House of Lords concluded that the Council had acted unreasonably. Unreasonableness is also a ground for holding that a discretion has been abused. In *Wednesbury Corp*[89] Lord Greene, MR considered the meaning of the term "unreasonable" and concluded that where an authority's decision "was so unreasonable that no reasonable authority" could ever come to the decision then it could be impugned by the courts. The courts are left with considerable discretion as to how to apply this direction. The question is whether a reasonable authority "could" ever come to the decision. What is the standard of the reasonable authority? On a narrow construction of the test, the courts should rarely intervene. As Lord Diplock recognised in the *Council of Civil Service Unions v Minister for the Civil Service*[90] the decision would have to be so outrageous or

---

87 [1925] A.C. 578 HL.
88 [1983] 1 A.C. 768; [1982] 2 W.L.R. 92 HL.
89 *Associated Provincial Picture Houses Ltd v Wednesbury Corp* [1948] 1 K.B. 223; [1947] 2 All E.R. 680 CA.
90 *Council of Civil Service Unions v Minister for the Civil Service* [1985] A.C. 374; [1984] 3 W.L.R. 1174 HL at [410].

in defiance of logic that no sensible person could come to such a decision. On this view, unreasonableness is unlikely to result in the courts intervening with the exercise of discretion. This appears to give decision-makers considerable latitude before offending against the criteria set by Lord Diplock. Unreasonableness will therefore provide a justification for upholding the exercise of discretion on the one hand but imposing self-restraint on the courts on the other. In *Nottingham C*,[91] the view of Lord Scarman was that the decision must be so absurd that the decision-maker "must have taken leave of his senses".

17-097

An alternative to the narrow interpretation of *Wednesbury* unreasonableness is that the courts are prepared to seek more active intervention on the grounds of unreasonableness defined in terms of review in discretion where it is found to be illogical or against good sense. The courts are free to consider as in *Padfield* whether the policy and objects of the statute have been frustrated. In *Wheeler v Leicester City Council*[92] Lord Roskill considered whether the local authority's decision to terminate the agreement with the Leicester Rugby Football Club to make use of the council's recreation ground was "unreasonable". The Council had responded to the Club's decision to take part in a rugby tour of South Africa. Lord Roskill concluded that the Council had used an unfair means to achieve its objectives. Although the judges had failed in the lower courts to classify the decision of the local authority as *Wednesbury* unreasonableness, Lord Roskill was prepared to hold that the local authority had acted unreasonably.

17-098

Unreasonableness may be used to impugn a byelaw or delegated rule-making function.[93] Statutory interpretation provides the main basis for adopting the test of unreasonableness, though it may be the basis of a tort action in negligence against a public body. In addition to unreasonableness, vagueness or a lack of fair hearing such as is implied in the rules of natural justice may result in the courts holding that discretion has been abused.

17-099

The concept of "unreasonableness" is difficult to categorise satisfactorily. The courts are reluctant to review decisions on their merits and the policy behind decisions very often falls outside the courts' remit. One way forward is to see the role of the courts as providing a more systematic guide to the development of principles of good administration. Avoiding arbitrariness or inconsistency and ensuring that fair decision-making takes place might be further assisted if "unreasonableness" were focused on what constitutes good administration.

17-100

There have been a number of cases that have provided further elaboration of the *Wednesbury* principle. There are three cases where the breadth and possible objective standards implied in the *Wednesbury* test are discussed. In *R v Chief Constable of the Devon and Cornwall Constabulary Ex p. Hay*,[94] Sedley J granted certiorari and *mandamus* directing the Chief Constable to hear and determine disciplinary charges. Some irrelevant and extraneous matters had been taken into account but "it was in the public interest" that where there was unfairness the disciplinary proceedings should be reinstated. In *R v Secretary of State for the*

---

91 *Nottingham C v Secretary of State for the Environment* [1986] A.C. 240; [1986] 2 W.L.R. 1; [1986] 1 All E.R. 199 HL at [247].
92 [1985] A.C. 1054; [1985] 3 W.L.R. 335 HL.
93 *Kruse v Johnson* [1898] 2 Q.B. 91 QBD.
94 [1996] 2 All E.R. 711; Times, February 19, 1996 QBD.

Home Department Ex p. Onibiyo,[95] the use of general *Wednesbury* principles was deployed in respect of an application for asylum. Sir Thomas Bingham noted that[96]

> "...the decision whether an asylum-seeker is a refugee is a question to be determined by the Secretary of State and the immigration appellate authorities whose determinations are susceptible to challenge only on *Wednesbury* principles."

17–101

In discussing *Wednesbury* principles Sir Thomas Bingham noted that[97] "on any *Wednesbury* ground of which irrationality is only one...". This is a useful reminder that strict categorisation of the grounds of review into self-contained compartments is to be avoided. *Wednesbury* principles may provide a "hard look" doctrine for the courts to discover if there is objectively any grounds for upholding a review. This approach favouring the overturning of any perverse decision-making may be found in *R v Wandsworth LBC Ex p. Mansor*,[98] a case on homeless persons.

17–102

The adequacy of *Wednesbury* unreasonableness was considered in the light of the Human Rights Act 1998. It is likely that over the coming years many of the grounds for judicial review will have to be considered within the broader canvass of Convention rights. Lord Steyn in *R v Secretary of State for the Home Department Ex p. Daly*[99] drew attention to the necessity for courts to take account of the Convention when considering the intensity of the review applicable. In cases where it was appropriate to apply the test of *Wednesbury* unreasonableness it may be necessary to adjust the criteria of what is unreasonable in the light of the subject matter under review. Lord Steyn approved *R (Mahmood) v Secretary of State for the Home Dept*[100] and the view of Laws LJ on the need to take account of the different "intensity of review" in a public law case. The courts may seek to adjust the scope of review available under *Wednesbury* and where appropriate expect a higher standard by public bodies. A broad based approach seems to be emerging, that is not determined by Convention rights or the application of EU law, but in favour of a more subtle understanding of the context of a particular case and the need to engage with the justice of the decision-maker and fairness to the applicant. The use of the heading of proportionality may provide the courts with the opportunity to further develop judicial review by taking into account the human rights dimension. It may even be possible to see an emerging fusion of proportionality and unreasonableness.[101]

---

95 [1996] Q.B. 768; [1996] 2 W.L.R. 490 CA (Civ Div).
96 [1996] Q.B. 768; [1996] 2 W.L.R. 490 CA (Civ Div) at [912C]–[912D].
97 [1996] Q.B. 768 at [912F].
98 [1997] Q.B. 953; [1996] 3 W.L.R. 282 CA (Civ Div).
99 [2001] UKHL 26; [2001] 2 A.C. 532 at [445G]–[445H].
100 [2001] 1 W.L.R. 840; [2001] 1 F.L.R. 756 CA (Civ Div).
101 See the views of Lord Sumption in *Pham v Secretary of State for the Home Department* [2015] UKSC 19; [2015] 1 W.L.R. 159.

D: Proportionality

17-103 Finally, in addition to the grounds of review already discussed consideration should be given to Lord Diplock's suggestion[102] that proportionality might be adopted as a ground for review in English law. Proportionality is fast emerging as an important way of developing judicial review, particularly along the lines of greater pragmatism and creating the potential for a more intrusive form of review. The principle of proportionality provides the courts with the opportunity to consider whether the harmful effects of a particular exercise of power are disproportionate to any benefits which may occur. Support for the adoption of such a doctrine into English administrative law focuses on the opportunity it may provide the courts in evaluating what is fair.[103] In *Ex p. Brind*[104] the Home Secretary under the Broadcasting Act 1981 and under the powers under the BBC's licence agreements issued an order prohibiting the broadcasting of words spoken by members of certain proscribed organisations or their supporters. The applicants sought judicial review of the ban and argued that the effects of the ban might produce greater harm than any good that might result. The House of Lords considered the concept of proportionality but refused to recognise proportionality as a distinct principle from *Wednesbury* unreasonableness. The outcome of the case was that the ban was upheld. However, the reticence of the House of Lords to develop more fully a doctrine of proportionality seems well placed given the nature of French administrative law which has helped develop the concept of proportionality. Differences between the French and English legal systems as to standard of proof, method of legal reasoning and the constitutional role of the courts require more careful consideration before the concept may be assessed as to its value in English administrative law.

17-104 As matters stand it appears that under the principles of *Wednesbury* unreasonableness, the courts might consider the reasonable relationship between the objective which is sought to be achieved and the means used to achieve it. Proportionality, as a principle of European Community law, is therefore part of the law of the UK. It is unlikely that this concept will be expanded into a separate heading for review. It is more likely to infiltrate the thinking and approach of judges when confronted with cases where it is felt that it is disproportionate to grant judicial review.[105] In *Ex p. Daly*,[106] Lord Steyn in the House of Lords canvassed the overlap between the traditional grounds for review and proportionality. The proportionality approach provided an intensity of review not available under the traditional headings of review. This suggests that the reviewing court may be required to "assess the balance which the decision maker has struck" and not merely consider if it falls within what is reasonable or unreasonable. The review court under the heading of proportionality may have to consider the "relative

---

102 *Council of Civil Service Unions v Minister for the Civil Service* [1985] A.C. 374; [1984] 3 W.L.R. 1174 HL.
103 See J. Jowell and A. Lester, "Beyond Wednesbury: Substantive Principles of Administrative Law" [1987] *P.L.* 368; and J. Jowell, "Beyond the Rule of Law: Towards Constitutional Judicial Review" [2000] *Public Law* 671.
104 [1991] 1 A.C. 696; [1991] 2 W.L.R. 58 HL.
105 S. Boyron, "Proportionality in English Administrative Law: A Faulty Translation?" [1992] *O.J.L.S.* 237. Proportionality is found in many countries such as Germany, France, the USA and Canada.
106 [2001] UKHL 26; [2001] 2 A.C. 532 at [445G]–[445H].

weight accorded to interests and considerations". Finally, consideration should be given to the question raised[107] by the intensity of review[108]:

> "In other words, the intensity of the review, in similar cases, is guaranteed by the twin requirements that the limitation of the right was necessary in a democratic society, in the sense of meeting a pressing social need, and the question whether the interference was really proportionate to the legitimate aim pursued."

17-105 Defining and setting the standards of proportionality has proved to be difficult. The House of Lords in *Huang v Home Secretary*[109] accepted that there were a number of steps to be taken to consider proportionality. These include: interpreting the legislative objective and finding that it is sufficiently justified to limit any fundamental rights; that the measures used to meet the legislative objectives are rationally connected to it; and that the means used are no more than necessary to accomplish the objective.[110] In *Huang*, a further point is added that the courts have always to strike a "fair balance" between the rights of the individual and the interests of the community as is appropriate in terms of Convention rights. Each case needs to be scrutinised with great care and an assessment of the consequences of interference undertaken. The Supreme Court has accepted this approach in *R (Quila) v Home Secretary*[111] with an emphasis on undertaking the process of evaluating proportionality carefully and engaging with the public authority by ensuring that their analysis is carefully considered. There are various ways to undertake the task but the courts have to make their own decision, weighing up, balancing and assessing the evidence. It is also relevant and important that convention rights are part of the evaluation. The House of Lords explained the importance of rights in *R (SB) v Governors of Denbeigh High School*.[112] Even when the decision-maker has taken into account Convention rights, it is possible that the court may examine and assess the decision, going behind the facts to establish if the decision is disproportionate. This may prove difficult to predict leaving public bodies with some uncertainty as to how best to make decisions when the balance of the issues are finely drawn.[113]

17-106 In *Pham*,[114] the Supreme Court has taken matters further by recognising that proportionality applies irrespective of EU or Convention rights. This perspective has been hinted in the past, but not made expressly clear until the *Pham* decision. The facts concerned the legality of the Home Secretary to remove the appellant's British citizenship and deport him to Vietnam

---

107 See *R v Ministry of Defence Ex p. Smith* [1996] Q.B. 517; [1996] 2 W.L.R. 305 CA (Civ Div).
108 [2001] UKHL 26 at [446H].
109 [2007] UKHL 1; [2007] 1 W.L.R. 320.
110 The main points are outlined by the Privy Council in *de Freitas v Permanent Secretary of the Ministry of Agriculture, Fisheries, Lands and Housing* [1999] 1 A.C. 69; [1998] 3 W.L.R. 675 PC (Antigua and Barbuda).
111 [2011] UKSC 45; [2012] 1 A.C. 6.
112 [2006] UKHL 15; [2007] 1 A.C. 100 HL.
113 *Belfast City Council v Miss Behavin' Ltd* [2007] UKHL 19; [2007] 1 W.L.R. 1420.
114 *Pham v Secretary of State for the Home Department* [2015] UKSC 19; [2015] 1 W.L.R. 1591.

under s.40(2) of the British Nationality Act 1981. Was the Home Secretary's decision lawful, when it would result in the statelessness of the appellant? There were some doubts about the full application and interpretation of EU law on the point but consensus on the point that proportionality would leave the decision potentially illegal. The Supreme Court adopted a flexible approach, the judges recognised that proportionality would assist in the case in ensuring that overall the courts would be able to assess the fairness of the decision. The context of the decision is important allowing the courts to engage with the full range of discretion enjoyed by the decision-maker. Proportionality offers a broader and more contextual shape to public law issues.

E: Legitimate Expectations

17–107

Since the 1980s, legitimate expectations has been developing as a ground of review. It was defined in the *Council for Civil Service Unions v Minister for the Civil Service*[115] by Lord Fraser as "the existence of a regular practice which the claimant can reasonably expect to continue". Laws LJ in *R (Nadarajah) v Secretary of State for the Home Department*[116] set out some of the main principles. In cases where public authority issues a promise or adopted a practice which represents how it proposes to act in a given area, then the law requires that the promise or practice should be honoured unless there are good reasons not to do so. *R V Ministry of Agriculture Ex p. Hamble Fisheries*[117] articulated two principles. First, that it was possible for a legitimate expectation to lead to a substantive benefit; and secondly, that the court must conduct a balancing exercise in considering the effect of a changed policy was "fair" or amounted to an abuse of power or whether the policy meets the *Wednesbury* test of unreasonableness.

17–108

The legitimate expectation doctrine is widely applicable in many countries and is often a product of constitutional interpretation drawing on principles of fairness and due process. This is a difficult area where not every representation will be regarded as legitimate or enforceable by law. The most practical application of the doctrine came in *R v North Devon Health Authority Ex p. Coughlan*.[118] The particular facts of the case were unusual. A Health Authority had built new disabled patient facilities in 1993 and the patients were given an assurance that they could live there as long as they chose. Events did not work out as the patients expected. In 1998, the Authority decided to close the facility and move the patients

---

115 [1985] A.C. 374; [1984] 3 W.L.R. 1174 HL at [401]. Also see *Nigel Rowe, David Worrall v The Commissioners for HM Revenue and Customs* [2015] EWHC 2293 (Admin); [2015] B.T.C. 27.
116 [2005] EWCA Civ 1363; Times, December 14, 2005.
117 [1995] 2 All E.R. 714; [1995] 1 C.M.L.R. 533 QBD.
118 [2001] Q.B. 213; [2000] 2 W.L.R. 622 CA (Civ Div).

to Local Authority care. The court held that there was a legitimate expectation given to the patients that gave the patients a substantive benefit. The promise was enforceable in law as not to do so was unfair and an abuse of power. There was no overriding public interest to depart from the original policy. The *Coughlan* case requires that the fairness or otherwise of departing from a substantive and legitimate expectation be considered. In such cases the standards expected of the review are set higher. It is for that reason the expectation relied upon must be "unambiguous and devoid of relevant qualification".[119] Since *Coughlan* understanding when a legitimate expectation may lead to a substantive remedy has been considered in a number of cases. In *R (Bibi) v Newham Council*,[120] the court articulated some principles that are practically based. The first question is whether the public body has, by practice or promise, committed itself, and the second, has the public body acted or proposed to act unlawfully in relation to its commitment? Finally, there is the question of what the court should do? The question of an assurance or practice may arise when taxpayers are dealing with HMRC.[121] The courts require that any assurance to taxpayers must be clear and where it would be "abusive" for the HMRC to go back on the promise or expectations made. Laws LJ in *R (Bhatt Murphy) v The Independent Assessor*[122] noted that "the promise of practice . . . must constitute a specific undertaking, directed at a particular individual or group by which the relevant policy's continuance is assured".

17–109 In *Mandalia v Home Secretary*,[123] the Supreme Court asked whether the UK Border Agency had acted lawfully when it refused the appellant's visa extension without first allowing him to submit certain information relevant to his application. The Border Agency's own policy permitted the information to be submitted, but this was not permitted. Lord Wilson gave the main decision of the Supreme Court. In the circumstances of the case, the appellant was not aware of the policy but the legitimate expectation existed, notwithstanding the appellant was unaware of it. This is an important case in drawing a distinction between what the appellant knew and relied on and what in fact was represented. Lord Wilson also endorsed the analysis in *R (Nadarajah) v Secretary of State for the Home Department*[124] and emphasised the legitimate expectation was drawn from a principle related to the doctrine of legitimate expectation was to be regarded as "free standing" and grounded in fairness. Consistency and fairness go the basic principles that underline judicial review. The consistent application of policy is an expectation that the courts place on all public bodies.

---

119 *R v Inland Revenue Commisisoners Ex p. MFK Underwriting Agents Ltd* [1990] 1 W.L.R. 1545; [1990] 1 All E.R. 91 QBD at [157B].
120 [2001] EWCA Civ 607; [2002] 1 W.L.R. 237.
121 *Nigel Rowe, David Worrall v The Commissioners for HM Revenue and Customs* [2015] EWHC 2293 (Admin).
122 [2008] EWCA Civ 755; (2008) 152(29) S.J.L.B. 29.
123 [2015] UKSC 59; [2015] 1 W.L.R. 4546.
124 [2005] EWCA Civ 1363; Times, December 14, 2005.

F: Natural Justice

17-110

The common law has developed principles of natural justice. Natural justice in administrative law is usually defined to include two rules. First there is the requirement to hear the other side of the case or give a fair hearing otherwise known as *audi alteram partem*. Secondly, there is the rule to avoid bias in the hearing or on the part of the decision-maker, known as *nemo judex in sua causa*. Both rules provide the basis for procedural standards to be applied by the courts in the supervision of public bodies. Lord Diplock in the *Council of Civil Service Unions v Minister for the Civil Service*,[125] the GCHQ case, referred to the rules of natural justice as procedural impropriety. In that case, procedural mistakes in not giving the Unions any consultation on the decision to ban Union membership at GCHQ were regarded as a breach of a legitimate expectation to be consulted, and were amenable to judicial review. However, considerations of national security outweighed such legitimate expectations and the courts declined relief. The Human Rights Act 1998 has strengthened principles of natural justice through the application of art.6(1) of the European Convention on Human Rights.[126] In general the common law operates consistently with art.6 particularly a robust approach to a hearing being undertaken by an "independent and impartial tribunal".

17-111

The sources of such rules of procedure vary according to the type of body and the relationship between the plaintiff and the decision-maker. In applying the rules of natural justice it is first necessary to inquire, does natural justice apply? The answer often depends on the nature of the body involved. Natural justice may be provided in a statutory form, or under contractual relations or through licences or even from a legitimate expectation that such rights may exist through the rather nebulous concept of private rights such as fiduciary relationships or quasi-contract. As Tucker LJ explained[127]:

> "The requirements of natural justice must depend on the circumstances of the case, the nature of the inquiry, the rules under which the tribunal is acting, the subject-matter that is being dealt with and so forth"

17-112

Natural justice is important in disciplinary hearings, employment disputes and in the rules of various regulatory authorities for sporting bodies.

---

125 [1985] A.C. 374; [1984] 3 W.L.R. 1174 HL.
126 ". . .everyone shall be entitled to a fair and public hearing within a reasonable time by an independent and impartial tribunal established by law".
127 *Russell v Duke of Norfolk* [1949] 1 All E.R. 109; 65 T.L.R. 225 CA.

The duty to act fairly

17-113 In the early development of natural justice, the courts developed principles on the basis of the common law. It was relatively easy to develop such principles when there was little statutory intervention. Gap-filling of this kind, however, is less common today. Statutory developments have become more comprehensive and often provide detailed rules relating to the conduct of hearings and the rights of parties.

17-114 The role of the courts has adapted to comprehensive statutory definitions setting out the principles of natural justice. This adaptation has been marked by a shift in focus from the rules of natural justice to the development by the courts of "the duty to act fairly". In *H (K) an infant, Re*,[128] Lord Parker considered the decision of an immigration officer to meet the requirements of having to act fairly when refusing entry to K who was entitled to enter the UK provided he satisfied the immigration officer that he was under 16. The immigration officer relied on medical evidence that K was at least 16 but Lord Parker considered that K was entitled to know what had determined the matter in the mind of the immigration officer so that K would have the opportunity to answer the evidence. In fact, the court found that the immigration officer had acted fairly.

17-115 The "duty to act fairly" may mark a shift in direction in judicial review through common law principles. Fairness is also supported through s.149 of the Equality Act 2010, which gives statutory recognition to all public authorities, having due regard to the need to eliminate all forms of discrimination and including the advancement of opportunity and fostering good relations between different races and ethnic groups. These are procedural as well as substantive responsibilities on public authority decision-makers.[129]

17-116 At times the courts have considered the duty to act fairly as a substitute for the rules of natural justice. Lord Diplock in *GCHQ*, discussed above, considered that natural justice was replaced by the duty to act fairly. At other times, such as in *Ex p. Hosenball*,[130] the courts continue to discuss the rules of natural justice.

17-117 The question arises as to whether the use of the duty to act fairly represents a substantive change in the approach by the courts to applying principles of natural justice. Fairness appears a broader and more flexible concept than the rules of natural justice. It might appear to offer the courts the opportunity to look behind procedural rules and consider whether the outcome is fair. An alternative interpretation is to deny any difference between natural justice and the duty to act fairly. It is unclear whether the courts will adopt the duty to act fairly as a general expression of natural justice and the terms will be interchangeable.

17-118 The right to a hearing is one of the rules of natural justice. This may take a number of forms: the right to put one's own side of the case, the right to be consulted, the right to make

---

128 [1967] 2 Q.B. 617; [1967] 2 W.L.R. 962 QBD. Also see *Pergamon Press Ltd, Re* [1971] Ch. 388; [1970] 3 W.L.R. 792 CA (Civ Div).
129 *R (MA) v Work and Pensions Secretary* [2013] EWHC 2213 (QB); [2013] P.T.S.R. 1521. See the views of Laws LJ.
130 *Bushell v Secretary of State for the Environment* [1981] A.C. 75; [1980] 3 W.L.R. 22 HL. Also *Pergamon Press Ltd, Re* [1971] Ch. 388.

representations, or to submit reasoned arguments rebutting any allegations are all considered as elements in the duty imposed upon all decision-makers to act in good faith and listen fairly to each side of the case.

17–119

In *Ridge v Baldwin*,[131] Ridge, a Chief Constable was subject to disciplinary action by the Watch Committee after he was acquitted of conspiracy to corrupt the course of justice. Remarks made by the trial judge critical of Ridge's conduct became the ground for disciplinary action. The Watch Committee decided to dismiss Ridge acting under s.191(4) of the Municipal Corporations Act 1882 without granting him a hearing. Ridge's solicitor requested and was granted a hearing and was permitted to appear before a later meeting of the Watch Committee. Ridge exercised his right of appeal to the Home Secretary, but his appeal failed. He applied to the courts arguing that he had been given no opportunity to be heard and was not allowed to make representations. The House of Lords found in his favour and granted him a declaration that the decision of the Watch Committee was void and breached the rules of natural justice.

17–120

In disciplinary hearings for students, doctors, dentists and prisoners the rules of natural justice have been applied. Natural justice may arise because the plaintiff's rights have been affected or because there is some legitimate expectation that consultation might take place. Particularly problematic has been a long established reticence on the part of the courts to review the internal disciplinary rules of sporting bodies. Examples of such bodies vary from the administration of boxing clubs by the British Board of Boxing Control, to the Jockey Club, and the Football Association. The courts' reluctance may stem from the rules themselves conforming to a certain minimum standard of natural justice and partly a concern that a large amount of litigation may result from active judicial intervention.[132]

17–121

Even where it may be established that natural justice applies it does not follow that this includes the right to legal representation. The question of representations may arise because of the nature of the proceedings. For example, in *Ex p. Hone*[133] the House of Lords considered whether legal representation was an absolute right. Lord Goff declined to accept that such a right existed in every case. The facts of *Hone* involved disciplinary charges against prisoners heard by the Board of Prison Visitors. The House of Lords accepted that there were circumstances where the need for legal representation might not be required. Matters which might be relevant in determining when to permit legal representation were outlined in *Ex p. Tarrant*,[134] cited in opinion by Lord Goff. The list includes: the serious nature of the charge; the question of whether any points of law are raised; the ability of the prisoner to make out his or her case; procedural questions of the difficulty of the rules; and the need for reasonable efficiency in decision-making and finally fairness between prisoners. However, while legal

---

131 [1964] A.C. 40; [1963] 2 W.L.R. 935 HL.
132 See "Mullan" (1975) 25 *University of Toronto Law Journal* 281.
133 *R v Board of Visitors of HM Prison the Maze Ex p. Hone* [1988] A.C. 379; [1988] 2 W.L.R. 177 HL.
134 *R v Secretary of State for the Home Department Ex p. Tarrant* [1985] Q.B. 251; [1984] 2 W.L.R. 613 Div Ct. *R v Secretary of State for the Environment Ex p. Kirkstall Valley Campaign Ltd* [1996] 3 All E.R. 304; [1997] 1 P.L.R. 8 QBD.

17-122 representation may be open to such considerations, the courts have maintained the view that cross-examination is an important element in a fair trial. Thus, the plaintiff is nearly always entitled to this right.

17-123 It is not a requirement that an inquiry or investigation should always be in public. This appears from two cases, one involving the inquiry into murders carried out by Dr Shipman[135] and the other arising from the setting-up of three independent inquiries into the foot-and-mouth epidemic.[136]

17-124 The giving of reasons is also an important aspect of natural justice. The courts have been reluctant to provide a general duty to give reasons, but have considered that there must be sufficient reasons for the parties to know the nature of the case that has been considered. In *R v Higher Education Funding Council Ex p. Institute of Dental Surgery*,[137] Sedley J, as he then was, considered whether the University Funding Council, as it then was, should be required to give reasons when making evaluations of the assessment of the quality of institutional research. He concluded that there was no general duty to give reasons but there are classes of case where a duty might arise. One example of such a class is where the subject matter is so highly regarded by the law, such as personal liberty, that reasons might be given as of right. Another class of case is where the decision appears aberrant. In the interests of fairness reasons may be required so that the recipient may know whether the aberration is in the legal sense real. In the case in question, a clear exercise of academic judgment does not fall within a decision which is challengeable only by reference to the reasons given for it.

An example where the House of Lords was prepared to require reasons is *Doody v Secretary of State for the Home Department*.[138] Prisoners convicted of murder and subject to a mandatory sentence of life imprisonment were entitled to be told by the Home Secretary what period or periods had been recommended by the judiciary to serve their sentence. The requirement to give reasons must therefore depend on the class of case involved and the role of the decision-maker under review. Some guidance as to the substantive details required when giving reasons to satisfy the requirements of natural justice may be found from the Court of Appeal decision in *English v Emery Reimbold and Strick Ltd*.[139]

17-125 The second rule of natural justice is the rule against bias. Pecuniary interests may disqualify a person from considering the case put before them. The courts have articulated this rule in the test of whether there is "a real likelihood of bias". Direct pecuniary advantage extends to other forms of bias. Prejudice or direct involvement with one party as against another may amount to sufficient interest to be regarded as a breach of natural justice. A judge must not be the accuser or the prosecutor. In *Franklin*,[140] the Minister appeared at a public meeting after

---

135 *R v Secretary of State for Health Ex p. Wagstaff* [2001] 1 W.L.R. 292; [2002] All E.R (D) 1021 Div Ct.
136 *Persey v Secretary of State for Environment, Food and Rural Affairs* [2002] EWHC 371 (Admin); [2002] All E.R (D) (March).
137 [1994] 1 W.L.R. 242; [1994] 1 All E.R. 651 Div Ct.
138 [1994] 1 A.C. 531; [1993] 3 W.L.R. 154 HL.
139 [2002] EWCA Civ 605; [2002] 1 W.L.R. 2409.
140 *Dimes v Grand Junction Canal* 10 E.R. 301; (1852) 3 H.L. Cas. 759 HL. *Metropolitan Properties v Lannon* [1969]

he had prepared a draft order under the New Towns Act 1946 which designated Stevenage as a new town, and after he had decided to hold a public inquiry. At the meeting, amid strong objections from those who attended he said "It is no good you jeering: it is going to be done". This raised a challenge to the fairness of the Minister's judgment. The House of Lords accepted that there was no evidence that the Minister had not made a genuine consideration of the matters put before him and they upheld the legality of the Minister's approval of the order. Thus it is possible for the courts to accept that Ministers may follow a certain policy but in making their mind up as to the particular application of the policy a genuine consideration must be given to any objections.

17-126
Difficulty in establishing a satisfactory test for bias may stem from the question of the perspective to take when judging bias. The assumption behind the "real likelihood of bias" test is that the matter is to be judged by the standards of the reasonable man. However, it may be necessary to consider a more subjective viewpoint. The perception of the plaintiff or others involved in the dispute may differ from the objective and balanced view of the hypothetical reasonable man. This may appear to be an equally valid perspective on the issue as the reasonable man. It may therefore appear necessary to consider both subjective and objective grounds as to whether there is bias or not.

17-127
The House of Lords in *Pinochet*[141] held that the issue of bias would apply where a judge might be thought to have a personal interest in the case. The real likelihood of bias test is set out in *R v Gough*[142] and suggests that the court has to consider whether there is a danger or possibility of bias or injustice by taking account of all the circumstances.[143] As a result great care must be directed at providing in the membership of any disciplinary committee clear distinctions between the different levels of decision-making when disciplinary hearings are involved. The complainant should not be part of the adjudication committee and the appeal committee should not be tainted by the membership of the first instance committee. A separation between each function is important in such cases, especially involving closely knit groups within employment or in educational establishments. Most universities have well established internal rules to adjudicate disciplinary matters with representation for students and if necessary legal representation. The rules of natural justice must be read alongside art.6 procedures.[144]

17-128
Given the problems that arose in the *Pinochet* case mentioned above, judges have become circumspect about how any interest in a case might give rise to a potential challenge. In *Taylor v Lawrence*[145] the Court of Appeal gave consideration to the question of when bias might occur, especially when contacts between the judiciary and the legal profession may be close

---

1 Q.B. 577; [1968] 3 W.L.R. 694 CA (Civ Div). *Franklin v Minister of Town and Country Planning* [1948] A.C. 87; [1947] 2 All E.R. 289 HL.
141 *R v Bow Street Metropolitan Stipendiary Magistrate Ex p. Pinochet Ugarte (No.2)* [2000] 1 A.C. 119; [1999] 2 W.L.R. 272 HL.
142 [1993] A.C. 646; [1993] 2 W.L.R. 883 HL.
143 *Nwabueze v General Medical Council* [2000] 1 W.L.R. 1760; (2000) 56 B.M.L.R. 106 PC (UK).
144 See *DG of Fair Trading v Proprietary Association of Great Britain* [2001] UKHR 429 [2001] All ER (D) 372.
145 [2002] EWCA Civ 90; [2003] Q.B. 528.

but in the normal way should not give rise to a possibility of bias. Where it was considered that "a fair minded and informed person" might regard the judge as biased it was important that disclosure should be made of any professional relationship or connection. In making a decision whether or not to withdraw from the case, the judge could hear from both parties and adopt the test of the perspective of a fair minded and informed person.

G: Excluding Judicial Review

17–129 The High Court's supervisory role in the development of judicial review is derived from its common law powers of supervising "inferior bodies". In some examples there may be reasons for attempting to exclude the courts from interfering with the exercise of power or the application of the discretion of an inferior court or public body. While there is a presumption at common law in favour of the supervisory role of the courts, there are occasions when the courts may decline jurisdiction.

17–130 Judicial self-restraint or self-limitation may mean the courts do not intervene in reviewing the legal powers or the exercise of discretion of a public body. The courts' recognition of ministerial accountability to Parliament may result in not intervening in ministerial discretion. Similarly, invoking national security or the interests of the State will usually exclude the courts. The courts may decline to review the merits, policy or political choices of the decision-maker.

17–131 The courts may regard the existence of an appeal or other grievance mechanism adequate to the needs of the plaintiff. This may arise, for example, when the jurisdiction to consider grievances is given to a tribunal or a special body entrusted with particular responsibility. In *R v Hull University Ex p. Page*,[146] the House of Lords declined to exercise review over the jurisdiction of the Visitor in determining disputes arising under the domestic law of Hull University. The Visitor's jurisdiction included questions of fact or law and provided such powers were exercised within jurisdiction that the adjudication of disputes fell within the University rules, then the courts would refrain from intervening. If the Visitor acted outside his jurisdiction and acted in a manner incompatible with his judicial role or in breach of the rules of natural justice, then the courts might intervene. Lord Browne-Wilkinson explained[147]:

> "It is not only modern universities which have visitors: there are a substantial number of other long-established educational, ecclesiastical and eleemosynary bodies which have visitors. The advantages of having an informal system which produces a speedy, cheap

---

146 [1993] A.C. 682; [1993] 1 All E.R. 97 HL.
147 [1993] A.C. 682 at [109]. See *Patel v University of Bradford Senate* [1978] 1 W.L.R. 1488; [1978] 3 All E.R. 841 Ch D; and *Thomas v University of Bradford* [1987] A.C. 795; [1987] 2 W.L.R. 677 HL at [850].

> and final answer to internal disputes has been repeatedly emphasised in the authorities..."

However as an illustration of an exception to the courts not reviewing such bodies, in *Ex p. Calder*[148] the Court of Appeal explained that judicial review was available against the disciplinary Tribunal of the Inns of Court. Judicial review jurisdiction also applied to the Visitors to the Inns of Court. In Calder's case the Visitors had misapprehended their role, and sat not as an appellate body but as a reviewing body.

The courts may decline to review on the basis that the right involves private law rights which are not susceptible to judicial review. In *R v Disciplinary Committee of the Jockey Club Ex p. Aga Khan*[149] the Court of Appeal considered the role of the Jockey Club, incorporated by Royal Charter since 1970. The issue was whether a decision by the Jockey Club disqualifying a steward from chairmanship of a local panel was susceptible to review. The Court of Appeal held that the Rules were based on contractual agreement between the parties and owed their existence to private law rights. Thus they were not susceptible to review by the courts on the basis of judicial review. Undoubtedly, if the Jockey Club had not provided such rules then Parliament would have had to intervene. This did not bring the matter within the category of a public body. Classification between public and private bodies provides a useful categorisation for the courts to decide whether the body is susceptible to review. However, this does not always lead to consistency in approach. In *Datafin*,[150] the takeover panel was susceptible to review notwithstanding that it was not created by statute or prerogative but because there was evidence that its powers would have been granted to the Department of Trade and Industry through legislation, rather than through the informal rules set by the takeover panel. In this context there are similarities between the Jockey Club and the takeover panel. The former is not susceptible to review while the latter is.

Various techniques may be invoked to make judicial review either difficult or excluded altogether. The exclusion of the courts may occur when the wording of the statute contains such widely phrased powers that are couched in subjective terms that make review impossible. The form of words adopted may vary, such as "as the minister thinks fit", or "the minister's decision shall be conclusive" or the powers may be exercised "in such circumstances as the minister may believe". Faced with the prospect of subjective wording and unlimited discretion conferred on a Minister or public body, the courts require that the decision is made in good faith and that the powers are exercised fairly. Even faced with very wide discretionary powers, the courts may consider there is scope to intervene. In *Tameside*,[151] the Secretary of State for Education directed a local authority under s.68 of the Education Act 1944 to implement a 1975 scheme for the introduction of comprehensive education. Following a change in the political power of the local authority from Labour to Conservative the direction under s.68 of the 1944 Act was

---

148 *R v Visitors to the Inns of Court Ex p. Calder; Ex p. Persaud* [1994] Q.B. 1; [1993] 3 W.L.R. 287 CA (Civ Div).
149 [1993] 1 W.L.R. 909; [1993] 2 All E.R. 853 CA (Civ Div).
150 *R v Panel on Take-overs and Mergers Ex p. Datafin* [1987] Q.B. 815; [1987] 2 W.L.R. 699 CA (Civ Div).
151 *Secretary of State for Education v Tameside MBC* [1977] A.C. 1014; [1976] 3 W.L.R. 641 HL.

intended to prevent the Conservative-controlled local authority from implementing a selection process and retaining a number of grammar schools. The terms of s.68 of the 1944 Act were expressed in subjective terms, namely "If the Secretary of State is satisfied. . ." and ". . .give such directions as appear to him to be expedient. . .". The House of Lords concluded that there were matters which the Secretary of State had to address his mind to, before the powers under s.68 could be invoked. Lord Salmon interpreted the section to mean that the Secretary of State had to ask, could "any reasonable local authority act in the way, in which this authority have acted or is proposing to act?" The Secretary of State had failed to ask the right questions and therefore the decision was reviewable by the courts and the House of Lords held that the Secretary of State had acted unlawfully.

17-135
A further technique of avoiding the jurisdiction of the courts is to attempt to oust their jurisdiction. The most clear attempt to use an ouster clause may occur with the words: "shall not be called in question" in any court of law. In *Anisminic*,[152] already discussed above, the nature of the ouster clause was that under s.4(4) of the Foreign Compensation Act, the Commission's determinations "should not be questioned in any court of law whatsoever". The House of Lords considered that the ouster clause only protected "real" determinations. The error of law made by the Commission in requiring Anisminic to be "a successor in title" resulted in the Commission's determination becoming a nullity and therefore the ouster clause was inoperative. Lord Reid regarded the purported determination of the Commission as in the eyes of the law one that had no existence. The courts had power to consider whether the determination made by the Commission was correct in law, notwithstanding the presence of an "ouster clause".

17-136
The success of ouster clauses may appear to be heavily qualified by the discretion of the courts in reviewing errors that go to the jurisdiction of the tribunal concerned. In *Johnston v Chief Constable of the Royal Ulster Constabulary*,[153] it was noted that statutory ouster clauses could not be used to oust the jurisdiction of the courts in matters of EC law. In Johnston, a reserve police officer claimed sex discrimination by the failure of the RUC to renew her contract of employment. The reason given was that the RUC had a policy that women police constables should not carry firearms and there were sufficient full-time RUC officers to carry out all the jobs designated to women officers. The Secretary of State issued a certificate "that was conclusive" that she had been dismissed in the interests of national security. The European Court of Justice ruled that the order was inconsistent with EC law.

17-137
An alternative formulation to ousting the jurisdiction of the courts may be attempted. Instead of expressly stating that the courts are excluded a subtler form of exclusion is used. Techniques of exclusion may vary but one method is to adopt the formula that a regulation or order "shall have effect as it enacted in this Act". A clause may provide that the confirmation of an order by a Minister is "conclusive evidence" of the requirements of the Act.

17-138
A widely used procedure is to limit the opportunity which allows a decision to be challenged in the courts. This may be achieved by specifying time limits for taking legal action. One

---

152 *Anisminic Ltd v Foreign Compensation Commission* [1969] 2 A.C. 147; [1969] 2 W.L.R. 163 HL.
153 (C-222/84) EU:C:1986:206; [1987] Q.B. 129.

example of the use of time limits is discussed in *Smith v East Elloe RDC*.[154] A person aggrieved with a compulsory purchase order made under the Acquisition of Land Act 1981 may apply to the High Court "within six weeks" for it to be quashed. Thereafter, the order could "not be questioned in any legal proceedings whatsoever". In the case of *Smith*, the order was made five years before Smith decided to sue the Council claiming that the order was made in bad faith and therefore invalid. The House of Lords was divided on the matter, but the majority held that the time limit effectively left the courts unable to review the order. Some of the judges advanced the view that had the proceedings been taken within the time limit of six weeks and even if bad faith were proven, the courts could not intervene.

Reconciling the principles in *Smith* and *Anisminic* has been complicated by the lack of clarity in the *Smith* decision. *Ex p. Ostler*[155] held that the authority of *Smith* had not been diminished by *Anisminic*. The *Ostler* case effectively distinguished the *Anisminic* case: the former raised the question of a time limit, while the latter was an ouster clause. The true interpretation of both the *Ostler* case and *Smith v East Elloe* rests on what is served by the public interest. Thus, time limits may retain their value as a protection in the public interest for some degree of finality to the judicial process. This leaves public bodies with some degree of certainty that projects once commenced may be safe from later review.

17-139

H: What is the Impact of Public Law Litigation?

17-140

Maurice Sunkin has considered the important question of the potential impact of public law litigation. If judicial review is a major contribution to the rule of law what are the practical effects of judicial review itself? Generalisations have to be treated with some caution:

> "Public bodies may not welcome judicial review and may find it inconvenient when their decisions are challenged, especially when this requires them to revisit budget priorities or alter habits of practice. However, evidence indicates that judicial review may lead to improvements in the quality of public services; that it may assist officials in their work by clarifying the law, setting standards for decision-making, and stimulating re-evaluation of services. Judicial review may also enable public bodies to better reconcile the

---

154 [1956] A.C. 736; [1956] 2 W.L.R. 888 HL.
155 *R v Secretary of State for the Environment Ex p. Ostler* [1977] Q.B. 122; [1976] 3 W.L.R. 288 CA (Civ Div).

> demands of the many with particular needs, including the needs of those unflavoured by populist pressures."[156]

17-141 Sunkin also notes how judicial review allows many issues to be raised by claimants with legitimate complaints that require a satisfactory remedy. Expense, delay, complexity and the use of appeals may leave some complainants frustrated as they may win their case in court but not necessarily in the way they hope. Overriding principles of upholding the rule of law makes judicial review an important protection for individual liberty. At the same time there are limitations on the scope of review. The Supreme Court in the *HSE v Wolverhampton City Council*[157] considered the responsibilities of public authorities when deciding to exercise a discretionary power to achieve a public objective. The main question was whether or not costs to the public ought to be taken into consideration. The Supreme Court considered the responsibilities on public bodies and their application to the case in question. Planning permission for a block of four student residences had been applied for and granted. In the course of construction, the Health and Safety Executive (HSE), concerned about gas storage on site, applied for an order to revoke planning permission against Wolverhampton Local Authority. In refusing the application, the Council considered costs and came to the view that the if planning permission were revoked the cost of compensation that would be payable would be high and consequently refused the HSE's application. The HSE brought judicial review proceedings against the Council. The High Court refused that part of the claim. The Court of Appeal allowed the HSE appeal and held that the Council has to make its decision in isolation from the economic circumstances of the decision. The Supreme Court adopted a different approach, and decided that a public authority was entitled to take into account the cost to the public purse. Section 97 required the authority to satisfy itself that revocation is expedient including consideration of the development plan and other "material considerations". As the payment of compensation is a relevant matter, the cost to the public purse has to be considered. As a general principle, a public body has to take into account public spending in assessing good value. The courts are unable to review policy merits even when faced with strong pressure to do so.

I: Summary and Conclusions

17-142 Judicial review has come of age and found in the judiciary a robust self-confidence about its future, that has defined the progress of the past 25 years. There remains, however, considerable uncertainty about the values that inform judicial decision-making. Indeed, uncertainty

---

156 M. Sunkin, "The Impact of public law litigation" in M. Elliott and D. Feldman (eds), *The Cambridge Companion to Public Law* (Cambridge: Cambridge University Press, 2015), pp.236–255.
157 *HSE v Wolverhampton CC* [2012] UKSC 34; [2012] 1 W.L.R. 2264.

characterises many aspects of public law at present.¹⁵⁸ This places the judiciary in the spotlight of speculation about the future, particularly when the Human Rights Act and EU membership is politically controversial. There are some signs, notably in the Supreme Court decision in *Pham v Secretary of State for the Home Department*,¹⁵⁹ that the common law principles of review are being developed that are not entirely reliant on the statutory arrangements under the Human Rights Act 1998 or EU law. This is a proactive approach that may anticipate changes in the rights available to UK Citizens through amendment to the Human Rights Act 1998.

17-143

In his path-breaking research on the case load of applications for judicial review, Sunkin¹⁶⁰ has noted how judicial review has developed into an important and essential means for the citizen to seek redress as well as for the courts to oversee the work of administrative decision-making. His research findings underline the breadth, diversity and range of issues which come before the courts. The statistical evidence in Sunkin's studies also shows the use of judicial review by local authorities against central government. A major proportion of judicial review cases come from litigation involving prisoners, housing disputes including homeless persons, planning and licensing disputes. Immigration cases are also significant over the refusal of entry or challenging asylum decisions. In two areas in particular, immigration and homelessness, judicial review has grown in size. In other areas judicial review has been used sparingly. Judicial review is used to challenge local government but its use in challenging the new generation of non-departmental public bodies is uncertain at present.¹⁶¹ Judicial review has the potential to change administrative and bureaucratic procedures and practices, alter the attitude of policy makers and influence citizens in setting their expectations about the value of the legal system.¹⁶²

17-144

Many of the conclusions to be drawn from Sunkin's study¹⁶³ underline the variables present in determining whether to seek judicial review. Variables include matters such as the availability of legal aid, the existence of alternative remedies, the ability of complainants to identify legal problems and lawyers to decide within the three-month time limit to seek an application for judicial review. The availability of evidence, its preparation and the willingness to litigate are all hidden factors in the availability of judicial review.

17-145

An additional question in using the courts is whether the adversarial nature of the English judicial system provides an adequate basis to lay down normative principles for the solution of administrative mistakes, inefficiencies or even in providing a grievance resolution for citizens.

---

158 A. Le Sueur and M.Sunkin, "Can Government Control Judicial Review?" (1991) 44 *Current Legal Problems* 161; and R. Gambitta, M. May and J. Forster (eds), *Governing Through Courts* (London: Sage, 1981).
159 [2015] UKSC 19; [2015] 1 W.L.R. 1591.
160 M. Sunlin, K. Calvo, L. Platt and T. Landman, "Mapping the Use of Judicial Review to Challenge Local Authorities in England and Wales" [2007] *Public Law* 545; and V. Bondy and M. Sunkin, *The Dyamics of Judicial Review Litigation* (London: Public Law Project, 2009).
161 *R (Consumer Council for the Postal Services) v Postal Setvices Commission* [2007] EWCA Civ 167; (2007) 104(12) L.S.G. 3. T. Prosser, "Regulation and Legitimacy" in D. Oliver, J. Jowell and C. O'Cinneide (eds), *The Changing Constitution* (Oxford: Oxford University Press, 2015), pp.329–349.
162 S. Halliday, "The Influence of Judicial Review on Bureaucratic Decision-making" [2000] *Public Law* 110.
163 M. Sunkin, "The Judicial Review Case-Load 1987–1989" [1991] *Public Law* 490–499; and M. Sunkin, "What is happening to Applications for Judicial review?" (1987) 50 *Modern Law Review* 432.

17-146

There is also the issue of how far formal legal rules may not only constrain officials but also condition or determine their behaviour. There is an increasing awareness among public authorities and judges of the principles of judicial review. Judicial approaches to substantive judicial review have become more nuanced and related to the context of the decision-maker. This may leave judges with a wider discretion than in the past; potentially innovative and creative in explaining doctrines and offering an analysis that provides for a deeper and richer jurisprudence of public law. This may have the inherent risk of creating an over complex case law that too often may depend only on the facts and not always related to the application of legal principles.

Further Reading

P. Craig, *Administrative Law*, 7th edn (London: Sweet and Maxwell, 2012).

T. Endicott, *Administrative Law* (Oxford: Oxford University Press, 2011).

K. D. Ewing, *Bonfire of the Liberties* (Oxford: Oxford University Press, 2011).

A. Horne and L. Maer, "From the Human Rights Act to a Bill of Rights" in A. Horne, G. Drewry and D. Oliver (eds), *Parliament and the Law* (Oxford: Hart, 2013), pp.251–280.

M. Loughlin, *Sword and Scales: An Examination of the Relationship between Law and Politics* (Oxford: Hart, 2000).

Lord Woolf, J. Jowell and A. P. Le Sueur, *Principles of Judicial Review* (London: Sweet & Maxwell, 1999).

M. Sunkin, "The Impact of public law litigation" in M. Elliott and D. Feldman (eds), *The Cambridge Companion to Public Law* (Cambridge: Cambridge University Press, 2015), pp.236–255.

H. W. R. Wade and C. F. Forsyth, *Administrative Law*, 8th edn (Oxford: Oxford University Press, 2000).

18 Remedies

A: Introduction

English law with its distinctive constitutional tradition, has developed throughout the centuries an extensive system of remedies rather than a system of positive rights. Rights may arise in English law through the development of the common law and in express statutory enactments. Often such rights are expressed as negative rights to be protected in a particular way. The Human Rights Act 1998 provides the courts with the opportunity to develop Convention rights supportive of the system of remedies. In many cases the availability of remedies is dependent on access to a lawyer. Often the availability of legal aid is one of the critical factors in determining whether or not an application for judicial review can be made. This chapter is focused on the role of the courts in the development of remedies. First, consideration is given to public law remedies and secondly, to remedies available in private law. The application for judicial review procedure, discussed below and in Ch.17, became Pt 54 of the Civil Procedures Rules from October 2000. In much of the literature it is still referred to as Order 53 and s.31 of the Senior Courts Act 1981. As noted previously, the other changes in line with the recent procedural changes introduced to the civil justice system include applicants becoming "claimants" and the nomenclature of the prerogative orders. In line with the case management approach to civil justice there is a Pre-Action Protocol for Judicial Review.[1] This includes good practice relevant to Alternative Dispute Resolution and the exchange of documents at the pre-action stage of proceedings. There are details of letters before claim and responses to a letter before claim as well as public funding adjustments for legal costs in judicial review proceedings. The Queen's Bench Division of the High Court also known as the Divisional Court is now the Administrative Court.

---

1 Ministry of Justice, *Pre-Action Protocol for Judicial Review* (London, 2015).

18-002 The outcome of austerity budgeting and cuts in public spending on legal aid[2] is to place more emphasis on remedies that do not involve litigation and avoiding litigation whenever possible.[3] The Civil Procedure Rules encourages mediation as an alternative way of resolving disputes and it is likely that in future years mediation for judicial review cases will increase in importance.[4] There is also an overriding discretion exercisable in public law cases.

B: Forms of Relief

18-003 Remedies may be statutory or non-statutory. In the case of statutory remedies, commonly this may take the form of an appeal to the High Court or of an application to a single judge of the High Court to quash or make an Order depending on the terms of the statute. For example, in the case of compulsory purchase orders there is an appeal to the High Court that the Order may be ultra vires. Supervision by the courts of the planning process is an important and significant influence over how the planning system operates. Such rights of appeal originated in the 1947 Town and Country Planning Act and have been maintained under the 1971 Town and Country Planning legislation and s.78 of the Town and Country Planning Act 1990.[5] Thus the validity of development plans and various other planning orders may be challenged in the High Court within a six-week period. In such cases the rights of appeal are usually available to "any person aggrieved" by the plan or its amendment.

18-004 The provision of remedies through the system of appeals allows for the quashing of the decision at first instance. Generally, appeals may be by rehearing, or on a point of law or by case stated. There are a number of procedural routes that may be taken to achieve an appeal. Many are derived from statutory provision or from the Rules of the Supreme Court. Appeals by way of rehearing under Order 53 give the appellate court powers to reverse the decision of the lower court. Appeals by way of case stated are usually from the magistrates' court to the High Court or specialist tribunals or the Crown Court to the High Court.

18-005 In the case of non-statutory remedies, the development of the various remedies available in administrative law may now be considered. In 1969 the Law Commission considered the law relating to the remedies available "for the judicial control of administrative acts or omissions with a view to evolving a simpler and more effective procedure". Following the Law Commission Report,[6] in 1977 the Order 53 procedure was introduced and took effect in 1978.

---

2 House of Lords, *Future of Legal Aid* LLN, Library Note, 2015/048 (7 December 2015).
3 *R (Cowl) v Plymouth Council* [2001] EWCA Civ 1935; [2002] 1 W.L.R. 803.
4 V. Bondy and M. Sunkin, "Settlement in Judicial Review Proceedings" [2009] *P.L.* 237.
5 See The Planning Inspectorate, *Procedural Guide on Planning Appeals—England* (2015)
6 *Report on Remedies in Administrative Law*, Law Commission Paper, No.73, Cmnd.6407. Also see Law

The importance of this reform, and afterwards in 1981 its modification by s.31 of the Supreme Court Act 1981 (now the Senior Courts Act 1981), was that the application for judicial review became the exclusive procedure for obtaining the prerogative writs. These arrangements have been supplemented with a pre-action protocol that brings the procedures into line with other civil case management systems.

18-006

Prerogative remedies have a long history in English law. Certiorari according to Lord Atkin in *R v Electricity Commissioners Ex p. London Electricity Joint Committee*[7] is available "whenever any body of persons having legal authority to determine questions affecting the rights of subjects, and having the duty to act judicially, act in excess of their jurisdiction". Certiorari is available to quash a decision in breach of the rules of natural justice or which is ultra vires. Prohibition is available to prevent action or the continuation of action which breaches the rules of natural justice or is in excess of jurisdiction. Mandamus compels the performance of a public duty. The prerogative remedies were first known as writs brought by the King against the offending official to compel the legal exercise of their powers. The Crown could ensure the performance of public duties and responsibilities by public authorities and inferior bodies kept within their jurisdiction. In 1933 the Administration of Justice (Miscellaneous Provisions) Act 1933 introduced a system whereby an ex parte motion had to be made to the High Court asking first for leave to apply for the remedy. The ex parte nature of the application resulted in only the applicant being represented and the other parties were not represented or given notice of the case. Rules of the Supreme Court laid down a time-limit of six months for seeking certiorari subject to the Court's discretion. The prerogative writs were subject to further change under s.7 of the Administration of Justice (Miscellaneous Provisions) Act 1938, which provided that the prerogative writs should be known as prerogative orders. Their development is part of the inherent supervisory jurisdiction of the High Court to review inferior bodies. Finally, there is also habeas corpus as a means of questioning the legality of detention exercised by administrative authorities and tribunals. The role of habeas corpus has diminished in use in recent years, but it still provides an important element of supervision over the detention powers of the Executive.

18-007

In addition to the prerogative orders the citizen may seek a declaration and injunction. Declarations set out the rights of the parties and could settle the legality of a particular cause or action, but it could not review cases where there was error of law on the face of the record. Injunctions provide the main remedy in private law prohibiting the commission of an unlawful act such as a breach of contract or a tort. It is a discretionary remedy and in origin owes its earlier existence to the Court of Chancery. The popularity of both declaration and injunction came to rival the use of the prerogative orders, specifically certiorari, traditionally regarded as the main Order for keeping public bodies within their legal powers.[8] Litigants found a

---

Commission Report No.226. Also see The Law Commission, *Administrative Law: Judicial Review and Statutory Appeals*, Consultation Paper, No.126 (London: HMSO, 1993).
7   [1924] 1 K.B. 171 CA at [205].
8   *Congreve v Home Office* [1976] Q.B. 629; [1976] 2 W.L.R. 291 CA (Civ Div). See S. A. de Smith, *Judicial Review of Administrative Action*, 4th edn (London: Stevens,1980), Ch.10.

number of procedural drawbacks with the prerogative orders which may, in part, account for this development. First, that the prerogative orders did not provide for any interrogatories, normally available in any private action. Interrogatories included the lack of discovery of documents. Secondly, it was not possible to "mix" remedies. This means it was impossible to seek a certiorari along with damages or an injunction or declaration. Thirdly, the rules of standing varied according to the remedy sought and the circumstances differed where one remedy was available and another was unavailable.

18-008 Declaration provided the basis for establishing some of the most important developments in administrative law and helped to shape and change the substantive law of judicial review. Declaration offered the litigant certain advantages. These included the absence of requirement of leave and the absence of a short time-limit for action such as the six-month time-limit for certiorari. Litigants' solicitors may have found the declaration a more attractive remedy because of its common use in many private law matters, whereas certiorari provided greater complexity concerning the nature of the decision that may be reviewed.

18-009 The Justice-All Souls Review[9] identified the problems that existed before the introduction of the Order 53 reforms as follows:

> "The applicant, however, could not get sight of the relevant files of the authority nor could he cross-examine its witnesses. The general rule was that discovery of documents and interrogatories were not available and that evidence was confined to affidavit material. Different time-limits applied in relation to each remedy. If the applicant applied for the wrong remedy the whole proceedings would fail and he would have to start again (if still in time). The court had no power to award the right remedy."

18-010 In addition to declaration and injunction there is also an action for damages arising out of a public authority's liability in tort or contract. Such remedies are discretionary and subject to rules relating to locus standi. Order 53 introduced significant reforms to the system of remedies. In public law matters an application for judicial review for mandamus, prohibition or certiorari, or declaration or injunction may be made to the High Court. Discovery may be ordered. Damages may be joined to the application for judicial review at the discretion of the Court. Before considering each of the remedies in more detail it is first necessary to explain the law of standing.

---

9 *Administrative Justice Report of the Committee of the Justice—All Souls Review of Administrative Law in the United Kingdom* (Oxford: Clarendon, 1988), p.143.

C: The Law of Standing

18–011 The law relating to standing, locus standi, is important in both private law claims and in the application made by claimants for judicial review. The rules of standing set out the entitlement of the aggrieved citizen to seek redress in the courts for the particular remedy sought. The rules of standing have a "gate-keeping" function as providing the means to exclude vexatious litigants or unworthy cases. Standing may appear as a procedural requirement but procedural rules in this instance are linked to substantive issues.

18–012 The arguments in favour of liberal rules of standing appear persuasive. Access to the courts should be open to the citizen as a means of complaint. Wide rules of standing permit the courts a large discretion in remedying the abuse of public power. Traditionally this fits Dicey's view that the rule of law requires that disputes as to the legality of acts of the Government ought to be decided by judges independent of the Executive. This implies that illegal conduct should be prevented or stopped which is a necessary corollary of enforcing the law. Flouting of the law may occur where the procedures for redress are inadequate. If illegality is not checked, then the law may be diminished in status.

18–013 What is the purpose of having rules of standing? One view is that standing rules provide administrators some protection against vexatious litigants and this protects the conduct of Government business to be carried on unrestricted from outside interference. Setting limits on who may litigate prevents government from an over-cautious and over-legalistic approach to problem-solving. Interest groups and organisations may be prevented from waging a political struggle by adopting legalistic techniques in order to challenge existing rules. There is a fear that politically motivated litigation may involve the courts in political struggles and the courts may regard such a use of judicial review as an unacceptable abuse of the courts' proper role. However, distinguishing acceptable from unacceptable motives in seeking litigation may not be easy and the need for flexible rules of standing may permit the courts a much needed discretion.

18–014 Standing may also permit public institutions to enforce the law. In the case of the Audit Commission, it is envisaged that under s.25(d) of the local Government Finance Act 1982 provided by s.30 and Sch.4 to the Local Government Act 1988, the auditor appointed in relation to the audit of accounts may apply for judicial review. This may arise where there is a failure by the body audited to act arising out of any decision where it might reasonably be considered that it would have an effect on the accounts of the local authority. Such powers to seek judicial review include the power to take action in anticipation of any breach of the law. In 1990, a Code of Audit Practice was published to facilitate the use of the auditor's legal powers and provides for consultation with the body under audit.

18–015 Local authorities under s.222(1) of the Local Government Act 1972 have, in respect of civil proceedings and where "it is expedient for the promotion or protection of the interests of their inhabitants", the right to institute proceedings. The use of injunctions in the case of the Sunday Trading laws is an example of this power.[10] In many instances such rights of standing have

---

10 *Kirklees MBC v Wickes Building Supplies Ltd* [1993] A.C. 227; [1992] 3 W.L.R. 170 HL.

been used to enforce the law in respect of nuisance through stop-notices. In criminal matters local authorities are given wide powers to institute prosecutions for specific breaches of the criminal law that fall within their jurisdiction.

18-016 The Attorney General occupies a unique role in terms of standing. As the guardian of the public interest, he has a special duty to enforce the law. The Attorney General may agree to lend his name to the actions of a private citizen in seeking redress in the courts. When a private individual is unable to establish sufficient standing for the institution of a private action, which may involve public rights, the Attorney General may permit the action to proceed as a "relator" action. Today the occasions to do this are rare as locus standi has been sufficiently broadened to permit the citizen direct access to the courts.[11] The use of the Attorney General has expanded the role of injunction and declaration as providing a protection arising from private law for many public law grievances. The case for having a flexible approach to standing appears well made. However, permissive rules of standing may give rise to serious administrative problems in the organisation of the courts. The courts may become overburdened with the flow of cases and delays in having cases heard may lead to injustice. Currently, there is a delay of at least 15 months before an application for judicial review may be heard by a single judge. There are also questions about the cost of administering the system. In many instances the opportunities for litigation may depend on the availability of legal aid which is paid out of public funds. The cost of legal aid may become a consideration in the expense of operating the system of judicial review and pressure to reduce costs may require adjustments to the present arrangements.

Standing in private law

18-017 The rules of standing may be considered with respect to private actions. The use of remedies available in private law for public law wrongs requires there to be standing. In general, in private law the entitlement to a remedy and the right to apply for the remedy are treated together. The most common remedies are the action for an injunction or declaration. In *Boyce v Paddington Corp*,[12] the plaintiff brought an action to restrain the Council from constructing a hoarding adjacent to a building site, which would obstruct the plaintiff's right to light. The right to sue was accepted in respect of a public wrong where the plaintiff suffered damage to his private rights. This is capable of both narrow or broad interpretation depending on the nature of the issue.

18-018 In the case of a private action against a public authority in *Steeples v Derbyshire CC*,[13] it was held that the plaintiff's action based on private propriety rights could provide sufficient locus standi when affected by the exercise of public law powers. The plaintiff was granted

---

11   Sir Harry Woolf, *Protection of the Public—A New Challenge* (Hamlyn Lecture, 1990). See *Gouriet v Union of Post Office Workers* [1978] A.C. 435; [1977] 3 W.L.R. 300 HL.
12   [1903] 1 Ch. 109 Ch D.
13   [1985] 1 W.L.R. 256; [1984] 3 All E.R. 468 QBD.

sufficient standing to challenge the grant of planning permission over two leisure complexes. The plaintiff claimed that his private rights such as enjoyment of his property as against nuisance caused by noise, or enjoyment of the use of a lane and the risk of vandals or litter were infringed. He also claimed that there was a breach of natural justice in the granting of the planning permission. The grounds for standing arising out of both private rights were equivalent to those available to him to make an application for judicial review if necessary.

The courts may wish to restrict the availability of private law remedies only to those directly affected rather than to any citizen's sense of public spirit. In cases where the private person may lack the necessary standing, the Attorney General may be requested to give his permission to a relator action. In *Gouriet*,[14] Lord Wilberforce explained how a relator action, which allowed the Attorney General at the suit of individuals to bring an action or assert a public right, might be used in a private action for an injunction to restrain a threatened breach of the criminal law by a trade union. However, such a relator action was at the discretion of the Attorney General and the courts were unwilling to review such a discretion.

Similarly, the courts are sensitive to the need to restrict the availability of remedies so as to exclude busybodies or unmeritorious cases. Invariably standing may be sought by ratepayers, taxpayers or "aggrieved citizens". Applying *Boyce v Paddington* such citizens may sue in their own name where a public right causes special damage. In *Barrs v Bethell*[15] some ratepayers from Camden sought an injunction against the local authority alleging that there had been various abuses of the discretion given to councillors and requiring that cuts should be made in services. It was decided that they could not sue in their own name but could seek a relator action through the Attorney General.

Standing in public law

The application for judicial review under Order 53 requires consideration of the applicant's standing. It will be remembered that the procedure under Order 53 is a two-stage process. At the first stage there is a leave requirement. Obtaining leave requires that an arguable case is made out and if this is not found, leave may be refused. In practice this sets a low threshold but it may be seen as a procedural sieve or hurdle to be surmounted before the full hearing of the issues is considered at the second stage.

Section 7 of the Human Rights Act 1998 provides that a claim that a public authority acted incompatibly with a Convention right such as a breach of s.6 is based on their being a "victim" within the meaning of art.34 of the European Convention on Human Rights. The victim test applies to a pressure group or group of individuals in order to rely on Convention rights. The victim test applies to ensuring that legislation is applied consistently with the Convention.

There is no equivalent leave requirement in ordinary civil actions and the leave requirement has been criticised as wrong in principle. However, the requirement of leave may be

---

14   *Gouriet v Union of Post Office Workers* [1978] A.C. 435.
15   [1982] Ch. 294; [1981] 3 W.L.R. 874 Ch D.

justified as an important way to exclude vexatious litigants or busybodies. The leave requirement acts as a means to filter out hopeless or unmeritorious cases. In *Ex p. Doorga*,[16] it was noted that leave should be granted where there are prima facie reasons for granting judicial review, but refused either when there is no prima facie case and where the case is wholly unarguable. In practical terms there are cases where the issues clearly appear arguable and those that require more detailed consideration to determine whether they are worth further consideration. In the former, leave will always be granted while the latter require more careful scrutiny.

18-024 At the first stage an application for leave normally is made ex parte to a single judge, usually on affidavits and subject to amendment at the discretion of the judge. The ex parte nature of the proceedings results in the absence of any representation from the defendant and this requires that the courts take time to ensure the accuracy of the affidavits. All relevant matters must be disclosed and there is a presumption of good faith on the part of the applicant. Thus, if material facts are suppressed or withheld, the court may dismiss the application without reference to the merits of the case. In cases where the judge is uncertain of whether an arguable case is made out, it is possible for the judge to invite the defendant to appear in person and make representations on the nature of the case. An application may be made under the general jurisdiction of the court to set aside leave which has been granted. The criterion is whether the judge is satisfied that the case has no reasonable prospect of success.

18-025 The Order 53 procedure permits applying in a single application, for the prerogative remedies of certiorari, mandamus and prohibition, together with declaration, damages or injunction. The requirement of standing is now part of the leave requirement for the application for judicial review and is contained in s.31(3) of the Senior Courts Act 1981, "that the applicant has a sufficient interest in the matter to which the application relates".

18-026 Originally, the Law Commission had envisaged that the standing rule should be part of the consideration of whether to grant any of the remedies sought. However, as matters presently stand, the question of standing may be raised as to the grant of leave to apply for judicial review under s.31(3) of the 1981 Act, but there remains the possibility that standing may be considered also at the second stage when there is a substantive hearing of the case. This possibility emerges from consideration given to the law of standing by the House of Lords in *R v Inland Revenue Commissioners Ex p. National Federation of Self-Employed and Small Businesses*,[17] which may be conveniently referred to as the *Fleet Street Casuals* case. An application for judicial review was made by an association of taxpayers who objected to the Inland Revenue waiving the arrears of income tax for 6,000 workers in the printing industry in Fleet Street. The association objected to preferential treatment which it viewed as condoning illegality in newspaper practices in hiring casual labour for the printing industry in Fleet Street.

---

16 *R v Secretary of State for the Home Department Ex p. Doorga* [1990] Imm. A.R. 98; [1990] C.O.D. 109 CA (Civ Div).
17 [1982] A.C. 617; [1981] 2 W.L.R. 722 HL.

This case raises important issues over the interpretation of the existing law of standing but the decision unfortunately leaves uncertainty as to the precise legal principles which may apply. The case favoured a flexible and liberal approach to standing but failed to set out clear principles, preferring to leave a large measure of judicial discretion and policy making.

The law of standing before the introduction of Order 53 varied according to the particular remedy sought. After the *Fleet Street Casuals* case there is still some doubt as to whether there is a single test for standing under the new procedures under Order 53. Thus it may still remain relevant to consider the nature of the particular remedy that is sought. However, it is generally accepted that in the *Fleet Street Casuals* case the general preference in judicial opinion was in favour of a uniform test for standing freed from any undue procedural or technical differences depending on the remedy sought. This preference emerges from the following opinions.

Lords Diplock, Scarman and Wilberforce agreed that standing had to be considered not in isolation but as part of the legal and factual context of the application. Lord Fraser dissented on this point but it was commonly agreed that the applicants had failed to show any breach of the duty of the Inland Revenue and that the Revenue had wide managerial powers which allowed them to make special agreements of this kind. Consequently, the association according to Lord Scarman had failed to show sufficient interest to justify any further proceedings.

On the general matter of standing, Lords Diplock, Scarman and Roskill agreed that the law on standing was the same for all remedies. Lords Diplock and Scarman considered that mandamus was not stricter than certiorari and that injunction and declaration are available where certiorari would lie. The consensus of opinion in favour of liberal rules of standing raises the question about the nature of the rules that should apply to determine standing.

The judges refer to standing being determined as a question of "mixed law and fact". Statutory interpretation and the general context of the application are relevant to determine the nature of the applicant's interest in the case. Legal principles are expected to be applied to determine standing rather than general discretion, though Lord Diplock admitted that he regarded the judges as having an unfettered discretion to decide what sufficient interest may mean in a particular case. Searching for legal principles from the *Fleet Street Casuals* case, it emerges that every person who has a good case has standing. This might be interpreted to mean that standing no longer forms a distinct category as every good case will fulfil the standing requirement on its merits. Standing only becomes a relevant issue for those cases where there is doubt about the merits of the decision. However, this view does not find universal acceptance and the matter remains uncertain.

The *Fleet Street Casuals* case, by joining the issue of the applicant's status and interest to the merits of the case, appears to move in favour of presuming that citizens have the right of legal redress. However, this does not always guarantee that the citizen's action is approved of by the courts. Consistent principles in this area of the law are difficult to formulate. Factors that contribute to uncertainty include the use of the discretion of the courts and the fact that in some cases the Crown will waive any consideration of standing when issues arise that the Crown considers require adjudication by the courts.

Pressure groups and standing

18-033

In *Covent Garden Community Association Ltd v Greater London Council*,[18] the Covent Garden Community Association was a company formed to protect the rights and interests of Covent Garden residents. Woolf J accepted that this gave the Association sufficient interest and therefore locus standi to challenge planning permission, but certiorari was refused on the merits of the case. A similar approach was evident in *R v Hammersmith and Fulham BC Ex p. People Before Profit*,[19] where a company limited by guarantee sought leave to object to the planning policy committee of the local borough's decision to grant planning permission after a planning report following a public inquiry had favoured objectors. Locus standi was established on the "legitimate" bona fide reason that any person was entitled to object to a planning matter. The status of a company did not provide sufficient ground to prevent standing. However, the application was refused because the case was not a reasonable one.

18-034

A more fundamental objection to citizens challenging decisions appears from *R v Secretary of State for the Environment Ex p. Rose Theatre Trust Co.*[20] Schiemann J considered the standing of a trust formed from local residents, well known and renowned archaeological experts and leading actors, who applied for judicial review to preserve the remains of a site in London which was claimed to be the remains of the Rose Theatre and of great historical interest.

18-035

The case raised the fundamental question of the role of a pressure group and the law of standing. Leave was granted to apply for judicial review but the question of standing became a central issue at the full hearing of the application. Schiemann J considered whether standing was established. He observed that, even after leave was granted, the court which hears the application ought to consider whether the applicant has sufficient interest. Whether an applicant has sufficient interest is not purely a matter for the court's discretion. Not every member of the public can complain of every breach of statutory duty. The fact that "some thousands of people join together and assert that they have an interest does not create an interest if the individuals did not have an interest". A company which has a particular power within its memorandum to pursue a particular objective does not create for a company an interest in the case. It remains to be seen whether this restrictive view of public interest litigation will be followed by the courts in future cases.

18-036

The *Rose Theatre Case* adopts an approach which emphasises the importance of establishing a sufficient interest even if the effect is to allow unchallenged the legality of the Secretary of State's powers. In deciding that the applicants failed to meet the standing requirement the question of who might have sufficient standing was also considered and it was concluded that "no individual has the standing to move for judicial review". This reasoning appears unduly protective of the powers of the Secretary of State, but it may arise from an unwillingness by the courts to become involved as an instrument of pressure group activity. This interpretation

---

18   [1981] J.P.L. 183.
19   80 L.G.R. 322; (1983) 45 P. & C.R. 364 QBD.
20   [1990] 1 Q.B. 504; [1990] 2 W.L.R. 186 QBD.

may arise from the particular statutory arrangements under s.1 of the Ancient Monuments and Archaeological Areas Act 1979 which did not envisage any appeal or review. However, there is also an apparent reluctance from the case to develop public interest litigation. Two reasons may contribute to this reluctance. First, administrative pressures on the courts to cope with the increased volume of judicial review. Secondly, a concern that policy formulation is best left to parliamentary supervision rather than judicial review.

Is the law of standing in a satisfactory state? The answer depends on the earlier discussion about the precise role of the rules of standing. Galligan distinguishes standing which concerns an individual's capacity to seek judicial review where his private interest is in some way affected, from the position where a person seeks to challenge simply on the basis of the public interest in not allowing official power to be used improperly.

The current state of the law allows great flexibility in the courts and even though there are doubts about public interest challenge, such challenges have been allowed by the courts albeit on a restrictive basis. It is useful, for example, to contrast the use of public challenge to local authority decisions when compared to the use of public challenge to matters involving central government. The former was expressly approved by the Widdicombe Report[21] as a means to control local authority activities.

The importance of pressure groups at both the national and international level includes such well known groups as Friends of the Earth, Greenpeace and the World Development Movement. They have been active campaigners and have been active in the lobbying process for better protection of the environment and in challenging government policy. In *R v Secretary of State for Foreign and Commonwealth Affairs Ex p. World Development Movement*,[22] the World Development Movement successfully challenged the payments from the overseas aid budget to build a dam in Malaysia.

The World Development Movement was described as "a non-partisan group, over 20 years old and limited by guarantee", that has 7,000 full voting members throughout the UK with a total supporter base of some 13,000. There are about 200 local groups, and campaign activities include letter writing and petitioning MPs.

The case marks an unusual and significant use of official documents and greater transparency in government decision-making. The pressure group relied on information obtained through a National Audit Office report and information gleaned from debates within, and evidence taken by, the Public Accounts Committee and the Foreign Affairs Committee.[23] The National Audit Office and the Public Accounts Committee assumed the legality of the aid but criticised aspects of its value for money. The National Audit Office regarded the allocation of money as falling under policy matters within the remit of Ministers. This excluded from its consideration the merits of the policy. However, it appeared that the Accounting Officer had serious reservations about the project.

---

21 *The Conduct of Local Authority Business*, Cmd.9797 (1986).
22 [1995] 1 W.L.R. 386; [1995] 1 All E.R. 611 Div Ct.
23 *Pergau Hydro-Electric Project*, HC 155 (1994–95). See F. White, I. Harden and K. Donnelly, "Audit, Accounting Officers and Accountability: The Pergau Dam Affair" [1994] *Public Law* 526.

18-042 As Rose LJ noted, the Accounting Officer's view was that the Pergau project was "an abuse of the aid programme in the terms that this is an uneconomic project" and that "it was not a sound development project".[24] Despite such reservations, written ministerial instructions were given to proceed with the financial aid. The Pergau project was funded, purportedly under s.1 of the Overseas Development and Co-operation Act 1980. Considering whether the aid for the Pergau Dam fell within the ambit of the 1980 Act, Rose LJ concluded that

> "[a]ccordingly, where, as here, the contemplated development is, on the evidence, so economically unsound that there is no economic argument in favour of the case, it is not, in my judgment, possible to draw any material distinction between questions of propriety and regularity on the one hand and questions of economy and efficiency of public expenditure on the other."[25]

18-043 The Secretary of State under s.1(1) of the 1980 Act had extensive powers as follows:

> "The Secretary of State shall have power, for the purpose of promoting the development or maintaining the economy of a country or territory outside the UK, or the welfare of its people, to furnish any person or body with assistance, whether financial, technical or of any other nature."

18-044 The case hinged on the interpretation of this section. Was the grant in question "for the purpose of promoting the development" of Malaysia? This depended on whether the aid flowed into a development that might be described, according to the Foreign Office test for funding development, as one that was "sound, financially viable and [would] bring economic benefits". As doubts had been expressed within the consultation process within the Government departments, the Divisional Court held that the provision of aid was ultra vires the 1980 Act. As a result of this decision, the Comptroller and Auditor General qualified his opinion of the aid on the basis of irregularity. Despite this finding and the decision of the Divisional Court, the Government found the necessary additional aid required to finance the Dam from a repayable charge on the Contingency Fund. Eventually the money was found from the Reserve Fund.

18-045 The World Development Movement were able to show how the dam project had limited use in terms of promoting development but had enormous potential for encouraging arms sales and potential markets for UK companies. The project also failed on the criteria of its potential damage to the environment and limited benefits for the community. Evidence used in the case provided a broad cost-benefit analysis of the project, beyond the narrow view of the Government in favour of economic trade.

---

24 [1995] 1 W.L.R. 386; [1995] 1 All E.R. 611 Div Ct at [617A]–[617B].
25 [1995] 1 All E.R. 611 at [626J]–[627B].

THE LAW OF STANDING

18-046

The case signifies that issues of the legality of public expenditure may involve questions of value for money. There is a stark warning here. As Rose LJ noted, the Government had taken no legal advice in the first instance on the legality of the aid; and as Daintith and Page observe:

> "The question of the relationship between the legislation and the Department's power to incur expenditure subject only to the authority of the Appropriation Act does not appear to have been raised or discussed."[26]

18-047

Greenpeace has also been particularly active in monitoring radioactive waste. Otton J in *R v Pollution Inspectorate Ex p. Greenpeace*[27] described how the organisation had nearly 5 million supporters worldwide with 400,000 supporters in the UK of whom about 2,500 lived in the Cumbria region where the British Nuclear Fuels plant was situated. In *R (SRM Global Master Fund LP) v Treasury Commission*[28] (The Nationalisation of Northern Rock), claimants sought judicial review of the decision to nationalise Northern Rock. The standing of the claimants was that they were all share-holders of Northern Rock. Their complaint was that the valuation of Northern Rock at the date of nationalisation was unfair. The case argued by the claimants was that through the economic device of loans and guarantees, the Bank of England secured for the taxpayers' expropriation through nationalisation of Northern Rock but without adequate compensation to the Northern Rock shareholders. The case made out by the claimants was rejected. Stanley Burnton LJ held that without Bank of England intervention Northern Rock would have ceased trading.[29]

18-048

The role of the pressure group or lobby group is often controversial. In recent years, their importance has become more significant in the area of legal challenge. In *R (on the application of Client Earth) v Secretary of State for the Environment, Food and Rural Affairs*[30] the pressure group Client Earth took proceedings against the UK Government in respect of failure to comply since 2010 with nitrogen dioxide levels set by European Law under Directive 2008/50. A recent House of Lords Paper has shown that air pollution in London has reached levels that are detrimental to health, with an estimated "mortality burden" of nearly 9,500 people per year.[31] The World Health Organisation (WHO) has established a link between air pollution and increased risk of disease. Two Supreme Court decisions, the first in 2013 and the

---

26 T. Daintith and A. Page, *The Executive in the Constitution* (New York: Oxford University Press, 1999), p.35.
27 [1994] 1 W.L.R. 570; [1994] 4 All E.R. 321 CA (Civ Div) at [349].
28 [2009] EWHC 227 (Admin); [2009] All E.R. (D) 139.
29 Dimitrios Kyritsis, "Constitutional Review in Representative Democracy" (2012) 32(2) *Oxford Journal of Legal Studies* 297–324. *R (Jackson) v Attorney General* [2005] EWCA Civ 126; [2005] Q.B. 579.
   The debate on the 42 detention period in 2009/10 is a good example. *Thoburn v Sunderland City Council* [2002] EWHC 195 (Admin); [2003] Q.B. 151; *R (Corner House) v Director of the Serious Fraud Office* [2007] EWHC 311 (Admin); [2007] Env. L.R. 29; and *R (Alconbury Developments Ltd) v Secretary of State for the Environment, Transport and the Regions* [2001] UKHL 23; [2003] 2 A.C. 295, p.980 at [70].
30 [2015] UKSC 28; [2015] 4 All E.R. 724.
31 House of Lords, *Air Quality and Health in the UK*, LIF 2015/024 (18 November 2014).

second in 2015, taken by the Charity Client Earth have ruled that the UK's non-compliance with European legal limits in certain zones is in breach of art.13 of the EU Directive 2008/50. The Supreme Court requested guidance from the Court of Justice of the EU on various matters including the extension of certain deadlines for compliance and the nature of the legal duty on the UK. In April 2015, the Supreme Court delivered a second decision, after receiving guidance from the Court of Justice, and required the Government to draw up plans by the end of 2015 to meet the requirements of EU law. The EU Commission has also launched an investigation. The postponement of the decision on the third runway at Heathrow until the Summer of 2016, for more time to undertake further environmental studies of air and noise pollution underlines the importance of the regulation of air quality. This case study of both Supreme Court decisions examines judicial decision-making in the context of sensitive policy and political issues and how legal interpretation may be influenced by the context of social and economic problems. The Government has issued draft plans for reducing nitrogen dioxide and a consultation process has been undertaken. It is clear that 40 out of 43 of the UK's air pollution monitoring zones have exceeded permitted pollution levels in 2011. Both Supreme Court decisions underline how judicial input into the policy making process can have serious consequences that may be regarded as necessary to uphold the rule of law. Interpreting EU law in the context of common law principles provides an important lens into the relationship between the Court of Justice of the EU and the UK's Supreme Court.

18-049 Concern arises out of the *Rose Theatre Case*, if interpreted to mean that the ordinary citizen in the absence of an express statutory right is debarred from challenging decisions, even where it appears that there may be a public interest served by such a challenge. This may leave a gap in the arrangements for public challenge. There may be a role for the Attorney General in such cases. But as Galligan notes, the traditional role of the Attorney General may be inappropriate to the needs of public interest litigation and therefore some means must be found for individuals to make a challenge:[32]

> "There is, however a serious flaw in the apparent symmetry between the object of review and the standing rules; the object of review is to ensure that officials act within their powers, while the point of standing is to determine who may bring an action. These are two different issues and the determination of the legality question is not linked in any logical way to the decision about who brings the action."

18-050 An important dimension to the law of standing in the UK is the development of European Community law. Article 230 (ex.art.173) provides standing for individuals or one who is directly concerned by a decision, to challenge decisions made by Community institutions. National rules set down by Member States of the Community may not be used to inhibit the enforcement of a Community right.

---

32 D. J. Galligan, *Discretionary Powers* (Oxford: Clarendon 1986), pp.379–382.

The extension of this right has been recognised in *Factortame* and in *Francovich*[33] where the European Court has created a remedy under Community law enforceable by individuals in their national courts against defaulting Member States. Thus any obstacle such as a restrictive view of standing may be placed to one side by the European Court in cases concerning Community law. In a particular context, for example European environmental law where Community environmental rights may be wider than domestic rights, the law on locus standi of the UK maybe more restrictive than that available under the law of the European Community. Inevitably reconciling domestic and European Community law may take some time, but in this particular example where the activities of pressure groups is high, there will be inevitable pressure to expand the rules of locus standi in favour of public interest litigation.

It is also inevitable that greater account will have to be taken of the provisions of European Community law in the interpretation of Order 53 and s.31 of the Supreme Court Act 1981 in cases involving rights conferred by Community law.

Rules of standing and the role of the courts

The law relating to standing, locus standi, is important in both private law actions and the application for judicial review. The rules of standing set out the entitlement of the aggrieved citizen to seek redress in the courts for the particular remedy sought. The rules of standing have a "gate-keeping" function: they provide the means to exclude vexatious litigants or unworthy cases. Standing may appear to be a procedural requirement, but procedural rules in this instance are linked to substantive issues. The arguments in favour of liberal rules of standing appear persuasive.

Access to the courts should be open to the citizen as a means of complaint. Wide rules of standing permit the courts a large discretion in remedying the abuse of public power. This fits Dicey's view, that the rule of law requires that disputes as to whether acts of the Government are legal ought to be decided by judges independent of the Executive. Upholding the rule of law is one of the most important values in the hands of the judiciary.

In the UK there are some notable examples[34] where an individual or pressure group has taken legal action. In *Gillick*,[35] the rights of an under-age schoolgirl to receive information on contraception were considered in a crusade against contraceptive advice being available to schoolgirls without the consent of their parents. The case was taken by Mrs Gillick and was broadly supported by religious groups and organisations. The pressure group tactic of pursuing legal cases is clear. The Pro-Life Alliance, an anti-abortion group, have pursued legal cases directly; recently, in an important legal case,[36] they were accepted as an intervention setting

---

33   *Francovich v Italy* (C-6/90) EU:C:1991:428; [1992] I.R.L.R. 84.
34   See Carol Harlow, "Public Law and Popular Justice" (2001) 65 *Modern Law Review* 1. Also see D. Feldman, "Public Interest Litigation and Constitutional Theory" (1992) *Modern Law Review* 44.
35   *Gillick v W. Norfolk and Wisbech AHA* [1986] A.C. 112; [1985] 3 W.L.R. 830 HL.
36   *A (children) (Conjoined Twins: Surgical Separation), Re* [2001] Fam. 147; [2001] 2 W.L.R. 480 CA (Civ Div).

out moral issues as part of the court's consideration of the legality of a decision. Such tactics are unmistakably to make use of the courts in an effort to protect the unborn and to advance that cause through legal rights.

18–056 Increasingly, the courts show willingness to allow interested parties or groups to represent their views in cases where the interpretation of law or international agreement might require explanation or expertise. The flexibility in allowing such a development appears from the introduction of new civil procedure rules. As Harlow has noted:

> "To sum up, we are seeing a shift away from the traditional bipolar and adversarial law suit familiar to common lawyers, to something more fluid, less formal and possibly less individualistic in character. By making access easier, judges are subtly changing the rules of the game. A novel public interest action is in the making, with the help of which campaigning groups are gaining entry to the legal process. No serious credentials in the form of 'democratic stake' are required of them."[37]

18–057 The "rules of the game" include the possibility that public interest challenges, when they raise public law issues and the claimant has no private interest in the outcome of the case,[38] may be heard by the courts. However, though the number of applications for judicial review[39] has increased to 5,398 for the year 2001, these do not reflect a marked increase in pressure group activity. In fact, judicial review cases neatly fall into three categories: those taken by homeless people; those arising out of immigration disputes; and those involving the Police in relation to criminal matters and local authority cases.[40] One reason for pressure groups' small role in litigation is that, despite the liberalisation of the rules of standing, there is general reluctance on the part of the judiciary to encourage a widespread use of judicial review to settle disputes. There is marked sensitivity to maintaining strict discipline in applying the rules of procedure. The rules of standing are therefore important as a procedural route of access to the Administrative Court.

18–058 The Human Rights Act 1998 introduced a fresh dimension to the rights that may be interpreted by the courts. Rights issues are now more openly addressed through legal action taken by pressure groups. Most noticeably there is a contrast between the "sufficient interest" test in judicial review, outlined above, and the restricted "victim" test for standing[41] adopted by s.7 of the Human Rights Act 1998 as part of the jurisprudence of the Strasbourg Court of Human Rights.[42] It would appear that various civil liberties groups or pressure groups may not meet

---

37 Harlow, "Public Law and Popular Justice", pp.7–8.
38 *R v Lord Chancellor Ex p. Child Poverty Action Group* [1999] 1 W.L.R. 347; [1998] 2 All E.R. 755 QBD.
39 *Practice Statement* [2002] 1 W.L.R. 810; [2002] 1 All E.R. 633 QBD.
40 L. Bridges, G. Meszaros and M. Sunkin, *Judicial Review in Perspective* (London: Cavendish, 1995).
41 Mark Elliott, "The Human Rights Act 1998 and the Standard of Substantive Review" (2001) *Cambridge Law Journal* 301.
42 N. Garnham, "A Sufficient Victim?: Standing and the Human Rights Act 1998" [1999] *J.R.* 39. See *R (Pelling) v Bow County Cour* [2001] U.K.H.R.R. 165; [2001] A.C.D. 1 QBD.

the more difficult hurdle of the victim test than the lower requirement of "sufficient interest". This restriction may apply to trade unions or professional groups. This does not prevent financial resources being made available to meet the costs of litigation.

D: Public Law Remedies

Procedural matters

18–059

In the previous chapter, attention was given to the exclusivity principle, namely that after *O'Reilly v Mackman* the courts have required the Order 53 procedure to be exclusively confined to public law matters. Linked to this principle is the requirement of a time-limit in English law in which to make the application. Before Order 53 was introduced, certiorari was the only prerogative remedy which required a time-limit, namely six months. While the courts had a limited discretion to review the six-month period this was rarely exercised. In the case of civil proceedings for declarations and injunction time-limits did not apply.

18–060

The law on time-limits for all applications for judicial review is contained in Order 53, r.4 and also s.31(6) and (7) of the Supreme Court Act 1981. Currently the time-limit is three months though there is a complexity in reconciling the terms of r.4 with s.31(6). Rule 4 applies only to applications for leave to apply for judicial review, whereas s.31(6) applies to both applications for leave and applications for substantive relief. This adds to the complexity of the issue when it is also considered that r.4 is concerned with good reasons for extending the three-month time-limit, whereas s.31(6) is confined to the effects of dealing with grounds for refusing relief either at the substantive stage or at the application stage.

18–061

Section 84(2) of the Criminal Justice and Courts Act 2015 amends ss.31 (3C–3F) of the Senior Courts Act 1981 by inserting a new section. Permission must be refused if it appears to the High Court to be highly likely that the outcome for the applicant would not have been substantially different. The "highly likely" to succeed test is acceptable to be applied if it is appropriate to do so for reasons of exceptional public interest. The discussion of this important reform in the House of Lords expressed some unease about any adjustment by statute of the judicial interpretation of such an important test to qualify for judicial review.[43] In addition, there are substantial fees to be paid for an application for judicial review.[44]

---

43 House of Commons Library, *Government Reforms in the 2010–15 Parliament*, Briefing Paper, No.6616 (4 June 2015).
44 Lodging an application is £140, a further £ 700 is paid if the permission is granted and if refused and there is another hearing, then another £350 is payable. Civil legal aid is available but in limited circumstances.

18-062 The importance of promptness has to be satisfied otherwise the application may be refused.[45] The three-month period is not a guarantee as the courts may still refuse in a case where it considers that the matter requires urgent action.[46]

The consideration of "promptness" was discussed in *Ex p. Caswell*.[47] The House of Lords affirmed the view that the three-month time-limit was not an entitlement. In cases where there is undue delay even within the three-month period, reasons must be given. Even where an extension of time is given at the first stage, that is, the application for leave, this may be considered at the full hearing after representations from both parties are heard. In *Ex p. Caswell* the applicants conceded that there had been undue delay. The House of Lords then had to consider whether the granting of relief would be likely to cause hardship or prejudice or would be detrimental to good administration. The answer to this question depended on the effect of whether after the lapse of time the Dairy Produce Quota tribunal's decision had been made in 1985—it would be detrimental to good administration to grant relief. The House of Lords concluded that it would, and dismissed the appeal.

18-063 Time-limits under Order 53 and s.31 of the Supreme Court Act 1981, appear too short and the ground of the courts discretion too vague. The question of whether it is desirable to retain a three-month time-limit or in general whether time-limits are needed is also under consideration.[48]

18-064 The question of time-limits was considered by the House of Lords in a planning case involving analysis of the rule about going to the courts promptly and its compatibility with the Human Rights Act 1998. In *R v Hammersmith and Fulham LBC Ex p. Burkett*,[49] the House of Lords adopted a sensitive approach to the question of "promptness". The case involved a complex series of facts regarding a planning application for outline planning permission. In September 1999 the local authority planning committee decided to refer the application to the Secretary of State to make use of his call in plans. In February 2000, the Secretary of State declined to call in the application and outline planning permission was granted in May 2000. In April, local residents issued judicial review proceedings to quash the decision to refer the matter in September 1999 to the Secretary of State. Their case rested on alleged failures on the part of the local authority planning committee to consider an environmental assessment.

18-065 The House of Lords reviewed the issues of promptness, as both the Court of Appeal and the High Court had considered this to be the main reason for dismissing the application for judicial review. The promptness rule, often interpreted to mean within three months, was considered by the House of Lords. Lord Steyn pointed out that going to court too quickly had often resulted in poorly considered cases and a reduction in the possibility of negotiated

---

45 *R v Dairy Produce Tribunal Ex p. Caswell* [1990] 2 A.C. 738; [1990] 2 W.L.R. 1320 HL.
46 *R (Camelot UK lotteries Ltd) v Gambling Commission* [2012] EWHC 2391 (Admin); [2013] P.T.S.R. 729.
47 [2012] EWHC 2391 (Admin).
48 *Law Commission Consultation Paper No.126*. On European Community law, see, *Ferriera Valsabbia* (C-209/83) EU:C:1984:274.
49 [2002] UKHL 23; [2002] 1 W.L.R. 1593.

settlements. The uncertainty surrounding the exact nature of what promptness had actually meant in practice might be inconsistent with the Convention under the Human Rights Act. Lord Steyn also acknowledged that complex cases needed time for preparation and expressed unhappiness with a rigid three-month rule. It would appear that while there remains a need to go to court and prepare a case, the question of promptness has been given some latitude by the House of Lords. The way forward seems to be to give some certainty to the law and, even if this means tighter time-limits, to allow the court to consider the merits of each case.

Is the UK requirement of promptness compatible with EU law or human rights? In the case of EU law the requirement of promptness may not apply as to do so might violate the principles of legal certainty and the requirement of having access to a legal remedy.[50] In the case of human rights the requirement was held to be compatible with Article 6 of the European Convention.[51]

18-066

The discretionary nature of remedies

All the remedies available under the application for judicial review fall under the discretionary jurisdiction of the Divisional Court. There are no simple criteria on which this discretion is based. Generally, the court will consider the availability of any alternative remedies such as appeals or the existence of a specialised tribunal before granting judicial review. As a general rule it is expected that the applicant will have attempted to make use of any available alternative remedies before coming to the court. In *Ex p. Calveley*,[52] Sir John Donaldson suggested that the courts would only rarely exercise their jurisdiction to grant judicial review in cases such as this one when there was an alternative appeal remedy available. Only in "exceptional circumstances" would review be accepted in preference to appeals available to the applicant. In *Ex p. Calveley*, in the case of Police officers subject to disciplinary proceedings, certiorari was granted notwithstanding the existence of rights of appeal under the Police (Appeal) Rules 1977.[53] This was a case where departure from the disciplinary procedures was such that on the merits, the courts would intervene by way of judicial review. But this exercise of judicial discretion is not always a predictable one. For example, in *Puhlhoffer*[54] a local authority's decision that a person is not entitled to accommodation under the Housing (Homeless Persons) Act 1977 was not open to appeal. The House of Lords was clear that judicial review should be confined only to exceptional cases. In *Ex p. Swati*,[55] a person refused leave to enter the UK was refused leave to apply for judicial review. The applicant would have to rely on his appeal rights

18-067

---

50   See *Uniplex (UK) Ltd v NHS Business Service Authority* (C-406/08) EU:C:2010:45.
51   *Lam v UK* App No.41671/98, 5 July 2001 ECJ.
52   *R v Chief Constable of the Merseyside Police Ex p. Calveley* [1986] Q.B. 424; [1986] 2 W.L.R. 144 CA (Civ Div).
53   Now see Police Regulations 1995 (SI 1995/215).
54   *Puhlhoffer v Hillingdon LBC* [1986] A.C. 484; [1986] 1 All E.R. 467 HL.
55   *R v Secretary of State for the Home Department Ex p. Swati* [1986] 1 W.L.R. 477; [1986] 1 All E.R. 717 CA (Civ Div).

only. However the circumstances which determined whether judicial review might be available appeared unquantifiable and appeared to "defy definition" in the case.

18–068 Considerations which may guide the exercise of the courts' discretion are very wide. It may be that there is concern for the workload generated by judicial review in certain areas such as immigration cases or homeless persons. The courts' preference for seeking alternative remedies is in part recognition of the degree of specialist advice available to appeal tribunals. It is also recognition of the nature of many of the disputes which cover multi-disciplinary issues that the courts may wish to confine their jurisdiction and not usurp the jurisdiction of appellate bodies.

18–069 Another approach is to consider the balance of convenience. This is where the courts regard proceedings taken by judicial review as an acceptable means to resolve the dispute because "in all the circumstances" it is the most cost-effective. Glidewell LJ took this view in a number of cases following from the *Royco Homes Case*[56] in 1974. Lord Widgery explained that while a planning condition could be challenged on the basis of the statutory appeal structure, certiorari might lie where it was more efficient and effectual.

18–070 In exercising their discretion, the courts may also consider matters of delay and the locus standi of the applicants. Both these matters may be considered at the full hearing stage as well as at the initial application for leave procedure. Indeed, the entire boundary between public law and private law rights invites consideration of a whole range of questions which also admit the discretion of the court. This may include the subject matter of the dispute, the nature of the remedy sought and the implications for administrative decision-making. In this area of judicial discretion, the courts find it difficult to explain why discretion is exercised in one case and not another. Consistency of approach should be important as well as the merits of the specific case, but courts are not always predictable.

18–071 There is an increasing judicial awareness of the cost-benefit analysis of judicial review. This may mean considering the question of whether good administration is encouraged by the outcome of the decision. In *Ex p. Argyll Group*[57] the courts' reluctance to quash the decision of the Chairman of the Monopolies and Mergers Commission, even though it was found to be illegal, was based on the needs of public administration. In assessing whether to exercise the courts' discretion it was noted that third parties had already acted on the decision and that the Commission would have made the same decision as its chairman. Lord Donaldson explained how the courts' discretion may be influenced by the following factors. Though not intended to be a complete catalogue they emphasise the importance of substance over form. These factors include a proper consideration: of the public interest; of the legitimate expectations of the individual citizens; of the financial interest involved; and finally, of decisiveness and finality in decision-making. The speed of decision-making is also relevant. Decisiveness and finality are important virtues in the process of good administrative decisions.

---

56 *R v Hillingdon LBC Ex p. Royco Homes Ltd* [1974] Q.B. 720; [1974] 2 W.L.R. 805 QBD.
57 *R v Monopolies and Mergers Commission Ex p. Argyll Group Plc* [1986] 1 W.L.R. 763; [1986] 2 All E.R. 257 CA (Civ Div).

18-072 A final issue for consideration is the grant of legal aid. Section 18(4) of the Legal Aid Act 1988 provides that the respondent must establish "severe financial hardship" unless an order is made. In matters involving judicial review there is consideration by both the courts when granting leave and the Legal Aid Board when considering legal aid, of the "appropriateness" of bringing the application. Two questions arise: first, whether public bodies when they are involved in litigation should be able to receive legal aid, when presently they may not because they do not fall under the heading of "severe financial hardship"; and secondly, whether the merits test as regards granting by the courts should be the same as the Legal Aid Board when granting legal aid. It is quite possible for the two different bodies to come to different conclusions when purporting to follow the same test.

Void and voidable administrative action

18-073 A related and important question when considering remedies and the grounds for challenge either through judicial review or appeal is the question of the effect of an ultra vires decision. This question arises in connection with the effects of two types of error of law. One is jurisdictional and the other is non-jurisdictional. The former may render the decision void and having no legal effect. When the court decides to quash the decision, it does so in a retrospective way. The latter may have had some legal effect but because of some mistake in the law, it does not remain valid once the court decides to exercise its discretion and quash the decision. This is described as a voidable, as opposed to a void, decision. The court when quashing a voidable decision does so prospectively, because the decision is valid until the time comes for the court to quash the decision.

18-074 While there remains some doubt as to whether there is a distinction between jurisdictional errors which render a decision void and not voidable, the concept of void and voidable is an additional element in judicial discretion. While it is not always easy to know whether an act is void or voidable, the categorisation may also have a direct result on a number of related issues. For example, the exercise of a right of appeal will not always cure the defect of a void act and the courts may wish not to consider an appeal against a void decision. A void act may be ignored by the person affected whereas a voidable act may not. If an act is potentially voidable, the courts may still regard the act as valid until it is declared invalid.

18-075 There are a variety of views as to the importance of the void and voidable distinction and there is a lack of consistency in the use of language when describing how void and voidable may apply to a decision. Judicial application of the distinction may not always be consistently applied. In *Anisminic*,[58] the House of Lords accepted that an ultra vires act was void and a breach of natural justice was similarly void.

18-076 For the reasons outlined above, the void and voidable distinction appears important when considering the legal position of the parties and may affect the outcome of the decision.

---

58 *Anisminic Ltd v Foreign Compensation Commission* [1969] 2 A.C. 147; [1969] 2 W.L.R. 163 HL.

Certiorari (a Quashing Order), Prohibition (a Prohibiting Order) and Mandamus (a Mandatory Order)

18-077 The main public law remedies may be briefly mentioned. Certiorari[59] has the effect of quashing a decision which may be done by an excess or abuse of power, whereas prohibition is intended to restrain a body from acting unlawfully in the future or preventing an excess or abuse of power. Certiorari and prohibition are similar and both are available as remedies in public law. The criteria for deciding which acts and decisions are subject to certiorari and prohibition was expressed by Lord Atkin in the *Electricity Commissioners case*[60]:

> "...Wherever any body of persons having legal authority to determine questions affecting the rights of subjects, and having the duty to act judicially, act in excess of their legal authority they are subject to the controlling jurisdiction of the King's Bench Division."

18-078 The interpretation of the duty to act judicially has been widened considerably since the case was decided. Since *Ridge v Baldwin*,[61] the courts have interpreted the phrase to include those bodies that have the power to decide and determine matters which affect the citizen. This means that certiorari generally may be available to review all administrative acts. This includes such variety of examples as a valuation officer, the grant of planning permission, the Criminal Injuries Compensation Board set up under the prerogative, and mandatory grants to students.[62] However certiorari was not available to quash a provisional order made by the Secretary of State for the compulsory purchase of land by the Hastings Board of Health.[63]

18-079 The formulation of acting judicially commonly used today is that favoured by Lord Diplock in *O'Reilly v Mackman* that it is enough to show that the body or person has legal authority to determine questions affecting the common law or statutory rights of other persons. Historically it was assumed that certiorari would not be available for contractual matters or purely domestic disputes.

18-080 *Certiorari* is available to quash decisions that are ultra vires, in breach of natural justice or where traditionally there has been an error of law on the face of the record. This includes most forms of ultra vires discussed in Ch.17. As Lord Slynn suggested in *Page v Hull University Visitor*,[64] the scope of certiorari may be interpreted widely:

---

59 *R v Electricity Commissioners Ex p. London Electricity Joint Committee Co (1920) Ltd* [1924] 1 K.B. 171 CA.
60 *R v Electricity Commissioners Ex p. London Electricity Joint Committee Co (1920) Ltd* [1924] 1 K.B. 171.
61 [1964] A.C. 40; [1963] 2 W.L.R. 935 HL.
62 *R v Paddington Valuation Officer Ex p. Peachey Property Corporation Ltd* [1966] 1 Q.B. 380; [1965] 3 W.L.R. 426 CA; *R v Hillingdon LBC Ex p. Royco Homes Ltd* [1974] Q.B. 720; [1974] 2 W.L.R. 805 QBD; *R v Criminal Injuries Compensation Board Ex p. Lain* [1967] 2 Q.B. 864; [1967] 3 W.L.R. 348 QBD; and *Ex p. Nilish Shah* [1983] 2 A.C. 309; [1983] 2 W.L.R. 16 HL.
63 *R v Hastings Board of Health* 122 E.R. 1243; (1865) 6 B. & S. 401 Ct of King's Bench.
64 [1993] A.C. 682; [1992] 3 W.L.R. 1112 HL at [114B].

> "If it is accepted, as I believe it should be accepted, that certiorari goes not only for such an excess or abuse of power but also for a breach of the rules of natural justice."

18-081 Prohibition shares a similar scope to certiorari but it lies to restrain such action rather than quash it. It is important to emphasise that both certiorari and prohibition are discretionary remedies. While the law on locus standi has been discussed above with respect to the changes introduced by Order 53 it is worthwhile mentioning the law before Order 53, was introduced, as there is still the possibility that the courts may wish to consider the old law. Locus standi for certiorari distinguished between "persons aggrieved" and strangers. This distinction was left to the courts to define. A person aggrieved was explained by Lord Denning in *Ex p. Liverpool Taxi*[65] as including any "person whose interests may be prejudicially affected". Strangers included busybodies interfering in matters which did not concern them.

18-082 Mandamus is a court order which commands the performance of a public duty. Public duty has been described as a concept which is "important but elusive". The courts have drawn attention to the distinction between a duty or a power. The former is enforced by mandamus, while the latter is not. The question of what constitutes a duty is inconclusively defined by the courts. Statutory interpretation may depend on the purpose for which duties are to be exercised. Invariably the public character of the duty is crucial in the courts' discretion to make mandamus available. The source of a public duty may arise from the common law, prerogative or statute. It may also arise in respect of licences or contracts or from legal powers through charters or customs. The bodies amenable to mandamus include local authorities, the Metropolitan Police Commissioner and Ministers.[66]

18-083 Mandamus may lie where there is a breach of procedural jurisdiction or even where there is a discretion that involves public duties. In *Padfield*,[67] the Minister was said by Lord Reid "to have a duty to act" even though such a duty was expressed in discretionary language, "if the minister in any case so directs". If such a power is used for an improper purpose or irrelevant considerations are taken into account, the courts may decide to grant mandamus to correct the misuse of power. Mandamus is a powerful remedy because it commands the performance of set obligations or responsibilities. Failure to obey the terms of mandamus may result in proceedings for contempt of court.

18-084 Mandamus usually required a strict rule of standing before Order 53 was introduced. In *R v Lewisham Union*[68] standing required there to be a "legal specific right". The case raised particular facts relating to the attempt to compel the guardians of the poor to undertake compulsory vaccination to prevent outbreaks of smallpox. A less strict view was favoured in

---

65 *R v Liverpool Corp Ex p. Liverpool Taxi Fleet Operators' Association* [1972] 2 Q.B. 299; [1972] 2 W.L.R. 1262 CA (Civ Div).
66 See *R v Camden LBC Ex p. Gillan* (1989) 21 H.L.R. 114; [1989] C.O.D. 196 QBD; and *R v Metropolitan Police Commissioner Ex p. Blackburn* [1968] 2 Q.B. 118; [1968] 2 W.L.R. 893 CA (Civ Div).
67 *Padfield v Minister of Agriculture* [1968] A.C. 997; [1968] 2 W.L.R. 924 HL.
68 [1897] 1 Q.B. 498 QBD.

Ex p. Blackburn[69] which favoured a public interest aspect to the enforcement of public rights created by the criminal law. This liberal trend has been further advanced by the House of Lords in the *Fleet Street Casuals* case discussed above.

18-085
Mandamus may not lie against the Crown. This is a rule that has also been interpreted to include servants of the Crown. The rationale behind this rule owes its origins historically to the role of the courts in not commanding the Sovereign to command her own performance of any duty.[70] Crown immunity, however, does not appear to prevent mandamus being taken against the activities of the Crown, for example the Income Tax Commissioners in their function of revenue collection. The development of the declaration has limited the restrictions such a rule might appear to hold. Mandamus will also be refused where there are circumstances that suggest that all steps that could be taken have been taken and thus the courts' intervention would be inappropriate.

Habeas Corpus

18-086
Habeas corpus is an ancient remedy which allows a person detained to challenge the legality of detention. The law relating to habeas corpus has been kept outside the reforms introduced under Order 53 and consequently the remedy has been given less attention in recent years compared to its historical importance. Application is made to a Divisional Court of the Queen's Bench Division. The remedy is technical and narrow in scope as invariably other remedies have been developed to allow the detention of the applicant to be tested, such as the right of appeal or appearance before a magistrate. However, there are circumstances where habeas corpus is the only remedy available to an applicant. In *X v UK*[71] the European Court of Human Rights expressed dissatisfaction about the procedures open to mental health patients to challenge their detention. The European Convention was not satisfied by the limited scope of the habeas corpus application.

18-087
Habeas corpus also appears to be useful in immigration cases. In *Khawaja*[72] the House of Lords considered that common principles might be applied to habeas corpus and judicial review, but failed to clarify the scope of the courts' inquiry.

18-088
The Law Commission has considered the restrictive nature of habeas corpus applications which are confined to the facts on which the detention is based. As Lord Donaldson noted in *Muboyai*,[73] the application for judicial review afforded a wider opportunity for challenging an administrative decision and this favoured using judicial review as opposed to habeas corpus. Perhaps the time has come to rationalise the relationship and set out the exact role that habeas corpus is expected to fulfil when reviewing powers of detention. One

---

69 [1968] 2 Q.B. 118; [1968] 2 W.L.R. 893 CA (Civ Div).
70 *R v Customs and Excise Commissioners Ex p. Cook* [1970] 1 W.L.R. 450; [1970] 1 All E.R. 1068 Div Ct.
71 (1981) 4 E.H.R.R. 188; [1981] E.C.H.R. 6 ECHR.
72 *R v Secretary of State for the Home Department Ex p. Khawaja* [1984] A.C. 74; [1983] 2 W.L.R. 321 HL.
73 *R v Secretary of State for the Home Department Ex p. Muboyai* [1992] Q.B. 244; [1991] 3 W.L.R. 442 CA (Civ Div).

suggestion is to allow interim relief at the leave stage to allow the legality of detention to be questioned.

E: Private Law Remedies

Remedies such as declaration, injunction and damages are available in ordinary civil proceedings. Order 53 provides that such remedies are added to the prerogative remedies of certiorari, prohibition and mandamus, and are available under the application for judicial review procedures in public law matters. In effect this gave the potential for an overlapping jurisdiction between the power to seek declaration and injunction in civil proceedings and under the application for judicial review. The limitations set by *O'Reilly v Mackman* have been considered in Ch.17. It is important to consider in this section not only the remedies of declaration and injunction but also the special position of the Crown and the availability of tort and restitution remedies against public authorities.

18-089

Declaration and injunction

A declaration or, as it is sometimes referred to, a declaratory judgment is an order of the court. The procedure by way of originating summons is under RSC 1965 Order 5 r.2, or under Order 15 r.16, and it is also available under Order 53 on the application for judicial review for public law matters as defined in *O'Reilly v Mackman*. The preferred means of obtaining a declaration raising a public law matter is under the Order 53 procedure. In the case of an originating summons there is no power to grant an interim declaration of rights but some broadening of this rule has occurred under Order 5 r.4. Such a limitation does not arise under the Order 53 procedure.

18-090

Declaration is a wide ranging remedy. In *Dyson*,[74] the applicant challenged the Inland Revenue's decision to require him under penalty to supply them with information. There was no cause of action and little authority for the use of the procedure under the then existing procedure, Order 25 r.5 which has since been amended by Order 15 r.16. The aim of providing a speedy and simple procedure in part underlines the reasons behind the *Dyson* decision. As a declaration is available against the Crown, this underlines the usefulness of this remedy.

18-091

The courts have not provided a complete list of situations or categories where a declaration may lie. In declaring rights there is the added implication that illegality will be established. This is useful in setting out the scope of a public body's duties, liabilities and lawfulness of decisions. In *Gillick*,[75] advice on contraception for girls under 16 was considered as to its legality

18-092

---
74 *Dyson v Attorney General* [1911] 1 K.B. 410 CA.
75 *Gillick v West Norfolk and Wisbech AHA* [1986] A.C. 112; [1985] 3 W.L.R. 830 HL.

and the House of Lords upheld the advice as legal. Thus declaration may be useful for settling many doubtful matters relating to the exercise of legal powers. Planning permission, the work of the Boundary Commission, reports of public inquiries and the like are typical examples of the versatility of a declaration.

18-093 Despite the potential width and scope of a declaration there are limitations to its availability. In general terms a declaration will not be granted where the court considers that the statute retains an exclusive jurisdiction to the tribunal or other body provided in the statute. In *Barraclough v Brown*[76] the House of Lords held that the plaintiff's claim for declaration was one which arose under a statute and the statute had provided a procedure for grievances. The courts were confined by the procedures laid down in the statute and therefore declaration was not available. In contrast, in *Pyx Granite*[77] the House of Lords distinguished *Barraclough*. A declaration might be available notwithstanding any statutory rights where there remained common law rights. These may be enforced through a declaration.

18-094 A declaration will not be granted by the courts if its effect is to usurp the authority of the body under review. A declaration is not based on a speculative or hypothetical basis, it only issues as a ground of relief where relief is real and is needed. Unlike some countries where a written constitution permits a form of judicial preview, English law has historically been reluctant to take abstract or moot points as part of the remit of the courts. A declaration is available to the Equal Opportunities Commission for the purposes of determining whether the relevant provisions of the Employment Protection (Consolidation) Act 1978 are compatible with Community law.

18-095 The question of whether a declaration is available for an error of law is problematic. Such an error is usually regarded as resulting in a voidable and not a void decision. This means that the decision remains valid until action is taken to control or remedy the error. As a declaration merely declares what the rights of the parties may be and does not alter their position, this suggests that declaration would not be a useful means to control such an error of law. However, this limitation may be less important with the availability of certiorari under the Order 53 procedure.

18-096 Injunctions are of equitable origin and may restrain a person or body from illegal action. The equitable nature of the remedy makes the injunction a discretionary remedy in common with the prerogative remedies. Thus an injunction may be refused if there are alternative remedies available or where the court regards the granting of the injunction unnecessary. Injunctions may be prohibitory, or mandatory and may be expressed in terms of positive obligations or in the form of negative prohibition. Injunctions may be interim or interlocutory, that is, pending the outcome of the full hearing of an action, an injunction may be granted to preserve existing arrangements. The injunction as a form of interim relief is important. Under Order 53, the applicant may seek an order of mandamus or declaration, the main form of interim relief is through an interim injunction. When granted in the form of an interim injunction, the plaintiff is normally required to give an undertaking to indemnify the defendant for any loss he suffers

---

76 [1897] A.C. 615 HL.
77 *Pyx Granite Ltd v Ministry of Housing and Local Government* [1960] A.C. 260; [1959] 3 W.L.R. 346 HL.

as a result of the interim order. This practice does not always apply in the case of the Crown seeking an injunction.

18-097
The test applicable when interim relief is sought is based on principles developed in the decision of the House of Lords in *American Cyanamid Co v Ethicon Ltd*.[78] The test is to decide if the applicant has a good arguable case and, if he has to take into account the balance of convenience when considering the duties owed by the public body and the interests of the public. An addition to this criterion is the inclusion of a prima facie case needed to justify the granting of relief when the court is exercising its discretion.

18-098
A good arguable case means one with a real chance of success, not necessarily a 51 per cent chance. The balance of convenience may take into account the interest of the public.

18-099
Injunctions may be perpetual and granted at the end of the action. Injunctions are available to one who has an arguable case, that is not frivolous or vexatious and that there is at least an arguable case which is likely to succeed. When considering such matters as the likelihood of success, the court may take account of the balance of convenience and the interests of the public.

18-100
The availability of injunctions may be by judicial review under Order 53 or in the following circumstances where an injunction may lie at the suit of a private individual. In a private action, injunctions are available on the same basis of locus standi as a declaration, where some private right appears to be affected or where special damage peculiar to the private individual arises from an interference with a public right.

18-101
Injunctions are also available at the suit of the Attorney General on behalf of the Crown. This may arise where the protection of public rights or the interests of the public require the Attorney General to take action to restrain breaches of the criminal law. Where a public body may be acting ultra vires the Attorney General may intervene to prevent a threatened or immediate breach of the law.

18-102
The Attorney General may take a relator action. Such action may arise where the Attorney General allows, at the suit of a private individual (the relator), his name to be joined to the action on the basis that he believes such action should be taken. The responsibility of the relator is to ensure that the Attorney General is satisfied on the evidence that such an action should be taken. In *Gouriet v Union of Post Office Workers*,[79] the House of Lords considered the refusal of the Attorney General to agree to a relator action to enforce an injunction restraining a threatened breach of the criminal law. It is considered unlikely that the courts may wish to review the discretion of the Attorney General in such matters.

18-103
The value of the relator action is less certain, since the general liberalisation of the rules of standing under Order 53, as the necessary standing may be given to the private individual in cases of judicial review. In the *Rose Theatre Case*[80] the Attorney General did not agree to a relator action and so recourse to judicial review was necessary.

---

78 [1975] A.C. 396; [1975] 2 W.L.R. 316 HL.
79 [1978] A.C. 435; [1977] 3 W.L.R. 300 HL.
80 [1990] 1 Q.B. 504; [1990] 2 W.L.R. 186 QBD.

The Crown

18–104 One of the often discussed limitations on the use of the injunction is that it is not traditionally available against the Crown. This rule has a long historical development. Sectopm 21(1) of the Crown Proceedings Act 1947 expressly provides that the court shall not grant an injunction against the Crown. It had been generally accepted that this prohibition also applied to servants of the Crown. The reforms introduced under s.31(2) and Order 53 r.3(10) had possibly given the courts powers to grant injunctions, including interim injunctions, against Officers of the Crown and against Government Ministers acting under statutory powers in their own names.

18–105 The House of Lords in *M, Re*[81] have, since *Factortame*,[82] considered the availability of injunctions against the Crown. Injunctions are generally available against departments or Ministers, although it was conceded that the use of injunctions against Government departments would be rare.

Discovery, damages and restitution

18–106 Discovery of documents forms an important pre-trial preliminary in ordinary civil proceedings. The availability of discovery in public law matters under Order 53 allows for the cross-examination and appearance of affidavits. This is regarded as an important inclusion under the application for judicial review procedures. Since *O'Reilly v Mackman* the courts have generally adopted a common approach to the granting of discovery but in judicial review applications the courts have favoured a more restrictive approach and the careful exercise of discretion on the merits of each case. Not all documents will be relevant to the judicial review and those that are not will not normally be included in the granting of discovery. An additional issue is that the Crown is able to claim public interest immunity arising out of certain documents or indeed rely on the confidential nature of the papers as a means to prevent disclosure.[83]

18–107 Under Order 53, claims for damages may be joined to the application for judicial review. In England and Wales there is no provision for restitution proceedings. In *Woolwich Building Society v I.R.C. (No.2)*,[84] the House of Lords considered the question of restitution proceedings after an application for judicial review had established that the regulations on which the Revenue based its demand for tax payment against the Woolwich Building Society were illegal. The approach adopted by the House of Lords established the right of the citizen to recover money paid by the citizen under regulations which are ultra vires. The Law Commission is considering whether the application for judicial review should include proceedings for restitution.

---

81   See *M, Re* [1994] 1 A.C. 377; [1993] 3 W.L.R. 433 HL. See Lord Donaldson in *M v Home Office* [1992] Q.B. 270; [1992] 2 W.L.R. 73 CA (Civ Div) at [306].
82   *R v Secretary of State for Transport Ex p. Factortame Ltd (No.2)* [1991] 1 A.C. 603; [1990] 3 W.L.R. 818 HL.
83   *Air Canada v Secretary of State for Trade* [1983] 2 A.C. 394; [1983] 2 W.L.R. 494 HL.
84   [1993] A.C. 70; [1992] 3 W.L.R. 366 HL.

Tort and contract liability of public authorities

18–108 A public body that acts ultra vires may be liable in tort in the same way as a private citizen, provided a cause of action is established. Section 2 of the Crown Proceedings Act 1947 permits the Crown to be sued on the same basis as private individuals, although the courts have a discretion whether to award damages or not, especially when policy issues may be concerned in the question of liability. Statutory interpretation is often difficult when it comes to the question of the application of tort principles to public bodies. When comparing public bodies to private individuals, the former usually possess wide statutory powers whereas the latter do not. Public bodies have to ensure that published policies are genuine and are not inconsistent with unpublished policies that may represent the reality of how decisions are being taken. In *R (Lumba) (Congo)v Home Secretary*,[85] the Supreme Court held that it was unlawful to operate inconsistent policies between the published and unpublished versions. It is not guaranteed that such illegality will give rise to damages, and the Supreme Court was divided on this question. There are widely divergent views on the availability of damages in such cases.

18–109 As a general principle, public bodies may be liable for the negligent exercise of their powers. In *R (SRM Global Master Fund LP) v Treasury Commission*[86] (The Nationalisation of Northern Rock). The applicant's complaint was that the valuation of Northern Rock at the date of nationalisation was unfair.[87] Valuations made at the time were regarded as being in the public interest and there was no proof that this was a negligent valuation. The applicants claim was rejected. The courts in their discretion have attempted to apply principles to the liability of public officials and authorities, as apply to private persons. In the interpretation of statutory duties, the courts may hold public bodies liable in damages for breach of their duty. For example, a breach of a duty to provide housing for homeless people under the housing legislation may give rise to liability in damages. However, it is a good defence to argue that the alleged tort is carried out according to express or implied statutory powers. In *Geddis*,[88] the court accepted that even if the Act was authorised by the legislature, if carried out negligently it may give rise to liability. It is not easy to categorise how the courts will respond in each individual case. The courts have not found it easy to lay down clear principles when decisions amount to ultra vires and when decisions are to be regarded as negligent policy decisions and reviewable by the courts, there is often uncertainty.

---

85 [2012] UKSC 19; [2012] 2 A.C. 337.
86 [2009] EWHC 227 (Admin); [2009] All E.R. (D) 139.
87 Dimitrios Kyritsis, "Constitutional Review in Representative Democracy" (2012) 32(2) *Oxford Journal of Legal Studies* 297–324. *R (Jackson) v Attorney General* [2005] EWCA Civ 126; [2005] Q.B. 579.
The debate on the 42 detention period in 2009/10 is a good example. *Thoburn v Sunderland City Council* [2002] EWHC 195 (Admin); [2003] Q.B. 151; *R (Corner House) v Director of the Serious Fraud Office* [2007] EWHC 311 (Admin); [2007] Env. L.R. 29; and *R (Alconbury Developments Ltd) v Secretary of State for the Environment, Transport and the Regions* [2001] UKHL 23; [2003] 2 A.C. 295, p.980 at [70].
88 *Geddis v Bann Reservoir Proprietors* (1878) L.R. 3 App. Cas. 430 HL.

18-110 Principles of liability on the basis of *Anns v Merton LBC*[89] were established by the House of Lords. The Council had statutory responsibility to regulate building regulations and requirements for the proper construction of property. The House of Lords accepted that the Council was liable in negligence for the cost of repairing buildings when the foundations had been improperly inspected or the inspector had negligently carried out inspections. Since *Anns* a more restrictive view of the extent of liability for economic loss has been accepted in *Murphy v Brentwood*,[90] which distinguished *Anns* on the basis that there can be no liability in tort for the cost of repairing defective premises in anticipation of any personal injury or property liability.

In a significant decision of Supreme Court in *Michael v Chief Constable of South Wales*,[91] the question of negligence against a Police force was considered. The question was whether the Police should be liable for a negligent act or omission to control the danger posed by a criminal act of a third party. The facts of the case arose when the family of a woman, murdered by her ex-boyfriend claimed damages of negligence against two police forces. The victim had dialled 999 where it was recorded as requiring immediate response by the first police force and then transferred to the second police force, where the victim lived. However, the call centre did not mention that there was a threat to kill and the call was graded as requiring a response within 60 minutes. The victim phoned the Police for a second time but the line went dead as she was being murdered. In previous cases, most notably *Hill v Chief Constable of West Yorkshire*,[92] the courts applied the principle that there was no duty of care to take reasonable steps where it is alleged that there could have prevented death or personal injury caused by a third party. This is known as the "Hill immunity." The reasoning was based the absence of a proximate relationship between the Police or the victim and that any liability was inconsistent with public policy. In the case of *Michael*, the majority considered that there was no general rule of liability on a defendant for injury caused to the claimant by a third party. There were some exceptions that the defendant was in a position of control over the third party and should have foreseen the likelihood of the third party causing damage to somebody in close proximity. There was liability if the defendant assumed a positive responsibility to safeguard the claimant. The Supreme Court dismissed the claim in negligence because the defendant was neither in a position of control and there was no assumption of responsibility towards the defendant. Lord Kerr, one of the judges in the minority, was unconvinced and argued that there was sufficient closeness between the information communicated by the victim and the defendant police forces. The case is evidence of strong public policy considerations that are at the heart of any decision on the liability of public authorities. Article 2 considerations resulted in the case being taken to trial. It is unlikely that after the case there will be any diminution in the approach to the case that liability will only arise in the most exceptional circumstances.

---

89   [1978] A.C. 728; [1977] 2 W.L.R. 1024 HL. See the development by the courts of foreseen damage in *Cambridge Water Co Ltd v Eastern Counties Leather Plc* [1994] 2 A.C. 264; [1994] 2 W.L.R. 53 HL.
90   [1991] 1 A.C. 398; [1990] 3 W.L.R. 414 HL.
91   [2015] UKSC 2; [2015] A.C. 1732,
92   [1989] A.C. 53; [1988] 2 W.L.R. 1049 HL.

Michael is a welcome approach to the much criticised decision of the Strasbourg Court in *Osman v UK*[93] that objected to any concept of police immunity, illustrating the potential for conflict between UK attitudes to litigation and the civil tradition of the European Court of Human Rights.[94] The Osman case has been criticised,[95] but it is illustrative of the differing perceptions about rules and their application in different legal cultures and constitutional traditions.

18-111
Public bodies may be liable for nuisance but there is a presumption that statutory powers are not intended to be exercised so as to cause nuisance. However, the question of whether a nuisance may be condoned in the exercise of statutory powers depends on the nature of the powers and their interpretation by the courts. In *Burgoin SA v Ministry of Agriculture*[96] the question arose out of the entitlement of a trader in a claim alleging liability because of a breach of European Community regulations against the Ministry of Agriculture. The courts were divided on the matter and decided in that instance that there was no liability; this is likely to become an important issue for the future. The basics of the tort is that there is dishonesty on the conduct of the official and is one of the intentional torts.

18-112
Powers to engage in contracts are an important element in the activities of both central and local government. Such powers may be statutory or through the development of the law of the EU subject to public procurement directives. Increasingly such contracting powers are a means to enforce standards and this may provide remedies for the citizen. The financial controls over public bodies in their role of entering contractual relations are an important element of scrutiny. Local government powers to undertake competitive contracting are carefully proscribed under Pt 2 of the Local Government Act 1992.

18-113
The courts rarely intervene through judicial review to review the terms of contracts but the legal powers to enter contracts are carefully scrutinised. This may be achieved in two ways. First, has the public body the requisite legal authority to enter into the contract? If the court finds that the body has acted ultra vires the contract is void. Secondly, where there are sufficient legal powers to enter into a contract and the contract is not ultra vires, the question then falls to be determined under principles of ordinary contract law that the public body may be liable for any breach of contract.

18-114
Finally, Convention rights may provide remedies when in the past the English common law was lacking in a remedy. In *Marcic v Thames Water Utilities Ltd*[97] the Court of Appeal held that Thames Water's refusal to take measures to prevent flooding of Mr Marcic's property amounted to an infringement of his rights under art.8 (the right to respect for private and family life). An award of damages in nuisance was available when in the past it is unlikely that any nuisance claim might have succeeded. This is a classic example of applying a rights-based formula to a minority of people who are liable to be flooded because of sewerage operations.

---

93   (1998) 29 E.H.R.R. 245 ECHR.
94   C. Gearty, "Unravelling *Osman*" (2001) 64 *M.L.R.* 159.
95   *Barrett v Enfield LBC* [2001] 2 A.C. 550; [1999] 3 W.L.R. 7 HL at [85]. Lord Browne-Wilkinson.
96   [1986] Q.B. 716; [1985] 3 W.L.R. 1027 CA (Civ Div).
97   [2002] EWCA Civ 64; [2002] Q.B. 929.

18-115 The case is anticipatory of Government proposals to undertake developments to prevent the increase in flooding.

Article 8, the respect for private and family life, arose in the Court of Appeal decision in *Anufrijeva v Southwark Council*[98] where there were inefficiency and delay by local authorities and the Home Office. Damages were not recoverable as of right, even where the Convention had been breached. While damages may not be recoverable, the possibility of judicial review is available for breaches of the Convention. In *R (TG) v Lambeth Council*,[99] a wrong decision of the Council in dealing with a claimant when aged 18 under the housing legislation was subject to judicial review, but not an award of damages. Similar cases[100] follow a pattern of reluctance to develop the law of tort around judicial review or the Human Rights Act 1998. Two Supreme Court cases have paved the way for a departure from this approach. In *Rabone v Pennine Care NHS Trust*,[101] the Supreme Court did award compensation arising out of a breach of art.2. The facts and circumstances were very special to the award of compensation. The parents' daughter after psychiatric care was released prematurely from a mental hospital on home leave and she committed suicide. Her parents had not been in favour of her release and warned of the dangers.

18-116 In *R (Faulkner) v Justice Secretary*[102] involving delays in the Parole Board hearing, the prisoners' tariffs had expired where they were serving indeterminate sentences. The lack of resources was the reason for their cases not to be heard. The Supreme Court relied on an earlier case, *R (Greenfield) v Home Secretary*,[103] where the House of Lords had rejected a claim for compensation arising out of a failure to have a fair hearing. The basic reasoning in Greenfield was that the Human Rights Act 1998 was not a tort statute and could only be interpreted following the interpretation of the Strasbourg Court. In *Faulkner*, the Supreme Court adapted a principle of "just satisfaction" as applicable and only in such rare circumstances will the court award damages. Certain Convention rights will be treated differently such as art.3 on the prohibition against torture or a breach of art.5 on the right to liberty. This is a welcome development as the restrictions in *Greenfield* are perhaps too restrictive of compensation claims. There is an emerging jurisprudence from military claims arguing that a Convention breach might give rise to compensation. In *Smith v Ministry of Defence*,[104] the Supreme Court, allowed cases involving "friendly fire" and inadequate military equipment were permitted to go to trial. The cases revolved around art.2 claims and the question of whether the claimants rights were breached.[105] The Supreme Court were unanimously of the view that Convention rights applied to military operations of the British armed forces outside the UK.[106] The question of the scope

---

98 [2003] EWCA Civ 1406; [2004] Q.B. 1124.
99 [2011] EWCA Civ 526; [2011] 4 All E.R. 453.
100 *R (Greenfield) v Home Secretary* [2005] UKHL 14; [2005] 1 W.L.R. 673.
101 [2012] UKSC 29; 2013 S.C. (U.K.S.C.) 1.
102 [2011] EWCA Civ 526; [2011] 4 All E.R. 453.
103 [2013] UKSC 23; [2013] 2 A.C. 254.
104 [2013] UKSC 41; [2014] A.C. 52.
105 See Lord Sumption, "The right to a court Article 6 of the Human Rights Convention", James Wood Lecture, University of Glasgow (13 November 2016).
106 See a critique offered by Jonathan Morgan, "Negligence: Into Battle" [2013] *Cambridge Law Journal* 14.

of human rights and serving soldiers has proved controversial and has convinced sceptics of the Human Rights Act 1998 that the scope of Convention rights is currently too widely drawn. Many military commanders fear that Convention rights will give rise to large damages paid to military service personnel.[107]

F: Summary and Conclusions

Applications for Judicial review face considerable pressure from the changes in legal aid that have reduced its availability to many citizens.[108] The House of Commons Justice Committee, has noted how real savings in the cost of legal aid have taken place, has harmed access to justice for some litigants.[109] The future of judicial review is often wholly dependent on the availability of legal aid.[110] Pressure groups or lobby groups often play a controversial role. In recent years their activities have become more significant in the area of legal challenge.[111] Concern arises out of the *Rose Theatre Case*, however, if interpreted to mean that in the absence of an express statutory right the ordinary citizen is debarred from challenging decisions, even where it appears that there may be a public interest served by such a challenge. This may leave a gap in the arrangements for public challenge and may restrict standing to a few.

18–117

The broad liberalisation of the rules of standing since the *Fleet Street Casuals* case raises the question of whether the special rules of standing are required. The Woolf and Jackson Reforms on civil procedure provide a case management system sufficient to act as a gatekeeper function. Standing may therefore be seen less as a substantive hurdle to be overcome, but more as an unnecessary procedural requirement. In terms of developing systems for the simplification of the procedures for judicial review, rules of standing may be substituted by the exercise of a straightforward judicial discretion on the merits of each case.

18–118

There is an inherent problem in shifting democratic participation from the parliamentary political process to courts. It might be argued in this context that, perhaps, the rules of standing are too liberal and require some refinement? That problem is exemplified in the *Pergau Dam* case, where government policy, however misconceived, eventually prevailed over the technical legal arguments accepted by the courts. The World Development Movement

18–119

---

107 See Richard Ekins, Jonathan Morgan and Tom Tugendhat, *Clearing the Fog of Law* (London: Policy Exchange, 2015).
108 House of Lords, *Future of Legal Aid*, Library Note, LLN2015/048 (2015).
109 House of Commons Justice Committee, *Impact of Changes to Civil Legal Aid under Part 1 of the Legal Aid, Sentencing and punishment of Offenders Act 2012*, HC 311 Session 2014–15 (12 March 2015), p.36; and House of Commons Justice Committee, *Courts and Tribunals Fees and Charges Terms of Reference Extended* (11 September 2015).
110 House of Lords Library, *Future of Legal Aid*, LLN 2015/048 (7 December 2014).
111 Law Commission, *Administrative Law: Judicial Review and Statutory Appeals*, Report No.226 (1994).

18–120 emerges as an effective group with international standing, and that can hardly be questioned, but as a representative group of the public at large it appears to be a small minority. However worthy its cause, pressure group activity has the potential for abuses of the legal process. Until the day the UK creates a constitutional court and a written constitution delineating the boundaries of legal and political power, the ultimate parliamentary authority and sovereignty vested in the government of the day prevails; meanwhile, confusion and lack of clarity remain over how legal and political authority may best be defined and where the boundaries between them should be drawn.

18–120 The system of remedies is largely discretionary, leaving the judiciary to develop principles and ideas largely on an ad hoc basis. There is a case for codification and perhaps a greater articulation of guiding principles. This is likely to become increasingly important when many litigants are unable to afford legal advice and have to rely on their own devices to make an application for judicial review. Advances over the last ten years have made judicial review, its procedures and remedies an important achievement in providing many citizens with remedies that in the past would not have been possible.

18–121 The Human Rights Act, although politically contentious, has enriched the jurisprudence of the Administrative Court and been influential in the UK's Supreme Court in helping to set the future of judicial review.[112] Paul Craig's analysis of the UK's system of public law as opposed to public laws. He admits, that "...it is clear that we have a system of public laws insofar as this connotes distinct statutory rules on subject matter as diverse as education, health, asylum and licensing".[113] Remedies are the means of ensuring standards and fairness that engage with good administration and encourage good policy makers to link sound policy with good decision-making.

Further Reading

H. Arthurs, *"Without the Law": Administrative Justice and Legal Pluralism in Nineteenth Century England* (Toronto: University of Toronto Press, 1985).

V. Bondy and M. Sunkin, *The Dynamics of Judicial Review Litigation* (London: Public Law Project, 2009).

P. P. Craig, *Administrative Law*, 7th edn (London: Sweet and Maxwell, 2012).

---

112 House of Commons Briefing Paper, *UK Cases at the European Court of Human Rights since 1975*, No.05611 (22 May 2015).

113 P. Craig, "Public law and Public Laws" in Mark Elliott and David Feldman, *The Cambridge Companion to Public Law* (Cambridge: Cambridge University Press, 2015), 153–170, p.170.

A. C. L. Davies, *The Public Law of Government Contracts* (Oxford: Oxford University Press, 2008).

M. Elliott and D. Feldman (eds), *The Cambridge Companion to Public Law* (Cambridge: Cambridge University Press, 2015).

C. R. Harlow and R. W. Rawlings, *Law and Administration*, 2nd edn (London: Butterworths, 1997).

Law Commission Report, *Remedies in Administrative Law*, No.73, Cmnd.6407 (1976).

Part V

Public Law and Conflict

Part V examines the role of law when tackling problems of public order, terrorism, and state secrecy. Chapter 19 addresses the issue of the law of public order. Chapter 20 is how secrecy is protected. The final chapter, Ch.21 attempts to assess the current state and future development of public law.

19

Public Order and the Freedom of Assembly

A: Introduction

The focus of this chapter is first, on how the law regulates public meetings, processions or demonstrations. The common law has been increasingly replaced by statutory arrangements as successive governments have sought to strengthen the legal regime applicable to public order and street protests. The protection of the common law in terms of the freedom of assembly has been addressed through the Human Rights Act 1998. Article 11 of the European Convention on Human Rights encompasses the right to freedom of association and assembly. The interconnection between the common law and the Convention is an important element in how democracy engages with rights. Parliament and the scrutiny of government is one of the most important checks on abuse of power. Too often, Parliament is unable to resist the Government's demands for emergency powers or additional regulation in the interests of the State. This is perhaps an inevitability of party politics, public opinion and the role of modern government. The role of the courts is often limited because of concerns of the legitimacy of judicial discretion when it opposes executive action. A second focus is to consider emergency powers in the context of civil disturbance. Historically, popular protest succeeded in gaining important constitutional rights such as: the broadening of the franchise; the right to vote for women; and in industrial relations, the rights of trades unions. Many rights gained through popular movements have endured. This is an important dimension to the discussion of public order. Freedoms associated with Convention rights under the Human Rights Act 1998 have now to be considered as part of the law. In particular, the right to freedom of peaceful assembly and association (art.11) and the right to free expression (art.10). Limitations on both freedoms must be prescribed by law but may be necessary in a democratic society. In addition the question of State interference with any freedom must be[1]

19–001

---

1   *Steel v UK* (1998) 28 E.H.R.R. 603 ECHR.

"proportionate to the legitimate aim pursued". The onus rests on the State to show that the law meets this obligation.

In a democratic and accountable society that is open to change, the freedoms enjoyed by any particular group or the majority are dependent on how the law treats protests in the context of public order.[2] A wide variety of political causes or beliefs may attract public protest which may take the form of public meeting, demonstration or protest. A responsibility rests on the police to fulfil their general function of keeping the peace. Their responsibility applies to a wide variety of public order problems as wide-ranging and as diverse as pop festivals, football crowds and political demonstrations.

As Lord Denning recognised in *Hubbard v Pitt*[3] "the right to demonstrate and the right to protest on matters of public concern. . . are often the only means by which grievances can be brought to the knowledge of those in authority". Detecting that the liberty of the individual to assemble is a hallmark of an open society, Lord Scarman noted[4] that while peaceful assembly is a fundamental right:

> "A balance has to be struck, a compromise found that will accommodate the exercise of the right to protest within a framework of public order which enables ordinary citizens who are not protesting to go about their business and pleasure without obstruction or inconvenience."

In this area of law, one of the most important questions is how police powers to maintain public order may be balanced in the interests of society to ensure freedom of assembly and association. Discussion of the freedom to protest, assemble or demonstrate within the context of the discussion of public order has undoubtedly facilitated more extensive powers to uphold public order. This fact reinforces the need to balance discussion of public order and the effect of those laws upon freedom of expression.

In recent years, one of the most notable periods for intense debate about public demonstrations was in the 1980s and the development of the peace movement as part of the Campaign for Nuclear Disarmament (CND). Another notable occasion for public protest which raised a number of public order issues came from an industrial conflict: a period of one year from March 1984–1985 when coal miners embarked on industrial action involved widespread picketing and protests at collieries throughout the country. The mobilisation of the police and the national co-ordination of police resources based on the National Reporting Centre at New Scotland Yard in London raised questions about policing in the

---

2 Defend the Right to Protest, *Threats to the right to freedom of peaceful assembly and of association* (London, 2014).
3 [1976] Q.B. 142; [1975] 3 W.L.R. 201 CA (Civ Div).
4 See D. G. T. Williams, *Keeping the Peace* (London: Hutchinson, 1967); R. Card, *Public Order The New Law* (London: Butterworths, 1987); and A. T. H. Smith, *Offences Against Public Order* (London: Sweet & Maxwell, 1987).

1980s. Subsequent prosecutions of the strikers were accompanied by the use of binding over orders and bail requirements to contain the activities of striking miners. The Public Order Act 1986 has been strengthened by the Criminal Justice and Public Order Act 1994.[5] Additional powers have been granted to the police when dealing with football disorder and young offenders. There are also a miscellaneous set of powers and responsibilities that overshadow freedoms and rights in the UK. This includes the Counter-Terrorism and Security Act 2015.[6]

B: Historical Perspectives

The setting up of Sir Robert Peel's new police force in the nineteenth century was greatly advanced by the need to regulate popular protest. The historical role of policing identified by Cornish[7] as covering a wide selection of popular issues and demands, including "strikes, elections, political demands and periods of poor trade each contributed to spasmodic unrest" and "also represented a significant opposition to military intervention in the internal maintenance of order in England". The lessons of policing developed through experience. Past mistakes were quickly overcome by a delicate mixture of Royal Commission and judicial oversight. The first attempt to provide comprehensive police powers to control public protest emerged in the Public Order Act 1936, which spearheaded the legal prohibition of "quasi-military organisations". The Act was passed at a period of high activity for the British Union of Fascists.

19–006

The importance of popular protest as providing pressure for reform had succeeded in gaining the vote for women, and greater trade union rights. Political authority gained from addressing the hustings and delivering directly to the electorate party political promises to gain election victory, has become an important feature of English democracy. Special arrangements are provided for policing the Metropolis with specific attention given to the rights of Parliament to sit unimpeded.

19–007

Policing is inextricably linked to public order. Public order requires high levels of intelligence and surveillance activities.

19–008

Maintaining public order may involve the State in the use of extreme powers at times of emergency or civil unrest. The benefits of Empire and the colonial experience informed English constitutional writing on martial law and states of emergency. Townshend noted[8]:

19–009

---

5   Cm.2263 (July 1993).
6   See Data Retention and Investigatory Powers Act 2014.
7   W. R. Cornish, *Law and Society in England 1750–1850* (London: Sweet & Maxwell, 1989); J. Stevenson and R. Qinault (ed), *Popular Protest and Public Order* (London: George Allen & Unwin, 1974).
8   C. Townshend, *Political Violence in Ireland* (Oxford: Clarendon, 1983) on the use of military in Ireland.

PUBLIC ORDER AND THE FREEDOM OF ASSEMBLY

> "The whole drift of thinking about martial law, or emergency powers in general, was concerned with the problem of legality, and of ethical or political acceptability, not with that of practicality. . ."

19-010 Martial law may be defined as the common law duty of the Executive to repel force with force. The courts, after the event, could determine what was justified on the basis of what was reasonable. Set against this extreme, some doubted if martial law—meaning a state of siege, and the partial transfer of powers to the military—might exist within English domestic law. Doubts about the effectiveness and acceptability of the use of the army in peacetime to control civil disorder on mainland Britain remain, and the onus is on the police as the primary agency to keep the peace.

19-011 Currently the law of public order is contained in the Public Order Act 1936 and detailed powers granted to the police in the Public Order Act 1986 and the Criminal Justice and Public Order Act 1994. Other measures such as the Highways Act 1980 and Police Act 1964 are also relevant. Common law powers such as breach of the peace have also survived.[9]

C: Police Powers

Public meetings and assemblies

19-012 Various freedoms such as the right to take part in public meetings, processions and demonstrations or to engage in political activities by joining trade unions or political clubs or associations may be discussed in the context of the powers the police have to preserve public order. For example the freedom to assemble and to engage in peaceful protest may be generally accepted as among[10] "our fundamental freedoms: they are numbered the touchstones which distinguish a free society from a totalitarian one. . ." However, the freedom to assemble is not unfettered. The law may regulate both the conduct and location of public assemblies. The policing of popular demonstrations and protests is often carried out in the glare of publicity with wide media coverage and reporting of meetings and demonstrations.

19-013 The various powers granted to the police to anticipate problems arising from organisations and associations are both common law and statutory. The Public Order Act 1936 provides a number of relevant powers. Section 1 prohibits the wearing of a uniform which has

---

9 House of Commons Library, *The Policing of Marches and Demonstrations*, Standard Note, SN/HA/5013 (2009).
10 *R v Jordan and Tyndall* [1963] Crim. L.R. 124 CCA.

political objectives, introduced to prohibit the increasing use of uniforms by political groups in the 1930s, with the rise of Fascists. In addition, s.2 of the 1936 Act prohibits the rise in quasi-military organisations by banning their organisation and association. Vigilante groups may fall within the category of proscribed organisation. In the absence of express statutory prohibition there is also the possibility of conspiracy offences arising out of an organisation set up to carry out illegal activities. The caveat to any prosecution is that the illegality must be capable of being committed by a single individual. There are various duties on UK higher education to uphold freedom of speech as far as it is practicable to within the law, under the Counter-Terrorism and Security Act 2015.[11] Fears of radicalisation of many educational institutions influenced the Education (No.2) Act 1986 that establishes educational institutions with a statutory duty to uphold the freedom of speech in their institutions. There is a *Prevent Strategy* that is designed to combat discrimination and racial hatred by operating best practice.[12] Section 43 of the 1986 Act requires that "shall take such steps as are reasonably practicable to ensure that freedom of speech within the law is secured for members, students and employees of the establishment and for visiting speakers". This is a difficult duty for educational institutions to apply in the context of lively debate, intellectual argument and often openly hostile and often critical views of the status quo. Creating the balance between freedom of debate and the prevention of extremism requires careful debate and delicate decisions.[13]

Public processions

Invariably many forms of public protest involve the use of the highway. There are both statutory and common law offences regulating the conduct involved. Section 137 of the Highways Act 1980 provides that "a person, without lawful authority or excuse, [who] in any way wilfully obstructs the free passage along the highway" is guilty of a criminal offence. The question of what constitutes a lawful excuse may be considered by the courts. In *Hirst v Chief Constable of West Yorkshire*,[14] animal rights supporters were convicted after they protested outside shops selling furs in Bradford city centre. Glidewell LJ in the Divisional Court considered their appeal against conviction. In the earlier decision of *Nagy v Weston*,[15] Lord Parker considered the obstruction of the highway by a hot dog vendor. The question of whether it was a reasonable use

19-014

---

11 House of Commons Library, *Freedom of Speech and preventing extremism in UK higher education institutions*, Briefing Paper, CBP 7199 (20 May 2015).
12 See *Prevent Duty Guidance for England and Wales* (March 2015); and Universities UK, *External speakers in higher education institutions*, revised edn (March 2014).
13 *R v University of Liverpool Ex p. Caesar Gordon* [1991] 1 Q.B. 124; [1990] 3 W.L.R. 667 QBD. Case law on this subject is likely to develop over the coming years. See B. Dickson, "Activism and Restraint within the UK Supreme Court" (2015) 21(1) *EJoCL* 1.
14 (1987) 85 Cr. App. R. 143; (1987) 151 J.P. 304 QBD.
15 [1965] 1 W.L.R. 280; [1965] 1 All E.R. 78 Div Ct.

> "depends upon all the circumstances, including the length of time the obstruction continues, the place where it occurs, the purpose for which it is done and of course whether it does in fact cause an actual obstruction as opposed to a potential obstruction."

19–015 Applying Lord Parker's dicta to the facts in *Hirst*, Glidewell LJ considered three questions to be posed in such cases and quashed the convictions on the basis that the issues were not properly considered in the Crown Court. First, was there an obstruction? Any stopping on the highway could amount to an obstruction whether it is on the footpath or carriageway. Secondly, was the obstruction wilful? If the stopping was deliberate this could amount to wilful obstruction. Thirdly, was the activity complained about lawful? Lawful excuse requires the court to consider that "lawful excuse embraces activities otherwise lawful in themselves which may or may not be reasonable in all the circumstances". This leaves unclear the exact balance to be struck between activity such as obstructing the highway when a group of friends meet to discuss their holidays for 20 minutes or so, which is lawful, and that which is not. In the case of distributors advertising material or free periodicals outside major rail stations, this may raise issues of legality because it may appear to be unreasonable. The courts may regard conduct which is ancillary to the use of the highway as acceptable and reasonable, and that which is not as unreasonable.

19–016 The obstruction of the highway may constitute a public nuisance and it may also involve private nuisance and trespass. In the case of public nuisance, at common law this is a misdemeanour triable in either the Crown Court or before magistrates. The exact terms of the common law offence are broadly described as Smith and Hogan note[16] to include obstructing the highway and:

> "...it also includes a wide variety of other interferences with the public; for example the carrying on of an offensive trade which impregnates the air 'with noisome offensive and stinking smoke' to the common nuisance of the public passing along the highway, polluting a river with gas so as to destroy the fish and render the water unfit for drinking..."

19–017 The interference in such cases must be substantial and unreasonable. The courts appear to have a discretion to decide where the limits lie between what is "reasonably incidental" to the right of passage on the highway and what is inconvenient. The degree of obstruction or inconvenience may determine the legality of what is permissible.

19–018 While it is not necessary to show that the defendant intended to create a nuisance, it is necessary to show that his actions constituted a nuisance. In criminal cases the defendant may be intentional or reckless in his actions. This may be more widely construed in the light

---

16 *Smith and Hogan's Criminal Law* (Oxford: Oxford University Press, 1992), p.762.

of the *Caldwell*[17] criteria for recklessness which implies some degree of criminal liability for acts which are not foreseen by the defendant to involve risk but are foreseen to the reasonable man. This may in effect provide for criminal negligence as a basis for liability. In criminal cases of nuisance, the prosecution must prove beyond a reasonable doubt, whereas in civil cases involving nuisance proof on a balance of probabilities is sufficient.

A public nuisance may be actionable in civil law, usually at the instance of the Attorney General or a private citizen who must show special loss that is particular to the individual and not the public at large. It is necessary to distinguish civil cases from criminal cases although there has been considerable overlap arising from the grounds of nuisance liability. In *Southport Corp v Esso Petroleum*,[18] Lord Denning observed how in a civil action once nuisance was proved and the defendant shown to have caused the act or omission constituting the nuisance, the legal burden shifts onto the defendant to justify or excuse his action.

A private nuisance is actionable at the instance of the private citizen who suffers a wilful interference with the enjoyment of land or rights over or in connection with the land. Sections 4 and 5 of the Protection of Harassment Act 1997 prevent harassment of a private citizen and may be used to prohibit conduct of a protestor. The Criminal Justice and Police Act 2001 restrains demonstrations outside a citizen's home.

Pt V of the Criminal Justice and Public Order Act 1994 gives additional and wide powers for the police to deal with squatters, large-scale trespass and those participating in raves or connected with hunt saboteurs. There is a new offence of aggravated trespass. This applies with trespass on land in the open air by those who seek to obstruct or disrupt those that are engaged in lawful activity.

There are powers to direct people to leave the land should the police have reasonable belief that the trespassers will disrupt a lawful activity. An offence is committed if a trespasser fails to obey a police direction. There are powers to prevent people attending raves or other events by stopping people and directing them to disperse. Failure to disperse is a criminal offence.

The police have powers to regulate what is called a "trespassery assembly". This is an assembly of 20 or more people on land to which the public has no right of access. There are powers to remove trespassers with six or more vehicles on land. Failure to comply with the directions of a police officer is a criminal offence.

There are extensive remedies available under the Act which permits owners or occupiers to go to the County Court to require the squatter to leave the occupation of the land within 24 hours. The police are empowered to enforce this order. Finally, local authorities are given powers to direct unauthorised campers to leave the land. Failure to comply with this request is a criminal offence. An enforcement order may be obtained from the magistrates and the police may take reasonable steps to enforce the order including entering on the land and removing any vehicles. Obstructing the police in carrying out their duties is an offence.

---

17 *Metropolitan Police Commissioner v Caldwell* [1982] A.C. 341; [1981] 2 W.L.R. 509 HL.
18 [1954] 2 Q.B. 182; [1954] 3 W.L.R. 200 at [197].

19-025 Injunctions may be sought to prevent any threatened illegal assembly or picket. This is a common remedy used to enforce employment law and the rules about picketing.

19-026 The carrying on of a meeting or demonstration may be the subject of legal restrictions as to where the meeting may be held. It is a common law trespass to hold meetings on highways or in public places. Restrictions on holding meetings in open spaces such as parks or recreation areas may depend on the geographical location and therefore the jurisdiction such open space comes under. Byelaws empower local authorities to regulate such open spaces according to whether there is conduct amounting to a nuisance or the use of specific statutory powers for the good government of the area. In addition to these powers conditions may be imposed on such meetings by the police under the Public Order Act 1986 discussed below.

19-027 Pt IV of the Criminal Justice and Public Order Act 1994 gives the police extended powers to stop and search for offensive weapons or dangerous instruments. This power is constrained to a particular area for a specific and limited time provided a senior police officer reasonably believes that violence may break out.

19-028 Parliamentary candidates at elections have specific protection afforded to the traditional meetings carried out during the election period. Similar provisions apply to the carrying on of local government elections.[19] There are special provisions for protests held within the vicinity of Parliament in London. Following protests against the war in Iraq in Parliament Square, it was decided to regulate public meetings around Parliament. The Serious Organised Crime and Police Act 2005 made it a criminal offence to demonstrate within the vicinity of Parliament without authorisation. Demonstrators have to give notice of their intention and the notice of intention has to conform to certain standards.[20]

19-029 The law also facilitates the carrying on of election meetings in public halls. The freedom of political discussion is an important responsibility which the governing bodies of universities and colleges of further education are expected to uphold, and take reasonable steps in order to ensure that there is freedom of speech afforded to visitors and members of the institution concerned. Interpretation of this provision can be extremely difficult when the university authorities are considering the likelihood of violence on the campus. In *Ex p. Caesar Gordon*,[21] the University of Liverpool granted permission to the student Conservative Association to hold a meeting. Restrictions were issued on the confidential nature of the organisational details of the meeting. The University considered that there was a threat of disorder because of the nature of the meeting and public feeling outside the University. These fears of disorder were in part because the University had little control over members of the public having access to University premises. Previously there had been widespread disorder in Toxteth, an area of Liverpool not

---

19 *Thomas v National Union of Mineworkers (South Wales Area)* [1986] Ch. 20; [1985] 2 W.L.R. 1081 Ch D; and *Newsgroup Newspapers Ltd v Society of Graphical and Allied Trades '82 (No.2)* [1987] I.C.R. 181; [1986] I.R.L.R. 337 QBD. See, for example: Open Spaces Act 1906 s.15; the various Public Health Acts 1875; and s.235 of the Local Government Act 1972; and the Parks Regulations Act 1872. In London see the Trafalgar Square Regulations 1952, SI 1952/776. See s.95 of the Representation of the People Act 1983; s.96 of the Representation of the People Act 1983 as amended by Sch.4 para.38 to the Representation of the People Act 1985.
20 House of Commons, *Protests around Parliament*, Standard Note, SN/HA/3658 (3 June 2010).
21 *R v University of Liverpool Ex p. Caesar-Gordon* [1991] 1 Q.B. 124; [1990] 3 W.L.R. 667 QBD.

far from the University. The Divisional Court granted a declaration and held that the University was not entitled to take account of the threat of disorder other than on the University campus. This did not however invalidate the conditions imposed by the University. Each University is expected to publicise its own rules of conduct as codes of practice for public meetings within its own premises in accordance with the Education (No.2) Act 1986.[22]

19-030
Extensive powers are provided under the Public Order Act 1936 to control public processions. Section 3 permits a chief officer of police who reasonably apprehends that a procession may "occasion serious public disorder" to apply in London to the Home Secretary for a banning order, or elsewhere, to a local authority; the order may be for a period up to three months. This power has been supplemented by Pt 1 of the Public Order Act 1986. The 1986 Act provides under s.11 for advance notice and s.12 regulates advance notice for processions. The Act includes the circumstances where there may be conditions attached to the permission to hold a procession, and under s.14 for the imposition of conditions on assemblies. Hitherto, the 1936 Public Order Act was silent as to the regulation of an assembly which is stationary and not engaged in a procession.

19-031
Imposing conditions on processions and assemblies arises out of the experience of past years. During the 1960s and 70s an increase in political agitation led to a greater number of public demonstrations with their opposing counter-demonstrations. Popular causes have included the Vietnam War, apartheid, and the activities of the CND. The National Front has also been actively contesting a number of parliamentary by-elections. Balancing the needs of each group to present its viewpoint requires careful judgment on the part of the police and the prosecuting authorities.

19-032
The police have at their disposal a wide range of possibilities. Rerouting processions away from counter-demonstrations may be adopted. Conditions on the route of the procession may include a ban on using certain streets or thoroughfares. Matters which may be considered in regulating processions or meetings include the question of whether there might be serious damage to property, serious disruption to the life of the community and intimidation. In making any tactical judgment on these matters there is an added consideration which is the cost of policing, the manpower involved and the question of the most effective deployment of police resources. Public meetings may distract the police from other activities, engage a large amount of police overtime and increase the workload on the courts in any prosecutions taken as a result of disorder.

19-033
There are a number of offences which may be committed by those who take part in or are engaged in the disruption of a public meeting or in certain circumstances carrying out a protest arising from a trade dispute. These include obstructing the police in the execution of their duty, criminal damage, the possession of offensive weapons, the use of threatening violence to enter premises, trespassing on premises, and failure to leave at the request of a displaced occupier, trespassing with an offensive weapon, and obstructing the court officers in the execution of their duty.

---

22 House of Commons Library, *Freedom of Speech and Preventing extremism in UK Higher Education Institutions*, Briefing Paper, CBP 7199 (20 May 2015).

19-034 During the Miners' Strike in 1984, the police made use of powers under the Road Traffic Act 1972 to stop vehicles. This was used to ascertain whether the occupants were engaged in picket duties. Failure to comply with a request by the police to re-route their journey and return home ran the risk of prosecution under s.51(3) of the Police Act 1964, namely obstructing a police officer in the execution of his duty.

19-035 The action taken by the police is usually left to their discretion. Even though the courts may review that discretion, there is a reluctance to overturn police tactical decision-making. This reluctance may be traced back to cases decided at an earlier period though the courts may occasionally interpret the law to protect demonstrators. In *Beatty v Gillbanks*,[23] members of the Salvation Army were subject to a binding over by magistrates not to assemble and hold a meeting. The binding over was the result of a police direction that the assembly might cause a breach of the peace because a rival and opposing organisation, the Skeleton Army, intended to counter-demonstrate against the Salvation Army. The Salvation Army appealed to the Divisional Court against the magistrates' order. Field J concluded that the Salvation Army were wrongly bound over. There were no grounds for saying that the Salvation Army were holding an illegal protest. Any disturbance that was caused in the past had come from the Skeleton Army, and the Salvation Army did not incite or intentionally provoke a breach of the peace.

19-036 The case may be regarded as establishing an important principle that an assembly that is legal does not become illegal merely because it causes a counter-demonstration or when others threaten illegality. However, in practice how far might this principle be applied? It was possible for the court in *Beatty v Gillbanks* to clearly distinguish the motives or good faith of the Salvation Army from the Skeleton Army, but where this is not possible the principle may not easily be upheld.

19-037 There is also in Field J's formulation of the law, that if the natural and probable consequences of the action of the lawful assembly is to create a disturbance then there could legally be a binding over. It is hardly convincing that the Salvation Army did not share some element of responsibility. If their meeting were not held it is at least arguable that there would be no counter-demonstration.

19-038 Counter-demonstrations or protests were considered in *Wise v Dunning*.[24] A Protestant pastor, George Wise, made provocative comments about Catholics in Liverpool and the majority of his meetings were held in Catholic areas of the city. He was bound over to keep the peace by magistrates and challenged the legality of the binding over. As breaches of the peace were likely to be the natural consequence of his meetings, the binding over was held by the Divisional Court to be legal.

19-039 In *Duncan v Jones*[25] Mrs Duncan, a communist, was about to make a speech at a public meeting in a quiet cul-de-sac in Deptford near the entrance to an unemployment centre.

---

23 (1882) 15 Cox C.C. 138; (1882) L.R. QBD 308 QBD.
24 [1902] 1 K.B. 167 KBD.
25 [1936] 1 K.B. 218 KBD. The case has been heavily criticised by Daintith ([1966] *P.L.* 248) and Williams, *Textbook of Criminal Law* (London: Sweet & Maxwell, 1983), p.203. See *Piddington v Bates* [1961] 1 W.L.R. 162; [1960] 3 All E.R. 660 QBD.

Duncan was convicted by magistrates of obstructing a police officer in the execution of his duty when she stepped on a box which she had placed on the road to deliver her speech. In a previous meeting held by Mrs Duncan 14 months previously, there had been some disturbances. The Divisional Court upheld her conviction at Quarter Sessions. The case raises the possibility that because the police may fear a breach of the peace, even if none occurs, a peaceful meeting may be amenable to prosecution for the offence of obstructing the police in the execution of their duty. The far-reaching potential of *Duncan v Jones* means that the police may make use of the obstruction offence to regulate and control the activities of lawful pickets involved in trade disputes. The courts have been reluctant to challenge the day-to-day operational decisions of the police in these matters. Thus there appears to be little requirement on the police to prove that a threat to the peace is apprehended.

19-040

The role of the courts has proved problematic. On the one hand, the courts may be invited to consider the legality of police powers, especially the powers to seek a ban on a public demonstration. On the other hand, the courts have not provided much oversight of police operational practices, such as deciding how many demonstrators to allow to attend a meeting or how many pickets to permit at the place of work of the strikers. A code of practice exists[26] for industrial disputes, stating that in general the number of pickets should not "exceed six at any entrance to a workplace; frequently a smaller number will be appropriate".

19-041

In recent years, an additional concern has been the policing of sports fixtures. The Sporting Events (Control of Alcohol, etc.) Act 1985 regulates the sale of alcohol inside sports grounds and at the entry to stadiums. Following the Hillsborough football disaster,[27] the Football Spectators Act 1989 was passed enabling the courts to make restriction orders preventing supporters from attending football matches if they have been involved in hooligan activity. The Football Offences Act 1991 further strengthens the law regulating crowds at football matches. Offences such as throwing missiles, chanting indecent and racial abuse, running onto the pitch without any reasonable excuse and selling tickets on the day of the match without the express authority of the home club, are intended to provide preventative powers as well as enabling the police to respond to incidents at football matches. There has been a spate of additional legislation aimed at tackling the problems of football hooliganism. The Football (Offences and Disorder) Act 1999 built on the foundations of the earlier legislation and provided additional powers and closed loopholes in the law. Sections 1–5 provide powers to tackle the international dimension of football hooligans, and banning orders are now possible to prevent someone convicted of a football-related offence from travelling to an international fixture. Additional powers are granted to the courts when dealing with domestic football matches: a strengthening of penalties for breach of court orders and a widening in the scope of the court orders available. Orders banning supporters from attending football matches may be for a minimum of 12 months up to a maximum of three years. The 1999 Act also clarifies various offences relating to racism, obscenity and ticket touting. The Football (Disorder) Act 2000

---

26 Section 15 of the Trade Union and Labour Relations Act 1974 as amended by s.16(1) of the Employment Act 1980. Code of Practice on Picketing, see s.3(8) of the Employment Act 1980.
27 *Report on the Hillsborough Disaster*, Cm.962 (1990).

makes further changes to the law as an immediate response to football violence at the Euro 2000 competition. Banning orders are strengthened and the surrender of passports may be required in connection with specific football matches held outside the UK. Additional powers are given for the National Criminal Intelligence Service to disclose information for the regulation of spectators. Section 2 of the 2000 Act inserts this power into the Police Act 1997.

19-042 Clarification of the scope and extent of the banning orders mentioned above is given in yet another Act to regulate the problem of hooliganism and football. The Football (Disorder) (Amendment) Act 2002 also deals with creating a new summary procedure to prevent people from leaving the country during a control period when the police become aware of likely disorder. The powers under the 2002 Act are broader than before as they include disorder at departure rather than confined to disorder at the football fixture. A limited power of detention of up to six hours may be used and the police may make a requirement to appear before a magistrates' court. The use of "kettling" powers to keep groups of people from moving about freely to prevent a breach of the peace are examined below.

Breach of the peace

19-043 The police have common law powers of arrest for breach of the peace. If the police reasonably apprehend that the holding of a meeting or a demonstration will give rise to a breach of the peace, then such powers may be invoked. In *R v Howell*[28] the Court of Appeal attempted to classify such powers, which have been distinctive in their breadth. Watkins LJ held that there is a power of arrest for breach of the peace:

> "(1) where a breach of the peace is committed in the presence of the person making the arrest, or (2) the arrestor reasonably believes that such a breach of the peace will be committed in the immediate future by the person arrested although he has not yet committed any breach or (3) where a breach has been committed and it is reasonably believed that a renewal of it is threatened."

19-044 Relying on *Halsbury*,[29] the Court of Appeal considered that a breach of the peace might be defined:

> "...where there is an actual assault, or where a public alarm and excitement are caused by a person's wrongful act. Mere annoyance and disturbance or insult to a person or abusive language or great heat and fury without personal violence are not generally sufficient."

---

28 [1982] Q.B. 416; [1981] 3 W.L.R. 501 CA. See *Colhoun v Friel* 1996 S.L.T. 1252 High Ct of Justiciary.
29 See *Halsbury's Laws of England*, 4th edn (London: Butterworths, 1976), Vol.11, para.108.

19-045 This leaves unanswered the exact nature of the arrest powers available to the police because of the difficulty in defining breach of the peace. The elusive nature of any satisfactory definition of breach of the peace has received criticism. Peaceful behaviour in a public place may fall within the remit of a breach of the peace if the nature of the activity commands public attention and therefore a larger attendance of the public than if it were ignored. Lord Denning in *Ex p. Central Electricity Generating Board*[30] considered that a breach of the peace might arise if someone who is lawfully carrying out his work, is unlawfully and physically prevented from doing so, illustrating the potential for a wide police discretion in terms of arrest powers.

19-046 It was also accepted by the court that a person making an arrest is entitled to rely on what he reasonably believes. This raises the question of whether that belief relates to an actual breach of the peace or an apprehended breach of the peace. In *Howell*, the possibility that an apprehended breach of the peace is sufficient considerably widens the arrest powers of the police.

19-047 In *Ex p. Central Electricity Generating Board*, the Court of Appeal refused an application for mandamus requested by the Central Electricity Generating Board (CEGB) to require the Chief Constable to remove protestors encamped on private land with the intention of preventing the CEGB from carrying out a survey of the land for a nuclear power station. The question of the powers of the police in respect of a breach of the peace was considered, but as no breach of the peace had actually occurred the discussion was largely an academic one. The police appeared to have sufficient powers to intervene but the court was unwilling to substitute its judgment for that of the operational decision of the police, hence the decision not to grant mandamus. The Court of Appeal approved the test of whether an apprehended breach of the peace existed as this would be sufficient to constitute arrest powers as discussed in *Howell*. However, at most this opinion is obiter dicta and the question of whether *Howell* will be followed remains unclear.

19-048 At common law the power of arrest for breach of the peace appears to extend to private property. This point has been indirectly accepted in *McConnell v Chief Constable of the Greater Manchester Police*[31] and Glidewell LJ rejected the idea that a breach of the peace on private premises had to have an external effect on public property before there could be an offence.

19-049 In addition to arrest powers for a breach of the peace, the police have powers of arrest under ss.24–26 of the Police and Criminal Evidence Act 1984 (PACE) which did not abolish the common law powers of arrest for breach of the peace, although it generally codified other arrest powers. Section 26 allows an arrest for causing unlawful obstruction of the highway provided the arrest is necessary to prevent the unlawful obstruction continuing. Miscellaneous arrest powers are provided under s.25 of PACE arising out of offences under s.28 of the Town Police Clauses Act 1847.

19-050 The scope of breach of the peace is also relevant in defining the basis of the powers of magistrates to bind over persons to keep the peace. This is a power of historical importance

---

30 *R v Chief Constable of the Devon and Cornwall Constabulary Ex p. Central Electricity Generating Board* [1982] Q.B. 458; [1981] 3 W.L.R. 967 CA (Civ Div). See K. D. Ewing and C. A. Gearty, *Freedom under Thatcher* (Oxford: Clarendon, 1990), p.90.
31 [1990] 1 W.L.R. 364; [1990] 1 All E.R. 423 CA (Civ Div).

to the development of the magistracy. The power to bind over is that the person remains of good behaviour. Binding over may be used where there is a reasonable apprehension that a breach of the peace may occur. It has been accepted that a binding over power may be used where it is considered that there is no threat to peace but that public morality or "a good way of life" is threatened. The person who is bound over must enter a recognisance to be of good behaviour. The recognisance is forfeited on a breach in the conditions of the binding over. Such an order is both subject to an appeal and to review by the courts under Order 53. Binding over is a frequently used power to attempt to restrict the movement of potential trouble-makers. An additional power vested in magistrates is to set conditions on the grant of bail. Such bail conditions may set limits on the movements of the individual.

19-051 In addition to the above powers there is also the offence of threatening behaviour under s.5 of the Public Order Act 1936. Section 5 has been replaced later by s.4 of the Public Order Act 1986. This was the main public order offence commonly used by the police for 50 years in preference to charges of riot, unlawful assembly and affray. Section 5 of the Public Order Act 1936 covered any person who in a public place or at any public meeting used threatening, abusive or insulting words or behaviour or distributed or displayed any writing, sign or other visible representation which was threatening, abusive or insulting. For a criminal offence to be proven, the conduct was required to be intended to be a breach of the peace or to be of such a nature that such a breach of the peace was threatened. This section has now been replaced by s.4 of the Public Order Act 1986 discussed below.

19-052 The powers of the police to enter private property are also related to the idea of preserving the peace. In *Thomas v Sawkins*,[32] Lord Hewart thought that the power of the police to enter and if necessary remain on private property arose when the police officer had "reasonable ground for believing that an offence is imminent or is likely to be committed". Such generalised powers appear to be too widely expressed. The powers are vague as to when the police must have grounds for belief or the nature of the offence which falls within the police powers. If widely interpreted an extension of police powers in this way seems beyond the proper remit of judicial discretion. The powers of the police to enter on land to deal with nuisance or collective trespass have been strengthened under Pt V of the Criminal Justice and Public Order Act 1994.

19-053 A variety of innovative powers have been adopted to curb rowdy behaviour in public. There are rules for child curfew and anti-social behaviour orders under the Crime and Disorder Act 1998. Local authorities are required to formulate strategies for the prevention of crime and disorder with particular attention being paid to youth justice. The Criminal Justice and Police Act 2001 has powers to combat public drinking including drink-free zones.

Offences under the Public Order Act 1986

19-054 The experience gained from the Miners' Strike in 1984 and the policing of the peace movement led to consideration of the law on public order. The Public Order Act 1986 is largely based on

---

32 [1935] 2 K.B. 249; [1935] All E.R. Rep. 655 KBD.

the recommendations of the Law Commission.[33] The law was believed to be too complex and fragmented. This fact led to consideration of a single statute providing for greater clarity. The 1986 Act creates new statutory offences and abolishes the common law offences of riot, unlawful assembly and affray, and the offence under s.5 of the Public Order Act 1936. In fact, the 1986 Act appears to add more powers to the police while retaining the miscellaneous powers outlined above and fails to clarify the concept of breach of the peace which remains largely dependent on judicial developments.

19-055
Each of the four new offences may be examined, namely: riot; violent disorder; affray; and causing fear or provocation of violence. At common law, riot consisted of three or more persons, together with a common purpose, with an intent to help one another by force if necessary against anyone who opposed their common purpose and such force or violence is displayed in such a manner as to cause alarm in at least one person of reasonable firmness and courage. Riot is one of the most serious offences and s.1 of the Public Order Act 1986 defines the offence in similar terms to the common law offence but with the requirement of 12 or more persons and not three. If 12 or more persons threaten violence through an unlawful purpose but only one person uses violence then there is a riot but only one rioter. The offence is indictable and punishable with ten years' imprisonment.

19-056
Riot may be committed where the 12 assemble without any pre-arranged plan or by chance. Once they form together, all that is required is that they have a common purpose and at some point unlawful violence is used or there is a threat of violence. The common purpose may be inferred from conduct and need not be an unlawful one.

19-057
Violence is generally defined in s.8 of the 1986 Act to include, except in the context of affray, "violent conduct towards property as well as violent conduct towards persons". Violence is not restricted to conduct causing or intended to cause injury or damage but includes any other violent conduct (for example throwing at or towards a person a missile of a kind capable of causing injury which does not hit or falls short). But the threat of violence or the use of violence must be unlawful, and this appears to allow the excuse of violence used in self-defence. The courts may have a difficult task in establishing whether such force is believed to constitute self-defence when the force is used against the police. It has been held that when the police use force lawfully and that force is reasonable in the circumstances, in the prevention of crime or in the apprehension of suspects, then self-defence is not available against such force. But if the defendant uses force because he suspects that the police are terrorists or criminals, the defence might be available, even where the police might act lawfully.

19-058
The offence of riot is intended to provide for serious disorder where there has been widespread civil unrest and the authorities are required to arrest large numbers of people. There remains considerable difficulty in obtaining convictions. This appears to stem from the mental element of the offence requiring proof of common purpose. It must be proved that the defendant intended to use violence or was aware that his conduct might be violent; being aware of whether one's conduct is violent or not appears a difficult concept to prove. This would appear to give the police evidential problems in proving the commission of the offence.

---

33   Law Commission No.123.

19-059 Compensation for riot under the Riot (Damages) Act 1886 is now construed under the definition of riot under the Public Order Act 1986. The majority of cases involving riot raise issues associated with claims for compensation under the 1986 Act. Compensation is payable under the 1986 Act and regard is given to the conduct of the claimant. Relevant considerations are whether adequate precautions were taken by the claimant or whether he participated in the riot. In such circumstance compensation may be reduced.

19-060 Violent disorder under s.2 of the Public Order Act 1986 replaces the common law offence of unlawful assembly, and is punishable on indictment or on summary conviction. This offence is commonly charged and used more frequently than the common law offence of unlawful assembly as a means to regulate crowd behaviour. For the offence to be proved there is a requirement that there is an assembly of three or more with a common purpose to commit a crime of violence or to achieve some other object whether lawful or not in such a way as to cause reasonable men to apprehend a breach of the peace. There need not be a common purpose as each of the three or more persons may have a different purpose or no purpose. The defendant must be proved to have threatened violence or must have been aware that his conduct might be violent and threaten violence. In *Mahroof*,[34] three defendants were charged jointly on one indictment with violent disorder. Mahroof alone was convicted and appealed with the result that his conviction was quashed but a conviction on an alternative offence under s.4 was substituted. It was assumed that if three defendants to a violent disorder are involved and one of the three is acquitted, the others invariably but not necessarily must be acquitted. Invariably the acquittal of one may cause the jury to re-consider the evidence and may lead to the acquittal of the others.

19-061 Section 3 of the Public Order Act 1986 replaces the common law offence of affray with a new statutory equivalent. Affray under s.3 is triable either on indictment or on summary trial. The offence of affray requires three persons: the person using or threatening unlawful violence; a person towards whom the violence is directed; and a person of reasonable firmness who need not be, or be likely to be, at the scene. The use of affray is common in prosecutions of fights. The overlap in charging between ss.2 and 3 gives the police discretion in terms of differentiating pre-meditated violence charged under s.2 and spontaneous violence under s.3. It is also possible to charge defendants with a wide range of offences under the Offences Against the Person Act 1861, arising out of the same incident such as assault or causing grievous bodily harm.

19-062 Section 4 of the Public Order Act 1986 contains the offence of using fear or provocation of violence. The purpose of s.4 was to replace the offence under s.5 of the Public Order Act 1936, noted above concerning using threatening behaviour. The new offence covers both private and public places, and is not confined to where a third party may be likely to be provoked into violence but where a third party fears violence. There is no requirement of proving that there is or has been a breach of the peace.

19-063 Section 57 of the Crime and Courts Act 2013 introduced a small, but important change, to s.5 of the Public Order Act. It is no longer an offence to use insulting words or behaviour on the only ground that they are insulting. The power of insulting behaviour only was thought to be

---

34 (1989) 88 Cr. App. R. 317 CA (Civ Div).

too much of an inhibition to free speech. This does not alter the prosecution of insulting words or behaviour and the delivery of insults by writing or other visible signs under ss.4 and 4a of the Act.

19–064 In addition to the four offences noted above, s.5 of the Public Order Act 1986 creates a summary offence of harassment, alarm or distress. This section was intended to deal with minor acts of hooliganism causing rowdy behaviour, shouting abuse or obscenities. The width of the offence is due to the unspecific nature of the activity which may fall under its ambit. A wide range of fairly innocuous behaviour, including noisy behaviour and high spirits, may come within its scope. This may be committed where a person uses abusive, threatening or insulting words or behaviour, or displays any writing sign or other visible representation which is threatening, abusive or insulting. The person who may be affected by the conduct could be a policeman or bystander, and therefore to be harassed or alarmed must have the act performed within hearing or sight. It must be proved that the defendant intended his conduct to be threatening, abusive or insulting or disorderly and must be aware that it might be so construed. When drawing up any prosecutions under the Act the purpose of the Public Order Act must be considered when framing charges and the courts have been reluctant to accept charges under the Act for acts which are not intended to be covered by the legislation.

19–065 The width of s.5 allows the prosecution of a wide variety of activities including the wearing of tee shirts with particular slogans, the distribution of posters with unusual captions or emotive words. All such activities may fall under the criminal law. This raises the question of whether it is satisfactory to use the criminal law in this way. There is a power of arrest which accompanies the use of s.5 after a warning has been given, which extends police powers quite considerably in this area. The Public Order (Amendment) Act 1996 amends s.5(4) of the Public Order Act 1986. This permits a constable the power to arrest a person without warrant if he engages in conduct which the constable warns him to stop. The offensive conduct is set out in the Public Order Act 1986.

19–066 One of the striking features of the 1986 Act is that it does not set out rights for demonstrators or protestors. In terms of preventative powers for the purposes of controlling meetings or demonstrations, the new Act builds on the old law. Under s.11 of the Public Order Act 1986, the police, subject to few exceptions, must be given written notice of all public processions at least six days before they are due to take place. Reflecting the increase in the carrying out of public processions and meetings, the new law is intended to give the police advance warning and information about organisers, the type of procession, the date, time, route and destination of the march.

19–067 Section 12 of the 1986 Act provides the police with powers to impose conditions on public assemblies, processions or meetings. The nature of the restrictions comes into operation once there is an assembly of 20 or more in a public place. The power to make conditions is a police power and not vested in magistrates, reflecting an emphasis on the operational control by the police of public meetings or assemblies. The grounds for imposing restrictions are much wider than the apprehension of a serious breach of the peace or public disorder. If the police reasonably believe that serious damage to property or serious disruption to the life of the community may occur, then restrictions may be lawfully imposed by the police. Also if the police fear that intimidation of others may occur this may mean that restrictions may be imposed. The intimidation provision is intended to allow the police to distinguish between marches which are intended to persuade rather than intimidate.

This distinction may not be at once apparent and thus the police have to make their own judgment in such matters. Intimidation may appear to follow from the size of the gathering rather than from the motive of those involved. In trades disputes picketing may seek to persuade but it may also have the effect of intimidating those that are a minority and are fearful of the results of refusing to strike. Line-drawing in these matters is exceptionally difficult. The police are in effect exercising a dual role. Facilitating processions may not be consistent with the maintenance of good order.

The Act also includes powers of arrest and it is a criminal offence to disregard the instructions of a police officer acting under the powers contained in the Act. Conditions may be imposed at the scene of the meeting or procession that extend even to a fairly junior police officer as powers are conferred on "the senior police officer" present at the scene, and such a junior officer may be the most senior officer present. Conditions may be such as appear to the police officer to be necessary "to prevent such disorder, damage, disruption or intimidation, including conditions as to the route of the procession".

The need for such powers may be justified in terms of the variety of public meetings and demonstrations the police are expected to regulate. The presumption built into the police powers under the Act is that disruption of the normal day-to-day lives of ordinary people should not be interfered with by public demonstrations. Thus there is an assumption that the police may need to regulate various forms of protest in favour of the more orthodox behaviour in society. Invariably this will mean that the unusual or unorthodox will receive little real protection under the law and are only free to demonstrate within the police tolerance of what is reasonable. Thus inconvenience will be tolerated only marginally subject to the availability of resources and the disposition of police policy.

One example of where the police have regarded the inconvenience factor of public meetings as too great and have sought to use their powers is in the annual ritual meeting of the Druids at Stonehenge. A ban under the Public Order Act 1986 was imposed on meetings and assemblies during a period in June to coincide with the summer solstice, the aim being to avoid disruption when travelling people descended on the area to take part in ceremonies at Stonehenge.

The management of demonstrations and techniques of "kettling"

Settling the balance between lawful and peaceful protest often involves preventative action in anticipation of violence or the threat of violence. On technique adopted by the police is the use of "kettling". This involves holding protestors in large groups for a period of time so that any risk of violence that the police may perceive to exist has passed. This technique has proved controversial and its legality has been considered by the courts. In *Austin v Metropolitan Police*

Commissioner,[35] the conduct of the police was held to be justified when they kept protestors in Oxford Circus for seven hours without toilet facilities and even though permission was refused to leave the scene by one protestor who wished to pick up their child and by a person who was not a protestor. The legality of the action is based on the police officer authorising the containment believing that a breach of the peace was imminent.[36] The legality of the police use of kettling was also upheld by the Strasbourg Court in *Austin v UK*[37] specifically upholding that there was no breach of art.5. Public disquiet about the use of kettling remains despite its necessity and the police perception that it is often the lesser of two problems: preventing violence even at the expense of the freedom of movement and the right to protest.[38]

Police organisation and accountability

19-073

The importance of the police in the control of public protest and their extensive powers of arrest, search, seizure and entry requires some consideration[39] At common law, the police have analogous powers to the ordinary citizen's powers of arrest. However, wide statutory powers such as those under the Public Order Act 1986 have resulted in the police acquiring a special status in terms of both organisation and resources.

19-074

Traditionally, the role of prosecution vested with the private citizen. Gradually the police acquired the prosecution of offences as part of their investigation of crime and the interrogation of suspects. The private citizen rarely prosecuted while the police for over 150 years dominated the prosecution of offences. In terms of prosecution, the Prosecution of Offences Act 1985 created the Crown Prosecution Service headed by the Director of Public Prosecutions and organised into 31 areas, each under a Chief Crown Prosecutor. The powers of the ordinary citizen to prosecute are still retained but according to published guidelines, prosecutions are undertaken by the Crown Prosecution Service. The Crown Prosecution Inspectorate Act 2000 provides an external inspectorate to inspect the operation of the Crown Prosecution System. It is modelled on similar inspectorates for prisons, probation, magistrates' courts and constabulary.

19-075

In historical terms the absence of any centralised and controlled national police force has allowed the police to develop a large degree of local autonomy within fairly clear structures of accountability. This doctrine of "constabulary independence" governs the operational independence of the police in their day-to-day functions. As noted above the doctrine has been implicitly accepted in the way the courts have shown a reluctance to interfere with police judgment arising out of the exercise of their discretion over crowd control and public order powers. However, as Lord Steyn explained in *O'Hara v Chief Constable of the RUC*,[40] where there is a

---

35 [2009] UKHL 5; [2009] 1 A.C. 564.
36 *R (Moos) v Metropolitan Police Commissioners* [2012] EWCA Civ 12.
37 [2012] ECHR 459.
38 See: House of Commons Library Briefing Paper: Policing and Crime Bill 2015–16 No. 07499 (2 March 2016)
39 D. Hay and F. Snyder, *Policing and Prosecution in Britain 1750–1850* (Oxford: Clarendon, 1989).
40 [1997] A.C. 286; [1997] 2 W.L.R. 1 HL.

19-076 power of arrest provided by legislation on an individual police officer, the fact that a superior officer has reasonable suspicion does not of itself provide the police officer the reasonable grounds that are required for a lawful arrest. The responsibility is an individual one and cannot be discharged through superior orders.

In London in the past the Metropolitan Police were uniquely accountable to the Home Secretary while other police forces were organised on a local authority basis and accountable to their respective police authority. Pts VI and VII of the Greater London Authority Act 1999 provided that the Metropolitan Police Service fitted within the overall framework laid down in the Police Act 1996. This meant replacing the role of the Home Secretary with a police authority. This resulted in the creation of a Metropolitan Police Authority and under devolution Assembly members may become members of that authority. This arrangement was abolished and the Mayor's Office for Policing and Crime Established and is fully operational.

19-077 Recently, the 43 police areas in England and Wales were reformed under the Police Reform and Social Responsibility Act 2011 and since 2012, the appointment of new Police and Crime Commissioners is also a significant step in providing direct community accountability over the police with a duty to produce a local policing plan. These new arrangements are taking shape and it is hard to know whether or not the new Police and Crime Commissioners are going to be effective. There are further police reforms being considered. The Government is considering changing the relationship between the police and the fire services in England. Their proposals are at the stage of negotiation and discussion. The main proposals include introducing a new statutory duty on the police, fire and ambulance services to collaborate to improve their effectiveness. In specific localities where the case was justified, Police and Crime Commissioners might be given responsibilities to take over fire and rescue services. This would require primary legislation, especially in the case of disagreements. There are also specific proposals to abolish the London Fire and Emergency Planning Authority to create a form of London Fire Commissioner.[41] The Policing and Crime Bill 2012–16 before Parliament contains details of the proposals.

19-078 The authority of the constable remains that he is a public officer. The theory of maintaining public order and the Queen's peace gives the police constable wide discretion under the command of a Chief Constable. In reality many of the decisions at the scene of public disturbances are made by fairly junior officers who are under the command of more senior officers. Police officers may be sued or prosecuted as any other citizen. In the cases of negligence claims, the principle of vicarious liability attaches to the Chief Constable who may be indemnified out of public funds.

19-079 The office of Chief Constable is an onerous responsibility with considerable discretionary powers. However, in legal terms the powers of the Chief Constable are often unclear and poorly defined. Reforms to the organisation and structure of the police under the Police Act 1964 leave questions about how the Chief Constable may be directed or made accountable. Each local police authority is composed of two-thirds local councillors, and one-third lay magistrates. The police authority appoints a Chief Constable, a deputy Chief Constable and assistant Chief

---

41 House of Commons Library, *Police and fire reforms 2016: The Government's proposals for England*, Briefing Paper, No.07494 (5 February 2016).

Constables, which are subject to the agreement of the Home Secretary. The police authority has the power to require the retirement of those senior officers in the interests of efficiency of the police force. An inquiry may be commissioned by the Home Secretary when such powers are adopted to investigate a compulsory retirement. The officer must be given the right to a hearing and the investigation must conform to the rules of natural justice. Powers under the Police Act 1964 permit the Home Secretary to require an authority to retire a Chief Constable. In 1985 this power was used to require the retirement of the Chief Constable of Derbyshire in the interests of efficiency. The newly elected system of Police Commissioners since the enactment of the Police Reform and Social Responsibility Act 2011 is gradually transforming the governance and management of the police. There is a new Police and Crime Bill 2015/16 before Parliament.

19–080

The Chief Constable may exercise disciplinary powers over senior officers, and has the power of promotion and the appointment of other ranks of officers in his force. Failure to give fair employment opportunities to women or ethnic minorities may result in legal action against the Chief Constable. A failure to promote the Assistant Chief Constable of Merseyside, Alison Halford, gave rise to allegations of unlawful discrimination.[42]

19–081

While the Home Secretary is answerable for the activities of the Metropolitan Police to Parliament, this does not extend to operational matters for that police force which are in the hands of the Commissioner of the Metropolitan Police. The Home Secretary has powers in relation to regulations covering pensions, training, duties and equipment, including the decision to issue CS gas or baton rounds, or matters of policy in the deployment of such equipment. In *R v Secretary of State for the Home Department, Ex p. Northumbria Police Authority*,[43] the Police Authority was opposed to the issuing of CS gas and plastic bullets and applied for judicial review to require withdrawal by the Home Secretary from issuing guidance in the form of a circular to Chief Constables on the availability of such equipment. The Court of Appeal refused the Police Authority's application and upheld the Home Office powers to issue baton rounds as part of a general power under s.41 of the Police Act 1964 to provide police colleges and forensic evidence for the police. In addition, the Court of Appeal recognised a prerogative power to keep the peace which might allow the Home Office to supply such equipment.

19–082

The contribution of the Home Office to the expenditure of police forces may represent 50 per cent of the net expenditure. The Home Secretary is advised by a Chief Inspector of Constabulary, who makes an annual report on matters such as the efficiency and effectiveness of the police force. If the Home Secretary is dissatisfied, grants may be withheld. If necessary through a system of investigations and inquiries the Home Secretary has the potential to widen the remit of parliamentary accountability for the police. There is a widely drawn power under s.28 of the Police Act 1964 that allows the Home Secretary to ensure that powers "...to such an extent as appears to him to be best calculated to promote the efficiency of the police". This power has been used sparingly as the traditional wisdom of Home Secretaries has been to allow police forces autonomy. However, there are signs that this attitude may change. Chief Constables come under considerable pressure from government controls over

---

42   *Halford v Sharples* [1992] 1 W.L.R. 736; [1992] 3 All E.R. 624 CA (Civ Div).
43   [1989] Q.B. 26; [1988] 2 W.L.R. 590 CA (Civ Div).

their expenditure. Increasingly seen like any other public sector body rather than a special case, police forces are becoming subject to more stringent financial controls. These may directly change the role of the police in their operational activities.

19–083 Such concerns about the efficiency of public expenditure on the police and the perceived increase in crime but reduction in detection and prosecution rates have resulted in the Home Secretary considering whether reform of the structure of the police is required. Criticism of the police in the interrogation of suspects led to the setting up of a Royal Commission on Criminal Justice and an internal review of the organisation and structure of the police. It is likely that each police force may be required to publish efficiency studies of crime detection and "clear-up rates". On the principle that centralisation may be adopted in order to reform, it is likely that pressure for a national police force may grow. The setting up of the National Reporting Centre in Scotland Yard in 1972 to co-ordinate the disposition of the police at times of crisis has set the trend for future development. The counter-intelligence tasks of the police have, since 1992, been delegated to MI5, which is intended to lead to better co-ordination of intelligence against terrorists. The National Criminal Intelligence Service, set up in 1992 is now regulated under the Police Act 1997.

19–084 The Criminal Justice and Public Order Act 1994 gives the police additional powers for cross-border co-operation between the police in Scotland and England and Wales. The police have in common with many other public bodies come under immense pressure to conform to the new style of public management. Two White Papers[44] in 1993 set out the basis for the Police and Magistrates' Courts Act 1994. The aims of the 1994 Act were to set performance standards for the police and instil a "business management" culture within policing. There are some examples of this new ethos in the Act such as provision for fixed-term contracts for the rank of superintendent and above. A movement in favour of free-standing police authorities removed from the necessity of local and elected control is finally consolidated in the new Police Act 1996. This 1996 Act consolidates the earlier law and introduces new statutory provisions for free-standing police authorities outside London. It maintains the distinction that Metropolitan Police forces are separately treated.

19–085 There was intense debate over the proposals for the composition of the new police authorities. Schedule 2 para.1(1) provides that nine members are to be drawn from the relevant councils, five are to be independent members, and three are to be justices of the peace. Independent members are to be chosen from a short-list prepared by the Secretary of State and after nomination the candidates are submitted to the Secretary of State before appointment.

19–086 It appears from research studies that in the area of public order[45] "the police put up with disorderliness only if it ceases on their arrival". The research has shown that police presence is usually effective; few arrests are made out of many of the disturbances attended by the police, but in periods of mass demonstrations such as the Miners' Strike, the powers of arrest are widely used.

---

44 *Police Reform: The Government's Proposals for the Police service in England and Wales*, Cm.2281 (1993); and *A New Framework for Local Justice*, Cm.1829 (1993).
45 McCabe et al., *Police, Public Order and Civil Liberties* (London: Routledge, 1988).

POLICE POWERS | **741**

19–087

One important aspect of police powers is the desire to see that the police have their own authority accepted by the public. While most police officers may seek to avoid confrontations, when the police feel that their authority may be challenged it is more likely that they will wish to intervene even if there is a risk of physical violence. Aggressive police tactics may therefore be seen as a legitimate way to exert police authority and therefore respect for the law. The Policing and Crime Bill 2016 has extensive reforms of the management of the police including collaborative powers with fire and rescue services. The Bill will further enhance the role of the Police and Crime Commissioners.

The Intelligence Services' functions and policing

19–088

There have been notable improvements in the way the intelligence services are organised and how they might be made accountable. The Security Services Act 1989 placed the activities of MI5 on a statutory basis. The Intelligence Services Act 1994 similarly places the Secret Intelligence Service MI6 and the Government Communications Headquarters (GCHQ) on a statutory basis. The security services are placed under the scrutiny of a tribunal, a Commissioner and a parliamentary committee, the Intelligence and Security Committee, which may not compel the attendance of witnesses and may not review operational matters. Policy is under the control of the Secretary of State. The Intelligence and Security Committee is required to make an annual report, but this is subject to vetting by the Prime Minister. There are powers for the Prime Minister to order a report from the committee and to exclude matters either from Parliament or from publication under s.10(7) of the 1994 Act. State security is accorded special protection. There are specific exclusions such as those related to the Parliamentary Ombudsman who may not investigate action under the authority of the Secretary of State thus excluding the Data Protection Act 1998.[46] Journalists are not able to protect their sources when the interests of national security are involved. The right of access under the Freedom of Information Act 2000 is excluded in matters of national security. There are also special provisions for national security to be protected under both civil and criminal cases. The Government's *Justice and Security Green Paper* (CM 8194, October 2011) and the resultant Justice and Security Act 2013, has proved highly controversial, Pt 2 permitting the extension of Closed Material Proceedings (CMP)[47] in civil litigation as well as criminal proceedings. Striking the balance in the interests of justice between human rights, national security and the rule of law has proved controversial.

19–089

The link between the security services in the collection of information and intelligence and policing is made in the important Security Service Act 1996. This Act amends the Security Services Act 1989 and provides statutory authority for the security services including "the func-

---

46 See the role of whistle blowing and its importance in accountability systems: House of Commons Library, *Whistleblowing and gagging clauses*, Briefing Paper, No.CBP 7442 (4 January 2016).
47 See House of Commons Library, *Special Advocates and Closed Material Procedures*, Standard Note, SN/HA/6285 (25 June 2012).

tion of acting in support of the prevention and detection of serious crime". This is interpreted to mean "organised crime" involving serious criminal offences. However, there is no definition of what serious crime is and the role of the security services is only generally outlined. This leaves the impression that the detail will not be made clear and will be left to the discretion of the police and the security services. As a result, the Act leaves little guidance on any checks or balances that may be in place to prevent abuse.

19-090 The 1996 Act is broadly drafted in another respect which gives a large discretion to the issuing of executive warrants. This is in principle contrary to the constitutional protection articulated in *Entick v Carrington*.[48] The general nature of the discretions contained in the Act may provide scope for its challenge as incompatible with the European Convention on Human Rights.

19-091 A variety of new statutory powers are in force intended to broaden the coordination of the different parts of the police and security services. In the 1990s the Security Service was also given responsibility for the protection of the State including its economic well being. The Security Services Act 1996 acknowledges this role. The Police Act 1997 and the Regulation of Investigatory Powers Act 2000 provide for a support function for the security services to act alongside the police. The Regulation of Investigatory Powers Act 2000 provides comprehensive regulation of the interception of communications and the processing of data. While the Act makes it a criminal offence to intercept a communication without lawful authority, lawful authority is very generously provided. Part of the rationale of the legislation was to fill the gap left when the European Court of Human Rights decided in *Khan v UK*[49] that the applicant's human rights under art.8 had been breached mainly because the law did not regulate the use of secret listening devices.

D: Military Powers, States of Emergency and Terrorism

19-092 Public protest may give rise to a complete breakdown in law and order. With the exception of Northern Ireland, particularly from 1969–2007, the UK experience has been rare and mainly confined to particular periods in history, when military power has been required to aid the civil power and restore order. Although the police are mainly unarmed, there is an increasing requirement for armed police to be involved where there is an emergency involving political terrorists. Terrorism poses a major threat to the lives of ordinary citizens and this factor may weigh heavily in the granting of additional powers to the police to maintain civil order. The UK, because of Northern Ireland and in the aftermath of the events in New York on 11 September 2001, has derogated from the European Convention on Human Rights (art.15). However, dero-

---

48 (1765) 19 St. Tr. 1030.
49 12 May 2000 and also [2000] Crim. L.R.

gation is not possible from art.2, the protection of life but not involving deaths from lawful acts of war; art.3, the prohibition against torture; art.4(1), which prohibits slavery; and art.7, which prohibits retrospective criminal laws.

19–093 The use of military assistance during periods of industrial disputes may involve troops in agricultural duties or in preserving public order as part of a general assistance to aid the civil power in preserving public order. The Emergency Powers Acts 1920 and 1964 permit the proclamation of a state of emergency where events have occurred or are likely to occur that are calculated to deprive the community, or a substantial part of the community, of the essentials of life by interference with the supply and distribution of food, water, fuel, or light, or the means of locomotion.

19–094 Industrial action in 1921, 1924 and 1926 at the time of the General Strike resulted in the proclamation of states of emergency. In more recent times, during the Heath Government in the 1970s, regulations were issued covering emergency supplies of electricity and powers to control the dock strike to ensure the essential supply of goods and services.[50] During widespread violence and disruption during the Miners' Strike in 1984–85, the police were utilised to the full and as already noted this brought to bear a wide variety of arrest powers which were later to prove controversial, especially the use of breach of the peace as the basis for stopping and re-directing strikers. The authorities appear reluctant to countenance the use of military powers for the purposes of industrial strikes. Largely this may be because the appearance of the use of the military is an emotive issue and may lose the government of the day much needed popular support.

19–095 Increasingly there is a preference for making use of the ordinary police to cope with civil disturbance and emergency. This is evidenced through the better training given to the police and the issuing of various riot control equipment. On the whole the police may prefer to take this responsibility as part of their general involvement in maintaining public order. However, the model of an unarmed civilian police force may become less credible if the police are required to make increasing use of their powers to control riots and civil disturbances.

19–096 In cases where there are serious breaches in the law and rioting becomes widespread and uncontrolled, resort may be had to the use of the military. Both the police and military may rely on the legal right to make use of force under s.3 of the Criminal Law Act 1967. This permits the use of reasonable force in all circumstances in the prevention of crime.

19–097 The judgment between when to make use of force by the police and when to consider the use of the army calls for careful consideration of the level of violence and its likely duration. During the Miners' Strike in 1984/85, the use of troops was considered by the Government but this was not implemented. A Chief Constable may then invite the Home Secretary, in consultation with the Prime Minister and Secretary of State for Defence, to consider the use of military aid to the civil power. Once the military are invited to restore order, then some form of martial law may be said to exist. Lord Diplock in *Attorney General for Northern Ireland's Reference* explained that at common law:[51]

---

50   Emergency Powers Act 1964. Also see G. Morris, *Strikes in Essential Services* (London: Mansell, 1986).
51   *Attorney General for Northern Ireland's Reference (No.1 of 1975)* [1977] A.C. 105; [1976] 3 W.L.R. 235 HL at [136]. See *Clifford, Re* [1921] 2 A.C. 570 HL.

> "There is little authority in English law concerning the rights and duties of a member of the armed forces of the Crown when acting in aid of the civil power; and what little authority there is relates almost entirely to the duties of soldiers when troops are called on to assist in controlling a riotous assembly."

19-098 In England, troops have been used when there was severe flooding in the North of England in the winter of 2015.

19-099 While there is a duty on the private citizen to assist in the maintenance of order, this becomes very difficult to put into practice when the nature of that duty is ill-defined and the citizen is acting under military command.

Martial law is in one sense the suspension of the ordinary law and the use of military command over the civil authorities. The term is therefore broad enough to cover the complete suspension of democratic government and its substitution by military orders. In the extreme example of the overthrow of the civilian authorities and the removal of democratic government, martial law may refer to the use of military law. This refers to the body of law under which military rules are administered by military officers through courts-martial. Such courts have military law powers and are subject to review and appeal to the ordinary courts. However, when courts-martial exercise martial law jurisdiction, they are not perceived of as "ordinary courts" but simply a form of military justice administered through a tribunal which may at a future date be subject to oversight by the ordinary courts. This may normally occur once civilian government has been restored.

19-100 The Armed Forces Act 1996 makes substantial changes to the military justice system. In general terms this is an attempt to modernise the military system, and improve the standards and quality of courts-martial procedures and the general powers of military investigation. The changes introduced under the 1996 Act occur partly because of the case of *Findlay v UK*[52] considered by the European Commission of Human Rights. It decided that Findlay had not received a fair hearing and this questioned the procedures of military discipline and courts-martial.

19-101 Similarly, a major revision of the law relating to reserve forces is contained in the Reserve Forces Act 1996. Taken together these changes provide an important modernisation of law and practice for the armed services. Consolidation and change in the law were introduced by the Armed Forces Discipline Act 2000. The Act regulates internal discipline within the armed forces and brings many of the procedures into compatibility with human rights requirements. Rules relating to trial and pre-trial and detailed rules about arrest, detention and the rules of procedure are provided in the Act.

19-102 The Act attempts to address some of the issues arising from the decision of the European Court of Human Rights in *Findlay v UK*[53] and *Hood v UK*.[54]

---

52 Application No.22107/93. (1996) 21 E.H.R.R. CD7 ECHR.
53 (1997) 24 E.H.R.R. 221; Times, February 27, 1997 ECHR.
54 (2000) 29 E.H.R.R. 365; Times, March 11, 1999 ECHR.

19–103 However, in civil emergencies, martial law may be used more generally to mean the state of affairs requiring the presence of the military under the direction of the civil authorities. This use of martial law has historical more than contemporary relevance. Given the extremely wide nature of emergency powers under the Emergency Powers Act 1920 and 1964, it is unnecessary for martial law to be resorted to in those circumstances. In addition, wide powers under the Prevention of Terrorism (Temporary Provisions) Act 1989 subject to annual renewal, provide comprehensive powers to deal with most emergencies from any acts of terrorism.

19–104 The legal authorities on the existence of martial law and its review by the ordinary courts appear confined to the period during the Irish rebellion in 1916 and its aftermath in the creating of the Irish Republic. It appears to be settled law that the courts may at a later date determine that martial law based on the facts of the case, existed. The question of martial law may settle the legality of the jurisdiction of the military and the question of whether necessity is established justifying recourse to martial law. An important question is whether the civil or military authorities are liable in civil law for their actions. Thus it is often the experience of emergency powers that there is some form of Act of Indemnity[55] restricting civil and even criminal liability for acts done during war or civil emergency.

19–105 There is a presumption in favour of the ordinary courts, while still sitting, to have the jurisdiction to determine whether a state of war or martial law is in existence. It is normal for the courts to wait for the cessation of hostilities before determining any proceedings brought by citizens who wish to determine their rights and the liability of the authorities. Military law is therefore seen as a last resort and not to be utilised when the ordinary civilian government is able to function.

19–106 War may require that the authorities exercise both prerogative and statutory powers. The declaration of war and the conduct of the war is subject to the prerogative powers of the Crown and international law. It has become common place for the Government of the day to inform Parliament whenever possible on the decision to commit military force abroad. A Parliamentary vote was held in December 2015 on the extension of aircraft bombing into Syria[56] in the coalition campaign against ISIS/Daesh. Various powers for requisitioning supplies, ships, vehicles and material are provided in legislation passed during wartime. Such powers may be found in the Emergency Powers (Defence) Acts 1939 and 1940. The trial of civilians by special military courts may also be authorised by statute.

19–107 The regulation of exports and dual-use material suitable for adaptation or re-sale for military purposes is tightly regulated. Historically, this area was regulated by the Import, Export and Customs Powers (Defence) Act 1939 and the Import Export Control Act 1990 provided the government of the day with powers to regulate through the issue of licences for manufactured goods intended for export. Sir Richard Scott in his report in 1996 recommended that

---

55 The Indemnity Act 1920.
56 House of Commons Library, *ISIS/Daesh: the military response in Iraq and Syria*, No.06995 (15 December 2015); *Legal basis for UK military action in Syria*, CBP 7404 (1 December 2015); and *UK drone attack in Syria: legal questions*, CBP 7332 (20 October 2015).

there should be reform of the law and a strengthening of policy making.[57] In May 1997, the Government introduced new licensing criteria adapting the voluntary EU Code of Conduct on Arms Exports. This became a *Consolidated EU and National Arms Export Licencing Criteria*. The Export Control Act 2002 replaced the previous legislation and came into force in 2004. Many of the main provisions are in the Export Control Order 2008. Under the Act and Order arrangements there is an annual report to Parliament known as the *Strategic Export Controls: Annual Report*, which provides a regular system for providing Parliament with information. Five years after the 2002 Act was introduced, a review was undertaken to report on the system of brokering, trafficking and licensed production building on the system of oversight. The House of Commons Committee, renamed the Committees on Arms Export Controls,[58] provides a system of accountability and analysis. The EU Code of Conduct on Arms Exports and Title V of the EU treaty has adopted *The Common Rules Governing the Control of Exports of Military, Technology and Equipment*.[59] The EU publish an annual *Common Military List of the European Union* (March 2014), setting out the arrangements in each Member State. In 2009, the EU also adopted Regulation 428/2009 on *Dual-use material* used to address exports with dual-use capabilities.

19–108

The export market is volatile and subject to changing global conditions. In 2010, the rules relating to export licences were further reviewed. Since 2011, there have been concerns that existing licences needed to be reviewed in the face of new evidence about their use. On 2 April 2013, a new Arms Trade Treaty was agreed at the United Nations. This has helped settle international criteria. There is a new version of the Consolidated Criteria and some disagreement over how far current UK practice is consistent with the 2008 EU Common Rules.[60] The export of arms and dual-use material remains an area of intense political debate.[61]

19–109

Wartime powers to requisition property may be subject to claims for compensation. Such claims may be subject to legislation which may deprive the citizen of any right of payment, as in the example of the War Damage Act 1965. Many of the major powers given to the authorities to protect the State may also be subject to judicial review by the courts. However, the courts have been reluctant to interfere with executive discretion when the interests of the State and national security are pre-eminent. In a number of wartime cases the courts have refused to review the exercise of executive powers.[62] The role of the courts and national security is examined in the next chapter.

---

57 Sir Richard Scott, *Inquiry into the Export of Defence Equipment and Dual-use Goods to Iraq and Related Prosecution*, HC 115 (15 February 1996).
58 Originally called the Quadrapartite Committee.
59 European Council Common Position, 2008/944/CFSP.
60 House of Commons Library, *UK arms export control policy*, Briefing Paper, No.02729 (8 May 2015).
61 Details of the arms trade are set out in House of Commons Standard Note, *The Arms Trade Treaty*, SN05802 (21 November 2014).
62 *Burmah Oil Co v Lord Advocate* [1965] A.C. 75; [1964] 2 W.L.R. 1231 HL. See *Liversidge v Anderson* [1942] A.C. 206; [1941] 3 All E.R. 338 HL; also R. F. V. Heuston "*Liversidge v Anderson* in Retrospect" (1970) 86 *L.Q.R.* 33; and *R v Home Secretary Ex p. Lees* [1941] 1 K.B. 72 CA. In more recent times this reluctance of the courts to intervene has continued, see *McEldowney v Forde* [1971] A.C. 632; [1969] 3 W.L.R. 179 HL.

Legal liability and the use of force

19-110 There have been a few successful prosecutions of members of the security forces. Two members of the Scots Guards regiment were convicted of the murder of Peter McBride in 1992 in Belfast. They unsuccessfully appealed to the House of Lords against conviction. It was held that they had had sufficient time to make a decision whether or not to use force and that Peter McBride when fired on posed no threat. Although convicted of murder the Army Board decided not to discharge the soldiers from the army; however, this decision was quashed on a judicial review taken by the deceased's mother.[63]

19-111 The findings of the Saville Inquiry in 2010 into the deaths of 13 citizens—shot dead and 14 seriously injured when troops in Londonderry opened fire with live rounds—was found to be the result of excessive force.[64] The Saville Inquiry determined that there was no justification for their shooting and none of the victims posed a threat of causing death or serious injury. Since 2010, the Chief Constable of the Police Service of Northern Ireland (PSNI) conducted an investigation of the events and the findings as part of a PSNI Legacy Investigation Branch. The PSNI is currently undertaking investigations including the decision to arrest and interview various soldiers involved. The High Court has recently rejected the PSNI's decision to arrest and detain the soldiers and question them in Northern Ireland. This does not prevent the interrogation under caution of the soldiers in England and Wales[65] and the soldiers are willing to agree an undertaking to do this. The outcome of the case places considerable operational burdens on the Northern Ireland Police to set up arrangements for the continued investigation of the cases.

19-112 Two analyses may be drawn from the state of the law in this area. First, clearer guidelines are needed to set out the general circumstances where lethal force may be used. Currently, members of the security forces have "yellow card" guidelines on the use of force, but the details of the guidelines are not published and they do not have the force of law. The need to clarify s.3 of the 1967 Act is apparent when it is realised that the section states a rule of both civil and criminal law. The justification of force on the basis of "reasonable in the circumstances" removes the possibility of a successful civil action or the prosecution of the defendant in criminal proceedings.

19-113 Secondly, the Criminal Law Act 1967 is unclear as to the use of force in self-defence or against an unjustifiable attack. Such a defence exists in common law, and there is a question of whether self-defence is governed by s.3. It is most likely the case that s.3 governs the law of self-defence, but this should be made more clear. There is also a remarkable difference between civil and criminal liability in terms of evidential burden. Hutton J in *McGuigan v Ministry of Defence*[66] noted that in criminal trials, once the accused raises a defence of reasonable force, the prosecution have the onus to prove beyond a reasonable doubt that the

---

63 *McBride's Application for Judicial Review, Re* [1999] N.I. 299 QBD.
64 Saville Inquiry, *The Bloody Sunday Inquiry Report* (2010); and earlier the *Widgery Report*, HC 220 (1971–72).
65 *B v The Chief Constable of the Police Service of Northern Ireland* [2015] EWHC 3691 (Admin); [2016] A.C.D. 30.
66 [1982] 19 N.I.J.B. CA (Civ Div).

force used was unreasonable. In a civil case the defence have to rely on establishing on the balance of probabilities that a defence of reasonable force is proved. The call for a review of the law is supported by the United Nations' *Instrument on Basic Principles on the use of Force and Firearms by Law Enforcement Officials*, 7 September 1990. This is an area of law of particular sensitivity in Northern Ireland.

19–114 Members of the security forces are also amenable to the civil law.[67] In the case of the shootings in Londonderry, out-of-court settlements were made in civil actions. In *Copeland v Ministry of Defence*[68] vicarious liability applied to the Ministry of Defence in connection with the shooting of the plaintiff arising out of negligence on the part of an army corporal.

19–115 Another area of great difficulty in assessing the use of force is in connection with the use of plastic baton rounds or CS gas. Serious injury, even death has been caused by the use of such devices which are primarily intended to avoid the use of lethal force. In the case of using excessive force it is the criminal and civil liability of the individual policeman or soldier that is involved. There is no direct authority clearly stating the principle of where the borderline between superior orders and individual responsibility may lie. It is thought that it is no defence to a criminal charge to plead a duty to obey the commands of a superior where the orders are so manifestly illegal that the soldier must have recognised they are unlawful. Only when the orders are legal may the individual responsible hope to plead superior orders.

19–116 Controversy surrounding the use of force came to the fore in the case of *R v Clegg*.[69] Over 350 deaths have been caused by the security forces in the course of their duties in Northern Ireland. This has caused enormous controversy. The *Clegg* case highlights the problems for the prosecution authorities if there are grounds to consider that the use of force is unreasonable. The defendants were members of the British Army manning a road check-point. The victims were teenage joy-riders in a stolen car. Police evidence was given which challenged the army's version of the shooting incident arising out of the failure of the stolen car to stop at an army check-point. At the trial the judge held that the army was justified in firing shots at the car when speeding towards them but not justified in shooting after the car had passed the patrol. Two soldiers were convicted of murder. The Court of Appeal dismissed the appeal of one defendant, Clegg, but in the case of Aindow, the other defendant, substituted a conviction for malicious wounding for that of murder. The case went on appeal to the House of Lords which dismissed the appeal.[70] The controversy following has led to the release of Corporal Clegg on licence in July 1995.

19–117 Finally, in *McCann v UK*[71] the European Court of Human Rights considered whether the shooting of IRA suspects in Gibraltar violated the rights of the deceased under art.2 of the European Convention. By a majority the Court held that there was no violation of art.2, but the Court found that the UK had breached art.2 in respect of the inadequacies of the

---

67 *McLaughlin v Ministry of Defence* (1978) 7 N.I.J.B.
68 Unreported Northern Ireland 19 May 1999.
69 4 June 1993, [1995] 1 A.C. 482; [1995] 2 W.L.R. 80 HL.
70 [1995] 1 A.C. 482; [1995] 2 W.L.R. 80 HL.
71 (1995) 21 E.H.R.R. 97 ECHR.

investigations. The case highlights the importance of the human rights aspects of the use of force. There have been a number of cases taken under the European Convention on Human Rights arising out of deaths in Northern Ireland which test the compatibility of the use of force and the human rights of the deceased.[72]

The Terrorism Act 2000

The Terrorism Act 2000 provides a consolidation and reform of the law relating to terrorism. It applies throughout the UK and covers terrorism whether at home, abroad or in relation to Northern Ireland. Some of the sections are entirely new while others are consolidations of previous law. Section 1 defines terrorism very broadly to include "the use or threat of action where it is directed to influence the Government or to intimidate the public or a section of the public and the use or threat is for the purpose of advancing a political, religious or ideological cause".

The Terrorism Act re-defines terrorism from previous legislation by considerably broadening the scope and remit of what may be categorised as terrorism. The original idea embedded in the Prevention of Terrorism Act 1989 and the Emergency Provisions Act 1996 was the definition containing "the use of violence for political ends". Section 1 of the Terrorism Act applies to serious violence but is all-embracing in the catalogue of causes that may be ideological and religious. This might include almost any organisation but what qualifies it as terrorism under the Act is ". . .action or threat of action which is designed to influence the Government or to intimidate the public or a section of the public". The action involved falls within the remit of the section if it:

- involves serious violence against a person;
- involves serious damage to property;
- endangers a person's life other than that of the person committing the action;
- creates a serious risk to the health or safety of the public or a section of the public; or
- is designed seriously to interfere with or seriously to disrupt an electronic system.

Despite assurances given in the debate on the Terrorism Bill, it is possible to see such a wide definition covering industrial disputes, animal rights groups, or active engagement by religious or political causes. The underlying assumption is that the section is intended to apply to those who are seeking to undermine democracy.

Schedule 6 to the Terrorism Act 2000 provides an extensive range of powers that cover financial institutions and ss.24 and 25 apply to the movement of cash between states, allowing

---

72   *McShane v UK*, Application No.43290/98.

the seizure of assets. The Act also retains the idea of proscribed organisations and under Pt II adds powers to Secretary of State to proscribe certain organisations connected with terrorism. There is a Proscribed Organisations Appeal Commission under s.5 to hear appeals against proscription. This provides an extensive set of procedures for de-proscription of a proscribed organisation. In the Northern Ireland context the IRA, the Ulster Freedom Fighters and other organisations were proscribed and continue to be proscribed under the Terrorism Act 2000. Following the Act's coming into force in March 2001 various international organisations were also proscribed. The Northern Ireland experience would suggest that few individuals have been successfully prosecuted for membership of a proscribed organisation alone. Proscription may assist in identifying the funds and organisational structure of terrorist groups. It also may help proscribe fund-raising activities and information is required to be disclosed in respect of individuals who have suspected involvement with a proscribed organisation. Pt III of the Act also covers terrorist property and fund-raising.

19–122 The Act is certified to be compatible with the Human Rights Act 1998, though throughout debate on the Terrorism Act some doubts were expressed about this. The courts will have to consider whether the Act is compatible with arts.10 and 11 of the European Convention on Human Rights. The Terrorism Act is extensive in range and scope. Various organisations are proscribed under Pt II, and Pt III of the Act sets out offences for the seizing of terrorist property and proscribes financial fund-raising for terrorism. Additional powers are granted under Pt V for the police to investigate terrorist acts and this includes search powers, setting up road-blocks and a raft of counter-terrorist powers especially at ports and borders. The Act also creates offences relating to paramilitary activities and incitement to terrorism overseas. Powers of extradition and penalties for the possession of information for terrorist purposes are also included. Financial institutions are required to provide information about terrorists during the investigation of any terrorist activities. There are powers under s.41 of the Act covering the detention and arrest of suspects.[73] One of the most controversial powers is under s.19, itself a replica of s.18A of the Prevention of Terrorism (Temporary Provisions) Act 1989, for disclosure of information about someone who the person may suspect of being a terrorist. This power may require journalists to disclose information and sources used in investigative journalism.

19–123 Part V of the Terrorism Act 2000 applies to the police powers of arrest that are applicable to someone who is a terrorist. This includes someone who is concerned in the commission, preparation or instigation of acts of terrorism. Section 41 gives the power to a constable to arrest without a warrant a person whom he reasonably suspects to be a terrorist. The person may be detained for up to 48 hours which is much greater than the non-terrorist detention period of 24 or 36 hours. Further detention must be authorised by a warrant. A suspect should not be detained in detention for more than 14 days in total from the time of his arrest. Debates about the necessary period of detention have been difficult to resolve. In 2006, the period of detention was extended to 28 days but the Protection of Freedoms Act 2012 reversed this. It is possible to reinstate the 28-day period in certain circumstances even when Parliament is not sitting.

---

73 *Legislation Against Terrorism*, Cm.3420 (1996).

In 2006 under the Terrorism Act 2006, the police were given additional powers to enter and search premises on the basis of an application for a warrant before a Magistrate if there is reasonable suspicion that a person is concerned with terrorism or is a terrorist. This is in addition to s.41 to search a person arrested under s.41 to find evidence that he is a terrorist.

Section 44 of the 2006 Act's controversial and highly debated powers, allowed the police to undertake stop and search powers with much wider than the limited powers under s.43. Such powers proved to be frequently used and controversially viewed by many citizens. Over 10,000 stop and search powers were routinely used each month. The powers proved to be in breach of the European Convention on Human Rights, although this was a finding of the European Court of Human Rights after the powers were upheld by the House of Lords.[74] The stop and search powers were replaced by a new s.59 of the Protection of Freedoms Act 2012. Stop and search was retained, but subject to an authorisation by a senior police officer. The requirement is that the officer must reasonably suspect that an act of terrorism will take place and that such an authorisation is necessary to prevent such an act. The geographical location and scope of the authorisation has to be established. The authorisation triggers a series of powers. Here the officer in uniform may stop and search a vehicle, including its driver and passengers (s.47A(2)). There are also powers to stop a pedestrian and search anything a pedestrian is carrying (s.47A(3)). There is a restriction that the stop and search power must be exercised in relation to terrorism and articles of any kind that could be used in connection with terrorism. Such powers may be exercised whether or not the police officer reasonably suspects that there is such evidence (see s.47A(5)). There are some restrictions on how the powers may be exercised in terms of what is permitted in public and what may be undertaken in private at a police station. The authorisation once granted is only for 14 days unlike the previous period of up to 28 days.

Police and Investigative powers in response to terrorism

Part IV of the Terrorism Act relates to carrying out investigations into terrorism. It covers a large range of activities and the powers include the investigation, commission and instigation of acts of terrorism. This includes all related activities including the resources used to undertake terrorism.

There are a variety of terrorist offences aimed to frustrate any terrorist activities. The provision of any instruction, training or making use of firearms and related weapons, of which there is a long list are all proscribed under s.54 of the Act. There is a defence under s.54(3) relating to the accused proving that there is a justified purpose other than assisting or participating in terrorism.

Past experience of terrorism has given rise to a number of offences related to the direction of the activities of an organisation concerned in the commission or acts of terrorism under

---

74   See *Gillan and Quinton v UK* [2009] ECHR 28 and the House of Lords decision in *R (Gillan) v MPC* [2006] UKHL 12; [2006] 2 A.C. 307.

19–129 s.56. Possession of any article for a purpose connected with the commission, preparation or instigation of acts of terrorism are also criminal offences under s.57. Again there are defences available under s.57(3) but the burden of proof is on the defendant to show that the possession was not for a purpose to assist prepare or participate in a terrorist offence.

There are also wide-ranging intelligence gathering powers—including powers granted under the Counter-Terrorism Act 2008. Under s.58 and 58A of the Terrorism Act 2000 makes it an offence for any person to collect or record information of any kind that may be useful to a terrorist. The same section might be widely interpreted to bring journalists or photographers within the terms of the section.[75]

19–130 Important additional powers include the use of cordons to control specific areas where there is suspicion of terrorism. Such powers may be applied up to 28 days and include requiring people to leave including the removal of vehicles from the area that is cordoned off.

19–131 There are also extensive powers to obtain information and search and seize documents or data files that are necessary for the investigation of terrorism.

The operation and policy are part of the overall 2015 National Security Strategy.[76] This is a complex document that contains national security risk assessment and the threat from different forms of terrorism. It is based around a global strategy and is proactive in form.

19–132 Schedule 8 to the Terrorism Act 2000 provides for the regulation and administration of detention. This means that a person detained under the Act will rely on those procedures rather than the procedures available under PACE. Included within the arrangements for detention under the Act are codes of practice for the use of audio arrangements in interrogation. Account is taken under Sch.8 of the right of access to a solicitor and for the future there is the possibility of video-recording of questioning. Wide powers to examine any person on arrival or departure from Great Britain or Northern Ireland, by ship or aircraft, in travelling by land between Northern Ireland and the Republic, were contained in s. 16 Sch.5 to the 1989 Act. Additional powers of investigation for the search of terrorist materials modelled on the Drugs Trafficking Offences Act 1986 are combined in s. 17 Sch.7 to the 1989 Act. Such powers find their way generally into Pt V of the Terrorism Act 2000. Sch.7 of the Act provides powers for the examination and questioning of suspects at ports and borders and Sch.8 for their detention and treatment during investigation of their conduct. The Terrorism Act provide a comprehensive set of rules and codes of practice for the detention and questioning of suspects.

19–133 Finally, internment powers, originally used in Northern Ireland for a limited period, have been retained but are not in use under Pt IV and Sch.3 to the 1991 Act. These may be brought into force by the Secretary of State through the laying of a statutory instrument. Detailed detention orders may be made under Pt IV of the Northern Ireland (Emergency Provisions) Act 1996. There is no internment power under the Terrorism Act 2000 although the detention powers under the Act may provide similar arrangements.

---

75 See Lord Carlisle Report on the Operation in 2008 of the Terrorism Act 2000 and Pt 1 of the Terrorism Act 2006 (2009).
76 House of Commons Library, *The UK National Security Strategy*, Briefing Paper, No.7431 (14 December 2015).

Control orders

The Prevention of Terrorism Act 2005 has introduced a new innovation in the form of control orders. These allow preventative and proactive measures to be taken against a suspect in order to protect members of the public from a risk of terrorism under s.1 of the Prevention of Terrorism Act 2005. Control orders are of two kinds, one is non-derogating control orders made by the Home Secretary consistent with art.5 of the ECHR; the second is derogating control orders which could be inconsistent with art.5 but could only be made by a court on the application of the Home Secretary. Invoking such powers requires a long list of s.6 requirements that in the end have never been utilised. The use of non-derogating orders are wide-ranging in their application and scope.[77] Their success, was however limited and operated as a form of effective house arrest. They were expensive and the Home Office spent over £10.8 million between April 2006 and August 2009 on their operation. Only 12 orders were in force by the end of 2009 and even more remarkable only 45 individuals were ever subject to a control order.[78] The Supreme Court in *Home Secretary v AP*[79] quashed a decision to require an individual to live over 150 miles away from their family to avoid contact with "racial elements".

The Terrorism Prevention and Investigation Measures Act 2011 replaced control orders with a new variation called a Terrorism Protection and Investigation Measure (TPIM). Their duration is normally up to 12 months and they may be renewed by the Home Secretary. The application has to be made to the High Court by the Home Secretary. The High Court has to consider the application and whether or not to grant permission as well as to consider whether the application is "obviously flawed". The procedure may be considered in the absence of the individual but the individual has to be notified of the application and under s.6(4) given the opportunity to make representations to the court. Rather oddly the application must apply the principles for judicial review. The various conditions include that there is reasonable belief that the individual is or has been involved in terrorism-related activity, that some or all of the relevant activity is new terrorism-related and that the Home Secretary considers that it is necessary for purposes connected with protecting members of the public from a risk of terrorism for a TIPIM to be imposed on the individual. In the case of all three conditions the Home Secretary's application must not be "obviously flawed". The Home Secretary has widely defined powers where it is considered reasonable for purposes connected with preventing or restricting the individual's involvement in terrorism-related activity for the specified for a TIPIM order to be made. Here, even if the conditions are obviously flawed the High Court may give directions to the Home Secretary about measures imposed on the individual under s.6(10).

A TIPIM notice may be issued without the individual being present. Under s.8 it is possible for a review of the notice to take place "as soon as reasonably practicable". The court's powers

---

77   See House of Commons Library, *Control Orders and the Prevention of Terrorism Act 2005*, Standard Note, SN/HA/3438 (19 December 2011).
78   *Control Orders and the Prevention of Terrorism Act 2005*, p. 2.
79   [2010] UKSC 24; [2011] 2 A.C. 1.

19-137 are similar to judicial review and the TIPIM may be quashed or directions may be given to the Home Secretary including a notice of revocation or variation in the conditions of the TIPIM.

Continuance of a TIPIM under s.9(6) requires the Home Secretary to consult the police about whether or not there are criminal charges possible against the individual. Whenever a TIPIM is issued the Home Secretary is to inform the police so that steps can be taken to secure the investigation of an individual and whether a prosecution might be possible. The various restraints on individuals are wide-ranging including their movement, communication, including electronic communication and their activities at work and home. These are extensive and wide-ranging powers that undoubtedly have major consequences on individual freedom.

19-138 The terrorist threat continues to intensify as the Government's advisors have warned about British nationals going abroad to join terrorist groups. This is perceived to be a growing problem with various estimates of around 2000 EU citizens to be around 2,000 in Iraq and Syria.[80] Counter-terrorism measures are likely to be an ongoing concern for the current and future governments. The threat level to the UK's security is alarmingly high and this has been the case for some time.[81] Consequently in August 2014, the Government decided to introduce various measures designed to pursue terrorists, prevent terrorist activities with the aim of protecting the UK. The Counter-Terrorism and Security Act 2015 contains details of various measures Pt 1 of the Act brings forward temporary measures on travel restrictions and gives immigration officers powers to search and seize passports and retain a passport when it is suspected that a person is travelling for the purpose of involvement in terrorism. Part 2 of the 2015 Act amends the Terrorism Prevention and Investigative Measures Act 2011 and tightens up the arrangements for TPIM. A TPIM notice must be necessary for purposes connected with protecting the public from a risk of terrorism. The content of the notice is quite extensive. Section 16 covers powers to ensure that an individual is required to conform to overnight residence in a location that the Secretary of State reasonably considers necessary and appropriate. This includes restrictions on travel outside a certain area and also prohibition on obtaining or possessing firearms or offensive weapons. Sections 16–20 contains detailed regulations on the conduct of an individual and prohibits on contact with individuals involved in conduct which facilitates or gives encouragement to the commission, preparation or instigation of acts of terrorism. There are also requirements for the individual to meet people or persons specified in the management of their activities.

19-139 The Act also makes amendments to the Data Retention and Investigatory Powers Act 2014 and allows the Secretary of State to require communications service providers to retain the data that allow individuals to be identified who are using a device and the internet. Part 5 of the

---

80 Estimates vary, but the total number of foreign fighters with Sunni extremist groups in Iraq and Syria are around 15,000 from 80 countries. See House of Commons Library, *The Counter-Terrorism and Security Bill*, Bill No.127 of 2014–15, Research Paper, 14/63 (27 November 2014).

81 There is an independent Joint Terrorism Analysis Centre (JTAC) that advises the Government on such matters. The UK has a counter-intelligence strategy for countering terrorism named CONTEST. There is also a 2015 National Security Strategy See House of Commons, *The 2015 UK National Security Strategy*, No.7421 (14 December 2015).

Act provides wide-ranging powers to address the risk of individuals being drawn into terrorism. There are various provisions in Pt 6 that relates to insurance claims relating to terrorism.[82]

Terrorism and human rights

The UK's in response to the 11 September 2001 (9/11) attacks in the USA resulted in the Anti-Terrorism, Crime and Security Act 2001 that addressed many security issues, but specifically the perceived threat that foreign Islamic extremists were the major threat to the UK's security. Traditional approaches to the threat from foreign nationals include criminal prosecution or deportation of suspects to their country of origin. Detention without trial after the Northern Ireland experience had proved controversial and ineffective so although possible but not the most favoured option. Criminal prosecutions faced the problem that evidence would be subject to judicial scrutiny and if held in open court would expose the security services to public scrutiny. Additional problems about the truthfulness of evidence arise if the evidence is not corroborated. Allegation of torture or oppressive interrogation might make evidence inadmissible. Deportation of suspects also faced legal problems as the risks of deportation related to concerns that suspects, once repatriated would face torture in their own countries. The ECHR specifically prohibits torture or ill-treatment and as a matter of international law prohibits deportation where there is a risk of torture. Part 4 of the 2001 Act allowed the Executive to imprison suspected terrorists who could not be deported. The suspicion required under the Act fell short of beyond a reasonable doubt needed for a criminal trial and rested largely on security service evidence based on only reasonable belief and not tested by the use of the normal criminal courts. Suspects as detainees have the right to appeal to a special tribunal, the Special Immigration Appeals Commission. However this is a limited right as suspects are not entitled to know the evidence against them or the reasons for the detention. Specially security vetted lawyers known as a special advocate are allowed to represent detainees.

The legislation was severely criticised and the subject of legal challenges. The famous *Belmarsh case*[83] in 2004 considered the human rights implications of the legislation. The House of Lords held that s.23 of the 2001 Act was incompatible with arts 5 and 14 ECHR and this resulted in a declaration of incompatibility being issued. The Government responded by introducing the Prevention of Terrorism Act 2005 which was also subject to strong parliamentary scrutiny and amendments. The objection made in the Belmarsh decision was that non-nationals were being treated less favourably than nationals. The aims of the 2005 Act were to introduce derogating and non-derogating control orders irrespective of the nationality of the suspects concerned. The aim is to attempt to achieve sufficient elements of compatibility

---

82 Part 7 of the Act relates to miscellaneous and general provisions including the powers of the Independent Reviewer of Terrorism. For a detailed analysis of the Counter-Terrorism and Security Act 2015. See House of Commons Library, *Counter-Terrorism and Security Bill*, No.127 of 2014–15, Research Papers, 14/63 (27 November 2014).
83 *A v Secretary of State for the Home Department* [2004] UKHL 56; [2005] 2 A.C. 68 HL.

with art.5 in order to ensure that the legislation is not impugned by the courts. The House of Lords has had the opportunity to consider many aspects of the 2005 Act. In general, the judges concluded that the control order regime was compatible with art.5. However, there are a large number of reservations made about the arrangements on the 2005 Act that raised issues about the compatibility with art.6, the right to a fair trial. The House of Lords[84] concluded that that the person under the Control Order should be given sufficient information about the allegations to allow the issues raised to be adequately addressed by their legal representative. In the case of open material, i.e. not secret in itself, the requirements of a fair trial would not be satisfied by general assertion rather than by specific allegations. This gives rise to a specific set of problems when the State seeks to withhold certain sensitive information. The results of judicial concerns about the use of control orders under the 2005 Act led to the Act's repeal.

UK Judicial Scrutiny over information obtained abroad and the Norwich Pharmacal Principle

19–142 Information obtained by torture or inhuman and degrading treatment is inadmissible in the UK Courts.[85] This is a principle that is often made more complicated when the information is obtained by detention abroad and the result of interrogation undertaken by authorities outside the UK or as a result of torture which does not fall under the direct control of the UK authorities. The case of *R (Mohamed) v Secretary of State for Foreign and Commonwealth Affairs*[86] is illustrative of the complexity of the issues involved. The facts of the case begin in 2008 when Binyan Mohamed, a UK resident, was detained in the US and held in custody at Guantanamo Bay. He sought judicial review against the Foreign Secretary, arising from his claim for disclosure of information that he alleged showed the details and conditions of his arrest that he claimed was in the possession of the UK Government. His allegations of torture included the time of his arrest in Pakistan in 2002 and subsequent detention. He was then taken to Morocco and Afghanistan before his transfer to Guantanamo in 2004. His main claim was also based on the allegation that those who tortured him received questions and materials from British intelligence officers. Mr Mohamed claimed disclosure of information, which he believed showed that he was tortured, to assist his defence in his trial before a US military commission.

19–143 Mr Mohamed's claim rested on the application of an important tort principle, known as the *Norwich Pharmacal case* and familiar in intellectual property disputes. The principle set out in

---

84 A. Kavanagh, "Judging the Judges under the Human Rights Act: Deterrence, Disillusionment and the 'War on terror'" [2009] *P.L.* 287. Also see A. Kavanagh, "Special Advocates, Control Orders and the Right to a Fair Trial" (2010) 73 *M.L.R.* 836; and M. Garrod, "Deportation of Suspected Terrorists with Real Risk of Torture: The House of Lords Decision in Abu Qatada" (2010) *M.L.R.* 631.

85 *R v H* [2004] UKHL 3; [2004] 2 A.C. 134 HL. See Stephen Sedley, *Ashes and Sparks* (Cambridge: Cambridge University Press, 2011), p.368. K. D. Ewing, *Bonfire of the Liberties* (Oxford: Oxford University Press, 2011), pp.228–234.

86 [2010] EWCA Civ 65; [2011] Q.B. 218.

Norwich Pharmacal Co v Customs and Excise Commissioners[87] is that an order for disclosure may be made by the courts in England and Wales or Northern Ireland, on the basis that if a wrong has been established then an order of disclosure might be made. The conditions for a *Norwich Pharmacal* order rest on showing that there is a wrong, carried out by an ultimate wrongdoer, that an order is needed, and that the person against whom an order is sought must be involved in the wrongdoing or facilitated the wrongdoing and that the information sought must be such as to enable the wrongdoer to be sued.

Mr Mohamad's case was a novel application of the *Norwich Pharmacal principle* in the security context. It was strongly argued by the Foreign Office that the *Pharmacal* principle was ill-suited to intelligence claims and might seriously jeopardise intelligence exchange between the US and the UK. The system underpinning the exchange of secret information operated under the doctrine of the "control principle". This doctrine assumed that exchanged intelligence would remain under the control of the originator of the information. The rationale of the doctrine assumed that only the originator could fully understand the nature of the information, why it should be treated as confidential and the exact basis on which the material might be treated. The doctrine was underpinned by a mutual appreciation and reciprocity of each country's intelligence system. The UK relied on such a doctrine when it shared intelligence with the USA. In court the UK Government advanced the claim of the doctrine of the control principle to argue that any information it possessed on Mr Mohamad should not be released.

19-144

The UK Courts faced a difficult task of considering whether the information that Mr Mohamad sought should be released to him under the application of the *Norwich Pharmacal* case. The Government sought Public Interest Immunity Certificates preventing disclosure. This was only partially successful as the trial judge chose to exercise a balancing test of whether to release the information if it was necessary in the interests of justice. Specifically, there were seven paragraphs of particular sensitive information that the Foreign Secretary did not want to release. The US authorities relaxed their objections and allowed some release of information when faced by similar claims in the US courts. It took some time for the case to be considered by the UK Court of Appeal in 2010. The Court of Appeal followed the *Norwich Pharmacal doctrine* and allowed disclosure of the relevant material. In the meantime, the US courts had already made available much of the information set out in the seven paragraphs that were so heavily contested by the UK Foreign Secretary. Following the outcome of the Court of Appeal decision, the Court allowed publication of the seven paragraphs but at the same time the US authorities insisted that the material was classified and should not be released.

19-145

The "stand off" in contrasting perspectives between the UK and US courts is not simply accounted for through differences in legal culture but also in approaches to judicial control over Executive influence in matters of security and intelligence. The US authorities adopted deference to US security matters while the UK Courts gave greater pre-eminence to rules against torture rather than national security.[88] The Coalition Government remained concerned

19-146

---

87 [1974] A.C. 133; [1973] 3 W.L.R. 164 HL.
88 See The FCO, Binyan Mohamed Case (10 February 2010); and House of Lords Library, *Justice and Security Bill*, Note, HL 27, 2012–13, LLN 2012/024 (June 2012).

about the application of the *Norwich Pharmacal* doctrine in security cases and the concern that as a consequence security material might not be exchanged between the UK and US governments. In its Green Paper there were proposals, later contained in cl.13 of the Justice and Security Bill, to limit the application of the *Norwich Pharmacal* doctrine and a ban on the disclosure of "sensitive information".

Closed Material Procedure and the Justice and Security Act 2013

19-147 The operation of a Closed Material Procedure (CMP) in matters of national security raise concerns of "secret justice" arising from the operation of hearings where sensitive information is partially heard in secret. CMP is one part of procedures that involve both closed and open sessions. The accused and legal representative are unable to be present during the closed part of the procedure while the open procedure follows normal court room procedures. Overall such proceedings require the appointment of a special advocate[89] who is specially vetted by the security services and is a specially trained barrister. The special advocate can attend both closed and open sessions. In open sessions he has access to the accused and his legal representative. The special advocate has access to confidential information but does not have the accused as a client. The appointment of a special advocate is intended to protect the accused's interests during the closed sessions where neither the defendant's advocate or the defendant is present. Special Advocates were originally created under the Special Immigration Appeals Act 1997 for immigration appeals involving sensitive materials. Their use became more widespread in cases involving security matters or requiring the protection of sensitive information. The appointment of the special advocate does not detract from the question of what is confidential and what may be disclosed. Such matters are for the Court and not the Secretary of State. The system of using closed sessions for the analysis of closed material has a long history from the system of immigration deportation sessions. Its use is part of the Special Immigration Appeals Commission and various other related bodies that have to handle sensitive information involving national security and terrorism cases.[90] The aims of the arrangements are clear. The special advocate system is intended to meet the requirements of various common law principles of natural justice as well as the case law under the European Convention on Human Rights. Broadly this includes fair representation and access to legal advice, a fair trial and procedures which address the rights of the individual. Interpreting such principles has to be considered in settling the balance between rights and protecting the national interest of the State.

---

89   See House of Commons Library, *Special Advocates and Closed Material Procedures*, SN/HA/6285 (25 June 2012).
90   The proscribed Organisations Appeal Commission; the Employment Tribunal in cases involving national security; control order cases under the Prevention of Terrorism Act 2005; financial restriction proceedings under the Counter-Terrorism Act 2008; and the Sentence Review Commission and Parole Commission in Northern Ireland.

19-148 In a number of important cases,[91] the operation of CMP has been considered in terms of alignment with the rules of natural justice, fairness to the accused and the interpretation of an accused person's rights. In *Secretary of State for the Home Department v MB*,[92] strong judicial support was given to the operation of a core minimum of procedural rights that were not capable of being negotiated under any regime for the disclosure of information. The ECtHR had agreed in *A v United Kingdom* that in cases of non-disclosure, the consequences might be to deny a person the knowledge of the main essence of the case against him. This defect might be mitigated to some degree by the operation of the special advocate scheme. Nevertheless, this might not be adequate to provide sufficient safeguards against the detained person not knowing the case against them. The cases are about the problems that arise under the operation of control orders and the necessity in such cases to furnish the detained person sufficient information to enable effective instructions to be given by the detained person to their legal representatives. The line to be drawn is likely to be difficult for the courts. There are core minimum standards that cannot be abrogated in terms of giving the accused an opportunity to make a realistic defence. This approach has been approved in *Bank Mellat v HM Treasury*[93] and settles the issue of how minimum standards are necessary. This gives a clear indication to the state authorities that the importance of protecting the public from the risk of terrorism has to be considered in the context of the risk of not disclosing sensitive material. This provides the opportunity for the judge to rule that disclosure of the information is required. Should the Government not wish to undertake this step, then it follows that the withdrawal of such information in a case will lead to its collapse. In the case where there is a control order in force the order would have to be quashed unless the material that the Government is willing to be disclosed is such to uphold the case.

19-149 There remains many ambiguities about the present arrangements, not least what is said to satisfy the test of "the essence" of the case or the "gist of the case" against the accused. The nature of the material under consideration may make drawing the line highly problematic. In *Tariq*[94] in 2011, an Employment Tribunal case, T was employed as an immigration officer by the Home Office. His brother was arrested on suspicion of terrorist offences but released without charge. There was no information that T was involved but the consequences of the arrest of his brother resulted in his security clearance being revoked. The Secretary of State argued that this was necessary in the national interest. The Employment Tribunal used the CMP in respect of the issues raised by T in his claim for unfair dismissal. T argued that the operation of CMP was incompatible with his art.6 rights.

19-150 The Supreme Court held that CMP was indeed compatible with art.6. CMP was justifiable in terms of national security. The main analysis that followed made clear that the Employment Tribunal was able to provide an overall supervision of the process including the operation of the special advocate procedure. The operation of the principle of the "gist" of the case had

---

91   *A v Secretary of State for the Home Department* [2004] UKHL 56; [2005] 2 A.C. 68.
92   [2007] UKHL 46; [2008] 1 A.C. 440.
93   [2010] EWCA Civ 483; [2012] Q.B. 91.
94   *Tariq v Home Office* [2011] UKSC 35; [2012] 1 A.C. 452.

to be considered in the context of national security and the public interest. Defining the boundaries of protecting the liberty of the subject is difficult. The case is primarily about the lifting of security clearance and employment rights that are associated as a result. This is a further example of the challenges in setting the appropriate standard between human rights and security. In one part the aim is to strengthen the oversight of the intelligence and security agencies. In the other and more controversial part is to allow for the first time the operation in the civil courts the use of closed material. The Justice and Security Green Paper[95] outlined the main issues of the Government's proposals that seek to use civil courts to make use of CMP for the consideration of national security cases. The Green Paper explained that there was an increasing number of civil cases arising out of claims in damages from former Guantanamo detainees or appeals against control orders or arising out of deportation and immigration decisions. In many cases the use of civil proceedings is the main way that some transparency or review of detention can be undertaken. The rationale for the proposals is to secure the exchange of information between the main governments, the UK and the USA, while permitting an element of judicial scrutiny. After much debate and public unease, Pt 2 of the Justice and Security Act 2013 allows the civil courts to consider a closed material application. Under s.6, the court is enabled to grant a CMP if they consider that the proceedings would require disclosure of material which would damage national security. The court is empowered to consider the sensitive information and focus on the relevance or otherwise of the material for the case in hand. This might include intercept evidence as well as consideration of what is precisely to be covered by the CMP order. The overall concern is whether disclosure is damaging to the national interest.

19–151   Section 9 of the Act provides for the appointment of special advocates. This is roughly similar to the arrangements already in place under the Special Immigration Appeals Commission Act 1997. It has been used more widely than ever before. Narrowly defined to address concerns over material from MI5, MI6 and GCHQ, the Government Communications gathering centre, it has been used in ordinary criminal proceedings to address intimidation of witnesses, for example in parole hearings in the East Midlands.[96] The use of special advocates is also a remarkable implication of the creeping effects of terrorism into the day-to-day operation of the justice system. The operation of special advocates is a general weakening of the protections afforded to individuals under the ordinary law and a reduction in the depth of judicial oversight that is available. Doubts about the effectiveness of the special advocates procedure were also expressed in the case of *A and other v UK*[97] in 2009 although the use of special advocates was upheld as legal. Section 12 of the Justice and Security Act 2013 introduces an obligation on the Secretary of State to make annual reports to Parliament on the use of s.6 powers on CMP applications. This is an attempt by the Government to address parliamentary concerns about accountability beyond judicial scrutiny of an individual case.

---

95 *Justice and Security Green Paper*, Cm 8194 (October 2011).
96 Justice, *Secret Evidence* (June 2009), para.184. See The Constitutional Affairs Committee, *The Operation of the Special Immigration Appeals Commission and Special Advocates*, HC 323-1 (2005).
97 *A v UK* Application No.3455/05 (19 February 2009).

19–152

The UK Supreme Court has yet to determine any case involving the direct interpretation of the new legislation. However there have been an important series of cases surrounding the UK's Government attempts to restrict the financial activities of Bank Mellat, a Bank it alleged had connections with Iran's nuclear programme, hence the role of CMP was considered when a case was appealed to the Supreme Court. Interestingly, the Supreme Court entered into a closed material consideration of the sensitive material to come to its own conclusions. The Supreme Court found that ministers had failed to convince Parliament as to why the Bank was subject to proceedings and that the Bank had not received notice of the Treasury's decision to restrict its access to the UK's financial markets. The Court, however accepted that there was a case to conduct a closed material procedure—and importantly that the Supreme Court was itself empowered to consider such a hearing where it was necessary.[98] Since the Supreme Court decision, the English Commercial Court[99] has decided that the UK is financially liable for the sanctions that are illegal when applied to a particular entity. The conclusions from the case are that the UK government had acted illegally in imposing sanctions on Bank Mellat and the amount of loss is recoverable from the Government. The exact amount has yet to be determined but Bank Mellat is known to be seeking £2.3 billion.

E: Summary and Conclusions

19–153

Many of the freedoms enjoyed by citizens in democratic countries have been hard won through centuries of case law amidst efforts to restrain over-zealous or badly motivated officials. The Human Rights Act 1998 has proved influential in ensuring that rights and public order are reconciled in a proportionate and fair manner. Ewing encapsulates the main debate as follows: "It is thus the supreme irony of the British constitution, that liberty and legality would be better served by politics rather than by law; or by power rather than by rights".[100]

19–154

The breadth and scope of terrorism legislation is also an ever present feature of the legal system and vests very wide discretion with public officials. The Counter-Terrorism and Security Act 2015 takes matter in the direction of increasing executive powers over suspected individuals. The aim is to take preventative measures in anticipation of terrorist acts. These are reactions to the threat high levels of likely terrorist activity in the UK and alarmingly they are likely to be required for some foreseeable time in the future.

19–155

The rule of law and protections against arbitrariness remain under judicial discretion and vigilance. In many ways the determination of liberty and the balance between the interests of

---

98 *Bank Mellat (Appellant) v Her Majesty's Treasury (Respondent) (No.1)* [2013] UKSC 38; [2014] A.C. 700; and (No.2) [2013] UKSC 39; [2014] A.C. 700.
99 *Bank Mellat v HM Treasury* [2015] EWHC 1258 (Comm).
100 K. Ewing, *Bonfire of the Liberties* (Oxford: Oxford University Press, 2010), p.284.

the State, its protection and security and the right of the individual remains as precarious today as it did in the past.

19-156 Conor Gearty encapsulates one of the overpowering fears of our times: "There is no need to accept the elision of security with state protection in the way that an exclusive preoccupation with terrorism seems to force us to do".[101] Modern states may "collapse freedom into security" that may underline democracy and law. As he explains:

> "The rule of law is an elusive and protean concept. It has no fixed meaning. It certainly no longer has the anglocentric self-assurance with which its originator, Dicey, clothed it."[102]

19-157 There is an ongoing debate between the flow of legislation intended to address emergency powers while retaining freedom of association and assembly. Balancing the interests of each is likely to be a continuous debate. The Justice and Security Act 2013 was passed amidst wide-ranging concerns that the adoption of CMP in civil cases was unjustified in terms of protecting the interests of justice rather than national security. The Act includes checks and balances such as the use of annual reports to Parliament detailing the extent and scope of the powers used by the Secretary of State. It is too soon to say whether the courts will interpret the Justice and Security Act 2013 very strictly. The Court of Appeal in *Sarkandi v Secretary of State for Foreign and Commonwealth Affairs*[103] considered the role of CMP in its use in placing the applicants' names on the EU's Iran asset freeze and travel ban. The Court of Appeal accepted that the Foreign Secretary was not required to disclose sensitive material and rejected the idea that there should be a presumption that CMP should be used as a measure of last resort. The CMP procedure had been originally approved in proceedings before the High Court.

19-158 More generally the use of CMP should be considered in a much wider context including the role of the State in surveillance. In a wide-ranging review of surveillance and investigatory powers, David Anderson QC has called for a new legal framework for all investigatory powers and the protection of national security through the use of specific warrants rather than as a generic executive power.[104] It is very important that emergency powers are examined holistically and not just in terms of individual powers. The newly established Intelligence and Security Committee (ISC) has made similar observations on how material is gathered by the various security services and how the reliability of the material is to be assessed.[105] The accusation of "secret courts" is a serious concern when problems raised by the allegations of torture in the USA may undermine the legality and reliability of evidence obtained under such circumstances. The material that might support claims of mistreatment may be subjected to

---

101 Conor Gearty, *Liberty and Security* (Cambridge: Polity Press, 2013), p.108.
102 S. Sedley, *Lions under the Throne* (Cambridge: Cambridge University Press, 2015), p.280.
103 [2015] EWCA Civ 687.
104 David Anderson QC, *A Question of Trust: Report of the Investigatory Powers Review* (June 2015).
105 ISC, *Privacy and Security: A Modern and Transparent Legal Framework* (March 2015).

exclusion and this may apply to cases that raise doubts about the interrogation practices and the rendition of suspects. It is far from clear what role if any the UK has played in both practices.

Striking appropriate balances between powers held by executive or judicial authorities has to ensure that the rule of law is upheld by the State even in the face of justifications arising from terrorism and the "war on terror". CMP and its procedures are likely to remain controversial. Efforts to ensure that the correct balance is struck under the new Justice and Security Act 2013 will require the UK's Supreme Court to consider how best justice is served. Court powers of review need to be strongly protected against any executive influence, if the rule of law is to be upheld and fairly applied. The UK's position on human rights remains uneven and unpredictable EU membership, the possible repeal of the Human Rights Act 1998 and a British Bill of Rights are actively being discussed with uncertain outcomes.[106]

Further Reading

T. R. S. Allan, *Constitutional Justice: A Liberal Theory of the Rule of Law* (Oxford: Oxford University Press, 2013).

Tom Bingham, *The Rule of Law* (London, Penguin, 2010).

T. Campbell, K. D. Ewing and A. Tomkins (eds), *Sceptical Essays on Human Rights* (Oxford: Oxford University Press, 2001).

M. Elliott and D. Feldman, *The Cambridge Companion to Public Law* (Cambridge: Cambridge University Press, 2015).

K. Ewing, *Bonfire of the Liberties* (Oxford: Oxford University Press, 2010).

C. Gearty, *Liberty and Security* (Cambridge: Polity Press, 2013).

S. Sedley, *Lions Under the Throne* (Cambridge: Cambridge University Press, 2015).

---

106 See Colm O'Cinneide, "Human Rights and the UK Constitution" in J. Jowell, D. Oliver and C. O'Cinneide (eds), *The Changing Constitution* (Oxford: Oxford University Press, 2015), pp.67–103.

20

Secrecy, Freedom of Expression and the State

A: Introduction

20–001

Governmental secrecy and the interests of the State are considered in this chapter in the context of freedom of information. Access to information has a crucial role in the various systems of government accountability. Information is required to make effective use of parliamentary questions and debate in the performance of select committees and in the work of pressure groups. Information is also an essential element in government decision-making and especially in the area of policy formulation. Evidenced based policy-making is essential to good government. An open style of government encourages debate and discussion, and is helpful in coming to a fully informed and reasoned analysis that is axiomatic to good decision-making.[1] Increasingly national security demands inhibit the degree of openness that many members of the public expect. The creation of the National Security Council (NSC) in 2010 was an attempt to oversee various aspects of security and defence. The NSC is made up of senior ministers, including the Prime Minister who acts as its chair, served by a National Security Secretariat to ensure that there is co-ordination of cross departmental security-related functions. In certain circumstances it is possible for the Leader of the Opposition to attend.[2] There is a comprehensive consolidation and codification of the law on surveillance under the Draft Investigatory Powers Bill 2015/16 that has yet to be finalised.

20–002

The Freedom of Information Act 2000 has the potential to change the culture of secrecy and how an open society is achieved while retaining the public interest. Government secrecy and freedom of information has to be considered in the context of the various Convention rights that are available under the Human Rights Act 1998. Article 10 recognises the freedom of expression, as well as the right to receive and impart information that is free from

---

1   See Max Hastings, *The Secret War: Spies, Codes and Guerrillas 1939–1945* (London: Harper Collins, 2015).
2   House of Commons Library, *The UK National Security* Council, Briefing Paper, No.7456 (11 January 2016).

interference from the State. There is also protection from international treaties such as art.19(2) of the United Nations Covenant on Civil and Political Rights that recognises the freedom of expression.

20-003
The impact of the Human Rights Act in areas of public controversy such as the media and press, or in the law relating to contempt, or official secrets has yet to be fully evaluated. The question of what restraints the State should impose on the media and press commensurate with freedom of information is one of the most challenging questions in public law.

20-004
The Human Rights Act 1998, has moved judicial approaches to develop a right to privacy. This is a good example of judicial creativity under the influence of Convention rights in the UK. Before the Human Rights Act 1998 was passed in *Kaye v Robertson*,[3] the Court of Appeal denied that there is a right to privacy in English law. This view was upheld by the House of Lords in *R v Brown*[4] by Lord Hoffman, in strong terms, who commented that the common law did not recognise such a right and that Parliament was reluctant to introduce one. In court decisions after the introduction of the Human Rights Act 1998, the courts have gone to great lengths to create such a right. In *Douglas v Hello! Ltd*[5] the courts acknowledged the possibility of an arguable right to privacy. This decision has the potential[6] of developing into a full right of privacy when in the past judges had been reluctant. This is an example of how the Human Rights Act may provide judges with new perspectives and allow the common law to be supplemented by a "rights" jurisprudence. There is, however, no easy solution when balancing the right of the private citizen, press freedom and media attention with privacy. The right to privacy is acknowledged in the Office of Communications (Ofcom) Broadcasting Code that attempts to set the balance between openness and respecting guarantees about confidentiality and anonymity.[7]

20-005
One pressure for greater openness comes from the widely available access to the international media through the internet. Territorial protection of confidential information is increasingly difficult. Attempts in the UK to make government more open resulted in the creation of a *Code of Practice on Access to Government Information* revised in 1997. There are a number of examples where the citizen has greater access to information than in the past such as through: the Local Government (Access to Information) Act 1985; the Access to Personal Files Act 1987; the Access to Medical Reports Act 1988; the Environment and Safety Information Act 1988; the Access to Health Records Act 1990; and the Data Protection Act 1998. The Freedom of Information Act 2000 from 2005 allowed individual applications for information. There is a requirement to provide information unless it falls within one or more exceptions under the Act.[8]

---

3 [1991] F.S.R. 62; Times, March 21, 1990 CA (Civ Div).
4 [1996] A.C. 543; [1996] 2 W.L.R. 203 HL.
5 [2001] Q.B. 967; [2001] 2 W.L.R. 992 CA (Civ Div).
6 See *Earl Spencer v UK* (1998) 25 E.H.R.R. CD 105 HL before the 1998 Act came into force.
7 Ofcom, *Broadcasting Code* (2013).
8 Section 2(2) states "in all the circumstances of the case, the public interest in maintaining the exemption outweighs the public interest in disclosing the information". There is also s.23 relating to the security services.

20–006

The focus of this chapter is on the restrictions and inhibitions which are placed on the freedom of expression and on the access to information which permits the State to retain secrecy. The Supreme Court in *R (Evans) v Attorney General*[9] allowing the publication of correspondence between the Prince of Wales and government departments is an important step in interpreting freedom of information in favour of greater transparency. The Supreme Court rejected the argument made by the Attorney General that he was entitled to issue a certificate under s.53 of the Freedom of Information Act 2000. The public are able to gain access to important correspondence between the heir to the Throne and the Government.

B: Open Government and Official Secrets

20–007

Openness is a necessary prerequisite for accountable and responsible government. An open style of government permits Parliament, pressure groups and interested members of the public to participate in policy decision-making. A government that is more open is likely to be better informed than a government that is restrictive. A consequence of openness in government is that the quality of decision-making may be improved. Participation in the democratic process should not end with an election vote, but should continue to allow citizens the opportunity to contribute to the system of government decision-making.

20–008

There is a variety of legal rules and techniques relevant to the secrecy of government.[10] For many years, there has been a secrecy culture in the Government and amongst public authorities in the UK. Before the Human Rights Act 1998 and latterly the passage of the Freedom of Information Act 2000, there was no legally enforceable right to information. But it would be misleading to attribute the culture of secrecy as owing to that single cause. Successive UK governments have maintained secrecy as the hallmark of Government decision-making. There are a number of factors that may contribute to this culture.

20–009

First, the civil service developed, during the Victorian era, the ethos of public service. Hierarchical in structure, disciplined through promotion and advancement through public service, civil servants were kept hidden from public view and their contribution to government preserved under secrecy and the responsibility of Ministers to Parliament. The civil service sought to achieve influence but maintain political neutrality. As a result, civil servants have contributed to the high degree of secrecy evident in government. Advice given to Ministers must remain confidential, sometimes because of the nature of the advice itself but also to protect the anonymity of the advice giver.

---

9 [2015] UKSC 21; [2015] A.C. 1787.
10 House of Commons Library, *The Official Secrets Act and Official Secrecy*, Briefing Paper, CB07422 (17 December 2015).

20-010 Secondly, the doctrine of collective Cabinet responsibility, intended to provide collective decision-making and collective deliberations, ensures that the climate of secrecy becomes built into every structure of government. There is in fact a secretive character to the political culture of the UK. This is reinforced by the use of Cabinet collective decision-making, which binds the civil service and Ministers to confidentiality. The ethos of secrecy is also underlined by the way information is disseminated to the media. Official leaks of information concerning government policy may quite legally be given to newspapers through the process known as "the lobby system". This system was in operation until 2002, when the Prime Minister took the initiative to meet the press on a regular basis for a press briefing, adopting a question and answer format. Ministers may be self-authorising in releasing to the press details of government policy that may affect their department. Thirdly, individual ministerial responsibility serves to preserve the secrecy of government departmental decision-making. Ministers are directly accountable to Parliament but civil servants are not. Thus, civil servants and Ministers may find secrecy the most effective buffer against outside intrusion or unwanted publicity.

20-011 Fourthly, governments are major providers of contracts. In the government's relationship with the private sector there is a high degree of secrecy in contractual relationships. Relations between commercial enterprises seek to preserve confidentiality and protection against competitors through patenting industrial processes or copyright which contributes to the need to preserve price sensitive and commercially valuable information. Confidentiality of the commercial variety permeates the relationship between the private and public sectors.

20-012 The greater use of select committees by both the House of Commons and the House of Lords provides a fascinating account of how modern government developed in the Victorian era. Reports from inspectors and the setting up of various inspectorates also increased access to the workings of government. Such developments did not prove successful against the culture of secrecy. Inspectors were subject to ministerial responsibility and confidentiality was retained. The Treasury through the issuing of treasury minutes and memoranda influenced civil service attitudes to secrecy by preventing the disclosure of any official information without proper authority. The Victorian preoccupation with confidential information provides a culture which was receptive to instructions requiring non-disclosure. Equally clear is that attempts to circumvent legal controls were made and often were successful.[11]

20-013 The Victorian legacy remains today. As there is no absolute public right to all official information various restrictions remain on the disclosure of information about the past activities of government. Public records in the Public Records Office are only available for inspection after a period of 30 years has elapsed. Section 5(1) of the Public Records Act 1958 as amended by the Public Records Act 1967, provides that the Lord Chancellor may also proscribe different time periods for the disclosure of documents at the request of the Minister "or other person". Certain categories of papers may be subject to a longer time-scale. These are: "exceptionally sensitive papers, the disclosure of which would be contrary to the public interest whether on security or

---

[11] C. Roberts, *The Growth of Responsible Government in Stuart England* (Cambridge: Cambridge University Press, 1966). See William Cobbet and his pamphlets ensuring a constant flow of information on state trials and prosecutions. Wilson Report, *Modern Public Records: Selection and Access*, Cmnd.8204 (1981).

other grounds"; documents which contain information "supplied in confidence", the disclosure of which would or might constitute a breach of good faith; and documents containing information about individuals, "the disclosure of which would cause distress or danger to living persons or their immediate descendants".

In fact, it is possible to prevent the disclosure of many documents by the simple expedient of "weeding" out those documents which may be too sensitive to publish, and their destruction amounts to their permanent removal from the records of government. Estimates as to the amount of weeding carried out are difficult to make with any degree of accuracy, but it is also possible for papers to be destroyed at departmental level before they are ever put into the hands of the staff of the Public Records Office. The responsibility for the Public Records Office was with the Lord Chancellor, but under the Transfer of Functions (Information and Public Records) Order 2015 this is with Secretary of State.[12] The assessment of the value of official papers in terms of their historical content is not included in the legislation. Thus it is possible and legal for government Ministers to order the destruction of official papers in the public interest. It is difficult to prevent the destruction of official papers. Would a longer time-limit beyond 30 years result in a different attitude towards publication? A longer time-limit may make the destruction of papers less likely but this may be at the expense of depriving the present generation of information about the activities of the government during their lifetime. Is this a price worth paying in the interests of preserving historical records? There is no guarantee that a longer time-limit would help to preserve official papers without some legal requirement of preservation.

20–014

While the 30-year rule is still in place, the Code of Practice on Access to Government Information has provided a more liberal attitude to opening up files. Recent examples of such an approach may be found in the release of files on the German occupation of the Channel Islands and the release of the Rudolf Hess and Roger Casement papers. However, there have been surprises such as the revelation that in 1957 there had been a government decision to keep the details of an accident at the Windscale nuclear plant secret. This was revealed in papers released in January 1988.

20–015

An important source of information are ministerial memoirs. Previous Prime Ministers and Cabinet Ministers often write biographies and memoirs of their period in office. Such publications usually obeyed certain conventions about confidential information. The advice tendered to the government of the day by the civil service usually fell into this category. However, the memoirs of the late Richard Crossman who had been a Cabinet Minister in the Wilson Government ten years previously created concerns about the revelation of official information. The text of the diaries contained detailed information about the deliberations of the Cabinet. Officials were identified as were the names and views of Ministers. Particularly significant was the advice given to Ministers by civil servants, which was also given in great detail. The Attorney General in 1976 attempted to prevent the publication of the diaries. The arguments made to prevent publication included the confidential nature of Cabinet information, that the public interest requires that publication should be restrained and that the courts had a duty

20–016

---

12   Transfer of Functions (Information and Public Records) Order 2015, No.1897.

to restrain publication. Lord Widgery took the unusual step of reading the diaries and concluded that publication ten years after the event would not inhibit Cabinet discussion and that publication would not harm the public interest. The result of the decision allowed publication of the Crossman Diaries and since then many ex-Cabinet Ministers have provided details of their period in office in a relatively short period after they left office. Such memoirs can often become an indispensable guide to the workings of government and the way in which modern government develops. Following the *Crossman* case,[13] Lord Radcliffe's Committee of privy counsellors considered the advice tendered to Ministers about publication of their memoirs. In general, the Committee took a restrictive perspective on the publication of information which might put in jeopardy the "confidential relationships" between Ministers within the government. The Committee concluded that the opinions or advice of civil servants or ministerial colleagues should not be revealed, nor should the advice of advisers, furthermore that criticism of policy or competence should not be made public. Such guidelines are much stricter than the *Crossman* case accepted. However, enforcement is left to the individual responsibility of each Minister and not through the courts. There is little sign that the Radcliffe view is being followed by Ministers today and it seems more commonly accepted that ministerial memoirs will be forthcoming and that their value as a means of understanding the work of government remains undiminished. The normal convention is that former Ministers or civil servants who wish to publish their memoirs should submit a full text to the Cabinet secretary in advance for clearance. Upon refusal of publication there is an appeal to the Prime Minister who has the final decision in the matter. There is a tacit acceptance that[14] after a period of 15 years, as the Government may no longer be in office, a fairly wide latitude may be shown to former Ministers.[15]

Official secrets legislation

20-017

Various laws and legal restrictions exist against the publication or dissemination of official information. At common law various offences such as blasphemy, sedition and conspiracy provided a structure for the prosecution of offences which were intended to limit the variety and content of published material available to the public. The criminal law exercised a crude form of censorship aimed at controlling booksellers, publishers and printers as well as authors. The nineteenth-century legacy of secrecy resulted in the passage of the Official Secrets Act 1889 which made it an offence to "improperly divulge official information" was so widely drawn that the requirement of proof of the mental elements of the crime made successful prosecutions difficult to achieve. At the end of the nineteenth century legal controls were ineffective whereby many breaches of the law went unpunished under the growing power and influence of newspapers. The need to tighten the law was recognised by the Official Secrets Act 1911. This Act

---

13   *Attorney General v Jonathan Cape Ltd* [1976] Q.B. 752; [1975] 3 W.L.R. 606 QBD.
14   *Attorney General v Guardian Newspapers Ltd (No.2)* [1990] 1 A.C. 109; [1988] 3 W.L.R. 776 HL.
15   Lord Radcliffe, *Committee of Privy Counsellors on Ministerial Memoirs*, Cmnd.6386 (1976).

was further refined and reformed by the Official Secrets Act 1920 and again reformed by the Official Secrets Act 1939.

20-018 Section 1(1) of the 1911 Act makes it an offence for any person for any purpose prejudicial "to the safety or interests of the state" to engage in a number of activities. Those which are covered by the 1911 Act include: approaching or entering a prohibited place; making a sketch or plan calculated or intended to be useful to an enemy; and obtaining, publishing, communicating such information, sketch, document or information which is calculated to or is intended to be useful to an enemy.

20-019 The purpose which is prejudicial to the interests of the State may be inferred from the circumstances. The purpose which is prejudicial refers to the intention of the accused and will be judged not on the actual effect but on what the accused intended. Thus in *Chandler v DPP*[16] demonstrators for the Campaign for Nuclear Disarmament who approached a military airfield were convicted under s.1 of the 1911 Act when it was proved that their intention was to disable the airfield. The House of Lords regarded a "prohibited place" as not confined to specific sites so designated by the Ministry of Defence but applied to places where information would be useful to an enemy. Thus the law, which was intended to cover acts during wartime, had a peacetime operational focus which included protestors, as well as spies, saboteurs or agitators. This broad construction of the Act seems perfectly consistent with the breadth of the language used in the legislation. However, was it correct to have brought such a prosecution under a section which was aimed at spies and saboteurs rather than protestors and demonstrators? This highlights one of the problems with broadly drafted and interpreted laws. Prosecutorial discretion seems to depend on whether the statute is broad enough to catch the undesirable activity, which in this case it was, rather than on whether the Official Secrets Act should be used for such a prosecution.

20-020 The defence in *Chandler* had argued that the purpose of the demonstrators was not to prejudice the interests of the State but to draw attention to the use of nuclear weapons and thereby disarm the aircraft. Such direct action was unjustified and the courts rejected the defendants' arguments. Obstructing the lawful purpose of the armed services was held as prejudicial to the State even when the demonstrators held strongly their conviction that they were acting in the State's interests. The decision has been strongly criticised but the legal interpretation of the legislation is consistent with the words of the statute.

20-021 Section 2 of the 1911 Act is intended to prevent the misuse of any sketch plan or model, document or information. The section is aimed first at the holders of official information and makes it an offence to communicate this information except to a person authorised to receive the communication. A person who receives such information is also guilty of an offence if he has reasonable cause to believe that the information is in contravention of the Act. In *Crisp*,[17] the scope of the section applied to a clerk in the War Office who handed to the Director of a firm of tailors a copy of the clothing contract for the army. The clerk was not directly employed by the War Office but worked under the direction of the office-holder and this was sufficient.

---

16 [1964] A.C. 763; [1962] 3 W.L.R. 694 HL.
17 (1919) 83 J.P. 121.

20-022 Section 2(1) of the 1911 Act was used to prosecute Sarah Tisdell, a civil service clerk in 1984 for leaking to a newspaper a memorandum setting out the plans drawn up by the Government for maintaining public order when cruise missiles arrived at Greenham Common. Tisdell was sentenced to six months imprisonment. Section 2(1) was used in a prosecution against Clive Ponting, an assistant secretary in the Ministry of Defence, after he leaked a memorandum relating to the sinking of the Argentine Battleship *General Belgrano*. Ponting admitted leaking the document but claimed that he owed a duty to the House of Commons, in their constitutional role to hold government accountable. The document contained highly embarrassing revelations which questioned the complete accuracy of the Prime Minister's account of the sinking to the House of Commons. Ponting[18] was acquitted after the jury were able to see the documents and the jury's verdict was a surprise to many after the judge's summing up pointed in favour of a conviction. Ponting had not been authorised to leak the documents. The trial judge explicitly rejected Ponting's argument that he was justified in leaking the documents as he could not be said to owe a duty to the House of Commons; such a duty was the duty of Ministers and not civil servants. This direction appears correct in constitutional law. Ponting had breached the confidential nature of his relationship with Ministers and, however altruistic his motives, this was not a breach that could be authorised in law. The Armstrong Memorandum[19] issued to civil servants soon after Ponting's acquittal provided civil servants with procedures for expressing concern including a direct access to the Head of the Civil Service as a form of appeal court to resort to after exhausting departmental means to remedy any conflict between the civil servant's duties and responsibilities and those of the Minister. The Armstrong Memorandum has been replaced by the Civil Service Code from January 1996, which was revised in 1999 to take account of devolution. However, another view is that Ponting exposed both the failure of the civil service to exercise sufficient control over Ministers in such cases of dispute and that civil servants ought to be able to appeal directly to Parliament as a means to hold Ministers to account. The latter is objected to because of the nature of the Minister's responsibility to Parliament. Undoubtedly Ponting's leak had the effect of breaching an important confidence between a civil servant and his Minister. Ponting's acquittal also highlighted patent defects in the Official Secrets Acts and this led to the Government's consideration of reform in preference to various private members' initiatives.

20-023 Criticism of s.2 had been of long standing, with the Franks Committee[20] (1972) having recommended its abolition. The broadly drafted legislation with its "catch-all" quality became so heavily criticised that it was seldom used. This Draconian law however was said to have a preventive effect and therefore was perceived as valuable. About one-third of prosecutions under the Act related to the use of police information improperly disclosed to journalists or private detectives. The Franks Committee made comprehensive proposals for replacing s.2 with a more modern and focused Act. Thus the use of criminal sanctions would be restricted to

---

18 C. Ponting, *The Right to Know* (London: Sphere, 1986).
19 Sir Robert Armstrong, *The Duties and Responsibilities of Civil Servants in relation to Ministers: Note by the Head of the Home Civil Service 1985*, HC Official Report, Vol.74, 1984–85 (London: HMSO, 1985).
20 *Departmental Committee on s.2 of the Official Secrets Act 1911*, Cmnd.5104 (1972).

areas of major significance such as wrongful disclosure of information relating to the defence, security, foreign relations and reserves, Cabinet documents and the use of official information for private gain or information supplied about particular individuals. This reform proposal was accompanied by proposals to regularise the classification of documents, long regarded as the product of an over-protective civil service. Top secret would be restricted to defence, security, foreign relations and reserves. Prosecution would require a certificate from the responsible Minister and there would be some form of advisory committee advising on matters of classification. The Franks proposals received belated attention in the aftermath of the Ponting trial and consideration given to implementing some part of them in a White Paper.[21] The result was the introduction of the Official Secrets Act 1989.

The 1989 Act replaced s.2 of the 1911 Act and narrowed the protection of official information considerably. The use of the criminal law under the Act is restricted to various categories of information. While all Cabinet documents are not automatically protected under the Act, documents or information which falls under the following categories are subject to the criminal law.

It is an offence for a Crown servant or government contractor to disclose information which falls under any one of the following categories. The categories under ss.1–4 of the 1989 Act are: security and intelligence; defence; international relations; information obtained in confidence from other states or international organisations; and information obtained by special investigations authorised by warrant. In the cases of security and intelligence information or where information is obtained by special investigations authorised by warrant, no damage need be proven for the offence to have been committed if the disclosure is made by an officer of the security and intelligence services. In cases where disclosure is made by a Crown servant or government contractor, damage must be proven for there to be an offence. However, in the remaining categories covering defence and international relations, damage must be proven to have occurred where disclosure is made by someone other than a member of the security and intelligence services.

The 1989 Act also makes it a criminal offence for any person to make without authority a damaging disclosure of information protected under the Act that has come into his possession following an unauthorised disclosure of information by a current Crown servant or government contractor. This applies to information which is made available in breach of a requirement of confidentiality or in breach of s.1 of the 1911 Official Secrets Act. While mere receipt of information is no longer an offence, it is an offence to make disclosure of information relating to security and intelligence, defence and international relations when the information is communicated in confidence by the UK to another State or international organisation.

Section 8 of the 1989 Act makes it an offence to retain or fail to take care of protected documents and articles or disclose information which may facilitate access to protected material.

In its effect, the 1989 Act means that there is a general prohibition against disclosure of information by members of the security services or disclosure of information received from any authorised use of telephone tapping, irrespective of any damage proven. In such cases there is

---

21   Cmnd.408 (1988) and the debates at *Hansard*, HC Vol.137, cols.1412–1481.

no public interest defence and no defence of prior publication. Raising a defence requires the burden of proof to rest on the accused and this may make a defence to such offences difficult to prove. The 1989 Act does not permit the disclosure of information even where it may reveal any unlawful behaviour. There is no general defence that disclosure was in the public interest thus excluding the type of defence argued by Ponting in his trial, but then rejected by the trial judge. Various defences under the 1989 Act are that, in general, it is a defence for the accused to prove that he did not know that any of the information fell into a prohibited category or, in certain circumstances indicated above where damage must be shown in relation to the disclosure, that damage did not occur.

20–029 The scope of the 1989 Act applies generally within the civil service and to some outside bodies. The 1989 Act appears to move in a more liberal direction to official secrets compared to s.2 of the 1911 Act which it replaced. However, the 1989 Act falls short of providing access to information and its scope is supplemented by an increasing reliance on legal devices and techniques other than the criminal law, to prevent disclosures. Very often such techniques involve the use of the civil law.

20–030 As mentioned above for civil servants, the Civil Service Pay and Conditions of Service Code has been revised to take account of the provisions of the 1989 Act and the details of the Armstrong Memorandum mentioned above. Thus civil servants are explicitly required under the terms and conditions of their employment as owing the Crown a duty of confidentiality. This duty applies even after the civil servant leaves his employment. In addition, there is an obligation not to frustrate the policies or decisions of Ministers by the use or disclosure of information to which civil servants have access. Such requirements are intended to prevent leaks of information from civil servants who wish to disagree with the government's policy.

20–031 Civil servants who prove to be unreliable and untrustworthy are subject to disciplinary procedures which may result in dismissal from the Service. Promotion prospects are severely restricted when civil servants engage in activities incompatible with their duty of confidence to Ministers.

20–032 Recourse to the civil law either on the basis of breach of confidence or through the use of injunctions to protect copyright ownership avoids some of the difficulties encountered with the application of the criminal law. The disadvantages of using criminal prosecutions to punish leaks of information may be attributable to the unpredictable nature of jury trials for serious breaches of the Official Secrets Act and the publicity of court proceedings even when the proceedings may be held *in camera* or where disclosure is a contempt of court. The scope of contempt laws allows for restrictions on the access to information available to the court. Documents obtained by a solicitor and read out in open court in the course of litigation could not be used for any collateral or ancillary purpose. In *Home Office v Harman*[22] Harman, a solicitor for one of the parties in a civil action obtained documents by way of discovery which she later revealed to newspapers, was held by the House of Lords to have been in contempt of court for so doing in breach of the undertaking given for the disclosure of the documents to the court.

---

22   [1983] 1 A.C. 280; [1982] 2 W.L.R. 338 HL.

Civil proceedings have other advantages over criminal prosecutions. The burden of proof in criminal cases is higher than in civil cases which rests not on the standard of beyond a reasonable doubt but on the balance of probabilities. In civil cases the judiciary, and not the jury, performs the fact-finding role and this may facilitate the proof of the case against the defendant. Normally, criminal proceedings are only used after the leak has occurred and the suspect detected. Civil proceedings can be activated in anticipation of any publication and offers prior restraint through the use of injunctions over any proposed publication. The ex parte nature of the interim injunction procedures means that the law may be readily applied and take effect as soon as the leak becomes apparent to the government.

However it is a mistake to assume that civil proceedings are a complete panacea when the government wishes to retain confidential information which has become available on a worldwide basis outside the UK and outside the jurisdiction of the UK's courts. The long running *Spycatcher* litigation exposed limitations in the use of law to enforce secrecy. The case is an example of the use of litigation to enforce the doctrine of breach of confidence. This doctrine owed its origins to private law and the enforcement of personal rights, including the enforcement of trade secrets and marital secrets. The potential for its use in public law owes its origins to the obiter dicta of Lord Widgery in the *Crossman Diaries Case*,[23] discussed above. Then it was suggested that a breach of confidence might occur when government information was made public. The opportunity to apply this doctrine to its full potential, as an alternative to the use of the criminal law, arose in the *Spycatcher* case.

The saga began in 1985 when the Attorney General commenced proceedings in Australia against Peter Wright and his publisher seeking an injunction to prevent publication of Wright's memoirs detailing the activities of the security services during the period when Wright was a member of MI5. In the UK ex parte injunctions were granted restraining the publication of extracts from the memoirs in the *Guardian* and the *Observer*. After the trial of the issues in the Australian court, the Attorney General's action was dismissed and Wright's memoirs allowed to be published. Publication also took place in the United States from May 1987 after extracts from the book were published in the *Washington Post*. The Attorney General continued to attempt to prevent publication in the UK and was granted further interim injunctions against the *Sunday Times* and the *Independent*, the *Evening Standard* and the *London Daily News*.

In the meantime, an appeal against permission to publish was heard in the New South Wales Court of Appeal where the Attorney General was unsuccessful. Finally, after the *Independent*, the *Sunday Times* and the *News on Sunday* were fined £50,000 each for contempt of court, the House of Lords in 1990 decided that no injunction would lie against the newspapers against any further serialisation of the book, nor would the newspapers be liable for any financial account of profits to the Government as the information contained in the *Spycatcher* book was now in the public domain and thus could not be restrained.

The House of Lords' decision to permit publication indicated the ineffectiveness of the law when attempting to restrain publication of information which has entered the international arena. The case also highlights a number of further possibilities open to the government

---

23 [1976] Q.B. 752; [1975] 3 W.L.R. 606 QBD.

interested in preventing publication. First, the House of Lords accepted that neither the publishers nor the author had copyright in the book as copyright vested with the Crown. This gives rise to the possibility that the Crown might seek damages and an account of profits to base its claim. In the future this is likely to be a useful remedy. It could be argued that if a claim had been based on this ground, the Government's attempts to prevent publication might have been more effective. It is unlikely that any publisher would be willing to take such a risk of publication if the profits from publication are put in jeopardy.

20-038 Secondly, the House of Lords considered whether reliance could be placed on Wright's main defence that it was in the public interest to publish. The book was claimed to establish wrongdoing and lack of accountability on the part of the security services claims which if proven might give rise to serious public concern about the operational controls over the security services. In particular, allegations were made that MI5 had engaged in activities to destabilise the government when Harold Wilson was Prime Minister. In the House of Lords, Lord Griffiths was prepared to concede that in an extreme case the confidential nature of the trust between security service operatives and the security services might be lifted so that the dangers of a serious abuse might be made public.[24] However, such a justification did not appear to arise in the *Spycatcher* case. The House of Lords appeared to accept that once the book was available in the public domain, publication could not be prevented by an injunction. Such an injunction would be "futile", as personal copies of the book had been purchased or received by many UK citizens abroad and were imported into the UK. Despite the fact that Wright had a life-long duty of confidence, the reality was that such a duty was in practical terms unenforceable. This gave rise to the surprising result that Wright might be free to return to the UK and publish his memoirs without any prior restraint. The reality was that he would be prosecuted under the Official Secrets Act.

20-039 The effects of the *Spycatcher* litigation were far-reaching. The Government was seriously embarrassed by the revelations in the book, and attempts to restrict its publication had been unsuccessful. In the earlier consideration of an interim injunction, Lord Bridge in the House of Lords pointed to the absence of any Bill of Rights in the UK, at that time, when compared to many other countries. He indicated that the European Convention would most likely result in the unenforceable nature of any ban.

20-040 The defence of public interest was used by David Shayler, a former member of the security services who was charged with unlawful disclosure of documents under ss.1 and 4 of the Official Secrets Act 1989 In *R v Shayler*,[25] the House of Lords approved the use of a preparatory hearing to decide whether there was a public interest defence. This procedure is available under the Criminal Procedure and Investigations Act 1996 and the House of Lords held that the 1989 Official Secrets legislation was compatible with the Human Rights Act 1998. The Attorney General is entitled to an account of the profits of former members of the security and intelligence services for publications that are in breach of contractual or confidential agreements.[26]

---

24   [1990] 1 A.C. 109; [1988] 3 W.L.R. 776 HL at [650]. See P. Wright, *Spycatcher* (New York: Viking, 1987), p.54.
25   [2002] UKHL 11; [2003] 1 A.C. 247 HL.
26   *Attorney General v Blake* [2001] 1 A.C. 268; [2000] 3 W.L.R. 625 HL.

C: The Security Services

20-041 The unwelcome glare of publicity resulting from the *Spycatcher* affair exposed many of the previously held secret activities of the security services. In particular the often quoted comment that Peter Wright and others "bugged and burgled our way across London at the State's behest, while pompous, bowler-hatted civil servants in Whitehall pretended to look the other way". In addition, allegations made by Cathy Massiter that the phones of prominent CND activists and trade unionists were bugged confirmed the suspicion of many commentators that the security services were not under complete control.

20-042 The question of control over the security services is itself often shrouded in secrecy. In the 1940s a system of positive vetting developed which was aimed at preventing persons with a communist interest or affiliation from joining the civil service or the security services. This procedure applied to personnel mainly charged with handling sensitive information. It also applied to contractors engaged in work which may be similarly regarded as involving sensitive material.

20-043 The system of positive vetting developed as a means to purge the public service and contractors of any communists or sympathisers. Revisions to the system have been continuous since it was introduced in 1952. In 1990 it was revised once more and a written statement made by the Prime Minister defended the operation of the system.[27] The increasing use of positive vetting reflects the growing complexity and sensitivity of government decision-making. Also the series of leaks by civil servants may cause a wider drawing of the boundaries as to who should or should not be included. The main focus of positive vetting is directed against anyone who might be involved in any activities which threaten national security, such as espionage, terrorism, sabotage, or actions "intended to overthrow or undermine parliamentary democracy by political, industrial or violent means". Different levels of clearance are necessary for the various categories of secret information ranging from top secret to merely confidential information.

20-044 Judicial review for someone who is refused positive vetting clearance is limited as the courts have shown reluctance to engage in any substantial examination of what is in the national interest, but there is an appeal procedure to the three advisers constituted to hear cases where there are allegations against a public servant. There is a procedure which relies on the use of three advisers who may take account of the representations of the person affected. The recommendations of the three advisers are made to the Minister who may consider further evidence in the matter including representations from the person concerned.[28] Government contractors may also make use of the three advisers procedure since 1956.

---

27 See *Hansard*, HC Vol.448, cols.1703–1704 (14 March 1948). See P. Hennessy and G. Brownfield, "Britain's Cold War Security purge: The Origins of Positive Vetting" (1982) 4(25) *The Historical Journal* 965–973. *Hansard*, HC Vol.177, cols.159–161 (24 July 1990).

28 *R v Director of Government Communications Headquarters Ex p. Hodges* Times, July 26, 1988; Independent, July 21, 1988 QBD. See Statement of the procedure to be followed when the reliability of a public servant is thought to be in doubt on security grounds (Cabinet Office, 1985), Cmnd.9715 (1956).

20-045 In the aftermath of the *Spycatcher* case, the Government responded. The outcome was first to establish a staff counsellor for the security services to deal with matters relating to concerns of officers about the nature of their work and, if necessary, the counsellor could have access to the Head of the Civil Service in order to allay fears. Setting up some form of internal grievance mechanism in order to deal with legitimate concerns about the operational responsibilities of the security services was partly intended to restore morale to the service and also to rebuild public confidence in the work of the service. The remit of the staff counsellor was later extended to include staff who were former members of the service. Dissatisfied members of the service could have recourse to the departmental Minister or the Prime Minister.

20-046 It is doubtful if such arrangements would be effective if they had been available to Peter Wright. In fact, many of his allegations, especially that the one-time Head of MI5 was a double agent, had been considered but rejected by his superior officers. It is hard to envisage that an aggrieved officer would be satisfied by a polite refusal internally to take no further action. Thus, the creation of a staff counsellor appears to have limited potential for effectiveness. However, the creation of this office further served to strengthen the secrecy binding all members of the security services. This culture of secrecy is further reinforced by the Official Secrets Act 1989.

20-047 In addition to the creation of a staff counsellor, the Government introduced a new Act, the Security Services Act 1989, to put the security services on a statutory basis. The new legislation marked an important departure in official recognition of MI5 under s.1 of the Act. However, this Act did not include any of the other elements in the security services such as MI6, responsible for overseas intelligence activity in liaison with the Foreign Office. There is no mention of the Government Communications Headquarters (GCHQ) at Cheltenham nor any statutory basis for its existence in the legislation. Plans to put the intelligence service and GCHQ on a statutory basis are contained in the Intelligence Services Act 1994. The remit covering the activities of the security services is widely drawn. It includes under s.1(2) of the 1989 Act:

> "...the protection of national security and in particular, its protection against threats from espionage, terrorism, sabotage, from the activities of agents of foreign powers and from actions intended to overthrow or undermine parliamentary democracy by political, industrial or violent means."

20-048 In addition under s.1(3) the function of the security services includes "the economic well-being of the UK against threats posed by the actions or intentions of persons outside the British Islands". This is so broadly drafted that it might include any industrial commercial activity of foreign or international companies; in fact, almost anything may be connected to this function. Criticism of this section has focused on the widely drawn nature of the section.

20-049 There is provision under the Act for the appointment of a Director General by the Secretary of State. The statutory responsibility of the Director includes "the proper discharge of the functions of the service, for the purpose of preventing or detecting serious crime". The Director has to ensure that under s.2(2)b, the "service does not take any action to further the interests of any political party". The legislation, however, is vague on the arrangements for ministerial responsibility. The Government is presently agreed that some form of committee should be set up composed of Privy Councillors to oversee the work of the security services. There is little guidance in the legislation as to when Ministers ought to be consulted or the relationship between the Minister and the Director. The implication is that the Director should have broad discretion in carrying out the various duties under the Act.

20-050

Prior to the passage of the Act, it was common practice for the security services to operate alongside the Special Branch officers designated for that purpose by each police force. In 1992 the Government announced that the main responsibility for detecting terrorists would be devolved to MI5 away from the Special Branch and the Anti-terrorist branch of the Metropolitan Police. The supremacy of the intelligence officers over the police may be in part a refocusing of their activities in the aftermath of the collapse of the Soviet Union and a perceived end to the military threat of the Soviet Union.

20-051

The Security Services Act 1989 also contains considerable legal powers for the security services to carry out their activities. Prior to 1989, doubt was expressed about the legal powers of the security services to engage in covert activities. Section 3 of the Act remedies such gaps which may have existed in the law by the use of warrants issued by the Home Secretary. A warrant may authorise entry onto property and the "taking of such action" as is specified in the warrant and thought to be necessary. The power to issue a warrant in such circumstances depends on whether the value of the information is likely "to be of substantial value in assisting the Service to discharge its functions" and "cannot reasonably be obtained by other means". This gives extremely wide powers first to the Home Secretary to authorise warrants and second to the security services to carry on their activities. Information obtained under a warrant may not be disclosed as the Security Services Act 1989 makes disclosures a criminal offence.

20-052

The 1989 Act was amended by the Security Service Act 1996 allowing the security services to support the activities of the police and other law enforcement agencies.[29]

20-053

It is noteworthy that the powers are Executive-based and there is no recourse to a judicial element which is customary in the granting of warrants for example under PACE 1984. This leaves judicial review as the main means to challenge the decision of the Home Secretary or the activities of the security services. Judicial review[30] is limited in such cases because historically judges have been reluctant to look behind the "national interest" and the opportunities for challenge will usually be confined to challenges after the warrants have been issued.

20-054

The procedure for granting warrants, which makes use of the Home Secretary's powers, is likened to any other delegated authority without any special procedure for obtaining the Home Secretary's permission. There is no requirement to check the nature of the information, its source, reliability, the period for which the warrant may be issued and the places or people that may be affected. Critics of the Act have pointed to the systems in operation in both Canada and Australia which have greater accountability built into the system of granting of authority to the security services.

---

29 The Modern Slavery Act 2015 and the Gangmasters (Licensing) Act 2004.
30 See I. Leigh and L. Lustgarten "The Security Service Act 1989" (1989) 52 *Modern Law Review* 801; see also Cmnd.2523 (1994).

20-055 Although the statutory authority for warrants is very extensive, there is the question of whether prerogative powers may co-exist with statutory authority. The scope of the prerogative is unclear and the question of whether prerogative powers remain after the statute is open to conjecture.

20-056 The Security Services Act 1989 also provides procedures for complaints. A tribunal for the investigation of complaints against the security services is created with the Security Services Commissioner to undertake investigations with a duty on every member of the security services and every official of the Home Office to "disclose or give to the Commissioner such documents or information" as he may require for the purpose of enabling him to discharge his functions. Reports, including an annual report may be made to the Prime Minister and the Prime Minister is under a duty to lay the annual report before Parliament.[31]

20-057 The Intelligence Services Act 1994 performs similar functions for the Secret Intelligence Service (MI6) and the Government Communications Headquarters (GCHQ) as outlined under the Security Service Act 1989 for MI5. The 1994 Act attempts to strike a balance between more openness and the protection of the national interest. Sections 1(1) and 3(1) are very widely drawn, setting out the remit of the operations of MI6 and their functions. Little information can be gained from the definition contained in the Act except its vagueness. For example, one function is to protect the "economic well-being of the United Kingdom" and this finds its place alongside the function of "support of the prevention or detection of serious crime".

20-058 The Act establishes a Committee composed of MPs and members of the House of Lords to examine the administration, expenditure and policy of the three services: MI5, MI6 and GCHQ. The Committee is called the Intelligence and Security Committee. However, its function is not to review operational matters and it may not summon witnesses. In addition, there is a tribunal for the purpose of investigating complaints against any one of the three services. The Tribunal has no powers to compel the attendance of witnesses, its reasoning is kept confidential and its decisions are not open to challenge in the courts. Section 9(4) of the 1994 Act stipulates that the decisions of the Tribunal and the Commissioner "shall not be subject to appeal or liable to be questioned in any court".

20-059 The Intelligence and Security Committee is intended to supplement the appointment of a Commissioner under the 1989 Act. The main functions are set out in the Justice and Security Act 2013.[32] The Act was path breaking in attempting to provide a link between Parliamentary oversight and Executive controls. The Act provides some clarification of how the Committee is expected to operate. The Committee has powers to examine or otherwise, the "expenditure, administration and operations" of the three main intelligence services. It may also investigate overseas work of other security services. There is also a Memorandum of Understanding between the Committee and the Prime minister. The secretariat is drawn from outside Parliament from the Cabinet Office. There are limitations in the work of the Committee

---

31 D. Cayley Chung (1985) 26 Harvard *International Law Journal* 234; J. L. J. Edwards (1985) *Oxford Journal of Legal Studies* 143; and H. P. Lee (1989) 38 *International and Comparative Legal Quarterly* 890. See K. D. Ewing and C. A. Gearty, *Freedom under Thatcher* (Oxford: Clarendon, 1990), pp.130–136.

32 See House of Commons, *Intelligence and Security Committee*, Standard Note, SN/HA/2178 (29 October 2013).

as the powers of the Committee to call for papers is subject to the veto by the Home Secretary if the information is sensitive. The Prime Minister has a statutory veto over the Committee's examination of ongoing operational matters.

20–060
The Security Services Commissioner provides annual independent reports to Parliament and may give evidence to the Intelligence and Security Committee as well as give interviews to the media and television. The Commissioner's reports are delivered to the Prime Minister who acts as a filter before the release of the report to Parliament. This allows the Prime Minister of the day to censor the contents of reports and clearly this provides an inadequate parliamentary check on the activities of the security services.

20–061
It remains unclear as to how effective the Intelligence and Security Committee is likely to be. The reports contain much redacted material and under current security problems it is likely that the pressures to retain confidential information will intense.

20–062
The Security Service Act 1996 adds a further dimension to the law. The 1996 Act gives freedom to the security services to become involved in the "prevention and detection of serious crime". This inclusion of policing functions brings the activities of the security services into line with what many regarded as present day practice. In response to al-Qaeda and Northern Ireland, the security services have refocused on the nature of domestic terrorism and this in turn has given way to the need for an overarching structure for the UK as a whole. The Metropolitan Police had responsibility for domestic terrorism under the National Domestic Extremism Unit. In 2006 the Serious Organised Crime Agency was established but more recently replaced by the National Crime Agency. There is a Director General, appointed by the Home Secretary entrusted with the duty to make an annual report to the Prime Minister and the Home Secretary.

20–063
As part of the programme to encourage a National Crime Squad the 1996 Act amends the Security Service Act 1989 and the Intelligence Services Act 1994. The Secretary of State may issue in certain specified circumstances general warrants to enter property or to interfere with wireless telegraphy in circumstances that would otherwise be unlawful. This represents a considerable extension of the legal powers of the security service but realistically it may only reflect the reality of how powers were exercised in the past.

20–064
The Regulation of Investigatory Powers Act 2000 has established a new Intelligence Services Commissioner that has oversight of all the intelligence services and powers, to keep under review how both ministers and members of the intelligence services exercise their powers under both Pts II and III of the Regulation of Investigatory Powers Act 2000. There is also an Investigatory Powers Tribunal to hear complaints and make adjudications. The complaints cover all aspects of the security services.

20–065
Reform of the law on surveillance such as telephone tapping and the interception of letters was introduced under the Interception of Communication Act 1985. The *Malone* case[33] established that telephone tapping was in violation of art.8 of the European Convention on Human Rights. The case drew attention to the regulation of such practices carried out in the UK through administrative practices. There was no direct statutory authority for phone

---

33   *Malone v UK*, ECHR, Series A, No.82 (2 August 1985); (1984) 7 E.H.R.R. 14.

tapping. It was argued that s.80 of the Post Office Act 1969 required the Post Office to make available to the police information gained through metering phone calls for the detection of criminal activity.

20-066 The 1985 Act creates a new offence of unlawful interception of communications by post or by means of a public telecommunications system. The offence is widely drawn and may be committed by journalists, newspapers or others in both the public or private sector. The assumption underlying the Act is that the Home Secretary will continue to make use of warrants authorising the interception of communications. Section 2 of the Act authorises such warrants for the purposes of the interests of national security, preventing or detecting serious crime or for the purposes of safeguarding the economic well-being of the UK. Although attempts were made in Parliament to restrict the scope of the issuing of warrants to specific purposes such as the defence of the realm or to prevent subversions of terrorism or espionage, this was rejected in favour of the catch-all quality of the legislation. One troublesome concept is "national security", a phrase that is ideally suited to exclude much judicial scrutiny of the discretion of the Executive.

20-067 Also noteworthy is that the issuing of warrants remains vested in the relevant Secretary of State. In the past there was no judicial or independent element in the decision whether or not to issue a warrant and this has been objected to on the basis that it would be more desirable to subject such a power to judicial control. Since 1966, the Prime Minister has given assurances that the telephones of MPs were immune from interception. The issuing of warrants and the coverage of information obtained in the warrants leaves many critics of the system uneasy. The scope of the warrant may specify a single individual or organisation, but this would not prevent the tapping of many phones over a protracted period of time without any further need to re-apply for a warrant. Bailey, Harris and Jones have noted that there were on average over 500 warrants, the majority for the interception of telephones[34]:

> "Most warrants concerned 'serious crime'. 60% of the warrants requested by the police related to the importation or distribution of drugs. Just under 50% of all warrants issued at the request of the police have resulted directly or indirectly in arrests and in some cases in the recovery of property."

20-068 Under the 1985 Act, there was a Commissioner appointed by the Prime Minister together with a quasi-judicial Tribunal to provide the main complaints procedures. The decision of the Tribunal is final and may not be reviewed by the courts though this may still leave open consideration by the European Convention on Human Rights. The membership of the Tribunal is for a limited fixed period of five years. The Tribunal has powers to determine whether a warrant to intercept information is properly issued under the Act. This refers to the question of whether there are adequate grounds for issuing the warrant and that statutory procedures are complied with. The means adopted to test the validity of the warrant procedure is akin to a court of law when exercising judicial review powers. This leaves considerable latitude with the security services,

---

34   S. H. Bailey, D. J. Harris and B. L. Jones, *Civil Liberties: Cases and Materials* (London: Butterworths, 1995), p.517.

as the courts are reluctant to apply more than a cursory consideration of national security matters. Indeed, on the basis of the *Wednesbury*[35] criteria of unreasonableness, in most cases ministerial discretion will be presumed to conform with the law unless it is so unreasonable that no reasonable Minister could have taken such a decision. The Commission has only found errors in the issuing of warrants of a minor and insubstantial nature. There has not been a finding that a warrant has been issued without cause.

20-069

The Commissioner must report to the Prime Minister on an annual basis. It appears that the remit of the 1985 Act does not cover electronic bugging devices. This leaves open the questions of what controls may exist and whether such devices should be used by the authorities. The Commissioner has three functions and responsibilities under the 1985 Act. First, to keep under review the various functions carried out by the Home Secretary conferred by the Act. Secondly, to keep under review the arrangements for restricting the use of information obtained under the intercepted material. Thirdly, to give assistance to the Tribunal to carry out its statutory functions. These arrangements have now been changed by recent legislation.

20-070

The Police Act 1997 has the limited objective of regulating surveillance that involves entry onto property or interference of property rights This regulates bugging devices where there is an interference in property rights. The Regulation of Investigatory Powers Act 2000 regulates the interception of communications that are made by postal service or telephone. Section 1 provides that it is an offence to "intentionally or without lawful defence to interfere without lawful authority" with any communication in the course of its transmission by means of a public or private telecommunications system in the UK. A warrant may be issued and there is, under Pt III of the Act, provision for an Interception of Communication Commissioner appointed by the Prime Minister, replacing the arrangements under the 1985 Act for a Commissioner. There is also an Intelligence Service Commissioner and an Investigatory Powers Commissioner for Northern Ireland.

20-071

Section 65 creates a Tribunal to hear complaints in respect of matters that fall under the Act. There is also a statutory tort under s.1(3) for any unlawful interception in communication.

The Draft Investigatory Powers Bill 2015/16

Codification of the law to update, consolidate and strengthen the way in which investigatory powers operate in a global context is the main aim of the Investigatory Powers Bill 2015/16. The Bill, published in November 2015 is an ambitious legislative project to place all the investigatory powers of the State into a consolidated form that are available to the security services and intelligence agencies. The Bill addresses all forms of communications and data retrieval. The Bill extends throughout the UK and is an attempt to move the system of security and intelligence into a coherent form.[36] This is a complex area of law as the rules relating to data

20-072

---

35 [1948] 1 K.B. 223; [1947] 2 All E.R. 680 CA.
36 The Wireless Telegraphy Act 2006; the Telecommunications Act 1984; the Police and Criminal Evidence Act 1984; the Terrorism Act 2000; and the Intelligence Services Act 1994.

retention are also part of European Union law.[37] Attempts to legislate in this area are difficult the Data Retention and Investigatory Powers Act 2014 was considered in a judicial review,[38] when s.1 of the Act allowing the Home Secretary to issue a retention notice to a service provider was found to be incompatible with EU law. The decision is under appeal. Part 3 of the Counter-Terrorism and Security At 2015 amended the 2014 Act to enable the Secretary of State to require internet service providers to retain data allowing the authorities to identify the person or device using a particular Internet Protocol (IP) address.

20-073 The Bill follows the outcome of various reports[39] on the subject of terrorism and how communications collection and it is planned that the Bill should be passed and in force in 2016.

20-074 The main parts of the Bill include the lawful interception of communications. This may be undertaken through the use of a targeted warrant interception and its counterpart a targeted examination warrant allowing access to communication data and this may relate to a particular person, organisation or premises or groups of connected subjects. The examination of material and a request for overseas assistance through a mutual assistance warrant provides very wide ranging and defined powers. There is approval through a Judicial Commissioner. Included in the communications may be MPs communications although before this might be authorised the Secretary of State would consult the Prime Minister.[40]

20-075 The Bill also provides extensive powers to obtain communications data through a process of authorisations that applies to a wide variety of law enforcement agencies, regulatory bodies and the NHS. There are specific limitations on the use of the powers. Perhaps the most controversial is Pt 4 of the Bill that allows for the retention of communications data. This will have a major implication for service providers and their responsibilities to gather and maintain a record of communication data. There are powers for the relevant security authorities to seek warrants for targeted interference with equipment in order to ascertain data records and communications. This is an important power for the purposes of security data gathering. Part 6 of the Bill contains details of the use of bulk warrants that may be used for the acquisition of information, its examination and collection. There are also provisions for bulk personal dataset warrants oversight of the main provisions of the Bill includes the setting up of a new Investigatory Powers Commission with Judicial Commissioners, appointed from only people who have held high judicial office. The Investigatory Powers Commissioner will replace the existing Intelligence Services Commissioner, Surveillance Commissioner and Interception of Communication Commissioner. Also included in the Bill are Codes of practice and the right of appeal from the IPC to the Court of Appeal on a point of law.

---

37 See the Draft Retention Directive and the Court of Justice decision in *Digital Rights Ireland* (C-293/12) EU:C:2014:238; [2015] Q.B. 127.
38 *David v SSHD* [2015] EWHC 2092 (Admin); [2016] 1 C.M.L.R. 13.
39 See the Report by David Anderson QC, *A Question of Trust* (June 2015). *Intelligence and Security Committee Press Release* (9 October 2014). White Paper, *Draft Investigatory Powers Bill*, Cmnd.9152 (November 2015). House of Commons Library, *Draft Investigatory Powers Bill*, Briefing Paper, No.7371 (19 November 2015). See David Pannick, "Safeguards provide a fair balance on surveillance powers", *The Times*, 12 November 2015.
40 The Wilson doctrine was an understanding under the previous Prime Minister, Harold Wilson, that MPs phones would be tapped. This has been set aside under the proposals in the Bill.

20-076 There are mixed reactions to the Bill. Its main attraction is that it brings into one organised Bill all the components of surveillance. The use of Parliament scrutiny and oversight through the Intelligence and Security Committee is important but the innovation of having a judicial element in the form of Judicial Commissioners is seen as welcome by some but not sufficient by others.[41]

20-077 The main issues raised in the Bill are likely to be the subject of intense debate in the context of the accountability and balance in defining the public interest and allowing free speech but protecting national security.

D: Press and Media

20-078 The press and media are subject to a wide variety of legal controls over what they may publish or broadcast. Newspapers are subject to the Defence Press and Broadcasting Committee. This Committee was formally referred to as "the D notice system". In 1979–80 the system of D notices was reviewed[42] by the Defence Select Committee and evidence given which indicated that the system was not working effectively. Chapman Pincher, a journalist, had revealed in 1978 that the D notice system was dependent on the Secretary of State indicating whether the story was covered by a D notice and if not then the journalist would not be prosecuted if the story was published. This had gained some press confidence in the system but once the Secretary of State declined to make any implied undertaking the system became virtually unused. As indicated in the discussion of the *Spycatcher* story, the international press makes it more difficult to retain stories within the national boundaries of the UK.

20-079 The Select Committee divided on the issue of whether the D notice system should be reformed. It agreed that some forms of secrecy required control over the press or broadcasting authorities. The Committee concluded that the essence of the D notice should be published as common practice was not to mention the use of the D notice system. After consideration of the Committee's report, the Government decided to retain the D Notice Committee reviewed its operation.

20-080 Today it is known as the Defence Advisory (DA) notices system. DA notices may be addressed to radio, television and national and provincial editors of newspapers. In essence, the system

---

41 David Pannick provides a well-balanced assessment in "Safeguards provide a fair balance of surveillance powers", *The Times* 12 November 2015.

42 3rd Report of the House of Commons Defence Committee, *The D Notice System: Observations Presented by the Secretary of State for Defence*, Cmnd.8129 (1981); 4th Report of the Defence Committee (1982–83), *Previous Recommendations of the Committee*, HC 55 (1982–83); the programme "My Country Right or Wrong", see D. Oliver and D. Kingsford-Smith (eds), *Economical with the Truth* (Oxford: ESC Publishing, 1990); *Justice Report on Privacy and the Law* (1970); The Younger Committee Report, *Report of the Committee on Privacy*, Cmnd.5012 (1972); and *Report of the Committee on Privacy and Related Matters*, Cmnd.1102 (1990).

advises that publication or broadcasting of information would not be in the public interest. The composition of the DA Notice Committee—known as the Defence, Press and Broadcasting Advisory Committee—provides different forms of notices to cover Military Operations; Plans and Capabilities (DA Notice 1); Nuclear and Non-Nuclear Weapons Equipment (DA Notice 2); Ciphers and Secure Communications (DA Notice 3); Sensitive Installations and Home Addresses (DA Notice 4); and finally, UK Security and Intelligence Services and Special Forces (DA Notice 5).

20–081 Broadly drafted and often vague the system provides general advice intended to guide editors and journalists. Even complying with the notices does not remove obligations under the Official Secrets legislation.

20–082 The advantage of the present system is that it allows representatives of the media to consider the matter in a responsible manner. The disadvantage is that there is little openness in how the system actually works and the criteria used are far from clear. A more fundamental weakness of the system was revealed some years ago when the BBC attempted to broadcast a programme on the *Spycatcher* book. The programme had received clearance from the secretary to the D Notice Committee on the basis that it did not provide any material which was a threat to national security. However, the Government sought and obtained injunctions to prevent the broadcast of interviews being held about the programme on the basis that there was a breach of confidence in the disclosure made in the programme. The explanation for the apparent disparity is that the Attorney General based his injunction on breach of confidence whereas the secretary to the D Notice Committee based his clearance on the basis of national security. There is therefore some doubt about the effectiveness of the D Notice Committee when the Government is actively pursuing greater use of civil remedies rather than the use of the criminal law.

20–083 There appears to be a case for maintaining some form of DA Notice. For the purposes of wartime expediency, it would appear to offer a reasonably effective means to preserve some balance between freedom of the press to publish information and the protection of the public interest. It would appear to have become an anachronism, although it is influential with many newspapers and their reporters but in fact largely ignored when the availability of news on an international basis facilitates the dissemination of information so easily available instantaneously on fax machines.

20–084 This raises the important question of the extent to which the right to privacy may exist in English law and how this right may be protected by the courts. The Calcutt Committee in 1990 concluded that the most appropriate definition of privacy might cover[43]:

> "The right of the individual to be protected against intrusion into his personal life or affairs, or those of his family, by direct physical means or by publication of information."

20–085 Following the recommendations of the Calcutt Report the Press Complaints Commission was established in 1991, replacing the Press Council established in 1953. The Commission is a

---

43 Calcutt Committee, *1st Report* (1990).

non-statutory body comprising a chairman and 15 members, one-third of whom are not associated with the press. Any person may complain to the press directly and the Commission may investigate and return findings such as an adverse adjudication which must be published by the newspapers in question. There is no legal obligation to publish and the criticism about the Commission is that it lacks sufficient legal powers and sanctions.

Further reforms of the law have been considered by a second report carried out by the Calcutt[44] Committee. The second report went much further than previous reports by recommending a statutory tribunal to replace the Press Commission. This favoured a move away from voluntary self-regulation towards statutory and legal regulation. The Tribunal might be presided over by a senior judge appointed by the Lord Chancellor with powers to fine and place injunctions on newspapers. In addition, Calcutt recommended that electronic eavesdropping and long-range photography on private property should be prohibited.

The press reacted unfavourably to proposals for tighter regulation. In that light the National Heritage Select Committee recommended that there should be a strengthening of both the civil and criminal law on privacy.[45] The Committee favoured the retention of some form of Press Complaints Commission but replacing the existing Press Complaints Commission with a Press Commission to uphold press freedom. The new commission should have powers to order fines and to order publication of apologies and in suitable cases the award of compensation. An appointed ombudsman to be appointed by the Lord Chancellor and funded by the Treasury is intended to supervise adjudications of disputes, with the statutory power to compel newspapers to print apologies in a particular way, including the power of fines. This is intended to strengthen supervision of the press. The Government rejected the idea of Calcutt's statutory Tribunal but is considering the best way forward in the light of the proposals. Recent newspaper articles on certain government ministers, and the private lives of the Royal Family and other public figures have drawn attention to the need to increase regulation of the press.

The call for tougher press regulation came about after a series of scandals surrounding the widespread use of "phone hacking" by journalists at the News of the World and other British newspapers. Lord Justice Leveson was invited to report on the "culture, practices and ethics of the press". The Leveson Report[46] published on 29 November 2012 made various recommendations for the regulation of the press while maintaining protection of free speech. Leveson's proposals included an element of self-regulation but that it has to be underpinned by statute and be independent. The Government's response was to opt for a new draft Royal Charter and embedded in part under statute. The Enterprise and Regulatory Reform Act 2013 and the Crime and Courts Act 2013 provide such a framework. This will allow there to be exemplary damages on any newspaper not subscribing to the new regulator. Discussion amongst newspapers and politicians led to compromises. There is a Recognition Panel that oversees the Charter established by the Panel under the Royal Prerogative. Major newspapers responded by producing their alternative Royal Charter of their own, and considered by the Privy Council ahead of the

---

44 Calcutt Committee, *2nd Report* (January 1993).
45 Report of the National Heritage Committee, *Privacy and Media Intrusion* (London: HMSO, March 1993).
46 HC Deb (13 July 2011), c.311.

Government's proposed Charter.[47] However, the newspapers own Charter was not accepted and this resulted in the setting up of a new Independent Press Standards Organisation, with the support of some "tabloid" newspapers but not the Broadsheet variety. It is not expected that the new Independent Press Standards Organisation, set up on 8 September 2014 to replace the Press Complaints Commission, will seek royal approval in the form of a charter.

20-089

The current arrangements are far from satisfactory. The Leveson Report[48] recommendations of a fully independent organisation from the publishers has not been realised and the new Independent Press Standards Organisation does not comply with the Leveson independence recommendations. The part that has been implemented namely the Royal Charter has been partly realised. The majority of the press refuse to submit to the Royal Charter and this may require further action in the future.

20-090

The press and media may come under considerable government influence in matters of national security. In the case of broadcasting, fear of prosecution under the Official Secrets Acts may result in television or radio programmes being withdrawn. In the same period as the Ponting trial, Channel 4 withdrew one of its television programmes "20/20 Vision", which contained detailed allegations made by Cathy Massiter about the use of MI5, but after a period of delay the programme was eventually shown.

20-091

The media is also subject to various search and seizure powers either under the Official Secrets Acts or under the ordinary law. For example there is a power for the police to search with a warrant under s.9 of the Official Secrets Act 1911 and this may be applied to discover journalists' information. In 1986, the BBC had commissioned a film series entitled "Secret Society" under the direction of Duncan Campbell, a journalist working in the intelligence field. The programme revealed the cost and extent of a secret Defence Ministry project to put a spy satellite into orbit. The programme was banned and an injunction obtained banning Campbell from publishing the story. A search of Campbell's home and offices, and also the Glasgow offices of the BBC allowed the police to remove substantial numbers of documents. In Scotland, powers under s.9 of the Official Secrets Act 1911 were used, while in England, a warrant was issued under PACE 1984.

20-092

Little of substance was achieved in the use of these powers. Campbell had already published the story in the *New Statesman* before the injunction had been granted. The BBC eventually broadcast an agreed version of the programme.

20-093

The media is also subject to ordinary civil action in the form of actions for libel and defamation. In *Joyce v Sengupta*,[49] the Court of Appeal accepted that a plaintiff could establish more than one cause of action against a defendant and this might include both a claim for defamation and a claim for malicious falsehood. The latter gave rise to the possibility of legal aid, while the former did not. The plaintiff's claim arose out of a newspaper article which asserted that the plaintiff, then in the employment of the royal household, had stolen certain letters of an

---

47 House of Commons Library, *The Leveson Report: Implementation*, SN/HA/6535 (27 March 2014).
48 House of Lords Select Committee on Communications, 3rd Report of Session 2014–15, *Press Regulation: where are we now?*, HL 135 (23 March 2015).
49 *Independent*, 11 August 1992.

intimate character and had handed them to the national press. In such a case, the plaintiff's intention in pursuing a claim in the courts was not dependent on the award of damages but the main means open to a plaintiff to clear her name.

The BBC

20–094

Broadcasting in the UK is also the focus of State influence. Preserving independence for broadcasters is equally important as preserving the freedom of the press. In the case of the British Broadcasting Corporation (BBC), since 1926 it has been constituted by Royal Charter. The BBC provides public broadcasting on a non-commercial basis, funded through a licence fee payable by the public who have television sets. The BBC operates under its Charter, its Licence and Agreement[50] and where appropriate it receives directions under the relevant authority of the Charter or its licence from the Home Secretary. Failure to comply with such a direction might result in the withdrawal of the BBC's licence. The BBC is expected and required to act in a politically impartial manner and its programmes must be consistent with good taste and public opinion. The courts may be invited to consider whether the broadcasting authorities have complied with the standards of good taste. The BBC's Charter was renewed in 2006 but expiries in 2016. The system of Charter is a form of Royal Prerogative and there is a question of whether legislation might be more appropriate. The main sources of revenue are a licence fee but this is seen as a public subsidy in the form of a tax and there is considerable pressure on the BBC to operate effectively and efficiently.[51] For the financial year 2014/15 the BBC's operating costs are £4.9 billion. Its income was £4.8 billion, of which £3.7 billion came from the licence fee revenues.[52] Its mission is to "inform, educate and entertain". Its independence is established since 1926 in its Charter.

20–095

The use of the Home Secretary's directions is rare. In 1927 in the early life of the BBC the corporation was forbidden to broadcast matters involving any religious, political or industrial controversy. There is a convention that the BBC should not derogate from the authority of Parliament in matters of public record. In recent years the televising of both Houses of Parliament has greatly assisted public information on the workings of Parliament and the broadcast of debates and the hearings of select committees is said to educate the public on the workings of democracy. This has been regarded as beneficial to the role of broadcasters.

20–096

In 1988 the Home Secretary announced a ban on the BBC and the independent broadcasting companies from broadcasting the spoken words of members of the IRA or its supporters including Sinn Fein. This ban was intended to prevent public support or sympathy for the IRA or like organisations.

20–097

The Government has been active in opposing programmes that in any way are regarded as promoting the cause of terrorism. Programmes which may be critical of the security

---

50 Cmnd.8313; and Cmnd.8233.
51 House of Commons Library Briefing Paper, *BBC Charter Renewal Number 3416* (3 December 2015).
52 The licence fee is pegged at £145.50 until 31 March 2017.

services may indirectly appear supportive of the terrorist cause and the drawing of boundaries in such cases as to what is or is not permissible is often controversial. The Government has removed the ban on the broadcasting of Sinn Fein in an effort to expedite the peace process. The ban was seen as counterproductive, as the television authorities interpreted the ban as allowing actors' voices to replace the words of Sinn Fein spokesmen while broadcasting interviews.[53]

20-098 The focus of attention on the BBC is on its governance. The 2007 Charter established the BBC Trust and the Executive Board. The two bodies are organised where the main role of the Trust is to set the overall strategic direction of the BBC and also establish a working relationship with the Executive Board. The Executive Board has responsibility for delivering the BBC's services in accordance with the priorities set by the Trust and for all aspects of operational management with the exception of finance. The current Chair of the BBC Trust is Rona Fairhead and the Chair of the Executive Board is Lord Hall, the Director General of the BBC.[54]

20-099 Political parties from all shades of opinion have from time to time alleged bias in reporting and presentation of political views. Particularly when the government of the day is loud in such accusations, the BBC has been placed on the defensive. The style and direction of the BBC is under pressure to provide greater accountability for the expenditure of public money. Quality assurance, better management style and greater attention to business principles have been encouraged in the run-up to the period for the renewal of the BBC's Charter.

20-100 In January 1993, the BBC Chairman and Deputy-Chairman were criticised for allowing the appointment of John Birt as a new Managing Director of the BBC to make his salary payable not under the PAYE scheme but to a company set up for this purpose. Resolution of this problem has called into question the organisation and structure of the management of the BBC.

20-101 Controversy surrounding the reporting of the war in Iraq and the capabilities of Saddam Hussein's weapons in the run-up to the war in 2003 created great tension between the Government of the day and the BBC especially the journalism of the BBC. The Hutton inquiry was highly critical of the BBC and this led to resignations within the BBC and questions about editorial decision-making and accountability.[55]

Charter renewal and the BBC

20-102 There is considerable debate about the future of the BBC. In July 2015, agreement was reached on certain aspects of the BBC's future funding. The licence fee for those over 75s is to be funded by the BBC rather than by the Department of Work and Pensions. This will be roughly equivalent to £200 million. Future BBC funding is to be tied to the consumer price index. This is subject to the conclusion of the Charter review on the purposes and scope of the BBC as well as the BBC demonstrating that it is undertaking efficiency savings equivalent to other parts of

---

53 *R v Secretary of State for the Home Department Ex p. Brind* [1991] 1 A.C. 696; [1991] 2 W.L.R. 588 HL.
54 House of Lords Library, *BBC Future Financing and Independence*, LLN 2015/026 (3 September 2015).
55 Lord Hutton, *Report of the Inquiry into the Circumstances Surrounding the death of Dr. David Kelly CMG* (2004).

the public sector. Legislation is also promised to ensure that using iPlayer is covered by the licence arrangements. The BBC's contribution to the rollout of superfast broadband is to be phased out. There is currently a Green Paper as a means of consultation and public discussion. There are also a number of ongoing reviews. The Perry Review[56] into penalties for failing to have a TV licence, the Clementi review[57] on the best model of governance for the BBC. The BBC is itself preparing for the review of its Charter and the Green Paper. It is likely that the BBC will be regulated by Ofcom with new arrangements for the BBC Trust.

Commercial broadcasting

20–103

In the case of commercial broadcasting, regulation is provided on a statutory basis. The Broadcasting Acts 1990 and 1996 together with the Communications Act 2003 provide the main statutory framework. The Office of Communications (Ofcom) is the main regulatory authority. Its aim is to ensure "the availability throughout the UK of a wide range of television and radio services which (taken as a whole) are both of high quality and calculated to appeal to a wide variety of tastes and interests". Ofcom is also an important standard setting organisation. There is the standard to protect the public from the inclusion of any "offensive and harmful material" in broadcasting services. There are standards to provide overall protection to the public and ensure that there is not unfair treatment in programmes or any unwarranted infringements of privacy by broadcasters. Such obligations are important oversight responsibilities while at the same time ensuring that Ofcom should act as a "buffer" ensuring that commercial television and radio have operational controls form day to day. There is no categorical protection of the independence of broadcasters. Implicitly the law on protecting free speech has to be upheld and certainly art.10 of the ECHR is applicable. Ofcom operates on standard setting and this is achieved through a code to promote statutory objectives. These are detailed covering programme content, advertisements and the overall requirements of impartiality on matters of political or industrial controversy. There is a vaguely expressed but significant requirement that the news is reported with "due accuracy" and that the public should be protected from obscene or offensive material.

20–104

Advertising and sponsorship through syndicated programmes and contracts provide the main revenues for commercial broadcasting. There are clear restraints on political advertising. The term "political advertising" is defined to mean an advertisement inserted by or on behalf of a political organisation, an advertisement directed towards a political end or an advertisement that has a connection with an industrial dispute. In April 2013, the Grand Chamber of the European Court of Human Rights accepted that the ban on political advertising did not amount to a disproportionate interference with the right to freedom of expression.[58]

---

56   David Perry QC under the Deregulation Act 2015.
57   Sir David Clementi, *An independent review of the governance and regulation of the BBC* (16 September 2015).
58   [2006] EWHC 3069 (Admin); [2007] E.M.L.R. 6. *Animal Defenders International v United Kingdom* [2013] E.M.L.R. 28; (2013) 57 E.H.R.R. 21 ECHR.

20-105 There is a standards code and Ofcom is required to establish procedures to deal with complaints if there are complaints. The licence holders are required to comply with the fairness code issued under the Broadcasting Act 1996—this obligation is now vested with Ofcom.

20-106 The Broadcasting Code is the most important standard setting device. It also applies in large part to the BBC. The aim is to balance the broadcaster's rights to freedom of expression with rights that are vested in viewers and listeners. In the case of commercial broadcasters there is also the matter of revenue and the need to engage with commercial advertisers is important. The boundaries set by the Code relating to fairness and standards. The latter includes protecting young people and all members of the public from harmful and offensive material and ensuring that the material likely to encourage disorder or crime is not included in broadcasts. Religion is also addressed in terms of due impartiality. There are specific responsibilities relating to elections and referendums. The responsibility is that due weight has to be given to the major parties during the election period. This includes the main national parties and outside England, to Scotland and Wales to include the principal nationalist parties. There is an overall discretion to ensure that broadcasters must give "appropriate coverage" to other parties and independent candidates with significant views and perspectives.

The prescription of fairness is also applicable to contributors of programmes and the need to have informed consent from participants who take part. The guidance is clear that contributors need to be told of the exact nature of the programme and why they are contributing. Confidentiality and guarantees of anonymity need to be respected and honoured. Aby breach of privacy has to be based on the public interest and its justification made clear that the public interest outweighs the right to privacy.

Ofcom operates a system of complaints but this does not extend to someone who lacks sufficient interest. Complaints are also not considered if the matter of the complaint is part of court proceedings or in Ofcom/s view there is an effective remedy by way of legal action.

20-107 The courts have only been involved in broadcasting challenges in a very limited number of cases.[59] The BBC sits in the position of being a public body and therefore covered by the Human Rights Act 1998 as well as being subject to judicial review.[60] However, in contrast to the limited number of challenges on general issues connected with broadcasting, the courts have been active in addressing issues connected with election issues.[61] The BBC is covered by a Code issued by the BBC Trust and Commercial broadcasting falls under the Ofcom Broadcasting Code under s.333 of the Communications Act 2003.[62]

---

59 *R v Broadcasting Standards Commission Ex p. BBC* [2001] Q.B. 885; [2000] 3 W.L.R. 1327 CA (Civ Div). It was held that a company does have activities even of aprovate nature that require protection from any unwarranted intrusion.
60 For example in *Houston v BBC* 1995 S.C. 433; 1995 S.L.T. 1305 Ct of Session. The BBC was subject to an interim injunction restraining it from broadcasting in Scotland an interview with the BBC three days before the local government elections.
61 Ofcom, *Rules on Party Political and Referendum Broadcasts* (2013). These rules do not apply to the BBC but the BBC Trust agrees a code before each election.
62 See House of Commons Library, *Party Political Broadcasts*, SN/PC/03354 (17 March 2015).

20–108 In common with the BBC, commercial television has found controversy in its desire to broadcast investigative programmes involving terrorist activities and the security services. In 1988, Thames Television broadcast "Death on the Rock", an investigative programme into the shooting of three members of the IRA by members of the SAS in Gibraltar. The programme received criticism from the then-Prime Minister and renewed debate began over whether there had been a shoot-to-kill policy on the part of the security forces. The criticism of the programme resulted in an inquiry into the objectivity and the factual basis of the programme. Programme makers are often under intense pressure to conform to political and other pressures.[63]

20–109 Broadcasters face a climate of opinion which may favour further restrictions on reporting of terrorist activities especially when they involve the activities of the security services. The ban on broadcasting the spoken words of terrorist groups and Sinn Fein has contributed to a greater degree of "self-censorship" within broadcasting. In fact, this has probably led to a more effective system of control than would have been possible through the passage of legislation prohibiting the broadcasting of a wide range of investigative programmes.

E: Freedom of Expression

The Public Interest Disclosure Act 1998 and the Freedom of Information Act 2000

20–110 Freedom of expression is commonly acknowledged to be a fundamental attribute of many Western-style democracies. Because of the absence of any written constitutional protection of this fundamental concept, its existence depends on the interpretation of various laws designed to protect the public including terms of blasphemy, defamation, obscenity and contempt of court. Street summarised the distinctive qualities of civil liberties in the UK[64]:

> "Civil liberties in Britain have been shown to be a patchwork. Some of them rest on the chance that citizens have sued each other and given the opportunity to declare some isolated legal rule. Some rest on

---

63 See *R (Pro-Life Alliance) v BBC* [2003] UKHL 23; [2004] 1 A.C. 185. The question arise over whether or not images of an aborted foetus should be broadcast at the request of the Pro-life alliance but objected to by the broadcasters. The House of Lords had to consider whether the banning of the broadcast amounted to censorship. The House of Lords reversed the Court of Appeal and held by a majority that it was not censorship.
64 H. Street, *Freedom, the Individual and the Law* (Harmondsworth: Penguin Books, 1963), p.307.

> sporadic legislation, often passed to meet some specific emergency real or imaginary. The extent of inroads on certain freedoms rests on the subtleties of ministerial responsibility and the muted insistence of Whitehall to be allowed to govern unhindered."

20-111 Secrecy and confidentiality discussed above operate in a society which is accustomed to legal controls over information in the form of censorship. In that context the criminal law and in certain circumstances the civil law, has developed an extensive jurisdiction over the citizen's freedom to see, hear and read matter which is deemed unsuitable. Such freedoms are constrained on the basis of providing legal restraints justified in the public interest. A difficult balance must be struck in such cases between providing a remedy for the citizen to protect his or her rights and the right of freedom of information for the public. The law may also extend to cover actions for breach of copyright or breach of confidence. This may also form the basis of civil actions which allow for the use of injunctions to restrain publication of the information and for damages by way of compensation.[65]

20-112 The acknowledgment that an open society is in the public interest is in part the reason for the Public Interest Disclosure Act 1998. The Act provides whistle-blowers with limited protection against dismissal or disciplinary action. Protection is provided by reading into the Employment Rights Act 1996 the protections as rights for employees. This means that a person who falls within the category of protection is regarded as unfairly dismissed or whose redundancy is regarded as unfair if based on the fact of disclosure. Not everyone in employment is included the police and security services are excluded. Protection is provided on the basis of the following:

- a protected disclosure is one where on the basis of reasonable belief, a criminal offence has been committed; or a legal obligation has been breached; or that health and safety of a worker has been endangered; or that the environment is likely to be damaged; and

- a qualified disclosure is one where it is made in good faith to the discloser's employer; or in the course of legal advice; or made to a proscribed person such as the Health and Safety Executive; or is of an exceptionally serious nature.

20-113 The Freedom of Information Act 2000 attempts to build on past efforts to promote greater openness in government through the *Code of Practice on Access to Government Information*. Wider use of web pages and the internet by government departments and transparency through Next Steps agencies publishing information on their activities are encouraged. The Act came into force in January 2005 and was gradually phased into law and applies to England, Wales and Northern Ireland. There is an enforceable right to access recorded information held

---

65 Copyright, Designs and Patents Act 1988.

by an estimated 100,000 public sector organisations.[66] The substantive change contained for the first time contained in s.1 is a general right of access to information held by public authorities. Rights under s.1 include the right to know if there is relevant information and, if it exists, the right to be given the information. There is a corresponding duty on public authorities to comply with these rights. Public authorities have been generally defined to cover local and central government and a list in Sch.1 may be further added to or amended by the Secretary of State. There is also a code of practice and Pt 1 of the Act relates to a code of good practice in the keeping, management and destruction of records. There is an Information Commissioner to whom complaints may be submitted and this role assumes responsibilities for the Data Protection Act 1998. However, encouraging this innovation may be, it is provided with restrictions and limitations. There are limits set for the cost of compliance and if the limits are exceeded the public authority may refuse to comply with the request. If the request for information is regarded as vexatious then this may also be a ground for refusal. The Information Commissioner[67] provide empowerment to individuals and through education and engagement with stakeholders advises sand encourages best practice. There is a requirement of an annual report and there is the Information Tribunal to hear appeals against the Information Commissioner.

Pt II of the Act provides details of circumstances where information is exempt from disclosure and the duty to confirm or deny the existence of information does not apply. These are ss.26–29, ss.32–35, ss.38–39, and ss.42–44 of the Act. The range of matters covered includes defence, international relations and relations within the UK, the economy, court and audit records, matters of parliamentary privilege, the formulation of government policy, communications with Her Majesty the Queen, health and safety, the environment, information protected by legal professional privilege, commercial interests and circumstances under s.44 where information may be prohibited from disclosure such as contempt of court.

20–114

The Freedom of Information Act 2000 is a significant legislative intervention that the House of Commons Justice Committee found had contributed significantly to the "enhancement of our democracy".[68] There are many exemptions and safeguards built into the Act but overall the Act has provided useful transparency on the working of government. The Freedom of Information Act allows a Cabinet Minister or the Attorney General to issue a veto which may override the Commissioner or the Tribunal. The Attorney General issued a veto in respect of letters from Prince Charles to various ministers. The Information Commissioner had ruled that disclosure was desirable and this ruling had been upheld by the Tribunal. The Supreme Court decision on the Prince of Wales letters to ministers upheld the decision of the Information Commissioner, and rejected the legality of the decision of the Attorney General to veto the

20–115

---

66 House of Commons Library, *Freedom of Information: changing the law?*, Briefing Paper, No.07400 (17 December 2015).
67 There are a variety of responsibilities that come under the responsibility of the Information Commissioner including: the Data Protection Act 1998; the Data Protection Monetary Penalty Regulations 2010; The Privacy and Electronic Communications (EC Directive) Regulations 2003; and the Information on Spatial Data in Europe Regulations.
68 House of Commons Justice Committee, *Post-legislative scrutiny of the Freedom of Information Act 2000* (3 July 2012).

information being made public.[69] This may well prove to be one of the most significant decisions as it clarifies the importance of transparency favoured by the Act. There is, however, considerable unease about burdens, costs and red tape that might divert resources away from other purposes. There is also concern that the veto exercised by the Attorney General might not be effective in the light of the Supreme Court decision.

20–116
The Government in July 2015 has set up an *Independent Commission on Freedom of Information*[70] under the chairmanship of Lord Burns. *The Independent Commission* has no remit to examine devolved legislation.[71] The Commission is expected to report as soon as possible after the end of January 2016 with two sessions on 20 and 25 January for oral evidence. The Commission is intended to review the operation of the Freedom of Information Act 2000 and consider the balance between transparency, accountability and the need for sensitive information to have robust protection. The Commission has also to consider

> "whether the Act adequately recognises the need for a safe space for policy development and frank advice. The Commission may also consider the balance between the need to maintain public access to information and the burden of the Act on public authorities and whether change is needed to moderate that while maintaining public access to information."

20–117
There are many reactions to the Government's decision to set up the Commission. There are concerns that the Government's intention is to water down the effectiveness of the Act. There are some concerns[72] that fees might be charged and that appeals against requests for information to the First-Tier Tribunal might be charged at full cost. It is argued that the introduction of fees might be a deterrent to making applications. It remains to be seen what the future of the Act will be, but it will be eagerly awaited in terms of setting the balance between confidentiality and transparency—a precondition of democratic decision-making. Overall, Birkinshaw regards the Act as "the most important provision on access to government information and thus on increased openness".[73] The Act has some limitations, in that in s.35 there is protection of the policy making process of decision-making and also there is privacy protection. These are broadly drafted and it remains to be seen how the Act is likely to be interpreted. One important indication of how interpretation may be approached is to be found in *DfES v*

---

69 *R (Evans) v Attorney General* [2015] UKSC 21; [2015] A.C. 1787 Sup Ct.
70 Lord Burns is chair, also included is the Rt Hon Jack Straw, Lord Howard of Lympe, Lord Carlile of Berriew and Dame Patricia Hodgson. There is a public all for evidence and a consultation process. The Commission is expected to report by the end of 2015 but the amount of evidence has included to date over 30,000 submissions.
71 In Scotland there is the Freedom of Information (Scotland) Act 2002.
72 The Ministry of Justice has floated this idea. See House of Commons Briefing Paper No.07400, p.3; and House of Commons Briefing Paper No.4169, *Fees for FOI requests*.
73 P. Birkinshaw, "Regulating Information" in D. Oliver, J. Jowell and C. O'Cinneide (eds), *The Changing Constitution*, 8th edn (Oxford: Oxford University Press, 2015), 378–409 at p.378.

IC and Evening Standard (AP).[74] Information requested including the budgets of schools in England and related information of the Policy Committee. The Tribunal distinguished between implementation of policy and the way policy was analysed. Minutes were not automatically exempted from information but the most sensitive information was protected. This approach allows the Tribunal to assess the information rather than adopt an automatic exemption category. The main matters that have to be considered are the balance between transparency and the weight of the information requested. The timing of the application is also relevant in terms of what is currently in the public interest.[75] The important point is that the scrutiny of information applications from an external perspective allows some consideration of how civil servants and officials may make decisions. Their perceptions of the public interest are not automatically followed or accepted by the Information Commissioner.

Birkinhshaw catalogues some examples where freedom of information applications have proved influential. Examples include: the MPs' expenses saga and other expenses[76]; the legality of the Iraq war; and the role of the Attorney General including disclosures over the dossiers on weapons of mass destruction.[77] Various Cabinet meetings and the ruling that private emails were covered by any disclosure requirements.[78]

20–118

The Evolving Criminal Law

Section 73 of the Coroners and Justice Act 2009 abolished the common law offences of seditious libel and blasphemous libel. The necessity to remove both offences is because they were not needed given the many other offences that may arise particularly a growth in the use of the law of contempt. This is particularly important in respect of publication of material that relates or may be regarded as calculated to prejudice a fair trial.

20–119

There are specific offences such as incitement to racial hatred. Section 17 of the Public Order Act 1986 replaced earlier arrangements under the Race Relations Act 1976 and the earlier the Race Relations Act 1965. Terrorism and the means of propagating or inciting terrorist acts is an important element in public order that is related to free speech. The Terrorism Act 2006 introduced regulation of speech that may be construed as supporting terrorism. Section 1 of the Act applies to any statement that is likely to be understood by some or all of the members of the public to whom it is published as a "direct encouragement or other inducement to them to the commission, preparation, or instigation of acts of terrorism".[79] Statements

20–120

---

74 EA/2006/006.
75 *R (Evans) v IC and MoD* (EA/2006/0064) on the consideration of the public interest at the time of the request. The public interest against disclosure may diminish over time.
76 *Corporate Officer of the HC v IC* [2008] EWHC 1084 (Admin); [2009] 3 All E.R. 403. Now see the Parliamentary Standards Act 2009.
77 *Foreign and Commonwealth Office v IC* (EA/2007/0047).
78 FS50422276 Decision (March 2012).
79 Public under s.20(3)(a) refers to any part of the UK or of a country or territory outside the UK.

may be interpreted as glorifying conduct that should be emulated. Glorification includes any praise or celebration that may be deemed as encouragement.

20–121 Section 2 of the Act addresses terrorist publications and it is an offence to disseminate. The criteria of what is a terrorist publication is very widely defined and it may mean any action or threat of action involving serious damage to property which is designed to influence the government or intimidate the public or a section of the public in order to advance an ideological cause. The breadth of the offence extends outside the UK and under s.2(13) and covers internet publication as well as more traditional forms of publication such a pamphlets or newspapers. Taken together, the way is open for quite a large field of information falling within the definition of terrorist publication. The parameters of the offence under s.2 require proof of intention that the dissemination takes place with the intention that it will have the effect of directly or indirectly encouraging or inducing the commission, preparation or instigation of acts of terrorism.[80] Home Office statistics show that of the 460 people charged with terrorist offences: 16 per cent relate to possession of an article of terrorist purposes; 16 per cent relate to preparation for terrorist acts; ten per cent relate to the collection of information useful for an act of terrorism; and ten per cent relate to fundraising.[81]

20–122 Freedom of Expression under art.10 of the Convention does admit the protection "of a reputation or rights of others". The law of defamation exists to protect citizens or the State against written or spoken words that expose the person to ridicule, or cause hatred or contempt. Defamatory words published in the course of a performance of a play amount to a criminal libel under ss.4 and 6 of the Theatres Act 1968. Defamatory matter usually consists of spoken words, but when written it is libel, and when accompanied by gestures is slander. Libel is writing which tends to vilify a person and bring them into hatred or contempt or ridicule.

20–123 Under s.5 of the Libel Act 1843, publication of a libel is a common law misdemeanour but it is rarely prosecuted. Normally criminal libel is focused only on serious matters. However sometimes, but not always, this may involve the question of whether a breach of the peace is involved. The use of the civil law is more frequent. The remedy usually lies in damages but the use of an interlocutory injunction may be more effective to prevent the dissemination of the offending material. It is a defence to show that the material published was true or was a fair comment or published in the public interest.

20–124 The Defamation Act 1996 categorises different protections in terms of privileged information. Absolute privilege at both common law and statute applies to circumstances whereby no proceedings may be brought in respect of them. Court proceedings or privileged statements such as the proceedings of the House of Commons will not allow for a civil action to be taken, but may well involve investigation by the Committee of Privileges should there be any abuse of the privileges of the House of Commons. Absolute privilege attaches to the judicial proceedings and communication between Officers of State.

20–125 Qualified privilege attaches to: the communications between members of the public and

---

80 See *R v Rahman* [2008] EWCA Crim 1465; [2008] 4 All E.R. 661.
81 Home Office Charges and offences relating to the Terrorism Act 2006 (2014).

MPs; between MPs and Ministers; in the proceedings of public meetings of local councils; and in the administration of tribunals and inquiries. Before the Human Rights Act 1998 came into force, the attempt to establish a new category of qualified privilege failed when Mr Reynolds, the former Irish Taoiseach (Prime Minister), sued the *Sunday Times* over a story suggesting he had lied to the Oireachtas (Irish Parliament) and misled his Cabinet colleagues. The jury found that the newspaper had not acted maliciously in publishing the story but found that the statements were defamatory and untrue. In the event he received damages. There is reluctance to develop new categories of qualified privilege. It will be difficult for the courts to balance the protections under art.10 of the Convention and the law on defamation.[82]

In *Loutchansky v Times (No.2)*[83] the Court of Appeal considered the question of qualified privilege within the context of whether there was a duty on journalists to publish defamatory words at large; the standard to be applied is that of responsible journalism. If the publication attracted qualified privilege this would provide publishers with a complete defence. However, in assessing journalists' standards, the court should consider that journalists should be rigorous and not lax in their approach to publication. However, it was important not to set the standard so high that newspapers would be unable to discharge their proper functions.

20–126

The Defamation Act 2013

The Defamation Act 2013 came into force on 1 January and introduced new arrangements relating to freedom of expression and the law on libel. Section 1 of the Act makes it a precondition of any libel that there should be serious harm, thus a publication will not be regarded as defamatory unless its publication has caused or is likely to cause serious harm to the reputation of the claimant. Claims made by bodies which trade for profit the threshold will not be met unless the publication has caused or is likely to cause serious financial loss. The defence of fair comment has been replaced by a new defence of honest opinion. There are three conditions that the defendant has to meet in order to rely on the defence, namely: that the statement complained of was a statement of opinion; that the statement complained of indicated whether in general or specific terms the basis of the opinion and that an honest person could have held the opinion on the basis of any fact which existed at the time the statement was published; or anything asserted to be a fact in a statement published before the statement complained of.[84]

20–127

Section 4 of the Act provides a new public interest defence, This puts into statutory form the decision in *Reynolds v Times Newspapers*[85] The defendant has to show that the statement was or formed part of a statement on a matter of public interest and that the defendant reasonably believed that publishing the statement complained of was in the public interest. The defence contains two elements that the defendant believed was in the public interest at the

20–128

---

82 *Loutchansky v Times Newspapers Ltd* [2001] EWCA Civ 536; [2002] Q.B. 321.
83 [2001] EWCA Civ 1805; [2002] Q.B. 783.
84 House of Commons Library, *The Defamation Act 2013*, Standard Note, SN/HA/6801 (21 January 2014).
85 [2001] 2 A.C. 127; [1999] 3 W.L.R. 1010 HL.

time of publication and that an objective element as established was a reasonable one. This is in the context of a common law doctrine of reportage namely that there should be neutral reporting of attributed allegations and not simply the adoption of the allegations by the newspaper. A reasonable belief may be established even though the publisher as not attempted to verify the truth of the allegations.

20-129 Section 5 has created a new defence for operators of websites hosting the third party content. The website operator must be able to show that they did not post the statement and follow a process designed to facilitate contact between the claimant and the author of the statement, in order that the clamant can pursue a claim against the author of the directly. If the website operator has failed to follow the set procedure and time limits then there is potential liability or the content.[86]

20-130 Section 6 of the Act extends the defence of qualified privilege to peer-reviewed material in scientific or academic journals. The defence is not applicable when it is shown that it is made with malice. The operation of absolute and qualified privilege has been so defined. There is also, under s.8, a single publication rule that prevents action for defamation being brought in relation to publication of the same material by the same publisher after a one-year limitation period from the date of the first publication of that material. This was introduced as a reflection of modern publishing and how it works in a practical world of modern downloading of publications. Section 11 of the Act removes the presumption in favour of jury trials in defamation cases.[87]

Contempt of court

20-131 Contempt of court provides protection for the administration of justice to ensure that it is free from interference and obstruction. The fear of contempt proceedings may cause newspapers or the media not to publish or broadcast the details of their stories and this may interfere with the freedom of expression. A distinction is drawn by the English courts between civil and criminal contempt: In the case of civil contempt, this may arise in disobedience of a court order such as an injunction. Criminal contempt may arise where there are publications prejudicial to a fair trial or civil proceedings, publications which interfere with the course of justice, contempt in the face of the court or acts which interfere with the course of justice. Newspapers may often find that contempt proceedings are used against them. In *Attorney General v Times Newspapers Ltd*,[88] the House of Lords considered contempt proceedings arising out of the publication by the *Sunday Times* of a series of investigative articles relating to the drug Thalidomide. The House of Lords held that the Attorney General was the proper person to institute contempt

---

86 The Defamation (Operators of Websites Regulations 2013. See House of Commons, *The Defamation Act 2013*, Standard Note, SN/HA/6801 (21 January 2014), pp.6–7.
87 There are also important amendments in terms of costs and their control through the Civil Justice Council.
88 [1974] A.C. 273; [1973] 3 W.L.R. 298 HL.

proceedings and that injunctions could be granted to restrain publication of any articles which may be prejudicial to a fair hearing of the case.

The law of contempt may severely inhibit the freedom of the press to publish articles. Some reform but not codification of the common law rules of contempt was provided in the Contempt of Court Act 1981. This followed recommendations for reform of the law, after the Phillimore Committee Report[89] in 1974 and after the Thalidomide case was considered by the European Court of Human Rights, where the court held[90] that art.10 of the Convention which concerns the right to freedom of expression had been infringed and the restrictions imposed by the injunction were not necessary in a democratic society.

Newspapers may attempt to protect their sources of information. In the case of Sarah Tisdell, the civil servant who copied documents relating to the defence arrangements for the reception of cruise missiles at RAF Greenham Common, and leaked the information to the *Guardian* newspaper, the identification of Tisdell followed after an investigation of the leak. The Government instituted proceedings for the return of the documents used by the newspaper. Section 10 of the Contempt of Court Act 1981 provides that the court may not require disclosure of information "unless it be established to the satisfaction of the court that disclosure is necessary in the interests of justice or national security or for the prevention of disorder or crime". The Court of Appeal required the newspaper to return the documents which enabled the identity of Sarah Tisdell to be known and she was later successfully prosecuted. Later on the basis of the legal principles involved, the newspaper appealed to the House of Lords.[91] Lord Diplock pointed out that s.10 did not contain any reference to "the public interest". A majority of 3 to 2 concluded that the need to find the identity of the person who leaked the documents was in the national interest. The claim of national security appears sufficiently strong to provide justification for the courts to require disclosure of information by the press. In the *Tisdell* case, national security was accepted by the courts on the basis of an affidavit sworn by the Ministry of Defence establishment officer that national security required the return of the leaked documents.

The courts have accepted that on general principle a liberal interpretation should be given to s.10. However, Lord Bridge in *X v Morgan-Grampian Publishers Ltd*[92] noted that in the balance to be struck between non-disclosure and disclosure, the courts would consider whether the information was obtained legitimately ("this will enhance the importance of protecting the source"), whereas if the information is obtained illegally, this will diminish "the importance of protecting the source", unless there are counterbalancing factors such as "a clear public interest in the publication of the information, as in the classic case where the source has acted for the purpose of exposing iniquity".

In this area, the courts focus their attention on the legality and the motives behind the giving of information to newspapers. The question of the content of the material, its reliabil-

---

89 Cmnd.5794 (1974).
90 *Sunday Times v UK* [1979] 2 E.H.R.R. 245 ECHR.
91 *Secretary of State for Defence v Guardian Newspapers Ltd* [1985] A.C. 339; [1984] 3 W.L.R. 986 HL.
92 [1991] 1 A.C. 1; [1990] 2 W.L.R. 1000 HL.

ity and whether, on the merits of the information contained in the material, disclosure of the source of information is in the public interest appears a secondary consideration.

20–136 Contempt of court protects the deliberations of jurors, the interference with witnesses and the course of justice. All are protected by the courts as part of their role in preventing any intentional contempt. In the case of jury deliberations, contempt of court proceedings were instituted after publication in the *New Statesman* of an interview carried out with a member of the jury in the trial of Jeremy Thorpe and others. Publications prejudicial to a criminal trial or civil proceedings are likely to fall within the remit of contempt.[93]

20–137 Journalists are aware of the potential problems that may arise when required to disclose their sources. Section 19 of the Terrorism Act 2000 may apply; thus this has the potential to restrict freedom of expression. There is a defence available under s.19(3) where there might be a reasonable excuse for not making the disclosure, for example if one's life is in danger but the scope of the defence is uncertain. Restrictions on freedom of expression that fall under s.19 must be read to be consistent with art.10 of the Convention.

20–138 Media attention in terms of phone hacking allegations and the subsequent Leveson inquiry into the press has increased tension between the media and the government. There have been some recent cases, prompted by intervention by the Attorney General in respect of press reporting of legal cases. Pre-trial publicity may be prejudicial to a fair trial. In *Attorney General v MGN Ltd*,[94] after a suspect was arrested on suspicion of murder considerable media attention focused on the suspect and this led to many press reports about the man's character. The man was not charged with any offence and the abuse of the man's character took place when proceedings were being actively considered. This was held to be a breach of s.2(2) of the 1981 Act. Similarly, a case was taken against Associated Newspapers Ltd over the press coverage of a murder trial, while the jury was still considering their verdict against the same defendant in another trial. In *Attorney General v Associated Newspapers Ltd*,[95] a contempt of court was found against several newspapers when they published an account of the conviction in the first trial. The holding of contempt was upheld but the proceedings in the second trial had to be halted and discontinued. There is a growing number of cases where the courts have taken a robust approach to requiring the disclosure of sources and information.[96] There are many instances when newspapers have had to reveal and help identify their sources even though the view of the Strasbourg Court may not be consistent with the approach taken by the UK courts.[97]

20–139 One area of protection where sensitive information has to be protected is the family courts where disclosure of information relating to the proceedings of the family court can have serious

---

93 *Attorney General v New Statesman* [1981] Q.B. 1; [1980] 2 W.L.R. 246 Div Ct. Contempt of Court Act 1981 ss.2, 32 and Sch.1. *Attorney General v News Groups Newspapers Plc* [1989] Q.B. 110; [1988] 3 W.L.R. 163 QBD. *Attorney General v Associated Newspapers Group Plc* [1989] 1 W.L.R. 322; [1989] 1 All E.R. 604 QBD.
94 [2011] EWHC 2074 (Admin); [2012] 1 W.L.R. 2408.
95 [2012] EWHC 2029 (Admin); [2012] A.C.D. 98.
96 See *British Steel Corporation v Granada Television Ltd* [1981] A.C. 1096; [1980] 3 W.L.R. 774 HL.
97 *John v Express Newspapers* [2000] 1 W.L.R. 1931; [2000] 3 All E.R. 257; *Broadmoor Hospital v Hyde* Times, March 18, 1994; Independent, March 4, 1994; and *Goodwin v UK* (1996) 22 E.H.R.R. 13 ECHR.

consequences.[98] The rules on confidentiality may also hide information that may help detect any miscarriage of justice. Drawing the line between opening up the courts to more public disclosure but protecting important confidentiality is complicated and a difficult decision to be made. There is an ongoing consultation process that is intended to ensure that there is an appropriate discussion of the issues.[99]

F: Summary and Conclusions

20-140 For many centuries, the climate of secrecy has been endemic to the culture of government in the UK.[100] Yet this must be set against a background of what many perceive to be a remarkably open and free society. This apparent contradiction appears to come from the fact that the UK had much less formal protection of fundamental rights and freedoms when compared to international standards. This situation is slowly changing. Reforms have been introduced in 2013 to regulate the Secret Services. The Freedom of Information Act 2000 and the Data Protection Act 1998 provide greater public access to information than in the past. The White Paper, *Open Data* (2012) is also important and the Human Rights Act 1998 has also contributed in creating a rights culture. However, there is no room for complacency. A major obstacle towards greater openness comes from the private sector and the need to preserve confidential commercial information which is market sensitive and to balance disclosure that is in the public interest. It is clear that access to information is a key element in any democratic system. There is a perceptible change in the direction of greater openness as demonstrated by many new initiatives, not least the greater use of electronic information and websites.

20-141 It is also clear that there are many uncertainties surrounding freedom of speech. The freedom of information is the subject of review; the regulation of the press largely unresolved and the BBC's Charter has to be renewed. Overarching the entire subject of freedom of information are issues surrounding national security and the prevention of terrorism.

20-142 Maintaining the rule of law and at the same time protecting the State is an ongoing debate. It is complex and often complicated and poses difficult challenges for policy makers and politicians. It is easy to respond to the latest terrorist threat or attack and make policy choices as a reaction to the latest public concern. This is understandable but may lead in unintended directions that maybe short term and counterproductive.

---

98 Family Procedure Rules 2010 (SI 2010/2955).
99 *Transparency in the Family Courts* January 2014 and *Transparency—the Next Steps* (August 2014). House of Commons Library, *Confidentiality and openness in the family courts: current rules and history of their* reform, Briefing Paper, No.07306 (29 September 2015).
100 See Christopher Moran, *Classified Secrecy and the State in Modern Britain* (London: Harper Collins, 2015).

SECRECY, FREEDOM OF EXPRESSION AND THE STATE

Freedom and security[101] are easily convoluted just as authoritarian government and democratically elected government[102] may sit uneasily together—the one masking the actions of the other. This may cause confused thinking that in the end may threaten the very nature of democracy upon which our liberties ultimately depend. The fickle nature of public opinion and the politics of the day may not appreciate the long term implications of how transparency and governing underpins accountability that is necessary in a democratic state.

Further Reading

C. Moran, *Classified Secrecy and the State in Modern Britain* (Cambridge: Cambridge University Press, 2013).

M. Hastings, *The Secret War: Spies, Codes and Guerrillas 1939–1945* (London: Harper Collins, 2015).

P. Birkinshaw, *Freedom of Information, The Law, the Practice and the Ideal*, 3rd edn (London: Weidenfeld & Nicolson, 2001).

P. Birkinshaw, "Regulating Information" in J. Jowell, D. Oliver and C. O'Cinneide (eds), *The Changing Constitution*, 8th edn (Oxford: Oxford University Press, 2015), pp.378–408.

P. Coppell, *Information Rights: Law and Practice*, 4th edn (Oxford: Hart, 2014).

---

101 Dimitrios Kyritsis, "Constitutional Review in Representative Democracy" (2012) 32(2) *Oxford Journal of Legal Studies* 297–324.
See Paul Craig, *Administrative* Law, 7th edn (London: Sweet and Maxwell, 2012), pp.628–636; and G. Huscroft "Constitutionalism from the Top Down" (2007) 45 *Osgoode Hall L.J.* 91.
John Gardner, *Can there be a written Constitution?*, Legal Research Papers Series, Paper No.17/2009, University of Oxford (May 2009); Kate Malleson, "The evolving role of the Supreme Court" (2011) *Public Law* 754; T.R.S. Allan, "Common Law reason and the Limits of Judicial Deference" in D. Dyzenhaus (ed), *The Unity of Public Law* (Oxford: Hart, 2004), p.7; and T. R. S. Allan, "Human Rights and Judicial Review: A Critique of 'Due Deference'" [2006] *C.L.J.* 671. See the useful discussion Jo Eric Khushai Murkens, "The quest for constitutionalism in UK public law discourse" (2009) *Oxford Journal of Legal Studies* 427; J. Jowell, "Judicial Deference and Human Rights: A Question of Competence" in P. Craig and R. Rawlings (eds), *Law and Administration in Europe: Essays in Honour of Carol Harlow* (Oxford: Oxford University Press, 2003).

102 T. J. Pempel (ed), *Uncommon Democracies: The One-Party Dominant Regimes* (Ithaca, NY: Cornell University Press, 1990); Arend Lijphart, *Democracies: Patterns of Majoritarian and Consensus Government in Twenty One Countries* (New Haven, CT: Yale University Press, 1984); and Jean Blondel, "Party Systems and patterns of Government in Western democracies" (1968) 1(2) *Canadian Journal of Political Science*, pp.180–203.

21

Public Law in the Twenty-First Century

A: Introduction

The final chapter in the book draws together an overall analysis about the future of public law in the UK, taking account of ongoing major constitutional change amidst a period distinguished by major uncertainties and challenges for the study of public law. Traditionally, the UK has followed an history-based constitution that has accommodated institutional and legal change, while formally maintaining degrees of continuity that from time to time faces re-adjustments to cope with reforms and modern developments.[1] The election of the Labour Government in 1997 brought constitutional reforms and these have been continued, albeit in many different directions, under a five-year period of Conservative-led Coalition Government and now under a Conservative Government, elected since May 2015.[2] Constitutional changes remain much in evidence in a time of marked economic and political uncertainty.

21-001

Overarching political considerations dominate much discussion about UK institutions and their potential for reform. This follows a developing pattern of constitutional reform that began at the end of the last century. Significant reforms under the Labour government included the coming into force of the Human Rights Act 1998, the creation of a new Supreme Court for the UK that acts as a final appellate court covering a range of matters including Human Rights and as a constitutional court involving devolution issues to the different nations, in Scotland, Wales and Northern Ireland. Reform of the House of Lords, and various changes to the way Parliamentary select committees operate including the election of chairs of select committees are also much in evidence. The Conservative-led Coalition Government from 2010–2015 contributed its own constitutional framework. This included the Fixed-Term Parliament Act 2011,

21-002

---

1 Nevil Johnson, *Reshaping the British Constitution: Essays in Political Interpretation* (Basingstoke: Palgrave Macmillan, 2014).
2 Vernon Bogdanor, *The Coalition and the Constitution* (Oxford: Hart, 2011).

the Localism Act 2011 and the European Union Act 2011, respectively introducing: five year fixed-term parliaments; greater potential autonomy to local authorities; and the use of a referendum to define the UK's relationship with the EU. The results of the Scottish referendum—which have led to substantial devolution to Scotland, Wales and Northern Ireland—are likely to have profound effects on the UK. The election of a majority Conservative government in May 2015 with election promises on renegotiation of the UK's membership of the EU, an in/out referendum and reform of the Human Rights Act 1998 or its replacement by a British Bill of Rights signal further substantial constitutional changes for the future.

21-003 Uncertainty surrounds many aspects of the future of the UK's constitution. There is uncertainty over EU membership and the future of the Human Rights Act 1998. The referendum decision in June 2016 to leave the EU will have considerable constitutional implications for the UK.

Reform of the House of Lords ebbs and flows. The Strathclyde Review[3] published In December 2015 considers the role of the House of Lords and the relationship between the Houses of Common and Lords.[4] The review arose after, on 26 October 2015, the House of Lords passed two separate amendments to the Government's motions to approve Statutory Instruments to implement their policy on tax credits. The decision of the House of Lords led to questions about whether the House of Lords had acted within existing convention regarding statutory instruments and financial privilege. Lord Strathclyde's review recommended that the Lords' powers over statutory instruments should be limited to one of delay with the Commons being able to insist on a Statutory Instrument following a Lords' defeat. Also included in the recommendations was the possibility of a Commons-only procedure for statutory instruments.

21-004 There are profound implications for the future role of the House of Lords and consideration of the Strathclyde review will inevitably involve discussion of the composition, role and functions of the House of Lords, particularly appointments and size of the Chamber. Membership of the House of Lords has steadily increased, making Parliament one of the largest in the world. Membership of the EU is likely to be highly contested in the planned in/out referendum before 2017 with uncertain outcomes. The possibility of a British Bill of Rights or abolished/ amended Human Rights Act 1998 is also being considered. There is discussion of the possibility of creating a new Constitutional Court and the emergence of a national sovereignty that unilaterally declares that the UK is sovereign.

21-005 Fundamental electoral reform is unlikely but remains an important issue to be resolved especially in relation to the funding of political parties and the conduct of elections. New planned boundary changes are likely to have political significance. The process of setting MPs pay and expenses based on a system of self- adjudication of MPs pay and expenses having failed, there is a new process of regulation through an independent regulatory system under the Independent Parliamentary Standards Authority (IPSA). IPSA struggles to gain acceptance in the political debate about the setting of salaries. Substantially more devolved powers to

---

3   Lord Strathclyde, *The Strathclyde Review: Secondary legislation and the primacy of the House of Commons*, CM 9177 (17 December 2015).
4   House of Commons Library, *Conventions on the relationship between the Commons and the Lords*, Briefing Paper, No.5996 (7 January 2016).

Scotland after the independence referendum in 2014 and further devolved powers to Wales and Northern Ireland as well as the English regions has raised questions about English Votes for English laws. This important issues remains to be fully worked out. The value and case for and against a written constitution has re-emerged but it is unclear with what results.

The shadow of the 2008 financial crisis[5] hangs over the budget deficit, bringing into question the role of the state, the extent of public spending and the economic face of the constitution that functions to regulate utilities, financial institutions and determines the size of the public sector. Austerity budgeting is gradually re-shaping the size, role and the functions of the state. In 2014 the UK's current account deficit was £106 billion—equivalent to 5.9 per cent of GDP—the highest since records began in 1948.

Events often determine constitutional issues. In the Autumn of 2015 the decision to bomb Syria took place against an intense Parliamentary debate and political disagreement. Uncertainty surround the outcome and findings of the long awaited Chilcot inquiry into the war in Iraq. This includes the time-scale of its publication which is promised for the Summer of 2016. Inquiries in general have come under considerable pressure, not least the Independent Inquiry into Child Abuse under a New Zealand judge, Goddard J. Parliament and its role in scrutiny of the executive is highly dependent on the work of MPs and their ability to withstand party allegiances.[6]

Assessing the future is particularly difficult. While there is overwhelming historical evidence of adaptation in the way the UK's public law has developed there is also increasing concern that instability in the major political parties and voter apathy may cause a vacillating and unchartered path for the UKs parliament and structures. There are also changes in the political parties and their relationship to each other with internal party political disagreements spilling over into the way in which Parliament functions. Inherent flexibility is one of the enduring characteristics of the Constitution. It has served the country well but this may change when confronted by doubts about EU membership. It is also not certain that the existing unitary constitution will endure as pressures for Scottish independence intensifies[7] amidst vocal concerns from voters in England that their needs are not being addressed. The Diceyan doctrine of the sovereignty of Parliament[8] remains remarkably resilient and adaptable to the UK's membership of the EU. At the same time there is considerable doctrinal debate about the future of public law and the rule of law. Normative and analytical approaches to public law are being contested especially over the role of sovereignty,[9] judicial review and administrative law. Parliament's role in holding the executive to account remains problematic and public confidence in parliamentary institutions low.[10] Much is unsure; we are in a time of major constitutional change.

---

5   House of Commons Library, *Background to the July 2015 Budget*, Briefing Paper, No.07244 (3 July 2015).
6   Anthony King and Ivor Crewe, *The Blunders of our Governments* (London: Oneworld, 2014).
7   C. D. Foster, *British Government in Crisis* (Oxford: Hart, 2005).
8   Michael Gordon, *Parliamentary Sovereignty in the UK Constitution* (Oxford: Hart, 2015).
9   T. R. S. Allan, *The Sovereignty of Law: Freedom, Constitution and Common Law* (Oxford: Oxford University Press, 2013). Also see Stuart Lakin, "Defending and Contesting the Sovereignty of Law: The Public Lawyer as Interpretivist" (2015) 78(3) *Modern Law Review* 549–570.
10 K. S. Ziegler, D. Baranger and A. Bradley (eds), *Constitutionalism and the Role of Parliaments Studies of the Oxford Institute of European and Comparative Law* (Oxford: Hart: 2008).

B: Continuity and Change—the Developing Constitution

21-009 A glance at how the UK's constitution has developed provides a useful insight into how constitutional principles evolve. In the absence of a written Constitution, continuity and change remain as enduring characteristics of constitutional arrangements within the UK for many centuries. Each century may be seen to have contributed to changes in public administration and in the constitution. The seventeenth century curtailed growth in the Royal Prerogative and developed an administrative system separate from the judiciary and episcopal influence. The eighteenth century reduced corruption among office holders and sought greater efficiency in the system of public administration. The nineteenth century, under the influence of the Northcote-Trevelyan reforms, introduced into the civil service greater professionalism and selection on merit. It also began a system of financial control for the accounting and authorisation of expenditure by Parliament that has endured.

21-010 The Committee on Standards in Public Life (formerly known as the Nolan Commission), provided codes and principles to apply to the behaviour of MPs, ministers and others in public life. Broadly, the Committee adopted a non-statutory approach to the setting of standards. Eventually this led to the Parliamentary Commissioner for Standards, created in 1995. This role has changed over time and recently comes within Standing Order No.150 (7 January 2013). Related to the role of the Commissioner is the Register of Members' Financial Interests.

21-011 The reality of MP corruption has signally changed attitudes to self-regulation. Fraudulent expenses claims in 2009 resulted in successful prosecutions of the Theft Act 1968. Significantly, the Parliamentary Standards Act 2009 provides a statutory structure for salaries and allowances with a new structure for salaries and allowances as well as a new regulatory body, The Independent Parliamentary Standards Authority (IPSA). The latter has adopted new and more robust arrangements for expenses intended to improve accountability and address public confidence in the system. This remains a work in progress.

Constitutional reforms and future directions

21-012 The UK's current constitutional arrangements are very much a product of the constitutional reforms and the policy underlying much of thinking behind the Labour Government in 1997, summed up in the phrase "modernisation". This term became a recurrent theme of many White Papers[11] and government documents covering central government, the civil service and the development of new regulation for privatised utilities. Examples include shifting the role of local government to a more community-based focus and the creation of a best value concept under the Local Government Act 1999.

---

11   *Modernizing Government*, Cmnd.4310 (1999).

21-013 Reforms introduced in 1998 on devolution to Scotland, Wales, Northern Ireland, London and some of the English regions have created an asymmetrical form to the Constitution. Under these arrangements, the sovereignty of Parliament is retained, while local administration is empowered through directly elected assemblies. Devolution increasingly rewards devolved nations with additional powers, especially since the Scottish referendum in 2015.

21-014 On human rights, Parliament tacitly accepted an accretion of judicial power—much of it judge-led, as well as judge-designed. Despite many concerns to the contrary, judicial interventions between the courts and Parliament has been remarkably conciliatory— especially when interpreting ss.3 and 4 of the Human Rights Act in the exercise of judicial discretion whether or not to issue a declaration of incompatibility.[12] Nevertheless, an increase in judicial power has been accomplished through innovative ideas and thinking about the development of judicial review and its application to the ordinary citizen. The transformation of judicial power has also involved assimilation of many European elements into UK law, including the enactment of the Human Rights Act 1998, incorporating most of the European Convention on Human Rights. In matters concerning the EU, the judiciary and not the UK Parliament has the final say.

21-015 The 2008 financial crisis, austerity and large scale public debt has resulted in a major decrease in public funding and a reduction, under the Coalition government and subsequent Conservative Government, in public spending. Economic austerity, characterised the period from 2010–2015 and is set to continue. The UK's current account deficit in 2014 of £106 billion, almost 5.5 per cent of GDP, is the largest since records began in 1948.[13] Consequently, public sector spending costs and a re-drawing of the boundaries between public and private in favour of more private sector engagement has changed the constitutional landscape of the UK. There is an increasingly critical analysis of existing laws and institutions and scepticism in the present constitutional arrangements has highlighted a number of specific areas of concerns, including the growth in judicial review and in the legal aid system provided for many to take action in the courts.

21-016 Parliament and the status of MPs has been greatly diminished by the MPs expenses scandal and this continues to set a framework about how the media and public opinion may be formed. There is concern that parliamentary control over government has been considerably weakened with the growth in, and the strength of, party government. Modern government, if endowed with a large majority, is said to have become insensitive to constitutional proprieties and resilient to criticism that is not weighted in parliamentary votes. Questions about the meaning and effectiveness of accountability over government have become an important theme in recent constitutional writing. One concern is that the "Next Steps" reforms in the civil service have moved institutions under democratic accountability to services commercially accountable to managers. It is questioned whether public services can be made commercially accountable. Is this form of accountability adequate? In theory, it is one that localises agency responsibility but in practice may weaken ministerial accountability because of its isolation

---

12　See *R (Chester) v Secretary of State for Justice* [2013] UKSC 63; and [2014] A.C. 271; *R (Nicklinson) v DPP* [2014] UKSC 38; [2015] A.C. 657.
13　House of Commons, *Background to the July 2015 Budget*, Briefing Paper, No.07244 (3 July 2015).

from responsibility for any particular agency. There is also the broader issue of whether government should be treated as a business? This tendency to emphasise the corporate image of government may enhance management accountability but may lessen the importance of parliamentary scrutiny and political decision-making.

21-017 There is a predisposition in every political party once in government to begin tinkering with existing constitutional arrangements. Often this is ad hoc but in the current climate of fundamental change and re-alignment, it is important that time is spent in evaluating the consequences of change and their effect on the traditional systems of checks and balances. Public law must meet that challenge and consider future directions.

C: A Written Constitution for the UK?

21-018 Historically, in many countries, the introduction of a written constitution has usually arisen out of a crisis, some form of political upheaval or an attempt by newly independent countries to establish independence through international recognition of the government and institutions. Any apparent "crisis" in the UK's Constitution would appear to fall short of the criteria offered by any historical examples. Few countries appear to reform existing constitutional arrangements through a thoughtful reflection on its shortcomings and a peaceful introduction of reforms to placate any discontent. At the same time, political discontent over the UK's constitutional arrangements may argue for reform, including some form of a written constitution.

21-019 Demands for a written constitution are long standing but their popularity ebbs and flows, despite the fact that they have attracted from time to time a wide spectrum of opinion raging from the Liberal Democrats,[14] the Institute of Public Policy Research and from the Charter 88 movement of many years ago. Contemporary writing of the 1980s and 90s is reminiscent of writing in the 1970s and even past diagnosis of the post-war period.[15] The popular imagination has not so far been attracted to a written constitution and the media are often sceptical. The House of Commons Political and Constitutional Reform Committee[16] published a codified UK Constitution with an assortment of accompanying draft Bills and Codes in 2015. The publication coincided with the celebration of eight hundred years since *Magna Carta* (1215). *Magna Carta* served an important purpose of addressing the political and social problems of

---

14 D. Brack (ed), *"We the people . . .": Towards a Written Constitution* (Liberal Democrat Publications, 1990); F. Mount, *The British Constitution Now* (London: Mandarin, 1993); and Institute of Public Policy Research, *The Constitution of the United Kingdom*, (London: IPPR, 1991). Also see R. Blackburn (ed), Constitutional Studies (London: Mansell, 1992).
15 D. Oliver, *Government in the United Kingdom* (Milton Keynes: Open University Press, 1991), pp.3–40.
16 The House of Commons Political and Constitutional Reform Committee, *Prospects for codifying the relationship between central and local government*, HC-656, 2012–13 (29 January 2013).

the time providing a mechanism for the King to continue in power albeit under accountability to the rule of law. *Magna Carta* provides historical precedent that has endured until the present day. The value of liberty and freedom ascribed to the *Magna Carta* continues to inspire generations and foster faith in civil and religious liberties as well as the law itself. The potential for a written constitution of some form may find new appeal. However well the academic case is made to justify a written or codified constitution, the decision rests with politicians and Parliament. The dominance of political perspectives makes it difficult to find an independent perspective that articulates legal and constitutional analysis of the case for an against a written constitution.

One argument in favour of a written constitution is that it might be a means to address a tendency for centralised power that has encouraged stronger central government as preferable to weak local authorities.[17] There are, however, attempts to address over-centralised powers through an increase in local authority autonomy. The Localism Act 2011 is a neat blend of the previous government's policies reinforced in the White Paper, *Open Public Services*, which is community based and focused on neighbourhood services. The Act brings together for England greater powers than those available in the devolved administrations in Scotland, Wales and Northern Ireland.[18] This adds an important dynamic to the way government is delivered and the autonomy of each locality. The Act also brings to local government directly enforceable EU responsibilities. This is deceptive, as the autonomy of local government is constrained by the imposition of tough financial controls. Consequently, it is arguable that Central Local relations are often intertwined as a consequence of contradictory and at times hard to comprehend policy making. Thus it is hard to discern logical or rational patterns of policy making. Austerity and poverty has had an uneven impact on regions in England. This leaves policy making on a pragmatic basis and often central government driven. The Localism Act 2011 is often cited as a step towards giving local decision-making priority and dispersing power from central government bureaucracy to local people and their communities. The political rhetoric of local community and the Big Society is high in the dynamics of a power shift from central government to people living in local communities. Localism meaning decentralisation is in vogue, although the reliance of local government on central government controls over their finance remains. Recent proposals in December 2015 for local government devolution may mark a new era of local government autonomy, but without any increase in public funding[19] or any additional tax raising powers. Public sector cuts are pre-eminent, minimising local authority duties owed to local communities will lead to wide divergences in the design

21-020

---

17 S. H. Bailey, and M. Elliott, "Taking Local Government Seriously: democracy, Autonomy and the Constitution" [2009] *C.L.J.* 436.
18 I. Leigh, "The Changing nature of Local and Regional Democracy" in J. Jowell and D. Oliver (eds), *The Changing Constitution* (Oxford: Oxford University Press, 2011); and Peter Leyland, "Multi-layered Constitutional accountability" in N. Bamforth and P. Leyland (eds), *Accountability in the Contemporary Constitution* (Oxford; Oxford University Press, 2013), p.328.
19 House of Commons Library, *The Voluntary sector and the Big Society*, SN/HA/5883 (21 March 2013); House of Commons Library, *Local Government: Shared services outsourcing, unitary authorities*, SN/PC/05950 (2 April 2014); House of Commons Library, *Combined Authorities*, SN/PC/06649 (3 April 2014); House of Commons

and implementation of local authority duties and a less coherent policy over key sectors such as energy, housing and health.[20]

21-021 Revitalising the local economy and developing around large cities what are known as "metro areas" is the policy of the Coalition Government.[21] Decentralisation may also prove popular in the North of England and opens up the potential for a new relationship between local and central government[22] through the influence of local income tax, independently funded activities and assigned revenue giving autonomy to local authorities.

21-022 The directly elected London Mayor is also an interesting model of local delegation. Directly elected Mayors were proposed under the Local Government Act 2000 but generally rejected by the public after various referendums were held[23] There are new proposals to introduce a local elected mayor in Manchester despite the fact that in a referendum in May 2012 it was decided against by a vote of 53 per cent to 47 per cent. The new proposal is to have a "metro mayor" but not subject to a prior referendum. This would make it easier to take the scheme forward but it is unclear if the absence of approval would make a difference to the success of the scheme.[24]

21-023 The asymmetry of the devolution arrangements raises major issues for the UK Parliament, particularly the fact that there is no separate legislature for England or its regions and that laws passed for England by the UK Parliament may be voted on by MPs sitting for constituencies in Scotland, Wales or Northern Ireland.

21-024 The most challenging issue for the UK Parliament is the so-called West Lothian question. Its origins lie in the 1880s in the debates on Home Rule for Ireland.[25] The question is whether it is right that MPs from areas where there is legislative devolution should be able to vote at Westminster on English domestic legislation. Tam Dalyell, MP for West Lothian, raised the question during discussions of devolution in the 1970s.[26]

Library, *Community budgets and city deals*, SN/PC/05955 (1 June 2014); and House of Commons Library, *The Greater London Authority*, SN/PC/05817 (9 July 2014).

20 Chris Bevan, "The Localism Act 2011: The Hollow Housing Law Revolution" (2014) 77(6) *Modern Law Review* 964–82.
21 M. J. Smith, "From Big Government to Big Society: Changing the State-Society balance" (2010) 639(4) *Parliamentary Affairs* 818–33.
22 Institute for Government, *What can elected mayors do for our cities?* (2005).
House of Commons Library, *Business Improvement Districts (BIDs)*, SN/PC/4591 (7 November 2012).
23 House of Commons Library, *The Greater London Authority*, SN/PC/ 05817 (9 July 2014); House of Commons Library, *Directly-Elected Mayors*, SN/PC/5000 (22 October 2014); and House of Commons Library, *Local Government devolution: fiscal proposals*, SN/PC/07046 (3 December 2014).
24 V. Lowndes and L. Pratchett, "Local Government under the Coalition Government: Austerity, Localism and the 'Big Society'" (2012) 34(1) *Local Government Studies* 21–40; and G. Mulgan, "Investing in Social Growth: Can the Big Society be more than a slogan?", *The Sunday Times*, 30 August 2010.
NAO, *Financial sustainability of Local Authorities*, HC 888, Session 2012–13 (30 January 2013).
25 There are excellent discussions in John Kendle, *Ireland and the Federal Solution* (Montreal: McGill-Queen's University Press, 1989), pp.57–86; and Roy Jenkins, *Gladstone* (London: MacMillan, 1989), pp.548–49.
26 Professor Vernon Bogdanor, *Evidence to the McKay Commission* (June 2012). See also M. Russell and G. Lodge, "The Government of England by Westminster" in R. Hazell (ed), *The English Question* (Manchester: Manchester

English votes of English laws and implications for the legislative process

The House of Commons has approved new Standing Order changes on 22 October 2015 to introduce English Votes for English Laws. The changes affect all Government Bills, specified motions and instruments. Government Bills that apply throughout the UK will not be affected. Bills that either wholly or in the case of only some provisions that may affect either England only or only England and Wales[27] will be subject to different procedures as they pass through the Commons aimed at ensuring that MPs in the affected constituencies in the UK have provisions that affect only them. This may result in discussion of a written constitution, if only to define and clarify the powers of central government.

Supporters of constitutional reform also highlight the weaknesses in parliamentary control over the Executive as evidenced by the accretion of centralised governmental power. In the aftermath of a period of strong government with large overall majorities, electoral reform is favoured, linked to the need for a fairer balance in the composition of the House of Commons. There is concern that set piece debates such as Prime Ministers Questions (PMQs) are evidence of bad parliamentary behaviour and poor scrutiny over the Executive. Debates on controversial issues such as the war in Iraq and the decision to take military action against Syria have exposed gaps in public expectation over what in reality Parliament is able to achieve.

The arguments against adopting a written constitution emphasise the flexibility inherent in existing arrangements. The tradition of an unwritten constitution has reinforced the supremacy of Parliament in both the narrow legal sense, and in the broader sense of political majoritarian government. Change may be accomplished without any general rethink of the constitutional arrangements. Adaptation may be seen as part of an organic growth unhindered by the restraint of a constitutional requirement to give the judiciary a final say in any change. The virtues of the present system must not be overlooked even if it is desirable to consider reforms. It is often conceded that many of the reforms mentioned above may be enacted without a written constitution. The strengths of a flexible unwritten constitution may be found in the primacy given to the political process. This may be weakened by entrenching in a written constitution those matters currently governed by convention or political choices. A written constitution might mark a shift from political decision-making to judicial scrutiny which may be too narrow and restrictive of the political choices on offer to the electorate.

Enacting a written constitution may not be a panacea for all constitutional law problems. The debate over whether a written constitution might be adopted or not provides an opportunity for students of the Constitution to analyse and critically examine existing arrangements which will undoubtedly contribute to a deeper understanding of the working of the UK's

---

University Press, 2006); and Jim Gallagher, *IPPR, England and the Union: How and Why to Answer the West Lothian Question* (London: IPPR, April 2012).
27 House of Commons Library, *English Votes for English Laws*, Briefing Paper, No.7339 (2 December 2015).

D: Public Law Scholarship[28]

21-029 What is public law and what are its aims? This is a recurring and important question. The question is asked of subjects such as tort, contract, criminal law or environmental law, yet this fundamental question as to the role and function of public law has been only fragmentally discussed.[29] As we have seen, public law has an endless variety of roles and functions including government contracting,[30] as well as providing for systems of accountability. The assortment of aims and objectives associated with defining how government is accountable and representative. This includes institutions and systems used for the controls necessary over government action. There are miscellaneous techniques and controls- some exercised by Parliament, others to be found through judicial action[31] through the courts that are intended to provide citizens with assurances about the way government makes decisions, and transparency is a key element in public confidence. There is an important initiative in terms of e petitions[32]. This is an important and fast growing activity. The commitment is that once 100,000 signatures are reached, the threshold secures consideration for debate allowing public access to parliamentary procedures in matters of public interest. Building on public engagement is an important way of attempting to create greater public confidence in the parliamentary system.[33]

21-030 Public law is required to provide that transparency through systems of accountability, both *a priori* and *ex post*, and is intended to ensure that citizens' rights are protected and good administration supported. Internal systems of accountability need to be distinguished from external systems. The former are concerned with internal systems of audit, rules and

---

28 The ideas expressed here are adapted from my public lectures delivered in the summer of 2001. See J. F. McEldowney, P. Havemann and J. Mackinnon (eds), *Modernizing Britain: Public Law and Challenges* (Hamilton, NZ: University of Waikato School of Law, 2002).
29 Martin Loughlin, *Foundations of Public Law* (Oxford: Oxford University Press 2010) provides the most scholarly and systematic analysis. Also see D. Oliver (ed), *Common Values and the Public-Private Divide* (London: Butterworths, 1999).
30 A. C. L. Davies, *The Public Law of Government Contracts* (Oxford: Oxford University Press, 2008).
31 Lord Judge, *The Safest Shield Lectures, Speeches and Essays* (Oxford: Hart, 2016).
32 House of Commons Petitions Committee. For an overview see House of Commons, *E-Petitions*, Briefing Paper, No.06450 (20 October 2015).
33 House of Commons Liaison Committee, *Building public engagement: Options for developing select committee outreach*, 1st Special Report, 2015–16, HC 470 (30 November 2015).

conventions that apply to the exercise of ministerial discretion.[34] The latter take the form of external controls through Parliament, the courts, the media, and public opinion.

21-031

There is also an enormous dependency on Executive self-restraint. In the absence of a written constitution, constitutional protections are undeniably weak against authoritarian decision-making, when compared to countries with written constitutions. This is largely due to the overwhelming presumption in English law, at least until relatively recently, that if an action or decision is not categorically prohibited, it is legal. Government authority and power are assumed on the basis that the Executive may do anything unless prohibited by statute. An equally familiar presumption was that rights are intended to protect minorities, while the protection of the majority is afforded by Parliament. Majoritarian democracy assumes that the casting of even one more vote for, rather than against, a particular proposition commands the respect of the losing side. Abuse of power is prevented by the spirit of compromise that government will act with self-restraint and find a way to accommodate minority interests. In the eighteenth and nineteenth centuries, cohesion was provided by deference to authority, including government and the Monarchy. In an age where deference has diminished, institutions have had to depend on persuasion rather than their status.

21-032

The liberty of the nation also depended on assuming good stewardship by the holder of public office. Today that assumption cannot be taken for granted, and in most cases the public interest requires that the holder of public office exercises power in an accountable way. News media intrude into the private and public lives of public figures. Increasing demands for transparency and verifiable outputs such as league tables arise out of public disquiet and mistrust.

21-033

Remedies available to the individual might take care of the exceptional case where there is a lapse of judgment or an error. The general presumption is that the ordinary law and self-restraint are sufficient to control arbitrariness. High dependency on Executive self-restraint is part of the history of the nation and the culture of the people. It is clear that the pre-eminent concern in Britain is political convenience, to allow the party in power to govern reflection of how the balance between the different elements of the constitution is expected to be struck.

21-034

Another dimension of public law is the setting of limits on economic power. Extensive economic powers, through instruments such as the system of budgeting and the borrowing of money, are in the hands of the executive. As Page and Daintith explain, economic powers are effectively under government control:

> "The executive can do this because basic principles of our constitution recognize it as an autonomous body which can manage its own resources save where Parliament ordains otherwise, and give it co-ordinate power with Parliament in the all-important area of public expenditure."[35]

---

34 J. F. McEldowney, "The Control of Public Expenditure" in J. Jowell and D. Oliver (eds), *The Changing Constitution*, 4th edn (Oxford: Oxford University Press, 2012), pp.190–198.
35 T. Daintith and A. Page, *The Executive in the Constitution* (Oxford: Oxford University Press, 1999), p.398. See T.

21-035 A striking feature of the UK's present-day constitutional arrangements is the growth in complex and all-inclusive legislation. It is remarkable that a "non-codified" common law system has developed in practice such comprehensive legislation. Skills in interpreting and reading statutes have not been given sufficient attention in the design of many courses and in the way public law is taught. Public law has developed beyond the accretion of political power and defining its limits. Having developed a system of remedies from medieval times and ensured the economic liberty of commerce and contractual relationships in the eighteenth and nineteenth centuries, legislation has pushed the frontiers of public law to develop individual rights.

21-036 The Human Rights Act 1998 defines public law in terms of individual rights and their protection through law. Giving legal priority to rights in this way marks a profound shift to the judicial element of the Constitution. This triumph of judicial power over the other parts of the Constitution vests legal rules with a higher authority than the political process.[36] In securing the promotion of legal rules, the question facing judges is how is judicial power in the hands of appointed judges to be made compatible with the democratic process?

21-037 Currently there is a highly contested discussion about the role and value of human rights.[37] Rights advanced since 1989 are largely defined around a neo-liberal perspective, few rights involve the interference with individual private property or alter public spending totals or protect education, health care and social security budgets. Rights have also been limited in setting boundaries on laws to address terrorism or inhibit the continued accretion of executive power. Many commentators[38] sense that the ambiguity in many rights leaves much to regret and there is a sense of frustration that rights have not reached their full potential.

21-038 Public law has also found its way into the study of what had been assumed to be discrete areas of private law, separate from administrative law or the European Community. Setting the boundaries of public law is going to be difficult as the human rights implications of legal powers spill over into private law cases.

21-039 Public law scholarship[39] has reflected the range and diversity of many recent developments in the changing shape of constitutional and administrative law. It is impossible to provide an exhaustive analysis of the formidable literature relevant to the subject and the student of the Constitution is referred to the bibliography for further references and additional reading. Many specialisms, often outside the traditional confines of law, are now required reading to understand some of the basics of public law. The question arises as to the future direction of change and the development of public law in the context of two apparently irrevocable trends. The first is the increasing influence of globalisation, with the pressure of the market

---

Daintith, "Law as a Policy Instrument: Comparative Perspectives'" in T. Daintith (ed), *Law as an Instrument of Economic Policy: Comparative and Critical Approaches* (Berlin: De Gruyter, 1988), pp.3–55.

36 M. Hunt, H. J. Hooper and P. Yowell (eds), *Parliament and Human Rights: Redressing the Democratic Deficit* (Oxford: Hart, 2015).
37 See C. Douzinas and C. Gearty (eds), *The Meanings of Rights* (Cambridge: Cambridge University Press, 2014).
38 Douzinas and Gearty, *The Meanings of Rights*.
39 See A. Horne and A. Le Sueur, *Parliament Legislation and Accountability* (Oxford: Hart Publishing, 2016).

economy and competition for scarce resources. This creates a tension between the national domestic interest and Britain's future role in the world. The second is the increasing influence and dependency on the part of the Member States on the economic and political power of the EU.[40] What is Britain's role? Will Britain stay in the EU and what if different regions vote differently for membership in any EU referendum? What impact will changes in the composition of the EU have on our future constitutional relations with the EU?

In considering the broader question of the future of the unwritten checks and balances in the UK's Constitution, it may be timely to consider a number of questions. What are the aims of public law? How effective is public law in achieving those aims? How may the future of public law be best delineated? Is it time for the UK to adopt a written Constitution? There appear to be many lessons to be gained for the future development of public law from studying how the UK has adapted to change thus far.

21–040

Diversity in public law scholarship[41] is partly a reflection of the unwritten constitution and the difficulties posed by the subject matter. The way forward is not easy to road-map. A growing body of public law literature moves from the traditional and often historical concerns of constitutional law to question the theoretical development of the subject and seek explanations rooted in legal theory. There is little convergence as to how best to achieve this ambitious task. Craig has considered some of the approaches which are open to the future study of public law and favours an approach which allows the lawyer to[42]

21–041

> "identify and assess the relevant background theory, consider the public law implications of it, and the political and social and economic background conditions within which it subsists."

While this methodology might not always find favour, it represents a growing interest among public lawyers of the wider social and political ramifications of how laws work, how they might be applied and whether the legal arrangements are relevant when other factors may be relevant to how decisions are taken. There is some caution in considering whether lawyers do in fact have much, if anything, to offer. Writing on the area of discretion and law, Lacey[43] points out limitations in legal methodology and the potential for turning a broadening and enlightening development "into a piece of intellectual and practical imperialism in which lawyers merely incorporate ever more inappropriate areas of activity into their own analytic and political framework". The dangers of what Lacey calls "the legal paradigm" is that legal methodology may tend to operate using generalisation; it tends to "pigeonhole" solutions, operates dichotomies

21–042

---

40 See House of Commons Library, *UK's EU reform negotiations: the Tusk package*, Briefing Paper, No.7497 (9 February 2016).
41 Nicholas Barber, Richard Ekins and Paul Yowell (eds), *Lord Sumption and the Limits of the Law* (Oxford: Hart Publishing, 2016).
42 P. P. Craig, "What Should Public Lawyers Do?: A Reply" (1992) 121(4) *Oxford Journal of Legal Studies* 565–577, p.565.
43 N. Lacey, "The Jurisprudence of Discretion" in K. Hawkins (ed), *The Uses of Discretion* (Oxford: Oxford University Press, 1992), 361–388, pp.361–363.

or opposites with either/or decisions, and may tend to assume that there are "right" answers found in some form of objectivity or truth. Furthermore, legal method may assume belief in its own self-importance and overestimate the value of the courts and the temptation to bring disputes within "a legal umbrella." Lacey's analysis calls for a pluralistic approach of pooling resources to problems. In the example of her study of discretion this means[44]:

> "The need to integrate empirical, interpretative and normative questions in an attempt to understand discretion and ultimately, to ensure the legitimacy and effectiveness of the exercise of social powers in particular contexts. Discretion must be taken, then primarily as a political question, and one whose centrality in contemporary society calls for the concerted attention of a number of related and interdependent disciplines."

21-043 Stuart Lakin takes the position that public lawyers are sometimes split between two schools of thought or approaches when interpreting public law. The first approach he describes as the empirical fact thesis. Broadly defined this is the attempt to describe the main rules of statutory interpretation, the dicta of judges and the standards and conduct of public life in much the same way as an anthropologist may study human behaviour. In contrast the second approach, is to deny that the "content of the law and the constitution depend wholly on empirical facts. It holds that the public lawyer, in common with judges, practitioners and citizens, must argue like a philosopher, rather than describe like a social scientist".[45] Inevitably, both approaches may appear attractive, but not all public lawyers will feel at ease being categorised into either approach.

21-044 Equally important is the consideration that no matter how much a forensic or objective approach is taken to understanding legal rules, in many instances this may reveal the "politics of the constitution" and the political choices that underpin many legal decisions. This is surely an inevitability as increasingly large areas of the Constitution are to be found in detailed legislation and statutory rules passed by one political party in government if only to be rejected by another political party when in power. Having established some form of methodology or approach, public lawyers are often uncertain as to how to establish principles rooted in constitutional law or theory. This problem is particularly acute when legislation is considered as to its policy and philosophy.

21-045 Assessing how to evaluate legislation may require consideration of the political issues underlying the law. In the last decade or so this has given rise to much public law literature concerning some of the changes introduced by both Conservative and Labour governments. The division between legal and non-legal opinion becomes difficult to draw as public lawyers examine the writings of political scientists and related disciplines. The burgeoning literature

---

44 Lacey, "The Jurisprudence of Discretion", p.388.
45 Stuart Lakin, "Defending and Contesting the Sovereignty of law: The Public Lawyer as Interpretivist" (2015) 78(3) *Modern Law Review* 549–70.

that reflects interest in the political as well as theoretical issues underlying constitutional change is also the result of political scientists finding legal analysis helpful.

Daintith has pointed out that public lawyers may have difficulty in finding a suitably clear constitutional principle or criteria to judge whether political changes have a constitutional impact. This difficulty is compounded by a[46] "prevailing descriptive and eclectic mode of writing about the UK Constitution and public law". Further difficulties arise because[47]

21-046

> "we have not formulated the twentieth- as opposed to nineteenth-century principles with which the recent legislation comes into conflict or which it purports to displace or modify."

Responses to the problems identified by Daintith have varied. Some have taken a critical view of the Constitution and sought to find expression through the value of "critique", and the need for reforms through the testing of the adequacy of existing arrangements. The political policies and ideology underlying law have also come under scrutiny, sometimes quite openly and directed at the ideology itself which is at the centre of government policy. Over the past few years, the judiciary have offered some interesting interpretations of constitutional principles in cases such as *Jackson v Attorney General*,[48] arising from a challenge to the validity of the Hunting Act 2004 and the Parliament Act 1949, the changing nature of sovereignty was recognised as Lord Hope acknowledged:

21-047

> "Our constitution is dominated by the sovereignty of Parliament. But parliamentary sovereignty is no longer, if it ever was, absolute . . . step by step, gradually but surely, the English principle of the absolute sovereignty of Parliament which Dicey derived from Coke and Blackstone is being qualified . . . The rule of law enforced by the courts is the ultimate controlling factor on which our constitution is based."

Judicial review is often a subject of intense debate when there are major policy implications. The Supreme Court in *R (on the application of Client Earth) v Secretary of State for Environment, Food and Rural affairs*[49] held that the UK was in breach of air quality regulations and ruled that the Government must take immediate action. The European Commission has started infraction proceedings that the UK has not achieved legal limits set for nitrogen dioxide. This comes

21-048

---

46 T. Daintith, "Political Programmes and the Constitution" in W. Finnie, C. M. G. Himsworth and N. Walker (eds), *Edinburgh Essays in Public Law* (Edinburgh: Edinburgh University Press, 1991), p.43.
47 Daintith, "Political Programmes and the Constitution", p.46; and T. Prosser, "Towards a Critical Public Law" (1982) 9 *Journal of Law and Society* 19.
48 *Jackson v Attorney General* [2005] UKHL 56; [2006] 1 A.C. 262.
49 [2015] UKSC 28; [2015] 4 All E.R. 724.

at a difficult time when the Paris agreement has just been reached. At a local level the UK government has to make a decision on the London Airport including the possibility of extending Heathrow. Air quality is a sensitive issue to be addressed in the decision that has to be made. There is also an ongoing question of emissions from diesel cars and the impact this may have on the environment and air quality.[50]

21-049 Cases such a *Thoburn v Sunderland City Council*[51] raise important constitutional issues. Laws LJ recognised the shifting changes in UK sovereignty and this had modified the doctrine of implied repeal when it came to EU law. The basis of the UK's relationship was a matter of the common law and the common law was the basis of any resolution. Consequently he reasoned that while ordinary statutes were subject to the implied repeal doctrine what he called "constitutional statutes" were not. Defining a constitutional statute was one which dealt with fundamental constitutional rights, including the European Communities Act 1972, and the only conditions where such a repeal might be possible arose from express words in the later statute. This is an area of judicial creativity[52] that may become a fertile ground for new developments.[53] The Supreme Court in *Pham v Secretary of State for the Home Department*[54] showed a willingness to adapt and analyse common law principles in terms of EU and human rights law with autonomy to the UK courts to develop in a pragmatic and principled way doctrines such as proportionality.

21-050 Prisoners' voting rights continue to give rise to issues regarding the UK's attitude to the Strasbourg Court's decisions. Since May 2015, the Council of the Europe's Committee of Ministers has on two occasions asked the UK to respond to the judgments in *Hirst (No.2)*[55] and *Green and MT*[56] decisions requiring votes for prisoners. In December 2015, the UK's Minister of Justice indicated that the UK Government would reply in 2016.[57]

21-051 The devolution settlement is likely to be a fruitful area for judicial scrutiny.[58] In cases such as *Axa General Insurance v The Lord Advocate*[59], the lawfulness of an Act of the Scottish Parliament, the Damages (Asbestos-related Conditions) (Scotland) Act 2009, was challenged. The UK Supreme Court held that the claimants were entitled to make such a claim and that the courts had an overarching power to ensure that the 2009 Act was legitimate in its aims and proportionate in its response. It is clear that the Court rejected the claimants' case and held that the legislation was compatible with the European Convention

---

50 *The Ends Report 490* (December 2015) pp.37–38.
51 *Thoburn v Sunderland City Council* [2002] EWHC 195 (Admin); [2003] Q.B. 151.
52 Paul S. Davies and Justine Pila, *The Jurisprudence of Lord Hoffman* (Oxford: Hart, 2015).
53 See *H v Lord Advocate* [2012] UKSC 24; [2013] 1 A.C. 413
54 [2015] UKSC 19; [2015] 1 W.L.R. 1591.
55 [2005] ECHR 681 ECHR.
56 (2010) 53 E.H.R.R. 710 ECHR.
57 House of Commons Library, *Prisoners' Voting rights: developments since May 2015*, Briefing Paper, No.CBP 7461 (12 January 2016).
58 See *Adams v Scottish Ministers* (2003) S.C. 17i in Scotland and the approach in *Axa* [2011] UKSC 46; [2012] 1 A.C. 868.
59 [2011] UKSC 46; [2012] 1 A.C. 868 and [2011] CSIH 31; 2011 S.C. 662.

and did not offend any of the other grounds for judicial review on which the claimants relied.[60]

Similarly, the UK Supreme Court has had to determine the legislative competence of the Welsh Assembly and its compatibility with the European Convention on Human Rights. In the *Recovery of Medical Costs for Asbestos Case*,[61] the Supreme Court unanimously concluded that the Welsh Assembly lacked the legislative competence to enact a Bill to address compensation for asbestos cases. One of the grounds for the decision was that the proposed Welsh Assembly Bill encroached upon the general fiscal powers to levy charges for the NHS in Wales that fell outside the powers of the Welsh Assembly. The development of a constitutional jurisdiction in devolution matters is likely to increase.

21–052

There has also been a notable growth in various specialist studies designed to highlight particular areas or problems traditionally not within the confines of public law. Innovative work in the area of discretion, regulation and on administration more generally sets new boundaries between the work of public lawyers and other related disciplines.

21–053

There appears to be common ground that the lawyer's task is to understand not merely legal doctrine but the wider context of its use, including the ideologies that underpin it and the variety of social forces that exert pressure for legal change.

21–054

An example of how this task might be taken forward is in the formulation of the principles of good administration, or the building up of principles containing the working practices of the Parliamentary Commissioner for Administration. The recurrent themes of accountability, control and scrutiny found in much public law literature require evaluation of different styles and techniques beyond a purely legal and court-orientated approach. For example, this may include scrutiny of the work of the National Audit Office and the useful reports from the Public Accounts Committee.

21–055

This may suggest an agenda for further research into public law. This may include consideration of the control and regulatory functions of government, investigating the dispute-resolving functions of government, and an examination of the legal implications and limitations of the delegation of government functions to private sector actors. Studying the work of tribunals and the effectiveness of informal grievance mechanisms are important in understanding the limits of legal rules and the potential for different methods of dispute resolution.

21–056

The future development of public law will benefit from the continuation of empirical studies into judicial review. From this model further research might be undertaken on the effects of judicial review on public bodies, and the potential impact of a code of guidance on good administration examined. In devising future strategies, it is essential that the problem-orientated and analytical tools of the common law tradition are continuously refreshed. The common law is inherently problem focused and the national legal culture reflects that pragmatic approach. A research register on public law is a good starting point, representing the diversity of interest

21–057

---

60 [2011] UKSC 46.
61 *Recovery of Medical Costs for Asbestos Diseases (Wales) Bill: reference by the Counsel General for Wales (Applicant) and the Association of British Insurers (Intervener)* [2015] UKSC 3; [2015] A.C. 1016.

in public law. Integrating empirical, interpretive and normative questions will set the future challenge for public law.

21-058 It is clear that the Human Rights Act has created a controversial subject for the future direction of rights in public law. This should not divert attention from the study of the many qualities and weaknesses of the parliamentary system and the diverse ways that government exercises power and is held to account. Public law is equally concerned with changes to our electoral system, Lords reform, the evolution of different approaches to regulation, the continued development of a comprehensive system of tribunals, the efficiency of the courts, the system for the appointment of judges, the evolving nature of devolution and local government and last, but most importantly, the changing nature of Parliamentary sovereignty to take account of Europe and a changing role of the judiciary.

21-059 Predicting the constitutional future of the UK is one of the most challenging questions.[62] One of the implications for the new procedures to address English Votes for English Laws is that for certain purposes the UK parliament is converted into an exclusively English body. This is another step in a re-drawing of the UK into different forms for different purposes. The UK may have to consider a written constitution to settle fairness in the financial arrangements between the nations, in addition to bringing some resolution to the devolution issues that are emerging since the Scottish referendum. Political and economic arrangements are not always resolvable on their own without the clarity of a legal text to guide the parties on how best to resolve any disputes.. Decentralization within England also has to be taken into account. The rule of law and citizen's rights require attention within the constitutional framework. The lessons of Magna Carta[63] are that law has to be given pre-eminence in the constitution. The future development of public law is likely to reflect its inherent pragmatic qualities: continuous change and steady growth with unpredictable results with results that appear rather unpredictable in a period of change and uncertainty.[64] Uncertainty hangs over the UK's constitutional institutions as the implications of leaving the EU are negotiated. This is likely to take two years if not longer.

Further Reading

Vernon Bogdanor, *The New British Constitution* (Oxford: Hart, 2009).
Mark Elliott and David Feldman (eds), *The Cambridge Companion to Public Law* (Cambridge: Cambridge University Press, 2015).

---

62 Matt Qvortrup (ed), *The British Constitution: Continuity and Change: A Festschrift for Vernon Bogdanor* (Oxford: Hart, 2015).
63 Andrew Blick, *Beyond Magna Carta: A Constitution for the United Kingdom* (Oxford: Hart, 2015).
64 David Feldman, *Law in Politics, Politics in Law* (Oxford: Hart, 2015).

Michael Emerson (ed), *Britain's Future in Europe: Reform, renegotiation or secession?* (March 2015).
A. Horne, G. Drewry and D. Oliver (eds), *Parliament and the Law* (Oxford: Hart, 2013).
House of Commons Library, *The UK and the EU: reform, renegotiation, withdrawal? A reading list*, Briefing Paper, No.07220 (15 September 2015).
Bill Jones and Philip Norton, *Politics UK*, 8th edn (Abingdon: Routledge, 2014).
J. Jowell, D. Oliver and C. O'Cinneide (eds), *The Changing Constitution*, 8th edn (Oxford: Oxford University Press, 2015).
Anthony King, *Who Governs Britain?* (London: Pelican, 2015).
Michael Moran, *Politics and Governance in the UK*, 2nd edn (Basingstoke: Palgrave Macmillan, 2011).

Select Bibliography

Ackerman, B., *Social Justice in the Liberal State* (New Haven: Yale University Press, 1980).
Adler, M., ed., *Administrative Justice in Context*, 2010
Adonis, A., *Parliament Today* (Manchester: Manchester University Press, 1994).
Allan, T.R.S., "Legislative Supremacy and the Rule of Law: Democracy and Constitutionalism" (1985) 44 Camb. L.J. 111.
__, "Dicey and Dworkin: the Rule of Law as Integrity" (1988) 8 *Oxford Journal of Legal Studies* 266.
__, "Pragmatism and Theory in Public Law" (1988) 104 *Law Quarterly Review* 422.
__, "Constitutional Rights and Common Law" (1991) 11 *Oxford Journal of Legal Studies* 453.
__, *Law, Liberty and Justice* (Oxford University Press, Oxford, 1993).
__, "Equality and Moral independence: public law and private morality" in *A Special Relationship* (I. Loveland ed., Clarendon Press, Oxford, 1995).
__, *Constitutional Justice: A Liberal Theory of the Rule of Law* (Oxford: Oxford University Press, 2001).
__, "Human Rights and judicial review: a critique of 'due deference'" [2006] CLJ 671
__ *Constitutional Justice: A Liberal Theory of the Rule of Law* (Oxford: Oxford University Press, 2013).
Allen, C.K., *Law in the Making* (London: Penguin, 1927).
__, *Democracy and the Individual* (London, 1943).
__, "Administrative Jurisdiction" [1956] *Public Law* 13.
Allen, M., Thompson, B. and Walsh, B., *Cases and Materials on Constitutional and Administrative Law*, 6th edn. (London: Blackstone, 2000).
Allison, J.W.F., *A Continental Distinction in the Common Law* (Oxford: Oxford University Press, revised edn, 2000).
__, "Theoretical and Institutional Underpinnings of a Separate Administrative Law" in *The Province of Administrative Law* M. Taggart ed. (Oxford: Oxford University Press, 1997), pp.71–89.
Allison, J.W.F., *The English Historical Constitution: Continuity, Change and European Effects*, 2007.
Alston, P., et al., *The EU and Human Rights* (Oxford: Oxford University Press, 1999).
Amery, L.S., *Thoughts on the Constitution* (Oxford: Oxford University Press, 1947; 2nd edn., 1953).
Amos, M., *The Science of Law* (London: University Press, 1870).
Andrews, J.A. (ed.), *Welsh Studies in Public Law* (London, 1970).
Anson, W.R., *The Law and Custom of the Constitution* (Oxford: Oxford University Press, 1886; 4th edn, 1909).

Arlidge, Anthony and others, *Magna Carta Uncovered* (Oxford: Hart Publishing, 2014)

Armstrong, W. (ed.), *Budgetary Reform in the United Kingdom* (London, 1980).

Arndt, H.W., "The Origins of Dicey's Concept of the Rule of Law" (1957) 31 *Australian Law Journal* 117.

Arnull, A., *The European Union and its Court of Justice* 2nd edn., 2006.

Arrowsmith, S., *The Law of Public and Utilities Procurement* 3rd edn. (London: Sweet and Maxwell, 2013)

Arthurs, H., *"Without the Law": Administrative Justice and Legal Pluralism in Nineteenth Century England* (Toronto: University of Toronto Press, 1985).

Atiyah, P.S., *The Rise and Fall of Freedom of Contract* (Oxford: Oxford University Press, 1979).

_, *From Principles to Pragmatism: Changes in the Function of the Judicial Process and the Law* (Oxford: Oxford University Press, 1978).

Attfield, R., *The Ethics of the Global Environment*, Edinburgh Studies in World Ethics, (Edinburgh: Edinburgh University Press, 1999).

Auburn, J., Moffett, J., and Sharland, A., Judicial Review: Principles and Procedures, 2013.

Austin, J., *The Province of Jurisprudence Determined* (1832) Hart ed. (London: H.L.A., 1954).

Bagehot, W., *The English Constitution* (Introduction by R.H.S. Crossman) (1963).

Bailey, S.H., Harris, D.J., and Jones, B.L., *Civil Liberties Cases and Materials* 6th edn. (London: Butterworths, 2009).

Baines, P., "Financial Accountability: Agencies and Audit" in *Parliamentary Accountability: A Study of Parliament and Executive Agencies*, P. Giddings ed. (London: Macmillan, 1995).

Bamforth, N., "The application of the Human Rights Act to public authorities and private bodies" (1999) *Cambridge LJ* 159–170.

Bamforth, N., and Leyland, P., *Accountability in the Modern Constitution* 2014

Bamforth, N., and Leyland, P., eds. *Public Law in a Multi-layered Constitution* 2014.

Barber, N.W., "The Rechstaat and the rule of law" (2003) 53 *University of Toronto Law Journal* 443.

Barendt, E., *Freedom of Speech* (Oxford: Oxford University Press, 1985).

_, *An Introduction to Constitutional Law* (Oxford: Oxford University Press, 1998).

Barendt, E. and Hitchens, L., *Media law: Cases and Materials* (London: Longman, 2000).

Beck, U., *Risk Society* (London: Sage, 1992).

Beer, S.H., *Treasury Control: The Co-ordination of Financial and Economic Policy in Great Britain*, 2nd edn. (Oxford: Clarendon Press, 1957).

Bell, S. and McGillivray, D., *Ball and Bell on Environmental Law*, 6th edn. (London: Blackstone Press, 2012).

Bennion, F., *Bennion on Statute Law*, 2nd edn. (London: Longman, 1990).

Benn, T., and Hood, A., *Common Sense: A New Constitution for Britain* (London: Hutchinson, 1993).

Bentham, J., *The Works of Jeremy Bentham* Vol. III, (J.L. Bowring ed., 1843).

_, *A Fragment on Government and An Introduction to the Principles of Morals and Legislation* (W. Harrison ed., Oxford, 1948).

Bew, P., *Conflict and Conciliation in Ireland 1890–1910* (Oxford: Oxford University Press, 1982).

Bew, P., Gibbon, P., Patterson, H., *Northern Ireland, 1921–1944: Political Forces and Social Classes* (London: Serif, 1995).

Bingham, Lord, "The old order changeth" (2006) 122 LQR 211.

"Bingham Centre, the Report of an Independent Commission, A Constitutional Crossroads: Ways forward for the United Kingdom", The Bingham Centre, London, May, 2015.

Binney, J.E.D., *British Public Finance and Administration 1774–92* (Oxford: Clarendon Press, 1958).

Birkinshaw, P., *Freedom of Information: The Law, the Practice and the Ideal* (London: Butterworths, 1988; 2nd edn., 1996; 3rd edn., 2001).

_, *Reforming the Secret State* (Milton Keynes: Open University, 1990).

Bishop, M., Kay, J., and Mayer C., (eds.), *The Regulatory Challenge* (Oxford: Oxford University Press, 1995).

_, *Privatization and Economic Performance* (Oxford: Oxford University Press, 1994).

Blackstone, W., *Commentaries on the Laws of England (1765–9)*, 4 vols., 15th edn. (London: Strahan, Cadell and Prince, 1809).

Blackburn, R., *The Electoral System in Britain* (London: Macmillan, 1995).

Blackburn, R., and Plant, R. (eds.), *Constitutional Reform: The Labour Government's Constitutional Reform Agenda* (London: Longman, 1999).

Blackburn, R., and Polakiewicz, J., *Fundamental Rights in Europe* (Oxford: Oxford University Press, 2001).

Blackburn, R., and Kennon, A., *Griffith and Ryle on Parliament: Functions, Practice and Procedures*, 2nd edn. (London: Sweet and Maxwell, 2003)

Blair, T., *A Journey* (London: Hutchinson, 2010).

Blick, A., Beyond Magna Carta: A Constitution for the United Kingdom Hart (Oxford: Oxford University Press, 2015)

Blom-Cooper, L., and Drewry, G., *Final Appeal: A Study of the House of Lords in its Judicial Capacity* (Oxford: Oxford University Press, 1972).

Bogdanor, V., *Devolution* (Oxford: Oxford University Press, 1979).

_, *Devolution in the United Kingdom* (Oxford: Oxford University Press, 1999).

_, *The People and the Party System. The Referendum and Electoral Reform in British Politics* (Cambridge: Cambridge University Press, 1981).

_, "Constitutional Law and Politics" (1987) 7 O.J.L.S. 454.

_, *The Monarchy and the Constitution* (Oxford: Clarendon Press, 1995).

_, *Power and the People: A Guide to Constitutional Reform* (London: Victor Gollancz, 1999).

_, *The New British Constitution in the Twentieth Century* 2003

_, " Our new constitution" (2004) 120 LQR 242

Bogdanor, V., and Summers, R., *The Law, Politics and the Constitution* (Oxford: Clarendon Press, 1999).

Bradley, A.W., "Applications for Judicial Review_the Scottish Model" [1987] *Public Law* 313.

_, "The Sovereignty of Parliament_In Perpetuity?", in *The Changing Constitution*, (J. Jowell and B. Oliver ed., (2nd edn, Oxford: University Press, 1989), pp.25–52.

_, "Justice, Good Government and Public Interest Immunity" [1992] *Public Law* 514.

__, and Ewing, K.D., and Knight, C.J.S., *Constitutional and Administrative Law* (16th ed., London: Longman, 2014).
Brady, A.D.P., *Proportionality and Deference under the UK Human Rights Act*, 2012
Brazier, R., *Constitutional Practice* (Oxford: Oxford University Press, 1988, 3rd edn., 1999).
__, *Constitutional Texts* (Oxford: Clarendon Press, 1990).
__, *Constitutional Reform*, 3rd edn. (Oxford: Oxford University Press, 2008).
Bridges, L., Meszaros, G., and Sunkin, M., *Judicial Review in Perspective* (2nd edn., 1995).
Bridges, Lord, *The Treasury* (London: Allen and Unwin, 1966).
Browning, P., *The Treasury and Economic Policy 1964–1985* (London: Longmans, 1986).
Browne-Wilkinson, N., "The Infiltration of a Bill of Rights" (1992) *Public Law* 397.
__, "The Independence of the Judiciary in the 1980s" [1988] *Public Law* 44–57.
Bryce, J., *Studies in History and Jurisprudence* 1901
Budge, I., Crewe, I., McKay, D., and Newton, K., *The New British Politics*, 2nd edn. (Harlow: Longman, 2001).
Burrows, N., *Devolution* (London: Sweet & Maxwell, 2000).
Butler, R., "The Evolution of the Civil Service_A Progress Report" (1993) 71 *Public Administration* 395–406.
Butler, D., Adonis A., Travers, T., *Failure in British Government: The Politics of the Poll Tax* (Oxford: Oxford University Press, 1994).
Byrne, Tony, *Local Government in Britain*, 7th edn. (London: Penguin, 2000).
Cabinet Office, *Public Bodies* (London: Stationery Office, 2001–).
__, *The Civil Service Yearbook 2001* (London: Stationery Office, 2001–).
Calvert, H., *Constitutional Law in Northern Ireland* (Belfast: Stevens, 1968).
Campbell, C., *Emergency Law in Ireland 1918–25* (Oxford: Clarendon Press, 1994).
Campbell, John, *Roy Jenkins: A Well-Rounded Life*, (London: Vintage Books, 2015).
Campbell, T., Ewing K.D., and Tomkins, A., (eds.) *The Legal Protection of Human Rights: Sceptical Essays on Human Rights* (Oxford: Oxford University Press, 2011).
Campion, *An Introduction to the Procedure of the House of Commons* (London, 1958).
Cane, P., *An Introduction to Administrative Law*, 5th edn. (Oxford: Clarendon Press, 2009).
Cappelletti, M., *The Judicial Process in Comparative Perspective* (Oxford: Oxford University Press, 1989).
Carr, C.T., *Delegated Legislation. Three Lectures* (Cambridge: Cambridge University Press, 1921).
Chrimes, S.B., *English Constitutional Ideas in the 15th Century* (London: Macmillan, 1966).
Clayton, R., " Judicial deference and "democratic dialogue": the legitimacy of judicial intervention under the Human Rights Act 1998" [2004] Public Law 33.
Cocks, R.C.J., *Sir Henry Maine: A Study in Victorian Jurisprudence* (Cambridge: Cambridge University Press, 1988).
Cohen, R, *Global Diasporas* (London: University College Press, 1999).
Cooke, Lord, *Turning Points of the Common Law The 47th Hamlyn Lectures*, (London: Sweet & Maxwell, 1997).
Cornish, W.R., and Clarke, de N., *Law and Society in England and Wales 1750–1950* (London: Sweet & Maxwell, 1989).

Cosgrove, R., *The Rule of Law: Albert Venn Dicey Victorian Jurist* (London: Macmillan, 1985).
Craig, P.P., *Administrative Law*, 7th edn. (London: Sweet & Maxwell, 2012).
__, *Public Law and Democracy in the United Kingdom and the United States of America* (Oxford: Oxford University Press, 1990).
Craig, P.P, "Public Law, Political Theory and Legal Theory" [2000] *Public Law* 211.
Craig, P.P. and De Burca, G., *EU LAW: Text, Cases and Materials*, 5th edn. (Oxford: Oxford University Press, 2011).
Craig, P., 2 The Stability, Cooridnation and Governanec Treaty: Principle,Politics and Pragmatism " (2012) 37 *European Law Review* 231–48.
Crick, B., *The Reform of Parliament Revised*, 2nd edn. (London: Weidenfeld and Nicholson, 1970).
Crick, M., *Michael Heseltine: A Biography* (London: Hamish Hamilton, 1997).
Crossman, R.H.S., *Inside View* (London: Jonathan Cape, 1972).
__, *Diaries of a Cabinet Minister*, Vol.2 (London: Hamish Hamilton and Jonathan Cape, 1977).
Cullen, M., *The Statistical Movement in Early Victorian Britain* (London: Hassocks, 1975).
Cullingworth, J., *Essays in Housing Policy* (London: Allen and Unwin, 1979).
Dahrendorf, R., "Citizenship and the Modern Social Conflict" in *1688–1988: Time for a New Constitution* (R. Holme and M. Elliott eds, London, 1988), Ch.7.
Daintith, T., "Public Law and Economic Policy" [1974] J.B.L. 9.
__, "The Functions of Law in the Field of Short-term Economic Policy" (1976) 92 L.Q.R. 62.
__, "Regulation by Contract: The New Prerogative" in *Current Legal Problems* (Lord Lloyd, R. Rideout and S. Guest ed., London: UCL, 1979).
__, (ed.), *Law as an Instrument of Economic Policy: Comparative and Critical Approaches* (Berlin: W. de Gruyter, 1988).
__, "Political Programmes and the Content of the Constitution" in *Edinburgh Essays in Public Law* (W. Finnie, C. Himsworth and N. Walker eds, Edinburgh: Edinburgh University Press, 1991).
__, "Between Domestic Democracy and an Alien Rule of Law? Some Thoughts on the Independence of the Bank of England" [1995] *Public Law* 118.
Daintith, T., and Page, A., *The Executive in the Constitution* (Oxford: Oxford University Press, 1999).
Dale, Sir William, *Legislative Drafting: A New Approach* (London: Butterworths, 1977).
De Burca, G., "The principle of proportionality and its application in EC law" (1993) *YEL* 105–130.
de Smith, S.A., *The Lawyers and the Constitution* (Inaugural Lecture, London School of Economics, 10 May 1960).
__, and Brazier, *Constitutional and Administrative Law*, 8th edn. (London: Penguin, 1998).
__, "The Boundaries between Parliament and the Courts" (1955) 18 M.L.R. 281.
de Smith, Woolf and Jowell's, *Principles of Judicial Review* (London: Sweet & Maxwell, 1999).
Davidson, Scott, *Human Rights* (Buckingham: Open University Press, 1993).
Dawson, J.P., *A History of Lay Judges* (Cambridge, Mass.: Harvard University Press, 1960).
Denning, A., *Freedom Under Law* (London: Butterworths, 1949).
Devlin, P., "The Common Law, Public Policy and the Executive" (1956) *Current Legal Problems* 1.

Devine, T.M., *The Scottish Nation 1700–2000* (London: Penguin, 1999).
Dicey, A.V., *Introduction to the Study of the Law of the Constitution* (London: Macmillan, 1885; 8th edn, 1915; 10th edn, 1959 with intro. by E.C.S. Wade).
__, "Droit Administratif in Modern French Law" (1901) 17 L.Q.R. 302.
__, *Lectures on the Relation between Law and Public Opinion in England During the Nineteenth Century* (London: Macmillan, 1905).
__, "The Development of Administrative Law in England" (1915) 31 L.Q.R. 148.
Dickson, B., and Carmichael, P., *The House of Lords: Its Parliamentary and Judicial Roles* (Oxford: Hart, 1999).
Diplock, Lord, "Administrative Law: Judicial Review Reviewed" (1975) *Cambridge Law Journal* 233.
Drewry, G., and Butcher, T., *The Civil Service Today* (Oxford: Blackwells, 1988).
Drewry, G., "Lawyers in the UK Civil Service" (1981) 59 *Public Administration* 15–46.
__, *The New Select Committees*, 2nd edn. (Oxford: Oxford University Press, 1989).
__, "The New Public Management" in *The Changing Constitution* (J. Jowell and D. Oliver ed., 4th edn., Oxford: Oxford University Press, 2001).
Dworkin, R., *Taking Rights Seriously* (Cambridge, Mass., 1977).
__, *A Matter of Principle* (Cambridge, Mass., and London, 1985).
__, *Law's Empire* (London, 1986).
__, *A Bill of Rights for Britain* (London, 1990).
__, *Freedom's Law: The Moral Reading of the American Constitution* (Oxford: Clarendon Press, 1996).
__, *Sovereign Virtue* (Cambridge, Mass.: Harvard University Press, 2000).
Efficiency Unit, *Improving Management in Government: The Next Steps* (London: Stationery Office, 1988).
__, *Making the Most of Next Steps: The Management of Ministers' Departments and their Executive Agencies* (London: Stationery Office, 1991).
Elliott, M., "The Human Rights Act 1998 and the Standard of Substantive Review" [2001] *Cambridge Law Journal* 301.
__, *The Constitutional Foundations of Judicial Review* (Oxford: Hart, 2001).
Ellis, E., (ed.), *The Principle of Proportionality in the Laws of Europe* (Oxford: Hart, 1999).
Erskine May, T., *Parliamentary Practice*, 22nd edn. (London: Butterworths, 1997).
Evans, A., *The EU Structural Funds* (Oxford: Oxford University Press, 1999).
Evans, P., *Handbook of House of Commons Procedures*, 2nd edn. (London: Vacher Dod Publishing, 1999).
Ewing, K., *The Funding of Political Parties* (Cambridge: Cambridge University Press, 1987).
__, *A Bill of Rights for Britain?* (London: Institute of Employment Rights, 1990).
__, "The Human Rights Act and Parliamentary Democracy" (1999) 62 *Modern Law Review* 79.
__, "A Theory of Democratic Adjudication: Towards a Representative, Accountable and Independent Judiciary" (2000) 38 *Alberta Law Review* 708.
Ewing, K.D., *Bonfire of the Liberties: New Labour, Human Rights and the Rule of Law* 2010

Ewing, K., and Gearty, C.A., *Freedom under Thatcher: Civil Liberties in Modern Britain* (Oxford: Clarendon Press, 1990).
__, *Democracy or a Bill of Rights* (London: Society of Labour Lawyers, 1991).
__, *The Struggle for Civil Liberties* (Oxford: Oxford University Press, 2000).
Faundez, J., (ed.), *Good Government and Law* (London: Macmillan in conjunction with the British Council, 1997).
Feldman, D., *Civil Liberties and Human Rights in England and Wales* (Oxford: Oxford University Press, 2002).
Feldman, D., J., ed., *English Public Law* 2nd edn., 2009.
Fenwick, H., *Civil Rights: New Labour, Freedom and the Human Rights Act* (Harlow, Essex: Longman, 2000).
Finer, S.E., "The Individual Responsibility of Ministers" (1956) 34 *Public Administration* 377.
Flegman, V., "The Public Accounts Committee: A Successful Select Committee?" (1980) *Parliamentary Affairs* 166.
Flinders, M., Gamble, A, Hay, C., and Kenny C., eds., *The Oxford Handbook of British Politics*, 2009
Flynn, N., *Public Sector Management*, 3rd edn. (London: Prentice Hall, 1997), pp.117–119.
Foley, M., *The Politics of the British Constitution* (Manchester: Manchester University Press, 1999).
Fordham, M., *Judicial Review Handbook*, 3rd edn. (Oxford: Hart, 2001).
Forsyth, C.F., "Beyond O'Reilly v. Mackman: the Foundations and Nature of Procedural Exclusivity" (1985) 44 *Cambridge Law Journal* 415.
__, "The Provenance and Protection of Legitimate Expectations", (1988) 47 *Cambridge Law Journal* 238.
Forsyth, C.F., and Hare, I., *The Golden Metwand and the Crooked Cord* (Oxford: Oxford University Press, 1998).
__, editor, *Judicial Review and the Constitution* (Oxford: Hart Publishing, 2000).
Foster, C., *Privatisation, Public Ownership and the Regulation of Natural Monopoly* (Oxford: Blackwell, 1992).
Foster, R.F., *Modern Ireland 1600–1972* (London: Allen Lane, 1988).
Francis, M., "The Nineteenth Century Theory of Sovereignty and Thomas Hobbes" (1980) 1 *History of Political Thought* 517.
Freedland, M., "Privatising Carltona: Part II of the Deregulation and Contracting Out Act 1994" (1995) *Public Law* 21–26.
Freedman, S., *Discrimination and Human Rights: The Case of Racism* (Oxford: Oxford University Press, 2001).
__, and Morris, G., "Civil Servants: A Contract of Employment" (1988) *Public Law* 58–77.
Gallagher, M., and Vincenzo Uleri, P., *The Referendum Experience in Europe* (London: Macmillan, 1996).
Galligan, D.J., *Discretionary Powers* (Oxford: Clarendon Press, 1986).
__, "Judicial Review and the Textbook Writers" (1982) 2 *Oxford Journal of Legal Studies* 257.
Ganz, G., *Administrative Procedures* (London: Sweet & Maxwell, 1974).

__, *Quasi-Legislation* (London: Sweet & Maxwell, 1987).
__, *Understanding Public Law*, 3rd edn. (London: Sweet & Maxwell, 2001).
Gearty, C., *Terror* (London: Faber and Faber, 1991).
__, ed., *European Civil Liberties and the European Convention on Human Rights* (London: Martinus Nijhoff Publishers, 1997).
__,C., *Civil Liberties* 2007
Gee, Graham, "The political constitutionalism of JAG Griffith" (2008) Legal Studies Vol 28 no 1 March 2008 pp.20–45.
Ghai, Y., *Hong Kong's New Constitutional Order* (Hong Kong: University Press, 1997).
Gordley, G., *The Philosophical Origins of Modern Contract Doctrine* (Oxford: Oxford University Press, 1991).
Gordon,R., and Street, A., *Select Committees and Coercive Powers: Clarity or Confusions?* 2012
Graham, C., and Prosser, T., "Privatising Nationalised Industries: Constitutional Issues and New Legal Techniques" (1987) 50 *Modern Law Review* 16–51.
__, *Privatising Public Enterprises: Constitutions, the State and Regulation in Comparative Perspective* (Oxford: Oxford University Press, 1999).
Graham, C., *Regulating Public Utilities: A Constitutional Approach* (Oxford: Hart, 2000).
Grant, Wyn, *Pressure Groups˙Politics and Democracy in Britain* (London: Philip Allan, 1989).
Green, T.H., *Lectures on the Principles of Political Obligation* (London, 1907).
Griffith, J.A.G., *Central Departments and Local Authorities* (London, 1966).
__, *Parliamentary Scrutiny of Government Bills* (London, 1974).
__, *The Politics of the Judiciary*, 5th edn. (London, 1997).
__, "Administrative discretion and the courts_the better part of valour?" (1955) 18 M.L.R. 159.
__, "Judges in Politics: England" (1968) 3 *Govt. and Oppos.* 485.
__, "Whose Bill of Rights?" *New Statesman* (14 November 1975).
__, "Standing Committees in the House of Commons" in *The Commons in the Seventies* (London: S.A. Walkland and M. Ryle ed., 1977).
__, "The Political Constitution" (1979) 42 *Modern Law Review* 1.
__, *Administrative Law and the Judges* (London: D.N. Pritt Memorial Lecture, 1978).
__, "Justice and Administrative Law Revisited" in *From Policy to Administration: Essays in Honour of William A. Robson* (London: J.A.G. Griffith ed., 1976).
__, "Constitutional and Administrative Law" in *More Law Reform Now* (Chichester: P. Archer and A. Martin ed., 1983).
__, "Judicial Decision-Making in Public Law" [1985] *Public Law* 564.
Griffith, J.A.G., and Ryle, M., *Parliament* (London: Sweet & Maxwell, 1989).
Hadfield, B., *The Constitution of Northern Ireland* (Belfast: SLS, 1989).
Hadfield B. (ed.), *Northern Ireland: Politics and the Constitution* (1992).
__, *Judicial Review: A Thematic Approach* (Dublin: Gill and Macmillan, 1995).
Hailsham, *The Dilemma of Democracy* (London, 1977).
__, "Elective Dictatorship" (The Richard Dimbleby Lecture, 1976), *Listener*, (21 October 1976), p.496.
Hamson, C.J., *Executive Discretion and Judicial Control* (London, 1954).

___, "The real lesson of Crichel Down" (1954) *Public Administration* 383–400.

Hansard Society, *Report of the Commission on Electoral Reform* (London: Hansard Society, 1976).

___, *Politics and Industry_The Great Mismatch* (London: Hansard Society, 1979).

___, *Paying for Politics: Report of the Hansard Society Commission upon the Financing of Political Parties* (London: Hansard Society, 1981).

___, *Report of the Hansard Society Commission on Parliamentary Scrutiny: The Challenge for Parliament: Making Government Accountable* (London: Hansard Society, Vacher Dod Publishing Ltd., 2001).

Harden, I., "Corporatism without Labour: The British Version" in *Waiving the Rules: The Constitution under Thatcherism* (C. Graham and T. Prosser ed., Milton Keynes: Open University Press, 1988).

Harden, I., Hollingsworth, K., and White, F., "Value for Money and Administrative Law" [1996] *Public Law* 661.

Harlow, C.R. and Rawlings, R.W., *Law and Administration*, 3rd edn. (London: Butterworths, 2009).

___, *Pressure Through Law* (London: Sweet & Maxwell, 1992).

Harlow, C., *Accountability in the European Union* (Oxford: Oxford University Press, 2002)

Harris, D.J., O'Boyle, M., and Warbrick, C., *Law of the European Convention on Human Rights* (London: Butterworths, 2009).

Hart, H.L.A., *The Concept of Law* (Oxford: Oxford University Press, 1961).

___, "Definition and Theory in Jurisprudence" (1954) 70 *Law Quarterly Review* 37.

___, "Positivism and the Separation of Law and Morals" (1958) 71 *Harv.Law Rev.* 593.

Hastings,M., *The Secret War: Spies,Codes and Guerrillas 1939–1945* (London: Harper Collins, 2015)

Hazell, R., ed., *The English Question* 2006

Hazell, R and Rawlings, R.W., *Devolution, Law Making and the Constitution* 2005

Hay, D., and Snyder, F., (eds.), *Policing and Prosecution in Britain 1750–1850* (Oxford: Oxford University Press, 1989).

Heald, D., "The Political Implications of Redefining Public Expenditure in the United Kingdom" (1991) 39 *Political Studies* 75–99.

___, and Steel, D., "Privatizing Public Enterprises: An Analysis of the Government's Case" (1982) 53 *Political Quarterly* 333–49.

___, and Georgiou, G., "Resource Accounting: Consolidation and Accounting Regulation" 73 (1995) *Public Administration* 571.

Heclo, H., and Wildavsky, A., *The Private Government of Public Money* (London: Macmillan, 1981).

Held, D., *Democracy and the Global Order* (Oxford: Blackwell, 1995).

Hennessy, P., *Whitehall* (London: Fontana Press, 1989; revised edn., 1990).

___, *Hidden Wiring* (London, 1995).

___, *The Blair Centre: A Question of Command and Control?* (London: Public Management Foundation, 1999).

_, *The Secret State: Whitehall and the Cold War* (London: Allen Lane, 2002).
Heuston, R.F.V., *Essays in Constitutional Law* (London: Stephens, 1964).
_, *Lives of the Lord Chancellors* (Oxford: Oxford University, 1989).
Hewart, G., *The New Despotism* (London, 1929).
Himsworth, C.M.G., and O'Neill, C.M., *Scotland's Constitution: Law and Practice* 2nd edn. 2009.
Hix, S., *The Political System of the European Union* (London: Macmillan Press, 1999).
Hogan, G., and Walker, C., *Political Violence and the Law in Ireland* (1989).
Holdsworth, W.S., *History of English Law* (A.C. Goodhart and H.S. London: Hanbury edn., 1956), Vol.5.
_, "The conventions of the Eighteenth Century Constitution" (1932) 17 *Iowa Law Review* 161.
Hoppen, T., *Ireland Since 1800* (London: Longman, 1992).
Horne, A., Drewry, G., and Oliver, D., eds., *Parliament and the Law*, 2013
Horwitz, M.J., *The Transformation of American Law 1780–1860* (Harvard: Harvard University Press, 1977) and *1870–1960* (Oxford: Oxford University Press, 1992).
House of Lords, Select Committee on the European Communities, *The Court of Auditors* (1986–87 HL 102).
_, *Financial Control and Fraud in the Community* (1993–94 HL 75).
_, Select Committee on the Constitution, *Reviewing the Constitution: terms of reference and methods of working*, First Report (2001–02 HL 11).
_, Select Committee on the Constitution, *Changing the Constitution: The Process of Constitutional Change*, (2001–02 HL 69).
Howe, Sir Geoffrey, *Conflict of Loyalty* (London: Macmillan, 1994).
Hughes, O.E., *Public Management and Administration*, 2nd edn. (London: MacMillan Press, 1998).
Ilbert, Sir Courtenay, *Legislative Methods and Forms* (Oxford: Clarendon Press, 1901).
Ibbetson, D.J., "What is legal history a history of?" in A. Lewis and A. M. Lobban, eds., *Law and History* (Oxford: Oxford University Press, 2004) pp.33–40.
Ingman, T., *The English Legal Process*, 5th ed. (Blackstone, London, 2000).
Institute for Fiscal Studies, The IFS Green Budget 2015 (London: Institute for Fiscal Studies, 2015)
Institute for Public Policy Research, *A British Bill of Rights* (London: IPPR, 1990).
_, *The Constitution of the United Kingdom* (London: IPPR, 1991).
Irvine, Lord of Lairg, Q.C., "Judges and Decision-Makers: The Theory and Practice of Wednesbury Review" (1996) *Public Law* 59–78.
Jacobs, F.G., White, R.C.A., and Ovey, C., *The European Convention on Human Rights* 5th edn., 2010.
Jaffe, L., and Henderson, E.G., "Judicial review and the Rule of Law: Historical Origins" (1956) 72 *Law Quarterly Review* 393.
Janis, M., Kay, R., and Bradley, A., *European Human Rights Law: Text and Materials*, 3rd edn. (Oxford: Oxford University Press, 2008).
Jenkins, R., *The Chancellors* (London: Macmillan, 1998).
_, *Churchill* (London: Macmillan, 2001).

Jennings, W.I., *The Law and the Constitution* (London: University of London, 1933).

__, *Parliament*, 2nd edn. (Cambridge: Cambridge University Press, 1957).

__, *Cabinet Government*, 3rd edn. (Cambridge: Cambridge University Press, 1959).

Johnson, N., *In Search of the Constitution: Reflections on State and Society in Britain* (Oxford: Pergamon Press, 1977).

Jones, B., Kavanagh, D., Moran, M., Norton, P., *Politics UK*, 4th edn. (Harlow: Longman, 2001).

Jones, Reginald, *Local Government Audit Law*, 2nd edn. (London: HMSO, 1985) with supplement, 1992).

Jowell, J., and Lester, A., "Beyond Wednesbury: Substantive Principles of Administrative Law" [1987] *Public Law* 368.

Jowell, J., "Proportionality: Neither Novel Nor Dangerous" in *New Directions in Judicial Review* (London: Sweet & Maxwell, J. Jowell and D. Oliver eds, 1988).

__, "Courts and Administration in Britain: Standards, Principles and Rights" (1988) Israel L.R. 409.

__, and Oliver, D. (eds.), *The Changing Constitution*, 8th edn. (Oxford: Oxford University Press, 2015).

__, and Woolf, *de Smith's Judicial Review & Administrative Action*, 5th edn. (London: Sweet & Maxwell, 1995).

Judson, M.A., *The Crisis of the Constitution: An Essay in constitutional and political thought in England 1603–1645* (New Brunswick, N.J.: Rutgers University Press, 1949).

Justice, *The Citizen and the Administration* (London, 1977).

__, *The Local Ombudsman: A Review of the First Five Years* (London, 1980).

__, *The Administration of the Courts* (London, 1986).

__, *All Souls, Review of Administrative Law in the United Kingdom* (London, 1988).

Kapetyn, P.J.G., and Verloren Van Themaat, *Introduction to the Law of the European Communities*, 3rd edn. (with Lawrence Gormley) (The Hague: Kluwer Law International, 1998).

Kay, J., and Thompson, D., "Privatisation: A Policy in Search of a Rationale", (1986) 96 *Economic Journal* 18–32.

Kay, J., Mayer, C., and Thompson, D., Privatisation and Regulation_the UK Experience 2nd edn. (Oxford: Oxford University Press, 1986).

Keir, D., and Lawson, F.H., *Cases in Constitutional Law*, 5th edn. (Oxford: University Press, 1967).

Keir, D.L., *The Constitutional History of Modern Britain 1585–1937*, 3rd edn. (London: Adam and Charles Black, 1948).

Kelly, J.M., *A Short History of Western Legal Theory* (Oxford: Oxford University Press, 1992).

Kelsey, J., *The New Zealand Experiment* (Auckland: Auckland University Press, 1995).

King, A., *Does the United Kingdom Still have a Constitution?* (London: Sweet & Maxwell, 2001).

__, *The British Constitution* 2007.

Kittichaisaree, K., *International Criminal Law* (Oxford: Oxford University Press, 2001).

Laffan, B., *Finances of the European Union* (London: MacMillan, 1997).

Landes, D., *The Wealth and Poverty of Nations* (London: Abacus, 1998).

Laski, H.J., *Studies in the Problem of Sovereignty* (London, 1917).
Law Commission, *Administrative Law: Judicial Review and Statutory Appeals*, Consultation Paper No.126 (HMSO, 1993).
Laundy, P., *The Office of Speaker* 1964
Lawson, Nigel, *The View from No. 11* (1992).
Layard, A., "The Localism Act 2011: what is 'local' and how do we (legally) construct it?" (2012) *Environmental Law Review* 134.
Leigh, D., *Betrayed, The Real Story of the Matrix Churchill Trial* (London: Macmillan, 1993).
Leigh, D., and Vulliamy, (eds), *Sleaze* (London: Fourth Estate, 1997).
Leigh, I., and Lustgarten, L., "The Security Service Act 1989" (1989) 52 *Modern Law Review* 801–40.
__, *In From the Cold: The Intelligence Services and National Security* (Oxford: Oxford University Press, 1994).
Lester,A., Pannick, D., and Herberg, J., eds., *Human Rights Law and Practice*, 3rd edn., 2009
Lewis, C.B., *Judicial remedies in Public Law*, 4th edn., 2009
Leyland, P., The Constitution of the United Kingdom, 2nd edn. (Oxford: Hart Publishers, 2012).
Lieberman, D., *The Province of Legislation Determined* (Cambridge: Cambridge University Press, 1989).
Likierman, A., *Public Expenditure* (London: Penguin Books, 1988).
__, "Resource Accounting and Budgeting: Rationale and Background" 73 (1995) *Public Administration* 562.
Lipsey, D., *In the Corridors of Power* (London: Biteback Books, 2012)
Lobban, M., *The Common Law and English Jurisprudence 1760–1850* (Oxford: Clarendon Press, 1991).
Locke, J., *Two Treatises of Government* (1690), (P. Laslett ed., Cambridge: Cambridge University Press, 1960).
Loughlin, M., *Local Government in the Modern State* (London: Sweet & Maxwell, 1986).
__, "Law, Ideologies and the Political-Administrative System" (1989) 16 *Journal of Law & Society* 21.
__, "Innovative Financing in Local Government: The Limits of Legal Instrumentalism" [1990] *Public Law* 372 (Pt. I); [1991] *Public Law* 568 (Pt. II).
__, *Public Law and Political Theory* (Oxford, 1992).
__, "The Pathways of Public Law Scholarship" in G.P. Wilson, (ed.), *Frontiers of Legal Scholarship* (G.P. Wilson ed., London: John Wiley, 1996) pp.163–188.
__, *Legality and Locality: The Role of Law in Central-Local Government Relations* (Oxford: Oxford University Press, 1996).
__, *Sword and Scales* (Oxford: Hart, 2000).
__, *The British Constitution* (Oxford: Oxford University Press, 2013)
Loveland, I., *Constitutional Law: A Critical Introduction* (London: Butterworths, 2012: 6th edn., 2012).
__, (ed.), *A Special Relationship? American Influences on Public Law in the UK* (Oxford: Clarendon Press, 1995).

Macpherson, C.B., *The Life and Times of Liberal Democracy* (Oxford: Oxford University Press, 1977).

McAuslan, P., "Administrative Law, Collective Consumption and Judicial Policy" (1983) 46 *Modern Law Review* 1.

__, "Dicey and his influence on public law" [1985] *Public Law* 721.

__, "Public Law and Public Choice" (1988) 51 *Modern Law Review* 681.

__, and McEldowney, J.F. (ed.), *Law, Legitimacy and the Constitution* (London: Sweet & Maxwell, 1985).

__, "Legitimacy and the Constitution: the Dissonance between Theory and Practice" in *Law, Legitimacy and the Constitution* (McAuslan and McEldowney eds, London: Sweet & Maxwell, 1985).

McEldowney, J.F., "The Contingencies Fund and the Parliamentary Scrutiny of Public Finance" [1988] *Public Law* 232–245.

__, "The National Audit Office and Privatisation" (1991) *Modern Law Review* 933–955.

__, "The Nationalisation Legislation of the 1940s and the Privatisation Legislation of the 1980s: A Constitutional Perspective", in *Constitutional Studies* (R. Blackburn ed., London: Mansell, 1992) pp.42–64.

__, "Administrative Justice" in *Rights of Citizenship* (R. Blackburn ed., London: Mansell, 1993), Ch.8, pp.156–78.

__, "The Control of Public Expenditure" in Jowell and Oliver ed., *The Changing Constitution* (3rd edn., 1994), pp.175–207; 4th edn. (Oxford: Oxford University Press, 2000), pp.190–228).

__, "Criminal Law and the development of Labour relations in Nineteenth-Century Ireland" in *Festschrift in honour of Paul O'Higgins* (Hepple, Ewing and Gearty eds, London: Mansell, 1994), Ch.12, pp.267–93.

__, "Public utilities: Is the British experience a model for developing countries? " in *Good Government and Law* (Julio Faundez ed., Macmillan in association with the British Council, London, 1997), pp.147–62.

__, (ed.), *National and International Perspectives on Law and Privatisation* (London: British Institute of International and Comparative Law, 1999).

__, *Modernizing Britain: Public Law and Challenges to Parliament* (New Zealand: University of Waikato Press, 2002) edited: J. Mackinnon and Paul Havermann.

McEldowney, J., and McEldowney, S., *Environment and the Law* (London: Longman, 1996).

__, *Environmental Law and Regulation* (London and Oxford: Blackstone and Oxford University Press, 2001).

McEldowney, J.F., "Debt Limits in German Constitutional Law – a UK Perspective" in Wolf-Georg Ringe and Peter H. Huber eds., *Legal Challenges in the Global Financial Crisis* (Oxford, 2014), pp.63–78.

McCrudden, C. (ed.), *Anti-Discrimination Law* (Aldershot: Dartmouth, 1991).

McCrudden, C., "Northern Ireland and the British Constitution" in *The Changing Constitution*, J. Jowell and D. Oliver eds, 2nd edn. (Oxford: Oxford University Press, 1989), pp.297–344.

McLean, I., *What's Wrong with the British Constitution?* 2010

McQuade, D., Fagon, J., *The Governance of Northern Ireland* (Belfast: Northern Whig, 2002).

Maitland, F.W., *The Constitutional History of England* (Cambridge: Cambridge University Press, 1908).

Marshall, G., *Constitutional Conventions. The Rules and Forms of Political Accountability* (Oxford: Oxford University Press, 1984).

__, (ed.), *Ministerial Responsibility* (Oxford: Oxford University Press, 1989).

__, and Moodie, G.C., *Some Problems of the Constitution*, 5th edn. (London: Hutchinson University Library, 1971).

Mayer, C., and Meadowcraft, S., "Selling Public Assets: Techniques and Financial Implications" in *Privatisation and Regulation: The UK Experience*, J. Kay, C. Mayer and D. Thompson, eds, (Oxford: Oxford University Press, 1986).

Mayer, C., "Public Ownership: Concepts and Applications" (1987) *Centre for Economic Policy Research Working Paper*, Vol.182.

Menski, W., *Comparative Law in a global context* (London: Platinium, 2000).

Metcalfe, Les and Richards, S., *Improving Public Management*, 2nd edn. (London: Sage, 1990).

Miers, D., and Page, A., *Legislation*, 2nd edn., 1990.

Milhaupt, C.J., Mark Ramseyer, J., and Young, M.K., *Japanese Law in Context* (Cambridge, Mass.: Harvard University Press, 2001).

Mill, J.S., *On Liberty* (1859) G. Himmelfarb ed., (London: Harmondsworth, 1974).

__, *Auguste Comte and Positivism* (1865): (Ann Arbor: Mich., 1961).

__, "Chapters on Socialism" (1879) 25 *Fortnightly Review* 226.

Miller, R., ed. *New Zealand Politics in Transition* (Auckland: Oxford University Press, 1998).

Milsom, S.F.C., *Historical Foundations of the Common Law*, 2nd edn. (London: Butterworths, 1980).

Mitchel, J., *Devolution in the United Kingdom*, 2009

Mitchell, J.D., *Constitutional Law*, 2nd edn. (Edinburgh: Edinburgh University Press, 1968).

__, "The state of public law in the United Kingdom" [1966] 15 I.C.L.Q. 133.

__, "The constitutional implications of judicial control of the administration in the United Kingdom" (1967) *Cambridge Law Journal* 46.

Moore, J., "Why Privatise?" *Privatisation and Regulation: The UK Experience*, J. Kay, C. Mayer, and D. Thompson ed., (Oxford: Oxford University Press, 1983).

Moore, V., *A Practical Approach to Planning Law*, 7th edn. (London: Blackstone, 2000).

Morrison, Lord, *Government and Parliament: A Survey from the Inside*, 3rd edn. (Oxford: Oxford University Press, 1964).

Mowbray, A.R., *Cases and Materials on the European Convention on Human Rights*, 3rd edn., 2012.

National Audit Office, *Pergau Hydro Electric Project* (1992–93 HC 908).

__, *Resource Accounting and Budgeting in Government* (1994–95 HC 123).

__, *The Work of the Directors of Telecommunications, Gas Supply, Water Service and Electricity Supply* (1995–96 HC 645).

__, *State Audit in the European Union* (London, 1996).

__, *Audit of Assumptions for the Pre-Budget Report* (1997–98 HC 361).

Nicolson, I.F., *The Mystery of Crichel Down* (1986).

Nolan, Lord, *First Report of the Committee on Standards in Public Life*, Cm.2850; *Second Report of the Committee on Standards in Public Life*, Cm.3270–1.

Nolan, Lord, and Sedley, Stephen, *The Making and Remaking of the British Constitution* (London: Blackstone Press, 1997).

Normanton, E.L., *The Accountability and Audit of Governments* (Manchester: Manchester University Press, 1966).

Norton, P., *The Constitution in Flux* (Oxford: Blackwell, 1982).

__, Parliament in British Politics, 2nd edn., 2005

O'Keffe, D., "The court of Auditors" in *Institutional Dynamics of European Integration* (D. Curtin and T. Heukels ed., London: Kluwer, 1984).

O'Leary, B., "What should Public Lawyers Do?" (1992) 12 O.J.L.S. No.3, pp.304–18.

O'Riordan, T., Kemp, R., and Purdue, M., *Sizewell B: An Anatomy of an Inquiry* (1988).

Oliver, D., *Government in the United Kingdom* (Milton Keynes: Open University Press, 1991).

__, and Austin, R., "Political and Constitutional Aspects of the Westland Affair" (1987) 40 *Parliamentary Affairs* 20–40.

__, "Common Values in Public and Private Law and the Public/Private Divide" [1997] *Public Law* 21.

Oliver, D., and Drewry, G., *Public Service Reform: issues of Accountability and Public Law* (London: Pinter, 1996).

__, (ed.), *Law and Parliament* (London: Butterworths, 1998).

Oliver, D., *Constitutional Reform in the UK* 2004

__ and Fusaro, C., *How Constitutions Change: A Comparative Study*, 2011

Olowofoyeku, A., *Suing Judges* (Oxford: Oxford University Press, 1993).

Palley, C., *The Constitutional History and Law of Southern Rhodesia 1888–1965* (Oxford: Oxford University Press, 1979).

__, *The Evolution, Disintegration and Possible Reconstruction of the Northern Ireland Constitution* (Chichester: Barry Rose Publishers, 1972). Also see (1972) 1 *Anglo-American L.Rev.* 368.

__, *The United Kingdom and Human Rights* (London: Sweet & Maxwell, 1991).

Pallot, J., and Ball, I., "Resource Accounting and Budgeting: The New Zealand Experience" 74 (1996) *Public Administration* 527.

Palmer, G., *Unbridled Power?* (Auckland: Oxford University Press, 1979).

Palmer, G., and Palmer, M., Bridled Power: New Zealand Government under MMP (Auckland: Oxford University Press, 1999).

Parris, H., *Constitutional Bureaucracy: The Development of British Central Administration since the Eighteenth Century* (London: Allen and Unwin, 1969).

Pattie, C., and Johnson, R., "How Big is the Big Society?" (2011) 64 *Parliamentary Affairs* 403.

Peacock, A.T., and Wiseman, J., *The Growth of Public Expenditure in the United Kingdom* (1961).

Plant, R., *The Plant Report* (London: IPPR, 1990).

Pliatzky, L., *The Treasury under Mrs Thatcher* (Oxford: Blackwell, 1989).

__, *Getting and Spending*, revised edn. (Oxford: Blackwell, 1984).

Pocock, J.G.A., *The Machiavellian Movement: Florentine Political Thought and the Atlantic Republican Tradition* (Princeton: Princeton University Press, 1975).

Pogany, Istvan, "Privatisation and Regulatory Change in Hungary" in *Privatization and Regulatory Change in Europe* (M. Moran and T. Prosser eds, Milton Keynes: Open University Press, 1994).

Pollack, A., *A Citizen's Inquiry: The Opsahl Report on Northern Ireland* (Dublin, 1993).

Pollard, D., and Hughes, D., *Constitutional and Administrative Law*, 3rd edn. (London: Butterworths, 2001).

Porter, Theodore, *The Rise of Statistical Thinking 1820–1900* (Princeton: Princeton University Press, 1986).

Poulter, S., *Ethnicity and Human Rights* (Oxford: Clarendon Press, 1998).

Pound, R., "Liberty of Contract" (1908–9) 18 *Yale L.J.* 454.

__, "Law in Books and Law in Action" (1910) 44 *American Law Rev.* 12.

__, "The Scope and Purpose of Sociological Jurisprudence" (1911) 24 Harv.L.Rev. 591; (1911) 25 Harv.L.Rev. 140; (1912) 25 Harv.L.Rev. 489.

__, "The Call for a Realist Jurisprudence" (1931) 44 Harv.L.Rev. 697.

Power, M., *The Audit Explosion* (London: Demos, 1995).

Priest, G.L., "The Common Law Process and the Selection of Efficient Rules" (1977) 6 *Journal of Legal Studies* 65.

Prime Minister's Efficiency Unit, Improving Management in Government: the Next Steps (London: (Ibbs Report), 1988).

Prosser, T., "Towards a Critical Public Law" (1982) *Journal of Law and Society* 9: 1–19.

__, *Nationalised Industries and Public Control* (Oxford: Oxford University Press, 1986).

Prosser, T., *The Economic Constitution* (Oxford: Oxford University Press, 2014).

Rawlings, R.W., *Delineating Wales: Constitutional, Legal and Administrative Aspects of National Devolution* 2003.

Rawls, J., *A Theory of Justice* (Oxford: Oxford University Press, 1972).

__, "Justice as Fairness: Political not Metaphysical" (1985) 14 *Philosophy and Public Affairs* 223.

__, "The Idea of an Overlapping Consensus" (1987) 7 O.J.L.S. 1.

Redlich, J. and Hirst, F. *A History of Local Government in England*, B. Keith-Lucas ed., (London: Macmillan, 1970).

Reports., *Report of the Committee on Ministers' Powers*, Cmd.4060 (1932) (Donoughmore Report).

__, *Report of the Committee on Tribunals and Enquiries* (1957) (Franks Report).

__, *Report of the Royal Commission on Legal Services* Cmnd.7448 (1980).

Ridley, F.F., "There is no British Constitution: A Dangerous case of the Emperor's Clothes" (1988) 41 *Parliamentary Affairs* 340–61.

Robertson, G., *Freedom, the Individual and the Law*, 7th edn. (London: Penguin, 1993).

__, *The Justice Game* (London: Chatto and Windus, 1998).

Robinson, O.F., Fergus, T.D., Gordon, W.M., *European Legal History*, 2nd edn. (London: Butterworths, 1994).

Robson, W.A., *Justice and Administrative Law*, 2nd edn., 1947; 3rd edn., 1951 (London: University of London, 1928).

__, *Public Administration Today* (London, 1948).

__, "The Report of the Committee on Ministers' Powers" (1932) 3 *Political Quarterly* 346.
__, "Administrative Law in England 1919–1948" in *British Government Since 1918*, G. Campion ed., (London, 1950).
__, "Administrative Justice and Injustice: A Commentary on the Franks Report" [1958] P.L. 12.
__, "Administrative Law" in *Law and Opinion in England in the Twentieth Century*, M. Ginsberg ed., (London, 1959).
__, "Justice and Administrative Law reconsidered" (1979) 32 *Current Legal Problems* 107.
Rogers, S., ed., The Hutton Inquiry and its Impact, 2004
Rosenfeld, M andSajo, *The Oxford Handbook of Comparative Constiutional Law*, 2012
Rose-Ackerman, S., *Corruption and Government* (Cambridge: Cambridge University Press, 1999).
Roseveare, H., *The Treasury 1660–1870* (London: Allen and Unwin, 1973).
Russell, M., *Reforming the House of Lords: Lessons from Overseas* (Oxford: Clarendon Press, 2000).
Rudden, B., and Wyatt, D. (eds.), *Basic Community Laws*, 6th edn. (Oxford, 1996).
Sands, P., *Lawless World*, revised edn., 2006.
Scott Report: *Return to an Address of the Honourable House of Commons dated 15th February 1996. Report of the Inquiry into the Export of Defence Equipment and Dual-use Goods to Iraq and Related Prosecutions*, The Rt Hon. Sir Richard Scott, The Vice-Chancellor (1996 HC 115) (London: HMSO, 1996).
Schwartz, B., and Wade, H.W.R., *Legal Control of Government: Administrative Law in Britain and the United States* (Oxford: Clarendon Press, 1972).
Sedley, Stephen, "The Sound of Silence: Constitutional Law without a Constitution" (1994) 110 *Law Quarterly Review* 270–91.
Sedley, Lord Justice, *Freedom, Law and Justice*, 50th Hamlyn Lectures (London: Sweet & Maxwell, 1999).
__, and Nolan, Lord, *The Making and Remaking of the British Constitution* (London: Blackstone, 1997).
Shell, D., *The House of Lords*, 2nd edn. (Oxford: Oxford University Press, 1992).
Shell, D., and Beamish, D., *The House of Lords at Work* (Oxford: Oxford University Press, 1993).
Silk, P., and Walters, R., *How Parliament Works*, 4th edn. (London: Longman, 1999).
Shortt, G, *Informations, Mandamus and Prohibitions* (London: Macmillan, 1887).
Simpson, B., *Human Rights and the End of Empire: Britain and the Genesis of the European Convention* (Oxford: Oxford University Press, 2001).
Skidelsky, R., *Politicians and the Slump: the Labour Government of 1929–31* (London, 1967).
__, John Maynard Keynes (London: Macmillan, 1983; Vol.3, London: Macmillan, 2000).
Skinner, Q., *The Foundation of Modern Political Thought*, 2 Vols., (Cambridge: Cambridge University Press, 1982).
Slapper, G. and Kelly, D., *The English Legal System*, 4th edn. (London: Cavendish, 1999).
Smith, L.B., "Accountability and Independence in the Contract State" in *The Dilemma of Accountability in Modern Government* (B. Smith and D. Hague eds, London, 1971).
Snyder, F., (ed.) *The Europeanisation of Law* (Oxford: Hart Publishing, 2000).

Stein, P., and Shand, J., *Legal Values in Western Society* (Edinburgh: Edinburgh University Press, 1974).

Steiner, H.J. and Alston, P., *International Human Rights in Context*, 2nd edn. (Oxford: Oxford University Press, 2000).

Sterett, S., *Creating Constitutionalism? The Politics of Legal Expertise and Administrative Law in England and Wales* (Ann Arbor: University of Michigan Press, 1997).

Stevens, R., *The Independence of the Judiciary: The View from the Lord Chancellor's Office* (Oxford: Clarendon Press, 1993).

__, *Law and Politics. The House of Lords as a Judicial Body 1800–1976* (London: Weidenfeld and Nicolson, 1979).

Stone Sweet, A., *Governing with Judges* (Oxford: Oxford University Press, 2000).

Sugarman, D., "Legal Theory, the Common Law Mind and the Making of the Textbook Tradition" in *Legal Theory and Common Law*, W. Twining ed. (Oxford: Oxford University Press, 1986), Ch.3.

__, "The Legal Boundaries of Liberty: Dicey, Liberalism and Legal Science" (1983) *Modern Law Review* 102.

Sunkin, M., Bridges, Lee, and Meszaros, G., *Judicial Review* (London: The Public Law Project, 1993).

__, and Le Sueur, A.P., "Can Government Control Judicial Review?" (1991) *Current Legal Problems* 161–83.

__, and Payne, S., *The Nature of the Crown* (Oxford: Oxford University Press, 1999).

Taggart, M., "Tugging on Superman's Cape: Lessons from the Experience with the New Zealand Bill of Rights Act 1990" [1998] *Public Law* 266.

Thain, C., "The Education of the Treasury: The Medium Term Financial Strategy, 1980–84", (1985) 63 *Public Administration* 261–85.

__, and Wright, M., "Planning and Controlling Public Expenditure in the United Kingdom (Part 1). The Treasury's Public Expenditure Survey" (1992) 70 *Public Administration* 3–24; Part II, (1992) 70 *Public Administration* 193–224.

__, *The Treasury and Whitehall: The Planning and Control of Public Expenditure 1976–1993* (Oxford: Clarendon Press, 1995).

Thompson, B., *Textbook on Constitutional and Administrative Law*, 3rd edn. (London: Blackstone Press, 1997).

Thring, H., *Practical Legislation* (London: John Murray, 1902).

Tomkins, A., "Public Interest Immunity after Matrix Churchill" [1993] *Public Law* 650.

Tomkins, A., *The Constitution after Scott: Government Unwrapped*, 1998.

Tomkins, A., *Our Republican Constitution* 2005

Tomlinson, J., *Public Policy and the Economy Since 1900* (Oxford: Oxford University Press, 1900).

Townshend, C., *Political Violence in Ireland* (Oxford: Oxford University Press, 1985).

Treasury and Civil Service Committee, *Eighth Report, Session 1987–88, Civil Service Management Reform: The Next Steps* (1987–88 HC 494).

Turpin, C., *British Government and the Constitution*, 4th edn. (London: Butterworths, 1999).

Van Caenegem, R.C., *An Historical Introduction to Western Constitutional Law* (Cambridge: Cambridge University Press, 1995).

Von Meheren, and Gordley, J., *The Civil Law System: An Introduction to the Comparative Study of Law*, 2nd edn. (Boston: University Press, 1977).

Vogel, D., *National Styles of Regulation* (Ithaca and London: Cornell University Press, 1986).

Vickers, J., and Yarrow, G., *Privatisation and the Natural Monopolies* (London, 1985).

__, *Privatisation: An Economic Analysis* (Boston, 1988).

Vile, M.J.C., *Constitutionalism and the Separation of Power* (Oxford, 1967).

Wade, E.C.S. and Phillips, G.G., *Constitutional and Administrative Law* (London, 1931; 11th ed., 1993 by A.W. Bradley and K. Ewing).

Wade, H.W.R., *Administrative Law*, 6th edn. (Oxford, 1988).

__, Constitutional Fundamentals (London, 1980).

__, "The Concept of Legal Certainty. A Preliminary Sketch" (1940–1) 4 M.L.R. 183.

__, "Quasi-judicial and its background" (1949) 10 Camb. L.J. 216.

__, "The Twilight of Natural Justice" (1951) 67 L.Q.R. 103.

__, "The Basis of Legal Sovereignty" (1955) Camb. L.J. 172.

__, "Law, Opinion and Administration" (1962) 78 L.Q.R. 188.

__, "Unlawful administrative action_void or voidable" (1967) 83 L.Q.R. 499 (Pt I); (1968) 84 L.Q.R. 95 (Pt II).

__, "Sovereignty and the European Communities" (1972) 88 L.Q.R. 1.

__, "Procedure and Prerogative in Public Law" (1985) 101 L.Q.R. 180.

__, "What has happened to the Sovereignty of Parliament?" (1991) 107 L.Q.R. 1.

Wadham, J., and Mountfield, H., *Blackstone's Guide to the Human Rights Act 1998* (London: Blackstone, 1999; 2nd edn., 2001).

Waldron, J., *The Law, Theory and Practices in British Politics* (London: Routledge, 1990).

Walker, C., *The Prevention of Terrorism in British Law*, 2nd edn. (Manchester: Manchester University Press, 1992).

Waller, R., "The 1983 Boundary Commission: Policies and Effects" (1983) 4 *Electoral Studies* 195.

Watt, B., *UK Election Law: A Critical Examination*, 2006.

Waters, M., *Globalization* (London: Routledge, 1995).

Weir, S., *Unequal Britain* 2006

Wheare, K.C., *Modern Constitutions* (2nd edn., 1966).

White, F., and Hollingsworth, K., "Resource Accounting and Budgeting: Constitutional Implications" [1997] *Public Law* 437.

__, *Audit, Accountability and Government* (Oxford: Clarendon Press, 1999).

Whittaker, E., *A History of Economic Ideas* (London: Longmans, 1940).

Wicks, E., *The Evolution of a Constitution: Eight Key Moments in British Constitutional History* 2006

Wildavsky, A., and Zapico-Goni, E., (eds) *National Budgeting for Economic and Monetary Union* (London: Institute of Public Administration, 1994).

Williams, D.G.T.,"Public local inquiries_formal administrative adjudication" (1980) 29 *International and Comparative Law Quarterly* 701.

__, "The Donoughmore Report in Retrospect" (1982) 60 *Public Administration* 273.
__, "The Council on Tribunals: the first twenty five years" [1984] *Public Law* 79.
Winch, D., and Burrow, J., *That Noble Science of Politics: A Study in Nineteenth Century Intellectual History* (Cambridge: Cambridge University Press, 1983).
Wistrich, E., "Restructuring Government New Zealand style" (1992) 70 *Public Administration* 119–35.
Woodhouse, D., "Ministerial Responsibility: Something Old, Something New" [1997] *Public Law* 262.
__, *The Office of Lord Chancellor* (Oxford: Hart, 2001).
__, *In Pursuit of Good Administration; Ministers, Civil Servants and Judges* (Oxford: Clarendon Press, 1997).
Woolf, H., "Public law_private law: Why the divide?" [1986] *Public Law* 220.
__, *Protection of the Public: A New Challenge?* (London: Stevens, 1990).
Woolf, Lord, Jowell, J., Le Sueur, A., Donnelly, C., and Hare, I., *De Smith's Judicial Review* 7th edition 2013.
Wraith, R.E., and Lamb, G.B., *Public Inquiries as an Instrument of Government* (1971).
Wright, M., *Treasury Control of the Civil Service 1854–1974* (Oxford: Oxford University Press, 1969).
Wyatt, D., and Dashwood, A., *Substantive European Community Law*, 4th edn. (London: Sweet & Maxwell, 2000).
Young, H., *This Blessed Plot: Britain and Europe from Churchill to Blair* (London: Macmillan, 1998).
Zellick, G., *Final Report of the Task Force on Student Disciplinary Procedures chaired by Professor Graham Zellick*, (CVCP, December 1994).
Ziegler, K., Baranger, D., and Bradley, A.W., Constituitonalism and the Role of Parliaments 2007.
Zimmermann, R., *Roman law, Contemporary Law, European Law: The Civilian Tradition Today* (Oxford: Oxford University Press, 2001).
Zweigert, K., and Kotz, H., *An Introduction to Comparative Law*, 2nd edn. (Oxford: Clarendon Press, 1994).

Index

This index has been prepared using Sweet and Maxwell's Legal Taxonomy. Main index entries conform to keywords provided by the Legal Taxonomy except where references to specific documents or non-standard terms (denoted by quotation marks) have been included. These keywords provide a means of identifying similar concepts in other Sweet & Maxwell publications and online services to which keywords from the Legal Taxonomy have been applied. Readers may find some minor differences between terms used in the text and those which appear in the index.

Suggestions to **taxonomy@sweetandmaxwell.co.uk**.

(All references are to paragraph number)

Abuse of discretion
    judicial review
        generally, 17–092—17–095
        Wednesbury unreasonableness, 17–096—17–102

Academic lawyers
    jurisprudence, 8–068—8–088

Accepted Practice regime
    see **Public expenditure**

Accidents
    inquiries, 15–037—15–038

Accountability
    BBC, 20–099—20–101
    civil service, 11–057—11–062
    Civil Service Code, 10–017
    constitutional conventions, 5–032
    Crown
        appointment of ministers, 10–080
        appointment of Prime Minister, 10–081
        Crown proceedings, 10–083
        dismissal of ministers, 10–082
        petitions of right, 10–083
        privileges, 10–084
        public interest immunity, 10–085—10–096
    economic regulation and, 10–008
    executive agencies, 11–034—11–051

    government
        public interest immunity, 10–079—10–111
        secrecy, 10–112—10–127
    introduction, 10–001—10–004
    local government, 13–096—13–102
    meaning, 10–005—10–018
    ministerial responsibility, 10–072—10–078
    Parliament
        generally, 10–037—10–040
        parliamentary reform, 10–070—10–071
        parliamentary scrutiny, 10–041—10–053
        select committees, 10–054—10–069
    parliamentary scrutiny, 10–041—10–053
    police powers and duties, 16–152—16–154, 19–073—19–087
    political parties, 10–023–10–036
    public interest immunity
        balancing of interests test, 10–110
        closed material, 10–111
        criminal prosecutions, 10–101—10–109
        Crown, 10–080—10–096
        generally, 10–079
        ministers, 10–097—10–100
        special advocates, 10–111

    Questions of Procedures for Ministers, 10–012—10–016
    redress schemes, 10–009
    responsible government, 10–011
    Scott Inquiry, 10–019—10–022
    secrecy and, 10–006
    select committees, 10–054—10–069
    summary, 10–128—10–131

Accounting officers
    public expenditure, 12–023—12–027, 12–066

Accounts
    elections, 7–070—7–071

Additional member system
    see **Elections**

Administration of justice
    role of courts, 6–109—6–141

Administrative decision-making
    judicial review, 17–008—17–013

Administrative law
    Administrative Law Court, 6–009
    aims of, 1–005—1–010
    central government, 6–093—6–108
    Commonwealth, influence of, 1–033
    contracts, 6–085—6–092
    courts
        administration of justice, 6–109—6–141
        judicial review, 6–142—6–155

EU law, 1-033
evolving nature of, 1-011—1-020, 1-037
executive agencies, 6-099—6-100
fringe organisations, 6-101—6-108
functions of, 1-005—1-010
future of
    constitutional reforms, 21-012—21-017
    developing constitution, 21-009—21-011
    English votes for English laws, 21-025—21-028
    introduction, 21-001—21-008
    public law scholarship, 21-029—21-059
    written UK constitution, 21-018—21-024
"green light" theory, 6-006
historical perspective
    allocation of functions, 6-060—6-064
    courts, 6-036—6-059
    generally, 6-014—6-022
    state intervention, 6-023—6-035
human rights, 1-010, 6-156—6-162
inquiries, 6-178—6-183
introduction, 1-001—1-004, 6-003—6-013
judicial review, 6-013, 6-142—6-155
legislation
    Church of England, 6-067
    delegated legislation, 6-068—6-069, 6-075
    generally, 6-065
    Orders in Council, 6-066
    quasi-legislation, 6-072—6-074
    regulatory reform, 6-070—6-071
    special procedure orders, 6-067
licences, 6-081—6-084
limits on economic power, 1-008
local government, 6-093—6-108
locus standi, 18-021—18-032
meaning, 6-003
political power and, 1-006—1-009
prerogative powers, 6-076—6-080
pressure groups, 6-004
private law distinguished, 1-003
"red light" theory, 6-006
scope of, 1-003—1-004, 1-038
summary, 6-184—6-185
tribunals, 6-163—6-177

Advertising
commercial broadcasting, 20-104

Advocates General
Court of Justice of the European Union, 9-052

Affray
public order offences, 19-055, 19-061

Agencies
see **Executive agencies**

Alternative vote
see **Elections**

Appropriation Acts
public expenditure, 12-053, 12-056

Armed forces
constitutional conventions
    Parliament authorising military action, 5-029
courts martial, 19-100
disciplinary procedures, 19-101—19-102
public order
    industrial action, 19-093—19-094
    introduction, 19-092
    rioting, 19-096

Arms trade
public order, 19-107—19-108

Arrest
parliamentary privilege, 3-167

Assemblies
see **Demonstrations; Public assemblies; Public order**

Assets Recovery Agency
executive agencies, 11-051

Asylum
human rights, 16-115—16-120

Asymmetrical constitution
see **Constitutional law; Constitutions; Devolution; Europe; Sovereignty**

Attorney General
separation of powers, 3-017—3-019

Auditor General for Scotland
public expenditure, 12-047

Auditor General for Wales
public expenditure, 12-047

Audits
local government, 13-096—13-102
public expenditure
    certification audits, 12-085—12-086
    internal audits, 12-067
    National Audit Office, 12-081—12-084
    Public Accounts Committee, 12-077—12-078
    Scrutiny Unit, 12-080
    select committees, 12-079
    value for money examinations, 12-077, 12-088—12-095

Austin
see **Jurisprudence**

Backbench Business Committee
see **Select committees**

Ballot Bills
introduction to Parliament of, 3-050

Bank of England
public expenditure, 12-032—12-036

Barnett Formula
see **Scotland**

BBC
accountability, 20-099—20-101
Charter renewal, 20-102
establishment, 20-094
governance, 20-098
Home Secretary's directions, 20-095—20-096
terrorism, 20-096—20-097

Bentham
see **Jurisprudence**

Big Society
see **Local government**

Blackstone
see **Jurisprudence**

Breach
constitutional conventions, 5-028, 5-033, 5-036

Breach of the peace
  police powers and duties, 19-043—19-053
British Telecom
  privatisation, 14-020—14-025
Broadcasting
  advertising, 20-104
  BBC
    accountability, 20-099—20-101
    Charter renewal, 20-102
    establishment, 20-094
    governance, 20-098
    Home Secretary's directions, 20-095—20-096
    terrorism, 20-096—20-097
  Calcutt Committee, 20-084—20-086
  commercial broadcasting
    advertising, 20-104
    Broadcasting Code, 20-106
    complaints, 20-105
    litigation, 20-107
    sponsorship, 20-104
    statutory regulation, 20-103
    terrorism, 20-108—20-109
  D notices, 20-078—20-079
  DA notices, 20-080—20-083
  defamation, 20-093
  generally, 20-078—20-093
  increased press regulation, 20-084—20-089
  Leveson Report, 20-089
  libel, 20-093
  national security, 20-090
  privacy, 20-087
  search and seizure, 20-091—20-092
  terrorism
    BBC, 20-096—20-097
    commercial broadcasting, 20-108—20-109
Cabinet
  Cabinet committees, 4-095—4-098
  collective responsibility
    confidentiality of Cabinet, 4-142—4-148
    division of responsibilities, 4-149—4-150
    meaning, 4-141
    publication of diaries or memoirs, 4-143—4-146
  constitution, 4-083—4-084
  executive power
    declining powers, 4-091—4-094
    exercise of, 4-077
    meaning, 4-075—4-076
    origins of, 4-078—4-79
    historical development, 4-079—4-082
    inner Cabinet, 4-099—4-100
    political parties' influence, 4-104
    Prime Ministerial influence, 4-099—4-106
    role of, 4-086—4-090
    secrecy of workings of, 4-085
    special advisers, 4-110
Cabinet Office
  Cabinet Office European Specialist, 9-010
  role of, 4-107
Calcutt Committee
  see **Broadcasting**
Calman Commission
  see **Scotland**
Cardinal rule
  statutory interpretation, 3-079
Cash for questions
  see **Parliament**
Causing fear or provocation of violence
  see **Fear or provocation of violence**
Causing harassment alarm or distress
  public order offences, 19-064—19-065
Certification audits
  see **Audits**
Certiorari
  public law remedies, 18-077—18-080
Chilcot Inquiry
  see **Inquiries**
Child sexual abuse
  inquiries, 15-039, 15-071
Child Support Agency
  executive agencies, 11-037
Citizen's grievances
  see **Complaints**
Citizenship
  European Convention on Human Rights, 16-066—16-077
  right of abode, 16-107—16-112
Civil list
  Crown relationship with Parliament, 3-116
Civil Service
  accountability, 11-057—11-062
  Civil Service Commission, 4-160
  crisis management, 11-063—11-073
  employment rights, 4-156—4-157
  employment status, 4-158—4-161
  evolution, 11-007—11-008
  executive agencies
    accountability, 11-034—11-051
    Assets Recovery Agency, 11-051
    Chief Executive, 11-080
    Child Support Agency, 11-037
    development of, 11-019—11-033
    financial management information, 11-019—11-020
    financial scrutiny, 11-044—11-045
    next step agencies, 11-022—11-026
    proliferation of, 11-078—11-079
    Passport Agency, 11-030
    Rural Payments Agency, 11-041—11-042
    trading funds, 11-046—11-050
    Vehicle Inspectorate, 11-027
  future developments, 11-074—11-085
  gender balance, 11-028
  introduction, 4-151
  legal status, 4-155
  lobbying and, 11-058
  management techniques, 11-012—11-018
  meaning, 4-152—4-153
  ministers and, 11-052—11-056
  new public management
    future of, 11-082—11-084
    original strategy, 11-012—11-018
  objectives, 11-003
  official secrets, 20-022, 20-029—20-031

reforms, 11-009—11-011
regulation of, 4-154
role of, 4-162—4-169, 11-003, 11-005
select committees, 3-098—3-099
special advisers, 11-059—11-062
statistics on size and composition, 11-001—11-002
statutory basis, 11-006
strategic planning, 11-004
summary, 11-086—11-092
Treasury and Civil Service Select Committee, 11-057

Closed material
public interest immunity, 10-111
terrorism, 19-147—19-152

Co-decision procedure
Council of the European Union, 9-032
European Parliament, 9-043

Commercial broadcasting
advertising, 20-104
Broadcasting Code, 20-106
complaints, 20-105
litigation, 20-107
sponsorship, 20-104
statutory regulation, 20-103
terrorism, 20-108—20-109

Committee on Standards and Privileges
parliamentary privilege, 3-173
role of, 3-008

Committee on Standards in Public Life
parliamentary privilege, 3-172

Common law
development of public law, 1-030
jurisprudence, 8-017—8-039

Commonwealth
influence of, 1-033

Competitive tendering
local government, 13-046—13-048

Complaints
informal mechanisms
access to information, 15-011—15-012
media, 15-011
Members of Parliament, 15-006—15-009
pressure groups, 15-010
trade unions, 15-010

inquiries
accidents, 15-037—15-038
Chilcot Inquiry, 15-070
child abuse, 15-039
compulsory purchase, 15-049
human rights, 15-057
Independent Inquiry into Child Sexual Abuse, 15-071
Inquiries Act 2005, 15-068—15-069
legal representation, 15-058
Lord Saville Inquiry, 15-048, 19-111
Lowell Goddard Inquiry, 15-071
planning appeals, 15-050—15-056, 15-067
role of, 15-034—15-036
rule for conduct of, 15-040
Scott Inquiry, 15-042—15-047
shortcomings, 15-059—15-066
statutory provisions, 15-041
inspectorates, 15-072
intelligence services, 20-056, 20-068
introduction, 15-001—15-005
Members of Parliament
e-petitions, 15-006
select committee contacts, 15-007
Early Day Motions, 15-008
Code of Conduct, 15-009
ombudsmen
central government, 15-073—15-100
European Ombudsman, 15-115
Health Service Commissioner, 15-080—15-082
Local Government Commissioner, 15-101—15-114
Lord Chancellor, 15-083
Parliamentary Commissioner for Administration, 15-075—15-100
reforms, 15-116—15-117
Parliamentary Commissioner for Administration

advice on administrative practices, 15-096
costs, 15-097
enforcement, 15-100
generally, 15-075—15-079
investigative techniques, 15-098
judicial review, 15-099
legal redress routes and, 15-084—15-085
maladministration, 15-086—15-089, 15-095
number of complaints, 15-089
remedies, 15-093
role of, 15-090—15-092
police powers and duties, 16-155—16-160
summary, 15-118
tribunals
advantages, 15-023—15-024
coherence of system of, 15-015
Council of Tribunals, 15-014
decision-making, 15-022
diversity of, 15-016
Legal Services Board, 15-017
Leggatt Review, 15-025
Prison Board of Visitors, 15-016—15-019
role of, 15-021
status, 15-020
Tribunals Courts and Enforcement Act 2007, 15-026—15-033
use of, 15-013

Comprehensive Spending Review
see **Public expenditure**

Comptroller and Auditor General
certification audits, 12-085—12-086
independence, 12-095
role of National Audit Office in relation to, 12-082
role of, 12-077—12-078
value for money examinations, 12-088

Compulsory purchase
inquiries, 15-049

Consolidated Fund
public expenditure, 12-054—12-062

Constituencies
boundaries, 7-045—7-065

Constitutional conventions
accountability, 5-032
adoption into statute, 5-035
breach, 5-028, 5-033, 5-036
codification, 5-030—5-031
collective responsibility of
individual ministers,
5-021
development of, 5-018
enforceability, 5-008
guidance, 5-019
introduction, 5-001—5-006
judicial recognition,
5-012—5-017
meaning, 5-007—5-011
military action, 5-029
ministerial resignations,
5-022—5-023
no confidence motions, 5-020
purpose of, 5-024—5-027
role of Parliament and courts,
5-037
significant conventions,
5-020—5-
sources, 5-007
subject matter, 5-034
summary, 5-076
value of, 5-038—5-042
Constitutional law
sources
England, 2-007—2-010
generally, 2-002—2-006
Ireland, 2-021—2-033
Scotland, 2-013—2-020
Wales, 2-011—2-012
Constitutional reform
Committee of the whole House,
1-031
evolution of public law and,
1-011
future of public law,
21-012—21-017
historical context, 1-021—1-026
parliamentary scrutiny, 1-031
Constitutions
asymmetrical constitution
composition of UK,
2-002—2-033
devolution, 2-034—2-125
Europe, 2-126—2-154
future constitutional
arrangements,
2-164—2-165
introduction, 2-001

sovereignty, 2-155—2-163
summary, 2-166—2-168
examples from abroad,
1-033—1-034
future of public law,
21-009—21-011
developing the constitution,
21-009—21-011
written UK constitution,
21-018—21-024
Japan, 1-033
Select Committee of the
House of Lords on the
Constitution, 1-035
South Africa, 1-033
UK constitution
characteristics of, 1-027—
1-032, 1-036
formalising, 1-018—1-020
multidimensional nature of,
1-011
sources, 1-032
"unconstitutional", 1-029
Contempt of court
freedom of expression,
20-131—20-139
Contingencies Fund
public expenditure,
12-073—12-076
Contracts
administrative law and,
6-085—6-092
Contractual liability
public authorities, 18-112—18-113
Control orders
terrorism, 19-134—19-139
COREPER
Council of the European Union,
9-031
Corruption
Court of Auditors, 9-090
Council of the European Union
co-decision procedure, 9-032
COREPER, 9-031
composition, 9-028
decision-making, 9-029
generally, 2-137—2-140
multiannual financial framework,
9-033
qualified majority voting, 9-030
Court Martial
military justice, 19-100
Court of Auditors
constitution, 9-086

corruption, 9-090
financial accountability of EU,
9-088—9-089
fraud, 9-090
generally, 2-151—2-154
role, 9-087
Court of Justice of the European Union
Advocates General, 9-052
delay, 9-050
generally, 2-146—2-150
jurisprudence, 9-053—9-069
parliamentary sovereignty,
9-068—9-069
preliminary rulings,
9-055—9-058
references to European Court,
9-059—9-067
remit, 9-047
review of measures adopted by
institutions, 9-051
structure, 9-049
workload, 9-048
Courts
see also **Court Martial; Court of Auditors; Court of Justice of the European Union; European Court of Human Rights**
evolution of public law and,
1-012—1-017
judicial scrutiny of legislation
hybrid Bills, 3-060
public expenditure,
12-096—12-098
Crown
abolition of monarchy, 4-069
accountability
appointment of ministers,
10-080
appointment of Prime
Minister, 10-081
Crown proceedings, 10-083
dismissal of ministers,
10-082
petitions of right, 10-083
privileges, 10-084
public interest immunity,
10-085—10-096
civil list, 3-116
freedom of information, 3-118
freedom of religion, 16-080
injunctions against, 4-035,
18-104—18-105

personal powers of Sovereign, 4-070—4-074
public interest immunity, 10-085—10-096
role of monarch, 4-067
Sovereign Grant, 4-068
succession, 3-115—3-116
taxation, 3-117

DA notices
broadcasting, 20-080—20-083

Damages
private law remedies, 18-107

Declarations
private law remedies, 18-090—18-095

Defamation
broadcasting, 20-093
freedom of expression, 20-127—20-130
parliamentary privilege, 3-165

Democracy
elections, 7-014—7-029

Demonstrations
police powers and duties
kettling, 19-072
public order offences, 19-066, 19-070

Deportation
human rights, 16-123—16-124

Deregulation
Better Regulation Framework, 3-090
Deregulation and Contracting Out Act 1994, 3-089
Regulatory Reform Act 2001, 3-091

Derogations
human rights, 16-042

Devolution
administrative devolution, 2-035—2-037
characteristics, 2-047—2-054
Commonwealth Charter, 2-124—2-125
constitutional implications, 2-118—2-120
coordinating, 2-101
Devolution Acts 1998, 2-041—2-044
devolution issues, 2-058—2-059
electorates
London, 2-057
Northern Ireland, 2-056
Scotland, 2-055
Wales, 2-055
England
generally, 2-065
London, 2-066—2-067
regions, 2-068
select committees, 2-117
English Votes for English Laws, 2-105—2-109
generally, 2-045—2-046
Grand Committee, 2-116
human rights, 2-060—2-062
introduction, 2-034
Judicial Committee of the Privy Council, 2-121—2-123
judicial review, 2-063—2-064
Law Officers, 2-058—2-059
legislative consent motions, 2-110—2-111
London
electorates, 2-057
generally, 2-066—2-067
Northern Ireland
electorates, 2-056
generally, 2-094
Grand Committee, 2-116
Northern Ireland Act 2998, 2-095—2-100
select committees, 2-114
parliamentary procedures, 2-112
proposals in the 1970s, 2-038—2-040
public expenditure
Auditor General for Scotland, 12-047
Auditor General for Wales, 12-047
Barnett Formula, 12-045
Calman Commission, 12-046
generally, 12-041—12-044
referendums, 7-156—7-157
statutory interpretation, 3-086
Scotland
electorates, 2-055
generally, 2-081
Grand Committee, 2-116
referendum, 2-090—2-091
role of courts, 2-089
Scotland Act 1998, 2-082—2-086
Scotland Act 2012, 2-087—2-088
Scotland Bill 2015, 2-092—2-093
select committees, 2-113
Smith Commission Agreement, 2-090—2-091
select committees, 2-112—2-115
Supreme Court, 2-122
Wales
draft Wales Bill, 2-080
electorates, 2-055
generally, 2-069—2-075
Grand Committee, 2-116
select committees, 2-112
Silk Commission Review, 2-076—2-079
West Lothian question, 2-102—2-109

Dicey
see **Jurisprudence**

Disability discrimination
human rights, 16-106

Discovery
private law remedies, 18-106

Discretion
judicial review
abuse of discretion, 17-092—17-102
fettering of discretion, 17-068—17-074

Donoughmore Committee
see **Jurisprudence**

Economic and monetary union
membership of EU and, 9-019—9-022

Ejusdem generis
statutory interpretation, 3-081

Election statements
mandate to govern and, 7-092—7-109

Elections
accounting requirements, 7-070—7-071
additional member system, 7-142—7-143
aims, 7-005—7-013
alternative vote, 7-146—7-152
conduct of, 7-068—7-069
constituencies, 7-045—7-065
democracy, 7-014—7-029
Electoral Commission, 7-066—7-067
electoral reform
additional member system, 7-142—7-143

INDEX

aims and objectives of electoral system, 7-130—7-136
alternative vote, 7-146—7-152
first past the post, 7-123—7-129
generally, 7-122
regional list system, 7-140—7-141
single transferable vote, 7-137—7-139
supplementary vote, 7-144—7-145
electorates
    generally, 7-039—7-044
    London, 2-057
    Northern Ireland, 2-056
    Scotland, 2-055
    Wales, 2-055
Europe, 7-088—7-091
expenses, 7-070—7-071
first past the post, 7-123—7-129
franchise, 7-030—7-038
introduction, 7-001—7-004
local government, 13-032—13-039
mandates, 7-093—7-097
manifestos, 7-092—7-109
media, 7-072—7-083
pressure groups, 7-110—7-121
"purdah", 7-084—7-087
referendums
    advantages of, 7-162
    devolution, 7-156—7-157
    electoral system, 7-158
    Europe, 7-155, 7-160
    generally, 7-153
    limitations, 7-161
    local authorities, 7-159
    Northern Ireland, 7-154
regional list system, 7-140—7-141
single transferable vote, 7-137—7-139
summary, 7-163—7-165
supplementary vote, 7-144—7-145

Electoral Commission
role of, 7-066—7-067

Electoral reform
see **Elections**

Electorates
see **Elections**

Electricity
privatisation, 14-045—14-056

Emergency powers
martial law
    generally, 19-099, 19-104
    jurisdiction, 19-105
public order
    industrial action, 19-094—19-095
    introduction, 19-092

Employment
human rights, 16-102—16-106

Energy
privatisation, 14-027

Enforcement
constitutional conventions, 5-008

England
constitutional law sources, 2-007—2-010
devolution
    generally, 2-065
    London, 2-066—2-067
    regions, 2-068
    select committees, 2-117

"English Votes for English Laws"
devolution, 2-105—2-109
enacting legislation, 3-049
future of public law, 21-025—21-028

Environmental Audit Committee
see **Select committees**

E-petitions
citizen's complaints, 15-006

Estimates
public expenditure, 12-058—12-059

Estoppel
judicial review, 17-075—17-082

EU law
drafting legislation, 3-068
hybrid Bills, 3-065—3-066
influence on public law, 1-033
sources, 9-070—9-085
statutory interpretation, 3-087

European Commission
aims, 9-034
composition, 9-036
generally, 2-130—2-136
powers, 9-037
remit, 9-038
role, 9-035
scrutiny by European Parliament, 9-044

European Convention on Human Rights
see also **European Court of Human Rights; Human rights**
citizenship, 16-066—16-077
Convention rights, 16-041
derogations, 16-042
individual petition procedure, 16-061
interpretation, 3-083
interrogation, 16-062
Northern Ireland, 16-063
prevention of terrorism, 16-064
reservations, 16-043

European Council
aims, 9-039
composition, 9-040
generally, 2-141

European Court of Human Rights
see also **European Convention on Human Rights; Human rights**
actions against States, 16-045
admissibility, 16-046
cases against UK, 16-049—16-060
commencement of proceedings, 16-044
composition, 16-048
future jurisprudence, 16-065
increase in case load, 16-047

European Ombudsman
citizen's grievances, 15-115

European Parliament
co-decision procedure, 9-043
composition, 9-041
future developments, 9-045
generally, 2-142—2-145
powers, 9-042
role, 9-046
scrutiny of Commission, 9-044

European Union
Cabinet Office European Specialist, 9-010
competitiveness, 9-005
Council of the European Union
    co-decision procedure, 9-032
    COREPER, 9-031
    composition, 9-028
    decision-making, 9-029
    generally, 2-137—2-140

multiannual financial framework, 9-033
qualified majority voting, 9-030
Court of Auditors
constitution, 9-086
corruption, 9-090
financial accountability of EU, 9-088—9-089
fraud, 9-090
generally, 2-151—2-154
role, 9-087
Court of Justice of the European Union
Advocate General's opinions, 9-052
delay, 9-050
generally, 2-146—2-150
jurisprudence, 9-053—9-069
parliamentary sovereignty, 9-068—9-069
preliminary rulings, 9-055—9-058
references to European Court, 9-059—9-067
remit, 9-047
review of measures adopted by institutions, 9-051
structure, 9-049
workload, 9-048
economic and monetary union, 9-019—9-022
economic governance, 9-004
elections
generally, 7-088—7-091
referendums, 7-155, 7-160
European Commission
aims, 9-034
composition, 9-036
generally, 2-130—2-136
powers, 9-037
remit, 9-038
role, 9-035
European Council
aims, 9-039
composition, 9-040
generally, 2-141
European Parliament
co-decision procedure, 9-043
composition, 9-041
future developments, 9-045
generally, 2-142—2-145
powers, 9-042

role, 9-046
scrutiny of Commission, 9-044
Europeanisation of UK law, 2-126—2-129
evolution of, 9-013—9-014
exchange rate mechanism, 9-021
freedom of movement, 9-007
human rights, 9-096—9-102
institutions
Council of the European Union, 9-028—9-033
Court of Justice of the European Union, 9-047—9-052
European Commission, 9-034—9-038
European Council, 9-039—9-040
European Parliament, 9-041—9-046
generally, 9-026—9-027
internal market, 9-017—9-018
introduction, 9-001—9-003
Lisbon Treaty, 9-011—9-012
membership
evaluation of, 9-023—9-025
generally, 9-015—9-022
parliamentary sovereignty, 9-006, 9-068—9-069
public law, 9-091—9-095
social benefits, 9-007
sources of EU law, 9-070—9-085
summary, 9-103—9-107
UK personnel in staff of EU institutions, 9-009
veto, 9-008
Euthanasia
human rights, 16-084—16-089
Exchange rate mechanism
membership of EU, 9-021
Executive agencies
accountability, 11-034—11-051
administrative law, 6-099—6-100
Assets Recovery Agency, 11-051
Chief Executive, 11-080
Child Support Agency, 11-037
development of, 11-019—11-033
financial management information, 11-019—11-020

financial scrutiny, 11-044—11-045
next step agencies, 11-022—11-026
proliferation of, 11-078—11-079
Passport Agency, 11-030
Rural Payments Agency, 11-041—11-042
trading funds, 11-046—11-050
Vehicle Inspectorate, 11-027
Expenses
elections, 7-070—7-071
Fairness
judicial review, 17-113—17-128
Fear or provocation of violence
public order offences, 19-055, 19-062
Fettering of discretion
judicial review, 17-068—17-074
First past the post
see **Elections**
Foreign affairs
see **International relations**
Formal reasoning
see **Jurisprudence**
Franchise
elections, 7-030—7-038
Fraud
Court of Auditors, 9-090
Freedom of assembly
see **Public order**
Freedom of expression
contempt of court, 20-131—20-139
criminal law, 20-119—20-126
defamation, 20-127—20-130
freedom of information
examples of applications, 20-118
Freedom of information Act 2000, 20-113—20-115
Independent Commission on Freedom of Information, 20-116—20-117
generally, 20-110—20-111
public interest, 20-112
Freedom of information
Crown, 3-118
evolution of public law and, 1-011
examples of applications, 20-118
Freedom of information Act 2000, 20-113—20-115

Independent Commission on
Freedom of Information,
20-116—20-117
parliamentary privilege, 3-174
Freedom of movement
European Union, 9-007
Freedom of religion
charitable status, 16-079
criminal law and,
16-090—16-092
Crown, 16-080
euthanasia, 16-084—16-089
meaning, 16-078
religious education in schools,
16-081—16-083
statutory protections for religious
beliefs, 16-083
Freedom of speech
parliamentary privilege,
3-159—3-166
Gas industry
privatisation, 14-028—14-044
Golden rule
see **Cardinal rule**
Government
accountability
geberally, 1-006
public interest immunity,
10-079—10-111
secrecy, 10-112—10-127
Cabinet
collective responsibility,
4-141—4-150
ministerial responsibility,
4-111—4-140
powers and functions,
4-075—4-109
special advisers, 4-110
Civil Service
introduction, 4-151
meaning, 4-152—4-161
role of, 4-162—4-169
Crown relationship with
abolition of monarchy, 4-069
personal powers of sovereign,
4-070—4-074
role of monarch, 4-067
sovereign grant, 4-068
introduction, 4-001—4-004
meaning, 4-019—4-027
prerogative powers
examples, 4-038—4-043
foreign affairs,
4-056—4-066

incorporation powers, 4-055
injunctions against the
Crown, 4-035
meaning, 4-028—4-031
nature of, 4-037
origins, 4-032
relevance of, 4-036
scope, 4-044—4-047
statutory powers
distinguished, 4-034
statutory powers in
preference to,
4-048—4-054
summary, 4-170
UK constitution, 4-005—4-018
**Government Communications
Headquarters**
intelligence services, 20-057
Government trading funds
executive agencies,
11-046—11-050
Grand Committee
devolution, 2-116
"Green light" theory
see **Jurisprudence**
Guillotines
enacting legislation, 3-046
Habeas corpus
public law remedies,
18-086—18-088
Hansard
statutory interpretation, 3-084
Harassment
see **Causing harassment alarm
or distress**
Health Service Commissioner
citizen's grievances,
15-080—15-082
Hereditary peers
House of Lords reforms, 3-142
House of Commons
see also **Government;
Parliament**
relationship with House of Lords,
3-119—3-122
Salisbury-Addison convention,
3-132—3-133
select committees
modernisation, , 3-039
reform, 3-040, 3-045
House of Lords
see also **Parliament**
composition, 3-151—3-152
Money Bills, 3-123—3-128

reforms
future reforms, 3-134
hereditary peers, 3-142
post-1999, 3-142—3-149
power of veto, 3-123—3-131
pre-1999, 3-135—3-141
Strathclyde Review (2015),
3-150
Wakeham Commission,
3-143—3-145
White Paper on Lords reform,
3-146
relationship with House of
Commons, 3-119—3-122
Salisbury-Addison convention,
3-132—3-133
select committees, 3-100,
3-153—3-155
veto, 3-123—3-131
Human rights
administrative law
aims of, 1-010
evolution of, 1-017,
6-156—6-162
asylum, 16-115—16-120
citizenship
European Convention
on Human Rights,
16-066—16-077
right of abode,
16-107—16-112
deportation, 16-123—16-124
derogations, 16-042
development of law,
1-027—1-028
devolution, 2-060—2-062
disability discrimination, 16-106
drafting legislation, 3-068
employment rights,
16-102—16-106
European Convention on Human
Rights
citizenship, 16-066—16-077
Convention rights, 16-041
derogations, 16-042
individual petition procedure,
16-061
interrogation, 16-062
Northern Ireland, 16-063
prevention of terrorism,
16-064
reservations, 16-043
European Court on Human
Rights

actions against States,
  16-045
admissibility, 16-046
cases against UK,
  16-049—16-060
commencement of
  proceedings, 16-044
composition, 16-048
future jurisprudence, 16-065
increase in case load, 16-047
European Union, 9-096—9-102
euthanasia, 16-084—16-089
freedom of religion
  charitable status, 16-079
  criminal law and,
    16-090—16-092
  Crown, 16-080
  euthanasia, 16-084—16-089
  meaning, 16-078
  religious education in
    schools, 16-081—16-083
  statutory protections for
    religious beliefs, 16-083
Human Rights Act 1998
  incorporation of ECHR,
    16-004—16-009
  interpretation,
    16-027—16-040
  Parliament and,
    16-010—16-011
  public authorities,
    16-021—16-026
  scope, 16-012—16-014
  territorial scope,
    16-015—16-020
  war, 16-015—16-020
hybrid Bills, 3-067
immigration
  asylum, 16-115—16-120
  deportation, 16-123—16-124
  humanitarian protection,
    16-121
  Immigration Bill, 16-122
  refugees, 16-121
  rules and procedure,
    16-113—16-114
influence on public law, 1-010
inquiries, 15-057
interrogation
  European Convention on
    Human Rights, 16-062
  police powers and duties,
    16-142—16-151
introduction, 16-001—16-003

jurisprudence, 8-014,
  8-111—8-120
Northern Ireland, 16-063
Parliament and, 16-010—16-011
police powers and duties
  accountability,
    16-152—16-154
  complaints against police,
    16-155—16-160
  generally, 16-125—16-130
  interrogation of suspects,
    16-142—16-151
  powers of arrest,
    16-131—16-138
  reform proposals, 16-161
  search and seizure,
    16-139—16-141
powers of arrest, 16-131—16-138
prevention of terrorism,
  16-064
public authorities, 16-021—
  16-026, 18-114—18-116
racial discrimination,
  16-093—16-101
refugees, 16-121
religious education,
  16-081—16-083
reservations, 16-043
rule of law, 5-064
search and seizure,
  16-139—16-141
secrecy, 20-003—20-004
sex discrimination,
  16-102—16-105
statutory interpretation, 3-082
summary, 16-162
terrorism, 19-140—19-141
Humanitarian protection
human rights, 16-121
Hybrid Bills
characteristics, 3-056
charges on public funds, 3-059
EU law, 3-065—3-066
growth in legislation,
  3-062—3-064
HS2, 3-057
human rights, 3-067
judicial scrutiny, 3-060
parliamentary scrutiny,
  3-065—3-067
select committees, 3-061
table of Bills, 3-058
Immigration
human rights

asylum, 16-115—16-120
deportation, 16-123—16-124
humanitarian protection,
  16-121
Immigration Bill, 16-122
refugees, 16-121
rules and procedure,
  16-113—16-114
**Independent Inquiry into Child
  Sexual Abuse**
see **Inquiries**
Industrial action
public order
  emergency powers,
    19-094—19-095
  use of military,
    19-093—19-094
Injunctions
Crown, 4-035, 18-104—18-105
private law remedies,
  18-096—18-101
Inquiries
accidents, 15-037—15-038
Chilcot Inquiry, 15-070
child abuse, 15-039
compulsory purchase, 15-049
historical development,
  6-178—6-183
human rights, 15-057
Independent Inquiry into Child
  Sexual Abuse, 15-071
Inquiries Act 2005,
  15-068—15-069
legal representation, 15-058
Lord Saville Inquiry, 15-048,
  19-111
Lowell Goddard Inquiry,
  15-071
planning appeals, 15-050—
  15-056, 15-067
role of, 15-034—15-036
rule for conduct of, 15-040
Scott Inquiry, 15-042—15-047
shortcomings, 15-059—15-066
statutory provisions, 15-041
**Intelligence and Security
  Committee**
role of, 20-058—20-061
Intelligence services
complaints, 20-056, 20-068
generally, 20-041—20-042
Government Communications
  Headquarters (GCHQ),
  20-057

Intelligence and Security
    Committee,
    20-058—20-061
Intelligence Services
    Commissioner, 20-064,
    20-068—20-069
interception of communications,
    20-065—20-066
interference with property rights,
    20-070—20-071
Investigatory Powers Bill,
    20-072—20-077
National Crime Agency, 20-062
National Crime Squad, 20-063
positive vetting,
    20-043—20-044
public order, 19-088—19-091
Secret Intelligence Service,
    20-057
Security Services Act 1989
    complaints, 20-056
    Director General, 20-049
    generally, 20-047—20-048
    judicial review, 20-053
    National Crime Agency,
        20-062
    National Crime Squad,
        20-063
    Special Branch liaison,
        20-050
    support of other agencies,
        20-052
    terrorism, 20-062
    warrants, 20-051,
        20-054—20-055
Security Services Commissioner,
    20-060
Special Branch liaison, 20-050
staff counsellors,
    20-045—20-046
terrorism, 20-062
warrants, 20-051, 20-054—
    20-055, 20-067
**Intelligence Services
    Commissioner**
role of, 20-064,
    20-068—20-069
Interception of communications
intelligence services,
    20-065—20-066
Internal audits
public expenditure, 12-067
Internal market
European Union, 9-017—9-018

International relations
prerogative powers,
    4-056—4-066
Interrogation
human rights
    European Convention on
        Human Rights, 16-062
    police powers and duties,
        16-142—16-151
Intimidation
public order offences, 19-068
Investigatory Powers Bill
see **Intelligence services**
Japan
constitutions, 1-033
Jennings
see **Jurisprudence**
**Judicial Committee of the Privy
    Council**
devolution, 2-121—2-123
Judicial independence
separation of powers, 3-019
Judicial review
abuse of discretion
    generally, 17-092—17-095
    Wednesbury
        unreasonableness,
        17-096—17-102
administrative decision-making,
    17-008—17-013
applications
    availability, 17-021
    distinguishing between
        public and private law,
        17-031—17-050
    exclusive nature of,
        17-029—17-030
    jurisdiction, 17-023
    pre-action protocols,
        17-022
    reform, 17-024—17-025
    time limits, 17-026—17-028
devolution, 2-063—2-064
evolution of public law and,
    1-015, 1-017
exclusion of, 17-129—17-139
fairness, 17-113—17-128
impact of public law litigation,
    17-140—17-141
intelligence services, 20-053
introduction, 6-013, 6-142—
    6-155, 17-001—17-007
legitimate expectation,
    17-107—17-109

local government,
    13-068—13-078
natural justice, 17-110—17-112
Parliamentary Commissioner for
    Administration, 15-099
policies, 17-051—17-058
proportionality, 17-103—17-106
review grounds
    estoppel, 17-075—17-082
    fettering of discretion,
        17-068—17-074
    generally, 17-059—17-061
    jurisdictional errors,
        17-087—17-091
    ultra vires, 17-062—17-067,
        17-083—17-086
rule of law and, 5-065—5-073
statutory appeals,
    17-014—17-020
summary, 17-142—17-146
trends, 17-051—17-058
Wednesbury unreasonableness,
    17-096—17-102
"Judicial scrutiny"
hybrid Bills, 3-060
information obtained abroad,
    19-142—19-146
statutory interpretation,
    3-088
Jurisdiction
judicial review, 17-023
Jurisprudence
academic lawyers,
    8-068—8-088
Austin, 8-059—8-062, 8-104
Bentham, 8-051, 8-056—
    8-059, 8-104
Blackstone, 8-046—8-047,
    8-051—8-052
common law tradition,
    8-017—8-039
contemporary issues,
    8-004—8-016
Dicey, 8-070—8-088,
    8-101—8-104
Donoughmore Committee,
    8-096—8-098
formal reasoning,
    8-020—8-022
future of public law,
    8-106—8-110
"green light" theory, 6-006,
    8-011—8-012
historical legacy, 8-040—8-050

human rights, 8-014,
    8-111—8-120
introduction, 8-001—8-003
Jennings, 8-091-8-092, 8-102
Laski, 8-093—8-096, 8-102
Montesquieu, 8-044—8-045
political change, 8-089—8-105
pragmatism, 8-023, 8-026
"red light" theory, 6-006, 8-011
"rights based" public law,
    8-015—8-016
Robson, 8-096, 8-102
science of law, 8-051—8-067
statutory law, 8-033—8-036
summary, 8-121—8-129

Laski
see **Jurisprudence**

Law Commission
drafting legislation,
    3-070—3-072

Law Officers
devolution, 2-058—2-059
separation of powers, 3-017,
    3-019

Legal representation
inquiries, 15-058

Legal thought
see **Jurisprudence**

Legislation
see also **Statutory interpretation**
drafting
    EU law, 3-068
    human rights, 3-068
    Law Commission,
        3-070—3-072
    Parliamentary Counsel,
        3-068—3-069
    statutory interpretation,
        3-073—3-088
enacting
    English Votes for English
        Laws, 3-049
    forms of legislation,
        3-044—3-048
    guillotine procedure, 3-046
    hybrid Bills, 3-056—3-067
    parliamentary procedure,
        3-039—3-040
    parliamentary scrutiny,
        3-041—3-043
    private Bills, 3-054—3-055
    Private Members' Bills,
        3-050—3-053

Legitimate expectation
judicial review, 17-107—17-109

Leveson Report
see **Broadcasting**

Liaison Committee
see **Select committees**

Libel
broadcasting, 20-093

Licences
administrative law and,
    6-081—6-084

Literal interpretation
legislation, 3-078

Lobbying
civil servants and, 11-058

Local authorities
referendums, 7-159

Local government
accountability, 13-096—13-102
administrative law,
    6-093—6-108
audits, 13-096—13-102
Big Society, 13-019
central-local government
    relations, 13-050
Cities and Local Government
    Devolution Act 2016,
    13-031
competitive tendering,
    13-046—13-048
elections, 13-032—13-039
functions, 13-024—13-030
historical developments
    1979-1997, 13-007—13-009
    1997-2002, 13-010—13-017
    Big Society, 13-019
    introduction, 13-006
    localism, 13-018
introduction, 13-001—13-005
judicial review, 13-068—13-078
local government finance,
    13-051—13-067
localism, 13-018
organisation
    England, 13-021—13-023
    generally, 13-020—13-021
    London, 13-021
private finance initiative,
    13-049
public expenditure,
    13-079—13-095
rule of law, 5-063
structure, 13-040—13-045
summary, 13-103—13-105

Local Government Commissioner
see **Ombudsmen**

Local government finance
generally, 13-051—13-067

Localism
see **Local government**

Locus standi
remedies
    generally, 18-011—18-016
    pressure groups,
        18-033—18-052
    private law, 18-017—18-020
    public law, 18-021—18-032
    role of courts,
        18-053—18-058

London
devolution
    electorates, 2-057
    generally, 2-066—2-067

Lord Chancellor
citizen's grievances, 15-083

Lord Saville Inquiry
see **Inquiries; Use of force**

Lowell Goddard Inquiry
see **Inquiries**

Maladministration
Parliamentary Commissioner for
    Administration, 15-086—
    15-089, 15-095

Mandamus
public law remedies,
    18-082—18-085

Mandates
see **Elections**

Mandatory orders
public law remedies,
    18-082—18-085

Manifestos
see **Election statements**

Martial law
generally, 19-099, 19-104
jurisdiction, 19-105

Media
see also **Broadcasting**
elections, 7-072—7-083

Members of Parliament
citizen's complaints
    e-petitions, 15-006
    select committee contacts,
        15-007
    Early Day Motions, 15-008
    codes of conduct, 15-009

Ministerial responsibility
accountability, 10-072—10-078

INDEX

collective responsibility
  confidentiality of Cabinet, 4–142—4–148
  division of responsibilities, 4–149—4–150
  meaning, 4–141
  publication of diaries or memoirs, 4–143—4–146
  Howe guidelines, 4–122—4–128
  meaning, 4–111
  purpose, 4–112
  resignation, 4–113—4–115
  Scott Inquiry, 4–116—4–140

Ministers
  civil servants and, 11–052—11–056

Mischief rule
  statutory interpretation, 3–080

Monarch
  see **Crown**

Money Bills
  House of Lords, 3–123—3–128

Montesquieu
  see **Jurisprudence**

National Audit Office
  public expenditure, 12–081—12–084

National Crime Agency
  intelligence services, 20–062

National crime squad
  intelligence services, 20–063

National security
  see also **Intelligence services**
  broadcasting, 20–090

National Security Council
  see **Secrecy**

Nationalisation
  privatisation of industries, 14–006—14–14–009

Natural justice
  judicial review, 17–110—17–112

Natural resources
  privatisation, 14–027

Negligence
  public authorities, 18–109—18–110

New Control Total
  see **Public expenditure**

Next step agencies
  executive agencies, 11–022—11–026

No confidence motions
  constitutional conventions, 5–020

Nolan Committee
  see **Parliamentary privilege**

Northern Ireland
  constitutional law sources, 2–021—2–033
  devolution
    electorates, 2–056
    generally, 2–094
    Grand Committee, 2–116
    Northern Ireland Act 2998, 2–095—2–100
    select committees, 2–114
  human rights, 16–063
  referendums, 7–154
  use of force, 19–110—19–111, 19–116

Nuisance
  public authorities, 18–111

OFCOM
  privatisation, 14–026

Offensive behaviour
  public order offences, 19–063

Official secrets
  civil remedies, 20–032—20–040
  civil servants, 20–022, 20–029—20–031
  generally, 20–017
  Official Secrets Act 1911, 20–018—20–023
  Official Secrets Act 1989, 20–024—20–029
  public interest, 20–040
  Spycatcher litigation, 20–034—20–039

Ombudsmen
  central government, 15–073—15–100
  European Ombudsman, 15–115
  Health Service Commissioner, 15–080—15–082
  Local Government Commissioner, 15–101—15–114
  Lord Chancellor, 15–083
  Parliamentary Commissioner for Administration, 15–075—15–100
  reforms, 15–116—15–117

Open government
  see **Secrecy**

Parliament
  see also **House of Lords**
  accountability
    generally, 10–037—10–040
    parliamentary reform, 10–070—10–071
    parliamentary scrutiny, 10–041—10–053
    select committees, 10–054—10–069
  cash for questions, 3–008
  Crown
    civil list, 3–116
    freedom of information, 3–118
    succession to throne, 3–115—3–116
    taxation, 3–117
  deregulation
    Better Regulation Framework, 3–090
    Deregulation and Contracting Out Act 1994, 3–089
    Regulatory Reform Act 2001, 3–091
  drafting legislation
    EU law and, 3–068
    human rights and, 3–068
    Law Commission, 3–070—3–072
    Parliamentary Counsel, 3–068—3–069
    statutory interpretation, 3–073—3–088
  enacting legislation
    English Votes for English Laws, 3–049
    forms of legislation, 3–044—3–048
    guillotine procedure, 3–046
    hybrid Bills, 3–056—3–067
    parliamentary procedure, 3–039—3–040
    parliamentary scrutiny, 3–041—3–043
    private Bills, 3–054—3–055
    Private Members' Bills, 3–050—3–053
  fixed-term Parliaments, 3–010
  human rights and, 16–010—16–011
  introduction, 3–001—3–009
  parliamentary debates, 3–092—3–104
  parliamentary privilege
    arrest in civil matters, 3–167

Committee on Standards and
  Privileges, 3-173
Committee on Standards in
  Public Life, 3-172
defamation, 3-165
freedom of information, 3-174
freedom of speech,
  3-159—3-166
nature of, 3-157—3-169
Nolan Committee, 3-171
regulating financial and other
  interests, 3-170—3-174
public expectations
  cash for questions, 3-008
  generally, 3-105—3-107
  public engagement, 3-108
"Queen in Parliament", 3-025
role of, 3-020—3-038
royal prerogative, 3-109—3-114
Salisbury-Addison convention,
  3-132—3-133
select committees
  Backbench Business
    Committee, 3-040,
    3-095
  bipartisan nature,
    3-103—3-104
  civil servants and,
    3-098—3-099
  Committee on Standards and
    Privileges, 3-008
  development of,
    3-093—3-094
  Environmental Audit
    Committee , 3-095
  House of Lords, 3-100
  impact of, 3-101
  Liaison Committee, 3-039,
    3-096
  Modernisation of the House
    of Commons, 3-039
  number of, 3-095
  powers, 3-097
  Public Accounts Committee,
    3-093, 3-095
  Reform of the House of
    Commons (Wright
    Committee), 3-040,
    3-045
  scrutiny of financial affairs of
    government, 3-102
separation of powers,
  3-010—3-019
summary, 3-175

**Parliamentary Commissioner for
  Administration**
  advice on administrative
    practices, 15-096
  costs, 15-097
  enforcement, 15-100
  generally, 15-075—15-079
  investigative techniques, 15-098
  judicial review, 15-099
  legal redress routes and,
    15-084—15-085
  maladministration, 15-086—
    15-089, 15-095
  number of complaints, 15-089
  remedies, 15-093
  role of, 15-090—15-092
Parliamentary Counsel
  drafting legislation,
    3-068—3-069
Parliamentary debates
  generally, 3-092—3-104
Parliamentary privilege
  arrest in civil matters, 3-167
  Committee on Standards and
    Privileges, 3-173
  Committee on Standards in
    Public Life, 3-172
  defamation, 3-165
  freedom of information, 3-174
  freedom of speech,
    3-159—3-166
  nature of, 3-157—3-169
  Nolan Committee, 3-171
  regulating financial and other
    interests, 3-170—3-174
Parliamentary procedure
  enacting legislation,
    3-039—3-040
Parliamentary scrutiny
  constitutional reform, 1-031
  enacting legislation,
    3-041—3-043
  hybrid Bills, 3-065—3-067
Parliamentary sovereignty
  EU law, 9-006, 9-068—9-069
  judicial review and,
    5-065—5-073
Passport Agency
  see **Executive agencies**
Planning appeals
  inquiries, 15-050—15-056,
    15-067
Police powers and duties
  accountability

human rights,
  16-152—16-154
public order,
  19-073—19-087
assistance by private citizens,
  19-098
complaints, 16-155—16-160
human rights
  accountability,
    16-152—16-154
  complaints against police,
    16-155—16-160
  generally, 16-125—16-130
  interrogation of suspects,
    16-142—16-151
  powers of arrest,
    16-131—16-138
  reform proposals, 16-161
  search and seizure,
    16-139—16-141
interrogation of suspects,
  16-142—16-151
powers of arrest, 16-131—16-138
public order
  accountability,
    19-073—19-087
  assistance of private citizens,
    19-098
  breach of the peace,
    19-043—19-053
  kettling, 19-072
  management of
    demonstrations,
    19-072
  offences against Public
    Order Act 1986,
    19-054—19-071
  police organisation,
    19-073—19-087
  public meetings,
    19-012—19-013
  public processions,
    19-014—19-042
  terrorism, 19-126—19-133
  use of force, 19-097
  search and seizure,
    16-139—16-141
Political parties
  accountability, 10-023-10-036
Powers of arrest
  human rights, 16-131—16-138
  public order offences, 19-069
Pragmatism
  see **Jurisprudence**

Pre-action protocols
  judicial review, 17–022
Preliminary rulings
  Court of Justice of the European Union, 9–055—9–058
Prerogative powers
  administrative law, 6–076—6–080
  examples, 4–038—4–043
  foreign affairs, 4–056—4–066
  incorporation powers, 4–055
  injunctions against the Crown, 4–035
  meaning, 4–028—4–031
  nature of, 4–037
  origins, 4–032
  relevance of, 4–036
  scope, 4–044—4–047
  statutory powers
    distinguished, 4–034
    preference for use of, 4–048—4–054
Pressure groups
  administrative law, 6–004
  elections, 7–110—7–121
Prevention of terrorism
  human rights, 16–064
Prime Minister
  increasing influence of, 4–099—4–106
  political staff and advisers, 4–108
  report on role of, 4–109
Privacy
  broadcasting, 20–087
Private Bills
  enacting legislation, 3–054—3–055
Private Finance Initiative
  local government, 13–049
  public expenditure, 12–037—12–040
Private Members' Bills
  introduction of
    Ballot Bills, 3–050
    special leave, 3–052
    Ten minute rule Bills, 3–051
  number of, 3–053
  subject matter, 3–053
Privatisation
  courts' role, 14–016—14–019
  introduction, 14–001—14–005
  nationalisation, 14–006—14–14–009

  policy and objectives, 14–010—14–013
  regulation
    generally, 14–014—14–015
    learning from experience, 14–074—14–081
  summary, 14–082—14–087
  utilities
    British Telecom, 14–020—14–025
    electricity, 14–045—14–056
    energy and natural resources, 14–027
    gas, 14–028—14–044
    OFCOM, 14–026
    Utilities Act 2000, 14–057—14–060
    water, 14–061—14–070
    Water Act 2014, 14–071—14–073
Processions
  police powers and duties, 19–014—19–042
  public order offences, 19–067
Prohibiting orders
  public law remedies, 18–081
Proportionality
  judicial review, 17–103—17–106
Proprietary rights
  intelligence services, 20–070—20–071
Public Accounts Committee
  public expenditure, 12–077—12–078
  role of, 3–093, 3–095
Public assemblies
  public order offences, 19–067
Public authorities
  see also **Local government**
  contractual liability, 18–112—18–113
  human rights, 16–021—16–026, 18–114—18–116
  tortious liability, 18–108—18–111
Public expenditure
  Accepted Practice regime, 12–069
  accounting officers, 12–023—12–027, 12–066
  Appropriation Acts, 12–053, 12–056
  audits
    certification audits, 12–085—12–086

    National Audit Office, 12–081—12–084
    Public Accounts Committee, 12–077—12–078
    Scrutiny Unit, 12–080
    select committees, 12–079
    value for money examinations, 12–077, 12–088—12–095
  Bank of England, 12–032—12–036
  Comprehensive Spending Review, 12–029, 12–061
  Comptroller and Auditor General
    certification audits, 12–085—12–086
    independence, 12–095
    role of National Audit Office in relation to, 12–082
    role of, 12–077—12–078
    value for money examinations, 12–088
  Consolidated Fund, 12–054—12–062
  Contingencies Fund, 12–073—12–076
  courts, 12–096—12–098
  devolution
    Auditor General for Scotland, 12–047
    Auditor General for Wales, 12–047
    Barnett Formula, 12–045
    Calman Commission, 12–046
    generally, 12–041—12–044
  estimates, 12–058—12–05900
  general principle, 12–049
  generally, 12–004—12–005
  historical development of, 12–050—12–051
  internal audits, 12–067
  introduction, 12–001—12–003
  local government, 13–079—13–095
  New Control Total, 12–030
  Private Finance Initiative, 12–037—12–040
  Public Expenditure Survey, 12–028, 12–060, 12–062
  public revenue, 12–006—12–012
  resource accounting, 12–070—12–072
  Standing Orders, 12–052, 12–057

summary, 12-099—12-105
supply procedure, 12-048
Total Managed Expenditure, 12-061
Treasury

Public Expenditure Survey
see **Public expenditure**

Public interest
freedom of information, 20-112
official secrets, 20-040

Public interest immunity
balancing of interests test, 10-110
closed material, 10-111
criminal prosecutions, 10-101—10-109
Crown, 10-080—10-096
generally, 10-079
ministers, 10-097—10-100
special advocates, 10-111

Public law
see **Administrative law**

Public meetings
police powers and duties, 19-012—19-013
public order offences, 19-067, 19-070, 19-071

Public order
see also **Public order offences**
arms trade, 19-107—19-108
emergency powers
 industrial action, 19-094—19-095
 introduction, 19-092
historical perspectives, 19-006—19-011
intelligence services, 19-088—19-091
introduction, 19-001—19-005
martial law
 generally, 19-099, 19-104
 jurisdiction, 19-105
military assistance
 industrial action, 19-093—19-094
 introduction, 19-092
 rioting, 19-096
police powers and duties
 accountability, 19-073—19-087
 assistance of private citizens, 19-098
 breach of the peace, 19-043—19-053

kettling, 19-072
management of demonstrations, 19-072
police organisation, 19-073—19-087
public meetings, 19-012—19-013
public processions, 19-014—19-042
use of force, 19-097
summary, 19-153—19-159
terrorism
 closed material, 19-147—19-152
 control orders, 19-134—19-139
 generally, 19-092, 19-118—19-125
 human rights, 19-140—19-141
 judicial scrutiny over information obtained abroad, 19-142—19-146
 police and investigatory powers, 19-126—19-133
use of force
 civil law, 19-114
 CS gas, 19-115
 legal liability, 19-110—19-117
 Northern Ireland, 19-110—19-111, 19-116
 plastic baton rounds, 19-115
 police powers and duties, 19-097
 right to life, 19-117
 Saville Inquiry, 15-048, 19-111
war
 prerogative powers, 19-106
 requisitions, 19-109

Public order offences
affray, 19-055, 19-061
causing harassment alarm or distress, 19-064—19-065
demonstrations, 19-066, 19-070
fear or provocation of violence, 19-055, 19-062
insulting words or behaviour, 19-063
intimidation, 19-068
powers of arrest, 19-069
processions, 19-067
protestors, 19-066

public assemblies, 19-067
public meetings, 19-067, 19-070, 19-071
Public Order Act 1986, 19-054
riot, 19-055—19-059
violent disorder, 19-055, 19-060

Public revenue
see **Public expenditure**

Purdah
see **Elections**

Purposive interpretation
legislation, 3-083

Qualified majority voting
Council of the European Union, 9-030

Quashing orders
public law remedies, 18-077—18-080

Racial discrimination
human rights, 16-093—16-101

"Red light" theory
see **Jurisprudence**

Redress schemes
accountability, 10-009
Parliamentary Commissioner for Administration, 15-084—15-085

References to European Court
jurisprudence, 9-059—9-067

Referendums
advantages of, 7-162
devolution, 7-156—7-157
electoral system, 7-158
Europe, 7-155, 7-160
generally, 7-153
limitations, 7-161
local authorities, 7-159
Northern Ireland, 7-154
Scottish independence, 2-090—2-091

Refugees
human rights, 16-121

Regional list system
see **Elections**

Regulatory reform
evolution of public law and, 1-016

Relator proceedings
private law remedies, 18-102—18-103

Religious education
human rights, 16-081—16-083

Remedies
forms of relief, 18-003—18-010

introduction, 18-001—18-002
locus standi
  generally, 18-011—18-016
  pressure groups, 18-033—18-052
  private law, 18-017—18-020
  public law, 18-021—18-032
  role of courts, 18-053—18-058
Parliamentary Commissioner for Administration, 15-093
private law remedies
  Crown, 18-104—18-105
  damages, 18-107
  declarations, 18-090—18-095
  discovery, 18-106
  generally, 18-089
  injunctions, 18-096—18-101
  relator proceedings, 18-102—18-103
  restitution, 18-107
public authorities
  contractual liability, 18-112—18-113
  human rights, 18-114—18-116
  tortious liability, 18-108—18-111
public law remedies
  certiorari, 18-077—18-080
  discretionary nature, 18-067—18-072
  habeas corpus, 18-086—18-088
  mandamus, 18-082—18-085
  mandatory orders, 18-082—18-085
  procedural matters, 18-059—18-066
  prohibiting orders, 18-081
  quashing orders, 18-077—18-080
  void and voidable administrative action, 18-073—18-074—18-076
summary, 18-117—18-121
Reservations
  human rights, 16-043
Resource accounting
  see **Public expenditure**
Restitution
  private law remedies, 18-107
Review grounds
  estoppel, 17-075—17-082

fettering of discretion, 17-068—17-074
generally, 17-059—17-061
jurisdictional errors, 17-087—17-091
ultra vires, 17-062—17-067, 17-083—17-086
Right to life
  use of force, 19-117
Riot
  public order offences, 19-055—19-059
  use of military, 19-096
Robson
  see **Jurisprudence**
Royal prerogative
  Parliament and, 3-109—3-114
Rule of law
  courts' approach, 5-057—5-060
  Dicey's analysis of, 5-054—5-056
  hierarchy of rights, 5-061—5-062
  historical background, 5-044—5-049
  human rights, 5-064
  judicial review, 5-065—5-073
  local government, 5-063
  meaning, 5-050—5-053
  nature of, 5-043
  summary, 5-074—5-075
Rural Payments Agency
  executive agencies, 11-041—11-042
Salisbury-Addison convention
  see **House of Commons**
Saville Inquiry
  see **Inquiries; Use of force**
Scholarships
  future of public law, 21-029—21-059
Scotland
  constitutional law sources, 2-013—2-020
  devolution
    electorates, 2-055
    generally, 2-081
    Grand Committee, 2-116
    referendum, 2-090—2-091
    role of courts, 2-089
    Scotland Act 1998, 2-082—2-086

Scotland Act 2012, 2-087—2-088
Scotland Bill 2015, 2-092—2-093
select committees, 2-113
Smith Commission Agreement, 2-090—2-091
public expenditure
  Auditor General for Scotland, 12-047
  Barnett Formula, 12-045
  Calman Commission, 12-046
  generally, 12-041—12-044
Scott Inquiry
  accountability, 10-019—10-022
  generally, 15-042—15-047
  ministerial responsibility, 4-116—4-140
Scrutiny Unit
  see **Audits**
Search and seizure
  broadcasting, 20-091—20-092
  human rights, 16-139—16-141
Secrecy
  access to information, 20-005
  accountability and, 10-006
  broadcasting
    BBC, 20-094—20-102
    commercial broadcasting, 20-103—20-109
    generally, 20-078—20-093
  freedom of expression
    contempt of court, 20-131—20-139
    criminal law, 20-119—20-126
    defamation, 20-127—20-130
    generally, 20-110—20-118
  human rights, 20-003—20-004
  intelligence services
    complaints, 20-056, 20-068
    generally, 20-041—20-042
    Government Communications Headquarters (GCHQ), 20-057
    Intelligence and Security Committee, 20-058—20-061
    Intelligence Services Commissioner, 20-064, 20-068—20-069

interception of communications, 20-065—20-066
interference with property rights, 20-070—20-071
Investigatory Powers Bill, 20-072—20-077
National Crime Agency, 20-062
National Crime Squad, 20-063
positive vetting, 20-043—20-044
Secret Intelligence Service, 20-057
Security Services Act 1989, 20-047—20-053
Security Services Commissioner, 20-060
Special Branch liaison, 20-050
staff counsellors, 20-045—20-046
terrorism, 20-062
warrants, 20-051, 20-054—20-055, 20-067
introduction, 20-001—20-006
National Security Council, 20-001
official secrets
civil remedies, 20-032—20-040
civil servants, 20-022, 20-029—20-031
generally, 20-017
Official Secrets Act 1911, 20-018—20-023
Official Secrets Act 1989, 20-024—20-029
public interest, 20-040
Spycatcher litigation, 20-034—20-039
open government
30-year rule, 20-014—20-015
Cabinet, 20-010
civil service, 20-009
contractual relationships, 20-011
generally, 20-007—20-008
ministerial memoirs, 20-016
public records, 20-013—20-015
select committees, 20-012
summary, 20-140—20-142

Secret Intelligence Service
role of, 20-057
Security Services Commissioner
see **Intelligence services**
Select committees
accountability, 10-054—10-069
Backbench Business Committee, 3-040, 3-095
bipartisan nature, 3-103—3-104
civil servants and, 3-098—3-099
Committee on Standards and Privileges, 3-008
development of, 3-093—3-094
devolution, 2-112—2-115
Environmental Audit Committee, 3-095
House of Lords
generally, 3-100, 3-153—3-155
Select Committee of the House of Lords on the Constitution, 1-035
hybrid Bills, 3-061
impact of, 3-101
Liaison Committee, 3-039, 3-096
Modernisation of the House of Commons, 3-039
number of, 3-095
Osmotherly Rules, 10-062
powers, 3-097
Public Accounts Committee, 3-093, 3-095
public expenditure, 12-079
Reform of the House of Commons (Wright Committee), 3-040, 3-045
scrutiny of financial affairs of government, 3-102
Treasury and Civil Service Select Committee, 11-057
Separation of powers
Parliament, 3-010—3-019
Sex discrimination
human rights, 16-102—16-105
Single transferable vote
see **Elections**
Solicitor General
separation of powers, 3-017
South Africa
constitutions, 1-033

Sovereign Grant
prerogative powers, 4-068
Sovereignty
EU law
sovereignty clause, 2-162
supremacy of EU law, 2-156—2-163
meaning, 2-155
Special advisers
civil servants and, 11-059—11-062
role of, 4-110
Special advocates
public interest immunity, 10-111
Special Branch
see **Intelligence services**
Standing orders
public expenditure, 12-052, 12-057
Statutory appeals
judicial review, 17-014—17-020
Statutory interpretation
constitutional statutes, 3-085—3-088
devolution legislation, 3-086
drafting legislation and, 3-073—3-077
ejusdem generis rule, 3-081
EU law, 3-087
golden rule, 3-079
Hansard, 3-084
human rights as aid to, 3-082
judicial discretion, 3-088
literal rule, 3-078
mischief rule, 3-080
purposive interpretation, 3-083
Strathclyde Review (2015)
House of Lords reforms, 3-150
Succession
Crown, 3-115—3-116
Supplementary vote
see **Elections**
Supply procedure
see **Public expenditure**
Taxation
Crown, 3-117
Ten minute rule Bills
introduction to Parliament of, 3-051
Terrorism
BBC, 20-096—20-097
commercial broadcasting, 20-108—20-109
intelligence services, 20-062

INDEX

public order
  closed material,
    19-147—19-152
  control orders,
    19-134—19-139
  generally, 19-092,
    19-118—19-125
  human rights,
    19-140—19-141
  judicial scrutiny over
    information obtained
    abroad, 19-142—19-146
  police and investigatory
    powers, 19-126—19-133

Tortious liability
  public authorities,
    18-108—18-111

Total Managed Expenditure
  see **Public expenditure**

Trading funds
  see **Government trading funds**

Treasury
  public expenditure
    financial control,
      12-013—12-022
    parliamentary control,
      12-063—12-069
    planning, 12-031

Tribunals
  advantages, 15-023—15-024
  coherence of system of, 15-015
  Council of Tribunals, 15-014
  decision-making, 15-022
  diversity of, 15-016
  evolution of public law and, 1-015
  historical development, 6-163—6-177
  Legal Services Board, 15-017
  Leggatt Review, 15-025
  Prison Board of Visitors, 15-016—15-019
  role of, 15-021
  status, 15-020
  Tribunals Courts and Enforcement Act 2007, 15-026—15-033
  use of, 15-013

Ultra vires
  judicial review, 17-062—17-067, 17-083—17-086

United Kingdom
  structure of
    introduction, 2-001

Use of force
  public order
    civil law, 19-114
    CS gas, 19-115
    legal liability, 19-110—19-117
    Northern Ireland, 19-110—19-111, 19-116
    plastic baton rounds, 19-115
    police powers and duties, 19-097
    right to life, 19-117
    Saville Inquiry, 15-048, 19-111

Utilities
  privatisation
    British Telecom, 14-020—14-025
    electricity, 14-045—14-056
    energy and natural resources, 14-027
    gas, 14-028—14-044
    OFCOM, 14-026
    Utilities Act 2000, 14-057—14-060
    water, 14-061—14-070
    Water Act 2014, 14-071—14-073

Value for money examinations
  see **Audits**

Vehicle Inspectorate
  see **Executive agencies**

Veto
  European Union, 9-008

Vetting
  intelligence services, 20-043—20-044

Violent disorder
  public order offences, 19-055, 19-060

Void transactions
  public law remedies, 18-073—18-074—18-076

Voidable transactions
  public law remedies, 18-073—18-074—18-076

Wakeham Commission
  House of Lords reforms, 3-143—3-145

Wales
  Auditor General for Wales, 12-047
  constitutional law sources, 2-011—2-012
  devolution
    draft Wales Bill, 2-080
    electorates, 2-055
    generally, 2-069—2-075
    Grand Committee, 2-116
    select committees, 2-112
    Silk Commission Review, 2-076—2-079

War
  prerogative powers, 19-106
  requisitions, 19-109

Warrants
  intelligence services, 20-051, 20-054—20-055, 20-067

Water
  privatisation
    generally, 14-061—14-070
    Water Act 2014, 14-071—14-073

Wednesbury unreasonableness
  judicial review, 17-096—17-102

West Lothian question
  see **Devolution**

Wright Committee
  see **Select committees**